IISS

THE MILITARY BALANCE

2005·2006

published by

Routledge
Taylor & Francis Group

for

The International Institute for Strategic Studies

ARUNDEL HOUSE | 13–15 ARUNDEL STREET | TEMPLE PLACE | LONDON | WC2R 3DX | UK

THE MILITARY BALANCE 2005·2006

The International Institute for Strategic Studies

ARUNDEL HOUSE | 13–15 ARUNDEL STREET | TEMPLE PLACE | LONDON | WC2R 3DX | UK

DIRECTOR **Dr John Chipman**
EDITOR **Col Christopher Langton**

DEFENCE ANALYSTS
GROUND FORCES **Nigel Adderley, Phillip Mitchell**
AEROSPACE **Wg Cdr Andrew Brookes**
MARITIME **Cdr Rodney Craig**
DEFENCE ECONOMIST **Mark Stoker**
ARMED CONFLICT **Hanna Ucko**

ASSISTANT EDITORS **Dr Ayse Abdullah, James Hackett**
DESIGN AND PRODUCTION **Jesse Simon, Shirley Nicholls**
CARTOGRAPHER **Steven Bernard**

RESEARCH ASSISTANTS **Stacy Pepper, Agnieszka Fitzclarence, Roland Friedrich, Rich Cowley, Kemal Alam, Chan Le, James McDaid, Nicholas Long**

This publication has been prepared by the Director of the Institute and his Staff, who accept full responsibility for its contents. The views expressed herein do not, and indeed cannot, represent a consensus of views among the worldwide membership of the Institute as a whole.

FIRST PUBLISHED October 2005

ISBN 0-415-37393-x
ISSN 0459-7222

The Military Balance (ISSN 0459-7222) is published annually in October by Routledge Journals, an imprint of Taylor & Francis, 4 Park Square, Milton Park, Abingdon, Oxfordshire OX14 4RN, UK. The 2005 annual subscription rate is: UK£88 (individual rate), UK£170 (institution rate); overseas US$145 (individual rate), US$280 (institution rate).

A subscription to the institution print edition, ISSN 0459-7222, includes free access for any number of concurrent users across a local area network to the online edition, ISSN 1479-9022.

Dollar rates apply to subscribers in all countries except the UK and the Republic of Ireland where the pound sterling price applies. All subscriptions are payable in advance and all rates include postage. Journals are sent by air to the USA, Canada, Mexico, India, Japan and Australasia. Subscriptions are entered on an annual basis, i.e. January to December. Payment may be made by sterling cheque, dollar cheque, international money order, National Giro, or credit card (Amex, Visa, Mastercard).

Please send subscription orders to: USA/Canada: Taylor & Francis Inc., Journals Department, 325 Chestnut Street, 8th Floor, Philadelphia, PA 19106, USA. UK/Europe/Rest of World: Routledge Journals, T&F Customer Services, T&F Informa UK Ltd., Sheepen Place, Colchester, Essex, CO3 3LP, UK.

The print edition of this journal is typeset by Techset Composition, Salisbury, UK and printed on ANSI conforming acid free paper by Bell & Bain, Glasgow, UK. The online edition of this journal is hosted by MetaPress.

CONTENTS

Index of **TABLES**

Index of **MAPS**

The Military Balance 2005·2006
Editor's Foreword

The challenges posed by the asymmetric character of contemporary conflict continue to dominate military thinking and defence planning. In particular, Iraq, Afghanistan and Chechnya demonstrate the limitations of modern conventional forces in complex environments that demand more of them than traditional warfighting (see essay p. 411). For the US and coalition forces, this has been demonstrated by the difficulties faced in Iraq and Afghanistan, where swift and successful warfighting phases have given way to more uncertain post-conflict environments, with practical and political reconstruction hindered by insurgent activities. As a result, in the run-up to the publication of the next Quadrennial Defense Review, the US is revisiting some of the conclusions of the 2001 review – not necessarily revising them, rather taking into account current realities. For instance, the 2005 National Defense Strategy says US planners 'have learned that an unrivalled capacity to respond to traditional challenges is no longer sufficient' and the concept of 'three dimensional warfare' has come under further examination. Furthermore, within this complex environment, the financial cost of conflict is placing the US economy – already carrying a deficit of some 4.25% of GDP – under growing pressure. One outcome has been a significant cut in the 2006–2011 defence programme.

Given the substantial cost of ongoing asymmetric operations, in terms of forces committed as well financial draws, harnessing international support is of growing importance. In Afghanistan, with NATO due to take an increasing share of the burden from US forces, the performance and contribution of member states will be placed under sharp scrutiny. In this operation, NATO's first with a combat dimension outside its traditional area of activity, the alliance cannot afford to fail. (see p. 224) In general, though, support of the volume and kind required is proving hard to find. Meanwhile, in Iraq, where an international coalition has been active since the invasion, developing the expertise of indigenous security forces to a level where they can take over security tasks from coalition forces is a priority, not least as it will enable coalition forces to begin the process of withdrawal. (see p. 173)

However, despite the limitations on the use of conventional military forces that are highlighted by the aforementioned ongoing operations, the rapid and large-scale response to aid South and Southeast Asian and East African countries afflicted by the tsunami disaster of 26 December 2004 demonstrated that such large-scale forces can still be of unrivalled utility. The substantial standing forces deployed across affected areas by a diverse array of nations, but particularly the Carrier Strike and Expeditionary Strike Groups despatched by the US, proved of great efficacy in disaster and humanitarian relief efforts (see pp. 14, 229, 264). The disaster relief efforts also showed how ad hoc military groupings can quickly coalesce and function together – and with civilian humanitarian organisations – in a common operating environment despite difficulties in language, operating procedures and communications.

Despite the continuing impact of asymmetric conflict, including in the north Caucasus republics of the Russian Federation (see pp. 153–6), and the attention devoted to this, development continues vis-à-vis conventional approaches to defence. China's military is rapidly modernising. This is of concern to the US and some countries in the Asia-Pacific region as the modernisation of the People's Liberation Army is no longer directed solely against Taiwan, but also has a force projection component. Moreover, there are increasing signs of a developing military relationship between China and Russia (see pp. 153, 260).

In Sub-Saharan Africa, the African Union (AU) continues to develop its capabilities in peace support operations with its deployment to Darfur, supported by NATO and the European Union (see pp. 46, 360). However, the continent continues to be heavily afflicted by the hardship resulting from disease and famine – which can themselves create and complicate local and regional security situations – notwithstanding the instability arising from political issues. However, at its July 2005 summit at Gleneagles, the G8 pledged that aid to Africa would be increased by $25 billion a year by 2010, while it restated its 'Sea Island commitment to train and equip, some 75,000 troops by 2010 to take part in peace support operations worldwide, with a sustained focus on Africa.' The G8 also said it would support the AU mission in Sudan.

Christopher Langton
Editor, *The Military Balance*
London

The Military Balance 2005·2006
Preface

The Military Balance is updated each year to provide an accurate assessment of the military forces and defence expenditures of 169 countries. The data in the current edition are according to IISS assessments as at August 2005. Inclusion of a country or state in *The Military Balance* does not imply legal recognition or indicate support for any government.

GENERAL ARRANGEMENT

Part I of *The Military Balance* comprises the regional trends, military capabilities and defence economics data for countries grouped by region. Thus North America includes the United States and Canada. Regional groupings are preceded by a short introduction describing the military issues facing the region. There are tables depicting major training exercises, nuclear delivery and warhead holdings and military satellites. Conventional Forces in Europe Treaty data are also shown. There is an essay on Complex Irregular Warfare.

Part II contains information on non-state armed groups and their activity. The loose wall-map is updated for 2005 to show data on recent and current armed conflicts, including fatalities and costs.

Part III comprises reference material.

USING THE MILITARY BALANCE

The country entries in *The Military Balance* are a quantitative assessment of the personnel strengths and equipment holdings of the world's armed forces. The strengths of forces and the numbers of weapons held are based on the most accurate data available or, failing that, on the best estimate that can be made.

The data presented each year reflect judgements based on information available to the IISS at the time the book is compiled. Where information differs from previous editions, this is mainly because of changes in national forces, but it is sometimes because the IISS has reassessed the evidence supporting past entries. An attempt is made to distinguish between these reasons for change in the text that introduces each regional section, but care must be taken in constructing time-series comparisons from information given in successive editions.

In order to interpret the data in the country entries correctly, it is essential to read the explanatory notes beginning on page 7.

The large quantity of data in *The Military Balance* has been compressed into a portable volume by extensive employment of abbreviations. An essential tool is therefore the alphabetical index of abbreviations, which appears at the back of the book.

ATTRIBUTION AND ACKNOWLEDGEMENTS

The International Institute for Strategic Studies owes no allegiance to any government, group of governments, or any political or other organisation. Its assessments are its own, based on the material available to it from a wide variety of sources. The cooperation of governments of all listed countries has been sought and, in many cases, received. However, some data in *The Military Balance* are estimates.

Care is taken to ensure that these are as accurate and free from bias as possible. The Institute owes a considerable debt to a number of its own members, consultants and all those who helped compile and check material. The Director and staff of the Institute assume full responsibility for the data and judgements in this book. Comments and suggestions on the data presented are welcomed. Suggestions on the style and method of presentation are also much appreciated.

Readers may use data from *The Military Balance* without applying for permission from the Institute on condition that the IISS and *The Military Balance* are cited as the source in any published work. However, applications to reproduce portions of text, complete country entries or complete tables from *The Military Balance* must be referred to the publishers. Prior to publication, applications should be addressed to: Taylor and Francis, 4 Park Square, Milton Park, Abingdon, Oxon, ox14 4RN, with a copy to the Editor of *The Military Balance*.

The Military Balance 2005·2006
Explanatory Notes

ABBREVIATIONS AND DEFINITIONS

Abbreviations are used throughout to save space and to avoid repetition. The abbreviations may have both singular or plural meanings; for example, 'elm' = 'element' or 'elements'. The qualification 'some' means up to, while 'about' means the total could be higher than given. In financial data, '$' refers to US dollars unless otherwise stated; billion (bn) signifies 1,000 million (m). Footnotes particular to a country entry or table are indicated by letters, while those that apply throughout the book are marked by symbols (* for training aircraft counted by the IISS as combat-capable, and † where serviceability of equipment is in doubt). A full list of abbreviations appears on the detachable laminated card at the back of the book.

COUNTRY ENTRIES

Information on each country is shown in a standard format, although the differing availability of information results in some variations. Country entries include economic, demographic and military data. Military data include manpower, length of conscript service, outline organisation, number of formations and units and an inventory of the major equipment of each service. This is followed, where applicable, by a description of the deployment of each service. Details of national forces stationed abroad and of foreign-stationed forces are also given.

ARMS ORDERS AND DELIVERIES

Tables in the regional texts show arms orders and deliveries listed by country buyer for the past and current years, together with country supplier and delivery dates, if known. Every effort has been made to ensure accuracy, but some transactions may not be fulfilled or may differ from those reported.

GENERAL MILITARY DATA

Manpower
The 'Active' total comprises all servicemen and women on full-time duty (including conscripts and long-term assignments from the Reserves). Under the heading 'Terms of Service', only the length of conscript service

is shown; where service is voluntary there is no entry. 'Reserve' describes formations and units not fully manned or operational in peacetime, but which can be mobilised by recalling reservists in an emergency. Unless otherwise indicated, the 'Reserves' entry includes all reservists committed to rejoining the armed forces in an emergency, except when national reserve service obligations following conscription last almost a lifetime. The Military Balance bases its estimates of effective reservist strengths on the numbers available within five years of completing full-time service, unless there is good evidence that obligations are enforced for longer. Some countries have more than one category of 'Reserves', often kept at varying degrees of readiness. Where possible, these differences are denoted using the national descriptive title, but always under the heading of 'Reserves' to distinguish them from full-time active forces.

Other forces
Many countries maintain paramilitary forces whose training, organisation, equipment and control suggest they may be used to support or replace regular military forces. These are listed, and their roles described, after the military forces of each country. Their manpower is not normally included in the Armed Forces totals at the start of each entry. Home Guard units are counted as paramilitary. Where paramilitary groups are not on full-time active duty, '(R)' is added after the title to indicate that they have reserve status. A list of non-state armed opposition groups which pose a significant threat to a state's security is provided in Part II.

Equipment
Quantities are shown by function and type, and represent what are believed to be total holdings, including active and reserve operational and training units and 'in store' stocks. Inventory totals for missile systems – such as surface-to-surface missiles (SSM), surface-to-air missiles (SAM) and anti-tank guided weapons (ATGW) – relate to launchers and not to missiles. Stocks of equipment held in reserve and not assigned to either active or reserve units are listed as 'in store'. However, aircraft in excess of unit establishment holdings, held to allow for repair and modification or immediate replacement, are not shown 'in store'.

Table 1 **Units and formation strength**

Company	100–200
Battalion	500–800
Brigade (regiment)	3,000–5,000
Division	15,000–20,000
Corps (Army)	60,000–80,000

This accounts for apparent disparities between unit strengths and aircraft inventory strengths.

Operational deployments

Where deployments are overseas, *The Military Balance* lists permanent bases and does not normally list short-term operational deployments, particularly where military operations are in progress. An exception is made in the case of peacekeeping operations. Recent developments are also described in the text for each regional section.

GROUND FORCES

The national designation is normally used for army formations. The term 'regiment' can be misleading. It can mean essentially a brigade of all arms; a grouping of battalions of a single arm; or a battalion group. The sense intended is indicated in each case. Where there is no standard organisation, the intermediate levels of command are shown as headquarters (HQs), followed by the total numbers of units that could be allocated to them. Where a unit's title overstates its real capability, the title is given in inverted commas, with an estimate given in parentheses of the comparable unit size typical of countries with substantial armed forces. For guidelines for unit and formation strengths, see Table 1.

Military formations

The manpower strength, equipment holdings and organisation of formations such as brigades and divisions differ widely from country to country. Where possible, the normal composition of formations is given in parentheses. It should be noted that where both divisions and brigades are listed, only independent or separate brigades are counted and not those included in divisions.

NAVAL FORCES

Categorisation is based on operational role, weapon fit and displacement. Ship classes are identified by the name of the first ship of that class, except where a class is recognised by another name (such as *Udalay*, *Petya*). Where the class is based on a foreign design or has been acquired from another country, the original class name is added in parentheses. Each class is given an acronym. All such designators are included in the list of abbreviations. The term 'ship' refers to vessels with over 1,000 tonnes full-load displacement that are more than 60

Principal Ground Equipment Definitions

The Military Balance uses the following definitions of equipment:

Main Battle Tank (MBT) An armoured, tracked combat vehicle, weighing at least 16.5 metric tonnes unladen, that may be armed with a turret-mounted gun of at least 75mm calibre. Any new-wheeled combat vehicles that meet the latter two criteria will be considered MBTs.

Armoured Combat Vehicle (ACV) A self-propelled vehicle with armoured protection and cross-country capability. ACVs include:

Armoured Infantry Fighting Vehicle (AIFV) An armoured combat vehicle designed and equipped to transport an infantry squad, armed with an integral/organic cannon of at least 20mm calibre. Variants of AIFVs are also included and indicated as such.

Armoured Personnel Carrier (APC) A lightly armoured combat vehicle, designed and equipped to transport an infantry squad and armed with integral/organic weapons of less than 20mm calibre. Variants of APCs converted for other uses (such as weapons platforms, command posts and communications vehicles) are included and indicated as such.

Artillery A weapon with a calibre of 100mm and above, capable of engaging ground targets by delivering primarily indirect fire. The definition covers guns, howitzers, gun/howitzers, multiple-rocket launchers and mortars.

Principal Naval Equipment Definitions

To aid comparison between fleets, the following definitions, which do not necessarily conform to national definitions, are used:

Submarines. All vessels equipped for military operations and designed to operate primarily below the surface. Those vessels with submarine-launched ballistic missiles are listed separately under 'Strategic Nuclear Forces'.

Principal Surface Combatant. This term includes all surface ships with both 1,000 tonnes full load displacement and a weapons system for other than self-protection. All such ships are assumed to have an anti-surface ship capability. They comprise: aircraft carriers (defined below); cruisers (over 8,000 tonnes) and destroyers (less than 8,000 tonnes), both of which normally have an anti-air role and may also have an anti-submarine capability; and frigates (less than 8,000 tonnes) which normally have an anti-submarine role. Only ships with a flight deck that extends beyond two-thirds of the vessel's length are classified as aircraft carriers. Ships with shorter flight decks are shown as helicopter carriers.

Patrol and Coastal Combatants. These are ships and craft whose primary role is protecting a state's sea approaches and coastline. Included are corvettes (500–1,500 tonnes with an attack capability), missile craft (with permanently fitted missile-launcher ramps and control equipment) and torpedo craft (with anti-surface-ship torpedoes). Ships and craft that fall outside these definitions are classified as 'patrol' and divided into 'offshore' (over 500 tonnes), 'coastal' (75–500 tonnes), 'inshore' (less than 75 tonnes) and 'riverine'. The prefix 'fast' indicates that the ship's speed is greater than 30 knots.

Mine Warfare. This term covers surface vessels configured primarily for mine laying or mine counter-measures (such as mine-hunters, minesweepers or dual-capable vessels). They are further classified into 'offshore', 'coastal', 'inshore' and 'riverine' with the same tonnage definitions as for 'patrol' vessels shown above.

Amphibious. This term includes ships specifically procured and employed to disembark troops and their equipment onto unprepared beachheads by means such as landing craft, helicopters or hovercraft, or directly supporting amphibious operations. The term 'Landing Ship' (as opposed to 'Landing Craft') refers to vessels capable of an ocean passage that can deliver their troops and equipment in a fit state to fight. Vessels with an amphibious capability but not assigned to amphibious duties are not included. Amphibious craft are listed at the end of each entry.

Support and Miscellaneous. This term covers auxiliary military ships. It covers four broad categories: 'underway support' (e.g., tankers and stores ships), 'maintenance and logistic' (e.g., sealift ships), 'special purposes' (e.g., intelligence collection ships) and 'survey and research' ships.

Merchant Fleet. This category is included in a state's inventory when it can make a significant contribution to the state's military sealift capability.

Weapons Systems. Weapons are listed in the following order: land-attack missiles, anti-surface ship missiles, surface-to-air missiles, guns, torpedo tubes, other anti-submarine weapons, and helicopters. Missiles with a range of less than 5km, and guns with a calibre of less than 76mm, are not included. Exceptions may be made in the case of some minor combatants with a primary gun armament of a lesser calibre.

Aircraft. All armed aircraft, including anti-submarine warfare and maritime-reconnaissance aircraft, are included as combat aircraft in naval inventories.

Organisations. Naval groupings such as fleets and squadrons frequently change and are often temporary; organisations are shown only where it is meaningful.

Principal Air Force Equipment Definitions

Different countries often use the same basic aircraft in different roles; the key to determining these roles lies mainly in aircrew training. In The Military Balance the following definitions are used as a guide:

Fixed Wing Aircraft

Fighter. This term is used to describe aircraft with the weapons, avionics and performance capacity for aerial combat. Multi-role aircraft are shown as fighter ground attack (FGA), fighter, reconnaissance and so on, according to the role in which they are deployed.

Bombers. These aircraft are categorised according to their designed range and payload as follows:

Long-range. Capable of delivering a weapons payload of more than 10,000kg over an unrefuelled radius of action of over 5,000km;

Medium-range. Capable of delivering weapons of more than 10,000kg over an unrefuelled radius of action of between 1,000km and 5,000km;

Short-range. Capable of delivering a weapons payload of more than 10,000kg over an unrefuel-led radius of action of less than 1,000km.

A few bombers with the radius of action described above, but designed to deliver a payload of less than 10,000kg, and which do not fall into the category of FGA, are described as light bombers.

Helicopters

Armed Helicopters. This term is used to cover helicopters equipped to deliver ordnance, including for anti-submarine warfare.

Attack. Helicopters with an integrated fire control and aiming system, designed to deliver anti-armour, air-to-ground or air-to-air weapons;

Combat. Support Helicopters equipped with area suppression or self-defence weapons, but without an integrated fire control and aiming system;

Assault. Armed helicopters designed to deliver troops to the battlefield.

Transport Helicopters. The term describes unarmed helicopters designed to transport personnel or cargo in support of military operations.

---

metres (m) in overall length; vessels of lesser displacement, but of 16m or more overall length, are termed 'craft'. Vessels of less than 16m overall length are not included. The term 'commissioning' of a ship is used to mean the ship has completed fitting out and initial sea trials, and has a naval crew; operational training may not have been completed, but otherwise the ship is available for service. 'Decommissioning' means that a ship has been removed from operational duty and the bulk of its naval crew transferred. Removing equipment and stores and dismantling weapons, however, may not have started. Where known, ships in long-term refit are shown as such.

AIR FORCES

The term 'combat aircraft' refers to aircraft normally equipped to deliver air-to-air or air-to-surface ordnance. The 'combat' totals include aircraft in operational conversion units whose main role is weapons training, and training aircraft of the same type as those in front-line squadrons that are assumed to be available for operations at short notice. Training aircraft considered to be combat capable are marked with an asterisk (*). Armed maritime aircraft are included in combat aircraft totals. Operational groupings of air forces are shown where known. Squadron aircraft strengths vary with aircraft types and from country to country.

DEFENCE ECONOMICS

Country entries in Part I include defence expenditures, selected economic performance indicators and demographic aggregates. There are also international comparisons of defence expenditure and military manpower, giving expenditure figures for the past three years in per capita terms and as a % of GDP. The aim is to provide an accurate measure of military expenditure and of the allocation of economic resources to defence. All country entries are subject to revision each year, as new information, particularly that regarding defence expenditure, becomes available. The information is necessarily selective.

Individual country entries show economic performance over the past two years, and current demographic data. Where these data are unavailable, information from the last available year is provided. Where possible, official defence budgets for the current year and previous two years are shown, as well as an estimate of actual defence expenditures for those countries where true defence expenditure is thought to be considerably higher than official budget figures suggest. Estimates of actual defence expenditure, however, are only made for those countries where there are sufficient data to justify such a measurement. Therefore, there will be several countries listed in *The Military Balance* for which only an official defence budget figure is provided but where, in reality, true defence-related expenditure is almost certainly higher.

All financial data in the country entries are shown both in national currency and US dollars at current year, not constant, prices. US dollar conversions are generally, but not invariably, calculated from the exchange rates listed in the entry. In a few cases, notably Russia, a US-dollar purchasing power parity (PPP) rate is used in preference to official or market-exchange rates.

Definitions of terms

Despite efforts by NATO and the UN to develop a standardised definition of military expenditure, many countries prefer to use their own definitions (which are often not made public). In order to present a comprehensive picture, *The Military Balance* lists three different measures of military-related spending data.

- For most countries, an official defence budget figure is provided.
- For those countries where other military-related outlays, over and above the defence budget, are known, or can be reasonably estimated, an additional measurement referred to as defence expenditure is also provided. Defence expenditure figures will naturally be higher than official budget figures, depending on the range of additional factors included.
- For NATO countries, an official defence budget figure as well as a measure of defence expenditure (calculated using NATO's definition) is quoted.

NATO's definition of military expenditure, the most comprehensive, is defined as the cash outlays of central or federal government to meet the costs of national armed forces. The term 'armed forces' includes strategic, land, naval, air, command, administration and support forces. It also includes paramilitary forces such as *gendarmerie*, the customs service and the border guard if these forces are trained in military tactics, equipped as a military force and operate under military authority in the event of war. Defence expenditures are reported in four categories: Operating Costs, Procurement and Construction, Research and Development (R&D) and Other Expenditure. Operating Costs include: salaries and pensions for military and civilian personnel; the cost of maintaining and training units, service organisations, headquarters and support elements; and the cost of servicing and repairing military equipment and infrastructure. Procurement and Construction expenditure covers national equipment and infrastructure spending, as well as common infrastructure programmes. It also includes financial contributions to multinational military organisations, host-nation support in cash and in kind, and payments made to other countries under bilateral agreements. R&D is defence expenditure up to the point at which new equipment can be put in service, regardless of whether new equipment is actually procured. Foreign Military Aid (FMA) contributions of more than US$1 million are also noted.

For many non-NATO countries the issue of transparency in reporting military budgets is a fundamental one. Not every UN member state reports defence budget (even fewer real defence expenditures) data to their electorates, the UN, the IMF or other multinational organisations. In the case of governments with a proven record of transparency, official figures generally conform to the standardised definition of defence budgeting, as adopted by the UN, and consistency problems are not usually a major issue. The IISS cites official defence budgets as reported by either national governments, the UN, the OSCE or the IMF.

For those countries where the official defence budget figure is considered to be an incomplete measure of total military related spending, and appropriate additional data are available, the IISS will use data from a variety of sources to arrive at a more accurate estimate of true defence expenditure. The most frequent instances of budgetary manipulation or falsification typically involve equipment procurement, R&D, defence industrial investment, covert weapons programmes, pensions for retired military and civilian personnel, paramilitary forces and non-budgetary sources of revenue for the military arising from ownership of industrial, property and land assets.

The principal sources for national economic statistics cited in the country entries are the IMF, the Organisation for Economic Cooperation and Development (OECD), the World Bank and three regional banks (the Inter-American, Asian and African Development Banks). For some countries basic economic data are difficult to obtain. This is the case in a few former command economies in transition and countries currently or recently involved in armed conflict. The Gross Domestic Product (GDP) figures are nominal (current) values at market prices. GDP growth is real not nominal growth, and inflation is the year-on-year change in consumer prices. Two different measures of debt are used to distinguish between OECD and non-OECD countries: for OECD countries, debt is gross public debt (or, more exactly, general government gross financial liabilities) expressed as a proportion of GDP. For all other countries, debt is gross foreign debt denominated in current US dollars. Dollar exchange rates relate to the last two years plus the current year. Values for the past two years are annual averages, while current values are the latest monthly value.

Calculating exchange rates

Typically, but not invariably, the exchange rates shown in the country entries are also used to calculate GDP and defence budget and expenditure dollar conversions. Where they are not used, it is because the use of exchange rate dollar conversions can misrepresent both GDP and defence expenditure. For former communist countries, PPP rather than market exchange rates are sometimes used for dollar conversions of both GDP and defence expenditures. Where PPP is used, it is annotated accordingly.

The arguments for using PPP are strongest for Russia and China. Both the UN and IMF have issued caveats concerning the reliability of official economic statistics on transitional economies, particularly those of Russia, some Eastern European and Central Asian countries. Non-reporting, lags in the publication of current statistics and frequent revisions of recent data (not always accompanied by timely revision of previously published figures in the same series) pose transparency and consistency problems. Another problem arises with certain transitional economies whose productive capabilities are similar to those of developed economies, but where cost and price structures are often much lower than world levels.

PPP dollar values are used in preference to market exchange rates in cases where using such exchange rates may result in excessively low dollar-conversion values for GDP and defence expenditure data.

Demographic data

Population aggregates are based on the most recent official census data or, in their absence, demographic statistics taken from US Census Bureau. Data on ethnic and religious minorities are also provided under country entries where a related security issue exists.

Chapter One
North America

US SECURITY AND DEFENCE POLICY

The Department of Defense (DoD) is soon to publish the 2005 Quadrennial Defense Review (QDR) (See past editions of *The Military Balance*). Mandated by Congress, this publication appears every four years and comprises a comprehensive review of US defence policies and programmes as well as present and emerging threats. One of the key statements of the Bush administration's first QDR (which appeared on 30 September 2001) was that new force sizing should enable US forces to 'swiftly defeat aggression in overlapping major conflicts while preserving for the President the option to call for a decisive victory in one of those conflicts – including the possibility of regime change or occupation'. The 2001 QDR also focused on the need for transformation of the US military, without which it would 'not be prepared to meet emerging challenges.' The *National Defense Strategy of the United States of America* (NDS), published in March 2005, continued many of these themes (such as the need to retain global freedom of action), but drew particularly on lessons from operations in Afghanistan, and it revealed that the context of past thinking has changed. The NDS asserts that US planners 'have learned that an unrivalled capacity to respond to traditional challenges is no longer sufficient' and that 'the Defense Department's capabilities are only one component of a comprehensive national and international effort. For example, battlefield success is only one element of our long-term, multi-faceted campaign against terrorism.' Moreover, in Iraq and Afghanistan, the type of conflict initially envisioned did not materialise as the reality of post-conflict operations, including reconstruction, prevented quick withdrawal. Moreover, both operations demand high numbers of troops over a protracted period. As the US prepares to deliver the 2005 QDR, therefore, a study into 'three block warfare' is ongoing (see pp. 15, 411).

NATIONAL MISSILE DEFENSE

Missile defence testing and research has continued, despite a $1 billion reduction in the programme's 2006 budget. Progress has continued on the construction of the sea-based X-band radar (SBX), with the radar mated to the former oil rig base unit in late April, the radome installed in June and the SBX dedicated in late July. The Missile Defense Agency (MDA) says that 'preparations are underway for further tests and the transit of the vehicle to its homeport of Adak, Alaska.'

December 2004 saw the sixth groundbased interceptor (GBI) installed at Fort Greely, Alaska, and the first installed at Vandenberg Air Force Base in California. But the last listed integrated flight test attempt relating to the GBI failed in late 2004, and testing in 2005 has so far focused on the *Aegis*-based standard Missile 3 interceptors, the airborne laser, Theatre High Altitude Area Defense and the SBX vehicle. The testing of air-launched targets has also taken place: on 8 April 2005, a medium-range missile was launched downrange of the Pacific Missile Range Facility on Kauai, Hawaii. MDA states that using air-launched targets enables better replication of the potential trajectories that could be taken by hostile ballistic missiles. In addition to these tests – and as a result of budget cuts and criticism in the Senate of missile defence programme costs – the Pentagon has re-examined programme priorities.

$870 million has been cut from the Kinetic Energy Interceptor (KEI) programme. In May 2005, MDA chief Lt Gen. Obering said, to the Defense Subcommittee of the Senate Appropriations Committee, that 'We restructured the Kinetic Energy Interceptor activity as risk mitigation for the Airborne Laser and focused it on development of a land-based mobile, high-acceleration booster' and that 'we have established the Airborne Laser as the primary boost phase defense element'. Development of the airborne laser programme is proceeding. Following a series of flight and system tests completed in July, the airborne laser aircraft is to be modified at a Boeing facility prior to the installation of the megawatt-class Chemical Oxygen–Iodine Laser. Following this, Obering continued, 'we will integrate the high-power laser into the aircraft and conduct a campaign of flight tests, including lethal shoot-down of a series of targets'.

INTERNATIONAL DEPLOYMENTS AND ASSISTANCE

Iraq (see pp. 173–4)

As at July 2005, there were 137,157 US troops in Iraq deployed on counter-insurgency, post-conflict reconstruction and stabilisation operations. The overall objective of policy, within the security environment, is to increase the capacity of Iraqi security forces and structures. Operationally, however, US forces continue an emphasis on counter-insurgency operations.

A major offensive took place in Fallujah starting on 8 November 2004, prior to the January parliamentary elections. *Operation Al Fajr* saw a reported 10–15,000 US and Iraqi personnel engage insurgent forces across the city. Although this operation largely concluded on 16 November, and the city's population are returning, insurgent activity continues in Fallujah, though at a much reduced level. A second offensive, called *Operation Matador*, took place between 7 and 14 May 2005 and involved some 1,000 marines and soldiers. US officials reported that the operation was aimed at interdicting 'smuggling routes and safe houses for foreign fighters arriving in Iraq through the western desert', near the border with Syria. Meanwhile, US, coalition and Iraqi forces have been engaged in numerous smaller-scale operations throughout the year as well as organising, training, equipping and mentoring Iraqi security forces, primarily through the operations of the Multi-National Security Transition Command Iraq.

Afghanistan (see pp. 224)

The US maintains strength of some 18,000 troops on *Operation Enduring Freedom* in Afghanistan. A resurgence in Taliban activity, aimed at de-stabilising the country in the run-up to the September 2005 parliamentary elections, has reinforced the need for a continued US military presence; not least because the Afghan National Army is far from ready to take over combat operations in the south without considerable support. The relatively high tempo of operations has also resulted in an increase in casualties for the US. In one incident, in July 2005, 17 US servicemen died when a *Chinook* helicopter was shot down by Taliban fighters as it attempted to rescue a special forces patrol which had been ambushed – with the further loss of three men. The incident, along with various rocket attacks and small arms engagements, served to show that the Taliban are still capable of mounting tactically sound military operations against technically superior coalition forces in Afghanistan.

Africa (see pp. 360, 364)

US military and security involvement in Africa continues to develop as large numbers of African jihadists are taking part in the insurgency in Iraq. The $100m East Africa Counterterrorism Initiative, announced by President Bush in June 2003, 'includes military training for border and coastal security, programmes to strengthen control of the movement of people and goods across borders' and police training, among other measures. Meanwhile, the Trans-Sahara Counter-Terrorism Initiative (TSCTI), formerly the Pan-Sahel Initiative, aims to 'develop the internal security forces necessary to control borders and combat terrorism and other illegal activity'. The US military part of the TSCTI, *Operation Enduring Freedom-Trans Sahara,* is carried out by EUCOM through military-to-military contacts and exercises 'designed to strengthen the ability of regional governments to police the large expanses of remote terrain in the trans-Sahara. The US has also been active in assisting the African Union in moving forces to Sudan's Darfur region, following NATO's agreements, in May and June, to support the AU Mission in Sudan (AMIS). On 14 July 2005, EUCOM began deploying staff to Kigali to facilitate the deployment of Rwandan troops in support of the AU mission. As of 10 August, US forces had transported 1,200 troops and 49 civilian police staff, while the UK had airlifted around 680 Nigerian troops. Airlift operations are planned to continue until eight AU battalions are in place.

Tsunami (see pp. 230, 263 and maps 257–258)

The US was quick to respond to the 26 December 2004 tsunami disaster, demonstrating its capability to deploy forces rapidly over distance. US naval elements were ready off the coast of Sumatra within five days of receiving orders. The USS *Abraham Lincoln* Carrier Strike Group was underway in the western Pacific (after a port visit to Hong Kong), while the USS *Bonhomme Richard* Expeditionary Strike Group was redirected to the area. With its helicopter air group, the *Abraham Lincoln* was able to supply significant amounts of manpower, drinking water, food and first aid to stricken areas in the early phases of the operation. In addition, it was also able to act as the HQ and base for NGO relief workers and journalists.

The ship also embarked a number of local (Indonesian) military liaison officers (LOs) who provided local advice and acted as a link between the ship and the Indonesian authorities ashore. However, there were three limitations which curtailed the full potential of the deployment. The carrier was denied permission to carry out essential fixed-wing flying training whilst in Indonesian territorial waters. In addition, the sheer numbers of unexpected NGO personnel who required air-lifting around the afflicted areas resulted in over-tasking of the ship's SH-60 *Seahawk* helicopters. Control of airspace was also a problem; the numerous military, NGO and press helicopters flying in the region led to safety concerns, and potential contentious issues were at times resolved on an ad-hoc basis.

OVERSTRETCH AND TRANSFORMATION

Extended commitments in Afghanistan and Iraq have forced the Pentagon to reconsider its manning strategy to ensure operational sustainability. Despite the continuation of 'stop-loss' and 'stop-move' programmes (see *The Military Balance 2004–2005*), numbers are declining. Reportedly, the percentage of Americans willing to consider army service has dropped from 11% in 2004 to 7% in 2005 while in May, the shortfall of active-duty army recruits reached 8,321 (for FY2005). Moreover, army recruit training camps are reported to be operating at 46% capacity compared with 91% at the same time in 2004. The immediate solution is the extensive use of reserve personnel in Iraq and an extension of tour length. Since 11 September 2001, 469,000 National Guard or reserve forces from the army, marines, navy and air force have been deployed on operations in Iraq and Afghanistan. However, although reservists help to overcome the manning problem, there are domestic repercussions. Prolonged use of reserve soldiers has affected small businesses, resulted in job losses and economic hardship for the families of some of those deployed.

Transformation

Washington's post-Cold War military policy was shaped by unipolar dominance and economic and technological superiority. However, the reality of asymmetric threats, including the possibility of nuclear, biological, and chemical terrorism by non-state actors, has undercut the feasibility of rapid, decisive victory. These non-traditional threats necessitate greater attention not only to the combat phase of operations, but also post-combat issues. The demands of this modern 'battlefield' are manpower intensive and require a broad range of non-military skills. Thus, the study into 'three-block warfare' – contingencies in which, according to former US Marine

Corps Commandant James Krulak, forces 'may be confronted by the entire spectrum of tactical challenges in the span of a few hours and within the space of a few city blocks', and possibly involving combat warfare, peacekeeping operations, and humanitarian assistance – is ongoing. (See essay p. 411)

GLOBAL FORCE POSTURE REVIEW CHANGES

The US is continuing to develop its global basing strategy, announced in August 2004. In addition to existing bases in Eastern Europe (Poland, Romania, Bulgaria) and Africa (Uganda, Gabon, Ghana, Senegal, and Zambia), there are plans for new bases in Afghanistan and Azerbaijan. To assist this process, the DoD is implementing measures suggested by the Base Realignment and Closure (BRAC) Commission (see *The Military Balance 2004–2005*). Although its final report is still pending, the Commission's most recent announcement suggests that 15 active Army bases, seven leased bases, 176 Army reserve installations, and 211 National Guard facilities are expected to close, including several in Germany, Japan and South Korea. Restructuring strives to consolidate strategic positioning, enabling the rapid deployment of forces to meet contingencies. One possible negative effect of realignment concerns US relations with Russia and China. The latter sees the plan as a form of encirclement, and the former is concerned about a NATO and US military presence on its borders in the South Caucusus and Central Asia (see p. 153). Moreover, following a deterioration in relations between the US and Uzbekistan the Khanabad-Farsi base, which was established to support operations in Afghanistan, is set to close by the end of 2005. (see p. 223).

The report of the Commission on the Review of the Overseas Military Facility Structure of the United States (the Overseas Basing Commission), submitted to Congress in May 2005, stated that the 'sequencing and pace of the proposed realignments could harm our ability to meet broader national security imperatives and could significantly impact both the military's ability to protect national interests and the quality of life of the servicemen and women affected by the realignment'. The commission was also critical of the feasibility of the realignment plan (which is planned to take place between 2006 and 2011) and its cost, which is estimated to be between $16 billion and $20bn, while also noting that some potential host communities may be unprepared to accommodate the increases in local military populations when tens of thousands of troops return to the US.

COUNTER-TERRORISM AND HOMELAND SECURITY

In December 2004, President Bush signed the **Intelligence Reform Bill**, reorganising US intelligence structures. This followed the release of the findings of the National Commission Report on Terrorist Attacks upon the United States (the 9/11 Commission) (see *The Military Balance 2004–2005*) Two key provisions are the creation of a National Counter-Terrorism Center and the appointment of a new Director of National Intelligence (DNI). This latter position will constitute the central authority uniting the 15 intelligence agencies. The DNI post-holder also acts as the president's chief intelligence advisor, a role formerly held by the CIA director whose direct influence on the president has been somewhat diminished.

In May 2005, the House of Representatives passed, and referred to the Senate Committee on Homeland Security and Governmental Affairs, the **Homeland Security Authorization Act for 2006**. The legislation allocates $34bn to Homeland Security, but also monitors the Department of Homeland Security (DHS), its programmes, structure and the resources needed to meet its objectives. These include: to prevent terrorist attacks; reduce vulnerability to terrorism; minimise damage and assist in recovery from terrorist attack; and be the focal point for handling natural and manmade crises and emergency planning.

The bill tasks DHS to submit to Congress a cohesive Terrorism Prevention Plan (TPP) and overhaul the colour-coded alert system. However, the proposed legislation's demand for the need for an Assistant Secretary for Cybersecurity was met by DHS Secretary Chertoff's 13 July announcement, in which he set out a 'six point agenda' for the DHS which would create a new Assistant Secretary for Cyber Security and Telecommunications within a Directorate for Preparedness (currently the Information Analysis and Infrastructure Protection Directorate). Moreover, the text calls for a 90-day deadline to set up the **Technology Clearinghouse** called for in the 2002 Homeland Security Act, which should among other duties aim 'to engage the technological solutions and expertise of the private sector' by identifying and preparing technologies that could be of use to federal, state, local and non-governmental

agencies in preventing, preparing for, and responding to, acts of terrorism. Furthermore, the proposed legislation calls for increased border control, risk-based cargo screening, and training for nuclear, biological and chemical contingencies.

Washington has continued to develop the **Container Security Initiative (CSI)** and the **Proliferation Security Initiative (PSI)** (for both, see past editions of *The Military Balance*). Thirty-six ports in North America, Europe, Asia and Africa currently participate in the CSI and the DHS plans to include 14 additional ports by the end of 2005. The new legislation charges DHS to implement a systematic, risk-based strategy for port selection in place of the original criteria for selection which was based on shipping volume. The proposed Homeland Security Authorization Act 2006 further sanctions DHS to purchase screening equipment for ports that are unable to procure inspection equipment themselves. Meanwhile, PSI membership expanded to 60 nations in 2004–05. However, the initiative is limited by the non-participation of major powers. Neither China nor India, growing naval powers in the Asia-Pacific region, have agreed to participate, and Russia has also remained outside PSI.

CANADA

The defence debate in Canada continues to be dogged by the lack of a threat-based approach and agreement over resources necessary for much-needed modernisation of the armed forces. However, the Disaster Assistance Response Team (DART) initiative has shown many other countries a pragmatic means of rapid reaction in response to humanitarian crises and disaster relief. Except in nuclear, biological, or chemical emergencies, DART can immediately respond to a crisis. Comprised of some 200 personnel, DART teams can remain in position for up to 40 days, offering basic, non-surgical medical care, water purification and engineering operations, as well as implementing command and control functions to facilitate relief until other elements mobilise to provide longer-term assistance. Canada has also continued to support the expansion of NATO-led operations with the deployment of 1,500 troops to Afghanistan including a 250-strong Provincial Reconstruction Team (PRT) to Kandahar – the first non-US PRT in the southern provinces (see p. 224).

Table 2 Selected US Training And Operational Activity 2004–05

Operation/ Exercise Date	Location	Aim	Principal Participants/ Remarks
Malabar 04 Oct 2004	Indian Coast	Interoperability	India, US
Talon Vision 05 Nov 2004	Philippines	Interoperability, combat readiness	Philippines, US
Flexible Leader 05 Nov 2004	Europe	Train US European Command (EUCOM) in command, control and communications	EUCOM
Reliant Mermaid VII Jan 2005	Israel	SAR, interoperability and humanitarian missions	Israel, Turkey, US
Cope Tiger 2005 Jan 2005	Thailand	C2, Interoperability	Singapore, Thailand, US
Balikatan 2005 Feb 2005	Philippines	Due to the tsunami, focused on Civil Military Operations (CMO) using Humanitarian and Civic Assistance (HCA) funding and supporting activities	Philippines, US
Joint Red Flag Mar-Apr 2005	US	Joint Service interoperability	US Joint Forces Command (USJFC)
Roving Sands 2005 Mar–Apr 2005	Texas	Joint training exercise to practice joint air defence interoperability incorporating lessons learned from Operation Iraqi Freedom	Netherlands, UK, Canada, Kuwait, US
African Lion 05 Apr 2005	Morocco	Interoperability	Morocco, US
Blue Game 05 Apr 2005	Denmark	NATO Response Force (NRF) training	US and other NATO countries
Combined Endeavor 05 May 2005	Germany	Communication and information systems exercise	US, 42 other NATO countries, South Africa
Cobra Gold 05 May 2005	Thailand	Interoperability, combat readiness, Non-combatant Evacuation Operations (NEO), disaster relief. Due to the tsunami, changed to a multinational workshop and staff exercise focusing on tsunami affected areas	Thailand, Singapore, US
CARAT 05 May–Aug 2005	South China Sea	AAW, ASuW, ASW, diving and salvage interoperability to counter seaborne terrorism and transnational crime at sea	Malaysia, Indonesia, Singapore, Thailand, Brunei, Philippines, US
Flintlock 2005 Jun 2005	Niger	Series of exercises to develop a partnership to halt the flow of illicit weapons, goods and human trafficking in the region	Algeria, Tunisia, Senegal, Mauritania, Mali, Niger, Chad, US
Blue Action 05 Jun 2005	Spain	PSI operations; Air/ground interdiction exercise	Spain (lead nation), Bulgaria, Croatia, Hungary, Latvia, Ukraine, Romania, Slovakia, US
Talisman Sabre 2005 Jun 2005	Australia	Combined Task Force (CTF) exercise	Australia, US
Immediate Response 2005 Jul 2005	Bulgaria	Bilateral live-fire exercise	Bulgaria, US
Peace Shield 05 Jul 2005	Ukraine	Field-training exercise on rapid reaction support operations	US and 21 NATO and partner countries
Northern Edge 2005 Aug 2005	Alaska	Homeland security exercise	US (units from all services)
Arctic Sarex 05 Sep 2005	Alaska	Interoperability, extreme cold weather rescue techniques	Canada, Russia, US
RESCUER/MEDCEUR (Medical Central Europe) 05 Sep 2005	Georgia	Medical exercise	US and partner countries
Active Endeavour (continuous)	Mediterranean	Counter-terrorism operations	STANAVFORLANT, STANAVFORMED (FF/DD from all NATO nations except Iceland and new members; not all countries have units permanently assigned)
CTF-150 (continuous)	Horn of Africa/ Arabian Sea/ North Indian Ocean	Counter-terrorism operations	Australia, Canada, France, Germany, Greece, Italy, New Zealand, Pakistan, Spain, UK, US (other coalition countries contribute from time to time; not all countries have units permanently assigned)

Canada Ca

Canadian Dollar $		2003	2004	2005
GDP	C$	1.21tr	1.29tr	
	US$	867bn	980bn	
per capita	US$	26,919	30,146	
Growth	%	2.0	2.8	
Inflation	%	2.8	1.8	
Public Debt	%	73.3	71.5	
Def exp	C$	14.1bn	15.0bn	
	US$	10.1bn	11.4bn	
Def bdgt	C$	12.2bn	13.2bn	13.8bn
	US$	8.75bn	10bn	10.9bn
US$1= C$		1.4	1.32	1.26

Population (2004)   32,507,874

Age	0 – 14	15 – 19	20 – 24	25 – 29	30 – 64	65 plus
Male	9%	3%	3%	3%	24%	6%
Female	9%	3%	3%	3%	24%	7%

Capabilities

ACTIVE 62,000 (Army 33,000 Navy 12,000 Air 17,000) Paramilitary 9,350

RESERVE 36,900 (Army 15,500 Navy 4,000 Air 2,600 Primary Reserve List 600 Supplementary Ready Reserve 14,700)

ORGANISATIONS BY SERVICE

Army (Land Forces) ε33,000

FORCES BY ROLE
1 Task Force HQ
Mech Inf   3 (bde) gp (*each:* 1 armd regt, 1 AD bty, 1 engr regt, 1 arty regt, 1 recce sqn, 1 lt inf bn, 2 inf bn)
Cdo   1 unit (Joint Task Force-2)
Spt / Engr 1 indep regt
AD   1 indep regt

EQUIPMENT BY TYPE
TK • MBT 114: 114 *Leopard* C2
RECCE 303: 100 *Cougar* in store; 203 LAV-25 *Coyote*
APC ε1,278
  APC (T) ε428: 78 Bv-206; ε289 M-113; 61 M-577
  APC (W) 850
    LAV-III 651: 651 *Kodiak* (incl variants)
    MILLAV *Bison* 199
ARTY 456
  TOWED • 105mm 213: 89 C2 (M-101); 96 C3 (M-101); 28 LG1 MK II
  SP • 155mm • M-109 76: 18 M-109A4; 58 in store
  MOR 167: 167 81mm
AT
  MSL 575: 425 *Eryx*
    TOW • TOW-2 150: 150 TOW-2A/TOW-2B (incl 71 TUA M-113 SP)

RCL • 84mm: • CARL GUSTAV 1,040: 1,040 M2/M3
RL • 66mm: some M-72 *LAW*
AD
SAM
  SP 34: 34 ADATS
  MANPAD: some *Starburst*
GUNS • 40mm • TOWED 57: 57 L40/60 in store

Reserve Organisations

Canadian Rangers
Army 144 (patrols) unit

Militia 15,500 reservists
Army   10 (bde) gp
Armd   18 unit (bn level)
Inf   51 unit (bn level)
Arty   15 unit (bn level)
Engr   12 unit (bn level)
Log   20 unit (bn level)
Medical 14 coy

Navy (Maritime Command) ε12,000

EQUIPMENT BY TYPE
SUBMARINES • TACTICAL • SSK 2:
  2 *Victoria* (UK *Upholder*, commisioned but not yet op.) each with 6 single TT each with Mk48 *Sea Arrow* HWT
PRINCIPAL SURFACE COMBATANTS 16
  DESTROYERS • DDG 4:
    3 mod *Iroquois* each with 1 76mm gun, 2 CH-124A (SH-3A) *Sea King* ASW hel each with Mk 46 LWT, 2 triple ASTT (6 eff.), 1 Mk 41 VLS with 29+ SM-2 MR SAM
    1 mod *Iroquois* in reserve with 1 76mm gun, 2 CH-124A (SH-3A) *Sea King* ASW hel each with Mk 46 LWT, 2 triple ASTT (6 eff.) each with 29+ SM-2 MR SAM, 1 Mk 41 VLS with 29+ SM-2 MR SAM
  FRIGATES • FFG 12:
    12 *Halifax* (capacity either 1 CH-124A (SH-3A) *Sea King* ASW hel or 1 SH-3B *Sea King* CH-124 (SH-3) ASW) each with 1 CH-124A (SH-3A) *Sea King* ASW hel with 2 Mk 46 LWT, 2 Twin 324mm ASTT (4 eff.) with 24 Mk 46 LWT, 2 quad (8 eff.) with 8 RGM-84 *Harpoon* tactical SSM, 2 octuple Mk 48 *Sea Sparrow* with 16 RIM-7P *Sea Sparrow* SAM
PATROL AND COASTAL COMBATANTS 14
  MCDV 12: 12 *Kingston*
  PCC 2: 2 *Fundy* (trg)

FACILITIES
Base 1 located at Esquimalt (Pacific), 1 located at Halifax (Atlantic), 1 located at Ottawa (National)

Logistic Support
LOGISTICS AND SUPPORT 6: 2 AGOR; 2 AO; 1 AOT; 1 diving tender/spt

Reserves 4,000 reservists

HQ	1 HQ located at Quebec
Navy	24 div (tasks: crew 10 of the 12 MCDV; harbour defence; naval control of shipping)

Air Force (Air Command) 14,500; 2,600 reservists (total 19,100)

Flying hours   210 hrs/year

FORCES BY ROLE

HQ (AF)	1 Air Div (13 air wg responsible for operational readiness, combat air-spt, air tpt, SAR, MR and trg)
Strategic Force	1 (NORAD Regional) HQ located at North Bay with 11 NORTH WARNING SYSTEM LONG RANGE; 36 NORTH WARNING SYSTEM SHORT RANGE; 4 Coastal; 2 Transportable
FGA	5 sqn with total 60 CF-18A (F/A-18A) Hornet/CF-18B (F/A-18B) Hornet
MP	4 sqn with 18 CP-140 Aurora; 3 CP-140A Arcturus (environmental patrol)
SAR / tpt	4 sqn with 7 CC-115 Buffalo; 4 CC-138 (DHC-6) Twin Otter
Tkr / tpt	4 sqn with 5 KC-130H Hercules; 19 CC-130E (C-130E) Hercules; 8 CC-130H (C-130H) Hercules; 1 sqn with 5 CC-137 (C-137); 3 CC-150 Polaris; 2 A-310MRTT
VIP	1 sqn with 8 CC-144B Challenger
Trials and testing / Trg / Rotational	some sqn with 62 CF-18A (F/A-18A) Hornet/CF-18B (F/A-18B) Hornet*
Hel	3 sqn with 15 CH-149 Cormorant; 8 sqn with 75 CH-146 Griffon; 3 sqn with 29 CH-124 (SH-3) Sea King

EQUIPMENT BY TYPE

AIRCRAFT 140 combat capable

FGA

F/A-18 122: 83 CF-18A (F/A-18A) Hornet; 39 CF-18B (F/A-18B) Hornet

Hawk **MK115** (First of 20 advanced wpns/tactics trg) delivered)

MP 21: 18 CP-140 Aurora; 3 CP-140A Arcturus (environmental patrol)

TKR • KCC-130 (KC-130) 5: 5 KC-130H Hercules

TPT 56

C-130 27: 19 CC-130E (C-130E) Hercules; 8 CC-130H (C-130H) Hercules

CC-115 *Buffalo* 7

CC-137 (C-137) 5

CC-138 (DHC-6) *Twin Otter* 4

CC-144B *Challenger* 8

CC-150 *Polaris* 5

TPT/TKR 2: 2 A-310MRTT

TRG 166: 26 CT-156 Harvard II/T-6A Texan II; 136 CT-114 Tutor; 4 CT-142 Dash 8 Nav Trainer

HELICOPTERS

SAR 15: 15 CH-149 Cormorant

ASW 29: 29 CH-124 (SH-3) Sea King

UTL 84: 9 CH-139 Jet Ranger; 75 CH-146 Griffon

RADAR 53

AD RADAR • NORTH WARNING SYSTEM 47: 11 NORTH WARNING SYSTEM LONG RANGE; 36 NORTH WARNING SYSTEM SHORT RANGE

STRATEGIC 6: 4 Coastal; 2 Transportable

MSL • TACTICAL • AAM

AIM-7: some AIM-7M Sparrow

AIM-9: some AIM-9L Sidewinder

FACILITIES

Radar Stn	47 with 11 NORTH WARNING SYSTEM LONG RANGE AD Radar; 36 NORTH WARNING SYSTEM SHORT RANGE AD Radar (North Warning) located in Canada
Centre	1 with 4 Coastal Strategic; 2 Transportable Strategic (Regional Op Control (ROCC) (2 Sector Op Control Centres (SOCC)) located in Canada
School	2 with 136 CT-114 Tutor trg ac; 4 CT-142 Dash 8 Nav Trainer trg ac; 9 CH-139 Jet Ranger utl hel (flying) located in Canada

NATO Flight Training Canada

AIRCRAFT

TRG 26: 26 CT-156 Harvard II/T-6A Texan II; first of 20 Hawk MK115 (advanced wpns/tactics trg) delivered

Paramilitary 9,350

Canadian Coast Guard has merged with Department of Fisheries and Oceans.

Canadian Coast Guard 4,700 (civilian)

PATROL AND COASTAL COMBATANTS 32: 18 PC; 10 PCI; 4 PCO

LOGISTICS AND SUPPORT 64

ACV 4

AGB 5

POLAR ICEBREAKER 1: 1 Gulf class Type 1300

RIVER ICEBREAKER 4: 1 Modified R class Type 1200; 3 R class Type 1200

AGOR 12 (fishery)

AGOS 11

Navaids 29

Trg 3

HELICOPTERS

UTL 27:

BO-105 16

BELL 206 6: 6 Bell 206L Longranger

Bell 212 5

Department of Fisheries and Oceans 4,650 (civilian)

PATROL AND COASTAL COMBATANTS 38: 38 PB

LOGISTICS AND SUPPORT 52: 17 AGB; 35 AGOR

DEPLOYMENT

AFGHANISTAN

NATO • ISAF 1,576

BOSNIA-HERZEGOVINA

EU • EUFOR II ε800

CYPRUS

UN • UNFICYP 1

DEMOCRATIC REPUBLIC OF CONGO

UN • MONUC 8

EGYPT

MFO 29

HAITI
UN • MINUSTAH 4

MIDDLE EAST
UN • UNTSO 8 obs

SERBIA AND MONTENEGRO
NATO • KFOR I 3-2

SIERRA LEONE
UN • UNAMSIL 5 obs

SUDAN
UN • UNMIS 11

SYRIA/ISRAEL
UN • UNDOF 185 (log unit)

FOREIGN FORCES

Italy Air Force: 12 (flying trg)

United Kingdom: 1 trg unit Air Force: F-3 *Tornado* ftr ac/*Tornado* GR4 Strike/FGA ac trg; *Jaguar* GR3 FGA ac trg; *Harrier* GR7 FGA ac/*Harrier* GR7A trg; 57 Army: 500

United States US

United States Dollar $		2003	2004	2005	2006
GDP	US$	11.0tr	11.7tr		
per capita	US$	37,900	40,047		
Growth	%	3.0	4.4		
Inflation	%	2.3	2.7		
Public Debt	%	62.6	63.4		
National Def Budget					
BA	US$	456bn	490bn	423bn	
Outlay	US$	404bn	455bn	465bn	
Request					
BA	US$				441bn
Outlay	US$				447bn

Population (2004)   293,027,571

Age	0 – 14	15 – 19	20 – 24	25 – 29	30 – 64	65 plus
Male	11%	4%	4%	3%	23%	5%
Female	10%	3%	3%	3%	23%	7%

Capabilities

ACTIVE 1,473,960 (Army 502,000 Navy 376,750 Air 379,500 US Marine Corps 175,350 US Coast Guard 40,360)

CIVILIAN 10,126 (US Special Operations Command 3,376 US Coast Guard 6,750)

RESERVE 1,290,988 (Army 676,150 Navy 155,350 Air 200,800 Marine Corps Reserve 92,000 Marine Corps Aviation Reserve 11,592 Marine Stand-by Reserve 700 US Coast Guard 1,546 Naval Reserve Force 152,850)

ORGANISATIONS BY SERVICE

US Strategic Command

Combined Service 1 HQ located at Offutt AFB (NE)

Five missions –   US nuclear deterent; missile defence; global strike; info ops; ISR

US Navy

SUBMARINES • STRATEGIC • SSBN 16: 6 *Ohio* SSBN 727 each with up to 24 UGM-93A *Trident* C-4 strategic SLBM; 10 *Ohio* (mod) *SSBN 734* each with up to 24 UGM-133A *Trident* D-5 strategic SLBM

US Air Force • Air Combat Command

Bbr 4 sqn each with 64 B-52 *Stratofortress* (56 combat ready); 2 sqn each with 21 B-2A *Spirit* (16 combat ready)

Air Force Space Command

Msl 11 sqn each with 50 LGM-118A *Peacekeeper* (capacity 10 MK21s); 500 LGM-30G *Minuteman III* (capacity 3 MK12/MK12As)

Reserve Organisations

Air Force Reserve
Bbr 1 sqn with 9 B-52H *Stratofortress*

Flight Test Centre

AIRCRAFT • LRSA 3: 1 B-2 *Spirit* in testing
B-52 2: 2 B-52H *Stratofortress* in testing

Strategic Recce/Intelligence Collection (Satellites)

SPACE BASED SYSTEMS 58+
SATELLITES 34+
IMAGERY 3+: ε3 *Improved Crystal* (visible and infra-red imagery, resolution 6 inches); some *Lacrosse* (formerly *Indigo*, radar imaging satellite resolution 1–2m)
ELINT/SIGINT 7: 2 *Orion* (formerly *Magnum*); 2 *Trumpet* (successor to *Jumpseat*); 3 unknown (launched Aug 1994, May 1995, Apr 1996)
ELECTRONIC OCEAN RECCE SATELLITE: some EORSAT (detection of shipping by use of infra-red and radar)
NAVIGATIONAL SATELLITE TIMING AND RANGING 24: 24 NAVSTAR Block 2R (components of Global Positioning System (GPS) accuracy 1m)
SENSORS • NUCLEAR DETONATION DETECTION 24: (detects and evaluates nuclear detonations. Sensors deployed in NAVSTAR satellites)

Strategic Defences – Early Warning

North American Aerospace Defense Command (NORAD), a combined US/Ca org.
SPACE BASED SYSTEMS • SATELLITES 4: 4 DEFENSE SUPPORT PROGRAMME *DSP* (Infra-red surveillance and warning system. Detects missile launches, nuclear detonations, ac in afterburn, spacecraft and terrestrial infra-red events. Approved constellation: 3 operational satellites; 1 operational on-orbit spare.)

NORTH WARNING SYSTEM 15 NORTH WARNING SYSTEM LONG RANGE (range 200nm); 40 NORTH WARNING SYSTEM SHORT RANGE (range 110–150km)

OTH-B 2: 1 AN/FPS-118 *OTH-B* (500–3000nm) located at Mountain Home AFB (ID); 1 non-operational located at Maine (ME)

STRATEGIC 2 BALLISTIC MISSILE EARLY WARNING SYSTEM *BMEWS* located at Thule, GL and Fylingdales Moor, UK; 1 (primary mission to track ICBM and SLBM; also used to track satellites) located at Clear (AK)

SPACETRACK SYSTEM 11: 8 Spacetrack Radar located at Incirlik (Tu), Eglin (FL), Cavalier AFS (ND), Clear (AK), Thule (GL), Fylingdales Moor (UK), Beale AFB (CA), Cape Cod (MA); 3 Spacetrack Optical Trackers located at Socorro (NM), Maui (HI), Diego Garcia

USN SPACE SURVEILLANCE SYSTEM *NAV SPASUR* 3 strategic transmitting stations; 6 strategic receiving sites in southeast USA

PERIMETER ACQUISITION RADAR ATTACK CHARACTERISATION SYSTEM *PARCS* 1 at Cavalier AFS, (ND)

PAVE PAWS 3 at Beale AFB (CA), Cape Cod AFS (MA), Clear AFS (AK); 1 (phased array radar 5,500km range) located at Otis AFB (MA)

DETECTION AND TRACKING RADARS Kwajalein Atoll, Ascension Island, Antigua, Kaena Point (HI), MIT Lincoln Laboratory (MA)

GROUND BASED ELECTRO OPTICAL DEEP SPACE SURVEILLANCE SYSTEM *GEODSS* Socorro (NM), Maui (HI), Diego Garcia

US Army 502,000; 131,630 reservists (total 633,630)

2 Armd, 4 Inf (Mech), 2 Lt Inf, 1 Air Assault, 1 AB Divs

FORCES BY ROLE

Comd	3 army HQ, 1 AB corps HQ, 3 corps HQ
HQ	2 (integrated div HQs (for peacetime trg)) (*total:* 6 enhanced (ARNG) – 3 bde HQ per div)
Armd	2 div HQ (*each:* 1 AD bn, 1 MLRS bn, 1 avn bde, 3 armd bde HQ (*total:* 3 SP arty bn, 4 mech inf bn, 5 armd bn))
Armd Cav	1 light regt; 1 regt (OPFOR); 1 heavy regt
Mech	1 div HQ (1 mech UA HQ (1 armd bn, 1 SP arty bn, 1 bde tp bn, 2 mech inf bn), 1 MLRS bn, 1 avn bde (1 atk bn, 3 avn bn), 2 engr bn, 3 mech UA HQ (*each:* 1 armd bn, 1 mech inf bn, 1 SP arty bn, 1 cav sqn, 1 bde tp bn)); 1 div HQ (1 avn bde, 1 AD bn, 1 HQ BCT HQ (1 SP arty bn, 3 lt inf bn), 2 HQ bde HQ (*total:* 2 mech inf bn, 2 SP arty bn, 2 armd bn, 2 air aslt bn)); 2 div HQ (*each:* 1 cav sqn, 1 ADA bn, 1 avn bde, 1 MLRS bn, 3 mech bde HQ (*total:* 3 SP arty bn, 4 mech inf bn, 5 armd bn))

Inf	1 lt div HQ (1 AD bn, 1 avn bde, 2 lt inf bde HQ (*each:* 1 arty bn, 3 inf bn)); 1 indep bde HQ; 1 lt div HQ (1 lt inf BCT HQ (1 arty bn, 3 BCT bn), 1 avn bde, 2 HQ bde HQ (*each:* 1 arty bn, 3 inf bn)); 1 bn (OPFOR); 1 (indep bn) bn
SF	5 gp opcon USSOCOM (*each:* 3 SF bn)
Ranger	1 regt opcon USSOCOM (3 Ranger bn)
Air Aslt	1 div HQ (2 avn bde (*total:* 1 comd bn, 1 med tpt bn, 3 ATK ac bn, 3 aslt bn), 3 BCT bde HQ (*total:* 3 arty bn, 9 air aslt bn))
AB	1 div HQ (1 air cav bde, 1 AD bn, 1 avn bde, 3 HQ bde HQ (*total:* 3 arty bn, 9 AB bn)); 1 (task force) bde HQ
Arty	3 bde (*each:* 1 SP arty bn, 2 MLRS bn); 1 bde (1 MLRS bn, 3 arty bn); 1 bde (1 MLRS bn); 1 bde (3 MLRS bn)
Sigs	1 bn opcon USSOCOM
Avn	1 regt opcon USSOCOM (3 avn bn); 5 bde (1 army spt bde, 3 corps spt bdes, 1 trg bde)
Psyops	1 gp opcon USSOCOM (5 psyops bn)
Civil Affairs	1 bn opcon USSOCOM (5 civil affairs coy)
AD	10 bn with MIM-104 *Patriot*

EQUIPMENT BY TYPE

TK • MBT • M-1 7,620+: 7,620+ M-1 *Abrams*/M1-A1 *Abrams*/M1-A2 *Abrams*

RECCE 96: 96 Tpz-1 *Fuchs*

AIFV 6,719: 6,719 M-2 *Bradley*/M-3 *Bradley* each with 2 TOW msl, 1 30mm gun

APC 14,900

APC (T) • M-113 14,300: 14,300 M-113A2/M-113A3

APC (W) • LAV-III 600: ε600 *Stryker*

ARTY 6,530

TOWED 1,547

105mm 850: 434 M-102; 416 M-119

155mm 697: 697 M-198

SP • 155mm • M-109 2,087: 2,087 M-109A1/M-109A2/M-109A6

MRL • 227mm 830: 830 MLRS (all ATACMS-capable)

MOR 2,066

81mm 990: 990 M-252

120mm 1,076: 1,076 M-120/M-121

AT

MSL 21,955

Javelin (**Fire and Forget**) 950

M47 *Dragon* (**Command Line Of Sight**) 19,000

TOW 2,005: 1,379 HMMWV; 626 M-901

RL • 84mm: some AT-4

AMPHIBIOUS • CRAFT 124+

LCU 45:

11 LCU-1600 (capacity either 2 M1-A1 *Abrams* M-1 MBT or 350)

34 LCU-2000

LC 79+:

6 *Frank Besson* (capacity 32 M-1 *Abrams* MBT)

73+ LCM-8 (capacity either 1 MBT or 200 troops)

AIRCRAFT

RECCE 60

ARL 9: 3 COMINT/ELINT; 3 COMINT; 3 IMINT

O-2 *Skymaster* 2
RC-12 49: 37 RC-12D *Guardrail*/RC-12H *Guardrail*/RC-12K *Guardrail*; 12 RC-12P *Guardrail*/RC-12Q *Guardrail*
EW • ELINT 9: 9 RC-7 *Dash 7*
TPT 208
  C-12 136: 46 C-12C *Huron*/C-12R *Huron*; 90 C-12D *Huron*/C-12F *Huron*/C-12J *Huron*
  C-20 *Gulfstream* 3
  C-23 47: 47 C-23A *Sherpa*/C-23B *Sherpa*
  C-26 *Metro* 11
  C-31 *Friendship* 2
  C-37 2
  Cessna 182 *Skylane* 2
  U-21 *Ute* 1
  UV-18 4: 4 UV-18A *Twin Otter*
  UTL 27: 26 UC-35 *Citation*; 1 UV-20A *Chiricahua*
  TRG 3: 3 T-34 *Turbo Mentor*
HELICOPTERS
  OBS • OH-58 463: 463 OH-58A *Kiowa*/OH-58C *Kiowa*
  SAR • HH-60 7: 7 HH-60L *Black Hawk*
  ATK 1,477
    AH-1 370: 370 AH-1S *Cobra*
    AH-64 732: 732 AH-64A *Apache*/AH-64D *Apache*
    OH-58D *Warrior* 375
  ASLT 36: 36 AH-6 *Little Bird*/MH-6 *Little Bird*
  SPEC OP 523
    MH-47 463: 440 MH-47D *Chinook*; 23 MH-47E *Chinook*
    MH-60 60: 60 MH-60K *Black Hawk*/MH-60L *Black Hawk*
  UTL 1,935
    UH-60 1488: 1,484 UH-60A *Black Hawk*/UH-60L *Black Hawk*/UH-60M *Black Hawk*; 4 UH-60Q *Black Hawk*
    UH-1H *Iroquois* utl/**UH-1V** *Iroquois* spt 447
  TRG 154: 154 TH-67 *Creek*
UAV • RECCE 42+
  TAC 18+: 12 RQ-5A *Hunter*; 6 in store; some *Raven* on lease
  STRATEGIC 24: 24 RQ-7A *Shadow*
AD • SAM 1281+
  SP 798: 703 FIM-92A *Avenger* (veh-mounted *Stinger*); 95 M-6 *Linebacker* (4 *Stinger* plus 25mm gun)
  TOWED 483: 483 MIM-104 *Patriot*
  MANPAD: some FIM-92A *Stinger*
RADAR • LAND 251: 98 AN/TPQ-36 *Firefinder* (arty); 56 AN/TPQ-37 *Firefinder* (arty); 60 AN/TRQ-32 *Teammate* (COMINT); 32 AN/TSQ-138 *Trailblazer* (COMINT); 5 AN/TSQ-138A *Trailblazer*

Reserve Organisations

Army Reserve National Guard 351,350 reservists
Capable of manning 8 divs after mobilisation
FORCES BY ROLE

Armd	1 div; 2 indep bde
Armd Cav	1 regt
Scout	1 gp
Medium	3 div
Mech	3 div; 5 indep bde
Inf	1 light div; 7 indep bde; 1 indep bn

SF	2 gp opcon USSOCOM (*total*: 3 SF bn)
Arty	42 indep bn
Fd Arty	17 bde HQ (mostly non-operational)
Engr	40 indep bn
Avn	32 indep bn
WMD	32 WMD-CST (Weapons of Mass Destruction Civil Support Teams)
AD	2 indep bn with MIM-104 *Patriot*; 9 indep bn with FIM-92A *Avenger*

Army Reserve 324,100 reservists

Atk hel	2 bn with AH-64 *Apache*
SH	2 bn with CH-47 *Chinook*; 1 coy with CH-47 *Chinook*
Aslt	2 coy with UH-60 *Black Hawk*
Inf	5 div (exercise); 7 div (trg)
ATK ac	2 bn
Psyops	2 gp opcon USSOCOM
Civil Affairs	36 (coys) bn opcon USSOCOM; 12 (4 comd, 8 bde) HQ opcon USSOCOM
Regional Spt	13 comd

Army Stand-by-Reserve 700 reservists
Trained individuals for mobilisation

US Navy 376,750
2 fleet areas, Atlantic and Pacific. Surface combatants divided in 5 fleets: 2nd - Atlantic; 3rd - Pacific; 5th - Indian - Ocean, Persian Gulf, Red Sea; 6th - Mediterranean; 7th - W Pacific; plus Military Sealift Command (MSC); Naval Special Warfare Command; Naval Reserve Force (NRF).
EQUIPMENT BY TYPE
SUBMARINES up to 80
  STRATEGIC • SSBN 16:
    6 *Ohio* SSBN 727 opcon US STRATCOM (SSBN-727) each with up to 24 UGM-93A *Trident* C-4 strategic SLBM
    10 *Ohio* (Mod) SSBN 734 opcon US STRATCOM each with up to 24 UGM-133A *Trident* D-5 strategic SLBM
  TACTICAL up to 64: up to 8 SSGN/SSN in refit
    SSGN 2:
      1 SSGN-726 mod *Ohio* SSBN with 154 *Tomahawk* tactical LAM
      1 SSGN-728 mod *Ohio* SSBN with 154 *Tomahawk* tactical LAM
    SSN 54:
      20 *Los Angeles* each with 4 single 533mm TT each with Mk48 *Sea Arrow* HWT/UGM-84 *Harpoon* tactical USGW
      23 *Los Angeles*, imp each with up to 12 *Tomahawk* tactical LAM, 4 single 533mm TT each with Mk48 *Sea Arrow* HWT/UGM-84 *Harpoon* tactical USGW
      8 *Los Angeles*, mod each with 12 *Tomahawk* tactical LAM, 4 single 533mm TT each with Mk48 *Sea Arrow* HWT/UGM-84 *Harpoon* tactical USGW
      2 *Seawolf* each with 8 x1 660mm TT each with up to 45 *Tomahawk* LAM/UGM-84C *Harpoon* USGW, Mk48 *Sea Arrow* HWT
      1 *Sturgeon* with 4 single 533mm TT each with Mk48 *Sea Arrow* HWT/*Tomahawk* tactical SLCM

PRINCIPAL SURFACE COMBATANTS 118
AIRCRAFT CARRIERS 12
CVN 9:

1 *Enterprise* (capacity 20 F-14 *Tomcat* ftr ac; 36 F/A-18 *Hornet* FGA ac; 4 EA-6B *Prowler* ELINT EW ac; 4 E-2C *Hawkeye* AEW ac; 6 S-3B *Viking* ASW ac; 4 SH-60F *Seahawk* ASW hel; 2 HH-60H *Rescue Hawk Seahawk* SAR hel) (CVN-65) with 3 Mk 29 *Sea Sparrow* octuple each with RIM-7M/RIM-7P, 2 Mk 49 RAM (may be fitted) with 21 RIM-116 RAM SAM

8 *Nimitz* (capacity 20 F-14 *Tomcat* ftr ac; 36 F/A-18 *Hornet* FGA ac; 4 EA-6B *Prowler* ELINT EW ac; 4 E-2C *Hawkeye* AEW ac; 6 S-3B *Viking* ASW ac; 4 SH-60F *Seahawk* ASW hel; 2 HH-60H *Rescue Hawk Seahawk* SAR hel) (CVN-68 (one in refit)) each with 2–3 Mk 29 *Sea Sparrow* octuple each with RIM-7M/RIM-7P, 2 Mk 49 RAM (Replaces *Phalanx* systems CVN 69,76 remainder due to fitted.) with 42 RIM-116 RAM SAM

CV 3:

1 *John F. Kennedy* (capacity 20 F-14 *Tomcat* ftr ac; 36 F/A-18 *Hornet* FGA ac; 4 EA-6B *Prowler* ELINT EW ac; 4 E-2C *Hawkeye* AEW ac; 6 S-3B *Viking* ASW ac; 4 SH-60F *Seahawk* ASW hel; 2 HH-60H *Seahawk* SAR hel) (CV-67) with 3 Mk 29 *Sea Sparrow* octuple each with RIM-7M/RIM-7P, 2 Mk 49 RAM with 42 RIM-116 RAM SAM

1 *Kitty Hawk* (capacity 20 F-14 *Tomcat* ftr ac; 36 F/A-18 *Hornet* FGA ac; 4 EA-6B *Prowler* ELINT EW ac; 4 E-2C *Hawkeye* AEW ac; 6 S-3B *Viking* ASW ac; 4 SH-60F *Seahawk* ASW hel; 2 HH-60H *Seahawk* SAR hel) (CV-63) each with 3 Mk 29 *Sea Sparrow* octuple each with RIM-7M/RIM-7P, 2 Mk 49 RAM with 42 RIM-116 RAM SAM

CRUISERS • CG • *TICONDEROGA* 27:

22 Aegis *Baseline* 2/3/4 (CG-52-CG-74) each with 2 SH-60B *Seahawk* ASW hel, 1 comd and control, 2 quad (8 eff.) each with RGM-84 *Harpoon* tactical SSM, 2 61 cell Mk 41 VLS (122 eff.) each with SM-2 ER SAM/*Tomahawk* tactical LAM, 2 127mm gun

3 Aegis *Baseline* 1 each with 2 SH-60B *Seahawk* ASW hel, 4 SM-2 MR SAM

8 RGM-84 *Harpoon* tactical SSM, 2 127mm gun

DESTROYERS • DDG 49

28 *Arleigh Burke* Flight I/II each with 2 triple ASTT (6 eff.) each with Mk 46 LWT, 2 quad (8 eff.) each with RGM-84 *Harpoon* tactical SSM, 2 Mk 49 RAM with 42 RIM-116 RAM SAM, 1 32 cell Mk 41 VLS (32 eff.) with ASROC tactical/ASSM SSM tactical/SM-2 ER SAM/*Tomahawk* tactical LAM, 1 64 cell Mk 41 VLS (64 eff.) with ASROC tactical/ASSM SSM tactical/SM-2 ER SAM/*Tomahawk* tactical LAM, 1 127mm gun, *Aegis* comd and control, 1 hel landing platform

11 *Arleigh Burke* Flight IIA each with 2 triple ASTT (6 eff.) each with Mk 46 LWT, 2 quad (8 eff.) each with RGM-84 *Harpoon* tactical SSM, 1 32 cell Mk 41 VLS (32 eff.) with ASROC tactical/ASSM SSM tactical/SM-2 ER SAM/*Tomahawk* tactical LAM, 1 64 cell Mk 41 VLS (64 eff.) with ASROC tactical/ASSM SSM tactical/SM-2 ER SAM/*Tomahawk* tactical LAM, 1 127mm gun, 1 *Aegis* comd and control , 1 hel landing platform

10 *Spruance* (capacity either 2 SH-60B *Seahawk* ASW hel or 2 SH-2G *Super Seasprite* ASW hel) (DD 963) each with 2 SH-60B *Seahawk* ASW hel, 2 triple ASTT (6 eff.) each with 14 Mk 46 LWT, 1 octuple (8 eff.) with 24 RIM-7M *Sea Sparrow* SAM, 2 quad (8 eff.) each with AGM-84 *Harpoon* ASM tactical, 1 Mk 49 RAM with 21 RIM-116 RAM SAM, 2 32 cell Mk 41 VLS (64 eff.) each with ASROC/ASSM SSM/*Tomahawk* LAM, 2 127mm gun

FRIGATES • FFG 30:

22 *Oliver Hazard Perry* (capacity 2 SH-60B *Seahawk* ASW hel) each with 2 triple 324mm ASTT (6 eff.) with 24 Mk 46 LWT, 1 Mk 13 GMLS with 36 SM-1 MR SAM, 4 RGM-84D *Harpoon*/RGM-84F

8 *Oliver Hazard Perry* (capacity 2 SH-60B *Seahawk* ASW hel) in reserve each with 2 triple 324mm ASTT (6 eff.) with 24 Mk 46 LWT, 1 Mk 13 GMLS with 4 RGM-84D *Harpoon* tactical SSM/RGM-84F tactical SSM, 36 SM-1 MR SAM, 1 76mm gun

PATROL AND COASTAL COMBATANTS 21:
PCI 8
PFC 13: 13 *Cyclone*
MINE WARFARE • MINE COUNTERMEASURES 26
MCM 14:

9 *Avenger* (MCM-1) each with 1 SLQ-48 MCM system, 1 SQQ-32(V)3 Sonar (mine hunting)

5 *Avenger* in reserve each with 1 SLQ-48 MCM system, 1 SQQ-32(V)3 Sonar (mine hunting)

MHC 12:

2 *Osprey* (MHC-1) each with 1 SLQ-48 MCM system, 1 SQQ-32(V)2 Sonar (mine hunting)

10 *Osprey* in reserve each with 1 SLQ-48 MCM system, 1 SQQ-32(V)2 Sonar (mine hunting)

Minelayers (none dedicated, but mines can be laid from attack SSN, aircraft and surface ships)

COMMAND SHIPS • LCC 2:

2 *Blue Ridge* (capacity 3 LCPL; 2 LCVP; 700 troops; 1 SH-3H *Sea King* utl hel)

AMPHIBIOUS
PRINCIPAL AMPHIBIOUS SHIPS 38
LHD 7:

7 *Wasp* (capacity 60 tanks; 1,890 troops; 5 AV-8B *Harrier II* FGA; 42 CH-46E *Sea Knight* spt hel; 6 SH-60B *Seahawk* ASW hel; 3 LCAC(L) ACV) each with 2 Mk 29 *Sea Sparrow* octuple with 32 RIM-7M/RIM-7P, 2 Mk 49 RAM with 42 RIM-116 RAM SAM

LHA 5:

5 *Tarawa* (capacity 100 tanks; 1,900 troops; 6 AV-8B *Harrier II* FGA ac; 12 CH-46E *Sea Knight* spt hel; 9 CH-53 *Sea Stallion* spt hel; 4 LCU) each with 2 Mk 49 RAM with 42 RIM-116 RAM SAM

LPD 12:

11 *Austin* (capacity 40 tanks; 788 troops; 2 LCAC(L) ACV/LCU; 6 CH-46E *Sea Knight* spt hel)

1 *San Antonio* (capacity 720 troops; 2 LCAC(L); 14 AAAV; 1 UA-53E *Sea Stallion* hel or 2 CH-46 *Sea Knight* or 1 MV-22 Osprey)

LSD 15:

    3 *Anchorage* (capacity 38 tanks; 330 troops; 3 LCAC(L) ACV) each with 1 hel landing platform

    4 *Harpers Ferry* (capacity 40 tanks; 500 troops; 2 LCAC(L) ACV) each with 1–2 Mk 49 RAM with 21–42 RIM-116 RAM SAM, 1 hel landing platform (for 2 Ch-35)

    8 *Whidbey Island* (capacity 40 tanks; 500 troops; 4 LCAC(L) ACV) each with 2 Mk 49 RAM with 42 RIM-116 RAM SAM, 1 hel landing platform (for 2 CH-53)

CRAFT 192+: some LCU

  LCU 37+: 37 LCU-1610 (capacity 1 MBT)

  LCVP 8

  LCM 75

  ACV 72: 72 LCAC(L) (capacity either 1 MBT or 60 troops)

SF EQUIPMENT 6: 6 DDS opcon USSOCOM

FACILITIES

Base	1 opcon EUCOM located at Makri, Gr, 1 opcon EUCOM located at Naples, It, 1 opcon EUCOM located at Soudha Bay, Gr, 1 opcon EUCOM located at La Maddalena, It, 1 opcon US Pacific Fleet located at Yokosuka, J, 1 opcon EUCOM located at Rota, Sp, 1 opcon US Pacific Fleet located at Sasebo, J
Naval airbase	1 opcon US Pacific Fleet (plus naval comms facility) located at Andersen AFB, 1 opcon US Pacific Fleet located at Diego Garcia, BIOT
SEWS	1 opcon US Pacific Fleet located at Pine Gap, Aus
Comms facility	1 opcon US Pacific Fleet located at NW Cape, Aus, 1 opcon USNORTHCOM located at Thurso, UK, 1 opcon USNORTHCOM located at Edzell, UK
SIGINT Stn	1 opcon US Pacific Fleet located at Pine Gap, Aus
Intel facility	1 opcon USNORTHCOM located at Thurso, UK, 1 opcon USNORTHCOM located at Edzell, UK
Support facility	1 opcon EUCOM located at Ankara, Tu, 1 opcon EUCOM located at Izmir, Tu, 1 opcon US Pacific Fleet located at Diego Garcia, BIOT, 1 opcon US Pacific Fleet located at Singapore, Sgp

Combat Logistics Force

LOGISTICS AND SUPPORT

AOE 5: 4 *Sacramento* (capacity 2 CH-46E *Sea Knight* spt hel); 1 *Supply* (capacity 3 CH-46E *Sea Knight* spt hel)

Naval Reserve Surface Forces

PRINCIPAL SURFACE COMBATANTS

FRIGATES 8: 8 FFG

MINE WARFARE • MINE COUNTERMEASURES 15: 5 MCM spt; 10 MHC

INSHORE UNDERSEA WARFARE 45: 45 HDS/IBU/ MIUW

Navy Stand-by-Reserve 2,500 reservists

Naval Inactive Fleet

PRINCIPAL SURFACE COMBATANTS 9

  AIRCRAFT CARRIERS 4: 4 CV

  BATTLESHIP 2: 2 BB

  DESTROYERS 4: 4 DD

AMPHIBIOUS

  LS 5: 5 LKA

  CRAFT 5: 5 LCT

LOGISTICS AND SUPPORT 9: 5 AG

  AO 2: 2 *Aditya*

Military Sealift Command (MSC) • Naval Fleet Auxiliary Force

LOGISTICS AND SUPPORT 35: 6 AE (ammo); 6 AF

  AH (MED) 2: 2 *Mercy* each with 1 hel landing platform

  ATF 5

  T-AO 13

  T-AOE (RAS) 3

Prepositioning Program/Maritime Prepositioning Program

LOGISTICS AND SUPPORT 36: 16 AVB (avn log) (MPS); 2 (USAF); 1 T-AK (USN); 2 (USAF); 4 (army)

  T-AKR • LMSR T-AKR 8: 8 *Watson* (army)

  T-AOT 3 (DLA)

Sealift Force

LOGISTICS AND SUPPORT 24

  T-AKR 19

    AKR 8: 8 *Algol*

    LMSR T-AKR 11: 11 *Bob Hope/Gordon/Shughart*

  T-AOT 5: 5 T5 type

Special Mission Ships

LOGISTICS AND SUPPORT 26: 1 T-AGF; 1 T-AG; 2 T-AGM; 12 T-AGOS; 9 T-AGS; 1 T-ARC

US Maritime Administration Support • National Defense Reserve Fleet

LOGISTICS AND SUPPORT 49

  T-AK 42: 39 T-AK (breakbulk); 3 T-AK (heavy lift)

  T-AO 7

Ready Reserve Force

Ships at readiness of 4/5/10/20 days

LOGISTICS AND SUPPORT 78: 2 AVB (Avn Log)

  T-ACS 10: 10 *Keystone State*

  T-AK 24: 17 T-AK (breakbulk); 7 T-AK (heavy lift)

  T-AKR 31

  T-AOT 9: 5; 4 T-AOT (OPDS)

  T-AP 2

Augmentation Force • Active

Cargo handling   1 bn

Reserve

Cargo handling   12 bn

Naval Aviation 98,588

Operates from 12 carriers, 11 air wings (10 active 1 reserve). Average air wing comprises 9 sqns: 3 with 12

F/A-18C, 1 with 10 F-14, 1 with 8 S-3B, 1 with 6 SH-60, 1 with 4 EA-6B, 1 with 4 E-2C, a spt with C-2.

FORCES BY ROLE

COMD	1 sqn with E-6A *Mercury TACAMO*
Air wing	11 wg
Ftr	4 sqn with F-14A *Tomcat*; 5 sqn with F-14B *Tomcat*; 3 sqn with F-14D *Tomcat*
FGA	23 sqn with F/A-18C *Hornet*; 1 sqn with F/A-18A *Hornet*
ASW	10 sqn with S-3B *Viking*; 10 sqn with SH-60B *Seahawk* (LAMPS Mk III); 10 sqn with HH-60H *Rescue Hawk*/SH-60F *Seahawk*
ELINT	2 sqn with EP-3 *Orion*; 2 sqn with EA-6B *Prowler*
MP	12 (land-based) sqn with P-3C *Orion*
AEW	10 sqn with E-2C *Hawkeye*
MCM	1 sqn with MH-53E *Sea Dragon*
ECM	14 sqn with EA-6B *Prowler*
Op spt tpt	4 sqn with CH-46 *Sea Knight*/MH-60S *Knight Hawk*; 1 sqn with MH-53E *Sea Dragon*
Tpt	2 sqn with C-2A *Greyhound*
Trg	2 sqn with TH-57B *Sea Ranger*/TH-57C *Sea Ranger*; 2 (Aggressor) sqn with F/A-18 *Hornet*; 14 sqn with T-2C *Buckeye*/T-34C *Turbo Mentor*/T-44 *Pegasus*/T-44A *Pegasus*

EQUIPMENT BY TYPE

AIRCRAFT 983 combat capable

FTR 178

  F-5 23: 20 F-5E *Tiger II* in store; 3 F-5F *Tiger II*

  F-14 155: 35 F-14A *Tomcat*; 13 in store; 62 F-14B *Tomcat*; 1 in store; 44 F-14D *Tomcat*

FGA • F/A-18 574: 49 F/A-18A *Hornet*; 14 in store; 1 in testing; 23 F/A-18B *Hornet*; 316 F/A-18C *Hornet*; 2 in testing; 43 F/A-18D *Hornet*; 3 in testing; 54 F/A-18E *Super Hornet*; 4 in store; 64 F/A-18F *Super Hornet*; 1 in store

ASW • S-3 108: 107 S-3B *Viking**; 1 in store

MP • P-3 225: 24 P-3B *Orion* in store; 177 P-3C *Orion**; 24 P-3B in store

EW • ELINT 103

  EA-6 91: 91 EA-6B *Prowler*

  EP-3 12: 11 EP-3E *Orion*; 1 EP-3J *Orion* in store

AEW • E-2 7: 7 E-2C *Hawkeye* in store

COMD • E-6 16: 1 E-6A *Mercury TACAMO*; 15 E-6B *Mercury*

TKR • KC-130 5: 5 KC-130F *Hercules*

TPT 65

  C-12 4: 4 C-12C *Huron*

  C-2 37: 36 C-2A *Greyhound*; 1 in store

  C-20 7: 1 C-20A *Gulfstream III*; 2 C-20D *Gulfstream III*; 4 C-20G *Gulfstream IV*

  C-26 7: 7 C-26D *Metro III*

  C-37 1

  CT-39 1: 1 CT-39G *Sabreliner*

  LC-130 3: 2 LC-130F *Hercules* in store; 1 LC-130R *Hercules* in store

  VP-3 5: 5 VP-3A *Orion*

UTL 37

  RC-12 4: 2 RC-12F *Huron*; 2 RC-12M *Huron*

  U-6 2: 2 U-6A *Beaver*

  UC-12 26: 22 UC-12B *Huron*; 4 in store

  UC-35 1: 1 UC-35D *Citation Encore*

  UP-3 4: 4 UP-3A *Orion*

TRG 689

  T-2 104: 91 T-2C *Buckeye*; 13 in store

  T-34 308: 303 T-34C *Turbo Mentor*; 5 in store

  T-38 *Talon* 9

  T-39 24: 1 T-39D *Sabreliner*; 8 T-39G *Sabreliner*; 15 T-39N *Sabreliner*

  T-44 55: 55 T-44A *Pegasus*

  T-45 149: 74 T-45A *Goshawk*; 75 T-45C *Goshawk*

  TA-4 17: 7 TA-4J *Skyhawk*; 10 in store

  TC-12 21: 21 TC-12B *Huron*

  TE-2 2: 2 TE-2C *Hawkeye*

TRIALS AND TEST 49

  NF-14 4: 1 NF-14A *Tomcat*; 1 NF-14B *Tomcat*; 2 NF-14D *Tomcat*

  NF/A-18 6: 1 NF/A-18A *Hornet*; 2 NF/A-18C *Hornet*; 3 NF/A-18D *Hornet*

  NP-3 12: 1 NP-3C *Orion*; 11 NP-3D *Orion*

  NT-34 1: 1 NT-34C *Mentor* in testing

  NU-1 1: 1 NU-1B *Otter* in testing

  QF-4 18: 2 QF-4N *Phantom II*; 16 QF-4S *Phantom II*

  X-26 2: 2 X-26A in testing

  X-31 1: 1 X-31A in testing

  YF-4J *Phantom II* 1 (prototype, FGA)

  YSH-60 *Seahawk* 1 (prototype)

  YSH-60 3: 1 YSH-60B *Seahawk* in store; 1 YSH-60F *Seahawk* in store

HELICOPTERS

MCM 33: 30 MH-53E *Sea Dragon*; 3 in store

OBS • OH-58 3: 3 OH-58A *Kiowa*

SAR 123

  HH-1 23: 18 HH-1N *Iroquois*; 5 in store

  HH-46 32: 32 HH-46D *Sea Knight*

  HH-60 23: 23 HH-60H *Rescue Hawk*

  UH-3 45: 44 UH-3H *Sea King*; 1 in store

ATK • AH-1 4: 3 AH-1Z *Super Cobra*; 1 in store

ASW • SH-60 213: 144 SH-60B *Seahawk*; 1 in store; 67 SH-60F *Seahawk*; 1 in store

SPEC OP • MH-60 50: 8 MH-60R *Strike Hawk*; 42 MH-60S *Knight Hawk*

SPT 28

  CH-46 10: 10 CH-46D *Sea Knight*

  CH-53 18: 9 CH-53D *Sea Stallion* in store; 9 CH-53E *Sea Stallion* in store

UTL 19

  UH-1 5: 1 UH-1N *Iroquois*; 2 UH-1Y *Iroquois*; 2 in store

  UH-46D *Sea Knight* 9

  UH-60 3: 3 UH-60L *Black Hawk*

  VH-3 2: 2 VH-3A *Sea King* (2 VIP, 1 trials)

TRG 132

  TH-57 126: 44 TH-57B *Sea Ranger*; 73 TH-57C *Sea Ranger*; 9 in store

  TH-6 6: 6 TH-6B in testing

TEST • N-SH-60 3: 3 N-SH-60B *Seahawk*

MSL • TACTICAL

  ASM

    AGM-45: some AGM-45 *Shrike*

AGM-84: some AGM-84A *Harpoon*
AGM-114: some AGM-114 *Hellfire*
AGM-119: some AGM-119A *Penguin 3*
AGM-88: some AGM-88A *HARM*
AAM
AIM-7: some AIM-7 *Sparrow*
AIM-9: some AIM-9 *Sidewinder*
AIM-54: some AIM-54A *Phoenix*
AIM-120: some AIM-120 *AMRAAM*

Naval Aviation Reserve

FORCES BY ROLE

Ftr   3 sqn with F/A-18D *Hornet*

ASW   1 sqn with HH-60F/SH-60F *Seahawk*; 1 sqn
            with SH-60B *Seahawk*

MR   7 sqn with P-3C *Orion*; EP-3J *Orion*

AEW   1 sqn with E-2C *Hawkeye*

MSC   1 sqn with UH-3H *Sea King*; 2 sqn with HH-
            60H *Rescue Hawk*

ECM   1 sqn with EA-6B *Prowler*

Log spt   1 wg (1 log spt sqn with C-40A *Clipper*,
            3 log spt sqn with C-20 *Gulfstream*,
            4 tactical tpt sqn with C-130T *Hercules*, 6 log
            spt sqn with C-9B *Nightingale*; DC-9)

Trg   1 (aggressor) sqn with F-5E *Tiger II*/F-5F *Tiger
            II*; 1 (aggressor) sqn with F/A-18 *Hornet*

EQUIPMENT BY TYPE
AIRCRAFT 99 combat capable
  FGA • F/A-18 52: 49 F/A-18A *Hornet*; 3 F/A-18B
  Hornet
  RECCE • DC-130 1: 1 DC-130A *Hercules*
  MP • P-3 47: 47 P-3C *Orion**
  EW • ELINT • EA-6 4: 4 EA-6B *Prowler*
  AEW • E-2 9: 9 E-2C *Hawkeye*
  TPT 49
    C-130 20: 20 C-130T *Hercules*
    C-40 6: 6 C-40A *Clipper*
    C-9 15: 15 C-9B *Nightingale*
    DC-9 8
    UTL • UC-12 22: 6 UC-12B *Huron*; 6 UC-12F *Huron*;
    10 UC-12M *Huron*
  HELICOPTERS
    MCM 8: 8 MH-53E *Sea Dragon*
    SAR 24
      HH-60 16: 16 HH-60H *Rescue Hawk*
      UH-3 8: 8 UH-3H *Sea King*
    ASW • SH-60 11: 5 SH-60B *Seahawk*; 6 SH-60F *Seahawk*

Naval Reserve Force 152,850 reservists

Delivery veh	1 det opcon USSOCOM
Naval special warfare	3 det opcon USSOCOM; 6 (Gp) det opcon USSOCOM; 1 det opcon USSOCOM
Special boat	2 sqn opcon USSOCOM; 2 unit opcon USSOCOM
HQ	1 (CINCSOC) det opcon USSOCOM
SEAL	5 det opcon USSOCOM

US Marine Corps 175,350; 11,311 reservists (total 186,661)

3 Marine Expeditionary Force (MEF), 2 Marine Expeditionary Brigade (MEB) drawn from 3 div.

FORCES BY ROLE

MARDIV   1st MARDIV (1 cbt engr bn, 1 recce
                    bn, 1 arty regt (4 arty bn), 1 amph aslt
                    bn, 1 armd bn, 2 (LAV-25) lt armd
                    recce bn, 3 inf regt (*each*: 3 inf bn));
                    2nd MARDIV (1 cbt engr bn, 1 amph
                    aslt bn, 1 recce bn, 1 arty regt (4 arty
                    bn), 1 lt armd recce bn, 1 armd bn, 3
                    inf regt (*each*: 3 inf bn));
                    3rd MARDIV (1 recce bn, 1 arty regt
                    (2 arty bn), 1 cbt engr bn, 1 cbt sp bn
                    (1 lt armd recce coy, 1 amph aslt coy),
                    2 inf regt (*each*: 3 inf bn))

Anti-terrorism   1 bde (1 anti terrorist bn, 1 Chemical
                    and Biological Incident Response
                    Force, 1 (1 HQ 7 region coys) Marine
                    Security Gd bn, 1 (Atlantic and Pacific)
                    Marine Corps Security Force bn)

Spec Ops   1 force (3 recce bn, 3 MEF recce coy)

Force Service Sp Gp 3 gp; 1 sqn

EQUIPMENT BY TYPE
TK • MBT • M-1 403: 403 M1-A1 *Abrams*
RECCE 252: 252 LAV-25 *Coyote* (25mm gun, plus 189 variants excluding 50 mor, 95 ATGW see below)
AAV • AAV-7 1,311: 1,311 AAV-7A1 (all roles)
ARTY 1,511
  TOWED 926
    105mm • M-101 331: 331 M-101A1
    155mm 595: 595 M-198
  MOR • 81mm 585: 50 LAV-M; 535 M-252
AT
  MSL 2,299
    Predator 1,121
    TOW 1,178: 1,083; 95 LAV-TOW
  RL 2,764
    83mm 1,650: 1,650 SMAW
    84mm 1,114: 1,114 AT-4
AD • SAM • MANPAD: some FIM-92A *Stinger*
RADAR • LAND 23: 23 AN/TPQ-36 *Firefinder* (arty)

Marine Corps Aviation 34,686

3 active Marine Aircraft Wings (MAW) and 1 MCR MAW

Flying hours   248 hrs/year on ac; 365 hrs/year on tpt ac; 277 hrs/year on hel

FORCES BY ROLE

Ftr   14 sqn with 168 F/A-18A *Hornet*/F/A-18C
            Hornet/F/A-18D *Hornet*

FGA   7 sqn with 112 AV-8B *Harrier II*

ECM   4 sqn with 20 EA-6B *Prowler*

Tkr   3 sqn with 36 KC-130F *Hercules*/KC-130R
            Hercules

Atk hel   4 sqn with 72 AH-1W *Cobra*;
            36 UH-1N *Iroquois*

Spt hel	4 sqn with 38 CH-53D *Sea Stallion*; 16 sqn with 174 CH-46E *Sea Knight*; 4 sqn with 80 CH-53E *Sea Stallion*
Trg	3 sqn with 36 CH-46E *Sea Knight*/CH-53D *Sea Stallion*/V-22 *Osprey*; 1 sqn with 15 CH-53E *Sea Stallion*; 1 sqn with 8 KC-130F *Hercules*; 1 sqn with 12 AV-8B *Harrier II*; 14 TAV-8B *Harrier*; 1 sqn with 34 AH-1W *Cobra*/HH-1N *Iroquois*/UH-1N *Iroquois*; 1 sqn with 40 F/A-18A *Hornet*/F/A-18B *Hornet*/F/A-18C *Hornet*/F/A-18D *Hornet*; 2 T-34C *Turbo Mentor*
AD	5 bty with FIM-92A *Avenger*; FIM-92A *Stinger*
UAV	2 sqn with RQ-2B *Pioneer*

EQUIPMENT BY TYPE
AIRCRAFT 344 combat capable
 FGA 344
  F/A-18 213: 28 F/A-18A *Hornet*; 4 F/A-18B *Hornet*; 86 F/A-18C *Hornet*; 95 F/A-18D *Hornet*
  AV-8 131: 131 AV-8B *Harrier II*
 EW • ELINT • EA-6 27: 27 EA-6B *Prowler*
 TKR • KC-130 48: 31 KC-130F *Hercules*; 4 KC-130J *Hercules*; 13 KC-130R *Hercules*
 TPT 3
  C-20 1: 1 C-20G *Gulfstream IV*
  C-9 2: 2 C-9B *Nightingale*
 UTL 8
  UC-12 7: 7 UC-12B *Huron*
  UC-35 1: 1 UC-35D *Citation Encore*
 TRG 17
  T-34 2: 2 T-34C *Turbo Mentor*
  TAV-8 15: 15 TAV-8B *Harrier*
HELICOPTERS
 SAR 14
  HH-1 9: 9 HH-1N *Iroquois*
  HH-46 5: 5 HH-46D *Sea Knight*
 ATK • AH-1 148: 144 AH-1W *Cobra*; 3 AH-1Z *Super Cobra*; 1 in store
 SPT 57
  CH-53 49: 40 CH-53D *Sea Stallion*; 9 in store
  VH-60N *Presidential Hawk* 8 (VIP tpt)
 UTL 85
  UH-1 74: 72 UH-1N *Iroquois*; 2 UH-1Y *Iroquois*
  VH-3 11: 11 VH-3D *Sea King* (VIP tpt)
UAV • RQ-2: some RQ-2B *Pioneer*
MSL • TACTICAL
 ASM: some AGM-114 *Hellfire*; some AGM-65 *Maverick*; some TOW
 AAM: some AIM-120 *AMRAAM*; some AIM-7 *Sparrow*; some AIM-9 *Sidewinder*

Reserve Organisations

Marine Corps Reserve 92,000 reservists

Marine	1 div (1 amph aslt bn, 1 arty bn (5 arty bn), 1 recce bn, 1 cbt engr bn, 1 (LAV-25) lt armd recce bn, 3 inf regt (*each*: 3 inf bn))
Spec Ops	1 force (1 MEF recce coy, 1 recce bn)
Force Service Sp Gp	1 gp

Marine Corps Aviation Reserve 11,592 reservists
FORCES BY ROLE

Ftr	4 sqn with 48 F/A-18A *Hornet*
Tkr	2 sqn with 28 KC-130T *Hercules*
Atk hel	2 sqn with 36 AH-1W *Cobra*; 18 UH-1N *Iroquois*
Spt hel	2 sqn with 24 CH-46E *Sea Knight*; 2 sqn with 32 CH-53E *Sea Stallion*
Trg	1 sqn with 13 F-5E *Tiger II* (aggressor)
AD	1 bn (2 Bty) with FIM-92A *Avenger*

EQUIPMENT BY TYPE
AIRCRAFT 64 combat capable
 FTR • F-5 13: 12 F-5E *Tiger II*; 1 F-5F *Tiger II*
 FGA • F/A-18 51: 51 F/A-18A *Hornet*
 TKR • KC-130 28: 28 KC-130T *Hercules*
 UTL 10
  RC-12 4: 4 RC-12M *Huron*
  UC-12 3: 3 UC-12B *Huron*
  UC-35 3: 2 UC-35C *Citation Ultra*; 1 UC-35D *Citation Encore*
HELICOPTERS
 ATK • AH-1 40: 40 AH-1W *Cobra*
 SPT 45
  CH-46 24: 24 CH-46E *Sea Knight*
  CH-53 21: 21 CH-53E *Sea Stallion*
 UTL • UH-1 20: 20 UH-1N *Iroquois*

Marine Stand-by Reserve 700 reservists
Trained individuals for mobilisation

US Coast Guard 40,360 (Military); 6,750 (civilian); 1,546 reservists (Coast Guard) (total 41,906 plus 6,750 civilians)
PATROL AND COASTAL COMBATANTS 131
 PBC 89: 40 *Marine Protector*; 49 *Farallon*
 PSO 2
 PSOH 40: 1 *Alex Haley*; 13 *Famous*; 12 *Hamilton*; 14 *Reliance*
LOGISTICS AND SUPPORT 92
 ABU 16: 16 *Juniper*
 AGB 3: 3 *Polar Icebreaker*
 Trg 2
 WLI 5
 WLIC 13
 WLM 15: 15 *Keeper*
 WLR 18
 WTGB 9
 YTM 11

US Coast Guard Aviation 7,960
AIRCRAFT
 MP 17: 17 HU-25 *Guardian*
 SAR • HC-130 22: 22 HC-130H *Hercules*
 TPT 4
  C-130 2: 2 C-130J *Hercules*
  C-37 1
  VC-4A 1
HELICOPTERS
 SAR 119: 35 HH-60J *Jayhawk*; 84 HH-65A (AS-366G1) *Dauphin II*
 UTL • A-109 8: 8 MH-68A (A-109E) *Power*

US Air Force (USAF) 379,500 (plus 183,200 ANG and Air Force Reserve)

Flying hours ftr 189, bbr 260, tkr 308, airlift 343

Air Combat Command (ACC)

Comprises of 4 air forces, 23 ac wings. Almost the entire USAF (plus active force ANG and AFR) is divided into 10 Aerospace Expeditionary Forces (AEF). Each AEF is on call for 90 days every 15 months, and at least 2 of the 10 AEFs are on call at any one time. Each AEF with 10,000–15,000 personnel comprises 90 multi-role ftr and bbr ac, 31 intra-theatre refuelling aircraft and 13 aircraft for intelligence, surveillance, reconnaissance and EW missions.

FORCES BY ROLE

HQ (AF) 1 HQ located at Langley AFB (VA)

Bbr	5 (non-STRATCOM mission capable) sqn each with 60+ B-1B *Lancer*; 4 sqn opcon US STRATCOM each with 64 B-52 *Stratofortress* (56 combat ready); 2 sqn opcon US STRATCOM each with 21 B-2A *Spirit* (16 combat ready)
Ftr	11 sqn with 198+ F-15 *Eagle*; 2 sqn with 36+ F-117 *Nighthawk*; 6 sqn with 108+ A-10 *Thunderbolt II*/OA-10 *Thunderbolt II*; 6 sqn with 66+ F-15E *Strike Eagle*; 1 sqn with 16 F/A-22A *Raptor*; 21 sqn with 378+ F-16C *Fighting Falcon*/F-16D *Fighting Falcon*
FAC	7 sqn with A-10 *Thunderbolt II*/OA-10A *Thunderbolt II*
Recce	3 sqn with RC-135/U-2S; 1 sqn with E-8 J-STARS
EW	2 sqn with EC-130 *Commando Solo*
AEW	1 wg (6 AEW sqn with E-3B *Sentry*/E-3C *Sentry*)
SAR	6 sqn with HC-130N *Hercules*/HC-130P *Hercules*/HH-60G *Pave Hawk*
Trg	1 (aggressor) sqn with 18+ F-16C *Fighting Falcon*/F-16D *Fighting Falcon*
UAV	3 sqn with RQ-1B *Predator*/RQ-4A *Global Hawk*

Air Mobility Command (AMC)

Provides strategic, tactical, special op airlift, aero medical evacuation, SAR and weather recce.

HQ (AF)	1 HQ located at Scott AFB (IL)
Air	2 Air Forces (*total:* 12 air wg)
Strategic tpt	4 sqn with C-5 *Galaxy*; 7 sqn with C-17 *Globemaster*; 1 sqn with C-141 *Starlifter*
Tactical tpt	9 sqn with C-130 *Hercules*
Op spt tpt	8 sqn with C-12 *Huron*; C-20 *Gulfstream*; C-21 *Learjet*; C-37; C-40 *Clipper*; C-9 *Nightingale*; VC-25 *Air Force One*; UH-1 *Iroquois*
Tkr	18 sqn with KC-135 *Stratotanker*; 4 sqn with KC-10A *Extender DC-10*
Medevac	3 sqn with C-9A *Nightingale*
Weather recce	some sqn with WC-135

ACC AND AMC EQUIPMENT SUMMARY

AIRCRAFT 1,577 combat capable

LRSA 191

B-1 88: 65 B-1B *Lancer*; 23 in store

B-2 21: 21 B-2A *Spirit*

B-52 82: 65 B-52H *Stratofortress*; 18 in store

BBR 184: 184 F-111 *Aardvark* in store

FTR 865

F-22 16: 16 F/A-22A *Raptor*

F-117 *Nighthawk* 51

F-16 399: 9 F-16A *Fighting Falcon*; 350 in store; 40 F-16B *Fighting Falcon* in store

F-15 399: 381 F-15A *Eagle*/F-15B *Eagle*/F-15C *Eagle*/F-15D *Eagle*; 18 in store

FGA 1,382

F-16 914: 586 F-16C *Fighting Falcon*; 118 F-16D *Fighting Falcon*; 212 F-15E *Strike Eagle*

A-10 229: 119 A-10A *Thunderbolt II*; 110 in store

F-4 237: 237 F-4D *Phantom II*/F-4E *Phantom II*/F-4G *Phantom II* in store

FAC • OA-10 85: 85 OA-10A *Thunderbolt II**

RECCE 252

E-8 J-STARS 17: 17 E-8C J-STARS

E-9 2: 2 E-9A

OC-135 *Boeing 707* 3

RC-135 21: 16 RC-135V *Rivet Joint*/RC-135W *Rivet Joint*; 3 RC-135S *Cobra Ball*; 2 RC-135U *Combat Sent*

RF-4 162: 162 RF-4C *Phantom II* in store

TU-2 4: 4 TU-2S

U-2 31: 30 U-2S; 1 on lease

WC-130 8: 8 WC-130H *Hercules* in store

WC-135 3: 2 WC-135C/WC-135W *Constant Phoenix*; 1 in store

AEW • E-3 31: 31 E-3B *Sentry*/E-3C *Sentry*

COMD 30

E-4 4: 4 E-4B

EC-135 26 in store

SEAD • EF-111 33: 33 EF-111A *Raven* in store

SPEC OPS • MC-130 25: 25 MC-130E *Combat Talon*/MC-130H *Combat Talon II*/MC-130P *Combat Shadow*

SAR • HC-130 17: 17 HC-130N *Hercules*/HC-130P *Hercules*

TKR 310: 255 KC-130J and KC-130R *Hercules*/KC-135A *Stratotanker*/KC-135E *Stratotanker*/KC-135T *Stratotanker*; 55 in store

TPT 541

C-12 19: 11 C-12C *Huron*/C-12D *Huron*/C-12F *Huron*/C-12J *Huron*; 8 in store

C-130 197: 182 C-130B *Hercules*/C-130E *Hercules*/C-130H *Hercules*/C-130J *Hercules*; 15 in store

C-135 5: 4 C-135B *Stratolifter*/C-135C *Stratolifter*/C-135E *Stratolifter*; 1 C-135C *Stratolifter* in store

C-141 4: 4 C-141B *Starlifter*/C-141C *Starlifter* in store

C-17 101: 101 C-17A *Globemaster*

C-20 15: 3 C-20A *Gulfstream III* in store; 5 C-20C *Gulfstream III*; 5 C-20G,C-20H (C-20B) *Gulfstream III*; 2 C-20H *Gulfstream IV*

C-21 76: 76 C-21A *Learjet*

C-22 2: 2 C-22B in store

C-32 4: 4 C-32A

C-38 10: 10 C-38A *Astra*

C-5 80: 28 C-5A *Galaxy*; 50 C-5B *Galaxy*; 2 C-5C *Galaxy*

C-9 23: 23 C-9A *Nightingale*/C-9C *Nightingale*

UV-18 3: 3 UV-18B *Twin Otter*

VC-25 2: 2 VC-25A

TPT/TKR • KC-10 59: 59 KC-10A *Extender DC-10*
TRG 1513
  AT-38 44: 15 AT-38 *Talon* trg ac/AT-38B *Talon*; 29 AT-38B *Talon* in store
  CT-43A 5 in store
  T-1 180: 180 T-1A *Jayhawk*
  T-3 111: 111 T-3A *Firefly* in store
  T-37 505: 317 T-37B *Tweet*; 188 in store
  T-38 545: 422 T-38A *Talon*/T-38C *Talon*; 123 in store
  T-41 *Mescalero* 6; 101 on lease
  T-43 11: 9 T-43A; 2 in store
  TC-135 2: 2 TC-135S/TC-135W
  TC-18 2: 2 TC-18E *Aria*
  TE-8A *JSTARS* 1
  RANGE INST • EC-18 5: 2 EC-18B *Aria*/EC-18D *Aria*; 3 in store
HELICOPTERS
SAR 76
  HH-1 11: 11 HH-1H *Iroquois* in store
  HH-60 65: 65 HH-60G *Pave Hawk*
  SPEC OP • MH-53 18: 7 MH-53J *Pave Low III*/MH-53M *Pave Low IV*; 11 in store
  UTL • UH-1 62: 62 UH-1N *Iroquois* in store
UAV • RECCE 20
  TAC • RQ-1 12: 11 RQ-1B *Predator*; 1 in testing
  STRATEGIC • RQ-4 8: 2 RQ-4A *Global Hawk*; 6 in testing
MSL • TACTICAL 41,120+
  ASM 26,120+
    AGM-129 400+: 400+ AGM-129A *Advanced Cruise Missile*
    AGM-130 400+: 400+ AGM-130A
    AGM-142 *Popeye* 150+
    AGM-65 17,000+: 17,000+ AGM-65A *Maverick*/AGM-65B *Maverick*/AGM-65D *Maverick*/AGM-65G *Maverick*
    AGM-84 70+: 70+ AGM-84B *Harpoon*
    AGM-86 1,600+: 900+ AGM-86B *ALCM*; 700+ AGM-86C *CALCM*
    ARM • AGM-88 6500+: 6,500+ AGM-88A *HARM*/AGM-88B *HARM*
  AAM 15,000+
    AIM-120 5,000+: 5,000+ AIM-120A *AMRAAM*/AIM-120B *AMRAAM*/AIM-120C *AMRAAM*
    AIM-7 3,000+: 3,000+ AIM-7M *Sparrow*
    AIM-9 7,000+: 7,000+ AIM-9M *Sidewinder*
BOMB • PGM • JSOW 130+: 130+ AGM-154

Air Education and Training Command

FORCES BY ROLE

Air	7 sqn (AFR personnel) trained to use ac; 2 air forces (*total*: 11 air wg)
Flying trg	8 wg with AT-38 *Talon*; T-1 *Jayhawk*; T-37 *Tweet*; T-38 *Talon*; T-43; T-6 *Texan II*
Mission trg	25 sqn with F-16 *Fighting Falcon*; F-15 *Eagle*; A-10 *Thunderbolt II*; OA-10 *Thunderbolt II*; E-3 *Sentry*; MC-130 *Hercules*; HC-130 *Hercules*; KC-135 *Stratotanker*; C-130 *Hercules*; C-135 *Stratolifter*; C-17 *Globemaster*; C-21 *Learjet*; C-5 *Galaxy*; HH-60 *Seahawk*; UH-1N *Iroquois*

Trials and testing	some unit with 2 B-1 *Lancer*; 1 B-2 *Spirit*; 2 B-52 *Stratofortress*; 10 F-22 *Raptor*; 1 F-117 *Nighthawk*; 38 F-16 *Fighting Falcon*; 11 F-15A *Eagle*/F-15B *Eagle*/F-15C *Eagle*/F-15D *Eagle*; 2 A-10 *Thunderbolt II*; U-2; 1 EC-130E *Commando Solo*; 1 E-3B *Sentry*; AC-130 *Spectre*; KC-135 *Stratotanker*; 4 C-12 *Huron*; C-135 *Stratolifter*; C-17 *Globemaster*; AT-38 *Talon*; T-3 *Firefly*; 3 T-38C *Talon*; T-39 *Sabreliner*; NC-130 *Hercules*; TG-10 *Glider*; 3 HH-60 *Seahawk*; UH-1 *Iroquois*

EQUIPMENT BY TYPE
AIRCRAFT 62 combat capable
  LRSA 5: 2 B-1 *Lancer* in testing; 1 B-2 *Spirit* in testing; 2 B-52 *Stratofortress* in testing
  FTR 60: 10 F-22 *Raptor* in testing; 1 F-117 *Nighthawk* in testing; 38 F-16 *Fighting Falcon* in testing; 11 F-15A *Eagle*/F-15B *Eagle*/F-15C *Eagle*/F-15D *Eagle* in testing
  FGA 2: 2 A-10 *Thunderbolt II* in testing
  EW • EC-130 1: 1 EC-130E *Commando Solo* in testing
  AEW • E-3 1: 1 E-3B *Sentry* in testing
  TKR: some KC-135 *Stratotanker* in testing
  TPT 4+: 4 C-12 *Huron* in testing; some C-135 *Stratolifter* in testing
  TRG • T-38 3: 3 T-38C *Talon* in testing
  TRIALS AND TEST: some TG-10 *Glider* in testing
HELICOPTERS • SAR 3: 3 HH-60 *Seahawk* in testing

Air Force Space Command

Provides ballistic missile warning, space control, worldwide satellite operations and maintains ICBM force

FORCES BY ROLE

HQ (AF)	1 HQ located at Petersen AFB (CO)
Msl	11 sqn opcon US STRATCOM each with 50 LGM-118A *Peacekeeper* (capacity 10 MK21s); 500 LGM-30G *Minuteman III* (capacity 3 MK12/MK12As)

EQUIPMENT BY TYPE
MSL • STRATEGIC • ICBM 550: 50 LGM-118A *Peacekeeper* (capacity 10 MK21 nuclear warheads); 500 LGM-30G *Minuteman III* (capacity 3 MK12 nuclear warheads/MK12A nuclear warheads)

Reserve Organisations

Air National Guard 108,100 reservists

FORCES BY ROLE

Ftr	3 sqn with F-15 *Eagle*; 1 sqn with F-16 *Fighting Falcon*
FGA	6 sqn with A-10 *Thunderbolt II*/OA-10 *Thunderbolt II*; 3 sqn with F-15A *Eagle*/F-15B *Eagle*; 23 sqn with F-16 *Fighting Falcon*
Special Ops	1 sqn opcon USSOCOM with 7 EC-130E *Commando Solo*/EC-130H *Compass Call*
SAR	3 sqn with HC-130 *Hercules*/MC-130 *Hercules*; HH-60 *Seahawk*

Strategic tpt	1 sqn with C-38 *Astra*; 1 sqn with C-21 *Learjet*; 1 sqn with C-17 *Globemaster*; 1 sqn with C-5 *Galaxy*; 1 sqn with C-141 *Starlifter*
Tactical tpt	24 sqn with C-130E *Hercules*/C-130H *Hercules*/C-130J *Hercules*
Tkr	11 sqn with KC-135E *Stratotanker*; 13 sqn with KC-135R *Stratotanker*
Mission trg	7 sqn with F-16 *Fighting Falcon*; F-15 *Eagle*; C-130 *Hercules*

EQUIPMENT BY TYPE
AIRCRAFT 733 combat capable
  FTR 169
    F-16 59: 36 F-16A *Fighting Falcon*; 23 F-16B *Fighting Falcon*
    F-15 110: 110 F-15A *Eagle*/F-15B *Eagle*/F-15C *Eagle*/F-15D *Eagle*
  FGA 546: 433 F-16C *Fighting Falcon*; 41 F-16D *Fighting Falcon*; 72 A-10A *Thunderbolt II*
  FAC • OA-10 18: 18 OA-10A *Thunderbolt II**
  EW • EC-130 7: 7 EC-130E *Commando Solo*/EC-130H *Compass Call*
  SPEC OPS • MC-130 4: 4 MC-130P *Combat Shadow*
  SAR • HC-130 9: 9 HC-130N *Hercules*/HC-130P *Hercules*
  TKR • KC-135 220: 220 KC-135A *Stratotanker*/KC-135E *Stratotanker*/KC-135R *Stratotanker*/KC-135T *Stratotanker*
  TPT 271+
    C-130 226+: 226 C-130B *Hercules*/C-130E *Hercules*/C-130H *Hercules*/C-130J *Hercules*
    C-130 *Hercules* some
    C-141 16: 16 C-141B *Starlifter*/C-141C *Starlifter*
    C-21 *Learjet* some
    C-21 2+: 2 C-21A *Learjet*
    C-26 11: 11 C-26B *Metro III*
    C-38 2: 2 C-38A *Astra*
    C-5 14: 14 C-5A *Galaxy*
  HELICOPTERS • SAR • HH-60 21: 21 HH-60G *Pave Hawk*

Air Force Reserve 75,100 reservists

FORCES BY ROLE

(▲ including associate sqn – personnel only)

Bbr	1 sqn opcon US STRATCOM with 9 B-52H *Stratofortress*
FGA	2 sqn with A-10 *Thunderbolt II*/OA-10 *Thunderbolt II*; 3 sqn with F-16C *Fighting Falcon*/F-16D *Fighting Falcon*
Special Ops	1 sqn ▲ MC-130P *Combat Shadow Hercules* SPEC OPS ac; 2 sqn opcon USSOCOM each with 14 MC-130E *Combat Talon*
SAR	3 sqn with HH-60 *Seahawk*; 2 sqn with HC-130 *Hercules*
Strategic tpt	1 sqn ▲ C-9 *Nightingale* tpt ac; 2 sqn with C-5A *Galaxy*; 5 sqn with C-141B *Starlifter*; 6 sqn ▲ C-17 *Globemaster* tpt ac; 4 sqn ▲ C-5A *Galaxy* tpt ac
Tactical tpt	11 sqn with C-130E *Hercules*/C-130H *Hercules*/C-130J *Hercules*

Tpt	4 sqn ▲ KC-10 *Extender DC-10* tpt/tkr ac
Tkr	2 sqn with KC-135E *Stratotanker*; 5 sqn with KC-135R *Stratotanker*; 1 sqn ▲ KC-135 *Stratotanker* tkr ac
Weather recce	1 sqn with WC-130H *Hercules*/WC-130J *Hercules*
Mission trg	3 sqn with F-16 *Fighting Falcon*; A-10 *Thunderbolt II*; C-130 *Hercules*

EQUIPMENT BY TYPE
AIRCRAFT 120 combat capable
  LRSA • B-52 9: 9 B-52H *Stratofortress*
  FGA 113: 63 F-16C *Fighting Falcon*; 11 F-16D *Fighting Falcon*; 39 A-10A *Thunderbolt II*
  FAC • OA-10 7: 7 OA-10A *Thunderbolt II**
  RECCE • WC-130 10: 10 WC-130H *Hercules*/WC-130J *Hercules*
  SPEC OPS • MC-130 14: 14 MC-130E *Combat Talon*
  SAR • HC-130 10: 10 HC-130N *Hercules*/HC-130P *Hercules*
  TKR • KC-135 70: 70 KC-135A *Stratotanker*/KC-135E *Stratotanker*/KC-135R *Stratotanker*/KC-135T *Stratotanker*
  TPT 209
    C-130 120: 120 C-130B *Hercules*/C-130E *Hercules*/C-130H *Hercules*/C-130J *Hercules*
    C-141 57: 57 C-141B *Starlifter*/C-141C *Starlifter*
    C-5 32: 32 C-5A *Galaxy*
  HELICOPTERS • SAR • HH-60 18: 18 HH-60G *Pave Hawk*

Air Force Stand-by-Reserve 17,600 reservists
Trained individuals for mobilisation

Civil Reserve Air Fleet
Commercial ac numbers fluctuate
AIRCRAFT • TPT 927: 252 B-747/DC-10/DC-8/L-1011 *Tristar*/MD-11 civil (long range cargo); 141 B-727/B-737/MD-80/83 civil (short range passenger); 15 A-300-B4F/B-727/DC-9/L-100 *Hercules* civil (short range cargo); 433 A-300-60ER/A-310/A-330/B-747/B-757/B-767/B-777/DC-10/L-1011 *Tristar*/MD-11 civil (long range passenger); 86 Aeromedical civil (domestic)

US Special Operations Command 31,496; 3,376 (civilian); 11,247 reservists (SOF) (total 42,743 plus 3,376 civilians)
Commands all active, reserve, and National Guard Special Operations Forces (SOF) of all services based in CONUS
FORCES BY ROLE
Combined Service 1 HQ located at MacDill AFB (FL)
FACILITIES
Centre 1 (Navy Special Warfare) no location

US Army

SF	5 gp (*each:* 3 SF bn)
Ranger	1 regt (3 Ranger bn)
Sigs	1 bn
Avn	1 regt (3 Avn bn)
Psyops	1 gp (5 Psyops bn)
Civil Affairs	1 bn (5 Civil Affairs coy)

Reserve Organisations

Army Reserve National Guard
SF 2 gp (*total:* 3 SF bn)

Army Reserve
Psyops   2 gp
Civil Affairs   12 (4 comd, 8 bde) HQ; 36 (coys) bn

US Navy

FORCES BY ROLE
Delivery veh   2 team
Naval Special Warfare   3 gp; 2 sqn; 1 comd
Special Boat   2 sqn
SEAL   8 team

EQUIPMENT BY TYPE
SF EQUIPMENT 6: 6 DDS

Naval Reserve Force
Delivery veh   1 det
Naval Special Warfare   6 (Gp) det; 3 det; 1 det
Special Boat   2 unit; 2 sqn
HQ   1 (CINCSOC) det
SEAL   5 det

US Air Force

FORCES BY ROLE
HQ (AF)   1 HQ
Air   1 wg
Special Ops 13 sqn each with 20 EC-130E *Commando Solo*/EC-130H *Compass Call*; 21 AC-130H *Spectre*/AC-130U *Spectre**; 20 MC-130E *Combat Talon*/MC-130H *Combat Talon II*/MC-130P *Combat Shadow*; 5 C-130E *Hercules*; 21 MH-53J *Pave Low III*/MH-53M *Pave Low IV*

EQUIPMENT BY TYPE
AIRCRAFT 273 combat capable
  EW • EC-130 20: 20 EC-130E *Commando Solo*/EC-130H *Compass Call*
  SPEC OPS • MC-130 20: 20 MC-130E *Combat Talon*/MC-130H *Combat Talon II*/MC-130P *Combat Shadow*
  TPT • C-130 5: 5 C-130E *Hercules*
HELICOPTERS • SPEC OP • MH-53 21: 21 MH-53J *Pave Low III*/MH-53M *Pave Low IV*

Reserve Organisations

Air National Guard
Special Ops 1 sqn with 7 EC-130E *Commando Solo*/EC-130H *Compass Call*

Air Force Reserve
Special Ops 2 sqn each with 14 MC-130E *Combat Talon*

DEPLOYMENT

AFGHANISTAN
United States Central Command 18,000 (*Op Enduring Freedom*)
NATO • ISAF 67

ANTIGUA AND BARBUDA
US Strategic Command
  Strategic Defences - Early Warning
  RADAR • STRATEGIC 1: 1 DETECTION AND TRACKING RADARS located at Antigua, AB

ASCENSION ISLAND
US Strategic Command
  Strategic Defences - Early Warning
  RADAR • STRATEGIC 1: 1 DETECTION AND TRACKING RADARS located at USAF Ascension

ATLANTIC
United States Northern Command • US Navy
  SUBMARINES 35
    STRATEGIC 10:
      10 SSBN each with 16 M-45 strategic SLBM/TN-75 nuclear warheads, SM-39 *Exocet* tactical USGW, 4 single 533mm TT, F-17/L5
    TACTICAL 25: 25 SSN
  PRINCIPAL SURFACE COMBATANTS 54
    AIRCRAFT CARRIERS 5:
      5 CVN/CV
    CRUISERS 13: 13 CG
    DESTROYERS 18: 18 DDG
    FRIGATES 18: 18 FFG
  COMMAND SHIPS • LCC 1:
    1 *Blue Ridge* (capacity 3 LCPL; 2 LCVP; 700 troops; 1 SH-3H *Sea King* utl hel)
  AMPHIBIOUS
    PRINCIPAL AMPHIBIOUS SHIPS 15: 2 LHA; 4 LPD; 4 LPH; 5 LSD
    LS 7: 1 LKA; 6 LST
United States Northern Command • HQ 2nd Fleet • US Navy
4–5 CVBG CVGP (2nd Fleet)

AUSTRALIA
United States Pacific Command • Marine Forces Pacific • US Marine Corps 31
United States Pacific Command • PACAF • US Air Force 59
United States Pacific Command • US Pacific Fleet • US Navy
SEWS   1 located at Pine Gap, Aus
Comms facility 1 located at NW Cape, Aus
SIGINT Stn   1 located at Pine Gap, Aus

BAHRAIN
United States Central Command 3,000 (Navy/USMC/Army)

BELGIUM
European Command
HQ Stuttgart-Vaihingen. Commander is SACEUR. (V Corps) Army Prepositioned Stocks (APS) for 2 armd/mech bdes, approximately 57% stored in Ge, remainder in Be (22%) Lux (21%) and NL.
US Army 788

US Navy 94
US Air Force 508

BERMUDA
United States Northern Command • US Navy 800

BRITISH INDIAN OCEAN TERRITORY
US Strategic Command

Strategic Defences - Early Warning
RADAR • STRATEGIC 2: 1 GROUND BASED ELECTRO OPTICAL DEEP SPACE SURVEILLANCE SYSTEM *GEODSS* located at Diego Garcia, BIOT

SPACETRACK SYSTEM 1: 1 Spacetrack Optical Trackers located at Diego Garcia, BIOT

United States Pacific Command • PACAF • US Air Force 701 located at Diego Garcia, BIOT

United States Pacific Command • US Pacific Fleet • US Navy 370 located at Diego Garcia, BIOT

FORCES BY ROLE
1 MPS sqn (MPS-2 with equipment for one MEB) located at Diego Garcia, BIOT with 5 logistics and support

FACILITIES
Naval airbase   1 located at Diego Garcia, BIOT
Support facility 1 located at Diego Garcia, BIOT

BOSNIA-HERZEGOVINA
EU • EUFOR II 839

COLOMBIA
United States Southern Command 400

CUBA
United States Northern Command • US Navy 510 located at Guantánamo, C

DJIBOUTI
United States Central Command 1,000 (USMC/Army/Air)

ECUADOR
United States Southern Command 290

EGYPT
MFO 1 Inf bn; 1 spt bn; 750

ETHIOPIA/ERITREA
UN 7 obs

GEORGIA
UN • UNOMIG 2 obs

GERMANY
European Command

US Armed Forces
1 Combined Service HQ (EUCOM) located at Stuttgart-Vaihingen, Ge

US Army 53,300
US Navy 330
US Air Force 15,900

US Army Europe
1 HQ (HQ US Army Europe (USAREUR)) located at Heidelberg, Ge

US Army

FORCES BY ROLE

1 armd corps HQ located at Heidelberg, Ge (1 armd div ((less 1 bde at Ft Riley)), 1 engr bde, 1 avn bde, 1 mech inf div, 1 arty bde, 1 AD bde)

EQUIPMENT BY TYPE
ARTY 312: 312 mor/MRL/SP
TK • MBT 568: 568 M-1 *Abrams*
AIFV 1266:
    1,266 M-2 *Bradley* each with 2 TOW msl, 1 30mm gun
HELICOPTERS: 115 atk

US Navy Europe
Commander is also CINCAFSOUTH

USMC • US Marine Corps 260
US Air Force Europe • US Air Force
1 HQ (AF) HQ (HQ US Airforce Europe (USAFE)) located at Ramstein AB, Ge

US Air Force Europe • 3rd Air Force
1 ftr wg located at Spangdahlem AB, Ge

US Air Force • Air Combat Command
1 airlift wg located at Ramstein AB, Ge with 16 C-130E *Hercules*; 2 C-20 *Gulfstream*; 9 C-21 *Learjet*; 6 C-9A *Nightingale*; 1 CT-43 *Boeing 737*

GREECE
European Command
US Army 52
US Navy 418 (Base facilities)
Base 1 located at Makri, Gr, 1 located at Soudha Bay, Gr

US Air Force 68
US Air Force Europe • 16th Air Force • US Air Force
Air base 1 located at Iraklion, Gr

GREENLAND
US Strategic Command

Strategic Defences - Early Warning
RADAR • STRATEGIC 2: 1 BALLISTIC MISSILE EARLY WARNING SYSTEM *BMEWS* located at Thule, GL

SPACETRACK SYSTEM 1: 1 Spacetrack Radar located at Thule, GL

GUAM
United States Pacific Command • PACAF • US Air Force 2,100
United States Pacific Command • PACAF • 13th Air Force • US Air Force • Air Combat Command 2,100
United States Pacific Command • US Pacific Fleet • US Navy 2,300

FORCES BY ROLE
1 MPS sqn (MPS-3 with equipment for one MEB) with 4 Logistics and Support

FACILITIES
Naval airbase   1 (plus naval comms facility) located at Andersen AFB

GUYANA
United States Southern Command 200

HAITI
UN • MINUSTAH 4

HONDURAS
United States Southern Command • US Army South • US Army 382

United States Southern Command • US Southern Air Force • US Air Force 205

ICELAND
United States Northern Command • US Navy 1,058
1 MR sqn with 6 P-3 *Orion*; 1 UP-3 *Orion*

IRAQ
United States Central Command 121,600 (OP IRAQ FREEDOM)
United States Central Command • US Army Central Command • US Army 85,600
1 armd bde; 1 armd div; 1 armd cav regt (cav regt is bde equivalent); 1 mech inf div; 1 Air aslt div

United States Central Command • US Navy Central Command • US Navy 2,850

United States Central Command • US Central Command Air Force • US Air Force 7,100

United States Central Command • US Marines Central Command • US Marine Corps 26,050
1 MEF HQ (1 MAW wg with up to 48 F/A-18A *Hornet*/F/A-18C *Hornet*; up to 36 F/A-18D *Hornet*; up to 64 AV-8B *Harrier II*; up to 12 KC-130 *Hercules*; up to 92 AH-1W *Cobra*; up to 90 CH-46E *Sea Knight*; up to 64 CH-53E *Sea Stallion*; up to 50 UH-1N *Iroquois*, 1 FSSG regt, 1 MARDIV div with up to 58 M-1 *Abrams*; up to 207 LAV-CP; up to 247 AAV; up to 72 M-198)

ITALY
European Command
US Army 3,070
US Navy 7,780
Base 1 located at Naples, It, 1 located at La Maddalena, It
US Air Force 4,550
US Army Europe
US Army
1 SETAF HQ Task Force located at Vicenza, It; 2 SETAF para bn located at Vicenza, It; 1 SETAF log unit (in store) (holds eqpt for Theater Reserve Unit (TRU)/Army Readiness Package South (ARPS)) with 116 M-1 *Abrams* MBT; 127 AIFV; 4 APC (T)

US Navy Europe
1 HQ located at Gaeta, It; 1 MR sqn located at Sigonella, It with 9 P-3C *Orion*
USMC • US Marine Corps 74
US Air Force Europe • 16th Air Force • US Air Force
1 (HQ 16th Air Force) HQ (AF) HQ; 1 ftr wg (2 ftr sqn each with 21 F-16C *Fighting Falcon*/F-16D *Fighting Falcon* located at Aviano, It)

JAPAN
US Air Force 14,700
United States Pacific Command • Marine Forces Pacific • US Marine Corps 17,850
1 elems MEF div
United States Pacific Command • PACAF • US Air Force 14,700
United States Pacific Command • PACAF • 5th Air Force
1 Special Ops gp located at Okinawa – Kadena AB, J
US Air Force

1 5th Air Force HQ (AF) HQ (5th Air Force) located at Okinawa – Kadena AB, J

Air Combat Command
1 ftr wg located at Okinawa – Kadena AB, J (1 SAR sqn with 8 HH-60G *Pave Hawk*, 1 AEW sqn with 2 E-3B *Sentry*, 2 ftr sqn each with 24 F-15C *Eagle*/F-15D *Eagle*); 1 ftr wg located at Okinawa - Kadena AB, J (2 ftr sqn each with 18 F-16 *Fighting Falcon* located at Misawa AB, J)

Air Mobility Command
1 airlift wg located at Yokota AB, J with 10 C-130E *Hercules*; 4 C-21 *Learjet*; 4 C-9 *Nightingale*

United States Pacific Command • US Army Pacific • US Army 28,000
1 HQ (9th Theater Army Area Command) located at Zama, J 1 HQ – HQ USARPAC

United States Pacific Command • US Pacific Fleet • US Navy
Base 1 located at Sasebo, J, 1 located at Yokosuka, J

United States Pacific Command • US Pacific Fleet • HQ 7th Fleet
1 HQ (7th Fleet) located at Yokosuka, J; 1 MCM sqn located at Sasebo, J

US Navy
> Principal Surface Combatants 9 at Yokosuka, J
> Amphibious 4 at Sasebo, J
> PRINCIPAL SURFACE COMBATANTS 10:
> 1 *Kitty Hawk* (capacity 20 F-14 *Tomcat* ftr ac; 36 F/A-18 *Hornet* FGA ac; 4 EA-6B *Prowler* ELINT EW ac; 4 E-2C *Hawkeye* AEW ac; 6 S-3B *Viking* ASW ac; 4 SH-60F *Seahawk* ASW hel; 2 HH-60H *Seahawk* SAR hel) (CV-63) each with 3 Mk 29 *Sea Sparrow* octuple each with RIM-7M/RIM-7P, 2 Mk 49 RAM with 42 RIM-116 RAM SAM
> COMMAND SHIPS • LCC 1: 1 *Blue Ridge* (capacity 3 LCPL; 2 LCVP; 700 troops; 1 SH-3H *Sea King* utl hel) located at Yokosuka, J

KOREA, REPUBLIC OF
United States Pacific Command • Eighth US Army • US Army
FORCES BY ROLE
1 (UN comd) HQ Eighth Army located at Seoul, ROK; 1 elems HQ 2ID located at Tongduchon, ROK (1 avn bde (1 aslt hel bn, 1 atk hel bn), 1 armd bde (1 armd inf bn, 2 tk bns), 1 air cav bde (2 atk hel bn), 2 SP arty bn, 2 fd arty bn with MLRS); 1 SAM bn located at Uijongbu, ROK with MIM-104 *Patriot*

EQUIPMENT BY TYPE
ARTY 45: 45 mor/MRL/SP
TK • MBT 116: 116 M-1 *Abrams*
AIFV 126:
> 126 M-2 *Bradley* each with 2 TOW Msl, 1 30mm Gun
APC 111: 111 APC (T)
United States Pacific Command • Marine Forces Pacific • US Marine Corps 180
United States Pacific Command • PACAF • US Air Force 8,900
United States Pacific Command • PACAF • 7th Air Force 8,900
> AIRCRAFT: 24 A-10 *Thunderbolt II* FGA/OA-10 *Thunderbolt II* FAC (12 of each type) located at Osan AB, ROK
US Air Force

1 HQ 7th Air Force HQ (AF) HQ (HQ 7th Air Force) located at Osan AB, ROK; 1 ftr wg located at Osan AB, ROK (1 ftr sqn with 20 F-16C *Fighting Falcon*/F-16D *Fighting Falcon*, 1 ftr sqn with 24 A-10 *Thunderbolt II*/OA-10 *Thunderbolt II* (12 of each type) located at Osan AB, ROK); 1 ftr wg located at Kusan AB, ROK (2 ftr sqn with 20 F-16C *Fighting Falcon*/F-16D *Fighting Falcon*); 1 Special Ops sqn

United States Pacific Command · US Army Pacific · US Army 25,000

United States Pacific Command · US Pacific Fleet · US Navy 40,360

KUWAIT

United States Central Command · US Army Central Command · US Army 19,700

United States Central Command · US Navy Central Command · US Navy 1,250

United States Central Command · US Central Command Air Force · US Air Force 2,700

United States Central Command · US Marines Central Command · US Marine Corps 1,600

KYRGYZSTAN

NATO 950

LIBERIA

UN · UNMIL 7 obs; 6

LUXEMBOURG

European Command
US Army 27

MACEDONIA, FORMER YUGOSLAV REPUBLIC

NATO · KFOR I 260

MEDITERRANEAN

European Command
US Navy 11,800
  US Navy Europe
US Marine Corps 2,200
  HQ 6th Fleet
US Navy
  FORCES BY ROLE
  (capacity 20 F-14 *Tomcat* ftr ac; 36 F/A-18 *Hornet* FGA ac; 4 EA-6B *Prowler* ELINT EW ac; 4 E-2C *Hawkeye* AEW ac; 6 S-3B *Viking* ASW ac; 4 SH-60F *Seahawk* ASW hel; 2 HH-60H *Seahawk* SAR hel)
  EQUIPMENT BY TYPE
  SUBMARINES · TACTICAL 3: circa 3 SSN
US Marine Corps 1 MEU gp

MIDDLE EAST

UN · UNTSO 3 obs

NETHERLANDS

European Command
US Air Force 303

NORWAY

European Command
US Air Force 50
US Army Europe
  US Army
    ARTY · SP · 155mm 36: 18 M-109 (Army Prepositioned Stocks (APS)); 18 M-198 (APS)

OMAN

United States Central Command · US Navy Central Command · US Navy 60

United States Central Command · US Central Command Air Force · US Air Force 210

PACIFIC

United States Pacific Command · US Pacific Fleet · US Navy
  SUBMARINES 35
    STRATEGIC 8:
      8 SSBN each with 16 M-45 strategic SLBM/TN-75 *nuclear warheads*, SM-39 *Exocet* tactical USGW, 4 single 533mm TT, F-17/L5
    TACTICAL 27: 27 SSN
  PRINCIPAL SURFACE COMBATANTS 58
    AIRCRAFT CARRIERS 6:
      6 CVN/CV
    CRUISERS 13: 13 CG
    DESTROYERS 24: 24 DDG
    FRIGATES 15: 15 FFG
  MINE WARFARE · MINE COUNTERMEASURES 2: 2 MCM
  COMMAND SHIPS 2: 2 LCC
  LOGISTICS AND SUPPORT 8: 8 AG
  Aircraft 1,400

PAKISTAN

United States Central Command 400 (Army/Air Force (*Op Enduring Freedom*))

PORTUGAL

European Command
US Air Force 1,008
United States Northern Command
Support facility 1 located at Lajes, Por

PUERTO RICO

United States Southern Command · Commander Naval Forces South · US Navy
1 HQ located at Roosevelt Roads

United States Southern Command · US Special Operations South
1 HQ (SOCSOUTH) located at Roosevelt Roads

QATAR

United States Central Command · US Army Central Command · US Army 800

United States Central Command · US Navy Central Command · US Navy 230

United States Central Command · US Central Command Air Force · US Air Force 5,350

United States Central Command · US Marines Central Command · US Marine Corps 160

REPUBLIC OF MARSHALL ISLANDS

US Strategic Command
  Strategic Defences - Early Warning
  RADAR · STRATEGIC 1: 1 DETECTION AND TRACKING RADARS located at US Army Kwajalein Atoll, RMI

SAUDI ARABIA

United States Central Command 300 (Army/Air Force. Trg personnel only)

SERBIA AND MONTENEGRO
NATO • KFOR I 1,800

SINGAPORE
United States Pacific Command • PACAF • US Air Force 39
1 log spt sqn located at Singapore, Sgp
United States Pacific Command • US Pacific Fleet • US Navy 50
Support facility 1 located at Singapore, Sgp

SPAIN
European Command
  US Navy
  Base 1 located at Rota, Sp
US Air Force 282

THAILAND
United States Pacific Command • Marine Forces Pacific • US Marine Corps 29
United States Pacific Command • PACAF • US Air Force 30
United States Pacific Command • US Pacific Fleet • US Navy 10

TURKEY
US Strategic Command
  Strategic Defences - Early Warning
  RADAR • STRATEGIC • SPACETRACK SYSTEM 1: 1
  Spacetrack Radar located at Incirlik, Tu
European Command
  US Navy
  Support facility 1 located at Ankara, Tu, 1 located at Izmir, Tu
US Air Force 1,650
US Air Force Europe • 16th Air Force • US Air Force
FORCES
1 air wg (ac on detachment only) located at Incirlik, Tu with F-16 *Fighting Falcon*; F-15E *Strike Eagle*; EA-6B *Prowler*; E-3B *Sentry*/E-3C *Sentry*; HC-130 *Hercules*; KC-135 *Stratotanker*; C-12 *Huron*; HH-60 *Seahawk*

FACILITIES
Air base 1 located at Incirlik, Tu

UNITED ARAB EMIRATES
United States Central Command • Air Force 1,300

UNITED KINGDOM
US Strategic Command
  Strategic Defences – Early Warning
  RADAR • STRATEGIC 2: 1 BALLISTIC MISSILE EARLY WARNING SYSTEM *BMEWS* located at Fylingdales Moor, UK
    SPACETRACK SYSTEM 1: 1 Spacetrack Radar located at Fylingdales Moor, UK

US Air Force
1 Special Ops gp located at Mildenhall, UK with 5 MC-130H *Combat Talon II*; 5 MC-130P *Combat Shadow*; 1 C-130E *Hercules*; 8 MH-53J *Pave Low III*

European Command
US Air Force 9,800
  US Navy Europe
  US Navy
  1 HQ (HQ US Navy Europe (USNAVEUR)) located at London, UK

US Air Force Europe • 3rd Air Force • US Air Force • Air Combat Command
1 HQ (AF) HQ (3rd US Air Force) located at Mildenhall, UK; 1 ftr wg located at Mildenhall (1 ftr sqn with 24 F-15C *Eagle*/F-15D *Eagle*, 2 ftr sqn each with 24 F-15E *Strike Eagle*); 1 tkr wg located at Mildenhall with 15 KC-135 *Stratotanker*

United States Northern Command
  US Navy 4,500 located at Thurso, UK
  Comms facility 1 located at Thurso, UK, 1 located at Edzell, UK
  Intel facility 1 located at Edzell, UK, 1 located at Thurso, UK

FOREIGN FORCES

Germany Air Force: some (joint jet pilot) trg sqn opcon NATO located at Sheppard AFB (TX) with 35 T-37B *Tweet*; 40 T-38A *Talon*; some (primary) trg sqn opcon NATO located at Goodyear AFB (AZ) with Beech F-33 *Bonanza* Army: 1 (battle) Army gp (trg) (Army trg area) with 35 *Leopard* 2; 26 *Marder* 1; 12 M-109A3G Air Force: 37 *Tornado* IDS Strike/FGA ac located at Fort Bliss (TX); 23 F-4F *Phantom II* FGA ac located at Fort Rucker (AL); 35 T-37 *Tweet* Trg ac located at Fort Rucker (AL); 40 T-38 *Talon* Trg ac located at Fort Rucker (AL); Missile trg located at Fort Bliss (TX); School (GAF Air Defence) located at Fort Bliss (TX); 812 (flying trg) located at Goodyear AFB (AZ); 812 (flying trg) located at Sheppard AFB (TX); 812 (flying trg) located at Holloman AFB (NM); 812 (flying trg) located at NAS Pensacola (FL); 812 (flying trg) located at Fort Rucker (AL)

Italy Air Force: 38 (flying trg)

Mexico Navy: base located at Mayport (FL)

United Kingdom Air Force: 519; 173

UNITED STATES – DEFENCE ECONOMICS

The economic expansion that began in the second half of 2003 continued at a solid pace in 2004 and incoming data, suggesting strong business and consumer confidence, indicates that the outlook for the US economy in 2005 is encouraging. With other regions of the world exhibiting varying levels of growth, the US economy has been underpinned by robust domestic demand and a steady improvement in employment, which, although rather muted by historic standards, has seen the unemployment rate fall to 5%. Despite the trend of higher energy prices and interest rate increases, real GDP grew by 4.4% in 2004 and is forecast to moderate only slightly in 2005.

However, despite high levels of confidence, employment growth and a buoyant stock market Federal Reserve Chairman Alan Greenspan continued to indicate that the economy faces 'significant uncertainties'. In particular, he drew attention to a slowdown in productivity, high energy prices, a 'frothy' housing market (fueled by an unusually low level of long-term interest rates), record consumer debt and 'evidence of anti-globalization sentiment and protectionist initiatives'.

In their 2005 Article IV review of the US economy, the International Monetary Fund (IMF) also high-lighted the extremely low level of national savings as a key policy challenge. As the domestic savings rate has fallen, foreign investment and corporate profits have increasingly had to finance government and household spending, leaving the economy vulnerable to any change in confidence by overseas investors. Tax cuts enacted between 2001 and 2003 and increased security-related spending since 11 September 2001 have resulted in a federal budget deficit of 4.25% of GDP in 2004, compared to a surplus of 2.5% of GDP in 2000. In addition to the government's fiscal deficit, sustained strong growth in real imports of consumer goods and higher oil prices have led to a ballooning of the trade deficit, which reached 5.7% of GDP in 2004. Whilst there has so far been little reluctance by the rest of the world to finance the US's twin deficits, the IMF warned that the imbalances posed 'systemic risks', particularly if productivity growth was to falter.

The Bush administration has pledged to cut the swollen federal budget deficit in half within five years, but despite an unexpected increase in tax revenues in 2005, no significant measures have been introduced to achieve that goal. Indeed, the published plan outlining how the budget deficit will be improved does not include three vital elements: it assumes that President Bush's tax cuts will be tempo-

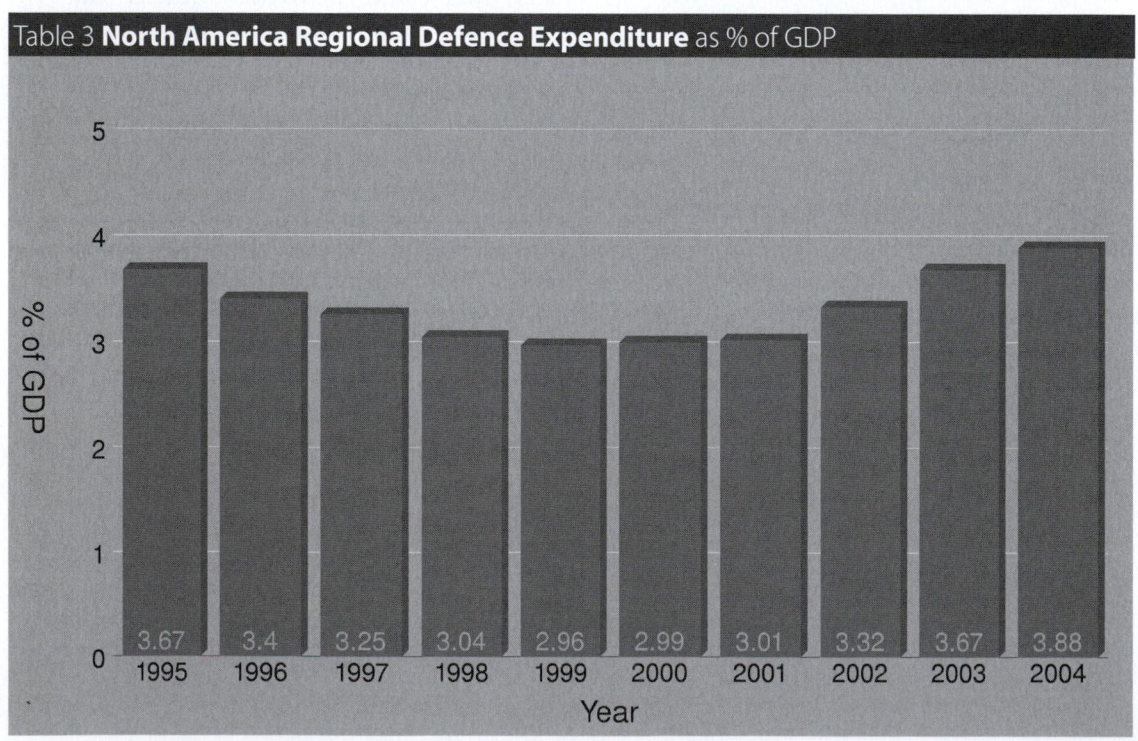

Table 3 **North America Regional Defence Expenditure** as % of GDP

Year	% of GDP
1995	3.67
1996	3.4
1997	3.25
1998	3.04
1999	2.96
2000	2.99
2001	3.01
2002	3.32
2003	3.67
2004	3.88

Table 4 National Defense Budget Authority, FY2004–FY2010

($million)	2004	2005 Estimate	2006 Request	2007 Plan	2008 Plan	2009 Plan	2010 Plan
Military Personnel	116,111	105,562	111,286	114,442	117,893	121,909	125,939
Operations & Maintenance	189,763	138,396	148,437	154.674	161,412	167,917	172,739
Procurement	83,073	78,260	78,041	91,618	101,418	105,273	111,306
R, D,T & E	64,641	68,798	69,356	66,762	66,499	72,404	68,786
Military Construction	6,137	6,098	7,809	12,290	13,647	11,148	10,515
Family housing	3,829	4,077	4,242	3,945	3,030	2,742	2,692
Revolving & Mgt Funds	7,978	2,383	3,120	2,415	1,613	3,748	3,335
Other	-521	-1,543	-1,175	-1,144	-1,102	-1,104	-998
Total Department of Defense	471,011	402,031	421,116	445,002	464,410	484,037	494,314
Department of Energy (defence-related)	16,822	17,962	17,489	17,154	16,065	16,301	16,137
Other (defence-related)	2,798	3,610	3,220	3,285	3,379	3,477	3,565
Total National Defense	490,621[a]	423,603	441,825	465,441	483,854	503,815	514,016

[a] Including US$66.1bn emergency and non-emergency supplementals

rary, despite the fact that he has indicated a desire to make them permanent; no provision for future war costs are included; and the projections do not include the borrowing that would be required for the president's proposal to establish private investment accounts for Social Security beginning in 2009. As a result, it is difficult to see how the goal of halving the deficit can be achieved without significant cuts in other discretionary spending programmes such as education, health and the environment. The non-partisan Congressional Budget Office has calculated that President Bush will fail to meet his objective and that the federal budget will still register a deficit, amounting to US$311 million in 2009.

DEFENCE BUDGET FY2006

Despite the troublesome fiscal position, the Bush administration's federal budget request for fiscal year (FY)2006, included a nominal 4.3% increase in funds (2.0% in real terms) for national defense (excluding FY2005 Iraq supplemental). The Future Years Defense Programme published at the same time indicates that planned national defense budget authority (excluding supplementals) will increase from US$441.8bn in FY2006 to US$514.0bn in FY2010. Since coming to office in 2001, President Bush has increased the non-war budget by about 45% in nominal terms or 22% after taking account of inflation.

However, due the size and allocation of recent supplemental appropriations it is becoming more difficult to assess the true budget position of the US armed forces. Commentators have noted that certain items included in the FY2005 supplemental would have occurred whether the US had been involved in overseas military operations or not and that this is obscuring analysis of the long-term funding requirements of the Department of Defense (DoD). Particular attention has been drawn to the Army Modularity Plan (AMP), intended to create new, more flexible and self-sufficient brigade-sized units, which is considered central to the long-term transformation of the ground forces, regardless of current operational commitments, and will receive US$5.0bn directly from the FY2005 supplemental and again from the as yet unsubmitted FY2006 supplemental rather than from regular defence budget appropriations, even though it is not a direct war-related cost.

The publication of the defence budget in February 2006 was foreshadowed by details of significant cuts in future military procurement outlined in a document which became public in early January 2005. The document, known as Program Budget Decisions 753 (PBD 753), revealed that, faced with mounting budget deficits and soaring costs for the 'global war on terror', the White House Office of Management and Budget (OMB) had instructed the Pentagon to trim its defence programme for the period FY2006–11 by US$55bn. However, given that the OMB also directed the Pentagon to add money to certain programmes, the largest being US$5bn annually for the AMP (which will be included in the regular defence budget from 2007, a total of US$25bn by FY2011), the DoD has in effect had to trim a net US$30bn from its six-year plan. Adjustments and cancellation are most evident in key air force and navy procurement programmes, a trend that is likely to continue with the publication of the next Quadrennial Defense Review in early 2006. However, as most of the major programme adjustments will occur beyond FY2006 and some beyond FY2008, there is scope for significant amendments by both the current or subsequent administrations.

In addition to the equipment cuts outlined in PBD 753 and the emphasis on restructuring the army, the budget also included plans to increase the Marine Corps by 2,400 and special operations forces by 1,200 personnel. The DoD will also spend US$9.9bn over five years to improve chemical and biological defences and US$9.5bn over the same period to pay for the military to play a larger role in homeland defence.

FY2005 SUPPLEMENTAL

In addition to the US$74.9bn requested for the DoD (see Table 5), the FY2005 supplemental included US$5.6bn for international activities. The majority of these funds cover State Department expenditure, including

- Embassy construction and operations in Iraq
- Police training and counter-drug activities in Afghanistan
- Support for Palestinian democracy building
- Peacekeeping missions in Haiti, Burundi, Côte d'Ivoire, the Congo and Sudan

The supplemental also includes a total of US$950m for multi-agency tsunami relief efforts and US$400m for other agencies, including the Department of Energy and the Department of Homeland Security.

An FY2006 supplemental is due to be presented in early 2006 and, given that the number of US troops in Iraq is not likely to be reduced before the middle of that year, a similar-size request is probable. The FY2005 supplemental included funds to cover the recruitment of an additional 30,000 troops that are being kept over and above normal 'end strength' levels. These additional troops are being maintained in part to provide a rotation base for Iraq, and also to help provide a buffer whilst the army reorganisation takes place. To date, since September 2001 a total of US$346bn has been appropriated for the 'global war on terror', of which US$268bn has been allocated to the DoD.

AIR FORCE

The air force requested US$127.4bn in FY2006, an increase in real terms of 5.75% from FY2005. Of that, US$32.5bn is for procurement, US$29.8bn for personnel costs, US$39.1bn for operations and maintenance activities and US$22.6bn for research and development.

The biggest equipment programme to suffer as a result of recommendations contained in PBD 753 was the F-22 fighter aircraft. At conception, the air force had planned to procure up to 750 F-22 platforms; however, repeated increases in the unit cost of each aircraft had slowly cut down the final number likely to be acquired and PBD 753 proposed that production of the platform be completely terminated in FY2009, a decision which, if implemented, would leave the air force with 170 aircraft compared to its revised target of 381 aircraft. The other major air force programme to come under scrutiny was the C-130J transport aircraft. PBD 753 indicated that procurement of both air force and Marine Corps aircraft would terminate in FY2006, 51 aircraft short of previously agreed targets. However, Congressional support for the C-130, which outfits National Guard units, has historically been very strong and in May 2005, Secretary of

US$m	Army	Navy	Marine Corps	Air Force	Defence Wide	Total
Table 5 FY2005 Supplemental Request (DoD)						
Military Operations	25,446	3,186	1,633	5,859	184	36,310
Maintenance of Equipment	3,218	682	612	758		5,270
Procurement and RDT&E	8,994	670	2,974	3,213	744	16,569
Military Construction	990	107		301		1,399
Revolving & Management Fund		32			1,311	1,343
Other Programmes	2,567	288	3	429	10,734	14,022
- Support to Allies/Coalition	400			27	1,570	1,997
- Security Forces Fund					6,985	6,985
- Classified & Other Programmes	2,167	288	3	402	2,179	5,040
Supplemental Request	41,216	4,967	5,222	10,561	12,974	74,943

Defense Donald Rumsfeld announced that the costs of terminating the programme were so prohibitive that another 42 aircraft would in fact be procured. This would, however, leave the air force with only 79 C-130Js, significantly short of its 168-aircraft requirement. The budget document also hit other air force programmes, ending the Wind Corrected Munitions Dispenser-Extended Range programme and cutting back on funds for the next-generation E-10A surveillance and battle-management aircraft programme.

Although escaping direct attention in PBD 753, concern has been expressed by DoD acquisition offi-

cials about the spiralling costs of unmanned aerial vehicles, whose price has risen in line with their increasing capability. The increased complexity of these platforms has seen the price of a *Global Hawk* climb from around US$16m per unit in 1997 to US$30m for the current RQ-4A vehicle, while the cost of the latest RQ-4B, currently in the early stages of production, could reach close to US$45m per vehicle. Although UAVs have repeatedly demonstrated their value in Iraq and Afghanistan, the air force has made it clear that increasing acquisition costs could force them into re-evaluating the need for unmanned versus manned platforms. The air force intends to purchase 51 production-version *Global Hawks*.

The FY2006 air force budget reflects the increasing trend of spending on space programmes with the budget request increasing from US$8.1bn in FY2005 to US$9.9bn in FY2006. The request is broad based and earmarks funds for the modernisation of communications, missile-launch-warning, navigation and surveillance satellites across the services and follows the provision of additional resources for space programmes outlined in PBD 753. The Transformational Satellite Communication (TSAT) programme request is US$836m in FY2006 to continue development of a system based on laser communications and greatly enhanced radio-frequency capability, which would free users from current bandwidth constraints and provide improved interoperability and connectivity to support net-centric operations First launch of the four-satellite constellation is due in FY2013. A total of US$226m is requested for the revamped Space Radar (SR) programme, formerly the Space Based Radar, up from US$75m in FY2005, to start preparations for the possible launch in FY2008 of two quarter-scale spacecraft equipped with synthetic aperture radar and moving target indicator. The first launch of the final SR system is scheduled for FY2015. And there is a US$1.2bn request for the Advanced Extremely High Frequency Satellite Communication System, due to replace the current Milstar communications system from FY2008.

NAVY

The navy's budget request for FY2006 totals US$125.4bn, including funds for the Marine Corps, of which US$37.7bn is for personnel costs, US$35.9bn for operations and maintenance, US$29.7bn for procurement and US$18bn for research and development.

Table 6 Major US Research & Development FY2004–FY2006

Service	Designation Classification	FY2004 Value ($m)	FY2005 Value ($m)	FY2006 Value ($m)
Joint				
FGA	JSF	4,102	4,326	4,867
UAV	Various	722	1,179	912
hel	V-22	482	342	275
tpt	C-130	116	183	239
SIGINT	Aerial Common Sensor	102	145	298
ASM	Small Diameter Bomb	118	85	96
Army				
hel	UH-60 *Blackhawk*	155	108	115
FCS	Future Combat System	1,624	2,800	3,404
Navy				
FGA	F/A-18E/F	164	128	89
CVN	Carrier Replacement	306	351	308
DDG	DDX	1,015	1,163	1,084
LCS	Littoral Combat Ship	158	452	576
SSN	*Virginia*	141	171	155
AEW	EC-2	328	590	629
sat	MUOS	84	389	470
hel	H-1 Upgrades	98	173	42
SAM	*Standard*	73	110	145
Air Force				
bbr	B-2	171	270	285
tpt	C-17	175	199	165
FGA	F-22	918	570	479
FGA	F-15	120	131	124
FGA	F-16	88	105	155
sat	AEHF	775	606	665
sat	NAVSTAR	234	289	401
sat	SBIRS	621	594	756
sat	TSAT	325	467	835
sat	Space Based Radar	165	73	225

Since 2003, the navy has been implementing its Fleet Response Plan designed to increase the effectiveness of naval forces available for deployment, at a time when personnel numbers and available platforms are both decreasing. During this process the number of active naval personnel has been reduced by nearly 10,000, with the reduction of a further 13,200 scheduled in FY2006. The size of the navy's fleet has also been falling steadily for several years and initiatives outlined in PBD 753 indicate that this trend will continue. According to Chief of Naval Operations Admiral Vernon Clark, speaking at the Senate Armed Services Committee, both crew numbers and platform numbers can be reduced through technology and by swapping crews on forward-deployed ships. He went on to indicate that transformational technology and new manning concepts will enable the navy to 'attain the desired future combat capability with a force posture of between 260 and 325 ships'. The fleet will drop to 285 ships in 2005 but rise to 289 in 2006.

The FY2006 naval budget reduced the number of new ships to be funded from a previously planned six to just four: procurement of one of two T-AKE dry cargo ammunition ships was delayed and one Littoral Combat Ship (LCS) was delayed until FY2007. The shipbuilding order in FY2006 will consist of one SSN-774 nuclear attack submarine, one LPD-17 amphibious transport dock, one LCS and one T-AKE. The budget also confirmed a number of programme adjustments that had first been outlined in PBD 753. Making the biggest headlines was the plan to retire the *John F. Kennedy* aircraft carrier in FY2006, thus reducing the size of the carrier force from 12 to 11 and saving an estimated US$1.2bn by FY11. Prior to this proposal, the navy's plan was to maintain a force of 12 carriers and keep the *Kennedy* in operation until 2018. The budget also pushed back procurement funding for the next aircraft carrier CVN 21 from FY2007 to FY2008. However, the plan to retire the *Kennedy* was not passed by either the House or Senate Armed Services Committee, who instructed that the navy retain all 12 carriers until at least 180 days after the publication of the 2006 Quadrennial Defence Review. The navy was forced to acknowledge concern that its new DD(X) destroyer programme was moving too fast and reduced procurement plans from five ships to three in the medium term, for a saving of some US$2.5bn. Further savings will be accrued by halting the procurement of the LPD-17 *San Antonio*-class amphibious ship in 2007, leaving a fleet of nine ships rather than 12 as originally planned. The submarine fleet is also likely to fall in number, from the current 54 vessels, following a revised procurement programme for the *Virginia*-class SSN. Under the new plan only one ship will be built per year, rather than three every two years, and in addition around US$600m will be allocated to design a 'future undersea superiority system alternative', suggesting that the buy rate for the *Virginia*-class ship will remain at the reduced rate in anticipation of a potentially newly designed submarine. For the marines the largest programme cut would be to the V-22 *Osprey* tilt-rotor aircraft. The service was instructed to delay moving to full production of the aircraft by one year, which will mean 22 fewer V-22s over the next five years, a saving of US$1.2bn.

The navy's main aircraft programme remains unchanged, with 42 F/A-18 *Super Hornets* due to procured each year through to FY2010 before dropping to 28 in FY2011.

ARMY

The US Army's budget request for FY2006 totals US$98.4bn, around US$1.7bn less than the previous

Table 7 **US Agency for International Development: International Affairs Budget**			
Budget Authority in US $ millions	FY2004 Actual	FY2005 Est.	FY2006 Request
Assistance to the New Independent States of the FSU	585	556	482
Support for East European Democracy	442	393	382
Voluntary Peacekeeping Operations	124	178	196
Economic Support Fund	3,288	2,481	3,036
International Military Education and Training	91	89	87
Foreign Military Financing	4,622	4,735	4,589
Global HIV/AIDS Initiative	488	1,374	1,970
Non-Proliferation, Anti-Terrorism and Related Programmes	396	399	440
Int Narcotics & Crime plus Andean Counterdrug Initiative	1,198	1,051	1,259
International Disaster and Famine Assistance	544	485	656
Migration and Refugee Assistance	781	764	893
Iraq Relief and Reconstruction Fund (IRRF)	19,316	-	-
Total International Affairs Budget	38,927	19,713	22,828

year. However, as noted above, the army will receive an additional US$41.2bn from the FY2005 supplemental, including US$5bn to begin the Army Modularity Plan which will convert the army's current 33 brigade combat teams into 43 units and equip them with new trucks, body armour, night-vision goggles, Blue-Force Tracking devices, radios and weapons.

The army has budgeted US$2.8bn for aircraft procurement, US$1.3bn for missiles and US$1.7bn for weapons and tracked vehicles. The major procurement programme remains the Future Combat System, for which US$3.4bn in R&D funds is requested (20% more than last year) and US$878m for 240 *Stryker* armoured fighting vehicles to equip a sixth *Stryker* Brigade Combat Team. In line with comments made last year following the cancellation of the RAH-66 *Comanche* armed reconnaissance helicopter, more money has been made available for other aviation programmes. Due to a new DoD policy that allows the individual services to cancel programmes with the assurance that any savings generated will be returned to their own modernisation accounts, rather than dispersed throughout the three services, the army announced upgrades to its CH-47 *Chinook* transport and AH-64 *Apache* attack helicopters, along with the acquisition of 41 UH-60 *Black Hawk* aircraft. In the medium term the army will allocate funds from the cancelled *Comanche* programme towards recapitalising other aspects of its ageing rotary-winged fleet particularly armed reconnaissance and utility models. In August 2005, the army announced that it had selected a militarised version of Bell Helicopters Model 407 to replace the army's fleet of OH-58D *Kiowa Warriors*, which have been in service since 1985. It is planned that up to 368 platforms will be procured with the first units ready in 2008. At about the same time, the army also issued a request for proposals for its next generation Light Utility Helicopter (LUH). It is expected that up to 322 LUHs will be procured for domestic roles such as civil search and rescue operations, damage assessment support, medical evacuation and counter-narcotics activities. Likely contenders for the programme include Bell's Model 210, AgustaWestland's A109, refurbished DynCorp UH-1s and the EADS EC-135.

MISSILE DEFENCE

As part of the OMB instruction to the Pentagon to reduce its future years defence programme, missile defence suffered the biggest cut, losing some US$5bn between FY2006 and FY2011. In order to make such significant cutbacks, the Missile Defense Agency (MDA) will all but halt development of a new high-acceleration rocket to intercept enemy missiles in the boost phase. Known as the Kinetic Energy Interceptor (KEI), the programme was seen as the one most likely to involve international participation and was central to the concept of a 'layered' defensive shield consisting of three major components:

- a ground-based mid-course missile defence programme, designed to shoot down long-range missiles at mid-flight in space;
- terminal defence systems including Theater High Altitude Area Defense (THAAD) and *Patriot* missiles; both are short- to medium-range systems;
- Airborne Laser and KEI boost-phase anti-missile systems, designed to intercept missiles still in powered flight and before they can deploy decoys.

Table 8 Missile Defense Budget Request FY2004–FY2006 US$m

Research, Development, Testing & Engineering	FY2004	FY2005	FY2006
Missile Defense Agency RDT&E			
RDT&E			
BMD Technologies	226	231	136
Advanced concepts	132	159	349
BMD Terminal Defence	860	928	1,143
BMD Midcourse Defence	3,711	4,501	3,234
BMD Boost Defence	475	476	483
BMD Sensors	417	577	537
BMD System Interceptors	114	279	236
BMD Test and Targets	612	718	617
BMD Products	309	383	455
BMD System Core	449	399	464
Other programmes	313	127	116
Subtotal	7,625	8,783	7,775
Army RDT&E			
Patriot/ MEADS	388	312	288
Patriot Improvement	45	32	16
The Joint Staff RTD&E			
JTAMDO	85	86	80
Military Construction	22	22	5
Procurement			
Patriot PAC-3	616	487	489
Patriot Mods	225	87	77
Total Missile Defence	9,066	9,900	8,844

Although funding for the KEI system was massively reduced and several key decisions regarding its future were delayed until 2008, following a successful first test in late 2004, the Airborne Laser programme emerged relatively unscathed.

In FY2006 the MDA requested US$8.8bn, down from US$9.9bn in FY2005 – the KEI programme which was expected to receive US$1.1bn in FY2006 had its budget cut to US$236m. Plans to deploy a second sea-based X-band radar were withdrawn. However, with savings accruing from the delay of the KEI system, the budget does provide consistent funding for other research activities (including THAAD and MEADS), the deployment of a further 11 sea-based interceptors and the Multiple Kill Vehicle project, and maintains the schedule for a two-satellite missile-tracking demonstration in 2007.

Table 9 **US National Defense Budget Function and other selected budgets, FY1992, 1998–2006**

FY	National Defense Budget Function1 BA	Outlay	Department of Defense BA	Outlay	Atomic Energy Defense Activities BA	Department of Homeland Security BA	Veterans Administration	Total Federal Government Expenditure	Total Federal Budget Surplus
1992	295.1	298.3	282.1	286.9	10.6	n.a.	33.9	1,381	-290
1998	271.3	268.5	258.5	256.1	11.3	n.a.	41.8	1,652	69
1999	292.1	274.9	278.4	261.3	12.4	n.a.	43.2	1,702	125
2000	304.1	294.5	290.5	281.2	12.2	n.a.	46.7	1,788	236
2001	335.5	305.5	319.4	290.9	13.0	19.7	47.6	1,863	127
2002	362.1	348.5	344.9	331.9	14.9	36.3	45.1	2,010	-157
2003	356.2	404.9	437.9	387.3	16.4	31.2	56.9	2,157	-375
2004	490.6	455.9	471.0	436.5	16.8	36.4	60.5	2,292	-412
2005	423.6	465.9	402.0	443.9	17.5	41.0	67.6	2,479	-427
2006	441.8	447.4	421.1	426.2	17.9	41.4	68.3	2,568	-390

Notes

FY = Fiscal Year (1 October-September)

[1] The National Defense Budget Function subsumes funding for the DoD, the DoE Atomic Energy Defense Activities and some smaller support agencies (including Federal Emergency Management and Selective Service System). It does not include funding for International Security Assistance (under International Affairs), the Veterans Administration, the US Coast Guard (Department of Transport), nor for the National Aeronautics and Space Administration (NASA). Funding for civil projects administered by the DoD is excluded from the figures cited here.

[2] Early in each calendar year, the US government presents its defence budget to Congress for the next fiscal year which begins on 1 October. It also presents its Future Years' Defense Program (FYDP), which covers the next fiscal year plus the following five. Until approved by Congress, the Budget is called the Budget Request; after approval, it becomes the Budget Authority.

[3] Definitions of US budget terms: Authorisation establishes or maintains a government programme or agency by defining its scope. Authorising legislation is normally a prerequisite for appropriations and may set specific limits on the amount that may be appropriated. An authorisation, however, does not make money available. Budget Authority is the legal authority for an agency to enter into obligations for the provision of goods or services. It may be available for one or more years. Appropriation is one form of Budget Authority provided by Congress for funding an agency, department or programme for a given length of time and for specific purposes. Funds will not necessarily all be spent in the year in which they are initially provided. Obligation is an order placed, contract awarded, service agreement undertaken or other commitment made by federal agencies during a given period which will require outlays during the same or some future period. Outlays are money spent by a federal agency from funds provided by Congress. Outlays in a given fiscal year are a result of obligations that in turn follow the provision of Budget Authority.

Table 10 Major US Equipment Orders, FY2004–FY2006

Classification	Designation	FY 2004 Units	FY 2004 Value ($m)	FY 2005 Units	FY 2005 Value ($m)	FY 2006 Units	FY 2006 Value ($m)
Joint trg	JPATS	54	295	55	119	54	235
UAV	various	27	584	24	691	14	579
hel	V-22	11	1,142	11	1,355	11	1,503
tpt	C-130J	8	745	15	1,411	12	1,382
AAM	AMRAAM	201	135	205	135	267	202
ASM	JASSM	240	100	288	139	300	150
ASM	JSOW	638	193	405	142	420	145
PGM	JDAM	32,666	689	29,757	665	11,400	305
Air Force tpt	C-17	11	3,494	15	4,058	15	3,497
FGA	F-15E		188		316		151
FGA	F-16 C/D		304		347		381
FGA	F-22	22	4,152	24	4,111	24	3,817
SFW	Sensor Fused Weapon	320	117	314	116	302	120
sat	DSP		108		105		42
sat	NAVSTAR GPS		252	3	327	3	318
launcher	EELV	4	624	2	506	5	838
sat	AEHF					1	529
Army hel	AH-64D		825		687		684
hel	CH-47		510		857		670
hel	UH-60	17	286	38	531	41	618
MRL	HIMARS		228		380		299
ATGW	Javelin	991	133	1,038	117	300	57
MBT	M1A2		297		418		450
AFV	Stryker	371	962	576	1,524	240	878
veh	FHTV		218		207		207
veh	FMTV		324		593		449
veh	HMMWV		1,338		432		224
SAM	Patriot PAC-3	135	616	108	487	108	489
SAM	Patriot Mods		225		87		77
Navy and Marines hel	MH-60S	13	402	15	399	26	589
hel	MH-60R	4	327	6	363	12	554
hel	H-1 Upgrades	9	308	7	198	10	307
ELINT	EA-6B		235		115		120
recce	E-2V Hawkeye	2	226	2	247	2	249
FGA	F/A-18 E/F	42	3,044	42	2,979	38	2,822
trg	T-45	14	339	10	304	6	239
SAM	Standard	75	146	75	1449	75	145
TCM	Tactical Tomahawk	322	352	298	279	379	353
SLBM	Trident II	12	640	5	715		932
CVN	Carrier replacement		1,162		623		564
DDG	AEGIS Destroyer	3	3,268	3	3,559		225
DDG	DD(X)				304		716
SSN	Virginia	1	2,690	1	2,520	1	2,401
LPD	LPD-17	1	1,575	1	1,227	1	1,344
RCOH	CVN refuelling		214		331		1,513
SSN	SSGN conversion	1	1,156	1	515		286
auxiliary	T-AKE	2	621	2	768	1	380

Table 11 **Arms orders and deliveries, Canada**

	Country Supplier	Classification	Designation	Quantity	Order date	Delivery date	Comment
Canada (Ca)	US	APC	M-113	400	1997	1998	Life extension update; deliveries continue
	UK	SSK	*Victoria*	4	1998	2000	
	UK	hel	EH-101 (*Merlin*)	15	1998	2001	Ca designation CH-149; deliveries from 2002
	dom		CP-140 (*Aurora*)	16	2000	2001	Upgrade
	dom	APC	*Grizzly*	246	2000	2002	Upgrade continues. Some to re-role
	dom	APC	MILLAV (*Bison*)	199	2000	2002	Upgrade continues. Existing fleet to re-role
	US	FGA	F/A-18C (*Hornet*)	80	2000	2003	Upgrade to C/D status
	US	SAM	*Sea Sparrow*		2001	2003	To equip *Halifax*-class FFG
	US	UAV	*Sperwer*	4	2003	2004	Being delivered
	US	MGS	*Stryker*	66	2003	2006	

Chapter Two
Europe

NATO

The European Union (EU) and NATO have continued to suffer from a lack of progress in forging a coherent and integrated defence and security policy. Member states hoping that the Constitutional Treaty might move defence initiatives forward in a more cooperative fashion were disappointed when France and the Netherlands voted against the treaty in separate referendums. Nevertheless, limited progress has been made, namely, the inauguration of the **European Defence Agency** (EDA), the 'battlegroups' initiative, and the EU's assumption of control in Bosnia-Herzegovina.

The ongoing operation in Afghanistan is a challenge for NATO's European members as the Alliance moves to take over *Operation Enduring Freedom* from US Combined Forces Command (CFC) in 2006. Meanwhile, NATO's KFOR operations continue in Kosovo.

With the **European Security Strategy** (ESS) dealing increasingly with 'neighbourhood' issues on the eastern, southeastern and southern borders of the Union, conflicts and conflict resolution in those areas are of increasing concern. Apart from the Balkans, and a new involvement in Africa, the resolution of so-called 'frozen conflicts' in the separatist territories of Transnistria in Moldova, and Abkhazia and South Ossetia in Georgia, are becoming increasingly important to the expanding European Union, which may also increase its role in the resolution of the conflict in Nagorno-Karabakh.

NATO operations

In December 2004, the Alliance handed over lead status in **Bosnia-Herzegovina** to the EU while retaining its mission to provide training to local police. At the same time, the Alliance took over command of the International Security Assistance Force (ISAF) in **Afghanistan** – the first NATO operation outside its traditional geographic area. Adding to the nine ISAF Provincial Reconstruction Teams (PRT) in place, NATO deployed an additional two teams in the west under Lithuanian command, while an additional PRT under Spanish command

is now deployed to Qal'eh-Now (see p.225). NATO ISAF forces in Afghanistan now number some 10,000 personnel. The next challenge for the Alliance is to take over the south of the country from US Combined Forces Command in 2006, when the UK assumes command of NATO forces in Afghanistan. At this time, it is planned to integrate the ISAF mission with the missions under *Operation Enduring Freedom* (see p. 225)

NATO is further expanding its involvement to Iraq, where it has pledged to annually train and equip 1,000 senior Iraqi officers within the country and 500 outside. Moreover, there is the possibility of building a security **Training and Education Centre** near Baghdad.

NATO is now engaged in providing logistical assistance to help the 8,000-strong African Union (AU) force in the humanitarian crisis in **Darfur**. At the June 2005 meeting of NATO Ministers of Defence, Secretary-General Jaap de Hoop Scheffer announced that NATO would aid AU peacekeepers in their *AMIS II* mission to protect some 2.6 million Sudanese internally displaced persons (IDPs) and returning refugees from the government-supported Janjaweed militias. He listed operational training, command-and-control and strategic airlift as areas of possible NATO assistance, but made clear that NATO would not send troops to the conflict zone. NATO's announcement followed a similar EU pledge of assistance, made in May 2005.

NATO–EU interface

NATO continues to endorse the EU's European Security and Defence Policy (ESDP), which is complementary to, but independent of, NATO. Moreover, the EU's troubled Constitutional Treaty contains a clause reiterating mutual defence and security cooperation with NATO as a priority. Both parties also use the 2003 **Berlin Plus Agreement** as the overarching guide for defence consolidation between the two, giving the EU access to NATO planning and asset capabilities for its crisis management operations (CMOs). So far, however, there is a lack of substance in the relationship. Despite some progress in Europe and evidence of coordinated activity between NATO and the EU, the schism over defence 'burden sharing' with the US continues to complicate transatlantic relations. With some justification, Washington criticises the EU and European NATO members for insufficient contributions to operations. For example, in Afghanistan, European nations are placing national caveats on the deployment of their forces which are due to take over some operational tasks from US forces. Such conditionality could not only reduce the effectiveness of *Operation Enduring Freedom*, but also worsen the transatlantic rift.

NATO–Russia

The possibility of further NATO expansion and Alliance activity in the South Caucasus and Black Sea region remains the greatest obstacle to a better NATO–Russia relationship. **Georgia** is proceeding with its Individual Partnership Action Plan (IPAP), ultimately aiming for membership of the Alliance. **Ukraine** is pursuing a similar plan, and this year attained 'Intensified Dialogue Status' – an intermediary position before full consideration for membership in April 2006. However, there is some doubt over Ukraine's ability to meet NATO requirements in the short or medium term. The intent to downsize the armed forces to a strength of 210,000 in 2005 is unlikely to be met, and although the merger of the Air and Air Defence Forces has been completed, there are questions over the command-and-control effectiveness of the new combined body. Nevertheless, under the programme for determining the future size and structure of the Ukrainian armed forces – 'Model 2015' – Kiev aims to have fully professional forces, at a strength of about 70,000 by 2015, with a rapid reaction capability and interoperability with NATO. Ukraine remains a major contributor to international peace-keeping operations. It contributed some 1,640 troops to *Operation Iraqi Freedom*; this deployment is due to end soon. Furthermore, there are some 742 Ukrainian troops deployed on UN missions.

Russia is also uncomfortable with what it deems encroachment by the US and NATO along its borders. However, despite some tensions, new initiatives were discussed at the NATO–Russia Council (NRC). At the NRC's December 2004 meeting, Russia agreed to participate in NATO's *Operation Active Endeavour*, the NATO maritime counter-terrorism operation to monitor shipping in the Mediterranean. This is the first time Russia has taken part in a NATO collective defence operation.

Transformation

Through its policy termed 'Comprehensive Political Guidance', NATO is slowly showing how it may evolve as its role changes and new defence and security tasks emerge. The 500-strong **Allied Command Transformation** (ACT) maintains its commitment to efficiency, striving to identify capabilities, streamline expenditures, and bridge the divide between the US and Europe, both technologically and operationally. The NATO Response Force (NRF), which retains the Alliance's high intensity combat role, (see *The Military Balance 2004–05*) reached initial operational capability in October 2004. Designed for rapid response, troops can be deployed within five days after the initial order, with a capability to maintain operations for up to one month. So far member states have contributed forces numbering 17,000. *Exercise Allied Reach* in February 2005 tested logistics and planning in the NRF programme. In March and April, NATO tested the NRF in *Exercise Noble Javelin* in the Canary Islands.

NON-NATO

Operations

In May 2005, the EU focused its attention on Africa. In addition to committing operational and logistical assistance to the AU's *AMIS II* mission to Darfur (see p. 360), the EU extended its presence in the Democratic Republic of Congo (DRC) under operation *EUSEC DR Congo*, which focuses on security sector reform. This is intended to follow up and complement *Operation Artemis*, the previous EU stabilisation and humanitarian mission in Bunia, northeastern Congo, as well as the ongoing EUPOL mission in the DRC, which is focused on police training and reform.

The EU relieved NATO of its primary peace-keeping role in Bosnia-Herzegovina in December 2004. *Operation Althea* transfers the lead responsibility to an EU force (EUFOR) (see *The Military Balance 2004–05*). Meanwhile, EU support to the UN mission in Kosovo (UNMIK) also continues.

EU initiatives

The European Defence Agency (EDA) became fully operational in early 2005 (see *The Military Balance 2004–05*). The agency is tasked with coordinating defence operations and capabilities among EU member states, and will provide the framework for aspirations for a unified foreign security policy. The **European Capabilities Action Plan** (ECAP) serves as the EDA's fundamental agenda, aiming to identify and redress shortfalls in the EU's military and defence capabilities. ECAP underscores interoperability and technological standardisation as being crucial to EU military transformation. Eliminating duplication of technical capabilities is also emphasised.

Another proposal aimed at increasing military capabilities in the EU is the battlegroup initiative announced in November 2004. By 2007, the EU plans to field 13 battlegroups, nine of them multi-national, and each comprising 1,500 troops. In May 2005, EU defence ministers accelerated the timeframe for their deployment from ten days after the initial order to five days. These battlegroups must be able to sustain the deployment for up to three months. The EU intends that, at full operability, it will be able to run two rapid-response missions simultaneously. However, the multinational character of the battlegroups presents challenges. Language barriers make command, control and communications difficult, and national constitutional restrictions on the deployment of troops, or parliamentary permission for deployment, complicate the preparation for, and the execution of operations. Moreover, in light of the NATO's NRF endeavour, critics have argued that the battlegroup initiative may be a duplication of effort, although the EU's project was conceived to enhance crisis management capacity beyond the geographic and institutional boundaries of NATO, and EU and NATO officials have said that the two initiatives are 'mutually reinforcing'.

By May 2005, Germany, Austria, the Czech Republic, Latvia, Lithuania, Poland, Spain and Estonia had organised additional, multinational battlegroups to supplement the two existing French and British battlegroups. Notably, despite their neutral stance, Sweden and Finland, together with Norway (which is not an EU member) will form a joint battlegroup, while Italy, Romania and Turkey will combine in an additional battlegroup by 2009.

Conflicts

East and South Europe. There has been little substantive progress in Europe's longest-running conflict in **Cyprus.** However, at a local level, inter-communal contacts strengthened, and at a meeting on 5 July between the Turkish Cypriot Republican Party and the Greek Cypriot Party (AKEL) discussed joint amendments to the 2004 Annan plan, which could include plans for a communal federation.

In **Moldova**, clashes between Moldovan farmers attempting to cross into the separatist region of Transnistria and Transnistrian authorities led Chisinau to boycott the Joint Control Commission (JCC) meeting on 19 April. This increase in tension between the two parties to the conflict proved to be temporary, however, and there is now fresh impetus to resolve the conflict between Moldova and Transnistria.

With the announcement of a **Ukrainian Peace Initiative** on 22 April 2005 at the summit meeting of the GUAM states – Georgia, Ukraine, Azerbaijan and Moldova – in Chisinau, the conflict resolution process has become increasingly internationalised. Ukrainian President Viktor Yushchenko presented a 'roadmap' for resolution that was received positively by both sides of the conflict as well as by the EU, which is beginning to play a more active role in finding a solution. Both parties to the conflict agreed to invite the EU and the US to join the negotiations, and Moldova has accepted that the Organization for Security and Cooperation in Europe (OSCE) should monitor the elections in Transnistria. Chisinau had previously rejected this idea, which it interpreted as de facto international recognition of the separatist territory.

The re-election of Vladimir Voronin as president of Moldova on 7 April ended some of the uncertainty over prospects for conflict resolution. His parliamentary majority depended on the support of the Democratic Party, whose eight-member faction left its previous alliance with the Democratic Moldova Bloc (BMD). The hitherto strongly oppositional Christian Democratic Popular Party announced on the day of the election that it would also support Voronin.

After further preparatory meetings, Ukraine presented a more detailed version of its plan to the parties and mediators during joint talks in Vinnytsya, Ukraine, on 16–17 May. The plan comprises a draft framework of seven steps towards a resolution of the conflict. The first three are: the democratisation of Transnistrian representative bodies; the joint monitoring of the Ukrainian–Moldovan border together with Ukrainian and possibly EU and other international observers; and demilitarisation of the conflict zone. The plan for joint border monitoring was accepted, and five border checkpoints were set up under Chisinau's control in July 2005. Two further checkpoints are planned at the Transnistrian-Ukrainian border section.

However, having initially accepted a demand from Moldova for democratisation, and with parliamentary elections planned for late 2005,

Tiraspol warned Chisinau against any attempt to impose its electoral law on the separatist region, and rejected Moldova's 10 June demands that Russian troops should withdraw by the end of 2005.

The Russian military base and ammunition depot at Cobasna, in the separatist zone, remain issues for negotiation. The Russian Foreign Ministry stated that Russia would be willing to remove ammunition and equipment, but that the Transnistrian authorities were preventing this from taking place. On 12 May, the Transnistrian authorities prevented an OSCE monitoring team from entering the depot. Subsequently, the OSCE mission stated it could not certify the security of the stockpiles any longer. Moreover, reports of weapons and ammunition being exported illegally from the territory have made it necessary to increase oversight of Transnistrian activities and to secure its borders.

BALKANS

On 2 December, 2004 the European Union deployed 7,000 troops (EUFOR) on *Operation Althea*, taking over from NATO's SFOR mission in **Bosnia-Herzegovina**. Although SFOR and now EUFOR have both had some success in fighting crime and corruption in the country, criminal networks and ethnic tensions still undermine its stability. Meanwhile, in an attempt to change Bosnia's image from a country still dependent on foreign peacekeepers to one able to contribute to international security and participate in Euro-Atlantic structures, a multi-ethnic unit was deployed from Bosnia to Iraq at the beginning of June to assist US-led forces in clearing unexploded ordnance. However, Sarajevo's aspiration to join NATO has been made conditional on the arrest of the two former Bosnian Serb leaders suspected of carrying out war crimes: Radovan Karadzic and Ratko Mladic. Both are believed to be hiding in neighbouring Serbia-Montenegro, which lies outside the jurisdiction of EUFOR.

Tensions remain in **Kosovo** following last year's ethnic clashes, which reached a peak in April 2004 when 20 Serbs were killed in the town of Mitrovica. Restrictions on freedom of movement and 60–70% unemployment contribute to an atmosphere of discontent and make a return to violence an ever-present possibility. However, when Kosovan prime minister Ramush Haradinaj, seen by many as a war hero, resigned and surrendered to the Hague War Crimes Tribunal in July 2004, the expected violence

did not materialise. Nevertheless, the assassination attempt on President Ibrahim Rugova on 15 March 2005 demonstrated the disputed province's continuing insecurity. As a result of this insecurity, only a small number of Serbs have returned to their homes. In October 2004, Serbs boycotted the elections, claiming that the UN and NATO had failed to create a safe environment for them.

There is international consensus that the conflict should be resolved via some form of independence for Kosovo. However the province's status remains unresolved, as the concept of independence frustrates both the Serbs, who want to keep Kosovo as an autonomous province under Belgrade's rule, and those Albanian Kosovars who want full independence. The ongoing failure to determine Kosovo's status can only delay Serbia's EU membership application. No viable solution for Kosovo can be sustained without the active participation and consent of Belgrade. Full-scale negotiations regarding Kosovo's status are due to start in autumn 2005.

While the French and Dutch rejection of the European Constitution has led to questions over the EU's intentions for further enlargement, **the Former Yugoslav Republic of Macedonia (FYROM)** believes that it can achieve candidate status by the end of 2005 along with Bulgaria, Croatia, Romania and Turkey. Moreover, as a signal of their desire for further integration into Europe, FYROM, Albania and Bulgaria signed a military cooperation agreement on 17 May 2005. The agreement demonstrates – to some extent – that these countries are prepared to put old enmities behind them and to work together on mutual security concerns, including transnational crime.

Albania has also shown its willingness to play a greater role in European security issues. On 7 March, it agreed to maintain its seven-strong SFOR contingent in Bosnia-Herzegovina as part of EUFOR's *Operation Althea*. Moreover, Tirana is being proactive in dealing with ethnic Albanian guerrillas who operate in FYROM and perhaps Kosovo. On 14 December, the Albanian government arrested Gafur Adilli, reportedly the current commander of the Albanian National Army (ANA, or AKSH), which is active in both Kosovo and FYROM.

South Caucasus. In the south Caucasus, Georgia's conflicts with its separatist regions remain unresolved. Changes in both Abkhazia and South Ossetia have brought new challenges. **Abkhazia** elected a new president after an electoral process dominated by the possibility of interfactional fighting between the parties of Moscow's favoured candidate, Raoul Xadzhimba, and Sergei Bagapsh. The latter was eventually elected president in January 2005. To maintain a relatively stable political establishment, a power-sharing arrangement was worked out whereby Xadzhimba and his supporters received virtual control of some of the defence and security agencies. Therefore, Bagapsh's leadership is restricted and it is hard for him either to initiate any meaningful reforms, or act against elites with agendas contrary to his objectives. Meanwhile, the UN-brokered peace talks continue in Geneva, but without any significant progress.

Georgia's relationship with **South Ossetia** remains confrontational. Since the armed clashes of summer 2004, which left several people dead on both sides, there has been relative calm in the zone of conflict despite incidents of hostage-taking: three Ossetians were taken hostage in May and one Georgian was killed in retaliation. An IISS initiative has successfully set up an informal dialogue between the two parties, and the Joint Control Commission (JCC) has resumed its work, having been suspended following the 2004 clashes.

Perhaps the biggest danger in the context of both these unresolved conflicts is the unpredictability of the Georgian government, whose inability to implement successful social and economic policies has led to a decline in its popularity. And, despite a view that President Mikhail Saakashvili is unlikely to sacrifice his ambitions for EU and NATO memberhip by launching military action against either separatist region, some members of his government are prone to making inflammatory remarks, giving the impression that they may be capable of taking such action. A series of propagandist television broadcasts depicting Georgia's armed forces as ready for combat has further increased overall tension in the region. Furthermore, the acquisition of T-72 main battle tanks, to replace the Georgian army 's T-55 fleet, can be viewed either as a normal modernisation, or as an unnecessary and expensive step by a government whose economy is in a poor state. Nevertheless, Saakashvili's offer of autonomy, delivered at the January 2005 Council of Europe meeting to both regional separatist governments, seemed to indicate that he is more disposed towards peaceful solutions. Meanwhile, these two conflicts in the South Caucasus are vulnerable to the possibility of a spillover from the spreading conflicts in the north Caucasus (see pp. 153–6).

Politics in both **Azerbaijan and Armenia** continue to be dominated by the issue of **Nagorno-Karabakh**. There is no real change in their positions, nor in the ability of the OSCE Minsk Group to move the peace process towards a resolution. In Baku, the main political focus remains on the issues of the 'occupied territories' and refugees. Neither side takes account of the fact that the realities inside the disputed territory have changed. Political and social structures are well-established, and elections were held in the territory on 19 June. Nevertheless, the Armenian and Azeri presidents, Robert Kocharian and Ilham Aliyev, met informally during a Council of Europe summit in Warsaw on 15 May. No details were released, but the two presidents talked for an hour and made concluding statements reflecting new optimism and progress. This positive atmosphere was echoed in subsequent public statements both in Yerevan and Baku. The two countries' foreign ministers met at the sidelines of an international conference in Brussels on 22 June.

Meanwhile, the 30 May 2005 agreement between **Russia and Georgia** for the remaining two Russian military bases at Batumi and Akalkhalaki to be closed by 1 October 2007 has become an issue between **Armenia** and **Azerbaijan.** Moscow has said that some 40% of equipment from the bases may be moved to the Russian base at Gyumri in Armenia, thus theoretically boosting Armenia's overall military capability in the eyes of Baku. The announcement of joint Russian–Armenian ground force exercises (to be held in Armenia in 2006) has further angered the Azeri government. The exercises, and the equipment withdrawal, are viewed as a reaction by Moscow to the increasing US and NATO influence in Georgia and Azerbaijan. In particular, the continuing US programme of assistance to Georgia's armed forces and the acceptance of the Georgian Individual Partnership Action Plan (IPAP) by NATO serve as justification to Moscow for its own policies in the South Caucasus.

TERRORISM & NON-STATE ACTIVITY

Terrorism once again became the main threat to European countries on 7 July 2005 when, in an attack reminiscent of the 11 March 2004 Madrid train bombings, four explosive devices – carried by suicide bombers – were detonated without warning in London during the rush hour. Three bombs exploded simultaneously on different London Underground trains, and one detonated later on a bus. Altogether, 56 people, including the bombers, were killed, and some 700 people were injured. The coordinated nature of the attack and the lack of warning were indicative of an al-Qaeda style operation, and a group calling itself the Secret Organisation of al-Qaeda in Europe claimed responsibility. Although it had long been expected that the UK could be a target of an incident of this type, the British security services were taken by surprise and there was no intelligence to suggest that an attack was imminent. The bombers were all British citizens. The two factors of radicalised British Muslims, and their links to executives of terror abroad, show the trans-national of the continuing terrorist threat to Europe (see *The Military Balance* 2004-05).

In **Northern Ireland** in September 2004, talks to restore the Catholic–Protestant power-sharing government, agreed in the 1998 Good Friday Accord, ended without resolution. Despite its continuing adherence to a 1997 ceasefire agreement, and having handed over some weapons as part of the decommissioning process, the IRA, during December 2004 negotiations, expressed willingness to disarm further, but only if Loyalist calls for photographic evidence of decommissioning were disregarded. The IRA labelled the photographs an attempt to humiliate the organisation, while Loyalist leaders made verifiable disarmament a precondition of a return to power-sharing. Another setback to progress was the theft of some £25 million from a Belfast bank by a group widely believed to be from the Provisional IRA (PIRA). The proceeds of the robbery were thought to have been laundered through fraudulent currency transactions, tobacco-smuggling operations and property purchases in the UK.

On the political front, the robbery raised tensions, not just between political groups in Northern Ireland, but also between the Irish government and Sinn Féin. In February 2005 the Minister of Justice publicly named three Sinn Féin politicians as leaders of the IRA's seven-member Army Council.

The UK general election in May 2005 produced a new hardline political configuration in Northern Ireland. The moderate leader of the Ulster Unionist Party (UUP), David Trimble, lost his seat; overall, his party only retained one seat, while the hardline Democratic Unionist Party (DUP), led by the Reverend Ian Paisley, captured the majority of unionist votes. Although the moderate republican party, the Social and Democratic Liberal Party (SDLP), retained its three seats, Sinn Féin, representing militant republicanism, gained one seat.

Following the December bank robbery, Ian Paisley – now the main Unionist representative – emphasised that he would not enter into a political arrangement with Sinn Féin. Therefore, with the political process in turmoil, and the retention of an armed capability by loyalist and republican paramilitary groups, any hope for a return to power-sharing seemed to be diminishing. However, on 27 July, the IRA Army Council announced that the 'armed struggle' was over and that 'volunteers' were being ordered to 'dump' their weapons. In a reciprocal move, the British Army started to dismantle observation posts in South Armagh, and Peter Hain, the UK Northern Ireland Secretary, announced that the number of British troops in the province would be reduced from 10,500 to 5,000 in the next two years, with three Home Service Force battalions being disbanded. However, the IRA statement renewed the organisation's commitment to a united Ireland and an end to British rule in Northern Ireland.

Loyalists are unlikely to agree to a return to power-sharing until substantial decommissioning of IRA weapons is verified, and until it can be shown that the organisation has ceased its criminal activities. It is through sophisticated criminal structures with global reach that the IRA, and other groups in Northern Ireland, obtain finance to maintain their organisations, their way of life, and the ability to return to violence.

Negotiations between **Spain** and the Basque separatist group Eusakdi ta Askatasuna (ETA) have stalled. ETA's last fatal attack occurred in 2003; however, terrorist bombings still occur, including one major bombing in Madrid on 25 May 2005. A week before the bombing, the Spanish Prime Minister José Luis Zapatero asked parliament to debate a motion to open opening a dialogue with ETA in order to find a resolution to the conflict. Despite parliament's endorsement of this proposal, hundreds of thousands of people publicly protested. Moreover, in June 2005, ETA announced it would end attacks on politically elected officials, but pledged neither to disarm nor to abandon fighting until Spain recognised the Basque right to self-determination. Meanwhile in an example of increasing cooperation between France and Spain, the French security services arrested a senior ETA figure, Mikel Albizu, known as 'Antza', on 3 October 2004.

In **Turkey**, a wave of terrorist attacks in July 2005 killed an estimated 15–20 people. Some nine people died in a bomb attack on a train in eastern Turkey on 2 July, and a further five died in an attack on a tourist bus on 16 July. Several other attacks failed, including one on 1 July in Ankara, in which a suicide bomber was shot by police. The attacks have mostly been claimed by Kurdish separatist groups – the People's Defence Force (HPG), the Freedom Hawks of Kurdistan (TAK), and the Partiya Karkeren Kurdistan (PKK), which Turkish officials believe now has a strength equivalent to its 1999 levels at the time of the arrest of Abdullah Ocalan. This includes some 2,500 PKK members who are believed to have entered Turkey from Iraq in the last two years.

Table 12 Selected NATO Exercises 2004–05

Date	Title	Location	Type	Participant Nations	Participant forces	Other
4–16 Sep 2004	*NATO Air Meet 2004*	Incirlik and Konya, Turkey	Tactical composite air operations, suppression of air defence and electronic warfare	16 NATO countries and 2 observer nations	About 1500 personnel and over 90 aircraft	
30 Sep–16 Oct 2004	*Destined Glory 2004*	Sardinia, Italy	NATO live-fire amphibious exercise to demonstrate initial operational capability for the NATO Response Force	Belgium, Canada, France, Germany, Greece, Italy, the Netherlands, Spain, Turkey, UK and US	About 9,500 personnel	
1–12 Nov 2004	*Arrcade Fusion 2004*	Sennelager Training Centre, Germany	Computer aided command post exercise for crisis management in Middle East scenario, focus on staff procedures and processes	Allied Rapid Reaction Corps (ARRC)	More than 2,500 NATO military experts (plus 1 [UK] Signal Brigade)	
8–24 Nov 2004	*Allied Warrior 2004*	Amersfoort, Ede and Harskamp, Netherlands and in Verona and Naples, Italy	NRF deployment and command, Combined Joint Task Force operation with rapid deployment of a Combined Joint Force Land Component Command Headquarters	Canada, Denmark, France, Germany, Greece, Hungary, Italy, the Netherlands, Norway, Poland, Portugal, Spain, Turkey, the United Kingdom and the United States of America	Approximately 900 personnel	
26 Jan–1 Feb 2005	*CMX 05*	Brussels and national capitals	NATO crisis management exercise to strengthen cooperation between NATO and its partners in the Political-Military Framework for NATO-led Partnership for Peace (PfP) operations	26 NATO Nations plus 9 Partner Nations. Observers: UN, EU, OSCE		
1–3 Feb 2005	*Allied Reach 2005*	Allied Command Trans-formation Joint Warfare Center's facilities in Stavanger, Norway	Joint Strategic Command Study Seminar; AR 05 will examine the planning, deployability, operational and capability issues that NATO Response Force (NRF) commanders may face in the year 2007	Allied Command Transformation (ACT) and Allied Command Operations (ACO/ SHAPE), supported by ACT's Joint Warfare Centre (JWC)	About 300 personnel	
24 Feb–9 Mar 2005	*Battle Griffin 05*	Bodø, Norway and surrounding area.	Norwegian invitational live joint combined Exercise to provide training along the lines of the NATO Deployed Forces concept, with a focus on high-intensity operations	Belgium, Denmark, Finland, France, Germany, Italy, Netherlands, Norway, Poland, Romania, Spain, Switzerland, Sweden, UK and US	About 14,000 personnel (8,000 Norwegian)	
3–16 Mar 2005	*Noble Marlin*	Ionian Sea, aircraft operating from Sicily	Anti-Submarine Exercise to demonstrate NATO's determination to maintain proficiency in coordinated ASW, AsuW, and costal surveillance operations using a multi-national force	Canada, France, Germany, Greece, Italy, Portugal, Spain, Turkey, UK and US	Submarines, Maritime Patrol Aircraft, Surface Vessels, personnel	

Table 12 Selected NATO Exercises 2004–05

Date	Title	Location	Type	Participant Nations	Participant forces	Other
6 Mar–13 Apr 2005 (First Phase)	*Determined Effort 2005*	Kosovo	Operational deployment, rapid reinforcement of in-theatre NATO forces to demonstrate NATO ability to reinforce KFOR or EUFOR at short notice with 'Over-the-horizon Forces'	Germany, KFOR contributing nations	Phase One: 600 German troops	
28 Mar–14 Apr 2005	*Noble Javelin 2005*	Canary Islands, Spain	Live training exercise/Field training exercise to evaluate the ability to activate, mount and deploy the NATO Response Force components in order to accomplish a combination of different NRF missions	Belgium, Canada, Denmark, France, Germany, Greece, Hungary, Italy, The Netherlands, Norway, Poland, Romania, Spain, Turkey, UK and US	About 3,000 personnel	
4–27 April 2005	*BLACKSEAFOR 2005*	Black Sea	Naval interoperability	Ships of the Black Sea Fleet and Turkish Navy: Russia, Bulgaria, Georgia, Romania, the Ukraine, and Turkey		
11–29 Apr 2005	*Loyal Mariner 2005*	North Sea, Skagerak, Kattegat and adjacent Danish, Norwegian and Swedish Territorial Waters	Live training exercise to provide Joint Warfare Interoperability training in a multi-threat environment for NATO Response Force Maritime Staff and Forces, and other National Maritime Forces, and enabling them to operate together in littoral waters	Belgium, Canada, Denmark, Estonia, France, Germany, Greece, Iceland, Italy, Latvia, Lithuania, The Netherlands, Norway, Poland, Portugal, Spain, Turkey, the UK and US. Non-NATO: Finland, Sweden, Ukraine.		
18–29 Apr 2005	*European Challenge 2005*	Wildflecken, Germany and other parts of Germany	Joint and combined command of EU-led crisis operations to understand Principles of Peace Support Operations (PSO) and to develop staff structures in multinational missions	17 EU and NATO states	over 4,000 (majority German)	
29 Apr–9 May 2005	*NATO Tiger Meet 2005*	Balikesir, Turkey	Live-flying exercise to train Composite Air Operations (COMAO) in multinational alliance to evaluate existing command structures	Turkey, the Czech Republic, UK, Germany, France, Belgium, Switzerland (Observer), Austria (Observer)	60 aircraft including helicopters and airborne early warning air craft	
10–12 May 2005	*Ample Train 2005*	Gran Canaria, Spain	Live logistics exercise to improve cooperation between the air forces of NATO countries and test land-based personnel's ability to supply fuel, flight security and the performance of weapons	Spain, Belgium, Denmark, Greece, Turkey, France and Germany	450 troops and 37 combat aircraft (+ 1 Spanish frigate)	
17 May–1 Jun 2005	*Allied Action 05*	France and Spain	Combined Joint Task Force command post exercise to mobilize and deploy NATO's Rapid Reaction Force, based on an imaginary scenario of a NATO-led operation in response to a crisis with a focus on rapid simultaneous mobilisation of ground, naval and air forces and their cooperation in the NATO Response Force	23 NATO member and 11 associate states	Over 3,400 personnel	
5–6 June 2005	*Baltops 2005*	Baltic Sea	Naval interoperability	A NATO exercise with Russian participation including a Russian landing ship and rescue tug. 40 warships, two submarines, and 28 aircraft from 11 nations participated overall. Co-hosted by Latvia and the US		

Table 12 Selected NATO Exercises 2004–05

Date	Title	Location	Type	Participant Nations	Participant forces	Other
19–30 June 2005	*Sorbet Royal 2005*	Gulf of Taranto, Italy	Naval: rescue a submarine at 50–200 meters	A NATO exercise including participation from Russia, GB, Greece, Spain, Italy, Canada, Germany, the Netherlands, Norway, Poland, Turkey, France, Israel, Egypt, and the US		
19–30 Jun 2005	*Cooperative Best Effort 2005*	Yavoriv Training Centre, L'viv, Ukraine	Land Live Exercise (LIVEX) and Field Training Exercise (FTX); securing sensitive points and assuring a safe and secure environment with a focus on anti-terrorism operations to prevent the destabilisation of a particular area	11 NATO countries, 11 partners, 2 'Mediterranean dialogue' countries, 2 'Istanbul Cooperation initiative' countries and 2 Balkan countries as observers	one light infantry squad per nation	Interoperability of PfP/MD forces using NATO standards
28 Jun–8 Jul 2005	*Clean Hunter*	Southern Germany to Denmark and from the United Kingdom to mid-Poland	Live-flying exercise for coordinated air operations	Belgium, the Czech Republic, Denmark, France, Germany, Greece, the Netherlands, Poland, Turkey, the United Kingdom and the United States of America	Estimated 250 aircraft including tankers and airborne early warning aircraft	

Belgium Be

Euro €		2003	2004	2005
GDP	€	267bn	282bn	
	US$	304bn	349bn	
per capita	US$	29,479	33,762	
Growth	%	1.3	2.7	
Inflation	%	1.5	1.9	
Public Debt	%	104.0	101.0	
Def exp [a]	€	3.5bn	3.53bn	
	US$	3.98bn	4.36bn	
Def bdgt	€	2.68bn	2.63bn	2.64bn
	US$	3.05bn	3.25bn	3.35bn
US$1=€		0.88	0.81	0.79

[a] including military pensions

Population	10,364,388					
Age	0–14	15–19	20–24	25–29	30–64	65 plus
Male	9%	3%	3%	3%	24%	7%
Female	8%	3%	3%	3%	24%	9%

Capabilities

ACTIVE 36,900 (Army 24,800 Navy 2,450 Air 6,350 Medical Service 1,800 Joint Service 1,500)

RESERVE 18,650 (Army 8,500 Navy 1,200 Air 1,600 Medical Service 850 Joint Service 2,200 Territorial Support Units 4,300)

ORGANISATIONS BY SERVICE

Joint Service 1,500; 2,200 reservists (total 3,700)

Army 24,800; 4,200 reservists (total 29,000)

FORCES BY ROLE

1 Joint Service Territorial Comd, 1 Comd HQ (COMOPSLAND)
Comd   2 bde HQ (*each:* 1 lt cbt bn, 1 arty bn, 1 recce bn, 1 engr bn, 3 med cbt bn (1 with straight-fire capability))
SF   1 gp
AB   1 (AB module) bde (2 para bn, 1 mne cdo bn)
ADA   1 bn

Reserves

Territorial Support Units 4,300 reservists

Army 11 unit

EQUIPMENT BY TYPE

TK • MBT • LEOPARD 1 52: 52 1A5
AIFV 104: 104 YPR-765 (25mm)
APC 223
  APC (T) 163: 163 M-113
  APC (W) 60: 60 *Pandur*
ARTY 132
  TOWED • 105mm • LG1 14: 14 LG1 MK II
  SP • 155mm 48: 48 M-109

MOR 70: **81mm** 22; **120mm** 48
AT • MSL 161: 161 *Milan*
AD • SAM • MANPAD 36: 36 *Mistral*
RADAR 12: 12 land (Battlefield Surveillance)

Navy 2,450; 600 reservists (total 3,050)

EQUIPMENT BY TYPE

PRINCIPAL SURFACE COMBATANTS • FRIGATES • FFG 2:
  2 *Wielingen* each with 2 single ASTT with 2 L5 HWT, 1 Mk 29 *Sea Sparrow* octuple with RIM-7P *Sea Sparrow* SAM, 2 twin (4 eff.) each with 1 MM-38 *Exocet* tactical SSM, 1 Mle 54 Creusot-Loire 375mm *Bofors* (6 eff.), 1 100mm gun
PATROL AND COASTAL COMBATANTS 1: 1 PCR
MINE WARFARE • MINE COUNTERMEASURES • MHC • FLOWER 6: 6 *Aster* (Tripartite)
LOGISTICS AND SUPPORT 9: 1 AG; 1 AGOR; 5 AT; 1 spt (log spt/comd, with hel platform)
  TRG 1: 1 YDT

FACILITIES

Base 1 located at Zeebrugge, 1 located at Ostend

Naval Aviation

HELICOPTERS • UTL • SA-316 3: 3 SA-316B *Alouette III*

Reserves 600 reservists

Air Force 6,350; 1,600 reservists (total 7,950)

Flying hours   165 hrs/year

FORCES BY ROLE

AD / FGA / Recce	2 (Tac) wg with 72 F-16 MLU *Fighting Falcon* (Mid-Life Update) (total: 1 AD/FGA/recce sqn, 1 AD/FGA/trg sqn, 2 AD/FGA sqn)
SAR	1 sqn with 5 *Sea King* MK48
Tpt	1 wg with 2 DA-20 *Falcon*; 2 A-310; 2 A-310-200; 11 C-130H *Hercules*; 2 ERJ-135 LR; 2 ERJ-145 LR; 2 *Falcon* 20 (VIP); 1 *Falcon* 900
Trg	1 wg (1 trg sqn with SF-260D/SF-260M, 2 trg sqn (1 trg flt with CM-170 *Magister*))
Hel	1 wg with 32 A-109 (obs); 12 SA-318 *Alouette II*

EQUIPMENT BY TYPE

AIRCRAFT 90 combat capable
  FGA 90: 72 F-16 MLU *Fighting Falcon* (Mid-Life Update); 18 in reserve
  EW • ELINT 2: 2 DA-20 *Falcon*
  TPT 36:
    A-310 4: 2; 2 A-310-200
    C-130 11: 11 **C-130H** *Hercules* 11
    ERJ-135 2: 2 ERJ-135 LR
    ERJ-145 4: 4 ERJ-145 LR
    Falcon 20 2 (VIP)
    FALCON 900 2: 1 *Falcon* **900B** 1
  TRG 62+: 29 *Alpha Jet*; some CM-170 *Magister*
    SF-260 33+: 33; some SF-260D/SF-260M
HELICOPTERS
  SAR 5: 5 *Sea King* MK48
  UTL 44: 32 A-109 (Obs); 12 SA-318 *Alouette II*
UAV 18: 18 *B-Hunter* systems
AD • SAM 24: 24 *Mistral*

MSL • **TACTICAL** • **ASM** • **AGM-65**: some AGM-65G *Maverick*
  AAM: some AIM-120 *AMRAAM*
    AIM-9: some AIM-9M *Sidewinder*
FACILITIES
Air base 1 located at Coxijde, 1 located at Kleine-Brogel, 1 located at Florennes, 1 located at Bierset, 1 located at Beauvechain, 1 located at Melsbroek

DEPLOYMENT

AFGHANISTAN
NATO • ISAF 250

BOSNIA/CROATIA
EU • EUFOR II 4

BURUNDI
UN • ONUB 2 obs

DEMOCRATIC REPUBLIC OF CONGO
UN • MONUC 8

FRANCE
NATO • Air Force
  AIRCRAFT • **TRG** 29: 29 *Alpha Jet* located at Cazaux/ Tours, Fr

GERMANY
Army 1 elems mech inf bde (withdrawal to be completed in 2005)

INDIA/PAKISTAN
UN • UNMOGIP 1 obs

MIDDLE EAST
UN • UNTSO 4 obs

SERBIA AND MONTENEGRO
NATO • KFOR I ε500
UN • UNMIK 1 obs

FOREIGN FORCES

NATO HQ NATO Brussels; HQ SHAPE Mons
United Kingdom Air Force: 183
United States EUCOM: Army 788; Navy 94; Air Force 508

Bulgaria Bg

Bulgarian Lev L		2003	2004	2005
GDP	L	34.3bn	37.9bn	
	US$	19.8bn	23.8bn	
per capita	US$	2,620	3,178	
Growth	%	4.3	5.7	
Inflation	%	2.3	6.1	
Debt	US$	13.2bn		
Def exp	L	814m	920m	
	US$	471m	579m	
Def bdgt	L	814m	897m	977m
	US$	471m	564m	630m
FMA (US)	US$	20.3m	9.91m	8.33m
US$1=L		1.73	1.59	1.55

Population   7,450,349

Ethnic groups: Turkish 9%; Macedonian 3%; Romany 3%

Age	0–14	15–19	20–24	25–29	30–64	65 plus
Male	7%	3%	4%	4%	23%	8%
Female	7%	3%	3%	4%	25%	10%

Capabilities

ACTIVE 51,000 (Army 25,000 Navy 4,370 Air 13,100 Joint 8,530) Paramilitary 34,000
Terms of service 9 months

RESERVE 303,000 (Army 250,500 Navy 7,500 Air 45,000)

ORGANISATIONS BY SERVICE

Army 25,000 (incl conscripts); 250,500 reservists **(total 275,500)**

FORCES BY ROLE
Mil District   1 corps HQ (1 armd bde, 1 Lt inf bde, 2 arty bde, 3 (Reserve and Territorial Comd) army regt, 4 army bde); 1 corps HQ (1 armd bde, 2 army bde, 4 (Reserve and Territorial Comd) army regt); 1 corps HQ (1 arty bde, 2 mech bde)
Armd recce   1 bde
SF   1 comd
Rocket   1 bde
Engr   1 bde; 2 regt
NBC   2 regt

EQUIPMENT BY TYPE
TK • **MBT** 1,474: 432 T-72; 1,042 T-55
RECCE • **BRDM** 18: 18 BRDM-1/BRDM-2 (non-op)
AIFV • **BMP** 214: 100 BMP-1; 114 BMP-23
APC 1,643
  APC (T) 1,025: 1,025 MT-LB (plus 1,144 look-a-likes)
  APC (W) • **BTR** 618: 618 BTR-60
ARTY 1,774+
  TOWED 501+

100mm 16: 16 M-1944 (BS-3)
122mm 220: 25 M-1931/37 (A-19); 195 M-30 *M-1938*
130mm 60: 60 M-46
152mm 205+: 205 D-20; some M-1937 (ML-20)
SP • 122mm 692: 692 2S1 *Carnation*
MRL • 122mm 222: 222 BM-21
MOR • 120mm 359: 359 2S11 SP *Tundzha*
AT
MSL 200+: 200 AT-3 *Sagger*; some AT-4 *Spigot*; some AT-5 *Spandrel*
GUNS • 85mm 150: 150 D-44
AD
SAM 67+: 20 SA-3 *Goa*
SP 47: 27 SA-4 *Ganef*; 20 SA-6 *Gainful*
MANPAD: some SA-7 *Grail*
GUNS 400
SP
23mm: ZSU23-4
TOWED
23mm: ZU-23
57mm: S-60
100mm: KS-19
RADAR • LAND: some GS-13 *Long Eye* (veh); some SNAR-1 *Long Trough* (arty); some SNAR-10 *Big Fred* (veh, arty); some SNAR-2/-6 *Pork Trough* (arty); some Small Fred/Small Yawn (veh, arty)

Navy ε2,370; ε2,000 conscript; 7,500 reservists (age LIMIT 55,officers 60 OR 65) (total 11,870)

EQUIPMENT BY TYPE
SUBMARINES • TACTICAL • SSK 1:
1 *Pobeda*† (FSU *Romeo*) with 8 single 533mm TT with 14 SAET-60 HWT
PRINCIPAL SURFACE COMBATANTS 8
FRIGATES • FF 1:
1 *Smeli* (FSU *Koni*) with 1 twin (2 eff.) with 2 SA-N-4 *Gecko* SAM, 2 RBU 6000 *Smerch* 2 (24 eff.), 2 x2 76mm gun (4 eff.)
CORVETTES 7
FSG 1:
1 *Tarantul* II with 2 quad (8 eff.) with 8 SA-N-5 *Grail* SAM, 2 twin (4 eff.) with 4 SS-N-2C *Styx* tactical SSM, 1 76mm gun
FS 6:
2 *Pauk* each with 1 SA-N-5 *Grail* SAM, 4 single 406mm TT, 2 RBU 1200 (10 eff.)
4 *Poti* each with 4 single ASTT, 2 RBU 6000 *Smerch* 2 (24 eff.)
PATROL AND COASTAL COMBATANTS 16
PFI 10: 10 *Zhuk* less than 100 tonnes
PFM 6:
6 *Osa* I/II each with 4 SS-N-2A *Styx*/SS-N-2B *Styx*
MINE WARFARE • MINE COUNTERMEASURES 20
MSC 8: 4 *Sonya*; 4 *Vanya*
MSI 12: 6 *Olya* less than 100 tonnes; 2 PO-2 less than 100 tonnes; 4 *Yevgenya* less than 100 tonnes
AMPHIBIOUS
LS • LSM 2:
2 *Polnochny* A (capacity 6 MBT; 180 troops) (FSU)
CRAFT 6: 6 LCU
LOGISTICS AND SUPPORT 16: 7 AG; 3 AGHS; 3 AO; 1 AT; 1 Diving tender/spt; 1 YDG

FACILITIES
Base 1 located at Atya, 1 located at Balchik, 1 located at Vidin, 1 located at Sozopol, 1 located at Burgas, 1 located at Varna

Naval Aviation
HELICOPTERS • ASW 10: 10 Mi-14 *Haze* (3 operational)

Coastal Arty
FORCES BY ROLE
Arty 2 regt; 20 bty
EQUIPMENT BY TYPE
MSL • TACTICAL • SSM: some SS-C-1B *Sepal*; some SS-C-3 *Styx*
GUN • GUN • 130mm 4: 4 SM-4-1

Naval Guard
Gd 3 coy

Air Force 13,100; 45,000 reservists (to age of 60) (total 58,100)
Flying hours   30 to 40 hrs/year

FORCES BY ROLE
1 AD Cmd,1 Tactical Aviation Cmd
Ftr / Recce	1 (Air Base) gp with 16 MiG-29A *Fulcrum A*; 18 MiG-21MF *Fishbed J*/MiG-21UM *Mongol B*; 59 MiG-21bis *Fishbed L & N*; 4 MiG-29UB *Fulcrum*
FGA	1 (Air Base) gp with 35 Su-25K *Frogfoot A*/Su-25UBK *Frogfoot B*; 4 Su-25UB *Frogfoot B*
Tpt	1 regt with 1 AN-2 *Colt*; 2 AN-24 *Coke*; 3 AN-26 *Curl*; 7 L-410 *Turbolet*; 1 TU-134B *Crusty*; 1 PC-12M
Survey	1 unit with 1 AN-30 *Clank* (Open Skies)
Hel	1 (Air Base) gp with 24 Mi-24D *Hind D* *; 6 Mi-24V *Hind E*; 8 Mi-8 *Hip*; 18 MI-17 (Mi-8MT) *Hip H*; 6 Bell 206 *JetRanger*

EQUIPMENT BY TYPE
AIRCRAFT 137 combat capable
FTR 35
MiG-29 17: 17 MiG-29A *Fulcrum A*
MiG-21MF *Fishbed J*/MiG-21UM *Mongol B Mongol A* trg 18*
FGA 94
MiG-21 59: 59 MiG-21bis *Fishbed L & N*
Su-25K *Frogfoot A* FGA/Su-25UBK *Frogfoot B* trg 35*
TPT 15: 1 AN-2 *Colt*; 2 AN-24 *Coke*; 3 AN-26 *Curl*; 1 AN-30 *Clank* (Open Skies); 7 L-410 *Turbolet*
TU-134 1: 1 TU-134B *Crusty*
UTL • PC-12 1: 1 PC-12M
TRG 26
L-39 12: 12 L-39ZA *Albatros* (advanced)
MiG-29U 4: 4 MiG-29UB *Fulcrum**
PC-9 6: 6 PC-9M (basic)
Su-25UB *Frogfoot B* 4*
HELICOPTERS
ATK • MI-24 30: 24 Mi-24D *Hind D* *; 6 Mi-24V *Hind E*
SPT 26:
MI-8 26: 8; 18 MI-17 (Mi-8MT) *Hip H*
UTL 6: 6 Bell 206 *JetRanger*

AD • SAM: some SA-10 *Grumble (quad)* SP/SA-2 *Guideline* Towed/SA-3 *Goa*/SA-5 *Gammon* static (20 sites, some 110 launchers)

MSL • TACTICAL • ASM: some AS-14 *Kedge*; some AS-7 *Kerry*

   AAM: some AA-11 *Archer*; some AA-2 *Atoll*; some AA-7 *Apex*; some AA-8 *Aphid*

FACILITIES

Air base   1 (ttr/recce), 1 (FGA)

Hel base   1 (hel)

School   2 with 12 L-39ZA *Albatros* trg ac (advanced); 6 PC-9M trg ac (basic) (trg)

Paramilitary 34,000

Border Guards 12,000
Ministry of Interior

FORCES BY ROLE

Paramilitary   12 regt

EQUIPMENT BY TYPE

PATROL AND COASTAL COMBATANTS up to 50

   MISC BOATS/CRAFT: up to 38 craft

   PCI 12: circa 12 PO2 (FSU, under 100 tonnes)

Railway and Construction Troops 18,000

Security Police 4,000

DEPLOYMENT

AFGHANISTAN

NATO • ISAF 34

BOSNIA-HERZEGOVINA

EU • EUFOR II 1 pl

ETHIOPIA/ERITREA

UN • UNMEE 2; 5 obs

IRAQ

Army ε466 (Peace Support)

LIBERIA

UN • UNMIL 2 obs

SERBIA AND MONTENEGRO

UN • UNMIK 1 obs

Czech Republic Cz

Czech Koruna Kc		2003	2004	2005
GDP	Kc	2.54tr	2.75tr	
	US$	90.7bn	106bn	
per capita	US$	8,852	10,406	
Growth	%	3.7	4.0	
Inflation	%	0.1	2.8	
Debt	US$	34.6bn		
Def exp	Kc	52.5bn	50.9bn	
	US$	1.86bn	1.97bn	
Def bdgt	Kc	51.2bn	50.5bn	52.8bn
	US$	1.85bn	1.95bn	2.19bn
FMA (US)	US$	27.8m	10.1m	7.85m
US$1=Kc		28.1	25.8	24.1

Population   10,241,138

Ethnic groups: Slovak 3%; Polish 0.6%; German 0.5%

Age	0–14	15–19	20–24	25–29	30–64	65 plus
Male	8%	3%	3%	4%	25%	6%
Female	7%	3%	3%	4%	25%	8%

Capabilities

ACTIVE 22,272 (Army 16,663 Air 5,609) Paramilitary 5,600

CIVILIAN 17,858 (Joint 17,858)

Conscription abandoned early 2005. Armed Forces being re-org; initial operational capabilities set for 2005-6 with full operational cap. by 2009-12.

ORGANISATIONS BY SERVICE

Army 16,663

FORCES BY ROLE

Rapid Reaction   1 bde (3 mech bn)

Mech   1 bde (2 mech bn, 1 tk bn)

SF   1 gp

Arty   1 bde (2 arty bn)

Engr rescue   1 bde (1 engr bn, 6 rescue bn)

SAM   1 bde

Reserves

FORCES BY ROLE

Territorial Def   14 comd; 1 region

Engr   1 regt

EQUIPMENT BY TYPE

TK • MBT • T-72 298: 298 T-72M

AIFV 647

   BMP 545: 370 BMP-1; 175 BMP-2

   BPzV 102

APC 100

   APC (T) 82: 82 OT-90

   APC (W) • OT 18: 18 OT-64

L-A-L • 388 AIFV/APC
ARTY 362
  SP • 152mm 209: 209 M-77 *Dana*
  MRL • 122mm 60: 60 RM-70 *Dana*
  MOR • 120mm 93: 85 M-1982; 8 SPM-85
AT • MSL 671: 3 9P133; 175 9P135 (AT-4) *Spigot*; 21 9P148; 472 9S428

FACILITIES
Trg base 4

Air Force 5,609 (incl AD)

Flying hours   60 hrs/year

FORCES BY ROLE
Integrated with Jt Forces

Ftr   1 sqn with 8 MiG-21 *Fishbed*
FGA   1 sqn with 18 L-159 *Albatros*; 12 JAS 39C *Gripen* (being delivered); 2 JAS 39D *Gripen* (being delivered)
Tpt   2 sqn with 2 An-24 *Coke*; 5 An-26 *Curl*; 1 CL-601 *Challenger*; 9 L-410 *Turbolet*; 3 Tu-154 *Careless*; 2 Yak-40 *Codling*
Trg   1 regt with 4 L-29 *Delfin*; 23 L-39C; 8 Z-142C; 4 PZL MI-2 *Hoplite*
Hel   2 (aslt/tpt/attack) sqn with 10 PZL W-3RM *Anakonda*; 32 Mi-24 *Hind* *; 2 Mi-8 *Hip*; 18 MI-17 (Mi-8MT) *Hip H*
AD   1 (missile) bde

EQUIPMENT BY TYPE
AIRCRAFT 40 combat capable
  FTR 32: 8 MiG-21 *Fishbed*; 24 in store
  FGA 76: **JAS 39** 14: first 12 JAS 39C *Gripen* (being delivered); 2 JAS 39D *Gripen* (being delivered); 18 L-159 *Albatros*; 53 in store; 5 Su-25 *Frogfoot* in store
  TPT 22: 2 An-24 *Coke*; 5 An-26 *Curl*; 1 CL-601 *Challenger*; 9 L-410 *Turbolet*; 3 TU-154 *Careless*; 2 Yak-40 *Codling*
  TRG 44: 4 L-29 *Delfin*; 4 in store
    L-39 28: 23 L-39C; 5 L-39ZA *Albatros* in store
    Z-142 8: 8 Z-142C
HELICOPTERS
  SAR 10: 10 PZL W-3RM *Anakonda*
  ATK 32: 32 Mi-24 *Hind* *
  SPT 24:
    MI-8 20: 2; 18 MI-17 (Mi-8MT) *Hip H*
    PZL MI-2 *Hoplite* 4
AD • SAM • SP: some SA-13 *Gopher*; some SA-6 *Gainful*; some SA-8 *Gecko*
  MANPAD: some SA-7 *Grail*
MSL • TACTICAL • AAM: some AA-2 *Atoll*; some AA-7 *Apex*; some AA-8 *Aphid*; some AIM-9 *Sidewinder*

FACILITIES
Air base 5 no location

Paramilitary 5,600

Border Guards 3,000; 1,000 conscript **(total 4,000)**

Internal Security Forces 100; 1,500 conscript **(total 1,600)**

DEPLOYMENT

AFGHANISTAN
NATO • ISAF 56

BOSNIA-HERZEGOVINA
EU • *Op Althea* 84
EU • EUFOR I 1 obs

DEMOCRATIC REPUBLIC OF CONGO
UN • MONUC 3 obs

ETHIOPIA/ERITREA
UN • UNMEE 2 obs

GEORGIA
UN • UNOMIG 5 obs

IRAQ
Armed Forces 10 medical (surgical team); 100 MP

LIBERIA
UN • UNMIL 3 obs

SERBIA AND MONTENEGRO
NATO • KFOR I 410
UN • UNMIK 1 obs

SIERRA LEONE
UN • UNAMSIL 2 obs

Denmark Da

Danish Krone kr		2003	2004	2005
GDP	kr	1.39tr	1.44tr	
	US$	212bn	239bn	
per capita	US$	39,387	44,224	
Growth	%	0.4	2.3	
Inflation	%	2.1	1.2	
Public Debt	%	51.9	49.4	
Def exp [a]	kr	21.1bn	21.4bn	
	US$	3.2bn	3.55bn	
Def bdgt	kr	17.6bn	17.6bn	18.7bn
	US$	2.67bn	2.91bn	3.17bn
US$1=kr		6.58	6.04	5.93

[a] including military pensions

Population   5,432,335

Age	0–14	15–19	20–24	25–29	30–64	65 plus
Male	10%	3%	3%	3%	25%	6%
Female	9%	3%	3%	3%	24%	8%

Capabilities

ACTIVE 21,180 (Army 12,500 Navy 3,800 Air 4,200 Joint 680)
Terms of service 10 months (to be 4 months)

CIVILIAN 7,400 (Joint 7,400)

RESERVE 129,700 (Army 46,000 Navy 7,300 Air 17,100 Home Guard (Hjemmevaernet) about 59,300 incl Army 46,400 Navy 4,500 Air Force 5,500 Service Corps 2,900)

ORGANISATIONS BY SERVICE

Armed Forces 680 (Joint Service personnel); 7,400 (civilian)

Army 7,300; 2,900 (civilian); 5,200 conscript; 46,000 reservists (total 58,500 plus 2,900 civilians)

FORCES BY ROLE

Army	1 (op) comd
Rapid Reaction	1 bde (1 SP arty bn, 1 tk bn, 2 mech inf bn (20% active cbt str))
Tk	1 bn
Recce	1 bn; 1 coy
Mech inf	1 div (3 mech inf bde (*each:* 1 SP arty bn, 1 tk bn, 2 mech inf bn))
SF	1 unit
Div arty	some bn
MLRS	1 coy
Engr	1 bn; 1 coy
Avn	1 gp (1 atk hel coy, 1 armd recce hel det)
Regt cbt	1 gp (1 mech inf bn, 1 engr coy, 1 mot inf bn)
AD	2 bn; 1 coy

Reserves

Army 5 (local def) region (*each:* up to 2 mot inf bn); 2 (regt cbt) gp (*each:* 1 arty bn, 3 mot inf bn)

EQUIPMENT BY TYPE

TK • MBT 231: 51 *Leopard* 2; 180 *Leopard* 1A5
RECCE 36: 36 *Eagle* (MOWAG)
APC 310
  APC (T) 288: 288 M-113 (plus 369 look-a-likes incl 55 SP mor)
  APC (W) 22: 22 *Piranha* III (incl variants)
ARTY 860
  TOWED 157
    105mm 60: 60 M-101
    155mm 97: 97 M-114/M-139
  SP • 155mm 76: 76 M-109
  MRL • 227mm 12: 12 MLRS
  MOR 615: **81mm** 455 (incl 53 SP)
    120mm 160: 160 Brandt
AT
  MSL 140: 140 TOW (incl 56 SP)
  RCL • 84mm 1131: 1,131 *Carl Gustav*
  RL • 84mm 10600: 10,600 AT-4
HELICOPTERS
  ATK 12: 12 AS-550C2 *Fennec* (with TOW)
  MD-500M utl/OH-6 *Cayuse* **OBS** 13
UAV: some *Sperwer*
AD • SAM • MANPAD: some FIM-92A *Stinger*
RADAR • LAND: some ARTHUR

Navy 3,300; 500 conscript; 7,300 reservists (**total** 11,100)

EQUIPMENT BY TYPE

PRINCIPAL SURFACE COMBATANTS • CORVETTES
• FSG 3:
  3 *Niels Juel* each with 2 Mk 141 *Harpoon* quad (8 eff.) each with 1 RGM-84C *Harpoon* tactical SSM, 2 6 cell Mk 48 VLS with 12 *Sea Sparrow* SAM, 1 76mm gun
PATROL AND COASTAL COMBATANTS 67
  PCC 12: 3 *Agdlek*; 9 *Barsoe*
  PCI 40 in reserve (Home Guard)
  PFC 4:
    4 *Flyvefisken* each with 1 76mm gun
  PFM 4:
    4 *Flyvefisken* (capacity 60) each with 2 Mk 141 *Harpoon* quad (8 eff.) each with 1 RGM-84C *Harpoon*/RGM-84L *Harpoon*/tactical SSM, 2 single 533mm TT, 1 6 cell Mk 48 VLS with 6 *Sea Sparrow* SAM, 1 76mm gun
  PFT 3:
    3 *Flyvefisken* (Patrol fit) each with 2 single 533mm TT, 1 Mk 48 *Sea Sparrow* VLS with 1 *Sea Sparrow* SAM, 1 76mm gun
  PCO 4:
    4 *Thetis* each with 1 hel (*Lynx*), 1 76mm gun
MINE WARFARE 6
  MINE COUNTERMEASURES • MHC 3: 3 *Flyvefisken*
  MINELAYERS • ML 3:
    1 *Falster* with up to 400 Mine
    2 *Lindormen* each with up to 50 Mine
LOGISTICS AND SUPPORT 5: 1 AE (Ammo); 3 AGB; 1 tpt

FACILITIES

Base	1 located at Korsøer, 1 located at Frederikshavn
Naval airbase	1 located at Kapur

Naval Aviation

HELICOPTERS • ASW 8: 8 *Lynx* MK80A/*Lynx* MK90A (up to 4 embarked)

Reserves

Home Guard (Navy) 4,500 reservists (to age 50)
PATROL AND COASTAL COMBATANTS • PCI 40: 40 *Attacker*

Air Force 4,100; 100 conscript; 11,600 reservists (**total** 15,800)

Four air bases
Flying hours   165 hrs/year

Tactical Air Comd

FORCES BY ROLE

Ftr / FGA	3 sqn with 60 F-16A *Fighting Falcon*/F-16B *Fighting Falcon*; 2 in reserve
SAR	1 sqn with 8 S-61A *Sea King*
Tpt	1 sqn with 3 C-130J-30 *Hercules*; 3 CL-604 *Challenger* (MR/VIP)

EQUIPMENT BY TYPE

AIRCRAFT 62 combat capable
  FTR • F-16 62: 60 F-16A *Fighting Falcon*/F-16B *Fighting Falcon*; 2 in reserve

TPT 6
    C-130 • **C-130J** 3: 3 C-130J-30 *Hercules*
    CL-604 *Challenger* 3 (MR/VIP)
TRG 28: 28 SAAB T-17
HELICOPTERS • **ASW** • **S-61** 8: 8 S-61A *Sea King*
MSL • **TACTICAL** • **ASM**: some AGM-65 *Maverick*
    AAM • **AIM-120**: some AIM-120A *AMRAAM*
    AIM-9 *Sidewinder* some
BOMB • **PGM** • **JDAM**: some GBU-31
    PAVEWAY • **PAVEWAY II**: some EGBU-12
    PAVEWAY III: some GBU-24
FACILITIES
School 1 with 28 SAAB T-17 trg ac (flying trg)

Control and Air Defence Group

FORCES BY ROLE
SAM 2 bn; 6 bty with FIM-92A *Stinger*; 36 I HAWK

EQUIPMENT BY TYPE
AD
    SAM • **TOWED**: some MIM-23 *HAWK*
    MANPAD: some FIM-92A *Stinger*
    LAUNCHER 216: 216 I HAWK
FACILITIES
Radar Stn 4, 1 located at Faroe Islands

DEPLOYMENT

AFGHANISTAN
Army 5 Obs Team (*Op Enduring Freedom*)
NATO • ISAF 185
UN • UNAMA 1 obs

BOSNIA-HERZEGOVINA
EU • EUFOR II 4

DEMOCRATIC REPUBLIC OF CONGO
UN • MONUC 1 obs

ETHIOPIA/ERITREA
UN • UNMEE 4 obs

GEORGIA
UN • UNOMIG 5 obs

INDIA/PAKISTAN
UN • UNMOGIP 6 obs

IRAQ
Army ε380; ε90 (det from L) (total 470)
1 (bn) inf gp (1 Scout sqn, 1 inf/SH coy)

KYRGYZSTAN
Army 75 (incl C-130 contingent. *Op Enduring Freedom*)

LIBERIA
UN • UNMIL 1 obs

MIDDLE EAST
UN • UNTSO 10 obs

SERBIA AND MONTENEGRO
NATO • KFOR I 1 inf gp (1 scout sqn, 1 inf coy); 370 obs
UN • UNMIK 1 obs

SIERRA LEONE
UN • UNAMSIL 1 obs

SUDAN
UN • UNMIS 40

FOREIGN FORCES

NATO HQ Joint Command North-East
UN HQ Standby High Readiness Brigade (SHIRBRIG)

Estonia Ea

Estonian Kroon kn		2003	2004	2005
GDP	kn	124bn	138bn	
	US$	9.05bn	10.9bn	
per capita	US$	6,706	8,157	
Growth	%	5.1	6.2	
Inflation	%	1.3	3.0	
Debt	US$	6.97bn		
Def exp	kn	2.37bn	2.18bn	
	US$	172m	172m	
Def bdgt	kn	2.14bn	2.30bn	2.57bn
	US$	155m	181m	207m
FMA (US)	US$	10.3m	7.38m	6.16m
US$1=kn		13.8	12.7	12.4

Population 1,332,893
Ethnic groups: Russian 28%; Ukrainian 3%; Belarussian 2%

Age	0–14	15–19	20–24	25–29	30–64	65 plus
Male	8%	4%	4%	3%	21%	6%
Female	8%	4%	4%	3%	24%	11%

Capabilities

ACTIVE 4,934 (Army 3,429 Navy 331 Air 193 Joint 981) **Paramilitary 2,600**

RESERVE 24,000 (Joint 24,000)
Terms of service 8 months, officers and some specialists 11 months.

ORGANISATIONS BY SERVICE

Army 2,000; 1,429 conscript (**total** 3,429)
FORCES BY ROLE
Def	4 region, 14 district
Recce	1 bn
Inf	3 bn
Arty	1 bde
Gd	1 bn
Peacekeeping	1 bn under strength

Reserves

Militia 8,700 reservists
Army 15 (Defence League) Kaitseliit unit

EQUIPMENT BY TYPE
RECCE • BRDM 7: 7 BRDM-2
APC 29+
  APC (T): some Bv-206
  APC (W) 29
    BTR 25: 5 BTR-60/BTR-70; 20 BTR-80
    XA SERIES 4: 4 XA-180 *Sisu*
ARTY 77
  TOWED • 105mm 19: 19 M 61-37
  MOR 58: 44 81mm
    120mm 14: 14 2S11 SP *Tundzha*
AT
  MSL 13: 10 MAPATS; 3 RB-56 *Bill*
  RCL 239
    106mm • M-40 30: 30 M-40A1
    84mm 109: 109 *Carl Gustav*
    90mm 100: 100 PV-1110
  RL • 82mm 200: 200 B-300
AD • GUNS • 23mm • TOWED 100: 100 ZU-23-2

FACILITIES
Centre 1 (peace ops)

Navy 208; 123 conscript (total 331)

Lat, Ea and L have set up a joint Naval unit BALTRON with bases at Liepaja, Riga, Ventspils (Lat), Tallinn (Ea), Klaipeda (L).

EQUIPMENT BY TYPE
PRINCIPAL SURFACE COMBATANTS • CORVETTES • FS 1:
  1 *Admiral Pitka* with 1 76mm gun
PATROL AND COASTAL COMBATANTS • PCC 2:
  2 *Rihtiniemi* each with Mine (capability)
MINE WARFARE • MINE COUNTERMEASURES 4
  MHC 2: 2 *Lindau*
  MSI 2: 2 *Frauenlob* (*Kalev*)

FACILITIES
Base 1 located at Tallinn, 1 (Navy and BALTRON) located at Miinisadam

Air Force 195

Flying hours 120 hrs/year

FORCES BY ROLE
Air base 1 air base, 1 surv wg

EQUIPMENT BY TYPE
AIRCRAFT
  TPT 2: 2 AN-2 *Colt*
  TRG 1: 1 PZL-104 *Wilga 35*
HELICOPTERS • UTL 4: 4 R-44

Paramilitary 2,600

Border Guard 2,430; 170 conscript (total 2,600)

Ministry of Internal Affairs

FORCES BY ROLE
maritime elm of Border Guard also fulfils task of Coast Guard
Paramilitary 1 regt; 3 (rescue) coy

EQUIPMENT BY TYPE
PATROL AND COASTAL COMBATANTS 31
  PCC 6: 1 *Maru*; 3 PVL-100; 1 *Pikker*; 1 *Torm*

  PCI 22: 11
    11 less than 100 tonnes
  PCO 3: 1 *Kou*; 1 *Linda*; 1 *Valvas*
AIRCRAFT • TPT • L-410 2: 2 L-410UVP *Turbolet*
HELICOPTERS • SPT 5: 5 Mi-8 *Hip* (in war, subordinated to Air Force staff)

DEPLOYMENT

AFGHANISTAN
Armed Forces 1 (METEO) spt team; 1 medical team; 1 (EDD) unit (Explosive Detective Dogs); 1 (ISAF HQ); 1 (Cross Service) team; 1 (EOD) team

BOSNIA-HERZEGOVINA
EU • EUFOR II 1 (NATO HQ); 3 (EUFOR)

IRAQ
Armed Forces 3 army (NTM-1, PAO, US CENTCOM); 1 inf pl (*Operation Iraqi Freedom*)

MIDDLE EAST
UN • UNTSO 2 obs

SERBIA AND MONTENEGRO
NATO • KFOR I 2 (offs.); 1 (MSU) pl (ESTPATROL)

France Fr

Euro €		2003	2004	2005
GDP	€	1.55tr	1.62tr	
	US$	1.77tr	2.0tr	
per capita	US$	29,437	33,201	
Growth	%	0.5	2.3	
Inflation	%	2.2	2.3	
Public Debt	%	71.1	73.2	
Def exp [a]	€	40.6bn	41.8bn	
	US$	46.2bn	51.6bn	
Def bdgt	€	31bn	32.4bn	32.8bn
	US$	35.3bn	40bn	41.6bn
US$1=€		0.88	0.81	0.79

[a] including military pensions

Population	60,656,178

Age	0–14	15–19	20–24	25–29	30–64	65 plus
Male	9%	3%	3%	3%	23%	7%
Female	9%	3%	3%	3%	23%	9%

Capabilities

ACTIVE 254,895 (Army 133,500 Navy 43,995 Air 63,600 Central Staff 5,200 Service de Santé 8,600) Paramilitary 104,275

CIVILIAN 44,465 (Army 28,500 Navy 10,265 Air 5,700)

RESERVE 21,650 (Army 11,350 Navy 6,000 Air 4,300) Paramilitary 40,000

ORGANISATIONS BY SERVICE

Strategic Nuclear Forces

Navy 2,200
SUBMARINES • STRATEGIC • SSBN 4
L'Inflexible **M4 S 615** 1 with 16 M-45 strategic SLBM each with 6 TN-75 nuclear warheads, 4 single 533mm TT each with up to 18 F-17 HWT/L5 HWT/SM-39 *Exocet* tactical USGW
Le Triomphant **S 616** 3 each with 16 M-45 strategic SLBM each with 6 TN-75 nuclear warheads, 4 single 533mm TT each with up to 18 F17 Mod 2 HWT/SM-39 *Exocet* tactical USGW
AIRCRAFT • STRIKE/FGA 24: 24 *Super Etendard*

Air Force 1,800

Air Combat Command
FGA / Strike   3 sqn with 60 M-2000N *Mirage* each with 2 tactical ASMP, R-550 *Magic* 2 tactical AAM

Air Mobility Command
Tkr 1 sqn with 11 C-135FR; 3 KC-135 *Stratotanker*
Trg 1 unit with 2 *Mystère* 20 (*Falcon* 20)

Paramilitary • Gendarmerie 41

Army 133,500; 28,500 (civilian)
FORCES BY ROLE
regt normally bn size
Army   4 (task force) HQ; 1 (land) comd HQ; 5 region HQ
Armd   1 elems bde (Fr/Ge bde 2500 personnel) (1 mech inf regt, 1 armd cav regt); 1 bde (1 armd regt, 2 armd inf regt, 1 SP arty regt, 1 engr rescue regt); 1 bde (1 SP arty regt, 1 engr regt, 2 armd inf regt, 2 armd regt)
Lt armd 2 bde (*each:* 1 arty regt, 1 engr regt, 2 armd cav regt, 2 (APC inf) mech inf regt)
Mech inf 2 bde (*each:* 1 SP arty regt, 1 armd inf regt, 1 armd regt, 1 engr regt, 1 (APC inf) mech inf regt)
Air mob 1 bde (4 cbt hel regt)
Mtn inf 1 bde (1 arty regt, 1 engr regt, 1 armd cav regt, 3 (APC) mech inf regt)
AB   1 bde (1 armd cav regt, 1 arty regt, 1 engr regt, 1 spt regt, 4 para regt)
Arty   1 bde (1 SAM regt with I-HAWK *MIM-23B*, 2 MLRS regt, 3 SAM regt with *Roland*)
Engr   1 bde
Sigs   1 bde
EW / Int 1 bde (1 Cav regt, 2 UAV regt, 1 EW regt, 1 Int bn)

Foreign Legion 7,700
Armd 1 regt
Inf 6 regt

Para 1 regt
Engr 2 regt (incl in units listed above)

Marines 14,700
Marine 14 regt (France); 4 regt (Africa); 10 regt (French overseas possession)

Special Operation Forces ε2,700
FORCES BY ROLE
HQ   1 comd
Para   1 regt
Cbt hel 1 sqn

FACILITIES
Training Centre   3

Reserves 11,350 reservists
Territorial defence forces
Army   1 coy
Spt / engr 14 coy

EQUIPMENT BY TYPE
TK • MBT 926: 312 *Leclerc*; 614 AMX-30
RECCE 1809: 337 AMX-10RC; 192 ERC-90F4 *Sagaie*
   VBL 1280: 1,280 VBL M-11
AIFV • AMX-10P 601: 601 AMX-10P/PC
APC • APC (W) 4413:
   VAB 4413: 3,906; 61 VAB BOA; 172 VAB *Eryx*; 134 VAB HOT; 113 VAB *Milan*; 27 VAB NBC
ARTY 787
   TOWED • 155mm 105: 105 TR-F-1
   SP • 155mm 266: 261 AU-F-1; 5 CAESAR
   MRL • 227mm 55: 55 MLRS
   MOR • 120mm 361: 361 RT-F1
AT • MSL 1195: 1,195 *Milan*
   RL • 84mm some AT-4
AIRCRAFT
   TPT 13: 5 PC-6 *Turbo-Porter*; 8 TBM-700
   UTL 2: 2 F406 *Caravan II*
HELICOPTERS
   ATK 2: 2 AS-665 *Tiger*
   RECCE 4: 4 AS-532 *Horizon*
   ASLT • SA-342 276: 276 SA-342M *Gazelle* (all variants)
   SPT 106: 106 SA-330 *Puma*
UAV 68
   AN/USD-502 50: 50 CL-289
   RECCE • TAC 18: 18 SDTI
AD • SAM 455+
   SP 98+:
      ROLAND 98+: some; 98 *Roland* II/*Roland* I
   TOWED 26+:
      MIM-23 26+: 26; some I-HAWK *MIM-23B*
   MANPAD 331: 331 *Mistral*
RADAR • LAND 75: 1 *Cobra*; 28 RASIT; 46 RATAC

Navy 43,995; 10,265 (civilian); 2,200 opcon Strategic Nuclear Forces (total 46,195 plus 10,265 civilians)
FORCES BY ROLE
Navy 1 HQ opcon HRF (N) located at Toulon; 1 HQ opcon ALFOST located at Brest

Europe (NATO)

EQUIPMENT BY TYPE
SUBMARINES 10
STRATEGIC • SSBN 4
L'Inflexible **M4 S 615** 1 opcon Strategic Nuclear Forces with 16 M-45 SLBM each with 6 TN-75 nuclear warheads, 4 single 533mm TT each with up to 18 F-17 HWT/L5 HWT/SM-39 *Exocet* tactical USGW

Le Triomphant **S 616** 3 opcon Strategic Nuclear Forces each with 16 M-45 SLBM each with 6 TN-75 nuclear warheads, 4 single 533mm TT each with up to 18 F17 Mod 2 HWT/SM-39 *Exocet* tactical USGW

TACTICAL • SSN 6:
6 *Rubis* each with 4 single 533mm TT each with 1+ SM-39 *Exocet* tactical USGW, 1+ F-17 HWT

PRINCIPAL SURFACE COMBATANTS 34
AIRCRAFT CARRIERS 2
CVN 1:
1 *Charles de Gaulle* (capacity 20 *Super Etendard* strike/FGA ac; 12 *Rafale* M ftr; 3 E-2C *Hawkeye* AEW ac; 2 SA-360 *Dauphin* SAR hel; 3 SA-321 *Super Frelon* SAR hel) (40, 600t) with 4 octuple VLS each with *Aster* 15 SAM, 2 *Sadral* sextuple each with *Mistral* SAM

CVH 1:
1 *Jeanne d Arc* (capacity 8 SA-319B *Alouette III* ASW hel) with 2 triple (6 eff.) each with 3 MM-38 *Exocet* tactical SSM, 2 100mm gun

DESTROYERS • DDG 12:
2 *Cassard* each with 1 AS-565SA *Panther* ASW hel, 2 single ASTT each with L5 HWT, 1 Mk 13 GMLS with 40 SM-1 MR SAM, 2 quad (8 eff.) with 8 MM-40 *Exocet* tactical SSM, 1 100mm gun

2 *Georges Leygues* each with 2 *Lynx* Mk4 (*Lynx* MK3) ASW hel each with 1+ Mk 46 LWT, 4 MM-38 *Exocet* tactical SSM, 2 single ASTT each with 1+ L5 HWT, 1 octuple (8 eff.) with 26 *Crotale* SAM, 1 100mm gun

5 *Georges Leygues* each with 2 *Lynx* utl hel each with 1+ Mk 46 LWT, 8 MM-40 *Exocet* tactical SSM, 2 single ASTT each with 1+ L5 HWT, 1 octuple (8 eff.) with 26 *Crotale* SAM, 1 100mm gun

1 *Suffren* (*Duquesne*) with 4 MM-38 *Exocet* tactical SSM, 4 single ASTT each with 1+ L5 HWT, 1 twin (2 eff.) with 48 *Masurca* SAM, 2 100mm gun

2 *Tourville* each with 2 *Lynx* Mk4 (*Lynx* MK3) ASW hel each with 1+ Mk 46 LWT, 6 MM-38 *Exocet* tactical SSM, 2 single ASTT each with 1+ L5 HWT, 2 100mm gun

FRIGATES 20
FFH 11:
6 *Floreal* each with 1 AS-565SA *Panther* ASW hel, 2 MM-38 *Exocet* tactical SSM, 1 100mm gun

5 *La Fayette* (capacity either 1 AS-565SA *Panther* ASW hel or 1 SA-321 *Super Frelon* SAR hel) (Space for fitting 16 VLS SAM launchers (ASTER 15/30)) each with 1 AS-565SA *Panther* ASW hel, 8 MM-40 *Exocet* tactical SSM, 1 octuple (8 eff.) with *Crotale* SAM, 1 100mm gun

FF 9:
3 *D'Estienne d'Orves* each with 2 MM-38 *Exocet* tactical SSM, 4 single ASTT, 6 single, 1 100mm gun

6 *D'Estienne d'Orves* each with 6 MM-40 *Exocet* tactical SSM, 4 single ASTT, 6 single, 1 100mm gun

PATROL AND COASTAL COMBATANTS 36
PCC 24: 1 *Arago*; 3 *Flamant*; 1 *Grebe*; 10 *L'Audacieuse*; 8

Leopard (Instruction); 1 *Sterne*

PCI 11: 5 less than 100 tonnes (manned by Gendarmarie Maritime); *Athos* 2 less than 100 tonnes; *Patra* 2 less than 100 tonnes; *Stellis* 2 less than 100 tonnes
PFM 1: 1 *Albatros* (Public Service Force)

MINE WARFARE • MINE COUNTERMEASURES 21
MCCS 1: 1 *Loire*
MCM SPT 7: 3 *Antares*; 4 *Vulcain*
MHC 13: 13 *Eridan*

AMPHIBIOUS
PRINCIPAL AMPHIBIOUS SHIPS 5
LHD 1: 1 *Mistral* (second (*Tonnerre*) due commissioning 2006)
LPD 4:
2 *Foudre* (capacity 22 tanks; 470 troops; 4 AS-532 *Cougar* utl hel; either 2 Edic LCT or 10 LCM)

2 *Ouragan* (capacity 22 tanks; 370 troops; 2 Edic LCT; either 2 SA-321 *Super Frelon* SAR hel or 4 SA-330 *Puma* spt hel) (to be replaced by *Mistral* Class)

LS • LSM 5: 5 *Champlain* (capacity 12 trucks; 140 troops)
CRAFT 20: 5 LCU; 15 LCM

LOGISTICS AND SUPPORT 23: 3 AGHS; 1 AGOR
AOR 4:
4 *Durance* (capacity either 1 SA-319 *Alouette III* utl hel or 1 AS-365 *Dauphin 2* utl hel or 1 *Lynx* utl hel)

AR 1:
1 *Jules Verne* (capacity 1 SA-319 *Alouette III* utl hel)

ATF 4 (Civil Charter)
TRG 2: 2 *Glycine*
Trial Ship 8

AIRCRAFT • STRIKE/FGA 24: 24 *Super Etendard* opcon Strategic Nuclear Forces

FACILITIES
Base | 1 (HQ) located at Toulon, 1 (HQ) located at Brest, 1 with 2 Frigates; 2 PCI (P 400); 1 *Champlain* LSM (capacity 12 trucks; 140 troops); 3 *Gardian* MP ac (HQ) located at Papeete, PF, 1 located at Dzaoudzi (Mayotte), 1 (HQ) located at Port-des-Galets, 1 located at Fort de France, 1 with 1 *Floreal* FFH; *Albatros* OPV; 2 *Gardian* MP ac located at Nouméa, NC, 1 with 2 PCI; 2 (P 400) located at Cayenne, Gf, 1 located at Lorient, 1 located at Cherbourg

Naval airbase | 1 located at Nimes-Garons, 1 located at Landivisiau, 1 located at Lann-Bihoue, 1 located at Hyères

Naval Aviation 6,443

Flying hours | 180 to 220 hrs/year on *Super Etendard* strike/FGA ac

FORCES BY ROLE

Nuclear Strike	2 sqn with 28 *Super Etendard* (incls Strategic Nuclear Forces)
Ftr	1 sqn with 10 *Rafale* M
ASW	2 regt with 18 *Lynx* Mk4 (*Lynx* MK3); 1 sqn with 12 AS-565SA *Panther*
MR	1 sqn with N-262 *Fregate*
MP	2 sqn with 16 *Atlantique* 2 *
AEW	1 sqn with 3 E-2C *Hawkeye*

SAR 1 sqn with 9 AS-365F *Dauphin 2*; 1 sqn with 7 SA-321 *Super Frelon*

Trg 1 sqn with 21 SA-319B *Alouette III*; 2 unit with N-262 *Fregate*; 7 CAP 10; 6 *Rallye* MS-880*

EQUIPMENT BY TYPE
AIRCRAFT 60 combat capable
 FTR 10: 10 *Rafale* M
 STRIKE/FGA 43: 28 *Super Etendard* (incl Strategic Nuclear Forces); 15 in store
 MP 33: 16 *Atlantique* 2 *; 9 * in store; 4 *Falcon* 50M; 4 *Gardian*
 AEW • E-2 3: 3 E-2C *Hawkeye*
 TPT 21: 8 EMB-121 *Xingu*; 13 N-262 *Fregate*
 TRG 18: 7 CAP 10; 5 *Falcon* 10 MER; 6 *Rallye* MS-880 *
HELICOPTERS
 SAR 7: 7 SA-321 *Super Frelon*
 ASW 64: 12 AS-565SA *Panther*; 18 *Lynx* Mk4 (*Lynx* MK3); 13 in store; 21 SA-319B *Alouette III*
 UTL • AS-365 9: 9 AS-365F *Dauphin 2*
MSL • TACTICAL • ASM: some AM-39 *Exocet*; some ASMP
 AAM: some AS 30 *Laser*; some MICA
  R-550: some R-550 *Magic 2*

Marines 2,050

Commando Units 500

Recce	1 gp
Aslt	2 gp
Atk Swimmer	1 gp
Raiding	1 gp

Fusiliers-Marin 1,550

Protection 14 (Naval Base) gp

Public Service Force

Naval personnel performing general coast guard, fishery protection, SAR, anti-pollution and traffic surv duties. Command exercised through Maritime Prefectures (Premar): Manche (Cherbourg), Atlantique (Brest), Mediterranee (Toulon)
Ships incl in naval patrol and coastal totals
PATROL AND COASTAL COMBATANTS 5
 PCC 4: 3 *Flamant*; 1 *Sterne*
 PFM 1: 1 *Albatros*
AIRCRAFT • TPT 4: 4 N-262 *Fregate*
HELICOPTERS • UTL 4: 4 AS-365 *Dauphin 2*

Reserves 6,000 reservists

Territorial Command • Atlantic
CECLANT
Navy 1 HQ located at Brest

Indian Ocean
ALINDIEN
Navy 1 (afloat) HQ located at Toulon

Mediterranean
CECMED
Navy 1 HQ located at Toulon

North Sea/Channel
COMAR CHERBOURG
Navy 1 HQ located at Cherbourg

Pacific Ocean
ALPACI
Navy 1 HQ located at Papeete, PF

Air Force 63,600; 5,700 (civilian); 1,800 opcon Strategic Nuclear Forces (total 65,400 plus 5,700 civilians)

Flying hours 180 hrs/year

Air Signals and Ground Environment Command
FORCES BY ROLE
Air 1 (Control) sqn with 4 E-3F *Sentry*
ADA 1 bty with 20mm
AD 11 (1 trg) sqn with *Crotale*; SATCP; ASPIC

EQUIPMENT BY TYPE
AIRCRAFT • AEW • E-3 4: 4 E-3F *Sentry*
AD • SYSTEMS: some STRIDA (Control)
 SAM: some *Crotale*; some SATCP
 GUNS: some 20mm
 LAUNCHER: some ASPIC
FACILITIES
Radar Stn 5 (Control)

Air Combat Command
FORCES BY ROLE

Ftr	5 sqn with 32 M-2000-5F *Mirage* (upgraded C); 65 M-2000C *Mirage*; 23 M-2000B *Mirage*
FGA	1 sqn with 4 *Rafale* F1-B; 1 *Rafale* F1-C; 3 sqn with 67 M-2000D *Mirage*; 2 sqn with 43 F-1CT *Mirage*
FGA / Strike	3 sqn opcon Strategic Nuclear Forces with 60 M-2000N *Mirage*
Recce	2 sqn with 43 F-1CR *Mirage*
EW	1 sqn with C-160G *Gabriel* (ESM)
OCU	1 sqn with M-2000B *Mirage*

EQUIPMENT BY TYPE
AIRCRAFT 295 combat capable
 FTR • M-2000-5 32: 32 M-2000-5F *Mirage* (upgraded C)
 STRIKE/FGA 43: 43 F-1CT *Mirage*
 FGA 137
  RAFALE 5: 4 *Rafale* F1-B; 1 *Rafale* F1-C
  M-2000 132: 65 M-2000C *Mirage*; 67 M-2000D *Mirage*
 RECCE 43: 43 F-1CR *Mirage*
 EW • ELINT: some C-160G *Gabriel* (ESM)
 TRG 33: 10 F-1B *Mirage*; 23 M-2000B *Mirage**
MSL • TACTICAL • ASM • AS-30: some AS-30L
 ASMP some *Apache* some SCALP EG *Storm Shadow*
 AAM: some MICA
  R-550: some R-550 *Magic 2*
  R530 • SUPER 530: some Super 530D

Air Mobility Command
FORCES BY ROLE

SAR / trg / tpt / utl	7 light sqn with A-319; C-160 *Transall*; 20 CN-235M; 6 DHC-6 *Twin Otter*; 1 *Mystère* 20 (*Falcon* 20); 4 *Falcon* 50 (VIP); 2 *Falcon* 900 (VIP); 17 TBM-700; 6 EC 725 *Cougar MKII*; AS-555 *Fennec*
Tkr / tactical tpt	6 sqn with 5 C-130H *Hercules*; 50 C-160 *Transall*; 15 Transall C-160NG
Tpt	1 heavy sqn with 3 A-310-300; A-319
Tkr	1 sqn opcon Strategic Nuclear Forces with 11 C-135FR; 3 KC-135 *Stratotanker*
OCU	1 sqn with 3 SA-330 *Puma*; 9 AS-555 *Fennec*; 1 unit with C-160 *Transall*
Trg	1 unit opcon Strategic Nuclear Forces with 2 *Mystère* 20 (*Falcon* 20)
Hel	5 sqn with 7 AS-332 *Super Puma*; 6 AS-355 *Ecureuil*; 26 SA-330 *Puma*; 3 AS-532 *Cougar* (tpt/VIP); 33 AS-555 *Fennec*

EQUIPMENT BY TYPE
AIRCRAFT
TKR 14: 11 C-135FR; 3 KC-135 *Stratotanker*
TPT 174
    A-310 3: 3 A-310-300
    A-319 2 (VIP)
    C-130 *Hercules* 14:
      C-130H 5 **C-130H-30** 9
    C-160 *Transall* 100
    CN-235 20: 20 CN-235M
    DHC-6 *Twin Otter* 6 *Falcon* 50 4 (VIP) *Falcon* 900 2 (VIP)*Mystère* 20 (*Falcon* 20) 1 TBM-700 17
    TPT/TKR 15: 15 *Transall* C-160NG
HELICOPTERS
    CSAR 6: 6 EC 725 *Cougar MKII*
    SPT 42: 7 AS-332 *Super Puma*; 6 AS-355 *Ecureuil*; 29 SA-330 *Puma*
    UTL 69: 24 AS-532 *Cougar*; 3 (tpt/VIP); 42 AS-555 *Fennec*

Air Training Command
FORCES BY ROLE
Trg some sqn with 31 EMB-121 *Xingu*; 113 *Alpha Jet*; 11 CAP 10B/CAP 231/CAP 232; 47 EMB-312 *Tucano*; 138 TB-30 *Epsilon*

EQUIPMENT BY TYPE
AIRCRAFT
    TPT 31: 31 EMB-121 *Xingu*
    TRG 309: 113 *Alpha Jet*; 11 CAP 10B/CAP 231/CAP 232; 47 EMB-312 *Tucano*; 138 TB-30 *Epsilon*

Reserves 4,300 reservists

Paramilitary 104,275

Gendarmerie 102,322; 3,884 (Administration); 2,078 (Maritime Air (personnel drawn from other departments)); 16,859 (Mobile); 4,741 (Republican Guard, Air Tpt, Arsenals); 5,049 (Schools); 66,537 (Territorial); 1,953 (civilian); 40,000 reservists; 41 opcon Strategic Nuclear Forces (**total** 241,511 plus 1,953 civilians)
TK • LT TK 28: 28 VBC-90
APC • APC (W) 153: 153 VBRG-170

ARTY • MOR 157+: 157 60mm; some 81mm
HELICOPTERS
    SPT • **AS-350** 32: 32 AS-350B *Ecureuil*
    UTL 17: 8 EC-135; 9 SA-316 *Alouette III*/SA-319 *Alouette III*

NON-STATE ARMED GROUPS
see Part II

DEPLOYMENT

AFGHANISTAN
NATO • ISAF 565

AFGHANISTAN AND INDIAN OCEAN
NATO 700 (*Operation Enduring Freedom*) army

BOSNIA-HERZEGOVINA
EU • EUFOR I • Air Force • Air Mobility Command
    AIRCRAFT • TPT 1: 1 TBM-700
EU • EUFOR II 500

CHAD
Army 950
FORCES BY ROLE
1 recce sqn with ERC-90F *Sagaie*; 2 inf coy
EQUIPMENT BY TYPE
RECCE: some ERC-90F *Sagaie*
Navy 400
Air Force • Air Combat Command
    AIRCRAFT: 6 F-1CR *Mirage* recce/F-1CT *Mirage* strike/FGA
Air Mobility Command
    AIRCRAFT • TPT 4: 1 C-135 *Stratolifter*; 3 C-160 *Transall*
    HELICOPTERS • SPT 3: 3 SA-330 *Puma*

CÔTE D'IVOIRE
Army 3,800
UN • UNOCI 186; 2 obs

DEMOCRATIC REPUBLIC OF CONGO
UN • MONUC 8; 1 obs

DJIBOUTI
Army 2,850
2 (combined) army regt (*total:* 1 engr coy, 1 arty bty, 2 recce sqn, 2 inf coy)
Air Force
1 Air sqn with 10 M-2000 *Mirage*; 1 C-160 *Transall*; 3 SA-342 *Gazelle*; 7 SA-330 *Puma*; 1 AS-555 *Fennec*; 1 SA-319 *Alouette III*

EGYPT
MFO
Air Force • Air Mobility Command
    AIRCRAFT • TPT 1: 1 DHC-6 *Twin Otter*
Armed Forces 15

ETHIOPIA/ERITREA
UN • UNMEE 1

FRENCH GUIANA

Army 1,300 2 army regt; 1 SMA regt

Navy 170

EQUIPMENT BY TYPE

PATROL AND COASTAL COMBATANTS 3: 3 PCI (P 400)

FACILITIES

Base 1 with 2 PCI; 2 (P 400) located at Cayenne

Naval Aviation
AIRCRAFT • MP 1: 1 *Atlantique*

Air Force • Air Mobility Command

FORCES BY ROLE

1 tpt unit

EQUIPMENT BY TYPE

HELICOPTERS
SPT 4: 4 SA-330 *Puma*
UTL 3: 3 AS-555 *Fennec*

Paramilitary • Gendarmerie

FORCES BY ROLE

3 Paramilitary coy

EQUIPMENT BY TYPE

HELICOPTERS • SPT 1: 1 AS-350 *Ecureuil*

FRENCH POLYNESIA

Army 800 (incl Centre d'Expérimentation du Pacifique)
1 marine inf bn; 3 SMA coy

Navy 710

EQUIPMENT BY TYPE

PRINCIPAL SURFACE COMBATANTS • FRIGATES 1:
1 FFH with 1 AS-565SA *Panther* ASW hel

PATROL AND COASTAL COMBATANTS 2: 2 PC

AMPHIBIOUS • LS 1: 1 LSM

FACILITIES

Base 1 with 2 Frigates; 2 PCI (P 400); 1 *Champlain* LSM
(capacity 12 trucks; 140 troops); 3 *Gardian* MP ac
(HQ) located at Papeete

Naval Aviation
AIRCRAFT • MP 2: 2 CASA 235 MPA

Territorial Command • Pacific Ocean
1 Navy HQ located at Papeete, PF

Air Force • Air Mobility Command

FORCES BY ROLE

1 tpt unit

EQUIPMENT BY TYPE

HELICOPTERS • SPT 2: 2 AS-332 *Super Puma*

FRENCH WEST INDIES

Army 800 2 marine inf regt; 2 SMA regt

Navy 450

PRINCIPAL SURFACE COMBATANTS • FRIGATES 1:
1 FFH

PATROL AND COASTAL COMBATANTS 2: 2 PCI

AMPHIBIOUS • LS 1: 1 LSM

Naval Aviation
AIRCRAFT • MP 3: 3 CASA 235 MPA
HELICOPTERS • ASW 1: 1 AS-555SN *Fennec*

Air Force • Air Mobility Command

FORCES BY ROLE

1 tpt unit

EQUIPMENT BY TYPE

HELICOPTERS • SPT 2: 2 SA-330 *Puma*

Paramilitary • Gendarmerie

FORCES BY ROLE

6 Paramilitary coy

EQUIPMENT BY TYPE

HELICOPTERS • SPT 2: 2 AS-350 *Ecureuil*

GABON

Army 700

FORCES BY ROLE

1 recce pl with ERC-90F *Sagaie*; 1 marine inf bn

EQUIPMENT BY TYPE

RECCE: some ERC-90F *Sagaie*

HELICOPTERS • RECCE 4: 4 AS-532 *Horizon*

Navy 1,560

Air Force • Air Mobility Command
AIRCRAFT • TPT 2: 2 C-160 *Transall*
HELICOPTERS • UTL 1: 1 AS-555 *Fennec*

GEORGIA

UN • UNOMIG 3 obs

GERMANY

Army 2,800 (incl elm Eurocorps and Fr/Ge bde (2500))
1 (Fr/Ge) army bde (1 army HQ, 1 recce regt, 1 inf regt)

INDIAN OCEAN

Army 1,000 (incl La Reunion and TAAF)

FORCES BY ROLE

1 marine inf regt; 1 SMA regt

EQUIPMENT BY TYPE

PRINCIPAL SURFACE COMBATANTS • FRIGATES 2:
2 FFH with 2 AS-555 *Fennec* utl hel

PATROL AND COASTAL COMBATANTS 3: 1 PC; 2 PCI

AMPHIBIOUS • LS 1: 1 LSM

Air Force • Air Mobility Command

FORCES BY ROLE

1 tpt unit

EQUIPMENT BY TYPE

AIRCRAFT • TPT 2: 2 C-160 *Transall*
HELICOPTERS: 1 spt
UTL 2: 2 AS-555 *Fennec*

Paramilitary • Gendarmerie

FORCES BY ROLE

5 Paramilitary coy

EQUIPMENT BY TYPE

HELICOPTERS • UTL 1: 1 SA-319 *Alouette III*

LA RÉUNION

Navy

EQUIPMENT BY TYPE

PRINCIPAL SURFACE COMBATANTS • FRIGATES •
FFH 1: 1 *Floreal*

PATROL AND COASTAL COMBATANTS 2: 2 PCI (P 400)

AMPHIBIOUS • LS 1: 1 LSM

FACILITIES
Base 1 located at Dzaoudzi (Mayotte), 1 (HQ) located at
   Port-des-Galets

LEBANON
UN • UNIFIL
Army 1 log bn (elm)
Armed Forces 204

LIBERIA
UN • UNMIL 1

MACEDONIA AND BOSNIA
EU 23 (*Op Proxima*)
EU • EUMM/EUPM 60

MARTINIQUE
Navy
Base   1 located at Fort de France
Naval airbase   1 located at Hyères, 1 located at Nimes-
                 Garons, 1 located at Lann-Bihoue, 1 located
                 at Landivisiau

MIDDLE EAST
UN • UNTSO 3 obs

NEW CALEDONIA
Army 1,030
FORCES BY ROLE
1 marine inf regt; 2 SMA coy
EQUIPMENT BY TYPE
RECCE 6: 6 ERC-90F *Sagaie*
Navy 510
Base 1 with 1 *Floreal* FFH; *Albatros* OPV; 2 *Gardian* MP
   aircraft located at Nouméa
Naval Aviation
   AIRCRAFT • MP 3: 3 CASA 235 MPA
Air Force • Air Mobility Command
   FORCES BY ROLE
   some air det; 1 tpt unit
   EQUIPMENT BY TYPE
   HELICOPTERS
      SPT 5: 5 SA-330 *Puma*
      UTL 2: 2 AS-555 *Fennec*
Paramilitary • Gendarmerie
   FORCES BY ROLE
   4 Paramilitary coy
   EQUIPMENT BY TYPE
   HELICOPTERS • SPT 2: 2 AS-350 *Ecureuil*

SENEGAL
Army 610
FORCES BY ROLE
1 marine inf bn (1 recce sqn with ERC-90F *Sagaie*)
EQUIPMENT BY TYPE
RECCE: some ERC-90F *Sagaie*
Navy 230

Naval Aviation
   AIRCRAFT • MP 1: 1 *Atlantique*
Air Force • Air Mobility Command
   AIRCRAFT • TPT 1: 1 C-160 *Transall*
   HELICOPTERS • UTL 1: 1 AS-555 *Fennec*

SERBIA AND MONTENEGRO
NATO • KFOR I 2,400
UN • UNMIK 57

TAJIKISTAN
Air Force • Air Mobility Command
   AIRCRAFT • TPT 2: 2 C-160 *Transall*
Armed Forces 120

WESTERN SAHARA
UN • MINURSO 25 obs (Gendarmerie)

FOREIGN FORCES

Belgium Air Force: 29 *Alpha Jet* trg ac located at Cazaux/
Tours
Germany Army: 209 (Ge elm Eurocorps)
Singapore Air Force: 200 Air; some trg sqn with 6 A-4SU
Super Skyhawk; 10 TA-4SU *Super Skyhawk*

Germany Ge

Euro €		2003	2004	2005
GDP	€	2.12tr	2.16tr	
	US$	2.41tr	2.67tr	
per capita	US$	29,361	32,472	
Growth	%	-0.1	1.7	
Inflation	%	1.0	1.8	
Public Debt	%	67.0	70.1	
Def exp [a]	€	31.0bn	30.6bn	
	US$	35.2bn	37.7bn	
Def bdgt	€	24.3bn	24.0bn	23.8bn
	US$	27.7bn	29.7bn	30.2bn
US$1=€		0.88	0.81	0.79

[a] including military pensions

Population	82,431,390

Age	0–14	15–19	20–24	25–29	30–64	65 plus
Male	7%	3%	3%	3%	25%	8%
Female	7%	3%	3%	3%	24%	10%

Capabilities

**ACTIVE 284,500 (Army 191,350 Navy 25,650 Air
67,500)**
Terms of service 9 months; 10–23 months voluntary. *Reserves:*
men to age 45 NCOs and officers to 60.

**RESERVE 358,650 (Army 297,300 Navy 11,500 Air
49,850)**

ORGANISATIONS BY SERVICE

Army 117,900; 73,450 conscript; 297,300 reservists (total 488,650)

I GE/NL Corps HQ, II GE/US Corps HQ

FORCES BY ROLE

Bde differ in their basic org, peacetime str, eqpt and mob capability; 4 (2 armd, 1 inf and Ge/Fr bde are allocated to the CRF, the remainder to Main Defence Forces (MDF). 1 armd inf div is earmarked for EUROCORPS, 1 armd div (incl 1 Pl bde) to Allied Rapid Reaction Corps (ARRC) and 1 armd inf div to the Multi-National Corps North East

Armd / Armd inf	5 div (3 armd, 2 armd inf) (*total:* 1 inf bde, 1 mtn inf bde, 13 armd/armd inf bde (and the GE elm of the GE/Fr bde), 4 mech bde, 7 engr bde, 7 arty regt, 7 AD regt)
Army	1 (SIGINT/ELINT) bde; 1 (battle) gp (trg) (army trg area) with 35 *Leopard* 2; 26 *Marder* 1; 12 M-109A3G
Air mob	1 div (1 air mech bde (4 regt), 1 avn bde (5 regt))
Spec Ops	1 div (1 SF comd (1 cdo/SF bde), 2 AB bde (1 Crisis Reaction Force (CRF)))
Spt	1 regt
Log	2 bde
Spt arms	1 comd (forming)

EQUIPMENT BY TYPE

TK • MBT 2,398: 1,728 *Leopard* 2 (350 to be upgraded to A6); 670 *Leopard* 1A1/1A3/1A4/1A5
RECCE 523: 409 SPz-2 *Luchs*; 114 Tpz-1 *Fuchs* (NBC)
AIFV 2,255: 2,122 1 A2 *Marder*/1 A3 *Marder*; 133 *Wiesel* (with **20mm** gun)
APC 3,123
  APC (T) 2067: 2,067 M-113 (incl 317 arty obs and other variants)
  APC (W) 1056: 147 APCV-2 *Dingo*; 909 TPz-1 *Fuchs* (incl variants)
ARTY 1,682
  TOWED 314
    105mm 118: 118 M-101
    155mm 196: 196 FH-70
  SP • 155mm 664
    M-109 499: 499 M-109A3G
    PzH 2000 165
  MRL 200
    110mm 50: 50 LARS
    227mm 150: 150 MLRS
  MOR • 120mm 504: 504 *Tampella*
AT • MSL 1,915: 1,519 *Milan*; 186 RJPz-(HOT) *Jaguar* 1; 210 *Wiesel* (TOW)
AMPHIBIOUS • CRAFT 13: 13 LCM (river engineers)
HELICOPTERS
  ATK 199: 199 BO-105,BO 105 M (PAH-1) (with HOT)
  RECCE 60: 60 BO-105M
  SPT • CH-53 107: 107 CH-53G *Stallion*
  UTL 159: 13 EC-135; 28 SE 3130 *Alouette II*
  UH-1 118: 118 UH-1D *Iroquois*
UAV • AN/USD-502: some AOLOS-289/CL-289
  Aladin some **X-2000** *LUNA* some

AD
  SAM • SP 143: 143 *Roland*
    MANPAD: some FIM-92A *Stinger* (incl some *Ozelot* SP)
  GUNS 1,509
    20mm • TOWED 1,155: 1,155 Rh 202
    35mm • SP 354: 354 *Gepard* (147 being upgraded)
RADAR • LAND 154+: some *Cobra*; 18 M-113 A1GE *Green Archer* (mor); 91 RASIT (veh, arty); 45 RATAC (veh, arty)

Navy 20,700; 4,950 conscript; 11,500 reservists (total 37,150)

Type Comds SS, FF, Patrol Boats, MCMV, Naval Aviation.

EQUIPMENT BY TYPE

SUBMARINES • TACTICAL 13
  SSK 12:
    11 Type 206 each with 8 x1 533mm ASTT each with DM2 HWT
    1 Type 212A (Sea Trials in Progress) with 6 single 533mm TT with 12 A4 *Seehecht* DM2 HWT
  SSC 1:
    1 Type 205 with 8 x1 533mm ASTT
PRINCIPAL SURFACE COMBATANTS 14
  FRIGATES 14
    FFGHM 2:
      2 *Sachsen* (capacity either 2 NH-90 utl hel or 2 *Lynx* utl hel) (Both under-going sea trials) each with 2 Mk 141 *Harpoon* quad (8 eff.) each with 1 RGM-84F tactical SSM, 1 32 cell Mk 41 VLS (32 eff.) with 24 SM-2 MR SAM, 32 RIM-162B *Sea Sparrow* SAM, 2 Mk 49 RAM with 21 RIM-116 *RAM* SAM
    FFG 12:
      4 *Brandenburg* (capacity either 2 MK88 *Sea Lynx* ASW hel or 2 *Sea Lynx* MK88A MK88 ASW) each with 4 x1 324mm ASTT each with Mk 46 LWT, 2 Mk 49 RAM with 21 RIM-116 *RAM* SAM, 2 with 21 RIM-116 *RAM* SAM, 2 twin (4 eff.) each with 1 MM-38 *Exocet* tactical SSM, 1 Mk 41 VLS with 16 RIM-7M/RIM-7P, 1 76mm gun
      8 *Bremen* (capacity either 2 MK88 *Sea Lynx* ASW hel or 2 *Sea Lynx* MK88A MK88 ASWs) each with 2 twin 324mm ASTT (4 eff.) each with Mk 46 LWT, 1 Mk 29 *Sea Sparrow* octuple with 16 RIM-7M/RIM-7P, 2 Mk 141 *Harpoon* quad (8 eff.) each with RGM-84A *Harpoon*/RGM-84C *Harpoon*, 2 Mk 49 RAM with 21 RIM-116 *RAM* SAM, 1 76mm gun
PATROL AND COASTAL COMBATANTS • PFM 14:
  4 *Albatros* each with 2 single 533mm TT, 2 twin (4 eff.) each with 1 MM-38 *Exocet* tactical SSM
  10 *Gepard* each with 1 Mk 49 RAM with 21 RIM-116 *RAM* SAM, 2 twin (4 eff.)
MINE WARFARE • MINE COUNTERMEASURES 23: 1 MCM spt/Type 742A MCD
  MHC 17: 12 *Frankenthal*; 5 *Kulmback*
  MSC 5:
    5 *Ensdorf* each with 4 MSD
LOGISTICS AND SUPPORT 38
  AE (AMMO) 1: 1 *Westerwald*
  AG 8: 3 *Schwedeneck* Type 748; 5 *Stollergrund* Type 745
  AGB 1: 1 *Eisvogel* (Civil)

AGHS 3 (civil manned for Ministry of Transport); **AGI** 3; **AGOR** 1
AO 2: 2 *Spessart*
AORH 2:
  2 *Berlin* (capacity either 2 NH-90 utl hel or 2 *Sea King* MK41 SAR hel; 2 RAMs)
AOT 2 (small (2,000t))
AR 1: 1 *Lüneburg*
AT 5
SPT 6: 6 *Elbe*
Trg 1 **Trial Ship** 2

FACILITIES
Base 1 located at Olpenitz, 1 located at Wilhelmshaven, 1 (Maritime HQ) located at Glücksburg, 1 located at Warnemünde, 1 located at Eckernförde, 1 located at Kiel

Naval Aviation 3,720
AIRCRAFT
MP 16: 16 *Atlantic* (12 armed MR, 4 int)
TPT 4: 4 DO-228 (2 pollution control, 2 tpt)
HELICOPTERS
SAR 21: 21 *Sea King* MK41 (SAR)
ASW • MK88 22: 22 *Sea Lynx* MK88A (ASW/ASUW)
MSL • TACTICAL • ASM: some AS-34 *Kormoran*; some *Sea Skua*
AAM • AIM-9: some AIM-9L *Sidewinder*

Air Force 51,400; 16,100 conscript; 49,850 reservists (**total** 117,350)
Flying hours   150 hrs/year
Missile trg   1 located at Fort Bliss (TX), US

Air Force Command
4 FGA, 4 ftr wg
FORCES BY ROLE
Air   4 div
Ftr   4 wg (*total:* 7 ftr sqn eq. with 145 F-4F *Phantom II*); 1 wg eq. with 9 *Typhoon*
FGA   1 wg (2 FGA sqn eq. with 35 *Tornado* ECR *); 3 wg (*total:* 6 FGA sqn eq. with 186 *Tornado* IDS)
Recce   1 wg (2 recce sqn eq. with 41 *Tornado* IDS (recce))
Radar   2 (tac air control) regt
SAM   6 (mixed) wg (*each:* 1 SAM gp eq. with MIM-104 *Patriot* (6 SAM sqn)); 1 gp eq. with MIM-23 HAWK (2 SAM sqn , 4 SAM sqn); 14 sqn eq. with *Roland*

EQUIPMENT BY TYPE
AIRCRAFT 417 combat capable
FTR 12 [B] : 9 *Typhoon* ; 2 MiG-23 *Flogger* in store; 1 MiG-21 *Fishbed*
STRIKE/FGA 227 [B] : 41 *Tornado* IDS (recce); 186 more
FGA 145 [B] :
  F-4 145 [B] : 145 F-4F *Phantom II*
SEAD 35 [B] : 35 *Tornado* ECR *
TRG 75 [B][A]
  T-37 35 [B] : 35 T-37B *Tweet*
  T-38 40 [B] : 40 T-38A *Talon*

AD • SAM • SP : some *Roland*
  TOWED : some MIM-104 *Patriot* ; some MIM-23 *HAWK*
MSL • TACTICAL • ASM : some AGM-65 *Maverick*
  ARM • AGM-88 : some AGM-88A *HARM*
  KEPD 350 *Taurus* some
  AAM : some AA-10 *Alamo* ; some AA-11 *Archer* ; some AA-8 *Aphid* ; some AIM-9 *Sidewinder*
FACILITIES
Radar Stn 1 no location (8), 1 no location (11, remote)

Transport Command
3 wg
FORCES BY ROLE
Tkr / tpt 1 (special air mission) wg eq. with 7 A-310 (incl tpt/tkr); 6 CL-601 *Challenger* ; 3 AS-532U2 *Cougar II* (VIP)
Tpt   3 wg (*total:* 4 tpt sqn eq. with 86 UH-1D *Iroquois* (82 SAR, tpt, liaison, 4 VIP)(*total:* 1 OCU), 3 tpt sqn eq. with 83 C-160 *Transall* (*total:* 1 OCU))

EQUIPMENT BY TYPE
AIRCRAFT • TPT 96 [B] : 7 A-310 (incl tpt/tkr); 83 C-160 *Transall* ; 6 CL-601 *Challenger*
TRG : some Beech F-33 *Bonanza*
HELICOPTERS • UTL 89 [B][A]
  AS-532 3 [B] : 3 AS-532U2 *Cougar II* (VIP)
  UH-1 86 [B] : 86 UH-1D *Iroquois* (82 SAR, tpt, liaison, 4 VIP)
FACILITIES
School 1 located at Fort Bliss (TX), US opcon KFOR I (GAF Air Defence)

Training
OCU 1 eq. with 30 F-4F *Phantom II* ; 1 eq. with 36 *Tornado* IDS

Euro NATO Joint Jet Pilot Training
AIRCRAFT • TRG 75 [B][A]
T-37 35 [B] : 35 T-37B *Tweet*
T-38 40 [B] : 40 T-38A *Talon*
  ARTY • SP • 155mm • M-109 10 [B] : 10 M-109A3G

DEPLOYMENT

AFGHANISTAN
NATO • ISAF 1,909
UN • UNAMA 1 obs

BOSNIA-HERZEGOVINA
EU • EUFOR II
FORCES BY ROLE
1,000
EQUIPMENT BY TYPE
RECCE 28: 28 SPz-2 *Luchs*
APC • APC (W): some TPz-1 *Fuchs*
HELICOPTERS
SPT 3: 3 CH-53 *Sea Stallion*
UTL • UH-1 4: 4 UH-1D *Iroquois*

DJIBOUTI
Armed Forces
HELICOPTERS
  SAR 2: 2 *Sea King* MK41
  UTL • UH-1 2: 2 UH-1D *Iroquois*
EU • EUFOR II/KFOR
  AIRCRAFT • SEAD 3: 3 *Tornado* ECR

ETHIOPIA/ERITREA
UN • UNMEE 2

FRANCE
Army 209 (Ge elm Eurocorps)

GEORGIA
UN • UNOMIG 12 obs

ITALY
Army
AIRCRAFT: 3 MP (in ELMAS/Sardinia)
EU • EUFOR II/KFOR 200 air force

LIBERIA
UN • UNMIL 15

POLAND
Army 67 (Ge elm Corps HQ (multinational))

SERBIA AND MONTENEGRO
NATO • KFOR I
Armed Forces
  FORCES BY ROLE
  3,900

  EQUIPMENT BY TYPE
  TK 28:
    MBT 28: 2; 26 *Leopard* C2
  RECCE 17: 17 SPz-2 *Luchs*
  AIFV 25: 25 *Marder* 1
  APC 75: 21 APC (T)
    APC (W) 54: 54 TPz-1 *Fuchs*
  ARTY • SP • 155mm • M-109 10: 10 M-109A3G
  AT • MSL 6: 6 *Wiesel* (TOW)
  HELICOPTERS
    SPT 3: 3 CH-53 *Sea Stallion*
    UTL • UH-1 9: 9 UH-1D *Iroquois*

SIERRA LEONE
UN • UNAMSIL 8

SUDAN
UN • UNMIS 2 obs

UNITED STATES
Army
FORCES BY ROLE
1 (battle) army gp (trg) (army trg area) with 35 *Leopard* 2;
26 *Marder* 1; 12 M-109A3G

EQUIPMENT BY TYPE
TK • MBT 35: 35 *Leopard* 2
AIFV 26: 26 *Marder* 1
ARTY • SP • 155mm • M-109 12: 12 M-109A3G
Air Force 812 (flying trg) located at Goodyear AFB (AZ),
US; 812 (flying trg) located at Sheppard AFB (TX), US; 812
(flying trg) located at Holloman AFB (NM), US; 812 (flying

trg) located at NAS Pensacola (FL), US; 812 (flying trg)
located at Fort Rucker (AL), US (total 4,060)

EQUIPMENT BY TYPE
AIRCRAFT 190 combat capable
  STRIKE/FGA 37: 37 *Tornado* IDS located at Fort Bliss
  (TX), US
  FGA • F-4 23: 23 F-4F *Phantom II* located at Fort Rucker
  (AL), US
  TRG 75: 35 T-37 *Tweet* located at Fort Rucker (AL), US; 40
  T-38 *Talon* located at Fort Rucker (AL), US
FACILITIES
Missile trg 1 located at Fort Bliss (TX), US
NATO • Air Force • Transport Command
  FORCES BY ROLE
  some (primary) trg sqn located at Goodyear AFB (AZ),
  US with Beech F-33 *Bonanza*; some (joint jet pilot) trg
  sqn located at Sheppard AFB (TX), US with 35 T-37B
  Tweet; 40 T-38A *Talon*

  EQUIPMENT BY TYPE
  AIRCRAFT • TRG: some Beech F-33 *Bonanza*
NATO • KFOR I
Air Force • Transport Command
School 1 (GAF Air Defence) located at Fort Bliss (TX), US

UZBEKISTAN
NATO • ISAF 163

FOREIGN FORCES

Belgium Army: 1 elems mech inf bde (withdrawal to be
completed in 2005)
France Army: 1 (Fr/Ge) army bde (1 army HQ, 1 recce regt,
1 inf regt); 2,800 (incl elm Eurocorps and Fr/Ge bde (2500))
Italy Air Force: 91 (NAEW Force)
Netherlands Air Force: 300 army: 1 mech inf bde (plus spt
elms) (1 armd bn, 1 tk bn); 2,300
United Kingdom Army: 1 army corps HQ (multinational);
1 army corps; 1 armd div; 22,000
United States Army: 1 armd corps HQ located at
Heidelberg (1 armd div ((less 1 bde at Ft Riley)), 1 engr bde,
1 avn bde, 1 mech inf div, 1 arty bde, 1 AD bde) EUCOM:
568 M-1 *Abrams* MBT; 1,266 M-2 *Bradley* AIFV each with
2 TOW msl, 1 30mm gun; 312 mor/MRL/SP; 115 atk hel;
1 Combined Service HQ (EUCOM) located at Stuttgart-
Vaihingen; 1 HQ (AF) HQ (HQ US Airforce Europe
(USAFE)) located at Ramstein AB; 1 HQ HQ (HQ US Army
Europe (USAREUR)) located at Heidelberg; 1 ftr wg located
at Spangdahlem AB (1 ftr sqn with 12 A-10 *Thunderbolt
II*; 6 OA-10 *Thunderbolt II*, 2 ftr sqn each with 21 F-16C
Fighting Falcon); 1 airlift wg located at Ramstein AB with
16 C-130E *Hercules*; 2 C-20 *Gulfstream*; 9 C-21 *Learjet*; 6 C-9A
Nightingale; 1 CT-43 *Boeing* 737; 53,300; 330; 15,900; 260

Greece Gr

Euro €		2003	2004	2005
GDP	€	152bn	163bn	
	US$	173bn	202bn	
per capita	US$	16,362	19,015	
Growth	%	4.7	4.2	
Inflation	%	3.4	3.0	
Public Debt	%	109.0	110.0	
Def exp [a]	€	4.26bn	4.75bn	
	US$	4.84bn	5.86bn	
Def bdgt	€	3.21bn	3.34bn	3.52bn
	US$	3.65bn	4.12bn	4.46bn
FMA (US)	US$			1m
US$1=€		0.88	0.81	0.79

[a] including military pensions and procurement

Population   10,668,354

Ethnic groups: Muslim 1%

Age	0–14	15–19	20–24	25–29	30–64	65 plus
Male	7%	3%	3%	4%	24%	8%
Female	7%	3%	3%	4%	24%	10%

Capabilities

ACTIVE 163,850 (Army 110,000 Navy 19,250 Air 23,000 Joint 11,600) Paramilitary 4,000

Terms of service Army up to 12 months, Navy up to 15 months, Air Force up to 14 months. Reserve service to age 50

RESERVE 325,000 (Army 234,500 Navy 24,000 Air 32,000 National Guard 34,500)

ORGANISATIONS BY SERVICE

Army 30,000; 80,000 conscript; 200,000 reservists (Field Army) **(total** 310,000)

FORCES BY ROLE

Field army to re-org. Units are manned at 3 different levels – Cat A 85% fully ready, Cat B 60% ready in 24 hours, Cat C 20% ready in 48 hours

Mil Region	3 region
Army	1 HQ; 5 corps HQ (incl 1 RRF – 2 HQ to disband)
Armd	1 div HQ; 5 indep bde (*each:* 1 mech inf bn, 1 SP arty bn, 2 armd bn)
Recce	4 bn
Mech inf	3 div HQ; 7 bde (*each:* 1 armd bn, 1 SP arty bn, 2 mech bn)
Inf	5 div (*each:* 1 armd bn, 1 arty regt, 3 inf regt); 1 div HQ; 5 bde
Spec Ops	1 comd (1 (cdo) amph sqn)
Cdo	1 bde (1 para sqn, 3 cdo sqn)
Marine	1 bde (Special Forces) (3 army bn)
Fd arty	5 bn
ADA	10 bn
Avn	1 bde (1 atk hel bn, 1 (tpt) hel bn, 3 avn bn); 1 indep coy
SAM	2 bn, with *I-HAWK*

National Guard 34,500 reservists

Internal security role

Gd 1 (National Guard. Internal security role) force

EQUIPMENT BY TYPE

TK • MBT 1723: 412 *Leopard 1*
  M-60 628: 628 M-60A1/M-60A3
  M-48 683: 683 M-48A5
RECCE 175: 130 M-8; 8 M1114 *HMMWV*; 37 VBL
AIFV • BMP 501: 501 BMP-1
APC • APC (T) 1640
  LEONIDAS 131: 131 *Leonidas* Mk1/*Leonidas* Mk2
  M-113 1509: 1,509 M-113A1/M-113A2
ARTY 4,660+
  TOWED 689
    105mm 463: 445 M-101; 18 M-56
    155mm 226: 226 M-114
  SP 400+
    155mm 207+
      M-109 195: 195 M-109A1B/M-109A2/M-109A3GEA1/M-109A5
      PzH 2000 some *Zuzana* 12
    175mm 12: 12 M-107
    203mm 181: 181 M-110A2
  MRL 151
    122mm 115: 115 RM-70 *Dana*
    227mm 36: 36 MLRS (incl ATACMS)
  MOR 3,420: 2,800 81mm
    107mm 620: 620 M-30 (incl 231 SP)
AT
  MSL 888: 262 AT-4 *Spigot*; 290 *Milan* (incl 42 HMMWV); 336 TOW (incl 320 M-901)
  RCL 4,605
    106mm • M-40 1291: 1,291 M-40A1
    84mm 2000: 2,000 *Carl Gustav*
    90mm 1314: 1,314 EM-67
  RL 29,220
    64mm 18520: 18,520 RPG-18 *Fly*
    66mm 10700: 10,700 M-72 *LAW*
AIRCRAFT • UTL • U-17 43: 43 U-17A
HELICOPTERS
  ATK • AH-64 20: 20 AH-64A *Apache*
  SPT • CH-47 9: 9 CH-47D *Chinook* (1 in store)
  UTL 121: 14 AB-206 (Bell 206) *JetRanger*
    BELL 205 31: 31 AB-205A (Bell 205A)
    UH-1 76: 76 UH-1H *Iroquois*
AD
  SAM 1,083+
    SP 41+: some SA-10 *Grumble (quad)* (in Crete, originally intended for Cy); 21 SA-15 *Gauntlet*
      SA-8 20: 20 SA-8B
    TOWED • MIM-23 42: 42 I-HAWK *MIM-23B*
    MANPAD 1000: 1,000 FIM-92A *Stinger*
  GUNS • 23mm • TOWED 506: 506 ZU-23-2
RADAR • LAND 12: 10 AN/TPQ-36 *Firefinder* (arty, mor)
  AN/TPQ-37 2: 2 AN/TPQ-37(V)3

Greek Navy 9,200; 9,800 conscript; 24,000 reservists **(total** 43,000**)**

EQUIPMENT BY TYPE
SUBMARINES • TACTICAL • SSK 13:
  8 *Glavkos* (Ge T-209/1100) each with 8 single 533mm TT each with UGM-84C *Harpoon* tactical USGW, SUT HWT
  1 *Glavkos* in refit (Ge T-209/1100) with 8 single 533mm TT each with tactical USGW
  4 *Poseidon* (Ge T-209/1200) each with 8 single 533mm TT each with UGM-84C *Harpoon* tactical USGW, SUT HWT
PRINCIPAL SURFACE COMBATANTS 18
  FRIGATES • FFG 14:
    10 *Elli* (capacity 2 AB-212 (Bell 212) utl hel) (EX *Kortenaer* Batch 2) each with 2 twin ASTT (4 eff.) each with Mk 46 LWT, 1+ Mk 29 *Sea Sparrow* octuple with 24 RIM-7M/RIM-7P, 2 Mk 141 *Harpoon* quad (8 eff.) each with RGM-84A *Harpoon*/RGM-84C *Harpoon*, 2 76mm gun
    4 *Hydra* (capacity 1 S-70B *Seahawk* ASW hel) (Ge MEKO 200) each with 2 triple ASTT (6 eff.) each with Mk 46 LWT, 2 quad (8 eff.) each with 1 RGM-84G *Harpoon* tactical SSM, 1 16 cell Mk 48 VLS with 16 RIM-7M *Sea Sparrow* SAM, 1 127mm gun
  CORVETTES • FS 4:
    4 *Niki* (ex-Ge *Thetis*) each with 2 triple 324mm ASTT (6 eff.) each with Mk 46 LWT, 2 twin 40mm gun (4 eff.)
PATROL AND COASTAL COMBATANTS 36
  PCC 2: 2 *Tolmi*
  PCI 4
  PFM 15:
    5 *Laskos* (Fr *La Combattante* II, III, IIIB) each with 6 RB 12 *Penguin* tactical SSM, 2 single 533mm TT each with SST-4 HWT
    4 *Laskos* (Fr *La Combattante* II, III, IIIB) each with 4 MM-38 *Exocet* tactical SSM, 2 single 533mm TT each with SST-4 HWT
    4 *Votsis* (Fr *La Combattante*) each with 2 Mk-141 *Harpoon* twin each with 1 RGM-84C *Harpoon* tactical SSM
    2 *Votsis* (Fr *La Combattante* IIA) each with 4 MM-38 *Exocet* tactical SSM
  PCM 1:
    1 *Stamou* with 4 SS 12M tactical SSM
  PFT 8:
    4 *Andromeda* (No *Nasty*) each with 4 single 533mm TT each with SST-4 HWT
    4 *Hesperos* (Ge *Jaguar*) each with 4 single 533mm TT each with SST-4 HWT
  PCO 4: 2 *Armatolos* (Dk *Osprey*); 2 *Pirpolitis*
MINE WARFARE 13
  MINE COUNTERMEASURES 10
    MHC 2: 2 *Evropi* (UK *Hunt*)
    MSC 8: 7 *Alkyon* (US MSC-294); 1 *Castagno* (US *Adjutant*)
AMPHIBIOUS
  LS • LST 6:
    5 *Chios* (capacity 4 LCVP; 300 troops) each with 1 hel landing platform (for med hel)
    1 *Inouse* (capacity 18 MBT; 400 troops; 4 LCVP) (US *County*)†
  CRAFT 61: 2 LCT; 6 LCU; 31 LCVP; 11 LCM; 7 LCA
  ACV 4:

4 *Pomornik* (*Zubr*) (capacity 230 troops; either 3 MBT or 10 APC (T)s)
LOGISTICS AND SUPPORT 19: 1 AE (ex-Ge *Luneburg*); 3 AGHS; 2 AOT; 4 (small); 6 AWT; 2 tpt; 1 trg
FACILITIES
Base 1 located at Salamis, 1 located at Patras, 1 located at Soudha Bay

Naval Aviation 250

FORCES BY ROLE
ASW   some sqn with 8 S-70B *Seahawk*; 8 AB-212 (Bell 212); 2 SA-319 *Alouette III*

SAR   some sqn with 2 AB-212 (Bell 212)

EQUIPMENT BY TYPE
HELICOPTERS
  ASW 8: 8 S-70B *Seahawk*
  UTL 12: 10 AB-212 (Bell 212); 2 SA-319 *Alouette III*
MSL • TACTICAL • ASM: some AGM-119 *Penguin*

Air Force 23,000 (incl some conscripts); 32,000 reservists **(total** 55,000**)**

Tactical Air Cmd

FORCES BY ROLE
AD / FGA   3 sqn with 25 M-2000-5 Mk 2 *Mirage*; M-2000EG (M-2000E) *Mirage*; total of 24 M-2000BG (M-2000B) *Mirage*/M-2000EG (M-2000E) *Mirage*; 2 sqn with F-4E *Phantom II*; 2 sqn with 96 A-7H *Corsair II*/TA-7H *Corsair II*; 2 sqn with 25 F-1CG (F-1C) *Mirage*; 7 sqn with 74 C-16CG (F-16C) *Fighting Falcon*/F-16DG (F-16D) *Fighting Falcon*
Recce   1 sqn with RF-4E *Phantom II*
AEW   1 sqn with 4 EMB-145H *Erieye* (being delivered); 2 SAAB 340H *Erieye* (on loan FROM Swe AF)

EQUIPMENT BY TYPE
AIRCRAFT 283 combat capable
  FTR 50
    M-2000-5 25: 25 M-2000-5 Mk 2 *Mirage*
    F-1 25: 25 F-1CG (F-1C) *Mirage*
  A-7H *Corsair II* FGA/TA-7H *Corsair II* trg 96*
  FGA 74+
    M-2000: some M-2000EG (M-2000E) *Mirage*
    C-16CG (F-16C) *Fighting Falcon*/**F-16DG (F-16D)** *Fighting Falcon* 74
  F-4E *Phantom II* FGA/RF-4E *Phantom II* RECCE 63*
  AEW 6
    EMB-145 4: 4 EMB-145H *Erieye* (being delivered)
    SAAB 340 2: 2 SAAB 340H *Erieye* (on loan FROM Swe AF)
  M-2000BG (M-2000B) *Mirage* **trg/ M-2000EG (M-2000E)** *Mirage* **FGA** 24
MSL • TACTICAL • ASM: some AGM-65 *Maverick*
  ARM: some AGM-88 *HARM*
  SCALP EG *Storm Shadow* some
  AAM: some AIM-120 *AMRAAM*; some AIM-7 *Sparrow*
    AIM-9: some AIM-9L *Sidewinder*/AIM-9P *Sidewinder*
    MICA some

R-550: some R-550 *Magic 2*
R530: some Super 530

Air Sup Cmd

FORCES BY ROLE

CSAR some sqn with 6 AS-332 *Super Puma**

Tpt 3 sqn each with 5 C-130B *Hercules*; 10 C-130H *Hercules*; 4 C-47 *Skytrain*; 13 DO-28; 2 *Gulfstream I/Gulfstream V*; 2 YS-11-200; 1 sqn with 12 C-27J *Spartan* (8 AT and 4 AAR)

hel 1 sqn with 4 AS-332 *Super Puma*; 13 AB-205A (Bell 205A) (SAR); 4 AB-212 (Bell 212) (VIP, tpt); 7 Bell 47G (liaison)

EQUIPMENT BY TYPE

AIRCRAFT • TPT 120
  C-130 45: 15 C-130B *Hercules*; 30 C-130H *Hercules*
  C-27 12: 12 C-27J *Spartan* (8 AT and 4 AAR)
  C-47 *Skytrain* 12 **DO-28** 39 *Gulfstream* **I**/*Gulfstream* **V** 6
  YS-11 6: 6 YS-11-200
HELICOPTERS
  SPT 10: 4 AS-332 *Super Puma*; 6*
  UTL 17: 4 AB-212 (Bell 212) (VIP, tpt)
    BELL 205 13: 13 AB-205A (Bell 205A) (SAR)
  TRG 7: 7 Bell 47G (liaison)
HELICOPTERS • UTL 1: 1 AB-206 (Bell 206) *JetRanger*

Air Defence

FORCES BY ROLE

SAM 2 sqn with MIM-14 *Nike Hercules*; 1 sqn with MIM-104 *Patriot*

SAM 1 bn with 36 MIM-14 *Nike Hercules*; 6 bty with PAC-3 *Patriot*; 12 bty each with 9 *Crotale*; 4 SA-15 *Gauntlet* (32 eff.); *Skyguard*

EQUIPMENT BY TYPE

AD • SAM • STATIC: some MIM-14 *Nike Hercules*
  GUNS • 35mm: some twin
AD
  SAM 192+: 108 *Crotale*; some PAC-3 *Patriot*
    SP 48: 48 SA-15 *Gauntlet*
    STATIC 36: 36 MIM-14 *Nike Hercules*
  GUNS 35+: 35+ 35mm

Air Training Command

FORCES BY ROLE

Trg 4 sqn with T-2C *Buckeye*/T-2E *Buckeye*; T-37B *Tweet*/T-37C *Tweet*; T-6A *Texan II*/T-6B *Texan II*/towed

EQUIPMENT BY TYPE

AIRCRAFT • TRG 124
  T-2 45: 10 T-2C *Buckeye*; 35 T-2E *Buckeye*
  T-37 34: 34 T-37B *Tweet*/T-37C *Tweet*
  T-6 45: 20 T-6A *Texan II*; 25 T-6B *Texan II*

Paramilitary • Coast Guard and Customs 4,000

PATROL AND COASTAL COMBATANTS 100: 100 PC
Patrol craft
AIRCRAFT • UTL 4
  CESSNA 172 2: 2 Cessna 172RG *Cutlass*
  TB-20 *Trinidad* 2

NON-STATE ARMED GROUPS

see Part II

DEPLOYMENT

AFGHANISTAN

NATO • ISAF 127

BOSNIA-HERZEGOVINA

EU • EUFOR I • EUFOR Air
  AIRCRAFT • TPT 1: 1 C-130 *Hercules*
EU • EUFOR II 250

CYPRUS

Army 950 (ELDYK army); ε200 (officers/NCO seconded to Greek-Cypriot National Guard) (total 1,150)

FORCES BY ROLE

1 armd bn; 1 (incl 950 (ELDYK) army) mech bde; 2 mech inf bn; 1 arty bn

EQUIPMENT BY TYPE

TK • MBT • M-48 • M-48A5 61: 61 M-48A5 MOLF
APC • APC (T) 80: 80 *Leonidas*
ARTY 24
  TOWED • 155mm 12: 12 M-114
  SP 12
    175mm 6: 6 M-107
    203mm 6: 6 M-110A2

ETHIOPIA/ERITREA

UN • UNMEE 3 obs

GEORGIA

UN • UNOMIG 5 obs

MIDDLE EAST

UN • UNTSO 3 obs

SERBIA AND MONTENEGRO

NATO • KFOR I 1,700

WESTERN SAHARA

UN • MINURSO 1 obs

FOREIGN FORCES

United States EUCOM: 52; 418 (Base facilities); 68 Navy: Base located at Makri; Base located at Soudha Bay USAF: Air base located at Iraklion

Hungary Hu

Hungarian Forint f		2003	2004	2005
GDP	f	18.5tr	20.2tr	
	US$	82.8bn	99.5bn	
per capita	US$	8,241	9,926	
Growth	%	3.0	4.0	
Inflation	%	4.7	6.7	
Debt	US$	45.7bn		
Def exp	f	314bn	310bn	
	US$	1.4bn	1.53bn	
Def bdgt	f	314bn	326bn	288bn
	US$	1.4bn	1.61bn	1.43bn
FMA (US)	US$	20.7m	8.98m	7.85m
US$1=f		224	203	201

Population	10,006,835

Ethnic groups: Romany 4%; German 3%; Serb 2%; Romanian 1%; Slovak 1%

Age	0–14	15–19	20–24	25–29	30–64	65 plus
Male	8%	3%	3%	4%	23%	6%
Female	8%	3%	3%	4%	25%	9%

Capabilities

ACTIVE 32,300 (Army 23,950 Air 7,500 Joint 850)
Paramilitary 12,000

RESERVE 44,000 (Army 35,200 Air 8,800)
Terms of service 6 months. Reservists to age 50.

ORGANISATIONS BY SERVICE

Army ε23,950
FORCES BY ROLE
being re-org
Army	1 (Land Forces) force HQ; 1 (garrison) comd; 1 (NBC) bn
Armd	1 bn
Recce	2 bn
Lt inf	2 bde (*total*: 7 Lt inf bn)
Maritime	1 wg
Engr	1 bde
Log	1 regt
MP	1 regt

Reserves 35,200 reservists
Mech inf 4 bde

EQUIPMENT BY TYPE
TK • MBT 238: 238 T-72
AIFV 178: 178 BTR-80A
APC • APC (W) • BTR 458: 458 BTR-80
ARTY 573+
   TOWED • 152mm 308: 308 D-20
   SP • 122mm 153+: 153+ 2S1 *Carnation* in store
   MRL • 122mm 62+: 62+ BM-21 in store
   MOR 50: 50 82mm

AT • MSL 110: 30 AT-4 *Spigot*; 80 AT-5 *Spandrel*
AD • SAM 121: 45 *Mistral*
   MANPAD 60: 60 SA-14 *Gremlin*
RADAR • LAND 15: 5 PSZNR-5B; 10 SNAR-10 *Big Fred* (SZNAR-10)
FACILITIES
Training Centre 2

Army Maritime Wing 60
EQUIPMENT BY TYPE
PATROL AND COASTAL COMBATANTS • MISC BOATS/CRAFT 4: 4 craft
MINE WARFARE • MINE COUNTERMEASURES • MSR 3: 3 *Nestin*
FACILITIES
Base 1 located at Budapest

Air Force Command 7,500; 8,800 reservists (to age 50) (total 16,300)
Flying hours   50 hrs/year

FORCES BY ROLE
FGA	1 (tac ftr) wg with 12 MiG-29B *Fulcrum*; 2 MiG-29UB *Fulcrum*
Tpt	1 (mixed) wg with 5 AN-26 *Curl*; 12 Mi-8 *Hip*; 5 MI-17 (Mi-8MT) *Hip H*
Atk hel	1 (cbt) sqn with 12 Mi-24 *Hind*
Trg	some sqn with 6 L-39ZO *Albatros*; 9 Yak-52
AD	1 (msl) bde; 1 (cmd and radar) regt
SAM	2 (mixed) regt with 45 *Mistral*; 20 SA-6 *Gainful* (60 eff.)

EQUIPMENT BY TYPE
AIRCRAFT 14 combat capable
   FTR • MiG-29 12: 12 MiG-29B *Fulcrum**
   TPT 5: 5 AN-26 *Curl*
   TRG 17
      L-39 6: 6 L-39ZO *Albatros*
      MiG-29U 2: 2 MiG-29UB *Fulcrum**
      Yak-52 9
HELICOPTERS
   ATK 12: 12 Mi-24 *Hind*
   SPT 17:
      MI-8 17: 12; 5 MI-17 (Mi-8MT) *Hip H*
AD • SAM 65: 45 *Mistral*
   SP 20: 20 SA-6 *Gainful*
MSL • TACTICAL 891
   ASM 597: 97 AT-2 *Swatter*; 500 AT-6 *Spiral*
   AAM 294: 84 AA-10 *Alamo*; 210 AA-11 *Archer*

Paramilitary 12,000

Border Guards 12,000 (to reduce)
Ministry of Interior
FORCES BY ROLE
Paramilitary 1 (Budapest) district (7 Rapid Reaction coy); 11 (regts/districts) regt

EQUIPMENT BY TYPE
APC • APC (W) • BTR 68: 68 BTR-80

DEPLOYMENT

AFGHANISTAN
NATO • ISAF 130

BOSNIA-HERZEGOVINA
EU • EUFOR II 150 engr; 4 obs

CYPRUS
UN • UNFICYP 84

EGYPT
MFO 41 MP

GEORGIA
UN • UNOMIG 7 obs

IRAQ
Army 293 (Peace Support)

SERBIA AND MONTENEGRO
NATO • KFOR I 1 mech inf bn; 294
UN • UNMIK 1

WESTERN SAHARA
UN • MINURSO 5 obs

Iceland Icl

Icelandic Krona K		2003	2004	2005
GDP	K	796bn	857bn	
	US$	10.3bn	11.8bn	
per capita	US$	35,700	40,425	
Growth	%	4.3	5.7	
Inflation	%	2.1	3.2	
Public Debt	%	42.1	36.3	
Sy Bdgt [a]	K	2.49bn	2.59bn	2.69bn
	US$	32.5m	36m	41.5m
US$1=K		76.7	72.2	65

[a] Iceland has no armed forces. Budget is mainly for coast guard.

Population   296,737

Age	0–14	15–19	20–24	25–29	30–64	65 plus
Male	11%	4%	4%	4%	22%	5%
Female	11%	4%	4%	4%	22%	6%

Capabilities

ACTIVE NIL Paramilitary 130

ORGANISATIONS BY SERVICE

Paramilitary

Iceland Coast Guard 130

EQUIPMENT BY TYPE
PATROL AND COASTAL COMBATANTS • PCO 3: 2
Aegir (with hel); 1 *Odinn* (with hel deck)
LOGISTICS AND SUPPORT • RESEARCH CRAFT 1:
1 *Baldur*

AIRCRAFT • TPT • F-27 1: 1 F-27-200 *Friendship*
HELICOPTERS
  SPT • AS-332 • AS-332L 1: 1 AS-322L1 *Super Puma*
  UTL • AS-365 1: 1 AS-365N *Dauphin 2*
FACILITIES
Base 1 located at Reykjavik

FOREIGN FORCES

NATO Island Commander Iceland (ISCOMICE), responsible to CINCEASTLANT
Netherlands Navy: 1 P-3C *Orion* MP ac
United States USNORTHCOM: 1 MR sqn with 6 P-3 *Orion*; 1 UP-3 *Orion*; 960 Navy; USMC 48; Air Force 650, 4 HH-60G

Italy It

Euro €		2003	2004	2005
GDP	€	1.30tr	1.34tr	
	US$	1.47tr	1.66tr	
per capita	US$	25,470	28,685	
Growth	%	0.3	1.2	
Inflation	%	2.8	2.3	
Public Debt	%	120.0	118.0	
Def exp [a]	€	26.7bn	24.7bn	
	US$	30.4bn	30.5bn	
Def bdgt	€	13.7bn	14.1bn	13.6bn
	US$	15.6bn	17.4bn	17.2bn
US$1=€		0.88	0.81	0.79

[a] including military pensions and carabinieri

Population   58,103,033

Age	0–14	15–19	20–24	25–29	30–64	65 plus
Male	7%	2%	3%	3%	25%	8%
Female	7%	2%	3%	3%	25%	10%

Capabilities

ACTIVE 191,875 (Army 112,000 Navy 34,000 Air 45,875) Paramilitary 254,300
Terms of service all services 10 months (to be all professional from 2005) 500,000 Army Reserves have commitment to age 45; Navy Reservists to 39 or in case of officers variable to age 73; Air Force reservists to the age of 25 or 45 for specialists

RESERVE 56,500 (Army 35,500 Navy 21,000)

ORGANISATIONS BY SERVICE

Army 110,000; ε2,000 conscript; 35,500 reservists **(total** 147,500**)**

FORCES BY ROLE
Op   1 comd HQ
Army 1 corps HQ; 1 (projection force) force HQ (1 mtn force (1 (alpine) AB bn, 2 mtn bde), 1 sigs bde)

EW 1 (CIS-EW) comd (1 (IEW) EW bde, 2 sigs bde)

Spt 1 comd (1 arty bde (1 hy arty regt, 1 NBC regt, 2 arty regt, 1 psyops regt), 1 AD bde (2 (*HAWK*) SAM regt, 2 SHORAD regt), 1 engr bde (4 engr regt), 1 avn bde (1 avn bn, 3 avn regt), 1 log div (8 log regt)

Def 1 div HQ (1 AB bde, 1 Air Mob bde, 1 armd bde, 1 armd Cav bde); 1 div HQ (5 mech bde)

EQUIPMENT BY TYPE

TK • MBT 320: 200 C1 *Ariete*
LEOPARD 1 120: 120 1A5
RECCE 300: 300 B-1 *Centauro*
AIFV 122: 122 VCC-80 *Dardo*
APC 2,036
APC (T) 1979: 90 Bv-206; 529 M-113 (incl variants); 1,360 VCC-1 *Camillino*/VCC-2
APC (W) 57: 57 Fiat 6614
AAV 14: 14 LVTP-7
ARTY 1,562
TOWED • 155mm 164: 164 FH-70
SP • 155mm • M-109 260: 260 M-109G/M-109L
MRL • 227mm 22: 22 MLRS
MOR 1116: 253 81mm
120mm 863: 724 Brandt; 139 RT-F1
AT
MSL 1,426: 1,000 *Milan*
TOW 426: 426 I-TOW
RCL • 80mm 434: 434 *Folgore*
RL • 110mm 1430: 1,430 Pzf 3 *Panzerfaust 3*
AIRCRAFT • TPT 6: 3 ACTL-1 (DO-228); 3 P-180
HELICOPTERS
ATK • A-129 60: 60 A-129EA *Mangusta*/A-129ESS *Mangusta*
SPT • CH-47 22: 22 CH-47C *Chinook*
UTL 186: 25 A-109
AB-205 (BELL 205) 71: 71 AB-205A (Bell 205A)
AB-206 (BELL 206) *JetRanger* 50 **AB-212 (Bell 212)** 18
AB-412 (Bell 412) *Twin Huey* 22
AD
SAM 148
TOWED 68: 36 MIM-23 *HAWK*
SKYGUARD 32: 32 *Skyguard*/*Aspide*
MANPAD 80: 80 FIM-92A *Stinger*
GUNS • 25mm • SP 64: 64 SIDAM

Navy 33,100; 900 conscript; 21,000 reservists (total 55,000)

FORCES BY ROLE

Fleet 1 Fleet Commander CINCNAV comd (also NATO COMEDCENT)

Navy 1 Ionian and Strait of Otranto comd; 1 Adriatic comd; 1 Rome comd; 1 Sicily comd; 1 Sardinia comd; 1 Upper Tyrrhenian comd

Maritime 1 High Readiness Forces HQ

EQUIPMENT BY TYPE

SUBMARINES • TACTICAL • SSK 6:
4 *Pelosi* (imp *Sauro*) each with 6 single 533mm TT each with 12 Type 184 HWT
1 *Sauro* with 6 single 533mm TT each with 12 Type 184 HWT

1 *Todaro* with 6 single 533mm TT each with 12 Type 184 HWT

PRINCIPAL SURFACE COMBATANTS 23
AIRCRAFT CARRIERS • CVS 1:
1 *G. Garibaldi* (capacity 6 AV-8B *Harrier II* FGA ac; 4 SH-3 *Sea King* ASW hel)
DESTROYERS • DDG 2:
2 *Luigi Durand de la Penne* (capacity 2 AB-212 (Bell 212) utl hel) (ex-*Animoso*) each with 2 triple 324mm ASTT (6 eff.) each with Mk 46 LWT, 1 Mk 13 GMLS with 40 SM-1 MR SAM, 1 *Albatros* octuple with 16 *Aspide* SAM, 2 quad (8 eff.) each with 8 *Milas* AS/Mk 2 *Otomat* SSM, 1 127mm gun
FRIGATES • FFG 12:
4 *Artigliere* (capacity 1 AB-212 (Bell 212) utl hel) each with 1 *Albatros* octuple with 8 *Aspide* SAM, 8 single each with 1 Mk 2 *Otomat* SSM, 1 127mm gun
8 *Maestrale* (capacity 2 AB-212 (Bell 212) utl hel) each with 2 triple 324mm ASTT (6 eff.) each with Mk 46 LWT, 2 x1 533mm ASTT each with A-184 *Black Shark* HWT, 1 *Albatros* octuple with 16 *Aspide* SAM, 4 single with 4 Mk 2 *Otomat* SSM, 1 127mm gun
CORVETTES • FS 8:
4 *Minerva* each with 1 *Albatros* octuple with *Aspide* SAM, 1 76mm gun
4 *Minerva* each with 1 76mm gun
PATROL AND COASTAL COMBATANTS 14
PCC 4: 4 *Esploratore*
PCO 10:
4 *Cassiopea* each with 1 AB-212 (Bell 212) utl hel, 1 76mm gun
4 *Comandante Cigala Fuligosi* each with 1 AB-212 (Bell 212) utl hel, 1 76mm gun
2 *Sirio* each with 1 AB-212 (Bell 212) utl hel, 1 76mm gun
MINE WARFARE • MINE COUNTERMEASURES 13: 1 MCCS (ex *Alpino*)
MHC 12: 8 *Gaeta*; 4 *Lerici*
AMPHIBIOUS
PRINCIPAL AMPHIBIOUS SHIPS • LPD 3:
2 *San Giorgio* (capacity 30 trucks; 350 troops; 2 SH-3D *Sea King* ASW hel; 1 CH-47 *Chinook* spt hel; 6 LCA; 36 APC (T)s)
1 *San Giusto* (capacity 350 troops; either 2 SH-3D *Sea King* ASW hel or 1 CH-47 *Chinook* spt hel; 6 LCA)
CRAFT 43: 15 LCVP; 8 LCM
LC 20: 20 RRC
LOGISTICS AND SUPPORT 94: 3 AGOR
AOR 2: 2 *Stromboli*
AORL 1: 1 *Etna*
ARS 1
AT 49: 33 (harbour)
7 more; 9 (coastal) **AWT** 3 **Research Craft** 3 tkr 7 tpt 11 (coastal)
TRG 9: 7 AXS; 2 YDT
Trial Ship 1 (AGE) **Water Tender** 4

FACILITIES

Base 1 (HQ) located at La Spezia, 1 (HQ) located at Taranto, 1 located at Brindisi, 1 located at Augusta

Naval Aviation 2,200

FORCES BY ROLE

FGA   1 sqn with 15 AV-8B *Harrier II*

ASW   5 sqn with 12 SH-3D *Sea King*; 15 EH-101 *Merlin*; 29 AB-212 (Bell 212)

Aslt hel   some sqn with 5 SH-3D *Sea King*; 5 AB-212 (Bell 212)

Trg   some sqn with 2 TAV-8B *Harrier*

EQUIPMENT BY TYPE
AIRCRAFT 15 combat capable
  FGA • AV-8 15: 15 AV-8B *Harrier II*
  TRG • TAV-8 2: 2 TAV-8B *Harrier*
HELICOPTERS
  ASW • SH-3 17: 17 SH-3D *Sea King*
  SPT 15: 15 EH-101 *Merlin*
  UTL 34: 34 AB-212 (Bell 212)
MSL • TACTICAL • ASM: some AGM-65 *Maverick*; some *Marte* Mk 2
    AAM: some AIM-120 *AMRAAM*
      AIM-9: some AIM-9L *Sidewinder*

Marines 2,000
FORCES BY ROLE
Op   1 San Marco regt (1,300 Marine)

Log   1 regt

LC   1 gp

EQUIPMENT BY TYPE
APC • APC (T) 40: 40 VCC-2
AAV 18: 18 AAV-7
ARTY • MOR 12
  81mm 8: 8 Brandt
  120mm 4: 4 Brandt
AT • MSL 6: 6 *Milan*
AD • SAM • MANPAD: some FIM-92A *Stinger*

Special Forces Command
FORCES BY ROLE
Diving   1 op

Navy SF   1 op

SF   1 comd

FACILITIES
Centre   1 (Research)

School   1

Air Force 44,723; 1,152 conscript (total 45,875)
FORCES BY ROLE
Ftr   2 sqn with 30 F-16A *Fighting Falcon* on lease; 4 F-16B *Fighting Falcon* on lease; 1 sqn with 5 *Typhoon*; 1 sqn with MB-339CD * (slow mover interceptor)

FGA   3 sqn with 69 *Tornado* IDS; 3 (50% of 1 sqn devoted to recce.) sqn with 44 AMX *Ghibli*; 1 sqn with 15 *Tornado* ECR

MR   1 sqn opcon Navy with 11 *Atlantic* *

EW   1 (ECM/recce) sqn with 2+ G-222VS; 4 P-166-DL3; 6 P-180

CSAR   1 sqn with 6 HH-3F

SAR   3 det with 15 HH-3F; 4 det with 31 AB-212 (Bell 212)

Tkr / CAL / tpt   1 sqn with 3 B-707-320C; 4 MB-339A RM; 4 G-222TM

Tpt   1 sqn with 3 G-222; 2 sqn with 19 C-130J *Hercules*

Liaison   2 sqn with 2 *Falcon* 50; 2 A-319CJ; 3 *Falcon* 900EX; 1 SH-3D *Sea King*

Trg   1 (aerobatic team) sqn with 17 MB-339A; 1 sqn with 44 NH-500D; 4 sqn with 18 AMX-T *Ghibli*; 41 MB-339A; 24 MB-339CD *; 31 SF-260M

AD   9 bty with *Spada*; 3 bty with MIM-14 *Nike Hercules*

UAV   1 sqn with 5 RQ-1B *Predator*

EQUIPMENT BY TYPE
AIRCRAFT 199 combat capable
  FTR 52: 5 *Typhoon*
    F-16 34: 30 F-16A *Fighting Falcon* on lease; 4 F-16B *Fighting Falcon* on lease
  STRIKE/FGA 69: 52 *Tornado* IDS; 22 in store
  FGA 79: 45 AMX *Ghibli*; 35 in store
  MP 18: 11 *Atlantic* *; 6 in store
  EW 2+
    ELINT 2+: 2+ G-222VS
  SEAD: 15 *Tornado* ECR*
  TPT 106
    A-319 3: 2 A-319CJ (plus 1 in store)
    B-707 3:
      B-707-320 3: 2 B-707-320C (plus 1 in store)
    C-130 22: 21 C-130J *Hercules* (plus 1 in store)
    FALCON 4: 2 *Falcon* 50 (plus 2 in store)
    FALCON 900 3: 2 *Falcon* 900EX (plus 1 in store)
    G-222 35: 9 RM/RM/VS (plus 26 in store)
    P-166 6: 5 P-166-DL3; 1 in store
    P-180 10: 6 (plus 4 in store)
    SIAI-208 20: 17 (liaison) (plus 3 in store)
  TRG 135: 9 AMX-T *Ghibli*; 14 in store
    MB-339 84: 17 MB-339A (aero team); 41 trg; 24 MB-339CD *; 2 in store
    SF-260 28: 26 SF-260M; 2 in store
HELICOPTERS
  SAR 33: 21 HH-3F (incl 6*); 12 in store
  ASW • SH-3 2: 1 SH-3D *Sea King**; 1 in store
  UTL 35: 31 AB-212 (Bell 212); 4 in store
  TRG • NH-500 50: 44 NH-500D; 6 in store
UAV • RECCE • TAC • RQ-1 5: 5 RQ-1B *Predator*
AD • SAM • TOWED: some *Spada*
  STATIC: some *Aspide*; some MIM-14 *Nike Hercules*
MSL • TACTICAL • ASM • ARM: some AGM-88 *HARM*
  AS-34 *Kormoran* some **SCALP EG** *Storm Shadow* some
  AAM: some AIM-120 *AMRAAM*
    AIM-9: some AIM-9L *Sidewinder*
    Sky Flash some

Flight Safety Inspectorate
HQ (AF)   1 HQ

Force Cmd
HQ (AF)   1 HQ

Logs Cmd

HQ (AF) 1 HQ

Naval Aviation Inspectorate

Air 1 HQ

Op Cmd

HQ (AF) 1 HQ
Air 2 (op) div; 3 (op) bde

Trg Cmd

HQ (AF) 1 HQ

Paramilitary 254,300

Carabinieri 111,367

Police Force with a military status and an all-encompassing jurisdiction, in permanent duty of public security and law enforcement
DEPENDENCE
Ministry of Defence; Ministry of Interior; other ministries (Public Health, Environment, Labour, Foreign Affairs, Cultural Activities and Arts)
RECCE 18: 18 Fiat 6616
APC 32
   APC (T) 26: 10 VCC-1 *Camillino*; 16 VCC-2
   APC (W) 6: 6 *Puma*
HELICOPTERS • UTL 92: 24 A-109; 38 AB-206 (Bell 206) *JetRanger*; 33 AB-412 (Bell 412) *Twin Huey*

Mobile and Specialised Branch

Mob / specialised unit	1 corps comd
Specialised unit	1 div (1 Ministry of Foreign Affairs Carabinieri Paramilitary HQ, 8 Paramilitary HQ (*each:* some Paramilitary tps), 1 hel gp)
Spec Ops	1 gp (ROS)
Hel	1 gp
Mobile div	1 div (1 (Special Intervention) GIS Paramilitary gp, 1 AB regt, 2 Mob bde, 1 (mounted) Cav regt, 11 Mob bn, 2 Mob regt)

Territorial

Inter-regional	5 comd
Region	19 comd
Provincial	102 comd

17 Territorial Depts; 1 Group Comd; 536 Company Comd; 37 Lieutenancy Comd; 4637 Station Comd

Training

FORCES BY ROLE
Paramilitary 1 HQ
FACILITIES
School 5

Harbour Control 8,700

Capitanerie di Porto

NON-STATE ARMED GROUPS

see Part II

DEPLOYMENT

AFGHANISTAN
NATO • ISAF 990; 256 (*Op Enduring Freedom*)

ALBANIA
NATO 498 (HQ Tirana)

BOSNIA-HERZEGOVINA
EU • *Op Althea* 1,126

CANADA
Air Force 12 (flying trg)

DEMOCRATIC REPUBLIC OF CONGO
EU • EUPOL KINSHASA 3

EGYPT
MFO 76

ETHIOPIA/ERITREA
UN • UNMEE 1

GERMANY
Air Force 91 (NAEW Force)

INDIA/PAKISTAN
UN • UNMOGIP 7 obs

IRAQ
Army 3,100 (Peace Suport)
1 (Carabinieri) army det; 1 mech inf; 1 marine coy

LEBANON
UN • UNIFIL 53

MACEDONIA, FORMER YUGOSLAV REPUBLIC
NATO 156 (HQ SKOPJE + EUPOL *Op Proxima*) (including logistic support for KFOR)

MALTA
Air Force 16
HELICOPTERS • UTL 2: 2 AB-212 (Bell 212)
Armed Forces
49 MIATM cbt Sp (Missione Italiana d'Assistenza Tecnico Militare)

MIDDLE EAST
UN • UNTSO 7 obs

PALESTINIAN AUTONOMOUS AREAS OF GAZA AND JERICHO
TIPH 15

SERBIA AND MONTENEGRO
NATO • KFOR I 2,471
UN • UNMIK 1 obs

SUDAN
UN • UNMIS 213

UNITED STATES
Air Force 38 (flying trg)

WESTERN SAHARA
UN • MINURSO 5 obs

FOREIGN FORCES

Germany 3 MP ac (in ELMAS/Sardinia); 200
Netherlands 4 F-16 *Fighting Falcon* ftr; 80
Spain 4 F/A-18 *Hornet* FGA; 1 KC-130 *Hercules* TKR
Turkey 4 F-16C *Fighting Falcon* FGA
United Kingdom 4 *Tornado* GR4 Strike/FGA; 2 E-3D *Sentry* AEW, periodic); 1 *Tristar* K1 tpt/tkr; 350
United States EUCOM: 1 HQ HQ located at Gaeta; 1 (HQ 16th Air Force) HQ (AF) HQ; 1 SETAF HQ Task Force located at Vicenza; 1 ftr wg (1 ftr sqn each with 21 F-16C *Fighting Falcon*/F-16D *Fighting Falcon* located at Aviano); 1 MR sqn located at Sigonella with 9 P-3C *Orion*; 2 SETAF Para bn located at Vicenza; 1 SETAF log unit (in store) (Holds eqpt forTheater Reserve Unit (TRU) /Army Readiness Package South (ARPS)) with 116 M-1 *Abrams*; 127 AIFV; 4 APC (T); 3,070 Army; 7,780 Navy; 4,550 Air Force; 74 USMC: Base located at Naples; Base located at La Maddalena

Latvia Lat

Latvian Lat L		2003	2004	2005
GDP	L	6.29bn	6.89bn	
	US$	11bn	13bn	
per capita	US$	4,758	5,644	
Growth	%	7.5	8.0	
Inflation	%	2.9	6.3	
Debt	US$	8.8bn		
Def bdgt	L	110m	123m	153m
	US$	194m	233m	278m
FMA (US)	US$	10.3m	7.83m	6.16m
US$1=L		0.57	0.53	0.55

Population   2,290,237

Age	0–14	15–19	20–24	25–29	30–64	65 plus
Male	7%	4%	4%	3%	22%	6%
Female	7%	4%	4%	3%	25%	11%

Capabilities

ACTIVE 5,238 (Army 1,817 Navy 685 Air 255 Administration and Command 759 Administration and Command 296 Central Support 590 Central Support 192 Other Forces (TRADOC) 457 Other Forces (TRADOC) 187)
Terms of service 12 months

RESERVE 11,204 (Army 11,204)

ORGANISATIONS BY SERVICE

Army 1,721; 96 conscript (total 1,817)

FORCES BY ROLE
Inf   1 bde (2 inf bn)
SF   1 unit
Fd arty   1 bty
Engr   1 bn

Reserves

National Guard 11,204 reservists
Inf 4 bde; 20 bn

EQUIPMENT BY TYPE
TK • **MBT** 3: 3 T-55 (trg)
RECCE • **BRDM** 2: 2 BRDM-2
ARTY 124
  TOWED • 100mm 26: 26 K-53
  MOR 98: 60mm 3; 71mm 40; 82mm 5; 120mm 50
AT
  RCL • 84mm 430: 430 *Carl Gustav*
  RL 1373
    64mm 2: 2 RPG-18 *Fly*
    68mm 162: 162 RPG-76 *KOMAR*
    73mm • **RPG-7** 407: 407 RPG-7V *Knout*
    82mm 3: 3 RPG-2
    84mm 799: 332 **AT-4** 467
  GUNS 143: 76mm 3; 90mm 140
AD
  SAM • **MANPAD** 5: 5 *Strela* 2M (SA-7) *Grail*
  GUNS 52
    14.5mm • **TOWED** • **ZPU** 2: 2 ZPU-4
    20mm • **TOWED** 10: 10 FK-20
    23mm • **TOWED** 16: 16 GSH-23
    30mm 2:
      TOWED 2: 1; 1 AK-230
    40mm • **TOWED** 22: 22 L/70

Navy 449; 236 conscript (total 685)

Lat, Ea and L have set up a joint Naval unit* BALTRON with bases at Liepaja, Riga, Ventspils (Lat), Tallinn (Ea), Klaipeda (L). *Each nation contributes 1–2 MCMVs

EQUIPMENT BY TYPE
PATROL AND COASTAL COMBATANTS • **PFB** 1:
  1 *Storm* with 1 L-70 40mm gun, 1 TAK-76 76mm gun
MINE WARFARE • **MINE COUNTERMEASURES** 3
  MHC 1: 1 *Lindau*
  MSC 2: 2 *Kondor*
LOGISTICS AND SUPPORT 2
  CL 1: 1 *Vidar*
  SPT 1: 1 *Buyskes* (C3 and support ship)

FACILITIES
Base 1 located at Liepaja, 1 located at Riga, 1 located at Ventspils

Air Force 255

AIRCRAFT
  TPT 14: 13 AN-2 *Colt*; 1 L-410 *Turbolet*
  TRG 5: 5 PZL-104 *Wilga* 35
HELICOPTERS • **SPT** 6: 4 Mi-8 *Hip*; 2 PZL MI-2 *Hoplite*

Administration and Command 759; 296 conscript (total 1,055)

Central Support 590; 192 conscript (total 782)
(LSC)

Other Forces (TRADOC) 457; 187 conscript (total 644)

DEPLOYMENT

AFGHANISTAN
NATO • ISAF 10

BOSNIA-HERZEGOVINA
EU • *Op Althea* 3

IRAQ
Army 120 (Peace Support)

SERBIA AND MONTENEGRO
NATO • KFOR I 12

Lithuania L

Lithuanian Litas L		2003	2004	2005
GDP	L	56.1bn	61.8bn	
	US$	18.3bn	22.1bn	
per capita	US$	5,073	6,127	
Growth	%	9.7	6.6	
Inflation	%	-1.2	1.2	
Debt	US$	8.34bn		
Def exp	L	1.02bn	872m	
	US$	335m	311m	
Def bdgt	L	815m	871m	915m
	US$	266m	311m	333m
FMA (US)	US$	11.5m	7.73m	6.65m
US$1=L		3.06	2.8	2.75

Population   3,596,617

Ethnic groups: Russian 8%; Polish 7%; Belarussian 2%

Age	0–14	15–19	20–24	25–29	30–64	65 plus
Male	8%	4%	4%	4%	22%	5%
Female	8%	4%	4%	3%	24%	9%

Capabilities

ACTIVE 13,510 (Army 11,600 Navy 710 Air 1,200)
Paramilitary 15,140
Terms of service 12 months.

RESERVE 6,700 (Army 6,700)

ORGANISATIONS BY SERVICE

Army 6,569; 3,531 conscript (total 10,100)
FORCES BY ROLE
1 mil region
Reaction 1 bde (1 arty bn, 2 mot inf bn, 2 mech inf bn)
SF   1 unit
Mot inf   1 indep bn
Jaeger   1 bn
Staff   1 bn
Engr   1 bn
Trg   1 regt

Reserves

National Defence Voluntary Forces 6,700
reservists; 1,500 active reservists (total 8,200)

Territorial Def 10 regt; 36 bn (*total:* 130 Territorial Def coy)

Avn   2 sqn

EQUIPMENT BY TYPE
RECCE • BRDM 10: 10 BRDM-2
APC 137
  APC (T) 104
    M-113 94: 94 M-113A1
    MT-LB 10
  APC (W) 33
    BTR 22: 22 BTR-60
    M/42 11: 11 m/42D *Pskbil*
ARTY 133
  TOWED • 105mm 72: 72 M-101
  MOR • 120mm 61: 61 M-43
AT
  MSL: some *Javelin*
  RCL 693
    84mm 273: 273 *Carl Gustav*
    90mm 420: 420 PV-1110
  RL 613+
    73mm 403: 403 RPG-7 *Knout*
    82mm 210: 210 RPG-2
    84mm: some AT-4

Navy 410; 300 conscript (total 710)
Lat, Ea and L have set up a joint Naval unit BALTRON with bases at Liepaja, Riga, Ventpils (Lat), Tallinn (Ea), Klaipeda (L), HQ at Tallinn

EQUIPMENT BY TYPE
PRINCIPAL SURFACE COMBATANTS • FRIGATES • FFL 2:
  2 *Grisha* III each with 2 twin 533mm ASTT (4 eff.), 1 twin (2 eff.), 2 RBU 6000 *Smerch* 2 (24 eff.)
PATROL AND COASTAL COMBATANTS • PFB 3: 3 *Storm*
MINE WARFARE • MINE COUNTERMEASURES • MHC 2: 2 *Suduvis*
LOGISTICS AND SUPPORT • AGOR 1: 1 *Valerian Uryvayev*

FACILITIES
Base 1 located at Klaipeda

Air Force 1,050; 150 conscript (total 1,200)
Flying hours   120 hrs/year

FORCES BY ROLE
Tpt some sqn with 6 AN-2 *Colt*; 3 AN-26 *Curl*; 2 L-410 *Turbolet*
Trg some sqn with 6 L-39 *Albatros*
Hel some sqn with 10 Mi-8 *Hip* (tpt/SAR); 2 PZL MI-2 *Hoplite*
AD 1 bn with 18 L/70; 1 bn (for mobilisation needs)

EQUIPMENT BY TYPE
AIRCRAFT
  TPT 11: 6 AN-2 *Colt*; 3 AN-26 *Curl*; 2 L-410 *Turbolet*
  TRG 6: 6 L-39 *Albatros*
HELICOPTERS • SPT 12: 10 Mi-8 *Hip* (tpt/SAR); 2 PZL MI-2 *Hoplite*
AD • GUNS • 40mm • TOWED 18: 18 L/70

FACILITIES

Air Surveillance and Control Centre	1 no location
Air base	2 no location
Radar Stn	1 (6) no location

Paramilitary 14,600

Riflemen Union 9,600

State Border Guard Service 5,000
Ministry of Internal Affairs

Coast Guard 540

DEPLOYMENT

AFGHANISTAN
NATO • ISAF 6

BOSNIA-HERZEGOVINA
EU • EUFOR II 97

IRAQ
Army 90 (Peace Support)

SERBIA AND MONTENEGRO
NATO • KFOR I 30

Luxembourg Lu

Euro €		2003	2004	2005
GDP	€	23.1bn	25.6bn	
	US$	26.2bn	31.7bn	
per capita	US$	57,469	68,573	
Growth	%	2.4	4.4	
Inflation	%	2.5	3.2	
Public Debt	%	7.1	7.5	
Def exp	€	176m	196m	
	US$	200m	243m	
Def bdgt	€	180m	195m	208m
	US$	205m	241m	264m
US$1=€		0.88	0.81	0.79

Population   468,571

Foreign citizens: ε124,000

Age	0–14	15–19	20–24	25–29	30–64	65 plus
Male	10%	3%	3%	3%	24%	6%
Female	9%	3%	3%	3%	24%	8%

Capabilities

ACTIVE 900 (Army 900) Paramilitary 612

ORGANISATIONS BY SERVICE

Army 900
FORCES BY ROLE
Recce 2 coy (1 to Eurocorps/BE div, 1 to NATO pool of
    deployable forces)

Lt inf 1 bn

EQUIPMENT BY TYPE
ARTY • MOR 6: 81mm 6
AT • MSL 6: 6 TOW
    RL • 66mm: some M-72 *LAW*

Air Force

FORCES BY ROLE
none, but for legal purposes NATO's E-3A AEW ac have
Lu registration
Air 1 sqn with 17 E-3A *Sentry* (NATO standard); 2 B-707
    (trg)

EQUIPMENT BY TYPE
AIRCRAFT
    AEW • E-3 17: 17 E-3A *Sentry* (NATO standard)
    TPT 2: 2 B-707 (trg)

Paramilitary 612

Gendarmerie 612

DEPLOYMENT

AFGHANISTAN
NATO • ISAF 9

BOSNIA-HERZEGOVINA
EU • EUFOR I • EUFOR Air
    AIRCRAFT • AEW • E-3 5: 5 E-3A *Sentry* (*Op Deliberate
    Forge*)
EU • EUFOR II 23

SERBIA AND MONTENEGRO
NATO • KFOR I 26

FOREIGN FORCES

United States EUCOM: 27

Netherlands Nl

Euro €		2003	2004	2005
GDP	€	453bn	465bn	
	US$	515bn	575bn	
per capita	US$	31,800	35,255	
Growth	%	-0.9	1.3	
Inflation	%	2.2	1.4	
Public Debt	%	54.8		
Def exp	€	7.40bn	7.78bn	
	US$	8.4bn	9.6bn	
Def bdgt	€	7.31bn	7.66bn	7.66bn
	US$	8.3bn	9.46bn	9.7bn
US$1=€		0.88	0.81	0.79

Population   16,407,491

Age	0–14	5–19	0–24	5–29	30–64	65 plus
Male	9%	3%	3%	3%	25%	6%
Female	9%	3%	3%	3%	25%	7%

Capabilities

ACTIVE 53,130 (Army 23,150 Navy 12,130 Air 11,050 Paramilitary 6,800)

RESERVE 54,400 (Army 22,200 Navy 5,000 Air 5,000 Reserves 22,200)
Men to age 35, NCOs to 40, officers to 45

ORGANISATIONS BY SERVICE

Army 23,150

FORCES BY ROLE

1 Corps HQ (GE/NL)	
Tk	3 bn
Armd recce	1 bn
Mech	1 div HQ
Mech inf	3 bde (2 cadre)
Armd inf	6 bn
Air Mob	1 bde (3 Air Mob bn)
SF	1 bn
Fd arty	1 gp (6 arty bn)
MLRS	1 bty
Engr	1 gp (3 Engr bn)
AD	1 bn

Reserves 22,200 reservists

National Command
Cadre bde and corps tps completed by call-up of reservists (incl Territorial Comd)

Inf 5 bn (Could be mob for territorial defence)

EQUIPMENT BY TYPE
TK • MBT 283: 258 *Leopard* 2; 25 *Leopard* 1
RECCE: some *Fennek*
AIFV 569: 224 YPR-765 (Used as APC); 345 more
APC • APC (W) 94: 22 TPz-1 *Fuchs*
  XA SERIES 72: 72 XA-188 *Sisu*
ARTY 407
  TOWED • 155mm 113: 13 FH-70 (trg); 20 M-114; 80 M-114/M-139
  SP • 155mm • M-109 120: 120 M-109A3
  MRL • 227mm 22: 22 MLRS
  MOR 152:
    81mm: 40
    120mm 112: 112 Brandt
AT • MSL 753+: 427 M47 *Dragon*
  SPIKE: some Gil/Spike
  TOW 326 (incl 92 YPR-765)
  RCL • 84mm: some *Carl Gustav*
  RL • 84mm: some AT-4
PATROL AND COASTAL COMBATANTS 6: 3 PBR; 3 PCC
LOGISTICS AND SUPPORT 1: 1 tpt (tk)
AD
  SAM • MANPAD 312: 312 FIM-92A *Stinger*
  GUNS • 35mm • SP 60: 60 *Gepard* (in store–for sale)
RADAR • LAND: some AN/TPQ-36 *Firefinder* (arty, mor); some *Squire*

Navy 8,080; 3,100 (Marines); 950 (Naval Avn); 5,000+ reservists (total 17,130)

EQUIPMENT BY TYPE
SUBMARINES • TACTICAL • SSK 4:
  4 *Walrus* each with 4 single 533mm TT with Mk48 *Sea Arrow* HWT/UGM-84C *Harpoon* tactical USGW (Equipped for *Harpoon* but not embarked)
PRINCIPAL SURFACE COMBATANTS 14
  DESTROYERS • DDG 6:
    2 *Van Heemskerck* each with 2 twin 324mm ASTT (4 eff.) each with Mk 46 LWT, 1 Mk 13 GMLS with 40 SM-1 MR SAM, 2 Mk 141 *Harpoon* quad (8 eff.) each with 1 RGM-84C *Harpoon* tactical SSM
    4 *Zeven Provincien* (capacity 1 *Lynx* MK86 ASW hel) (2 under construction) each with 2 twin ASTT (4 eff.) each with Mk 46 LWT, 2 Mk 141 *Harpoon* quad (8 eff.) each with 8 RGM-84F tactical SSM, 1 40 cell Mk 41 VLS (40 eff.) with 32 SM-2 MR SAM, 32 enhanced *Sea Sparrow* SAM (quad pack), 1 Otobreda 127mm gun
  FRIGATES • FFG 8:
    8 *Karel Doorman* (capacity 1 *Lynx* utl hel) each with 2 twin 324mm ASTT (4 eff.) each with Mk 46 LWT, 2 Mk 141 *Harpoon* quad (8 eff.) each with 1 RGM-84A *Harpoon*/RGM-84C *Harpoon*, 1 Mk 48 VLS with 16 RIM-7P *Sea Sparrow* SAM, 1 76mm gun
MINE WARFARE • MINE COUNTERMEASURES • MHC 12: 12 *Alkmaar* (tripartite)
AMPHIBIOUS
  PRINCIPAL AMPHIBIOUS SHIPS • LPD 1:
    1 *Rotterdam* (capacity 600 troops; either 6 *Lynx* utl hel or 4 NH-90 utl hel; either 170 APC (T)s or 33 MBT; either 6 LCVP or 4 LCU or 4 LCM) (could be used as SAR or in disaster relief roles)
  CRAFT 11: 5 LCU; 6 LCA
LOGISTICS AND SUPPORT 12: 1 AGHS; 1 AGOR
  AO 1:
    1 *Zuideruis* with 2 *Lynx*/NH-90
  AORH 1: 1 *Amsterdam*
  Research Craft 4
  SPT 1: 1 *Pelikaan*
  TRV 1: 1 *Murcuur*
  Trg 2
FACILITIES

Base	1 (MPA) located at Valkenburg, 1 located at Den Helder, 1 located at Willemstad
Naval airbase	1 (hel) located at De Koy

Naval Aviation 950
AIRCRAFT • MP • P-3 10: 10 P-3C *Orion**
HELICOPTERS • UTL 21: 21 SH-14D *Lynx** (ASW/SAR)

Marines 3,100
FORCES BY ROLE

Marine	3 bn (1 cadre); 1 bn (integrated with UK 3 Cdo Bde to form UK/NL Amph Landing Force)
Spt	1 bn (1 recce coy, 2 mor coy)

EQUIPMENT BY TYPE
AIFV 22: 11 YPR-765; 11 look-a-like
APC • APC (W) • XA SERIES 17: 17 XA-188 *Sisu*
ARTY • MOR 32:

81mm: 18
120mm 14: 14 Brandt
AT • **MSL**: some M47 *Dragon*
  RCL • **84mm**: some *Carl Gustav*
  RL • **84mm**: some AT-4
AD • **SAM** • **MANPAD**: some FIM-92A *Stinger*

Air Force 11,050; 5,000 reservists (men to age 35, NCOs to 40, officers to 45, immediate recall) (total 16,050)

Flying hours   180 hrs/year

FORCES BY ROLE

COMD	1 logistics HQ; 1 Tac Air HQ; 1 Education HQ
Ftr / FGA / recce	5 (swing role) sqn with 108 F-16 MLU AM *Fighting Falcon*/F-16 MLU BM *Fighting Falcon*
SAR	1 sqn with 3 AB-412SP *Griffon*
Tpt	1 sqn with 2 KDC-10; 2 C-130H-30 *Hercules*; 2 Fokker 50; 4 Fokker 60; 1 *Gulfstream* IV
Trg	1 sqn with 13 PC-7 *Turbo Trainer*
Hel	1 sqn with 13 CH-47D *Chinook*; 1 sqn with 17 AS-532U2 *Cougar II*; 4 SA-316 *Alouette III*; 2 sqn with 30 AH-64D *Apache*; 1 flt with 5 BO-105
AD	4 sqn (*total:* 7 AD Team with FIM-92A *Stinger*, 4 AD bty with MIM-104 *Patriot* (TMD capable))

EQUIPMENT BY TYPE

AIRCRAFT 108 combat capable
  FGA • **F-16 MLU** 137: 108 F-16 MLU AM *Fighting Falcon*/F-16 MLU BM *Fighting Falcon*; 29 in store
  TKR 2: 2 KDC-10
  TPT 9
    C-130 • **C-130H** 2: 2 C-130H-30 *Hercules*
    Fokker 50 2 **Fokker 60** 4 *Gulfstream* **IV** 1
  TRG 13: 13 PC-7 *Turbo Trainer*
HELICOPTERS
  ATK • **AH-64** 30: 30 AH-64D *Apache*
  SPT • **CH-47** 13: 13 CH-47D *Chinook*
  UTL 29: 3 AB-412SP *Griffon*
    AS-532 17: 17 AS-532U2 *Cougar II*
    BO-105 5 **SA-316** *Alouette III* 4
AD • **SAM** • **TOWED**: some MIM-104 *Patriot* (TMD capable)
  MANPAD: some FIM-92A *Stinger*
MSL • **TACTICAL** • **ASM** • **AGM-114**: some AGM-114K *Hellfire*
  AGM-65: some AGM-65G *Maverick*
  AAM • **AIM-120**: some AIM-120B *AMRAAM*
    AIM-9: some AIM-9 *Sidewinder* tactical AAM/AIM-9L *Sidewinder*/AIM-9M *Sidewinder*
BOMB • **PGM** • **PAVEWAY** • **PAVEWAY II**: some GBU-10 (supported by LANTIRN); some GUB-12 (supported by LANTIRN)
  PAVEWAY III: some GBU-24 (supported by LANTIRN)

FACILITIES

Air base 3 with 108 F-16 MLU AM *Fighting Falcon*/F-16 MLU BM *Fighting Falcon*

Paramilitary 6,800

Royal Military Constabulary 6,800

FORCES BY ROLE

Paramilitary 6 district (*total:* 60 Paramilitary 'bde')

EQUIPMENT BY TYPE

AIFV 24: 24 YPR-765

Reserves 22,200 reservists

men to age 35, NCOs to 40, officers to 45

National Command

Cadre bde and corps tps completed by call-up of reservists (incl Territorial Comd)
Inf 5 bn (Could be mob for territorial defence)

DEPLOYMENT

AFGHANISTAN
NATO • ISAF 153

BOSNIA-HERZEGOVINA
EU • EUFOR II ε1,000

BURUNDI
UN • ONUB 1

DEMOCRATIC REPUBLIC OF CONGO
UN • MONUC 1 obs

GERMANY
Army 2,300
1 mech inf bde (plus spt elms) (1 armd bn, 1 tk bn)
Air Force 300

ICELAND
Navy • Naval Aviation
  AIRCRAFT • **MP** • **P-3** 1: 1 P-3C *Orion*

IRAQ
Armed Forces ε1,100 (Peace Support)
Navy • Marines 1 (bn) Marine gp
Air Force
HELICOPTERS • **SPT** • **CH-47** 3: 3 CH-47D *Chinook*

ITALY
Air Force
AIRCRAFT • **FTR** 4: 4 F-16 *Fighting Falcon*
EU • EUFOR I • EUFOR Air
Armed Forces 80
Air Force
  AIRCRAFT • **FTR** 4: 4 F-16 *Fighting Falcon*

NETHERLANDS ANTILLES
Navy 20 (to expand). NI, Aruba and the Netherlands Antilles operate a Coast Guard Force to combat org crime and drug smuggling. Comd by Netherlands Commander Caribbean. HQ Curaçao, bases Aruba and St. Maarten)
PRINCIPAL SURFACE COMBATANTS • **FRIGATES**
• **FFG** 1: 1 *Kortenaer* (capacity 2 *Lynx* utl hel) with 2 twin 324mm ASTT (4 eff.) each with Mk 46 LWT, 2 Mk 141 *Harpoon* quad (8 eff.) each with 1 RGM-84A *Harpoon*/RGM-

84C *Harpoon*, 8 Mk 29 VLS each with 24 RIM-7M/P *Sea Sparrow* SAM, 1 76mm gun

Naval Aviation
AIRCRAFT • MP • P-3 3: 3 P-3C *Orion*
Marines 1 (cbt) amph det; 1 (2 coy) marine bn
Base 1 located at Willemstad

Air Force
AIRCRAFT • TPT 2: 2 Fokker 60

FOREIGN FORCES

NATO HQ Allied Forces Europe
United Kingdom Air Force: 120
United States EUCOM: 303

Norway No

Norwegian Kroner kr		2003	2004	2005
GDP	kr	1.56tr	1.68tr	
	US$	220bn	243bn	
per capita	US$	48,399	53,305	
Growth	%	0.4	2.9	
Inflation	%	2.5	0.5	
Public Debt	%	50.4	51.1	
Def exp	kr	31.8bn	30.6bn	
	US$	4.50bn	4.43bn	
Def bdgt	kr	29.6bn	29.3bn	30.3bn
	US$	4.18bn	4.25bn	4.69bn
US$1=kr		7.08	6.91	6.47

Population 4,593,041

Age	0–14	15–19	20–24	25–29	30–64	65 plus
Male	10%	3%	3%	3%	24%	6%
Female	10%	3%	3%	3%	23%	7%

Capabilities

ACTIVE 25,800 (Army 14,700 Navy 6,100 Air 5,000)
Terms of service 12 months with 4-5 refresher trg periods.

RESERVE 219,000 (Army 172,000 Navy 22,000 Air 25,000)
Reserves: 219000 on 24-72hr readiness; obligation to age of 44, (conscripts remain with fd army units to age of 35, officers to 55, regulars to 60)

ORGANISATIONS BY SERVICE

Army 6,000; 8,700 conscript (**total** 14,700)
2 Joint Comd, 4 Land Comd
FORCES BY ROLE
Territorial 14 regt

North Norway

Army	1 div (cadre and trg units for, 1 armd bde, 2 mot inf bde)
Mech inf	1 indep bde

Ranger 1 bn
Border Guard some unit

South Norway

Armd	1 bde (armd cadre units)
Mech inf	1 bde (mech inf cadre untis)
Inf	2 (incl Royal Guard) bn

Land Home Guard 73,000 reservists
18 districts each divided into 2-6 sub-districts (bn) comprising a total of 480 units (coy)

Reserves 83,000 reservists (on mobilisation)

Reserves 89,000 reservists
Ranger 3 bn
Jaeger 17 bn
Arty 1 bn
Engr some unit
Sigs some unit
Log some unit
AD some unit

EQUIPMENT BY TYPE
TK • MBT 165: 52 *Leopard* 2A4; 113 *Leopard* 1 (2 1A1NO, 111 1A5NO)
AIFV 157
  CV90 • CV9030 104: 104 CV9030N
  NM-135 53 (M-113/20mm)
APC 189
  APC (T) 109: 109 M-113 (incl variants)
  APC (W) • XA SERIES 80: ε80 XA-186 *Sisu*/XA-200 *Sisu*
ARTY 634
  TOWED • 155mm • M-114 46: 46 M-114/39
  SP • 155mm • M-109 126: 126 M-109A3GN
  MRL • 227mm 12: 12 MLRS
  MOR 450
    81mm 450 (incl 40 SP)
      M-125 12: 12 M-125A2
    107mm • M-106 24: 24 M-106A1
AT
  MSL 744: 424 *Eryx*
    TOW 320: 320 TOW msl/TOW-2 (incl 97 NM-142 (M-901))
  RCL • 84mm 2517: 2,517 *Carl Gustav*
  RL • 66mm: some M-72 *LAW*
AD
  SAM • MANPAD 300: 300 RBS-70 (120 in store)
  GUNS • 20mm • TOWED 252: 252 Rh 202 (192 in store)
RADAR • LAND 12+: 12 ARTHUR; some *Cymbeline* (mor)

Navy 2,370; 3,300 conscript; 22,000 reservists (**total** 27,670)
2 Joint Commands, COMNAVSONOR (South Norway) and COMNAVNON (North Norway) with regional naval commanders and 7 regional Naval districts
EQUIPMENT BY TYPE
SUBMARINES • TACTICAL • SSK 6:
  6 *Ula* each with 8 single 533mm TT each with A3 *Seal* DM2 HWT
PRINCIPAL SURFACE COMBATANTS • FRIGATES • FFG 3:

3 *Oslo* each with 4 RB 12 *Penguin* tactical SSM, 2 Mk32 triple 324mm each with 6 *Sting Ray* LWT, 1 Mk 29 *Sea Sparrow* octuple with 8 RIM-7M/P *Sea Sparrow* SAM, 1 *Terne* III Rocket Depth charge, 1 x2 76mm gun (2 eff.)

PATROL AND COASTAL COMBATANTS • PFM 15:
11 *Hauk* each with 1 twin 533mm ASTT (2 eff.) with 2 T-61 HWT, 1 SIMBAD x2 manual with 2 *Mistral* SAM, 6 single each with 1 RB 12 *Penguin* tactical SSM
1 *Skjold*
3 mod *Hauk* each with 1 twin 533mm ASTT (2 eff.) with 2 T-61 HWT, 1 SIMBAD x2 manual with 1 *Mistral* SAM, 6 single each with 1 RB 12 *Penguin* tactical SSM

MINE WARFARE 10
MINE COUNTERMEASURES • MSC 8: 4 *Alta*; 4 *Oskoy*
MINELAYERS • ML 2: 1 *Tyr*; 1 *Vidar*

AMPHIBIOUS • CRAFT 25
LCT 3: 3 *Tjeldsund*
LCA 22: 22 S90N

LOGISTICS AND SUPPORT 29
AGI (INT) 1: 1 *Marjata*
AS 22: 22 *Horten*
Diving tender/spt 2 **RY** *Royal Yacht* 1
TRV 1: 1 *Valkyrien*
TRG 2: 2 *Hessa*

FACILITIES
Base 1 located at Bergen, 1 located at Horten, 1 located at Tromsø

Coast Guard 270
PATROL AND COASTAL COMBATANTS 16
MISC BOATS/CRAFT 6: 6 cutters (for fishery dept)
PCI 7 (4 on lease)
PCO 3:
3 *Nordkapp* each with 1 *Lynx* utl hel (SAR/recce), 6 single (fitted for but not embarked) each with 1 RB 12 *Penguin* tactical SSM
HELICOPTERS • ASW 6: 6 *Lynx* MK86 (Air Force-manned)

Coastal Defence 160
FORCES BY ROLE
Navy 3 bty with ε 18 torpedoes; 5 bty with ε 30 tactical (lt) msl

EQUIPMENT BY TYPE
ARTY • COASTAL 9: 120mm 3; 75mm 6
MSL ε 30: 5 tactical (lt) msl bty
TORPEDO: ε 18: 3 torpedo bty
MINE 3: 3 cable mine

FACILITIES
Coastal fortress 1

Naval Home Guard 4,900 reservists on mobilisation
assigned to 10 HQ Sectors icl 31 areas
235 Naval Vessels; 77 less than 100 tonnes

Air Force 1,800; 3,200 conscript; 25,000 reservists (total 30,000)
OPERATIONAL COMMANDS 2 joint with COMSONOR and COMNON
Flying hours 180 hrs/year

FORCES BY ROLE
FGA   4 sqn with F-16A *Fighting Falcon*/F-16B *Fighting Falcon*
MR   1 sqn with 4 P-3C *Orion* * (UIP (MR)); 2 P-3N *Orion* (pilot trg)
SAR   1 sqn with *Sea King* MK43B
ECM / CAL   1 sqn with 1 *Falcon* 20C (Flight Inspection Service); 2 (EW)
Tpt   1 sqn with C-130 *Hercules*
ADA   8 bty (org into 5 gps) with L/70 (with Fire-Control System 2000)
Trg   some sqn with MFI-15 *Safari*
Hel   2 sqn with Bell 412SP *Twin Huey*
AD   2 bn with NM-45
SAM   10 bty with RB-70; 6 bty with NASAMS

EQUIPMENT BY TYPE
AIRCRAFT 61 combat capable
FTR • F-16 57: 57 F-16A *Fighting Falcon*/F-16B *Fighting Falcon*
MP • P-3 6: 4 P-3C *Orion* * (UIP (MR)); 2 P-3N *Orion* (pilot trg)
TPT 15
C-130 6: 6 C-130H *Hercules*
DHC-6 *Twin Otter* 3
FALCON 20 6: 2 *Falcon* 20C (EW); 3 (EW/FIS); 1 (Flight Inspection Service)
TRG 15: 15 MFI-15 *Safari*
HELICOPTERS
SAR 12: 12 *Sea King* MK43B (SAR)
UTL • BELL 412 18: 18 Bell 412SP *Twin Huey* (12 tpt, 6 SF)
AD • SAM: some NASAMS
SP: some RB-70
GUNS • 20mm • TOWED: some NM-45
40mm • TOWED: some L/70 (with Fire-Control System 2000)
MSL • TACTICAL • ASM • AGM-119: some AGM-119A *Penguin 3*
CRV-7 some
AAM: some AIM-120 *AMRAAM*
AIM-9: some AIM-9L *Sidewinder*/AIM-9N *Sidewinder*

AA Home Guard 2,500 reservists on mobilisation
on mob under comd of Air Force

FORCES BY ROLE
Army 2 bn (*total:* 9 army bty)

EQUIPMENT BY TYPE
AD • GUNS • 20mm • TOWED: some NM-45

DEPLOYMENT

AFGHANISTAN
NATO • ISAF 1+ army coy; 147

BOSNIA-HERZEGOVINA
EU • EUFOR II 125

EGYPT
MFO 4 Staff

ETHIOPIA/ERITREA
UN • **UNMEE** 5 obs

IRAQ
Army 12 (Staff Officers, Peace Support)

MIDDLE EAST
UN • **UNTSO** 12 obs

SERBIA AND MONTENEGRO
NATO • **KFOR I** ε60
UN • **UNMIK** 1

SUDAN
UN • **UNMIS** 2 obs

FOREIGN FORCES

NATO HQ Joint Command North Europe (JC North)
United States EUCOM: 18 M-109 155mm SP (Army
Prepositioned Stocks (APS)); 18 M-198 155mm SP (APS); 50

Poland Pl

Polish Zloty z		2003	2004	2005
GDP	z	814bn	884bn	
	US$	209bn	241bn	
per capita	US$	5,431	6,243	
Growth	%	3.8	5.3	
Inflation	%	0.8	3.4	
Debt	US$	95.2bn		
Def exp	z	15.4bn	16.9bn	
	US$	3.97bn	4.60bn	
Def bdgt	z	14.8bn	16.2bn	17.1bn
	US$	3.82bn	4.42bn	5.16bn
FMA (US)	US$	30m	34.7m	67.4m
US$1=z		3.88	3.67	3.33

Population   38,557,984

Ethnic groups: German 1.3%; Ukrainian 0.6%; Belarussian 0.5%

Age	0–14	15–19	20–24	25–29	30–64	65 plus
Male	8%	4%	4%	4%	23%	5%
Female	8%	4%	4%	4%	23%	8%

Capabilities

ACTIVE 141,500 (Army 89,000 Navy 14,300 Air
30,000 Joint 8,200) **Paramilitary 21,400**
Terms of service 12 months (to be 9 months from 2005)

RESERVE 234,000 (Army 188,000 Navy 12,000 Air
19,000 Joint 15,000)

ORGANISATIONS BY SERVICE

Army ε40,100; ε48,900 conscript; 188,000
reservists **(total 277,000)**
To reorg: 2 Mil Districts/Army HQ; 1 Multi-national Corps
HQ (Pl/Ge/Da); 2 Corps HQ

FORCES BY ROLE

Territorial Def	7 bde
Armd	1 bde
Armd Cav	1 div
Air Cav	1 bde
Recce	1 regt
Mech inf	3 div; 2 bde (1 coastal)
Mtn inf	1 bde
Spec Ops	1 regt
Air aslt	1 bde
Arty	2 bde
Cbt hel	2 regt
SSM	1 regt
Engr	2 bde
Gd	1 regt
AD	3 regt

EQUIPMENT BY TYPE

TK • MBT 947
  LEOPARD 2 128: 128 2A4
  PT-91 *Twardy* 233
  T-72 586: 586 T-72 MBT/T-72M1D/T-72M1
RECCE • BRDM 435: 435 BRDM-2
AIFV 1,281
  BMP 1248: 1,248 BMP-1
  BRM-1 33
APC • APC (W) • OT 33: 33 OT-64 SKOT (OT-64)
L-A-L 693: 693 APC
ARTY 1,482
  TOWED 362
    122mm 227: 227 M-30 *M-1938*
    152mm 135: 135 M-1938 (ML-20)
  SP 652
    122mm 533: 533 2S1 *Carnation*
    152mm 111: 111 M-77 *Dana*
    203mm 8: 8 2S7
  MRL • 122mm 249: 219 BM-21; 30 RM-70 *Dana*
  MOR • 120mm 219: 15 2B11/2S12; 204 M-120
AT • MSL 258: 129 AT-3 *Sagger*; 104 AT-4 *Spigot*; 18 AT-5
Spandrel; 7 AT-7 *Saxhorn*
HELICOPTERS
  ATK 65
    MI-24 43: 43 Mi-24D *Hind* D/Mi-24V *Hind* E
    PZL MI-2URP *Hoplite* 22
  SPT 80
    PZL W-3 35: 34 PZL W-3A *Sokol*/PZL W-3W *Sokol*
      PZL W-3A 1: 1 PZL W-3A *Sokol* spt hel/PZL W-3A-1
      Sokol (tpt)
    MI-8 11: 11 (tpt)
  Mi-8T *Hip* spt/Mi-8U *Hip* trg 18
  SPT 80:
    PZL MI-2 34: 29 (tpt); 5 PZL MI-2URN *Hoplite*
  Mi-17T *Hip* spt/Mi-17U *Hip* H trg 6
AD
  SAM 952
    SP 376: 80 SA-6 *Gainful*; 64 SA-8 *Gecko*; 232 SA-9
    Gaskin
    MANPAD 576: 576 SA-7 *Grail*
  GUNS 644
    23mm 420
      SP 44: 44 ZSU-23-4
      TOWED 376: 376 ZU-23-2

57mm • TOWED 224: 224 S-60
RADAR • LAND: some SNAR-10 *Big Fred* (veh, arty)
MSL • TACTICAL • SSM 4: 4 SS-21 *Scarab* (*Tochka*)

Navy 12,300 (incl some conscripts); 12,000 reservists (up to age 50) (total 24,300)

EQUIPMENT BY TYPE
SUBMARINES • TACTICAL 3
SSK 1:
1 *Sokol* with 8 single 533mm TT
SS 2:
1 *Orzel* with 6 single 533mm TT with 12 T-53/T-65
1 *Wilk* (RF *Foxtrot*, expected to be decommissioned late 2002) with 10 single 533mm TT with 12 T-53 HWT
PRINCIPAL SURFACE COMBATANTS 8
DESTROYERS • DDG 1:
1 *Warszawa* with 1 quad (4 eff.) with 1 SS-N-2C *Styx* tactical SSM, 1 x5 533mm TT (5 eff.) with 1 T-53 HWT, 2 x16 (32 eff.) each with 1 SA-N-1 *Goa* SAM, 2 RL, 1 hel landing platform
FRIGATES 3
FFG 2:
2 *Pulawski* (capacity 2 SH-2G *Super Seasprite* ASW hel) each with 2 triple 324mm ASTT (6 eff.) each with 24 A244 LWT, 1 Mk 13 GMLS with 36 SM-1 MR SAM, 4 RGM-84D/F *Harpoon* tactical SSM, 1 76mm gun
FF 1:
1 *Kaszub* with 2 twin 533mm ASTT (4 eff.) each with SET-53 HWT, 1 quad (4 eff.) with SA-N-5 *Grail* SAM, 2 RBU 6000 *Smerch* 2 (24 eff.), 1 76mm gun
CORVETTES • FSG 4:
4 *Gornik* each with 1 x4 manual with SA-N-5 *Grail* SAM, 2 twin (4 eff.) each with 4 SS-N-2C *Styx* tactical SSM, 1 76mm gun
PATROL AND COASTAL COMBATANTS 19
PCC 3:
3 *Sassnitz* each with 1 x4 Manual with SA-N-5 *Grail* SAM, 2 quad (8 eff.) (Refit programme in progress) each with 1 RBS-15M tactical SSM, 1 76mm gun
PCI 11: 11 *Pilica*
PFM 5:
5 *Osa* each with 4 SS-N-2A *Styx* tactical SSM
MINE WARFARE • MINE COUNTERMEASURES 22
MHC 7: 3 *Krogulec*; 4 *Mamry*
MSC 13: 13 *Goplo*
MSI 2: 2 *Leniwka*
AMPHIBIOUS
LS • LSM 5: 5 *Lublin* (capacity 9 tanks; 135 troops)
CRAFT • LCU 3:
3 *Deba* (capacity 50 troops)
LOGISTICS AND SUPPORT 18
AGF 1: 1 *Polnochny* C (mod)
AGHS 3
AGI 2: 2 *Moma*
AOT 1 **ARS** 5
TRG 6: 5 **AXS** 1

FACILITIES
Base 1 located at Kolobrzeg, 1 (HQ) located at Gdynia, 1 located at Swinoujscie, 1 located on the Hel Peninsula, 1 located at Gdynia-Babie Doly

Naval Aviation 2,000

Flying hours   60 hrs/year on MiG-21 *Fishbed* ftr

FORCES BY ROLE

Air	1 sqn with M-28 *Bryza E*
Ftr	2 sqn with MiG-21 *Fishbed*
ASW	1 sqn with Mi-14PL *Haze A*
Recce	1 sqn with M-28 *Bryza R*; PZL TS-11R *Iskra*
SAR	1 sqn with Mi-14PS *Haze C*; PZL W-3RM *Anakonda*
Tpt	1 sqn with PZL W-3 *Sokol*; MI-17 (Mi-8MT) *Hip H*; PZL MI-2 *Hoplite*

EQUIPMENT BY TYPE
AIRCRAFT 18 combat capable
FTR 18: 18 MiG-21 *Fishbed*
MP 12: 12 PZL TS-11R *Iskra*
TPT 8: 1 AN-2 *Colt*; 3 AN-286; 4 M-28 *Bryza TD*
UTL 4: 4 M-28 *Bryza E*
HELICOPTERS
SAR 8: 3 Mi-14PS *Haze C*; 5 PZL W-3RM *Anakonda*
ASW • MI-14 13: 13 Mi-14PL *Haze A*
SPT 9
PZL W-3 2: 2 PZL W-3S *Sokol*
MI-8 2: 2 MI-17 (Mi-8MT) *Hip H*
PZL MI-2 *Hoplite* 5

Air Force 30,000 (incl some conscripts); 19,000 reservists (up to age 60) (total 49,000)

2 AD Corps- North and South
Flying hours   60 to 180 hrs/year

FORCES BY ROLE

Ftr	1 sqn with 37 MiG-29A *Fulcrum*; 8 MiG-29UB *Fulcrum*
FGA / recce	5 sqn with 53 Su-22M-4 (Su-17M-4) *Fitter K*; 9 Su-17UM-3 *Fitter G*; 4 sqn with 27 MiG-21M *Fishbed J*/MiG-21MF *Fishbed J*/MiG-21R *Fishbed H*; 28 MiG-21bis *Fishbed L & N*; 26 MiG-21UM *Mongol B*
Tpt	1 regt; 3 sqn with 25 AN-2 *Colt*; 5 AN-26 *Curl*; 2 AN-28 *Cash*; 8 CASA C-295M; 2 M-28 *Bryza TD*; 2 TU-154 *Careless*; 9 Yak-40 *Codling*
Trg	some sqn with 105 PZL TS-11 *Iskra*; 35 PZL-130 *Orlik*
Hel	some sqn with 18 PZL W-3 *Sokol*; 12 MI-17 (Mi-8MT) *Hip H*/Mi-8 *Hip*; 67 PZL MI-2 *Hoplite*; 1 Bell 412 *Twin Huey*
SAM	3 bde; 1 indep regt (25 SAM bty each with 20 SA-3 *Goa*; 3 SA-4 *Ganef* (6 eff.); 2 SA-5 *Gammon*)

EQUIPMENT BY TYPE
AIRCRAFT 142 combat capable
FTR • MiG-21 28: 28 MiG-21bis *Fishbed L & N*
FGA 53: 53 Su-22M-4 (Su-17M-4) *Fitter K*: 27 MiG-21M *Fishbed J* MiG-21 ftr/MiG-21MF *Fishbed J* MiG-21 ftr/MiG-21R *Fishbed H* recce*
TPT 53: 25 AN-2 *Colt*; 5 AN-26 *Curl*; 2 AN-28 *Cash*
CASA C-295 8: 8 CASA C-295M
M-28 *Bryza TD* 2 **TU-154** *Careless* 2 **Yak-40** *Codling* 9
TRG 220
MiG-21U 26: 26 MiG-21UM *Mongol B**
MiG-29 45: 37 MiG-29A *Fulcrum*; 8 MiG-29UB *Fulcrum**
PZL TS-11 *Iskra* 105 **PZL-130** *Orlik* 35

Su-17U 9: 9 Su-17UM-3 *Fitter G*
HELICOPTERS
SPT 97: 18 PZL W-3 *Sokol*
  MI-8 12: 12 MI-17 (Mi-8MT) *Hip H*/Mi-8 *Hip* spt hel
  PZL MI-2 *Hoplite* 67
  UTL 1: 1 Bell 412 *Twin Huey*
AD • SAM 625: 500 SA-3 *Goa*
  SP 75: 75 SA-4 *Ganef*
  STATIC 50: 50 SA-5 *Gammon*
MSL • TACTICAL • ASM: some AS-7 *Kerry*
  AAM: some AA-11 *Archer*; some AA-2 *Atoll*; some AA-3 *Anab*; some AA-8 *Aphid*

Paramilitary 21,400

Border Guards 14,100
Ministry of Interior and Administration

Maritime Border Guard
PATROL AND COASTAL COMBATANTS 12: 6 PCC; 6 PCO

Prevention Units of Police 6,300; 1,000 conscript (total 7,300)
OPP-Ministry of Interior

DEPLOYMENT

AFGHANISTAN
Army 87 (*Op Enduring Freedom*)
NATO • ISAF 22
UN • UNAMA 1 obs

BOSNIA-HERZEGOVINA
EU • EUFOR II 2 inf coy; 287
UN • UNMIBH 1 obs

CÔTE D'IVOIRE
UN • UNOCI 2 obs

DEMOCRATIC REPUBLIC OF CONGO
UN • MONUC 2 obs

ETHIOPIA/ERITREA
UN • UNMEE 6

GEORGIA
UN • UNOMIG 5 obs

IRAQ
Army
FORCES BY ROLE
1 mech inf bde
EQUIPMENT BY TYPE
HELICOPTERS
SPT 8: 8 PZL W-3 *Sokol*
  Mi-17U *Hip H* trg/Mi-8 *Hip* spt 4

LEBANON
Armed Forces
Military Hospital 1 located in Lebanon
UN • UNIFIL 1 inf bn; 236

LIBERIA
UN • UNMIL 2 obs

SERBIA AND MONTENEGRO
NATO • KFOR I 1 inf bn; 574
UN • UNMIK 1

SUDAN
UN • UNMIS 2

SYRIA/ISRAEL
UN • UNDOF 1 inf bn; 340

WESTERN SAHARA
UN • MINURSO 1 obs

FOREIGN FORCES
Germany Army: 67 (Ge elm Corps HQ (multinational))

Portugal Por

Euro €		2003	2004	2005
GDP	€	129bn	134bn	
	US$	147bn	166bn	
per capita	US$	14,096	15,836	
Growth	%	-1.2	1.0	
Inflation	%	3.3	2.5	
Public Debt	%	69.3	72.3	
Def exp[a]	€	2.09bn	2.29bn	
	US$	2.37bn	2.83bn	
Def bdgt	€	1.65bn	1.71bn	1.92bn
	US$	1.88bn	2.12bn	2.43bn
US$1=€		0.88	0.81	0.79

[a] including military pensions

Population   10,566,212

Age	0–14	15–19	20–24	25–29	30–64	65 plus
Male	9%	3%	4%	4%	22%	7%
Female	8%	3%	3%	4%	24%	10%

Capabilities

ACTIVE 44,900 (Army 26,700 Navy 10,950 Air 7,250)
Paramilitary 47,700
Terms of service 4 months, conscription is being phased out.

RESERVE 210,930 (Army 210,000 Navy 930)
Reservist obligation to age of 35

ORGANISATIONS BY SERVICE

Armed Forces 9,100 conscript

Army 26,700
5 Territorial Comd (2 mil region, 1 mil district, 2 mil zone)
FORCES BY ROLE

Army	2 (Task Forces – Azores and Madeira) unit (*total*: 2 AD bty, 3 inf bn)
Mech inf	1 bde (1 SP arty bty, 1 tk gp, 1 engr coy, 1 AD bty, 1 recce sqn, 2 mech inf bn)
Lt inf	1 bde (1 fd arty bn, 2 inf bn)

Spec Ops 1 unit
Cdo   1 bn
AB   1 bde (1 AT coy, 1 engr coy, 1 AD bty, 1 fd arty
          bn, 1 recce sqn, 2 Para bn)
MP   1 regt

Reserves

Territorial Def 3 bde (on mob)

EQUIPMENT BY TYPE
TK • MBT 187:
  M-60 101: 7; 86 M-60A3; 8 M-60A4
  M-48 86: 86 M-48A5
RECCE 40: 15 V-150 *Chaimite*
  VBL 25: 25 ULTRAV M-11
APC 353
  APC (T) 280: 240 M-113; 40 M-557
  APC (W) 73: 73 V-200 *Chaimite*
ARTY 350+
  TOWED 135
    105mm 97: 21 L-119; 52 M-101; 24 M-56
    155mm • M-114 38: 38 M-114A1
  SP • 155mm • M-109 20: 6 M-109A2; 14 M-109A5
  COASTAL 21: **150mm** 9; **152mm** 6; **234mm** 6 (inactive)
  MOR 174+: **81mm** some (incl 21 SP)
    107mm 76: 76 M-30 (incl 14 SP)
    120mm 98: 98 *Tampella*
AT
  MSL 118: 68 Milan (incl 6 ULTRAV-11); 50 TOW (incl 18
  M-113, 4 M-901)
  RCL 402
    106mm 128: 128 M-40
    84mm 162: 162 *Carl Gustav*
    90mm 112
AD
  SAM • MANPAD 52: 37 *Chaparral*; 15 FIM-92A *Stinger*
  GUNS 93
    20mm • TOWED 31: 31 Rh 202
    40mm • TOWED 62: 62 L/60

Navy 8,480; 360 conscript; 930 reservists (obligation to age 35); 130 active reservists (recalled) (total 9,900)

EQUIPMENT BY TYPE
SUBMARINES • TACTICAL • SSK 2:
  2 *Albacora* each with 12 single 550mm TT (8 bow, 4 stern)
  each with 12 E14/E15
PRINCIPAL SURFACE COMBATANTS • FRIGATES 6
  FFG 3:
    3 *Vasco Da Gama* (capacity 2 *Lynx* MK95 (*Super Lynx*)
    utl hel) each with 2 Mk 36 triple 324mm each with Mk
    46 LWT, 1 Mk 29 *Sea Sparrow* octuple with RIM-7M *Sea
    Sparrow* SAM, 2 Mk 141 *Harpoon* quad (8 eff.) each with
    1 RGM-84C *Harpoon* tactical SSM, 1 100mm gun
  FF 3:
    3 *Commandante Joao Belo* each with 2 Mk32 triple
    324mm each with Mk 46 LWT, 2 100mm gun, 1 hel
    landing platform
PATROL AND COASTAL COMBATANTS 29
  PCC 8: 8 *Cacine*
  PCI 9: 5 *Argos*; 4 *Centauro*
  PCR 4: 3 *Albatroz*; 1 *Rio Minho*

PCO 8:
  3 *Baptista de Andrade* each with 1 100mm gun, 1 hel
  landing platform
  5 *Joao Coutinho* each with 2 76mm gun
AMPHIBIOUS • CRAFT 1: 1 LCU
LOGISTICS AND SUPPORT 8: 4 AGS
  AORLH 1:
    1 *Bérrio* with 1 hel landing platform (for medium hel)
  TRG 3: 3 AXS

FACILITIES
Base   1 located at Lisbon
Naval airbase 1 located at Montido
Support base 1 (North) located at Leca da Palmeira,
              1 (South) located at Portimao, 1 located
              at Funchal (Madiera), 1 located at Ponta
              Delgada (Azores)

Marines 1,980

FORCES BY ROLE
Police   1 det
Lt inf   2 bn
Spec Ops 1 det
Fire spt 1 coy

EQUIPMENT BY TYPE
ARTY • MOR 36: 36 120mm

Naval Aviation
HELICOPTERS • UTL 5: 5 *Lynx* MK95 (*Super Lynx*)

Air Force 7,250

Flying hours   180 hrs/year on F-16 *Fighting Falcon* ftr

FORCES BY ROLE
Air   1 (op) COFA comd; 5 (op) gp
FGA   1 sqn with *Alpha Jet*; 1 sqn with F-16A
             Fighting Falcon/F-16B *Fighting Falcon*
Surv   1 sqn with CASA 212 *Aviocar*
MR   1 sqn with 6 P-3P *Orion* *
CSAR/SAR   1 sqn with SA-330 *Puma*; 1 sqn with CASA
             212 *Aviocar*; SA-330 *Puma*; 1 sqn with EH101
Tpt   1 sqn with CASA 212 *Aviocar*; 1 sqn with
             Falcon 20; *Falcon* 50; 1 sqn with C-130H
             Hercules
Liaison / utl 1 sqn with SA-330 *Puma*; 1 sqn with FTB337
             Skymaster
Trg   1 sqn with TB-30 *Epsilon*; 1 sqn (hel and
             multi-engine trg provided by SA-316 and
             one of C-212) with *Alpha Jet*

EQUIPMENT BY TYPE
AIRCRAFT 50 combat capable
FTR 19:
  F-16 19: 16; 3 F-16B *Fighting Falcon*
  RECCE 2: 2 CASA 212B *Aviocar* (survey)
  MP • P-3 6: 6 P-3P *Orion* *
TPT 42+
  C-130 6: 6 C-130H *Hercules* (tpt/SAR)
  CASA 212 20: 20 CASA 212A *Aviocar* (12 tpt/SAR, 1
  Nav trg, 2 ECM trg, 5 fisheries protection)
  Cessna 337 *Skymaster* 12 (utility)**FTB337** *Skymaster*
  some *Falcon* **20** 1 (tpt, cal) *Falcon* **50** 3

TRG 41: 25 *Alpha Jet* (FGA/trg)*; 16 TB-30 *Epsilon*
HELICOPTERS
  SPT 10: 10 SA-330 *Puma* (SAR/tpt) 6 EH101 (CSAR), another 6 being delivered
  UTL 18: 18 SA-316 *Alouette III* (trg, utl)
MSL • TACTICAL • ASM • AGM-65: some AGM-65B *Maverick*/AGM-65G *Maverick*
  AGM-84: some AGM-84A *Harpoon*
  AAM • AIM-9: some AIM-9Li *Sidewinder*

Paramilitary 47,700

National Republican Guard 26,100
APC • APC (W): some *Commando* Mk III (*Bravia*)
HELICOPTERS • UTL 7: 7 SA-315 *Lama*

Public Security Police 21,600

DEPLOYMENT

AFGHANISTAN
NATO • ISAF 8

BOSNIA-HERZEGOVINA
EU • EUFOR II 1 inf bn under strength; 330

BURUNDI
UN • ONUB 2 obs

DEMOCRATIC REPUBLIC OF CONGO
UN • MONUC 5

EAST TIMOR
UN • UNOTIL 3 obs

IRAQ
Army 128 (Peace Support) 1 Sy coy

SAO TOME AND PRINCIPE
Air Force 5
AIRCRAFT • TPT 1: 1 CASA 212 *Aviocar*

SERBIA AND MONTENEGRO
NATO • KFOR I 313
UN • UNMIK 2 obs

FOREIGN FORCES

United States EUCOM: 1,008 USNORTHCOM: Support facility located at Lajes

Romania R

Lei		2003	2004	2005
GDP	lei	1,903tr	2,387tr	
	US$	57.3bn	72.1bn	
per capita	US$	2,561	3,225	
Growth	%	5.2	8.3	
Inflation	%	15.3	11.9	
Debt	US$	21.2bn		
Def exp	lei	43.6tr	50.1tr	
	US$	1.31bn	1.51bn	
Def bdgt	lei	44.6tr	49.9tr	60.6tr
	US$	1.34bn	1.51bn	2.10bn
FMA (US)	US$	26.5m	10.4m	12.4m
US$1=lei		33.2k	33.1k	28,827

Population   22,329,977
Ethnic groups: Hungarian 9%

Age	0–14	15–19	20–24	25–29	30–64	65 plus
Male	8%	4%	4%	4%	22%	6%
Female	8%	4%	4%	4%	23%	9%

Capabilities

ACTIVE 97,200 (Army 66,000 Navy 7,200 Air 14,000 Joint 10,000) **Paramilitary 79,900**
Terms of service All services 12 months

RESERVE 104,000 (Joint 104,000)

ORGANISATIONS BY SERVICE

Armed Forces 10,000 (centrally controlled units); ε29,600 conscript; 104,000 reservists **(total** 143,600)

Army 47,500; 18,500 conscript (total 66,000)
FORCES BY ROLE
1 Joint Ops Comd (corps), 2 Ops Comd (div), 1 Land Forces HQ.
Readiness is reported as 80-90% for Active bde and 20-40% for Territorial bde
Territorial 2 corps comd (10 active bde: (1 AD bde, 1 engr bde, 1 log bde, 1 arty bde, 1 tk bde, 1 mtn inf bde, 1 AB bde, 3 mech bde), 14 territorial bde (1 engr bde, 1 tk bde, 2 arty bde, 2 mtn inf bde, 2 AD bde, 6 mech bde)

EQUIPMENT BY TYPE
TK • MBT 1258: 314 TR-85 M1; 717 T-55; 227 TR-580 *TR-77*
RECCE • BRDM 4: 4 BRDM-2
AIFV 177: 177 MLI-84
APC 1,583
  APC (T) 88: 88 MLVM
  APC (W) 1495: 70 B33 *TAB Zimbru*; 881 TAB-71; 166 TAB-77; 378 TABC-79
L-A-L • 1119: 1,119 APC look-a-like
ARTY 1,238

TOWED 661
  122mm 163: 163 M-30 *M-1938* (A-19)
  152mm 498: 54 M-1937; 330 M-1981 Model 81; 114 M1985 gun/how 85
SP • 122mm 48: 6 2S1 *Carnation*; 42 Model 89
MRL • 122mm 171: 171 APR-40
MOR • 120mm 358: 358 M-1982
AT
  MSL 227: 53 9P122; 120 9P133; 54 9P148
  GUNS • 100mm 933: 72 M1975 gun 75; 777 M1977 gun 77; 84 Su-100 SP
AD
  SAM 64: 64 SA-6 *Gainful* SP/SA-7 *Grail* MANPAD/SA-8 *Gecko* SP (64-384 eff.)
  GUNS 675+: **100mm** 213
    35mm • SP 4: 4 *Gepard*
      TOWED • GDF: some GDF-003
    37mm 230 **57mm** 216 **85mm** 12
RADAR • LAND 10: 10 SNAR-10 *Big Fred* (veh, arty)
MSL • TACTICAL • SSM 9: 9 FROG (in store)

Navy 7,200

Navy HQ with 1 Naval Operational Command (fleet level), 1 (Danube based) Riverine Flotilla

EQUIPMENT BY TYPE
PRINCIPAL SURFACE COMBATANTS 7
  FRIGATES • FFG 1:
    1 *Marasesti* (capacity 2 IAR-316 (SA-316) *Alouette III* utl hel) with 2 triple 533mm ASTT (6 eff.) each with Russian 53-65 ASW, 4 twin (8 eff.) with 8 SS-N-2C *Styx* tactical SSM, each with SA-N-5 *Grail* SAM, 2 RBU 6000 *Smerch* 2 (24 eff.), 2 x2 76mm gun (4 eff.)
  CORVETTES • FS 6:
    4 *Tetal* I each with 2 twin 533mm ASTT (4 eff.) each with Russian 53-65 ASW, 2 RBU 2500 *Smerch* 1 (32 eff.), 2 x2 76mm gun (4 eff.)
    2 *Tetal* II (capacity 1 IAR-316 (SA-316) *Alouette III* utl hel) each with 2 twin 533mm ASTT (4 eff.), 2 RBU 6000 *Smerch* 2 (24 eff.), 1 76mm gun
PATROL AND COASTAL COMBATANTS 38
  PC 3:
    3 *Zborul* each with 2 twin (4 eff.) each with 4 SS-N-2C *Styx* tactical SSM, 1 76mm gun
  PCR 20:
    5 *Brutar* each with 1 BM-21 MRL RL, 1 100mm gun
    3 *Kogalniceanu* each with 2 100mm gun
    12 VB 76
  PFM 3:
    3 *Osa* I each with 4 single each with 4 SS-N-2C *Styx* tactical SSM
  PFT 6:
    6 *Epitrop* each with 4 single 533mm TT
  PHT 6:
    6 *Huchuan* each with 2 single 533mm TT†
MINE WARFARE 12
  MINE COUNTERMEASURES 10
    MSI 6: 6 VD141
    MSO 4: 4 *Musca*
  MINELAYERS • ML 2:
    2 *Cosar* each with up to 100 mine
LOGISTICS AND SUPPORT 11: 2 AGF; 2 AGOR; 1 AK; 3 AOT; 2 AT
  TRG 1: 1 AXS

FACILITIES
Base 1 (Danube) located at Tulcea, 1 (Danube) located at Braila, 1 (coastal) located at Mangalia, 1 (coastal) located at Constanta

Naval Infantry

FORCES BY ROLE
Naval inf 1 bn
EQUIPMENT BY TYPE
APC • APC (W) 13
  TAB-71 10: 10 TAB-71M
  TABC-79 3

Air Force 10,200; 3,800 conscript (total 14,000)

Flying hours   120 hrs/year

FORCES BY ROLE
HQ (AF) some HQ HQ (*total:* 1 Air div, 1 (op) Air comd)
Ftr   2 sqn MiG-21 *Lancer* C
FGA   3 sqn MiG-21 *Lancer* A
Tpt   some sqn with 2 AN-24 *Coke*; 6 AN-26 *Curl*; 4 C-130B *Hercules*; 9 IAR-330 (SA-330) *Puma*; 3 Mi-8 *Hip*
Survey   some sqn with 3 AN-30 *Clank*
Spt hel some (Combat) sqn with 8 IAR-330 SOCAT *Puma*; 32 IAR-330 (SA-330) *Puma*; 22 IAR-316B (SA-316B) *Alouette III*
Trg   some sqn with 15 IAR-99 *Soim*; 16 L-29 *Delfin*; 13 L-39 *Albatros*
AD   1 bde; 2 regt

EQUIPMENT BY TYPE
AIRCRAFT 106 combat capable
  FTR 25: 25 MiG-21 *Lancer* C
  FGA 68: 68 MiG-21 *Lancer* A
  TPT 11: 2 AN-24 *Coke*; 6 AN-26 *Curl*; 3 AN-30 *Clank*
    C-130 4: 4 C-130B *Hercules*
  TRG 83: 15 IAR-99 *Soim*; 16 L-29 *Delfin*; 26 in store; 13 L-39 *Albatros*; 13 MiG-21 *Lancer* B (two-seat trainers) *
HELICOPTERS
  ASLT 8: 8 IAR-330 SOCAT *Puma*
  SPT 92: 41 IAR-330 (SA-330) *Puma*; 39 in store; 3 Mi-8 *Hip*; 9 in store
  UTL 22:
    IAR-316 (SA-316) 22: 22 IAR-316B (SA-316B) *Alouette III*
UAV: some *Shadow* 600
AD • SAM • TOWED 42: 42 SA-2 *Guideline*
MSL • TACTICAL • ASM: some AS-7 *Kerry*
  AAM: some AA-11 *Archer*; some AA-2 *Atoll*; some AA-8 *Aphid*; some *Python* III; some R-550 *Magic*
FACILITIES

Air base	1 with 25 MiG-21 *Lancer* C ftr (AD), 4 with 68 MiG-21A *Fishbed* ftr (air-to-gd); 13 MiG-21 *Lancer* B trg ac (two-seat trainers), 1
Surface-to-air missile site	7 with 42 SA-2 *Guideline* Towed SAM
Trg base	1

Paramilitary 79,900

Border Guards 22,900 (incl conscripts)
Ministry of Interior

Gendarmerie ε57,000
Ministry of Interior

DEPLOYMENT

AFGHANISTAN
Army 418 (*Op Enduring Freedom*) 1 inf bn; 1 NBC coy
NATO • ISAF 32
UN • UNAMA 2 obs

BOSNIA-HERZEGOVINA
EU • EUFOR II 106

BURUNDI
UN • ONUB 3 obs

CÔTE D'IVOIRE
UN • UNOCI 6 obs; 2

DEMOCRATIC REPUBLIC OF CONGO
UN • MONUC 22 obs

ETHIOPIA/ERITREA
UN • UNMEE 7 obs

GEORGIA
UN • UNOMIG 1 obs

IRAQ
Army ε730 1 mech inf bn

LIBERIA
UN • UNMIL 3 obs

SERBIA AND MONTENEGRO
NATO • KFOR I 2 inf coy; 226
UN • UNMIK 1 obs

SUDAN
UN • UNMIS 4

Slovakia Slvk

Slovak Koruna Ks		2003	2004	2005
GDP	Ks	1.20tr	1.32tr	
	US$	32.7bn	41.0bn	
per capita	US$	6,041	7,563	
Growth	%	4.5	5.5	
Inflation	%	8.5	7.5	
Debt	US$	18.3bn		
Def bdgt	Ks	22.9bn	23.1bn	25.6bn
	US$	625m	717m	828m
FMA (US)	US$	15.4m	7.67m	5.91m
US$1=Ks		36.7	32.3	31

Population   5,431,363

Ethnic groups: Hungarian 11%; Romany ε5%; Czech 1%

Age	0–14	5–19	20–24	25–29	30–64	65 plus
Male	9%	4%	4%	4%	23%	5%
Female	8%	4%	4%	4%	24%	7%

Capabilities

ACTIVE 20,195 (Army 12,860 Air 5,160 Joint 2,175)
Terms of service 6 months

ORGANISATIONS BY SERVICE

Army 12,860 (incl some conscripts)
1 Land Forces Comd HQ, 1 tri-national bde HQ

FORCES BY ROLE

Rapid Reaction	1 bn
Mech inf	1 bde (1 tk bn, 1 engr coy, 1 arty bn, 1 recce bn, 2 mech inf bn)
Lt inf	1 bde (1 engr coy, 1 arty bn, 3 inf bn)
Arty	1 regt
Engr	1 coy

Reserves ε20,000 on mobilisation

National Guard Force
1 mob base (to form 2 inf bde on mob)

EQUIPMENT BY TYPE
TK • MBT • T-72 271: 271 T-72M
RECCE 291: 72 BPVZ; 129 BRDM; 90 OT-65
AIFV • BMP 404: 311 BMP-1; 93 BMP-2
APC 120
  APC (T) 113: 113 OT-90
  APC (W) • OT 7: 7 OT-64
ARTY 374
  TOWED • 122mm 76: 76 D-30
  SP 199
    122mm 49: 49 2S1 *Carnation*
    152mm 134: 134 M-77 *Dana*
    155mm 16: 16 M 200
  MRL • 122mm 87: 87 RM-70 *Dana*
  MOR • 120mm 12: 8 M-1982; 4 SPM-85
AT • MSL 466: 466 AT-3 *Sagger*/AT-5 *Spandrel* (incl BMP-1/-2 and BRDM mounted)
AD
  SAM • SP 48: ε48 SA-13 *Gopher*
    MANPAD: some SA-16 *Gimlet*; some SA-7 *Grail*
  GUNS 200: 200 M-53/59SP SP 30mm/S-60 towed 57mm
RADAR • LAND: some SNAR-10 *Big Fred* (veh, arty)

Air Force 5,160 (Incl some conscripts)
Flying hours   45 hrs/year

FORCES BY ROLE

Ftr	1 wg with 22 MiG-29 *Fulcrum*/MiG-29UB *Fulcrum* (12 Modernised); 29 MiG-21MF *Fishbed J*/MiG-21UB *Mongol*
FGA / recce	1 wg with 12 Su-25K *Frogfoot A*/Su-25UBK *Frogfoot B*; 8 Su-22M-4 (Su-17M-4) *Fitter K*/Su-22UM-3K (Su-17UM-3) *Fitter G*
Tpt	1 wg with 2 AN-24 *Coke*; 2 AN-26 *Curl*; 7 L-410M *Turbolet*
Trg	some sqn with 11 L-29 *Delfin*; 15 L-39 *Albatros*
Hel	1 wg with 19 Mi-24D *Hind D*/Mi-24V *Hind E**; 6 Mi-8 *Hip*; 14 MI-17 (Mi-8MT) *Hip H*; 2 PZL MI-2 *Hoplite*

AD   1 bde with S-125 *Neva*; SA-10B *Grumble*; SA-6
          Gainful; SA-7 *Grail*

EQUIPMENT BY TYPE
AIRCRAFT 71 combat capable
    22 MiG-29 *Fulcrum* ftr/MiG-29UB *Fulcrum* MiG-29U
    trg; 29 MiG-21MF *Fishbed J* MiG-21 ftr/MiG-21UB
    Mongol Mongol A trg; 12 Su-25K *Frogfoot A* FGA/Su-
    25UBK *Frogfoot B* trg
    TPT 11: 2 AN-24 *Coke*; 2 AN-26 *Curl*
    L-410 7: 7 L-410M *Turbolet*
    TRG 26: 11 L-29 *Delfin*; 15 L-39 *Albatros*
    Su-22M-4 (Su-17M-4) *Fitter K* **Su-17M** *Fitter C* FGA/Su-
    22UM-3K (Su-17UM-3) *Fitter G* **Su-17U** trg 8
HELICOPTERS
    ATK • MI-24 19: 19 Mi-24D *Hind D*/Mi-24V *Hind E* *
    SPT 22:
        MI-8 20: 6; 14 MI-17 (Mi-8MT) *Hip H*
        PZL MI-2 *Hoplite* 2
    AD • SAM: some S-125 *Neva*
        SP • SA-10: some SA-10B *Grumble*
        SA-6 *Gainful* some
        MANPAD: some SA-7 *Grail*
MSL • TACTICAL • AAM: some AA-10 *Alamo*; some AA-
11 *Archer*; some AA-2 *Atoll*; some AA-8 *Aphid*
FACILITIES
Air base 3

DEPLOYMENT

AFGHANISTAN
Army 40 (*Op Enduring Freedom*)
NATO • ISAF 17

BOSNIA-HERZEGOVINA
EU • EUFOR I 29

CYPRUS
UN • UNFICYP 205

IRAQ
Army 82 (Peace Support)

MIDDLE EAST
UN • UNTSO 2 obs

SERBIA AND MONTENEGRO
NATO • KFOR I 100

SIERRA LEONE
UN • UNAMSIL 1 obs

SYRIA/ISRAEL
UN • UNDOF 95

Slovenia Slvn

Slovenian Tolar t		2003	2004	2005
GDP	t	5.74tr	6.19tr	
	US$	27.7bn	31.7bn	
per capita	US$	13,801	15,783	
Growth	%	2.5	4.4	
Inflation	%	5.6	3.6	
Debt	US$	14.6bn		
Def bdgt	t	78.1bn	99.6bn	110bn
	US$	377m	511m	580m
FMA (US)	US$	4.93m	2.92m	2.43m
US$1=t		207	195	190

Population   2,011,070

Ethnic groups: Croat 3%; Serb 2%; Muslim 1%

Age	0–14	15–19	20–24	25–29	30–64	65 plus
Male	7%	3%	4%	4%	25%	6%
Female	7%	3%	3%	4%	25%	9%

Capabilities

ACTIVE 6,550 (Army 6,550) **Paramilitary 4,500**

RESERVE 20,000 (Army 20,000) **Paramilitary 5,000**

ORGANISATIONS BY SERVICE

Army 5,973
1 Force Comd
FORCES BY ROLE
Inf 1 bde (1 MP bn, 1 engr bn, 2 mot inf bn)

Reserves
Inf 2 bde (on mob) (*each:* 1 tk bn, 1 arty bn, 1 recce bn, 2
    inf bn)

EQUIPMENT BY TYPE
TK • MBT 70: 40 M-84
    T-55 30: 30 T-55S1
RECCE • BRDM 8: 8 BRDM-2
AIFV 26: 26 M-80
APC • APC (W) 64
    BOV 28: 28 BOV-3MD
    BTR • BTR-50 2: 2 BTR-50PU
    Valuk 34 (*Pandur*)
ARTY 140
    TOWED 24
        105mm • M-2 6: 6 M-2A1
        155mm 18: 18 TN-90
    MOR 116: **82mm** 60
        120mm 56: 8 M-52; 16 M-74; 32 MN-9
AT • MSL: some AT-3 *Sagger* (incl 12 BOV-3SP); some AT-4
Spigot (incl 12 BOV-3SP)

Army Maritime Element 47
FORCES BY ROLE
Maritime 1 bn (part of Sp Comd)

EQUIPMENT BY TYPE
PATROL AND COASTAL COMBATANTS • PB 1: 1
Super Dvora MKII
FACILITIES
Base 1 located at Koper

Air Element 530

FORCES BY ROLE
Air 1 regt
AD 1 regt

EQUIPMENT BY TYPE
AIRCRAFT
TPT 3: 1 L-410 *Turbolet*; 2 PC-6 *Turbo-Porter*
TRG 12:
PC-9 12: 3; 9 PC-9M (armed trainer)
HELICOPTERS
RECCE 2: 2 AS-532 *Horizon*
UTL 11: 3 AB-206 (Bell 206) *JetRanger*; 8 Bell 412 *Twin Huey* *
AD
SAM 138
SP • ROLAND 6: 6 *Roland* II
MANPAD 132: 36 SA-16 *Gimlet*; 96 SA-18 *Grouse (Igla)*
GUNS 24
12.7mm • TOWED 12: 12 M-55
20mm • SP 12: 12 BOV-3 SPAAG

Paramilitary 4,500

Police 4,500 (armed); 5,000 reservists (**total 9,500**)
HELICOPTERS • UTL 5: 1 A-109; 2 AB-206 (Bell 206) *JetRanger*; 1 AB-212 (Bell 212); 1 Bell 412 *Twin Huey*

DEPLOYMENT

AFGHANISTAN
NATO • ISAF 18

BOSNIA-HERZEGOVINA
EU • EUFOR II 158

MIDDLE EAST
UN • UNTSO 2 obs

SERBIA AND MONTENEGRO
NATO • KFOR I 2

Spain Sp

Euro €		2003	2004	2005
GDP	€	742bn	799bn	
	US$	844bn	986bn	
per capita	US$	20,993	24,488	
Growth	%	2.5	2.7	
Inflation	%	3.1	3.1	
Public Debt	%	57.4	55.2	
Def exp[a]	€	9.57bn	10.10bn	
	US$	10.8bn	12.5bn	
Def bdgt	€	6.21bn	6.74bn	6.98bn
	US$	7.0bn	8.3bn	8.8bn
US$1=€		0.88	0.81	0.79

Population   40,341,462

Age	0–14	15–19	20–24	25–29	30–64	65 plus
Male	7%	3%	3%	4%	24%	7%
Female	7%	3%	3%	4%	24%	9%

Capabilities

ACTIVE 147,255 (Army 95,600 Navy 19,455 Air 22,750 Joint 9,450) **Paramilitary 73,360**

RESERVE 319,000 (Army 265,000 Navy 9,000 Air 45,000)

ORGANISATIONS BY SERVICE

Army 95,600
4 Area Defence Forces

Manoeuvre Force (FMA)

Reaction	1 div (1 AB bde, 1 (Legion) inf bde, 1 HQ div, 1 HQ bn, 1 Sigs regt, 1 Cav regt, 1 fd arty regt)
HQ	1 NRDC-SP HQ (1 NRDC-SP HQ bn)
Cav	1 bde (1 HQ bde, 2 light Cav regt, 1 armd Cav regt, 1 fd arty regt, 1 HQ bn, 1 log bn, 1 engr unit)
Mech inf	1 div (1 armd bde, 1 engr regt, 1 ADA regt, 1 SP arty regt, 2 mech inf bde, 1 HQ div, 1 HQ bn, 1 Sigs regt, 1 Cav regt, 1 log regt)
Mtn inf	1 bde (1 HQ bde, 2 mtn inf regt, 1 HQ bn, 1 fd arty bn, 1 engr unit, 1 log bn)
Spec Ops	1 comd (3 Spec Ops bn, 1 HQ bn, 1 HQ bde)
Fd arty	1 bde (1 HQ bde, 2 fd arty regt)
Engr	1 bde (1 HQ bde, 1 engr regt, 1 engr bridging regt, 1 railway regt, 1 NBC regt)
Sigs	1 bde (1 HQ bde, 1 sigs regt, 1 EW regt)
Avn	1 FAMET bde (1 HQ bde, 1 sigs bn, 6 hel bn, 1 log coy)

Land Force (FT)

Coast arty	1 comd (2 coast arty regt, 1 HQ bde, 1 sigs unit)

Army	1 (General) Melilla comd (1 HQ div, 1 HQ bn, 2 inf regt, 1 cav regt, 1 fd arty regt, 1 ADA bn, 1 coast arty bn, 1 engr regt, 1 Sigs bn, 1 log unit); 1 Balearic comd (1 HQ div, 1 HQ bn, 1 inf regt, 1 engr unit, 1 fd arty regt, 1 log unit); 1 Ceuta comd (1 HQ div, 1 HQ bn, 2 inf regt, 1 cav regt, 1 fd arty regt, 1 ADA bn, 1 coast arty bn, 1 engr regt, 1 sigs bn, 1 log unit); 1 Canary comd (1 HQ corps, 1 HQ bn, 3 inf regt, 2 fd arty regt, 1 engr bn, 1 log unit)
Inf	2 bde (*each:* 1 HQ bde, 1 HQ bn, 2 inf regt, 1 engr unit, 1 fd arty bn, 1 log unit)
ADA	1 comd (1 HQ bn, 1 ADA regt)

Logistic Operational Force (FLO)

HQ	1 corps
Log	2 div HQ (operations); 1 op (force) (1 HQ div, 4 log regt)
Medical	1 bde (1 HQ bde, 3 medical regt, 1 log unit, 1 Field Hospital)

Reserves

cadre units

Railway	1 regt
Armd Cav	1 bde
Inf	3 bde

EQUIPMENT BY TYPE
TK • MBT 323
  LEOPARD 2 126: 108 2A4
    2A5 18: 18 2A5E
  M-60 • M-60A3 184: 184 M-60A3TTS
  M-48 • M-48A5 13: 13 M-48A5E
RECCE 270: 42 B-1 *Centauro*; 228 VEC-3562 *BMR-VEC*
AIFV 144: 144 *Pizarro* (incl variants)
APC 2,022
  APC (T) 1,337: 1,337 M-113 (incl variants)
  APC (W) 685: 130 BMR-600 (incl variants); 555 BMR-600M1
ARTY 2,013
  TOWED 290
    105mm 226: 56 L-118 light gun; 170 Model 56 pack howitzer
    155mm 64: 52 M-114; 12 SBT-1
  SP 170
    105mm 34: 34 M-108
    155mm • M-109 96: 96 M-109A5
    203mm 40: 40 M-110A2
  COASTAL 50
    155mm 8: 8 SBT 52
    305mm 3 **381mm** 3 **6in** 36
  MRL • 140mm 14: 14 Teruel
  MOR 1,489: **81mm** 1,040 (incl 446 SP); **120mm** 449 (incl 110 SP)
AT
  MSL 632: 28 HOT; 404 *Milan* (incl 106 SP); 200 TOW (incl 68 SP)
  RCL 507: 507 106mm
HELICOPTERS
  OBS 9: 9 OH-58 *Kiowa*

SPT • CH-47 17: 17 HT-17D (CH-47D) *Chinook*
UTL 96: 28 BO-105; 6 HU-18 (Bell 212)
  HU.21 (AS-532) 31: 15 AS-532UC *Cougar*; 16 AS-532UL *Cougar*
  UH-1 31: 31 UH-1H *Iroquois*
AD
  SAM 247
    SP 18: 18 *Roland*
    TOWED 49
      MIM-23 • I-HAWK 36: 36 I HAWK Phase III *MIM-23B*
      SKYGUARD 13: 13 *Skyguard/Aspide*
    MANPAD 180: 180 *Mistral*
  GUNS 267
    20mm • TOWED 175: 175 GAI-B01
    35mm • TOWED • GDF 92: 92 GDF-002
RADAR • LAND 2: 2 AN/TPQ-36 *Firefinder* (arty, mor)

Navy 19,455 (incl Naval Aviation and Marines); 9,000 reservists (total 28,455)

FORCES BY ROLE
Navy 1 comd HQ located at Madrid

EQUIPMENT BY TYPE
SUBMARINES • TACTICAL • SSK 5:
  1 *Delfin* with 12 single 550mm TT (8 bow, 4 stern) with 12 F17 Mod 2/L5
  4 *Galerna* each with 4 single 533mm TT each with 20 F17 Mod 2/L5
PRINCIPAL SURFACE COMBATANTS 13
  AIRCRAFT CARRIERS • CVS 1:
    1 *Principe de Asturias* (capacity 10 AV-8B *Harrier II* FGA ac/AV-8B *Harrier II Plus* FGA ac; 8 SH-3 *Sea King* ASW hel; 2 HU-18 (Bell 212) utl hel)
  FRIGATES • FFG 12:
    4 *Alvaro de Bazan* (capacity 1 SH-60B *Seahawk* ASW hel) each with 2 twin 324mm ASTT (4 eff.) with 24 Mk 46 LWT, 2 Mk 141 *Harpoon* quad (8 eff.) each with 1 RGM-84F tactical SSM, 1 48 cell Mk 41 VLS (LAM capable) with 32 SM-2 MR SAM, 64 RIM-162B *Sea Sparrow* SAM (quad packs), 1 127mm gun; *Aegis* Baseline 5
    2 *Baleares* each with 2 twin ASTT (4 eff.) each with Mk 46 LWT, 1 Mk 22 GMLS with 16 SM-1 MR SAM, 1 Mk 112 octuple (8 eff.) with 16 tactical ASROC, 2 Mk 141 *Harpoon* quad (8 eff.) each with 1 RGM-84C *Harpoon* tactical SSM, 1 127mm gun
    6 *Santa Maria* (capacity 2 SH-60B *Seahawk* ASW hel) each with 2 Mk32 triple 324mm each with 6 Mk 46 LWT, 1 Mk 13 GMLS with 32 SM-1 MR SAM, 8 RGM-84C *Harpoon* tactical SSM, 1 76mm gun
PATROL AND COASTAL COMBATANTS 36
  PCC 9: 9 *Anaga*
  PCI 9: 3 *Conejera* 4 *Toralla* 2
  PFI 5: 5 *Barcelo*
  PCO 13: 4 *Chilreu*; 5 *Descubierta*; 4 *Serviola*
MINE WARFARE • MINE COUNTERMEASURES 7
  MCCS 1: 1 *Diana*
  MHO 6: 6 *Segura*
AMPHIBIOUS
  PRINCIPAL AMPHIBIOUS SHIPS • LPD 2: 2 *Galicia*
  LS • LST 2: 2 *Pizarro*

LOGISTICS AND SUPPORT 29: 2 AGHS; 2 AGOR; 2 AGS; 3 AK; 1 AO; 1 AOR (*Patino*); 4 AT; 2 AWT; 1 Diving tender/spt

TRG 11: 1 AX; 5 AXL; 5 AXS
MSL • TACTICAL • AAM • AIM-120: some AIM-120A *AMRAAM*

FACILITIES
Base   1 located at El Ferrol, 1 (Fleet HQ) located at Rota, 1 (ALMART HQ, Maritime Action) located at Cartagena, 1 located at Las Palmas (Canary Islands)

Naval Station   1 located at Mahón (Menorca), 1 located at Porto Pi (Mallorca)

Naval Aviation 814

Flying hours   150 hrs/year on AV-8B *Harrier II* FGA ac; 200 hrs/year on hel

FORCES BY ROLE
COMD / tpt   1 sqn with 9 HU-18 (Bell 212)
FGA   1 sqn with 12 AV-8B *Harrier II Plus*; 4 AV-8B *Harrier II*
ASW   1 sqn with 8 SH-3D *Sea King*; 1 sqn with 12 SH-60B *Seahawk*
EW   1 flt with 3 SH-3D *Sea King* (AEW)
Liaison   1 sqn with 3 CE-550 *Citation II*
Trg   1 sqn with 1 TAV-8B *Harrier* on lease (USMC); 10 Hughes 500

EQUIPMENT BY TYPE
AIRCRAFT 16 combat capable
   FGA • AV-8 16: 12 AV-8B *Harrier II Plus*; 4 AV-8B *Harrier II*
   TPT 3: 3 CE-550 *Citation II*
   TRG • TAV-8 1: 1 TAV-8B *Harrier* on lease (USMC)
HELICOPTERS
   ASW 23
      SH-3 11: 3 SH-3D *Sea King* (AEW); 8 more
      SH-60 12: 12 SH-60B *Seahawk*
   UTL 19: 9 HU-18 (Bell 212); 10 Hughes 500
MSL • TACTICAL • ASM: some AGM-119 *Penguin*
   AGM-65: some AGM-65G *Maverick*
   AAM: some AIM-120 *AMRAAM*
   AIM-9: some AIM-9L *Sidewinder*
TORPEDOES • LWT: some Mk 46

Marines 5,300

FORCES BY ROLE
Marine   1 bde (2500) (1 mech inf bn, 2 inf bn, 1 arty bn)
Marine Garrison   5 gp

EQUIPMENT BY TYPE
TK • MBT • M-60 • M-60A3 16: 16 M-60A3TTS
APC • APC (W) 18: 18 *Piranha*
AAV • AAV-7 19: 16 AAV-7A1/AAVP-7A1; 2 AAVC-7A1; 1 AAVR-7A1
ARTY 18
   TOWED • 105mm 12: 12 M-56 (pack)
   SP • 155mm • M-109 6: 6 M-109A2
AT • MSL • TOW 24: 24 TOW-2
   RL • 90mm: some C-90C
AD • SAM • MANPAD 12: 12 Mistral

Air Force 22,750; 45,000 reservists (total 67,750)

Flying hours   120 hrs/year on hel/tpt ac; 180 hrs/year on FGA/ftr

FORCES BY ROLE
Ftr   1 sqn with 4 *Typhoon*; 2 sqn with 48 F-1CE (F-1C) *Mirage*/F-1EDA/Mirage F-1EE (F-1E)
Ftr / OCU   6 sqn with 91 EF-18A (F/A-18A) *Hornet*/EF-18B (F/A-18B) *Hornet* (First of 67 MLU EF-F18 delivered)
MP   1 sqn with 2 P-3A *Orion* *; 5 P-3B *Orion* * (MR)
EW   1 sqn with 1 B-707; CASA 212 *Aviocar*; 2 *Falcon* 20 (EW); 1 *Falcon* 50 (EW)
SAR   1 sqn with 3 F-27 *Friendship* (SAR); 3 HU-21 (AS-332) *Super Puma*; 1 sqn with CASA 212 *Aviocar*; 3 HU-21 (AS-332) *Super Puma*; 1 sqn with CASA 212 *Aviocar*; 5 AS-330 (SA-330) *Puma*
Spt   1 sqn with CASA 212 *Aviocar*; 2 Cessna 550 *Citation V* (recce); 15 Canadair CL-215
Tkr / tpt   1 sqn with 5 KC-130H *Hercules*
Tpt   2 sqn with 20 CN-235 (18 tpt, 2 VIP); 1 sqn with 7 C-130H *Hercules*/C-130H-30 *Hercules*; CASA 212 *Aviocar*; 1 sqn with 3 Falcon 20 (VIP); 2 Falcon 900 (VIP); 1 sqn; 1 sqn with 6 HU-21 (AS-332) *Super Puma*
Tkr   1 sqn with 2 A-310; 2 B-707
OCU   1 sqn with EF-18A (F/A-18A) *Hornet*/EF-18B (F/A-18B) *Hornet*
Lead-in trg   2 sqn with 23 F-5B *Freedom Fighter*
Trg   2 sqn with 78 CASA C-101 *Aviojet*; 1 sqn with CASA 212 *Aviocar*; 1 sqn with CASA 212 *Aviocar*; 1 sqn with 22 Beech F-33C *Bonanza* (trg); 2 sqn with 15 EC-120 *Colibri*; 8 S-76C; 1 sqn with 37 E-26 (T-35) *Pillan*

EQUIPMENT BY TYPE
AIRCRAFT 177 combat capable
   FTR 75
      F-5 23: 23 F-5B *Freedom Fighter*
      Typhoon 4
      F-1 48: 48 F-1CE (F-1C) *Mirage*/F-1EDA *Mirage* F-1EE (F-1E)/*Mirage* F-1EE (F-1E)
   FGA • EF-18 (F/A-18) 91: 91 EF-18A (F/A-18A) *Hornet*/EF-18B (F/A-18B) *Hornet* (First of 67 MLU EF-F18 delivered)
   MP • P-3 7: 2 P-3A *Orion* *; 5 P-3B *Orion* * (MR)
   TKR • KC-130 5: 5 KC-130H *Hercules*
   TPT 109: 2 A-310; 3 B-707
      C-130 • C-130H 7: 7 C-130H *Hercules* tpt ac/C-130H-30 *Hercules*
      CASA 212 *Aviocar* 57 **CASA C-295** 7 (9 on order to replace some CASA 212)**CN-235** 20 (18 tpt, 2 VIP)**Cessna 550** *Citation V* 2 (recce)**F-27** *Friendship* 3 (SAR)
      FALCON 20 5: 3 (VIP)
      2 (EW) *Falcon 50* 1 (EW) *Falcon 900* 2 (VIP)
   SPT 15: 15 Canadair CL-215
   TRG 162: 78 CASA C-101 *Aviojet*; 21 DO-27 (liaison/trg)
      E-24 (BEECH F-33) 22: 22 Beech F-33C *Bonanza* (trg)
      E-26 (T-35) *Pillan* 37 **F-1DDA** *Mirage* 1 ***Mirage F-1BE (F-1B)** 3 *

HELICOPTERS
SPT 17: 5 AS-330 (SA-330) *Puma*; 12 HU-21 (AS-332) *Super Puma*
UTL 23: 15 EC-120 *Colibri*; 2 AS-532 (VIP)
  S-76 8: 8 S-76C
AD • SAM: some *Mistral*; some R-530
  TOWED • SKYGUARD: some *Skyguard/Aspide*
MSL • TACTICAL • ASM • AGM-65: some AGM-65G *Maverick*
  AGM-84: some AGM-84A *Harpoon*; some AGM-84D *Harpoon*
  AAM: some AIM-120 *AMRAAM*; some AIM-7 *Sparrow*; some AIM-9 *Sidewinder*

Central Air Command
4 Wg

Ftr 2 sqn with EF-18 (F/A-18) *Hornet*
Spt 1 sqn with CASA 212 *Aviocar*; Cessna 550 *Citation V*; 1 sqn with Canadair CL-215; 1 sqn with B-707; CASA 212 *Aviocar* (EW); *Falcon* 20; 1 sqn with CASA 212 *Aviocar*; HU-21 (AS-332) *Super Puma* (SAR)
Tpt 1 sqn with A-310; B-707 (tkr/tpt); 1 sqn with HU-21 (AS-332) *Super Puma* (tpt); 2 sqn with CN-235; 1 sqn with CASA C-295; 1 sqn with *Falcon 20/Falcon 50/Falcon* 900
Trg 1 sqn with CASA C-101 *Aviojet*; 1 sqn with E-24 (Beech F-33) *Bonanza*; 1 sqn with CASA 212 *Aviocar*

Eastern Air Command
2 Wg

Ftr 2 sqn with EF-18 (F/A-18) *Hornet*
Spt 1 sqn with CASA 212 *Aviocar*; AS-330 (SA-330) *Puma*
Tpt 1 sqn with CASA 212 *Aviocar*; 1 sqn with KC-130H *Hercules* (tkr/tpt); C-130H *Hercules*; 1 sqn
OCU 1 sqn with EF-18 (F/A-18) *Hornet*

Strait Air Command
4 Wg

Ftr 1 sqn with EF-18 (F/A-18) *Hornet*; 1 sqn with *Typhoon*; 2 sqn with F-1CE (F-1C) *Mirage*/Mirage F-1BE (F-1B)
MP 1 sqn with P-3A *Orion*/P-3B *Orion*
Lead-in trg 2 sqn with F-5B *Freedom Fighter*
Trg 2 sqn with EC-120B *Colibri*; S-76C; 1 sqn with E-26 (T-35) *Pillan*; 1 sqn with CASA C-101 *Aviojet*; 1 sqn with CASA 212 *Aviocar*

Canary Island Air Command
1 Wg

FGA 1 sqn with EF-18 (F/A-18) *Hornet*
SAR 1 sqn with F-27 *Friendship*; HU-21 (AS-332) *Super Puma*
Tpt 1 detachment with 2 CN-235

Logistic Support Air Command
Trials and Testing 1 sqn with F-5A *Freedom Fighter* test; F-1 *Mirage* test; EF-18 (F/A-18) *Hornet* test; CASA 212 *Aviocar* test; CASA C-101 *Aviojet* test

Paramilitary 73,360

Guardia Civil 72,600
9 regions
FORCES BY ROLE
Inf   19 (Tercios) regt (*total:* 56 Rural bn)
Spec Op 6 (rural) gp
Sy   6 (traffic) gp; 1 (Special) bn
EQUIPMENT BY TYPE
APC • APC (W) 18: 18 BLR
HELICOPTERS
  ARMED 26: 26 BO-105ATH
  UTL 9: 8 BK-117; 1 EC135P2

Guardia Civil Del Mar 760
PATROL AND COASTAL COMBATANTS 32: 32 PCI
Patrol craft inshore

NON-STATE ARMED GROUPS
see Part II

DEPLOYMENT

AFGHANISTAN
NATO • ISAF 125
Army 400 (*Op Enduring Freedom*)
Air Force
AIRCRAFT 177 combat capable
  MP 1: 1 P-3 *Orion*
  TPT 13: 5 C-130 *Hercules*; 8 CN-235

BOSNIA-HERZEGOVINA
EU • EUFOR II 1 Cav sqn; 2 inf coy; 935

DEMOCRATIC REPUBLIC OF CONGO
UN • MONUC 2 obs; 1

ETHIOPIA/ERITREA
UN • UNMEE 3 obs

HAITI
UN • MINUSTAH 202

ITALY
EU • EUFOR I • EUFOR Air
  AIRCRAFT
    FGA 4: 4 EF-18 (F/A-18) *Hornet* (*Op Deliberate Forge*)
    TKR 1: 1 KC-130 *Hercules*

SERBIA AND MONTENEGRO
NATO • KFOR I ε800
UN • UNMIK 2 obs

SUDAN
UN • UNMIS 3

FOREIGN FORCES
United States EUCOM: 282 Navy: Base located at Rota

Turkey Tu

New Turkish Lira L		2003	2004	2005
GDP	L	359qd	430qd	
	US$	239bn	297bn	
per capita	US$	3,521	4,322	
Growth	%	5.9	8.0	
Inflation	%	25.3	10.6	
Debt	US$	145bn		
Def exp [a]	L	13.5qd	14.6qd	
	US$	9.03bn	10.10bn	
Def bdgt	L	12.1qd	12.2qd	13.4bn
	US$	8.10bn	8.48bn	9.81bn
FMA (US)	US$	20.1m	40m	37.7m
US$1=L		1.5m	1.4m	1.37[b]

[a] including coast guard and gendarmerie
[b] New Turkish Lira from 2005

Population 69,660,559

Ethnic groups: Kurds ε20%

Age	0–14	15–19	20–24	25–29	30–64	65 plus
Male	13%	5%	5%	5%	20%	3%
Female	13%	5%	5%	5%	19%	4%

Capabilities

ACTIVE 514,850 (Army 402,000 Navy 52,750 Air 60,100) **Paramilitary 102,200**
Terms of service 15 months. Reserve service to age of 41 for all services. Active figure reducing

RESERVE 378,700 (Army 258,700 Navy 55,000 Air 65,000) **Paramilitary 50,000**

ORGANISATIONS BY SERVICE

Army ε77,000; ε325,000 conscript; 258,700 reservists **(total** 660,700)

FORCES BY ROLE
2 armd bde, 1 mech inf bde, 1 inf bde to be disbanded
Inf	4 bde
Army	4 HQ HQ; 10 corps HQ
Armd	17 bde
Mech inf	15 bde
Inf	2 div
Trg / inf	4 bde
Inf	11 bde
SF	1 comd HQ
Cdo	5 bde
Cbt hel	1 bn
Avn	4 regt; 3 bn (*total:* 1 tpt bn, 2 trg bn)
Trg / arty	4 bde

EQUIPMENT BY TYPE
TK • MBT 4,205
   LEOPARD 1 397: 170 1A1; 227 1A3

M-60 932: 274 M-60A1; 658 M-60A3
M-48 • M-48A5 2876: 2,876 M-48A5T1/M-48A5T2 (1300 to be stored)
RECCE 250+: some ARSV *Cobra*; ε250 *Akrep*
AIFV 650: 650 AIFV
APC • APC (T) 3,643: 830 AAPC
   M-113 2,813: 2,813 M-113 APC (T)/M-113A1/M-113A2
ARTY 7,450+
   TOWED 685+
      105mm • M-101: some M-101A1
      155mm 523
         M-114 517: 517 M-114A1/M-114A2
         Panter 6
      203mm 162: 162 M-115
   SP 868+
      105mm 391
         M-108 26: 26 M-108T
         M-52 365: 365 M-52T
      155mm • M-44 222: 222 M-44T1
         TU SpH Storm (K-9) *Thunder* some
      175mm 36: 36 M-107
      203mm 219: 219 M-110A2
   MRL 84+: **107mm** 48
      122mm: some T-122
      227mm 12: 12 MLRS (incl ATACMS)
      70mm 24
   MOR 5,813: **81mm** 3,792 (incl SP)
      107mm 1,264: 1,264 M-30 (some SP)
      120mm 757 (some 179 SP)
AT
   MSL 1,283: 186 *Cobra*; ε340 *Eryx*; 392 *Milan*; 365 TOW (SP)
   RCL 3,869
      106mm 2,329 M-40A1
      57mm 923: 923 M-18
      75mm 617
   RL • 66mm: some M-72 *LAW*
AIRCRAFT
   TPT 7: 4 Beech 200 *Super King Air*; 3 Cessna 421
   UTL • U-17 98: 98 U-17B
   TRG 63: 34 7GCBC *Citabria*
      T-41 25: 25 T-41D *Mescalero*
      T-42 4: 4 T-42A *Cochise*
HELICOPTERS
   OBS • OH-58 3: 3 OH-58B *Kiowa*
   ATK • AH-1 37: 37 AH-1P *Cobra*/AH-1W *Cobra*
   SPT • S-70 50: 50 S-70A *Black Hawk*
   UTL 153: 2 AB-212 (Bell 212)
      AS-532 10: 10 AS-532UL *Cougar*
      BELL 204 12: 12 AB-204B (Bell 204B)
      BELL 205 64: 64 AB-205A (Bell 205A)
      Bell 206 *JetRanger* 20
      UH-1 45: ε45 UH-1H *Iroquois*
   TRG • HUGHES 300 28: 28 Hughes 300C
UAV 100+: some AN/USD-501 *Midge*; some *Falcon* 600/ *Firebee*; some *Gnat* 750
   RECCE • TAC 100: ε100 *Harpy*
AD
   SAM • MANPAD 897: 789 FIM-43 *Redeye* (being withdrawn); 108 FIM-92A *Stinger*
   GUNS 1664

20mm • **TOWED** 439: 439 GAI-D01
35mm • **TOWED** • **GDF** 120: 120 GDF-001/GDF-003
40mm 1105
  SP • **M-42** 262: 262 M-42A1
  TOWED 843: 803 L/60/L/70; 40 T-1
RADAR • **LAND**: some AN/TPQ-36 *Firefinder* (arty, mor)

Navy 14,100; 34,500 conscript; 55,000 reservists (total 103,600)

FORCES BY ROLE
HQ 1 (Ankara) Naval Forces Command HQ (1
(Altinovayalova) Training HQ, 1 (Gölcük) Fleet HQ
HQ with UGM- 84 *Harpoon*, 1 (Istanbul) Northern Sea
Area HQ, 1 (Izmir) Southern Sea Area HQ)

EQUIPMENT BY TYPE
SUBMARINES • TACTICAL 13
SSK 10:
  6 *Atilay* (Ge Type 209/1200) each with 8 x1 533mm
  ASTT each with 14 SST-4 HWT
  4 Type 209/1400 (Ge Type 209/1400) each with 8 x1
  533mm ASTT each with UGM- 84 *Harpoon* tactical
  USGW, *Tigerfish* HWT
SSC 3:
  1 *Canakkale* (US *Guppy*, sid) with 10 x1 533mm ASTT (6
  forward, 4 aft) each with 24 Mk 23/Mk 37
  2 *Hizirreis* (US *Tang*) each with 8 single 533mm TT each
  with Mk 37 HWT
PRINCIPAL SURFACE COMBATANTS • FRIGATES 19
FFG 18:
  2 *Barbaros* (MOD Ge MEKO 200 F244, F245) each with
  1 AB-212 (Bell 212) utl hel, 2 Mk32 triple 324mm each
  with Mk 46 LWT, 1 Mk 29 *Sea Sparrow* octuple with 24
  Aspide SAM, 2 Mk 141 *Harpoon* quad (8 eff.) each with 1
  RGM-84C *Harpoon* tactical SSM, 1 127mm gun
  2 *Barbaros* (MOD Ge MEKO 200 F246, F247) each with
  2 Mk32 triple 324mm each with Mk 46 LWT, 2 Mk 141
  Harpoon quad (8 eff.) each with 1 RGM-84C *Harpoon*
  tactical SSM, 1 8 cell Mk 41 VLS with 24 Aspide SAM,
  1 127mm gun
  2 *Burak* (Fr *d'Estienne d'Orves*) each with 4 single ASTT
  each with 4 L5 HWT, 1 x2 Manual with SIMBAD x2
  Manual, 2 single each with 4 MM-38 *Exocet* tactical
  SSM, 1 100mm gun
  6 *Gaziantep* (capacity 1 S-70B *Seahawk* ASW hel) (US
  Perry) each with 2 Mk32 triple 324mm each with 24 Mk
  46 LWT, 1 Mk 13 GMLS with 36 SM-1 MR SAM, 4+
  RGM-84C *Harpoon* tactical SSM, 1 76mm gun
  2 *Muavenet* (capacity 1 AB-212 (Bell 212) utl hel) (US
  Knox-class) each with 2 twin 324mm ASTT (4 eff.)
  each with 22+ Mk 46 LWT, 1 Mk16 Mk 112 octuple
  with ASROC/RGM-84C *Harpoon* SSM (from ASROC
  launcher), 1 127mm gun
  4 *Yavuz* (Ge MEKO 200 F244, F245) each with 1 AB-212
  (Bell 212) utl hel, 2 Mk32 triple 324mm each with Mk
  46 LWT, 1 Mk 29 *Sea Sparrow* octuple with 24 *Aspide*
  SAM, 2 Mk 141 *Harpoon* quad (8 eff.) each with 1 RGM-
  84C *Harpoon* tactical SSM, 1 127mm gun
FF 1:
  1 *Berk* with 6 Mk32 triple 324mm, 2 x24 123mm (48 eff.)
  each with Mk 11 Hedgehog, 4 76mm gun

PATROL AND COASTAL COMBATANTS 55
PCC 26: 4 AB-21; 10 AB-25; 4 PGM-71; 6 *Sultanhisar*; 2
Trabzon
PFC 2: 1 *Bora* (US *Asheville*); 1 *Girne*
PFM 27:
  8 *Dogan* (Ge *Lurssen*-57) each with 1 76mm gun, 2
  quad (8 eff.) each with RGM-84A *Harpoon*/RGM-84C
  Harpoon
  8 *Kartal* (Ge *Jaguar*) each with 4 single each with RB 12
  Penguin tactical SSM, 2 single 533mm TT
  3 *Kilic* each with 2 Mk 141 *Harpoon* quad (8 eff.) each
  with 1 RGM-84C *Harpoon* tactical SSM, 1 76mm gun
  8 *Yildiz* each with 1 76mm gun, 2 quad (8 eff.) each with
  RGM-84A *Harpoon*/RGM-84C *Harpoon*
MINE WARFARE 35
MINE COUNTERMEASURES 31: 8 MCM spt (tenders)
  MHC 5: 5 *Edineik* (Fr *Circe*)
  MSC 14: 6 *Karamursel* (Ge *Vegesack*); 8 *Samsun* (US
  Adjutant)
  MSI 4: 4 *Foca* (US *Cape*)
MINELAYERS 4: 3 (Tenders)
  ML 1: 1 *Nusret* (400 mines)
AMPHIBIOUS
LS 8
  LSM 1: 1 *Cakabey* (capacity 9 tanks; 400 troops)
  LST 7:
    2 *Bayraktar* (capacity 16 tanks; 200 troops) (US LST-
    512)
    2 *Ertugru* (capacity 18 tanks; 400 troops) (US
    Terrebonne Parish)
    1 *Osman Gazi* (capacity 17 tanks; 980 troops; 4 LCVP)
    2 *Sarucabey* (capacity 11 tanks; 600 troops)
  CRAFT 59: 35 LCT; 2 LCU; 22 LCM
LOGISTICS AND SUPPORT 27: 2 AGHS
  AO 1: 1 *Akar*
  AR 2 **ARS** 3 **AT** 5 **Diving tender/spt** 1 **spt** 2 (Ge *Rhein*) **tkr**
  5 (spt tkr) **tpt** 3 **depot ship** 3
FACILITIES
Base 1 located at Gölcük, 1 located at Erdek, 1 located at
  Canakkale, 1 located at Eregli, 1 located at Bartin,
  1 located at Izmir, 1 located at Istanbul, 1 located
  at Foka, 1 located at Aksaz, 1 located at Antalya, 1
  located at Mersin, 1 located at Iskenderun

Marines 3,100

Arty	1 bn (18 guns)
Marine	1 HQ; 1 regt; 3 bn
Spt	some unit

Naval Aviation

FORCES BY ROLE

ASW	some sqn with 3 AB-204AS (Bell 204AS); 13 AB-212 (Bell 212)
Trg	some sqn with 7 TB-20 *Trinidad*

EQUIPMENT BY TYPE
AIRCRAFT • UTL 7: 7 TB-20 *Trinidad*
HELICOPTERS
  ASW 3: 3 AB-204AS (Bell 204AS)
  UTL 13: 13 AB-212 (Bell 212)*

Naval Forces Command
HQ 1 HQ located at Ankara

Fleet
HQ 1 HQ located at Gölcük

Northern Sea Area
HQ 1 HQ located at Istanbul

Southern Sea Area
HQ 1 HQ located at Izmir

Training
HQ 1 HQ located at Altinovayalova

Air Force 28,600; 31,500 conscript; 65,000 reservists (total 125,100)
2 tac air forces (divided between east and west)
Flying hours   180 hrs/year

FORCES BY ROLE
Ftr   3 sqn with F-16C *Fighting Falcon*/F-16D *Fighting Falcon*; 2 sqn with F-4E *Phantom II*; 2 sqn with F-5A *Freedom Fighter*/F-5B *Freedom Fighter*

FGA   5 sqn with F-16C *Fighting Falcon*/F-16D *Fighting Falcon*; 3 sqn with F-4E *Phantom II*

Recce   1 sqn with RF-4E *Phantom II*

SAR   some sqn with AS-532 *Cougar*

Tpt   1 (VIP) sqn with C-20 *Gulfstream*; CN-235; UC-35 *Citation*; 2 sqn with CN-235; 1 sqn with C-160 *Transall*; 1 sqn with C-130B *Hercules*/C-130E *Hercules*

Tkr   some sqn with KC-135R *Stratotanker*

Liaison   10 base flt with CN-235 (sometimes); UH-1H *Iroquois*

OCU   1 sqn with F-4E *Phantom II*; 1 sqn with F-16C *Fighting Falcon*/F-16D *Fighting Falcon*; 1 sqn with F-5A *Freedom Fighter*/F-5B *Freedom Fighter*

Trg   1 sqn with T-37B *Tweet*/T-37C *Tweet*; T-38A *Talon*; 1 sqn with SF-260D; 1 sqn with T-41 *Mescalero*

SAM   4 sqn with 92 MIM-14 *Nike Hercules*; 2 sqn with 86 *Rapier*; 8 (firing) unit with MIM-23 *HAWK*

EQUIPMENT BY TYPE
AIRCRAFT 445 combat capable
   FTR • F-5 87: 87 F/NF-5A/B *Freedom Fighter*; (48 being upgraded as lead-in trainers)
   FGA 358: 193 F-16C *Fighting Falcon*; 30 F-16D *Fighting Falcon*
      F-4 135: 135 F-4E *Phantom II* (88 FGA, 47 ftr (52 upgraded to *Phantom* 2020));
   RECCE • RF-4 35: 35 RF-4E *Phantom II* (recce);
   TKR • KC-135 7: 7 KC-135R *Stratotanker*
   TPT 77
      C-130 13: 13 C-130B *Hercules*/C-130E *Hercules*
      C-160 16: *Transall* **C-160D** 16
      C-20 *Gulfstream* some
      CN-235 46: 46 (tpt/EW)
      2 Cessna *Citation* **VII** 2 (VIP)
   UTL: some UC-35 *Citation*
   TRG 198

SF-260 40: 40 SF-260D (trg);
T-37 60: 60 T-37B *Tweet*/T-37C *Tweet* some
T-38 70: 70 T-38A *Talon* some
T-41 *Mescalero* 28
HELICOPTERS
UTL 40+: 20 AS-532 *Cougar* (14 SAR/6 CSAR)
   UH-1 20+: 20 UH-1H *Iroquois* (tpt, liaison, base flt, trg schools); some more
UAV 1: 1 *Gnat* 750
AD • SAM 178+: 86 *Rapier*
   TOWED: some MIM-23 *HAWK*
   STATIC 92: 92 MIM-14 *Nike Hercules*
MSL • TACTICAL • ASM: some AGM-142 *Popeye*; some AGM-65 *Maverick*
   ARM: some AGM-88 *HARM*
   Popeye I some
   AAM: some AIM-120 *AMRAAM*
      AIM-7: some AIM-7E *Sparrow*
      AIM-9: some AIM-9S *Sidewinder*

Paramilitary

Gendarmerie/National Guard 100,000; 50,000 reservists (total 150,000)
Ministry of Interior, Ministry of Defence in war
FORCES BY ROLE
Army   1 (Border) div; 2 bde
Cdo   1 bde

EQUIPMENT BY TYPE
RECCE: some *Akrep*
APC • APC (W) 560
   BTR 535: 535 BTR-60/BTR-80
   Condor 25
AIRCRAFT
   RECCE • OBS: some Cessna O-1E *Bird Dog*
   TPT • Do-28 2: 2 Do-28D
HELICOPTERS
   SPT 33
      S-70 14: 14 S-70A *Black Hawk*
      MI-8 19: 19 MI-17 (Mi-8MT) *Hip H*
   UTL 23: 1 AB-212 (Bell 212)
      BELL 204 8: 8 AB-204B (Bell 204B)
      BELL 205 6: 6 AB-205A (Bell 205A)
      BELL 206 8: 8 AB-206A (Bell 206A) *JetRanger*

Coast Guard 800 (Coast Guard Regular element); 1,050 (from Navy); 1,400 conscript (total 3,250)
PATROL AND COASTAL COMBATANTS 64: 16 PCI (small); 48 more
LOGISTICS AND SUPPORT 2: 2 tpt

NON-STATE ARMED GROUPS
see Part II

DEPLOYMENT

AFGHANISTAN
NATO • ISAF 161

BOSNIA-HERZEGOVINA
EU • EUFOR II 1 inf gp; 1,200

CYPRUS (northern)

Army ε36,000

FORCES BY ROLE

1 army corps HQ; some air det; 1 armd bde; 1 indep mech inf bde; 2 inf div; 1 cdo regt; 1 arty bde; 1 avn comd

EQUIPMENT BY TYPE

TK • MBT • M-48 449: 8 M-48A2 training
 M-48A5 441: 441 M-48A5T1/M-48A5T2
APC • APC (T) 627: 361 AAPC (incl variants); 266 M-113 (incl variants)
ARTY 648
 TOWED 102
  105mm • M-101 72: 72 M-101A1
  155mm • M-114 18: 18 M-114A2
  203mm 12: 12 M-115
 SP • 155mm • M-44 90: 90 M-44T
 MRL • 122mm 6: 6 T-122
 MOR 450: 175 81mm
  107mm 148: 148 M-30
  120mm 127: 127 HY-12
AT
 MSL 114: 66 *Milan*; 48 TOW
 RCL • 106mm • M-40 192: 192 M-40A1
  90mm: some M-67
 RL • 66mm: some M-72 *LAW*
AD • GUNS 64+
 20mm • TOWED: some Rh 202
 35mm • TOWED • GDF 16: 16 GDF-003
 40mm • TOWED 48: 48 M-1
AIRCRAFT • UTL 3: 3 U-17
HELICOPTERS • UTL 4
 AS-532 1: 1 AS-532UL *Cougar*
 UH-1 3: 3 UH-1H *Iroquois*
PATROL AND COASTAL COMBATANTS 1: 1 PCI less than 100 tonnes

GEORGIA

UN • UNOMIG 5 obs

ITALY

EU • EUFOR I • EUFOR Air
AIRCRAFT • FGA 4: 4 F-16C *Fighting Falcon*

SERBIA AND MONTENEGRO

NATO • KFOR I 940

SUDAN

UN • UNMIS 3

FOREIGN FORCES

Israel Air Force: up to 1 ftr det (occasional) located at Akinci with F-16 *Fighting Falcon*
United States EUCOM: 1 air wg (ac on detachment only) located at Incirlik with F-16 *Fighting Falcon*; F-15E *Strike Eagle*; EA-6B *Prowler*; E-3B *Sentry*/E-3C *Sentry*; HC-130 *Hercules*; KC-135 *Stratotanker*; C-12 *Huron*; HH-60 *Seahawk*; 1,650 Navy: Support facility located at Izmir; Support facility located at Ankara US STRATCOM: 1 Spacetrack Radar SPACETRACK SYSTEM Strategic located at Incirlik USAF: Air base located at Incirlik

United Kingdom UK

British Pound £		2003	2004	2005
GDP	£	1.09tr	1.15tr	
	US$	1.80tr	2.13tr	
per capita	US$	29,980	35,488	
Growth	%	2.2	3.1	
Inflation	%	1.4	1.3	
Public Debt	%	42.0	44.2	
Def exp	£	26.4bn	26.7bn	
	US$	43.3bn	49.6bn	
Def bdgt	£	25.5bn	26.4bn	27.5bn
	US$	41.9bn	49bn	51.1bn
US$1=£		0.61	0.54	0.54

Population 60,441,457

Ethnic groups: Northern Ireland 1,600,000; Protestant 56%; Roman Catholic 41%

Age	0–14	15–19	20–24	25–29	30–64	65 plus
Male	9%	3%	3%	3%	24%	7%
Female	9%	3%	3%	3%	23%	8%

Capabilities

ACTIVE 205,890 (Army 116,760 Navy 40,630 Air 48,500)

RESERVE 272,550 (Army 201,150 Navy 28,500 Air 42,900)

Includes both trained and untrained Regular Forces.

ORGANISATIONS BY SERVICE

Strategic Forces 1,000

Armed Forces
RADAR • STRATEGIC 1: 1 BALLISTIC MISSILE EARLY WARNING SYSTEM *BMEWS* located at Fylingdales Moor

Royal Navy
SUBMARINES • STRATEGIC • SSBN 4:
 4 *Vanguard S 28* each with up to 16 UGM-133A *Trident D-5* strategic SLBM (Each boat will not deploy with more than 48 warheads, but each missile could carry up to 12 MIRV, some *Trident* D5 configured for sub strategic role)
MSL • STRATEGIC 58: 58 SLBM (Fewer than 200 operational warheads.)

Army 112,010; 3,700 (Gurkhas); 160,800 reservists; 1,050 active reservists (to be 750) (total 277,560)

regt normally bn size
FORCES BY ROLE
1 Land Comd HQ, 3 (regenerative) div HQ (former mil districts) and UK Spt Comd (Germany), 1 tri-service joint hel comd.

Europe (NATO)

Armd inf	9 bn (*Warrior*)
Army	1 (ARRC Corps) tps (1 engr regt (EOD), 2 AD regt, 2 MLRS regt, 3 armd recce regt)
Armd	1 div (1 avn bn, 1 AD regt, 3 armd bde, 3 arty bn, 4 engr bn); 6 regt
Armd recce	4 regt
Recce	1 bde HQ
Mech	1 div (1 AD regt, 3 arty regt, 3 mech bde (*Warrior/Saxon*), 4 engr regt)
Mech inf	6 bn (*Saxon*)
Inf	14 bde HQ (3 contol ops in N. Ireland, remainder mixed regular and TA for trg/ administrative purposes only)
SF	1 (SAS) regt
Gurkha	2 light bn
Lt inf	20 bn
Air aslt	1 bde (incorporated in tri-service joint hel comd)
AB	3 light bn
Arty	1 bde HQ; 1 regt (trg)
SP arty	6 regt
Fd arty	2 regt (1 cdo, 1 air aslt)
MLRS	2 regt
Engr	12 regt
Avn	5 regt (incl 1 trg)
Hel	4 indep flt
NBC	1 (joint) regt (army/RAF)
Log	2 bde
AD	1 bde HQ; 3 regt (1 *Rapier*, 2 HVM)

Home Service Forces • Gibraltar 200 reservists; 150 active reservists (**total** 350)

Northern Ireland 1,290 reservists; 2,100 active reservists (**total** 3,390)

Reserves

Territorial Army 40,350 reservists

Amph recce	4 light bn
Inf	15 bn
SF	2 regt (SAS)
Obs	1 regt
Fd arty	1 regt
MLRS	1 regt
Engr	5 regt
Avn	1 regt
AD	4 regt

EQUIPMENT BY TYPE
TK • MBT 543: 386 CR2 *Challenger 2*; 156 CR1 *Challenger 1*; 1 *Chieftain*
RECCE 475: 137 *Sabre*; 327 *Scimitar*; 11 Tpz-1 *Fuchs*
AIFV 575: 575 MCV-80 *Warrior*
APC 2503
 APC (T) 1,853: 1,121 AFV 432; 597 FV 103 *Spartan*; 135 FV4333 *Stormer*
 APC (W) 650: 649 AT105 *Saxon*; 1 FV603 *Saracen*

L-A-L • UK 1,675: 1,675 AIFV/APC
ARTY 877
 TOWED • 105mm 166: 166 L-118 light gun/L-119
 SP • 155mm 178: 178 AS-90 *Braveheart*
 MRL • 227mm 63: 63 MLRS
 MOR 470: **81mm** 470 (incl 110 SP)
AT • MSL 800+: 740 *Milan*; 60 *Swingfire* (FV 102 *Striker* SP); some TOW
 RL • 94mm: some LAW-80
HELICOPTERS
 ATK • AH-64 17: 17 WAH-MK1 (AH-64D) *Apache Lynx* **AH MK1 atk/*Lynx* AH MK7 atk/*Lynx* AH MK9 aslt** 109*
 SPT 148: 133 SA-341 *Gazelle*; 15 Westland *Scout*
UAV 8: 8 *Phoenix*
AD • SAM 339+
 SP 135: 135 HVM (SP)
 TOWED 57+: 57+ *Rapier* C (some 24 SP)
 MANPAD 147: 147 *Starstreak* (LML)
RADAR • LAND 4+: ε4 MAMBA (ARTHUR); some MSTAR
PATROL AND COASTAL COMBATANTS • MISC BOATS/CRAFT 4: 4 workboats
AMPHIBIOUS • CRAFT 4: 4 LCVP
LOGISTICS AND SUPPORT 6: 6 RCL

Land Command

Assigned to ACE Rapid Reaction Corps
Corps cbt spt tps in the UK

Mech inf	1 div
SF	2 SAS regt
Air aslt	1 bde
AD	3 regt
Territorial	8 (inf) bn; some unit

Royal Navy 26,430; 23,500 reservists (incl Royal Marine reserves); 1,000 active reservists (Full Time Reserve Service) (**total** 50,930)

Typical 'expeditionary air group' comprises 8 *Sea Harrier* FA-2, 8 RAF *Harrier* GR-7, 2 *Sea King* ASW, 4 *Sea King* AEW 2/7. Support and Miscellaneous – most mannned and maintained by Royal Fleet Auxiliary (RFA), a civilian fleet, owned by the UK MoD, which has 2,400 manpower; type cmd under CINCFLEET. Fleet (CinC is also CINCEASTLANT and COMNAVNORTHWEST): almost all regular RN forces are declared to NATO, split between SACLANT and SACEUR.

EQUIPMENT BY TYPE
SUBMARINES 15
 STRATEGIC • SSBN 4:
  4 *Vanguard S 28* opcon Strategic Forces each with up to 16 UGM-133A *Trident D-5* strategic SLBM (Each boat will not deploy with more than 48 warheads, but each missile could carry up to 12 MIRV, some *Trident D5* configured for sub strategic role)
 TACTICAL • SSN 11:
  1 *Swiftsure* (*Spartan*) with 5 single 533mm TT each with *Spearfish* HWT/*Tigerfish* HWT/*Tomahawk* tactical LAM/ UGM- 84 *Harpoon* tactical USGW
  3 *Swiftsure* each with 5 single 533mm TT each with

Spearfish HWT/*Tigerfish* HWT/UGM – 84 *Harpoon* tactical USGW

7 *Trafalgar* each with 5 single 533mm TT each with *Spearfish* HWT/*Tigerfish* HWT/Tomahawk tactical LAM/UGM 84 *Harpoon* tactical USGW

PRINCIPAL SURFACE COMBATANTS 34

AIRCRAFT CARRIERS • CVS 3:

2 *Invincible* (capacity 9 *Merlin* HM MK1 ASW hel; 3 *Sea King* AEW MK2 AEW hel) (mod)

1 in refit (mod, extended refit)

DESTROYERS • DDGH 11:

7 Type 42 1/2 (capacity 1 *Lynx* utl hel) each with 2 x1 MK 15 *Phalanx* CIWS, 1 twin (2 eff.) with 22 *Sea Dart* SAM, 1 114mm gun

4 Type 42 3 (capacity 1 *Lynx* utl hel) each with 2 x1 MK 15 *Phalanx* CIWS, 1 twin (2 eff.) with 22 *Sea Dart* SAM, 1 114mm gun

FRIGATES • FFG 20:

4 *Cornwall* (capacity either 2 *Lynx* utl hel or 1 SH-3 *Sea King* ASW hel) (Type 22 Batch 3) each with 1 *Goalkeeper* CIWS guns, 2 Mk 141 *Harpoon* quad (8 eff.) each with 1 RGM-84C *Harpoon* tactical SSM, 2 sextuple (12 eff.) each with 1 *Sea Wolf* SAM, 1 114mm gun

16 *Norfolk* (capacity either 1 *Lynx* utl hel or 1 *Merlin* HM MK1 ASW hel) (Type 23) each with 2 twin 324mm ASTT (4 eff.) each with *Sting Ray* LWT, 2 Mk 141 *Harpoon* quad (8 eff.) each with 1 RGM-84C *Harpoon* tactical SSM, 1 32 canister *Sea Wolf* VLS with *Sea Wolf* SAM, 1 114mm gun

PATROL AND COASTAL COMBATANTS 24: 2 LPV

PBC 2: 2 WPB

PCI 16: 16 *Archer* (incl 8 trg)

ICE PATROL 1: 1 *Endurance* (RN Manned)

OPV 1: 1 *River*

PCO 2: 2 *Castle*

MINE WARFARE • MINE COUNTERMEASURES 22

MCC 11: 11 *Hunt* (incl 4 mod *Hunt* MCC/PCC)

MHO 11: 4 *Sandown* Batch 1; 7 *Sandown* Batch 2

AMPHIBIOUS

PRINCIPAL AMPHIBIOUS SHIPS 3

LPD 2: 2 *Albion*

LPH 1:

1 *Ocean* (capacity 800 troops; 18 hel; 4 LCVP)

LS • LSLH 4:

4 *Sir Bedivere* (capacity 16 tanks; 340 troops; 1 hel) (RFA manned)

CRAFT 24: 10 LCU; 14 LCVP

LOGISTICS AND SUPPORT 26

AFS 4: 4 *Fort Rosalie* (RFA manned)

AGHS 3: 1 *Gleaner* (RN manned); 1 *Roebuck* (RN manned); 1 *Scott* (RN manned)

AGS 2: 2 *Echo*

AO 4: 2 *Fort Victoria* (RFA manned); 2 *Wave Knight* (RFA manned)

AOT 4: 4 *Leaf* (RFA manned)

AR 1: 1 *Diligence*

ATS 1: 1 *Argus* (RFA manned)

RoRo 4

TANKER LIGHT 3: 3 *Rover*

MSL • STRATEGIC 58: 58 SLBM opcon strategic forces (Fewer than 200 operational warheads.)

FACILITIES

Base	1 located at Faslane, 1 located at Devonport, 1 located at Portsmouth, 1 located at Yeovilton, 1 located at Gibraltar, GI
Naval airbase	1 located at Prestwick, 1 located at Culdrose

Naval Aviation (Fleet Air Arm) 6,200

Flying hours   275 hrs/year on *Harrier*

FORCES BY ROLE

A typical CVS air group consists of 8 *Sea Harrier* FA-2, 7 *Sea King* (ASW), 3 *Sea King* (AEW) (can carry 8 RAF *Harrier* GR-7 instead of 4 *Sea King*)

Ftr	2 sqn with 10 *Sea Harrier* F/A MKII
ASW	1 sqn with *Sea King* HAS MK6; 1 sqn with *Merlin* HM MK1
ASW / atk hel	1 sqn with *Lynx* MK3 (in indept flt); 23 *Lynx* MK8
Recce	1 flt with 8 AH MK1 (SA-341B) *Gazelle* (incl in Marines entry)
AEW	1 sqn with 11 *Sea King* AEW MK2
SAR	1 sqn with *Sea King* HAS MK5 Utility
Spt	some (Fleet) sqn with 1 Beech 55 *Baron* (civil registration); 1 Cessna 441 *Conquest* (civil registration); 19 *Falcon* 20 (civil registration); 5 *Grob* 115 (op under contract); 2 (cdo) sqn with *Sea King* HC MK4; 1 (cdo) flt with 6 *Lynx* AH MK7 (incl in marines entry)
Trg	1 sqn with *Sea King* HC MK4; 1 sqn with 13 *Jetstream* T MK2; 1 sqn with *Lynx* MK3; 2 sqn with *Merlin* HM MK1

EQUIPMENT BY TYPE

AIRCRAFT 15 combat capable

FGA • SEA HARRIER FRS MKI 29: 10 *Sea Harrier* F/A MKII; 19 in store

TPT 21: 1 Beech 55 *Baron* (civil registration); 1 Cessna 441 *Conquest* (civil registration); 19 *Falcon* 20 (civil registration)

TRG 39: 5 *Grob* 115 (op under contract); 5 *Harrier* T MK4/*Harrier* T MK8 *; 2 in store; 14 *Hawk* T MK1 (spt); 13 *Jetstream* T MK2

HELICOPTERS

AEW 13: 11 *Sea King* AEW MK2; 2 *Sea King* AEW MK7

ATK 14: 8 AH MK1 (SA-341B) *Gazelle* (incl in Marines entry); 6 *Lynx* AH MK7 (incl in Marines entry)

ASW 61: 23 *Lynx* MK8; 38 *Merlin* HM MK1

Sea King **HAS MK5 Utility SAR**/*Sea King* **HAS MK6 ASW** 42

MSL • TACTICAL • ASM: some *Sea Skua*

AAM • AIM-120: some AIM-120C *AMRAAM*

AIM-9 *Sidewinder* some

Royal Marines Command 7,000 (incl RN and Army elements)

FORCES BY ROLE

LCA	2 sqn opcon Royal Navy; 1 sqn

Sy	1 gp opcon Royal Navy
Navy	3 det opcon Royal Navy (Naval Parties)
SF	1 sqn opcon Royal Navy
Cdo	1 (declared to SACLANT) bde (1 cdo arty regt (army), 3 cdo regt)
Cdo AD arty	1 bty (army)
Cdo engr	2 sqn (1 army, 1 TA)
Cdo lt hel	1 sqn opcon Royal Navy

EQUIPMENT BY TYPE
APC • APC (T) 24+: 24+ BvS-10 *Viking*
ARTY • MOR: some 81mm
AMPHIBIOUS • CRAFT 28
  ACV 4: 4 *Griffon* 2000 TDX(M)
  LC 24: 24 RRC
HELICOPTERS
  ATK 6: 6 *Lynx* AH MK7
  SPT 12: 9 SA-341 *Gazelle*; 3 in store
AD • SAM • SP: some HVM (SP)
RADAR • LAND: some MAMBA (Arthur)

Air Force 48,140; 40,300 reservists; 360 active reservists (total 88,800)

Flying hours	218 hrs/year on *Harrier* GR7 FGA; 215 hrs/year on *Jaguar* GR3 FGA; 188 hrs/year on *Tornado* GR1 FGA/*Tornado* GR4 strike/FGA; 208 hrs/year on *Tornado* F-3 ftr

FORCES BY ROLE

FGA / bbr	5 sqn with *Tornado* GR4
Ftr	2 sqn with *Typhoon*; 4 sqn with *Tornado* F-3
FGA	3 sqn with *Harrier* GR7/*Harrier* GR7A/*Harrier* T10; *Harrier* GR7A; 1 sqn with *Jaguar* GR3/*Jaguar* GR3A
ELINT	1 sqn with *Nimrod* R1
Recce	1 sqn with 1 *Sentinel* RMK1 (First of 5); 1 sqn with *Jaguar* GR3/*Jaguar* GR3A; 1 sqn with *Canberra* PR-9; 2 sqn with *Tornado* GR4A
MR	2 sqn with *Nimrod* MR2*
AEW	2 sqn with E-3D *Sentry*
SAR	2 sqn with *Sea King* HAR-3A/*Sea King* HAR-3
Tkr / tpt	1 sqn with *Tristar* C2; *Tristar* K1; *Tristar* KC1; 1 sqn with VC-10C1K; VC-10K3/VC-10K4
Tpt	4 sqn with C4 (C-130J) *Hercules*/*Hercules* C Mk1 (C-130K); 1 (comms) sqn with BAe-125; BAe-146; AS-355 *Ecureuil*; 1 sqn with C-17 *Globemaster*
OCU	4 sqn with F-3 *Tornado*; *Tornado* GR4; *Jaguar* T-4A; *Harrier* GR7/T10; *Nimrod* MR2
CAL	1 sqn with *Hawk* T MK1A/*Hawk* T MK1W/*Hawk* T MK1
Trg	some sqn (including postgraduate training on 203(R) sqn) with *Sea King* HAR-3; some sqn with Beech 200 *Super King Air*; *Dominie* T1; Grob 115E *Tutor*; *Hawk* T MK1A/*Hawk* T MK1W/*Hawk* T MK1; *Tucano* T MK1 (Shorts 312); T67 *Firefly*; *Sea King* HAR-3A

Hel	1 sqn with CH-47 *Chinook*; *Sea King* HAR-3; 1 sqn with CH-47 *Chinook*; HT MK3 (SA-341D) *Gazelle*; 1 sqn with *Merlin* HC MK3; 2 sqn with CH-47 *Chinook*; 2 sqn with SA-330 *Puma*
UAV	1 Flt with *Predator*

EQUIPMENT BY TYPE
AIRCRAFT 339 combat capable
  FTR 128: 17 *Typhoon*; 91 *Tornado* F-3; 20 in reserve
  STRIKE/FGA 117: 88 *Tornado* GR4; 29 in reserve
  FGA 74 : 24 *Jaguar* GR3/GR3A; *Harrier* GR7 50
  RECCE 29: 24 *Tornado* GR4A; 4 *Canberra* PR-9; 1 *Sentinel* RMK1 (First of 5)
  MP 21: 1 *Nimrod* MR2 in reserve; 20 *
  EW • ELINT 3: 3 *Nimrod* R1
  AEW • E-3 7: 6 E-3D *Sentry*; 1 in reserve
  TPT 66+
    BAE-125 6: 5 BAe-125 CC-3 (comms); 1 in reserve (comms)
    BAE-146 2: 2 BAe-146 MKII
    Beech 200 *Super King Air* 7 on lease
    C-130 45: 20 C MK3 (C-130H-30) *Hercules* C-130H/*Hercules* C Mk1 (C-130K)
      C4 (C-130J) 25: 25 C4 (C-130J) *Hercules* C-130 tpt/**C5 (C-130J-30)** *Hercules*
    C-17 4: 4 C-17A *Globemaster*
    CC2,CC2A (BN-2 ISLANDER) 2: 2 BN-2A *Islander*/CC2,CC2A (BN-2 *Islander*)
  TPT/TKR 25: 3 *Tristar* C2 (pax); 1 *Tristar* K1 (tkr/pax); 1 in reserve; 4 *Tristar* KC1 (tkr/pax/cgo)
    VC-10 16: 9 VC-10C1K (tkr/cgo); 4 VC-10K3; 3 VC-10K4
  TRG 278: 9 *Dominie* T1; 2 in reserve
    GROB 115 91: 91 Grob 115E *Tutor*
    HAWK T MK1 99: 99 *Hawk* T MK1 trg ac/*Hawk* T MK1A/*Hawk* T MK1W
    T-27 67
    1 **T-4** *Canberra* 2 **T-4** *Jaguar*
    T10 9
HELICOPTERS
  SPT 119
    AS-350B *Ecureuil* 28 **AS-355** *Ecureuil* 3 **CH-47** *Chinook* 34 *Merlin* HC MK3 21 SA-330 *Puma* 33
    SEA KING HAR-3 21
    3 *Griffin* HAR 2
UAV • RECCE • TAC: some RQ-1 *Predator*
MSL • TACTICAL • ASM • AGM-65 • AGM-65G: some AGM-65G2 *Maverick*
  AGM-84 • AGM-84D: some AGM-84D-1 *Harpoon*
  ARM: some ALARM
  SCALP EG *Storm Shadow* some
  AAM: some AIM-120 *AMRAAM*
    AIM-9: some AIM-9L *Sidewinder*; some AIM-9L *Sidewinder*/AIM-9M *Sidewinder*
    ASRAAM some *Sky Flash* some
BOMB • PGM • PAVEWAY • PAVEWAY II: some GBU-10
PAVEWAY III: some GBU-24 **PAVEWAY IV** some

Royal Air Force Regiment
FORCES BY ROLE
Air 3 (tactical Survival To Operate (STO)) HQ; 6 (fd) sqn

Trg 1 (joint) unit (with army) with *Rapier* C
AD 4 (gd based) sqn with 24 *Rapier* C

EQUIPMENT BY TYPE
AD • SAM • TOWED 24+: 24+ *Rapier* C

Strike Command

Responsible for all RAF front-line forces. Day-to-day control delegated to 3 Gps: No. 1 (all fast jet ac); No. 2 (all AT, AAR and Force Protection); No.3 (all ISTAR, Maritime and SAR)

Tri-Service Defence Hel School

HELICOPTERS • SPT: 28 AS-350 *Ecureuil*; 11 Bell 412 *Twin Huey* utl helicopters

Volunteer Reserve Air Forces

(Royal Auxiliary Air Force/RAF Reserve)

Air 1 (air movements) sqn; 2 (intelligence) sqn; 3 (field) sqn; 1 (HQ augmentation) sqn; 1 (C-130 Reserve Aircrew) flt

Medical 1 sqn
AD 1 (gd based) sqn

Reserve Organisations

Volunteer Reserve 2,600 reservists

Gibraltar 200 reservists; 150 active reservists **(total** 350**)**

Northern Ireland 1,290 reservists; 2,100 active reservists **(total** 3,390**)**

NON-STATE ARMED GROUPS

see Part II

DEPLOYMENT

AFGHANISTAN
Air Force
HELICOPTERS • SPT 3: 3 CH-47 *Chinook*
NATO • ISAF
Armed Forces 315
Air Force
  FORCES BY ROLE
  270
  EQUIPMENT BY TYPE
  HELICOPTERS: 3 spt; 2 utl

ASCENSION ISLAND
Air Force 23

BELGIUM
Air Force 183

BELIZE
Army 30

BOSNIA-HERZEGOVINA
EU • EUFOR II 1 (multinational) HQ bde; 1 recce sqn; 1 mech inf bn; 1 hel det; 1,100

BRITISH INDIAN OCEAN TERRITORY
Air Force 720 (*Op Veritas*)
AIRCRAFT 234 combat capable
  MP 3: 3 *Nimrod* MR2
  AEW • E-3 2: 2 E-3D *Sentry*
  TPT/TKR 2: 2 *Tristar* K1

BRUNEI
Army ε1,120
FORCES BY ROLE
1 Gurkha bn; 1 hel flt with 3 hel
EQUIPMENT BY TYPE
Helicopters 3

CANADA
Army 500 1 trg unit
Air Force 57
AIRCRAFT: some *Tornado* F-3 Ftr/*Tornado* GR4 strike/FGA trg
  FGA: some *Jaguar* GR3 training
    GR7: some *Harrier* GR7 FGA/*Harrier* GR7A trg

CROATIA
EU • EUFOR II spt tps; spt/log tps

CYPRUS
Army 2,110
2 inf bn; 1 (spt) engr sqn; 1 hel flt

Royal Navy 25
Air Force 1,140
FORCES BY ROLE
1 SAR sqn with Bell 412 *Twin Huey*; 1 hel sqn with 4 Bell 412 *Twin Huey*
EQUIPMENT BY TYPE
Aircraft some (on det)
HELICOPTERS • UTL 4+: 4+ Bell 412 *Twin Huey*
RADAR 1: 1 land (on det)
UN • UNFICYP 1 inf bn; 1 (spt) engr sqn; 282

DEMOCRATIC REPUBLIC OF CONGO
UN • MONUC 6

FALKLAND ISLANDS
Army 450
Air Force 750
FORCES BY ROLE
1 Ftr flt with F-3 *Tornado*; 1 SAR sqn with *Sea King* HAR-3A/*Sea King* HAR-3; 1 tkr/tpt flt with C-130 *Hercules*; VC-10 K3/4
EQUIPMENT BY TYPE
AIRCRAFT 234 combat capable
  FTR 4+: 4+ F-3 *Tornado*
  TPT 1+: 1+ C-130 *Hercules*
  TPT/TKR 1+: 1 KC-10 *Extender* DC-10; some VC-10
HELICOPTERS • SPT 3+: 1 CH-47 *Chinook*; 2 *Sea King* HAR-3
  SEA KING HAR-3 2+: some *Sea King* HAR-3 spt hel/*Sea King* HAR-3A
AD • SAM 1: 1 *Rapier*

GEORGIA

UN • UNOMIG 7 obs

GERMANY

Army 22,000
1 Army corps; 1 army corps HQ (multinational)

Land Command 1 armd div

GIBRALTAR

Army 235 (incl 175 men of Gibraltar regt)
Home Service Forces 1 army regt
Air Force 105 some (periodic) AEW det
Royal Navy
Base 1 located at Gibraltar, GI

ITALY

EU • EUFOR I • EUFOR Air
  FORCES BY ROLE
    350

  EQUIPMENT BY TYPE
  AIRCRAFT
    STRIKE/FGA 4: 4 GR4 *Tornado*
    AEW • E-3 2: 2 E-3D *Sentry*
    TPT/TKR 1: 1 Tristar K1

IRAQ

Army 9,200 (Peace Support)
1 (composite) Army HQ; 1 armd bde; some spt unit

KENYA

Army 20

KUWAIT

Army

LIBERIA

UN • UNMIL 4

NEPAL

Army 63 (Gurkha trg org)

NETHERLANDS

Air Force 120

NORTHERN IRELAND

Army • **HQ Northern Ireland** 10,700 (incl 31 RN and 1000 RAF) up to 13 (in inf role) major army bn (5 in province,

1 committed reserve, up to 4 roulement inf bn, 3 Home Service inf bn); 3 inf bde HQ; 1 engr regt; 1 avn regt

Home Service Forces 3 inf bn

OMAN

Air Force 132

SERBIA AND MONTENEGRO

NATO • KFOR I
  FORCES BY ROLE
    1 armd inf bn; 1 armd bde; 1 inf bn; 1 engr regt; 1,400

  EQUIPMENT BY TYPE
  HELICOPTERS • **SPT** 2: 2 SA-341 *Gazelle*
UN • UNMIK 1 obs

SIERRA LEONE

Army ε100 (incl trg team, tri-service HQ and spt)
UN • UNAMSIL 7 obs; 5

SUDAN

UN • UNMIS 4

UNITED STATES

Air Force 692

FOREIGN FORCES

United States EUCOM: 1 HQ (AF) HQ (3rd US Air Force) located at Mildenhall; 1 HQ HQ (HQ US Navy Europe (USNAVEUR)) located at London; 1 ftr wg located at Mildenhall (1 Ftr sqn with 24 F-15C *Eagle*/F-15D *Eagle*, 2 Ftr sqn each with 24 F-15E *Strike Eagle*); 1 tkr wg located at Mildenhall with 15 KC-135 *Stratotanker*; 9,800 US STRATCOM: 1 BALLISTIC MISSILE EARLY WARNING SYSTEM *BMEWS* Strategic located at Fylingdales Moor; 1 Spacetrack Radar SPACETRACK SYSTEM Strategic located at Fylingdales Moor USAF: 1 Special Ops gp located at Mildenhall with 5 MC-130H *Combat Talon II*; 5 MC-130P *Combat Shadow*; 1 C-130E *Hercules*; 8 MH-53J *Pave Low III* USNORTHCOM: Comms facility located at Edzell; Comms facility located at Thurso; intel facility located at Thurso; intel facility located at Edzell; 4,500 located at Thurso; 820 located at Thurso

Albania Alb

Albanian Lek		2003	2004	2005
GDP	lek	744bn	820bn	
	US$	6.1bn	8.2bn	
per capita	US$	1,729	2,313	
Growth	%	6.0	5.9	
Inflation	%	2.4	2.9	
Debt	US$	1.4bn		
Def bdgt	lek	9.29bn	10.74bn	11.54bn
	US$	76m	107m	116m
FMA (US)	US$	8.85m	6.19m	3.87m
US$1=lek		122	100	99

Population (2004)   3,544,808

Age	0 – 14	15 – 19	20 – 24	25 – 29	30 – 64	65 plus
Male	14%	5%	4%	4%	20%	4%
Female	13%	5%	4%	4%	19%	4%

Capabilities

ACTIVE 21,500 (Army 16,000 Navy 2,000 Air 3,500)
Paramilitary 500
Terms of service conscription 12 months.

ORGANISATIONS BY SERVICE

Army 16,000+
The Alb armed forces are being re-constituted. Restructuring is now planned to be completed by 2010

FORCES BY ROLE
The army is to consist of:
Rapid Reaction   1 bde
Tk   1 bn
Inf   5 bde
Cdo   1 regt
Arty   1 bn
Engr   1 bn

EQUIPMENT BY TYPE
TK • MBT 373: 373 Type-59
APC • APC (T) 123: 37 M-113; 86 Type-531 (Type-63)
ARTY 1,197
  TOWED 270: 198 122mm; 18 130mm; 54 152mm
  MRL 18: 18 130mm
  MOR 909
    82mm 259
    120mm 550: 550 M-120
    160mm 100: 100 M-43
AT • MSL 30: 30 HJ-73
AD • GUNS 125: 125 M-1939 towed 37mm/S-60 towed 57mm

Navy ε2,000
EQUIPMENT BY TYPE
PATROL AND COASTAL COMBATANTS 20

PB 5: 5 Mk3 (US, for Coast Guard use)
PFC 1: 1 *Shanghai* II† (PRC)
PFI 3: 3 Po-2† (FSU)
PHT 11: 11 *Huchuan*† (PRC) each with 2 single 533mm TT
MINE WARFARE • MINE COUNTERMEASURES 4
  MSC 2: 2 T-301† (FSU)
  MSO 2: 2 T-43 in store
LOGISTICS AND SUPPORT 2: 1 AGOR; 1 AT†

FACILITIES
Base   1 located at Durrës, 1 located at Vlorë

Air Force 3,500 (incl conscripts)
Flying hours   10 to 15 hrs/year

FORCES BY ROLE
FGA   2 regt with 6 MiG-21 *Fishbed*†; 9 MiG-17 *Fresco*†; 11 MiG-19 *Farmer*†
Tpt   1 sqn with 4 An-2 *Colt*
Trg   some sqn with 7 CJ-6
Hel   1 regt with 8 Mi-4 *Hound*; 7 AB-205A; 7 AB-206C

EQUIPMENT BY TYPE
AIRCRAFT 26 combat capable
  FTR 15: 6 MiG-21 *Fishbed*†; 9 MiG-17 *Fresco*†
  FGA 11: 11 MiG-19 *Farmer*†
  TPT 4: 4 An-2 *Colt*
  TRG 13: 7 CJ-6
HELICOPTERS • SPT 22: 8 Mi-4 *Hound*; 7 AB-205A; 7 AB-206C

Paramilitary

Border Police ε500
Ministry of Public Order

Special Police
Internal Security Force
MP 1 ((Tirana)) bn (plus pl sized units in major towns)

DEPLOYMENT

AFGHANISTAN
NATO • ISAF 81

BOSNIA-HERZEGOVINA
EU • EUFOR II 70

GEORGIA
UN • UNOMIG 3 obs

IRAQ
Army 70 (Peace Support)

FOREIGN FORCES

NATO (COMMZW): a small number of spt trps for KFOR

Armenia Arm

Armenian Dram d		2003	2004	2005
GDP	d	1.61tr	1.72tr	
	US$[a]	11.0bn	12.8bn	
per capita	US$[a]	3,664	4,278	
Growth	%	13.9	10.1	
Inflation	%	4.7	7.0	
Debt	US$	1.1bn		
Def exp	US$[a]	700m	810m	
Def bdgt	d	43.2bn	52.5bn	61.0bn
	US$	74.9m	98.5m	135m
FMA (US)	US$	5.65m	3.35m	8.68m
US$1=d		578	533	449

[a] = ppp estimate

Population (2004)   2,991,360

Age	0 – 14	15 – 19	20 – 24	25 – 29	30 – 64	65 plus
Male	12%	5%	5%	4%	17%	4%
Female	11%	5%	5%	4%	22%	6%

Capabilities

ACTIVE 48,160 (Army 45,000 Air 3,160) **Paramilitary 1,000**

Terms of service conscription 24 months. Reserves some mob reported, possibly 210,000 with military service within 15 years.

ORGANISATIONS BY SERVICE

Armed Forces 30,064 conscript

Army 45,000 (incl conscripts)

5 Army Corps HQ

FORCES BY ROLE

Army	1 corps HQ with 2 fortified areas (1 indep MRR, 1 indep rifle regt)
	1 corps HQ with 1 (mixed) arty bn, 4 MRR;
	1 corps HQ with 1 indep rifle regt, 1 recce bn, 2 indep MRR
	1 corps HQ with 1 indep recce bn, 1 indep tk bn, 1 MRL bn, 1 indep arty bn, 1 indep rifle regt, 1 maint bn, 4 MRR
	1 corps HQ with 1 maint bn, 1 indep recce bn, 1 indep tk bn, 2 indep MRR
AD / air	1 (Joint) comd
MRR	1 bde (trg)
SF	1 regt
Arty	1 regt
SP arty	1 regt
AT	1 regt
Engr	1 regt
SAM	1 bde; 2 regt

EQUIPMENT BY TYPE

TK • MBT 110: 102 T-72; 8 T-54

AIFV 104
  BMP 92: 80 BMP-1; 7 BMP-1K; 5 BMP-2
  BRM-1K 12
APC • APC (W) • BTR 140: 11 BTR-60; 21 BTR-70; 4 BTR-80; 104 look-a-like
ARTY 229
  TOWED 121
    122mm 59: 59 D-30
    152mm 62: 26 2A36; 2 D-1; 34 D-20
  SP 38
    122mm 10: 10 2S1 *Carnation*
    152mm 28: 28 2S3
  MRL 51
    122mm 47: 47 BM-21
    273mm 4: 4 WM-80
  MOR • 120mm 19: 19 M-120
AT • MSL 22: 13 9P149; 9 AT-5 *Spandrel*
AD
    SAM: some SA-3 *Goa*
    SP: some SA-4 *Ganef*; some SA-6 *Gainful*
    TOWED: some SA-2 *Guideline*
    GUNS • 23mm: some ZSU-23-4 SP/ZU-23-2 towed
RADAR • LAND 4: 4 SNAR-10 *Big Fred*

Air and Defence Aviation Forces 3,160

FORCES BY ROLE

FGA	1 sqn with 1 MiG-25 *Foxbat*; 15 Su-25 *Frogfoot*
Tpt	some sqn with 1 An-32 *Cline*; 2 Il-76 *Candid*
Trg	some sqn with 4 L-39 *Albatros*; 10 Yak-52
Hel	1 sqn with 12 Mi-24P *Hind-F** (attack); 2 Mi-24K *Hind G2* **(recce)**; 2 Mi-9 *Hip G* (cbt spt); 2 Mi-24R *Hind G1* (cbt spt); 7 Mi-8MT *Hip H* (cbt spt); 9 PZL MI-2 *Hoplite* (utl)

EQUIPMENT BY TYPE

AIRCRAFT 16 combat capable
  FTR 1: 1 MiG-25 *Foxbat*
  FGA 15: 15 Su-25 *Frogfoot*
  TPT 3: 1 An-32 *Cline*; 2 Il-76 *Candid*
  TRG 14: 4 L-39 *Albatros*; 10 Yak-52
HELICOPTERS
  ATK 12: 12 Mi-24P *Hind-F** (atk)
  RECCE 2: 2 Mi-24K *Hind G2*
  COMD 2: 2 Mi-9 *Hip G* (cbt spt)
  SPT 18: 2 Mi-24R *Hind G1*; 7 Mi-8MT *Hip H* (cbt Spt); 9 PZL MI-2 *Hoplite* (utl)
FACILITIES

Air base	2 located in Armenia
Demining centre	1 located in Armenia

Paramilitary 1,000

Ministry of Internal Affairs

FORCES BY ROLE

Paramilitary 4 bn

EQUIPMENT BY TYPE

AIFV 55
  BMD 5: 5 BMD-1
  BMP 45: 44 BMP-1; 1 BMP-1K

BRM-1K 5
APC • APC (W) • BTR 24: 24 BTR-152/BTR-60/BTR-70

Border Troops
Ministry of National Security
AIFV 43
    BMD 5: 5 BMD-1
    BMP 35: 35 BMP-1
    BRM-1K 3
APC • APC (W) • BTR 23: 5 BTR-60; 18 BTR-70

DEPLOYMENT

IRAQ
Armed Forces 46

SERBIA AND MONTENEGRO
Armed Forces 34

FOREIGN FORCES
Russia 3,500: **Army:** 1 mil base (div) with arty 84 mor/
MRL/; 224 ACV; 14 APC (T)/APC (W); 74 MBT **Military Air
Forces:** 1 ftr sqn with 14 MiG-29 *Fulcrum*; 1 SAM bty with
SA-6 *Gainful*; 2 SAM bty with SA-12A *Gladiator*

Austria A

Euro €		2003	2004	2005
GDP	€	223bn	234bn	
	US$	254bn	290bn	
per capita	US$	31,178	35,487	
Growth	%	0.8	2.0	
Inflation	%	1.3	2.0	
Public Debt	%	69.4	66.9	
Def bdgt	€	1.72bn	1.73bn	1.81bn
	US$	1.95bn	2.14bn	2.29bn
US$1=€		0.88	0.81	0.79

Population (2004)   8,174,762

Age	0 – 14	15 – 19	20 – 24	25 – 29	30 – 64	65 plus
Male	8%	3%	3%	3%	25%	6%
Female	8%	3%	3%	3%	25%	10%

Capabilities

ACTIVE 39,900 (Army 33,200 Air 6,700)

CIVILIAN 9,500 (Joint 9,500)
Air Service forms part of the army. Some 66,000 reservists a
year undergo refresher trg, a proportion at a time. *Terms of
service* 7 months recruit trg, 30 days reservist refresher trg
during 8 years (or 8 months trg, no refresher); 60–90 days
additional for officers, NCOs and specialists.

ORGANISATIONS BY SERVICE

Army 16,000; ε17,200 conscript (total 33,200)

FORCES BY ROLE
Army	1 (land forces) comd (1 mech inf bde (1 armd recce bn, 1 tk bn, 1 AT bn, 1 SP arty bn, 2 mech inf bn), 1 inf bde (1 engr bn, 3 inf bn), 1 mech inf bde (1 SP arty bn, 1 mech inf bn, 2 tk bn, 2 armd recce bn), 2 inf bde (*each:* 1 engr bn, 1 arty bn, 3 inf bn))
provincial mil	8 comd (*total:* 15 inf bn); 1 comd (1 inf regt (bn), 5 inf bn)

EQUIPMENT BY TYPE
TK 334
    MBT 114: *Leopard* 2A4
    LT TK 220: 120 SK-105 *Kuerassier*; 100 in store
APC 637
    APC (T) 566
        4K4 454: 454 4K4E *Saurer*/4K4F *Saurer* (incl look-a-likes)
        Ulan 112 (being delivered)
    APC (W) 71: 71 *Pandur*
ARTY 684
    TOWED 105
        105mm 85: 85 IFH (deactivated)
        155mm • M-1 20: 20 M-1A2 (deactivated)
    SP • 155mm • M-109 189: 189 M-109A2/M-109A3/M-109A5Ö
    MRL • 128mm 16: 16 M-51 in store
    MOR 374
        107mm 133
        120mm 241: 241 M-43
AT
    MSL 461: 372 RB-56 *Bill*; 89 RJPz-(HOT) *Jaguar 1*
    RCL 2361
        106mm • M-40 374: 374 M-40A1 in store
        84mm 1987: 1,987 *Carl Gustav*
AD • GUNS 499: 166 20mm; 333 in store

Marine Wing
under School of Military Engineering
PATROL AND COASTAL COMBATANTS 2: 2 PCR less
than 100 tonnes

Air Force 3,300; 3,400 conscript (total 6,700)
Flying hours	180 hrs/year on hel/tpt ac; 130 hrs/year on FGA/ftr

AF Comd
HQ (AF) 1 HQ

FORCES BY ROLE
Air	3 regt
Ftr / FGA	1 wg with 12 F-5E *Tiger II* on lease
Recce / liaison	some sqn with 11 OH-58B *Kiowa**
SAR / utl	some sqn with 24 SA-319 *Alouette III*
Tpt	some sqn with 3 C-130K *Hercules*; 2 SC.7 3M *Skyvan*
Hel	9 S-70A *Black Hawk*; 24 AB-212 (Bell 212)
Liaison	some sqn with 12 PC-6B *Turbo Porter*

| Trg | some sqn with 16 PC-7 *Turbo Trainer*; 28 Saab 105Ö*; 11 AB-206A (Bell 206A) *JetRanger* |
| AD | 3 regt |

EQUIPMENT BY TYPE
AIRCRAFT 40 combat capable
FTR • F-5 12: 12 F-5E *Tiger II* on lease
TPT 17
    C-130 3: 3 C-130K *Hercules*
    PC-6 12: 12 PC-6B *Turbo Porter*
    SC.7 3M *Skyvan* 2
    TRG 44: 16 PC-7 *Turbo Trainer*; 28 Saab 105Ö*
HELICOPTERS
OBS • OH-58 11: 11 OH-58B *Kiowa**
SPT • S-70 9: 9 S-70A *Black Hawk*
UTL 59
    BELL 212 24: 24 AB-212 (Bell 212)
    BELL 206 11: 11 AB-206A (Bell 206A) *JetRanger*
    SA-319 *Alouette III* 24
AD
SAM 76: 76 *Mistral* each with RAC 3D land
GUNS 144
    20mm 72
    35mm 72 each with 30 *Skyguard* land
RADAR • AD RADAR 1: 1 *Goldhaube* (1 3DLRR in delivery) with MRCS-403 *Selenia* land, RAC 3D land
MSL • TACTICAL • AAM • AIM-9 • AIM-9P: some AIM-9P3 *Sidewinder*

Armed Forces 9,500 (civilian)

DEPLOYMENT

AFGHANISTAN
NATO • ISAF 3
UN • UNAMA 2 obs

BOSNIA-HERZEGOVINA
EU • ALTHEA 291

CROATIA
UN • RACVIAC 1 obs

CYPRUS
UN • UNFICYP 4

ETHIOPIA/ERITREA
UN • UNMEE 3

FORMER YUGOSLAVIA/ALBANIA
EU • EUMM 5 obs

GEORGIA
UN • UNOMIG 2 obs

MIDDLE EAST
UN • UNTSO 5 obs

SERBIA AND MONTENEGRO
NATO • KFOR I 532

SUDAN
UN • UNAMIS 5 obs

SYRIA/ISRAEL
UN • UNDOF 1 inf bn; 376

WESTERN SAHARA
UN • MINURSO 2 obs

Azerbaijan Az

Azerbaijani Manat m		2003	2004	2005
GDP	m	35.1tr	36.4tr	
	US$[a]	29.3bn	34.6bn	
per capita	US$[a]	3,741	4,397	
Growth	%	10.8	10.1	
Inflation	%	2.2	8.1	
Debt	US$	1.68bn		
Def exp	US$[a]	950m	1,100m	
Def bdgt	m	680bn	ε899bn	1.48tr
	US$	138m	183m	310m
FMA (US)	US$	5.87m	3.56m	8.68m
US$1=m		4,910	4,915	4,784

[a] = ppp estimate

Population (2004) 7,868,385

Age	0 – 14	15 – 19	20 – 24	25 – 29	30 – 64	65 plus
Male	14%	5%	5%	4%	18%	3%
Female	13%	5%	4%	4%	20%	5%

Capabilities

ACTIVE 66,490 (Army 56,840 Navy 1,750 Air 7,900)
Paramilitary 15,000
Terms of service 17 months, but can be extended for ground forces.

RESERVE 300,000
Reserves some mobilisation, 300,000 with military service within 15 years

ORGANISATIONS BY SERVICE

Army 56,840
5 Army Corps HQ
FORCES BY ROLE
MRR 23 bde
Arty 1 bde
MRL 1 bde
AT 1 regt
EQUIPMENT BY TYPE
TK • MBT 220: 120 T-72; 100 T-55
AIFV 127
    BMD 20: 20 BMD-1
    BMP 86: 44 BMP-1; 41 BMP-2; 1 BMP-3
    BRM-1 21
APC 468
    APC (T) 404: 11 BTR-D; 393 MT-LB
    APC (W) • BTR 64: 25 BTR-60; 28 BTR-70; 11 BTR-80

ARTY 270

TOWED 132

122mm 80: 80 D-30

152mm 52: 22 2A36; 30 D-20

SP • **122mm** 12: 12 2S1 *Carnation*

GUN/MOR • **120mm** 26: 26 2S9 *NONA*

MRL • **122mm** 53: 53 BM-21

MOR • **120mm** 47: 47 PM-38

AT • **MSL** 250: ε250 AT-3 *Sagger*/AT-4 *Spigot*/AT-5 *Spandrel*/AT-7 *Saxhorn*

AD • **SAM** • **SP** 40: ε40 SA-13 *Gopher*/SA-4 *Ganef*/SA-8 *Gecko* (80–240 eff.)

RADAR • **LAND**: some SNAR-1 *Long Trough*/SNAR-2/-6 *Pork Trough* (arty); some *Small Fred*/*Small Yawn*/SNAR-10 *Big Fred* (veh, arty); some GS-13 *Long Eye* (veh)

Navy 1,750

EQUIPMENT BY TYPE

PATROL AND COASTAL COMBATANTS 6

PCC 1: 1 *Turk*

PCI 2: 1 *Svetlyak*; 1 *Zhuk*

PFI 2: 2 *Stenka*

PFM 1: 1 *Osa* II (no SSM)

MINE WARFARE • **MINE COUNTERMEASURES** 5

MSC 3: 3 *Sonya*

MSI 2: 2 *Yevgenya*

AMPHIBIOUS

LS • **LSM** 2: 2 *Polnochny* A (capacity 180 troops; 6 MBT)

CRAFT • **LCU** 2: 2 *Vydra* (capacity either 100 troops or 3 AMX-30 MBT)

LOGISTICS AND SUPPORT • **AG** 2: 1 *Balerian Uryvayev* (research); 1 *Vadim Popov* (research)

FACILITIES

Base 1 located at Baku

Air Force and Air Defence 7,900

FORCES BY ROLE

Ftr   1 sqn with 23 MiG-25 *Foxbat*; 3 MiG-25U *Foxbat*

FGA   1 regt with 4 MiG-21 *Fishbed*; 6 Su-25 *Frogfoot*; 5 Su-24 *Fencer*; 4 Su-17 *Fitter*; 2 Su-25UB *Frogfoot B*

Tpt   some sqn with 1 An-12 *Cub*; 3 Yak-40 *Codling*

Trg   some sqn with 28 L-29 *Delfin*; 12 L-39 *Albatros*; 1 Su-17U *Fitter*

Hel   1 regt with 15 Mi-24 *Hind**; 13 Mi-8 *Hip*; 7 PZL MI-2 *Hoplite*

EQUIPMENT BY TYPE

AIRCRAFT 47 combat capable

FTR 37: 23 MiG-25 *Foxbat* (+9 in store); 4 MiG-21 *Fishbed* (+1 in store)

FGA 15: 6 Su-25 *Frogfoot*; 5 Su-24 *Fencer*; 4 Su-17 *Fitter*

TPT 4: 1 An-12 *Cub*; 3 Yak-40 *Codling*

TRG 50: 28 L-29 *Delfin*; 12 L-39 *Albatros*; 3 MiG-25U* *Foxbat*; 1 Su-17U *Fitter*; 2 Su-25UB *Frogfoot B**

HELICOPTERS

ATK 15: 15 Mi-24 *Hind**

SPT 20: 13 Mi-8 *Hip*; 7 PZL MI-2 *Hoplite*

AD • **SAM** 100: 100 SA-2 *Guideline* towed/SA-3 *Goa*/SA-5 *Gammon* static

Paramilitary ε15,000

Border Guard ε5,000

Ministry of Internal Affairs

AIFV • **BMP** 168: 168 BMP-1/BMP-2

APC • **APC (W)** • **BTR** 19: 19 BTR-60/BTR-70/BTR-80

PATROL AND COASTAL COMBATANTS 2: 2 PCI (US)

Militia 10,000+

Ministry of Internal Affairs

APC • **APC (W)** • **BTR** 7: 7 BTR-60/BTR-70/BTR-80

DEPLOYMENT

AFGHANISTAN

NATO • ISAF 22

IRAQ

Armed Forces 150 (Peace Support)

SERBIA AND MONTENEGRO

NATO • KFOR II 34

NON-STATE ARMED GROUPS

see Part II

Belarus Bel

Belarusian Ruble r		2003	2004	2005
GDP	r	35.9bn	43.2bn	
	US$[a]	59.5bn	67.9bn	
per capita	US$[a]	5,764	6,585	
Growth	%	6.8	11.0	
Inflation	%	28.4	18.1	
Debt	US$	2.69bn		
Def exp	US$[a]	2.4bn	2.7bn	
Def bdgt	r	376bn	404bn	539bn
	US$	183m	186m	251m
US$1=r		2,053	2,163	2,148

[a] = ppp estimate

Population (2004)   10,310,520

Age	0 – 14	15 – 19	20 – 24	25 – 29	30 – 64	65 plus
Male	8%	4%	4%	4%	22%	5%
Female	8%	4%	4%	4%	24%	10%

Capabilities

ACTIVE 72,940 (Army 29,600 Air 18,170 Joint 25,170) **Paramilitary 110,000**

Terms of service 9–12 months

RESERVE 289,500 (Joint 289,500 with mil service within last 5 years)

ORGANISATIONS BY SERVICE

Armed Forces 25,170 (Centrally controlled units and MOD staff)

Army 29,600

FORCES BY ROLE

MoD Comd Tps

SF	1 bde
SSM	2 bde
Sigs	2 bde

Ground Forces

Arty	1 gp (5 bde) (5 arty bde)
Cbt engr	1 bde
Engr bridging	1 bde
NBC	1 regt
Mob	2 bde

North Western Op Comd

Mech	1 indep bde
Arty	2 regt
MRL	1 regt
SAM	1 bde

Western Op Comd

Mech	2 indep bde
Arty	2 regt
MRL	1 regt
Engr	1 regt
SAM	1 bde

EQUIPMENT BY TYPE
TK • MBT 1,586: 92 T-80; 1,465 T-72; 29 T-55
AIFV 1,588
  BMD 154: 154 BMD-1
  BMP 1,273: 109 BMP-1; 1,164 BMP-2
  BRM 161
APC 916
  APC (T) 88: 22 BTR-D; 66 MT-LB
  APC (W) • BTR 828: 188 BTR-60; 446 BTR-70; 194 BTR-80
ARTY 1,499
  TOWED 452
    122mm 202: 202 D-30
    152mm 250: 50 2A36; 136 2A65; 58 D-20; 6 M-1943
  SP 578
    122mm 246: 246 2S1 *Carnation*
    152mm 296: 13 2S19 *Farm*; 163 2S3; 120 2S5
    203mm 36: 36 2S7
  GUN/MOR • 120mm 54: 54 2S9 *NONA*
  MRL 338
    122mm 213: 5 9P138; 208 BM-21
    132mm 1: 1 BM-13
    220mm 84: 84 9P140 *Uragan*
    300mm 40: 40 9A52 *Smerch*
  MOR • 120mm 77: 77 2S12
AT • MSL 480: 480 AT-4 *Spigot*/AT-5 *Spandrel*/AT-6 *Spiral*/AT-7 *Saxhorn* (some SP)
AD • SAM • SP 350: 350 SA-11 *Gadfly*/SA-12A *Gladiator*/SA-12B *Giant (Twin)*/SA-13 *Gopher*/SA-8 *Gecko* (700–2,100 eff.)

RADAR • LAND: some GS-13 *Long Eye*/SNAR-1 *Long Trough*/SNAR-2/-6 *Pork Trough* (arty); some *Small Fred/Small Yawn*/SNAR-10 *Big Fred* (veh, arty)
MSL • TACTICAL • SSM 96: 36 FROG/SS-21 *Scarab* (*Tochka*); 60 *Scud*

Air Force and Air Defence Forces 18,170

Flying hours   15 hrs/year

FORCES BY ROLE

Ftr	some sqn with 23 Su-27P *Flanker-B*/Su-27UB *Flanker C*; 35 MiG-23MLD *Flogger K*/MiG-23UB *Flogger C*; 41 MiG-29S *Fulcrum C*/MiG-29UB *Fulcrum*
FGA / recce	some sqn with 35 Su-24MK *Fencer D*/Su-24MR *Fencer-E*; 76 Su-25 *Frogfoot*/Su-25UB *Frogfoot B*
Tpt	some sqn eith 3An-12 *Cub*; 1 An-24 *Coke*; 6 An-26 *Curl*; 4 IL-76 *Candid*; 1 Tu-134 *Crusty*
Trg	some sqn with L-39 *Albatros*
Atk hel	some sqn with 50 Mi-24 *Hind*; 1 Mi-24K *Hind G2*; 4 Mi-24R *Hind G1*
Spt hel	some (combat) sqn with 8 Mi-24K *Hind G2*; 29 Mi-6 *Hook*; 4 Mi-24R *Hind G1*; 125 Mi-8 *Hip*
Trg	some sqn

EQUIPMENT BY TYPE
AIRCRAFT 210 combat capable
  23 Su-27P *Flanker-B* ftr/Su-27UB *Flanker C* trg; 35 Su-24MK *Fencer D* FGA/Su-24MR *Fencer-E* recce; 35 MiG-23MLD *Flogger K* MiG-23 ftr/MiG-23UB *Flogger C* trg; 41 MiG-29S *Fulcrum C* MiG-29 FTR/MiG-29UB *Fulcrum* MiG-29U trg; 76 Su-25 *Frogfoot* FGA/Su-25UB *Frogfoot B* trg
  TPT 27: 3 An-12 *Cub*; 1 An-24 *Coke*; 6 An-26 *Curl*; 4 Il-76 *Candid*; 12 Il-76 civil (available for mil use); 1 Tu-134 *Crusty*
  TRG: some L-39 *Albatros*
HELICOPTERS
  ATK 50: 50 Mi-24 *Hind*
  RECCE 9: 9 Mi-24K *Hind G2*
  SPT 176: 14 Mi-26 *Halo*; 29 Mi-6 *Hook*; 8 Mi-24R *Hind G1*; 125 Mi-8 *Hip*
MSL • TACTICAL • ASM: some AS-10 *Karen*; some AS-11 *Kilter*; some AS-14 *Kedge*
  AAM: some AA-10 *Alamo*; some AA-11 *Archer*; some AA-7 *Apex*; some AA-8 *Aphid*

Air Defence

Consists of SAM/AAA units, ECM/ECCM units
AD • SAM 175: 175 SA-10 *Grumble* (quad) SP/SA-3 *Goa*/SA-5 *Gammon* static (175-700 eff.)

Paramilitary 110,000

Border Guards 12,000

Ministry of Interior

Militia 87,000

Ministry of Interior

Ministry of Interior Troops 11,000

Bosnia-Herzegovina BiH

Converted Mark		2003	2004	2005
GDP	mark	12.2bn	12.8bn	
	US$	7.1bn	8.1bn	
per capita	US$	1,779	2,021	
Growth	%	4.0	5.2	
Inflation	%	0.6	0.8	
Debt	US$	2,920		
Def bdgt	mark	269m	253m	223m
	US$	155m	159m	143m
FMA (US	US$	3.19m	19.39m	3.38m
US$1=mark		1.73	1.59	1.55

Population (2004) 4,007,608

Age	0 – 14	15 – 19	20 – 24	25 – 29	30 – 64	65 plus
Male	10%	4%	4%	4%	25%	5%
Female	9%	4%	4%	4%	24%	6%

Capabilities

ACTIVE 24,672 (Army 16,400 Joint 8,200 Other 72)

In accordance with the Dayton Peace Accords, BiH is composed of two entities: The (Muslim–Croat) 'Federation of Bosnia and Herzegovina' and The (Serbian) 'Republika Srpska'. The predominant view until 2003 was that the constitution would have precluded state command and control over armed forces, and attributed most competencies regarding defence and military matters to the two entities. There have thus been no armed forces (except Border Guards and Brcko District police) at the state level. The two entities have kept the armed forces they had established throughout the armed conflict until the 1995 Dayton Peace Accord. The armed forces of the entities are subject to an arms-limitation regime established under the Dayton Peace Accord. An agreement signed by BiH, its two entities, Cr and FRY on 14 June 1996, established ceilings for the arms of the parties. In May 2003 the High Representative established a Defence Reform Commission which recommended in September 2003 the establishing of state-level command and control, including a State Ministry of Defence and a State Joint Staff, and a further reduction of the Entities' armed forces. In December 2003, the Parliamentary Assembly of BiH adopted a law on defence, which established the recommended state structures. The chain of command now goes from the State Presidency via the State Ministry of Defence and the Joint Staff and a joint Operational Command to the respective forces within the Entities. A Presidential Decree in March 2004 established new ceilings for the armed forces of BiH. There will be a total of 12,000 professional soldiers (8,000 for the Federation and 4,000 for the RS), 12,600 conscripts (8,400 for the Federation and 4,200 for the RS), and 60,000 reserves (40,000 for the Federation and 20,000 for the RS).

ORGANISATIONS BY SERVICE

State Joint Staff 44

State Joint Operational Command 28

Forces of the Federation of Bosnia Herzegovina • Army (VF) 8,000 (VF-B 5,576, VF-H 2,424); 8,400 conscript (VF-B 6,416, VF-H 1,984); 40,000 reservists (VF-B 28,750, VF-H 11,250) **(total 56,400)**

FORCES BY ROLE

Army 4 div

Air 1 comd

Mech inf 2 bde

EQUIPMENT BY TYPE

(Mostly held under EUFOR control in weapon storage sites)

TK 189

  MBT 188: 6 M-84; 50 AMX-30; 45 M-60A3; 69 T-55; 13 T-54; 5 T-34

  LT TK 1: 1 PT-76

AIFV 35: 25 AMX-10P; 10 M-80

APC 129

  APC (T) • M-113 80: 80 M-113A2

  APC (W) 49

    BTR 5: 2 BTR-50; 3 BTR-70

    OT 37: 37 OT-60

    BOV 3, 4 look-a-like

ARTY 946+

  TOWED 384+

    105mm 89: 36 L-118 Light Gun; 4 M-18/61 27 M-2A1; 22 M-56

    122mm 118: 118 D-30

    130mm 36: 23 M-46; 13 M-82

    152mm 18+: 18 D-20; some M-84

    155mm 123: 119 M-114A2; 4 M-1

  SP • 122mm 3: 3 2S1 *Carnation*

  MRL 106+

    107mm 28: 28 Type-63

    122mm 41: 36 APR-40; 5 BM-21

    128mm 37+: some M-63 *Plamen*; 37 M-91

  MOR 453+

    82mm 62: 62 M-69

    120mm 391+: some M-38; 13 M-74; 350 M-75; 28 UBM 52

AT

  MSL 260: 157 AT-3 *Sagger*/Milan; 52 AT-4 *Spigot*; 51 HJ-8

  GUNS • 100mm 30: 30 MT-12/T-12

AIRCRAFT

  TRG 3: 3 UTVA-75

HELICOPTERS

  SPT • MI-8 3: 3 MI-17 (Mi-8MT) *Hip H*/Mi-8 *Hip* spt

  UTL • UH-1 15: 15 UH-1H *Iroquois*

AD

  SAM: some SA-14 *Gremlin* MANPAD/SA-16 *Gimlet* MANPAD/SA-7 *Grail* MANPAD/SA-9 *Gaskin* SP

  GUNS 19+: some BOV-3 SPAAG SP 20mm/M-53 towed 30mm/M-55 towed 20mm/S-60 towed 57mm

    20mm • SP: some BOV-3 SPAAG

    23mm • TOWED 19: 19 ZU-23

Republika Srpska Armed Forces • Army 4,000; 4,200 conscript; 20,000 reservists (total 28,200)

FORCES BY ROLE

Air   1 comd
Mech inf 1 bde
Inf   1 bde (plus spt); 2 div HQ (res)

EQUIPMENT BY TYPE (mostly held under EUFOR control in weapon storage sites)

TK • **MBT** 137: 65 M-84; 72 T-55
AIFV 74: 74 M-80
APC 74
  APC (T) 15: 15 M-60
  APC (W) 59
    BOV 15: 15 BOV-M
    BTR • **BTR-50** 44: 9 BTR-50PK; 35 look-a-like
ARTY 500
  TOWED 348
    105mm 74: 74 M-56
    122mm 150: 150 D-30
    130mm 38: 38 M-46
    152mm 12: 9 D-20; 3 M-84
    155mm 74: 74 M-1
  SP • **122mm** 24: 24 2S1 *Carnation*
  MRL 58
    122mm 1: 1 BM-21
    128mm 56: 36 M-63 *Plamen*; 20 M-77 *Organj*
    262mm 1: 1 M-87 *Orkan*
  MOR • **120mm** 70: 70 M-52/M-74/M-75
AT
  MSL 650: 650 AT-3 *Sagger*
  GUNS • **100mm** 128: 128 T-12
AIRCRAFT • **TRG** 3: 3 UTVA-75
AD
  SAM: some SA-2 *Guideline* Towed/SA-6 *Gainful* SP/SA-7B *Grail* MANPAD/SA-9 *Gaskin* SP
  GUNS 975: 975 20mm/90mm/M-53/59SP SP 30mm/ZSU-23-4 SP 23mm/ZSU-57-2 SP 57mm
MSL • **TACTICAL** • **SSM** 8: 8 FROG-7

Air Wing

AIRCRAFT 14 combat capable
  FGA 13: 6 J-21 (J-1) *Jastreb* (attack); 7 J-22 *Orao 1*
  RECCE 2: 2 IJ-21 (RJ-1) *Jastreb* (recce)
  TRG 6: 1 G-4 *Super Galeb**; 3 NJ-21 (TJ-1) *Jastreb* (attack/trg); 2 UTVA-75
HELICOPTERS
  ASLT 22: 15 HO-42 *Partizan*/HO-45 *Partizan*; 7 HN-45M *Partizan*
  SPT 11: 11 Mi-8 *Hip*

DEPLOYMENT

DEMOCRATIC REPUBLIC OF CONGO
UN • **MONUC** 5 obs

ETHIOPIA/ERITREA
UN • **UNMEE** 9 obs

FOREIGN FORCES

Albania 70 opcon EUFOR
Austria 291 opcon ALTHEA
Bulgaria 1 pl opcon EUFOR
Canada ε800 opcon EUFOR
Czech Republic 84 opcon ALTHEA; 1 obs opcon EUFOR
Denmark 4 opcon EUFOR
Estonia 3 (EUFOR) opcon EUFOR; 1 (NATO HQ) opcon EUFOR
Finland 200 opcon ALTHEA
France 500 opcon EUFOR Air Force: 1 TBM-700 tpt ac opcon EUFOR
Germany 1,000 opcon EUFOR; 28 SPz-2 *Luchs* recce opcon EUFOR; TPz-1 *Fuchs* APC (W) opcon EUFOR; 3 CH-53 *Sea Stallion* spt hel opcon EUFOR; 4 UH-1D *Iroquois* utl hel opcon EUFOR
Greece 250 opcon EUFOR; 1 C-130 *Hercules* tpt ac opcon EUFOR air
Hungary 150 engr opcon EUFOR; 4 obs opcon EUFOR
Ireland 50 opcon EUFOR
Italy 979 opcon EUFOR
Latvia 12 opcon KFOR I; 3 opcon ALTHEA
Lithuania 97 opcon EUFOR
Luxembourg 23 opcon EUFOR; 5 E-3A *Sentry* AEW ac opcon EUFOR Air
Morocco 1 mot inf bn opcon EUFOR; ε800 opcon EUFOR
Netherlands ε1,000 opcon EUFOR
New Zealand 12 opcon EUFOR
Norway 125 opcon EUFOR
Poland 2 inf coy opcon EUFOR; 1 obs opcon UNMIBH; 287 opcon EUFOR
Portugal 1 inf bn under strength opcon EUFOR; 330 opcon EUFOR
Romania 106 opcon EUFOR
Slovakia 29 opcon EUFOR
Slovenia 158 opcon EUFOR
Spain 1 cav sqn opcon EUFOR; 2 inf coy opcon EUFOR; 935 opcon EUFOR
Sweden 7 opcon EUFOR
Turkey 1 inf gp opcon EUFOR; 1,200 opcon EUFOR
United Kingdom 1 (multinational) HQ bde opcon EUFOR; 1 recce sqn opcon EUFOR; 1 mech inf bn opcon EUFOR; 1 hel det opcon EUFOR; 1,100 opcon EUFOR
United States 839 opcon EUFOR

Croatia Cr

Croatian Kuna k		2003	2004	2005
GDP	k	189bn	200bn	
	US$	28.3bn	33.6bn	
per capita	US$	6,291	7,471	
Growth	%	4.3	3.8	
Inflation	%	1.8	2.1	
Debt	US$	23.4bn		
Def bdgt	k	3.98bn	3.58bn	3.65bn
	US$	595m	598m	626m
US$1=k		6.70	5.98	5.83

Population (2004) 4,496,869

Age	0 – 14	15 – 19	20 – 24	25 – 29	30 – 64	65 plus
Male	9%	3%	4%	3%	23%	6%
Female	8%	3%	3%	3%	24%	10%

Capabilities

ACTIVE 20,800 (Army 14,050 Navy 2,500 Air 2,300 Joint 1,950) Paramilitary 10,000

The armed forces of Croatia are subject to arms limitations established under the Dayton Peace Accord. An agreement signed by BiH, its two entities, Cr and FRY on 14 June 1996, established ceilings for holdings of the armed forces of the parties. *Terms of service* 6 months. The active total is reported to be up to 31,500.

RESERVE 108,200 (Army 95,000 Navy 8,300 Air 4,900)

ORGANISATIONS BY SERVICE

Armed Forces 1,950 (General Staff); ε7,000 conscript (total 8,950)

Army ε9,200; ε4,850 conscript; 95,000 reservists (total 109,050)

FORCES BY ROLE
Army 4 corps
Armd 1 bde
SF 1 bn
MRL 1 bde
AT 1 bde
ADA 3 bde
Engr 3 bde
Gd 3 bde (org varies)
MP 1 bn
Reserves 22 inf bde, 4 arty, 2 AT bde

EQUIPMENT BY TYPE
TK • MBT 291: 66 M-84; 3 T-72M; 222 T-55
RECCE • BRDM 1: 1 BRDM-2
AIFV 104: 104 M-80
APC 53
  APC (T) • M-60 8: 8 M-60PB

APC (W) 45
  BOV 29: 9 BOV-VP; 20 look-a-like
  BTR 16: 16 BTR-50
ARTY 1,452
  TOWED 411
    105mm 146
      M-2 90: 90 M-2A1
      M-56 56: 48; 8 M-56H1
    122mm 85: 42 D-30; 43 *M-1938*
    130mm • M-46 79: 79 M-46H1
    152mm 42: 21 D-20; 18 M-84; 3 M-84H1
    155mm 37: 19 M-1; 18 M-1H1
    203mm 22: 22 M-2
  SP • 122mm 8: 8 2S1 *Carnation*
  MRL 224
    122mm 40: 40 BM-21
    128mm 182: 2 M-63 *Plamen*; 180 M-91
    262mm 2: 2 M-87 *Orkan*
  MOR 809
    82mm 486
    120mm 323: 317 M-75; 6 UBM 52
AT
  MSL: some AT-3 *Sagger*/AT-4 *Spigot*/AT-7 *Saxhorn*; some *Milan* (reported)
  RL
    73mm: some RPG-22 *Net*/RPG-7 *Knout*
    90mm: some M-79
  GUNS • 100mm 132: 132 T-12
AD • GUNS 448+
  20mm
    SP 315: 315 BOV-1SP
    TOWED: some M-55
  30mm 17+
    SP: some BOV-30 SP
    TOWED 17: 17 M-53/M-59
  40mm 116

Navy 1,850; 650 conscript; 8,300 reservists (total 10,800)

FORCES BY ROLE
Navy 1 HQ located at Split

EQUIPMENT BY TYPE
SUBMARINES • TACTICAL • SSI 1:
  1 *Velebit* (Mod *Una*, for SF ops) with 4 SDV
PRINCIPAL SURFACE COMBATANTS • CORVETTES • FSG 2:
  2 *Kralj Petar* each with 2–4 twin (8 eff.) each with 1 RBS-15B tactical SSM
PATROL AND COASTAL COMBATANTS 5
  PCC 4: 4 *Mirna*
  PFM 1:
    1 *Rade Koncar* with 2 twin (4 eff.) each with 1 RBS-15B tactical SSM
AMPHIBIOUS • CRAFT 5: 5 LCU
LOGISTICS AND SUPPORT 17
  AGS 1: 1 Moma (FSU, trg)
  Craft 16
FACILITIES

Base 1 located at Split, 1 located at Pula, 1 located at Sibenik, 1 located at Dubrovnik, 1 located at Ploce

Minor Base 1 located at Lastovo, 1 located at Vis

Coastal Defence

FORCES BY ROLE

SSM 3 bty with RBS-15K

Arty 21+ bty

EQUIPMENT BY TYPE

MSL • TACTICAL • SSM • **RBS-15**: some RBS-15K

Marines

Inf 2 indep coy

Air Force and Air Defence 2,300 incl 630 conscript

Flying hours 50 hrs/year

FORCES BY ROLE

Ftr / FGA 2 sqn with 20 MiG-21bis *Fishbed L & N*; 7 MiG-21UM *Mongol B*

EQUIPMENT BY TYPE

AIRCRAFT 27 combat capable

FTR • **MiG-21** 20: 20 MiG-21bis *Fishbed L & N*

TPT 11: 6 An-2 *Colt*; 4 An-32 *Cline*

PA-31 1: 1 PA-31P *Pressurized Navajo*

UTL 2: 2 PC-12

SPT 10

AT-802 4: 4 AT-802F *Air Tractor*

Canadair CL-215 2 (fire fighting)

Canadair CL-415 4

TRG 35

MiG-21U 7: 7 MiG-21UM *Mongol B**

PC-9 18

UTVA-75 10

HELICOPTERS

ATK • **MI-24** 9: 9 Mi-24V *Hind E*

SPT 19: 6 Mi-8 *Hip*; 13 Mi-8MTV *Hip H*

UTL • **BELL 206** 8: 8 Bell 206B *JetRanger II*

AD • SAM • SP: some SA-10 *Grumble (quad)*; some SA-9 *Gaskin*

MANPAD: some SA-14 *Gremlin*/SA-16 *Gimlet*; some SA-7 *Grail*

MSL • TACTICAL • AAM: some AA-2 *Atoll*; some AA-8 *Aphid*

Paramilitary 10,000

Police 10,000 armed

DEPLOYMENT

AFGHANISTAN

NATO • ISAF 22

CÔTE D'IVOIRE

UN • ONUCI 3 obs

EAST TIMOR

UN • UNOTIL 1

ETHIOPIA/ERITREA

UN • UNMEE 7 obs

GEORGIA

UN • UNMIG 1

HAITI

UN • MINUSTAH 1

INDIA/PAKISTAN

UN • UNMOGIP 3 obs

LIBERIA

UN • UNMIL 3

SERBIA AND MONTENEGRO

UN • UNAMSIL 2 obs

SIERRA LEONE

UN • UNAMSIL 6 obs

SUDAN

UN • UNMIS 3

WESTERN SAHARA

UN • MINURSO 2 obs

FOREIGN FORCES

Austria 1 obs opcon RACVIAC

United Kingdom spt tps opcon EUFOR II; spt/log tps opcon EUFOR II

Cyprus Cy

Cypriot Pound C£		2003	2004	2005
GDP	C£	6.78bn	7.19bn	
	US$	13.3bn	15.3bn	
per capita	US$	17,235	19,718	
Growth	%	1.9	3.7	
Inflation	%	4.1	2.3	
Debt	US$	5.9bn		
Def bdgt	C£	126m	129m	128m
	US$	247m	274m	280m
US$1=C£		0.51	0.47	0.46

Population (2004) 775,927

Age	0 – 14	15 – 19	20 – 24	25 – 29	30 – 64	65 plus
Male	11%	4%	4%	3%	22%	5%
Female	10%	4%	4%	3%	22%	6%

Capabilities

ACTIVE 10,000 (National Guard 10,000)

Paramilitary 750

Terms of service conscription, 25 months, then reserve to age 50 (officers 65)

RESERVE 60,000 (National Guard 60,000)

Europe (Non-NATO)

ORGANISATIONS BY SERVICE

National Guard 1,300; 8,700 conscript; 60,000 reservists (all branches) (total 70,000)

FORCES BY ROLE

Home Guard 1 comd HQ

Army 1 corps HQ

Navy 1 comd HQ

Air 1 comd HQ

Armd 1 bde (3 armd bn)

SF 1 comd (regt) (3 SF bn)

Lt inf 2 div HQ; 2 bde HQ

Arty 1 comd (regt)

Spt 1 (svc) bde

EQUIPMENT BY TYPE

TK • MBT 154

T-80 41: 41 T-80U

AMX-30 113: 61; 52 AMX-30 B2

RECCE 139: 15 EE-3 *Jararaca*; 124 EE-9 *Cascavel*

AIFV • BMP 43: 43 BMP-3

APC 310

APC (T) 184: 16 AMX-VCI; 168 *Leonidas*

APC (W) 126: 126 VAB (incl variants)

ARTY 562+

TOWED 140

88mm 36: 36 25-pdr in store

100mm 20: 20 M-1944

105mm 72: 72 M-56

155mm 12: 12 TR-F-1

SP • 155mm 24: 12 Mk F3; 12 *Zuzana*

MRL 22

122mm 4: 4 BM-21

128mm 18: 18 M-63 *Plamen*

MOR 376+

81mm 240+: 70+ M-1/M-29 in store; 170 E-44

107mm 20: 20 M-2/M-30

120mm 116: 116 RT61

AT

MSL 67: 22 HOT; 45 *Milan*

RCL 184

106mm • M-40 144: 144 M-40A1

90mm 40: 40 EM-67

RL 1,850+

112mm 1,000: 1,000 APILAS

66mm: some M-72 *LAW*

73mm 850: 850 RPG-7 *Knout*

AD

SAM 90

SP 6: 6 SA-15 *Gauntlet*

STATIC 24: 24 *Aspide*

MANPAD 60: 60 *Mistral* (some SP)

GUNS 80

20mm • TOWED 36: 36 M-55

35mm • TOWED • GDF 24: 24 GDF-003 (with *Skyguard*)

40mm • TOWED 20: 20 M-1 in store

Maritime Wing

FORCES BY ROLE

SSM 1 (coastal defence) bty with 3 MM-40 *Exocet*

EQUIPMENT BY TYPE

PATROL AND COASTAL COMBATANTS 15

MISC BOATS/CRAFT 11: 11 boats

PCC 4: 1 *Kyrenia* (Gr *Dilos*); 2 *Rodman* 55; 1 *Salamis*

MSL • TACTICAL • SSM 3: 3 MM-40 *Exocet*

Air Wing

AIRCRAFT

TPT 1: 1 BN-2 *Islander*

TRG 2: 2 PC-9

HELICOPTERS

ATK 16: 12 Mi-35P *Hind;* 4 SA-342 *Gazelle* (with HOT)

SPT 2: 2 PZL MI-2 *Hoplite* in store

UTL 4

BELL 206 2: 2 Bell 206C *JetRanger III*

UH-1 2: 2 UH-1H *Iroquois*

Paramilitary 750+

Armed Police 500+

FORCES BY ROLE

Mech 1 (rapid-reaction) unit

EQUIPMENT BY TYPE

APC • APC (W) • VAB 2: 2 VAB VTT

AIRCRAFT • TPT 1: 1 BN-2A *Defender*

HELICOPTERS • UTL 2: 2 Bell 412 *Twin Huey*

Maritime Police 250

PATROL AND COASTAL COMBATANTS 8

PCC 5: 5 SAB-12

PFI 3: 2 *Evagoras*; 1 *Shaltag*

FOREIGN FORCES

Argentina 1 inf bn; 298

Austria 4

Canada 1

Finland 1

Greece Army: 1 armd bn; 1 (incl 950 (ELDYK) army) mech bde; 2 mech inf bn; 1 arty bn; 61 M-48A5 MOLF MBT; 80 *Leonidas* APC (T); 12 M-114 155mm towed; 6 M-107 175mm SP; 6 M-110A2 203mm SP; 950 (ELDYK army); ε200 (officers/NCO seconded to Greek-Cypriot National Guard)

Hungary 84

Slovakia 205

United Kingdom Air Force: 1 SAR sqn with Bell 412 *Twin Huey;* 1 hel sqn with 4 Bell 412 *Twin Huey;* 282 UNFICYP; Army: 2 inf bn; 1 (spt) engr sqn; 1 hel flt Air Force: ac (on det); 1 land (on det); 1,140 Army: 2,110 Royal Navy: 25

Uruguay 1

AREAS WHERE THE GOVERNMENT DOES NOT EXERCISE EFFECTIVE CONTROL

Data presented here represent the de facto situation on the island. This does not imply international recognition as a sovereign state.

Capabilities

ACTIVE 5,000 (Army 5,000) **Paramilitary 150**
Terms of service conscription, 24 months, then reserve to age 50.

RESERVE 26,000 (first line 11,000 second line 10,000 third line 5,000)

ORGANISATIONS BY SERVICE

Army ε5,000

FORCES BY ROLE
Inf 7 bn

EQUIPMENT BY TYPE
ARTY • MOR 73: **120mm** 73
AT
    MSL 6: 6 *Milan*
    RCL 36: **106mm** 36

Paramilitary

Armed Police ε150
SF 1 (Police) unit

Coast Guard
PATROL AND COASTAL COMBATANTS 6
    PCC 5: 2 SG45/SG46; 1 *Rauf Denktash*; 2 US Mk 5
    PCI 1

FOREIGN FORCES

TURKEY
ARMY ε36,000
    1 army corps HQ, some air det, 1 armd bde, 1 indep mech inf bde, 2 inf div, 1 cdo regt, 1 arty bde, 1 avn comd
EQUIPMENT BY TYPE
    MBT 8: 8 M-48A2 MBT
    TRG 441: 441 M-48A5T1/M-48A5T2
    APC 627: 361 AAPC (T) (incl variants); 266 M-113 (T) (incl variants)
    TOWED 102
        105mm 72: 72 M-101A1
        155mm 18: 18 M-114A2
        203mm 12: 12M-115
    SP ARTY • **155mm** 90: 90 M-44T
    MRL • **122mm** 6: 6 T-122
    MOR 450
        81mm 175
        107mm 148: 148 M-30
        120mm 127: 127 HY-12
    MSL 114: 66 *Milan*; 48 TOW
    RCL
        106mm 192: 192 M-40A1
        90mm M-67
    RL: **66mm** M-72 *LAW*
    PATROL CRAFT: 1 PCI less than 100 tonnes
    AC 3: 3 U-17 Utl
    HEL 4: 1 AS-532UL *Cougar* Utl; 3 UH-1H *Iroquois* Utl
    TOWED
        20mm Rh 202
        35mm 16: 16 GDF-003
        40mm 48: 48 M-1

Finland SF

Euro €		2003	2004	2005
GDP	€	143bn	149bn	
	US$	162bn	184bn	
per capita	US$	31,223	35,286	
Growth	%	2.4	3.7	
Inflation	%	1.3	0.1	
Public Debt	%	52.1	53.3	
Def exp	€	2.02bn	2.01bn	
	US$	2.3bn	2.5bn	
Def bdgt	€	2.02bn	2.07bn	2.14bn
	US$	2.3bn	2.5bn	2.7bn
US$1=€		0.88	0.81	0.79

Population (2004)   5,214,512

Age	0 – 14	15 – 19	20 – 24	25 – 29	30 – 64	65 plus
Male	9%	3%	3%	3%	24%	6%
Female	9%	3%	3%	3%	24%	10%

Capabilities

ACTIVE 28,300 (Army 20,500 Navy 5,000 Air 2,800)
Paramilitary 3,100
Terms of Service 6-9-12 months (12 months for officers NCOs and soldiers with special duties. 35,000 reservists a year do refresher training: total obligation 40 days (75 for NCOs 100 for officers) between conscript service and age 50 (NCOs and officers to age 60). Reserve total reducing to 340,000.

RESERVE 237,000 (Army 202,000 Air 35,000)
Paramilitary 18,900

ORGANISATIONS BY SERVICE

Armed Forces

Army 4,900; 15,600 conscript (total 20,500)

FORCES BY ROLE
all brigades reserve, re-org underway to be complete by 2008
Mil 1 comd (2 provincial mil bde); 1 comd (4 provincial mil bde); 1 comd (6 provincial mil bde)

EQUIPMENT BY TYPE
TK • MBT 226: 226 *Leopard* 2A4/T-72
AIFV 263: 263 BMP-1PS/BMP-2/CV9030 (incl l-a-l)
APC 614: 614 BTR-50 APC (W)/BTR-60 APC (W)/MT-LB APC (T)/XA-180 *Sisu* XA series APC (W)/XA-185 *Sisu* XA series APC (W)/XA-200 *Sisu* XA series APC (W)
ARTY 1,446
    TOWED 714: 714 H 55 (D-20) **152mm**/H 63 (D-30) **122mm**/H 88-37 (ML-20) *M-1937* **152mm**/H 88-38 **152mm**/H 88-40 **152mm**/K 54 **130mm**/K 83 **155mm**/K 89 **152mm**/K 98 **155mm**
    SP 90: 90 PsH 74 (2S1) *Carnation* **122mm**/*Telak* 91 (2S5) **152mm**
    MOR • **120mm** 642: 642 KRH 92
HELICOPTERS

SPT 7: 7 Mi-8 *Hip*
UTL • HUGHES 500 2: 2 Hughes 500D
AD • SAM • SP • some ITO 90 (*Crotale* NG); some ITO 96 (SA-11) *Gadfly*
   MANPAD: some ITO 86 (SA-16) *Gimlet*; some ITO 86M (SA-18) *Grouse (Igla)*
   GUNS: some 23mm; some 30mm; some 35mm; 57mm

Reserve Organisations

Reserves 100,000 reservists on mobilisation; 75,000 reservists on mobilisation (local forces); 27,000 reservists on mobilisation (territorial) (total 202,000)

Army   230+ bn (and coys)
Armd   2 bde
Jaeger   9 bde
Inf   11 bde
Engr   16 bn
AD   3 regt

Navy 2,300; 2,700 conscript (total 5,000)

EQUIPMENT BY TYPE
PATROL AND COASTAL COMBATANTS • PFM 11:
   3 *Hamina* each with 2 twin (4 eff.) with 4 15SF (RBS-15M) RBS-15 SSM, 1 *Sadral* sextuple with *Mistral* SAM
   4 *Helsinki* each with 4 twin (8 eff.) with 8 15SF (RBS-15M) RBS-15 SSM, 2 *Sadral* sextuple each with *Mistral* SAM
   4 *Rauma* each with 2 single with 2 15SF (RBS-15M) RBS-15 SSM, 2 twin (4 eff.) with 4 15SF (RBS-15M) RBS-15 SSM, 1 *Sadral* sextuple with *Mistral* SAM
MINE WARFARE 19
   MINE COUNTERMEASURES • MSI 13: 7 *Kiiski* less than 100 tonnes; 6 *Kuha* less than 100 tonnes
   MINELAYERS • ML 6:
      2 *Hameenmaa* each with 1 *Sadral* sextuple with *Mistral* SAM, 2 RBU 1200 (10 eff.), up to 150–200 mine
      3 *Pansio* each with 50 mine
      1 *Pohjanmaa* with up to 100-150 mine
AMPHIBIOUS • CRAFT • LCU 6: 3 *Kala*; 3 *Kampela*
LOGISTICS AND SUPPORT 35: 7 AGB *Icebreaker* (Board of Navigation control)
   AGF (COMD) 1: 1 *Kustaanmiekka*
   AGOR 1: 1 *Aranda* (Ministry of Trade Control)
   AGS 9: 9 *Prisma*
   AKSL 15: 6 *Hauki*; 4 *Hila*; 5 *Valas*
   TPT 2: 2 *Lohi*

FACILITIES
Base   1 located at Upinniemi (Helsinki)
Naval airbase 1 located at Turku

Coastal Defence

ARTY • COASTAL 226+
   100mm: some 56 tank turrets
   130mm: 226+: 31 K-53tk (static); 195 K-54 RT; some K90 60
MSL • TACTICAL • SSM • RBS-15 4: 4 RBS-15K

Air Force 1,800; 1,000 conscript (total 2,800)

Wartime strength – 35,000
3 Air Comds: Satakunta (West), Karelia (East), Lapland (North). Each Air Comd assigned to one of the 3 AD areas into which SF is divided. 3 ftr wings, one in each AD area.
Flying hours   120 hrs/year

FORCES BY ROLE

FGA	3 wg with 56 F/A-18C *Hornet*; 7 F/A-18D *Hornet*
Advanced AD / Attack trg /recce	some sqn with 49 *Hawk* MK50/*Hawk* MK51A (1 F-27 *Maritime Enforcer* (ESM/ Elint))
Tpt	1 sqn with 2 F-27 *Friendship*; 3 *Learjet* 35A
Liaison	some sqn with 8 PA-28RT *Arrow IV*; 6 PA-31-350 *Navajo Chieftain*; 9 L-90 *Redigo*
Survey	some sqn with 3 *Learjet* 35A (survey, ECM trg, target-towing)
Trg	some sqn with 28 L-70 *Vinka*

EQUIPMENT BY TYPE
AIRCRAFT 63 combat capable
   FGA • F/A-18 63: 56 F/A-18C *Hornet*; 7 F/A-18D *Hornet*
   ASW 1: 1 F-27 *Maritime Enforcer* (ESM/Elint)
   TPT 22: 2 F-27 *Friendship*
      LEARJET 35 6: 3 *Learjet* 35A; 3 (survey, ECM trg, target-towing)
      PA-28RT *Arrow IV* 8
      PA-31 6: 6 PA-31-350 *Navajo Chieftain*
   TRG 86: 49 *Hawk* MK50/*Hawk* MK51A; 28 L-70 *Vinka*; 9 L-90 *Redigo*
UAV 1 (tactical)
MSL • TACTICAL • AAM: some AIM-120 *AMRAAM*; some AIM-9 *Sidewinder*

Reservists 35,000 reservists

Paramilitary

Frontier Guard 3,100

Ministry of Interior. 4 Frontier and 3 Coast Guard Districts

FORCES BY ROLE

Coast Guard	6 (offshore patrol) sqn; 2 (coastal patrol) sqn with 7 ACV; 60 PB
Air	1 (patrol) sqn with 2 Do-228 (maritime surv); 3 AS-332 *Super Puma*; 4 AB-206L (Bell 206L) *LongRanger*; 4 AB-412 (Bell 412) *Twin Huey*; 1 AB-412EP (Bell 412EP) *Twin Huey*

EQUIPMENT BY TYPE
ACV 7
PATROL AND COASTAL COMBATANTS 60: 60 PB
AIRCRAFT • TPT 2: 2 Do-228 (maritime surv)
HELICOPTERS
   SPT 3: 3 AS-332 *Super Puma*
   UTL 9: 4 AB-412 (Bell 412) *Twin Huey*; 1 AB-412EP (Bell 412EP) *Twin Huey*; 4 AB-206L (Bell 206L) *LongRanger*

Reserve 18,900 reservists on mobilisation

DEPLOYMENT

AFGHANISTAN
NATO • ISAF 83

BOSNIA-HERZEGOVINA
EU • ALTHEA 200

CYPRUS
UN • UNFICYP 1

ETHIOPIA/ERITREA
UN • UNMEE 7 obs

INDIA/PAKISTAN
UN • UNMOGIP 5 obs

LIBERIA
UN • UNMIL 2

MIDDLE EAST
UN • UNTSO 13 obs

SERBIA AND MONTENEGRO
NATO • KFOR I 510
UN • UNMIK 2 obs

SUDAN
UN • UNMIS 3 obs

Georgia Ga

Georgian Lari		2003	2004	2005
GDP	lari	8.4bn	9.2bn	
	US$[a]	13.1bn	13.5bn	
per capita	US$[a]	2,780	2,876	
Growth	%	11.1	8.5	
Inflation	%	4.8	5.7	
Debt	US$	1.93bn		
Def exp	US$[a]	350m	365m	
Def bdgt	lari	60m	ε70m	ε80m
	US$	28.2m	36.6m	44.0m
FMA (US)	US$	8.08m	13.22m	13.10m
US$1=lari		2.14	1.91	1.82

[a] = ppp estimate

Population (2004)   4,693,892

Age	0 – 14	15 – 19	20 – 24	25 – 29	30 – 64	65 plus
Male	10%	4%	4%	3%	21%	6%
Female	9%	4%	4%	3%	23%	9%

Capabilities

ACTIVE 11,320 (Army 7,042 Navy 1,350 Air 1,350 National Guard 1,578) **Paramilitary 11,700**

Terms of service **conscription,** 18 months

ORGANISATIONS BY SERVICE

Army 1,470; 5,572 conscript (total 7,042)

FORCES BY ROLE
1 land forces HQ
Recce   1 bn
MRR   2 bde

SF   1 bn
Marine inf   2 bn (1 cadre)
Arty   1 regt
Peacekeeping   1 bn

EQUIPMENT BY TYPE
TK • MBT 86: 31 T-72; 55 T-55
AIFV 89
  BMP 78: 65 BMP-1; 13 BMP-2
  BRM-1K 11
APC 91
  APC (T) 72: 72 MT-LB
  APC (W) • BTR 19: 1 BTR-60; 15 BTR-70; 3 BTR-80
ARTY 109
  TOWED 74
    122mm 60: 60 D-30
    152mm 14: 3 2A36; 11 2A65
  SP 2
    152mm 1: 1 2S3
    203mm 1: 1 2S7
  MRL • 122mm 16: 16 BM-21
  MOR • 120mm 17: 17 M-120
AT: ε10 msl; ε40 guns
AD • SAM • SP: some SA-13 *Gopher*

National Guard 1,578 active reservists

Navy 860; 490 conscript (total 1,350)

FORCES BY ROLE
Navy 1 HQ located at Tbilisi

EQUIPMENT BY TYPE
PATROL AND COASTAL COMBATANTS 11
  PCC 4: 2 *Dilos*; 1 *Lindau*; 1 *Turk*
  PCI 4 less than 100 tonnes
  PCI 5: 1 *Zhuk* less than 100 tonnes
  PFC 1: 1 *Stenka*
  PHM 1: 1 *Matka*
AMPHIBIOUS • CRAFT 6: 2 LCT; 4 LCM

FACILITIES
Base 1 located at Tbilisi, 1 located at Poti

Air Force 860; 490 conscript (total 1,350)

AIRCRAFT 7 combat capable
  FGA 11: 1 Su-25 *Frogfoot*; 5 Su-25K *Frogfoot A*; 5 Su-17 *Fitter* non-operational
  TPT 9: 6 An-2 *Colt*; 1 Tu-134A *Crusty* (VIP); 2 Yak-40 *Codling*
  TRG 15: 9 L-29 *Delfin*; 1 Yak-18T *Max*; 4 Yak-52; 1 Su-25UB *Frogfoot B* 1*
HELICOPTERS
  ATK 3: 3 Mi-24 *Hind*
  SPT 6: 4 Mi-8 *Hip*; 2 PZL MI-2 *Hoplite* trg
  UTL • UH-1 8: 8 UH-1H *Iroquois*
AD • SAM 75: 75 SA-2 *Guideline* towed/SA-3 *Goa*/SA-4 *Ganef* SP/SA-5 *Gammon* static/SA-7 *Grail* MANPAD (75–150 eff.)

National Guard 1,578 active reservists opcon Army

MRR   1 bde (plus trg centre)

Paramilitary

Border Guard 5,400

Coast Guard

PATROL AND COASTAL COMBATANTS • PCI 2: 2 *Zhuk*

Ministry of Interior Troops 6,300

DEPLOYMENT

IRAQ
Army 156 (Peace Support)

SERBIA AND MONTENEGRO
NATO • KFOR I 1 inf coy; 140

NON-STATE ARMED GROUPS

see Part II

FOREIGN FORCES

All UNOMIG unless otherwise specified
Albania 3 obs
Austria 2 obs
Bangladesh 7 obs
Croatia 1 obs
Czech Republic 5 obs
Denmark 5 obs
Egypt 4 obs
France 3 obs; Army: 800
Germany 12 obs
Greece 5 obs
Hungary 7 obs
Indonesia 4 obs
Jordan 9 obs
Pakistan 8 obs
Poland 5 obs
Republic of South Korea 7 obs
Romania 1 obs
Russia 3 obs. Army ε3,000: 2 mil bases; 139 120mm Mor/2S1 *Carnation* 122mm SP/2S3 152mm SP/BM-21 122mm MRL/D-30 122mm towed; 200 ACV; 65 T-72 MBT; Air ε500: 5 atk hel
Sweden 3 obs
Switzerland 4 obs
Turkey 5 obs
Ukraine 5 obs
United Kingdom 7 obs
United States 2 obs
Uruguay 3 obs

Ireland Irl

Euro €		2003	2004	2005
GDP	€	134bn	145bn	
	US$	152bn	180bn	
per capita	US$	38,812	45,395	
Growth	%	3.7	5.1	
Inflation	%	4.0	2.3	
Public Debt	%	32.0	29.9	
Def bdgt	€	711m	734m	758m
	US$	808m	907m	959m
US$1=€		0.88	0.81	0.79

Population (2004) 3,969,558

Age	0 – 14	15 – 19	20 – 24	25 – 29	30 – 64	65 plus
Male	11%	4%	4%	4%	22%	5%
Female	10%	4%	4%	4%	22%	6%

Capabilities

ACTIVE 10,460 (Army 8,500 Navy 1,100 Air 860)

RESERVE 14,875 (Army 14,500 Navy 300 Air 75)

ORGANISATIONS BY SERVICE

Army ε8,500

FORCES BY ROLE

Lt tk	1 sqn
Inf	3 bde (*each*: 1 fd arty regt (2 fd arty bty), 1 cav recce sqn, 1 fd engr coy, 3 inf bn)
Ranger	1 coy
Arty	1 bty
Fd Engr	1 coy
AD	1 regt (1 AD bty, 3 reserve AD bty)

EQUIPMENT BY TYPE
TK • LT TK 14: 14 *Scorpion*
RECCE • AML 33: 18 AML-20; 15 AML-90
APC • APC (W) 42: 40 *Piranha* III (incl variants); 2 XA-180 *Sisu*
ARTY 537
   TOWED 66
      88mm 42: 42 25-pdr
      105mm 24: 24 L-118 Light Gun
   MOR 471: 400 81mm; 71 120mm
AT
   MSL 57: 36 *Javelin*; 21 *Milan*
   RCL • 84mm 444: 444 *Carl Gustav*
   RL • 84mm: some AT-4
AD
   SAM • MANPAD 7: 7 RBS-70
   GUNS • 40mm • TOWED 30: 30 L/70 each with 8 *Flycatcher* firecon land

Reserves 500 reservists (first line); 14,000 reservists (second line) (total 14,500)
4 army groups (garrisons)

Cav	3 sqn
Inf	18 bn
Fd arty	6 regt
Engr	3 sqn
AD	3 bty

Navy 1,100

EQUIPMENT BY TYPE
PATROL AND COASTAL COMBATANTS • PCO 8: 1 *Eithne* with 1 hel landing platform (for *Dauphin*); 3 *Emer*; 2 *Orla* (UK *Peacock*) each with 1 76mm gun; 2 *Roisin* each with 1 76mm gun

FACILITIES
Base 1 located at Cork, 1 located at Haulbowline

Air Corps 860

FORCES BY ROLE
Air   2 (ops) wg; 2 (spt) wg

FACILITIES
School   1 (trg)

EQUIPMENT BY TYPE
AIRCRAFT
MP 2: 2 CASA 235 MPA
TPT 3: 1 Beech 200 *Super King Air*; 1 Gulfstream IV; 1 *Learjet* 45 (VIP)
UTL: 1 squadron with 5 Cessna FR-172H; 1 Cessna FR-172K
TRG • SF-260 7: 7 SF-260W *Warrior* (being replaced by 8 Pilatus 9M)
HELICOPTERS:
ASLT • SA-342 2: 2 SA-342L *Gazelle*
SAR (navy spt) some
UTL 11: 4 AS-365 *Dauphin 2* (army spt); 7 SA-316B *Alouette III*

FACILITIES
School   1 (trg)

DEPLOYMENT

AFGHANISTAN
NATO • ISAF 11

BOSNIA-HERZEGOVINA
EU • EUFOR II 50

CÔTE D'IVOIRE
UN • UNOCI 1 obs

CYPRUS
UN • UNFICYP 18

DEMOCRATIC REPUBLIC OF CONGO
UN • MONUC 1; 2 obs

LEBANON
UN • UNIFIL 5

LIBERIA
UN • UNMIL 413

MIDDLE EAST
UN • UNTSO 14 obs

SERBIA AND MONTENEGRO
NATO • KFOR I 104
UN • UNMIK 4 obs

WESTERN SAHARA
UN • MINURSO 4 obs

Macedonia, Former Yugoslav Republic FYROM

Macedonian Denar d		2003	2004	2005
GDP	d	255bn	266bn	
	US$	4.7bn	5.3bn	
per capita	US$	2,309	2,597	
Growth	%	3.2	2.3	
Inflation	%	1.2	-0.3	
Debt	US$	1.83bn		
Def bdgt	d	7.4bn	7.0bn	6.3bn
	US$	136m	139m	129m
FMA (US)	US$	12.57m	8.80m	5.85m
US$1=d		54.3	50.3	48.5

Population (2004)	2,040,085

Age	0 – 14	15 – 19	20 – 24	25 – 29	30 – 64	65 plus
Male	11%	4%	4%	4%	22%	5%
Female	10%	4%	4%	4%	22%	6%

Capabilities

ACTIVE 10,890 (Army 9,760 Air Force 1,130)
Paramilitary 7,600
Terms of service 6 months

ORGANISATIONS BY SERVICE

Army 9,760

FORCES BY ROLE
2 Corps HQ (cadre)
Tk	1 bn
Inf	2 bde
SF	1 (Special Purpose) unit (1 SF bn, 1 Ranger bn)
Arty	1 (mixed) regt
Engr	1 regt
Border	1 bde

EQUIPMENT BY TYPE
TK • MBT 61: 31 T-72A; 30 T-55A
RECCE 51
  BRDM 10: 10 BRDM-2
  M-1114 HMMWV 41
AIFV • BMP 11: 10 BMP-2; 1 BMP-2K
APC 207
  APC (T) 48: 8 *Leonidas*; 30 M-113A ; 10 MT-LB

APC (W) 159
BTR 70: 58 BTR-70; 12 BTR-80
TM-170 *Hermelin* 89
ARTY 944
TOWED 209
76mm 65: 55 M-48 *M-1948*; 10 ZIS-3 *M-1942*
105mm 36: 18 M-2A1; 18 M-56
122mm 108: 108 M-30 *M-1938*
MRL 18
122mm 6: 6 BM-21
128mm 12
MOR 717: **60mm** 234; **82mm** 340; **120mm** 143
AT • MSL 12+: some AT-3 *Sagger*; 12 *Milan*
RCL: some 57mm
82mm: some M60A

Reserves

Inf   8 bde
Arty 1 regt
AT   1 regt
AD   1 regt

Marine Wing
PATROL AND COASTAL COMBATANTS 5: 5 PCR

Air Force 1,130
FORCES BY ROLE
FGA   1 sqn with 3 Su-25K *Frogfoot A*; 1 Su-25UB
         Frogfoot B
Atk hel 1 sqn with 10 Mi-24V *Hind E*; 2 Mi-24K *Hind G2*
Tpt hel 1 sqn with 3 MI-17 (Mi-8MT) *Hip H*; 4 Mi-8MTV
         Hip H

EQUIPMENT BY TYPE
AIRCRAFT 4 combat capable
FGA • Su-25 3: 3 Su-25K *Frogfoot A*; 1 Su-25UB *Frogfoot B*
TPT 1: 1 Cessna 337 *Skymaster* on lease (surv)
TRG 5: 1 Z-143L; 3 Z-242
HELICOPTERS
ATK 10: 10 Mi-24V *Hind E*
RECCE 2: 2 Mi-24K *Hind G2*
SPT 7: 3 MI-17 (Mi-8MT) *Hip H*; 4 Mi-8MTV *Hip H*
UTL 2: 2 UH-1H *Iroquois* trg
AD • SAM 67
SP 8: 8 SA-13 *Gopher*
MANPAD 59: 5 SA-16 *Gimlet*; 54 SA-7 *Grail*

Paramilitary

Police 7,600 (some 5,000 armed)
incl 2 SF units
APC: some BTR APC (W)/M-113A APC (T)
HELICOPTERS • UTL 3: 1 AB-212 (Bell 212)
BELL 206 1: 1 AB-206B (Bell 206B) *JetRanger II*
BELL 412 1: 1 Bell 412EP *Twin Huey*

DEPLOYMENT

AFGHANISTAN
NATO • ISAF 48

IRAQ
Army 28 (Peace Support - to be deployed)

NON-STATE ARMED GROUPS
see Part II

FOREIGN FORCES
United States 260 opcon KFOR I

Malta M

Maltese Lira ML		2003	2004	2005
GDP	ML	1.77bn	1.83bn	
	US$	4.8bn	5.4bn	
per capita	US$	12,146	13,607	
Growth	%	-1.8	1.5	
Inflation	%	1.9	2.7	
Def bdgt	ML	14.9m	17.8m	16.4m
	US$	40.5m	52.4m	48.5m
FMA (US)	US$	5.29m		
US$1=ML		0.37	0.34	0.34

Population (2004)   396,851

Age	0 – 14	15 – 19	20 – 24	25 – 29	30 – 64	65 plus
Male	9%	4%	4%	4%	23%	6%
Female	9%	3%	4%	4%	23%	8%

Capabilities

ACTIVE 2,237 (Joint 2,237)

ORGANISATIONS BY SERVICE

Armed Forces of Malta 2,149
Comd HQ
Spt tps

No 1 (Infantry) Regt
Inf 1 bn (1 spt coy, 3 rifle coy, 1 HQ coy)

No 2 (Composite) Regt
FORCES
HQ   1 coy
Air   1 sqn with 2 BN-2B *Islander*; 5 *Bulldog* T MK1;
          2 Hughes 500M; 5 SA-316B *Alouette III*; 2 Bell 47G2
Maritime 1 sqn with 2 *Cantieri Vittoria*; 2 Marine
          Protector; 2 *Bremse*; 2 *Swift*
AD   1 bty

No 3 (Support) Regt
Airport   1 coy
Ordnance   1 coy
Workshop   1 coy
HQ   1 coy
Engr   1 sqn

Reserves

Emergency Volunteer Reserve Force 40

Individual Reserves 48

EQUIPMENT

PATROL AND COASTAL COMBATANTS 8

  PB 2: 2 *Cantieri Vittoria*

  PBC 2: 2 *Marine Protector*

  PCI 4: 2 *Bremse*; 2 *Swift*

AIRCRAFT

  TPT 2: 2 BN-2B *Islander*

  TRG 5: 5 *Bulldog* T MK1

HELICOPTERS

  UTL 7

    HUGHES 500 2: 2 Hughes 500M

    SA-316 5: 5 SA-316B *Alouette III*

  TRG • **BELL 47G** 2: 2 Bell 47G2

AD • **GUNS** 90

  14.5mm • **TOWED** • **ZPU** 50: 50 ZPU-4

  40mm • **TOWED** 40: 40 L/70

FOREIGN FORCES

Italy 49 MIATM cbt Sp (Missione Italiana d'Assistenza Tecnico Militare) 16: Air Force 2 Bell 212 Utl Helicopters

Moldova Mol

Moldovan Leu L		2003	2004	2005
GDP	L	22bn	26bn	
	US$ᵃ	6.3bn	7.3bn	
per capita	US$ᵃ	1,419	1,641	
Growth	%	6.3	7.0	
Inflation	%	11.7	12.3	
Debt	US$	1.9bn		
Def exp	US$ᵃ	150m	175m	
Def bdgt	L	115m	116m	115m
	US$	8.3m	9.8m	9.2m
FMA (US)	US$	1.98m	2.21m	1.34m
US$1=L		13.9	11.9	12.6

ᵃ = ppp estimate

Population (2004) 4,446,455

Age	0 – 14	15 – 19	20 – 24	25 – 29	30 – 64	65 plus
Male	10%	5%	4%	4%	20%	4%
Female	10%	5%	4%	4%	23%	6%

Capabilities

ACTIVE 6,750 (Army 5,710 Air 1,040) **Paramilitary 3,279**

Terms of service 12 months

RESERVE 66,000 (Joint 66,000)

ORGANISATIONS BY SERVICE

Army 1,671; 4,039 conscript (total 5,710)

FORCES BY ROLE

MRR   3 bde

SF   1 bn

Arty   1 bde

Engr   1 indep bn

Gd   1 indep unit

EQUIPMENT BY TYPE

AIFV • **BMD** 44: 44 BMD-1

APC 266

  APC (T) 15: 9 BTR-D; 6 MT-LB

  APC (W) 251

    BTR 11: 11 BTR-80

    TAB-71 91; 149 look-a-like

ARTY 227

  TOWED 69

    122mm 17: 17 *M-1938*

    152mm 52: 21 2A36; 31 D-20

  GUN/MOR • **120mm** 9: 9 2S9 *NONA*

  MRL • **220mm** 11: 11 9P140 *Uragan*

  MOR 138

    82mm 79

    120mm 59: 59 M-120

AT

  MSL 117: 71 AT-4 *Spigot*; 19 AT-5 *Spandrel*; 27 AT-6 *Spiral*

  RCL • **73mm** 138+: 138+ SPG-9

  GUNS • **100mm** 36: 36 MT-12

AD • **GUNS** 37

  23mm • **TOWED** 26: 26 ZU-23

  57mm • **TOWED** 11: 11 S-60

RADAR • **LAND** 1+: some GS-13 *Long Eye*/SNAR-1 *Long Trough* (arty); some *Small Fred*/*Small Yawn*/SNAR-10 *Big Fred*/SNAR-2/-6 *Pork Trough* (veh, arty); 1 L219/200 *PARK-1* (arty)

Air Force 1,040

(incl air defence)

FORCES BY ROLE

Trg/tpt   2 An-2 *Colt*; 1 An-26 *Curl*; 2 An-72 *Coaler*; 8 Mi-8 *Hip*

SAM   1 bde with 12 SA-3 *Goa*

EQUIPMENT BY TYPE

AIRCRAFT • **TPT** 5: 2 An-2 *Colt*; 1 An-26 *Curl*; 2 An-72 *Coaler*

HELICOPTERS • **SPT** 8: 8 Mi-8 *Hip*

AD • **SAM** 12: 12 SA-3 *Goa*

Paramilitary

  Ministry of Interior

  Internal troops 2,379

OPON 900 (riot police)

  Ministry of Interior

DEPLOYMENT

CÔTE D'IVOIRE
UN • UNOCI 4 obs

LIBERIA
UN • UNMIL 1 (staff officer); 3 obs

SUDAN
UN • UNAMIS 1 obs

NON-STATE ARMED GROUPS
see Part II

FOREIGN FORCES
Russia ε1,400 Army: 1 (op) army gp (subord. to Moscow MD) (1 SAM regt, 1 MRR bde); 125 mor/MRL; 214 ACV; 108 MBT; Air: 7 hel

Serbia and Montenegro FRY

Serbian Dinar d		2003	2004	2005
GDP	d	1.22tr	1.26tr	
	US$	21.3bn	21.4bn	
per capita	US$	1,967	1,976	
Growth	%	2.7	7.2	
Inflation	%	11.3	9.5	
Debt	US$	14.8bn		
Def bdgt	d	36.2bn	ε40.0bn	45.7bn
	US$	630m	678m	706m
US$1=d		57.4	59	64.8

Population (2004)   10,825,900

Age	0 – 14	15 – 19	20 – 24	25 – 29	30 – 64	65 plus
Male	9%	4%	4%	4%	22%	6%
Female	9%	4%	4%	4%	23%	8%

Capabilities

ACTIVE 65,300 (Army 55,000 Navy 3,800 Air 6,500)
Paramilitary 45,100
Terms of service 9 months

RESERVE 250,000 (Army 250,000)

ORGANISATIONS BY SERVICE

Army 30,000; 25,000 conscript (total 55,000)
FORCES BY ROLE
6 Corps HQ
Armd	6 bde
Mech	1 bde
Inf	1 bde
SF	1 bde
Mot inf	7 bde
AB	1 bde
Arty	5 (mixed) bde
Engr	3 regt
Gd	1 bde under strength
MP	2 bn

EQUIPMENT BY TYPE
TK • MBT 962: 206 M-84; 62 T-72; 694 T-55
AIFV 525: 525 M-80
APC 288
  APC (T) • M-60 70: 70 M-60P
  APC (W) • BOV 218: 57 M-86 (BOV-VP); 161 look-a-like
ARTY 2,729
  TOWED 790
    105mm 162: 162 M-56
    122mm 271: 271 D-30
    130mm 217: 217 M-46
    152mm 68: 18 D-20; 50 M-84
    155mm 72: 66 M-1; 6 M-65
  SP • 122mm 72: 72 2S1 *Carnation*
  MRL • 128mm 110: 48 M-63 *Plamen*; 62 M-77 *Organj*
  MOR 1,757
    81mm 1,090
    120mm 667: 89 M-74; 578 M-75
AT
  MSL 142+: 142 AT-3 *Sagger* (incl SP- BOV-1, BRDM-1/2); some AT-4 *Spigot*
  RCL 3,700
    105mm 650: 650 M-65
    57mm 1,550
    82mm 1,500: 1,500 M-60PB SP
  GUNS • 100mm 283: 283 T-12
AD
  SAM 960
    SP 60: 60 SA-13 *Gopher*/SA-6 *Gainful*/SA-9 *Gaskin* (180–240 eff.)
    MANPAD 900: 900 SA-14 *Gremlin*/SA-16 *Gimlet*/SA-18 *Grouse (Igla)*/SA-7 *Grail*
  GUNS 2,000: 2,000 BOV-3 SP (BOV-3 SPAAG) SP 20mm/ BOV-30 SP SP 30mm/M-53 towed 30mm/M-53/59SP SP 30mm/M-55 towed 20mm/M-75 towed 20mm/ZSU-57-2 SP (ZSU-57-2) SP 57mm
MSL • TACTICAL • SSM 7: 7 FROG

Reserve Organisations

Reserves 250,000 reservists
Inf	9 bde
Mot inf	5 bde
Arty	2 bde
Arty / rocket	1 bde
Engr	4 regt
SAM	1 bde

Navy 2,900; 9,000 Marines (total 3,800)
EQUIPMENT BY TYPE
SUBMARINES • TACTICAL 8: 2 SSK (midget); 3 non-operational (midget); 1 *Sava* with 6+ Single 533mm TT with 10 Test-71ME HWT; 2 non-operational
PRINCIPAL SURFACE COMBATANTS • FRIGATES •

FFG 3:

2 *Kotor* each with 4 single each with 1 SS-N-2C *Styx* tactical SSM, 1 twin (2 eff.) with SA-N-4 *Gecko* SAM, 2 RBU 6000 *Smerch 2* (24 eff.)

1 *Split* (FSU *Koni*) with 4 single each with 1 SS-N-2C *Styx* tactical SSM, 1 twin (2 eff.) with SA-N-4 *Gecko* SAM, 2 RBU 6000 *Smerch 2* (24 eff.)

PATROL AND COASTAL COMBATANTS 31

PCC 4: 4 *Mirna*

PCR 18

PFM 9:

4 *Mitar Acev* (FSU *Osa* I) each with 4 single each with 1 SS-N-2B *Styx* tactical SSM

5 *Rade Koncar* each with 2 single each with 1 SS-N-2B *Styx* tactical SSM

MINE WARFARE • MINE COUNTERMEASURES 10

MHC 2: 2 *Vukov Klanac*

MSI 2: 2 *Ham* (UK)

MSR 6: 6 *Nestin*

AMPHIBIOUS • CRAFT 23

LCT 1:

1 *Silba* (capacity either 6 medium tk or 7 APCs or 4 towed 130mm or 300 troops) with 1 quad (4 eff.) with SA-N-5 *Grail* SAM, up to 94 mine

LCU 4 (Type MZ); 5 more; 5 (Type 501); 8 (Type 601)

LOGISTICS AND SUPPORT 7: 2 AK; 4 AT

TPT 1: 1 *Lubin* (PO-91)

FACILITIES

Base   1 located at Kumbor, 1 (river comd) located at Novi Sad, 1 located at Bar, 1 located at Tivat

Marines 900

FORCES BY ROLE

Coast Arty   1 bde with 36 M-46 *Catapult*

MP   1 bn

Mot Inf   2 bde (*each*: 2 army regt (*each*: 2 army bn))

Lt inf   1 bde

EQUIPMENT BY TYPE

ARTY • SP • 130mm 36: 36 M-46 *Catapult*

Air Force 6,500

FORCES BY ROLE

1 Air and 1 AD Corps

Ftr   2 sqn with 4 MiG-29A *Fulcrum A* (1 MiG-29U *Fulcrum*); 28 MiG-21bis *Fishbed L & N*; 6 MiG-21UM *Mongol B*

FGA   4 sqn with 17 J-22 *Orao 1*; 34 G-4 *Super Galeb*

Recce   1 sqn with 10 I-22 *Orao 1**; 1 MiG-21R *Fishbed H**

ADA   15 regt

SAM   6 bn with 2 SA-3 *Goa*; 4 SA-6 *Gainful* (12 eff.)

EQUIPMENT BY TYPE

AIRCRAFT 101 combat capable

FTR 39

MiG-29 5: 4 MiG-29A *Fulcrum A*; **1** MiG-29U *Fulcrum*

MiG-21 34: 28 MiG-21bis *Fishbed L & N*; 6 MiG-21UM *Mongol B*

FGA 51: 17 J-22 *Orao 1*; 34 G-4 *Super Galeb*

RECCE 11: 10 I-22 *Orao 1**; 1 MiG-21R *Fishbed H**

TPT 17: 11 An-26 *Curl*; 2 Do-128 *Skyservant*; 2 *Falcon 50*; 2 Yak-40 *Codling*

TRG 9

UTVA-75 9

HELICOPTERS

ARMED 17: 17 H-45M (SA-342) *Partizan (Gazelle)*; 24 H-42M (SA-341) (AT); 2 Mi-24 *Hind*, 2 Mi-17

SPT 58: 29 Mi-8, 25 H-42, 17 K-45, 3 Hi-42 (recce/trg)

AD • SAM 6: 2 SA-3 *Goa*

SP 4: 4 SA-6 *Gainful*

MSL • TACTICAL • ASM: some AGM-65 *Maverick*; some AS-7 *Kerry*

AAM: some AA-10 *Alamo*; some AA-11 *Archer*; some AA-2 *Atoll*; some AA-8 *Aphid*

Paramilitary 45,100

Ministry of Interior Personnel 35,000

(internal security)

AIFV 63

ARTY 166: 166 mor

Helicopters 16 each with 2 Mi-24 *Hind* atk hel

Montenegrin Ministry of Interior Personnel ε6,000

Special Police Units ε4,100

DEPLOYMENT

BURUNDI

UN • ONUB 1

CÔTE D'IVOIRE

UN • UNOCI 3 obs

DEMOCRATIC REPUBLIC OF CONGO

UN • MONUC 6

LIBERIA

UN • UNMIL 6 obs

NON-STATE ARMED GROUPS

see Part II

FOREIGN FORCES

Argentina 113 opcon KFOR I; 1 obs opcon UNMIK

Armenia 34

Austria 532 opcon KFOR I

Azerbaijan 34 opcon KFOR II

Bangladesh 1 opcon UNMIK

Belgium ε500 opcon KFOR I

Bolivia 1 obs opcon UNMIK

Canada 3-2 opcon KFOR I

Czech Republic 1 obs opcon UNMIK; 410 opcon KFOR I

Denmark 1 inf gp opcon KFOR I (1 scout sqn, 1 inf coy); 370 obs opcon KFOR I; 1 obs opcon UNMIK

Estonia 2 opcon KFOR I (offs.); 1 (MSU) pl opcon KFOR I (ESTPATROL)

Finland 2 obs opcon UNMIK; 510 opcon KFOR I

France 2,400 opcon KFOR I; 57 opcon UNMIK

Georgia 1 inf coy opcon KFOR I; 140 opcon KFOR I

Germany 3,900 opcon KFOR I; 26 C2 *Leopard* MBT; 17

Europe (Non-NATO)

SPz-2 *Luchs* recce ; 25 *Marder* 1 AIFV; 21 APC (T) ; 54 TPz-1 *Fuchs* APC (W); 10 M-109A3G 155mm SP; 6 *Wiesel* (TOW) msl; 3 CH-53 *Sea Stallion* spt hel; 9 UH-1D *Iroquois* utl hel

Greece 1,700 opcon KFOR I

Hungary 1 mech inf bn opcon KFOR I; 1 opcon UNMIK; 294 opcon KFOR I

Ireland 4 obs opcon UNMIK; 104 opcon KFOR I

Italy 1 obs opcon UNMIK; 2,530 opcon KFOR I

Jordan 99 opcon KFOR I; 2 obs opcon UNMIK

Kenya 1 obs opcon UNMIK

Lithuania 30 opcon KFOR I

Luxembourg 26 opcon KFOR I

Malawi 1 obs opcon UNMIK

Malaysia 1 obs opcon UNMIK

Morocco 279 opcon KFOR I

Namibia 1 (staff officer) army (Kosovo)

Nepal 2 obs opcon UNMIK

New Zealand 1 obs opcon UNMIK

Norway 1 opcon UNMIK; ε60 opcon KFOR I

Pakistan 1 obs opcon UNMIK

Poland 1 inf bn opcon KFOR I; 574; 1 obs opcon UNMIK

Portugal 313 opcon KFOR I; 2 obs UNMIK

Romania 2 inf coy opcon KFOR I; 1 obs opcon UNMIK; 226 opcon KFOR I

Russia 2 obs opcon UNMIK

Slovakia 100 opcon KFOR I

Slovenia 2 opcon KFOR I

Spain 2 opcon UNMIK; ε800 opcon KFOR I

Sweden ε650 opcon KFOR I

Switzerland 220 opcon KFOR I; 1+ coy opcon KFOR I

Turkey 940 opcon KFOR I

Ukraine 325 opcon KFOR I; 2 obs opcon UNMIK

United Kingdom 1 armd inf bn opcon KFOR I; 1 armd bde opcon KFOR I; 1 inf bn opcon KFOR I; 1 engr regt opcon KFOR I; 1 obs opcon UNMIK; 1,400 opcon KFOR I; 2 SA-341 *Gazelle* spt hel opcon KFOR I

United States 1,800 opcon KFOR I

Zambia 1 obs opcon UNMIK

Sweden Swe

Swedish Krona Skr		2003	2004	2005
GDP	Skr	2.43tr	2.54tr	
	US$	301bn	340bn	
per capita	US$	33,633	37,923	
Growth	%	1.5	3.5	
Inflation	%	1.9	0.4	
Public Debt	%	60.6	62.1	
Def bdgt	Skr	41.2bn	39.5bn	40.6bn
	US$	5.1bn	5.3bn	5.6bn
US$1=Skr		8.08	7.46	7.31

Population (2004) 8,986,400

Age	0 – 14	15 – 19	20 – 24	25 – 29	30 – 64	65 plus
Male	9%	3%	3%	3%	24%	7%
Female	8%	3%	3%	3%	23%	10%

Capabilities

ACTIVE 27,600 (Army 13,800 Navy 7,900 Air 5,900) Paramilitary 600 Inactive Other 35,000
Terms of service Army, Navy 7–15 months Air Force 8–12 months

RESERVE 262,000 (Army 225,000 Navy 20,000 Air 17,000)

ORGANISATIONS BY SERVICE

Army 5,200; 8,600 conscript; 225,000 reservists (obligation to age 47, incl Local Defence and Home Guard); some active reservists (total 238,800)

FORCES BY ROLE
1 Joint Forces Comd, 4 Military Districts (incl Gotland - trg establishments-on mob to form 6 mech bde with 16 mech inf bn, 6 rifle bn, 1 AB bn, 4 arty bn, 4 AD bn, 4 engr bn)

Armd   4 regt

Inf   2 regt

Arty   1 regt

EQUIPMENT BY TYPE
TK • MBT • LEOPARD 2 280
  2A5 120: 120 Strv-122 *Leopard 2 (S)*
  2A4 160: 160 Strv-121
AIFV 705
  CV90 355: 355 Strv9040 (CV9040)
  Pbv-501 350
APC 1,521
  APC (T) 1,104: 433 Pbv 401A; 170 look-a-like; 501 Pbv-302
  APC (W) • XA SERIES 417: 122 XA-180 *Sisu*/XA-203 *Sisu*; 295 look-a-like
ARTY 820
  TOWED • 155mm • FH-77 155: 105 FH-77A; 50 FH-77B
  SP • 155mm 26: 26 BK-1C
  MOR 639: **81mm** 160; **120mm** 479
AT • MSL: some RB-55; some RB-56 *Bill*
  RCL • 84mm: some *Carl Gustav*
  RL • 84mm: some AT-4
AIRCRAFT
  TPT 1: 1 CASA 212 *Aviocar*
  UAV 3: 3 *Sperwer*
AD
  SAM • TOWED • MIM-23: some Rb-87 (I-HAWK) *MIM-23B*
    RBS-90 some
    MANPAD: some RBS-70
  GUNS 200: 170 40mm
    SP 30: 30 Strv 90LV
RADAR • LAND: some ARTHUR (arty); some M-113 A1GE *Green Archer* (mor)

Navy 4,280; 1,300 (Coastal Defence); 320 (Naval Avn); 2,000 conscript; 20,000 reservists (obligation to age 47) (total 27,900)

EQUIPMENT BY TYPE
SUBMARINES • TACTICAL • SSK 7:

3 *Gotland* (AIP powered) each with 2 x1 400mm TT with 6 Tp 432/Tp 451, 4 single 533mm TT with 12 Tp 613/Tp 62
4 *Västergötland* (2 being fitted with AIP) each with 6 single 533mm TT with 12 Tp 613/Tp 62, 6 Tp 432/Tp 451

PATROL AND COASTAL COMBATANTS 36: circa 18 PCI less than 100 tonnes

PFM 18:

4 *Göteborg* each with 4 twin (8 eff.) each with 1 RBS-15M tactical SSM, 4 Saab 601

8 *Kaparen* each with 6 single each with 1 RB 12 *Penguin* tactical SSM

2 *Stockholm* each with 4 single ASTT (may not be fitted) each with Tp 431 LWT, 4 twin (8 eff.) each with 1 RBS-15M tactical SSM, 4 Saab 601

4 *Ystad* each with up to 6 x1 533mm ASTT (Fitted at expense of SSM launchers) each with Tp 613 HWT, 4 twin (8 eff.) each with 1 RBS-15M tactical SSM

MINE WARFARE 21

MINE COUNTERMEASURES 20

MCD 5: 4 *Hisingen*; 1 *Skredsvic*
MCMV 5: 4 *Styrso*; 1 *Uto*
MHC 7: 7 *Landsort*
MSO 3: 2 *Gassten*; 1 *Vicksten*
MINELAYERS • ML 1:
1 *Carlskrona* (trg, mines can be layed by all SS classes) with 1 hel landing platform

AMPHIBIOUS • CRAFT 120: circa 120 LCU

LOGISTICS AND SUPPORT 17: 1 AGI (int); 1 AK

AK 2: 1 *Visborg*
AR 1
ARS 1
AT 8
TRV 2
Trg 2 (sail)

FACILITIES

Base   1 located at Muskö, 1 located at Karlskrona
Support base   1 located at Göteborg

Coastal Defence 1,300

FORCES BY ROLE

Amph   2 bde (trg establishments - on mob to form 1 amph bde with 3 amph bn)

EQUIPMENT BY TYPE

APC • APC (W) 3+: 3+ *Piranha*
ARTY • MOR 70+: **81mm** some; **120mm** 70
PATROL AND COASTAL COMBATANTS 12 less than 100 tonnes
MINE WARFARE 5 (inshore)
AMPHIBIOUS • CRAFT 191: 52 LCU; 139 LCM
AD • SAM: some RBS-70
MSL • TACTICAL • SSM 96
RBS-15 6: 6 RBS-15KA
RBS-17 *Hellfire* 90
GUN • GUN 24+
105mm some
120mm 24: 24 CD-80 *Karin* (mobile)
40mm some
40mm: some L-70
75mm some

Air Force 5,900 incl 1,500 conscript; 17,000 reservists; 1,600 active reservists (total 22,900)

Flying hours   110 to 140 hrs/year

FORCES BY ROLE

COMD	1 HQ (8 (air base) Air bn)
Ftr / FGA / recce	1 (*Gripen*) sqn (declared for Rapid Reaction Force); 6 sqn with 110 JAS 39A *Gripen*; 14 JAS 39B *Gripen*; 20 JAS 39C *Gripen*; 7 JAS 39D *Gripen*
Recce	1 sqn with 13 Saab AJSF 37 *Viggen*/Saab AJSH 37 *Viggen*; 1 (OCU/EW trg) unit with 6 SK 37E *Skolviggen*
ASW / MP	some sqn with 1 CASA 212-400 *Aviocar*
SIGINT	some sqn with 2 S-102B (Gulfstream IV SRA-4)
AEW	some sqn with 6 S-100B *Argus*
Tpt	6 sqn with 3 Tp-101 (Beech 200) *Super King Air*; 8 C-130E *Hercules*/Tp-84 (C-130H) *Hercules* (7 tpt, 1 tkr); 1 Tp-103 (Cessna 550) *Citation V*; 1 Tp-102A (Gulfstream IV); 1 Tp-100A (VIP)
Trg	some sqn with 103 SK-60
AD	3 (fighter control and air surv) bn

EQUIPMENT BY TYPE

AIRCRAFT 170 combat capable

FGA • SAAB 37 13: 13 Saab AJSF 37 *Viggen*/Saab AJSH 37 *Viggen*

MULTIROLE • JAS 39 151: 110 JAS 39A *Gripen**; 14 JAS 39B *Gripen**; 20 JAS 39C *Gripen**; 7 JAS 39D *Gripen**

MP 1: 1 CASA 212-400 *Aviocar*

EW • ELINT 2: 2 S-102B (Gulfstream IV SRA-4)

AEW 6: 6 S-100B *Argus*

TPT 14

C-130 8: 8 C-130E *Hercules*/Tp-84 (C-130H) *Hercules* (7 tpt, 1 tkr)

Tp-100A 1 (VIP)

Tp-101 (Beech 200) *Super King Air* 3

Tp-102A (Gulfstream IV) 1

Tp-103 (Cessna 550) *Citation V* 1

TRG 109

SK 37 6: 6 SK 37E *Skolviggen**

SK-60 103

MSL • TACTICAL • ASM: some RB-15F; some RB-75 (AGM-65) *Maverick*

AAM • AIM-120: some RB-99 (AIM-120B) *AMRAAM*

AIM-9: some RB-74 (AIM-9L) *Sidewinder*

RB-71 *(Sky Flash)* some

BOMB: some BK-39

Armed Forces Hel Wing 800 (from all three services); 250 conscript (total 1,050)

FORCES BY ROLE

Hel   2 bn with 11 HKP-10 (AS-332) *Super Puma* (SAR); 14 HKP-4 (Boeing Vertol 107) (ASW/tpt/SAR); 20 HKP-9A (BO-105CB) training; 5 HKP-11 (Bell 412) *Twin Huey* (SAR)

EQUIPMENT BY TYPE
HELICOPTERS
   SPT 25: 11 HKP-10 (AS-332) *Super Puma* (SAR); 14 HKP-4 (Boeing Vertol 107) (ASW/tpt/SAR)
   UTL 25
      BO-105 • BO-105C 20: 20 HKP-9A (BO-105CB) trg
      HKP-11 (Bell 412) *Twin Huey* 5 (SAR)

Paramilitary 600

Coast Guard 600
PATROL AND COASTAL COMBATANTS 67
   PCC 1: 1 KBV-171 (fishery protection)
   PCI 65
   PCO 1: 1 *Gotland*

Air Arm
AIRCRAFT • TPT 2: 2 CASA 212 *Aviocar* (maritime recce)

Voluntary Auxiliary Organisations 35,000+

DEPLOYMENT

AFGHANISTAN
NATO • ISAF 19
UN • UNAMA 1 obs

BOSNIA-HERZEGOVINA
EU • EUFOR II 7

DEMOCRATIC REPUBLIC OF CONGO
UN • MONUC 5 obs

ETHIOPIA/ERITREA
UN • UNMEE 5 obs

GEORGIA
UN • UNOMIG 3 obs

INDIA/PAKISTAN
UN • UNMOGIP 6 obs

LIBERIA
UN • UNMIL 233

MIDDLE EAST
UN • UNTSO 6 obs

SERBIA AND MONTENEGRO
NATO • KFOR I ε650

SIERRA LEONE
UN • UNAMSIL 1 obs

SUDAN
UN • UNMIS 2 obs

Switzerland CH

Swiss Franc fr		2003	2004	2005
GDP	fr	430bn	444bn	
	US$	320bn	361bn	
per capita	US$	43,316	48,450	
Growth	%	-0.4	1.7	
Inflation	%	0.6	0.8	
Def bdgt	fr	4.67bn	4.86bn	4.7bn
	US$	3.48bn	3.95bn	3.82bn
US$1=fr		1.34	1.23	1.23

Population (2004)   7,450,867

Age	0 – 14	15 – 19	20 – 24	25 – 29	30 – 64	65 plus
Male	9%	3%	3%	3%	25%	6%
Female	8%	3%	3%	3%	25%	9%

Capabilities

ACTIVE 4,300

RESERVE 210,000 (Army 153,200 Air 32,900 Joint 10,000 Command Support Organisation 14,000) Paramilitary 105,000

Terms of service After reformation of armed forces: 18–21 weeks compulsory recruit trg at age 19–20. Followed by 6-7 refresher trg courses (3 weeks each) over a 10-year period between ages 20–30. Approx 113,200 of all ranks were trained in 2004.

ORGANISATIONS BY SERVICE

Armed Forces 4,300+ (career officers and NCOs, surveillance wing, mil sy, contracted military personnel)

Armed Forces Logistic Organisation ε10,000 on mobilisation
Log 1 bde

Command Support Organisation ε14,000 on mobilisation
Spt 1 (comd) bde

Land Forces (Army) ε153,200 on mobilisation
With the exception of military security all units are non-active – being re-org
FORCES BY ROLE
Army   1 Land Forces Comd (1 sy unit, 2 armd bde, 3 mtn inf bde, 4 inf bde, 4 Territorial Regions)

Trg   1 Land Forces Trg Comd (1 spt/sigs unit, 1 inf trg unit, 1 armd trg unit, 1 arty trg unit, 1 engr/rescue trg unit, 1 log trg unit)

EQUIPMENT BY TYPE
TK • MBT • LEOPARD 2 355: 355 Pz-87 *Leo*

RECCE • EAGLE 446: 446 *Eagle* II/*Eagle* I
AIFV • CV90 127: 127 CV9030 (being delivered)
APC 1,049
  APC (T) 534: 534 M-63/73 (M-113) (incl variants)
  APC (W) 515: 515 *Piranha* (incl variants)
ARTY 1,008
  SP • 155mm • M-109 348: 348 PzHb 79/95 (M-109A1)/
  PzHb 88/95 (M-109U)
  MOR 660
    81mm 528: 528 M-72
    120mm 132: 132 M-64
AT
  MSL 685: 565 M47 *Dragon*
    TOW • TOW-2 120: 120 TOW-2 SP *Mowag Piranha*
  RL • 67mm 3,335: 3,335 PZF 44 *Panzerfaust*
AD • SAM • MANPAD: some FIM-92A *Stinger*

Marine
PATROL AND COASTAL COMBATANTS • PCR 10:
10 *Aquarius*

Air Force ε32,900 on mobilisation
6 air base cmd, 1 air force trg cmd
Flying hours   200–250 hrs/year

FORCES BY ROLE
incl AD units, mil airfield guard units
Ftr   3 sqn with 26 F/A-18C *Hornet*; 7 F/A-18D *Hornet*; 3
      sqn with 45 F-5E *Tiger II* (12 on lease to Austria)
Tpt   1 sqn with 1 *Learjet 35A*; 15 PC-6 *Turbo-Porter*;
      2 Do-27; 1 *Falcon-50*
Trg   some sqn with 12 F-5F *Tiger II*; 1 sqn with 37 PC-7
      Turbo Trainer; 1 sqn with 11 PC-9 (tgt towing)
Hel   6 sqn with 15 AS-332 *Super Puma*; 12 AS-532 *Cougar*;
      35 SA-316 *Alouette III*
UAV 1 bn with 4 ADS 95 *Ranger*

EQUIPMENT BY TYPE
AIRCRAFT 90 combat capable
  FTR • F-5 57: 45 F-5E *Tiger II*; 12 F-5F *Tiger II*
  FGA • F/A-18 33: 26 F/A-18C *Hornet*; 7 F/A-18D *Hornet*
  TPT 16
    LEARJET 35 1: 1 *Learjet 35A*
    PC-6 *Turbo-Porter* 15
    Falcon-50 1
  TRG 50: 2 Do-27; 37 PC-7 *Turbo Trainer*; 11 PC-9 (tgt
  towing)
HELICOPTERS
  SPT 15: 15 AS-332 *Super Puma*
  UTL 47: 12 AS-532 *Cougar*; 35 SA-316 *Alouette III*
UAV • RECCE • TAC 4: 4 ADS 95 *Ranger*
MSL • TACTICAL • AAM: some AIM-120 *AMRAAM*;
some AIM-9 *Sidewinder*

Air Defence
FORCES BY ROLE
ADA 1 unit (trg) (15 AD bn with *Rapier*; FIM-92A
      Stinger; 35mm; *Skyguard*

EQUIPMENT BY TYPE
AD • SAM: some *Rapier*
  MANPAD: some FIM-92A *Stinger*
  GUNS: some 35mm
RADAR • LAND: some *Skyguard*

Paramilitary

Civil Defence 105,000 reservists
(not part of armed forces)

DEPLOYMENT

AFGHANISTAN
NATO • ISAF 4 (KMNB and PRT Kunduz)

AUSTRIA
OSCE • HQ Vienna

DEMOCRATIC REPUBLIC OF CONGO
UN • MONUC 2

ETHIOPIA/ERITREA
UN • UNMEE 4 obs

GEORGIA
UN • UNOMIG 4 obs

KOREA, DEMOCRATIC PEOPLES REPUBLIC OF
NNSC 5 Staff

MIDDLE EAST
UN • UNTSO 10 obs

SERBIA AND MONTENEGRO
NATO • KFOR I 220 (military volunteers)
EU • ALTHEA 2 officers; 8 liaison and observation
teams (LOT)

Ukraine Ukr

Ukrainian Hryvnia h		2003	2004	2005
GDP	h	263bn	2.98bn	
	US$[a]	264bn	303bn	
per capita	US$[a]	5,493	6,347	
Growth	%	9.6	12.1	
Inflation	%	5.2	9.0	
Debt	US$	16.3bn		
Def exp	US$[a]	5.5bn	6.0bn	
Def bdgt	h	4.49bn	5.39bn	5.53bn
	US$	843m	1.01bn	1.09bn
FMA (US)	US$	6.19m	6.83m	4.67m
US$1=h		5.33	5.32	5.06

[a] = ppp estimate

Population (2004)   47,732,079

Ethnic groups: Russian 22%; Polish 4%; Jewish 1%

Age	0 – 14	15 – 19	20 – 24	25 – 29	30 – 64	65 plus
Male	8%	4%	4%	4%	21%	5%
Female	8%	4%	4%	4%	25%	10%

Capabilities

**ACTIVE 187,600 (Army 125,000 Navy 13,500 Air
49,100 (excl Black Sea Fleet and 95,000 civilian
personnel) Paramilitary 84,900**
Terms of Service Army, Air Force 18 months, Navy 2 years

RESERVE 1,000,000 (Joint 1,000,000)
mil service within 5 years

ORGANISATIONS BY SERVICE

Ground Forces (Army) 125,000
FORCES BY ROLE
3 op comd (1 to disband by end 2005; All corps HQ (except one) to disband by end of 2005
Army   1 (MoD) tps (1 engr bde, 1 sy bde); 1 (ground forces) comd (1 comd corps (1 arty regt, 1 SAM regt, 1 msl bde, 1 air mob bde, 1 MRL regt, 1 SSM div (3 SSM bde (SS-21)), 2 mech bde))

Northern Op Comd
To be disbanded
Comd 1 tps (1 trg bde, 1 avn bde, 1 engr bde, 1 mech bde, 1 tk div)

Southern Op Comd
Comd 1 tps (1 SAM regt, 1 engr regt, 1 mech bde, 1 air mob regt, 1 avn bde)
Army 1 corps (1 SAM regt, 1 arty regt, 1 air mob div (1 arty regt, 2 mech bde), 1 engr regt, 1 arty bde, 1 AB bde, 1 tk div, 1 arty div (2 arty bde, 2 MRL regt), 2 mech bde)

Western Op Comd
Comd 1 tps (1 air mob regt, 1 SAM regt, 1 avn regt, 1 avn bde, 1 mech inf regt, 1 SF bde, 1 engr bde, 1 SSM bde)
Army 1 corps (1 SAM regt, 1 mech div (1 SAM regt, 1 arty regt, 1 tk regt, 3 mech regt), 1 arty bde, 1 engr regt, 1 mech div (1 tk regt, 1 SAM regt, 2 mech regt), 1 arty div (1 MRL regt, 1 MRL bde, 2 arty bde), 2 mech bde)

EQUIPMENT BY TYPE
TK • **MBT** 3,784: 271 T-80; 6 T-84; 1,180 T-72; 2,215 T-64; 112 T-55
RECCE • **BRDM** 600+: 600+ BRDM-2
AIFV 3,043
   BMD 139: 61 BMD-1; 78 BMD-2
   BMP 2446: 1,008 BMP-1; 1,434 BMP-2; 4 BMP-3
   BRM-1K 458
APC 8,492
   APC (T) 6,834: 44 BTR-D; 6,790 MT-LB (incl 4,700 L-a-L)
   APC (W) • **BTR** 1,658: 176 BTR-60; 1,026 BTR-70; 456 BTR-80
ARTY 3,705
   TOWED 1,143
      122mm 446: 443 D-30; 3 M-30 *M-1938*
      152mm 697: 289 2A36; 185 2A65; 216 D-20; 7 M-1937
   SP 1,298
      122mm 638: 638 2S1 *Carnation*
      152mm 560: 40 2S19 *Farm*; 496 2S3; 24 2S5
      203mm 100: 100 2S7
   GUN/MOR • **120mm** 76: 2 2B16 *NONA-K*; 74 2S9 *NONA*
   MRL 588

   122mm 352: 20 9P138; 332 BM-21
   132mm 3: 3 BM-13
   220mm 139: 139 9P140 *Uragan*
   300mm 94: 94 9A52 *Smerch*
   MOR 600
      120mm 599: 342 2S12; 257 PM-38
      160mm 1: 1 M-160
AT
   MSL: some AT-4 *Spigot*/AT-5 *Spandrel*/AT-6 *Spiral*
   GUNS • **100mm** 500: ε500 MT-12/T-12
HELICOPTERS
   ATK 205: 205 Mi-24 *Hind*
   SPT 357: 42 Mi-6 *Hook*; 315 Mi-8 *Hip*
AD
   SAM • **SP** 435: 60 SA-11 *Gadfly*; ε150 SA-13 *Gopher*; 100 SA-4 *Ganef*; 125 SA-8 *Gecko*
   GUNS 470
      30mm • **SP** 70: 70 2S6
      57mm • **TOWED** 400: ε400 S-60
   RADAR • **LAND**: some *Small Fred/Small Yawn/SNAR-10 Big Fred* (arty)
   MSL • **TACTICAL** • **SSM** 212: 50 FROG; 90 SS-21 *Scarab* (*Tochka*)
      SCUD 72: 72 *Scud*-B

Navy ε11,500; 2,000 conscript (total 13,500)
On 31 May 1997, RF President Boris Yeltsin and Ukr Presidnt Leonid Kuchma signed an inter-governmental agreement on the status and terms of the Black Sea Fleet's deployment on the territory of Ukr and parameters for the fleet's division. The RF Fleet will lease bases in Sevastopol for the next 20 years. It is based at Sevastopol and Karantinnaya Bays and jointly with Ukr warships at Streletskaya Bay. The overall serviceability of the fleet is very low.
EQUIPMENT BY TYPE
SUBMARINES • **TACTICAL** • **SSK** 1: 1 *Foxtrot* (T-641)†
PRINCIPAL SURFACE COMBATANTS 6
   CRUISERS • **CG** 1: 1 *Ukraina* non-operational (RF *Slava*, laid up)
   FRIGATES 2
      FFG 1:
         1 *Mikolair* non-operational (RF *Krivak* I, laid up) with 1 quad (4 eff.) with 4 SS-N-14 *Silex* tactical SSM, 8 single 533mm TT, 2 twin (4 eff.) with 20 SA-N-4 *Gecko* SAM, 4 76mm gun
      FF 1:
         1 *Sagaidachny* (capacity 1 Ka-27 *Helix* ASW hel) (RF *Krivak* III) with 2 quad 533mm ASTT (8 eff.) each with T-53 HWT, 1 Twin (2 eff.) with 20 SA-N-4 *Gecko* SAM, 1 100mm gun
   CORVETTES • **FS** 3:
         3 *Grisha* (II/V) each with 2 twin 533mm ASTT (4 eff.) each with SAET-60 HWT, 1 twin (2 eff.) with 20 SA-N-4 *Gecko* SAM, up to 2 RBU 6000 *Smerch* 2 (24 eff.), 1 76mm gun
PATROL AND COASTAL COMBATANTS 5
   PCI 1: 1 *Zhuk*†
   PHM 2:
         2 *Matka* each with 2 single with 2 SS-N-2C *Styx*/SS-N-2D *Styx*, 1 76mm gun

PFT 2:

2 *Pauk* I each with 1 x 4 manual with 8 SA-N-5 *Grail* SAM, 4 Single 406mm TT, 1 76mm gun

MINE WARFARE • MINE COUNTERMEASURES 5

MHC 1: 1 *Yevgenya*

MSC 2: 2 *Sonya*

MSO 2: 2 *Natya*

AMPHIBIOUS

LS 3

LSM 1: 1 *Polnochny* A (capacity 180 troops; 6 MBT)/ *Polnochny* C (capacity 180 troops; 6 MBT)

LST 2:

1 *Alligator* (capacity 20 tanks; 300 troops) with up to 3 x1 manual each with SA-N-5 *Grail* SAM

1 *Ropucha* (capacity either 190 troops or 10 MBT; either 24 APC (T)s or 170 troops) with 4 quad (16 eff.) each with SA-N-5 *Grail* SAM, 2 57mm twin gun (4 eff.), 92 mine

CRAFT • ACV 2:

2 *Pomornik* (*Zubr*) (capacity 230 troops; either 3 MBT or 10 APC (T)s) each with 2 x 4 manual each with SA-N-5 *Grail* SAM

LOGISTICS AND SUPPORT 9

AG 1: 1 *Kashtan*

AGI (INT) 2: 1 *Moma* (mod); 1 *Primore*

AGOS 1

AK 2: 2 *Vytegrales*

AO 1

ASR 1: 1 *Elbrus*

SPT 1: 1 *Lama* (msl spt)

FACILITIES

Base	1 located at Sevastopol, 1 located at Kerch, 1 located at Donuzlav, 1 located at Chernomorskoye, 1 located at Odessa, 1 located at Ochakov
Construction and Repair Yard	1 located at Nikolaev, 1 located at Balaklava

Naval Aviation up to 2,500

AIRCRAFT 11 combat capable

ASW 11: 11 Be-12 *Mail*

TPT 16: 5 An-12 *Cub*; 1 An-24 *Coke*; 8 An-26 *Curl*; 1 Il-18 *Coot*; 1 Tu-134 *Crusty*

HELICOPTERS

ASW 72: 28 Ka-25 *Hormone*

KA-27 2: 2 Ka-27E *Helix*

Mi-14 *Haze* 42

SPT 5: 5 Mi-6 *Hook*

Naval Infantry 3,000

Naval inf 1 bde

Air Forces and Air Defence Forces 49,100

Air	2 corps (5th and 14th AVK); 1 (multi-role rapid reaction) gp (35th AVG); 1 Trg Aviation Cmd

FORCES BY ROLE

Bbr	1 regt with 26 Tu-22M *Backfire A*
FGA / bbr	3 regt with 71 Su-24 *Fencer*

Ftr	7 regt with 199 MiG-29 *Fulcrum*; 2 training; 60 Su-27 *Flanker*
FGA	2 regt with 63 Su-25 *Frogfoot*
Recce	2 regt with 29 Su-24 *Fencer**; 20 Su-17 *Fitter**
CCT	1 regt with 2 MiG-29 *Fulcrum**; 1 MiG-23 *Flogger**; 4 Su-24 *Fencer**
Tpt	3 regt with Il-78 *Midas*; 45 An-12 *Cub*/An-24 *Coke*/An-26 *Curl*/Tu-134 *Crusty*; 60 Il-76 *Candid*
Spt hel	some sqn with 23 Mi-6 *Hook*; 170 Mi-8 *Hip*; 111 PZL MI-2 *Hoplite*
Trg	1 regt with 16 Mi-8 *Hip*; 5 regt with 120 L-39 *Albatros*

EQUIPMENT BY TYPE

AIRCRAFT 444 combat capable

BBR 26: 26 Tu-22M *Backfire A*

FTR 280: 199 MiG-29 *Fulcrum*; 2 trg; 2*; 16 in store; 60 Su-27 *Flanker*; 1 MiG-23 *Flogger**

FGA 187: 63 Su-25 *Frogfoot*; 71 Su-24 *Fencer**; 20 Su-17 *Fitter**

TKR: some Il-78 *Midas*

TPT 105: 45 An-12 *Cub*/An-24 *Coke*/An-26 *Curl*/Tu-134 *Crusty*; 60 Il-76 *Candid*

TRG 120: 120 L-39 *Albatros*

HELICOPTERS

SPT 320: 23 Mi-6 *Hook*; 170 Mi-8 *Hip*; 16 more; 111 PZL MI-2 *Hoplite*

AD • SAM 825: 825 SA-10 *Grumble* (quad) SP/SA-11 *Gadfly* SP/SA-12A *Gladiator* SP/SA-2 *Guideline* towed/SA-3 *Goa*/SA-5 *Gammon* static/SA-6 *Gainful* SP (825-3300 eff.)

MSL

ASM: some AS-10 *Karen*; some AS-11 *Kilter*; some AS-12 *Kegler*; some AS-13 *Kingbolt*; some AS-14 *Kedge*; some AS-15 *Kent*; some AS-7 *Kerry*; some AS-9 *Kyle*

AAM: some AA-10 *Alamo*; some AA-11 *Archer*; some AA-7 *Apex*; some AA-8 *Aphid*; some AA-9 *Amos*

Paramilitary

MVS ε39,900 active

(Ministry of Internal Affairs)

FORCES BY ROLE

Mil Region	4 tps
MP	1 (Internal Security) tps

Border Guard 45,000 active

Maritime Border Guard

The Maritime Border Guard is an independent subdivision of the State Comission for Border Guards and is not part of the navy.

FORCES BY ROLE

Air Wing	1 (gunship) sqn
Air	3 sqn
MCM	1 sqn
Paramilitary	2 (river) bde; 1 (aux ship) gp; 4 (cutter) bde
Trg	1 div

Europe
(Non-NATO)

EQUIPMENT BY TYPE
PATROL AND COASTAL COMBATANTS 36
  PCI 20: 20 *Zhuk*
  PFC 10:
    10 *Stenka* each with 4 single 406mm TT,
    4 30mm gun
  PFT 3:
    3 *Pauk* I each with 4 SA-N-5 *Grail* SAM, 4 single
    406mm TT, 1 76mm gun
  PHT 3:
    3 *Muravey* each with 2 single 406mm TT,
    1 76mm gun
  AIRCRAFT • TPT: some An-24 *Coke*; some An-26 *Curl*;
  some An-72 *Coaler*; some An-8 *Camp*
  HELICOPTERS • ASW: some Ka-27 *Helix*

Coast Guard 14,000 (civilian)
PATROL AND COASTAL COMBATANTS 5
  MISC BOATS/CRAFT 1: 1 water jet boat
  PB 3
  OPV 1
AMPHIBIOUS: 1 LS
  CRAFT 1: 1 ACV
EQUIPMENT BY TYPE
ACV 85
Aircraft 6
Helicopters 8

Civil Defence Troops 9,500+ (civilian)
(Ministry of Emergency Situations)
Army   4 indep bde; 4 indep regt

DEPLOYMENT

DEMOCRATIC REPUBLIC OF CONGO
UN • MONUC 12 obs

ETHIOPIA/ERITREA
UN • UNMEE 7 obs

GEORGIA
UN • UNOMIG 5 obs

IRAQ
Ground Forces (army) 1,640 (Peace Support)

LEBANON
UN • UNIFIL 197

LIBERIA
UN • UNMIL 300

SERBIA AND MONTENEGRO
NATO • KFOR I 325
UN • UNMIK 2 obs

SIERRA LEONE
UN • UNAMSIL 3 obs

FOREIGN FORCES

Russia 1,100 Navy: 1 navy HQ located at Sevastopol;
1 naval inf regt; 102 AIFV/APC (T)/APC (W); 24 arty

NATO EUROPE – DEFENCE ECONOMICS

The modest recovery that had begun in the euro zone in 2003 carried through into early 2004, but momentum slowed in the second half of the year and by early 2005 economic indicators throughout the region were showing a distinctly mixed picture. As a result, eurozone GDP growth, which accelerated from 0.5% in 2003 to 2.0% in 2004, is projected to fall to 1.6% in 2005. Export growth, which had led the recovery in the first half of 2004, was negatively affected by the continued appreciation of the euro and the global slowdown that emerged in the second half of the year. On the domestic front, high unemployment together with subdued demand in the wake of high and volatile oil prices held back consumption, while business investment remained subdued as companies continued to focus on restructuring their balance sheets. Prospects for 2005 remain heavily dependent on global developments and their impact on eurozone exports, particularly in countries like Germany where external demand accounted for three-quarters of growth in 2004.

Low economic growth continues to have a negative impact on many countries' fiscal position, with Germany, France, Italy and Greece again failing, in 2004, to maintain budget deficits below 3% of GDP. And although government budgets for 2005 show varying degrees of fiscal consolidation, the one-off nature of many of these initiatives, particularly in France and Germany, have lead the International Monetery Fund (IMF) to question whether policies are in place to achieve and sustain targets. In Italy, the budget position is projected to deteriorate at an even faster pace. In its 2005 World Economic Outlook, the IMF urged countries with weak budget positions to implement a 'faster-than-currently-planned pace of fiscal consolidation … based on high quality measures'.

The continuing inability of major countries to adhere to the fiscal targets laid down in the Stability and Growth Pact (governing membership of the single currency) finally led to a series of reforms to the original rules, providing governments with significant additional fiscal policy flexibility. However, financial market practitioners and other observers pointed out that these reforms do not include any strengthening of supposed enforcement mechanisms, leaving the credibility of the framework down to individual governments' willingness to adopt often unpopular policies. Therefore, without a sustained boost to economic growth in the region, it appears unlikely that fiscal balances in the medium term will improve dramatically.

Budget problems, combined with a lack of public support for increased spending on defence, make

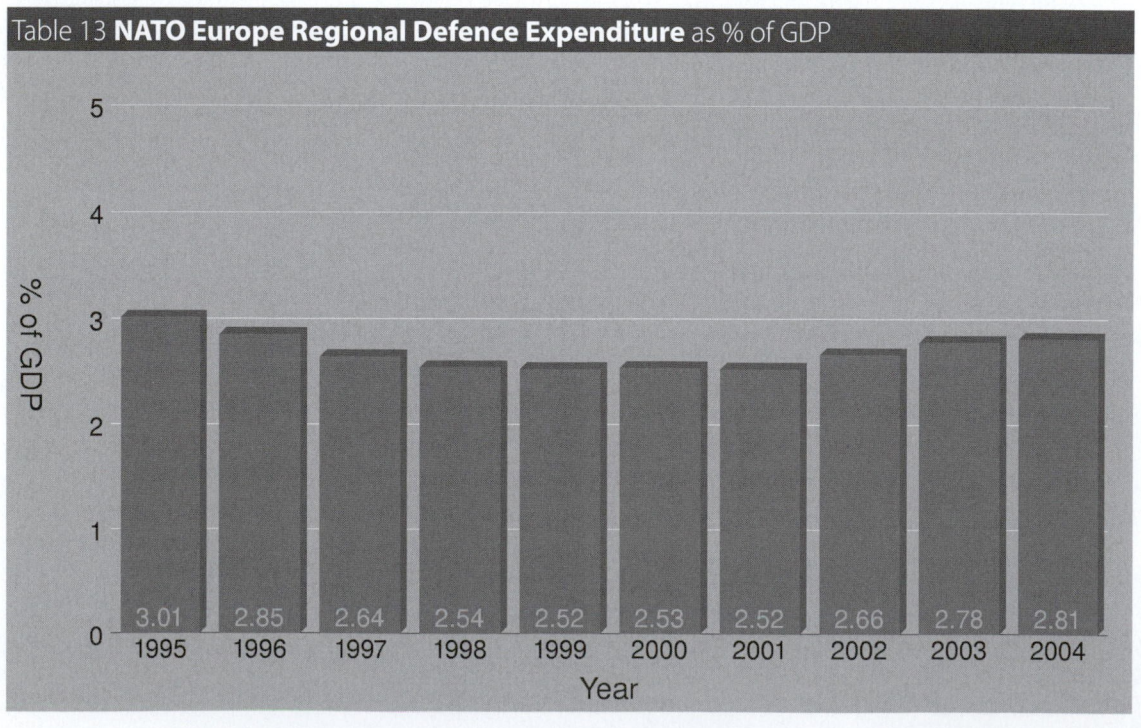

Table 13 **NATO Europe Regional Defence Expenditure** as % of GDP

Year	% of GDP
1995	3.01
1996	2.85
1997	2.64
1998	2.54
1999	2.52
2000	2.53
2001	2.52
2002	2.66
2003	2.78
2004	2.81

the need for greater efficiency and value for money in the European defence sector ever more necessary. However, the current lack of industry and government cooperation is well illustrated in the field of Armoured Fighting Vehicles (AFV). At present, there are 20,000 AFVs in service across Europe, with a procurement need for another 10,000, at a cost of €30bn, over the next decade. However, there are currently up to 23 separate national AFV programmes running to fill the requirement with, according to the European Defence Agency, 'almost no international cooperation between member states', leading Javier Solana, head of the European Defence Agency, to declare that pooling resources on research, development, acquisition and maintenance of equipment as 'the only way European armed forces can get interoperable equipment at a price they can afford'. Currently only 5% of European countries' research and development budgets are spent on collaborative projects.

Once again, the **UK** economy was the best performing among major European countries, growing by 3.1% in 2004; however, the government's fiscal position has deteriorated following several budgets notable for their increased expenditure on health and education. The 2005 defence budget rose in line with the three-year spending plan unveiled by the chancellor in 2004, which outlined a real-terms annual increase in the defence budget of 1.4% between 2004–05 and 2006–07, although the worsening outlook for government finances suggest that this trend may come to a halt in the following three-year cycle. In cash terms, the 2005–06 budget rises to £27.0bn before increasing to £28.7bn in 2006–07. (In recent years the MoD has introduced a different method of accounting known as Resource Account Budgeting [RAB], which takes into account the depreciation of military assets and a cost of capital, and by this standard the 2005–06 budget measures over £37.9bn. For purposes of comparison, *The Military Balance* will continue to publish figures based on the previous cash accounting basis, where possible). In addition to the increase in the defence budget itself, the chancellor announced further funds to help pay for the armed forces' operations in Iraq. While details about the overall cost to the UK of its involvement in Iraq are not available, the 2004 Pre-Budget Report included an additional £520m for 2004–05 and £400m for 2005–06.

Following the publication in June 2004 of government plans to implement the biggest cuts in a generation to both manpower and equipment, in November the Ministry of Defence (MoD) revealed a package of efficiency measures intended to save almost £6bn between 2005 and 2007. The biggest savings will come from the logistics budget where some £2.4bn is hoped to be saved, mainly through the concentration of aircraft maintenance at a smaller number of sites, cuts in staff and reductions in holdings of stocks and fixed assets. It is believed that £250m can be saved in the way the army manages its armoured fleet, by storing vehicles in humidity-controlled environments, and a further £960m can be saved in general operating costs by reducing the size of front-line fleets of aircraft, submarines, ships and armoured vehicles. In addition to savings in logistics, a target of nearly £1bn in procurement savings was outlined, including an improved strategy for the acquisition of the Future Offensive Air System, replacing the *Tornado* GR4 fleet, and changes to the army's Future Rapid Effects System assessment phase.

New procurement decisions included the eventual go-ahead for Tranche 2 of the Eurofighter *Typhoon*, given on 14 December 2004 after months of protracted negotiations. Of the 236 aircraft to be built under Tranche 2, the UK will acquire 89 at a cost of some £5bn. The other significant aircraft decision during the year was the selection of AugustaWestland's *Future Lynx* as the preferred option for the £1bn British Army scout/utility and Royal Navy attack helicopter programmes. Still to be decided is the £2bn Future Rotorcraft Capability programme that will furnish the armed forces with new medium- and heavy-lift helicopters. Further details emerged about the UK MoD's ISTAR programmes. There is a change to the operating concept of the £800m *Watchkeeper* intelligence, surveillance, target acquisition and reconnaissance unmanned aerial vehicle system, which will replace the current *Phoenix* system. Originally, the system, being developed by Thales, comprised two complementary but differently sized fleets of *Hermes* UAVs; however, under the new plan only medium-altitude *Hermes* 450 UAV platforms will be acquired. In addition, a major upgrade of the UK's E-3D *Sentry* AWACS fleet, which will transform the aircraft into the hub of the UK's network-centric warfare capability, was revealed for the end of the decade. Following experiences in Kosovo, Iraq and Afghanistan, it has become clear that the E-3 is being used as more of an airborne warning and control system rather than an early warning platform At the heart of the upgrade will be the improvement of battle-management capabilities, including incorporation of the US Network-Centric Collaborative Targeting (NCTT) technology which compresses sensor-to-shooter time by allowing a much wider range of information on ground targets to be displayed to crew members.

The flagship £13bn Private Finance Initiative programme to replace the RAF's ageing fleet of air-to-air refuelling aircraft moved further ahead. The project had stalled for several months over protracted negotiations between the MoD, the Treasury and the AirTanker consortium over whether the company was taking on enough risk to categorise the arrangement as a true PFI, and how the revenue gained by leasing the 17 Airbus A330 aircraft to third parties when not being used by the RAF would be shared. With these problems apparently resolved, the Defence Procurement Agency declared in February 2005 that the programme could proceed to final contract negotiations based on AirTanker's proposals.

Despite its difficult fiscal position, and lack of support from the then Finance Minister Nicolas Sarkozy, **France** once again increased its defence budget in line with its medium-term defence plan. Sarkozy had insisted that defence spending be cut in 2005 to help the government reduce its budget deficit closer to 3% of GDP – it was estimated to have been 3.7% in 2004 – and asked that the MoD bear the full cost of France's overseas military operations in 2004. However, President Jacques Chirac sided with the defence ministry in rejecting these demands and ruled that the majority of spending on foreign operations would come from outside the defence budget.

Under the terms of the six-year plan, covering the period 2003–08, a total of €88bn has been allocated to new equipment procurement. In 2005, procurement spending was increased to €15.2bn and included a long-expected order for 59 *Rafale* combat aircraft and funds to acquire 70 SCALP cruise missiles and eight *Tiger* helicopters as well as initial funding for eight multi-role frigates and €500m for continuing development of the M51 submarine-launched nuclear missile. However, despite the much needed increase in procurement funding, problems remain with the budget process. In March 2005, the parliamentary all-party defence committee revealed that up to 20% of funds earmarked for military procurement in 2004 had remained unspent, and under the French system there is no guarantee that the unspent credits will be brought forward for future use by the MoD. The shortfall in spending is thought to be due to lengthy delays in big-ticket programmes: in 2004 only three out of five *Rafale* aircraft were supplied while just 12 out of 50 *Leclerc* main battle tanks were delivered to the French

army. In addition to problems with the existing budget process, the defence ministry had to abandon plans to introduce its first-ever private finance initiative to secure external funding for 17 multi-role frigates that it intended to develop with Italy and bring into service between 2008 and 2017. Private funding had been sought in an effort to keep the €5.1bn purchase off the government's budget and hence ease pressure on the deficit. However, after 18 months of negotiations, the proposed deal proved too complicated and expensive, and so the ships will be funded from the regular defence budget, with the result that the in-service date will slip by at least two years.

Although growth in **Germany** climbed to 1.7% in 2004, the economy remains mired in debt and high unemployment. The government once again failed to meet the guidelines laid out in the original Stability and Growth Pact, recording a budget deficit of -3.7% of GDP, and was forced to introduce a package of measures, known as 'Agenda 2010', to try and remedy the problem. These fiscal reforms are wide ranging and include unpopular measures to alter pension and health care provisions, labour market regulations and initiatives to cut taxes and subsidies. As a result, the defence budget fell for the second year running, despite a pledge by the government in 2003 that the defence funding would be fixed at €24.0bn for a period of four years. In 2004, the budget fell to €24.1bn, and in 2005 it has fallen further to €23.8bn. Personnel expenditures, representing 50% of total defence spending, account for a smaller proportion of the budget than in 2004, whereas procurement spending has increased from €3.99bn in 2004 to €4.21bn in 2005 and R&D spending has been boosted from €786m to €964m in the same time period. The massive reorganisation of the Bundeswehr that will see the armed forces reduced to 250,000 personnel and divided into three distinct functions – an intervention force, a stabilisation force and a supporting force – continued in what Defence Minister Peter Struck referred to as a 'year of decisiveness' in the transformation schedule. Under the long-term transformation plan 'Structure 2010', the army will reduce its fleet of main battle tanks from 2,500 to 350, infantry fighting vehicles from 2,050 to 401, and helicopters from 530 to 240, while the air force will reduce its number of combat aircraft from 450 to 260. The navy will retain all its current capabilities, although the number of platforms will be reduced. The major procurement decision in 2005 saw government approval for Germany's participation in the Medium Extended Air Defense System (MEADS) with Italy and the US. Germany will contribute around €1bn towards development costs and 25% of the total costs of the $18bn missile programme. Other significant procurement allocations during the year included €350m for the first batch, out of a total of 410, of five *Puma* IFVs, €4.6bn for Germany's share of 68 Tranche 2 Eurofighter *Typhoons* and €270m for the acquisition of eight second-hand P-3C *Orion* maritime patrol aircraft from the Netherlands.

Of the major economies in the eurozone, **Italy** is facing the biggest challenge in trying to bring government spending closer to the notional 3% of GDP limit. In 2004 the budget deficit breached this level and is projected to climb as high as 4.3% of GDP in 2006. On current trends, the IMF estimates that Italy will still exceed the guideline in 2010. The Italian MoD submitted a budget (excluding military pensions and funding for the carabinieri) for 2005 that would have boosted defence spending by around 8%; however, in light of the government's worsening deficit, this was later amended and parliament approved a final budget that reduced core defence spending from €14.1bn in 2004 to €13.6bn in 2005, a reduction of 3.6%. Because of the ongoing switch to all-professional forces, personnel costs are currently fixed at over 60% of the total budget, meaning that the bulk of the cut will be felt in investment accounts – procurement will fall to €2.0bn, down 22% from the previous year and R&D funding will be reduced by 5% to €346m. In light of the budget reductions, the MoD announced that it would sell off property during 2005 worth up to €1.3bn in an attempt to restore funds to weapons acquisitions. The budget cut means that additional programmes have been added to the list of those already indefinitely delayed. New programmes that join airborne early warning and surveillance aircraft, submarines, an amphibious assault ship and maritime patrol aircraft on the delayed list include the *Centauro* IFV and 100 *Dardo* IFVs. In September 2004, **Poland**

unveiled a new six-year defence plan for the period 2005--10 that outlines a substantial increase in defence procurement funding and a large reduction in the service length and number of conscripts. Total defence spending during the period will be Zl116bn (€35.1bn) including Zl25bn (€7.5bn) for procurement, which will increase its proportion of defence funding from 15% of the total budget in 2005 to 23% in 2010. In addition to the official defence budget, Poland is also in the process of procuring 48 F-16 aircraft from the US. Such is the scale of the procurement that the aircraft had to be purchased via a separate $3.5bn special 15-year loan provided under the US Foreign Military Financing (FMF) programme. The procurement package, which is accompanied by a significant offsets arrangement, covers the delivery of the aircraft, plus their associated air-launched weapons, precision-guided equipment, mission systems and a detailed support package. To accommodate the aircraft, a major upgrade of the Posnan-Krzesiny and Lask airbases is underway. Other significant investments to be completed by 2010 include: 446 *Patria* wheeled vehicles, 205 *Spike*-LR anti-tank missile launchers, a *Meko* A100 guided missile corvette as well as the upgrade of *Orkan* fast missile craft and transport helicopters.

In contrast to much of the rest of the continent, the **Spanish** economy enjoyed another positive year, recording real GDP growth of 2.7% and a budget deficit of just -0.3% of GDP. The government was able to increase defence expenditure (excluding military pensions and some investment) in 2005 to €6.99bn; however, this represents just 0.85% of GDP and as such is one of the lowest in NATO. The budget included a 3.6% boost to procurement spending, which rose to €1.77bn, and was followed later in the year by the go-ahead for four major new acquisitions with a combined total value of €2.5bn. The procurement package includes the purchase of a fifth *Alvaro de Bazan*-class F-100 frigate, four new-design offshore maritime intervention vessels, a new combat logistics vessel, an initial batch of 45 NH90 transport helicopters and short-range anti-tank guided missiles. In addition to this procurement package, Spain also confirmed its order for 33 Tranche 2 Eurofighter *Typhoons*.

Turkey continued to make good progress towards recovery following the economic crisis that struck in 2000–01, which had resulted in a $19bn loan package from the IMF. Under the terms of the agreement, the Turkish authorities have been obliged to follow a strict government expenditure programme designed to reduce the budget deficit to more manageable levels.

Table 14 **Major Italian Equipment Programmes 2004**	
Eurofighter	€ 451 m
NH90 helicopters	€ 310 m
Horizon frigate	€ 194m
Anfrea Doria	€ 177m
B767 Tankers	€ 137m
JSF	€ 107m
U212 submarines	€ 83m
AMX upgrade	€ 73m

As a result, defence expenditure in Turkey has fallen from around 5.0% to 3.4% of GDP and is on course to reach the government's declared target of 3% of GDP. The official defence budget in Turkey does not accurately reflect total resources devoted to national defence, as it excludes significant allocations made to the Gendarmerie, Coast Guard and at least $1bn that is made available to the Turkish Defence Industry (SSM) for major arms co-production projects. In 2005, following the first ever parliamentary debate about military spending (part of a drive to improve public scrutiny of overall government spending), the official defence budget increased by 9.6% to YTL (New Turkish Lira) 13.4bn. At a later stage, it is intended to further improve transparency by scrapping the separate SSM procurement budget and incorporating it into the official Ministry of National Defence budget. Given the new budget environment, the Turkish Armed Forces have revised their own long-term acquisition programmes. New priorities include:

- Four long-range regional air defence systems
- Four advanced air/missile defence systems
- Eight Improved HAWK medium-range air-defence units
- Upgrades to four *Ay*-class submarines
- 12 Sikorsky *Seahawk* anti-submarine helicopters
- Four air independent propulsion submarines
- 120 Joint Strike Fighters
- Three air-defence frigates
- Seven *MilGem* corvettes

In a separate development, the SSM reopened the multi-billion dollar attack helicopter tender in a request for proposals for the purchase of an initial 50 aircraft together with the option of a further 41. Turkey's major procurement deal during the year was the $1bn upgrade of over 200 F-16 aircraft, a much-reduced programme originally valued at close to $4bn but which had to be scaled back because of budget restrictions.

In a new initiative to improve Turkey's trade deficit, the government has announced a policy that will see R&D spending significantly increase in coming years, particularly in the defence sector, making the armed forces less dependent on imported weapons systems. The target is to increase total R&D spending (including defence) from its current level of one quarter of a percent of government spending, or 0.7% of GNP, to 2% of GNP by 2010.

Despite indicating an intention to boost defence expenditure to 1.8% of GDP in its 2003 Strategic Defence Review (SDR), economic problems forced the **Hungarian** government instead to cut the 2005 defence budget by 12%, closer to 1.3% of GDP. As a result, NATO's Defence Review panel issued a strongly critical report, concluding that Hungary has 'only limited ability to share in high intensity operations'. The budget cuts, which are unlikely to be reversed in the medium term, illustrate the problem that several other NATO member countries who are also planning to join the EU face: a requirement by the EU to maintain a budget deficit of no more than 3% of GDP while also meeting NATO's defence spending target of 2% of GDP. As a result of budget difficulties, the Hungarian MoD has announced further reductions and rationalisations within the department and its support organisations, together with the cancellation of certain equipment projects such as the upgrading of the Mi-24 attack helicopter fleet. Even before the cuts were announced, the SDR had recognised that Hungary would have insufficient resources to acquire all the equipment and capabilities that it would ideally require, and indicated that the armed forces would, in addition to becoming more readily deployable, concentrate on developing niche capabilities, including engineering, civil affairs, medical nuclear, biological and chemical defence and military police.

The **Canadian** government revealed a five-year boost to defence spending as well as plans to increase the number of active and reserve personnel. Additional defence funds will amount to C$12.8bn over the next five years, a larger increase than expected, while an extra 5,000 troops and 3,000 reserves will be brought into service during the period. For practical and operational reasons, most of the extra funds will be allocated between 2008 and 2010, and as such, the 2005 defence budget will only increase by C$500m to C$13.8bn. Following the announcement of the five-year spending boost, of which C$2.8bn is earmarked for procurement, the Department of National Defence (DND) published its plans for the acquisition of military equipment. Priorities, which have not yet been detailed include: a new fixed-wing search and rescue aircraft to replace the Canadian air force's seven de Havilland *Buffalo* and some of its CC-130 transports; GPS-guided air-to-ground weapons for the air force's fleet of F-18A/B fighters; acquisition of UAVs and satellites; the conversion of two Airbus aircraft into tankers; acquisition of medium- to heavy-lift helicopters and modernisation of combat systems on board *Halifax*-class frigates.

Late in 2004, before the announcement of the budget boost, the DND concluded a C$5bn deal with

Sikorsky for the purchase of 28 H-92 medium-lift helicopters as its new maritime aircraft. However, the deal may still face a legal challenge by AugustaWestland, which is querying the selection process that saw its EH101 lose out in the competition.

NON-NATO EUROPE – DEFENCE ECONOMICS

The 2005 defence budget in **Switzerland** continued the steady decline that has seen it fall from around 2% of GDP to just 1% of GDP in 2004. In 2005, defence expenditure will fall to Sfr4.70bn from Sfr4.86bn in 2004. As a consequence of the falling budget, the Ministry of Defence announced the first wave of sweeping cuts affecting both the army and air force, which will see a total of 2,500 military posts disappear by 2010. The army lost over 500 positions in 2004 and a further 1,100 will be lost during 2005. Reductions in air force personnel will not come into effect for a couple of years. Under the Army XXI reform plan, approved in a national referendum in 2003, Switzerland's militia army will be reduced from 350,000 to 220,000 and obligatory military service will be reduced from 300 to 260 days. Under the first wave of cuts 18 logistics bases and four airbases will be closed. The Ministry has indicated that expects to save Sfr240m a year as a result of these measures.

Despite a pick up in economic activity that saw GDP grow by 3.5% in 2004, **Sweden** pressed ahead with plans to reduce defence spending by around 10% over the next three years and reallocate the money towards domestic security requirements. The 2005 defence budget (excluding civil defence and provisions for accidents and emergencies) is set at Skr39.5bn, down from Skr40.1bn in 2004, but under the new Swedish Defence Policy 2005–07, the budget will be cut by a further SEK3bn by 2007. The new policy states that the potential threat facing Sweden has changed and that with the risk of an armed military attack on Sweden diminishing, a comprehensive restructuring of the armed forces is necessary. The first impact of the budget cuts will be the reduction of 500 officers and 1,500 civilians from the payroll, a halt in recruitment and a scaling-back of international exercises. Conscription will be retained, but there will be an increased emphasis on volunteers with additional short-term contracts offered to trained personnel willing to deploy on international operations. The defence bill outlines five strategic niches upon which Sweden will focus – aerospace, armoured vehicles, network-centric capabilities, robust communications and short-range systems – but contains no reference to naval innovations, which have formed a significant element of Swedish expenditure in recent years, raising the possibility that future naval programmes

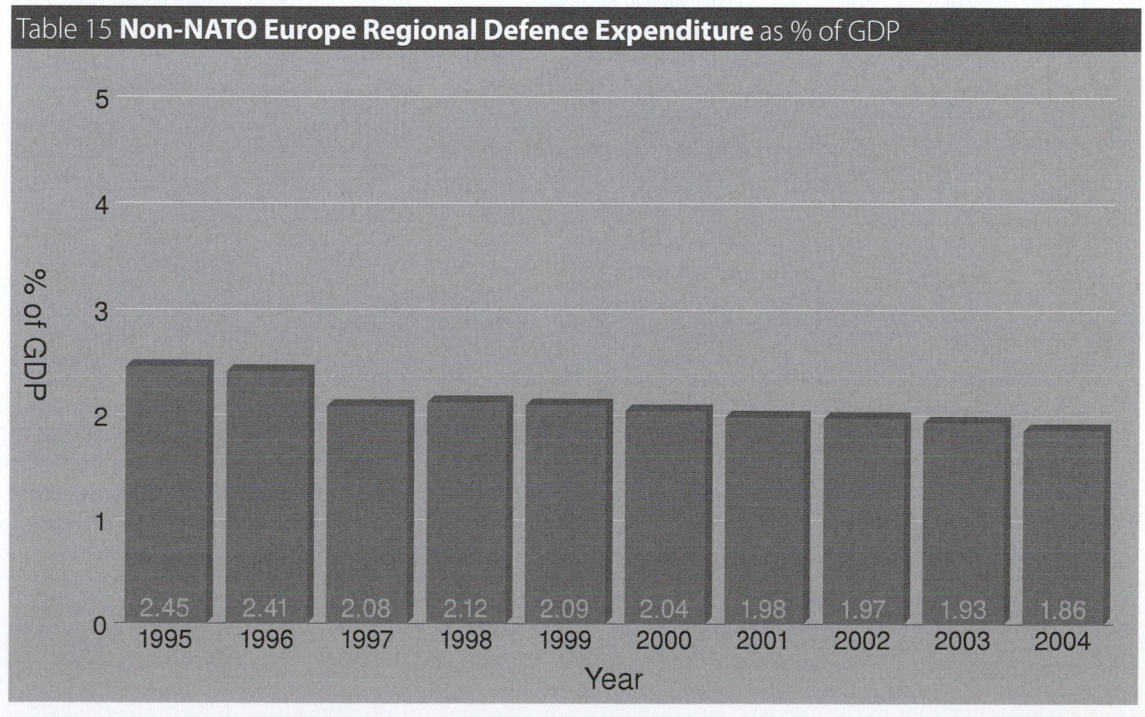

Table 15 **Non-NATO Europe Regional Defence Expenditure** as % of GDP

Year	% of GDP
1995	2.45
1996	2.41
1997	2.08
1998	2.12
1999	2.09
2000	2.04
2001	1.98
2002	1.97
2003	1.93
2004	1.86

may be under threat. The air force is likely to suffer a cut in the number of *Gripen* JAS-39 aircraft that it will acquire.

Finland announced a 3.4% increase in its defence budget to €2,140m, including €572m for the procurement of equipment. The Finnish government has announced plans to reduce the numbers in the armed forces and alter their orientation away from territorial defence towards creating a highly mobile well-equipped force that can be rapidly deployed to meet specific crises. By 2012, 1,200 jobs are to be eliminated mainly by retirements and natural wastage. This will be partly achieved by disbanding the Helsinki Air Defence Regiment, the Savo Brigade and the Turku Coastal Artillery Battalion, and moving the army's headquarters to the north of the country. Admiral Juhani Kaskeala, the Commander of the Finnish Defence Forces, has warned that the armed forces are drifting into a financial crisis that will be exacerbated by planned cuts of some €100m over the next two years.

Ukraine enjoyed another year of strong economic activity that boosted GDP by 12.1% in 2004. The economy was driven primarily by external factors, most notably booming metals prices and strong demand from China and Russia. Although growth should moderate in 2005, as measures to suppress economic overheating are implemented, it will likely remain strong. Improvements in economic activity were not matched by developments in the government's finances, which slipped into the red, recording a budget deficit of -4.6% in 2004. As a result of tight government finances, the defence budget in 2005 was increased by just 2.6%, significantly less than the rate of inflation that reached 9% in 2004. Following his election victory in December 2004, President Victor Yushchenko declared that he wanted the Ukraine to be 'integrated into both the EU and NATO' and called for military reforms to enable that process, leading to all-professional armed forces by 2010. Earlier in the year Lt Gen. Ivan Marko, chief of the Ukrainian Defence Ministry's financial and economic division, indicated that the minimal funding for the armed forces would be around h7.05bn compared to the 2005 allocation of h5.53bn.

Table 16 Arms orders and deliveries, NATO Europe

	Country Supplier	Classification	Designation	Quantity	Order date	Delivery date	Comment
Belgium (Be)	US	FGA	F-16 (*Fighting Falcon*)	110	1993	1998	Mid-life update. 88 AMRAAM on order
	Il	UAV	B-*Hunter* systems	18	1998	2000	
	US	FGA	F-16 (*Fighting Falcon*)	18	1999	2000	Upgrade; option on 18 exercised
	Br	trg	*Alpha Jet*	4	2000	2001	
	Int'l	tpt	A-400M	7	2003	2009	
	Ge	tpt	Truck	220	2005	2005	($222m)
Bulgaria (Bg)	US	hel	Bell 206 (*JetRanger*)	6	1998	2002	2 delivered
	RF	trg*	MiG-29UB (*Fulcrum*)	21	2001	2004	Upgrade
	It	trg	C-27J (*Spartan*)	8	2005	2006	($257.7m)
Czech Republic (Cz)	dom	trg	L-39 (*Albatros*)	27	1997	1999	Originally for Nga; delivery to Cz airforce delayed
	dom	FGA	L-159 (*Albatros*)	72	1997	2000	Completes 2003
	Hu	UAV	*Sojka 3*	8	1998	2000	Upgraded *Sojka III*. Dev with Hu
	dom	MBT	T-72CZ M4	30	2002	2006	To be upgraded to T-72CZ M4 standard
	RF	atk hel	Mi-24 (*Hind*)	7	2002	2006	Part of debt payment
	RF	tpt	An-70 (*Antanov*)	3	2002	2006	Part of debt payment
	RF	atk hel	Mi-24V (*Hind E*)	10	2004		Part of debt repayment. Likely to replace the current fleet of older aircraft.

Table 16 **Arms orders and deliveries, NATO Europe**

Country Supplier	Classification	Designation	Quantity	Order date	Delivery date	Comment
RF	hel	Mi-171S	16	2004	2005	Part of gov to gov debt repayment. M-171S has improvements on Mi-17: airborne operable rear ramp and redesigned doors, winch and night vision capability. Endurance of 6hrs triple that of M-17. Likely to replace all Czech Republic's Mi-17 fleet.
Swe	FGA	*Gripen*	14	2004	2005	10 year lease
Denmark (Da) Ca	tpt	CL-604 (*Challenger*)	3	1998		
UK	hel	*Super Lynx*	8	1998	2000	Upgrade to *Super Lynx* standard
US	PGM	JDAM	400	2000	2000	Deliveries to 2004
US	tpt	C-130J (*Hercules*)	3	2000	2003	Option on 4th
dom	AG	Stanflex S3	2	2000	2006	
UK	hel	EH-101 (*Merlin*)	14	2001	2004	
Estonia (Ea) US	hel	R-44	4	2000	2000	
France (Fr) dom	FFG	Frigates	8-17			($5bn) Multi mission frigates. target price $341m each ISD 2010
dom	FGA	*Rafale*	234	1984	1999	ISD 2005
Ge	hel	AS-665 (*Tiger*)	215	1984	2003	With Ge; 1st batch of 60 ordered 1999
dom	MBT	*Leclerc*	406	1985	1992	370 delivered by 2003
Ge	ASSM	ANNG		1985	2005	In dev with Ge
dom	SSBN	*Le Triomphant* (S 616)	3	1986	1997	Deliveries to 2004; 4th order 2000 for 2010
Ge	Radar	*Cobra*	10	1986	2002	Counter-bty radar; dev with UK, Ge. Delivery began 2004
It	hel	NH-90	160	1987	2003	With Ge, It, Nl; prod orders delayed.
Ge	ATGW	*Trigat*		1988	2004	With Ge
Por	tpt	A-400M	52	1989	2009	
dom	hel	EC-120 (*Colibri*)	5	1990	1996	Deliveries to 2003
UK	SAM	FSAF (Future surface-to-air-family)		1990	2006	Future surface-to-air-family; with It, UK
dom	FGA	M-2000D (*Mirage*)	86	1991	1994	Deliveries to 2000
Ge	torp	MU-90	150	1991	2000	With It and Ge. Deliveries 2000-02
dom	FGA	M-2000-5F (*Mirage*)	37	1993	1998	*Mirage* 2000-C upgrade, deliveries to 2002
UK	ALCM	SCALP	600	1994	2000	2 orders for delivery over 11 years
dom	sat	*Helios*-2a	1	1994	2004	Dev with Ge
Ge	hel	AS-532 (*Cougar*)	4	1995	1999	Combat SAR, requirement for 6
dom	SAM	*Mistral*	1130	1996	2008	Deliveries to 2002
dom	SLBM	M51		1996	2008	To replace M-45; dev continues
dom	recce	*Falcon 50*	4	1997	1998	Deliveries to 2000

Table 16 Arms orders and deliveries, NATO Europe

Country Supplier	Classification	Designation	Quantity	Order date	Delivery date	Comment
UK	ASM	*Vesta*		1997	2005	In dev
UK	AAM	MICA	225	1998	1999	Further 1,537 to be delivered from2004
UK	sat	*Skynet 5*	4	1998	2005	Comms; dev in 1998 with Ge, UK
dom	APC	VBCI	65	1998	2006	Up to 700 req
dom	SSN	SSN	6	1998	2012	Design studies approved Oct 1998
dom	AIFV	AMX-10P	300	1999	2001	Upgrade continues. First deliveries 2008/2009
It	FFG	mod *Horizon*	2	1999	2007	Joint It/Fr project
dom	MHC	*Eridan*	13	2000		Upgrade
dom	MBT	*Leclerc*	38	2000	2002	Upgrade to Mk2 standard continues
dom	sat	*Syracuse 3*	3	2000	2003	Comms
dom	LHD	*Mistral*	2	2000	2006	
Il	UAV	*Eagle*		2001	2009	
dom	FFG	FFG	17	2002	2008	First 4 ordered
Int'l	tpt	A-400M	50	2003	2009	
Germany (Ge) dom	hel	AS-665 (*Tiger*)	80	1984	2003	Reduced from 212
UK	FGA	*Typhoon*	180	1985	2004	Tranche 1 order 44
dom	SP arty	PzH 2000	185	1986	1998	Req 594 units; 165 delivered by 2003
dom	ATGW	*Trigat*		1988	2004	Confirmed in 2004
Nl	recce	*Fennek*	164	1994	2000	Joint dev with Nl. Prod in 2000
dom	sat	*Helios*-2a	1	1994	2001	Dev with Fr, It
dom	SSK	Type 212a	4	1994	2004	Deliveries to 2006
Fr	sat	*Horus*	1	1994	2005	Dev with Fr
UK	hel	*Lynx*	7	1996	1999	
dom	FFG	Type F 124	3	1996	2004	Deliveries 2002-05
dom	hel	EC-135	15	1997	1998	For *Tiger* hel trg. Del start mid-1998
dom	hel	AS-365 (*Dauphin 2*)	13	1997	1998	Delivery 1998-2001
Ca	AAM	IRIS-T		1997	2003	Dev with It, Swe, Gr, Ca, No
UK	sat	*Skynet 5*	4	1997	2005	With UK, Fr
UK	APC	*Boxer*	200	1998		UK withdrew. No order yet
US	SAM	PAC-3 (*Patriot*)	12	1998		Being delivered 2004
US	SAM	PAC-3 (*Patriot*)	7	1998		Upgrade to PAC-3 configuration
It	torp	MU-90	600	1998	2000	
UK	hel	*Super Lynx*	17	1998	2000	Upgrade to *Super Lynx* standard
Swe	ASM	KEPD 350 (*Taurus*)	600	1998	2004	Dev with Swe (KEPD-350)
dom	AG	Type 751	1	1999	2002	Defence research and test ship
dom	FFG	Type F 125	10	1999	2010	Feasibility study stage
dom	MBT	2A5	225	2000	2001	Upgrade to 2A6 continues
dom	MRTT	A-310	4	2001	2004	

Table 16 Arms orders and deliveries, NATO Europe

Country Supplier	Classification	Designation	Quantity	Order date	Delivery date	Comment
dom	FSG	Type 130k	5	2001	2007	Deliveries to 2008
Swe	AFV	Bv-206	31	2002	2002	Deliveries to be complete in 2004
Nl	recce	*Fennek*	206	2002	2003	Complete by 2007
Por	tpt	A-400M	60	2003	2009	
dom	AFV	*Mungo*	388	2004		4x4 Lt inf veh rapid reaction units
Nl	hel	NH-90	160	2004		
dom	AFV	APCV-2 (*Dingo*)	130	2004		Poss total of 1,300
dom	APC	*Duro*	100	2004		
Nl	MPA	P-3C (*Orion*)	8	2004		
dom	LAV	*Wiesel 2*	32	2004	2005	Option on further 16
dom	APC	*Puma*	410	2004	2006	First production batch in 2006
Fr	C2	Communications		2005	2008	($1.2bn) Military, global secure satcoms. awaiting parliamentary approval 2005.
Greece (Gr) US	hel	CH-47D (*Chinook*)	7	1995	2001	In addition to 9 in inventory
US	FGA	F-4 (*Phantom II*)	38	1996	1999	Upgrade in Ge; deliveries to 2000
US	trg	T-6A (*Texan II*)	45	1998	2000	Deliveries complete 2003
UK	MCMV	*Hunt*	2	1998	2000	
US	SAM	PAC-3 (*Patriot*)	5	1998	2001	5 batteries, option for 1 more
Br	AEW	ERJ-145	4	1998	2002	Interim lease from Swe of Saab 350 *Argus*
Ge	SSK	Type 214	3	1998	2005	Deliveries to 2008
Fr	SAM	*Crotale* NG	11	1999	2001	9 for air force; 2 for navy
Fr	hel	AS-532 (*Cougar*)	4	1999	2002	Option on further 2
Fr	FGA	M-2000-5 (*Mirage*)	15	1999	2003	Option on 3 more
It	AK	*Etna*	1	1999	2003	
US	FGA	F-16C (*Fighting Falcon*)	60	1999	2004	
Fr	FGA	M-2000 (*Mirage*)	10	1999	2004	Upgrade 10 of existing 35
US	AAM	AIM-120 (AMRAAM)	560	2000		
Fr	AAM	MICA	200	2000		Additional 100 ordered in 2004
Fr	ALCM	SCALP	56	2000		Additional 36 ordered in 2004
US	hel	S-70B (*Seahawk*)	8	2000		Upgrade including *Penguin* AAM
US	recce	C-12 (*Huron*)	2	2000		Option on further 2
RF	SAM	SA-15 (*Gauntlet*)	29	2000	2001	Aka Tor-M1; Additional 29. Original order for 21 units completed.
Fr	ASSM	MM-40 (*Exocet*)	27	2000	2001	Deliveries to 2004
RF	LCAC	*Pomornik* (*Zubr*)	4	2000	2001	Final delivery 2001
Ge	SP arty	PzH 2000	24	2000	2003	Deliveries to 2004
dom	PCO	PCO	4	2000	2003	
dom	PFM	*Super Vita*	3	2000	2003	Option on further 4

Table 16 **Arms orders and deliveries, NATO Europe**

	Country Supplier	Classification	Designation	Quantity	Order date	Delivery date	Comment
	dom	AO	AO	1	2000	2003	
	RF	ATGW	AT-14 (*Kornet*)	278	2001		Two phase purchase
	Ge	MBT	Leopard 2A5	170	2002		
	Fr	FFG	*Kortenaer*	6	2002		Upgrade
	It	tpt	C-27J (*Spartan*)	12	2002	2004	
	Nl	hel	NH-90	20	2002	2005	
	dom	PFM	*Super Vita*	2	2003		follow on to 2000 order
	Nl	FFG	*Kortenaer*	1	2003	2004	The 9th *Kortenaer* transferred
	Ge	IFV	*Kentaurus*	150	2003	2005	Option on further 130
	Nl	hel	NH-90	20	2003	2005	Option on further 14
	US	atk hel	AH-64D (*Apache*)	12	2003	2007	
		FGA	F-16C Block 50	30	2005	2009	
Hungary (Hu)	RF	FGA	MiG-29 (*Fulcrum*)	14	2001		Upgrade
	Swe	FGA	*Gripen*	14	2003	2006	Leased for 12 years
Italy (It)	UK	FGA	*Typhoon*	121	1985	2003	Tranche 1 order 29
	Nl	hel	NH-90	117	1987	2003	With Fr, Ge, Nl; prod order delayed
	Int'l	tpt	A-400M	44	1989	2009	With Fr, Ge, Sp, Be, Por, Tu, UK
	UK	SAM	FSAF (Future surface-to-air-family)		1990	2006	Future surface-to-air-family, with Fr, UK
	dom	PCO	*Esploratore*	4	1993	1997	Deliveries to 2004
	UK	hel	EH-101 (*Merlin*)	16	1993	1999	With UK; 4 more ordered in 2002 for amph spt
	dom	CV	*Conte di Cavout*	1	1996	2007	
	US	tpt	C-130J (*Hercules*)	22	1997	2000	Options on further 2
	Ge	SSK	Type 212a	2	1997	2005	Licence-built in It; options for 2 more
	dom	AIFV	VCC-80 (*Dardo*)	200	1998	2000	First ordered 1998; aka *Dardo*. Delivery to be complete end 2004
	dom	AGI	AGI (*Int Vsl*)	2	1998	2000	1 only
	dom	hel	A-129I (*Mangusta*)	15	1998	2001	New multi-role configuration
	dom	tpt	C-27J (*Spartan*)	12	1999	2001	
	dom	PCO	*Aliscarfi*	4	1999	2001	1st batch of 4; 2nd expected after2003
	dom	LPD	*San Giorgio*	2	1999	2001	Upgrade to carry 4 hel
	dom	APC	*Puma*	540	1999	2003	Deliveries continue.
	Ge	SP arty	PzH 2000	70	1999	2004	Joint production
	Fr	FFG	mod *Horizon*	2	1999	2007	Joint It/Fr project
	US	SAM	*Standard* SM-2	50	2000		
	dom	hel	A-129 (*Mangusta*)	45	2000		Upgrade to A-129I standard
	Sp	AAM	*Meteor*	400	2001		
	US	tkr	B-767	4	2001		Option on further 2
	US	UAV	*Predator*	6	2001	2002	
	US	FGA	F-16 (*Fighting Falcon*)	34	2001	2003	7-year lease
	dom	FFG	FFG	10	2002	2008	

Table 16 Arms orders and deliveries, NATO Europe

	Country Supplier	Classification	Designation	Quantity	Order date	Delivery date	Comment
	dom	trg	SF-260EA	30	2003		
	UK	APC	Bv-206	146	2003	2004	Possible further 43
Latvia (Lat)	Ge	MSC	*Lindau*	1	1999	1999	Free transfer
Lithuania (L)	US	ATGW	*Javelin*	10	2001	2004	Delivered
Luxembourg (Lu)	Int'l	trg	A-400M	1	2003	2009	
Netherlands (Nl)	It	hel	NH-90	20	1987	2003	With Fr, Ge, It
	US	FGA	F-16 (*Fighting Falcon*)	136	1993	1997	Update programme continues to 2001
	dom	LPD	*Rotterdam*	2	1993	1998	Second due to be delivered 2007
	US	atk hel	AH-64D (*Apache*)	30	1995	1998	4 delivered 1998
	dom	FFG	*Zeven Provincien*	4	1995	2003	2 ordered 1995; 2 more ordered 1997
	US	MPA	P-3C (*Orion*)	7	1999	2001	Upgrade
	Ge	SP arty	PzH 2000	60	2000	2004	Delivery 2004 to 2009
	dom	APC	*Boxer*	200	2000	2006	Joint Programme
	Ge	MBT	*Leopard* 2A5	180	2001		Upgrade to 2A6 continues
	Il	ATGW	*Gil/Spike*	300	2001	2002	Being delivered
	dom	recce	*Fennek*	410	2002	2003	Completed by 2007
	US	tpt	KDC-10	2	2004	2004	
	UK	C2	Comd and control	1405	2005	2005	($121m) *Bowman* digital communications for Royal Netherlands Marines. Pending Parliamentary approval
	Swe	APC	BvS-10 (*Viking*)	74	2005	2006	($76.6m) for Royal Netherlands Marines fitted with *Bowman* digital communications.
	US	SAM	PAC-3 (*Patriot*)	32	2005	2006	Part of 136 msls ($532m lot 6) procured for US Army allocated for foreign sales.
Norway (No)	US	AAM	AIM-120 (AMRAAM)	500	1993	1995	84 delivered 1998; del to 2000
	US	FGA	F-16A (*Fighting Falcon*)	58	1993	1997	Mid-life update prog to 2001
	Sp	FFG	*Fridtjof Nansen*	5	2000	2005	
	Nl	hel	NH-90	14	2001	2004	
	US	ATGW	*Javelin*	90	2003	2006	incl. 526 missiles
Poland (Pl)	Il	ATGW	NT-D (*Dandy*)		1997		For W-3 *Huzar* attack helicopters.
	UK	SP arty	AS-90 (*Braveheart*)	80	1999		Licence to produce turret system. Not yet in quantity production
	US	hel	SH-2G (*Super Seasprite*)	2	1999	2000	2 more due 2001
	Ge	FGA	MiG-29 (*Fulcrum*)	22	1999	2002	Upgrade
	Il	FGA	Su-17 (*Fitter*)	20	2000	2003	Upgrade
	No	SSK	*Kobben*	4	2001	2002	2 in 2002, 1 in 2004, + 1 for spares
	RF	atk hel	Mi-24 (*Hind*)	40	2001	2003	To be completed by 2006
	Indo	tpt	CASA C-295M	8	2001	2003	

Table 16 Arms orders and deliveries, NATO Europe

Country Supplier	Classification	Designation	Quantity	Order date	Delivery date	Comment
Ge	FGA	MiG-29 (*Fulcrum*)	23	2002	2004	Second-hand
US	FGA	F-16 (*Fighting Falcon*)	48	2002	2006	Licence
Fr	ATGW	*Spike*-LR	264	2003		To be built in Poland under license
SF	APC	*Patria* AMV	690	2003	2004	Deliveries between 2004-13. 1st nine accepted into service Jan 2005 ($21m) 2005 budget allocates $200m for 89 more vehicles.
US	tpt	C-130K (*Hercules*)	5	2004	2006	ex-UK RAF
Portugal (Por) Sp	hel	EC-635	9	2000	2001	Cancelled
US	FGA	F-16 (*Fighting Falcon*)	20	2000	2003	Upgrade
UK	hel	EH-101 (*Merlin*)	12	2001	2004	
Romania (R) dom	trg	IAR-99 (*Soim*)	33	1998	2000	6 delivered 2000
dom	FGA	MiG-29 (*Fulcrum*)	18	2001	2003	Upgrade
UK	FFG	*Cornwall*	2	2002		Second-hand
Slovakia (Slvk) RF	FGA	MiG-29 (*Fulcrum*)	12	2004		
Slovenia (Slvn) Ge	hel	AS-532 (*Cougar*)	2	2001	2003	
Spain (Sp) dom	MHC	*Segura*	4	1989	1999	Deliveries to 2000
dom	FFG	*Alvaro de Bazan*	4	1992	2002	Deliveries to 2006
UK	FGA	*Typhoon*	87	1994	2003	Tranche 1 order 20
Fr	hel	AS-532 (*Cougar*)	18	1995	1996	1st delivery 1996. Deliveries to 2003
It	SAM	*Spada* 2000	2	1996	1998	First of 2 batteries delivered
dom	arty	SBT-1		1997	2000	Dev
dom	MPA	P-3 (*Orion*)	7	1997	2002	Upgrade
Ge	MBT	*Leopard* 2	235	1998		Built in Sp. Includes 16 ARVs. Production from 2004
US	ATGW	*Javelin*	12	1999		
Swe	APC	Bv-206	10	2000		Total requirement of 50
dom	tpt	CASA C-295	9	2000		To be delivered by 2004
Fr	trg	EC-120B (*Colibri*)	12	2000	2000	Deliveries Jul 2000-Jul 2001
Sgp	trg	EC-120B (*Colibri*)	15	2000	2001	Training
No	SAM	NASAMS	4	2000	2002	
US	hel	SH-60B (*Seahawk*)	6	2000	2004	Also upgrade of existing 6
dom	MPA	P-3B (*Orion*)	5	2001	2003	Upgrade
dom	SSK	S-80	4	2003		
dom	LP	LP (*Landing Platform*)	1	2003		Multipurpose platform
dom	AIFV	*Pizarro*	212	2003	2005	Follow on order from 1996
Ge	hel	AS-665 (*Tiger*)	24	2003	2007	
Int'l	tpt	A-400M	27	2003	2009	
dom	AOR	AOR	1	2005	2008	($210m) similar to *Patiño* class

Table 16 **Arms orders and deliveries, NATO Europe**

	Country Supplier	Classification	Designation	Quantity	Order date	Delivery date	Comment
Turkey (Tu)	US	FGA	F-16 (*Fighting Falcon*)	80			($1.1bn) Upgrade of 70 block 50s and 4 Block 40ac. original deal included purchase of 295 *Sidewinder* (AIM-9X). Offset commitments are included.
	Ge	SSK	Type 209/1400	8	1987	1987	Delivery of first 5 to 2003
	Sp	tpt	CN-235	43	1990	1992	41 delivered by 1998
	Ge	PCM	*Kilic*	3	1993	1998	1st built Ge; 2nd and 3rd Tu; to 1999
	Il	FGA	F-4 (*Phantom II*)	54	1996	1999	Upgrade; deliveries to 2002
	Fr	hel	AS-532 (*Cougar*)	30	1996	2000	To be completed by 2003
	dom	APC	RN-94	5	1997		Dev complete. No production order yet placed
	Il	AGM	*Popeye* I	50	1997	1999	For use with upgraded F-4 ac
	US	AAM	AIM-120B (AMRAAM)	138	1997	2000	
	Sp	MPA	CASA 235 MPA	52	1997	2000	
	US	hel	SH-60B (*Seahawk*)	14	1997	2000	
	Il	FGA	F-5 (*Tiger*)	48	1998	2001	IAI awarded contract to upgrade 48 Tu F-5
	It	hel	Bell 412 (*Twin Huey*)	5	1998	2001	
	US	hel	CH-53E (*Sea Stallion*)	8	1998	2003	
	UK	SAM	*Rapier* Mk 2	840	1999	2000	Licence; 80 a year for 10 years
	US	FGA	F-16 (*Fighting Falcon*)	32	1999	2002	Licence; following orders of 240 in 2 batches
	US	hel	S-70B (*Seahawk*)	8	2000		Heavy lift
	US	radar	*Sentinel* RMK1	7	2000		Including HAWK missiles
	US	AEW	AEW	6	2000		
	US	APC	M-113	551	2000	2001	Deliveries to 2004
	Ge	tpt	B-737	6	2000	2003	1st to be built in Ge, 5 in Tu. Last delivery 2007
	Ge	SSK	Type 214	4	2000	2006	
	US	SAM	FIM-92A (*Stinger*)	146	2001		
	ROK	SP arty	K-9 (*Thunder*)	20	2001		300 required
	RF	hel	Ka-62	5	2001	2002	
	Il	MBT	M-60A1	170	2002		Upgraded by Il. First delivery in 2006
	Int't	tpt	A-400M	10	2003	2009	
	US	hel	SH-60B (*Seahawk*)	12	2005	2005	($389m) Naval order, $200m offset from Sikorsky
United Kingdom (UK)	US	SLCM	SLCM (*Tomahawk*)	64		2004	Block IV
	US	EW	*Soothsayer*			2006	($237m) battlefield electronic warfare system. First increment ($130m) delayed to 2008
	It	hel	EH-101 (*Merlin*)	44	1979	1999	With It; for RN; aka *Merlin* HM Mk 1

Table 16 Arms orders and deliveries, NATO Europe

Country Supplier	Classification	Designation	Quantity	Order date	Delivery date	Comment
dom	FGA	*Typhoon*	232	1984	2003	Tranche 1 order 55
dom	SSN	*Trafalgar*	7	1988	2000	Upgrade to carry TLAM
dom	SSN	*Astute*	3	1991	2006	Deliveries to 2008, 3 more may be ordered
dom	sat	*Skynet 5*	4	1993	2005	With Fr and Ge
dom	FGA	GR4 (*Tornado*)	142	1994	1998	Upgrade; deliveries to 2003
US	tpt	C-130J (*Hercules*)	25	1994	1999	Option for 20 more
dom	SAM	PAAMS		1994	2003	Dev with Fr, It. Part of FSAF prog
US	atk hel	WAH-64D (*Apache Longbow*)	67	1996	2000	Deliveries continue
dom	AGM	*Brimstone*		1996	2001	1st 12 to be delivered 2001
dom	ALCM	SCALP EG (*Storm Shadow*)	900	1996	2003	
dom	MPA	*Nimrod* MRA4	12	1996	2005	Reduced from 21
Ca	recce	*Sentinel* RMK1 (*ASTOR*)	5	1997	2004	
Ge	trg	Grob 115D (*Heron*)	85	1998	2000	
US	SLCM	SLCM (*Tomahawk*)	30	1999	2002	
dom	AAM	*Meteor*		2000		To provide BVRAAM capability
US	tpt	C-17 (*Globemaster*)	4	2000	2001	Originally leased before purchase
dom	AGHS	*Echo*	2	2000	2002	Deliveries 2002 and 2003
dom	ALSL	*Bay*	4	2000	2003	Alternate landing ship logistics
dom	AKR	T-AKR	6	2000	2004	
dom	UAV	*Watchkeeper*	21	2000	2006	Mid-life upgrade programme
dom	ro-ro	FSTA	6	2000	2009	
US	SLCM	SLCM (*Tomahawk*)	48	2001	2001	Block IIIC
Swe	APC	BvS-10 (*Viking*)	108	2001	2003	($100m) 24 delivered by 2004. Order completed by Sep 2005
dom	DDG	Type 45	6	2001	2005	2 further to be ordered
dom	CET	*Terrier*	60	2002	2008	20 vehs to be delivered by late 2008.
dom	trg	*Hawk* Mk 128	20	2003	2003	Option on further 24
dom	FCLV	*Alvis* MLV	486	2003	2006	In development phase
dom	FCLV	*Panther* FCLV	401	2003	2006	*Panther* is to fill a number of task, command at tp/pl level, recce, liaison and comms rebroadcast. £166m contract to BAE. 326 vehs to fitted with remote weapon station (AEI Enforcer). Additional option for futher 400 vehs.
US	ATGW	*Javelin*	300	2003	2006	Up to 5,000 missiles
US	PGM	*Paveway* IV	2000	2003	2007	

Table 16 Arms orders and deliveries, NATO Europe

Country Supplier	Classification	Designation	Quantity	Order date	Delivery date	Comment
Int'l	tpt	A-400M	25	2003	2009	
Ge	tpt	A-330	16	2004		27-year PFI
US	tpt	C-17 (*Globemaster*)	1	2004		
Ge	tpt	Truck	4,851	2005	2007	($1.9bn) MAN ERF Final delivery 2013.
dom	hel	*Sea King* AEW MK7	4	2005	2007	($56m) 2 ac are to be converted from ASW role, 2 being to built to replace Gulf War losses
dom	atk hel	WAH-64 (*Apache Longbow*)		2005	2009	($354m) *Apache* upgrade of sighting and targeting system, completion planned for 2010.

Table 17 Arms orders and deliveries, Non-NATO Europe

	Country Supplier	Classification	Designation	Quantity	Order date	Delivery date	Comment
Armenia (Arm)	Slvk	FGA	Su-25 (*Frogfoot*)	10	2004		
	RF	tpt	Il-76 (*Candid*)	2	2004		
Austria (A)	dom	APC	*Ulan*	112	1999	2002	Delivery to 2004. aka ASCOD
	US	hel	S-70A (*Black Hawk*)	9	2000	2001	Option for 3 more
	UK	tpt	C-130K (*Hercules*)	3	2002	2003	
	UK	FGA	*Typhoon*	18	2003	2009	
	CH	FGA	F-5E (*Tiger II*)	12	2004	2004	Leased until *Typhoon* delivery
Belarus (Bel)	RF	SAM	SA-10 (*Grumble* (quad))		2003		
Croatia (Cr)	dom	MBT	M-95 (*Degman*)		1995	2001	Trials. Expected to enter production soon
	dom	PCI	*Kralj Petar*	2	1996	2002	
	RF	FGA	MiG-21bis (*Fishbed L & N*)	28	1999		Upgrade
	US	FGA	F-16 (*Fighting Falcon*)	18	1999	2001	Ex-US inventory
Cyprus (Cy)	RF	hel	Mi-35 (*Hind*)	12	2002	2003	
Finland (SF)	US	FGA	F/A-18C (*Hornet*)	64	1992	1995	Delivered by 2000. 57 made in SF
	dom	PFM	*Hamina*	3	1997	1998	Delivery to 2005
	dom	AIFV	CV9030	57	1998	2002	Being delivered
	Il	UAV	ADS 95 (*Ranger*)	3	1999	2001	9 ac and 6 ground stations
	US	ATGW	*Javelin*	242	2000		3,190 msl
	dom	ATGW	*Spike*	100	2000	2001	Option on further 70. Being delivered
	Nl	hel	NH-90	20	2001	2004	
	dom	AMV	*Patria* AMV	100	2003	2005	
	dom	AIFV	CV9030	45	2004	2006	
Ireland (Irl)	UK	PCO	*Roisin*	2	1997	1999	2nd delivered 2001

Table 17 Arms orders and deliveries, Non-NATO Europe

Country Supplier	Classification	Designation	Quantity	Order date	Delivery date	Comment
US	hel	S-92 (*Superhawk*)	3	2001	2003	option on further 2
CH	trg	Pilatus PC-9M	8	2003	2004	
Macedonia, Former Yugoslav Republic (FYROM) Tu	FGA	F-5A (*Freedom Fighter*)	20	1998	1999	Free transfer
Ukr	hel	Mi-24 (*Hind*)	10	2001	2001	
Ukr	hel	Mi-8MTV (*Hip H*)	8	2001	2001	
Ukr	FGA	Su-25 (*Frogfoot*)	4	2001	2001	
Sweden (Swe) dom	FGA	JAS 39 (*Gripen*)	204	1981	1995	Deliveries to 2007; 112 del to date
dom	AIFV	CV90	600	1984	1993	To 2004. Extra 40 ordered 2001
dom	MCM	*Styrso*	4	1994	1996	Deliveries to 1998
US	AAM	AIM-120 (AMRAAM)	110	1994	1998	Option for a further 700
dom	FSG	*Visby*	5	1995	2001	Deliveries to 2007
Ge	AAM	IRIS-T		1997	2003	Dev with Ge
dom	ASM	KEPD 350 (*Taurus*)		1997	2003	Dev with Ge to 2002. Also KEPD 150
Fr	hel	AS-532 (*Cougar*)	12	1998	2001	Deliveries 2002
SF	APC	XA-203 (*Sisu*)	104	2000	2001	
dom	APC	Bv-206	15	2001		
It	hel	A-109	20	2001	2002	
Switzerland (CH) Fr	hel	AS-532 (*Cougar*)	12	1997	2000	Deliveries to 2002
US	AD	*Florako*	1	1999	2007	Upgrade
UK	AIFV	CV90	186	2000	2002	Deliveries to run to 2005
Sp	tpt	CASA C-295	2	2000	2003	
US	AAM	AIM-9X (*Sidewinder*)	200	2002	2003	
Ge	ARV	*Buffel*	25	2002	2004	
RF	FGA	Su-25 (*Frogfoot*)			2001	Upgrade
RF	tpt	An-70	5	1991	2003	Up to 65 req
RF	FGA	Su-24 (*Fencer*)	4	1996	2000	Final 2 delivered 2000

Chapter Three
Russia

REFORM

Russia's armed forces have continued to undergo much-needed reform and modernisation. While President Vladimir Putin's administrative reforms introduced new institutional challenges to the management of security, most of the so-called 'power' ministries (the Ministry of Defence [MoD], the Interior Ministry, the Federal Security Service, the External Intelligence Service and the Ministry for Emergencies) received more funding and more support from the Kremlin than at any time since the collapse of the Soviet Union.

However, efforts to modernise and transform the security sector at federal level have been complicated by an increasing number of challenges to security. Among these are continuing internal security threats, including escalating instability in the republics of the north Caucasus, which remain poorly governed and dominated by militant groups and clans. The conflict in Chechnya is now in its seventh year, and shows no sign of being resolved. Following major terrorist attacks in Beslan (North Ossetia) in September 2004, and in Nazran (Ingushetia) in July 2004, internal security is now also a major problem in Dagestan.

Focusing on challenges to the defence establishment, a recent report by the Council on Foreign Defence and Policy, a Russian NGO, has highlighted the need for a reappraisal of the national defence policy, saying that the threat to Russia is from conflict in the neighbourhood of Russia, terrorism and the proliferation of weapons of mass destruction, and not from another country. However, President Vladimir Putin emphasised, during a speech in July 2005, that the country's armed forces should be ready to counter any attempts by other states putting political and military pressure on Russia – possibly referring to the perception of a victory by pro-Western parties in the Ukraine and Georgia, and the increasing military involvement of the US in the South Caucasus.

The main question for the Russian MoD in the reform programme is how far to introduce professionalisation and how far to reduce conscription. Some senior officers have said that they cannot afford to reduce the size of the armed forces below the current strength of an estimated 1.2 million – a number that implies retaining a large conscript component – without putting the defence of the homeland at risk. This view not only demonstrates that old-style thinking remains at the heart of defence planning in Russia, but also that such thinking is at odds with the aspirations of Minister of Defence Sergei Ivanov, who wants to press ahead with large-scale professionalisation. He intends to have 50% of all army personnel as professional forces by 2007. According to a Russian MoD assessment, however, the number of contract servicemen is unlikely to reach 150,000 by 2007 – also the year when it is intended to cut conscription from two years to one. Moreover, at present, the numbers volunteering for contract service are not reaching annual targets. At the end of 2004, the number of contracts signed in the Moscow Military District (MD) was 17% of the target figure; in the North Caucasus MD it was 45%; and in the Volga–Ural MD 25%

One reason for the unpopularity of contract service is that it is poorly paid, with 5,000–6,000 roubles the average monthly wage for soldiers serving in home-base locations within the Russian Federation, and 15,000 roubles for those in conflict zones within the Commonwealth of Independent States (CIS). Operational service outside the CIS attracts a wage of approximately $1,000. On top of poor pay, social conditions for servicemen deteriorated when a number of benefits were cancelled as part of nationwide social and economic reforms in 2005. Moreover, some new benefits are barely adequate for their purpose, such as the entitlement of a monthly payment of 1,000 roubles (approximately $35) for service personnel disabled during their military service, which was announced in July 2005 by the Ministry of Health and Social Development.

One of the drivers behind calls for professionalisation is the apparent inability of military district commissariats to enforce the call-up of many young men of draft age. There are a number of ways to avoid conscription legally, including enrolment in a university degree course. In October 2004, military commissariats conscripted less than 10% (176,000) of all eligible men of conscript age and a large percentage of draftees are found to be physically and mentally unfit for service and have to be discharged. Of the spring draft in 2005 some 30% of conscripts were found to be unsuitable for military service. The continuing decline in Russia's population (see *The Military Balance* 2004–05) also supports the argument in favour of a predominantly volunteer force, as the retention of an army with a large conscript component may be unsustainable purely for demographic reasons.

The growing unpopularity of conscription also emphasises the need for voluntary service. Continuing reports of *dedovschina* (bullying) contribute to this unpopularity, but another factor is the dire living conditions endured by young soldiers. The Defence Committee of the Duma has expressed concern at MoD figures showing that 126 servicemen committed suicide in the first half of 2005, and that 98 servicemen died as a result of crimes and incidents in June alone, with a total of 445 for the first half of the year, ten of which were the result of 'hazing'.

Moreover, despite an MoD policy, announced in October 2004, that conscripts can only serve in Chechnya in emergencies requiring the deployment of extra troops, there are still many conscripts serving there, particularly in construction and other logistic units. However, some units in Shali and Borzoye districts in Chechnya are now fully professional and 75% of the manpower element of 42 Motor Rifle Division is made up of contract servicemen.

Despite these problems, manpower reforms and the modernisation of units are slowly taking place, particularly in elite and specialist units. For example, as a sign of a reconciliation of the manning levels in the airborne forces, the 119 Airborne regiment of the 116 Airborne division was disbanded on 1 September 2005, and the personnel have been reallocated to other airborne units to boost their strengths. At the same time, the total strength of the airborne forces has been preserved.

As part of the ongoing experiment in full professionalisation, permanent readiness units in the 76 Airborne Division in Pskov have been equipped with modern weapons and undergo fully professional training and development. By the end of 2005, two additional converted battalions will be added to the division, and in 2006 it is planned that there will be four such battalions and, in 2007, four fully converted regiments. 98 Airborne Division at Ivanovo and 21 Airborne Battalion at Ulyanovsk will then start the transformation process.

On 1 December 2004, two regiments of 27 Motor Rifle Division Second Army, which is stationed in Chernorech'e, was transformed into the first fully contract special peace-keeping brigade, and became operational on 1 February 2005. The brigade is trained for service on peacekeeping missions in Abkhazia, South Ossetia and Transnistria; in the future, it could be deployed to multinational peacekeeping operations. This is a positive change from the previous practice of manning peacekeeping forces mainly from airborne units.

CAPABILITY ISSUES

Russia continues to concentrate significant resources on the maintenance and development of strategic forces which remain the government's priority in its defence policy. As the draw-down of strategic missile divisions from 15 to 13 continues, plans to convert the ageing ICBM arsenal by 2010 progressed with the deployment of silo-launched SS-27 *Topol*-M missiles to the Tamanskaya missile division at Tatishchevo. The missiles currently carry a single warhead, but have the capability to carry 3 to 6. Enhancement of ground-based systems will be complete once the mobile SS-27 variants are deployed, possibly in 2006. Meanwhile, it is reported that flight-testing of the SLBM variant of *Topol*-M (SS-NX-30), *Bulava*, could be completed in 2006, thus bringing strategic military development near to completion. The nuclear-fuelled submarine (SSBN) *Dmitri Donskoy* is undergoing trials after being modernised over a ten-year period to enable it to carry the *Bulava* system. Meanwhile, a second new SSN, the *Yuri Dolgoruki*, is expected to enter service in 2006.

Considerable assets are being allocated to developments in space. It is expected that under the new allocation of $10.65bn for the Russian space programme in the period 2006–15, the number of military satellites will increase from 11 to 18 by 2006, thus expanding the military component of the Russian GLONASS orbital navigation system.

An upgrade in strategic theatre missile defence capability has begun with the deployment of the *Iskander*-M missile system. The first of the new systems has been deployed in a missile brigade of the Siberian Military District. With a range of between 50 and 280km, the *Iskander*-M is equipped with an inertial guidance system, and is reported to be difficult to intercept as it has an unpredictable flight path, flies most of the way to the target unpowered and operates without electronic emission.

In 2005 a regiment consisting of two battalions of S-400 surface-to-air missile (SAM) systems will enter service in the Russian Air Force and will be deployed in Moscow region. The system can destroy targets at altitudes of up to 185km, at distances of up to 450km, and is reported to be capable of engaging ground and sea-surface targets.

DISARMAMENT

The dismantlement programme of Russia's Soviet-era surplus nuclear submarines, which is to be complete by 2010, continues with assistance from Western countries. On 1 July, the State Duma ratified a cooperation agreement between Russia and Canada for the disposal of decommissioned submarines, which was signed in 2004.

The Russian state commission for **chemical disarmament** issued a report stating that the chemical arsenal, estimated at 40,000 tonnes of chemical weapons, was secure and in a stable condition. Under the terms of the Convention on the Prohibition of Chemical Weapons (CPCW) Russia is to dismantle some 20% of its chemical arsenal in 2007; 45% by the end of 2009; 100% by 2012. However, a reported $55.9m shortfall in funding and delays in completing the disposal facilities at Kambarka and Maradykovsky mean that the programme is behind schedule.

The US–Russia **Highly Enriched Uranium to Low-Enriched Uranium** (HEU–LEU) programme, which aims to reprocess weapons grade uranium, processed the equivalent of 10,000 nuclear warheads. The $12bn programme finishes in 2013.

TACTICAL CAPABILITY ENHANCEMENTS

Moves away from old-style thinking have been in evidence, with several training exercises, both national and multi-national, focusing on training to counter non-traditional threats, such as terrorism, illegal trafficking and local conflicts. High technology enhancements are concentrated on precision-guided munitions and communications, command, control, computers, intelligence, surveillance, and reconnaissance (C4ISR). To give one example, on 26 May 2005, a precision-guided long-range cruise missile engaged a target at a range of 200km.

Moreover, among other signs of replacing and modernising equipment to meet the demands of the modern tactical environment, the Russian Air Force (RFAF) has ordered 200 Yak-130 training aircraft and intends to field 12 by 2007. The Yak-130 is designed principally for low-intensity combat situations.

The RFAF also received 7 Su-27CM this year, and it is expected that another 17 aircraft will be delivered in 2006. Furthermore, as a sign of improving budgetary conditions, the MiG-29 modernisation programme has restarted, having been 'frozen' for financial reasons. On 21 January it was announced that some 300 Mi-28H *Night Hunter* helicopters are being purchased, 50 of which will enter service by 2010. A statement by the commander-in-chief of the Russian Federal Air Force (RFAF), Army General Vladimir Mikhailov, suggests that cuts will be made elsewhere in the helicopter fleet, with a move away from Kamov's Ka-50 *Black Shark*, whose production has been frozen, to the Mi-28H.

In the maritime sphere, too, there have been developments in tactical and littoral capability. In the Caspian Sea, a second vessel designed for anti-trafficking, counter-terrorism and littoral patrolling has been introduced into the Caspian Flotilla. The *Kaspisk* artillery cutter joins the *Astrakhan*, which came into service more than two years ago.

In 2005 capability enhancements in the Ground Forces will include 40 T-90 MBTs to re-equip one battalion. Two motor rifle battalions will receive 45 BTR-80 each, and a third motor rifle battalion will be equipped with 24 BMP-3 armoured personnel carriers.

MILITARY AND SECURITY COOPERATION

(SEE PP. 46, 223)

President Putin continues to concentrate on building collective security, both through the Shanghai Co-operation Organisation (SCO) and within the framework of the Collective Security Treaty Organization (CSTO). Both organisations have developed their political and military structures, and, although progress has been slow towards developing a viable military capability, training exercises under the auspices of both organisations indicate a concentration on the deployment of combined forces for counter-terrorist operations (see p. 155) with an emphasis on the Central Asia region. Moreover, there are initiatives underway to integrate certain parts of the military structure of the Collective Rapid Deployment Force (CRDF) comprising elements from Russia, Kazakhstan, Kyrgyzstan and Tajikistan. The plans include the possible formation of a single logistic support system, and a common training system.

The lower house of the Tajik parliament ratified the agreement, signed in October 2004 by President

Putin and President Emomali Rakhmonov, for the establishment of a new Russian base in **Tajikistan**. There is also the possibility of a CRDF base being set up in the south of **Kyrgyzstan** in Osh region near the Ferghana valley. This facility would be in addition to the CRDF airbase in Kant.

The Russia–China relationship is deepening in the military sphere. Apart from continuing Russian arms sales to China, which include the possibility of more strategic equipment, such as the Tu-160 strategic bomber, bilateral training has taken place. Exercise *Peace Mission 2005*, the first-ever joint training exercise, was held in three stages between 18 and 25 August. The first phase took place in Vladivostok, Russia while the other two were executed on China's Shandong Peninsula. Some 3,000 Russian troops and an estimated 6,000 Chinese troops participated, focusing on peacekeeping operations and cooperation in dealing with regional crises.

As a sign that it wishes to consolidate security on its periphery through cooperative arrangements, Russia proposed, at a July conference in Astrakhan on the security of the **Caspian Sea**, the establishment of a force similar to BLACKSEAFOR – the joint maritime force of the Black Sea littoral states – comprising maritime elements from all littoral Caspian states. The main task of the force would be the control of illicit trafficking through the region, and counter-terrorism.

The increasing military involvement of Russia in Central Asia makes its relationship with the US more competitive. A statement by the SCO in Astana at its July 2005 summit questioned the need for a continued US military presence in Uzbekistan, revealing a unity of opinion within the organisation concerning this issue. The statement coincided with the strong criticism voiced by the US of the Uzbek authorities' handling of the May protests in Andijon, which resulted in mass civilian casualties (see p. 223). On 27 July, Uzbek President Islam Karimov formally called for the withdrawal of all US forces from the Khanabad-Farsi base within six months.

Despite the increasing rivalry between Moscow and Washington in Central Asia and the South Caucasus, there is ongoing cooperation within the framework of the **NATO–Russia Council.** A Council meeting in Moscow on 15 March 2005 was followed up with the signing of a Status of Forces Agreement in Vilnius in April. The agreement paves the way for conducting joint training exercises on Russian territory. Joint anti-terrorist exercises with Russian,

American, British and French special forces will take place in Pskov in 2006. At the NATO–Russia Council meeting in Brussels in June 2005, the Russian Defence Minister Sergei Ivanov proposed holding a joint command-and-staff Theatre Missile Defense (TMD) exercise in Russia in 2006. The proposal followed a TMD command post exercise in the Netherlands on 14–23 March 2005 in order to test plans for the concept termed Operational Theatre Missile Defence (OTMD), comprising force components from NATO and Russia. Overall, the number of programmes to develop interoperability between NATO and Russian forces and command structures increased in 2004 by more than 150% compared with 2003. For the first time, Moscow has deployed its forces on a NATO operation: two ships from the Russian Navy have been deployed on *Operation Active Endeavour 2005* in the Mediterranean.

NORTH CAUCASUS

Spreading instability in the North Caucasus region, resulting from both criminal and insurgent violence, is the major security concern for Russia. The violence is widespread, not just in Chechnya, but also, increasingly, in the other North Caucasus republics: Dagestan, Ingushetia, Kabardino-Balkaria and Karachai-Cherkessia. Moreover, it is increasingly difficult to distinguish criminal from insurgent activity, as many clans (*teips*) and groups throughout the region are involved in both.

Crucially, Moscow does not seem to have altered its approach, particularly in Chechnya. The declared policy of the Russian government in Chechnya combines a strong military presence with the socio-economic development of the region; however, in practice it has given priority to the military suppression of the secessionist forces, following a strategy of arrests and targeted killings of rebel leaders, and has neglected much-needed social and economic measures to rebuild the republic. In the first seven months of 2005, there were more than 230 terrorism-related incidents in Chechnya, killing 67 servicemen and policemen and 80 civilians, and injuring over 350 people. In the same time period, federal forces and Chechen police conducted around 400 major anti-terrorist operations in which over 200 alleged terrorists were killed and 194 arrested. Many weapons and explosives were confiscated. (see map, p. 157). President Putin's request to the EU, during his visit to Germany in December 2004, for socio-economic assistance in the North Caucasus,

Table 18 Selected Exercises involving Russia, Collective Security Treaty Organisation, and China

Exercise Date	Name	Location	Aim	Principal Participants/Remarks
28–30 September 2004		NATO Headquarters, Brussels	Procedural training for joint peacekeeping operations	NATO, Russia
14–18 February 2005	Allied Security 2005		Command and control	Joint forces of Belarus and Russia
14–23 March 2005		De Peel Airbase, Netherlands	Operational theatre missile defence (OTMD) and interoperability	Joint Russia–NATO exercise
April 2005	Rubezh 2005	Tajikistan	Anti-terrorism, rapid deployment, interoperability	Collective Security Treaty Organization members: Kazakhstan, Kyrgyzstan, Russia, and Tajikistan
5 April 2005		Armenia, Belarus, Kazakhstan and Russia	Air Force (combat readiness, defence capabilities, hostile aircraft interception and rescue operations)	Commonwealth of Independent States (CIS) countries (Armenia, Belarus, Kazakhstan, Kyrgyzstan, Russia, Tajikistan, Uzbekistan and Ukraine)
4–27 April 2005	BLACKSEAFOR 2005	Black Sea	Naval interoperability	Ships of the Black Sea Fleet and Turkish Navy: Russia, Bulgaria, Georgia, Romania, the Ukraine, and Turkey
23 May–3 June 2005	Torgau 2005	Moscow, Germany	Interoperability	Russia, US
7 June 2005		Command Post Exercise (CPX) Medvezhyi Ozera	Command and control coordination between Air Force units, land forces, and law-enforcement	Russia
9 June 2005		Primorsk Port, Bay of Finland	Anti-terrorism	Russia, Estonia, Finland; Azerbaijan, Armenia, Belarus, Latvia, Lithuania, Poland, Germany, Norway and Ukraine observed
13–14 June 2005		Baltic Sea	Joint minesweeper exercise	Russia and France
20–25 June 2005		CPX Siberia (Irkutsk region and internal republic of Buryatia)	Command and control, skill proficiency	Russia (included drafted reservists)
25 June 2005	Combat Commonwealth 2005 (Phase 1)	Trans-Baikal region, Russia	Airforce training for anti-terrorism, armed conflict, and defence; command and control coordination; and interoperability	Russia, Armenia, Belarus, Tajikistan. Six anti-aircraft brigades and regiments, six aviation units, two electronic warfare units including Su-27 fighters, Su-24 bombers, as well as S-300 and S-125 Buk surface-to-air missile systems.
6 July 2005		Tuapse, Krasnodar region	Air force (ejection, parachuting, and search and rescue)	Russia
7 July 2005		Yangshan Port in Shanghai, China	Counter-terrorism, pollution prevention, and search and rescue	2,000 troops from 10 regional nations including Korea, China, Japan, and Russia. One aircraft, two helicopters, and 32 patrol boats, including Korea's Jemin 5 Coast Guard cutter
11 July 2005		Ionian Sea	Training for embargo operations, tactical maneuvering and command and control	The Moskva cruiser and the Pytlivy escort boat of the Black Sea Fleet; the Italian Navy's frigate Espero
18 July 2005	Vostok 2005	Far East Russia	Air defence operations, command and control	Russia; new Su-27SM fighters used in exercise for the first time
22 July 2005		Barents Sea	Submarine tactics; live firing conditions	Russia (10 nuclear submarines and Northern Fleet surface ships)
28 July–11 August 2005	Kaspiy-Antiterror 2005	Kazakhstan	Anti-terrorism: counter sabotage at power-stations	Collective Security Treaty Organisation
5–12 August 2005	Combat Commonwealth 2005 (Phase 2)	Kazakh Saryshagan Firing Range	See Phase 1	See Phase 1. Also, Kazakhstan and Kyrgyzstan to participate
18–25 August 2005	Peace Mission 2005	Vladivostok, Russia and Shandong Peninsula, China	Counter-terrorism; regional crisis response	Russia: some 3,000 personnel from the Air Force, Airborne Troops and Navy. 5,000 Chinese troops.
22–31 August 2005	Combat Commonwealth 2005 (Phase 3)	Ashuluk Firing Range in the Astrakhan region	See Phase 1	See Phase 1
19–24 September 2005		Uzbekistan	Joint airborne training in mountainous terrain	Troops from 76 ABD

provides some hope that more international attention will be given to this increasingly volatile region within the EU's neighbourhood.

CHECHNYA

Insurgent and terrorist activity

(see map, opposite)

Violence intensified in the period leading up to the 31 August 2004 presidential elections, won by Kremlin-supported candidate Alu Alkhanov. On 24 August 2004, showing a continuing ability to carry out attacks outside the republic, the so-called Islambouli Brigades claimed responsibility for two simultaneous suicide bomb attacks on Russian airliners flying from Moscow's Domodedovo airport, killing 89 people. A week later the same group claimed responsibility for a car-bomb attack in Moscow which killed 10 people. However, many experts believe that attacks were in fact orchestrated by rebel leader Shamil Basaev. The worst attack, also outside Chechnya, took place on 1 September 2004 in neighbouring North Ossetia. Terrorists took some 1,600 adults and children hostage at School No.1 in Beslan. After a siege lasting three days, a gun battle ensued between hostage-takers, who had started killing hostages, and Russian forces. During the violence an estimated 330 hostages, including 172 children, were killed and 339 injured. Over 30 Russian servicemen and 31 terrorists also died in the incident

Russian authorities have accused Saudi-born terrorist leader Abu Dzeit, widely believed to have links to al-Qaeda, of being behind the Beslan attack. Abu Dzeit was subsequently killed in Ingushetia on 16 February 2005 by security forces.

Following the Beslan incident, there was widespread criticism of the Russian authorities. The high number of casualties and the lack of coordination between security and military authorities led to a special inquiry by a Russian Parliamentary Commission, which has yet to publish its report.

Counterinsurgency (see map, opposite)

Russian forces targeted and killed a number of key Chechen rebel commanders during the reporting period. In December 2004, rebel leaders Aslan Barayev and Yunadi Turchayev, the second in command of Shamil Basayev, were both killed in February 2005. Most significant was the assassination in March 2005 of rebel leader and former Chechen president Aslan Maskhadov by secu-

rity forces, following an intelligence tip-off as to his whereabouts. The little-known Abdul Khalim Saidulayev was nominated to succeed Maskhadov as the head of the rebel leadership's 'State Defence Council', but he does not have the same authority as Maskhadov, and the more radical leaders, including Shamil Basaev, seem to have almost unchallenged authority. While Maskhadov repeatedly sought some form of dialogue with Moscow, the new leadership is unlikely to be able pursue any political track and will continue to use violence and terrorism as the only means of achieving its objective. Moscow has ruled out any negotiations with radical groups which carry out major acts of terrorism.

Apart from the strategy of targeted assassination, 'cleansing operations' (*chistki*) and wide-scale arrests have continued. These have been accompanied by widespread abuses by Chechen militias loyal to Moscow, who are under command of deputy prime minister and son of a former president of Chechnya, Ramzan Kadyrov. Some of these Chechen militias are known to conduct arrests, torture and murder and engage in 'blood feud' assassinations. Some Chechen units serving alongside the Russian federal forces have also been accused of human-rights violations. On 4 July 2005 troops from the 'Vostok' special forces (GRU) battalion under the command of Sulim Yamadaev were found to be responsible for beating up, intimidation and the abduction of 11 residents of Borozdinovskaya settlement. Following the incident, over 600 remaining residents fled into neighbouring Dagestan. The incident provoked widespread criticism from the local population and Dagestani authorities, and resulted in the withdrawal of troops from the mountains surrounding the town.

The policy of 'Chechenisation' of the security forces in the republic has had mixed results. Although many former rebels switched sides, they often operate in the same uncontrolled way, but as part of the Russian federal forces, or as pro-Russian militias. This undermines Russian attempts to gain the confidence of the population and so work towards the successful reconstruction of Chechnya. Moreover, Russian forces suspect that the pro-Russian Chechen militias have been infiltrated by fighters who pass information to rebel commanders and in some cases, help to prepare terrorist attacks. Chechen groups who work with the federal forces also seek to marginalise the role of the Russian troops, in some cases defending local population against their excessive violence. This complex, and increasingly uncooperative, relationship is likely

INSURGENT AND TERRORIST ACTIVITY IN THE NORTH CAUCASUS (JANUARY 2004–JULY2005)

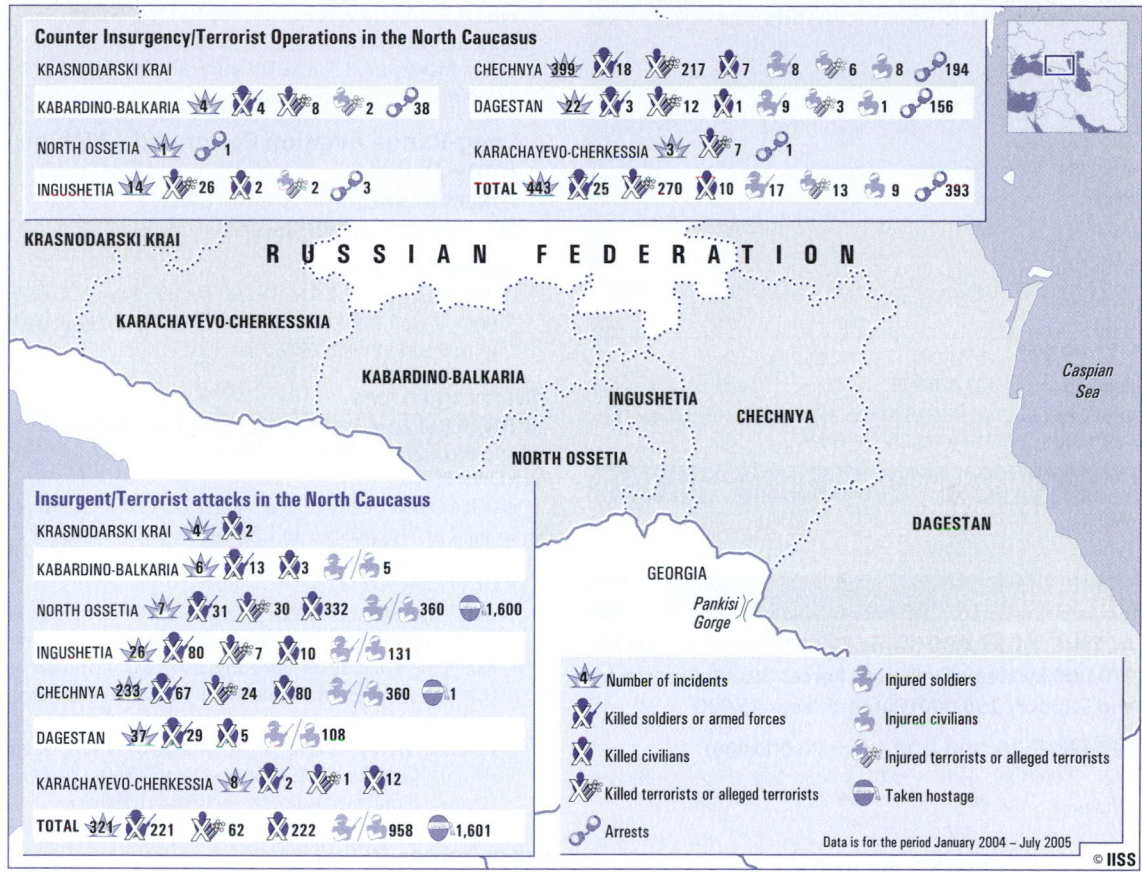

Counter Insurgency/Terrorist Operations in the North Caucasus

	Incidents	Killed soldiers	Killed civilians	Killed terrorists	Injured soldiers	Injured civilians	Injured terrorists	Taken hostage	Arrests
KRASNODARSKI KRAI									
KABARDINO-BALKARIA	4	4	8		2				38
NORTH OSSETIA	1								1
INGUSHETIA	14	26	2		2				3
CHECHNYA	399	18	217	7	8	6		8	194
DAGESTAN	22	3	12	1	9	3		1	156
KARACHAYEVO-CHERKESSIA	3		7						1
TOTAL	443	25	270	10	17	13		9	393

Insurgent/Terrorist attacks in the North Caucasus

	Incidents	Killed soldiers	Killed civilians	Killed terrorists	Injured soldiers	Injured civilians	Injured terrorists	Taken hostage
KRASNODARSKI KRAI	4	2						
KABARDINO-BALKARIA	6	13	3			5		
NORTH OSSETIA	7	31	30	332		360		1,600
INGUSHETIA	26	80	7	10		131		
CHECHNYA	233	67	24	80		360		1
DAGESTAN	37	29	5			108		
KARACHAYEVO-CHERKESSIA	8	2	1	12				
TOTAL	321	221	62	222		958		1,601

Legend:
- 4 — Number of incidents
- Killed soldiers or armed forces
- Killed civilians
- Killed terrorists or alleged terrorists
- Arrests
- Injured soldiers
- Injured civilians
- Injured terrorists or alleged terrorists
- Taken hostage

Data is for the period January 2004 – July 2005

© IISS

Map labels: KRASNODARSKI KRAI, RUSSIAN FEDERATION, KARACHAYEVO-CHERKESSKIA, KABARDINO-BALKARIA, INGUSHETIA, NORTH OSSETIA, CHECHNYA, DAGESTAN, GEORGIA, Pankisi Gorge, Caspian Sea

to complicate further the re-establishment of law and order in the Chechen republic.

DAGESTAN

While the level of violence in Chechnya has not increased, instability in neighbouring Dagestan has been growing. In the first seven months of 2005, more than 35 major incidents targeting law enforcement and government personnel in Dagestan took place; over 30 people were killed and more than 100 were injured. The Russian Prosecutor General's Office reported that there were more than 100 attempts on the lives of law enforcement officers in the same period. Deputy Interior Minister Magomed Omarov was killed in a bomb attack in December 2004. On 20

May 2005, the republic's National Policy, Information and External Relations Minister Zagir Arukhov was also killed. Ten servicemen were killed in a bomb attack on 1 July 2005. There are at least two major groups responsible for attacks in Dagestan. The first group, *Jennet* (Arabic for 'paradise') was headed by Rasul Makasharipov, and is dedicated to the creation of a Muslim *sharia* state in the Caucasus. Makashiripov was killed during a security operation in July together with 17 of his men. The second group is headed by Shamil Abubakarov, but the aims of this group are not known. A similar trend is emerging in other republics of the North Caucasus as well. As a result, the federal government is reinforcing Interior Ministry troops with special units trained in counter-terrorist tactics.

Russia RF

Russian Rouble r		2003	2004	2005
GDP	r	13.2tr	16.7tr	
	US$[a]	1.31tr	1.40tr	
per capita	US$[a]	9,115	9,779	
Growth	%	7.3	7.1	
Inflation	%	13.7	10.9	
Debt	US$	175bn		
Def exp	US$[a]	65.2bn	61.9bn	
Def bdgt	r	325bn	411bn	529bn
	US$	10.6bn	14.1bn	18.8bn
US$1=r		30.6	29.0	28.0

[a] PPP estimate

Population   143,420,309

Ethnic groups: Tatar 4%; Ukrainian 3%; Chuvash 1%; Bashkir 1%; Belarussian 1%; Moldovan 1%; Other 8%;

Age	0–14	15–19	20–24	25–29	30–64	65 plus
Male	7%	4%	4%	4%	22%	4%
Female	7%	4%	4%	4%	25%	10%

Capabilities

ACTIVE 1,037,000 (Army 395,000 Navy 142,000 Air 170,000 Strategic Deterrent Forces 80,000 Command and Support 250,000) Paramilitary 415,000

RESERVE 20,000,000 (Joint 20,000,000)

some 2,000,000 with service within last 5 years; Reserve obligation to age 50

ORGANISATIONS BY SERVICE

Strategic Deterrent Forces ε129,000 (includes 11,000 assigned from the Navy and 38,000 assigned from the Air Force)

Navy 11,000
SUBMARINES • STRATEGIC • SSBN 15: 6 *Delta* III† opcon Pacific Fleet (96 msl) each with 16 single each with 1 RSM-54 (SS-N-23) *Skiff* strategic SLBM; 3 *Delta* IV† opcon Northern Fleet (96 msl) each with 16 single each with 1 RSM-50 (SS-N-18) *Stingray* strategic SLBM; 3 *Delta* IV† in reserve opcon Northern Fleet (96 msl) each with 16 single each with 1 RSM-50 (SS-N-18) *Stingray* strategic SLBM; 2 *Typhoon* opcon Northern Fleet (60 msl) each with 20 single each with 1 RSM-52 (SS-N-20) *Sturgeon* strategic SLBM; 1 *Typhoon*† in reserve opcon Northern Fleet with 20 single each with 1 *Bulava* (SS-N-30) strategic SLBM

Strategic Missile Force Troops ε40,000
3 Rocket Armies operating silo and mobile missile lauchers. 570 Lauchers with 2035 nuclear warheads organised in 13 divs. Launcher gps normally with 10 silos (6 for SS-18) and one control centre
MSL • STRATEGIC 670

ABM 100: 64 9M96 (S-400)/SH-08 *Gazelle*; 36 SH-11 *Gorgon*
ICBM 570: 80 RS-20 (SS-18) *Satan* (at 4 fields; mostly mod 4/5, 10 MIRV per msl.); 300 RS12M (SS-25) *Sickle* (mobile single warhead); 150 RS18 (SS-19) *Stiletto* (at 4 fields; mostly mod 3, 6 MIRV per msl.); 40 *Topol*-M (SS-27) (4 regts each with 10 launchers)

Long-Range Aviation Command • 37th Air Army 38,000
FORCES BY ROLE
Bbr   4 (START Accountable) heavy regt

EQUIPMENT BY TYPE
AIRCRAFT • LRSA 80: 16 Tu-160 *Blackjack* each with 8 KH-101/KH-555; 1 test; 56 Tu-95 *Bear* each with 8 KH-101/KH-555; 7 test

Warning Forces
ICBM/SLBM launch-detection capability others include photo recce and ELINT
RADAR 22
AD RADAR 3: 2 OTH-B (covering US and Polar areas) located at Mukachevo and Nikolaev; 1 (covering PRC) located at Yeniseysk
STRATEGIC 19
ABM RADAR 12: 1 ABM Engagement System located at Pushkino (Moscow); 11 *Dnepr Hen House* (Range 6,000km, 6 locations covering covering approaches from West and South West,North East and South East, and partially South)
Phased Array Radar 7 at Moscow, Olenegorsk (Kola), Gaballa (Az), Baranovichi (Bel), Pechora (Urals), Balkhash (Kaz), Mishelevka (Irkutsk)

Space Forces 40,000
Formations and units withdrawn from Strategic Missile and Air Defence Forces to detect missile attack on the RF and its allies, to implement BMD, and to be responsible for military/dual-use spacecraft launch and control.

Army ε205,000; ε190,000 conscript (total 395,000)
FORCES BY ROLE
6 Mil Districts (MD), 1 Op Strategic Gp; 8 Army HQ, 2 Corps HQ, 7 District trg centre (each = bde–1 per MD)

Tk	5 div (*each:* some spt unit, 1 arty regt, 1 MRR, 1 SAM regt, 1 armd recce bn, 3 tk regt)
MRR	16 div (*each:* some Spt unit, 1 indep tk bn, 1 armd Recce bn, 1 tk regt, 3 MRR, 1 SAM regt, 1 AT bn, 1 arty regt); 10 indep bde; 1 (cadre) div (3 MRR, 2 tk regt, 1 arty regt, 1 indep tk regt, 1 AT regt, 1 armd recce bn, some spt unit, 1 SAM regt); 2 indep regt
SF	7 (Spetsnaz) bde
AB	4 div (*each:* 2–3 para regt, 1 arty regt); 3 indep bde; 1 (trg centre) bde
Arty	5 div (*each:* 1 MRL bde, 1 AT bde, up to 4 arty bde); 18 indep bde (incl MRL)
Arty / MG	6 div (converting to Motor Rifle)

AT   5 bde
SSM   14 bde with SS-21 *Scarab (Tochka)* (replacement by *Iskander*-M missile system began during 2005.)
arty loc   6 regt
SAM   4 bde with SA-11 *Gadfly*; 2 bde with SA-4 *Ganef*; 12 bde; 1 bde with S-300V (SA-12A) *Gladiator*/SA-12B *Giant (twin)*

Reserves
cadre formations, on mobilisation form

Tk   2 div; 2 bde
MRR   13 div; 6 bde
Arty   4 indep bde
Hy arty   1 bde

EQUIPMENT BY TYPE
TK 22,950+
MBT 22,800+: 400 T-90
  T-80 4,500: 4,500 T-80/T-80UD/T-80UM/T-80U
  T-72 9,700: 9,700 T-72L/T-72M
  T-64 4,000: 4,000 T-64A/T-64B
  T-62 3,000 **T-55** 1,200 **T-34** some
  LT TK 150: 150 PT-76
RECCE • BRDM 2,000+: 2,000+ BRDM-2
AIFV 15,090+
  BMD 1,500+: 1,500+ BMD-1/BMD-2/BMD-3
  BMP 12,890: 8,100 BMP-1; 4,600 BMP-2; 190 BMP-3
  BRM-1K 700 **BTR-80A** some
APC 9,900+
  APC (T) 4,000: 700 BTR-D; 3,300 MT-LB
  APC (W) • BTR 5,900+: 1,000 BTR-50; 4,900 BTR-60/BTR-70/BTR-80; some BTR-90
ARTY 30,045+
  TOWED 12,765
    122mm 8,350: 4,600 D-30; 3,750 M-30 *M-1938*
    130mm 650: 650 M-46
    152mm 3,725: 1,100 2A36; 750 2A65; 1,075 D-20; 700 M-1943; 100 ML-20 *M-1937*
    203mm 40: 40 B-4M
  SP 6010
    122mm 2,780: 2,780 2S1 *Carnation*
    152mm 3,100: 550 2S19 *Farm*; 1,600 2S3; 950 2S5
    203mm 130: 130 2S7
  GUN/MOR • 120mm 820+: some 2B16 *NONA-K*; 30 2S23 *NONA-SVK*; 790 2S9 SP *NONA-S*
  MRL 4,350: 374 some in store
    122mm 2,970: 420 9P138; 2,500 BM-21; 50 BM-16
    132mm: some BM-13
    140mm: some BM-14
    220mm 900: 900 9P140 *Uragan*
    300mm 106: 106 9A52 *Smerch*
  MOR 6,100: 3,550 some in store
    120mm 1,820: 920 2S12; 900 PM-38
    160mm 300: 300 M-160
    240mm 430: 430 2S4 SP
AT
  MSL: some AT-10; some AT-2 *Swatter*; some AT-3 *Sagger*; some AT-4 *Spigot*; some AT-5 *Spandrel*; some AT-6 *Spiral*; some AT-7 *Saxhorn*; some AT-9

RCL
  73mm: some SPG-9
  82mm: some B-10
RL
  105mm: some RPG-27/RPG-29
  64mm: some RPG-18 *Fly*
  73mm: some RPG-16/RPG-22 *Net*/RPG-26/RPG-7 *Knout*
GUNS
  57mm: some ASU-57 SP
  85mm: some ASU-85 SP; some D-44/SD44
  100mm 526: 526 T-12A/M-55 towed/T-12
AD • SAM
  SP 2,465+: 200 S-300V (SA-12A) *Gladiator*/SA-12B *Giant (twin)* (400–800 eff.); some S-400 (SA-20) *Triumph*; 350 SA-11 *Gadfly* (replacing SA-4/-6); 120 SA-15 *Gauntlet* (replacing SA-6/SA-8); some SA-19 *Grison* (8 SAM, plus twin 30mm gun); 220 SA-4 A/B *Ganef (twin)* (Army/Front wpn–most in store); SA-6 *Gainful* 225 (div wpn); SA-8 *Gecko* 550 (div wpn); SA-13 *Gopher*/SA-9 *Gaskin* 800 (3,200 eff.) (regt wpn)
  MANPAD: some 9K310 (SA-16) *Gimlet*/SA-18 *Grouse (Igla)*; some SA-14 *Gremlin*/SA-7 *Grail* (being replaced by -16/-18)
  GUNS
    100mm • TOWED: some KS-19
    130mm • TOWED: some KS-30
    23mm • SP: some ZSU-23-4
      TOWED: some ZU-23
    30mm • SP: some 2S6
    57mm • SP: some ZSU-57-2
      TOWED: some S-60
    85mm • TOWED: some M-1939 *KS-12*
MSL • TACTICAL • SSM 200+: some FROG/*Scud* in store; ε200 SS-21 *Scarab (Tochka)*

FACILITIES
Base   2 (each = bde+; subord. to North Caucasus MD) located in Georgia, 1 located in Tajikistan, 1 located in Armenia
Training Centre 7 (District (each = bde–1 per MD)), 1 (AB (bde))

Navy 142,000
SUBMARINES 54
  TACTICAL 46
    SSGN 8:
      7 *Oscar* II each with 2 single 650mm TT each with T-65 HWT, 1 VLS with 24 SS-N-19 *Shipwreck* tactical USGW
      1 *Oscar* II in reserve with 2 single 650mm TT each with T-65 HWT, 1 VLS with 24 SS-N-19 *Shipwreck* tactical USGW
    SSN 18:
      AKULA 10:
        2 *Akula* II each with 4 single 533mm TT each with SS-N-21 *Sampson* tactical SLCM, 4 single 650mm TT each with single 650mm TT
        6 *Akula* I each with 4 single 533mm TT each with SS-N-21 *Sampson* tactical SLCM, 4 single 650mm TT each with T-65 HWT
        2 in reserve

SIERRA 3:

1 *Sierra* II with 4 single 533mm TT each with SS-N-21 *Sampson* tactical SLCM, T-53 HWT, 4 single 650mm TT each with T-65 HWT

1 *Sierra* II in reserve

1 *Sierra* I in reserve

VICTOR 5:

4 *Victor* III each with 4 single 533mm TT each with SS-N-15 *Starfish* tactical SSM, T-65 HWT

1 in reserve

SSK 20:

14 *Kilo* each with 6 single 533mm TT each with T-53 HWT

5 *Kilo* in reserve each with 6 single 533mm TT each with T-53 HWT

1 *St Petersburg* in reserve

SUPPORT • SSAN 8: 1 *Delta Stretch*; 1 *Losharik*; 2 *Paltus*; 3 *Uniform*; 1 *X- Ray*

PRINCIPAL SURFACE COMBATANTS 66

AIRCRAFT CARRIERS • CV 1:

1 *Kuznetsov* (capacity 20 Su-33 *Flanker D* FGA ac; either 15–17 ASW hel or 36 Su-33 *Flanker D* FGA ac) (67,500t) with 1 12 cell VLS (12 eff.) with 1 SS-N-19 *Shipwreck* tactical SSM, 4 sextuple VLS (24 eff.) each with 8 SA-N-9 *Gauntlet* SAM

CRUISERS 6

CGN 2:

2 *Kirov* (capacity 3 Ka-28 (Ka-27) *Helix* ASW hel) each with 3 Ka-25 *Hormone*/Ka-28 (Ka-27) *Helix*, 10 x1 533mm ASTT, 1 single ASTT with 1 SS-N-15 *Starfish* ASW, 2 twin (4 eff.) each with 20 SA-N-4 *Gecko* SAM, 12 single VLS each with 8 SA-N-6 *Grumble* SAM, 10 twin VLS (20 eff.) each with 1 SS-N-19 *Shipwreck* tactical SSM, 1 twin 130mm gun (2 eff.)

CG 4:

1 *Kara* (capacity 1 Ka-28 (Ka-27) *Helix* ASW hel) with 1 Ka-25 *Hormone* ASW hel, 2 x5 ASTT (10 eff.), 2 quad (8 eff.) each with SS-N-14 *Silex* tactical SSM, 2 twin (4 eff.) each with 36 SA-N-3 *Goblet* SAM, 2 (4 eff.) each with 20 SA-N-4 *Gecko* SAM

3 *Slava* (capacity 1 Ka-28 (Ka-27) *Helix* ASW hel) each with 1 Ka-25 *Hormone*/Ka-28 (Ka-27) *Helix*, 8 x1 533mm ASTT, 8 twin (16 eff.) each with 1 SS-N-12 *Sandbox* tactical SSM, 8 octuple VLS each with 8 SA-N-6 *Grumble* SAM, 1 twin 130mm gun (2 eff.)

DESTROYERS • DDG 15:

1 *Kashin* (mod) with 5 x1 533mm ASTT, 2 quad (8 eff.) each with 1 SS-N-25 *Switchblade* tactical SSM, 2 twin (4 eff.) each with SA-N-1 *Goa* SAM, 2 76mm gun

6 *Sovremenny* (capacity 1 Ka-28 (Ka-27) *Helix* ASW hel) each with 2 quad (8 eff.) each with SS-N-22 *Sunburn* tactical SSM, 2 twin 533mm TT (4 eff.), 2 twin (4 eff.) each with 22 SA-N-7 SAM, 2 twin 130mm gun (4 eff.)

7 *Udaloy* (capacity 2 Ka-28 (Ka-27) *Helix* ASW hel) each with 2 quad 533mm ASTT (8 eff.), 2 quad (8 eff.) each with SS-N-14 *Silex* tactical AS, 8 single VLS each with SA-N-9 *Gauntlet* SAM, 2 100mm gun

1 *Udaloy* II (capacity 2 Ka-28 (Ka-27) *Helix* ASW hel) with 8 SA-N-11 *Grisson* SAM, 2 x2 CADS-N-1 CIWS (4 eff.), 10 x1 533mm ASTT, 2 quad (8 eff.) each with 1 SS-N-22 *Sunburn* tactical SSM, 8 octuple VLS each with 1 SA-N-9 *Gauntlet* SAM, 2 100mm gun

FRIGATES 19

FFG 7:

1 *Gepard* with 2 x1 30mm CIWS, 2 quad (8 eff.) each with 1 SS-N-25 *Switchblade* tactical SSM, 1 twin (2 eff.) with 1 SA-N-4 *Gecko* SAM (Pop Group), 1 76mm gun

3 *Krivak* I (capacity 1 Ka-28 (Ka-27) *Helix* ASW hel) each with 2 quad 533mm ASTT (8 eff.), 1 quad (4 eff.) with SS-N-14 *Silex* tactical SSM, 1 twin (2 eff.) with 20 SA-N-4 *Gecko* SAM, 2 x12 RL (24 eff.), 2 100mm gun, 2 x2 76mm gun (4 eff.)

2 *Krivak* II each with 2 quad 533mm ASTT (8 eff.), 1 quad (4 eff.) with SS-N-14 *Silex* tactical SSM, 2 twin (4 eff.) each with 10 SA-N-4 *Gecko* SAM, 2 x12 RL (24 eff.), 2 100mm gun

1 *Neustrashimyy* (capacity 1 Ka-28 (Ka-27) *Helix* ASW hel) with 6 x1 533mm ASTT, 4 octuple (32 eff.) each with 4 SA-N-9 *Gauntlet* SAM, 1 RBU 12000 (10 eff.), 1 100mm gun

FF 12:

12 *Parchim* II each with 2 twin 533mm ASTT (4 eff.), 2 quad (8 eff.) each with 1 SA-N-5 *Grail* SAM, 2 RBU 6000 *Smerch* 2 (24 eff.), 1 76mm gun

CORVETTES 25:

1 *Grisha* III with 2 twin 533mm ASTT (4 eff.), 1 twin (2 eff.) with 20 SA-N-4 *Gecko* SAM, 2 RBU 6000 *Smerch* 2 (24 eff.)

1 *Grisha* IV with 2 twin 533mm ASTT (4 eff.), 1 twin (2 eff.) with 20 SA-N-4 *Gecko* SAM, 2 RBU 6000 *Smerch* 2 (24 eff.)

23 *Grisha* V each with 2 twin 533mm ASTT (4 eff.), 1 twin (2 eff.) with 20 SA-N-4 *Gecko* SAM, 1 RBU 6000 *Smerch* 2 (12 eff.)

PATROL AND COASTAL COMBATANTS 72

PFC 23:

3 *Pauk* each with 4 x1 533mm ASTT, 2 RBU 1200 (10 eff.)

ε20 *Stenka*

PFM 35

12 *Nanuchka* III each with 2 triple (6 eff.) each with 1 SS-N-9 *Siren* tactical SSM

1 *Nanuchka* IV with 2 triple (6 eff.) each with 1 SS-N-9 *Siren* tactical SSM

2 *Tarantual* II each with 2 twin (4 eff.) each with SS-N-2C *Styx*/SS-N-2D *Styx*

20 *Tarantual* III each with 2 twin (4 eff.) each with 1 SS-N-22 *Sunburn* tactical SSM

PHM 5:

2 *Dergach* each with 2 quad (8 eff.) each with 1 SS-N-22 *Sunburn* tactical SSM, 1 twin (2 eff.) with 1 SA-N-4 *Gecko* SAM, 1 76mm gun

3 *Matka* each with 2 single each with quad/SS-N-2C *Styx* tactical SSM/SS-N-2D *Styx* tactical SSM

PHT 9:

1 *Mukha* with 2 quad 406mm TT (8 eff.)

8 *Turya* each with 4 x1 533mm ASTT

MINE WARFARE • MINE COUNTERMEASURES 41

MCO 2: 2 *Gorya*

MSC 10: 10 *Sonya*

MSI ε20 less than 100 tonnes

MSO • NATYA 9: 9 *Natya* II/*Natya*

AMPHIBIOUS: 80 (smaller)

PRINCIPAL AMPHIBIOUS SHIPS • LPD 1:

1 *Ivan Rogov* (capacity 20 tanks; 520 troops; 4–5 Ka-28 (Ka-27) *Helix* ASW hel)

LS 21

LSM 1:

1 *Polnochny* B (capacity 180 troops; 6 MBT) (may be non-op)

LST 20:

5 *Alligator* (capacity 20 tanks; 300 troops)

15 *Ropucha* II (capacity either 190 troops or 10 MBT or 24 APC (T)s or 170 troops)/*Ropucha* LST (capacity either 190 troops or 10 MBT; either 24 APC (T)s or 170 troops)

CRAFT 30

LCM 6: circa 6 *Ondatra*

ACV 24:

6 *Aist* (capacity 4 lt tk)

9 *Lebed*

2 *Orlan*

2 *Pomornik* (*Zubr*) (capacity 230 troops; either 3 MBT or 10 APC (T)s)

3 *Tsaplya*

1 *Utenko*

1 *Utka*

LOGISTICS AND SUPPORT 436: 24 AGB civil; 17 AGI (Int) (some armed); 19 AGOR; 61 civil; 4 AH (Med); 17 AK; 22 AO; 6 AOR (1 *Berezina*; 5 *Chilikin*); 20 AOT; 38 AR; 7 ARC; 13 ARS; 46 ARS/AT; 15 AS; 90 AT; 8 AWT; 12 SPT (8 msl spt/resupply; 4 *Delvar* (specialist)); 9 tkr (special liquid carriers); 7 trg; 1 msl range instrumentation

Merchant Fleet

aux/augmentation for sealift, RF-owned ships

LOGISTICS AND SUPPORT 1,628: 1,139 RCL (over 1,000t); 340 tkr (over 1,000t); 33 container (over 1,000t); 116 dry bulk (over 1,000t)

Naval Aviation ε35,000

4 Fleet Air Forces, each organised in air div; each with 2–3 regt of HQ elm and 2 sqn of 9–10 ac each; recce, ASW, tpt/utl org in indep regt or sqn

Flying hours   40 hrs/year

FORCES BY ROLE

Bbr	some sqn with 58 Tu-22M *Backfire A*
FGA	some sqn with 49 Su-27 *Flanker*; 10 Su-25 *Frogfoot*; 58 Su-24 *Fencer*
ASW	some sqn with 120 Ka-28 (Ka-27) *Helix*; some sqn with 20 Be-12 *Mail*; 43 Il-38 *May*; 28 Tu-142 *Bear*
MR / EW	some sqn with 18 An-12 *Cub*; some sqn with 8 Mi-8 *Hip*
Tpt	some sqn with 37 An-12 *Cub*/An-24 *Coke*/An-26 *Curl*
Aslt hel	some sqn with 11 Mi-24 *Hind*; 30 Ka-29 *Helix*
Tpt hel	some sqn with 66 Mi-8 *Hip*

EQUIPMENT BY TYPE

AIRCRAFT 266 combat capable

BBR 58: 58 Tu-22M *Backfire A*

FTR 49: 49 Su-27 *Flanker*

FGA 68: 10 Su-25 *Frogfoot*; 58 Su-24 *Fencer*

ASW 91: 20 Be-12 *Mail**; 43 Il-38 *May**; 28 Tu-142 *Bear**

TPT 55: 18 An-12 *Cub*; 37 An-12 *Cub*/An-24 *Coke*/An-26 *Curl*

HELICOPTERS

ATK 11: 11 Mi-24 *Hind*

ASW 120: 120 Ka-28 (Ka-27) *Helix*

ASLT 30: 30 Ka-29 *Helix*

SPT 74: 74 Mi-8 *Hip*

MSL • TACTICAL • ASM: AS-10 *Karen*; some AS-11 *Kilter*; some AS-12 *Kegler*; some AS-4 *Kitchen*; some AS-7 *Kerry*; some KH-59 (AS-13) *Kingbolt*

Coastal Defence • Naval Infantry (Marines) 9,500

FORCES BY ROLE

Naval inf	3 indep bn; 3 regt; 1 indep regt; 3 indep bde (*total*: 1 AT bn, 1 arty bn, 1 MRL bn, 1 tk bn, 4 naval inf bn)
Inf	1 div HQ (Pacific Fleet) (3 inf bn, 1 tk bn, 1 arty bn)
SF	3 (fleet) bde (1 op, 2 cadre) (*each*: 1 para bn, 1 spt elm, 2–3 underwater bn)

EQUIPMENT BY TYPE

TK • MBT 160: 160 T-55M/T-72/T-80

RECCE • BRDM 60: 60 BRDM-2 each with AT-3 *Sagger* msl

AIFV

BMP 150+: ε150 BMP-2; some BMP-3

BRM-1K some

APC 750+

APC (T) 250: 250 MT-LB

APC (W) • BTR 500+: 500+ BTR-60/BTR-70/BTR-80

ARTY 367

TOWED • 122mm 45: 45 D-30

SP 113

122mm 95: 95 2S1 *Carnation*

152mm 18: 18 2S3

GUN/MOR • 120mm 113: 18 2B16 *NONA-K*; 20 2S23 *NONA-SVK*; 75 2S9 SP *NONA-S*

MRL • 122mm 96: 96 9P138

AT

MSL 72: 72 AT-3 *Sagger*/AT-5 *Spandrel*

GUNS • 100mm: some T-12

AD

SAM 320

SP 70: 20 SA-8 *Gecko*; 50 SA-13 *Gopher*/SA-9 *Gaskin* (200 eff.)

MANPAD 250: 250 SA-7 *Grail*

GUNS • 23mm • SP 60: 60 ZSU-23-4

Coastal Defence Troops 2,000

FORCES BY ROLE

(All units reserve status)

Coastal Def	1 bde; 1 div
Arty	2 regt
AD	1 regt with 28 Su-27 *Flanker*
SAM	2 regt

EQUIPMENT BY TYPE
TK • MBT 350: 350 T-64
AIFV 450: 450 BMP
APC 320
  APC (T) 40: 40 MT-LB
  APC (W) • BTR 280: 280 BTR-60/BTR-70/BTR-80
ARTY 364
  TOWED 280
    122mm 140: 140 D-30
    152mm 140: 50 2A36; 50 2A65; 40 D-20
  SP • 152mm 48: 48 2S5
  MRL • 122mm 36: 36 BM-21
AIRCRAFT • FTR 28: 28 Su-27 *Flanker*
AD: 50 SAM

Military Air Forces ε170,000 (incl conscripts)

The Military Air Forces comprise Long Range Aviation (LRA), Military Transport Aviation Comd (VTA), 5 Tactical/Air Defence Armies comprising 49 air regts. Tactical/Air Defence roles includes air defence, interdiction, recce and tactical air spt. LRA (2 div) and VTA (9 regt) are subordinated to central Air Force comd. A joint CIS Unified Air Defence System covers R, Arm, Bel, Ga, Kaz, Kgz, Tjk, Tkm, Ukr and Uz.

Long-Range Aviation Command • 37th Air Army

FORCES BY ROLE

Bbr 4 heavy regt (non-strategic); 4 (START accountable) heavy regt

Tkr some sqn with 20 Il-78 *Midas*/Il-78M *Midas*

Trg 1 hvy bbr trg centre with 8 Tu-22M-3 *Backfire C*; 30 Tu-134 *Crusty*

EQUIPMENT BY TYPE
AIRCRAFT 124 combat capable
  BBR
    Tu-22M 8:
    Tu-22M-3/Tu-22MR *Backfire C* 116
  TKR • Il-78 20: 20 IL-78 *Midas* TKR/Il-78M *Midas*
  TPT 30: 30 Tu-134 *Crusty*

Tactical Aviation

Flying hours 20 to 25 hrs/year

FORCES BY ROLE

FGA / bbr some sqn with 275 Su-25 *Frogfoot*; 400 Su-24 *Fencer*, 1 Su-34 (Su-27IB) (slow rate of delivery to replace Su-24)

Ftr some sqn with 279 MiG-31 *Foxhound*; 314 MiG-29 *Fulcrum*; 350 Su-27 *Flanker*; 1 Su-27P *Flanker-B*/Su-34 (Su-27IB) *Fullback*; 40 Su-27SMK *Flanker*; 30 MiG-25 *Foxbat*

Recce some sqn with 160 MiG-25R *Foxbat*/Su-24E *Fencer*

AEW some sqn with 20 A-50 *Mainstay*/A-50U *Mainstay*

ECM some sqn with 60 Mi-8(ECM) *Hip J*

SAM 37 regt with 1,900+ S-300 (SA-10) *Grumble* (quad) (7,600 eff.). First SA-20/S-400 (*Triumph*) regt (2 bn) deployed near Moscow.

EQUIPMENT BY TYPE
AIRCRAFT 1,852 combat capable
  FTR 1,094: 279 MiG-31 *Foxhound*; 374 MiG-29 *Fulcrum*; 371 Su-27; 40 Su-27SMK *Flanker*; 30 MiG-25 *Foxbat*; 1 Su-34 (Su-27IB) *Fullback*
  FGA 757: 305 Su-25 *Frogfoot*; 451 Su-24 *Fencer*; 1 Su-27P *Flanker-B*/Su-34 (Su-27IB) *Fullback*
  RECCE 160: 160 MiG-25R *Foxbat*/Su-24E *Fencer*
  AEW • A-50 20: 20 A-50 *Mainstay* AEW/A-50U *Mainstay*
  Trg 383
HELICOPTERS • ECM 60: 60 Mi-8(ECM) *Hip J*
AD • SAM • SP 1,900+: 1,900+ S-300 (SA-10) *Grumble* (quad) some S-400 (SA-20) *Triumph*
MSL • TACTICAL
  ASM: some AS-11 *Kilter*; some AS-12 *Kegler*; some AS-14 *Kedge*; some AS-15 *Kent*; some AS-16 *Kickback*; some AS-17 *Krypton*; some AS-4 *Kitchen*; some AS-7 *Kerry*; some KH-101; some KH-555; some KH-59 (AS-13) *Kingbolt*
  AAM: some R-27T (AA-10) *Alamo*; some R-60T (AA-8) *Aphid*; some R-73M1 (AA-11) *Archer*
FACILITIES
Centre 2 with 20+ ac; 20 MiG-29 *Fulcrum* ftr ac; 15 Su-25 *Frogfoot* FGA ac; 35 Su-24 *Fencer* FGA ac (op conversion), 2 with 40 MiG-29 *Fulcrum* ftr ac; 21 Su-27 *Flanker* ftr ac; 15 Su-25 *Frogfoot* FGA ac; 16 Su-24 *Fencer* FGA ac (instructor trg)

Military Transport Aviation Command • 61st Air Army

FORCES BY ROLE

Air 9 regt incl. 5 indep regt; 1 div with An-124 *Condor*; An-22 *Cock* (Under MoD control); Il-76 *Candid*

Civilian Fleet some (medium and long-range passenger) sqn

EQUIPMENT BY TYPE
AIRCRAFT
  TPT 293+: 50 An-12 *Cub*; 12 An-124 *Condor*; 21 An-22 *Cock* (Under MoD control); 210 Il-76M/MD/MF *Candid*

Army Aviation Helicopters

Under VVS control. Units organic to army formations.

FORCES BY ROLE

Atk hel some sqn with Ka-50 *Hokum*; ε620 Mi-24 *Hind*; Mi-28N *Havoc*

Hel some sqn with ε252 hel; 600 in store

Recce / hel some sqn with Ka-52 *Hokum*; 140 Mi-24 *Hind*

Tpt some sqn with Mi-26 *Halo* (hy); Mi-6 *Hook*; MI-17 (Mi-8MT) *Hip H*/Mi-8 *Hip* (Some armed)

EQUIPMENT BY TYPE
HELICOPTERS: ε1,520
  ATK 628+: 8 Ka-50 *Hokum*; some 620 Mi-24 *Hind* D/V/P; some Mi-28N *Havoc*
  RECCE 140+: 140 Mi-24; some Ka-52 *Hokum*
  SPT: some Mi-26 *Halo* (hy); some Mi-6 *Hook*; some MI-17 (Mi-8MT) *Hip H*/Mi-8 *Hip* Spt

Air Force Aviation Training Schools

EQUIPMENT BY TYPE
AIRCRAFT: 980+
    FTR: some MiG-29 *Fulcrum*; some Su-27 *Flanker*; some MiG-23 *Flogger*
    FGA: some Su-25 *Frogfoot*
    TPT: some Tu-134 *Crusty*
    TRG: some L-39 *Albatros*

FACILITIES

Aviation Institute	5 with 980+ ac; MiG-29 *Fulcrum* ftr ac; Su-27 *Flanker* ftr ac; MiG-23 *Flogger* ftr ac; Su-25 *Frogfoot* FGA ac; Tu-134 *Crusty* tpt ac; L-39 *Albatros* trg ac (subordinate to Air Force HQ)

ATTU

The following combat effectiveness assessment of units within the ATTU region is based on the latest available information. Above 75% – possibly 1 TD, 6 MRD, 1 ABD, 1 arty bde. The remainder are assessed as 20–50%. Units outside the ATTU are likely to be at a lower level. All bde are maintained at or above 50%. TLE in each MD includes active and trg units and in store.

Tk	2 div
MRR	7 bde; 8 div
AB	ε4 div
Arty	1 div; 9 (indep) bde
MRL	3 bde
SSM	8 bde
SAM	12 bde

Operation Combat Aircraft

based west of the Urals (for all air forces other than maritime)
AIRCRAFT
    BBR 92: 29 Tu-22 *Blinder*; 63 Tu-22M *Backfire A*
    FTR 1,418: 237 MiG-31 *Foxhound*; 445 MiG-29 *Fulcrum*; 296 Su-27 *Flanker*; 81 MiG-25 *Foxbat*; 359 MiG-23 *Flogger* in store
    FGA 924: 172 Su-25 *Frogfoot*; 93 MiG-27 *Flogger* in store; 413 Su-24 *Fencer*; 246 Su-17 (194 in store); 52 Su-17M-2 *Fitter D* in store
    HELICOPTERS: ε700 aslt

Kaliningrad Operational Strategic Group
10,500 (Ground and Airborne); 1,100 (Naval Infantry) (total 11,600)

These forces are operated by The Ground and Coastal Defence Forces of the Baltic Fleet

Army

FORCES BY ROLE

MRR	1 bde; 1 div (cadre) (3 MRR, 2 tk regt, 1 arty regt, 1 SAM regt, 1 indep tk regt, 1 AT regt, 1 armd recce bn, some spt unit); 1 indep regt (trg)
SSM	1 bde with 18 SS-21 *Scarab (Tochka)*
SAM	1 regt

EQUIPMENT BY TYPE
TK 811: 811 MBT

ACV 865; 374 look-a-like
ARTY 345: 345 mor/MRL

Naval Infantry

Naval inf 1 regt with 26 MBT; 220 ACV; 52 MRL

Coastal Defence

FORCES BY ROLE

Arty	2 regt with 133 arty
SSM	1 regt with 8 SS-C-1B *Sepal*
AD	1 regt with 28 Su-27 *Flanker* (Baltic Fleet)

EQUIPMENT BY TYPE
AD: 50 SAM

Russian Military Districts • Leningrad MD
33,000 (Ground and Airborne); 1,300 (Naval Infantry–subordinate to Northern Fleet) (total 34,300)

HQ St Petersburg

Army

FORCES BY ROLE

MRR	2 indep bde
SF	1 (Spetsnaz) bde
AB	1 div (1 arty regt, 2 para regt)
Arty	2 bde
MRL	1 regt
AT	1 regt
SSM	1 bde with 18 SS-21 *Scarab (Tochka)*
SAM	4 bde

EQUIPMENT BY TYPE
TK 300: 300 MBT
ACV 100; 2,250 look-a-like
ARTY 690: 690 mor/MRL/

Naval Infantry

Naval inf 1 regt with 74 MBT; 209 ACV; 44 arty

Coastal Defence

Coastal Def	1 bde with 360 MT-LB; 134 arty
SAM	1 regt

Military Air Force

6th Air Force and AD Army
FORCES BY ROLE

PVO	2 corps
Bbr	1 div with 58 Su-24 *Fencer*
Ftr	1 div with 85 MiG-31 *Foxhound*; 116 Su-27 *Flanker*
Recce	1 regt with 18 Su-24 *Fencer*; 28 MiG-25R *Foxbat*
ECM / hel	1 sqn with 35 Mi-8(ECM) *Hip J*

EQUIPMENT BY TYPE
AD: 525 SAM

Moscow MD 86,200 (Ground and Airborne)
HQ Moscow

Army

2 Army HQ

FORCES BY ROLE

Tk   2 div (*each:* some spt unit, 1 armd recce bn, 1 MRR, 1 SAM regt, 1 arty regt, 3 tk regt)

MRR   2 div (*each:* some spt unit, 1 indep tk bn, 1 SAM regt, 1 AT bn, 1 armd recce bn, 1 tk regt, 1 arty regt, 3 MRR); 1 indep bde

SF   1 (Spetsnaz) bde

AB   2 div (*each:* 1 arty regt, 2 para regt)

Arty 3 indep bde (incl MRL); 1 div HQ (1 MRL bde, 1 AT bde, up to 4 arty bde (incl 1 trg))

SSM   2 bde each with 36 SS-21 *Scarab* (*Tochka*)

SAM   4 bde

EQUIPMENT BY TYPE

TK 2,000: 2,000 MBT

ACV 2,100; 1,000 look-a-like

ARTY 1,600: 1,600 mor/MRL/

Military Air Force

Moscow Air Defence and Air Army has 1 corps. Due to have additional AD regt (2 bn) equiped with S-400 SAM system. And 16th Air Army (tactical)

FORCES BY ROLE

395 cbt ac

PVO   1 (32 PVO) corps

Hel   2 sqn each with 46 Mi-8(ECM) *Hip J*

EQUIPMENT BY TYPE

AIRCRAFT

   FTR 299: 62 MiG-31 *Foxhound*; 106 MiG-29 *Fulcrum*; 90 Su-27 *Flanker*; 41 MiG-25 *Foxbat*

   FGA 80: 46 Su-25 *Frogfoot*; 34 Su-24 *Fencer*

   RECCE 16: 16 Su-24MR *Fencer-E*

AD: 600 SAM

Volga–Ural MD 66,000 (Ground and Airborne)

HQ Yekaterinburg

Army

1 Army HQ

FORCES BY ROLE

Tk   1 div (some spt unit, 1 armd recce bn, 1 SAM regt, 1 arty regt, 1 MRR, 3 tk regt)

MRR   2 div (*each:* some spt unit, 1 SAM regt, 1 arty regt, 1 tk regt, 1 indep tk bn, 1 AT bn, 1 armd recce bn, 3 MRR); 1 indep bde

SF   1 (Spetsnaz) bde

AB   1 bde

Arty 3 regt

MRL   1 bde

SSM   2 bde each with 36 SS-21 *Scarab* (*Tochka*)

SAM   1 bde

EQUIPMENT BY TYPE

TK 3,000: 3,000 MBT

ACV 2,700

ARTY 2,700: 2,700 mor/MRL

Military Air Force

5th AF and AD Army has no ac subordinated, incl storage bases

EQUIPMENT BY TYPE

AIRCRAFT • TRG 383: 383 L-39 *Albatros*

HELICOPTERS • SPT: some Mi-8 *Hip* (comms); some PZL MI-2 *Hoplite*

FACILITIES

Storage base   1

School   1 with 383 L-39 *Albatros* Trg ac; PZL Mi-2 *Hoplite* Spt hel

North Caucasus MD 101,000 (Ground And Airborne); ε1,400 (Naval infantry) (total 102,400)

HQ Rostov-on-Don; including South Caucasus Group of Forces

Army

1 Army HQ

FORCES BY ROLE

MRR   2 indep bde; 1 regt; 3 div (*each:* some spt unit, 1 arty regt, 1 tk regt, 1 armd recce bn, 1 indep tk bn, 1 SAM regt, 1 AT bn, 3 MRR)

SF   1 (Spetsnaz) bde

AB   1 div (1 arty regt, 2 para regt)

Arty   2 bde

AT   2 regt

SSM   2 bde each with 18 SS-21 *Scarab* (*Tochka*)

SAM   3 bde

EQUIPMENT BY TYPE

TK 620: 620 MBT

ACV 2,000

ARTY 875: 875 mor/MRL/

Naval Infantry

Naval inf 1 regt with 59 ACV; 14 arty

Military Air Force

4th AF and AD Army

FORCES BY ROLE

391 cbt ac

Bbr   1 div with 84 Su-24 *Fencer*

Ftr   1 corps (4 Air regt with 103 MiG-29 *Fulcrum*; 75 Su-27 *Flanker*)

FGA   1 div with 99 Su-25 *Frogfoot*

Recce 1 regt with 30 Su-24 *Fencer*

ECM   1 sqn with 52 Mi-8(ECM) *Hip J*

Trg   some regt (of tac aviation)

FACILITIES

School 1

Siberian MD 50,000 (Ground and Airborne)

HQ Chita

Army

3 Army HQ

FORCES BY ROLE

Tk	2 div (*each:* some spt unit, 1 arty regt, 1 MRR, 1 SAM regt, 1 armd recce bn, 3 tk regt)
MRR	4 bde; 4 div (*each:* some spt unit, 1 indep tk bn, 1 armd recce bn, 1 tk regt, 1 MRR, 1 SAM regt, 1 AT bn, 3 arty regt)
SF	2 (Spetsnaz) bde
AB	1 bde
Arty	10 regt; 1 div (1 AT bde, 1 MRL bde, up to 4 arty bde)
Arty / MG	2 div
AT	4 bde
SSM	2 bde each with 36 SS-21 *Scarab (Tochka)*
SAM	2 bde

EQUIPMENT BY TYPE

TK 4,000: 4,000 MBT
ACV 6,300
ARTY 2,600: 2,600 mor/MRL/

Military Air Force

14th AF and AD Army (HQ Novosibirsk)
200 cbt ac

FGA / bbr	some sqn with 30 Su-25 *Frogfoot*; 56 Su-24M *Fencer*
Ftr	some sqn with 39 MiG-31 *Foxhound*; 46 MiG-29 *Fulcrum*
Recce	some sqn with 29 Su-24MR *Fencer-E*

Far Eastern MD 73,500 (Ground and Airborne); 2,500 (Naval infantry) (total 76,000)

HQ Khabarovsk; incl Pacific Fleet and Joint Command of Troops and Forces in the Russian Northeast (comd of Pacific Fleet)

Army

2 Army HQ, 1 Corps HQ

FORCES BY ROLE

MRR	1 bde; 5 div (2 trg) (*each:* some spt unit, 1 indep tk bn, 1 AT bn, 1 SAM regt, 1 arty regt, 1 tk regt, 1 armd recce bn, 3 MRR)
SF	1 bde
Arty	1 div (1 AT bde, 1 MRL bde, 4 arty bde); 9 regt
Arty / MG	4 div (Converting to Motor Rifle)
AT	1 bde
SSM	3 bde each with 54 SS-21 *Scarab (Tochka)*
SAM	5 bde

EQUIPMENT BY TYPE

TK 3,000: 3,000 MBT
ACV 3,800
ARTY 3,500: 3,500 mor/MRL

Naval Infantry

Inf 1 div HQ (Pacific Fleet) (1 arty bn, 1 tk bn, 3 inf bn)

Coastal Defence

Coastal Def 1 div

Military Air Force

11th AF and AD Army (HQ Khabarovsk)
345 cbt ac

FGA / bbr	1 regt with 20 Su-27M; some sqn with 60 Su-25 *Frogfoot*; 97 Su-24M *Fencer*
Ftr	some sqn with 26 MiG-31 *Foxhound*; 111 Su-27 *Flanker*
Recce	some sqn with 51 Su-24MR *Fencer-E*

Paramilitary 415,000

Federal Border Guard Service ε160,000 active

Directly subordinate to the President

FORCES BY ROLE

10 regional directorates
Frontier 7 gp

EQUIPMENT BY TYPE

BMP AIFV/BTR APC (W) 1,000
ARTY 90: 90 2S1 *Carnation* 122mm SP/2S12 120mm mor/2S9 *NONA* 120mm gun/mor
PRINCIPAL SURFACE COMBATANTS • FRIGATES 23
  FFG 7:
    7 *Krivak* III (capacity 1 Ka-28 (Ka-27) *Helix* ASW hel; 1 100mm gun)
  FFL 16: 12 *Grisha* II; 4 *Grisha* III
PATROL AND COASTAL COMBATANTS 214
  PBR 7: 7 *Piyavka*
  PCI 35: 15 *Svetlyak*; 20 *Zhuk*
  PCR 77: 60 *Shmel*; 7 *Vosh*; 10 *Yaz*
  PFC 85: 20 *Pauk*; 65 *Stenka*
  PHT 10: 10 *Muravey*
LOGISTICS AND SUPPORT 26
  AGB 8: 8 *Ivan Susanin*
  ATF 18: 18 *Sorum*
AIRCRAFT • TPT 86+: 70+ An-24 *Coke*/An-26 *Curl*/An-72 *Coaler*/Il-76 *Candid*/Tu-134 *Crusty*/Yak-40 *Codling*; 16 SM-92
HELICOPTERS: 200+ Ka-28 (Ka-27) *Helix* ASW/Mi-24 *Hind* Atk/Mi-26 *Halo* Spt/Mi-8 *Hip* Spt

Interior Troops 170,000 active

FORCES BY ROLE

7 districts

Paramilitary	5 (special purpose) indep div (ODON) (*each:* 2–5 paramilitary regt); 6 div; 65 regt (bn – incl special motorised units); 10 (special designation) indep bde (OBRON) (*each:* 1 mor bn, 3 mech bn); 19 indep bde
Avn	some gp

EQUIPMENT BY TYPE

all hy eqpt to be phased out by 2005
TK 9: 9 MBT
BMP-1 AIFV/BMP-2 AIFV/BTR-80 APC (W) 1,650
ARTY 35

TOWED • 122mm 20: 20 D-30
MOR • 120mm 15: 15 PM-38
HELICOPTERS • ATK 4: 4 Mi-24 *Hind* (all hy eqpt to be phased out by 2005)

Federal Security Service ε4,000 active (armed)

Cdo some unit (incl Alfa, Beta, Zenit units)

Federal Protection Service ε10,000-30,000 active

org include elm of ground forces (mech inf bde and AB regt)

Mech inf	1 bde
AB	1 regt
Presidential Guard	1 regt

Federal Communications and Information Agency ε54,000 active

MOD • Railway Troops ε50,000

Paramilitary 4 (rly) corps; 28 (rly) bde

Special Construction Troops 50,000

DEPLOYMENT

ARCTIC AND ATLANTIC
Navy • Northern Fleet

FORCES BY ROLE

1 Navy HQ located at Severomorsk

EQUIPMENT BY TYPE

SUBMARINES 43
   STRATEGIC 11: 7 SSBN; 4 in reserve
   TACTICAL 24: 3 SSGN; 14 SSN; 7 SSK
   SUPPORT 8: 3 SSAN (other roles); 5 in reserve (other roles)
PRINCIPAL SURFACE COMBATANTS 11
   AIRCRAFT CARRIERS 1: 1 CV
   CRUISERS 3: 3 CGN/CG
   DESTROYERS 5: 5 DDG
   FRIGATES 2: 2 FFG
Patrol and Coastal Combatants circa 26
MINE WARFARE • MINE COUNTERMEASURES 18: 18 MCMV
Amphibious 8 **Logistics and Support** 130+
Naval Aviation
   AIRCRAFT
      BBR 38: 38 Tu-22M *Backfire A*
      FTR 23: 23 Su-27 *Flanker* (FGA)
      FGA 10: 10 Su-25 *Frogfoot*
      ASW 31: 17 Il-38 *May*; 14 Tu-142 *Bear*
      TPT 27: 2 An-12 *Cub* (MR/EW); 25 An-12 *Cub*/An-24 *Coke*/An-26 *Curl*
   HELICOPTERS
      ASW 42: 42 Ka-28 (Ka-27) *Helix*
      ASLT 16: 16 Ka-29 *Helix*
      SPT 24: 24 Mi-8 *Hip* (TPT)

ARMENIA
Army 3,500

EQUIPMENT BY TYPE

TK 74: 74 MBT
ACV 224
APC 14: 14 APC (T)/APC (W)
ARTY 84: 84 mor/MRL

FACILITIES

Base 1 located in Armenia

Military Air Forces • Tactical Aviation

FORCES BY ROLE

1 AD sqn with 14 MiG-29 *Fulcrum*; 2 SAM bty with S-300V (SA-12A) *Gladiator*; 1 SAM bty with SA-6 *Gainful*

EQUIPMENT BY TYPE

AIRCRAFT • FTR 14: 14 MiG-29 *Fulcrum*
AD • SAM • SP: some S-300V (SA-12A) *Gladiator*; some SA-6 *Gainful*

BALTIC
Navy • Baltic Fleet

FORCES BY ROLE

1 Navy HQ located at Kaliningrad

EQUIPMENT BY TYPE

SUBMARINES • TACTICAL 2: 2 SSK
PRINCIPAL SURFACE COMBATANTS 6: 2 DDG; 4 FFG
PATROL AND COASTAL COMBATANTS circa 26
MINE WARFARE • MINE COUNTERMEASURES 13: 13 MCMV
AMPHIBIOUS 5
LOGISTICS AND SUPPORT 130+
Naval Aviation
   AIRCRAFT
      FTR 23: 23 Su-27 *Flanker*
      FGA 26: 26 Su-24 *Fencer*
      TPT 14: 12 An-12 *Cub*/An-24 *Coke*/An-26 *Curl*; 2 An-12 *Cub* (MR/EW)
   HELICOPTERS
      ATK 11: 11 Mi-24 *Hind*
      ASW 19: 19 Ka-28 (Ka-27) *Helix*
      ASLT 8: 8 Ka-29 *Helix*
      SPT 17: 17 Mi-8 *Hip* (TPT)

BLACK SEA
Navy • Black Sea Fleet

The RF Fleet is leasing bases in Sevastopol and Karantinnaya Bays, and, jointly with Ukr warships, at Streletskaya Bay. The Fleet's overall serviceability is low.

FORCES BY ROLE

1 Navy HQ located at Sevastopol, Ukr

EQUIPMENT BY TYPE

SUBMARINES • TACTICAL 1: 1 SSK
PRINCIPAL SURFACE COMBATANTS 6: 2 CG; 2 DDG; 2 FFG
PATROL AND COASTAL COMBATANTS circa 15
MINE WARFARE • MINE COUNTERMEASURES 14: 14 MCMV
AMPHIBIOUS 5

LOGISTICS AND SUPPORT 90+: 90+ ACV
Naval Aviation
  AIRCRAFT
    FGA 18: 18 Su-24 *Fencer*
    ASW 14: 14 Be-12 *Mail*
    TPT 4: 4 An-12 *Cub* (MR/EW)
  HELICOPTERS
    ASW 33: 33 Ka-28 (Ka-27) *Helix*
    SPT 9: 1 Mi-8 *Hip* (TPT); 8 (MR/EW)

BURUNDI
UN • ONUB 1; 7 obs

CASPIAN SEA
Navy • Caspian Sea Flotilla
  The Caspian Sea Flotilla has been divided between Az (about 25%), RF, Kaz, and Tkm, which are operating a joint flotilla under RF comd currently based Astrakhan.
PRINCIPAL SURFACE COMBATANTS • FRIGATES •
FFG 1: 1 *Gepard*
PATROL AND COASTAL COMBATANTS 11: 10
  PC 1: 1 *Astrakhan* Project 21630 (First of 5–7 on order)
MINE WARFARE • MINE COUNTERMEASURES 5: 5
MCMV
AMPHIBIOUS 6+
LOGISTICS AND SUPPORT circa 15

CÔTE D'IVOIRE
UN • UNOCI 11 obs

DEMOCRATIC REPUBLIC OF CONGO
UN • MONUC 1; 22 obs

ETHIOPIA/ERITREA
UN • UNMEE 8 obs

GEORGIA
Army ε3,000
EQUIPMENT BY TYPE
TK • MBT 65: 65 T-72
ACV 200
ARTY 139: 139 120mm mor/2S1 *Carnation* 122mm SP/2S3 152mm SP/BM-21 122mm MRL/D-30 122mm Towed
FACILITIES
Base 2 (each = bde+; subord. to North Caucasus MD) located in Georgia
Military Air Forces • Tactical Aviation
  HELICOPTERS: 5 atk
UN • UNOMIG 3 obs

GEORGIA/ABKHAZIA
Armed Forces ε1,600

GEORGIA/SOUTH OSSETIA
Armed Forces 530

KYRGYZSTAN
Military Air Forces ε500
  Tactical Aviation
  Mi-8 *Hip* Spt hel/Su-24 *Fencer* FGA ac/Su-25 *Frogfoot* FGA ac/Su-27 *Flanker* ftr ac 20+

LIBERIA
UN • UNMIL 6 obs

MIDDLE EAST
UN • UNTSO 4 obs

MOLDOVA
Army ε1,400
FORCES BY ROLE
1 (op) Army gp (subord. to Moscow MD) (1 SAM regt, 1 MRR bde)
EQUIPMENT BY TYPE
TK 108: 108 MBT
ACV 214
ARTY 125: 125 mor/MRL
Military Air Forces • Tactical Aviation
  Helicopters 7

MOLDOVA/TRANSDNESTR
Army 1 MR bn
Armed Forces 500

PACIFIC
Navy • Pacific Fleet
  SUBMARINES 15
    STRATEGIC • SSBN 4:
      4 *Delta* III each with 16+ single each with RSM-50 (SS-N-18) *Stingray* SLBM Strategic
    TACTICAL 11
      SSGN 5: 4 *Oscar* II; 1 in reserve
      SSN 6: 2 in reserve; 3 *Akula*; 1 in reserve
  PRINCIPAL SURFACE COMBATANTS 8: 1 CG; 5 DDG; 2 FFG
  PATROL AND COASTAL COMBATANTS circa 30
  MINE WARFARE 8
  AMPHIBIOUs 4
  LOGISTICS AND SUPPORT 57+: 57+ ABU
Naval Aviation
  AIRCRAFT
    BBR 14: 14 Tu-22M *Backfire A*
    ASW 36: 24 Il-38 *May*; 12 Tu-142 *Bear*
    TPT 10: 10 An-12 *Cub* (MR/EW)
  HELICOPTERS
    ASW 31: 31 Ka-28 (Ka-27) *Helix*
    ASLT 6: 6 Ka-29 *Helix*
    SPT 26: 26 Mi-8 *Hip* (TPT)

SERBIA AND MONTENEGRO
UN • UNMIK 2 obs

SIERRA LEONE
UN • UNAMSIL
4 Mi-24 *Hind*
15 obs; 109

SUB-SAHARAN AFRICA
Army 100

SUDAN
UN • UNAMIS 5 obs

SYRIA
Army 150

TAJIKISTAN
Army 7,800; 14,500 conscript (Frontier Forces; RF officers, Tajik conscripts) (total 22,300)

FORCES BY ROLE

1 MRR div (subord to Volga-Ural MD)

EQUIPMENT BY TYPE

TK 128: 128 MBT

ACV 314

ARTY 180: 180 mor/MRL

FACILITIES

Base 1 located in Tajikstan

Military Air Forces • Tactical Aviation

   AIRCRAFT • FGA 5: 5 Su-25 *Frogfoot*

UKRAINE

Navy • Coastal Defence • Naval Infantry (Marines) 1,100

FORCES BY ROLE

1 indep Naval inf regt

EQUIPMENT BY TYPE

AIFV/APC (T)/APC (W) 102

lost equip type: 24 arty

WESTERN SAHARA

UN • MINURSO 26 obs

RUSSIA – DEFENCE ECONOMICS

Russia's impressive economic performance continued in 2004, on the back of high oil prices and sound economic policies. However, the IMF noted in its 2004 Article IV Consultation that the oil-driven boom has led to growing macroeconomic tensions, explaining that 'while the near-term outlook is strong, based on current projections for oil prices, and external vulnerabilities are generally low, recent nervousness in the banking sector and uncertainty related to the Yukos affair highlight the fragility of confidence'. Real GDP growth measured 7.1% in 2004, mainly as a result of higher investment and increased oil export volumes.

For the fifth year running, Russia is expected to post a budget surplus, amounting to 3.1% of GDP in 2004. Following a suggestion from the IMF, in 2003 Russia established a $3.6bn stabilisation fund with revenues from high oil prices, intended to protect the economy against future resource-price volatility and the demands on public resources that will arise from future planned structural reforms. By 2005 this had risen to $18.8bn. In recent years, the government has resisted the temptation to plough revenue windfalls into additional expenditure; however, there are signs that it is planning to loosen fiscal policy in 2005. The IMF has instead urged the authorities to increase the cap on the collection of windfall oil revenues in the oil stabilisation fund and to consider the use of some revenues in the fund to reduce debt rather than increasing expenditure.

Russia began 2005 on a positive note, fully repaying its outstanding $3.3bn debt to the IMF and receiving an investment-grade credit rating from Standard and Poor's. However, despite high oil prices, GDP growth is set to slow to 6.0% and the government's medium-term goals of doubling real GDP in the next decade and reducing excessive dependence on the energy sector remain dependent on whether investor confidence and reform momentum can be restored.

THE 2005 DEFENCE BUDGET

Over the past decade, Russian defence reforms have focused primarily on manpower cuts across the five branches of the armed forces: the Strategic Missile Force, Space Forces and Air, Land and Naval forces. During this time, the number of military personnel has fallen from 4.8m to 1.2m, closer to the longer-term target of around 800,000. At a conference in November 2003, Defence Minister Sergei Ivanov indicated that the bulk of the 'complex structural changes' were now complete and that attention would turn to the everyday issues of 'combat training and improving

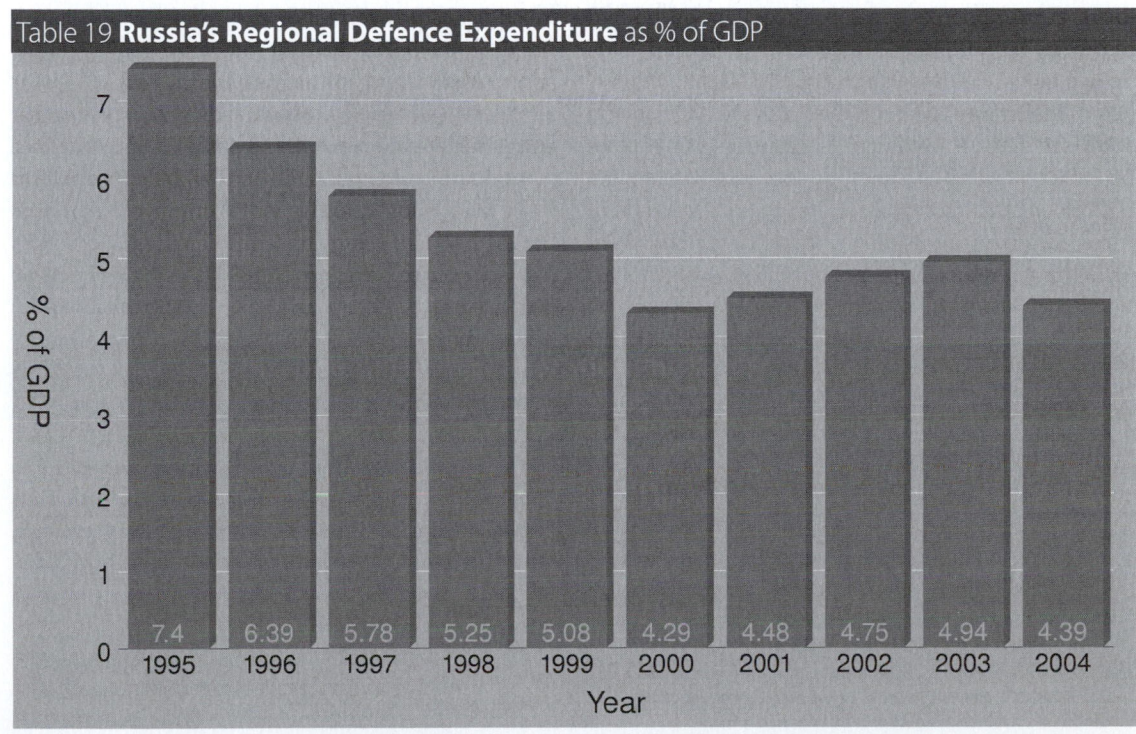

Table 19 **Russia's Regional Defence Expenditure** as % of GDP

Year	1995	1996	1997	1998	1999	2000	2001	2002	2003	2004
% of GDP	7.4	6.39	5.78	5.25	5.08	4.29	4.48	4.75	4.94	4.39

combat readiness'. In terms of future equipment and readiness capability, guidelines are set out in the 2002-10 rearmament programme that heavily weights funds towards R&D activities from 2002 to 2006, after which the focus will switch to actual procurement of new weapons systems.

In the 2005 State Budget, National Defence spending was set at R529bn, around 3.15% of GDP or 17.36% of total government expenditure (the budget was later increased by R2bn in October 2004 and R18.5bn in June 2005). However, the transparency of both the State Budget and National Defence Budget was significantly reduced and several budget

lines were dropped, making comparison with earlier years difficult. For example, in 2004, the State Budget comprised 31 different line items, but this was reduced to just 11 in 2005. Composition of the National Defence element of the State Budget was also altered, ostensibly bringing together all the various elements that relate to National Defence, which had previously been dispersed throughout different parts of the State Budget. However, of the total National Defence allocation of R529bn, only R303bn was declassified; as a result, it is not now possible to isolate the exact allocation to the Defence Ministry from within the overall National Defence Budget.

In addition to these changes in the presentation of budget data, the Defence Ministry is also proceeding with widespread reform of the procurement system in an effort to improve efficiency. When the current Defence Minister Ivanov took up his position over 50 different sub-departmental units were entitled to make procurement decisions; by the beginning of 2004, this number had been reduced to 20 and during 2005, all the previous bodies will be absorbed in one single unit. However, despite these measures and the trend in recent years that has seen the National Defence Budget increase from R149bn in 2000 to R529 in 2005, the defence minister stated that current resources would only cover the 'minimum requirements' of the armed forces and that talk of 'modernisation' under such circumstances was misleading.

Increases were spread evenly across all areas of the budget and included extra money for pay and allowances, research and development, and procurement. As part of the ongoing process to make the armed forces more attractive to potential recruits, salaries were increased by around 30%, and hazardous duty pay and pensions were also increased. A pledge was made to fully finance the transition to contracted personnel that will see the length of conscripted service reduced to 12 months from 2008. The State Defence Order (a combination of funds earmarked for procurement, R&D, repair and modernisation of equipment) was increased to R199bn. In recent years, the State Defence Order has undergone rapid growth, measuring R53bn in 2001, R80bn in 2002, R118bn in 2003 and 148bn in 2004. Of more importance, however, is the fact that in each year the Order has been virtually fully funded, with the exception of 2003, when it was reported that a more significant underspend of around 10% occurred. The government has indicated that its

Table 20 Official Russian National Defence Budget 2005 (Rbm)

National Defence Budget	2005
Armed Forces of which	384,043
- Salaries	109,800
- Procurement	82,800
- Maintenance	42,100
- Food	17,800
- Clothing	5,700
Mobilisation of troops	1,895
Mobilisation of the economy	3,500
Peacekeeping	61
Military nuclear programmes	8,693
International treaty obligations	6,231
Applied research and development	81,175
Miltary reform	7,194
Chemical weapons liquidation	10,916
Disposal of weapons and equipment	6,488
Unprogrammed investments	10,918
Others	8,018
Total National Defence Budget*	**529,132**
GDP	19,000,000
Nat Defence as % of GDP	2.78
Total Federal Budet Expenditure	3,047,000
Nat Defence as % of total expenditure	17.37
Other defence related security expenditure	
Internal Troops	23,893
State Security	61,827
Border Troops	31,684
Military Pensions	105,807
Total	**223,211**
Total Defence-related expenditure	**752,343**

* 2005 budget later reportedly increased by R2bn in October 2004 and a further R18.5bn in June 2005.

long-term aim is to split the defence budget so that 50% is earmarked for operational costs and 50% for investment and combat training.

Despite the increasing trend in the State Defence Order, debate continues about the likelihood of fulfilling the 2002-12 state armaments programme. Andrei Nikolaev, chairman of the State Duma defence committee, has indicated in the past that if the procurement budget is not increased to at least R250bn, from the current level of R82.5bn, then the timetable set out in the armament programme will not be achieved. The procurement list for 2005 include:

- 17 T-90 main battle tanks;
- One squadron of *Iskander*-M SRBMs;
- Three battalions of BTR-80 armoured personnel carriers;
- Two surface warships;
- Nine defence satellites; and
- Seven upgraded Su-27SM fighter aircraft.

There are also extra funds for the *Topol-M* intercontinental ballistic missile and development of the navy's next-generation *Bulava* submarine-launched ballistic missile, which will be carried by the new *Borey*-class nuclear-powered submarines. Equipment modernisation programmes will focus on counter-insurgency, in particular, the upgrading of 50 Mi-24 attack helicopters with night vision equipment, laser designators and precision-guided missiles. The air force is to continue with the modernisation of its Su-25 ground attack aircraft, enabling it to provide close air support to infantry units operating in urban and mountainous environments, and expects its share of the defence budget to double from 15 to 30% in 2006.

DEFENCE INDUSTRY/EXPORTS

Russian arms manufacturers enjoyed another successful year in 2004. Exports of Russian-made military hardware amounted to $4.5bn while new orders signed during the year reached $6.1bn, slightly higher than the average of $5.4bn achieved over the previous four years. Major deliveries during 2004 included the last of three Project 11356 frigates and a further 10 Su-30MKI fighter aircraft to India, and a Project 636 diesel-electric submarine and 24 Su-30MK2 fighter aircraft to China. While India and China remain the core market for Russian military equipment, other significant deliveries were made to Vietnam, Sudan and Yemen. In recent years, aerospace companies have led the field in terms of the value of exports; however, with China not now

Table 21 **2005 Russia State Defence Order (Rbm)**	
Ministry of Defence	**2005**
Procurement	82,531
Maintenance	42,115
R&D	63,136
of which	
Airforce	*11,413*
Navy	*7,051*
Army vehicles	*7,156*
Artillery	*2,151*
Light weapons	*1,552*
Electronics & Comms	*25,287*
Ammunition	*5,861*
Total	**187,783**
Interior Ministry	6,816
Federal Security Service	4,459
Total State Defence Order	**199,058**

expected to proceed with additional purchases of Su-30MK2 aircraft and terminating its licensed production of Su-27SK aircraft in favour of the acquisition of further submarines, naval companies, in particular, Admiralty Shipyards of St Petersburg, are expected to climb the export league table.

As noted in *The Military Balance* 2004–05, the relationship between China and Russia in the trade of military equipment is set to change. It is known that China wants to acquire more licences and undertake joint development of military hardware rather than continue with the historic policy of simply purchasing completed weapons systems. At present, the export of military technologies from Russia to China accounts for just 30% of the weapons trade between the two countries, and it is believed that Beijing would like to increase this share to 70%.

In recent years, Russia has made robust efforts to develop new markets, particularly in South East Asia and the Middle East, in an effort to reduce reliance on her traditional military partners. In the drive to open up new overseas markets, Sergey Chemezov, director general of Rosobornoexport, Russia's biggest military exporter by far, indicated that the company plans to open offices in Belgium, Italy, Myanmar and Venezuela. Major contracts finalised during 2004 included the $900m contract with India to modernise the aircraft carrier *Admiral Gorshkov* and a separate $700m deal to equip the aircraft carrier with 12 MiG-29K and four MiG-29K-UB aircraft, to be delivered in

2008. In a separate $1.5bn deal, Russia will supply the Indian navy with a further 30 fighter aircraft some time after 2008. China agreed a $1bn plan to acquire eight battalions of S-300PMU-2 air defence systems and Morocco contracted to purchase armoured vehicles and *Tunguska* short-range air-defence systems for an undisclosed amount.

As ever, estimating the real scale of Russian military spending is fraught with difficulty. When taken at face value, the official National Defence Budget heading in the 2004 State Budget corresponds to 2.44% of GDP; however, this figure excludes military pensions, funding for military reform, paramilitary forces and several other items that are clearly defence-related costs but are funded from outside the National Defence Budget (from 2005 several of these items will be included under the National Defence Budget heading).

When military-related spending outside the National Defence Budget is taken into account, total military spend is significantly boosted. Once included, these extra funds bring overall military related expenditure to around R683bn or 4.07% of 2004 GDP. On top of this, there is also revenue from arms exports, $4.6bn in 2004, much of which finds its way into the military coffers, further inflating the total.

Translated into dollars at the market exchange rate, Russia's official National Defence Budget for 2004 amounts to $14.2bn – roughly equivalent to South Korea's annual defence expenditure. Including the additional defence related items referred to above boosts the figure to $23.5bn, significantly lower than that suggested by the size of the armed forces or the structure of the military-industrial complex, and thus, neither of these figures are useful for comparative analysis.

For this reason, *The Military Balance* makes an estimate of actual defence expenditure in Russia based on purchasing power parity (PPP) rates. Using this methodology we estimate that total military related expenditure in 2004 (including funds from arms exports) was equivalent to $61.9bn.

Chapter Four
Middle East and North Africa

IRAQ

Despite some progress in building democratic institutions in Iraq following the 30 January 2005 elections, the ongoing insurgency continues to hamper reconstruction of the state infrastructure and the establishment of a working economy essential to the future success of the political and security efforts. The insurgency, which is being conducted by Sunni fundamentalists, Ba'ath loyalists and foreign fighters, has continued to focus its attacks on US, coalition and Iraqi security forces and, increasingly, on the Shia population, with a number of attacks on Shia mosques and rising Shia casualties. The possibility of a civil war has so far been avoided by the considerable restraint exercised by Shia community leaders, as well as by a more moderate position being adopted by the leader of the 2003–04 Shia insurgency, the radical young cleric Moqtada al-Sadr.

Suicide bombers have become the insurgents' weapon of choice. On the Shia holy day of Ashura, 19 February 2005, 17 people were killed when a suicide bomber blew up a bus in Baghdad. On 28 February in Hilla, a suicide bomb attack on people waiting to apply for government jobs killed 125 and injured 130. Another attack occurred on 18 July when, following a weekend of intensified bombings, a suicide bomber drove a petrol tanker into the centre of the town of Al-Musayyib, killing some 71 people and injuring over 100. Some reports estimate that, by July 2005, some 25,000 Iraqi civilians had been killed since the beginning of hostilities in 2003.

While the suicide bombings have done much to destabilise the country by creating fear and uncertainty, kidnapping and murder are also tactics frequently used by the insurgents, and particularly by foreign fighters led by Abu Musab al-Zarqawi, who claims to be the leader of al-Qaeda in Iraq. Moreover, al-Qaeda claimed responsibility for the assassination of the Egyptian ambassador to Baghdad, Ihab el-Sherif, on 8 July 2005. There have also been attacks on diplomats from Pakistan and Bahrain. Internet broadcasts of hostages have augmented the shock effect of these kidnappings and assassinations. For example, in May 2005, pictures of the body of Akihiko Saito,

a Japanese national working for a British security company, were posted on the Internet after he had been kidnapped and subsequently murdered.

In addition to attacks on civilians, insurgents continue to target **Iraqi security forces**. The main purpose of these attacks is to deter Iraqis from joining the counterinsurgency effort and to frustrate coalition plans to hand over some areas and tasks to indigenous security elements. Insurgents have carried out targeted assassinations of security officials: the deputy police chief of Samarra and the deputy police chief of Baghdad were killed within a day of each other on 9 and 10 January. Police stations, checkpoints and recruitment and training centres have also been attacked. A typical attack occurred on 10 July 2005, when a suicide bomber targeted an army recruitment centre in Baghdad, killing 20 Iraqi men. Earlier in the year, a car bomb in Baghdad killed 15 people when it exploded outside a security forces' academy. Altogether, some 1,174 Iraqi policemen and soldiers were killed in the first six months of 2005.

The ability of the Iraqi forces to conduct counterinsurgency operations and stabilisation efforts independently is in question. The Pentagon reported in July 2005 that the Iraqi armed forces had reached a strength of 77,700, and that police and paramilitary units totalled 93,800. The US Department of Defense expects the numbers to rise to a total of 270,000 by summer 2006, when ten 14,000-strong divisions will be equipped and operational. However, it was reported in January 2005 that of the 135,000 Iraqi forces on the security payroll, only two-thirds consistently reported for duty; and in July 2005, it was reported that half of the new police units were in training and not ready to deploy, while the other half, plus two-thirds of Iraqi Army battalions, could not carry out operations without coalition assistance.

In an attempt to overcome part of this problem and to augment the indigenous security forces in the counterinsurgency effort, the US has begun raising irregular brigades. Altogether, these units comprise some 15,000 Iraqi irregular personnel who make up local brigades in addition to the 77,000 troops of the Iraqi Army. There is some doubt as to the loyalty of these brigades, but despite this concern, the US has funded the project, constructing bases and equipping the units with vehicles, ammunition, radios and weapons.

Attacks on **coalition forces** increased in early 2005. Attacks on convoys and checkpoints worsened traffic conditions, making convoys more vulnerable. By July 2005, US forces had suffered 1,795 deaths since the beginning of conflict, the UK had lost 90 troops overall, and the other members of the coalition had collectively lost some 100 troops.

The burden of the protracted conflict and domestic dissatisfaction in a number of coalition countries led to the withdrawal of some troop contingents. In March 2005, Ukraine announced it would begin withdrawing its 1,650 troops in three stages beginning that month; Italy announced plans to withdraw its troops by September 2005, although President Silvio Berlusconi later said that the September date was an 'aspiration', not a deadline. In April 2005, Poland announced that it would withdraw its contingent when the UN mandate for stabilisation expires at the end of 2005 and, in May 2005, Bulgaria confirmed that it too would withdraw all 450 of its troops by the end of the year. Meanwhile, there are some indications that there is an intention to hand over 14 of the 18 Iraqi provinces to Iraqi control by mid-2006. The UK and the US are considering reducing coalition forces to 66,000 from the 160,000 currently deployed, of which 138,000 are American. Although UK and US officials have emphasised publicly that no deadline for withdrawal will be set, and that withdrawal will only occur when Iraq's security forces are able to take over operations, a US statement of 26 July indicated that it was hoped that troop withdrawals could start in 2006.

Despite the considerable problems faced in countering the insurgency, coalition and Iraqi troops carried out successful **counterinsurgency operations** throughout the year. In particular, in November 2004, an estimated 10,000–15,000 American troops and some 2,000 Iraqi troops participated in *Operation Phantom Fury* – later renamed *Operation al-Fajr* – to retake Fallujah from an estimated 3,000 insurgents who had taken control of the city. Thirty eight US troops and 1,200 insurgents were killed in the battle. Nine US marines and over 125 insurgents were killed in *Operation Matador*, carried out on 7–14 May with the aim of stemming the flow of foreign jihadists crossing the Syrian border to join the insurgency. *Operation Lightning* was launched on 29 May in Baghdad against increasing insurgent activity. 40,000 Iraqi soldiers and police took part in the operation, which was backed by the 10,000 US troops stationed in the capital.

Three further operations designed to follow up *Operation Matador* were launched in Anbar province in late June 2005. *Operation Spear,* a joint operation of 1,000 US marines and Iraqi soldiers targeting the insurgent routes between Syria and Iraq near Karbala, took place on 17–21 June. On 18–22 June, 800 US and Iraqi forces participated in *Operation Dagger*, which focused upon locating explosive materials and insurgent cells in the deserts north of Fallujah. Between 28 June and 6 July, an interdiction operation, *Operation Sword*, took place along the Euphrates River Hit–Haditha corridor.

Table 22 **Iraq – Selected Counter-Insurgency Operations**

Date	Name of Op	Participants	Aims	Location
8–16 November 2004	*Operation Phantom Fury/Operation al-Fajr*	10,000–15,000 US troops and some 2,000 Iraqi troops	Retake Fallujah from an estimated 3,000 insurgents controlling the city	Fallujah
7–14 May 2005	*Operation Matador*	Some 1,000 US troops	Stop foreign jihadists crossing the Syrian border to join the insurgency	Al Anbar Province
29 May	*Operation Lightning*	40,000 Iraqi soldiers and police backed by 10,000 US troops stationed in the capital.	Counter increasing insurgent activity in the capital	Baghdad
17–21 June 2005	*Operation Spear*	Joint deployment of 1,000 US marines and Iraqi soldiers	Targeted the insurgent routes between Syria and Iraq	Near Karbala
18–22 June	*Operation Dagger*	Joint deployment of 800 US and Iraqi troops	Focused upon explosive materials and insurgent cells	Deserts north of Fallujah
28 June– 6 July 2005	*Operation Sword*	Joint deployment of 1,000 US marines and Iraqi soldiers	Targeted the insurgent routes between Syria and Iraq	Along the Euphrates River in the Hit-Haditha corridor

IRAN

The nuclear issue

In November 2004, Iran voluntarily suspended enrichment processes under the Paris Agreement with the EU-3 (Britain, France and Germany). Under the accord, Tehran agreed to halt all enrichment-related activities, including production of feed material (uranium hexafluoride), manufacture and assembly of centrifuges, and installation, testing and operation of centrifuges at the Natanz facility. The EU-3 were due to offer a new package of incentives to Iran in August 2005, including the possibility of assistance for Iran's nuclear power programme. However, any new moves by the international community are being made in the knowledge that the new president, Mahmoud Ahmadinejad, who was elected in June, has made it clear that the Iranian nuclear research and development programme for enrichment will continue. On 27 July 2005, Tehran announced that it intended to restart its nuclear programme, despite a statement by the EU-3 that this would result in the end of their attempts to find a solution to the crisis, indicating that Tehran may feel strong enough to withstand Security Council sanctions and the risk of a possible US military response.

Teheran argues that development of the nuclear fuel-cycle for civilian purposes is guaranteed under Article IV of the Non-Proliferation Treaty, to which Iran has been a signatory since 1970. But the EU-3 are concerned that Iran will exploit its civilian nuclear programme to develop nuclear weapons. In particular, the Natanz enrichment facility and the Arak 40MW heavy water research reactor project are capable of producing fissile materials for nuclear weapons. The EU-3 demanded that Iran 'permanently cease' its enrichment programme and abandon the Arak project in favour of a smaller light-water research reactor. Iran rejected these demands, proposing instead to defer completion of an industrial-scale centrifuge plant for the time being, if the EU-3 accepted Iran's right to finish a smaller pilot-scale enrichment plant, which would not be capable of producing significant quantities of weapons-grade uranium. The EU-3 rejected this proposal because it believes that Iran will use a pilot-scale plant as a basis for pursuing a covert enrichment programme or as a basis to eventually build a larger overt facility, which would give Iran a rapid nuclear break-out capability. Thus, it appears unlikely that the EU-3-Iran talks will produce a diplomatic solution. (For comprehensive detail on this topic, see the IISS Dossier, *Iran's Strategic Weapons Systems: A Net Assessment*, published September 2005).

Missile developments

Iran is believed to still be producing the original version of the *Shahab*-3 intermediate-range missile – possibly at a rate of about 10 missiles a year with three launcher variants. A modified nose section has also been developed, which allows the missile to carry a lighter warhead with increased range, and provides an airburst capability and more stability following separation of the warhead.

It was reported that on 11 August 2004 and again on 20 October, Iran tested the latest version of the liquid-fuelled *Shahab*-3A/M, also known as the *Ghadr*-101. The missile is reported to have achieved an estimated range of 1,700km. In another development, in May 2005, Tehran claimed to have tested a solid-fuel missile engine.

The US regards Iran's cruise missile capability as a major concern in Gulf security. Iran is working on several new cruise missiles and, once they are developed, Teheran could employ a combination of anti-ship and land-attack cruise missiles as well as ballistic missiles.

Coalition operations in neighbouring Iraq and Afghanistan are affecting Iranian thinking on how to conduct homeland defence. Tactics and doctrine are being adapted to take account of new threats, as witnessed by a statement in November 2004 by the commander of the ground forces of the Iranian Revolutionary Guard Council (IRGC), Brigadier General Jafari, who announced that training programmes would be changed to take account of threats posed by 'global arrogance'.

The *Ashura-5* exercise series in Hamdan, Kurdestan and Zanjan provinces in September 2004 was designed to test a new defence strategy and doctrine with an asymmetric component while retaining a conventional element, as demonstrated by the airlifting of a number of T-72 main battle tanks (MBTs). Furthermore, exercises that took place in the Persian Gulf in November with regular navy and IRGC units also included irregular tactics; and the *Payrovan-e Velayat* exercise series in Lurestan, Hamedan, Ilam, Kermanshah and Khuzestan provinces in December 2004 continued the theme set in the *Ashura-5* exercises. (For comprehensive detail on this topic, see *Iran's Strategic Weapons Systems: A Net Assessment*).

In the Caspian Sea, Iran is cooperating with Russia in proposing that all littoral states combine to form a joint rapid-reaction force to counter the growing threat of illicit trafficking in the region. However, the issue of delimitation of the Caspian remains unresolved.

ISRAEL'S SEPARATION BARRIER

Israel has continued construction of the Separation Barrier, a measure aimed at preventing attacks on Israel from the West Bank. As of February 2005, approximately 210km out of the barrier's envisaged 670km had been completed, with new segments added south of Ramallah and around East Jerusalem. On 20 February, following a decision of the Israeli Supreme Court, the Israeli cabinet approved a revised route which brings the barrier closer to the 1949 armistice line in some parts of the West Bank, particularly in the Hebron area. The question of including the large settlement blocks of Ariel and Ma'ale Adumim was subject to further government decision.

Israeli counter-insurgency strategy and renewed Israeli-Palestinian security cooperation

Before the 8 February ceasefire, Israel continued its counter-terrorist strategy of military incursions into Palestinian territory in conjunction with the targeted assassinations of militant leaders. On 26 September 2004, a Hamas leader, Izz ad-Din as-Sheikh Khalil, was assassinated in Damascus, the first targeted killing of a Hamas leader by Israel in Syria.

Between 29 September and 15 October 2004, the Israeli Defence Force (IDF) launched *Operation Days of Penitence* after two Israeli children died in a Palestinian *Qassam* rocket attack on the Israeli town of Sderot. The operation, in which some 104 Palestinians were killed, including 18 children, and 77 houses were demolished and hundreds more damaged, represented the most extensive Israeli incursion into the Gaza Strip since the beginning of the second Palestinian uprising in 2000 and was aimed at preventing Palestinian militants from using the northern Gaza Strip as a launching pad for rocket attacks on Israeli border towns.

Following the death of Yasser Arafat on 10 November 2004, the election of Mahmoud Abbas as Palestinian Authority (PA) president on 9 January 2005 heralded the emergence of a moderate Palestinian leadership and paved the way for the renewal of security cooperation between Israel and the Palestinians. Beginning in January 2005, the PA, for the first time since 2000, deployed security personnel throughout the Gaza

Strip, and on 23 January the Palestine National Army (PNA) took over responsibility for the security of parts of northern Gaza that had been used for the launching of *Qassam* rockets against Israeli targets. On 26 January, Israel announced the suspension of targeted assassinations at the request of President Abbas. Two days later, the IDF were ordered to stop all offensive operations in Gaza areas where Palestinian security forces were deployed and to restrict offensive operations in the West Bank to the interception of suicide bombers.

The Sharm el-Sheikh summit of February 2005 cemented the renewed security cooperation between the parties, mostly by establishing a joint committee to deal with the release of some 900 Palestinian prisoners, and by drawing up a timetable for the handover of five major West Bank cities – Jericho, Tulkarm, Qalqilyah, Bethlehem and Ramallah – to Palestinian control. Authority over Jericho and Tulkarm was handed over on 19 March and 21 March respectively. Moreover, more progress was made when a bill was finally passed on 16 February 2005 authorising prime minister Ariel Sharon's "Disengagement Plan" for the withdrawal of the IDF and 'settlers' from the Gaza Strip. Some 50,000 members of the IDF and Israeli police force, including three armoured brigade groups were to be deployed to facilitate the withdrawal. In addition, the Palestinian Authority was expected to provide some 5,000 Palestinian troops to prevent violence surrounding Gaza by insurgent groups and Egypt was expected to deploy some 750 border guards along the Philadelphi corridor to replace the Israeli security forces, once they withdraw. Furthermore, on 20 February, as a conciliatory gesture, Israel released 500 Palestinian prisoners. However, the implementation of the Sharm el-Sheikh commitments slowed, largely because of Israeli preconditions that the further release of prisoners was dependent on the ability of the PA to clamp down on militant factions.

Militant groups, in particular the armed wing of Hamas, the Palestinian Islamic Jihad (PIJ) and the factions operating under the umbrella of the al-Aqsa Martyrs Brigades, have continued to launch suicide bombings, mortar, rocket and small-arms attacks against Israel. The second half of 2004 and January 2005 witnessed three major attacks: a Hamas double suicide bombing of an Israeli bus in Beersheva on 31 August 2004 which killed 16 Israelis; the detonation of a booby-trapped tunnel under an IDF observer post near the Egyptian–Gaza border on 12 December 2004 by Hamas and the Fatah *Hawks*, which killed five IDF soldiers; and the combined shooting and bombing attack on the Karni border crossing in Gaza by Hamas and al-Aqsa factions on 14 January 2005, which killed six Israelis. Following, the election of Abbas as president in January 2005, the number of attacks dropped. However, a suicide attack on the Stage Club in Tel Aviv on 25 February, which was instigated by an Islamic Jihad cell, killed five Israelis, raised once again the spectre of a return to violence and prompted the Israeli authorities to freeze the process of transferring West Bank cities to PA control.

President Abbas lacks the means to deal comprehensively with the militant factions by disarming them, and instead has undertaken a strategy of cooperation, which has achieved some success. On 16 March 2005, Hamas, PIJ and 11 smaller groups agreed to a ceasefire conditioned upon Israeli reciprocity, which is to remain in place until the end of 2005. In exchange, Hamas and Islamic Jihad were expected to become part of the Palestine Liberation Organisation (PLO). Furthermore, Abbas has achieved some positive results with the disarming of militants wanted by Israel. In exchange for an Israeli commitment to remove them from its wanted list, some one hundred fighters – notably from the al-Aqsa Brigades – handed in their weapons and pledged to renounce violence before joining the Palestinian security forces as part of a re-integration process. Implementation of the programme started in Jericho and Tulkarm, and on 23 June, it was extended to several hundred militants in the Nablus area.

This ceasefire has proven to be fragile. Sporadic mortar and rocket fire on Jewish settlements in Gaza and shooting attacks on Israelis in the West Bank continued in the period April–July 2005. Israel, for its part, has continued to assassinate operatives of militant factions in the West Bank and Gaza, and the PIJ increased its operations in June 2005, prompting the IDF to announce the resumption of targeted killings and arrests of PIJ operatives on 21 June.

PALESTINIAN SECURITY REFORM

President Abbas made **security reform** a key component of his programme. Having announced a policy of 'one authority, one gun', on 14 April 2005, Abbas ordered the merger of the 13 independent Palestinian security forces into three new organisations: General Security (police and internal security), General Intelligence and National Security Forces. On 22 April, Abbas retired some 1,100 security officials,

among them many of the longest-serving and most corrupt commanders, and replaced them with former mid-level officials. However, the implementation of these reforms is being undermined by powerful figures within the security services and within Abbas' own Fatah movement, and lawlessness and anarchy are growing throughout the West Bank and Gaza. Gunmen – some associated with the al-Aqsa Brigades, some members of criminal gangs – have increasingly preyed on the population and regularly attacked PNA institutions: for example, on 22 June, militants in Nablus opened fire on Prime Minister Ahmad Qurei after another group had raided his winter home in Jericho three days before. On 12 July, the PA reintroduced the death penalty, executing four convicted criminals in Gaza, drawing harsh criticism from Palestinian human-rights groups. Moreover, enduring infighting within Fatah, coupled with the rising strength of Hamas, have compelled Abbas to postpone elections to the Palestinian Legslative Council (PLC), scheduled for 17 July.

Third-party role

Members of the Quartet, which comprises the UN, the US, the EU and Russia, have been very keen to support the new Palestinian leadership and to ensure that the disengagement from Gaza is linked to the Quartet's peace plan, the 'road map'. US Lieutenant-General William Ward was sent to oversee security matters and former World Bank President James Wolfensohn was sent to be a 'civilian coordinator' for the disengagement.

The UK and Egypt have continued to play important roles in security matters. London became strongly involved in Palestinian security reforms: on 1 March, Prime Minister Tony Blair hosted a meeting in London attended by the Palestinian leadership and UN Secretary-General Kofi Annan, on the subject supporting the PA with its governance and security reforms. Meanwhile, Cairo proceeded to mediate between Palestinian factions and agreed to deploy some 750 troops on the Egyptian side of the Philadelphi route, which crosses into Egypt from southern Gaza, in order to curb arms smuggling.

SYRIA–LEBANON–ISRAEL

Following the assassination of former Lebanese Prime Minister Rafiq al-Hariri in February 2005, intense international pressure and the formation of a broad Lebanese opposition movement forced Syria to end its

29-year military presence in Lebanon. The first phase of the withdrawal, comprising some 4,000 troops, was completed on 19 March, and the second and final stage, which was overseen by UN envoy Terje Roed-Larsen, involved an estimated 10,000 troops and was completed on 26 April 2005. Also in April, and in addition to the withdrawal of Syrian troops, the Lebanese opposition forced several pro-Syrian security officials to resign, such as the head of the General Security Department, Major General Jamil Sayyed, and the commander of the Internal Security Forces, Major General Ali Hajj.

However, Syrian influence in Lebanon has remained strong, not least due to the close links between Syrian and Lebanese intelligence services. Several bombings, among them two attacks on 23 and 27 March 2005 which killed six people in mainly Christian northern Beirut, were widely seen as a reminder that Syria still considers Lebanon to be part of its sphere of influence. Also on 2 June 2005, the prominent anti-Syrian journalist Samir Qasir was killed by a car bomb outside his home in east Beirut, and on 22 June 2005, the former head of the Lebanese Communist Party, George Hawi, was also killed in a car bomb attack. In response to the killings – attributed to Syrian and Lebanese intelligence services – the UN agreed on 10 June to send a team of inspectors to Lebanon to assess whether Syrian intelligence still operated in the country.

Israeli–Lebanon border

Artillery exchanges and skirmishes between the IDF and Hizbollah and Palestinian groups have continued. Fighting centred on the disputed Shebaa Farms area. The Israeli Air Force carried out occasional air strikes and regularly entered Lebanese air space to prevent Hizbollah attacks on northern Israel. In November 2004 and again in May 2005, Hizbollah sent an Iranian-made *Mersad* 1 Unmanned Aerial Vehicle (UAV) into northern Israeli airspace. Israel responded with increased surveillance flights over south Lebanon.

Syria–Israel

On 31 November 2004, President al-Assad offered to resume peace talks with Israel, continuing from the point at which negotiations broke off in 2000. However, this was rejected by Israel, which is demanding effective Syrian steps to curb the activities of Palestinian militant groups and to rein in Hizbollah before restarting peace negotiations.

GULF COOPERATION COUNCIL (GCC)

Counter-terrorism

Saudi Arabia hosted the first International Counter-Terrorism Conference in Riyadh on 5–8 February 2005. Fifty-one countries took part as well as representatives from the UN, the Gulf Cooperation Council (GCC), Interpol, the EU, the African Union (AU) and the Organisation of Islamic Countries (OIC). Crown Prince Abdullah bin Abdulaziz – who became king following the death of King Fahd on 1 August 2005 – made a proposal, known as the Riyadh Declaration, to set up an international counter-terrorism centre.

Pressure on al-Qaeda elements in Saudia Arabia was increased with a strategy of targeted arrests and leadership killings. On 1 January 2005, security forces killed Abdullah Saud al-Sebaie, who had been involved in the attack in Khobar on 29 May 2004. On 5 April 2005, eight militants were killed in a two-day gun battle in al-Ras, some 200km north of Riyadh; among the dead were two suspected al-Qaeda leaders, Abdulkarim al-Mejjat and Saud Homoud al-Oteibi. The former was linked to the Casablanca bombings in May 2003 and the Madrid train bombings in March 2004. On 5 August 2004 security forces captured Faris al-Zahrani in the southern Abha province. Al-Zahrani was believed to have played a leading role in the group calling itself the al-Qaeda Organisation in the Arabian Peninsula. In what was possibly the most significant anti-terrorist operation in the kkingdom, police killed Saleh Awfi during a raid in Medina on 18 August 2005. Saleh Awfi was believed to be the leader of al-Qaeda in Saudi Arabia.

Capability enhancements

In April 2005, **Saudi Arabia** signed a memorandum of understanding with France to purchase 48 *Rafale* jets. Riyadh also plans to purchase 12-24 Sikorsky *Black Hawk* helicopters to augment their existing fleet of 20.

The **United Arab Emirates** (UAE) Air Force (UAEAF) started the process of selecting new advanced trainer and tanker aircraft, and received its first batch of F-16 Block 60 fighters. The first 10 of 80 F-16 Block 60 fighter aircraft, purchased in a $6.4 billion deal signed in March 2000, arrived on 3 May. On 18 February, Bell/Agusta Aerospace Company announced that the UAEAF had awarded the company a contract for eight AB139 medium-twin helicopters. The UAE is also planning to develop a missile defence system. However, UAEAF plans to acquire Northrop Grumman E-2C

Hawkeye 2000 early-warning aircraft were shelved after the US State Department refused to fully release the Link-16 communication relay system.

The Royal Air Force of **Oman** ordered 20 NH90 tactical transport helicopters and six AB139 utility and transport helicopter.

On 6 August, the US approved a $19m sale of 436 TOW-2A/B anti-tank missiles to **Kuwait** to augment its anti-armour capability. Kuwait also began work on a fence along the 200km border with Iraq, in compliance with UN Security Council Resolution 833, adopted in 1993, which demarcated the borders between the two countries.

In November and December 2004, Alessandro Minuto Rizzo, NATO deputy secretary-general, visited GCC member states Bahrain, Kuwait, Oman, Qatar, Saudi Arabia and the UAE to promote the Istanbul Cooperative Initiative (ICI). On 29 November, at a conference in London, Minuto Rizzo told a conference on NATO, the Mediterranean and the Middle East that the ICI offered GCC members 'practical cooperation in defence reform, interoperability and the fight against terrorism'.

YEMEN

Government forces put down a rebellion by the Shia cleric Sheikh al-Houthi in the northern Sa'ada province. The month-long offensive, which claimed the lives of hundreds of troops and rebels, ended on 6 August 2004 with the seizure of Houthi's last stronghold in the mountainous Maran area. Clashes between Yemeni troops and supporters of al-Houthi continued, and on 10 September 2004 he was killed with a number of his aides near the border with Saudi Arabia. On 28 March 2005 further clashes erupted between Yemeni security forces and supporters of al-Houthi, after five months of relative calm. The resurgence in violence, blamed on the father of the late cleric, killed scores of soldiers and rebels, and in August 2005 led to 30 rebels being charged with belonging to an armed group.

On 5 February an appeals court in **Yemen** sentenced to death the leader of a group of 15 suspected members of al-Qaeda accused of bombing the oil tanker *Limburg* in October 2002. They were also accused of plotting to kill the US ambassador to Sana'a and involvement in a number of other attacks on Western targets.

Meanwhile, the government's campaign to reduce the carrying of arms in public met with resistance in February 2005 as Yemeni troops began to disarm tribesmen in the remote region of Marib.

NORTH AFRICA

In **Egypt,** a series of bomb attacks by extremist Islamist groups threatened a return to the violence of the 1990s. On 8 October 2004, a suicide car bomber killed at least 32 people, mostly Israeli and Russian tourists, at the Hilton hotel in Taba near the Israeli border. Two other people died in the Nuweiba resort in Ras al-Shitan, further south on the Sinai Peninsula. The incidents represented the first major attacks since 58 tourists were killed in 1997 at Luxor.

Two more attacks occurred in Cairo on 10 and 30 April when terrorists detonated two nail bombs. Three people lost their lives in the first incident and 11 were injured in the second. The worst attack occurred on 23 July when at least 88 people died in three separate bomb attacks in the resort of Sharm el-Sheikh. One of the explosions resulted from a suicide car bomber ramming a car into a hotel; the other bombs were left in a car and a suitcase a short distance away from the targets.

Although claimed by a previously unknown group calling itself the Abdullah Azzam Brigades of al-Qaeda in Syria and Egypt, it is unclear exactly who perpetrated the Sharm el-Sheikh attacks. Previously active groups, such as al-Gamaa al-Islamiya, who were responsible for attacking tourists in the 1990s, have renounced violence, having been all but destroyed by counter-terrorism operations late in the decade. Moreover, they have condemned the recent attacks. Hamas and Islamic Jihad, accused of attacking Israeli targets, especially in the October 2004 Taba bombings, have also denied any involvement, and it is unlikely that either group would stage terrorist attacks inside Egypt and risk worsening relations with Cairo.

Israel was quick to suggest the involvement of al-Qaeda in the bombings, given scale of the Taba and the Sharm el-Sheikh attacks. However, Egyptian officials ruled out the theory on the basis of evidence gathered and the confessions of suspects. Authorities initially arrested five Egyptians charged with plotting the bomb blasts in Taba, and identified the mastermind as a Palestinian man who died in the explosion at the hotel.

The renewed targeting of tourists and Cairo's arguably heavy-handed hunt for those responsible have both occurred amid a movement for democratic reform in Egypt. In a surprise announcement on 26 February, President Hosni Mubarak asked parliament to amend the constitution to permit more than a single candidate to take part in the presidential elections. The request was approved by referendum on 25 May. Meanwhile, hundreds of people were arrested between March and May in a series of illegal demonstrations protesting against the prospect of a fifth term for President Mubarak; and riot police were criticised by human-rights groups for their actions. On 22 March Ayman Nour, an Egyptian opposition leader intending to stand against Mubarak in forthcoming elections, was charged with forgery. However, his trial has been postponed until after the presidential poll which took place on 7 September 2005.

In **Libya**, steps have been taken to continue the normalisation of relations with the West following last year's breakthrough in non-proliferation negotiations. A report by the International Atomic Energy Agency (IAEA) on 30 August 2004 praised Libya for its cooperation in revealing the details of its terminated atomic-weapons programme. In addition, on 3 September 2004 Tripoli signed an agreement to pay $35m in compensation to the victims of a bomb attack at a West Berlin nightclub in 1986. The deal was the latest in a string of admissions and compensation deals aimed at paving the way to the restoration of trade and aid links between Libya and the European Union. Washington welcomed the agreement despite Tripoli's refusal to extend the deal to include American victims of the attack. Libya, meanwhile, is demanding Washington compensate it for the losses sustained during US retaliatory air strikes.

On 20 September, US President George W. Bush formally revoked all trade sanctions on **Libya** and lifted a freeze on Libyan assets in the US, in recognition of Tripoli's decision to give up weapons of mass destruction (WMD). The move, largely symbolic given that the majority of such sanctions had been suspended since April, reflected Washington's confidence that Tripoli was sincere in its abandonment of WMD programmes. However, several terrorism-related sanctions have remained in place.

The European Union (EU) has been slower to respond to Libya's efforts, but followed the US lead by agreeing to lift its sanctions against Libya on 11 October 2004. The Italian government fronted the drive to lift EU sanctions, threatening on 17 August to do so unilaterally. The cancellation of the EU sanctions has allowed Italy to provide supplies to Libya, including helicopters, military vehicles and night-vision equipment, to train Libyan police, and to

undertake joint patrols with the Libyan Navy and coastguard in an effort to stem illegal immigration.

Libya appears to be taking steps to prevent terrorist groups operating on its soil. On 11 October, Libyan authorities announced the arrest of 17 members of a group believed to be linked to al-Qaeda, but despite the ongoing thawing of relations, Libya remains on the US list of 'state sponsors of terrorism'.

In **Algeria**, President Abdelaziz Bouteflika has remained a strong counter-terrorism partner for the US by focusing its efforts on the al-Qaeda-related Salafist Group for Preaching and Combat (GSPC). On 28 October 2004, Algeria detained one of its most wanted terror suspects. Amar Saifi. Saifi, accused of being responsible for the kidnapping of European tourists in June 2003, was arrested in Chad. The Algerian National People's Army (ANP) has undertaken extensive military operations against the GSPC, which have resulted in the surrender or killing of hundreds of militants, including a number of senior insurgent leaders.

Algerian security forces detained the leader of the GIA, Nourredine Boudiafi, in eastern Algiers, and killed his deputy, Chaabane Younes, west of Algiers in early January 2005. Furthermore, on 29 April, security forces captured Boulenouar Oukil, the new leader of the GIA, during operations that following the death of 14 people at a roadblock manned by GIA militants near Algiers. The losses further weakened the group, which was already considered to be of minimal threat to Algeria's security.

On 13 October 2004, the African Union (AU) opened the Algerian-hosted regional counter-terrorism centre in Algiers. The centre is aimed at strengthening the AU member states' collective efforts in combating terrorism on the African continent.

Thousands of suspected Islamic militants have been arrested in **Morocco** since the 2003 Casablanca suicide bomb attacks on tourist sites. Relations between Morocco and Algeria remain poor, primarily as a result of differences of opinion on how to resolve the Western Saharan issue. Such rifts were exemplified when King Mohammed VI of Morocco refused to attend the Arab Maghreb Union meeting, because of Algeria's support for the Saharan independence movement, the Polisario Front, thereby causing the meeting to be postponed indefinitely. Due to take place in Tripoli, the summit would have been the first meeting of North African heads of state in more than a decade.

Algeria Ag

Algerian Dinar D		2003	2004	2005
GDP	D	5.12tr	5.49tr	
	US$	66.2bn	77.4bn	
per capita	US$	2,087	2,411	
Growth	%	6.9	5.3	
Inflation	%	2.6	3.6	
Debt	US$	23.3bn		
Def bdgt	D	170bn	201bn	209bn
	US$	2.20bn	2.84bn	2.87bn
US$1=D		77	71	73

Population 32,531,853

Age	0–14	15–19	20–24	25–29	30–64	65 plus
Male	15%	6%	6%	5%	17%	2%
Female	14%	6%	6%	5%	17%	2%

Capabilities

ACTIVE 137,500 (Army 120,000 Navy 7,500 Air 10,000) Paramilitary 181,200
Terms of service Army 18 months (6 months basic, 12 months civil projects)

RESERVE 150,000 (Army 150,000) to age 50

ORGANISATIONS BY SERVICE

Army 45,000; ε75,000 conscript; 150,000+ reservists (to age 50) **(total** 270,000)

FORCES BY ROLE
6 Mil Regions; re-org into div structure on hold

Armd	2 div (*each:* 1 mech regt, 3 tk regt); 1 indep bde
Mech	3 div (*each:* 1 tk regt, 3 mech regt)
Mech Inf / Mot Inf	5 indep bde
Inf	20 indep bn
AB	1 div (5 AB regt)
Arty	2 regt
ADA	6 bn
AD	5 bn

EQUIPMENT BY TYPE
TK • MBT 920: 350 T-72; 300 T-62; 270 T-54/T-55
RECCE 139
  BRDM 90:
    26 BRDM-2
    64 BRDM-2 each with AT-3 *Sagger* msl
  Saladin 49 (status uncertain)
AIFV • BMP 1084: 680 BMP-1; 304 BMP-2; 100 BMP-3
APC • APC (W) 910: 110 BTR-50/OT-62
  BTR 550: 400 BTR-60; 150 BTR-80
  OT 150: 150 OT-64
  TH 390 *Fahd* 100
ARTY 1019
  TOWED 375

122mm 345: 160 D-30; 25 D-74; 100 M-1931/37; 60 M-30 *M-1938*
130mm 10: 10 M-46
152mm 20: 20 ML-20 *M-1937*
SP 170
  122mm 140: 140 2S1 *Carnation*
  152mm 30: 30 2S3
MRL 144:
  122mm 48: 48 BM-21
  140mm 48: 48 BM-14/16
  240mm 30: 30 BM-24
  300mm 18: 18 9A52 *Smerch*
MOR 330
  82mm 150: 150 M-37
  120mm 120: 120 M-1943
  160mm 60: 60 M-1943
AT
  MSL: some AT-3 *Sagger*; some AT-4 *Spigot*; some AT-5 *Spandrel*
  RCL 180
    107mm 60: 60 B-11
    82mm 120: 120 B-10
  GUNS 300
    57mm 160: 160 ZIS-2 *M-1943*
    85mm 80: 80 D-44
    100mm 60: 50 SU-100 SP (in store); 10 T-12
AD
  SAM 288+
    SP 68: ε48 SA-8 *Gecko*; ε20 SA-9 *Gaskin*
    MANPAD 220+: some SA-14 *Gremlin*/SA-16 *Gimlet*
      SA-7 220: ε220 SA-7A *Grail*/SA-7B *Grail*
  GUNS 875
    14.5mm • TOWED • ZPU 100: 60 ZPU-2; 40 ZPU-4
    20mm: 100
    23mm: 325
      SP 225: ε225 ZSU-23-4
      TOWED 100: ε100 ZU-23
    37mm • TOWED 100: ε100 M-1939
    57mm • TOWED 70: 70 S-60
    85mm • TOWED 20: 20 M-1939 *KS-12*
    100mm • TOWED 150: 150 KS-19
    130mm • TOWED 10: 10 KS-30

Navy ε7,500 (incl 500 officers)

EQUIPMENT BY TYPE
SUBMARINES • TACTICAL • SSK 2:
  2 *Kilo* (FSU) each with 6 single 533mm TT with 18 Test-71ME HWT
PRINCIPAL SURFACE COMBATANTS 9
  FRIGATES • FF 3:
    3 *Mourad Rais* (FSU *Koni*) each with 1 twin (2 eff.) with 20 SA-N-4 *Gecko* SAM, 2 RBU 6000 *Smerch* 2 (24 eff.), 4 76mm gun
  CORVETTES 6
    FSG 3:
      2 *Rais Hamidou* (FSU *Nanuchka* II) each with 4 single each with 1 SS-N-2C *Styx* tactical SSM, twin with 20 SA-N-4 *Gecko* SAM
      1 *Rais Hamidou* (FSU *Nanuchka* II) with 4 quad (16 eff.) with 16 SS-N-25 *Switchblade* tactical SSM, 1 twin (2 eff.) with 20 SA-N-4 *Gecko* SAM

FS 3:

3 *Djebel Chinoise* each with 2 twin (4 eff.) each with 1 CSS-N-8 *Saccade* tactical SSM, 3 76mm gun

PATROL AND COASTAL COMBATANTS 24

PFC 13: 13 *Kebir*

PFM 11:

9 *Osa* II each with 4 single each with 1 SS-N-2B *Styx* tactical SSM

2 *Osa* II non-operational each with 4 single each with 1 SS-N-2B *Styx* tactical SSM

AMPHIBIOUS • LS 3

LSM 1:

1 *Polnochny* A (capacity 6 MBT; 180 troops)

LST 2:

2 *Kalaat beni Hammad* (capacity 7 tanks; 240 troops) each with 1 hel landing platform (for *Sea King*)

LOGISTICS AND SUPPORT 3

AGHS (SVY) 1: 1 *El Idrissi*

Spt 1 (div)

TRV 1: 1 *Poluchat*

FACILITIES

Base 1 located at Mers el Kebir, 1 located at Algiers, 1 located at Annaba, 1 located at Jijel

Coast Guard ε500

PATROL AND COASTAL COMBATANTS 31+

MISC BOATS/CRAFT: some boats

PCC 15: 4 Baglietto; 11 Chui- E (PRC)

PCI 16 less than 100 tonnes

LOGISTICS AND SUPPORT 1: 1 Spt

Air Force ε10,000

Flying hours   150 hrs/year

FORCES BY ROLE

Ftr	2 sqn each with 20 MiG-25 *Foxbat*; 2 sqn with 48 MiG-21bis *Fishbed L & N*/MiG-21MF *Fishbed J*; 26 MiG-23B *Flogger* F/MiG-23E *Flogger*; 10+ MiG-29C *Fulcrum*/MiG-29UB *Fulcrum*
FGA	1 sqn with 8 MiG-23F *Flogger*; 2 sqn each with 17 Su-24M *Fencer*/Su-24MK *Fencer D*
Recce	1 sqn with 4 Su-24E *Fencer*; 1 sqn with 8 MiG-25R *Foxbat*
Surv	2 sqn each with 12 Beech 1900D
MR	2 sqn with 15 Beech 200T *Maritime Patrol*
Tpt	2 sqn with 9 C-130H *Hercules*; 8 C-130H-30 *Hercules*; 4 Gulfstream IV-SP; 1 Gulfstream V; 3 Il-76MD *Candid B*; 6 Il-76TD *Candid*; 2 L-100-30; 2 (VIP) sqn with 3 F-27 *Friendship*; 2 *Falcon* 900
Tkr	1 sqn with 6 Il-78 *Midas*
Atk hel	some sqn with 33 Mi-24 *Hind*; 42 Mi-171; 30 Mi-17 (Mi-8MT) *Hip* H/Mi-8 *Hip*
Tpt hel	some sqn with 8 AS-355 *Ecureuil*; 34 Mi-8 *Hip*
Trg	1 sqn with 10 Mi-8 *Hip*; 1 sqn with misc ac; 6 sqn with 28 PZL Mi-2 *Hoplite*; 2 sqn with Z-142; 2 sqn with 44 L-39ZA *Albatros*
AD	3 bde with 725 100mm/130mm/85mm
SAM	3 regt with ε140 SA-2 *Guideline*/SA-3 *Goa*/SA-6 *Gainful*/SA-8 *Gecko* (140-840 eff.)

EQUIPMENT BY TYPE

AIRCRAFT: 178 combat capable

FTR 88: 40 MiG-25 *Foxbat*

MiG-21 48: 48 MiG-21bis *Fishbed L & N*/MiG-21MF *Fishbed J*

FGA

Su-24 34: 34 Su-24M *Fencer*/Su-24MK *Fencer D*

MiG-23B *Flogger* F FGA/MiG-23E *Flogger* FTR 34

MiG-23 8: 8 MiG-23F *Flogger*

RECCE 12: 8 MiG-25R *Foxbat*; 4 Su-24E *Fencer**

MP 15: 15 Beech 200T *Maritime Patrol*

TKR 6: 6 Il-78 *Midas*

TPT 62

BEECH 1900 24: 24 Beech 1900D

C-130 17:

C-130H 17: 9; 8 C-130H-30 *Hercules*

F-27 *Friendship* 3 *Falcon* 900 2

GULFSTREAM IV 4: 4 Gulfstream IV-SP

Gulfstream V 1

Il-76 9: 3 Il-76MD *Candid B*; 6 Il-76TD *Candid*

L-100 2: 2 L-100-30

TRG • L-39 44: 44 L-39ZA *Albatros*

MiG-29C *Fulcrum* MiG-29 FTR/MiG-29UB *Fulcrum* MiG-29U Trg 10+*

TRG 44+: some Z-142

HELICOPTERS

ATK 33: 33 Mi-24 *Hind*

SPT 152: 8 AS-355 *Ecureuil*; 42 Mi-171; 34 Mi-8 *Hip*

Mi-8 74: 30 Mi-17 (Mi-8MT) *Hip* H/Mi-8 *Hip* spt hel

Mi-8 *Hip* 10 PZL Mi-2 *Hoplite* 28

AD

SAM 140: ε140 SA-2 *Guideline* Towed/SA-3 *Goa*/SA-6 *Gainful* SP/SA-8 *Gecko* SP (140–840 eff.)

GUNS 725: 725 100mm/130mm/85mm

MSL • TACTICAL • ASM: some AS-10 *Karen*; some AS-12 *Kegler*; some AS-14 *Kedge*; some AS-17 *Krypton*; some AS-7 *Kerry*

AAM: some AA-10 *Alamo*; some AA-11 *Archer*; some AA-2 *Atoll*; some AA-6 *Acrid*; some AA-7 *Apex*; some AA-8 *Aphid*

Paramilitary ε181,200

Gendarmerie 20,000

Ministry of Defence

FORCES BY ROLE

Army 6 region

EQUIPMENT BY TYPE

RECCE AML-60 /110 M-3 *Panhard* **APC (W)**

APC • APC (W) 100: 100 TH 390 *Fahd*

HELICOPTERS • SPT: some PZL Mi-2 *Hoplite*

National Security Forces 16,000

Directorate of National Security. Small arms

Republican Guard 1,200

RECCE • AML: some AML-60

APC • APC (T): some M-3

Legitimate Defence Groups ε150,000

Self-defence militia, communal guards (60,000)

NON-STATE ARMED GROUPS

see Part II

DEPLOYMENT

BURUNDI
UN • ONUB 2; 1 obs

DEMOCRATIC REPUBLIC OF CONGO
UN • MONUC 8 obs

ETHIOPIA/ERITREA
UN • UNMEE 8 obs

Bahrain Brn

Bahraini Dinar D		2003	2004	2005
GDP	D	3.59bn	4.09bn	
	US$	9.47bn	10.7bn	
per capita	US$	14,198	15,916	
Growth	%	5.7	5.5	
Inflation	%	1.6	4.9	
Debt	US$	4.6bn		
Def bdgt[a]	D	174m	180m	ε200m
	US$	460m	473m	526m
FMA (US)	US$	90.4m	25.2m	19.4m
US$1=D		0.38	0.38	0.38

[a] excluding procurement

Population   688,345

Ethnic groups: Nationals 64%; Asian 13%; other Arab 10%; Iranian 8%; European 1%)

Age	0–14	15–19	20–24	25–29	30–64	65 plus
Male	14%	4%	4%	4%	28%	2%
Female	14%	4%	4%	3%	17%	2%

Capabilities

ACTIVE 11,200 (Army 8,500 Navy 1,200 Air 1,500)
Paramilitary 10,160

ORGANISATIONS BY SERVICE

Army 8,500

FORCES BY ROLE

Armd   1 bde under strength (1 recce bn, 2 Tt bn)

Inf   1 bde (1 mot inf bn, 2 mech inf bn)

SF   1 bn

Arty   1 bde (1 lt arty bty, 1 hy arty bty, 1 MRL bty, 2 med arty bty)

Gd   1 (amiri) bn

AD   1 bn (1 ADA bty, 2 SAM bty)

EQUIPMENT BY TYPE
TK • MBT • M-60 180: 180 M-60A3
RECCE 46
    AML 22: 22 AML-90
    Ferret 8 (in store)

S52 *Shorland* 8
Saladin 8 (in store)
AIFV 25: 25 YPR-765 (with 25mm)
APC 235+
    APC (T) • M-113 115: 115 M-113A2
    APC (W) 120+: 10+ AT105 *Saxon*; 110 M-3 *Panhard*
ARTY 69
    TOWED 26: 8 105mm (lt)
        155mm 18: 18 M-198
    SP • 203mm 13: 13 M-110
    MRL • 227mm 9: 9 MLRS (est. 30 ATACMS)
    MOR 21: 12 81mm; 9 120mm
AT
    MSL • TOW • TOW-2 15: 15 TOW-2A/TOW-2B
    RCL 31
        106mm • M-40 25: 25 M-40A1
        120mm 6: 6 MOBAT
AD
    SAM 93
        SP 7: 7 *Crotale*
        TOWED • MIM-23 8: 8 I-HAWK *MIM-23B*
        MANPAD 78: 18 FIM-92A *Stinger*; 60 RBS-70
    GUNS 27
        35mm • TOWED 15: 15 Oerlikon
        40mm • TOWED 12: 12 L/70

Navy 1,200

EQUIPMENT BY TYPE
PRINCIPAL SURFACE COMBATANTS 3
    FRIGATES • FFG 1:
        1 *Sabah* (capacity either 1 BO-105 utl hel or 2 SH-2G *Super Seasprite* ASW hel) (US *Oliver Hazard Perry*) with SM-1 MR SAM, 4+ RGM-84C *Harpoon* tactical SSM, 2 triple ASTT (6 eff.), 1 76mm gun
    CORVETTES • FSG 2:
        2 *Al Manama* (capacity 1 BO-105 utl hel) (Ge *Lurssen* 62m with hel deck) each with 2 twin (4 eff.) each with 1 MM-40 *Exocet* tactical SSM, 1 76mm gun
PATROL AND COASTAL COMBATANTS 8
    PCI 2: 2 *Swift* less than 100 tonnes (FPB-20)
    PFC 2: 2 *Al Riffa* (Ge *Lurssen* 38m)
    PFM 4:
        4 *Ahmed el Fateh* (Ge *Lurssen* 45m) each with 2 twin (4 eff.) each with 1 MM-40 *Exocet* tactical SSM, 1 76mm gun
AMPHIBIOUS • CRAFT • ACV • UTILITY CRAFT AIR CUSHION 1: 1 *Tiger*
LOGISTICS AND SUPPORT • SPT 4: 4 *Ajeera* (LCU-type)

FACILITIES
Base 1 located at Mina Salman

Air Force 1,500

FORCES BY ROLE

Ftr   2 sqn with 17 F-16C *Fighting Falcon*; 4 F-16D *Fighting Falcon*

FGA   1 sqn with 8 F-5E *Tiger II*; 4 F-5F *Tiger II*

Tpt   some sqn with 1 B-727; 1 Gulfstream II; 1 Gulfstream III (VIP); 1 RJ-85

VIP   1 unit with 1 S-70A *Black Hawk*; 3 BO-105; 1 UH-60L *Black Hawk*

Trg   some sqn with 3 T67M *Firefly*

Hel   3 sqn with 24 AH-1E *Cobra*; 6 TAH-1P *Cobra**; 1 sqn with 12 AB-212 (Bell 212)

EQUIPMENT BY TYPE
AT • MSL: some TOW
AIRCRAFT 33 combat capable
    FTR • F-5 12: 8 F-5E *Tiger II*; 4 F-5F *Tiger II*
    FGA 21: 17 F-16C *Fighting Falcon*; 4 F-16D *Fighting Falcon*
    TPT 4: 1 B-727; 1 Gulfstream II; 1 Gulfstream III (VIP); 1 RJ-85
    TRG • T67 3: 3 T67M *Firefly*
HELICOPTERS
    ATK • AH-1 24: 24 AH-1E *Cobra*
    SPT • S-70 1: 1 S-70A *Black Hawk*
    UTL 16: 12 AB-212 (Bell 212); 3 BO-105
      UH-60 1: 1 UH-60L *Black Hawk*
    TRG • TAH-1 6: 6 TAH-1P *Cobra**
MSL • TACTICAL • ASM • AGM-65: some AGM-65D *Maverick*/AGM-65G *Maverick*
    AS-12 *Kegler* some
    AAM: some AIM-7 *Sparrow*
      AIM-9: some AIM-9P *Sidewinder*

Paramilitary ε10,160

Police 9,000
Ministry of Interior
HELICOPTERS • UTL 5: 1 BO-105; 2 Bell 412 *Twin Huey*; 2 Hughes 500

National Guard ε2,000
Paramilitary 3 bn

Coast Guard 260
Ministry of Interior
PATROL AND COASTAL COMBATANTS 21+: 1 PCI; 20+ less than 100 tonnes
AMPHIBIOUS • CRAFT • ACV • UTILITY CRAFT AIR CUSHION 1: 1 *Tiger*
LOGISTICS AND SUPPORT 2: 2 spt (also landing craft)

FOREIGN FORCES
United States USCENTCOM: 1 HQ HQ (USNAVCENT) located at Manama; 3,000 (Navy/USMC/Army)

Egypt Et

Egyptian Pound E£		2003	2004	2005
GDP	E£	416bn	473bn	
	US$	67.8bn	76.2bn	
per capita	US$	907	1,001	
Growth	%	3.1	4.1	
Inflation	%	3.2	8.1	
Debt	US$	31.3bn		
Def exp	E£	16.7bn	21.9bn	
	US$	2.73bn	3.53bn	
Def bdgt	E£	12.6bn	13.9bn	ε14.5bn
	US$	2.05bn	2.24bn	2.5bn
FMA (US)	US$	1.29bn	1.29bn	1.29bn
US$1=E£		6.15	6.22	5.80

Population	77,505,756

Age	0–14	15–19	20–24	25–29	30–64	65 plus
Male	17%	5%	5%	4%	17%	2%
Female	16%	5%	5%	4%	17%	3%

Capabilities

ACTIVE 468,500 (Army 340,000 Navy 18,500 Air 30,000 Air Defence Command 80,000) **Paramilitary 330,000**
Terms of service 12 months-3 years (followed by refresher training over a period of up to 9 years)

RESERVE 479,000 (Army 375,000 Navy 14,000 Air 20,000 Air Defence 70,000)

ORGANISATIONS BY SERVICE

Army 90,000–120,000; 190,000–220,000 conscript; 375,000 reservists (**total** 655,000–715,000)

FORCES BY ROLE
Armd   4 div (*each*: 1 arty bde, 1 mech bde, 2 armd bde); 1 (Republican Guard) bde; 4 indep bde
Mech   4 indep bde
Mech Inf   8 div (*each*: 1 arty bde, 1 armd bde, 2 mech inf bde)
Air Mob   1 bde
Inf   2 indep bde
SF   1 gp
Cdo   1 gp HQ (5-7 cdo gp, 1 Counter-Terrorist unit (Unit 777 (Thunderbolt Force (El Saiqa)), str 300.)
Para   1 bde
Arty   15 indep bde
SSM   1 bde with 9 FROG-7; 1 bde with 9 *Scud*-B

EQUIPMENT BY TYPE
TK • MBT 3,855
    M-1 755: 755 M1-A1 *Abrams*

M-60 1500: 300 M-60A1; 1,200 M-60A3
T-62 500 in store
Ramses II 260 (mod T-54/55)
T-54/T-55 840 in store
RECCE 412
  BRDM 300: 300 BRDM-2
  Commando Scout 112
AIFV 520
  BMP 220: 220 BMP-1 (in store)
  YPR-765 300 (with 25mm) with 210 TOW-2 msl
APC 4750
  APC (T) • **M-113** 2100: 2,100 M-113A2 (incl variants)
  APC (W) 2650: 250 BMR-600P; 500 BTR-50/OT-62 (most in store)
    BTR 250: 250 BTR-60
    Fahd-30/TH 390 *Fahd* 1,000 *Walid* 650
ARTY 4348
  TOWED 946
    122mm 526
      D-30 190: 190 D-30M
      M-1931/37 36 **M-30** *M-1938* 300
    130mm 420: 420 M-46
  SP 489
    122mm 124: 124 SP 122
    155mm • **M-109** 365: 164 M-109A2; 201 M-109A2/M-109A3 (surplus US stock, delivered Nov 2005)
  MRL 498
    122mm 356: 96 BM-11; 60 BM-21
      SAKR 200: 50 *Sakr*-10; 50 *Sakr*-18; 100 *Sakr*-36
    130mm 36: 36 *Kooryong*
    140mm 32: 32 BM-14
    227mm 26: 26 MLRS
    240mm 48: 48 BM-24 in store
  MOR 2415
    81mm • **M-125** 50: 50 M-125A2
    82mm 500
    120mm 1835: 35 M-106A2; 1,800 M-1943
    160mm 30: 30 M-160
AT
  MSL 2152: 1,200 AT-3 *Sagger* (incl BRDM-2); 200 *Milan*
  TOW 752: 52 M-901; 700 TOW-2
  RCL • **107mm** 520: 520 B-11
UAV: some R4E-50 *Skyeye*
AD
  SAM 2096+
    SP 96: 50 FIM-92A *Avenger*; 26 M-54 *Chaparral*; 20 SA-9 *Gaskin*
    MANPAD 2000+: some FIM-92A *Stinger*; 2,000 *Ayn al-Saqr*/SA-7 *Grail*
  GUNS 705+
    14.5mm • **TOWED** • **ZPU** 300: 300 ZPU-4
    23mm 365
      SP 165: 45 *Sinai*-23; 120 ZSU-23-4
      TOWED 200: 200 ZU-23-2
    57mm • **SP** 40: 40 ZSU-57-2
      TOWED: some S-60
RADAR • **LAND**: some AN/TPQ-36 *Firefinder*; some AN/TPQ-37 *Firefinder* (arty/mor)
MSL • **TACTICAL** • **SSM** 42+: 9 FROG-7; 24 *Sakr*-80; some (trials)
  SCUD 9: 9 *Scud*-B

Central Zone
Mil Region 1 zone HQ located at Cairo

Eastern Zone
Mil Region 1 zone HQ located at Ismailiya
Armd 1 div
Mech Inf 2 div

Northern Zone
Mil Region 1 zone HQ located at Alexandria
Armd 1 div
Mech Inf 2 div

Southern Zone
Mil Region 1 zone HQ located at Aswan
Armd Cav 1 div
Mech Inf 2 div

Western Zone
Mil Region 1 zone HQ located at Mersa Matruh
Armd 1 div
Mech Inf 2 div

Navy ε8,500 (incl 2000 Coast Guard); 10,000 conscript; 14,000 reservists (total 32,500)

Two Fleets: Mediterranean and Red Sea. Naval Organisation: 1 Submarine Bde, 1 Destroyer Bde, 1 Patrol Bde, 1 Fast Attack Bde, and 1 Special Ops Bde.

FORCES BY ROLE
Navy 1 HQ located at Alexandria; 1 HQ located at Safaqa

EQUIPMENT BY TYPE
SUBMARINES • **TACTICAL** • **SSK** 4:
  4 *Romeo* each with 1+ single 533mm TT with UGM-84C *Harpoon* tactical USGW
PRINCIPAL SURFACE COMBATANTS 11
DESTROYERS • **DD** 1:
  1 *El Fateh* training (UK 'Z') with 2 quad 533mm ASTT (8 eff.), 4 114mm gun
FRIGATES • **FFG** 10:
  2 *Abu Qir* (Sp *Descubierta*) each with 2 triple ASTT (6 eff.) each with *Sting Ray* LWT, 2 Mk 141 *Harpoon* quad (8 eff.) each with 1 RGM-84C *Harpoon* tactical SSM, 1 2 tube *Bofors* 375mm (2 eff.), 1 76mm gun
  2 *Damyat* (capacity 1 SH-2G *Super Seasprite* ASW hel) (US *Knox*) each with 1 Mk16 Mk 112 octuple with 8 RGM-84C *Harpoon* tactical SSM, tactical ASROC, 2 twin 324mm TT (4 eff.), 1 127mm gun
  4 *Mubarak* (capacity 2 SH-2G *Super Seasprite* ASW hel) (ex-US *Oliver Hazard Perry*) each with 1 Mk 13 GMLS with 36 SM-1 MR SAM, 4 RGM-84C *Harpoon* tactical SSM, 1 76mm gun
  2 *Najim Al Zaffir* (PRC *Jianghu* I) each with 2 twin (4 eff.) each with 1 HY-2 (CSS-N-2) *Silkworm* tactical SSM, 2 RBU 1200 (10 eff.)
PATROL AND COASTAL COMBATANTS 48
PFC 18:
  4 *Hainan* (PRC) each with 2 triple 324mm TT (6 eff.), 4 x1 RL

4 *Hainan* in reserve (PRC) each with 2 triple 324mm TT (6 eff.), 4 x1 RL

4 *Shanghai* II (PRC)

4 *Shershen* each with 1+ SA-N-5 *Grail* SAM (manual aiming), 1 12 tube BM-24 MRL (12 eff.)

2 *Shershen* (FSU) each with 4 single 533mm TT, 1 8 tube BM-21 MRL (8 eff.)

PFM 30:

6 *5th October* each with 2 single each with 1 Otomat tactical SSM

6 *Hegu* (*Komar* type) (PRC) each with 2 single each with 1 SY-1 tactical SSM

3 *Komar* (FSU) each with 2 single each with 1 SY-1 tactical SSM

4 *Osa* I (FSU, 1 may be non-op) each with 4 single each with 1 SS-N-2A *Styx* tactical SSM

6 *Ramadan* each with 4 single each with 1 Otomat tactical SSM

5 *Tiger*

MINE WARFARE • MINE COUNTERMEASURES 15

MSC 4: 4 *Aswan* (FSU *Yurka*)

MSO 6: 6 *Assiout* (FSU T-43 class)

MHC 3: 3 *Dat Assawari*

MHI 2: 2 *Safaga Swiftships*

AMPHIBIOUS

LS • LSM 3:

3 *Polnochny* B (capacity 180 troops; 6 MBT) (FSU)

CRAFT • LCU 9:

9 *Vydra* (capacity either 100 troops or 3 AMX-30 MBT)

LOGISTICS AND SUPPORT 20: 7 AOT (small); 6 AT; 1 spt (diving)

TRG 6: 5; 1 *Tariq* (ex-UK FF)

FACILITIES

Base 1 located at Alexandria, 1 located at Port Said, 1 located at Mersa Matruh, 1 located at Port Tewfig, 1 located at Safaqa, 1 located at Hurghada, 1 located at Suez, 1 located at Al Ghardaqah

Coastal Defence

Army tps, Navy control

MSL • TACTICAL • SSM: some SSC-2b *Samlet*

LNCHR 3:

3 twin each with 1 Mk 2 Otomat SSM

GUN: some 100mm

130mm: some SM-4-1

152mm some

Naval Aviation

AIRCRAFT • TPT • BEECH 1900 2: 2 Beech 1900C (maritime surveillance)

HELICOPTERS (armed, operated by Air Force)

ATK 12: 12 SA-342 *Gazelle*

ASW 15:

10 SH-2G *Super Seasprite* each with Mk 46 LWT

5 *Sea King* MK47

UAV 2: 2 *Camcopter* 5.1

Air Force 20,000; 10,000 conscript; 20,000 reservists (total 50,000)

FORCES BY ROLE

Ftr	2 sqn with 53 *Mirage* 5DE; 2 sqn with 26 F-16A *Fighting Falcon*; 1 sqn with 15 M-2000C *Mirage*; 7 sqn with 113 F-16C *Fighting Falcon*; 6 sqn with 74 MiG-21 *Fishbed*; 3 sqn with 53 J-7 (MiG-21F) *Fishbed C*
FGA	2 sqn with 29 F-4E *Phantom II*; 2 sqn with 44 J-6 (MiG-19S) *Farmer B*; 2 sqn with 42 *Alpha Jet**; 1 sqn with 16 *Mirage* 5E2
ASW / hel	some sqn with 10 SH-2G *Super Seasprite**; 5 *Sea King* MK47*; 5 SA-342L *Gazelle**
Tac / hel / tpt	some sqn with 3 CH-47C *Chinook*; 16 CH-47D *Chinook* (medium); 3 *Commando* (VIP); 22 more; 12 Mi-6 *Hook*; 2 S-70 *Black Hawk* (VIP, light); 40 Mi-8 *Hip*; 2 AS-61; 2 UH-60A *Black Hawk*; 5 UH-60L *Black Hawk* (VIP); 17 UH-12E
Recce	2 sqn with 14 MiG-21R *Fishbed H**; 6 *Mirage* 5SDR (*Mirage* 5R)*
MR	some sqn with 4 Beech 1900C
EW	some sqn with 1 Beech 1900 (ELINT); 2 C-130H *Hercules* (ELINT); 4 *Commando* 2E (ECM)
AEW	some sqn with 4 E-2C *Hawkeye*
Tpt	some sqn with 3 B-707-366C; 1 B-737-100; 1 Beech 200 *Super King Air*; 22 C-130H *Hercules*; 5 DHC-5D *Buffalo*; 3 *Falcon* 20; 3 *Gulfstream* III; 3 *Gulfstream* IV
Atk hel	6 sqn with 36 AH-64A *Apache*; 74 SA-342K *Gazelle* (44 with HOT, 30 with 20mm)
Trg	some sqn with 12 F-16B *Fighting Falcon**; 6 F-16D *Fighting Falcon**; 4 DHC-5 *Buffalo*; 70 *Alpha Jet*; 34 EMB-312 *Tucano*; 36 *Gomhouria*; 74 Grob 115EG; 80 K-8 (being delivered to replace L-29); 26 L-29 *Delfin*; 10 L-39 *Albatros*; 35 L-59E *Albatros**; 3 M-2000B *Mirage**; 15 MiG-21U *Mongol A**; 6 JJ-6 (MiG-19UTI) *Farmer*; 16*
UAV	some sqn with 20 R4E-50 *Skyeye*; 29 Teledyne-Ryan 324 *Scarab*

EQUIPMENT BY TYPE

AIRCRAFT 572 combat capable

FTR 218: 53 *Mirage* 5ED

F-16 38: 26 F-16A *Fighting Falcon*; 12 F-16B *Fighting Falcon**

MiG-21 127: 74 **J-7 (MiG-21F)** *Fishbed C* 53

FGA 223

M-2000 15: 15 M-2000C *Mirage*

F-16C *Fighting Falcon* 113 **F-16D** *Fighting Falcon* 6 *Mirage* 5E2 16

F-4 29: 29 F-4E *Phantom II*

MiG-19 44: 44 J-6 (MiG-19S) *Farmer B*

RECCE 20: 14 MiG-21R *Fishbed H**; 6 *Mirage* 5SDR (*Mirage* 5R)*

AEW • E-2 4: 4 E-2C *Hawkeye*

TPT 52

B-707 3: 3 B-707-366C

B-737 1: 1 B-737-100

BEECH 1900 5: 1 (ELINT)**Beech** 1900C 4

Beech 200 *Super King Air* 1

C-130 24: 2 C-130H *Hercules* (ELINT); 22 more

DHC-5 9: 4 **DHC-5D** *Buffalo* 5

Falcon 20 3 Gulfstream III 3 Gulfstream IV 3
TRG 447: 70 *Alpha Jet*; 42*; 34 EMB-312 *Tucano*; 36 *Gomhouria*
    GROB 115 74: 74 Grob 115EG
    JJ-6 (MiG-19UTI) *Farmer* 6; 16***K-8** 80 (being delivered to replace L-29)**L-29** *Delfin* 26 **L-39** *Albatros* 10
    L-59 35: 35 L-59E *Albatros**
    M-2000B *Mirage* 3***MiG-21U** *Mongol A* 15*

HELICOPTERS
  ELINT 4: 4 *Commando* 2E (ECM)
  ATK 115
    AH-64 36: 36 AH-64A *Apache*
    SA-342 79: 74 SA-342K *Gazelle* (44 with HOT,30 with 20mm); 5 SA-342L *Gazelle**
  ASW 15: 10 SH-2G *Super Seasprite**; 5 *Sea King* MK47*
  SPT 98
    CH-47 19: 3 CH-47C *Chinook*; 16 CH-47D *Chinook* (Medium)
    Commando 22; 3 (VIP)**Mi-6** *Hook* 12 **S-70** *Black Hawk* 2 (VIP, light) **Mi-8** *Hip* 40
  UTL 9: 2 AS-61
    UH-60 7: 2 UH-60A *Black Hawk*; 5 UH-60L *Black Hawk* (VIP)
  TRG • UH-12 17: 17 UH-12E
UAV 49: 20 R4E-50 *Skyeye*; 29 Teledyne-Ryan 324 *Scarab*
MSL • TACTICAL • ASM 245+: some AGM-119 *Penguin*
  AGM-65 245: 80 AGM-65A *Maverick*; 123 AGM-65D *Maverick*; 12 AGM-65F *Maverick*; 30 AGM-65G *Maverick*
  AGM-84 *Harpoon* some **AM-39** *Exocet* some
  ARM: some *Armat*
  AS-12 *Kegler* some
  AS-30: some
    AS-30L: some AS-30L HOT
  AAM: some AA-2 *Atoll*
    AIM-7: some AIM-7E *Sparrow*/AIM-7F *Sparrow*/AIM-7M *Sparrow*
    AIM-9: some AIM-9F *Sidewinder*/AIM-9L *Sidewinder*/AIM-9P *Sidewinder*
    R-550 *Magic* some **R530** some

Air Defence Command 30,000; 50,000 conscript; 70,000 reservists (total 150,000)

FORCES BY ROLE
AD 5 div (geographically based) (*total:* 12 SAM bty with M-48 *Chaparral*, 12 radar bn, 12 ADA bde (*total:* 100 ADA bn), 12 SAM bty with I-HAWK MIM-23B, 14 SAM bty with *Crotale*, 18 SAM bn with *Skyguard*, 110 SAM bn with *Pechora* (SA-3A) *Goa*/SA-3 *Goa*; SA-6 *Gainful*; SA-2 *Guideline*)

EQUIPMENT BY TYPE
AD
  SYSTEMS 72+:
    72+ *Amoun* each with RIM-7F *Sea Sparrow* SAM, 36+ quad SAM (144 eff.), *Skyguard* towed SAM, 36+ twin 35mm guns (72 eff.)
  SAM 702+: some *Crotale*
    SA-3 212+: 212+ *Pechora* (SA-3A) *Goa*/SA-3 *Goa* SAM
    SP 130+: 24+ *Crotale*; 50+ M-48 *Chaparral*; 56+ SA-6 *Gainful*

  TOWED 360+
    MIM-23 78+: 78+ I-HAWK *MIM-23B*
    SA-2 *Guideline* 282+ *Skyguard* some
  GUNS 1566+
    23mm • SP 266+:
      36+ *Sinai-23* (SPAAG) each with *Ayn al-Saqr* MANPAD SAM, Dassault 6SD-20S land
      230 ZSU-23-4
    57mm • TOWED 600: 600 S-60
    85mm • TOWED 400: 400 M-1939 *KS-12*
    100mm • TOWED 300: 300 KS-19

Paramilitary ε330,000 active

Central Security Forces 325,000
Ministry of Interior; Includes conscripts
APC • APC (W) 100+: 100 *Hussar*; some *Walid*

National Guard 60,000
Lt wpns only
FORCES BY ROLE
Paramilitary 8 (cadre status) bde (*each:* 3 paramilitary bn)

EQUIPMENT BY TYPE
APC • APC (W) 250: 250 *Walid*

Border Guard Forces 12,000
Ministry of Interior; lt wpns only
Gd 18 (Border Guard) regt

Coast Guard 2,000 (incl in Naval entry)
PATROL AND COASTAL COMBATANTS 99+
  MISC BOATS/CRAFT 60+: 60+ boats
  PB 7: 7 *Bertram*
  PCI 26: 5 *Nisr* (sid); 9 *Swiftships*; 12 *Timsah* less than 100 tonnes
  PFI 6: 6 *Crestitalia* less than 100 tonnes

Egyptian Armed Forces
Advisers in O, Sau, DROC
Engr 1 det opcon UNMIS

NON-STATE ARMED GROUPS
see Part II

DEPLOYMENT

BURUNDI
UN • ONUB 2 obs

DEMOCRATIC REPUBLIC OF CONGO
UN • MONUC 15; 8 obs

GEORGIA
UN • UNOMIG 4 obs

LIBERIA
UN • UNMIL 8 obs

SERBIA AND MONTENEGRO
UN • UNMIK 21 civ police

SIERRA LEONE
UN • UNAMSIL 5 obs

SUDAN
UN • UNMIS 1 air elm; 1 tpt pl; 1 engr det; 1 minesweeping det; 98; 2 obs

WESTERN SAHARA
UN • MINURSO 21 obs

FOREIGN FORCES

Australia 25 staff

Canada 29

Colombia 1 inf bn; 358

Fiji 1 Inf bn; 338

France Air Force: 1 DHC-6 *Twin Otter* tpt ac 15

Hungary 41 MP

Italy 76

New Zealand 26

Norway 4 staff

United States 1 inf bn; 1 spt bn; 750

Uruguay 60

Iran Ir

Iranian Rial r		2003	2004	2005
GDP	r	1,107tr	1,282tr	
	US$	135bn	148bn	
per capita	US$	2,012	2,196	
Growth	%	6.6	6.6	
Inflation	%	15.6	15.6	
Debt	US$	11.6bn		
Def bdgt[a]	r	30.1tr	35.5tr	ε40.0tr
	US$	3.61bn	4.1bn	4.41bn
US$1=r		8,193	8,645	8,935

[a] excluding defence industry funding

Population   68,017,860

Ethnic groups: Persian 51%; Azeri 24%; Gilaki/Mazandarani 8%; Kurdish 7%; Arab 3%; Lur 2%; Baloch 2%; Turkman 2%

Age	0–14	15–19	20–24	25–29	30–64	65 plus
Male	14%	6%	7%	5%	17%	2%
Female	13%	6%	6%	5%	16%	2%

Capabilities

ACTIVE 420,000 (Army 350,000 Navy 18,000 Air 52,000) **Paramilitary 40,000**
Armed Forces General Staff co-ordinates two parallel organisations: Regular Armed Forces and Revolutionary Guard Corps

RESERVE 350,000 (Army 350,000, ex-service volunteers)

ORGANISATIONS BY SERVICE

Army 130,000; 220,000 conscript (**total 350,000**)

FORCES BY ROLE
4 Corps HQ
Armd 4 div; some indep bde
Inf   6 div; some indep bde
SF   1 bde
Cdo   2 div; some indep bde
AB   1 bde
Arty   6 gp
Avn   some gp

EQUIPMENT BY TYPE
Totals incl those held by Islamic Revolutionary Guard Corps Ground Forces. Some equipment serviceability in doubt
TK 1693+
   MBT 1613+: ε100 *Zulfiqar*; 480 T-72
     M-60 150: 150 M-60A1
     T-62 75+
     Chieftain 100: 100 Mk3/Mk5
     T-54/T-55/Type-59 540 M-47/M-48 168
   LT TK 80+: 80 *Scorpion*; some *Towsan*
RECCE 35: 35 EE-9 *Cascavel*
AIFV • BMP 610: 210 BMP-1; 400 BMP-2
APC 640
   APC (T) 340: 140 *Boragh*; 200 M-113
   APC (W) • BTR 300: 300 BTR-50/BTR-60
ARTY 8196+
   TOWED 2010
     105mm • M-101 130: 130 M-101A1
     122mm 640: 540 D-30; 100 Type-54 (M-30) *M-1938*
     130mm 985: 985 M-46
     152mm 30: 30 D-20
     155mm 205: 120 GHN-45; 70 M-114; 15 Type 88 *WAC-21*
     203mm 20: 20 M-115
   SP 310+
     122mm 60+: 60 2S1 *Carnation*; some *Thunder* 1
     155mm 180+: 180 M-109; some *Thunder* 2
     170mm 10: 10 M-1978
     175mm 30: 30 M-107
     203mm 30: 30 M-110
   MRL 876+
     107mm 700+: some *Fadjr* 1; some HASEB; 700 Type-63
     122mm 157: 7 BM-11; 100 BM-21; 50 ARASH/HADID/NOOR
     240mm 19: ε10 *Fadjr* 3; 9 M-1985
     333mm: some *Fadjr* 5
   MOR 5000: 5,000 incl 60mm/81mm/82mm /107mm M-30 /120mm M-65.
AT
   MSL 75: 75 AT-3 *Sagger*/AT-4 *Spigot*/AT-5 *Spandrel*/*Saeqhe* 1/*Saeqhe* 2/*Toophan*/TOW (AT-3 some SP, AT-5 on *Towsan*, *Saeqhe*1/2 (*Dragon*), *Toophan* (TOW))
   RCL • 106mm 200: ε200 M-40
     107mm: some B-11
     75mm: some M-20
     82mm: some B-10
   RL • 73mm: some RPG-7 *Knout*

AIRCRAFT • TPT 17: 10 Cessna 185; 2 F-27 *Friendship*; 1 *Falcon* 20; 4 Rockwell *Turbo Commander* 690

HELICOPTERS

ATK • AH-1 50: 50 AH-1J *Cobra*

SPT 45

CH-47 20: 20 CH-47C *Chinook*

Mi-8 25: 25 Mi-17 (Mi-8MT) *Hip H*/Mi-8 *Hip* spt hel

UTL 128

AB-205 (BELL 205) 68: 68 AB-205A (Bell 205A)

AB-206 (Bell 206) *JetRanger* 10 **Bell 214** 50

UAV: some *Mohajer* III/*Mohajer* II/*Mohajer* IV

AD

SAM • SP: some HQ-7 (reported)

MANPAD: some SA-14 *Gremlin*/SA-16 *Gimlet*/SA-7 *Grail*

GUNS 1700: 1,700 35mm/M-1939 towed 37mm/S-60 towed 57mm/ZPU-2 towed 14.5mm/ZPU-4 towed 14.5mm/ZSU-23-4 SP 23mm/ZSU-57-2 SP 57mm/ZU-23 towed 23mm

MSL • TACTICAL • SSM 42+: ε30 CSS-8 (175 msl); some *Nazeat*; some *Oghab*

SCUD 12+: 12+ *Scud-B*/*Scud-C* (Up to 18. launchers/launch vehicles. 300 msl)

Shaheen-1 *Hatf-4*/*Shaheen*-2 some

Islamic Revolutionary Guard Corps 125,000+

Controls Basij (paramilitary) when mob

Islamic Revolutionary Guard Corps Ground Forces 100,000+

Controls Basij (paramilitary) when mob

Very lightly manned in peacetime. Primary role: internal security; secondary role: external defence, in conjunction with regular armed forces.

Inf up to 20 div (Some divs are designated as armd or mech but all are predominantly infantry.); some indep bde

AB 1 indep bde

Islamic Revolutionary Guard Corps Naval Forces 20,000+ (incl 5,000 Marines)

FORCES BY ROLE

Navy some (coast-defence) elm (*total:* some SSM bty with HY-2 (CSS-C-3) *Seerseeker*, some arty bty)

EQUIPMENT BY TYPE

PATROL AND COASTAL COMBATANTS 50+

PB 40+:

40+ Boghammar Marin (Swe) each with AT (ATGW), RCL, gun (machine guns)

PFM 10:

10 *Houdong* each with C-802 (CSS-N-8) *Saccade* tactical SSM

MSL • TACTICAL • SSM: some HY-2 (CSS-C-3) *Seerseeker*

FACILITIES

Base 1 located at Bandar-e Abbas, 1 located at Khorramshahr, 1 with 40+ Boghammar Marin PB (Swe) each with AT (ATGW), RCL, gun (machine guns) located at Larak, 1 located at Abu Musa, 1 located at Al Farsiyah, 1 located at Halul (oil platform), 1 located at Sirri

Islamic Revolutionary Guard Corps Marines 5,000+

Marine 1 bde

Islamic Revolutionary Guard Corps Air Force

Controls Iran's strategic missile force.

FORCES BY ROLE

Msl ε1 bde *Shahab*-1/2 with 12–18 lauchers; ε1 bn with ε6 single launchers each with ε4 *Shahab*-3 strategic IRBM

EQUIPMENT BY TYPE

LNCHR 6: ε6 single each with ε4 *Shahab*-3 strategic IRBM

Navy 18,000

FORCES BY ROLE

Navy 1 HQ located at Bandar-e Abbas

EQUIPMENT BY TYPE

SUBMARINES • TACTICAL • SSK 3:

3 *Kilo* (RF Type 877) each with 6 single 533mm TT

PRINCIPAL SURFACE COMBATANTS 5

FRIGATES • FFG 3:

3 *Alvand* (UK Vosper Mk 5) each with 3 twin (6 eff.) each with CSS-N-4 *Sardine* tactical SSM, 1 x1 RL, 1 114mm gun

CORVETTES • FS 2:

2 *Bayandor* (US PF-103) each with 2 76mm gun

PATROL AND COASTAL COMBATANTS 254+

MISC BOATS/CRAFT 200+: 200+ small craft

PCC 3: 3 *Parvin*

PCI 6: 3 *China Cat* less than 100 tonnes; 3 *Zafar* less than 100 tonnes

PFI 35 less than 100 tonnes

PFM 10:

5 *Kaman* (Fr *Combattante* II) each with up to 2-4 CSS-N-4 *Sardine* tactical SSM

5 (Fr *Combattante* II)

MINE WARFARE • MINE COUNTERMEASURES 5

MSC 3: 2 292; 1 *Shahrokh* (in Caspian Sea as trg ship)

MSI 2: 2 *Riazi* (US Cape)

AMPHIBIOUS

LS 12

LSM 3: 3 *Iran Hormuz* 24 (capacity 9 tanks; 140 troops) (ROK)

LST 6:

2 *Hejaz* (also mine layers)

4 *Hengam* (capacity 9 tanks; 225 troops) each with up to 1 hel

LSL 3: 3 *Fouque*

CRAFT 23+: 3 LCT

ACV 20+: 14+ some non-operational (under 100 tonnes)

UTILITY CRAFT AIR CUSHION 6: 6 *Wellington* (BH7)

LOGISTICS AND SUPPORT 25

AO 3: 2 *Bandar Abbas*; 1 *Kharg*

AT 1 **AWT** 2

SPT 17: 5 *Delvar*; 12 *Hendijan*

Trg 2 (craft)

Middle East and North Africa

FACILITIES
Base 1 located at Bandar-e Abbas, 1 located at Bushehr, 1 located at Kharg Island, 1 located at Bandar-e Anzelli, 1 located at Bandar-e Khomeini, 1 located at Bandar-e Mahshahr, 1 located at Chah Bahar

Marines 2,600
Marine 2 bde

Naval Aviation 2,600
AIRCRAFT
MP • P-3 5: 5 P-3F *Orion*
EW • ELINT 3: 3 Da-20 *Falcon*
TPT 13: 5 Do-228; 4 F-27 *Friendship*; 4 Rockwell *Turbo Commander* 680
HELICOPTERS
MCM • RH-53 3: 3 RH-53D *Sea Stallion*
ASW • SH-3 10: ε10 SH-3D *Sea King*
UTL 17
    AB-205 (BELL 205) 5: 5 AB-205A (Bell 205A)
    AB-206 (Bell 206) *JetRanger* 2 **AB-212 (Bell 212)** 10

Air Force ε52,000 (incl 15,000 Air Defence)
FORCES BY ROLE
some 281 cbt ac (serviceability probably about 60% for US ac types and about 80% for PRC/Russian ac). Includes Islamic Revolutionary Guard Corps Air Force equpment

Ftr	1 sqn with 24 F-7M *Airguard*; 2 sqn with 25 MiG-29A *Fulcrum A*/MiG-29UB *Fulcrum* (incl former Iraq ac); 2 sqn with 25 F-14 *Tomcat*
FGA	1 sqn with 24 F-1E *Mirage* (former Iraq ac); 7 Su-25K *Frogfoot A* (former Iraq ac); 30 Su-24MK *Fencer D* (including former Iraq ac); 4 sqn total with 65+ F-4D *Phantom II*/F-4E *Phantom II*; 4 sqn total with 60+ F-5E *Tiger II*/F-5F *Tiger II*
Recce	1 (det) sqn with 6+ RF-4E *Phantom II**
MR	some sqn with 5 P-3MP *Orion**
AEW	some sqn with 1 Il-76 *Candid* (former Iraq ac)
Tkr / tpt	1 sqn with 3 B-707; 1 B-747
Tpt	5 sqn with 2 Y-7 (An-24) *Coke*; 1 B-727; 4 B-747F; 18 C-130E *Hercules*/C-130H *Hercules*; 10 F-27 *Friendship*; 1 *Falcon* 20; Il-76 *Candid* (former Iraq ac); total of 2 *Jetstar*; 10 PC-6B *Turbo Porter*; 3 Rockwell *Turbo Commander* 680; 9 Y-12, 40+ Iran-140
Trg	some sqn with 20 F-5B *Freedom Fighter**; 4 TB-200 *Tobago*; 8 TB-21 *Trinidad*; 20 Beech F-33A *Bonanza*/Beech F-33C *Bonanza*; 15 EMB-312 *Tucano*; 15 JJ-7 *Mongol A**; 22 MFI-17 *Mushshak*; 40 PC-7 *Turbo Trainer*; 7 T-33 *Shooting Star*
Hel	some sqn with 2 CH-47 *Chinook*; *Shabaviz* 2-75 (indigenous versions in production); *Shabaviz* 2061; 2 AB-206A (Bell 206) *JetRanger*; 30 AB-214C
SAM	16 bn each with ε150 I-HAWK MIM-23B; 5 sqn with FM-80 (*Crotale*); total of 30 *Rapier*; 15 *Tigercat*; 45 SA-2 *Guideline*; 10 SA-5 *Gammon*; FIM-92A *Stinger*; SA-7 *Grail*

EQUIPMENT BY TYPE
AIRCRAFT 281 combat capable
  FTR 153

F-5 80: 20 F-5B *Freedom Fighter**; 60+ F-5E *Tiger II*/F-5F *Tiger II*
F-7M *Airguard* 24 **F-14** *Tomcat* 25
F-1 24: 24 F-1E *Mirage* (former Irq ac)
FGA 102
  Su-25 7: 7 Su-25K *Frogfoot A* (former Iraq ac)
  Su-24 30: 30 Su-24MK *Fencer D* (including former Iraq ac)
  F-4 260+: 65 F-4D *Phantom II*/F-4E *Phantom II*
RECCE • RF-4 6+: 6+ RF-4E *Phantom II**
MP • P-3 5: 5 P-3MP *Orion**
TPT 65+: 3 B-707; 1 B-727
  B-747 5: 1; 4 B-747F
  C-130 18: 18 C-130E *Hercules*/C-130H *Hercules*
  F-27 *Friendship* 10 *Falcon* 20 1 **Il-76** *Candid* 1+ (former Irq ac) *Jetstar* 2
  PC-6 10: 10 PC-6B *Turbo Porter*
  Rockwell *Turbo Commander* 680 3 **Y-12** 9 **Y-7 (An-24)** *Coke* 2
UTL 12: 4 TB-200 *Tobago*; 8 TB-21 *Trinidad*
TRG 119
  BEECH F-33 20: 20 Beech F-33A *Bonanza*/Beech F-33C *Bonanza*
  EMB-312 *Tucano* 15 **JJ-7** *Mongol A* 15***MFI-17** *Mushshak* 22
  MiG-29A *Fulcrum A* MiG-29 FTR/MiG-29UB *Fulcrum* MiG-29U Trg 25 (incl former Irq ac)
TRG 119: 40 PC-7 *Turbo Trainer*; 7 T-33 *Shooting Star*
HELICOPTERS
SPT 2+: 2 CH-47 *Chinook*
  SHABAVIZ: some *Shabaviz* 2-75 (indigenous versions in production); some *Shabaviz* 2061
UTL 32
  AB-206 (BELL 206) 2: 2 AB-206A (Bell 206A) *JetRanger*
  BELL 214 30: 30 AB-214C
AD • SAM 2500+: some FM-80 (*Crotale*); 30 *Rapier*; 15 *Tigercat*
  TOWED 2445
    MIM-23 2400: ε2,400 I-HAWK MIM-23B
    SA-2 *Guideline* 45
  STATIC 10: 10 SA-5 *Gammon*
  MANPAD: some FIM-92A *Stinger*; some SA-7 *Grail*
  GUNS • 23mm • TOWED: some ZU-23
  37mm • TOWED: some Oerlikon
MSL • TACTICAL • ASM up to 3000: up to 3,000 AGM-65A *Maverick*/AS-10 *Karen*/AS-11 *Kilter*/AS-14 *Kedge*/C-801K (CSS-N-4) *Sardine* ALCM
  AAM: some AA-10 *Alamo*; some AA-11 *Archer*; some AA-8 *Aphid*; some AIM-54 *Phoenix*; some AIM-7 *Sparrow*; some AIM-9 *Sidewinder*
    PL-2: some PL-2A
    PL-7 some

Paramilitary 40,000

Law-Enforcement Forces 40,000 (border and security troops); 450,000 on mobilisation (incl conscripts) (total 40,000–490,000)
part of armed forces in wartime
PATROL AND COASTAL COMBATANTS 130
  MISC BOATS/CRAFT 40: 40 harbour craft
  PCI circa 90
AIRCRAFT • TPT: some Cessna 185/Cessna 310
HELICOPTERS • UTL 24: ε24 AB-205 (Bell 205)/AB-206 (Bell 206) *JetRanger*

Basij Resistance Force up to ε1,000,000 on mobilisation

paramilitary militia, part of the Islamic Revolutionary Guard Corps, with claimed membership of 10 million, including women and children; perhaps 1 million combat capable Militia 2,500 bn (claimed); some (full time)

NON-STATE ARMED GROUPS

see Part II

DEPLOYMENT

ETHIOPIA/ERITREA
UN • UNMEE 1 obs

Iraq Irq

Iraqi Dinar D		2003	2004	2005
GDP	US$	23bn	23bn	
per capita	US$	931	906	
Growth	%	-30	35	
Inflation	%	36.3	55	
Debt	US$	93.9bn		
US$1=D		0.31	1,456	1,471

Population   26,074,906

Ethnic groups: Arab 75-80% (of which Shi'a Muslim 55%, Sunni Muslim 45%) Kurdish 20-25%

Age	0–14	15–19	20–24	25–29	30–64	65 plus
Male	20%	6%	5%	4%	14%	1%
Female	20%	6%	5%	4%	13%	2%

Capabilities

ACTIVE 179,800 (Army 79,000 Navy 700 Air 200 Iraqi Police Service 67,000 Ministry of Interior Forces 32,900)

ORGANISATIONS BY SERVICE

Security Forces ε179,800

(These are estimated figures for the Iraqi security forces organisations which reflect ongoing changes occuring within the Iraqi security forces)

The target strength of the security forces is 273,889

Army ε79,000 (Includes National Guard)

Navy ε700 (total numbers unconfirmed)

Iraqi Coastal Defence Force (ICDF)

ICDF crews being trained by UK RN

EQUIPMENT BY TYPE
PATROL AND COASTAL COMBATANTS 10:
   PC 10: 5 (RIB); 5 27m (Chinese-built)

FACILITIES
Base 1 located at Umm Qasr

Department of Border Enforcement

Iraqi Air Wing ε200

FORCES BY ROLE
Recce   1 sqn located at Basra with 8 CH-2000 SAMA; 1 sqn located at Kirkuk with 8 SB7L-360 *Seeker*

Tpt   1 sqn located at Baghdad with 6 C-130B *Hercules*/C-130E *Hercules*

Tpt / utl 1 sqn located at Basra with 4 Bell 206 *JetRanger*; 16 UH-1H *Iroquois*

EQUIPMENT BY TYPE
AIRCRAFT
   RECCE 16: 8 CH-2000 SAMA; 8 SB7L-360 *Seeker*
   TPT • C-130 6: 6 C-130B *Hercules*/C-130E *Hercules*
HELICOPTERS
   SPT 36: 24 Mi-17-1V; 10 Mi-17-V5 (incl 1 VIP)
      PZL W-3 • PZL W-3W 2: 2 PZL W-3WA *Salamandra* (to arrive by end 2005)
   UTL 20: 4 Bell 206 *JetRanger*
      UH-1 16: 16 UH-1H *Iroquois*

Ministry of Interior Forces ε32,900 (Includes Civil Intervention Force, Emergency Response Unit, Border Enforcement and Dignitary Protection)

excluding Police

Iraqi Police Service 67,000 (including Highway Patrol)

FOREIGN FORCES

Albania Army: 70 (Peace Support)
Armenia 46
Australia Air Force: 1 P-3C *Orion* MP ac Army: 850 (Peace Support)
Azerbaijan 150 (Peace Support)
Bulgaria Army: ε466 (Peace Support)
Czech Republic 10 medical (surgical team); 100 MP
Denmark Army: 1 (bn) Inf gp (Peace Support) (1 scout sqn, 1 inf/SH coy); ε380 (Peace Support); ε90 (det from L)
El Salvador Army: 360 (Peace Support)
Estonia 3 Army (NTM-1, PAO, US CENTCOM); 1 inf pl (Operation Iraqi Freedom)
Georgia 156 (Peace Support) Army: 156 (Peace Support)
Hungary Army: 293 (Peace Support)
Italy Army: 1 (Carabinieri) Army det; 1 mech inf; 1 marine coy; 3,100 (Peace Suport)
Japan Air Self-Defense Force: 200 (Peace Support - in Kuwait) Ground Self-Defense Force: ε560 (Peace Support) Maritime Self- Defense Force: ε300 (Peace Support)
Latvia Army: 120 (Peace Support)
Lithuania Army: 90 (Peace Support)
Macedonia, Former Yugoslav Republic Army: 28 (Peace Support - to be deployed)
Mongolia Army: 130 (Peace Support)
Netherlands Air Force: 3 CH-47D *Chinook* spt hel ε1,100 (Peace Support) Navy: 1 (bn) marine gp
New Zealand Army: 61 (Peace Support) some
Norway Army: 12 (staff officers, Peace Support)

Poland Army: 8 PZL W-3 *Sokol* spt hel; 4 Mi-17U *Hip H* Trg/Mi-8 *Hip* spt; 1 mech inf bde; to be 2,300 (Peace Support)

Portugal Army: 1 sy coy; 128 (Peace Support)

Romania Army: 1 mech inf bn; ε730

Slovakia Army: 82 (Peace Support)

Thailand Army: ε400 (Peace Support - to withdraw Sep 2004)

Ukraine Ground Forces (Army): 1,640 (Peace Support)

United Kingdom Army: 1 (composite) Army HQ; 1 armd bde; some spt unit; 9,200 (Peace Support)

United States USCENTCOM: 1 MEF HQ (1 MAW with up to 48 F/A-18A *Hornet*/F/A-18C *Hornet*; up to 36 F/A-18D *Hornet*; up to 64 AV-8B *Harrier II*; up to 12 KC-130 *Hercules*; up to 92 AH-1W *Cobra*; up to 90 CH-46E *Sea Knight*; up to 64 CH-53E *Sea Stallion*; up to 50 UH-1N *Iroquois*, 1 FSSG regt, 1 MARDIV div with up to 58 M-1 *Abrams*; up to 207 LAV-CP; up to 247 AAV; up to 72 M-198); 1 armd div; 1 armd bde; 1 armd cav regt (cav regt is bde equivalent); 1 mech inf div; 1 air aslt div; 85,600; 2,850; 7,100; 26,050; 121,600 (*Op Iraqi Freedom*)

Israel Il

New Israeli Shekel NS		2003	2004	2005
GDP	NS	501bn	525bn	
	US$	110bn	117bn	
per capita	US$	18,002	18,982	
Growth	%	1.3	4.3	
Inflation	%	0.7	-0.4	
Debt	US$	71.2bn		
Def exp	NS	46.9bn	43.2bn	
	US$	10.3bn	9.68bn	
Def bdgt	NS	32.8bn	34.9bn	34.3bn
	US$	7.22bn	7.82bn	7.87bn
FMA (US)	US$	3.08bn	2.14bn	2.2bn
US$1=NS		4.55	4.47	4.37

Population   6,276,883

Ethnic groups: Jewish 82%; Arab 19% (incl Christian 3%, Druze 2%) Circassian ε3,000

Age	0–14	15–19	20–24	25–29	30–64	65 plus
Male	14%	4%	4%	4%	20%	4%
Female	13%	4%	4%	4%	20%	6%

Capabilities

ACTIVE 168,300 (Army 125,000 Navy 8,300 Air 35,000) **Paramilitary 8,050**

RESERVE 408,000 (Army 380,000 Navy 3,500 Air 24,500)

Terms of service officers 48 months other ranks 36 months women 24 months (Jews and Druze only; Christians, Circassians and Muslims may volunteer). Annual trg as cbt reservists to age 41 (some specialists to age 54) for men, 24 (or marriage) for women

ORGANISATIONS BY SERVICE

Strategic Forces

Il is widely believed to have a nuclear capability
Aircraft some
MSL • STRATEGIC • IRBM: some *Jericho 2*
  SRBM: some *Jericho 1*
WARHEADS up to 200 nuclear warheads

Army 20,000; 105,000 conscript; 500,000+ on mobilisation; (total 125,000–625,000)

Organisation and structure of formations may vary according to op situations

FORCES BY ROLE

3 regional commands (each with:) 2 regular divs, 1-2 regional/territorial divs, 2 regular bdes

Armd	2 div; 15 bde
Inf	4 div; 12 bde
Para	8 bde
Arty	4 regt
SP arty	8 regt

Regional/Territorial Forces

Can be mobilised in 72hrs
Inf 11 (territorial/regional) bde

Reserve Organisations

Reserves ε380,000 **reservists**

Armd   8 div (*total:* 15 armd bde, 6 arty regt, 4 inf bde, 6 mech inf bde)

Air Mob 1 div (3 air mob bde, 1 para bde)

EQUIPMENT BY TYPE

TK • MBT 3,657:
  Merkava 1681: 441; 407 Mk1; 375 MkII; 378 MkIII; 80 MkIV
  Magach-7 111 **Ti-67** 261 (T-55 mod)
  M-60 711: 711 M-60 MBT/M-60A1/M-60A3
  Centurion 206 **T-54/T-55/T-62S** 126
  M-48 561: 561 M-48A5
RECCE 408: ε400 RBY-1 RAMTA; ε8 Tpz-1 *Fuchs*
APC 10,419+
  APC (T) 10373+: 276 *Achzarit* (T-55)
    M-113 6131: 6,131 M-113A1/M-113A2
    M-2 180 some in store
    M-3 3,386 some in store
    Nagmachon ε400 (*Centurion* chassis)
    Nakpadon some
  APC (W) 46
    BTR 40: 34 BTR-152; 6 BTR-40
    Puma 6 (*Centurion*)
ARTY 5432
  TOWED 456
    105mm • M-101 70: 70 M-101A1
    122mm 5: 5 D-30
    130mm 100: 100 M-46
    155mm 281
      M-114 50: 50 M-114A1 in reserve
      M-46 100 **M-68/M-71** 50 **M-839P/M-845P** 81

SP 620
155mm 548: 148 L-33
    M-109 350: 350 M-109A1
    M-50 50
175mm 36: 36 M-107
203mm 36: 36 M-110
MRL 224
122mm 58: 58 BM-21
160mm 50: 50 LAR-160
227mm 60: 60 MLRS
240mm 36: 36 BM-24
290mm 20: 20 LAR-290
MOR 4132: 2,000 52mm; 1,358 81mm; 652 120mm (towed)
    160mm 122: 104 M-43 in reserve; 18 M-66 *Soltam*
AT
MSL 1225+: some AT-3 *Sagger*; 900 M47 *Dragon*; 25 MAPATS
    SPIKE: some *Gil/Spike*
    TOW • TOW-2 300: 300 TOW-2A/TOW-2B (incl Ramta (M-113) SP)
RCL • 106mm • M-40 250: 250 M-40A1
RL • 82mm: some B-300
AD • SAM • MANPAD 1250: 1,000 FIM-43 *Redeye*; 250 FIM-92A *Stinger*
RADAR • LAND: some AN/PPS-15 (arty); some AN/TPQ-37 *Firefinder* (arty); some EL/M-2140 (veh)
MSL 107
    STRATEGIC 100: ε100 Jericho 1 SRBM/*Jericho* 2 IRBM
    TACTICAL • SSM 7: 7 *Lance* (in store)

Navy ε5,500; 11,500 on mobilisation; 2,500 conscript; 3,500 reservists (total 11,500–23,000)

EQUIPMENT BY TYPE
SUBMARINES • TACTICAL • SSK 3:
3 *Dolphin* (Ge Type-212 variant) each with 6 single 533mm TT each with 5 UGM-84C *Harpoon* tactical USGW, 16 HWT, 4 single 650mm TT
PRINCIPAL SURFACE COMBATANTS • CORVETTES • FSG 3:
3 *Eilat* (capacity either 1 AS-565SA *Panther* ASW hel or 1 AS-366G *Dauphin II* SAR hel) (*Sa'ar* 5) each with 2 Mk 140 *Harpoon* quad (8 eff.) each with 1+ RGM-84C *Harpoon* tactical SSM, 2 triple (6 eff.) each with Mk 46 LWT, 2 32 cell VLS (64 eff.) each with up to 64 *Barak* SAM, 1 76mm gun
PATROL AND COASTAL COMBATANTS 51
MISC BOATS/CRAFT • SPECIAL WARFARE SUPPORT CRAFT 1: 1 *Katler*
PCC 3: 3 Type-1012 *Bobcat* catamaran
PCI 3: 3 *Nashal*
PFI 32:
1 *Alligator*
18 *Dabur* less than 100 tonnes each with 2 x1 324mm TT each with Mk 46 LWT
13 *Super Dvora* less than 100 tonnes (SSM, and TT may be fitted) each with 2 x1 324mm TT each with Mk 46 LWT
PFM 12:
2 *Aliya* each with 4 single each with 1 GII *Gabriel II* tactical SSM, 2 Mk 140 twin each with 4 RGM-84C *Harpoon* tactical SSM

8 *Hetz* (*Sa'ar* 4.5) each with 6 single each with 1 GII *Gabriel II* tactical SSM, 2 Mk 140 twin each with 1 RGM-84C *Harpoon* tactical SSM, 1 32 Cell/Mk 56 (1-32 eff.) with *Barak* SAM, 1 76mm gun
2 *Reshef* (*Sa'ar* 4) each with 4–6 single each with 1 GII *Gabriel II* tactical SSM, 1 Mk 140 twin with 1 RGM-84C *Harpoon* tactical SSM, 1 76mm gun
AMPHIBIOUS • CRAFT 2
LCT 1: 1 *Ashdod*
LCM 1: 1 US type
FACILITIES
Base 1 located at Haifa, 1 (naval commandos) located at Atlit, 1 located at Eilat, 1 located at Ashdod

Naval Aviation
HELICOPTERS • ASW 5: 5 AS-565SA *Panther*

Naval Commandos ε300

Air Force 35,000; 24,500 reservists (total 59,500)
Responsible for Air and Space Coordination

FORCES BY ROLE

Air	some (Strategic Reserve) sqn with A-4 *Skyhawk*/F-4 *Phantom II*/*Kfir* C-7
Ftr / FGA	2 sqn with 29 F-15A *Eagle*; 7 F-15B *Eagle*; 17 F-15C *Eagle*; 11 F-15D *Eagle*; 8 sqn with 90 F-16A *Fighting Falcon*; 20 F-16B *Fighting Falcon*; 52 F-16C *Fighting Falcon*; 74 F-16D *Fighting Falcon*; 1 sqn with 12 F-16I *Sufa* (102 being delivered at rate of 2/month); 3 sqn with 39 A-4N *Skyhawk*; 1 sqn with 25 F-15I *Ra'am*
ASW	some sqn with AS-565SA *Panther* (missions flown by IAF but with some in non-rated aircrew)
MR	some sqn with 3 IAI-1124 *Seascan*
EW	some sqn with 5 RC-12D *Guardrail*; 3 B-707 (ELINT/ECM); 4 Beech 200CT *Super King Air*; 2 C-130H *Hercules* (ELINT); 8+ Do-28; 3 Gulfstream G-550 (ELINT); 6 IAI-202 *Arava*
AEW	some sqn with 2 B-707 (with *Phalcon* system)
Tpt	some sqn with 5 B-707 (transport/tanker); 11 C-47 *Skytrain*
Tkr	some sqn with 5 KC-130H *Hercules*
Liaison	some sqn with 2 BN-2 *Islander*; 8 Beech 80 *Queen Air*; 22 Cessna U-206 *Stationair*
Atk hel	some sqn with 16 AH-1E *Cobra*; 39 AH-1F *Cobra*; 40 AH-64A *Apache*; *Sarat* (AH-64D) *Apache* (First of 18)
Tpt hel	some sqn with 41 CH-53D *Sea Stallion*; 24 S-70A *Black Hawk*; 43 Bell 206 *JetRanger*; 34 Bell 212; 10 UH-60A *Black Hawk*; 14 UH-60L *Black Hawk*
Trg	some sqn with 4 Beech 80 *Queen Air*; 43 CM-170 *Magister* (being replaced for lead-in ftr trg by A-4N); 17 Grob 120; 10 TA-4H *Skyhawk**; 16 TA-4J *Skyhawk**

UAV some sqn with *Delilah; Firebee; Harpy;* RQ-5A *Hunter; Samson; Scout; Searcher* MK II; Silver Arrow *Hermes* 450

SAM 2 bty each with 9 Arrow II; 3 bty each with 16 PAC-2; 17 bty with MIM-23 *HAWK*; 3 bty with MIM-104 *Patriot*

EQUIPMENT BY TYPE
AIRCRAFT 402 combat capable
FTR 199
F-16 110: 90 F-16A *Fighting Falcon*; 20 F-16B *Fighting Falcon*
F-15 89: 29 F-15A *Eagle*; 7 F-15B *Eagle*; 17 F-15C *Eagle*; 11 F-15D *Eagle*; 25 F-15I *Ra'am*
FGA 177+
A-4 39: 39 A-4N *Skyhawk*
F-16C *Fighting Falcon* 52 **F-16D** *Fighting Falcon* 74 **F-16I** *Sufa* 12 (102 being delivered at rate of 2/month)**A-4 Skyhawk/F-4 Phantom II/Kfir C-7** some
RECCE • RC-12 5: 5 RC-12D *Guardrail*
MP 3: 3 IAI-1124 *Seascan*
TKR • KC-130 5: 5 KC-130H *Hercules*
TPT 63+: 2 B-707 (with *phalcon* system); 5 (tpt/tkr); 3 (ELINT/ECM); 2 BN-2 *Islander*
BEECH 200 4: 4 Beech 200CT *Super King Air*
Beech 80 *Queen Air* 12
C-130 7: 2 C-130H *Hercules* (ELINT); 5 more
C-47 *Skytrain* 11 **Do-28** 8+ **Gulfstream G-550** 3 (ELINT)**IAI-202** *Arava* 6
UTL • CESSNA 206 22: 22 Cessna U-206 *Stationair*
TRG 86: 43 CM-170 *Magister* (being replaced for lead-in ftr trg by A-4N); 17 Grob 120
TA-4 26: 10 TA-4H *Skyhawk**; 16 TA-4J *Skyhawk**
HELICOPTERS
ATK 95+
AH-1 55: 16 AH-1E *Cobra*; 39 AH-1F *Cobra*
AH-64 40+: 40 AH-64A *Apache*; some *Sarat* (AH-64D) *Apache* (First of 18)
ASW: some AS-565SA *Panther* (missions flown by IAF but with some in non-rated aircrew)
SPT 65
CH-53 41: 41 CH-53D *Sea Stallion*
S-70 24: 24 S-70A *Black Hawk*
UTL 101: 43 Bell 206 *JetRanger*; 34 Bell 212
UH-60 24: 10 UH-60A *Black Hawk*; 14 UH-60L *Black Hawk*
UAV 22+: some *Delilah*; some *Firebee*
RECCE • TAC: some *Harpy*; some RQ-5A *Hunter*, some *Samson*, some *Scout*, 22+ *Searcher* MK II (some, 22 in store); some Silver Arrow *Hermes* 450
AD
SAM 66+: 18 *Arrow* II; 48 PAC-2
M-163 *Vulcan* SP 20mm/M-163 *Machbet Vulcan* SP 20mm/M-48 *Chaparral* SP SAM 35 each with 4 FIM-92A *Stinger* MANPAD SAM
SAM 66+
TOWED: some MIM-104 *Patriot*; some MIM-23 HAWK
GUNS 815
23mm 210
SP 60: 60 ZSU-23-4

TOWED 150: 150 ZU-23
M-167 *Vulcan* towed 20mm/M-1939 towed 37mm/TCM-20 towed 20mm 455
40mm • TOWED 150: 150 L/70
MSL • TACTICAL • ASM: some AGM-114 *Hellfire*; some AGM-45 *Shrike*
AGM-62: some AGM-62B *Walleye*
AGM-65: some *Maverick*
AGM-78: some AGM-78D *Standard*
POPEYE I: some *Popeye* I tactical ASM/*Popeye* II
AAM: some AIM-120 *AMRAAM*; some AIM-7 *Sparrow*; some AIM-9 *Sidewinder*; some *Python* III; some *Python* IV; some *Shafrir*
BOMB • PGM • JDAM: some GBU-31

Airfield Defence 3,000 active; 15,000 reservists **(total 18,000)**

Paramilitary ε8,050

Border Police ε8,000
APC • APC (W): some Walid

Coast Guard ε50
PATROL AND COASTAL COMBATANTS 4: 3 PC; 1 PCR (US)

DEPLOYMENT

TURKEY
Air Force
FORCES BY ROLE
up to 1 ftr det (occasional) located at Akinci, Tu with F-16 *Fighting Falcon*
EQUIPMENT BY TYPE
AIRCRAFT • FTR: some F-16 *Fighting Falcon*

Jordan HKJ

Jordanian Dinar D		2003	2004	2005
GDP	D	7.1bn	7.8bn	
	US$	10.0bn	10.9bn	
per capita	US$	1,831	1,957	
Growth	%	3.3	6.7	
Inflation	%	2.3	3.4	
Debt	US$	8.33bn		
Def bdgt	D	648m	652m	678m
	US$	914m	919m	956m
FMA (US)	US$	606m	208m	207m
US$1=D		0.71	0.71	0.71

Population	5,759,732

Ethnic groups: Palestinian ε50-60%

Age	0–14	15–19	20–24	25–29	30–64	65 plus
Male	18%	5%	5%	5%	18%	2%
Female	17%	5%	5%	4%	15%	2%

Capabilities

ACTIVE 100,500 (Army 85,000 Navy 500 Air 15,000)
Paramilitary 10,000

RESERVE 35,000 (Army 30,000 Joint 5,000)

ORGANISATIONS BY SERVICE

Army 85,000; 30,000 reservists (obligation to age 40) (total 115,000)

FORCES BY ROLE

Army | 1 (Northern) comd (1 inf bde, 1 arty bde, 1 AD bde, 2 mech bde); 1 (Southern) comd (1 armd bde, 1 inf bde); 1 (Eastern) comd (1 AD bde, 1 arty bde, 2 mech bde); 1 (Central) comd (1 AD bde, 1 lt inf bde, 1 mech bde, 1 arty bde)

Reserve | armd 1 (Royal) div (1 arty bde, 1 AD bde, 3 armd bde)

Spec Ops | 1 comd (1 Ranger bn, 1 (counter-terrorism) army bn, 2 SF bde)

EQUIPMENT BY TYPE
TK 1139
  MBT 1120: 390 CR1 *Challenger 1* (*Al Hussein*); 274 FV4030/2 *Khalid*
    M-60 288: 288 M-60A1/M-60A3
    Tariq Centurion 90 (*Centurion* in store)
    M-47/M-48A5 78 (in store)
  LT TK 19: 19 *Scorpion*
AIFV 226+
  BMP 26+: 26+ BMP-2
  FSV 90 • **MK III-20** 200: ε200 *Ratel-20*
APC 1350
  APC (T) 1300: ε100 FV 103 *Spartan*
    M-113 1200: 1,200 M-113A1/M-113A2
  APC (W) • **BTR** 50: 50 BTR-94 ((BTR-80))
ARTY 1233
  TOWED 94
    105mm 54: 36 M-102; 18 MOBAT (being delivered)
    155mm 36: 18 M-1/M-59; 18 M-114
    203mm 4: 4 M-115
  SP 399
    105mm 35: 35 M-52
    155mm 282
      M-109 253: 253 M-109A1/M-109A2
      M-44 29
    203mm 82: 82 M-110A2
  MOR 740: 450 81mm (incl 130 SP)
    107mm 60: 60 M-30
    120mm 230: 230 Brandt
AT
  MSL 670: 30 *Javelin*; 310 M47 *Dragon*
    TOW 330: 330 TOW msl/TOW-2A (incl 20 M-901 ITV)
  RL 4800+
    112mm 2300: 2,300 APILAS
    73mm: some RPG-26
    94mm 2500: 2,500 LAW-80
AD
  SAM 992+
    SP 152: 92 SA-13 *Gopher*; 60 SA-8 *Gecko*
    MANPAD 840+: 250 FIM-43 *Redeye*; 300 SA-14 *Gremlin*;

240 SA-16 *Gimlet*; some SA-18 *Grouse* (*Igla*)
    SA-7 50: 50 SA-7B2 *Grail*
  GUNS 395
    20mm • **SP** 139: 139 M-163 *Vulcan*
    23mm • **SP** 40: 40 ZSU-23-4
    40mm • **SP** 216: 216 M-42 (not all op)
RADAR • **LAND**: some AN/TPQ-36 *Firefinder*/AN/TPQ-37 *Firefinder* (arty, mor)

Navy ε500

EQUIPMENT BY TYPE
PATROL AND COASTAL COMBATANTS 20
  PB 7: 3 *Al Hashim* (*Rotork*); 4 *Bertram* (normally civilian)
  PCC 10 less than 100 tonnes
  PFI 3: 3 *Al Hussein* less than 100 tonnes (Vosper 30m)
FACILITIES
Base 1 located at Aqaba

Air Force 15,000 (incl 3,400 AD)

Flying hours | 180 hrs/year

FORCES BY ROLE

Ftr | 1 sqn with 15 F-1CJ (F-1C) *Mirage*/*Mirage* F-1BJ (F-1B); 1 sqn with 12 F-16A *Fighting Falcon*; 4 F-16B *Fighting Falcon*

FGA / Recce | 1 sqn with 15 *Mirage* F-1EJ (F-1E); 3 sqn with 54 F-5E *Tiger II*/F-5F *Tiger II*

Surv | some sqn with 2 RU-38A *Twin Condor*

Tpt | 1 sqn with 4 C-130H *Hercules*; 2 CASA 212A *Aviocar*; 2 CL-604 *Challenger*; 2 CN-235; 2 TB-20 *Trinidad*

VIP | 1 (Royal) flt with 1 A-340-211; 2 Gulfstream IV; 1 L-1011 *Tristar*; 3 S-70A *Black Hawk*

Atk hel | 2 sqn each with 20+ AH-1F *Cobra* each with TOW tactical ASM

Tpt hel | 1 sqn with 12 AS-332M *Super Puma*; 3 BO-105 (operated on behalf of the police); 9 EC-635 (utl/SAR); 36 UH-1H *Iroquois*

Trg | 3 sqn with 15 *Bulldog* 103 (being replaced by 16 T-67M); 13 CASA C-101 *Aviojet*; 8 Hughes 500D

AD | 2 bde (*total*: 14 AD bty each with 80 I-HAWK MIM-23B, 3 AD bty with PAC-2)

EQUIPMENT BY TYPE
AIRCRAFT 100 combat capable
  FTR 85
    F-5 54: 54 F-5E *Tiger II*/F-5F *Tiger II*
    F-16 16: 12 F-16A *Fighting Falcon*; 4 F-16B *Fighting Falcon*
    F-1 15: 15 *Mirage* F-1EJ (F-1E)
  MP • **RU-38** 2: 2 RU-38A *Twin Condor*
  TPT 14
    A-340 1: 1 A-340-211
    C-130 4: 4 C-130H *Hercules*
    CASA 212 2: 2 CASA 212A *Aviocar*
    CL-604 *Challenger* 2 **CN-235** 2 **Gulfstream IV** 2 **L-1011** *Tristar* 1
    UTL 2: 2 TB-20 *Trinidad*
  TRG 28: 15 *Bulldog* 103 (being replaced by 16 T-67M firefly); 13 CASA C-101 *Aviojet*
  F-1CJ (F-1C) *Mirage* **FTR**/*Mirage* **F-1BJ (F-1B) Trg** 15*

HELICOPTERS
ATK • AH-1 40+:
40+ AH-1F *Cobra* each with TOW tactical ASM
SPT 15
AS-332 12: 12 AS-332M *Super Puma*
S-70 3: 3 S-70A *Black Hawk*
UTL 56: 3 BO-105 (operated on behalf of the police); 9 EC-635 (ult/SAR)
HUGHES 500 8: 8 Hughes 500D
UH-1 36: 36 UH-1H *Iroquois*
AD • SAM 1120+: some PAC-2
TOWED • MIM-23 1120: 1,120 I-HAWK MIM-23B
MSL • TACTICAL • ASM • AGM-65: some AGM-65D *Maverick*
TOW some
AAM: some AIM-7 *Sparrow*; some AIM-9 *Sidewinder*; some R-550 *Magic*; some R530

Paramilitary 10,000 active

Public Security Directorate ε10,000 active
Ministry of Interior
FORCES BY ROLE
Sy 1 (Police Public) bde
EQUIPMENT BY TYPE
TK • LT TK: some *Scorpion*
APC • APC (W) 55+: 25+ EE-11 *Urutu*; 30 FV603 *Saracen*

Reserve Organisations

Civil Militia 'People's Army' ε35,000 reservists
men 16–65, women 16–45

DEPLOYMENT

BURUNDI
UN • ONUB 62; 5 obs

CÔTE D'IVOIRE
UN • UNOCI 210; 7 obs

DEMOCRATIC REPUBLIC OF CONGO
UN • MONUC 20 obs; 6

EAST TIMOR
UN • UNOTIL 1 obs

ETHIOPIA/ERITREA
UN • UNMEE 7 obs; 962

HAITI
UN • MINUSTAH 755

GEORGIA
UN • UNOMIG 9 obs

LIBERIA
UN • UNMIL 7 obs; 124

SERBIA AND MONTENEGRO
NATO • KFOR I 99
UN • UNMIK 2 obs

SIERRA LEONE
UN • UNAMSIL 4 obs; 84

SUDAN
UN • UNMIS 3 obs

Kuwait Kwt

Kuwaiti Dinar D		2003	2004	2005
GDP	D	12.4bn	15.7bn	
	US$	40.3bn	50.9bn	
per capita	US$	18,469	22,576	
Growth	%	9.7	7.2	
Inflation	%	1.0	1.8	
Debt	US$	14bn		
Def bdgt	D	1.20bn	1.23bn	ε1.32bn
	US$	3.88bn	3.99bn	4.27bn
US$1=D		0.31	0.31	0.31

Population   2,335,648

Ethnic groups: Nationals 35%; other Arab 35%; South Asian 9%; Iranian 4%; other 17%

Age	0–14	15–19	20–24	25–29	30–64	65 plus
Male	14%	4%	7%	9%	25%	2%
Female	13%	4%	5%	5%	11%	1%

Capabilities

ACTIVE 15,500 (Army 11,000 Navy 2,000 Air 2,500)
Paramilitary 6,600
Terms of service voluntary

RESERVE 23,700 (Joint 23,700)
Terms of service obbligation to age 40

ORGANISATIONS BY SERVICE

Army 7,300; up to 3,700 (foreign personnel) (total 11,000)

FORCES BY ROLE

Army	1 (reserve) bde
Armd	3 bde
Mech / Recce	1 bde
Mech Inf	2 bde
SF	1 unit (forming)
Cdo	1 bn
Arty	1 (force) bde
Engr	1 (force) bde
Gd	1 (Amiri) bde
AD	1 comd (some (small number of *Stinger*) AD bty, 4 (HAWK Phase III) AD bty, 5 (*Patriot* PAC-2) AD bty, 6 (*Amoun* (*Skyguard/Aspide*)) AD bty)

EQUIPMENT BY TYPE
TK • MBT 368
M-1 218: 218 M1-A2 *Abrams*
M-84 75; 75 in store
AIFV up to 450
BMP up to 196: up to 76 BMP-2; up to 120 BMP-3
254 *Desert Warrior* (incl variants)
APC 321
APC (T) 270

M-113 230: 230 M-113A2
M-577 40
APC (W) 51: 40 TH 390 *Fahd* in store; 11 TPz-1 *Fuchs*
ARTY 218
SP • 155mm 113: 18 AU-F-1 in store
M-109 23: 23 M-109A3
Mk F3 18 **PLZ45** 54
MRL • 300mm 27: 27 9A52 *Smerch*
MOR 78: 60 81mm
107mm 6: 6 M-30
120mm 12: ε12 RT-F1
AT
MSL 118+: some M47 *Dragon*
TOW 118: 44 TOW Msl/TOW-2; 66 HMMWV; 8 M-901
RCL • 84mm 200: ε200 *Carl Gustav*
AD • SAM 84
TOWED • MIM-23 • I-HAWK 24: 24 I HAWK Phase III *MIM-23B*
STATIC 12: 12 *Aspide*
MANPAD 48: 48 *Starburst*
GUNS • 35mm • TOWED: some Oerlikon

Navy ε2,000 (incl 500 Coast Guard)

EQUIPMENT BY TYPE
PATROL AND COASTAL COMBATANTS 40
MISC BOATS/CRAFT 30: circa 30 boats
PFM 10:
1 *Al Sanbouk* (Ge *Lurssen* TNC-45) with 2 twin (4 eff.) each with 1 MM-40 *Exocet* tactical SSM
1 *Istiqlal* (Ge *Lurssen* FPB-57) with 2 twin (4 eff.) each with 1 MM-40 *Exocet* tactical SSM
8 *Um Almaradim* (Fr P-37 BRL) each with 2 twin (4 eff.) each with 1 *Sea Skua* tactical SSM, 1 sextuple (6 eff.) (launcher only)
AMPHIBIOUS • CRAFT 2: 2 LCM
LOGISTICS AND SUPPORT 4: 4 spt
FACILITIES
Base 1 located at Ras al Qalaya

Air Force ε2,500

Flying hours   210 hrs/year

FORCES BY ROLE
Ftr   some sqn with 14 F-1CK (F-1C) *Mirage/Mirage* F-1BK (F-1B) non-operational
Ftr / FGA   some sqn with 31 F/A-18C *Hornet*; 8 F/A-18D *Hornet*
CCT   1 sqn with 11 *Hawk* MK64; 8 *Tucano* T MK52 (Shorts 312); 8†
Tpt   some sqn with 1 DC-9; 3 L-100-30; 4 AS-332 *Super Puma* (tpt/SAR/atk); 9 SA-330 *Puma*
Trg / atk hel some sqn with 16 SA-342 *Gazelle* each with HOT tactical ASM
Atk hel   some sqn with 16 AH-64D *Apache*

EQUIPMENT BY TYPE
AIRCRAFT 50 combat capable
FGA • F/A-18 39: 31 F/A-18C *Hornet*; 8 F/A-18D *Hornet*
TPT 4: 1 DC-9
L-100 3: 3 L-100-30
TRG 27: 11 *Hawk* MK64*

F-1CK (F-1C) *Mirage* **FTR**/*Mirage* **F-1BK (F-1B) trg** 14 non-operational
TRG 27: 8 *Tucano* T MK52 (Shorts 312); 8†
HELICOPTERS
ATK • AH-64 16: 16 AH-64D *Apache*
ASLT 16: 16 SA-342 *Gazelle** each with HOT tactical ASM
SPT 13: 4 AS-332 *Super Puma* (tpt/SAR/attack); 9 SA-330 *Puma*

Paramilitary ε6,600 active

National Guard ε6,600 active

FORCES BY ROLE
Armd   1 (armd car) bn
SF   1 bn
Paramilitary 3 (national guard) bn
MP   1 bn

EQUIPMENT BY TYPE
RECCE 20: 20 VBL
APC • APC (W) 92: 70 *Pandur*; 22 S600 (incl variants)

Coast Guard 500

PATROL AND COASTAL COMBATANTS 35+
MISC BOATS/CRAFT 30+: 30+ armed boats
PCC 5: 1 *Al Shaheed*; 4 *Inttisar* (Aust 31.5m)
AMPHIBIOUS • CRAFT 3: 3 LCU

Armed Forces 23,700 reservists

obligation to age 40; 1 month annual trg

FOREIGN FORCES

United Kingdom Army:
United States USCENTCOM: 19,700; 1,250; 2,700; 1,600
Germany (*Op Enduring Freedom*): 50

Lebanon RL

Lebanese Pound LP		2003	2004	2005
GDP	LP	27.4tr	25.6tr	
	US$	18.2bn	17.0bn	
per capita	US$	4,886	4,507	
Growth	%	3.0	5.0	
Inflation	%	1.3	3.0	
Debt	US$	18.5bn		
Def bdgt	LP	772bn	795bn	ε800bn
	US$	512m	528m	530m
US$1=LP		1,507	1,507	1,507

Population   3,826,018

Ethnic groups: Christian 30%; Druze 6%; Armenian 4%, excl ε300,000 Syrian nationals and ε350,000 Palestinian refugees

Age	0–14	15–19	20–24	25–29	30–64	65 plus
Male	14%	4%	5%	6%	17%	3%
Female	13%	4%	5%	5%	20%	4%

Capabilities

ACTIVE 72,100 (Army 70,000 Navy 1,100 Air 1,000)
Paramilitary 13,000
Terms of Service 1 year

ORGANISATIONS BY SERVICE

Army 70,000 (incl conscripts)
FORCES BY ROLE

Region	5 comd
Mech inf	11 bde under strength
Mne cdo	1 regt
SF	5 regt
Cdo / Ranger	1 regt
Air aslt	1 regt
Arty	2 regt
Presidential Guard	1 bde
MP	1 bde

EQUIPMENT BY TYPE
TK • MBT 310: 200 T-54/T-55
 M-48 110: 110 M-48A1/M-48A5
RECCE 60: 60 AML
APC 1257
 APC (T) • M-113 1164: 1,164 M-113A1/M-113A2
 APC (W) 93: 12 M-3/VTT
 VAB 81: 81 VAB VCI
ARTY 541
 TOWED 147
 105mm • M-101 13: 13 M-101A1
 122mm 56: 24 D-30; 32 M-30 *M-1938*
 130mm 16: 16 M-46
 155mm 62
 M-114 15: 15 M-114A1
 M-198 32 **Model-50** 15
 MRL • 122mm 25: 25 BM-21
 MOR 369: 158 81mm; 111 82mm
 120mm 100: 100 Brandt
AT
 MSL 70: 30 ENTAC; 16 *Milan*; 24 TOW
 RCL • 106mm • M-40 50: 50 M-40A1
 RL • 73mm: some RPG-7 *Knout*
 89mm: some M-65
AD
 SAM • MANPAD • SA-7 20: 20 SA-7A *Grail*/SA-7B *Grail*
 GUNS 10+: some 20mm
 23mm • TOWED: some ZU-23
 40mm • SP • M-42 10: 10 M-42A1

Navy 1,100
EQUIPMENT BY TYPE
PATROL AND COASTAL COMBATANTS 32
 MISC BOATS/CRAFT 25: 25 armed boats
 PCI 7: 5 *Attacker* (UK, under 100 tonnes); 2 *Tracker* (UK, under 100 tonnes)
AMPHIBIOUS • LS • LST 2: 2 *Sour* (capacity 96 troops) (Fr *Edic*)

FACILITIES
Base 1 located at Jounieh, 1 located at Beirut

Air Force 1,000
Many ac grounded and in store
AIRCRAFT
 FGA • HAWKER HUNTER 6: 6 *Hawker Hunter* FGA MK9 in store
 TRG 8: 3 *Bulldog* 127 in store; 5 CM-170 *Magister* in store
HELICOPTERS
 ATK 2: 2 SA-342 *Gazelle*
 SPT 3: 3 SA-330 *Puma*
 UTL 35: 5 Bell 212; 2 R-44 (utl/trg); 3 SA-316 *Alouette III*; 1 SA-318 *Alouette II*
 UH-1 24: 24 UH-1H *Iroquois*

Paramilitary ε13,000 active

Internal Security Force ε13,000
Ministry of Interior
FORCES BY ROLE

Police	1 (Judicial) unit
Regional	1 coy
Paramilitary	1 (Beirut Gendarmerie) coy

EQUIPMENT BY TYPE
APC • APC (W) 60: 60 V-200 *Chaimite*

Customs
PATROL AND COASTAL COMBATANTS • PCI 7: 5 *Aztec* less than 100 tonnes; 2 *Tracker* less than 100 tonnes

NON-STATE ARMED GROUPS
see Part II

FOREIGN FORCES
France 204 Army: 1 log bn (elm)
Ghana 1 inf bn; 652
India 648
Ireland 5
Italy 53
Poland 1 inf bn; 236
Syria Army: (Before withdrawal of troops, Syria maintained the following forces in Lebanon.) 1 armd bde; 1 mech div HQ; 4 mech inf bde; 10 SF regt (elm); 2 arty regt (elm); 16,000
Ukraine 197

Libya LAR

Libyan Dinar D		2003	2004	2005
GDP	D	29.3bn	34.8bn	
	US$	22.4bn	26.6bn	
per capita	US$	4,081	4,730	
Growth	%	5.3	0.9	
Inflation	%	-2.1	-1.0	
Debt	US$	4.1bn		
Def exp	D	625m	ε700m	ε800m
	US$	477m	534m	620m
US$1=D		1.31	1.31	1.29

Population   5,765,563

Age	0–14	15–19	20–24	25–29	30–64	65 plus
Male	17%	5%	5%	5%	16%	2%
Female	17%	5%	5%	5%	15%	2%

Capabilities

ACTIVE 76,000 (Army 45,000 Navy 8,000 Air 23,000)
Terms of service selective conscription, 1–2 years

RESERVE some 40,000 (People's Militia)

ORGANISATIONS BY SERVICE

Army 20,000; ε25,000 conscript (total 45,000)

FORCES BY ROLE
11 Border Def and 4 Sy Zones
Army	1 (elite) bde (regime sy force)
Tk	10 bn
Mech inf	10 bn
Inf	18 bn
Cdo / para	6 bn
Arty	22 bn
SSM	4 bde
ADA	7 bn

EQUIPMENT BY TYPE
TK • MBT 2025+: 200 T-72; 115 in store; 100 T-62; 70 in store; 500 T-55; 1,040+ T-54/T-55 in store
RECCE 120
  BRDM 50: 50 BRDM-2
  EE-9 *Cascavel* 70
AIFV 1000+: some BMD
  BMP 1000: 1,000 BMP-1
APC 945
  APC (T) 28: 28 M-113
  APC (W) 917
    BTR 750: 750 BTR-50/BTR-60
    EE-11 *Urutu* 100
    OT 67: 67 OT-62/OT-64
ARTY 2421+
  TOWED 647+
    105mm 42+: 42+ M-101
    122mm 250: 190 D-30; 60 D-74
    130mm 330: 330 M-46

  152mm 25: 25 M-1937
  SP 444
    122mm 130: 130 2S1 *Carnation*
    152mm 140: 60 2S3; 80 M-77 *Dana*
    155mm 174: 14 M-109; 160 VCA 155 *Palmaria*
  MRL 830
    107mm 300: ε300 Type-63
    122mm 530: ε200 BM-11; ε230 BM-21; ε100 RM-70 *Dana*
  MOR 500: 428 82mm
    120mm 48: ε48 M-43
    160mm 24: ε24 M-160
AT
  MSL 3000: 3,000 AT-3 *Sagger*/AT-4 *Spigot*/AT-5 *Spandrel*/Milan (AT-3 (incl BRDM SP)
  RCL • 106mm • M-40 220: 220 M-40A1
    84mm: some *Carl Gustav*
  RL • 73mm: some RPG-7 *Knout*
AD
  SAM • SP 24: 24 *Crotale* (quad)
    SA-13 *Gopher* SP/SA-7 *Grail* MANPAD/SA-9 *Gaskin* SP some
  GUNS 600: 600 M-53/59SP SP 30mm/S-60 towed 57mm/ZSU-23-4 SP 23mm/ZU-23 towed 23mm
RADAR • LAND: some RASIT (veh, arty)
MSL • TACTICAL • SSM 125: 45 FROG-7
  SCUD 80: 80 *Scud-B* (SSM msl totals est 450–500)

Navy 8,000 (incl Coast Guard)

EQUIPMENT BY TYPE
SUBMARINES • TACTICAL • SSK 5:
  4 *Al Badr* non-operational (FSU *Foxtrot*)
  1 *Al Badr†* (FSU *Foxtrot*) with 4+ single 406mm TT (stern), 6+ single 533mm TT (bow)
PRINCIPAL SURFACE COMBATANTS 6
  FRIGATES • FFG 2:
    1 *Al Hani* (FSU *Koni*) with 2 twin 406mm ASTT (4 eff.) each with USET-95 Type 40 LWT, 2 twin (4 eff.) each with 1 SS-N-2C *Styx* tactical SSM, 1 RBU 6000 *Smerch* 2 (12 eff.)
    1 non-operational (FSU *Koni*)
  CORVETTES • FSG 4:
    1 *Ean al Gazala* (FSU *Nanuchka* II) with 4 single each with 1 SS-N-2C *Styx* tactical SSM
    3 non-operational (FSU *Nanuchka* II)
PATROL AND COASTAL COMBATANTS • PFM 23:
  3 *Al Katum* (FSU *Osa* II) each with 4 single each with 1 SS-N-2C *Styx* tactical SSM
  12 non-operational (FSU *Osa* II)
  5 *Sharaba* (Fr *Combattante* II) each with 4 single each with 1 Mk 2 Otomat SSM, 1 76mm gun
  3 non-operational (Fr *Combattante* II)
MINE WARFARE • MINE COUNTERMEASURES • MSO 8: 2 *Ras al Gelais* (FSU *Natya*); 6 non-operational (FSU *Natya*)
AMPHIBIOUS
  LS 5
    LSM 3:
      1 *Polnochny* D (capacity 180 troops; 6 MBT) (FSU)
      2 non-operational (FSU)
    LST 2:
      2 *Ibn Ouf* (capacity 1 SA-316B *Alouette III* utl hel; 11

MBT; 240 troops)

CRAFT 3: 3 LCT

LOGISTICS AND SUPPORT 9: 1 ARS

SPT 2: 1 (diving); 1 *Zeltin* (log)

TPT 6: circa 5 (ro-ro) *El Temsah* 1

FACILITIES

| Base | 1 located at Tripoli, 1 located at Benghazi, 1 located at Tobruk, 1 located at Khums |
| Minor base | 1 located at Derna, 1 located at Zuwurah, 1 located at Misonhah |

Coastal Defence

FORCES BY ROLE

Msl 1 bty with SS-C-3 *Styx*

EQUIPMENT BY TYPE

MSL • TACTICAL • SSM: some SS-C-3 *Styx*

Customs/Coast Guard

PATROL AND COASTAL COMBATANTS • MISC BOATS/CRAFT: some armed boats

Naval Aviation

HELICOPTERS • SAR 7: 7 SA-321 *Super Frelon* (air force assets)

Air Force 10,000; ε13,000 conscript (total 23,000)

Flying hours 85 hrs/year

FORCES BY ROLE

Bbr	1 sqn with 6 Tu-22 *Blinder*
Ftr	9+ sqn with 15 *Mirage* F-1ED (F-1E); 94 MiG-25 *Foxbat*; 75 MiG-23 *Flogger*; 45 MiG-21 *Fishbed*; 3 *Mirage* F-1BD (F-1B); 3 MiG-25U *Foxbat*
FGA	7 sqn with 6 Su-24MK *Fencer D*; 14 *Mirage* F-1AD (F-1A); 40 MiG-23BN *Flogger H*; 53 Su-17M-2 *Fitter D*/Su-20 (Su-17M) *Fitter C*; 15 MiG-23U *Flogger*
Recce	2 sqn with 7 MiG-25R *Foxbat*; 4 *Mirage* 5DP30
Tpt	7 sqn with 2 An-124 *Condor*; 23 An-26 *Curl*; 7 C-130H *Hercules*; 6 G-222; 25 Il-76 *Candid*; 2 L-100-20; 3 L-100-30; 15 L-410 *Turbolet*
Atk hel	some sqn with 29 Mi-25 *Hind D*; 31 Mi-35 *Hind*
Tpt hel	some sqn with 4 CH-47C *Chinook* (hy); 34 Mi-17 (Mi-8MT) *Hip H*/Mi-8 *Hip* (med); 5 AB-206 (Bell 206) *JetRanger* (lt); 11 SA-316 *Alouette III* (lt)
Trg	some sqn with 1 Tu-22 *Blinder*; 90 G-2 *Galeb*; 115 L-39ZO *Albatros*; 20 SF-260WL *Warrior*; 50 PZL Mi-2 *Hoplite*

EQUIPMENT BY TYPE

(many non-operational, many ac in store)

AIRCRAFT 374 combat capable

BBR 7: 7 Tu-22 *Blinder*

FTR 229

F-1 15: 15 *Mirage* F-1ED (F-1E)

MiG-25 *Foxbat* 94

MiG-23 *Flogger* 75

MiG-21 *Fishbed* 45

FGA 113

Su-24 6: 6 Su-24MK *Fencer D*

Mirage **F-1AD (F-1A)** 14

MiG-23B 40: 40 MiG-23BN *Flogger H*

Su-17 • Su-20 (Su-17M) 53: 53 Su-17M-2 *Fitter D*/Su-20 (Su-17M) *Fitter C* Su-17 FGA

RECCE 7: 7 MiG-25R *Foxbat*

TPT 83: 2 An-124 *Condor*; 23 An-26 *Curl*

C-130 7: 7 C-130H *Hercules*

G-222 6 **Il-76** *Candid* 25

L-100 5: 2 L-100-20; 3 L-100-30

L-410 *Turbolet* 15

TRG 250: 90 G-2 *Galeb*

L-39 115: 115 L-39ZO *Albatros*

MiG-23U *Flogger** 15

MiG-25U *Foxbat** 3

MIRAGE 5D 4: 4 *Mirage* 5DP30*

Mirage **F-1BD (F-1B)** 3

SF-260 • SF-260W 20: 20 SF-260WL *Warrior*

HELICOPTERS

ATK 60: 29 Mi-25 *Hind D*; 31 Mi-35 *Hind*

SPT 88

CH-47 4: 4 CH-47C *Chinook* (hy)

Mi-8 34: 34 Mi-17 (Mi-8MT) *Hip H*/Mi-8 *Hip* spt hel (med)

PZL Mi-2 *Hoplite* 50

UTL 16: 5 AB-206 (Bell 206) *JetRanger* (lt); 11 SA-316 *Alouette III* (lt)

MSL • TACTICAL • ASM: some AS-11 *Kilter*; some AS-7 *Kerry*; some AS-9 *Kyle*; some AT-2 *Swatter*

AAM: some AA-2 *Atoll*; AA-6 *Acrid*; AA-7 *Apex*; AA-8 *Aphid*; R-550 *Magic*; R530

Air Defence Command

Senezh AD comd and control system

FORCES BY ROLE

AD 5 region (*each:* ε3 AD bde each with 20–24 SA-6 *Gainful*/SA-8 *Gecko* (72-144 eff.), 2–3 AD bde each with 12 SA-3 *Goa*, 5–6 AD bde each with 18 SA-2 *Guideline*); 4 bde with SA-5A *Gammon* (*each:* 1 radar coy, 2 AD bn each with 6 launcher, 4+ ADA bn with guns)

EQUIPMENT BY TYPE

AD

SAM 216+: 36 SA-3 *Goa*

SP 72: 20-72 SA-6 *Gainful*/SA-8 *Gecko* (216-432 eff.)

TOWED 108: 108 SA-2 *Guideline*

STATIC • SA-5: some SA-5A *Gammon*

GUNS some **Launcher** 12

NON-STATE ARMED GROUPS

see Part II

Mauritania RIM

Mauritanian Ouguiya OM		2003	2004	2005
GDP	OM	292bn	325bn	
	US$	1.11bn	1.22bn	
per capita	US$	382	407	
Growth	%	6.6	5.2	
Inflation	%	5.5	10.4	
Debt	US$	2.36bn		
Def bdgt	OM	ε5.0bn	ε5.2bn	ε5.4bn
	US$	19m	19.4m	20.1m
US$1=OM		263	267	268

Population	3,086,859

Age	0–14	15–19	20–24	25–29	30–64	65 plus
Male	23%	5%	4%	4%	12%	1%
Female	23%	5%	4%	4%	13%	1%

Capabilities

ACTIVE 15,870 (Army 15,000 Navy 620 Air 250)
Paramilitary 5,000
Terms of service conscription 24 months authorised

ORGANISATIONS BY SERVICE

Army 15,000
FORCES BY ROLE
6 Mil Regions
Army	2 (camel corps) bn
Armd	1 bn (T-54/55 MBTs)
Armd recce	1 sqn
Inf	8 (garrison) bn
Mot inf	7 bn
Cdo / para	1 bn
Arty	3 bn
ADA	4 bty
Engr	1 coy
Gd	1 bn

EQUIPMENT BY TYPE
TK • MBT 35: 35 T-54/T-55
RECCE 70
   AML 60: 20 AML-60; 40 AML-90
   Saladin 10
APC • APC (W) 25: 5 FV603 *Saracen*; ε20 M-3 *Panhard*
ARTY 194
   TOWED 80
      105mm 36: 36 HM-2/M-101A1
      122mm 44: 20 D-30; 24 D-74
   MOR 114: 24 60mm; 60 81mm
      120mm 30: 30 Brandt
AT
   MSL 24: 24 *Milan*
   RCL 114
      106mm • M-40 90: ε90 M-40A1
      75mm 24: ε24 M-20
   RL • 73mm 48: ε48 RPG-7 *Knout*
AD
   SAM 104
      SP 4: ε4 SA-9 *Gaskin* (reported)
      MANPAD 100: ε100 SA-7 *Grail*
   GUNS 82
      14.5mm • TOWED • ZPU 28: 16 ZPU-2; 12 ZPU-4
      23mm • TOWED 20: 20 ZU-23-2
      37mm • TOWED 10: 10 M-1939
      57mm • TOWED 12: 12 S-60
      100mm • TOWED 12: 12 KS-19

Navy ε620
EQUIPMENT BY TYPE
PATROL AND COASTAL COMBATANTS 10
   PCC 1: 1 *El Nasr* (Fr *Patra*)
   PCI 4: 4 *Mandovi* less than 100 tonnes
   PCR 1: 1 *Huangpu*
   PCO 4: 1 *Abourbekr Ben Amer* (Fr OPV 54); 1 *Arguin*; 1 Large Patrol Craft *Voum-Legleita*; 1 *N'Madi* (UK *Jura*, fishery protection)
FACILITIES
Base 1 located at Nouadhibou, 1 located at Nouakchott

Air Force 250
FORCES BY ROLE
MR	some sqn with 2 Cessna 337 *Skymaster*
Tpt	some sqn with 2 PA-31T *Navajo/Cheyenne II*; 2 Y-12(II)
COIN	some sqn with 2 FTB-337 *Milirole*; 5 BN-2 *Defender*; 1 Basler Turbo-67

EQUIPMENT BY TYPE
AIRCRAFT
   RECCE 2: 2 FTB-337 *Milirole*
   TPT 12: 5 BN-2 *Defender*; 1 Basler Turbo-67; 2 Cessna 337 *Skymaster*
      PA-31 2: 2 PA-31T *Navajo/Cheyenne II*
      Y-12 2: 2 Y-12(II)
   TRG • SF-260 4: 4 SF-260E

Paramilitary ε5,000 active

Gendarmerie ε3,000
Ministry of Interior
Regional 6 coy

National Guard 2,000
Ministry of Interior
Aux 1,000

Customs
PATROL AND COASTAL COMBATANTS • PB 1: 1 *Dah Ould Bah* (Fr *Amgram 14*)

Morocco Mor

Moroccan Dirham D		2003	2004	2005
GDP	D	417bn	468bn	
	US$	43.6bn	52.4bn	
per capita	US$	1,378	1,628	
Growth	%	5.2	3.5	
Inflation	%	1.2	2.0	
Debt	US$	18.7bn		
Def bdgt	D	17.4bn	17.6bn	18.1bn
	US$	1.82bn	1.97bn	2.07bn
FMA (US)	US$	6.41m	11.9m	17.0m
US$1=D		9.57	8.94	8.79

Population   32,725,847

Age	0–14	15–19	20–24	25–29	30–64	65 plus
Male	16%	5%	5%	4%	16%	2%
Female	16%	5%	5%	4%	17%	3%

Capabilities

ACTIVE 200,800 (Army 180,000 Navy 7,800 Air 13,000) **Paramilitary 50,000**

Terms of service conscription 18 months authorised; most enlisted personnel are volunteers

RESERVE 150,000 (Army 150,000)

Terms of service obligation to age 50

ORGANISATIONS BY SERVICE

Army ε80,000; 100,000 conscript; 150,000 reservists (obligation to age 50) **(total 330,000)**

FORCES BY ROLE

2 Comd (Northern Zone, Southern Zone)

Sy	1 light bde
Armd	12 indep bn
Mech / mot inf	8 regt
Mech inf	3 bde
Inf	38 indep bn
Mot inf	3 (camel corps) bn
Mtn inf	1 (indep) bn
Cdo	4 indep unit
Para	2 bde; 2 (indep) bn
Arty	11 indep bn
Engr	7 indep bn
AD	1 indep bn

Royal Guard 1,500

Army	1 bn
Cav	1 sqn

EQUIPMENT BY TYPE

TK 656

  MBT 540

    M-60 340: 220 M-60A1; 120 M-60A3

    M-48 200: ε200 M-48A5 in store

  LT TK 116: 5 AMX-13; 111 SK-105 *Kuerassier*

RECCE 384

  AML 228: 38 AML-60-7; 190 AML-90

  AMX-10RC 80

  EBR-75 16 *Eland* 40

  M1114 *HMMWV* 20

AIFV 70: 10 AMX-10P

  FSV 90 60

    MK III-20 30: 30 Ratel-20

    MK III-90 30: 30 Ratel-90

APC 765

  APC (T) • **M-113** 400: 400 M-113A1

  APC (W) • **VAB** 365: 45 VAB VCI; 320 VAB VTT

ARTY 2892

  TOWED 118

    105mm 50: 30 L-118 Light Gun; 20 M-101

    130mm 18: 18 M-46

    155mm 50: 30 FH-70; 20 M-114

  SP 199: 5 105mm

    155mm 134

      M-109 • **M-109A1** 44: 44 M-109A1B

      Mk F3 90

    203mm 60: 60 M-110

  MRL • **122mm** 35: 35 BM-21

  MOR 2540:

    81mm 1970: 870; 1,100 Expal model LN

    120mm 570: 20 (Mounted on a VAB APC) **Brandt** 550

AT

  MSL 790: 40 AT-3 *Sagger*; 440 M47 *Dragon*; 80 *Milan*

    TOW 230: 150; 80 M-901

  RCL • **106mm** • **M-40** 350: 350 M-40A1

  RL 700

    66mm 500: 500 M-72 *LAW*

    89mm 200: 200 M-20

  GUNS 36

    100mm 8: 8 SU-100 SP

    90mm 28: 28 M-56

UAV: some R4E-50 *Skyeye*

AD

  SAM 107

    SP 37: 37 M-48 *Chaparral*

    MANPAD 70: 70 SA-7 *Grail*

  GUNS 457

    14.5mm • **TOWED** • **ZPU** 200: 180 ZPU-2; 20 ZPU-4

    20mm 100

      SP 60: 60 M-163 *Vulcan*

      TOWED 40: 40 M-167 *Vulcan*

    23mm • **TOWED** 140: 140 ZU-23-2

    100mm • **TOWED** 17: 17 KS-19

RADAR • **LAND:** some RASIT (veh, arty)

Navy 7,800 (incl 1500 Marines)

EQUIPMENT BY TYPE

PRINCIPAL SURFACE COMBATANTS • **FRIGATES** • **FFG** 3:

1 *Lt Col Errhamani* (Sp *Descubierto*) with 2 triple ASTT (6 eff.) each with Mk 46 LWT, 1 *Albatros* octuple with 24 *Aspide* SAM, 2 twin (4 eff.) each with 1 MM-38 *Exocet* tactical SSM V (capacity 1 AS-565 aslt hel) (Fr mod *Floreal*) each with 2 single each with 1 MM-38 *Exocet* tactical SSM, 1 76mm gun

PATROL AND COASTAL COMBATANTS 27

  PCC 17:

    4 *El Hahiq* (Dk *Osprey* 55, incl 2 with customs)

    6 LV *Rabhi* (Sp 58m B-200D)

    2 *Okba* (Fr PR-72) each with 1 76mm gun

    5 *Rais Bargach* (under control of fisheries dept)

  PFI 6: 6 *El Wacil* (Fr P-32, under 100 tonnes, incl 4 with customs)

  PFM 4:

    4 *Cdt El Khattabi* (Sp *Lazaga* 58m) each with 4 single each with 1 MM-40 *Exocet* tactical SSM, 1 76mm gun

AMPHIBIOUS

  LS 4

    LSM 3: 3 *Ben Aicha* (capacity 7 tanks; 140 troops) (Fr *Champlain* BATRAL)

    LST 1: 1 *Sidi Mohammed Ben Abdallah* (capacity 400 troops) (US *Newport*)

    CRAFT • LCT 1:

      1 *Edic* (capacity 96 troops; 8 APCs)

LOGISTICS AND SUPPORT 4: 1 AGOR (US lease); 2 spt (log); 1 tpt

FACILITIES

Base 1 located at Casablanca, 1 located at Agadir, 1 located at Al Hoceima, 1 located at Dakhla, 1 located at Tangier

Marines 1,500

Naval inf 2 bn

Naval Aviation

  HELICOPTERS • ASLT 3: 3 AS-565

Air Force 13,000

Flying hours 100 hrs/year on F-1 *Mirage*/F-5A *Freedom Fighter Tiger*

FORCES BY ROLE

Ftr 1 sqn with 19 F-1CH (F-1C) *Mirage*

FGA 1 sqn with 8 F-5A *Freedom Fighter*; 2 F-5B *Freedom Fighter*; 2 sqn with 20 F-5E *Tiger II*; 3 F-5F *Tiger II*; 2 sqn with 14 *Mirage* F-1EH (F-1E)

Recce some sqn with 4 OV-10 *Bronco**; 2 C-130H *Hercules* (with side-looking radar)

EW some sqn with 2 C-130 *Hercules* (ELINT); 2 *Falcon* 20 (ELINT)

Tpt some sqn with 4 Beech 100 *King Air*; 3 Beech 200 *Super King Air*; 15 C-130H *Hercules*; 6 CN-235; 2 Do-28; 2 *Falcon* 20; 1 *Falcon* 50 (VIP); 2 Gulfstream II (VIP); some sqn

Tkr some sqn with 2 KC-130H *Hercules* (tpt/tkr); 1 B-707

Liaison some sqn with 2 Beech 200 *Super King Air*

Atk hel some sqn with 19 SA-342 *Gazelle* (with HOT, 12 with cannon)

Tpt hel some sqn with 8 CH-47D *Chinook* (hy); 24 SA-330 *Puma* (med); 25 AB-205A (Bell 205A); 11 AB-206 (Bell 206) *JetRanger* (lt); 3 AB-212 (Bell 212) (lt); 2 UH-60 *Black Hawk*

Trg some sqn with 7 AS-202 *Bravo*; 19 *Alpha Jet**; 2 CAP 10; 9 T-34C *Turbo Mentor*; 14 T-37B *Tweet* (being replaced by K-8); 4 CAP-231

EQUIPMENT BY TYPE

AIRCRAFT 89 combat capable

  FTR 66

    F-5 33: 8 F-5A *Freedom Fighter*; 2 F-5B *Freedom Fighter*; 20 F-5E *Tiger II*; 3 F-5F *Tiger II*

    F-1 33: 19 F-1CH (F-1C) *Mirage*; 14 *Mirage* F-1EH (F-1E)

  FAC 4: 4 OV-10 *Bronco**

  TKR • KC-130 2: 2 KC-130H *Hercules* (tpt/tkr)

  TPT 44: 1 B-707; 4 Beech 100 *King Air*; 5 Beech 200 *Super King Air*

    C-130 19: 2 (ELINT); 15 C-130H *Hercules*; 2 (with side-looking radar)

    CN-235 6 **Do-28** 2 *Falcon* 20 2; 2 (ELINT) *Falcon* 50 1 (VIP) **Gulfstream II** 2 (VIP)

  TRG 51: 7 AS-202 *Bravo*; 19 *Alpha Jet**; 2 CAP 10

    T-34 9: 9 T-34C *Turbo Mentor*

    T-37 14: 14 T-37B *Tweet* (being replaced by K-8)

  TRIALS AND TEST 4: 4 CAP-231

HELICOPTERS

  ASLT 19: 19 SA-342 *Gazelle* (with HOT, 12 with cannon)

  SPT 32

    CH-47 8: 8 CH-47D *Chinook* (hy)

    SA-330 *Puma* 24 (med)

  UTL 41: 11 AB-206 (Bell 206) *JetRanger* (lt); 3 AB-212 (Bell 212) (lt)

    BELL 205 25: 25 AB-205A (Bell 205A)

    UH-60 *Black Hawk* 2

MSL • TACTICAL • ASM • AGM-62: some AGM-62B *Walleye* (For F-5E)

  HOT some

  AAM • AIM-9: some AIM-9B *Sidewinder*/AIM-9D *Sidewinder*/AIM-9J *Sidewinder*

    R-550 *Magic* some **R530** some

Paramilitary 50,000 active

Gendarmerie Royale 20,000

FORCES BY ROLE

Coast Guard 1 unit

Para 1 sqn

Paramilitary 1 bde; 4 (mobile) gp

Avn 1 (air) sqn

EQUIPMENT BY TYPE

PATROL AND COASTAL COMBATANTS • MISC BOATS/CRAFT 18: 18 boats

AIRCRAFT • TRG 2: 2 *Rallye* 235 *Guerrier*

HELICOPTERS

  SAR 2: 2 SA-360 *Dauphin*

  ASLT • SA-342 6: 6 SA-342K *Gazelle*

  SPT 6: 6 SA-330 *Puma*

  UTL 8

    SA-315 3: 3 SA-315B *Lama*

    SA-316 *Alouette III* 3 **SA-318** *Alouette II* 2

Force Auxiliaire 30,000 (incl 5000 Mobile Intervention Corps)

Customs/Coast Guard
PATROL AND COASTAL COMBATANTS 39
  MISC BOATS/CRAFT 35: 3 SAR craft; 32 boats
  PCI 4: 4 *Erraid*

NON-STATE ARMED GROUPS

see Part II

DEPLOYMENT

BOSNIA-HERZEGOVINA
EU • **EUFOR II** 1 mot inf bn; ε800

CÔTE D'IVOIRE
UN • **ONUCI** 734; 1 obs

DEMOCRATIC REPUBLIC OF CONGO
UN • **MONUC** 804; 1 obs

HAITI
UN • **MINUSTAH** 167

SERBIA AND MONTENEGRO
NATO • **KFOR I** 279

Oman O

Omani Rial R		2003	2004	2005
GDP	R	8.29bn	9.19bn	
	US$	21.8bn	24.2bn	
per capita	US$	7,780	8,339	
Growth	%	1.4	2.5	
Inflation	%	-0.4	1.6	
Debt	US$	3.88bn		
Def bdgt	R	937m	973m	1.14bn
	US$	2.46bn	2.56bn	3.02bn
FMA (US)	US$	81.5m	25.6m	20.9m
US$1=R		0.38	0.38	0.38

Population   3,001,583
Expatriates: 27%

Age	0–14	15–19	20–24	25–29	30–64	65 plus
Male	22%	5%	4%	4%	20%	1%
Female	21%	4%	4%	3%	10%	1%

Capabilities

ACTIVE 41,700 (Army 25,000 Navy 4,200 Air 4,100
Joint 2,000 Royal Household 6,400) **Paramilitary 4,400**

ORGANISATIONS BY SERVICE

Army 25,000

FORCES BY ROLE
(Regt are bn size)
Armd   1 bde HQ; 2 regt (*each:* 3 tk sqn)
Armd recce 1 regt (3 armd recce sqn)

Recce   2 indep coy
Inf   2 bde HQ; 8 regt
Rifle   1 indep coy (Musandam Security Force)
AB   1 regt
Inf recce   1 regt (3 recce coy)
Med arty   1 regt (2 Med arty bty)
Fd arty   2 regt
ADA   1 regt (2 ADA bty)
Fd Engr   1 regt (3 fd engr sqn)

EQUIPMENT BY TYPE
TK 154
  MBT 117: 38 CR2 *Challenger 2*
    M-60 79: 6 M-60A1; 73 M-60A3
  LT TK 37: 37 *Scorpion*
RECCE 145: 13 *Sultan*; 132 VBL
APC 191
  APC (T) 16: 6 FV 103 *Spartan*; 10 FV4333 *Stormer*
  APC (W) 175: 175 *Piranha* (incl variants)
ARTY 233
  TOWED 108
    105mm 42: 42 ROF lt
    122mm 30: 30 D-30
    130mm 24: 12 M-46; 12 Type-59-I
    155mm 12: 12 FH-70
  SP • 155mm 24: 24 G-6
  MOR 101: 69 81mm
    107mm 20: 20 M-30
    120mm 12: 12 Brandt
AT • MSL 50: 32 *Milan*
  TOW 18: 18 TOW msl/TOW-2A (some SP)
  RL • 73mm: some RPG-7 *Knout*
    94mm: some LAW-80
AD
  SAM • MANPAD 54+: 20 *Javelin*; some *Mistral* 2 (SP);
  34 SA-7 *Grail*
  GUNS 26
    23mm • TOWED 4: 4 ZU-23-2
    35mm • TOWED • GDF 10: 10 GDF-005 (with
    Skyguard)
    40mm • TOWED 12: 12 L/60

Navy 4,200

FORCES BY ROLE
Navy 1 HQ (exercise) located at Seeb

EQUIPMENT BY TYPE
PRINCIPAL SURFACE COMBATANTS • CORVETTES
• **FSG** 2: 2 *Qahir Al Amwaj* each with 1 octuple (8 eff.) with
16 *Crotale* SAM, 2 quad (8 eff.) each with 1 MM-40 *Exocet*
tactical SSM, 2 triple 324mm TT (6 eff.) non-operational
each with 1 MM-40 *Exocet* tactical SSM, 1 76mm gun, 1 hel
landing platform (for *Super Lynx* type)
PATROL AND COASTAL COMBATANTS 8
  PCC 3: 3 *Al Bushra* (Fr P-400) each with 4 single 406mm
  TT, 1 76mm gun
  PCI 4: 4 *Seeb* (Vosper 25m, under 100 tonnes)
  PFM 4: 1 *Dhofar* with 2 triple (6 eff.) (not fitted); 3 *Dhofar*
  + *SSM* each with 1 MM-40 *Exocet* SSM tactical, 2 quad (8
  eff.)
AMPHIBIOUS
  LS • LST 1: 1 *Nasr el Bahr* (capacity 7 tanks; 240 troops)
  (with hel deck)

CRAFT 4: 1 LCU; 3 LCM
LOGISTICS AND SUPPORT 4: 1 AGHS
 AK 1: 1 *Al Sultana*
 TRG 1: 1 *Al Mabrukah* (with hel deck, also used in offshore patrol role)
 supply 1

FACILITIES
Base 1 located at Seeb, 1 located at Alwi, 1 (main base) located at Wudam, 1 located at Ghanam Island, 1 located at Mussandam, 1 located at Salalah

Air Force 4,100
FORCES BY ROLE

FGA 1 sqn with 12 F-16C *Fighting Falcon*/F-16D *Fighting Falcon*; 2 sqn with 4 T Mk2 *Jaguar* (upgraded to S(O)1 GR-3 standard); 16 *Jaguar* S(O) MK 1 (*Jaguar* S International)
FGA / recce some sqn with 12 *Hawk* MK203
CCT 1 sqn with 4 *Hawk* MK103*; 12 PC-9*
Tpt 2 sqn with 3 C-130H *Hercules*; 10 SC.7 3M *Skyvan* (7 radar-equipped, for MR); 1 sqn with 3 BAC-111
Tpt hel 2 (med) sqn with 19 AB-205 (Bell 205); 3 AB-206 (Bell 206) *JetRanger*; 3 AB-212 (Bell 212); 16 Lynx Srs 300 *Super Lynx* (maritime/SAR)
Trg some sqn with 4 AS-202-18 *Bravo*; 8 MFI-17B *Mushshak*
AD 2 sqn with 40 *Rapier*; 6 *Blindfire*; S713 *Martello*

EQUIPMENT BY TYPE
AIRCRAFT 48 combat capable
 FGA 36: 4 T Mk2 *Jaguar* (upgraded to S(O)1 GR-3 standard); 12 F-16C *Fighting Falcon*/F-16D *Fighting Falcon*; 16 *Jaguar* S(O) MK 1 (*Jaguar* S International); 4 *Hawk* MK103*
 TPT 16: 3 BAC-111
  C-130 3: 3 C-130H *Hercules*
  SC.7 3M *Skyvan* 10 (7 radar-equipped, for MR)
 TRG 36
  AS-202 4: 4 AS-202-18 *Bravo*
  Hawk MK203 12*
  MFI-17 8: 8 MFI-17B *Mushshak*
  PC-9 12*
HELICOPTERS • UTL 41: 19 AB-205 (Bell 205); 3 AB-206 (Bell 206) *JetRanger*; 3 AB-212 (Bell 212); 16 Lynx Srs 300 *Super Lynx* (maritime/SAR)
AD • SAM 40: 40 *Rapier*
RADAR • LAND 6+: 6 *Blindfire*; some S713 *Martello*
MSL • TACTICAL • AAM • AIM-9: some AIM-9M *Sidewinder*

Royal Household 6,400
(incl HQ staff)
SF 2 regt (1,000 men)

Royal Guard bde 5,000
TK • LT TK 9: 9 VBC-90
APC • APC (W) 73: ε50 Type-92
 VAB 23: 14 VAB VCI; 9 VAB VDAA
ARTY • MRL • 122mm 6: 6 Type-90A
AT • MSL: some *Milan*

AD • SAM • MANPAD 14: 14 *Javelin*

Royal Yacht Squadron 150
PATROL AND COASTAL COMBATANTS • MISC BOATS/CRAFT • DHOW 1: 1 *Zinat Al Bihaar*
LOGISTICS AND SUPPORT 2: 1 Royal Yacht (3,800t with hel deck)
 TPT 1: 1 *Fulk Al Salamah* (also veh tpt) with up to 2 AS-332C *Super Puma* spt hel

Royal Flight 250
AIRCRAFT • TPT 5
 B-747 2: 2 B-747SP
 DC-8 1: 1 DC-8-73CF
 Gulfstream IV 2
HELICOPTERS • SPT 6: 3 AS-330 (SA-330) *Puma*
 AS-332 3: 2 AS-332F *Super Puma*; 1 AS-332L *Super Puma*

Paramilitary 4,400 active

Tribal Home Guard 4,000
org in teams of est 100

Police Coast Guard 400
PATROL AND COASTAL COMBATANTS 17
 MISC BOATS/CRAFT 14: 14 craft
 PCI 3: 3 CG 29 less than 100 tonnes

Police Air Wing
AIRCRAFT • TPT 4
 BN-2 ISLANDER 1: 1 BN-2T Turbine *Islander*
 CN-235 2: 2 CN-235M
 Do-228 1
HELICOPTERS • UTL 5
 AB-205 (BELL 205) 2: 2 Bell 205A
 BELL 214 3: 3 AB-214ST

Armed Forces ε2,000 (foreign)

FOREIGN FORCES
United Kingdom Air Force: 99; 33
United States USCENTCOM: 60; 210

Palestinian Autonomous Areas of Gaza and Jericho PA

New Israeli Shekel NS		2002	2003	2004
GDP	US$	3.4bn	3.6bn	
per capita	US$	1,004	1,025	
Growth	%	-14.5	4.5	
Inflation	%	5.7	4.4	
US$1=NS		4.73	4.55	4.47

Capabilities
ACTIVE 0 Paramilitary 56,000
Personnel strength figures for the various Palestinian groups are not known

ORGANISATIONS BY SERVICE

Paramilitary

National Forces ε56,000 (reported)
GENERAL SECURITY
  Police
  Preventative Security
ARMY
NAVY
AIR FORCE

NON-STATE ARMED GROUPS

see Part II

FOREIGN FORCES

Italy 15

Qatar Q

Qatari Riyal R		2003	2004	2005
GDP	R	71bn	102bn	
	US$	19.4bn	28.2bn	
per capita	US$	23,805	33,674	
Growth	%	8.5	9.9	
Inflation	%	2.3	7.5	
Debt	US$	16.9bn		
Def bdgt	R	ε7.0bn	ε7.5bn	ε8.0bn
	US$	1.92bn	2.06bn	2.19bn
US$1=R		3.64	3.64	3.64

Population   863,051

Ethnic groups: Nationals 25%; Expatriates 75% of which Indian 18%; Iranian 10%; Pakistani 18%

Age	0–14	15–19	20–24	25–29	30–64	65 plus
Male	12%	4%	4%	5%	37%	3%
Female	12%	4%	3%	3%	12%	1%

Capabilities

ACTIVE 12,400 (Army 8,500 Navy 1,800 Air 2,100)

ORGANISATIONS BY SERVICE

Army 8,500

FORCES BY ROLE
Tk	1 bn
Mech inf	4 bn
SF	1 bn (coy)
Fd arty	1 regt
Mor	1 bn
AT	1 bn
Royal Guard	1 regt

EQUIPMENT BY TYPE
TK • MBT 30: 30 AMX-30
RECCE 68: 12 AMX-10RC; 20 EE-9 *Cascavel*; 12 *Ferret*; 8 V-150 *Chaimite*; 16 VBL
AIFV 40: 40 AMX-10P
APC 226
  APC (T) 30: 30 AMX-VCI
  APC (W) 196: 36 *Piranha* II; 160 VAB
ARTY 89
  TOWED • 155mm 12: 12 G-5
  SP • 155mm 28: 28 Mk F3
  MRL 4: 4 ASTROS II
  MOR 45
    81mm 30: 30 L16 (some SP)
    120mm 15: 15 Brandt
AT
  MSL 148: 48 HOT (incl 24 VAB SP); 100 *Milan*
  RCL • 84mm 40: ε40 *Carl Gustav*

Navy 1,800 (incl Marine Police)

FORCES BY ROLE
Navy 1 HQ located at Doha

EQUIPMENT BY TYPE
PATROL AND COASTAL COMBATANTS 27+
  MISC BOATS/CRAFT: 20+ small craft (operated by Marine Police)
  PFM 7: 4 *Barzan* (UK *Vita*) each with 2 quad (8 eff.) each with 1 MM-40 *Exocet* tactical SSM, 1 sextuple (6 eff.) with *Mistral* SAM, 1 76mm gun; 3 *Damash* (Fr *Combattante* III) each with 2 quad (8 eff.)

FACILITIES
Base 1 located at Doha, 1 located at Halul Island

Coastal Defence

FORCES BY ROLE
Navy 1 bty with 3 quad (12 eff.) each with MM-40 *Exocet* tactical SSM

EQUIPMENT BY TYPE
LNCHR 3: 3 quad each with MM-40 *Exocet* tactical SSM

Air Force 2,100

FORCES BY ROLE
Ftr / FGA	1 sqn with 6 *Alpha Jet*; 1 sqn with 3 M-2000D *Mirage*; 9 M-2000ED *Mirage*
Tpt	1 sqn with 1 A-340; 2 B-707; 1 B-727; 2 *Falcon* 900
Atk hel	some sqn with 8 *Commando* MK 3 (*Exocet*); 11 SA-342L *Gazelle* (with HOT)
Tpt hel	some sqn with 3 *Commando* MK 2A; 1 *Commando* MK 2C; 2 SA-341 *Gazelle*

EQUIPMENT BY TYPE
AIRCRAFT 18 combat capable
  FGA • M-2000 12: 3 M-2000D *Mirage*; 9 M-2000ED *Mirage*
  TPT 6: 1 A-340; 2 B-707; 1 B-727; 2 *Falcon* 900
  TRG 6: 6 *Alpha Jet**
HELICOPTERS

ASUW 8: 8 *Commando* MK 3 (*Exocet*)
ATK • SA-342 11: 11 SA-342L *Gazelle** (with HOT)
SPT 6
   COMMANDO 4: 3 *Commando* MK 2A; 1 *Commando* MK 2C
   SA-341 *Gazelle* 2
AD • SAM 75: 24 *Mistral*
   SP • ROLAND 9: 9 *Roland* II
   MANPAD 42: 10 *Blowpipe*; 12 FIM-92A *Stinger*; 20 SA-7 *Grail*
MSL • TACTICAL • ASM: some AM-39 *Exocet*; some *Apache*; some HOT
   AAM: some MICA; some R-550 *Magic*

FOREIGN FORCES

United States USCENTCOM: 800; 230; 5,350; 160

Saudi Arabia Sau

Saudi Riyal R		2003	2004	2005
GDP	R	804bn	885bn	
	US$	214bn	236bn	
per capita	US$	8,522	9,159	
Growth	%	7.2	5.3	
Inflation	%	0.6	0.2	
Debt	US$	32.5bn		
Def bdgt[a]	R	70.3bn	72.4bn	79.9bn
	US$	18.7bn	19.3bn	21.3bn
US$1=R		3.75	3.75	3.75

[a] defence and security budget

Population   26,417,599

Ethnic groups: Nationals 73% of which Bedoiun up to 10%, Shi'a 6%, Expatriates 27% of which Asians 20%, Arabs 6%, Africans 1%, Europeans <1%

Age	0–14	15–19	20–24	25–29	30–64	65 plus
Male	19%	5%	6%	6%	17%	1%
Female	19%	5%	4%	4%	12%	1%

Capabilities

ACTIVE 199,500 (Army 75,000 Navy 15,500 Air 18,000 Air Defence 16,000 National Guard 75,000) Paramilitary 15,500

ORGANISATIONS BY SERVICE

Army 75,000

FORCES BY ROLE

Armd	3 bde (*each*: 1 mech bn, 1 fd arty bn, 1 recce bn, 1 AD bn, 1 AT bn, 3 tk bn)
Mech	5 bde (*each*: 1 fd arty bn, 1 AD bn, 1 spt bn, 1 tk bn, 3 mech bn)
AB	1 bde (2 AB bn, 3 SF coy)
Arty	8 bn

Avn	1 comd (2 avn bde)
Royal Guard	1 bde (3 Royal Guard bn)

EQUIPMENT BY TYPE
TK • MBT 1055
   M-1 315: 115 M1-A2 *Abrams*; 200 in store
   AMX-30 145; 145 in store
   M-60 450: 450 M-60A3
RECCE • AML 300: 300 AML-60/AML-90
AIFV 970+:
   570+ AMX-10P
   400 M-2 *Bradley* each with 2 TOW msl, 1 30mm gun
APC 3190
   APC (T) • M-113 3000: 3,000 M-113A1/M-113A2/M-113A3 (incl variants)
   APC (W) 190: ε40 AF-40-8-1 *Al-Fahd*; 150 M-3 *Panhard*
ARTY 868
   TOWED 238
      105mm 100: 100 M-101/M-102 in store
      155mm 130: 40 FH-70 in store; 50 M-114; 40 M-198 in store
      203mm 8: 8 M-115 in store
   SP • 155mm 170: 60 AU-F-1
   M-109 110: 110 M-109A1B/M-109A2
   MRL 60: 60 ASTROS II
   MOR 400
      81mm: (incl 70 SP)
      107mm: M-30 (incl 150 SP)
      120mm 110: 110 Brandt
AT
   MSL 1950+: some HOT (incl 100 AMX-10P SP); 1,000 M47 *Dragon*
      TOW 950: 950 TOW msl/TOW-2A (incl 200 VCC-1 SP)
   RCL 450
      106mm • M-40 50: 50 M-40A1
      84mm 300: 300 *Carl Gustav*
      90mm 100: 100 M-67
   RL • 112mm 200: ε200 APILAS
HELICOPTERS
   ATK 12: 12 AH-64 *Apache*
   SPT 27
      S-70 • S-70A 12: 12 S-70A-1 *Desert Hawk*
      SCOUT 15: 15 Bell 406 CS *Combat Scout*
   UTL 28
      AS-365 6: 6 AS-365N *Dauphin* 2 (medevac)
      UH-60 22: 22 UH-60A *Black Hawk* (4 medevac)
AD • SAM 1,000+
   SP: some *Crotale*
   MANPAD 1000: 500 FIM-43 *Redeye*; 500 FIM-92A *Stinger*
RADAR • LAND: some AN/TPQ-36 *Firefinder*/AN/TPQ-37 *Firefinder* (arty, mor)
MSL • TACTICAL • SSM 10+: 10+ CSS-2 (40 msl)

Navy 15,500

FORCES BY ROLE
Navy 1 HQ (HQ Eastern Fleet) located at Jubail; 1 HQ (HQ Western Fleet) located at Jeddah; 1 HQ (HQ Naval Forces) located at Riyadh

EQUIPMENT BY TYPE
PRINCIPAL SURFACE COMBATANTS 11

FRIGATES • FFG 7:

3 *Al Riyadh* (Mod *La Fayette*, currently being acquired) each with 1 hel landing platform (plus hanger for *Cougar*-sized hel)

4 *Madina* French F-2000 (capacity 1 AS-365F *Dauphin 2* utl hel) (Fr F-2000) each with 4 x1 533mm ASTT each with F17P HWT, 1 octuple (8 eff.) with 26 *Crotale* SAM, 2 quad (8 eff.) each with 1 Mk 2 *Otomat* SSM, 1 100mm gun

CORVETTES • FSG 4:

4 *Badr* (US *Tacoma*) each with 2 triple ASTT (6 eff.) each with Mk 46 LWT, 2 Mk 140 *Harpoon* quad (8 eff.) each with 1 RGM-84C *Harpoon* tactical SSM, 1 76mm gun

PATROL AND COASTAL COMBATANTS 66

MISC BOATS/CRAFT 40: 40 craft

PCI 17 (US *Halter Marine*, under 100 tonnes, some with the Coast Guard)

PFM 9:

9 *Al Siddiq* (US 58m) each with 2 Mk 140 twin each with 1 RGM-84C *Harpoon* tactical SSM, 1 76mm gun

MINE WARFARE • MINE COUNTERMEASURES 7

MCC 4: 4 *Addriyah* (US MSC-322, sid)

MHO 3: 3 *Al Jawf* (UK *Sandown*)

AMPHIBIOUS • CRAFT 8: 4 LCU; 4 LCM

LOGISTICS AND SUPPORT 7

AO 2:

2 *Boraida* (capacity either 2 AS-365F *Dauphin 2* utl hel or 1 AS-332C *Super Puma* spt hel) (mod Fr *Durance*)

ARS 1 **ATF** 3 **Royal Yacht** 1

FACILITIES

Base 1 (HQ Eastern Fleet) located at Jubail, 1 (HQ Eastern Fleet) located at Jizan, 1 (HQ Western Fleet) located at Jeddah, 1 (HQ Naval Forces) located at Riyadh, 1 located at Dammam, 1 located at Al Wajh, 1 located at Ras al Mishab, 1 located at Ras al Ghar

Naval Aviation

HELICOPTERS

ASLT 19: 15 AS-565* each with AS-15TT tactical ASM; 4 (SAR)

SPT 25

AS-332 12: 6 AS-332B *Super Puma*/AS-332F *Super Puma* each with AM-39 *Exocet* tactical ASM; 6 (tpt)*

SCOUT 13: 13 Bell 406 CS *Combat Scout*

Marines 3,000

FORCES BY ROLE

Inf 1 regt (2 Inf bn)

EQUIPMENT BY TYPE

APC • APC (W) 140: 140 BMR-600P

Air Force 18,000

FORCES BY ROLE

Ftr   1 sqn with 22 *Tornado* ADV; 5 sqn with 66 F-15C *Eagle*; 18 F-15D *Eagle*

FGA   3 sqn with 85 *Tornado* IDS (incl 10 IDS recce); 1 sqn with 15 F-5B *Freedom Fighter*/F-5F *Tiger II*/RF-5E *Tigereye*; 3 sqn with 71 F-15S *Eagle*

AEW   1 sqn with 5 E-3A *Sentry*

Tpt   3 sqn with 7 C-130E *Hercules*; 29 C-130H *Hercules*; 2 C-130H-30 *Hercules*; 4 CN-235; 3 L-100-30HS (hospital ac)

Tkr   some sqn with 8 KC-130H *Hercules* (tkr/tpt); 3 KE-3A

OCU   2 sqn with 14 F-5B *Freedom Fighter**

Trg   3 sqn with 25 *Hawk* MK65 (incl aerobatic team); 18 *Hawk* MK65A; 1 sqn with 1 Jetstream MK31; some sqn with 20 MFI-17 *Mushshak*; 1 sqn with 13 Cessna 172; 2 sqn with 45 PC-9

Hel   2 sqn with 10 AS-532 *Cougar* (CSAR); 22 AB-205 (Bell 205); 13 AB-206A (Bell 206A) *JetRanger*; 17 AB-212 (Bell 212); 16 AB-412 (Bell 412) *Twin Huey* (SAR)

EQUIPMENT BY TYPE

AIRCRAFT 291 combat capable

FTR 191

F-5 14: 14 F-5B *Freedom Fighter**

F-5B *Freedom Fighter Tiger* **FTR/F-5F** *Tiger II* **FTR/RF-5E** *Tigereye* **RECCE** 15*

F-15 155: 66 F-15C *Eagle*; 18 F-15D *Eagle*; 71 F-15S *Eagle Tornado* **ADV** 22

STRIKE/FGA 85: 85 *Tornado* IDS (incl 10 IDS recce)

AEW • E-3 5: 5 E-3A *Sentry*

TKR 11

KC-130 8: 8 KC-130H *Hercules* (tkr/tpt)

KE-3A 3

TPT 45

C-130 38: 7 C-130E *Hercules*

C-130H 31: 29; 2 C-130H-30 *Hercules*

CN-235 4

L-100 3: 3 L-100-30HS (hospital ac)

UTL 13: 13 Cessna 172

TRG 109:

HAWK MK65 43: 25 (incl aerobatic team); 18 *Hawk* MK65A

Jetstream MK31 1 **MFI-17** *Mushshak* 20 **PC-9** 45

HELICOPTERS

UTL 78: 22 AB-205 (Bell 205); 17 AB-212 (Bell 212); 16 AB-412 (Bell 412) *Twin Huey* (SAR); 10 AS-532 *Cougar* (CSAR); 13 AB-206A (Bell 206A) *JetRanger*

MSL • TACTICAL • ASM: some AGM-65 *Maverick*

ARM: some ALARM

Sea Eagle some

AAM: some AIM-7 *Sparrow*; some AIM-7M *Sparrow*/AIM-9J *Sidewinder*/AIM-9L *Sidewinder*/AIM-9P *Sidewinder*; some *Sky Flash*

Royal Flt

AIRCRAFT • TPT 16

B-737 1: 1 B-737-200

B-747 2: 2 B-747SP

BAE-125 4: 4 BAe-125-800

Cessna 310 1 **Gulfstream III** 2 *Learjet* **35** 2

VC-130 4: 4 VC-130H

HELICOPTERS

SPT 1: 1 S-70 *Black Hawk*

UTL 3+: some AB-212 (Bell 212); 3 AS-61

Air Defence Forces 16,000

FORCES BY ROLE

SAM   2-4 bn each with 160 PAC-2; 17 bn each with 68 *Shahine*; 50 AMX-30SA; 73 unit (static defence) with *Crotale/Shahine*; 16 bty each with 128 I-HAWK MIM-23B

EQUIPMENT BY TYPE

AD

SAM 5284: 500 *Mistral*; 640 PAC-2; *Crotale/Shahine*; 1,156 Shahine
SP 440: 40 *Crotale*; 400 FIM-92A *Avenger*
TOWED • MIM-23 2048: 2,048 I-HAWK MIM-23B
MANPAD 500: 500 FIM-43 *Redeye*
GUNS 1140
20mm • SP 92: 92 M-163 *Vulcan*
30mm • SP 850: 850 AMX-30SA
35mm 128
40mm • TOWED 70: 70 L/70 in store
RADAR • AD RADAR 17: 17 AN/FPS-117

National Guard 75,000 active; 25,000 (tribal levies) (total 100,000)

FORCES BY ROLE

Cav   1 (ceremonial) sqn
Mech Inf 3 bde (*each:* 4 army bn (all arms))
Inf   5 bde

EQUIPMENT BY TYPE

RECCE 514: 384 LAV-25 *Coyote*; 130 LAV-AG
APC • APC (W) 1953+:
LAV 1513+: 47 (plus 190 spt vehs); 290+ LAV-150 *Commando*; 810 in store; 111 LAV-AT; 182 LAV-CP; 73 LAV-M
Piranha 440
ARTY • TOWED 70
105mm 40: 40 M-102
155mm 30: 30 M-198
MOR: some 81mm; some 120mm (incl 73 on LAV-M)
AT • MSL • TOW • TOW-2: some TOW-2A (incl 111 on LAV)
RCL • 106mm • M-40: some M-40A1

Paramilitary 15,500+ active

Frontier Force 10,500

Coast Guard 4,500

EQUIPMENT BY TYPE

PATROL AND COASTAL COMBATANTS 384
MISC BOATS/CRAFT 350: circa 350 armed boats
PCI circa 30 less than 100 tonnes
PFI 4: 4 *Al Jouf*
AMPHIBIOUS • CRAFT 16: 16 ACV
LOGISTICS AND SUPPORT 2: 1 RY (5,000t); 1 Trg

FACILITIES

Base 1 located at Azizam

General Civil Defence Administration Units

HELICOPTERS • SPT 10: 10 Boeing Vertol 107

Special Security Force 500

APC • APC (W): some UR-416

FOREIGN FORCES

United States USCENTCOM: 300 (army/air force trg personnel only)

Syria Syr

Syrian Pound S£		2003	2004	2005
GDP	S£	1.04tr	1.08tr	
	US$	22.6bn	22.2bn	
per capita	US$	1,286	1,237	
Growth	%	2.6	3.4	
Inflation	%	5.0	3.5	
Debt	US$	21.5bn		
Def bdgt	S£	74bn	ε80bn	ε90bn
	US$	1.61bn	1.64bn	1.72bn
US$1=S£		46.0	48.5	52.2

Population	18,448,752

Age	0–14	15–19	20–24	25–29	30–64	65 plus
Male	19%	6%	5%	4%	14%	2%
Female	18%	6%	5%	4%	14%	2%

Capabilities

ACTIVE 307,600 (Army 200,000 Navy 7,600 Air 100,000) Paramilitary 108,000

RESERVE 354,000 (Army 280,000 Navy 4,000 Air 70,000)

Terms of service conscription, 30 months

ORGANISATIONS BY SERVICE

Army 200,000 (incl conscripts); 280,000 reservists (to age 45) (total 480,000)

FORCES BY ROLE

3 Corps HQ

Armd	7 div (*each:* 1 mech bde, 1 arty regt, 3 armd bde)
Mech	3 div under strength (*each:* 1 arty regt, 2 mech bde, 2 armd bde)
Inf	4 indep bde
SF	1 div (3 SF regt); 10 indep regt
Arty	2 indep bde
AT	2 indep bde
SSM	1 bde (with SS-21) (3 SSM bn); 1 bde (with *Scud*-B/-C) (3 SSM bn); 2 (coastal def) bde (SS-C-1B *Sepal* and SS-C-3 *Styx*); 1 bde (with FROG-7) (3 SSM bn)
Border Guard	1 bde
Republican Guard	1 div (1 arty regt, 1 mech bde, 3 armd bde)

Reserves

Armd 1 div HQ; 4 bde; 2 regt
Inf   31 regt
Arty 3 regt

EQUIPMENT BY TYPE

TK • MBT 4,600
T-72 1,600: 1,600 T-72 MBT/T-72M some in store

T-62 1,000: 1,000 T-62K/T-62M some in store
T-55 2,000: 2,000 T-55 MBT/T-55MV some in store
RECCE • BRDM 800: 800 BRDM-2
AIFV • BMP 2200: 2,100 BMP-1; 100 BMP-2
APC • APC (W) • BTR 1600+: 1,600+ BTR-152/BTR-50/BTR-60/BTR-70
ARTY 3,150
  TOWED 1,530
    122mm 850: 600 D-30; 100 M-1931/37 (in store); 150 M-30 M-1938
    130mm 600: 600 M-46
    152mm 70: 20 D-20; 50 M-1937
    180mm 10: 10 S23
  SP 430
    122mm 380: 380 2S1 *Carnation*
    152mm 50: 50 2S3
  MRL 480
    107mm 200: 200 Type-63
    122mm 280: 280 BM-21
  MOR 710: 200 82mm
    120mm 400: 400 M-1943
    160mm 100: 100 M-160
    240mm 10: 10 M-240
AT • MSL 4190+: 800 AT-10; some AT-14 *Kornet*; 3,000 AT-3 *Sagger* (incl 2500 SP); 150 AT-4 *Spigot*; 40 AT-5 *Spandrel*; some AT-7 *Saxhorn*; 200 Milan
  RL • 105mm: some RPG-29
    73mm: some RPG-7 *Knout*
AD
  SAM 4,335+
    SP 235: 20 SA-11 *Gadfly*; 35 SA-13 *Gopher*; 160 SA-8 *Gecko*; 20 SA-9 *Gaskin*
    MANPAD 4,100+: 100 SA-14 *Gremlin*; some SA-18 *Grouse (Igla)*; 4,000 SA-7 *Grail*
  GUNS 2,050
    100mm • TOWED 25: 25 KS-19
    23mm 1,050
      SP 400: 400 ZSU-23-4
      TOWED 650: 650 ZU-23-2
    37mm • TOWED 300: 300 M-1939
    57mm • TOWED 675: 675 S-60
MSL • TACTICAL • SSM 72+: 18 FROG-7; 18+ SS-21 *Scarab (Tochka)*; 4 SS-C-1B *Sepal*; 6 SS-C-3 *Styx* (SSM msl totals est 850)
  SCUD 26: 26 *Scud-B/Scud-C/Scud-D*

Navy 7,600; 4,000 reservists (total 11,600)

EQUIPMENT BY TYPE
PRINCIPAL SURFACE COMBATANTS • FRIGATES • FF 2:
  2 FSU *Petya* III each with 1 triple 533mm ASTT (3 eff.) with SAET-60 HWT, 4 RBU 2500 *Smerch* 1 (64 eff.)†, 2 76mm twin gun
PATROL AND COASTAL COMBATANTS 20
  PFI 8: 8 *Zhuk* less than 100 tonnes
  PFM 12:
    12 *Osa* I/II each with 4 single each with 1 SS-N-2C *Styx* tactical SSM
MINE WARFARE • MINE COUNTERMEASURES 5

MSC 1: 1 *Sonya*
MSI 3: 3 *Yevgenya*
MSO 1: 1 T-43 (FSU)
AMPHIBIOUS • LS • LSM 3:
  3 *Polnochny* B (capacity 180 troops; 6 MBT)
LOGISTICS AND SUPPORT 4: 1 AGOR; 1 spt; 1 (div); 1 trg
FACILITIES
Base 1 located at Latakia, 1 located at Tartus, 1 located at Minet el-Baida

Naval Aviation
HELICOPTER 25 atk hel
ASW 25
  KA-27 5: 5 Ka-28 (Ka-27PL) *Helix A* (air force manpower)
  Mi-14 *Haze* 20

Air Force 40,000; 70,000 reservists (total 110,000)

Flying hours   15 to 25 hrs/year on FGA/ftr; 70 hrs/year; 50 hrs/year on MBB-223 *Flamingo* trg ac

FORCES BY ROLE
Ftr   4 sqn with 30 MiG-25 *Foxbat*; 4 sqn with 80 MiG-23 *Flogger*; 9 sqn with 160 MiG-21 *Fishbed*; 1 sqn with 80 MiG-29A *Fulcrum A*

FGA   2 sqn with 60 MiG-23BN *Flogger H*; 1 sqn with 20 Su-24 *Fencer*; 5 sqn with 50 Su-22 (Su-17M-2) *Fitter D*

Recce   4 sqn with 40 MiG-21H *Fishbed*/MiG-21J *Fishbed**; 8 MiG-25R *Foxbat**

Tpt   some sqn with 1 An-24 *Coke*; 6 An-26 *Curl*; 2 *Falcon* 20; 1 *Falcon* 900; 4 Il-76 *Candid*; 6 Yak-40 *Codling*; 100 Mi-17 (Mi-8MT) *Hip H*/Mi-8 *Hip*; 20 PZL Mi-2 *Hoplite*

Atk hel   some sqn with 36 Mi-25 *Hind D*; 35 SA-342L *Gazelle*

Trg   some sqn with 6 Su-22 (Su-17M-2) *Fitter D**; 2 PA-31 *Navajo*; 70 L-39 *Albatros**; 35 MBB-223 *Flamingo* (basic); 6 MFI-17 *Mushshak*; 20 MiG-21U *Mongol A**; 6 MiG-23UM*; 2 MiG-25U *Foxbat**

EQUIPMENT BY TYPE
AIRCRAFT 632 combat capable
  FTR 390
    MiG-29 80: 80 MiG-29A *Fulcrum A*
    MiG-25 *Foxbat* 30 **MiG-23** *Flogger* 80
    MiG-21 200: 160 **MiG-21H** *Fishbed*/**MiG-21J** *Fishbed* 40*
  FGA 136: 20 Su-24 *Fencer*
    MiG-23B 60: 60 MiG-23BN *Flogger H*
    Su-17 • Su-17M 56: 50 Su-22 (Su-17M-2) *Fitter D*; 6*
  RECCE 8: 8 MiG-25R *Foxbat**
  TPT 22: 1 An-24 *Coke*; 6 An-26 *Curl*; 2 *Falcon* 20; 1 *Falcon* 900; 4 Il-76 *Candid*; 2 PA-31 *Navajo*; 6 Yak-40 *Codling*
  TRG 139: 70 L-39 *Albatros**; 35 MBB-223 *Flamingo* (basic); 6 MFI-17 *Mushshak*; 20 MiG-21U *Mongol A**
    MiG-23U 6: 6 MiG-23UM*
    MiG-25U *Foxbat* 2*
HELICOPTERS

ATK 71
   Mi-25 36: 36 Mi-25 *Hind D*
   SA-342 35: 35 SA-342L *Gazelle*
SPT 120
   Mi-8 100: 100 Mi-17 (Mi-8MT) *Hip H*/Mi-8 *Hip* spt hel
   PZL Mi-2 *Hoplite* 20
MSL • TACTICAL • ASM: some AS-7 *Kerry*; some HOT
   AAM: some AA-10 *Alamo*; some AA-2 *Atoll*; some AA-6
   Acrid; some AA-7 *Apex*; some AA-8 *Aphid*

Air Defence Command ε60,000

FORCES BY ROLE
AD   2 div (*total*: 25 AD bde (*total*: 150 SAM bty with
     148 SA-3 *Goa*; 195 SA-6 *Gainful* (585 eff.); 320 SA-2
     Guideline, some ADA bty with 4,000 SA-7A *Grail*/SA-
     7B *Grail*))
SAM 2 regt with 44 SA-5 *Gammon* (*each*: 2 SAM bn (*each*: 2
     SAM bty))

EQUIPMENT BY TYPE
AD • SAM 4707: 148 SA-3 *Goa*
  SP 195: 195 SA-6 *Gainful*
  TOWED 320: 320 SA-2 *Guideline*
  STATIC 44: 44 SA-5 *Gammon*
  MANPAD • SA-7 4000: 4,000 SA-7A *Grail*/SA-7B *Grail*

Paramilitary ε108,000

Gendarmerie 8,000
Ministry of Interior

Workers' Militia ε100,000
People's Army (Ba'ath Party)

FOREIGN FORCES
Russia: Army 150

Tunisia Tn

Tunisian Dinar D		2003	2004	2005
GDP	D	32.2bn	35.1bn	
	US$	25.1bn	28.3bn	
per capita	US$	2,547	2,837	
Growth	%	5.6	5.8	
Inflation	%	2.8	3.6	
Debt	US$	15.5bn		
Def bdgt	D	525m	540m	ε550m
	US$	410m	435m	436m
FMA (US)	US$	6.4m	11.7m	11.7m
US$1=D		1.28	1.24	1.26

Population   10,074,951

Age	0–14	15–19	20–24	25–29	30–64	65 plus
Male	13%	5%	5%	5%	19%	3%
Female	12%	5%	5%	5%	19%	3%

Capabilities

ACTIVE 35,300 (Army 27,000 Navy 4,800 Air 3,500)
Paramilitary 12,000
Terms of service 12 months selective

ORGANISATIONS BY SERVICE

Army 5,000; 22,000 conscript (total 27,000)

FORCES BY ROLE
Mech 3 bde (*each*: 1 arty regt, 1 AD regt, 1 armd regt, 2
     mech inf regt)
SF   1 (Sahara) bde; 1 bde
Engr 1 regt

EQUIPMENT BY TYPE
TK 132
  MBT • M-60 84: 30 M-60A1; 54 M-60A3
  LT TK 48: 48 SK-105 *Kuerassier*
RECCE 60
  AML 40: 40 AML-90
  Saladin 20
APC 268
  APC (T) • M-113 140: 140 M-113A1/M-113A2
  APC (W) 128: 18 EE-11 *Urutu*; 110 Fiat 6614
ARTY 276
  TOWED 115
    105mm • M-101 48: 48 M-101A1/M-101A2
    155mm 67
      M-114 12: 12 M-114A1
      M-198 55
  MOR 161: 95 81mm; 48 107mm (some SP)
    120mm 18: 18 Brandt
AT
  MSL 590: 500 *Milan*; 90 TOW (incl 35 M-901 ITV)
  RL • 89mm 600: 300 LRAC; 300 M-20
AD
  SAM 86
    SP 26: 26 M-48 *Chaparral*
    MANPAD 60: 60 RBS-70
  GUNS 127
    20mm • TOWED 100: 100 M-55
    37mm • TOWED 15: 15 Type-55 (M-1939)/Type-65
    40mm • SP 12: 12 M-42
RADAR • LAND: some RASIT (veh, arty)

Navy ε4,800

EQUIPMENT BY TYPE
PATROL AND COASTAL COMBATANTS 19+
  PCC 3: 3 *Utique* (mod PRC *Shanghai* II)
  PCI 10+ less than 100 tonnes
  PFM 6:
    3 *Bizerte* (Fr P-48) each with 8 SS 12M tactical SSM
    3 *La Galite* (Fr *Combattante* III) each with 2 Mk 140
    Harpoon quad (8 eff.) each with 1 MM-40 *Exocet* tactical
    SSM, 1 76mm gun
LOGISTICS AND SUPPORT 2: 1 AGS
  TRG 1: 1 *Salambo* (US *Conrad*, survey)

FACILITIES
Base 1 located at Bizerte, 1 located at Sfax, 1 located at
   Kelibia

Air Force 2,800; 700 conscript (**total** 3,500)

FORCES BY ROLE

FGA	some sqn with 12 F-5E *Tiger II*/F-5F *Tiger II*
CCT	some sqn with 3 MB-326K; 3 MB-326L
Tpt	some sqn with 8 C-130B *Hercules*; 1 C-130E *Hercules*; 2 C-130H *Hercules*; 1 *Falcon* 20; 5 G-222; 3 L-410 *Turbolet*
Liaison	some sqn with 2 S-208A
Tpt hel	1 wg with 6 AS-350B *Ecureuil*; 1 AS-365 *Dauphin* 2; 15 AB-205 (Bell 205); 6 SA-313; 3 SA-316 *Alouette III*; 10 UH-1H *Iroquois*; 2 UH-1N *Iroquois*
Trg	some sqn with 12 L-59 *Albatros**; 4 MB-326B; 14 SF-260
Hel	some (armed) sqn with 11 HH-3 *Jolly Green Giant* (ASW); 5 SA-341 *Gazelle* (atk)

EQUIPMENT BY TYPE

AIRCRAFT 27 combat capable
FTR • F-5 12: 12 F-5E *Tiger II*/F-5F *Tiger II*
FGA 3: 3 MB-326K
TPT 20
   C-130 11: 8 C-130B *Hercules*; 1 C-130E *Hercules*; 2 C-130H *Hercules*
   Falcon 20 1 **G-222** 5 **L-410 *Turbolet*** 3
   UTL • S-208 2: 2 S-208A
TRG 33: 12 L-59 *Albatros**; 4 MB-326B; 3 MB-326L; 14 SF-260
HELICOPTERS
   SAR 11: 11 HH-3 *Jolly Green Giant** (ASW)
   SPT 11
     AS-350 6: 6 AS-350B *Ecureuil*
     SA-341 *Gazelle** 5 (atk)
   UTL 37: 15 AB-205 (Bell 205); 1 AS-365 *Dauphin* 2; 6 SA-313; 3 SA-316 *Alouette III*
     UH-1 12: 10 UH-1H *Iroquois*; 2 UH-1N *Iroquois*
MSL • TACTICAL • AAM • AIM-9: some AIM-9J *Sidewinder*

Paramilitary 12,000

National Guard 12,000

Ministry of Interior
PATROL AND COASTAL COMBATANTS 25
   PCC 6: 6 *Kondor* I (ex-GDR)
   PCI 19: 10 (other, under 100 tonnes) *Bremse* 5 (ex-GDR, under 100 tonnes) *Gabes* 4 less than 100 tonnes
   HELICOPTERS • UTL 8: 8 SA-318 *Alouette II*/SA-319 *Alouette III*

DEPLOYMENT

BURUNDI
UN • ONUB 9 obs

CÔTE D'IVOIRE
UN • ONUCI 2 obs

DEMOCRATIC REPUBLIC OF CONGO
UN • MONUC 168; 22 obs

ETHIOPIA/ERITREA
UN • UNMEE 2 obs

United Arab Emirates UAE

Emirati Dirham D		2003	2004	2005
GDP	D	286bn	328bn	
	US$	78.2bn	89.6bn	
per capita	US$	31,471	35,518	
Growth	%	7.0	5.7	
Inflation	%	2.8	3.8	
Debt	US$	21.5bn		
Def bdgt[a]	D	9.23bn	9.49bn	9.74bn
	US$	2.51bn	2.58bn	2.65bn
US$1=D		3.67	3.67	3.67

[a] excluding extra-budgetary procurement funding

Population   2,563,212

Ethnic groups: Nationals 24%; Expatriates 76% of which Indian 30%, Pakistani 20%; other Arab 12%; other Asian 10%; UK 2%; other European 1%

Age	0–14	15–19	20–24	25–29	30–64	65 plus
Male	13%	6%	5%	4%	29%	3%
Female	12%	5%	5%	3%	14%	1%

Capabilities

ACTIVE 50,500 (Army 44,000 Navy 2,500 Air 4,000)
The Union Defence Force and the armed forces of the UAE (Abu Dhabi, Dubai, Ras Al Khaimah, Fujairah, Ajman, Umm al-Qaywayn and Sharjah) were formally merged in 1976 and centred on Abu Dhabi. Dubai still maintains independent forces, as do other emirates to a lesser degree.

ORGANISATIONS BY SERVICE

Army 44,000 (incl Dubai 15000)
FORCES BY ROLE
GHQ Abu Dhabi

Armd	2 bde
Mech inf	3 bde
Inf	2 bde
Arty	1 bde (3 arty regt)
Royal Guard	1 bde

Dubai Independent Forces

Mech inf 2 bde

EQUIPMENT BY TYPE

TK 545
   MBT 469: 388 *Leclerc*; 36 OF-40 Mk2 (*Lion*); 45 AMX-30
   LT TK 76: 76 *Scorpion*
RECCE 113
   AML 49: 49 AML-90
   Ferret 20 in store *Saladin* 20 in store **VBL** 24
AIFV 430: 15 AMX-10P
   BMP 415: 415 BMP-3
APC 860
   APC (T) 136: 136 AAPC (incl 53 engr plus other variants)
   APC (W) 724
     BTR 90: 90 BTR-3U *Guardian*
     EE-11 *Urutu* 120

M-3 *Panhard* 370
TPz-1 *Fuchs* 64
VCR 80 (incl variants)
ARTY 501+
TOWED 93
105mm 73: 73 ROF lt
130mm 20: 20 Type-59-I
SP • 155mm 181: 78 G-6
M-109 85: 85 M-109A3
Mk F3 18
MRL 72+
122mm 48+: 48 Firos-25 (est 24 op); some Type-90 (reported)
300mm 6: 6 9A52 *Smerch*
70mm 18: 18 LAU-97
MOR 155
81mm 134: 20 Brandt; 114 L16
120mm 21: 21 Brandt
AT
MSL 305+: 50 HOT (20 SP); 230 *Milan*; 25 TOW; some *Vigilant* in store
RCL 262
106mm 12: 12 M-40
84mm 250: 250 *Carl Gustav*
AD
SAM • MANPAD 40+: 20+ *Blowpipe*; 20 *Mistral*
GUNS 62
20mm • SP 42: 42 M3 VDAA
30mm • TOWED 20: 20 GCF-BM2
MSL • TACTICAL • SSM • SCUD 6: 6 *Scud*-B (up to 20 msl)

Navy ε2,500

EQUIPMENT BY TYPE
PRINCIPAL SURFACE COMBATANTS 4
FRIGATES • FFG 2:
2 *Abu Dhabi* (NL *Kortenaer*) each with 2 AS-565 aslt hel, 1 Mk 29 *Sea Sparrow* octuple with 24 RIM-7F/M *Sea Sparrow* SAM, 2 Mk 141 *Harpoon* quad (8 eff.) (no weapons embarked) each with 1 AGM-84A *Harpoon* tactical ASM, 2 Twin 324mm TT (4 eff.) each with A244/Mk 46, 1 76mm gun
CORVETTES • FSG 2:
2 *Muray Jip* (Ge *Lurssen* 62m) each with 1 SA-316 *Alouette III* utl hel, 2 quad (8 eff.) each with 1 MM-40 *Exocet* tactical SSM
PATROL AND COASTAL COMBATANTS 14
PCC 6: 6 *Ardhana* (UK Vosper 33m)
PFM 8:
6 *Ban Yas* (Ge *Lurssen* TNC-45) each with 2 twin (4 eff.) each with 1 MM-40 *Exocet* tactical SSM, 1 76mm gun
2 *Mubarraz* (Ge *Lurssen* 45m) each with 2 twin (4 eff.) each with 1 MM-40 *Exocet* tactical SSM, 1 76mm gun
AMPHIBIOUS • CRAFT 5:
LCT 5: 2 (other); 3 *Al Feyi*
LOGISTICS AND SUPPORT 2: 1 AT; 1 spt (div)
FACILITIES
Base 1 (Sharjah) located at Mina Sakr, 1 located at Mina Rashid, 1 located at Khor Fakkan, 1 (Dubai) located at Mina Zayed, 1 located at Dalma, 1 (Main base) located at Abu Dhabi, 1 located at Mina Khalid, 1 (Ras-al-Khaimah) located at Mina Jabal

Naval Aviation

AIRCRAFT • TPT • LEARJET 35 2: 2 *Learjet* 35A
HELICOPTERS
ASLT 7: 7 AS-565
ASW/ASUW • AS-332 7: 7 AS-332F *Super Puma* (in ASUW role)
UTL 4: 4 SA-316 *Alouette III*

Air Force 4,000

incl Police Air Wing
Flying hours 110 hrs/year

FORCES BY ROLE

Ftr	1 sqn with 20 M-2000EAD (M-2000E) *Mirage*
FGA	1 sqn with first of 80 F-16E *Falcon* Block 60/F-16F *Falcon* Block 60/FGA (being delivered); 18 M-2000DAD (M-2000ED) *Mirage*; 44 M-2000 RAD *Mirage*; 1 sqn with 17 *Hawk* MK63A/*Hawk* MK63C/*Hawk* MK63; 1 sqn with 13 *Hawk* MK102
Recce	1 sqn with 7 M-2000 RAD *Mirage**
SAR	some sqn with 3 A-109K2; 6 AB-139
Tpt	some sqn with 1 An-124 *Condor*; 4 C-130H *Hercules*; 2 C-130H-30 *Hercules*; 7 CASA 235M-100; 1 DHC-6-300 *Twin Otter*; 4 Il-76 *Candid* on lease; 2 L-100-30
OCU	some unit with 6 M-2000DAD (M-2000ED) *Mirage**; 5 *Hawk* MK61*
Atk hel	some sqn with 30 AH-64A *Apache*; AS-550C3 *Fennec*; 10 SA-342K *Gazelle* each with HOT tactical ASM
Tpt hel	some sqn with 2 Beech 350 *Super King Air* (VIP); 12 CH-47C *Chinook* (SF); 15 IAR-330 SOCAT *Puma*/SA-330 *Puma*; 2 AB-139 (VIP); 4 AS-365F *Dauphin 2* (VIP); 9 Bell 206 *JetRanger* trg; 3 Bell 214; 1 Bell 407; 9 Bell 412 *Twin Huey*
Trg	some sqn with 12 Grob 115TA; 30 PC-7 *Turbo Trainer*

EQUIPMENT BY TYPE
AIRCRAFT 146 combat capable
FGA 57+: first of 80 F-16E *Falcon* Block 60/F-16F *Falcon* Block 60/FGA ac (being delivered)
M-2000 44: 24 M-2000DAD (M-2000ED) *Mirage*; 20 M-2000EAD (M-2000E) *Mirage*
Hawk **MK102** 13
RECCE 51: 51 M-2000 RAD *Mirage*
TPT 23: 1 An-124 *Condor*; 2 Beech 350 *Super King Air* (VIP)
C-130 6:
C-130H 6: 4; 2 C-130H-30 *Hercules*
CN-235 • CN-235M 7: 7 CASA 235M-100
DHC-6 1: 1 DHC-6-300 *Twin Otter*
Il-76 *Candid* 4 on lease
L-100 2: 2 L-100-30
TRG 64
GROB 115 12: 12 Grob 115TA
Hawk **MK61** 5*
HAWK MK63 17: 17 *Hawk* MK63 Trg ac/*Hawk* MK63A/*Hawk* MK63C*
PC-7 *Turbo Trainer* 30

Middle East and North Africa

HELICOPTERS

ATK • AH-64 30: 30 AH-64A *Apache*
   AS-550C3 *Fennec* some
ASLT • SA-342 10:
   10 SA-342K *Gazelle* each with HOT tactical ASM
SPT • CH-47 12: 12 CH-47C *Chinook* (SF)
IAR-330 SOCAT *Puma* aslt/SA-330 *Puma* spt 15
UTL 37
   A-109 3: 3 A-109K2
   AB-139 6; 2 (VIP)
   AS-365 4: 4 AS-365F *Dauphin 2* (VIP)
   Bell 206 *JetRanger* 9 trg **Bell 214** 3 **Bell 407** 1 **Bell 412** *Twin Huey* 9
MSL • TACTICAL • ASM: some AGM-114 *Hellfire*; some AS-15 *Kent*; some *Hydra-70*; some PGM-1 *Hakeem 1*; some PGM-2 *Hakeem 2*
   AAM • AIM-9: some AIM-9L *Sidewinder*
      MICA some **R-550** *Magic*

Air Defence

FORCES BY ROLE

AD   2 bde (*each:* 3 AD bn); 3 bn with I-HAWK MIM-23B

SAM 3 short-range bn with *Crotale; Mistral; Rapier;* RB-70; *Javelin;* SA-18 *Grouse (Igla)*

EQUIPMENT BY TYPE

AD • SAM: some *Crotale*; some *Mistral*; some *Rapier*
   SP: some RB-70
   TOWED • MIM-23: some I-HAWK MIM-23B
   MANPAD: some *Javelin*; some SA-18 *Grouse (Igla)*

Paramilitary • Coast Guard

Ministry of Interior
PATROL AND COASTAL COMBATANTS 40+
   MISC BOATS/CRAFT: some boats
   PCI 40+

Air Defence

FORCES BY ROLE

AD   2 bde (*each:* 3 AD bn); 3 bn with I-HAWK MIM-23B

SAM 3 short-range bn with *Crotale; Mistral; Rapier;* RB-70; *Javelin;* SA-18 *Grouse (Igla)*

EQUIPMENT BY TYPE

AD • SAM: some *Crotale*; some *Mistral*; some *Rapier*
   SP: some RB-70
   TOWED • MIM-23: some I-HAWK MIM-23B
   MANPAD: some *Javelin*; some SA-18 *Grouse (Igla)*

FOREIGN FORCES

United States USCENTCOM: 1,300

Yemen, Republic of Ye

Yemeni Rial R		2003	2004	2005
GDP	R	2.08tr	2.54tr	
	US$	11.3bn	13.8bn	
per capita	US$	587	690	
Growth	%	3.1	2.7	
Inflation	%	10.8	12.5	
Debt	US$	5.37bn		
Def bdgt	R	ε148bn	ε159bn	ε179bn
	US$	809m	869m	942m
FMA (US)	US$	2.53m	15.7m	11m
US$1=R		183	184	191

Population   20,727,063
Ethnic groups: North 79%; South 21%

Age	0–14	15–19	20–24	25–29	30–64	65 plus
Male	24%	6%	5%	4%	11%	1%
Female	23%	6%	5%	4%	11%	1%

Capabilities

ACTIVE 66,700 (Army 60,000 Navy 1,700 Air 5,000)
Paramilitary 70,000
Terms of service conscription, 2 years

ORGANISATIONS BY SERVICE

Army 60,000 (incl conscripts)

FORCES BY ROLE

Armd	8 bde
Mech	6 bde
Inf	16 bde
SF	1 bde
Cdo / AB	2 bde
Arty	3 bde
SSM	1 bde
Gd / Central Guard	1 force
AD	6 bde (*each:* 1 SAM bn, 4 ADA bn)

EQUIPMENT BY TYPE

TK • MBT 790: 60 T-72
   M-60 50: 50 M-60A1
   T-62 200 **T-54/T-55** 450 **T-34** 30
RECCE 130
   AML 80: 80 AML-90
   BRDM 50: 50 BRDM-2
AIFV • BMP 200: 200 BMP-1/BMP-2
APC 710
   APC (T) 60: 60 M-113
   APC (W) • BTR 650: 650 BTR-152/BTR-40/BTR-60 (150 op)
ARTY 1167
   TOWED 310
      105mm • M-101 25: 25 M-101A1
      122mm 200: 130 D-30; 30 M-1931/37; 40 M-30 *M-1938*
      130mm 60: 60 M-46
      152mm 10: 10 D-20
      155mm 15: 15 M-114
   SP • 122mm 25: 25 2S1 *Carnation*

COASTAL • 130mm 36: 36 SM-4-1
MRL 294
   122mm 280: 280 BM-21 (150 op)
   140mm 14: 14 BM-14
MOR 502: 200 81mm
   82mm 90: 90 M-43
   107mm 12 **120mm** 100 **160mm** ε100
AT
  MSL 71: 35 AT-3 *Sagger*; 24 M47 *Dragon*; 12 TOW
  RCL • 107mm: some B-11
   75mm: some M-20
   82mm: some B-10
  RL • 66mm: some M-72 *LAW*
   73mm: some RPG-7 *Knout*
  GUNS • 100mm 50: 20 M-1944; 30 SU-100 SP
   85mm: some D-44
AD
  SAM 800: ε800 SA-13 *Gopher* SP/SA-14 *Gremlin* MANPAD/SA-7 *Grail* MANPAD/SA-9 *Gaskin* SP (800-3200 eff.)
  GUNS 530
   20mm 70
    SP 20: 20 M-163 *Vulcan*
    TOWED 50: 50 M-167 *Vulcan*
   23mm 150
    SP 50: 50 ZSU-23-4
    TOWED 100: 100 ZU-23-2
   37mm • TOWED 150: 150 M-1939
   57mm • TOWED 120: 120 S-60
   85mm • TOWED 40: 40 M-1939 *KS-12*
MSL • TACTICAL • SSM 28: 12 FROG-7; 10 SS-21 *Scarab* (*Tochka*)
  SCUD 6: 6 *Scud*-B (est 33 msl)

Navy 1,700

EQUIPMENT BY TYPE
PATROL AND COASTAL COMBATANTS 19
  MISC BOATS/CRAFT 6: 6 boats
  PFI 5: 2 *Sana'a* (US *Broadsword* 32m, 1 non-op); 3 *Zhuk* (FSU, under 100 tonnes)
  PFM 8:
   3 *Huangfen* (Y-1 (CSS-N-4) capable) each with 4 single with 3 YJ-1 (CSS-N-4) *Sardine* tactical SSM
   1 *Huangfen* with 4 single with 3 YJ-1 (CSS-N-4) *Sardine* tactical SSM
   2 *Osa* II each with 2 SS-N-2C *Styx* tactical SSM
   1 *Tarantul* with 2 twin (4 eff.) with 4 SS-N-2C *Styx* tactical SSM
   1 *Tarantul* non-operational with 2 twin (4 eff.) with 4 SS-N-2C *Styx* tactical SSM
MINE WARFARE • MINE COUNTERMEASURES 6
  MHC 5: 5 *Yevgenya* (FSU)
  MSO 1: 1 *Natya* (FSU)
AMPHIBIOUS
  LS • LST 1:
   1 *Ropucha* (capacity either 190 troops or 10 MBT; either 24 APC (T)s or 170 troops)
  CRAFT 6
   LCU 4: 4 PI NS-717
   LCM 2: 2 *Ondatra* (FSU)
LOGISTICS AND SUPPORT • AOT 2: 2 *Toplivo*
FACILITIES
Base   1 located at Aden, 1 located at Hodeida
Minor 1 (these have naval spt eqpt) located at Socotra, 1
Base   located at Al Mukalla, 1 located at Perim Island

Air Force 5,000 (incl Air Defence)

FORCES BY ROLE
Ftr   some sqn with 10 F-5E *Tiger II*; 14 MiG-29SMT *Fulcrum*; 15 MiG-21 *Fishbed*; 2 MiG-29UBT *Fulcrum*
FGA some sqn with 30 Su-20 (Su-17M) *Fitter C*/Su-22 (Su-17M-2) *Fitter D*
Tpt   some sqn with 2 An-12 *Cub*; 6 An-26 *Curl*; 3 C-130H *Hercules*; 4 Il-14 *Crate*; 3 Il-76 *Candid*
Trg   some sqn with 2 F-5B *Freedom Fighter*†*; 12 L-39C; 4 MiG-21U *Mongol A**; 14 Yak-11 *Moose*; 12 Z-242
Hel   some sqn with 8 Mi-35 *Hind* (attack); 1 AB-47 (Bell 47); 9 Mi-8 *Hip*; 2 Bell 212

EQUIPMENT BY TYPE
AIRCRAFT 75 combat capable
  FTR 41
   F-5 12: 2 F-5B *Freedom Fighter*†; 10 F-5E *Tiger II*
   MiG-29 14: 14 MiG-29SMT *Fulcrum*
   MiG-21 *Fishbed* 15
  FGA • Su-17 • Su-20 (Su-17M) 30: 30 Su-20 (Su-17M) *Fitter C* Su-17 FGA/Su-22 (Su-17M-2) *Fitter D*
  TPT 18: 2 An-12 *Cub*; 6 An-26 *Curl*
   C-130 3: 3 C-130H *Hercules*
   Il-14 *Crate* 4 **Il-76** *Candid* 3
  TRG 44
   L-39 12: 12 L-39C
   MiG-21U *Mongol A* 4*
   MiG-29U 2: 2 MiG-29UBT *Fulcrum*
   Yak-11 *Moose* 14 **Z-242** 12
HELICOPTERS
  ATK 8: 8 Mi-35 *Hind* (atk)
  SPT 10: 1 AB-47 (Bell 47); 9 Mi-8 *Hip*
  UTL 2: 2 Bell 212

Air Defence 2,000

AD • SAM: some SA-3 *Goa*
  SP: some SA-13 *Gopher*; some SA-6 *Gainful*; some SA-9 *Gaskin*
  TOWED: some SA-2 *Guideline*
  MANPAD: some SA-14 *Gremlin*; some SA-7 *Grail*
MSL • TACTICAL • AAM: some AA-2 *Atoll*; some AIM-9 *Sidewinder*

Paramilitary 70,000

Ministry of the Interior Forces 50,000

Tribal Levies 20,000+

Coast Guard

slowly being established
PATROL AND COASTAL COMBATANTS • PCI 5: 5 French *Interceptor* less than 100 tonnes

NON-STATE ARMED GROUPS

see Part II

DEPLOYMENT

BURUNDI
UN • ONUB 5 obs

CÔTE D'IVOIRE
UN • ONUCI 5 obs

MIDDLE EAST & NORTH AFRICA – DEFENCE ECONOMICS

Countries in the Middle East and North Africa enjoyed another year of strong economic growth, driven primarily by continuing high energy prices. Regional GDP growth in 2004 registered 5.7%, slightly lower than in 2003, and with strong demand from emerging major oil consumers, including India and China, growth is forecast to remain above 5% in 2005. Growth in the non-oil-producing countries also picked up as they benefited from strong growth among their oil-producing neighbours.

Once again, the IMF urged Middle Eastern leaders to seize the opportunity afforded by high energy prices to build stronger macroeconomic foundations, increase savings for future generations and, most importantly, diversify their economies to promote sustainable economic growth that will meet the needs of a rapidly rising employment pool. One of the biggest challenges facing the region is how to improve employment growth without falling victim to the boom-and-bust cycle generated by fluctuating oil prices. In particular, the region is facing a burgeoning youth population for whom jobs are not being created fast enough. The number of young people entering the labour market will rise by an average of 3% per annum over the next ten years. Although the fertility rate is declining, population growth, particularly in the Persian Gulf, is nearly twice that of East Asia and four times that of developed nations.

After similar oil-driven booms in the 1970s and 1980s, there is some evidence that this time, governments are responding in a more responsible and disciplined fashion, particularly in terms of public expenditure. So far, where government spending has risen, the tendency has been to focus on infrastructure development and public services such as schools and hospitals. In addition, windfall revenues are being diverted into oil funds to provide for future generations or helping the repayment of national debt that ballooned following the oil crash in 1998, when prices fell to $10 a barrel. As yet, despite the uncertain regional security environment, there is little evidence that budget surpluses are being diverted into the purchase of expensive foreign weapons systems or defence expenditure in general. So, although regional defence expenditure increased from $55.5bn in 2003 to $59.6bn in 2004, as a proportion of GDP, spending continued to decline falling to 5.65%.

Not surprisingly, as the biggest oil producer in the region, **Saudi Arabia** recorded a massive budget surplus in 2004 enabling the government to further reduce debt to 66% of GDP (it had been 119% in

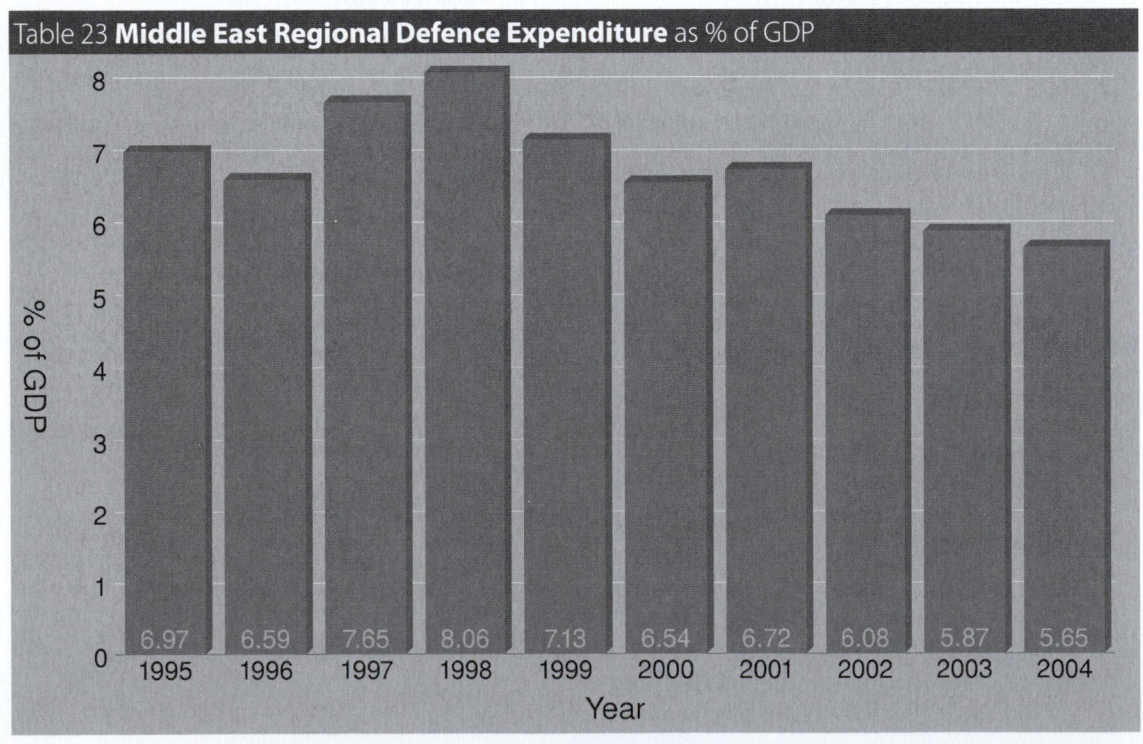

Table 23 **Middle East Regional Defence Expenditure** as % of GDP

Year	% of GDP
1995	6.97
1996	6.59
1997	7.65
1998	8.06
1999	7.13
2000	6.54
2001	6.72
2002	6.08
2003	5.87
2004	5.65

1999) and increase the central bank's foreign assets to $85bn. In its original budget proposal for 2004, the Ministry of Finance forecast revenues of SR200bn and expenditures of SR230bn; however, by the end of the year actual revenues amounted to SR393bn and expenditures to SR295bn, producing a surplus of SR98bn, the second largest in the Kingdom's history. However, as is standard practice, no details are provided for the allocation of additional expenditure. For 2005, the state budget has been calculated on an average price of $25 a barrel and production of 8.8 million barrels a day, and as such, a balanced budget is forecast. However, both the oil price and Saudi production have been significantly higher than budgeted levels for the first 6 months of 2005, and another surplus seems guaranteed. So far, few details about the 2005 budget have emerged although the available information shows that the focus on human resources, such as education and infrastructure projects remains, with the allocation to human resources rising by 25% and funds for health and social development increasing by 51%, compared to the original 2004 budget allocations.

In April 2005, it was reported that France and Saudi Arabia had signed a Memorandum of Understanding (MoU) that could lead to the sale of 48 Dassault *Rafale* multi-role fighter aircraft to the Royal Saudi Air Force (RSAF) together with a comprehensive border surveillance system. It is well-known that the RSAF has been keen to replace its fleet of aging F-5 aircraft as well as find a replacement for the *Tornado* in due course; however, the reported MoU has yet to be confirmed. In the past, Saudi Arabia has often signed similar agreements that have never materialised or been rolled over into other sets of negotiations.

Following years of disagreement that had soured defence relations between **Syria** and Russia, a solution to the outstanding debt owed by Syria was formulated during Syrian President Bashar al-Assad's visit to Moscow in January 2005. Russia has maintained that it was owed around $14.5bn for weapons supplied to the Syrian armed forces during the Cold War era; however, Syria has always argued that not only would it be unable to repay a debt of this size debt, but that the weapons in question were delivered in the context of the strategic relationship that existed between the two countries at the time. A compromise was reached during the January summit, both sides agreeing to reduce the size of the debt to just $3.6bn, which Syria will pay off over the following decade. Agreement on the issue now opens the way for Syria to conclude major weapons deals that it has been trying to secure since 1999. In particular, it is thought that Syria wishes to improve its air-defence capabilities with the acquisition of the Russian-made S-300 air defence system and SA-18 *Igla* surface-to-air missiles. Both the US and Israel have expressed their concern over the prospect of Syria acquiring the *Igla* missile system and have asked Russia not to proceed with any sale.

The 2003 disarmament deal negotiated by the US and UK that resulted in **Libya** abandoning its weapons of mass destruction capabilities, in return for improved economic and political relations, was followed in October 2004 by the lifting of the EU's 18-year arms embargo. At present, very little information about Libya's defence expenditure is available. Budget figures would suggest that in recent years the military has received around $500m a year; however, this amount would only be sufficient to pay for ongoing operational activities. If there are to be any major procurements, then this figure would need to increase dramatically. It is known that the EU has been keen for Libya to invest in improving its maritime patrol capabilities and other border control facil-

Table 24 **Saudi Arabia: original budget allocations by sector**

(SRbn)	2002	2003	2004	2005
Human resources and development	47.0	49.6	55.8	70.1
Transport and communication	5.4	5.6	6.3	8.9
Health and social development	18.9	16.7	17.9	27.1
Defence and security	69.4	70.3	78.4	80.0a
Water, agriculture & infrastructure	15.5	14.8	15.1	19.2
Public administration	39.3	44.8	49.9	n.a.
Other	6.5	7.2	6.6	n.a.
Total	202	209	230	280
a estimate				

ities to stem the flow of illegal immigrants heading for Italy and Malta. Another early priority could be the purchase of military transport aircraft, possibly the An-26 or Indonesian-built CN-235, which would be used to support African Union forces and help demonstrate Tripoli's increasing ties with African as well as Arab states. Libya has a considerable amount of Soviet-made arms and military equipment, which is thought to be in poor condition, and the lifting of the arms embargo has enabled resumption of military-technical cooperation between the two countries. It is thought likely that Libya will prioritise the upgrading of its existing weapons inventory before embarking on the wide-scale acquisition of new equipment. As part of the national plan aimed at ushering the country into the modern economic era, the 2005 state budget introduced sweeping economic reforms. The multi-pronged initiative will streamline government, speed up privatisation and liberalise the media sector in a bid to begin the transition from what remains essentially an authoritarian regime to a more liberal economy that is competitive in the region.

The recovery that began in the **Israeli** economy in 2003 accelerated in 2004 with real GDP growth climbing to 4.3%. However, despite the improving economy, the intifada has had a serious impact on the government's finances, leaving the budget deficit at 4% of GDP in 2004. To address the deteriorating budget position, the Knesset implemented an economic recovery law in 2003 that comprised a raft of initiatives, including expenditure cuts and tax reforms. As a result, the 2005 defence budget was cut to NIS34.3bn, down from NIS34.9bn in 2004, although it is thought that the 2005 budget includes a 'loan' of around NIS600m transferred from the separation fence budget (completion of the 'Seam Zone' and the implementation of the Gaza Disengagement Plan are not funded from the defence budget). Israel is also the recipient of a substantial amount of US Foreign Military Financing, in 2005 amounting to $2.28bn, which must be used to purchase US military equipment. The Israeli Defence Force (IDF) continues to allocate its funds based on the perceived reduction of a conventional threat to Israel, concentrating instead on operations at both ends of the conflict spectrum: low technology urban operations against Palestinian militants and the growing threat of advanced non-conventional missile technology in Iran. This policy, together with budget constraints, has led to a five-year plan to reduce the army by 25% and retire many of its older platforms. After years of investment in

heavy platforms, the current focus is on updating infantry capabilities. For many years the IDF has used the M113 as the backbone of its Armoured Personnel Carrier inventory; however, developments in Gaza have indicated that the platform is not robust enough to deal with the growing use of anti-tank missiles and rocket-propelled grenades. As a result, the army has procured more than 100 *Dingo* 2 4×4 vehicles and is investigating converting Mk1 *Merkava* tanks into APCs or upgrading existing M113s. The IDF has also taken delivery of three US *Stryker* light armoured vehicles for evaluation, although experience in Iraq suggests that these vehicles lack sufficient protection for urban operations.

Also under development is an expensive and ambitious plan to comprehensively integrate and digitise the Ground Forces' existing C4I capabilities. Known as Project Tsayad, the five-year $900m Digital Army Programme will create an all-IDF network, enabling land, air and naval forces to interconnect through secured broadband communications. The air force's main investment at present is the ongoing acquisition of 18 AH-64D *Apache Longbow* attack helicopters as well as continued development of the *Arrow* anti-ballistic missile Weapon System. Non-US procurement funds will be allocated to the local development of a wide variety of Unmanned Aerial Vehicles. It remains unclear if plans to acquire new tankers, early-warning aircraft and C-130 transports have been indefinitely deferred. In recent years the navy has fared less well than the other two services in financial terms, and plans to acquire new platforms have been subject to regular revisions. Current plans that need funding are the acquisition of additional submarine and two multi-mission corvettes equipped with phased array radar. Due to a lack of procurement funds, the purchase of a further two *Dolphin* submarines is dependent on the conclusion of a financing arrangement between Germany and Israel. The first three Israeli submarines were financed mainly by Germany.

Among the major oil-producing countries of the Middle East, **Iran** has one of the strongest performing economies and in 2004, GDP growth of 6.6% was again at the higher end of performance for the region. In comparison with other Gulf countries, the Iranian economy is much more successfully diversified – its manufacturing and agricultural sectors comprise one-third of GDP and services account for about half of GDP. However, there is growing concern that Iran is failing to make the best use of its current economic fortunes and that much needed structural reforms are being avoided. The IMF has expressed concern that revenue windfalls, rather than being invested, are being used to increase government spending on public sector projects and subsidies of essential goods such as bread and fuel. There is no accurate way of determining real defence expenditure in Iran. Although the IMF has published figures quoting an official defence budget, it also commented that the true figure is almost certainly higher when other factors, such as the substantial subsidies to the domestic defence industry, not to mention the possible costs of a nuclear weapons programme, are included. In addition the official budget probably does not include expenditure on R&D, the Revolutionary Guards and other paramilitary forces. When these additional elements are considered, the real level of military-related expenditure could be at least double the official budget. The Iranian regime has made no secret of its intention to build up Iran's defence industrial capability in order to reduce dependency on external arms suppliers, and claims to have numerous ongoing conventional weapons programmes across a range of land, sea and air applications. Many of these are either licensed (from Russia), or indigenous efforts to copy foreign equipment without a licence, and as a result R&D outlays are likely to be fairly substantial, certainly in regional terms.

Algeria has achieved a strong macroeconomic performance in recent years, marked by rising economic growth, low inflation and rapidly growing international reserves. Although Algeria is still facing the challenge of high unemployment, compounded by a growing workforce, the IMF, in its 2004 Article IV survey, indicated that Algeria's economic outlook in the medium term remains 'favourable'. Defence expenditure, as measured by the official National Defence budget, has remained stable at around 3–4% of GDP since 1993. However, the National Defence budget is only thought to cover ongoing operational expenditure, and no provision for significant military procurement, which could add another 50% to total defence outlays, is made public. Since 2000, modernisation of the air force has become a priority, with the delivery of over 30 MiG-29Cs, 42 Mi-17 hel and 17 L-39 jet trainers from the Czech Republic. Future plans include the acquisition of up to 80 Franco-Russian MiG-AT advanced jet trainers and replacement of MiG-29Cs by 42 Mig-29SMT aircraft. In addition to acquiring Russian weapons systems in coming years, Algeria should also be in a position to resume direct defence cooperation with France, following the cancellation of a French policy banning exports to Algeria on the grounds of its human-rights record.

Table 25 Arms orders and deliveries, Middle East and North Africa

	Country Supplier	Classification	Designation	Quantity	Order date	Delivery date	Comment
Algeria (Ag)	RF	ASSM	KH-35	96	1998	1999	For FACs. 2 batches of 48 ordered
	RSA	hel	Mi-24 (*Hind*)	33	1999	2001	Upgrade
	US	ESM	Beech 1900	6	2000		For SIGINT role
	RF	FGA	SU-24 (*Fencer*)	22	2000	2001	
	Cz	FGA	L-39ZA (*Albatros*)	17	2001		
	RF	FGA	MiG-29 (*Fulcrum*)	49	2004		
Bahrain (Brn)	US	FGA	F-16C (*Fighting Falcon*)	10	1998	2000	AMRAAM-equipped; option for 2 more
	US	AAM	AIM-120 (AMRAAM)		1999		
	UK	trg	*Hawk* T MK1	6	2003		Option on further 6
Egypt (Et)	US	hel	SH-2G (*Super Seasprite*)	10	1994	1997	Deliveries to 1999
	US	FGA	F-16C (*Fighting Falcon*)	21	1996	1999	
	US	SP arty	SP 122	24	1996	2000	2nd order
	US	hel	CH-47D (*Chinook*)	4	1997	1999	Also updates for 6 CH-47Cs to D
	US	SAM	PAC-3 (*Patriot*)	384	1998		384 msl; 48 launchers
	dom	AIFV	*Al-Akhbar*		1998	2001	Development continues through 2004
	SF	arty	GH-52	1	1999		Produced under license in Egypt
	Ge	trg	Grob 115EG	74	1999	2000	Deliveries to 2002
	US	MBT	M-1A1	200	1999	2001	Kits for local assembly
	PRC	trg	K-8	80	1999	2001	
	US	FGA	F-16 (*Fighting Falcon*)	24	1999	2001	12 x 1 seater; 12 x 2 seater
	US	AEW	E-2C (*Hawkeye*)	5	1999	2002	Upgrade
	RF	SAM	SA-3A (*Goa*)	50	1999	2003	Upgrade to *Pechora*-2 aka SA-3A Goa continues
	US	atk hel	AH-64A (*Apache*)	35	2000		Upgrade to *Longbow* standard
	It	AAM	AIM-120 (AMRAAM)	6	2000		Upgraded Comd & Control systems
	Nl	SSK	*Moray*	2	2000	2006	
	US	ASM	AGM-84 (*Harpoon*)	53	2001		Block II
	US	arty	MLRS	26	2001		Incl. 2,850 rockets. Deliveries continue
	A	UAV	Camcopter (.)	2	2001	2002	
	US	AAM	AIM-9 (*Sidewinder*)	414	2003		
	US	MBT	M-1A1	125	2003		Kits for local assembly
	US	arty	M-109A	201	2003	2003	US army surplus
	US	ARV	M88A2 (*Hercules*)	21	2004		co-production
	US	PCGF	*Ambassador* MK III	3	2004		
Iran (Ir)	dom	SSI	*Al-Sabehat 15*	1		2000	Mini-sub
	dom	SSM	*Shahab-2*		1994	1998	Dom produced *Scud*
	dom	SSM	*Shahab-3*		1994	1999	Reportedly based on DPRK *No-dong* 1
	PRC	tpt	An-24 (*Coke*)	14	1996	1998	Deliveries 1998-2006
	PRC	FGA	MIG-21F (*Fishbed C*)	10	1996	1998	
	dom	hel	*Shahed-5*	20	1999		
	RF	hel	Mi-8 (*Hip*)	4	1999	2000	Potential for further 20
	RF	ATGW	*Saeqhe 1*	30	2001	2002	
Iraq (Irq)	Pl	hel	Mi-171V5	24			

Table 25 Arms orders and deliveries, Middle East and North Africa

Country Supplier	Classification	Designation	Quantity	Order date	Delivery date	Comment
PI	hel	Mi-17-V5	10			
HKJ	UAV	*Seeker*	2	2004		For air surveillance
CH	APC	Spz 63/89	180	2005	2006	Original order was from UAE (blocked by Swiss Parliament) Given by UAE to Iraq.
Israel (il)						
US	BMD	*Arrow*	2	1986	1999	Deployment to begin 1999; with US
dom	MBT	MkIV		1991	2002	In production
US	BMD	*Nautilus*		1992	2000	Joint dev with US
Fr	hel	AS-565	8	1994	1997	5 delivered 1997
US	FGA	F-15I (*Ra'am*)	25	1994	1998	Deliveries: 4 in 1998, continue to 2000
US	hel	S-70A (*Black Hawk*)	15	1995	1998	1st 2 deliveries complete
dom	sat	*Ofeq 5*	1	1995	2003	Dev slowed by lack of funds
dom	UAV	*Silver Arrow Hermes 450*		1997		Prototype unveiled April 1998
US	AAM	AIM-120B (AMRAAM)	64	1998	1999	
US	ASM	AGM-114 (*Hellfire*)	480	1999		
US	FGA	F-16I (*Sufa*)	50	1999	2003	With *Popeye* 2 and *Python* 4 AAM
US	AAM	AIM-120 (AMRAAM)	57	2000		
US	hel	UH-60L (*Black Hawk*)	35	2000		
US	tpt	Beech 200 (*Super King Air*)	5	2000		
US	hel	S-70A (*Black Hawk*)	24	2001	2002	
US	hel	WAH-64 (*Apache Longbow*)	3	2001	2005	($640m) 3 AH-64D of possible 9 contract includes upgrade of 3 Israeli AH-64A to D.
US	FGA	F-16I (*Sufa*)	52	2001	2006	deliveries 2003-06
dom	PFC	*Super Dvora* MKII	6	2002	2003	Option on further five
dom	PFC	*Shaldag*	2	2002	2003	Option on further two
US	tpt	*Gulfstream* G-550	4	2003	2005	For EAW
US	ASM	JDAM	5000	2004		
dom	FGA	F-15 (*Eagle*)	110	2004		
US	hel	AH-64A (*Apache*)	3	2004		Upgrade to D standard. Poss total of 9
US	hel	AH-64D (*Apache*)	9	2004	2005	
US	ASM	*Paveway III*	100	2005		($30m) GBU-28B laser guided for F-15I *Thunderer*
dom	C2	Comd and control		2005	2008	($900m) Digital Army Programme (DAP) 2 Divs equiped by 2008
Jordan (HKJ)						
UK	ASSM	*Sea Skua*	60	1997	1998	
US	atk hel	AH-64 (*Apache*)	16	1997	2000	*Longbow* radar not fitted
Tu	tpt	CN-235	2	1999	2001	One year lease
US	FGA	F-16 (*Fighting Falcon*)	17	2003		Surplus US stock plus upgrade kits
US	hel	UH-60L (*Black Hawk*)	8	2003		
RF	tpt	IL-76MF (*Candid*)	2	2005		
Kuwait (Kwt)						
UK	ASSM	*Sea Skua*	60	1997	1998	
Ge	hel	EC-135	2	1999	2001	

Table 25 Arms orders and deliveries, Middle East and North Africa

Country Supplier	Classification	Designation	Quantity	Order date	Delivery date	Comment
US	hel	AH-64D (*Apache*)	16	2001	1999	
It	PFB	PFB (*Fast Patrol Boat*)	12	2004	2005	P46 for Coastgurd. First delivered Mar 2005 Order to be completed June 2006.
Mauritania (RIM) It	trg	SF-260E	5		2000	
Oman (O) UK	radar	S743D		1999	2002	
UK	hel	*Super Lynx*	20	2001		
US	FGA	F-16 (*Fighting Falcon*)	12	2001	2005	
Saudi Arabia (Sau) Fr	FFG	*Al Riyadh*	3	1994	2001	1st delivery 2002, 2nd 2003, 3rd 2004
US	ASW	AEW	5	1997	2000	Upgrade
US	AAM	AIM-120 (AMRAAM)	475	2000		
RF	FGA	SU-27 (*Flanker*)			2000	Deliveries from previously unannounced order
RF	SAM	SA-10 (*Grumble* (quad))		1997		Unconfirmed
RF	SAM	SA-18 (*Grouse* (*Igla*))		2005		Undisclosed number of vehicle mounted version of *Igla* SA-18
Tunisia (Tn) US	hel	HH-3 (*Jolly Green Giant*)	4	1996	1998	
United Arab Emirates (UAE) It	hel	CH-47C (*Chinook*)	12		2003	($68.3m) Upgrade of ex Libyan hels to CH-47C+
Fr	MBT	*Leclerc*	390	1993	1994	Final Delivery May 2005 final quantity 288.
Fr	hel	AS-565	6	1995	1998	For *Kortenaer* frigates
Fr	hel	AS-332 (*Super Puma*)	5	1996	1998	Upgrade of anti-ship and ASW eqpt
US	hel	AH-64A (*Apache*)	10	1997	1999	
Fr	hel	SA-341 (*Gazelle*)	5	1997	1999	Option for further 5
Fr	FGA	M-2000 (*Mirage*)	33	1997	2000	Upgrade to 2000-9 standard
Indo	tpt	CASA 235 MPA	4	1998		
Fr	ASM	*Black Shaheen*		1998	2000	For new and upgraded *Mirage* 2000-9
Fr	hel	AS-350B (*Ecureuil*)	14	1999	2001	
RF	SAM	*Pantsyr*-S1	50	2000	2002	
US	FGA	F-16 (*Fighting Falcon*)	80	2000	2004	With AMRAAM, HARM and *Hakeem* msl
Sp	tpt	CASA C-295	4	2001		
US	atk hel	AH-64D (*Apache*)	30	2002		Upgrade from AH-64A to D standard
Fr	FGA	M-2000-9 (*Mirage*)	33	2003	2005	
dom	FAC	*Baynunah*	6	2003	2008	
Ge	NBC	Tpz-1 (*Fuchs*)	32	2005		($205m)
dom	HMTV	Tpt	500	2005	2005	($41m) High mobility tactical vehicles
US	hel	AB-139	8	2005	2005	(£83m) SAR role
Yemen, Republic of (Ye) Fr	PCI	*Vigilante*	6	1996	1997	Commissioning delayed
Cz	trg	L-39C	12	1999	1999	Deliveries began late 1999
RF	FGA	SU-27 (*Flanker*)	14	1999	2001	
RF	FGA	MiG-29 (*Fulcrum*)	15	2001	2002	
Aus	PC	PCI	10	2003	2004	Contract includes crew training

Chapter Five
Central and South Asia

CENTRAL ASIA

Central Asia and **Afghanistan** are the focus of an increasingly competitive relationship among the countries of the region, the Shanghai Cooperation Organization (SCO) and the US. A statement issued at the July summit of the SCO in Astana, Kazakhstan challenged the need for a continued US presence at Khanabad in Uzbekistan and the Manas airbase in Kyrgyzstan. At the end of July, Uzbek President Islam Karimov ordered the US out of the Khanabad base within six months. Kyrgyz President Kurmanbek Bakiev said the US could use the Manas airbase as long as military operations in Afghanistan required it. At the same time, the US may establish more permanent facilities in **Afghanistan**, at Bagram and Kandahar, as part of the US Global Posture Review (see p. 15) and under a 'Strategic Partnership' between Washington and Kabul.

As its demand for energy increases and its concerns over encirclement by the US deepen, **China** seeks, through the SCO, to increase its influence in Central Asia. The SCO also helps to maintain cooperation between Russia and China with regard to their policies in Central Asia. However, this strategic partnership has its limits. For example, the SCO failed in attempts to establish a free-trade zone. Russia is also concerned about Chinese investment in a prospective oil pipeline from Kazakhstan, which presents a minor, but real, alternative to Russia's own eastward pipeline into China.

The Collective Security Treaty Organisation (CSTO) also continues to improve its institutional structures and regional defence capabilities by carrying out a number of military training exercises (see p. 155). Moreover, following an agreement between Russia and Tajikistan on the establishment of a military base for 201 Motor Rifle Division, there are reports of another military base, possibly in the south of Kyrgyzstan, being given to the CSTO. This would add to the CSTO airbase at Kant, close to the US-led coalition's persence at the Manas airbase.

However, internal security in some Central Asian states is providing new challenges to old-style and increasingly fragile regimes. On 13 May, at Andijon in Uzbekistan's Ferghana Valley – the traditional heartland of Uzbek opposition movements – there were widespread protests against President Karimov's government. The protests followed an attack on a prison and several other municipal and local government buildings by armed groups who succeeded in releasing a large number of prisoners and took a number of hostages, some of whom are believed to have been killed. In the riots which followed, government forces and rebels exchanged fire, leading to substantial casualties. The Uzbek authorities gave a figure of 173 dead. However, estimates by international sources and NGOs were as high as 700. Some experts and officials accuse government forces of initiating the use of force and killing many civilians. Uzbek authorities claim that fighters, trained by external terrorist groups, were the first to initiate violence and government troops had to use force in response. Europe and the US demanded an independent inquiry to determine the exact cause of the casualties; however, Uzbek authorities have so far been reluctant to agree on such external monitoring, with Russia and China backing their interpretation of events.

Whether or not an independent inquiry takes place, Tashkent's reaction to the protests has been widely condemned by the international community, and has deepened internal opposition to the Karimov administration, despite his readiness to use force against any opposition. Moreover, there is growing speculation about possible divisions within the government itself. The Uzbek administration's fear of opposition deepened further with the overthrow of President Askar Akaev in neighbouring **Kyrgyzstan.**

On 24 March 2005, a group of Kyrgyz opposition leaders, backed by a small group of mainly young protesters, successfully forced Akaev to leave the country. As in Georgia and Ukraine, protests were provoked by allegations of electoral fraud by the government; and, although the protests in Bishkek were largely peaceful, instability followed with looting and confusion in the process of interim political succession. A new interim government led by Kurmanbek Bakiev, with former political prisoner Felix Kulov, is trying to re-establish the rule of law in the country. The make-up of the leadership, with Bakiev coming from the south of Kyrgyzstan and Kulov from the north, reflects the divisions in the country. The south, with the potentially volatile regions of Osh and Batken bordering the Uzbek Ferghana valley, is where Bishkek most fears the emergence of some kind of volatile opposition.

The presidential elections in **Afghanistan** on 9 October 2004 resulted in victory for incumbent Hamid Karzai. Some eight million people (over 80% of registered voters) participated in the elections, which took place without serious incident. Elections for the lower house of the National Assembly (Wolesi Jirga) and the Provincial Councils were held on 18 September 2005. By 26 May, some 6,000 candidates had been registered – including 636 women. Moreover, some of the more moderate members of

the Taliban have accepted an amnesty from President Karzai and are taking part in the elections; it is not clear whether this is in order to be part of a democratic government of Afghanistan, or to prove that they still attract support. Regardless of Taliban political ambitions, the democratisation of Afghanistan attracts widespread popular support in the country at large. The process now depends on the ability of the new assembly to properly represent those who elected it, and on the government to carry out much-needed reforms, as well as to increase security.

Widespread anti-US protests, in response to reports of abuse of the Koran by US troops at Guantanamo Bay, took place in Jalalabad in May 2005 and spread quickly to other towns across the country. The incident showed that there may be growing unease

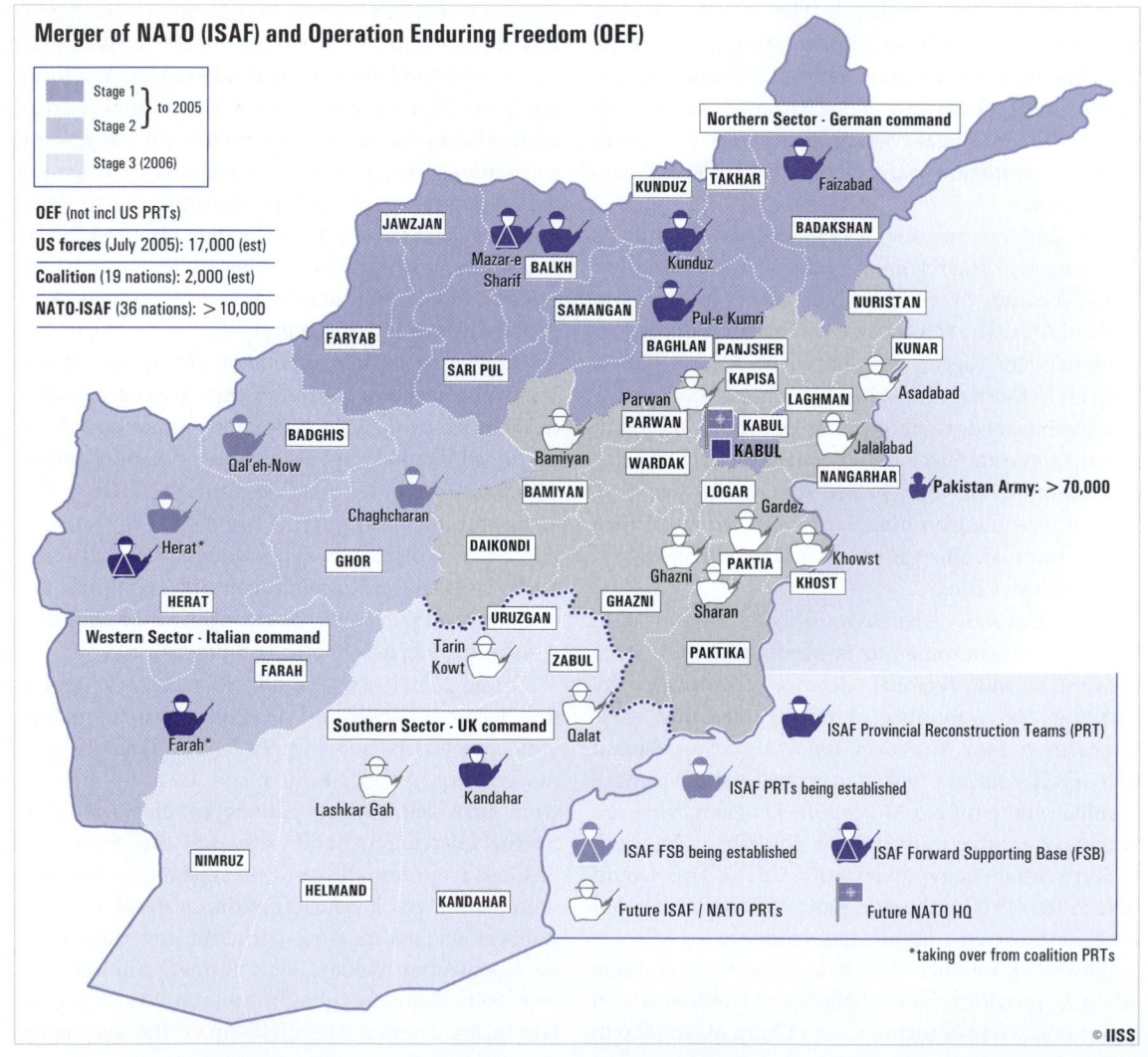

Merger of NATO (ISAF) and Operation Enduring Freedom (OEF)

Stage 1 } to 2005
Stage 2
Stage 3 (2006)

OEF (not incl US PRTs)
US forces (July 2005): 17,000 (est)
Coalition (19 nations): 2,000 (est)
NATO-ISAF (36 nations): > 10,000

Northern Sector - German command

ISAF Provincial Reconstruction Teams (PRT)
ISAF PRTs being established
ISAF FSB being established
ISAF Forward Supporting Base (FSB)
Future ISAF / NATO PRTs
Future NATO HQ

Pakistan Army: > 70,000

*taking over from coalition PRTs

© IISS

at the presence of foreign troops in the country, as well as, perhaps, the perceived inability of the government to bring about much-needed social and economic reform. The need for public-sector reform to bring public confidence and employment, and the establishment of the rule of law to bring lasting stability, are central to the future of Afghanistan. A viable justice system is also critical to this end, but currently, the difficulties of bringing together the three existing justice systems – Pushtoonwali, *sharia* law and secular state law, make this a long-term and complex process, perhaps one not fully understood by the international community.

Meanwhile, the Afghan National Army (ANA) continues to develop. By June 2005, the ANA's total strength was 24,700 troops. However, progress has been hampered by low volunteer rates and high levels of desertion, believed to be caused partly by the increasing intensity of combat missions. The increase in private security companies also hinders efforts to build an army as this provides an alternate form of service which is perhaps more lucrative and comfortable. One company employs 25,000 private security guards – equal to the total strength of the ANA and equivalent to half the number of soldiers that have gone through the disarmament, demobilisation and re-training (DDR) process under the Japanese-led Afghanistan New Beginnings Programme (ANBP).

NATO, which took command of the International Security Assistance Force (ISAF) in December 2004, is expanding its deployment of Provincial Reconstruction Teams (PRTs) so that, by late 2005, there were a total of 11 PRTs in the west and north of the country. NATO has also expanded its military presence in the western provinces of Afghanistan. On 31 May, the ISAF PRTs in Herat and Farah became fully operational. The deployment includes a Forward Support Base in Herat which serves as a logistical hub and provides emergency support to the PRTs in western Afghanistan. Another ISAF PRT was established under Lithuanian command in Chagcharan by mid-July. Its area of responsibility encompasses the Chagcharan and Ghor provinces. Expansion in the west was completed in Qal'eh-Now with the deployment of a Spanish-led PRT, while a 250-strong Canadian PRT was deployed in the south to Kandahar in July – the first NATO PRT in the US area of operations. Meanwhile, the US has some 15 PRTs deployed in the southern provinces. In 2006, NATO's role is to expand further to take over some operations from US Combined Forces Command in the south.

Under this new arrangement, the intention – still subject to the political caveats of individual member states in supplying sufficient numbers of troops – is for the UK to command the southern sector, Italy the west, Germany the north, and the US to maintain command in the south-east. Ideally, the concept envisages an amalgamation of *Operation Enduring Freedom* with ISAF (see map, opposite) and NATO carrying a greater share of the burden of military operations. However, the US is unlikely to reduce its military presence in the short term, particularly the provision of combat and logistic air support, which is crucial to the success of ground operations against the Taliban. In the longer term, Washington is seeking to establish two bases in Afghanistan under the terms of the so-called 'Strategic Partnership' signed by President Bush and President Karzai on 24 May.

The DDR programme ended in June 2005, having disarmed some 60,000 members of armed groups. A new programme, Disarmament of Illegal Armed Groups (DIAG), started on 11 June against a background of a rise in the number of irregular armed formations (estimated to number 1,800 with some 60,000–100,000 members) serving the interests of local leaders. The programme, under which unregistered weapons have been declared illegal, aims to disarm these groups. The Afghan police, supported by the ANBP, are tasked with collecting weapons. Kabul is also seeking to disenfranchise local strongmen by placing strict requirements on those wishing to run for office in the upcoming elections: candidates must disarm and formally renounce security-related posts. Should the voluntary DIAG process fail to achieve its objectives through the police, the ANA will take over the task. Coalition forces will be used as a last resort in the DIAG process.

The success of this new phase of disarmament will depend on the ability and robustness of Afghan security forces, and, in particular, the weak and corrupt police, to deal effectively with armed groups who are likely to protect their vested interests for as long as they can. The DIAG programme does not have incentives that are likely to wean long-established local leaders away from an armed way of life.

Part of this way of life is the continuing and widespread cultivation of poppy for the illicit production of opium and heroin, possibly including a low grade variant of heroin mentioned in the International Narcotics Control Board's 2004 report, in the context of India. Attempts to reduce the poppy crop have been slow to take hold, and the UK-led programme has been criticised by the US. Nevertheless, there is widespread recognition that, until sufficient incentives are found to wean growers away from their traditional source of income, meaningful progress cannot be made. For example, in Thailand, with a much smaller crop than Afghanistan, it took 20 years to bring poppy production under control. The linkage of poppy to armed groups, including the Taliban, is central to efforts to improve security, as well as to the democratisation process.

In months leading up to the elections, groups of Taliban fighters (some numbering more than 50) were able to move with relative freedom from Pakistan across the south of Afghanistan, seeking to disrupt the electoral process. The Tripartite Commission of Pakistan, Afghanistan and the US seeks to address the cross-border security issue, but terrain, and the ability of the Taliban to merge with the population, hinder this effort. There have been frequent clashes between Taliban and ANA forces, while the US lost 37 soldiers in combat in Afghanistan between April and June 2005. On 29 June, a *Chinook* helicopter was shot down by Taliban fighters using a rocket-propelled grenade, killing 17 US special forces troops on a rescue mission. This incident showed the Taliban's continuing ability to carry out tactically sophisticated and coordinated operations.

SOUTH ASIA

Internal conflicts

In an address to the nation in December, President Musharraf of **Pakistan** declared that he would stay on as army chief until 2007, as any change in internal policies could be extremely dangerous. This followed far-reaching changes in key corps commanders and senior appointments in October 2004. Two of Musharraf's trusted aides – Inter-Services Intelligence (ISI) directorate chief Lieutenant-General Ehsan ul-Haq and Karachi corps commander Lieutenant-General Ehsan Salim Hayat – were promoted to four-star rank and appointed as chairman of the Joint Chiefs of Staff Committee and army vice-chief respectively. Relatively junior officers were appointed as corps commanders, succeeding a half-dozen senior three-star army officers.

Addressing the nation in March 2005, Musharraf pointed out that the main threats Pakistan faced were terrorism, religious extremism and sectarianism, adding that the country did not face any external threat. Both Sunni and Shi'ite armed groups continued to target religious sites and to carry out

assassinations. In October 2004, a car bomb killed more than 40 people outside a Sunni mosque in Multan. In March 2005 more than 30 people were killed in a bomb blast at a Shi'ite shrine in Fatehpur, followed by a suicide bomb attack at the Bari Imam shrine in Islamabad in late May.

Since January 2005, Baluchistan has seen several small-scale attacks on security forces and rail, power and communications infrastructure, reportedly carried out by the nationalist Baluchistan Liberation Army (BLA). A clash between the security forces and Baloch nationalists in March in Dera Bugti left some 45 people dead, and led the government to instruct a parliamentary committee to make recommendations addressing the grievances of the Baluch people.

Following the London bombings of 7 July 2005, Islamabad came under international pressure to act more vigorously against extremism. In response, Musharraf announced in mid-July a new crackdown on extremist and jihadist groups, including banning groups operating under new names and registering all madrassas (estimated at over 15,000) by December 2005. This was followed by the order to expel all foreign students – conservatively estimated at 5,000 – studying in the madrassas. Towards the end of July, more than 300 people were arrested in a country-wide crackdown on Islamist extremism, giving rise to protests and demonstrations by right-wing religious parties.

Musharraf reiterated that al-Qaeda no longer had a command structure in Pakistan, although isolated pockets in the mountainous tribal areas of North Waziristan may still exist, and in June, three Pakistanis were arrested in Afghanistan for allegedly planning to assassinate former US Ambassador Zalmay Khalilzad. Nonetheless by mid-2005, Pakistan had arrested about 700 al-Qaeda activists, including a senior operative, Abu Faraj al-Libbi, who was alleged to have planned an attack on President Musharraf in December 2003.

Amidst continuing insurgent violence in the northeast, the government of **India** made progress on ceasefires on several fronts. Following the Memorandum of Understanding with the Bru National Liberation Front in Mizoram in April, a ceasefire with the National Democratic Front of Bodoland (NDFB) in Assam was signed in May. According to the terms of the agreement, all insurgency and counter-insurgency operations are to be suspended for a year from 1 June 2005. In July, India extended ceasefires with two separatist groups – the Achik National Volunteers Council of Meghalaya and the United People's

Democratic Solidarity of Assam – for another year. It also extended the ceasefire with the National Socialist Council of Nagaland-Isak-Muivah (NSCN-IM) for six months from 1 August, to consolidate peace talks and resolve the five-decade-old insurgency in Nagaland. This is the first time that the ceasefire with the NSCN-IM – signed in 1997 which is renewed every year – has been extended by only six months, signaling a higher stake in the peace talks.

Left-wing extremism is a growing source of concern for India. By February 2005, Naxalites were reportedly active in 170 districts in 15 states, an increase from 55 districts in nine states in November 2003. In September, the two major factions - the People's War Group and the Maoist Communist Centre – united under the banner of the CPI-Maoist. In April, peace talks with the Naxalites in Andhra Pradesh ended after a ten-month ceasefire. In response to this growing threat, Indian paramilitary forces will shortly be able to call for air power in support of counter-insurgency operations.

The December 2004 tsunami caused widespread destruction in the eastern and northern parts of **Sri Lanka**, claiming the lives of some 30,000 people and displacing some 850,000. Although the separatist Liberation Tigers of Tamil Eelam (LTTE) and Sri Lankan government troops worked side by side in some areas to provide immediate relief and rehabilitation, prospects for a peace dividend were soon belied with an LTTE demand that Sri Lankan troops withdraw from Tamil relief camps and accusations that the government was blocking aid to LTTE-controlled areas. In June, the government and the LTTE signed the much-delayed Memorandum of Understanding on the Post-Tsunami Operational Management Structure to ensure equitable distribution of international assistance. This led to the Sinhalese nationalist Janatha Vimukthi Peramuna (JVP) party pulling out of the coalition government. In mid-July, the Supreme Court suspended the memorandum by blocking four key provisions, to await a review in mid-September 2005. Despite reports to the contrary, the tsunami does not appear to have had a major long-term impact on the LTTE's military strength and capabilities.

Although the ceasefire formally continues to hold, violence has escalated in northeast Sri Lanka. Besides incidents between Sri Lankan troops and the LTTE, tit-for-tat assassinations by the LTTE and its breakaway faction have continued. In April, the LTTE was suspected of having attacked a Sri Lankan navy patrol boat near Trincomalee. In late 2004 the Sri Lankan government alleged that the LTTE was in violation of the ceasefire agreement by operating a light aircraft on a 1.2-km airstrip at Iranamadu, near Vavuniya. The LTTE air wing reportedly possesses a single light aircraft, possibly similar to the Czech-built Zlin Z-143, at least one Robinson helicopter, and a dozen micro-lites, causing unease in Colombo. The LTTE is the only insurgent group with an army, navy and an infant air force. However, the LTTE maintains that it acquired its air capability before the 2002 ceasefire and is, therefore, not obliged to dismantle it. In early 2005, the LTTE also refused to grant the Norwegian Peace Monitoring Mission access to the airstrip. However, the greatest setbacks to the peace process were the killings of top LTTE leader, E. Kaushalyan in February, near Batticaloa, and the assassination of the Sri Lankan Foreign Minister, Lakshman Kadirgamar, on 12 August 2005.

In a surprise move on 1 February 2005, King Gyanendra of **Nepal** dismissed Prime Minister Sher Bahadur Deuba's government and declared a state of emergency. Although the emergency was lifted three months later, the king has advocated a tough policy against the Maoists. With the Royal Nepalese Army increasingly occupied with maintaining law and order in Kathmandu, the Maoists have reportedly gained ground in rural areas, although their logistics are such as to hamper effective future advances. Following a landmine explosion that killed 38 civilians on a bus in early June, Maoist leader Prachanda announced the cessation of attacks on unarmed people. However, in August 2005, a major attack by Maoists killed more than 40 soldiers in western Nepal.

The power struggle in **Bangladesh** between the governing Bangladesh Nationalist Party (BNP) and the main opposition party, the Awami League, has resulted in considerable violence and encouraged the growth of Islamist extremism. In May, a senior member of the Awami League, Khorshed Alam, was shot dead in Dhaka, following the killing of former Finance Minister Shah A.M.S. Kibria in January 2005. In August 2004, the leader of the Awami League, Sheikh Hasina, narrowly escaped an assassination attempt at a rally in Dhaka. In February 2005, the Bangladeshi government banned two Islamic groups – Jagrata Muslim Janata and Jamaat-ul-Mujahideen – following their involvement in an attack on two Bangladeshi NGOs. The Indian government cited security reasons for postponing the 13th SAARC Summit in Bangladesh in February 2005. This is now to be held in November 2005 in Dhaka. However, on 17 August 2005 more than 300 explosions took place simultaneously in 50 cities and towns across Bangladesh, including Dhaka. In each incident, the explosive devices were set off in crowded places – mainly at government offices and courts. Two people were killed and more than 100 injured in the explosions. In leaflets left at some of the bomb sites, Jamaat-ul-Mujahideen (Bangladesh) claimed responsibility

India and **Pakistan** are engaging in their most wide-ranging and comprehensive talks in decades. Since June 2004, two rounds of a 'composite' dialogue on eight disputes and issues – including 'peace & security' and 'Jammu & Kashmir' – have been held. The third round will begin in January 2006. Technical and expert-level talks have dramatically broadened to include transportation and communication links, nuclear risk-reduction measures, energy security and narcotics-control issues. The most significant progress so far has been on confidence-building measures, focusing on enhancing people-to-people contacts and economic and commercial cooperation. The resumption in April 2005, after nearly 60 years, of a bus service between Srinagar and Muzzafarabad – across the Line of Control (LoC) – boosted the fragile peace process. The joint statement by Indian Prime Minister Manmohan Singh and Pakistan's President Pervez Musharraf in April 2005 aimed to enhance cross-LoC cooperation, including trade, increase the fortnightly frequency of the Srinagar-Muzzafarabad bus service, and start additional cross-LoC bus routes.

In **Kashmir**, the ceasefire along the LoC and the Siachen Glacier has held for over 20 months, notwithstanding allegations of minor violations in January-February and June 2005. Not since 1989 has a ceasefire on the LoC lasted so long, and, at the second round of talks on confidence-building measures (CBMs) in August 2005, both side agreed to keep the ceasefire and to hold monthly meetings between local army commanders in the four LoC sectors.

The 600-km fence on the Indian side of the LoC, completed in early 2005, was damaged in places by heavy snowfall. Cross-border infiltration substantially diminished in late 2004 and early 2005, but infiltration bids reportedly increased in mid-2005. In July 2005, India alleged that militant camps in Pakistan-administered Kashmir continued to operate and had not been dismantled. Pakistan dismissed these claims. With Kashmir becoming calmer, a reduction of 10,000–30,000 army troops took place in late 2004. Musharraf's bold suggestions on identifying, demilitarising and changing

the status of appropriate regions on both sides of the LoC was rejected by Singh on the basis that a 'second partition' of the country was not feasible. Sharp divergences emerged over the flow of water in Kashmir, with the World Bank appointing a neutral expert in May 2005 to resolve differences over the design of the Indian Baglihar hydroelectric power project on the Chenab river. In June 2005, Singh became the first Indian prime minister to visit Siachen, and spoke of converting it into a 'mountain of peace', though he emphasised that there would be no redrawing of boundaries.

MILITARY DEVELOPMENTS

In August 2004, **India** carried out the third flight-test of the *Agni* II medium-range (2,000 km) ballistic missile. It was reported that the first test of the longer-range *Agni* III missile (estimated at 3,000 km) could take place in late 2005/early 2006, although this has already been postponed twice in the past two years. India reportedly started inducting its *Agni* I and *Agni* II missiles into the recently established Strategic Forces Command. Two tests of the *Prithvi* III short-range ballistic missile took place in October and November 2004. This test was followed by the test of a surface-to-surface version of the *Prithvi* II missile in May 2005. In addition, India carried out three tests of the joint Indo-Russian supersonic cruise missile, *BrahMos*. In November 2004, it tested a *BrahMos* missile aboard a warship in the Bay of Bengal, followed by the first test of its land version in December 2004. In April 2005, the tenth test of the *BrahMos* missile took place in the Arabian Sea, with a live warhead for the first time. In mid-2005, the first Indian naval ship was fitted with the 290-km *BrahMos* missile; production had begun in late 2004. The *BrahMos* is currently being fitted alongside Russian-origin *Klub* anti-ship missiles (220–300 km) on major surface warships. The air force version of the *BrahMos* is to begin testing in 2006, with plans for deployment on the Su-30 MKI.

In March 2005, **Pakistan** carried out the second test, towards the Arabian Sea, of its *Shaheen* II medium-range (2,000–2,500 km) ballistic missile. It had tested two other medium-range ballistic missiles, the *Ghauri* I (1,300 km) and *Shaheen* I (750 km) over land in October and December 2004. Following the test of the *Ghaznavi* missile (280 km) in March 2004, Pakistan carried out a test of its short-range *Abdali* missile (190 km) in March 2005. At the third round of India–Pakistan talks on nuclear confidence-building measures in August 2005, both sides agreed to a prospective arrangement to provide advance notice of ballistic missile flight tests in a 'structured format' which would be formalised by the Foreign Ministers in October 2005, and to activate a hotline.

India's Ballistic Missile Development (BMD) programme is at an early stage. US assistance remains limited to technical briefings and presentations, though recently it agreed to provide technical inputs on the *Patriot* Advanced Capability (PAC)-3 anti-missile system.

In April, construction of **India**'s first air defence ship (ADS) was begun. To be built by Cochin Shipyard Ltd in southern India, the 37,500-tonne aircraft carrier is planned to be ready by 2012. It is planned to replace the *Viraat*, and along with the *Gorshkov* (to be deployed in 2008-09), will enable the navy to operate a two-carrier-centred naval force into the next decade. In May, India's largest naval base, INS Kadamba, was commissioned at Karwar in southern India. The first phase of the project – the most advanced in Asia – accommodates 11 ships,

Table 26 Selected Missile Flight Tests, South Asia, 2004–05

Date	Missile	Role	Range (km)	Payload (kg)	Test site	Status
India is developing						
• *Agni* III: a surface-to-surface ballistic missile with a range of 3,000km and unknown payload.						
• *Sagarika*: a submarine-launched-ballistic missile with a range of 300–350km and unknown payload.						
Pakistan is developing						
• *Ghauri* III: a surface-to-surface ballistic missile with an estimated range of 3,000km and unknown payload.						
India: ballistic missiles						
29 August 2004	*Agni*-II	Surface-to-surface	2,000 km	1,000 kg	From a mobile launcher at Wheeler Island, 10 km off the eastern coast (70 km south of Chandipur-on-sea), Orissa, eastern India	Development/Test
27 October 2004	*Prithvi* III (*Dhanush*)	Surface-to-surface	350 km	1,000 kg	At sea, off ITR, Chandipur-on-sea, from artificial underwater platform	Development/Test
7 November 2004	*Prithvi* III (*Dhanush*)	Surface-to-surface	350 km	1,000 kg	At sea, off ITR, Chandipur-on-sea, from INS *Subhadra*	Development/Test
12 May 2005	*Prithvi* II	Surface-to-surface	250 km	500 kg	Mobile launcher at ITR, Chandipur-on-sea	Development/Test
India: cruise missiles						
3 November 2004	*BrahMos*	Cruise	290 km	300 kg	At sea, Bay of Bengal, from INS *Rajput*	Serial production – to be deployed in Navy on surface warships in 2005
21 December 2004	*BrahMos*	Cruise	290 km	300 kg	Mobile launcher at ITR, Chandipur-on-Sea	First test of land version
16 April 2005	*BrahMos*	Cruise	290 km	300 kg	At sea, Arabian Sea, from INS *Rajput*	First test with a live warhead
Pakistan: ballistic missiles						
12 October 2004	*Ghauri* I (*Hatf* V/*No-dong*)	Surface-to-surface	1,300 km	1,000 kg	Mashhood Test Firing Range, Tilla Jogian, Jhelum (25 km west of Jhelum city, Punjab)	Inducted into the Army's Strategic Force Command in January 2003
29 November 2004	*Hatf* III (*Ghaznavi/M-11*)	Surface-to-surface	280 km	500 kg	Flight Test Range, Sonmiani Beach (50 km west of Karachi, Sindh)	Inducted into the Army's Strategic Force Command
8 December 2004	*Shaheen* I (*Hatf* IV)	Surface-to-surface	750 km	500 kg	Flight Test Range, Sonmiani Beach	Inducted into the Army's Strategic Force Command in March 2003
19 March 2005	*Shaheen* II (*Hatf* VI)	Surface-to-surface	2,000–2,500 km	1,000 kg	Flight Test Range, Sonmiani Beach (second missile test towards the Arabian Sea)	Development/Test
31 March 2005	*Hatf* II (*Abdali*)	Surface-to-surface	190 km	500 kg	Flight Test Range, Sonmiani Beach	Inducted into the Army's Strategic Force Command
Pakistan: cruise missiles						
11 August 2005	*Babur* (*Hatf* VII)	Cruise	ε500 km	Unknown	New Test Range, Baluchistan	Development/Test

including an aircraft carrier. It is aimed at reducing congestion at India's largest naval and commercial port at Mumbai, and providing an exclusive port for India's western fleet.

In March 2005, the Indian government approved the acquisition of 11 Dornier 228 maritime surveillance aircraft for the coast guard. The Indian navy is keen to purchase P-3C *Orion* maritime surveillance aircraft and submarine-rescue vessels from the US and Tu-22 long-range bombers from Russia.

In November, the first phase of the new deep-sea port at Gwadar in **Pakistan**'s Baluchistan province – with three functional berths and related port infrastructure – was completed. A 70,000-tonne Chinese vessel was the first to be berthed at Gwadar. Built with Chinese funding and technical support, this primarily commercial port could also serve naval ships.

In November, the first of 140 licensed-produced Sukhoi-30 MKI multi-role fighter aircraft built in **India** was handed over to the Indian air force. Following the tsunami disaster in December, the air force station at Car Nicobar was partly submerged and the runway was damaged. However, by mid-April, for the first time, Su-30Ks and *Jaguar* strike aircraft were able to deploy to the base for training.

Meanwhile, India continued its attempts to purchase 12 *Mirage* fighter aircraft from Qatar to replace over 300 ageing MiG aircraft which are to be phased out in the next three years. With an eye on the $5 billion Indian order for 126 multi-role combat aircraft, the US announced in March that it would allow India to purchase F-16/F-18 aircraft, along with a co-production agreement.

Moreover, in a significant development, the Bush administration, in March 2005, authorised the sale of F-16 fighter aircraft to **Pakistan**. Such sales had been barred by the US Congress for 15 years in view of Pakistan's then-clandestine nuclear weapons programme. It is reported that the US will provide 24 new Block-52 F-16 C/D aircraft – fourth-generation F-16s – and provide a mid-life update to its existing fleet of Block-15 F-16s to enhance their capability to the level of third-generation planes. Pakistan is reportedly keen to increase its existing fleet of F-16s to 111 by 2015. The Pakistan Air Force is shortly to receive two F-16s. In November 2004, Washington also proposed a $1.2bn arms package to Pakistan, including eight P-3C *Orion* maritime surveillance aircraft, anti-tank missiles and *Phalanx* rapid-fire guns.

In November, **India** announced plans to increase its special forces to 10–15 battalions and to modernise their equipment. The army also commissioned an additional command – Southwestern Command.

DEFENCE COOPERATION

In a significant development in June 2005, **India** and the **US** signed a 10-year defence cooperation framework agreement.While increasing military-to-military cooperation, including training, joint exercises and disaster response, it encourages joint weapons collaboration, co-production and R&D cooperation. For the first time, Delhi agreed to multinational military operations with the US without a UN mandate. This significant policy shift – a marked change from India's rationale in refusing to send troops to Iraq in mid-2004 – appears to be the prelude to Indian participation in US-led counter-proliferation and counter-terrorism initiatives. The India–US nuclear deal three weeks later – whereby the two countries agreed to develop 'full civil nuclear energy cooperation' – also created better conditions for improving strategic ties. However, Pakistan has expressed concern over the transfer of missile defence technology to India.

In December 2004, **India** and **Russia** agreed to protocols relating to intellectual property rights on jointly developed weapon systems (including a fifth-generation combat aircraft and a heavy multi-role transport aircraft), as well as the provision of spares and upgrades for Russian arms and equipment and technology transfers for the licensed production of the T-90 main battle tank in India. Russian investment in the joint venture *BrahMos* project was increased to 60%, with both countries agreeing to market the missile together in third countries.

In April 2005, **India** and **China** agreed to a three-stage process to resolve their border dispute, and an 11-point agreement on 'political guiding principles' was signed. The agreement details military confidence-building measures including the avoidance of large-scale military exercises in close proximity to the Line of Actual Control, and mechanisms for dealing with air intrusions. Moreover, following the visit of India's army chief to Beijing in December 2004, the PLA Chief of General Staff, General Liang Guanglie, visited India in May 2005, the first such high-level military visit in seven years.

Despite being the third worst-hit country in the tsunami disaster, Indian naval ships were the first to reach **Sri Lanka** and **the Maldives** with medical and other relief supplies. India also provided support to **Indonesia**, and overall India's international relief mission involved over 20,000 military personnel and 32 warships (including three coast guard vessels).

India actively continued its programme of naval and air exercises. In June 2005, the Indian Air Force carried out a fortnight-long joint exercise with the French Air Force (*Garuda* II) at the Istres base in France. In November 2005, the Indian Navy will carry out its first exercises with nuclear-powered aircraft carriers – in the US *Malabar*-series of exercises in the Arabian Sea and the *Varuna* IV exercises with the French in the Gulf of Aden. For the second year running, the Indian Navy will conduct exercises with a Russian naval flotilla in the Bay of Bengal (*Indra* exercises). The IAF is scheduled to carry out an exercise with the US Air Force in November. The Indian and Chinese armies plan to hold joint counter-terrorism and peacekeeping training programmes for the first time, along with a second round of bilateral naval exercises.

Following a freeze on Indian military aid to **Nepal** in February – with the royal coup and emergency in the country – India resumed non-military aid to Kathmandu three months later.

Pakistan and **China** launched two major licensed-production defence projects. In April, the JF-17 *Thunder* multi-role fighter aircraft, jointly developed with China, was launched. Production is expected to begin at the Pakistan Aeronautical Complex at Kamra at the end of 2006, with serial production in 2008. A few aircraft would be inducted into the Pakistan Air Force in 2007. This was followed in July by the joint project to build four F22P frigates in Pakistan. Earlier, in April, an agreement on technology transfer to Pakistan to build these ships had been signed. The first vessel is planned to be available in 2009, with the last in 2013. China will also provide six ship-based medium-sized Z-9C helicopters to Pakistan's navy.

In May, **Pakistan** and the **UK** signed a memorandum of understanding to increase defence collaboration and open up new avenues of cooperation to facilitate the procurement of arms and transfer of technology. Both sides agreed to hold joint exercises, exchange observers and jointly fight the 'war on terror'. In June, the Pakistan–US joint naval exercise, *Inspired Union*, was held in the north Arabian Sea. Pakistani naval ships have been participating in the Coalition Maritime Campaign Plan (CMCP) in the Persian Gulf.

Table 27 Selected Pakistani Exercises, August 2004–July 2005

Date	Exercise	Countries and Name	Service	Location
21–28 June 2005	Bilateral	Pakistan-US, *Inspired Union*	Navy	Arabian Sea.
16–17 June 2005	Bilateral	Pakistan-France	Navy	Red Sea/Gulf of Aden and the Mediterranean Sea
4–5 May 2005	Bilateral	Pakistan-France	Navy	Arabian Sea.
April 2005	Bilateral	Pakistan-US, *Inspired Venture*	Army	Cherat, North West Frontier Province, Pakistan
27 September–8 October 2004	Multilateral	Pakistan,Germany, Italy, the Netherlands, Turkey and US, *Anatolian Eagle*	Air force	Konya, Turkey
3–6 August 2004	Bilateral	Pakistan-China, *Friendship 2004*	Army (anti-terrorist)	Xinjiang, China

Table 28 Selected Indian Exercises, August 2004–July 2005

Date	Exercise	Countries and Name	Service	Location
15 June–1 July 2005	*Garuda* II	India-France	Air force	Istres, France
10–22 March 2005	*Emerald Mercury*	India-UK	Army (peace-enforcement)	Hyderabad, India
February–March 2005	*India-Singapore*	India-Singapore	Army	Babina (armoured) and Deolali (artillery), India
27 February–7 March 2005	*Varuna*	India-France	Navy	The Arabian Sea
24 February–5 March 2005	*Simbex* VII	India-Singapore	Navy	South China Sea
20–22 February 2005	*Thammar-Al-Thayib*	India-Oman	Navy	The Gulf of Oman
14–18 December 2004	*Eksath*	India-Sri Lanka	Navy/Coast Guard	Indian Ocean
1–6 November 2005	*India-Japan*	India-Japan	Coast Guard	Arabian Sea
11–26 October 2004	*Sindex*	India, Singapore, South Africa and US	Air force	Gwalior, India
1–10 October 2004	*Malabar VI*	India-US	Navy	Arabian Sea
27 September–3 October 2004	*Golden Eagle*	India, South Africa, UK, US, Germany	Air force	Hoedspruit, South Africa
1–30 September 2004	*INDINDOCORPAT*	India-Indonesia	Navy (4th coordinated patrol)	Indian Ocean

Afghanistan Afg

New Afghan Afghani Afs		2003	2004	2005
GDP	US$	4.1bn	4.6bn	
per capita	US$	151	161	
Growth	%	15.7	7.5	
Inflation	%	10.3	13.0	
FMA (US)	US$	191m	413m	396m
US$1=Afs				43

Population   29,928,987

Ethnic groups: Pashtun 38%; Tajik 25%; Hazara 19%; Uzbek 12%; Aimaq 4%; Baluchi 0.5%

Age	0–14	15–19	20–24	25–29	30–64	65 plus
Male	23%	5%	5%	4%	13%	1%
Female	22%	5%	4%	4%	13%	1%

Capabilities

ACTIVE 27,000 (Army 27,000)

The Afghan Transitional Administration aims to establish control over the country by forming a national army and a national police force encompassing all ethnic and tribal groups. The new Afghan Army (ANA), HQ in Kabul, currently comprises some 27,000 troops. Planned org and national strength of the ANA and national police is outlined below. *Operation Enduring Freedom* comprises 17,000 US and 2,000 coalition forces. The NATO ISAF strength is >10,000. ISAF will take on reconstruction and some combat measures from US Combined Forces Command (CFC).

ORGANISATIONS BY SERVICE

Proposed National Army/Security Services
ε27,000

FORCES BY ROLE
4 regional comd
Army 1 (central) corps (3 army bde (*total:* 21+ army bn))

EQUIPMENT BY TYPE
TK • MBT: some T-62; some T-54/T-55
RECCE • BRDM: some BRDM-1/BRDM-2
AIFV • BMP: some BMP-1/BMP-2
APC • APC (W) • BTR: some BTR-152/BTR-40/BTR-60/BTR-70/BTR-80
ARTY • TOWED • 76mm: some M-1938; some ZIS-3 *M-1942*
  100mm: some M-1944
  122mm: some D-30/M-30 *M-1938*
  130mm: some M-46
  152mm: some D-1; some D-20; some M-1937
  MRL • 122mm: some BM-21
    140mm: some BM-14
    220mm: some 9P140 *Uragan*
  MOR • 82mm: some M-37
    107mm some
    120mm: some M-43

AT • RCL • 73mm: some SPG-9
  82mm: some B-10
  GUNS • 85mm: some D-48
AD • SAM: some SA-13 *Gopher* SP/SA-7 *Grail* MANPAD
  GUNS • 100mm • TOWED: some KS-19
    14.5mm some
    23mm • SP: some ZSU-23-4
      TOWED: some ZU-23
    37mm • TOWED: some M-1939
    57mm • TOWED: some S-60
    85mm • TOWED: some M-1939 *KS-12*
MSL • TACTICAL • SSM: some FROG-7; some *Scud*

Air Force

FORCES BY ROLE
FGA some sqn with up to 5 FGA
Tpt some sqn with An-24 *Coke*
Trg some sqn with 2 L-39 *Albatros*
Hel some sqn with 5 Mi-24 *Hind* *; 8 Mi-8 *Hip*/Mi-8MT *Hip H*

EQUIPMENT BY TYPE
AIRCRAFT up to 5 combat capable
  FGA: up to 5
  TPT: some An-24 *Coke*
  TRG 2: 2 L-39 *Albatros*
HELICOPTERS
  ATK 5: 5 Mi-24 *Hind**
  SPT • MI-8 8: 8 Mi-8 *Hip* spt hel/Mi-8MT *Hip H*

NON-STATE ARMED GROUPS

see Part II

FOREIGN FORCES

Australia 1 obs
Austria 2 obs
Bangladesh 1 obs
Canada 1,576
Croatia 22
Czech Republic 56
Denmark 1 obs; 185 Army: 5 obs team (*Op Enduring Freedom*)
Estonia 1 (METEO) spt team; 1 medical team; 1 (EDD) unit (Explosive Detective Dogs); 1 (ISAF HQ); 1 (EOD) team; 1 (Cross Service) team
Finland 83
France 565
Germany 1,909; 1 obs
Greece 127
Hungary 130
Ireland 11
Italy 256 (*Enduring Freedom*); 990
Korea, Republic of: 1 obs
Latvia 10
Lithuania 6
Luxembourg 9
Macedonia, Former Yugoslav Republic 48

Mongolia Army: 21 Army (instructors)

Netherlands 153

New Zealand ε50 SF; 131 (for Provincial Reconstruction Team and various ISAF posts); 1 obs

Norway 1+ Army coy; 147

Poland 1 obs; 22 Army: 87 (*Op Enduring Freedom*)

Portugal 8

Republic of Korea 1 obs

Romania 2 obs; 32 Army: 1 inf bn; 1 NBC coy; 418 (*Op Enduring Freedom*)

Slovakia 17 Army: 40 (*Op Enduring Freedom*)

Slovenia 18

Spain Air Force: 1 P-3 *Orion* MP ac; 5 C-130 *Hercules* tpt ac; 8 CN-235 tpt ac 125 Army: 400 (*Op Enduring Freedom*)

Sweden 19; 1 obs

Switzerland 4 officer (KMNB and PRT Kunduz)

Turkey 161

United Kingdom Air Force: 3 spt hel; 3 CH-47 *Chinook* spt hel; 2 utl hel; 270 1 obs; 315

United States 67 USCENTCOM: 18,000 (*Op Enduring Freedom*)

Uruguay 1 obs

Bangladesh Bng

Bangladeshi Taka Tk		2003	2004	2005
GDP	Tk	3.0tr	3.3tr	
	US$	51.7bn	56.3bn	
per capita	US$	373	398	
Growth	%	6.5	7.0	
Inflation	%	5.4	6.1	
Debt	US$	18.7bn		
Def exp	Tk	37.4bn	46.1bn	
Def exp	US$	644m	777m	
Def bdgt	Tk	35.0bn	44.1bn	50.0bn
	US$	603m	744m	785m
FMA (US)	US$			1.14m
US$1=Tk		58.1	59.3	63.7

Population 144,319,628

Ethnic groups: Hindu 12%

Age	0–14	15–19	20–24	25–29	30–64	65 plus
Male	17%	6%	6%	4%	16%	2%
Female	16%	6%	6%	4%	15%	2%

Capabilities

ACTIVE 125,500 (Army 110,000 Navy 9,000 Air 6,500) **Paramilitary 126,200**

ORGANISATIONS BY SERVICE

Army 110,000

Some equipment†

FORCES BY ROLE

Armd	1 bde (2 armd regt); 2 regt
Inf	7 div HQ; 17 bde (*total:* 26+ Inf bn)
Cdo	1 bn
Arty	1 div (6 arty regt)
Engr	1 bde
Avn	2 sqn
AD	1 bde

EQUIPMENT BY TYPE
TK 220+
  MBT 180: 80 Type-59/Type-69; 100 T-54/T-55
  LT TK 40+: 40+ Type-62
APC 180+
  APC (T) 50+: some MT-LB; ε50 Type-63
  APC (W) • **BTR** 130: 60 BTR-70; 70 BTR-80
ARTY 190+
  TOWED 140+
    105mm 80: 50 M-101; 30 Model 56 pack howitzer
    122mm 20: 20 Type-54 (M-30) *M-1938*
    130mm 40+: 40+ Type-59 (M-46)
  MOR 50+: some 81mm
    82mm: some Type-53 (M-1937)
    120mm 50: 50 Type-53 (M-1943)
AT
  RCL • **106mm** • **M-40** 30: 30 M-40A1
  GUNS 68
    57mm 18: 18 6-pdr
    76mm 50: 50 Type-54 (ZIS-3)
AIRCRAFT • **TPT** 6: 4 Cessna 152
  CESSNA 337 2: 2 Cessna 337F *Skymaster*
AD
  SAM • **MANPAD** • **HN-5**: some HN-5A
  GUNS • **37mm** • **TOWED** 16: 16 Type-55 (M-1939)
    57mm • **TOWED**: some Type-59 (S-60)

Navy† ε9,000

FORCES BY ROLE
Navy 1 HQ located at Chittagong

EQUIPMENT BY TYPE
PRINCIPAL SURFACE COMBATANTS • **FRIGATES** 5
FFG 2:
  1 *Bangabandhu*† in refit (ROK mod *Ulsan*) with 2 B515 *ILAS-3* triple 324mm each with A244 LWT, 4 single each with 1 Otomat tactical SSM, 1 76mm gun, 1 hel landing platform (And hangar for operation of *Lynx* sized helicopter)
  1 *Osman*† (PRC *Jianghu* I) with 2 twin (4 eff.) each with 1 HY-2 (CSS-N-2) *Silkworm* tactical SSM, 2 RBU 1200 (10 eff.), 4 100mm gun
FF 3:
  2 *Abu Bakr*† (UK *Leopard*) each with 2 115mm twin gun (4 eff.)
  1 *Umar Farooq*† training (UK *Salisbury*) with 3 *Squid*, 2 115mm twin gun (4 eff.)
PATROL AND COASTAL COMBATANTS 33
PCC 4: 2 *Karnaphuli*†; 2 *Meghna*† (fishery protection)
PCI 4: 2 *Akshay*† less than 100 tonnes; 1 *Bakarat* less than 100 tonnes; 1 *Bishkali* less than 100 tonnes

PCR 5: 5 *Pabna†* less than 100 tonnes
PFC 4: 4 *Shahead Daulat†*
PFM 10:
5 *Durbar†* less than 100 tonnes (PRC *Hegu*) each with 2 single with 2 SY-1 tactical SSM
5 *Durdarsha†* (PRC *Huangfeng*) each with 4 single each with 1 HY-2 (CSS-N-2) *Silkworm* tactical SSM
PHT 4:
4 *Huchuan†* less than 100 tonnes (PRC) each with 2 single 533mm TT each with 2 YU 1 Type 53 HWT
PCO 2:
1 *Durjoy* (PRC *Hainan*) with 4 RBU 1200 (20 eff.)
1 *Madhumati†* (*Sea Dragon*) with 1 76mm gun
MINE WARFARE • MINE COUNTERMEASURES 4
MSI 3: 3 *Shapla†* (UK *River*)
MSO 1: 1 *Sagar†*
AMPHIBIOUS • CRAFT 14: 7 LCU†; 3 LCVP†; 4 LCM†
LOGISTICS AND SUPPORT 8
AGHS (SVY) 2: 2 *Yuch'in†*
AGOR 1: 1 *Shaibal†* (UK *River*, MCM capable)
AOT 1† (coastal)AR 1†AT 1†ATF 1†
TRG 1: 1 *Shaheed Ruhul Amin†*

FACILITIES
Base 1 located at Chittagong, 1 located at Dhaka, 1 located at Kaptai, 1 located at Khulna, 1 located at Mongla

Air Force† 6,500
Flying hours   100 to 120 hrs/year

FORCES BY ROLE
Ftr / FGA   4 sqn with 6 MiG-29 *Fulcrum*; 23 F-7M *Airguard/J-7II Fishbed*; 18 A-5C (Q-5III) *Fantan*; 16 F-6 (MiG-19S) *Farmer B†*; 2 MiG-29UB *Fulcrum* (*total*: 1 OCU sqn with 8 L-39ZA *Albatros*; 10 FT-6 (MiG-19UTI) *Farmer*)

Tpt   some sqn with 3 An-32 *Cline*

Hel   3 sqn with 1 Mi-8 *Hip*; 15 MI-17 (Mi-8MT) *Hip H*; 3 Mi-171; 11 Bell 212

Trg   Some sqn with 20 PT-6 (CJ-6); 8 CM-170 *Magister*; 31 T-37B *Tweet*; 2 Bell 206L *LongRanger*

EQUIPMENT BY TYPE†
AIRCRAFT 83 combat capable
FTR 29: 6 MiG-29 *Fulcrum†*; 23 F-7M *Airguard/J-7II Fishbed*
FGA 34: 18 A-5C (Q-5III) *Fantan*
MiG-19 16: 16 F-6 (MiG-19S) *Farmer B*
TPT 3: 3 An-32 *Cline†*
TRG 79: 8 CM-170 *Magister†*; 10 FT-6 (MiG-19UTI) *Farmer**
L-39 8: 8 L-39ZA *Albatros**
MiG-29U 2: 2 MiG-29UB *Fulcrum**
PT-6 (CJ-6) 20
T-37 31: 31 T-37B *Tweet*
HELICOPTERS
SPT 16:
MI-8 16: 1†; 15 MI-17 (Mi-8MT) *Hip H*
UTL 13
BELL 206 2: 2 Bell 206L *LongRanger*
Bell 212 11†
MSL • TACTICAL • AAM: some AA-2 *Atoll*

Paramilitary 63,200

Ansars 20,000+ (a further 180,000 unembodied)
Security Guards

Armed Police 5,000
rapid action force (forming)

Bangladesh Rifles 38,000
border guard
Paramilitary 41 bn

Coast Guard
PATROL AND COASTAL COMBATANTS • PCI 1: 1 *Bishkali* less than 100 tonnes (force in infancy and expected to expand)

NON-STATE ARMED GROUPS
see Part II

DEPLOYMENT

AFGHANISTAN
UN • UNAMA 1 obs

BURUNDI
UN • ONUB 2 obs

CÔTE D'IVOIRE
UN • UNOCI 10 obs; 3,025

DEMOCRATIC REPUBLIC OF CONGO
UN • MONUC 15 obs; 1,301

ETHIOPIA/ERITREA
UN • UNMEE 7 obs; 174

GEORGIA
UN • UNOMIG 7 obs

LIBERIA
UN • UNMIL 17 obs; 3,199

SERBIA AND MONTENEGRO
UN • UNMIK 1; 60 civ police

SIERRA LEONE
UN • UNAMSIL 8 obs; 240

SUDAN
UN • UNMIS 691; 13 obs

WESTERN SAHARA
UN • MINURSO 8 obs

Central and South Asia

India Ind

Indian Rupee Rs		2003	2004	2005
GDP	Rs	27.7tr	29.6tr	
	US$	596bn	648bn	
per capita	US$	567	609	
Growth	%	7.5	7.3	
Inflation	%	3.8	3.8	
Debt	US$	113bn		
Def exp	Rs	721bn	897bn	
	US$	15.5bn	19.6bn	
Def bdgt	Rs	770bn	890bn	958bn
	US$	16.5bn	19.4bn	22.0bn
US$1=Rs		46.5	45.7	43.4

Population   1,080,264,388

Ethnic groups: Hindu 80%; Muslim 14%; Christian 2%; Sikh 2%

Age	0–14	15–19	20–24	25–29	30–64	65 plus
Male	16%	5%	5%	5%	18%	2%
Female	15%	5%	4%	4%	18%	2%

Capabilities

ACTIVE 1,325,000 (Army 1,100,000 Navy 55,000 Air 170,000) **Paramilitary 1,721,586**

RESERVE 1,155,000 (Army 960,000 Navy 55,000 Air 140,000) **Paramilitary 1,293,229**

Army first line reserves (300,000) within 5 years of full time service, further 500,000 have commitment to the age of 50.

ORGANISATIONS BY SERVICE

Strategic Forces Command

In charge of all nuclear assets

FORCES BY ROLE

Msl 3 regt each with 15 SS-150 *Prithvi*/SS-250 *Prithvi*/SS-350 *Prithvi*; 1 gp with 8-12 *Agni*-3; 1 gp with 8-12 *Agni*-2

EQUIPMENT BY TYPE

MSL • STRATEGIC 69
  IRBM • AGNI 24: 8-12 *Agni*-2; 8-12 *Agni*-3
  SRBM • PRITHVI 45: 45 SS-150 *Prithvi*/SS-250 *Prithvi*/SS-350 *Prithvi*

Army 1,100,000

FORCES BY ROLE

6 Regional Comd HQ (Northern, Western, Central, Southern, Eastern, South Western), 1 Training Comd (ARTRAC), 11 corps HQ (3 strike corps, 8 'holding' corps – incl 1 Desert Corps)

Armd	3 div (*each:* 1 SP arty bde (1 medium regt, 2 SP arty regt), 2–3 armd bde); 8 indep bde; 13 regt each with 55 T-55; 35 regt each with 55 T-72M1; 6 regt each with 55 T-90S; 14 regt each with 72 *Vijayanta*
Mech inf	25 bn

Inf	4 RAPID div (*each:* 1 mech inf bde); 18 div (*each:* 1 arty bde, 2–5 Inf bde); 8 indep bde; 319 bn
Mtn inf	10 div (*each:* 1+ arty regt, 3–4 mtn inf bde); 2 indep bde
Cdo / AB	1 indep bde
Cdo	3 bn
AB	8 bn
Arty	2 div (*each:* 3 arty bde); 44 (reported) regt
Med arty	84 regt (bn)
SP med Arty	11 regt (bn)
Fd arty	185 regt
SP fd arty	3 regt (bn)
Mtn arty	39 regt (bn)
MRL	9 regt (bn)
SSM	2 regt (bn); 2 (*Prithvi*) regt
ADA	45 regt
Engr	3 bde
Hel	17 sqn
Atk hel	5 sqn
AD	4 bde; 5 'flak' regt with 320 ZU-23-2 (some SP); 30 'flak' regt with 1,920 L40/70 (*each:* 4 AD bty); 12+ regt
SAM	12 regt; 2 gp (*each:* 2–5 SAM bty)

Reserve Organisations

Reserves 300,000 reservists (1st line res within 5 years full time service); 500,000 reservists (commitment until age of 50) **(total 800,000)**

Territorial Army 160,000 reservists (only 40,000 regular establishment)

Army	3–4 Ecological bn; 29 Departmental unit (raised from government ministries)
Inf	25 bn
AD	20 'flak' regt with 1,280 L40/60

EQUIPMENT BY TYPE

TK 4,168
  MBT 3,978 (ε1,133 in reserve)
    T-90 330: 330 T-90S (to be 1,000+ to replace *Vijayanta* and T-55)
    Arjun ε14
    T-72 • **T-72M** 1925: 1,925 T-72M1 (modification program in progress, incl. thermal sights)
    1,008 **Vijayanta** (modified with night-fighting equipment and new fire control systems); 715 **T-55** (modifications similar to *Vijayanta*) (ε67 in reserve)
  LT TK 190: 90 AMX-13 in store; ε100 PT-76 (being phased out)
RECCE • BRDM 110:
    110 BRDM-2 each with AT-4 *Spigot*/AT-5 *Spandrel*
    some *Ferret* (used for internal security duties along with some locally built amoured cars)
AIFV • BMP 1700+: 700 BMP-1; 1,000+ BMP-2
APC 817+: 500+ in reserve in store (Czech and Soviet types)
  APC (W) 317+: ε160 *Casspir*
    OT 157+: 157+ OT-62/OT-64 (mainly used for 2nd line duties, such as towing mortars)

ARTY up to 12,675+
  TOWED up to 5,625+
    75mm 1,115: 900 75/24 mtn; 215 M-48 Tito Gun
    105mm up to 1,350+
      IFG 600+: 600+ Mk1/Mk2/Mk3 (being replaced)
      LFG up to 700 **M-56** 50
    122mm 550: 550 D-30
    130mm 2,200: 1,200 M-46; 500 (in process of upgrading to 155mm); 500 in reserve in store
    155mm • FH-77 410: 410 FH-77B
  SP 150+
    105mm 80: 80 *Abbot* in store
    130mm 70: ε70 M-46 *Catapult* in store
    152mm: some 2S19 *Farm*
  MRL 180
    122mm 150: ε150 BM-21/LRAR
    214mm 30: 30 *Pinaka*
  MOR 6720+
    81mm 5000+: 5,000+ E1
    120mm 1500+: some (SP)**AM-50/E1** ε1,500 (some E1 are SP)
    160mm 220: 20 M-58 Tampella; 200 in store
AT
  MSL: some AT-3 *Sagger* (being phased out); some AT-4 *Spigot* (some SP); some AT-5 *Spandrel* (some SP); some *Milan*
  RCL • 106mm • M-40 3,000+: 3,000+ M-40A1 (10 per inf bn)
    84mm: some *Carl Gustav* (one per inf section)
HELICOPTERS
  ASLT 12: 12 *Lancer*
  UTL 150
    SA-315 50: 50 HAL *Cheetah* (SA-315B) *Lama*
    SA-316 100: 100 HAL *Chetak* (SA-316B) *Alouette III*
UAV: some *Nishant*
  RECCE • TAC: some *Searcher*
AD
  SAM 3,500+
    SP 880+: 250 SA-13 *Gopher*; 180 SA-6 *Gainful*
      SA-8 50+: 50+ SA-8B
      SA-9 *Gaskin* 400
    MANPAD 2,620+: 2,000+ SA-16 *Gimlet*; 620 SA-7 *Grail* (being phased out)
  GUNS 2,339+
    20mm • TOWED: some Oerlikon (reported)
    23mm 395
      SP 75: 75 ZSU-23-4
      TOWED 320: 320 ZU-23-2 (some SP)
    30mm • SP 24: 24 2S6 (60+ more on order)
    40mm • TOWED 1,920: 1,920 L40/70
  RADAR • LAND 12+: 12 AN/TPQ-37 *Firefinder*; some BSR Mk.2; some *Cymbeline*; some EL/M-2140; some M-113 A1GE *Green Archer* (mor); some MUFAR; some *Stentor*
  AMPHIBIOUS • CRAFT 2: 2 LCVP

Navy 55,000 (incl 7,000 Naval Avn and 1,200 Marines)

FORCES BY ROLE
Navy 1 Fleet located at Mumbai (Bombay); 1 Fleet located at Vishakhapatnam

EQUIPMENT BY TYPE
SUBMARINES • TACTICAL • SSK 19:
  2 *Kursura*† (FSU *Foxtrot*) each with 10 single 533mm TT (6 forward,4 aft)

3 *Kursura*† in reserve (FSU *Foxtrot*) each with 10 single 533mm TT (6 forward 4 aft)
4 *Shishumar* (Ge T-209/1500) each with 1 single 533mm TT (+ 2 Type 1500 ordered locally)
9 *Sindhughosh* (FSU *Kilo*) each with 6 single 533mm TT (all *Kilos* to be fitted with SS-N-27)
1 *Sindhughosh* (FSU Type 636 *Kilo*) with 6 single 533mm TT each with SS-NX-27 *Club-S* tactical SSM
PRINCIPAL SURFACE COMBATANTS 54
  AIRCRAFT CARRIERS • CV 1:
    1 *Viraat* (UK *Hermes*) (capacity 30 *Sea Harrier* FRS MK51 (*Sea Harrier* FRS MKI) FGA ac each with *Sea Eagle* tactical ASM; 7 Ka-27 *Helix* ASW hel/*Sea King* MK42B ASW hel)
  DESTROYERS • DDG 8:
    3 *Delhi* (capacity either 2 *Sea King* MK42A ASW hel or 2 ALH utl hel) each with 5 x1 533mm ASTT, 4 quad (16 eff.) each with 4 SS-N-25 *Switchblade* tactical SSM, 2 single with 24 SA-N-7 SAM, 1 100mm gun
    5 *Rajput* (FSU *Kashin*) each with 1 Ka-25 *Hormone*/KA-28, 5 x1 533mm ASTT, 2 Twin (4 eff.) each with 1 SS-N-2C *Styx* tactical SSM, 2 (4 eff.) each with 16 SA-N-1 *Goa* SAM, 2 RBU 6000 *Smerch 2* (24 eff.), 2 76mm gun
  FRIGATES 17
    FFG 9:
      3 *Brahmaputra* (capacity either 2 HAL *Chetak* (SA-316B) *Alouette III* SA-316 Utl/*Sea King* MK42 ASW hel or 2 *Sea King* MK42 ASW hel) (2 awaiting full weapons fit) each with 20 SA-N-4 *Gecko* SAM, 2 triple 324mm ASTT (6 eff.), 4 quad (16 eff.) each with 4 SS-N-25 *Switchblade* tactical SSM, 1 76mm gun
      3 *Godavari* (capacity either 2 *Sea King* MK42 ASW hel or 2 HAL *Chetak* (SA-316B) *Alouette III* SA-316 Utl/*Sea King* MK42 ASW hel) each with 2 triple 324mm ASTT (6 eff.), 4 single each with 1 SS-N-2D *Styx* tactical SSM, 1 twin (2 eff.) with 20 SA-N-4 *Gecko* SAM
      3 *Talwar* (capacity either 1 KA-31 *Helix B* AEW hel/ KA-28 ASW hel or 1 ALH utl hel) (undergoing sea trials) each with SS-N-27 *Club* tactical SSM
    FF 8:
      1 *Arnala* (FSU *Petya*) with 3 x1 533mm ASTT, 4 RBU 2500 *Smerch 1* (64 eff.), 4 76mm gun
      1 *Krishna* in reserve (UK *Leander*; trg role)
      4 *Nilgiri* (UK *Leander*) each with 1 *Limbo* ASW Mor (triple), 1 HAL *Chetak* (SA-316B) *Alouette III* SA-316 Utl, 2 triple 533mm ASTT (6 eff.), 2 114mm gun
      2 *Nilgiri* in reserve (UK *Leander*) each with 1 *Limbo* ASW mor (triple), 1 HAL *Chetak* (SA-316B) *Alouette III* SA-316 utl, 2 triple 533mm ASTT (6 eff.), 2 114mm gun
  CORVETTES 28
    FSG 24:
      4 *Khukri* each with 1 76mm gun, 2 twin (4 eff.) each with 2 SS-N-2C *Styx* tactical SSM, 1 hel landing platform (For ALH/*Chetak*)
      4 *Kora* each with 1 quad (4 eff.) with SA-N-5 *Grail* SAM, 4 (16 eff.) each with 4 SS-N-25 *Switchblade* tactical SSM, 1 76mm gun, 1 hel landing platform (For ALH/*Chetak*)
      6 *Veer* (FSU *Tarantul*) each with 2 quad (8 eff.) (quad manual aiming) each with SA-N-5 *Grail* SAM, 4 single each with 1 SS-N-2D *Styx* tactical SSM, 1 76mm gun

6 *Vibhuti* (mod *Veer*) each with 1 quad (4 eff.) (quad manual aiming) with SA-N-5 *Grail* SAM, 4 (16 eff.) with 16 SS-N-25 *Switchblade* tactical SSM, 1 76mm gun

2 *Vibhuti* (advanced version) each with 4 quad (16 eff.) each with SA-N-5 *Grail* SAM, 16 SS-N-25 *Switchblade* tactical SSM, 1 (4 eff.) (quad manual aiming) with SA-N-5 *Grail* SAM, 16 SS-N-25 *Switchblade* tactical SSM, 1 76mm gun with SA-N-5 *Grail* SAM, 16 SS-N-25 *Switchblade* tactical SSM

1 *Vijay Durg* (FSU *Nanuchka* II) with 1 twin (2 eff.) (twin) with 20 SA-N-4 *Gecko* SAM, 2 (4 eff.) each with 1 SS-N-2C *Styx* tactical SSM

1 non-operational

FS 4:

4 *Abhay* (FSU *Pauk* II) each with 2 x1 533mm ASTT (twin), 1 quad (4 eff.) (quad manual aiming) with SA-N-5 *Grail* SAM, 2 RBU 1200 (10 eff.), 1 76mm gun

PATROL AND COASTAL COMBATANTS 41

MISC BOATS/CRAFT 17: 17 boats

PCI 6: 6 SDB Mk 3

PFI 4: 4 *Super Dvora* less than 100 tonnes (+1 under construction)

PFM 8: 8 *Osa* II

PCO 6: 6 *Sukanya*

MINE WARFARE • MINE COUNTERMEASURES 18

MSI 6: 6 *Mahe* less than 100 tonnes (FSU *Yevgenya*)

MSO 12:

12 *Pondicherry* (FSU *Natya*)

AMPHIBIOUS

LS 7

LSM 5: 5 *Ghorpad* (FSU *Polnocny* C)

LST 2: 2 *Magar*

CRAFT • LCU 10: 10 *Vasco da Gama*

LOGISTICS AND SUPPORT 32

AGHS (SVY) 12: 4 *Makar*; 8 *Sandhayak*

AGOR 1: 1 *Sagardhwani*

AH (med) 1

AO 3: 1 *Aditya* (mod *Deepak*); 1 *Deepak*; 1 *Jyoti*

AOT 6 (small) **AWT** 2 **Diving tender/spt** 3 **TRV** 3

TRG 1: 1 *Tir*

FACILITIES

Base   1 (under construction) located at Madras, 1 located at Mumbai (Bombay), 1 (under construction) located at Karwar, 1 (under construction) located at Calcutta, 1 located at Vishakhapatnam, 1 located at Port Blair (Andaman Is), 1 located at Kochi (Cochin)

Naval airbase 1 located at Arakonam, 1 located at Goa

Naval Aviation 7,000

Flying hours   180 to 240 hrs/year on T-60 trg Aircraft; 180 hrs/year on *Sea Harrier* FRS MK51 (*Sea Harrier* FRS MKI) FGA ac

FORCES BY ROLE

Air   1 HQ located at Arakonam

FGA   1 sqn with 15 *Sea Harrier* FRS MK51 (*Sea Harrier* FRS MKI); 2 T-60 *

ASW   6 sqn with 9 Ka-31 *Helix B*; 7 Ka-25 *Hormone*; 18 Ka-28 (Ka-27PL) *Helix A*; 35 *Sea King* MK42A/*Sea King* MK42B; 26 HAL *Chetak* (SA-316B) *Alouette III*

MR   3 sqn with 6 Il-38 *May*; 11 Tu-142M *Bear F*; up to 20 Do-228-201; 15 BN-2 *Defender*

SAR   1 sqn with 6 *Sea King* MK42C; HAL *Chetak* (SA-316B) *Alouette III* (several in SAR role)

Tpt   1 sqn with 10 HAL-784M (HS-748M)

Comms   1 sqn with 10 Do-228

Trg   2 sqn with 6 HJT-16 MKI *Kiran*; 6 HJT-16 MKII *Kiran II*; 8 HPT-32 *Deepak*

EQUIPMENT BY TYPE

AIRCRAFT 34 combat capable

FGA 15: 15 *Sea Harrier* FRS MK51 (*Sea Harrier* FRS MKI)

ASW 17: 6 Il-38 *May**

Tu-142 11: 11 Tu-142M *Bear F**

MP up to 20: up to 20 Do-228-201

TPT 35: 15 BN-2 *Defender*; 10 Do-228

HS-748 10: 10 HAL-784M (HS-748M)

TRG 22:

HJT-16 MKI 12: 6; 6 HJT-16 MKII *Kiran II*

HPT-32 *Deepak* 8 **T-60** 2 *

HELICOPTERS

AEW 9: 9 KA-31 *Helix B*

SAR 6: 6 *Sea King* MK42C

ASW 25: 7 Ka-25 *Hormone*

KA-27 18: 18 Ka-28 (Ka-27PL) *Helix A*

Sea King **MK42A ASW**/*Sea King* **MK42B ASW/ASUW** 35*

UTL 51+

SA-316 26+: 26 HAL *Chetak* (SA-316B) *Alouette III*; some (several in SAR role)

SA-319 *Alouette III* 25

MSL • TACTICAL • ASM: some *Sea Eagle*; some KH-35/*Sea Skua* (*Bear* and *May* a/c now cleared to fire *Sea Eagle* and Kh-35)

AAM • R-550: some R-550 *Magic* 2/R-550 *Magic* tactical AAM

Marines 1,200

Amph 1 bde

Cdo   1 (marine) force

Western Command

Navy 1 HQ located at Mumbai (Bombay)

Southern Command

Navy 1 HQ located at Kochi (Cochin)

Eastern Command

Navy 1 HQ located at Vishakhapatnam

Andaman and Nicobar Command

Navy 1 HQ located at Port Blair (Andaman Is)

Air Force 170,000

Flying hours   180 hrs/year

FORCES BY ROLE

Ftr	3 sqn with 74 MiG-29B *Fulcrum*; 1 sqn with 45 MiG-23MF *Flogger E*/MiG-23UM; 1 sqn with 18 MiG-21FL *Fishbed E*
FGA	3 sqn with 48 M-2000H (M-2000E) *Mirage*/M-2000TH (M-2000ED) *Mirage* (secondary ECM role); 10 sqn with 165 MiG-21bis *Fishbed L & N* (250 being upgraded); 4 sqn with 55 MiG-21MF *Fishbed J*/MiG-21PFMA *Fishbed*; 4 sqn with 100 *Jaguar* S(I) (*Jaguar* S International); 2 sqn with 42 Su-30 MKI *Flanker*; 8 Su-30K *Flanker*; 7 sqn with 120 MiG-27M *Flogger J2*; 3 sqn with 72 MiG-23BN *Flogger H*
Maritime attack	1 sqn with 16 *Jaguar* S(I) (*Jaguar* S International) each with *Sea Eagle* tactical ASM
ELINT	some sqn with 2 B-707; 2 B-737; 5 HS-748
Recce	1 sqn with 3 MiG-25R *Foxbat* *; 2 MiG-25U *Foxbat* *
MR / survey	some sqn (all operated by Aviation Research Centre – Intelligence Wing) with 2 Gulfstream IV SRA-4; 3 An-32 *Cline*; 2 B-707; 2 *Learjet* 29
ECM	1 sqn with 24 MiG-23BN *Flogger H*; 1 sqn with 24 MiG-21M *Fishbed J*; 1 sqn with 3 B(I) MK 58 *Canberra*; 2 PR-57 *Canberra*; 2 PR-67 *Canberra*; 2 T-54 *Canberra*; 3 TT-18 *Canberra* (tgt towing)
Tpt	3 sqn with 3 ALH; 60 HAL *Cheetah* (SA-315B) *Lama*/HAL *Chetak* (SA-316B) *Alouette III*; 6 sqn with 119 An-32 *Cline*; 2 sqn with 43 Do-228; 16 sqn with 43 Mi-8 *Hip*; 100 MI-17 (Mi-8MT) *Hip H*; 1 sqn with 10 Mi-26 *Halo* (hy tpt); 2 sqn with 30 Il-76 *Candid*; 2 sqn with 40 HS-748
Tkr	some sqn with 6 Il-78 *Midas*
VIP	1 sqn HQ with 2 B-707; 4 B-737; 7 HS-748
Atk hel	3 sqn with 40-60 Mi-25 *Hind D*/Mi-35 *Hind*
Trg	some sqn with 27 BAe-748 (trg/tpt); 120 HJT-16 MKI *Kiran*; 56 HJT-16 MKII *Kiran II*; 88 HPT-32 *Deepak*; 40 MiG-21U *Mongol A* *; 9 MiG-29UB *Fulcrum* *; 15 MiG-27UM*; 44 PZL TS-11 *Iskra*; 14 *Jaguar* B(I) (SEPECAT *Jaguar* International B) *; 20 HAL *Chetak* (SA-316B) *Alouette III*
UAV	some sqn with *Searcher* MK II .
SAM	30 sqn with S-125 (SA-3B) *Goa*; 8 sqn with SA-8B; 4 flt with SA-16 *Gimlet*

EQUIPMENT BY TYPE

AIRCRAFT 852 combat capable

FTR 386

  Su-30 50: 42 Su-30 MKI *Flanker*; 8 Su-30K *Flanker*

  MiG-29 74: 74 MiG-29B *Fulcrum*

 MiG-23MF *Flogger E* FTR/**MiG-23UM** *Flogger* **Trg** 45

  MiG-21 262: 18 MiG-21FL *Fishbed E*

   MiG-21M 24: 24

   MiG-21MF *Fishbed* **J**/**MiG-21PFMA** *Fishbed* 55

   MiG-21bis *Fishbed L & N* 165 (250 being upgraded)

 STRIKE/FGA 3: 3 B(I) MK 58 *Canberra*

FGA 380

  M-2000 48: 48 M-2000H (M-2000E) *Mirage*/M-2000TH (M-2000ED) *Mirage* (secondary ECM role)

  MiG-27 120: 120 MiG-27M *Flogger J2*

  Jaguar **S(I)** (*Jaguar* **S International**) 16 each with *Sea Eagle* tactical ASM; 100 more

  MiG-23B 96: 96 MiG-23BN *Flogger H*

RECCE 9

 MR 2: 2 Gulfstream IV SRA-4

 MiG-25R *Foxbat* 3 ***PR-57** *Canberra* 2 **PR-67** *Canberra* 2

TKR 6: 6 Il-78 *Midas*

TPT 288: 122 An-32 *Cline*; 6 B-707; 6 B-737; 27 BAe-748 (trg/tpt); 43 Do-228; 52 HS-748; 30 Il-76 *Candid*; 2 *Learjet* 29

TRG 378:

 HJT-16 MKI 176: 120; 56 HJT-16 MKII *Kiran II*

 HPT-32 *Deepak* 88 *Jaguar* **B(I)** (**SEPECAT** *Jaguar* **International B**) 14* **MiG-21U** *Mongol A* 40* **MiG-25U** *Foxbat* 2* 15 **MiG-27UM** **MiG-29U** 9: 9 MiG-29UB *Fulcrum**

 PZL TS-11 *Iskra* 44 **T-54** *Canberra* 2 **TT-18** *Canberra* 3 (tgt towing)

HELICOPTERS

 ATK 60: 40–60 Mi-25 *Hind D*/Mi-35 *Hind*

 SPT 153: 10 Mi-26 *Halo* (hy tpt)

  MI-8 143: 43; 100 MI-17 (Mi-8MT) *Hip H*

 UTL 83: 3 ALH; 60 HAL *Cheetah* (SA-315B) *Lama* SA-315/HAL *Chetak* (SA-316B) *Alouette III* SA-316

  SA-316 20: 20 HAL *Chetak* (SA-316B) *Alouette III*

UAV: some *Searcher* MK II .

AD • SAM • SA-3: some S-125 (SA-3B) *Goa*

 SP • SA-8: some SA-8B

 MANPAD: some SA-16 *Gimlet*

MSL • TACTICAL • ASM: some AM-39 *Exocet*

 AS-11: some AS-11B (ATGW)

 AS-12 *Kegler* some **AS-17** *Krypton* some **AS-30** some **AS-7** *Kerry* some *Sea Eagle* some

 SSM: some *Prithvi* MK II

 AAM: some AA-10 *Alamo*; some AA-11 *Archer*; some AA-12 *Adder*; some AA-7 *Apex*; some AA-8 *Aphid*; some R-550 *Magic*

  R530 • SUPER 530: some Super 530D

Paramilitary 1,293,229

Assam Rifles 63,883

Ministry of Home Affairs. Security within north-eastern states, mainly army-officered; better trained than BSF

FORCES BY ROLE

Equipped to roughly same standard as an army inf bn
Paramilitary 7 HQ HQ; 40 bn each with 6 81mm

EQUIPMENT BY TYPE

ARTY • MOR 240: 240 81mm

Border Security Force 208,422

Ministry of Home Affairs.

FORCES BY ROLE

Paramilitary 157+ bn each with 6 81mm

EQUIPMENT BY TYPE

Small arms, lt arty, some anti-tank weapons

ARTY • MOR 942: 942 81mm

AIRCRAFT: some tpt (air spt)

Central Industrial Security Force 94,347
(lightly armed security guards only)
Ministry of Home Affairs. Guards public-sector locations

Central Reserve Police Force 229,699
Ministry of Home Affairs. Internal security duties, only lightly armed, deployable throughout the country
Paramilitary 2 Mahila (women) bn; 125 bn; 13 rapid action force bn

Coast Guard 8,000+
FORCES BY ROLE
Air 3 sqn
EQUIPMENT BY TYPE
PATROL AND COASTAL COMBATANTS 50: 17 PB
  PCC 21: 7 *Jija Bai*; 14 *Jija Bai* Mod 1
  PCO 12: 3 *Samar*; 9 *Vikram*
AIRCRAFT • TPT 24: 24 Do-228
HELICOPTERS • UTL • SA-316 17: 17 HAL *Chetak* (SA-316B) *Alouette III*

Defence Security Corps 31,000
provides security at Defence Ministry sites

Indo–Tibetan Border Police 36,324
Ministry of Home Affairs. Tibetan border security SF/guerrila warfare and high altitude warfare specialists
Paramilitary 30 bn

National Security Guards 7,357
Anti-terrorism contingency deployment force, comprising elements of the armed forces, CRPF and Border Security Force

Railway Protection Forces 70,000

Rashtriya Rifles 57,000
Ministry of Defence
Paramilitary 55 bn (in 15 sector HQ. 8 more forming)

Sashtra Seema Bal 31,554
Guards Indo-Nepal/Bhutan borders

Special Frontier Force 10,000
Mainly ethnic Tibetans

Special Protection Group 3,000
Protection of VVIP

State Armed Police 450,000
For duty primarily in home state only, but can be moved to other states. Some bn with GPMG and army standard infantry weapons and equipment
Paramilitary 24 (India Reserve Police (cdo-trained)) bn

Reserve Organisations

Civil Defence 500,000 reservists
Fully train in 225 categorised towns in 32 states. Some units for NBC defence

Home Guard 487,821 reservists (actual str (515,000 authorised str))

In all states except Arunachal Pradesh and Kerala; men on lists, no trg. Not usually armed in peacetime–weapons held in state armouries. Used for civil defence, rescue and fire-fighting teams in wartime.
Paramilitary 6 bn (Special battalions created to protect tea plantations in Assam)

NON-STATE ARMED GROUPS
see Part II

DEPLOYMENT

BURUNDI
UN • ONUB 2; 7 obs

CÔTE D'IVOIRE
UN • UNOCI 5; 7 obs

DEMOCRATIC REPUBLIC OF CONGO
UN • MONUC 3,514; 36 obs

ETHIOPIA/ERITREA
UN • UNMEE 1,556; 8 obs

LEBANON
UN • UNIFIL 648

SUDAN
UN • UNMIS 332; 5 obs

TAJIKISTAN
IAF Forward Op Base, Farkhar

Kazakhstan Kaz

Kazakhstani Tenge t		2003	2004	2005
GDP	t	4.5tr	5.5tr	
	US$[a]	97.7bn	112bn	
per capita	US$[a]	6,466	7,395	
Growth	%	9.3	9.4	
Inflation	%	6.4	6.9	
Debt	US$	22.8bn		
Def exp	US$[a]	1.5bn	1.7bn	
Def bdgt	t	41.3bn	49.9bn	54.9bn
	US$	277m	362m	419m
FMA (US)	US$	3.77m	4.21m	5.96m
US$1=t		149	138	131

[a] PPP estimate

Population   15,185,844

Ethnic groups: Kazak 51%; Russian 32%; Ukrainian 5%; German 2%; Tatar 2%; Uzbek 2%

Age	0–14	15–19	20–24	25–29	30–64	65 plus
Male	12%	6%	5%	4%	19%	3%
Female	12%	5%	5%	4%	21%	6%

Capabilities

ACTIVE 65,800 (Army 46,800 Air 19,000)
Paramilitary 34,500

ORGANISATIONS BY SERVICE

Army 46,800
FORCES BY ROLE

Mil   1 district (1 MRR bde, 1 arty bde); 1 district (1 mech div, 1 MRL bde, 1 indep army bde, 2 MRR bde); 1 district (with nil formation); 1 district (1 MRR div, 1 engr bde, 1 MRR bde)

Air Aslt 1 bde

Arty   1 bde

SSM   1 bde

EQUIPMENT BY TYPE

TK • MBT 930: 650 T-72; 280 T-62

RECCE 140: 140 BRDM

AIFV 573

  BMP 508: 508 BMP-1/BMP-2

  BRM 65

APC 770

  APC (T) 686: 686 MT-LB (plus some 1000 in store)

  APC (W) • BTR 84: 84 BTR-70/BTR-80

ARTY 986

  TOWED 505

    122mm 161: 161 D-30

    152mm 344: 180 2A36; 90 2A65; 74 D-20

  SP 163

    122mm 74: 74 2S1 *Carnation*

    152mm 89: 89 2S3

  GUN/MOR • 120mm 26: 26 2S9 *NONA*

  MRL 147

    122mm 57: 57 BM-21

    220mm 90: 90 9P140 *Uragan*

  MOR • 120mm 145: 145 2B11/M-120

AT

  MSL: some AT-4 *Spigot*; some AT-5 *Spandrel*; some AT-6 *Spiral*

  RL • 73mm: some RPG-7 *Knout*

  GUNS • 100mm 68: 68 MT-12/T-12

MSL • TACTICAL • SSM 12: 12 SS-21 *Scarab (Tochka)*

FACILITIES

Training centre   1

Air Force 19,000 (incl Air Defence)
1 air force div, 164 cbt ac, 14 atk hel

Flying hours   100 hrs/year

FORCES BY ROLE

Comd   some regt with Tu-134 *Crusty*; Tu-154 *Careless*

Ftr   1 regt with 40 MiG-29 *Fulcrum*; 1 (AD) regt with 43 MiG-31 *Foxhound*; 16 MiG-25 *Foxbat*

FGA   1 regt with 14 Su-24 *Fencer*; 1 regt with 14 Su-25 *Frogfoot*; 1 regt with 25 Su-27 *Flanker*

Recce   1 regt with 12 Su-24 *Fencer* *

Atk hel   some regt with 14 Mi-171V5

Trg   some regt with 12 L-39 *Albatros*; 4 Yak-18 *Max*

Hel   some regt with Mi-8 *Hip*, 6 UH-1H

SAM   some regt with 100 SA-2 *Guideline*/SA-3 *Goa*; SA-10 *Grumble (quad)*; 27 SA-4 *Ganef*/SA-5 *Gammon* (27-54 eff.); 20 SA-6 *Gainful* (60 eff.)

EQUIPMENT BY TYPE

AIRCRAFT 164 combat capable

  FTR 124: 43 MiG-31 *Foxhound*; 40 MiG-29 *Fulcrum*; 25 Su-27 *Flanker*; 16 MiG-25 *Foxbat*

  MiG-23 *Flogger* FTR/MiG-23UB *Flogger C* Trg/MiG-25 *Foxbat* FTR/MiG-27 *Flogger* FGA/MiG-29 *Fulcrum* FTR/Su-27 *Flanker* FTR 75 in store

  FGA 40: 14 Su-25 *Frogfoot*; 14 Su-24 *Fencer*; 12 *

  TPT: some Tu-134 *Crusty*; some Tu-154 *Careless*

  TRG 16: 12 L-39 *Albatros*; 4 Yak-18 *Max*

HELICOPTERS

  SPT • MI-171 14: 14 Mi-171V5

  some **Mi-8 *Hip*,** 6 UH-1H

AD • SAM 147+: 100 SA-2 *Guideline* Towed/SA-3 *Goa*

  SP 20+: some SA-10 *Grumble (quad)*

  SA-4 *Ganef* SP/SA-5 Gammon static 27 (27-54 eff.)

  SP 20+: 20 SA-6 *Gainful*

MSL • TACTICAL • ASM: some AS-10 *Karen*; some AS-11 *Kilter*; some AS-7 *Kerry*; some AS-9 *Kyle*

  AAM: some AA-6 *Acrid*; some AA-7 *Apex*; some AA-8 *Aphid*

Paramilitary 34,500

Government Guard 500

Internal Security Troops ε20,000
Ministry of Interior

Presidential Guard 2,000

State Border Protection Forces ε12,000
Ministry of Interior. Incl

Maritime Border Guard 3,000
PATROL AND COASTAL COMBATANTS 15

  MISC BOATS/CRAFT 5: 5 boats (sid)

  PCI 10: 4 *Almaty* less than 100 tonnes; 1 *Dauntless* less than 100 tonnes; 5 *Guardian* less than 100 tonnes

FOREIGN FORCES
Korea, Republic of Army: 205 engr/medical (*Op Enduring Freedom*)

Central and South Asia

Kyrgyzstan Kgz

Kyrgyzstani Som s		2003	2004	2005
GDP	s	83bn	94bn	
	US$[a]	8.6bn	9.8bn	
per capita	US$[a]	1,713	1,928	
Growth	%	6.9	6.0	
Inflation	%	3.1	4.1	
Debt	US$	2.0bn		
Def exp	US$[a]	220m	255m	
Def bdgt	s	2.4bn	2.7bn	3.0bn
	US$	55.2m	63.5m	73.1m
FMA (US)	US$	4.96m	5.12m	3.08m
US$1=s		43.6	42.5	41

[a] PPP estimate

Population   5,146,281

Ethnic groups: Kyrgz 56%; Russian 17%; Uzbek 13%; Ukrainian 3%

Age	0–14	15–19	20–24	25–29	30–64	65 plus
Male	16%	6%	5%	4%	15%	3%
Female	15%	6%	5%	4%	17%	4%

Capabilities

ACTIVE 12,500 (Army 8,500 Air 4,000) Paramilitary 5,000

ORGANISATIONS BY SERVICE

Army 8,500

FORCES BY ROLE
MRR 1 div; 2 (mtn) indep bde
SF   3 bn
ADA 1 regt
AD   1 bde

EQUIPMENT BY TYPE
TK • MBT 215: 215 T-72
RECCE • BRDM 30: 30 BRDM-2
AIFV • BMP 387: 274 BMP-1; 113 BMP-2
APC • APC (W) • BTR 63: 53 BTR-70; 10 BTR-80
ARTY 246
  TOWED 141
    100mm 18: 18 M-1944
    122mm 107: 72 D-30; 35 M-30 *M-1938*
    152mm 16: 16 D-1
  SP • 122mm 18: 18 2S1 *Carnation*
  GUN/MOR • 120mm 12: 12 2S9 *NONA*
  MRL • 122mm 21: 21 BM-21
  MOR • 120mm 54: 6 2S12; 48 M-120
AT
  MSL 26+: 26 AT-3 *Sagger*; some AT-4 *Spigot*; some AT-5 *Spandrel*
  RCL • 73mm: some SPG-9
  RL • 73mm: some RPG-7 *Knout*
  GUNS • 100mm 18: 18 MT-12/T-12

AD
  SAM • MANPAD: some SA-7 *Grail*
  GUNS 48
    23mm • SP 24: 24 ZSU-23-4
    57mm • TOWED 24: 24 S-60

Air Force 4,000

FORCES BY ROLE
Air   1 (comp a vn) regt with 48 MiG-21 *Fishbed*; 2 An-12 *Cub*; 2 An-26 *Curl*
Ftr   1 regt with 4 L-39 *Albatros*
Hel   1 regt with 9 Mi-24 *Hind*; 23 Mi-8 *Hip*
SAM some regt with SA-3 *Goa*; SA-4 *Ganef*; SA-2 *Guideline*

EQUIPMENT BY TYPE
AIRCRAFT 52 combat capable
  FTR 72: 48 MiG-21 *Fishbed*; 24 in store
  TPT 4: 2 An-12 *Cub*; 2 An-26 *Curl*
  TRG 28: 4 L-39 *Albatros**; 24 in store
HELICOPTERS
  ATK 9: 9 Mi-24 *Hind*
  SPT 23: 23 Mi-8 *Hip*
AD • SAM: some SA-3 *Goa*
  SP: some SA-4 *Ganef*
  TOWED: some SA-2 *Guideline*

Paramilitary ε5,000

Border Guards ε5,000 (Kgz conscripts, RF officers)

National Guard
reported

DEPLOYMENT

BURUNDI
UN • ONUB 1 obs

LIBERIA
UN • UNMIL 4 obs

SIERRA LEONE
UN • UNAMSIL 4 obs

SUDAN
UN • UNMIS 5 obs

FOREIGN FORCES

Denmark Army: 75 (incl C-130 contingent. *Op Enduring Freedom*)

Russia Military Air Forces: 20+ Mi-8 *Hip* spt hel/Su-24 *Fencer* FGA ac/Su-25 *Frogfoot* FGA ac/Su-27 *Flanker* ftr ac; ε500

United States 950

Nepal N

Nepalese Rupee NR		2003	2004	2005
GDP	NR	453bn	493bn	
	US$	5.96bn	6.75bn	
per capita	US$	225	249	493bn
Growth	%	3.1	3.5	
Inflation	%	4.7	4.0	
Debt	US$	3.25bn		
Def exp	NR	8.4bn	9.7bn	
Def exp	US$	110m	132m	
Def bdgt	NR	7.4bn	8.0bn	10.4bn
	US$	97.5m	109m	151m
FMA (US)	US$	3.5m	4.5m	2.1m
US$1=NR		76.1	73.1	69.5

Population   27,676,547

Ethnic groups: Hindu 90%; Buddhist 5%; Muslim 3%

Age	0–14	15–19	20–24	25–29	30–64	65 plus
Male	20%	6%	5%	4%	14%	2%
Female	19%	5%	5%	4%	14%	2%

Capabilities

ACTIVE 69,000 (Army 69,000) Paramilitary 62,000

ORGANISATIONS BY SERVICE

Army 69,000

FORCES BY ROLE

Army	3 div HQ; 1 (valley) comd
Inf	7 bde (*total:* 16 Inf bn); 44 indep coy
SF	1 bde (1 AB bn, 1 (*Ferret*) cav sqn, 2 indep SF coy)
Ranger	1 bn
Arty	1 bde (1 arty regt, 1 AD regt)
Engr	1 bde (4 engr bn)
Royal Guard	1 bde (1 MP bn)

EQUIPMENT BY TYPE

RECCE 40: 40 *Ferret*

APC • APC (W) 40: 40 *Casspir*

ARTY 95+

  TOWED 25

    75mm 6: 6 pack

    94mm 5: 5 3.7in mtn (trg)

    105mm 14: 8 L-118 Light Gun; 6 pack howitzer non-operational

  MOR 70+: some 81mm

    120mm 70: 70 M-43 (est 12 op)

AD • GUNS 32+

  14.5mm • TOWED • ZPU 30: 30 Type-56 (ZPU-4)

  37mm some (PRC)

  40mm • TOWED 2: 2 L/60

Air Wing 320

AIRCRAFT • TPT 2: 1 BAe-748; 1 SC.7 3M *Skyvan*

HELICOPTERS

  SPT 7

    AS-332 3:

      AS-332L 3: 1; 2 AS-322L1 *Super Puma*

    AS-350 *Ecureuil* 1

    MI-8 3: 3 MI-17 (Mi-8MT) *Hip H*

  UTL 5

    BELL 206 2: 2 Bell 206L *LongRanger*

    SA-315 1: 1 HAS-315B (SA-315B) *Lama*

    SA-316 2: 2 SA-316B *Alouette III*

Paramilitary 62,000

Armed Police Force 15,000

Ministry of Home Affairs

Police Force 47,000

NON-STATE ARMED GROUPS

see Part II

DEPLOYMENT

BURUNDI

UN • ONUB 937; 6 obs

CÔTE D'IVOIRE

UN • UNOCI 3 obs

DEMOCRATIC REPUBLIC OF CONGO

UN • MONUC 19 obs; 1,126

ETHIOPIA/ERITREA

UN • UNMEE 5 obs

HAITI

UN • MINUSTAH 758

LIBERIA

UN • UNMIL 42; 3 obs

MIDDLE EAST

UN • UNTSO 2 obs

SERBIA AND MONTENEGRO

UN • UNMIK 2 obs

SIERRA LEONE

UN • UNAMSIL 5 obs

SUDAN

UN • UNMIS228

SYRIA/ISRAEL

UN • UNDOF 3

FOREIGN FORCES

United Kingdom Army: 63 (Gurkha trg org)

Pakistan Pak

Pakistani Rupee Rs		2003	2004	2005
GDP	Rs	4.0tr	5.5tr	
	US$	69.6bn	93.9bn	
per capita	US$	446	590	
Growth	%	5.6	6.5	
Inflation	%	2.9	6.7	
Debt	US$	36.3bn		
Def exp	Rs	180bn	193bn	
	US$	3.12bn	3.33bn	
Def bdgt	Rs	160bn	193bn	222bn
	US$	2.77bn	3.33bn	3.74bn
FMA (US)	US$	225m	75.9m	150m
US$1=Rs		57.7	58.1	59.5

Population 162,419,946

Ethnic groups: Hindu less than 3%

Age	0–14	15–19	20–24	25–29	30–64	65 plus
Male	20%	6%	5%	4%	14%	2%
Female	19%	5%	5%	4%	14%	2%

Capabilities

ACTIVE 619,000 (Army 550,000 Navy 24,000 Air 45,000) **Paramilitary 302,000**

ORGANISATIONS BY SERVICE

Army 550,000 (to reduce by 50,000 in 2004)

FORCES BY ROLE
Army 9 corps HQ
Armd 2 div; 7 (indep) bde
Mech 1 (indep) bde
Inf 18 div; 1 (area) comd; 6 bde
SF 1 gp (3 SF bn)
Arty 9 (corps) bde; 5 bde
Engr 7 bde
Avn 1 (VIP) sqn; 5 (comp) sqn
Hel 10 sqn
AD 1 comd (3 AD gp (total: 8 AD bde))

EQUIPMENT BY TYPE
TK • MBT 2,461+: 45 MBT 2000 Al-Khalid
 T-80 320: 320 T-80UD
 400 Type-69 275+ Type-85 1,100 Type-59 51 T-54/T-55
 M-48 270: 270 M-48A5 in store
APC 1,266
 APC (T) 1,100: 1,100 M-113
 APC (W) 166
  BTR 120: 120 BTR-70/BTR-80
  UR-416 46
ARTY 4,291+
 TOWED 1,629
  105mm 329: 216 M-101; 113 M-56

 122mm 570: 80 D-30 (PRC); 490 Type-54 M-1938
 130mm 410: 410 Type-59-I
 155mm 292: 144 M-114; 148 M-198
 203mm 28: 28 M-115
 SP 260
  155mm • M-109 200: 200 M-109 155mm SP/M-109A2
  203mm 60: 60 M-110A2/M-110
 MRL • 122mm 52: 52 Azar (Type-83)
 MOR 2,350+: 81mm; 120mm AM-50, M-61
AT
 MSL 10,500: 10,500 HJ-8/TOW (TOW incl M-901 SP)
 RCL 3,700: 75mm Type-52/106mm M-40A1
 RL • 73mm: some RPG-7 Knout
  89mm: some M-20
 GUNS • 85mm 200: 200 Type-56 (D-44)
AIRCRAFT
 RECCE • OBS 30: 30 Cessna O-1E Bird Dog
 TPT 4: 1 Cessna 421
  Y-12 3: 3 Y-12(II)
 UTL 90: 90 SAAB 91 Safrai (50 obs, 40 liaison)
HELICOPTERS
 ATK 22
  AH-1 21: 21 AH-1F Cobra (TOW)
  Mi-24 Hind 1
 SPT 54: 31 SA-330 Puma
  MI-8 23: 10; 13 MI-17 (Mi-8MT) Hip H
 UTL 55
  BELL 205 • BELL 205A 5: 5 AB-205A-1 (Bell 205A-1)
  BELL 206 13: 13 Bell 206B JetRanger II
  SA-315 12: 12 SA-315B Lama
  SA-319 Alouette III 20
  UH-1 5: 5 UH-1H Iroquois
 TRG 22: 12 Bell 47G
  HUGHES 300 10: 10 Hughes 300C
UAV: some Bravo; some Jasoos; some Vector
AD
 SAM • MANPAD 2,990+
  ANZA 2500: 2,500 Mk1/Mk2
  FIM-92A Stinger 60
  HN-5: some HN-5A
  Mistral 230 RBS-70 200
 GUNS 1900: 14.5mm 981
  35mm • TOWED • GDF 215: 215 GDF-002/GDF-005
  37mm • TOWED 310: 310 Type-55 (M-1939)/Type-65
  40mm • TOWED 50: 50 L/60
  57mm • TOWED 144: 144 Type-59 (S-60)
  85mm • TOWED 200: 200 Type-72 (M-1939) KS-12
RADAR • LAND: some AN/TPQ-36 Firefinder (arty, mor); some RASIT (veh, arty)
MSL • TACTICAL • SSM 166: 95 Hatf 1; 50 Hatf 3 (PRC M-11); 15 Hatf 5 Ghauri (up to 20); 6 Shaheen 1 Hatf-4

Navy 24,000 (incl estimated 1400 Marines and estimated 2000 Maritime Security Agency (see Paramilitary))

EQUIPMENT BY TYPE
SUBMARINES • TACTICAL 11
 SSK 8:
  4 Hangor (Fr Daphne) each with up to 12 x1 533mm ASTT (8 bow, 4 stern) with 12 L5 HWT/UGM-84A Harpoon tactical USGW
  2 Hashmat (Fr Agosta 70) each with 4 x1 533mm ASTT

each with 20+ F17P HWT/UGM-84 *Harpoon* tactical USGW

2 *Khalid* (Fr *Agosta* 90B) each with x1 533mm ASTT (unknown quantity) each with SM-39 *Exocet* tactical USGW

SSI 3: 3 MG110 (SF delivery)

PRINCIPAL SURFACE COMBATANTS • FRIGATES 7

FFG 6:

4 *Tariq* (UK *Amazon*) (capacity 1 *Lynx* utl hel) each with 2 single each with TP 45 LWT, 2 Mk-141 *Harpoon* twin each with 1 RGM-84D *Harpoon* tactical SSM, 1 114mm gun

2 *Tariq* (capacity 1 *Lynx* utl hel) (D184, D186) each with 2 triple 324mm ASTT (6 eff.) each with Mk 46 LWT, 1 sextuple (6 eff.) with LY-60 (Aspide) SAM, 1 114mm gun

FF 1:

1 *Zalfiquar* (UK *Leander*) (capacity 1 SA-319 *Alouette III* utl hel) with 3 Mk 10 *Limbo*, 2 114mm gun

PATROL AND COASTAL COMBATANTS 10

PCC 3: 1 *Larkana*; 2 *Quetta* (PRC *Shanghai*, operated by the Maritime Security Agency)

PCI 1: 1 *Rajshahi* less than 100 tonnes

PFM 6:

3 *Jalalat* II each with 2 twin (4 eff.) each with 1 C-802 (CSS-N-8) *Saccade* tactical SSM

3 *Sabqat* (PRC *Huangfeng*) each with 2 twin (4 eff.) each with 1 HY-2 (CSS-N-3) *Seersucker* tactical SSM

MINE WARFARE • MINE COUNTERMEASURES • MHC 3: 3 *Munsif* (Fr *Eridan*)

LOGISTICS AND SUPPORT 9

AGHS (SVY) 1: 1 *Behr Paima*

AO 2:

1 *Fuqing* with 1 SA-319 *Alouette III* utl hel

1 *Moawin* (capacity 5 *Lynx* utl hel) with 1 *Sea King* MK45 ASW hel

AOT 3: 1 *Attock*; 2 *Gwadar*

AT 3

FACILITIES

Base 1 (under construction) located at Ormara, 1 (under construction) located at Gwadar, 1 located at Karachi

Marines ε1,400

Cdo 1 gp

Naval Aviation

AIRCRAFT 9 ac combat capable

MP 9: 3 *Atlantic* (also ASW); 4 F-27 MK 200MPA

P-3 2: 2 P-3C *Orion* (operated by Air Force)

TPT • F-27 1: 1 F-27-400M *Troopship* (ASW/MR)

HELICOPTERS

ASW 12: 6 *Lynx* MK3

SEA KING MK45 6: 6 *Sea King* MK45 ASW hel/*Sea King* MK45C

UTL 14: 7 SA-319 *Alouette III*; 7 (SAR)

MSL • TACTICAL • ASM: some AM-39 *Exocet*

Air Force 45,000

FORCES BY ROLE

3 regional comds: Northern (Peshawar) Central (Sargodha) Southern (Faisal). The Composite Air Tpt Wg, Combat Cadrs School and PAF Academy are Direct Reporting Units.

Ftr	2 sqn with 43 *Mirage* IIIEP (*Mirage* IIIE); 7 *Mirage* IIIOD (*Mirage* IIID); 1 sqn with F-16A *Fighting Falcon*/F-16B *Fighting Falcon*; 5 sqn with F-7P *Skybolt*/FT-7 (JJ-7) *Mongol A*; 2 sqn with F-7PG (F-7MG) *Airguard*
FGA	1 sqn with 13 *Mirage* IIIEP (*Mirage* IIIE) each with AM-39 *Exocet* tactical ASM; 3 *Mirage* IIIB (trg); 2 sqn with 41 A-5C (Q-5III) *Fantan*; 2 sqn with *Mirage* 5PA3; *Mirage* 5PA2/*Mirage* 5PA; *Mirage* 5DPA (*Mirage* 5D)/*Mirage* 5DPA2
ELINT / ECM	some sqn with 2 Da-20 *Falcon*
Recce	1 sqn with 15 *Mirage* IIIRP (*Mirage* IIIR) *
SAR	7 sqn with SA-316 *Alouette III*
Tpt	some sqn with 1 An-26 *Curl*; 3 B-707; 1 Beech 200 *Super King Air*; 2 C-130 *Hercules*; 11 C-130B *Hercules*/C-130E *Hercules*; 4 CN-235; 2 F-27-200 *Friendship* (1 with navy); 1 *Falcon* 20; 1 L-100 *Hercules*; 1 Y-12; 1 Beech F-33 *Bonanza*
OCU	1 sqn with F-7PG (F-7MG) *Airguard*; 1 sqn with F-7P *Skybolt*/FT-7 (JJ-7) *Mongol A*; 1 sqn with F-16A *Fighting Falcon*/F-16B *Fighting Falcon*; 1 sqn with *Mirage* 5PA3; *Mirage* 5PA2/*Mirage* 5PA; *Mirage* 5DPA (*Mirage* 5D)/*Mirage* 5DPA2
Trg	some sqn with 12 K-8; 80 MFI-17B *Mushshak* *; 25 FT-5 (MiG-17U) *Fresco*; 15 FT-6 (MiG-19UTI) *Farmer*; 20 T-37C *Tweet*
SAM	1 bty with 6 CSA-1 (SA-2) *Guideline*; SA-16 *Gimlet*; 6 bty each with 24 *Crotale*

EQUIPMENT BY TYPE

AIRCRAFT 331 combat capable

FTR 143

F-7M 55: 55 F-7PG (F-7MG) *Airguard*

Mirage **IIIEP (*Mirage* IIIE)** 13 each with AM-39 *Exocet* tactical ASM; 43 more

F-16 32: 21 F-16A *Fighting Falcon*; 11 F-16B *Fighting Falcon*; some F-16A *Fighting Falcon*/F-16B *Fighting Falcon*; up to 24 F-16C/D on order

FGA 51+: 41 A-5C (Q-5III) *Fantan*; 10 *Mirage* 5PA3 (ASuW)

Mirage **5PA FGA/*Mirage* 5PA2 FTR** 40

RECCE 15: 15 *Mirage* IIIRP (*Mirage* IIIR) *

EW • ELINT 2: 2 Da-20 *Falcon*

TPT 27: 1 An-26 *Curl*; 3 B-707; 1 Beech 200 *Super King Air*

C-130 13: 2; 11 C-130B *Hercules*/C-130E *Hercules*

CN-235 4

F-27 2: 2 F-27-200 *Friendship* (1 with navy)

Falcon 20 1 **L-100 *Hercules*** 1 **Y-12** 1

TRG 165+: 1 Beech F-33 *Bonanza*; 25 FT-5 (MiG-17U) *Fresco*; 15 FT-6 (MiG-19UTI) *Farmer*

F-7P *Skybolt* FTR/FT-7 (JJ-7) *Mongol A* Trg 77*: 12 K-8

MFI-17 80: 80 MFI-17B *Mushshak*

Mirage **5DPA (*Mirage* 5D)/*Mirage* 5DPA2** 2+ *Mirage* IIIB 3 (trg) *Mirage* **IIIOD (*Mirage* IIID)** 7

T-37 20: 20 T-37C *Tweet*

HELICOPTERS • UTL: some SA-316 *Alouette III*

AD • SAM 150+: 144 *Crotale*
  TOWED 6: 6 CSA-1 (SA-2) *Guideline*
  MANPAD: some SA-16 *Gimlet*
RADAR • LAND 51+: 6 AR-1 (AD radar low level); some *Condor* (AD radar high level); some FPS-89/100 (AD radar high level)
  MPDR 45: 45 MPDR 45/MPDR 60/MPDR 90 (AD radar low level)
  TPS-43G some (AD radar high level)**Type 514** some (AD radar high level)
MSL • TACTICAL • ASM: some AGM-65 *Maverick*; some AM-39 *Exocet*
  AAM • AIM-9: some AIM-9L *Sidewinder*/AIM-9P *Sidewinder*
    R530: some Super 530

FACILITIES

Radar air control sectors	4
Radar control and reporting station	7

Paramilitary up to 302,000 active

Coast Guard
PATROL AND COASTAL COMBATANTS • MISC BOATS/CRAFT: up to 23 craft

Frontier Corps up to 65,000 (reported)
Ministry of Interior
FORCES BY ROLE
Armd recce 1 indep sqn
Paramilitary 11 regt (*total:* 40 paramilitary bn)
EQUIPMENT BY TYPE
APC • APC (W) 45: 45 UR-416

Maritime Security Agency ε2,000
PRINCIPAL SURFACE COMBATANTS • DESTROYERS • DD 1: 1 *Alamgir* (US *Gearing*, no ASROC or TT)
PATROL AND COASTAL COMBATANTS 6: 2 PCC (PRC Shanghai)
  PCO 4: 4 *Barkat*

National Guard 185,000
incl
  JANBAZ FORCE
  MUJAHID FORCE
  NATIONAL CADET CORPS
  WOMEN GUARDS

Northern Light Infantry ε12,000
Paramilitary 3 bn

Pakistan Rangers up to 40,000
Ministry of Interior

NON-STATE ARMED GROUPS
see Part II

DEPLOYMENT

BURUNDI
UN • ONUB 1,190; 5 obs

CÔTE D'IVOIRE
UN • UNOCI 10 obs; 374

DEMOCRATIC REPUBLIC OF CONGO
UN • MONUC 25 obs; 3,770

EAST TIMOR
UN • UNOTIL 1 obs

GEORGIA
UN • UNOMiG 8 obs

LIBERIA
UN • UNMIL 16 obs; 2,749

SERBIA AND MONTENEGRO
UN • UNMIK 1 obs

SIERRA LEONE
UN • UNAMSIL 8 obs; 1,267

SUDAN
UN • UNMIS 8 obs

WESTERN SAHARA
UN • MINURSO 7 obs

FOREIGN FORCES

United Kingdom some (fwd mounting base) air elm located at Karachi
United States USCENTCOM: 400 (army/air force (*Op Enduring Freedom*))

Sri Lanka Ska

Sri Lankan Rupee Rs		2003	2004	2005
GDP	Rs	1.8tr	2.0tr	
	US$	18.2bn	19.6bn	
per capita	US$	923	988	
Growth	%	5.9	5.2	
Inflation	%	6.3	7.6	
Debt	US$	10.2bn		
Def bdgt	Rs	49.7bn	52.0bn	56.2bn
	US$	515m	510m	564m
FMA (US)	US$		3.0m	1.0m
US$1=Rs		96.5	102	99.8

Population   20,064,776

Ethnic groups: Sinhalese 74%; Buddhist 69%; Tamil 18%; Hindu 15%; Christian 8%; Muslim 8%; Moor 7%;

Age	0–14	15–19	20–24	25–29	30–64	65 plus
Male	13%	4%	5%	4%	20%	3%
Female	12%	4%	5%	4%	22%	4%

Capabilities

ACTIVE 111,000 (Army 78,000 Navy 15,000 Air 18,000) Paramilitary 88,600

RESERVE 5,500 (Army 1,100 Navy 2,400 Air Force 2,000) Paramilitary 30,400

ORGANISATIONS BY SERVICE

Army 78,100; 39,900 reservists (recalled) (total 118,000)

FORCES BY ROLE

9 Div HQ

Armd	3 regt
Armd recce	3 regt (bn)
Air mob	1 bde
Inf	33 bde
SF	1 indep bde
Cdo	1 bde
Fd arty	1 light regt; 2 (med) regt
Fd engr	3 regt

EQUIPMENT BY TYPE

TK • MBT • T-55 62: 62 T-55AM2/T-55A

RECCE 15: 15 Saladin

AIFV • BMP 62: 13 BMP-1; 49 BMP-2

APC 192

  APC (T) 35: 35 Type-85

BTR-80 APC (W)/BTR-80A AIFV 25

APC 192

  APC (W) 157: 31 Buffel; 21 FV603 Saracen; 105 Unicorn

ARTY 963

  TOWED 157

    88mm 3: 3 25-pdr

    122mm 74

    130mm 40: 40 Type-59-I

    152mm 40: 40 Type-66 (D-20)

  MRL • 122mm 22: 22 RM-70 Dana

  MOR 784: 520 81mm; 209 82mm

    120mm 55: 55 M-43

AT

  RCL 40

    105mm 10: ε10 M-65

    106mm 30: ε30 M-40

  GUNS • 85mm 8: 8 Type-56 (D-44)

UAV 1: 1 Seeker

AD • GUNS 27

  40mm • TOWED 24: 24 L/40

  94mm • TOWED 3: 3 3.7in

RADAR • LAND 2: 2 AN/TPQ-36 Firefinder (arty)

Navy 15,000 (incl 2400 recalled reservists)

FORCES BY ROLE

Navy 1 HQ (HQ and Western comd) located at Colombo

EQUIPMENT BY TYPE

PATROL AND COASTAL COMBATANTS up to 113

  MISC BOATS/CRAFT up to 52: up to 52 boats

  PCC 10: 3 Abeetha (PRC mod Shanghai); 2 Prathapa (PRC mod Haizhui); 2 Ranajaya (PRC Haizhui); 1 Ranarisi (PRC Shanghai II); 2 Weeraya (PRC Shanghai)

  PFI 46: 19 Colombo less than 100 tonnes; 3 Dvora less than 100 tonnes; 3 Killer less than 100 tonnes (ROK); 7 Shaldag less than 100 tonnes; 5 Trinity Marine less than 100 tonnes; 9 Super Dvora less than 100 tonnes

  PFM 2:

    2 Nandimithra (Il Saar 4) each with 3 single each with 1 GII Gabriel II tactical SSM, 1 76mm gun

  PCO 3: 1 Jayesagara; 1 Parakrambahu; 1 Sayura (In Sukanya)

AMPHIBIOUS: 4 Fast Personnel Carrier

  LS • LSM 1: 1 Yuhai (capacity 2 tanks; 250 troops)

  CFT 5

    LCU 2: 2 Yunnan

    LCM 2

    ACV 1: 1 M 10 (capacity 56 troops)

FACILITIES

Base 1 (Northern Comd) located at Kankesanthurai, 1 (Southern Comd) located at Galle, 1 (North Central Comd) located at Medawachiya, 1 (HQ and Western Comd) located at Colombo, 1 (Main base and Eastern Comd) located at Trincomalee

Air Force 18,000

FORCES BY ROLE

FGA	1 sqn with 4 MiG-27M Flogger J2; 1 FT-7 (JJ-7) Mongol A, 3F-7M; 2 FT-5 (MiG-17U) Fresco; 1 MiG-23UB Flogger C (conversion trg); 1 sqn with 7 Kfir C-2; 2 Kfir C-7; 1 Kfir TC-2
Tpt	1 sqn with 7 An-32B Cline; 2 BAe-748; 1 Beech 200 Super King Air; 2 C-130K Hercules; 1 Cessna 421C Golden Eagle; 3 Y-12; 5 Cessna 150; 6 Bell 412 Twin Huey (VIP)
Atk hel	some sqn with 1 Mi-24V Hind E; 13 Mi-35P Hind; 10 Bell 212
Trg	some sqn with 10 PT-6 (CJ-6); 3 K-8; 5 SF-260TP; 6 Bell 206 JetRanger
Hel	some sqn with 3 MI-17 (Mi-8MT) Hip H; 6 Bell 206 JetRanger
Reserves	Air Force Regt, 3 sqn; airfield construction, 1 sqn

EQUIPMENT BY TYPE

AIRCRAFT 21 combat capable

  FGA 13: 7 Kfir C-2; 2 Kfir C-7

  MiG-27 4: 4 MiG-27M Flogger J2, 3 F-7M

  TPT 16

    An-32 7: 7 An-32B Cline

    BAe-748 2 Beech 200 Super King Air 1

    C-130 2: 2 C-130K Hercules

    CESSNA 421 1: 1 Cessna 421C Golden Eagle

    Y-12 3

  TRG 28: 5 Cessna 150; 2 FT-5 (MiG-17U* Fresco); 1 FT-7* (JJ-7) Mongol A; 3 K-8; 1 Kfir TC-2*

    MiG-23U 1: 1 MiG-23UB Flogger C (conversion trg)*

    PT-6 (CJ-6) 10

    SF-260 5: 5 SF-260TP

HELICOPTERS

  ATK 14

    MI-24 1: 1 Mi-24V Hind E

    MI-35 13: 13 Mi-35P Hind

  SPT • MI-8 7: 3 MI-17 (Mi-8MT) Hip H; 4 in store

  UTL 28: 12 Bell 206 JetRanger; 10 Bell 212; 6 Bell 412 Twin Huey (VIP)

UAV 3

  RECCE • TAC 2: 2 Searcher

  Scout 1

Paramilitary ε88,600

Home Guard 13,000

National Guard ε15,000

Police Force 30,200; 1,000 (women); 30,400 reservists (total 61,600)
Ministry of Defence

Special Task Force 3,000
anti-guerrilla unit

NON-STATE ARMED GROUPS

see Part II

DEPLOYMENT

BURUNDI
UN • ONUB 1 obs

DEMOCRATIC REPUBLIC OF CONGO
UN • MONUC 2 obs

HAITI
UN • MINUSTAH 754

WESTERN SAHARA
UN • MINURSO 2 obs

Tajikistan Tjk

Tajikistani Somoni Tr		2003	2004	2005
GDP	Tr	4.1bn	5.1bn	
	US$[a]	7.0bn	7.7bn	
per capita	US$[a]	1,019	1,098	
Growth	%	10.2	10.6	
Inflation	%	16.4	7.1	
Debt	US$	1.16bn		
Def exp	US$[a]	150m	160m	
Def bdgt	Tr	105m	124m	139m
	US$	34.6m	44.9m	50.3m
FMA (US)	US$		2.34m	
US$1=Tr		3.06	2.78	2.78

[a] PPP estimate

Population   7,163,506

Ethnic groups: Tajik 67%; Uzbek 25%; Russian 2%; Tatar 2%

Age	0–14	15–19	20–24	25–29	30–64	65 plus
Male	19%	6%	5%	4%	13%	2%
Female	19%	6%	5%	4%	14%	3%

Capabilities

ACTIVE 7,600 (Army 7,600) **Paramilitary 5,300**
Terms of service 24 months

ORGANISATIONS BY SERVICE

Army 7,600
FORCES BY ROLE
MRR   2 bde (incl 1 trg)
SF   1 bde: 1 det (bn+)
Mtn inf 1 bde
Arty   1 bde
SAM   1 regt

EQUIPMENT BY TYPE
TK • MBT 44: 44 T-72
AIFV • BMP 34: 9 BMP-1; 25 BMP-2
APC • APC (W) • BTR 29: 1 BTR-60; 2 BTR-70; 26 BTR-80
ARTY 31
  TOWED • 122mm 12: 12 D-30
  MRL • 122mm 10: 10 BM-21
  MOR • 120mm: 9
AD • SAM 20+
  MANPAD: some FIM-92A *Stinger* (reported)
  SA-2 *Guideline* towed/SA-3 *Goa*/SA-7 *Grail* MANPAD 20

Air Force 800+
FORCES BY ROLE
Tpt some sqn with 1 Tu-134A *Crusty*
Hel sqn with 5-4 Mi-24 *Hind*; 14-12 Mi-17TM *Hip H/ Mi-8 Hip*

EQUIPMENT BY TYPE
AIRCRAFT • TPT • Tu-134 1: 1 Tu-134A *Crusty*
HELICOPTERS
  ATK 4: 5-4 Mi-24 *Hind*
  SPT 12: 14-12 Mi-17TM *Hip H*/Mi-8 *Hip*

Paramilitary ε5,300

Border Guards ε5,300
Ministry of Interior

Islamic Movement of Tajikistan 5,000+
signed peace accord with govt on 27 June 1997. Integration with govt forces slowly proceeding

FOREIGN FORCES

France Air Force: 2 C-160 *Transall* tpt ac 120
India Air Force: 1 Fwd Op Base
Russia Army: 128 MBT; 314 ACV; 180 mor/MRL /; 1 MRR div (subord to Volga-Ural MD); 7,800; 14,500 conscript (Frontier Forces; RF officers, Tajik conscripts) Military Air Forces: 5 Su-25 *Frogfoot* FGA ac

Turkmenistan Tkm

Turkmen Manat TMM		2003	2004	2005
GDP	TMM	47.1tr	58.7tr	
	US$[a]	28.1bn	34.6bn	
per capita	US$[a]	5,884	7,114	
Growth	%	16.9	7.5	
Inflation	%	5.6	5.9	
Debt	US$	1.51bn		
Def exp	US$[a]	350m	415m	
Def bdgt	TMM	829bn	859bn	899bn
	US$	83m	165m	173m
FMA (US)	US$			1.14m
USD1=TMM		10,000	5,200	5,200

[a] PPP estimate

Population   4,952,081

Ethnic groups: Turkmen 77%; Uzbek 9%; Russian 7%; Kazak 2%

Age	0–14	15–19	20–24	25–29	30–64	65 plus
Male	18%	6%	5%	4%	15%	2%
Female	17%	6%	5%	4%	16%	3%

Capabilities

ACTIVE 26,000 (Army 21,000 Navy 700 Air 4,300)
Terms of service 24 months

ORGANISATIONS BY SERVICE

Army 21,000

FORCES BY ROLE
5 Mil Districts
MRR   3 div; 1 div (trg)
Air aslt   1 indep bn
Arty   1 bde
MRL   1 regt
AT   1 regt
Engr   1 regt
SAM   2 bde

EQUIPMENT BY TYPE
TK • MBT 702: 702 T-72
RECCE • BRDM 170: 170 BRDM recce/BRDM-2
AIFV 942
  BMP 930: 930 BMP-1/BMP-2
  BRM 12
APC • APC (W) • BTR 829: 829 BTR-60/BTR-70/BTR-80
ARTY 488
  TOWED 269
    122mm 180: 180 D-30
    152mm 89: 17 D-1; 72 D-20
  SP • 122mm 40: 40 2S1 *Carnation*
  GUN/MOR • 120mm 17: 17 2S9 *NONA*
  MRL • 122mm 65: 9 9P138; 56 BM-21
  MOR 97: 31 82mm
    120mm 66: 66 PM-38
AT

MSL 100+: 100 AT-3 *Sagger*; some AT-4 *Spigot*; some AT-5 *Spandrel*; some AT-6 *Spiral*
RL • 73mm: some RPG-7 *Knout*
GUNS • 100mm 72: 72 MT-12/T-12
AD
  SAM • SP 53: 13 SA-13 *Gopher*; 40 SA-8 *Gecko*
    MANPAD: some SA-7 *Grail*
  GUNS 70
    23mm • SP 48: 48 ZSU-23-4
    57mm • TOWED 22: 22 S-60

Navy ε700

Has announced intention to form a navy/coast guard and has minor base at Turkmenbashy with 5 boats. Caspian Sea Flotilla (see Russia) is operating as a joint RF, Kaz, Tkm flotilla under RF comd based at Astrakhan.

EQUIPMENT BY TYPE
PATROL AND COASTAL COMBATANTS • MISC BOATS/CRAFT 5: 5 boats

FACILITIES
Minor base 1 located at Turkmenbashy

Air Force 4,300

incl Air Defence
FORCES BY ROLE
Ftr / FGA   2 sqn with 22 MiG-29 *Fulcrum*; 65 Su-17 *Fitter*; 2 MiG-29U *Fulcrum*
Tpt / utl   1 sqn with 1 An-26 *Curl*; 10 Mi-24 *Hind*; 8 Mi-8 *Hip*
Trg   1 unit with 3 Su-7B; 2 L-39 *Albatros*
SAM   some sqn with 50 SA-2 *Guideline*/SA-3 *Goa*/SA-5 *Gammon*

EQUIPMENT BY TYPE
AIRCRAFT 92 combat capable
  FTR 22: 22 MiG-29 *Fulcrum*
  FGA 66: 65 Su-17 *Fitter*
    1 Su-25MK (+42 more being refurbished)
  TPT 1: 1 An-26 *Curl*
  TRG 7: 2 L-39 *Albatros*; 2 MiG-29U *Fulcrum**; 3 Su-7B*
HELICOPTERS
  ATK 10: 10 Mi-24 *Hind*
  SPT 8: 8 Mi-8 *Hip*
AD • SAM 50: 50 SA-2 *Guideline* towed/SA-3 *Goa*/SA-5 *Gammon* static

Uzbekistan Uz

Uzbekistani Som s		2003	2004	2005
GDP	s	8.3tr	9.5tr	
	US$[a]	44.4bn	48.5bn	
per capita	US$[a]	1,708	1,836	
Growth	%	1.5	7.1	
Inflation	%	14.6	8.8	
Debt	US$	5.0bn		
Def exp	US$[a]	2.2bn	2.4bn	
Def bdgt	s	53bn	54.9bn	59.9bn
	US$	53m	55m	60m
FMA (US)	US$	9.7m		11.7m
US$1=s		1,003	1,002	1,097

[a] PPP estimate

Population   26,851,195

Ethnic groups: Uzbek 73%; Russian 6%; Tajik 5%; Kazak 4%; Karakalpak 2%; Tatar 2%; Korean <1%; Ukrainian <1%

Age	0–14	15–19	20–24	25–29	30–64	65 plus
Male	17%	6%	5%	4%	15%	2%
Female	16%	6%	5%	4%	16%	3%

Capabilities

ACTIVE some 55,000 (Army 40,000 Air 15,000)
Paramilitary 36,000

Terms of service conscription 12 months

ORGANISATIONS BY SERVICE

Army 40,000

FORCES BY ROLE
4 Mil Districts; 2 op comd; 1 Tashkent Comd
Tk   1 bde
MRR   10 bde
Mtn Inf   1 (lt) bde
Air Aslt 1 bde
AB   1 bde
Arty   4 bde
EQUIPMENT BY TYPE
TK • MBT 340: 70 T-72; 100 T-64; 170 T-62
RECCE • BRDM 13: 13 BRDM-2
AIFV 405
    BMD 129: 120 BMD-1; 9 BMD-2
    BMP 270: 270 BMP-2
    BRM 6
APC 309
    APC (T) 50: 50 BTR-D
    APC (W) • BTR 259: 24 BTR-60; 25 BTR-70; 210 BTR-80
ARTY 487+
    TOWED 200
        122mm 60: 60 D-30
        152mm 140: 140 2A36
    SP 83+
        122mm 18: 18 2S1 *Carnation*
        152mm 17+: 17 2S3; some 2S5 (reported)
        203mm 48: 48 2S7
    GUN/MOR • 120mm 54: 54 2S9 *NONA*

MRL 108
    122mm 60: 24 9P138; 36 BM-21
    220mm 48: 48 9P140 *Uragan*
    MOR • 120mm 42: 5 2B11; 19 2S12; 18 PM-120
AT
    MSL: some AT-3 *Sagger*; some AT-4 *Spigot*
    GUNS • 100mm 36: 36 MT-12/T-12

Air Force 10,000–15,000

FORCES BY ROLE
7 fixed wg and hel regts.
FGA / bbr   1 regt with 23 Su-24 *Fencer*; 11 Su-24MP
             Fencer F (recce); 1 regt with 20 Su-25 *Frogfoot*/
             Su-25BM *Frogfoot*; 26 Su-17MZ (Su-17M)
             Fitter C/Su-17UMZ (Su-17UM-3) *Fitter G*
Ftr   1 regt with 30 MiG-29 *Fulcrum*/MiG-29UB
             Fulcrum; 25 Su-27 *Flanker*/Su-27UB *Flanker C*
ELINT /tpt   1 regt with 26 An-12 *Cub*/An-12PP *Cub*; 13
             An-26 *Curl*/An-26RKR *Curl*
Tpt   some sqn with 1 An-24 *Coke*; 1 Tu-134 *Crusty*
Trg   some sqn with 1 Su-17 *Fitter*; 5 L-39 *Albatros*
Hel   1 regt with 29 Mi-24 *Hind* (attack); 1 Mi-26
             Halo (tpt); 23 Mi-8 *Hip* (aslt/tpt); 1 regt with 2
             Mi-6AYa *Hook* (cmd post); 26 Mi-6 *Hook* (tpt);
             29 Mi-8 *Hip* (aslt/tpt)
EQUIPMENT BY TYPE
AIRCRAFT 136 combat capable
    FTR 75: 30 MiG-29 *Fulcrum* FTR/MiG-29UB *Fulcrum*
    MiG-29U Trg; 30 in store; 25 Su-27 *Flanker* FTR/Su-27UB
    Flanker C Trg*; 20 Su-25 *Frogfoot* FGA/Su-25BM *Frogfoot*
    Trg*
    FGA 50: 23 Su-24 *Fence* Su-17 1: 1 Su-17MZ (Su-17M)
    Fitter C FGA/Su-17UMZ (Su-17UM-3) *Fitter G* trg 26
    EW • ECM 11: 11 Su-24MP *Fencer F* (recce)*
    An-12 *Cub* Tpt/An-12PP *Cub* ECM EW 26
    TPT 2: 1 An-24 *Coke*
    An-26 *Curl* Tpt/An-26RKR *Curl* ELINT EW 13
    TPT 2: 1 Tu-134 *Crusty*
    TRG 14: 5 L-39 *Albatros*; 9 in store
HELICOPTERS
    ATK 29: 29 Mi-24 *Hind* (atk)
    COMD 2: 2 Mi-6AYa *Hook* (cmd post)
    SPT 79: 1 Mi-26 *Halo* (tpt); 26 Mi-6 *Hook* (tpt); 52 Mi-8
    Hip (aslt/tpt)
AD • SAM 45: 45 SA-2 *Guideline* towed/SA-3 *Goa*/SA-5
Gammon static
MSL • TACTICAL • ASM: some AS-10 *Karen*; some AS-11
Kilter; some AS-12 *Kegler*; some AS-7 *Kerry*; some AS-9 *Kyle*
    AAM: some AA-10 *Alamo*; some AA-11 *Archer*; some AA-
    8 *Aphid*

Paramilitary up to 20,000

Internal Security Troops up to 19,000
Ministry of Interior

National Guard 1,000
Ministry of Defence

NON-STATE ARMED GROUPS
see Part II

FOREIGN FORCES
Germany 163

CENTRAL AND SOUTH ASIA – DEFENCE ECONOMICS

Following a marked recovery in 2003, economic activity in South Asia maintained its upward momentum, recording GDP growth of 7.1% in 2004. In the second half of the year, however, the emergence of a global slowdown together with higher oil prices suggested that regional growth will weaken to around 6.5% in 2005. While the devastating December 2004 tsunami will lead to substantial reconstruction costs and corresponding fiscal challenges, particularly in Sri Lanka, the impact on growth is likely to be minimal since the affected areas accounted for a small proportion of national output and the adverse economic effects will be largely offset by rebuilding activities.

Economic growth in **India** slowed modestly from 7.5% in 2003 to 7.3% in 2004 and is projected to ease to 6.7% in 2005. The impacts of an uneven monsoon and higher oil prices were offset by buoyant industrial activity and strong investment. However, with a general government deficit of close to 10% of GDP, fiscal consolidation remains a key challenge, particularly given the ambitious social agenda set out in the government's Common Minimum Programme. Plans to address the imbalance were laid down in the 2003 Fiscal Responsibility and Budget Management Act, which outlined plans to balance the current budget by 2008, via a range of measures that will attempt to improve revenue rather than reduce expenditure.

In line with the growth in the economy, the ruling Congress Party increased India's defence budget by 7.7% from Rs890bn in 2004 to Rs958.5bn in 2005. However, given that inflation in the defence sector is probably running at around 5.5%, the increase in real terms is not sufficient to allow for any significant new acquisitions. Once again the Ministry of Defence's procurement process came in for heavy criticism with the publication of a report by India's parliamentary standing committee on defence. The committee criticised the MoD for undermining the country's military preparedness by failing to ensure that it spent all the funds allocated to it from the state budget. In the last five years, the committee revealed that 'tedious, cumbersome and time-consuming defence procurement procedures' had resulted in Rs327bn that had been allocated to capital expenditure having to be returned unspent to the Treasury due to MoD procrastination. The report also questioned the wisdom of the new Congress Party-led coalition's decision to cancel the previous government's plan to address the problem with an Rs250bn three-year non-lapsable defence modernisation fund to provide stability for procurement projects. The plan was scrapped shortly after the Congress Party assumed power following their surprise victory in the 2004 general election.

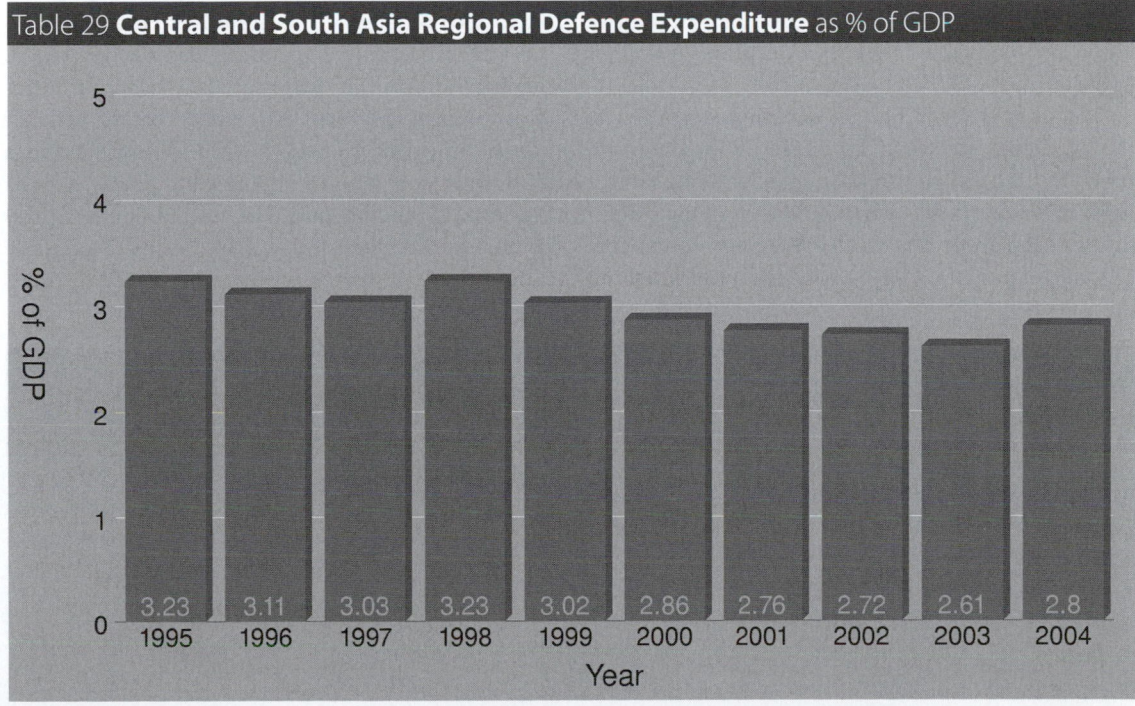

Table 29 **Central and South Asia Regional Defence Expenditure** as % of GDP

Year	1995	1996	1997	1998	1999	2000	2001	2002	2003	2004
% of GDP	3.23	3.11	3.03	3.23	3.02	2.86	2.76	2.72	2.61	2.8

Having relied historically on a mixture of foreign and domestic suppliers of military equipment, there is now a growing impetus within Indian government circles to try to increase the capacity and technical ability of the domestic defence industry with the goal of producing an increasing proportion of military equipment in India itself and moving some way towards the declared goal of achieving 70% self-reliance in defence needs. As noted, India's ability in recent years to implement much-needed acquisition programmes both domestically and overseas has been lamentable – it took 10 years to finalise the contract to purchase *Hawk* Advanced Jet Trainers and production of the domestic Light Combat Aircraft is at least a decade behind schedule. In April 2005, a panel set up by set up by Defence Minister Pranab Mukherjee, to look into ways of improving the procurement process and boosting domestic industry, issued a report recommending that the MoD establish a 15-year acquisition plan and encourage more cooperation between the military and industry. The report argued that a long-term procurement plan would help industry plan and budget for infrastructure changes and future production cycles and also suggested that a new professional agency should be established to improve the defence acquisition process. The report also included a controversial 'offset clause' suggestion which would require overseas defence suppliers to buy a certain amount of defence equipment from Indian companies or provide a certain amount of work on a contract if they wish to supply weapons to India.

The 2005 defence budget allocated Rs217.8bn to the air force, including Rs127.8bn in procurement funds to fund structured payments for its two major acquisitions in recent years: 66 BAE *Hawk* aircraft for $1.77bn and three *Phalcon* AEW aircraft for $1.1bn. The major procurement decision now facing the air force is the plan to acquire 126 combat aircraft to replace its aging fleet of MiG-21 fighters. At present the candidates to fill the requirement include Saab's *Gripen* JAS-39, RSK's MiG-29, Dassualt's *Mirage* 2000-5, Lockheed Martin's F-16 and Boeing's F/A-18E/F (this last following US approval in early 2005 for the renewed sale of fighter aircraft to India and Pakistan). However, recent history suggests that it may be several years before this decision is made, and during that time the air force intends to push ahead with the development of an indigenous Medium Combat Aircraft (MCA). Should this project move ahead successfully, before any other procurement decision is made, then it may become a contender itself for the combat aircraft requirement.

The growing importance of the domestic aerospace industry was further illustrated by two other programme developments. Firstly, following years of costly development and delays, the air force has finally ordered an initial 20 locally designed Light Combat Aircraft (LCA) for Rs20bn with an option to purchase a further 20. And secondly, the government has given approval for the development of an Indian-designed Airborne Early Warning system, likely to be based on the Embraer EMB-145 aircraft. In a separate development, India agreed terms with Qatar for the purchase of 12 used Dassualt *Mirage* 2000-5 for a sum of around $700m.

The Indian navy was allocated Rs147.8bn, up 10% on its 2004 budget and, in contrast to the other two services, procurement spending was also increased, rising by 15.7%. During the year, the navy introduced a new doctrine that called for the acquisition of a nuclear ballistic missile submarine and a blue-water fleet capable of projecting power into the Persian Gulf and beyond. The 2005 budget was also notable for specifically allocating funds to upgrade state-owned shipyards so that ship building rates

Table 30 **Indian defence budget by service/department, 2002–05**

Constant 2005 Rsbn	Outturn		Outturn		Outturn		Budget	
	2002	%	2003	%	2004	%	2005	%
Army	355.1	48.0	347.8	45.2	378.4	40.7	396.5	42.7
Navy	93.3	12.6	108.8	14.1	133.0	14.3	147.8	15.9
Air Force	137.3	18.6	148.6	19.3	240.6	25.9	217.8	23.4
R&D	35.3	4.8	36.9	4.8	41.3	4.4	53.5	5.8
Pensions	111.7	15.1	117.3	15.3	123.3	13.3	124.5	13.4
Other	7.0	0.9	9.5	1.2	12.5	1.3	18.4	2.0
Total	739.7		768.9		929.1		958.5	
% change	-4.6		4.0		20.8		3.2	

Table 31 **Indian defence budget by function, 2002–05**

Current Rsbn	2002 outurn	2003 outurn	2004 outurn	2005 budget
Personnel, Operations & Maintenance				
MoD	7.9	6.8	10.0	15.0
Defence Pensions	100.9	110.0	119.2	124.5
Army	271.9	282.7	278.2	312.4
Navy	43.6	49.1	52.9	60.3
Air Force	74.2	78.4	84.7	90.0
Defence Services-Research and Development	24.3	27.0	23.4	28.1
Defence ordnance factories	63.3	66.4	65.3	68.3
Recoveries & receipts	-66.9	-68.1	-69.8	-74.0
Sub-Total	519.2	552.3	563.9	624.6
Procurement and Construction				
Tri-Service Defence R&D	7.6	7.6	16.5	25.4
Army	48.9	43.5	87.5	84.1
Navy	40.7	52.9	75.6	87.5
Air Force	49.8	61.0	147.8	127.8
Other	2.0	3.8	6.6	9.1
Sub-Total	149	169	334	334
Total Defence Budget	668.2	721.1	897.9	958.5
Total US$bn	13.7	15.5	19.6	22.

can keep pace with naval requirements. In the past two years, 19 naval vessels have been ordered from various domestic shipyards. In addition to calling for a maritime ballistic missile capability, which many analysts see as more of long-term project, the new Indian Maritime Doctrine emphasises the increase in expeditionary capabilities that will become available with the future delivery of the MiG-29K-equipped re-fitted *Admiral Gorshkov* aircraft carrier and outlines plans for the ongoing development of the indige-nously-designed Air Defence Ship (ADS). Go ahead for the 37,500-tonne ADS was finally approved in early 2005, and it is expected to enter service in 2012. The ship will be 225m long and operate 12 MiG-29K multi-role fighters together with eight locally designed Light Combat Aircraft, *Sea Harriers* and up to 10 helicopters. Although no estimate of the final cost of the ship is available, it is thought that costs to date are in the order of Rs32bn.

As the largest of the three services, the Indian army received Rs396.5bn, nearly 43% of the total budget. In recent years the army has noted that the 'combat ratio', a capability measure used by India to deter-mine its military advantage over Pakistan, has fallen to 1.22:1 compared to a high of 1.75:1 in the mid-1970s. As a result, the army is keen to acquire a whole range of weapons systems, from artillery systems to electronic warfare capabilities, and has suggested that

it will require an additional $5bn over the next five years to fulfil its requirements.

Continuing the trend towards local procurement outlined above, the MoD announced that it was dramatically downsizing the number of multi-role hel that it intends to buy from the international market in order to buy local aircraft instead. Originally, the army had indicated a requirement for 198 helicop-ters, primarily for use on the Siachen glacier and in the Kargil area; however, the requirement will now be met by the indigenous Light Combat Helicopter project and just 35 aircraft will be procured internationally.

The relative stability of the internal and external security situation helped **Pakistan** record another year of solid growth. Real GDP increased by a healthy 6.5% in 2004, while fiscal adjustments – supported by official inflows and debt relief - have led to a substan-tial improvement in public and external debt posi-tions. The Asian Development Bank has expressed confidence that sound macro-economic fundamen-tals, together with reforms successfully implemented in the past 5 years, will lead to annual growth of over 7% in the medium term.

The government's improving economic fortunes allowed for a 15% increase in the 2005 defence budget, which rose from Rs194bn in 2004 to Rs223bn. In addition to the allocation from the state budget, the Pakistan armed forces will also receive an additional

$148m in 2005, rising to $300m in 2006, via the United States Foreign Military Financing programme. It is likely that the army's anti-terrorist operations on the western border may push final 2004 defence outlays as high as Rs216bn against the original Rs194 budget.

The most significant development in Pakistan during the past year was the decision by the US government to approve the sale of F-16 aircraft to the Pakistan Air Force (PAF). The PAF already has about 30 older F-16s and had arranged to buy 71 further aircraft in 1988, before Congress quashed the move in 1995 following the disclosure that Pakistan was developing a nuclear weapons programme. It is believed that Pakistan has already set aside $800m for the purchase of an initial 25 aircraft and additional purchases cannot be ruled out. Another longstanding aerospace requirement appears to have been filled with the selection of the Swedish *Erieye* airborne early warning and control radar system. Although a final decision on the number of platforms and a contract

price is yet to be agreed, it is thought that Pakistan would like to acquire up to seven Saab 2000 aircraft fitted with the *Erieye* radar. Naval developments were highlighted by the signing of a contract with China for the supply of four F-22P frigates. The first ship will be built in China; work on the second will be shared while the final two platforms will be built in Pakistan.

The **Nepalese** Ministry of Defence proposed a budget of R18bn for 2005/6, more than double the budget of the previous year. Although the hike in the budget is likely to be reduced during negotiations with the Ministry of Finance, to a figure probably closer to R12–13bn, the MoD has indicated that it is seeking annual budget increases of at least 10% over the next three years. The additional funding is needed to finance the army's plan to recruit an additional 13,000 men in the near future and to buy hel and other equipment. The new recruitment is being planned to form corps in eastern and western development regions.

Table 32 **Arms orders and deliveries, Central and South Asia**

Country Supplier	Classification	Designation	Quantity	Order date	Delivery date	Comment
Bangladesh (Bng) Cz		L-39ZA (*Albatros*)	4	1999	2000	Following delivery of 8 in 1995
India (Ind) dom	SSN	ATV	1	1982	2007	
dom	SSM	*Prithvi* MK II	100	1983		Naval variant aka *Danush*, still on trial
dom	MRBM	*Agni-2*	5	1983	2000	Range 2,000km; under test
dom	SLCM	*Sagrika*		1983	2003	300km range. May be ballistic
dom	MRBM	*Agni-3*	50	1983	2012	Air force variant
dom	FGA	LCA		1983	2012	
dom	hel	ALH	12	1984	2000	Tri-service requirement for 300 Delivery may slip to 2001
dom	DD	*Delhi*	3	1986	1997	1st in 1997, 2nd in 1998, 3rd in 2001
dom	FFG	*Brahmaputra*	3	1989	2000	Last delivered in 2004
dom	FSG	*Kora*	4	1990	1998	4th delivered in 2001
dom	LST	*Magar*	3	1991	1997	1 more under construction
dom	UAV	*Nishant*	14	1991	1999	Dev. 3 prototypes built. 14 pre- prod units on order
dom	AGHS	*Sandhayak*	8	1995	1999	All operational
RF	ASSM	SS-N-25 (*Switchblade*)	16	1996	1997	Deliveries continue
Il	PFC	*Super Dvora* MKII	5	1996	1998	3 delivered
RF	FGA	MiG-21bis (*Fishbed L & N*)	125	1996	2001	Upgrades
RF	FGA	Su-30 MKI (*Flanker*)	32	1996	2001	To be completed by 2003
UK	trg	*Harrier* T MK4	2	1997	1999	2 ex-RN ac for delivery 1999
RF	hel	KA-31 (*Helix B*)	12	1997	2001	To operate from *Krivak* III frigates
RF	MPA	P-3C (*Orion*)	3	1997	2002	All operational

Table 32 Arms orders and deliveries, Central and South Asia

	Country Supplier	Classification	Designation	Quantity	Order date	Delivery date	Comment
	UK	FGA	GR3 (*Jaguar*)	18	1998	2001	Potential upgrade for up to 60
	RF	ASSM	SS-N-27 (*Club*)		1998	2004	For *Krivak* 3 frigate. First export
	RF	FGA	MiG-29K (*Fulcrum D*)	24	1999		Possibly 60. To equip CV *Gorshkov*
	dom	MPA	DO-228	7	1999		Deliveries completed by 2003
	Pl	trg	PZL TS-11 (*Iskra*)	12	1999	2000	Option on 8 more
	dom	CV	*Viraat*	1	1999	2001	Upgrade (ex-UK *Hermes*)
	RF	AAM	*Astra*	125	1999	2002	Upgrade. Fr and Il avionics
	dom	MBT	*Arjun*	124	1999	2002	Low-rate production May not enter service as an MBT
	dom	trg	HJT-36	200	1999	2004	
	RF	CV	*Admiral Gorshkov*	1	1999	2008	Memo. of understanding signed. Oprl date 2008
	dom	ICBM	*Surya*		1999	2012	Dev. 1st test planned Jul 1999
	RF	MBT	T-90	310	2000		186 to be built in Ind. 124 delivered by 2004
	RF	hel	Mi-171	40	2000	2001	
	RF	FGA	Su-30 MKI (*Flanker*)	140	2000	2002	Licensed Production
	RF	recce	Tu-142M (*Bear F*)	8	2000	2002	Upgrades
	Fr	FGA	M-2000 (*Mirage*)	10	2000	2003	Originally approved 1996
	Il	hel	Mi-8 (*Hip*)	80	2001		Upgrades
	dom	FGA	MiG-27M (*Flogger J2*)	40	2001	2004	Upgrades
	RF	SSK	*Sindhughosh*	2	2002	2005	($160m) Upgrade (3rd in class to be upgraded - *Sindhugosh* completed 2005 another due to start May 2005.
	dom	MBT	T-72 VT	1300	2003		To be complete by 2005
	Q	FGA	M-2000-5 (*Mirage*)	12	2003		
	Fr	SSK	*Scorpene*	6	2003	2010	(First hull)
	Pl	ARV	WZT-3	228	2004	2004	Delivery thorugh to 2005
	Il	AEW	IAI-707 (*Phalcon*)	3	2004	2007	
	RF	FGA	MiG-29K (*Fulcrum D*)	16	2004	2008	($740m) incl 4 two seat MiG-29KUB. To equip INS *Vitramaditya* (ex CV *Gorshkov*). First delivery expected 2007 order complete by 2009.
Kazakhstan (Kaz)	RF	FGA	Su-27 (*Flanker*)	16	1997	1999	+ Su-27 & Su-29 exch. for 40 Tu-95M
	RF	SAM	SA-10 (*Grumble (quad)*)		1997	2000	
	Ind	hel	Mi-8 (*Hip*)	2	2001	2001	
Pakistan (Pak)	dom	sat	*Badr 1*				Multi-purpose sat. In operation.
	dom	sat	*Badr 2*				Development
	dom	sat	*Badr 2*		1993		Dev. Range 3,000km. Based on *Taepo-dong* 2
	dom	MRBM	*Hatf 6*		1993	1999	Dev. Range 2-3,000km. Test 4/99 Aka *Hatf* 6
	PRC	FGA	FC-1 (*Xiaolong*)	150	1993	2006	In co-development with PRC
	Fr	SSK	*Khalid*	3	1994	1999	1st in 1999, 2nd 2003, 3rd 2005
	dom	SSM	*Shaheen 2*		1994	1999	In prod mid-1999. Range 750km. Based on M-9. Aka *Hatf* 4

Table 32 Arms orders and deliveries, Central and South Asia

Country Supplier	Classification	Designation	Quantity	Order date	Delivery date	Comment
dom	PFM	*Larkana*	1	1996	1997	Commissioned 14 Aug 1997. 2 more planned.
PRC	FGA	F-7MG (*Airguard*)	30-50	1999	2002	Stop gap until S-7 completed
PRC	tpt	CN-235–220	4	2001	2008	
RF	hel	Mi-171	12	2002	2003	
LAR	FGA	*Mirage 5D*	40	2004	2004	
RF	FGA	MiG-23UB (*Flogger C*)	2		2000	
RF	FGA	MiG-27M (*Flogger J2*)	4		2001	

Pakistan
Forces included:

Sri Lanka:

• 6x C-130 flights • AORH PNS *Moawin*, a supply ship w/ 2x *Sea King* (then to Indonesia) • FFGH PNS *Khaibar*, a guided missile destroyer w/ 1x *Alouette* (then to Indonesia)

On goodwill mission to Maldives when Tsunami struck:
• FFGH PNS *Tariq* w/ helo • AORH PNS *Nasr* (supply ship w/ helo) • 1x C-130 flight

UK: *Operation Garron*
Forces included:

• Liaison and Reconnaissance Teams to Sri Lanka, Indonesia and Thailand • 1x FFGH (HMS *Chatham* + 2x *Lynx*) • 1x ARH RFA *Diligence* • 1x AGSH HMS *Scott* • 2x C-17 • 1x *Tristar* KC-1 • 2x Bell 212 (from Brunei) • Medical and engineering personnel

France: *Operation Beryx*
Forces included: • CVHG *Jeanne d'Arc* (1x *Alouette*; 2x *Gazelle*; 2x *Puma*) • DDGHM *Georges Leygues* (1x *Alouette*) • DDGH *Dupleix* (w/ *Lynx*) - Maldives • Command and Replenishment Ship *La Marne* (w/ *Alouette*) off Meulaboh • 7x *Puma* based at Sabang • 2x C-160 *Transall* based at Medan • 1x *Atlantique* 2 at Surat Thani in Thailand • 1x *Fennec* off Thailand • 1x A-310 • 1x C-135

Bangladesh: *Operation SAARC Bandhan*
Forces included: • Medical and engineering teams • 2 x C-130 • 3 Bell -212 • BNS *Turag*, BNS *Sangu* to Sri Lanka and the Maldives

Canada: *Operation Structure*
Forces included: • Disaster Assistance Response Team (DART) - to eastern Sri Lanka

Belgium *Operation Tsunami Solidarity*
Forces included: • Army, naval, aviation and medical specialists (to Sri Lanka) • 1xA-310

India
Forces included:

Indian mainland: *Operation Madad*

• Various elements of the Indian army • Various elements of the Indian air force • LSM INS *Sharabh*, DDGHM INS *Ranjit* w/ Ka-28 Helix, DDGHM INS *Ranvijay* w/Ka-28 *Helix*, PC INS SDB-57, AGS INS *Mithun*, FSGHM INS *Khukri* w/*Chetak*, FSGHM INS *Khanjar* w/*Chetak*, various helo and fixed-wing a/c, varying small craft • ICG aviationL 747,800, 848 sqn

Sri Lanka (*Operation Rainbow*): • Army FD HOSP, ENGR teams • 5x Mi-17 and Mi-8; 2x Il-76, 1x Do-228 a/c, 1x *Islander* a/c • AORH INS *Aditya* (1x helo, medical and dive teams), also to Maldives • FFH INS *Taragiri* w/ helo • PSOH CGS *Samar* (w/ helo) • AGSH INS *Sandhayak* (hospital ship) • PSOH INS *Sukanya* • FSGSM Corvette INS *Kirch* (w/ *Chetak*), LST INS *Ghorpad* and LCU 33 • AGSH INS Sutlej (w/ *chetak*) • PSOH INS *Sharada* • AGSH INS *Jamuna* (hospital ship w/ *Chetak*) • AGSH INS *Nirdeshak* (w/ helo and divers) • AGSH INS *Sarvekshak* (hospital ship w/ *Chetak*) • LCU-33

The Maldives (*Operation Castor*): Two mobile surgical teams, communications assistance and general reconstruction assistance
• Mi-17 helo flights • DDGHM INS *Mysore* • FFH INS *Udaygiri* • PSOH CGS *Sagar* • PSOH CGS *Vigraha*

Transport aircraft: • Il-76 flights • Coastguard Do-228 • 2x IAF BAe-748

Andaman and Nicobar Islands *Operation Sea Waves*

• Bde HQ, engineers, medical, infantry and logistics staff • IAF Il-76, IAF Do-228, An-32, Mi-8 • LST INS *Gharial* w/*Sea King* and LCVP • LST INS *Magar* w/*Sea King* and LCVP • DDGHM INS *Rajput* w/Ka-28 *Helix* • FFGHM INS *Brahmaputra* w/helo • AO INS *Jyoti* • LSM INS *Kumbhir* • LSM INS *Cheetah* • AGSH INS *Sandhayak* (hospital ship – also to Sri Lanka) • AGSH INS *Darshak* • PCO INS *Trinkat* • PCO INS *Tillanchang* • LCU-32, -34, -35, -38, -39 • ICGS *Kanaklata Barua*, ICGS *Vivek* w/ *Chetak* • ICGS *Bikhaji Cama* • ICGS *Akka devi* • ICGS *Ganga Devi* • elements of 745 Sqn ICG (Do-228 and *Cheetak* helos)

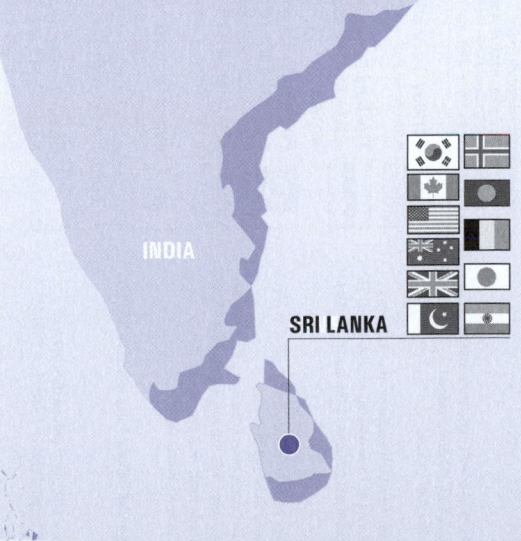

INDIA

SRI LANKA

ANDAMAN ISLANDS

NICOBAR ISLANDS

MALDIVES

Worst-affected districts

Central and South Asia

© IISS

© IISS

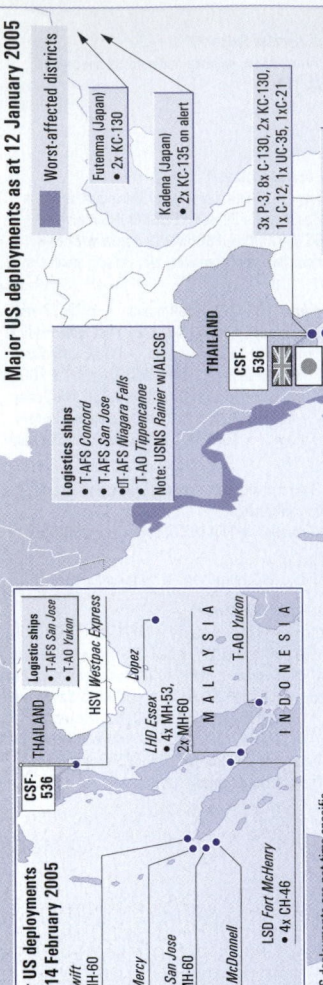

Major US deployments as at 12 January 2005

- Worst-affected districts

Futema (Japan) • 2x KC-130
Kadena (Japan) • 2x KC-135 on alert
3x P-3, 8x C-130, 2x KC-130, 1x C-12, 1x UC-35, 1x C-21
T-AGS McDonnell ETA Singapore 13 Jan
Martin, Hauge, Anderson
4x CH-46, 4x C,2, 2x C-130 (USCG)

Logistics ships
- T-AFS Concord
- T-AFS San Jose
- T-AFS Niagara Falls
- T-AO Tippecanoe
- Note: USNS Rainier w/ALCSG

HSV Westpac Express

JAKARTA 4 x C-130

5 x MC-130
BUTTERWORTH AIR BASE
MALAYSIA
SINGAPORE
INDONESIA
MEDAN
THAILAND
SURAT THANI — CSF-536
PHUKET
BELAWAN
LHOKSEUMAWE
SABANG
BANDA ACEH
MEULABOH
T-AFS San Jose
T-AFS Niagara Falls
2x MH-60
T-AO Tippecanoe

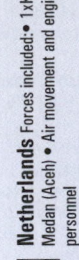
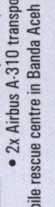

Major US deployments as at 14 February 2005

HSV Swift • 2x MH-60
T-AH Mercy
T-AFS San Jose • 2x MH-60
T-AGS McDonnell
LSD Fort McHenry • 4x CH-46

THAILAND CSF-536

Logistic ships
- T-AFS San Jose
- T-AO Yukon

HSV Westpac Express
Lopez
LHD Essex • 4x MH-53, 2x MH-60
T-AO Yukon
MALAYSIA
INDONESIA

- Non-US deployments are not time-specific
- Other nations not detailed may also have furnished valuable assistance
- CSG: Carrier Strike Group
- ESG: Expeditionary Strike Group

T-AFS Concord
LSD Fort McHenry • 4x CH-46

CSG AL
- CVN Lincoln (10x SH-60)
- CG Shiloh (2x SH-60)
- DDG Shoup (2x SH-60)
- DDG Benfold
- T-AGE Rainier (2x MH-60)

MPS Pless
CSG A. Lincoln
ESG B. Richard

ESG BHR
- LHD Bonhomme Richard (18x helos)
- LPD Duluth (3x CH-46) • LSD Rushmore
- DDG Milius • CG Bunker Hill (2x SH-60)
- FFG Thach (2x SH-60) • WHEC Munro

MEULABOH

Diego Garcia • 3x P-3

US *Operation Unified Assistance.* US assets were deployed from Hawaii, South Korea and Japan, as well as from the US and forces afloat, and included army, navy, air force, marine corps and coast guard personnel. Marines were deployed from III Marine Division, out of Okinawa, while in Sri Lanka, marines from the 7th Marine Expeditionary Support Battalion and sailors from the 7th Seabee Battalion provided engineering support. At 12 January 2005, the US had 15,455 personnel participating in *Operation Unified Assistance.* By the time CSF-536 ceased operations in tsunami-affected countries, on 14 February, US forces had drawn down to 683 personnel.

Australia and New Zealand *Operation Sumatra Assist*
Forces included: • LPD HMAS *Kanimbla* with 2x *Sea King* and 2x army LCM8 landing craft • 8x C-130 *Hercules* (2 from New Zealand); 4 in-theatre and 2 as air bridge between Darwin and Sumatra • 150 army engineers and equipment • Logistics personnel; water purification plant • ATC personnel • ANZAC field hospital (with New Zealand personnel) • 4x UH-1 *Iroquois* helo at Banda Aceh • 1x Boeing 707; 1x Boeing 757; 1x Beech 350 *King Air*

Mexico *Operación Fraternidad Internacional* Forces included: • LST ARM *Usumacinta* w/ Mi-17 helo (-to Banda Aceh), LST ARM *Papaloapan* (Belawan, Sumatra), ARM *Zapoteco* w/ Bo-105 helo (– to Lhokseumawe) w/Mexican army personnel

Switzerland Forces included: • 3 x Puma helicopters and around 50 personnel to Sumatra (Meulaboh)

Brunei *Operation Badai Berlalu* Forces included: • Around 50 personnel from Royal Brunei Armed Forces to Aceh • 2x Black Hawk • 1x CN-235 aircraft

Malaysia Forces included: • Over 400 pers, army assets, 2x S-61 helo, CN-235, several C-130, KD *Mahawangsa* and KD *Sri Indera Sakti*, KD *Musytari* to Aceh

Indonesia Forces included: • PACOM estimates that Indonesia deployed 28 ships, 2 helicopters and 15 fixed-wing aviation types. The TNI deployed various army, naval and air units to the region, on top of forces already in Aceh.

Singapore *Operation Flying Eagle* Forces included: • 1,057 in Medan (with OC Ops, Cdr 21 Div), Banda Aceh and Meulaboh
North Sumatra: Ships: • 3x LST *Endurance, Endeavour, Persistence*
Aircraft: • 6x CH-47D *Chinook* • 2x *Super Puma* • C-130 *Hercules*/Fokker 50: 76 missions • 2x fd hosp at Meulaboh and Banda Aceh • 2 engr teams (heavy equipment) • 2x ATC coordination teams (Medan, Banda Aceh) • 1x mobile ATC tower (Banda Aceh)
Phuket, Thailand: • 121, incl 80 Singapore Civil Defence Force and some SAF (2x *Super Puma*).

India (domestic response) Forces included: Indonesia (Operation *Gambhir*): • AGSH INS *Nirupak* (hospital ship w/ *Chetak*) • FSGHM Corvette INS *Khukri*

Norway Forces included: • 2xC-130 (Singapore)
• Around 50 Pers – in Indonesia, Sri Lanka and Thailand

Thailand Forces included: • 7x C-130 flights • PACOM estimates 7 vessels deployed, including CV HTMS Chakrinaruebet, assorted aviation incl C-130 and various helo types

Pakistan Forces included: Indonesia • 7x C-130 flights • 250-strong team deployed in 1x field hospital in Lammo (80km SW of Banda Aceh); naval medical facility in Samolanga (75km west of Lhokseumawe) and other locations • AORH PNS *Moawin*, a supply ship w/ 2x *Sea King* • FFGH PNS *Khaibar*, a guided missile destroyer w/ 1x *Alouette*

Japan Forces included: **Offshore Thailand** • 2x DDGHM *Kirishima* and *Takanami*; • AOE *Hamana* **Offshore Aceh** • LPD *Kunisaki* • DDHM *Kurama* • Medical units in Banda Aceh • 3x CH-47 • 2x UH-60JA • AOE *Tokiwa* • 2x LCAC • 1x C-130 • 1 x SH60-J • 1x C-130

Spain *Operación Respuesta Solidaria.* Forces included: LPD *Galicia* with 3x Agusta Bell 212, dive teams, 2x landing craft a field hospital and assorted medical and reconstruction materials • 3x C-235 • 2x C-130

Netherlands Forces included: • 1xKDC-10 – Medan (Aceh) • Air movement and engineering personnel

Germany Forces included: • 1x AORH *Berlin* – outfitted as hospital ship with 2x *Sea King* • 2x Airbus A-310 transport a/c • Mobile rescue centre in Banda Aceh

South Korea Forces included: • 1x C-130 to Sri Lanka • 2xLST (*Birobong* to Colombo, Sri Lanka; *Hyangrobong* to Banda Aceh)

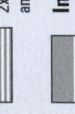

Chapter Six
East Asia and Australasia

EAST AND NORTH-EAST ASIA

The modernisation and reform of **China**'s armed forces, challenging the US and its allies, is one of the main defence and security issues in east and northeast Asia. Washington has had concerns about the growth in Chinese military power for some time. The US Department of Defense Report 'The Military Power of the People's Republic of China', released 19 July 2005, demonstrated Washington's concern at what it sees as a Chinese military build-up, not only directed towards Taiwan, but also aimed at developing force projection capabilities beyond Chinese waters.

However, this concern was not, initially, mirrored in Europe, and the European Union (EU) was fully prepared to lift the embargo on sales of arms and equipment to Beijing, imposed after the Tiananmen Square incident in 1989. Nevertheless, opposition to the lifting of the embargo recently increased following US pressure and a greater realisation in EU member states of the possible dangers of allowing China access to certain technologies. Moreover, the anti-secession law passed by the National People's Congress in March, which allows the use of force following a declaration of independence by Taiwan, also caused some European governments to change their view on the lifting of the embargo.

Before the release of the Pentagon's report, US Secretary of Defense Donald Rumsfeld, speaking at the IISS *Shangri-la Dialogue* in Singapore in June, said that China's increased military spending threatens stability in the Asia-Pacific region. He also said that 'China appears to be expanding its missile forces, allowing them to reach targets in many areas in the world'. Following this statement, it was reported that China had tested a new long-range submarine-launched ballistic missile (SLBM) on 16 June. The *Ju Lang-2* missile, which is believed to be a sea-launched version of the *Dong Feng-31*, was said to have achieved an estimated range of 8,000km, thus allowing Chinese missiles to reach areas of the continental US from China's littoral waters.

As a sign that reform of the Chinese armed forces is a priority for Beijing, the Central Military Commission (CMC) underwent a far-reaching re-shuffle following the resignation of former President Jiang Zemin from the chairmanship in September 2004. Furthermore, in an unprecedented move, President Hu Jintao appointed three military officers to the committee – Admiral Zhang Dingfa, the commander of the People's Liberation Army Navy (PLAN), the commander of the People's Liberation Army Air Force (PLAAF), and the commander of the Second Artillery. Subsequently, in December 2004, the new CMC issued its annual defence policy statement which laid out the main areas for modernisation.

Although Beijing has established links with Taiwanese opposition parties, another focus of the CMC policy was emphasised by a statement that relations with **Taiwan** are 'grim'. Consequently, a Chinese strategy of deploying overwhelming missile superiority against the island has developed. In addition to the DF-11 missiles deployed in Jiangxi province, and the DF-15 missiles in Fujian, Taipei estimates that, by 2006, there will be an additional 200 land-attack cruise missiles deployed, giving a total of some 1,000 missiles ranged against the island. In response, Taiwan is reported to have test-fired a cruise missile, *Hsiung Feng*, in Spring 2005, and the Taiwanese defence ministry is basing its future missile defence on the purchase of PAC-3 systems; but these will not come into service until 2012. Moreover, China is believed to be developing 'smart' systems to counter any ballistic defence missile systems that Taiwan might deploy. So-called *Shashoujian* weaponry aims to give the People's Liberation Army (PLA) a lead over the US and its regional allies in missile technology.

As the PLA starts its 11th Five Year Defence Plan, transformation draws on lessons from coalition operations in Iraq and Afghanistan, particularly in the areas of information and cyber warfare. It is expected that eight new surveillance satellites – four HJ1A/B electro-optical satellites and 4 HJ1C radar satellites – will be launched between 2006 and 2008. Moreover, as a partner in the European 'Galileo' project, and with its own analogous projects, China is building an extensive navigation satellite system.

Meanwhile, enhancements in the ground forces are concentrated on amphibious, special forces and airborne formations. In particular, a second Airborne

Army may be formed, whilst the first Airborne Army is receiving a new type of armoured vehicle which can be dropped by parachute.

The PLAAF is due to receive more aircraft from Russia, in particular Su-30MKK and Su-27 fighter aircraft. And the PLAN is due to acquire more amphibious assault ships, fast-attack craft, and two Project 965EM missile destroyers equipped with the *Moskit* anti-ship missile system which will enhance the anti-ship capability already available on the Russian *Sovremenny*-class destroyers equipped with SSN-22 *Sunburn* missiles. Moreover, as a sign of the importance of the submarine fleet in Beijing's strategy, the PLAN is to bring some eight new Russian *Kilo*-class SSKs equipped with SS-N-27 missiles into service in the next two years; and there are developments in the SSN fleet with the introduction of the Type 093 expected in 2005. A further indication of the priority which is given to the submarine fleet was the appointment of a nuclear submariner, Rear Admiral Sun Jianguo, as Chief of the Naval Staff in January 2005. The commander of the PLAN, Admiral Zhang Dingfa, is also a submariner.

Russia remains the main defence partner for China, not just in the supply of new equipment, but also, increasingly, as a regional security partner. Working through the Shanghai Cooperation Organisation (SCO), both countries seek to extend their influence in Central Asia, and to curb US influence in the region. Moreover, from 18 to 25 August 2005, exercise *Peace Mission 2005* was the first bilateral joint training exercise to have taken place involving forces of both countries. Some 10,000 Russian and PLA military personnel took part in the exercise on the Shandong Peninsula.

Meanwhile, as **China** builds its relationship with Russia, its relations with **Japan** have deteriorated. Anti-Japanese protests started in China in March and led to calls by Tokyo for an official apology, which was not forthcoming. The cause of the anti-Japanese sentiment appears to be Japanese Prime Minister Junichiro Koizumi's annual visit to the Yakuzuni shrine (a memorial to the war dead), seen by Beijing as a sign that Japan is unrepentant for its war record. However, this public argument can be seen against the wider regional political background with China's economic and military development increasingly challenging Japan's position in the region, its aspiration to membership of the UN Security Council, and its close alliance with the US – another competitor for China in the Asia-Pacific region.

In what was seen as an act of provocation, on 10 November 2004 a Chinese *Han*-class submarine entered Japanese territorial waters near Taramajima island. Subsequently, on 16 November, Beijing apologised for the incident, which had resulted in Tokyo declaring a 'maritime security operation' for only the second time since 1945. However, the incident highlighted the increasing activity of the PLAN in the region.

The naming of **China** as a possible threat in **Japan's** bold *National Defense Program Guideline for FY 2005 and After* an official document published by Tokyo in December 2004, further exacerbated tensions between the two countries. Prior to this, in October, there were indications that Japan would join the US Missile Defence Initiative (MDI), and in November 2004 the US agreed to the Japanese production of the PAC-3 interceptor by Mitsubishi Heavy Industries, due to start in 2006. The deployment of land-based PAC-3 systems as part of a layered ballistic missile defence system could start in 2008 to be followed by the deployment of *Aegis* sea-based systems.

At the centre of the defence debate in Japan is Article 9 of the Constitution, which restricts the deployment of the Self-Defense Forces (SDF) on operations. At a time when there is increasing pressure to take part in operations overseas, the restrictions are increasingly difficult to reconcile with the international role Japan envisages for itself as an aspirant member of the UN Security Council.

As an example of the difficulties caused by Article 9 conditions, the Iraq Reconstruction Special Measures Law, passed in August 2003, authorised the Japanese Ground Self-Defense Forces (JGSDF) to deploy on a non-combatant mission in Samawah, but the law has to be renewed in December 2005, and a decision in favour of extending the JGSDF mandate will depend on the security situation. At the same time, the coalition in Iraq is considering handing over areas of the country, including Samawah, to Iraqi security forces – a fact that will bear heavily on the decision of the Diet whether to extend the mandate.

However, the *National Defense Program Guideline for FY 2005 and After* indicated a shift in defence thinking. The relationship with the US is to be strengthened with commonly agreed objectives, technology exchange, joint training and information-sharing amongst the areas to be developed. Indicating the way forward, the SDF participated in the *Cobra Gold 2005* exercise held in Thailand between 2 and 13 May 2005, the first time its ground forces have joined a multilateral training event.

As part of the growing strategic relationship, a US Army corps headquarters is to be re-located from Washington State to Kanagawa Prefecture. Meanwhile, the future re-alignment of US forces in Japan, which currently number some 41, 000, is under review, with the emphasis on Okinawa Prefecture, where 75% of the US force is stationed.

US base re-alignment plans in **South Korea** have caused civil protest. On 10 July 2005 the US military's plan to expand its Camp Humphrey base at Pyongtaek met with opposition by some 12,000 locals and anti-war activists demanding the withdrawal of US troops from the country; and plans to build bases for the future deployment of PAC-3 missiles on the west coast met with more demonstrations. But with the re-alignment moving troops and bases away from the centre of Seoul – the main focus of anti-US sentiment – it is hoped that there will be less protest.

In September 2004 the US deployed F-117 stealth fighter-bombers, and a squadron of F-15E fighter-bombers, to South Korea to exercise its capability to respond to a crisis on the Korean Peninsula. Another deployment from the continental US took place in March 2005 when some 17,000 troops deployed on Exercise *Foal Eagle*. The exercise is an annual joint training event, with US and South Korean forces, to test defensive plans against an invasion from North Korea.

South Korea is planning to use robots to enhance its ability to secure its border with North Korea, and to carry out better surveillance of the 240-km-long and 4-km-wide Demilitarised Zone (DMZ). A study to examine the feasibility of the project, believed to cost some $2bn, is to be completed this year; and, if a decision to develop the systems is taken, they could be deployed in 2011.

Following the third round of six-party talks in June 2004, the process of persuading **North Korea** to give up its nuclear programme through negotiation stalled. Pyongyang persistently accused the Bush administration of adopting a 'hostile policy' and said it would not return to negotiation until this ceased. Moreover, the announcement by the International Atomic Energy Agency (IAEA) in August 2004 that South Korea had carried out uranium enrichment experiments in the past had the potential to further exacerbate the situation. However, in the event, the IAEA's inspection report on the South Korean experiments prevented the issue becoming a significant factor in the context of the North Korean question.

In January 2005 North Korea announced that it was prepared to re-start talks on its nuclear programme. However, following US Secretary of State Condoleezza Rice's naming of North Korea as 'an outpost of tyranny' in February 2005, Pyongyang once again declared that it was not prepared to negotiate, and announced on 10 February that it had constructed nuclear weapons, and would suspend its participation in the six-party talks indefinitely.

In April 2005 Seoul expressed concern that North Korea had shut down the Yongbyon reactor, which could allow more nuclear material to be extracted for its weapons programme. On 11 May, Pyongyang confirmed that this was happening and that it had completed extraction of spent fuel rods in order to increase its nuclear arsenal. In a further act of provocation, North Korea fired a short-range missile into the Sea of Japan on the eve of a meeting of members of the International Non-Proliferation Treaty (NPT) on 1 May.

However, on 16 May North and South Korea held their first bilateral talks for nearly a year against the background of a growing food crisis in the north, which resulted in a request by Pyongyang for food aid from Seoul. At the same time, North Korea was preparing to announce its readiness to return to negotiation; and on 25 July 2005 the fourth round of the six-party talks started in Beijing, to be adjourned after 13 days with very little sign of meaningful progress, and with no agreement on establishing a framework for negotiation despite numerous draft documents submitted by China. However, there was agreement to re-convene in September 2005

SOUTHEAST ASIA AND AUSTRALASIA

During 2004–05, several Southeast Asian states' armed forces remained focussed on low-intensity operations against insurgent groups. In **Indonesia**, although the government had ended martial law in the province of Aceh in May 2004, replacing it with a 'civil emergency', the armed separatist movement Gerakan Aceh Merdeka (GAM) continued to challenge Jakarta's rule. After being elected Indonesia's president in September 2004, Susilo Bambang Yudhoyono (a retired general) expressed his determination to end the conflict. Although at the time there seemed little immediate prospect of negotiations, the outlook for peace improved in the wake of the tsunami that devastated Aceh in late December 2004. The Indonesian armed forces quickly resumed counter-insurgency operations despite the reported loss of thousands of military personnel in the natural disaster, but international donors of relief and reconstruction aid persuaded the Indonesian government and GAM to recommence peace negotiations. After five rounds of talks brokered by a Finnish NGO in Helsinki between late January and mid-July 2005, the two sides agreed a memorandum of understanding aimed at ending hostilities and scheduled to be signed on 15 August. The memorandum covered the ending of armed activities by GAM and the withdrawal of Indonesian troops, apart from garrison forces, from Aceh. While this appeared to indicate a breakthrough, the key question of whether or not the settlement would allow GAM participation in provincial politics was apparently still undecided, and it remained to be seen whether the Indonesian armed forces and GAM field commanders would support the agreement's implementation. However, on 15 August GAM rebels and the Indonesian government signed the peace accord as planned, ending over 30 years of conflict in Aceh. According to the peace agreement, Aceh will have local self-government and up to 70% of the revenue from Aceh's natural resources. Additionally, the Indonesian government agreed to allow Aceh to establish local political parties and to withdraw some 30,000 Tentara Nasional Indonesia (TNI) troops from the province. In return, GAM agreed to disarm and demobilise some 3,000 rebels. Meanwhile, the European Union and Association of Southeast Asian Nations (ASEAN) have sent representatives to Aceh to monitor the implementation of the peace accord. In the southern **Philippines** in October 2004, an international monitoring team comprising 50 Malaysian and 10 Bruneian military observers, commanded by a Malaysian major-general, deployed to Mindanao in support of the fragile ceasefire between the Armed Forces of the Philippines (AFP) and the Moro Islamic Liberation Front (MILF). In December, a small number of Libyans joined the team. However, along with continuing disagreement over the political format of any settlement, alleged links between MILF elements on the one hand and terrorist groups – notably Jemaah Islamiah (JI) and the Abu Sayyaf Group (ASG) - on the other, continued to complicate the peace process. The AFP mounted airstrikes against the severely depleted ASG and its JI associates in November 2004 and January 2005, but failed to eliminate its leadership. In February, an attack by the renegade 'Nur Misuari faction' of the Moro National Liberation Front provoked a major 'punitive action' by the AFP, which subdued the rebellion. In late July 2005, a ninth round of peace talks between the government and

the MILF was postponed, against the background of a renewed AFP offensive (reportedly supported by US special forces) aimed at capturing or killing ASG leader Khadaffy Janjalani and his followers, as well as a major political crisis in Manila threatening the position of President Gloria Macapagal-Arroyo.

While there appeared to be some prospect of peaceful settlements in Aceh and the southern Philippines, the situation in southern **Thailand** deteriorated and it became clear that the wave of violence that began in early 2004 indicated a new upsurge in separatist activism by Malay-Muslim groups including the Gerakan Mujahideen Islam Pattani (Pattani Islamic Warriors' Movement). During 2004-05, there were frequent lethal attacks on Thai security forces, officials and ordinary Buddhist citizens. Heavy-handedness on the part of the Thai security forces, evident in the 'Tak Bai incident' in October 2004 when almost 80 Muslim demonstrators died after being 'stacked like bricks' in army trucks, did little to bring the growing conflict under control. In order to boost military strength in the south while enhancing the army's capacity for hearts-and-minds operations, in February 2005 the Thai cabinet authorised the reactivation of the 15th Infantry Division. In July 2005, by which time almost 900 people had been killed over the previous 17 months, the government declared an emergency zone, covering Narathiwat, Yala and Pattani provinces, together with four districts in neighbouring Songkhla province, in which it would have the power to conduct search and arrest operations without warrants, tap phones, impose curfews, ban public gatherings, censor news, restrict travel and expel foreigners.

Separatist insurgency continued to challenge the authority of **Myanmar**'s State Peace and Development Council (SPDC) regime. The ousting of the relatively pragmatic chief of military intelligence (MI) and prime minister, General Khin Nyunt, in October 2004, followed by the subsequent purge of the MI apparatus, threatened to worsen the internal security situation. From 1989, Khin Nyunt had negotiated ceasefires in border regions with 17 ethnic minority insurgent groups including the United Wa State Army (UWSA), the Kachin Independence Organisation and the New Mon State Army. Some 'ceasefire groups', including the UWSA and the Democratic Karen Buddhist Army (DKBA), even agreed to fight alongside the regime's forces. In return for halting their open rebellions, the ceasefire groups were allowed to keep their weapons, control territory and operate business concessions with extensive cross-border trade. Approximately two dozen insurgent groups continued their rebellions; though, at the time of Khin Nyunt's removal, a delegation from the Karen National Union, the oldest and largest ethnic rebel group, was in Yangon for ceasefire talks. While the SPDC claimed there would be no change in policy towards the ceasefire groups, the regime presented them with a 13-point memorandum demanding a formal ceasefire, under which they would be forced to renounce armed struggle, cease recruiting, end military training, stop collecting revenue and assist Yangon's anti-narcotics campaign. In return, they would receive subsistence funding and would be given roles as local armed police. In the face of this ultimatum and the loss of familiar MI contacts, some ceasefire groups began considering resuming their insurgencies. There were particular problems with Karen, Karenni and Shan groups. Ceasefire talks with the KNU broke down in April 2005 and by early June fighting had reignited. In April, the SPDC – in conjunction with the UWSA – launched a major offensive against the Shan State Army (SSA). The SPDC blamed the KNU and SSA for bomb attacks in Yangon in May, but these may have resulted from continuing factional disputes within the SPDC.

The military contingents from the **Phillipines** and **Thailand** were withdrawn from **Iraq** in July and September 2004, respectively. **New Zealand**'s 60-strong military engineer detachment was also witdrawn in September 2004 on expiry of its mandate. **Singapore** deployed a KC-135 tanker aircraft to the Gulf from June to September 2004, and an amphibious vessel from December 2004 to March 2005.

Australia demonstrated its staunch support for its US and British allies in Iraq, deploying an additional 450 troops and 40 ASLAV APCs to protect Japanese military engineers and train Iraqi security forces in the southern province of al-Muthana in April 2005. This deployment brought total Australian troop numbers in Iraq to approximately 950, most of the forces already present being involved in protecting diplomats and training Iraqi forces. Reports in July 2005 suggested that Britain was negotiating with Canberra to transfer its military command in southern Iraq to Australia in order to free UK forces for redeployment to Afghanistan.

In July, Canberra announced that it would be sending troops to Afghanistan again, after a two-and-a-half-year hiatus. Plans called for 150 Special Air Service personnel and commandos to deploy in September 2005 for 12 months, with 200 engineering

troops likely to follow in April 2006. In January 2005, New Zealand deployed a fresh 120-strong military contingent to the Provincial Reconstruction Team in Afghanistan's Bamiyan province.

In March 2005, **Thailand** despatched 177 military engineers to the UN peacekeeping mission in Burundi for a six-month tour.

The tsunami which followed the major earthquake off Aceh on 26 December 2004 had disastrous consequences for several parts of Southeast Asia, most importantly Aceh in **Indonesia**, and the area around Phuket in southern **Thailand** (where the Royal Thai Navy's major Phang Nga base was hard hit, leaving a frigate and other vessels badly damaged). The disaster provoked unprecedentedly large relief efforts spearheaded by military forces from within and without the region, incidentally highlighting their rapid deployment capabilities. The US made the most important contribution, deploying more than 15,000 personnel under *Operation Unified Assistance*. Though US forces also played significant roles in **Sri Lanka**, the **Maldives** and **Thailand**, American relief operations – in which US Navy and Marine Corps helicopters played prominent parts – were centred on Aceh. Under Operations *Sumatra Assist* and *Flying Eagle*, respectively, **Australia** and **Singapore** each deployed more than 1,000 personnel to Aceh. **Japan** also despatched approximately 1,000 personnel to Aceh, in the country's largest overseas military deployment since 1945. France, Germany, Malaysia, New Zealand, Pakistan, Spain and the UK were prominent amongst other countries sending forces to Aceh (for more details see *Strategic Survey 2004/5*, pp. xxvi–xxvii). US, Australian and Singapore forces were also involved in relief operations after a major earthquake struck the Indonesian island of Nias, off Sumatra, in late March 2005.

In the wake of the controversial US proposal for a Regional Maritime Security Initiative (RMSI) during the first half of 2004 (for details see *The Military Balance 2004–2005*, p. 165), Southeast Asian states continued to indicate their recognition of the need to counter piracy and potential maritime terrorism, particularly in the Malacca Strait, more effectively. Significant measures involving regional states included two Japanese initiatives: the Asia Maritime Security Initiative 2004 (AMARSECTIVE 2004), under which the heads of Asian coast guards, meeting in Tokyo in June 2004, agreed to intensify collaboration against piracy, sea robbery and maritime terrorism; and the Regional Cooperation Agreement on Combating

East Asia and Australasia

Piracy and Armed Robbery against Ships in Asia (ReCAAP), concluded in Tokyo in November 2004. Under ReCAAP, an Information Sharing Centre will be established in Singapore. In March 2005, the Malaysian Maritime Enforcement Agency (effectively the country's coast guard) became operational under the command of a one-star naval officer and assumed responsibility for law enforcement in Malaysia's territorial waters and Exclusive Economic Zone. Also in March, Singapore introduced tighter maritime security regulations, under which escort teams including armed naval personnel will board commercial vessels assessed as vulnerable to terrorist attack, while they are in national waters. Meanwhile, piracy has remained a serious problem in the Malacca Strait. Although no attacks were reported in the two months following the December 2004 tsunami, possibly because of the deterrent effect of the large international naval presence in the strait, violent attacks resumed in March 2005.

At the beginning of 2005, Australia's government announced an initiative aimed at strengthening national maritime security and particularly at reducing the threat from seaborne terrorism. Through a Joint Offshore Protection Command, established in April 2005, the Australian Defence Force will be tasked with all offshore counter-terrorist prevention, interdiction and response; the Customs Coastwatch organisation will remain responsible for maritime and coastal surveillance. Security patrols in the vicinity of Australia's oil and gas fields in the Timor Sea and on the North West Shelf have been introduced urgently, and two additional *Armidale*-class patrol vessels will be acquired for patrolling the latter area. Intrinsic to Canberra's initiative is the concept of a 1,000 nautical miles Maritime Identification Zone around Australia, aimed at providing early warning of potential maritime terrorist threats. The concept provoked criticism by Indonesia and Malaysia because of its apparent implications for their sovereignty.

Incremental modernisation of regional armed forces continued during 2004–05. In **Indonesia**, however, continuing restrictions on defence spending caused postponement of plans to expand the air force's fleet of Su-30MK combat aircraft. Five additional Korean-built KT-1B basic trainers were ordered. The December 2004 tsunami highlighted severe shortcomings in the Indonesian armed forces' logistic capabilities, and prompted the US government to relax its arms embargo to allow direct commercial sales of some defence items and services, including spares for C-130 transport aircraft. But while there were

few major equipment purchases, Indonesia's defence ministry is planning to reinforce substantially military deployments in hitherto relatively lightly defended eastern Indonesia. A third Kostrad (army strategic reserve) division will be formed, with its headquarters in Papua, which will also provide the base (to be completed in 2008) for a fourth marine brigade. Air defence facilities in Papua will also be expanded.

The Ninth Malaysia Plan (covering the 2006-10 period) will mainly fund equipment already ordered for **Malaysia**'s armed forces, including Su-30MKM fighters, PT-91 main battle tanks, and *Scorpene* submarines. While additional funds may be made available to purchase F/A-18F combat aircraft and A-400M transport aircraft, other planned procurement programmes – notably for AWACS aircraft – will probably be deferred until after 2010.

Singapore's defence ministry announced in April 2005 that the Eurofighter *Typhoon* had been dropped from the shortlist of types competing to fill the air force's Next Fighter Replacement (NFR) requirement; this left the Boeing F-15T and Dassault *Rafale* in the competition. If the F-35 Joint Strike Fighter is delayed, Singapore's air force might require more than the 20 NFR aircraft originally envisaged. A second air force competition involves provision of a commercially operated basic flying training school in Australia from 2008. Singapore's navy is also preparing for new equipment: the first two of its six 3,200-tonne *Formidable*-class frigates had been launched by early 2005; the type will enter service from 2007. The frigates will carry S-70B multi-mission helicopters, six of which were ordered in January 2005. In mid-2005, Singapore reportedly began negotiations for two Swedish *Västergötland*-class submarines. Singapore's seven F-16A/B fighter aircraft were transferred to **Thailand** in late 2004. Under a memorandum of understanding signed in November 2004, Singapore's air force will be allowed to deploy as many as 20 aircraft for training at Thailand's Udon Thani air base for up to six months annually.

Since 1995, the AFP Modernisation Act has guided development of the Armed Forces of the **Philippines**. However, progress towards upgrading capability has been painfully slow, mainly because of funding shortages. In light of urgent operational requirements imposed by the need to counter both Muslim separatist rebels and Maoist insurgents belonging to the New People's Army, in early 2005 the AFP began implementing a five-year Capability Upgrade Program (CUP), focussed on acquiring basic individual and unit equipment, aimed particularly at enhancing the mobility, firepower and communications of counter-insurgency forces and costing approximately US$600mn between 2005 and 2010.

Vietnam took delivery of a further four Su-30MK2V multi-role combat aircraft in November 2004. Two Polish-built PZL M28 *Skytruck* maritime patrol aircraft were delivered the following month; up to 10 more may follow by 2007.

Australia's 2005–06 defence budget, announced in May 2005, included provision for tactical UAVs for the army, upgrades for F/A-18 combat aircraft, new special forces equipment, and the initial stages of the navy's acquisition of new amphibious transport vessels and air warfare destroyers. It will also fund up to 2,560 stand-off air-to-ground missiles to equip the air force's F/A-18 and AP-3C combat aircraft from 2007. A decision on whether to acquire the F-35 Joint Strike Fighter will be deferred from 2006 to 2008. According to Defence Minister Robert Hill, the option of purchasing some STOVL variants of the F-35 for potential operation from the new amphibious ships has not been ruled out. Deliveries of the army's 22 Eurocopter *Tiger* attack helicopters began in December 2004. In June 2005, 12 NH90 utility helicopters were ordered for the army for delivery from 2007; New Zealand has selected the same type to replace its UH-1s from 2009.

Australia Aus

Australian Dollar A$		2003	2004	2005
GDP	A$	783bn	837bn	
	US$	512bn	598bn	
per capita	US$	25,968	30,059	
Growth	%	3.4	3.2	
Inflation	%	2.8	2.3	
Public Debt	%	19.5	20.5	
Def exp	A$	18.6bn	20bn	
	US$	12.2bn	14.3bn	
Def bdgt	A$	15.8bn	16.3bn	17.4bn
	US$	10.3bn	11.6bn	13.2bn
US$1=A$		1.53	1.4	1.32

Population   20,090,437

Ethnic groups: Asian 4%; Aborigines <1%

Age	0–14	15–19	20–24	25–29	30–64	65 plus
Male	10%	4%	3%	3%	24%	6%
Female	10%	3%	3%	3%	23%	7%

Capabilities

ACTIVE 52,872 (Army 26,035 Navy 13,167 Air 13,670)

RESERVE 20,800 (Army 17,200 Navy 1,600 Air 2,000)

ORGANISATIONS BY SERVICE

Army 26,035

Land Command

FORCES BY ROLE

1 Land HQ, 1 Deployable Joint Force HQ, 1 Logistic Support Force HQ

Air Lift	1 regt
Army	2 bde HQ; 1 bde HQ (intergrated)
Armd	1 regt (integrated)
Recce	1 regt (integrated); 1 regt
Armd recce hel	1 regt
Surv	3 (regional force) unit (integrated)
Mech inf	1 bn
EW	1 regt
Mot Inf	1 bn; 1 bn (integrated)
APC	1 indep sqn
Lt inf	2 bn
Para	1 bn
Med arty	1 regt
Fd arty	1 regt (integrated); 1 regt
Avn	1 bde HQ; 1 (surv) sqn
Spt	1 (joint support) regt (CIS)
Cbt engr	1 regt (integrated); 2 regt
Force Support	2 bn; 1 bn (integrated)
Combat Service Support	3 regt (CIS); 2 bn; 1 bn (integrated)
Joint Support	1 regt (CIS)
AD	1 regt

Special Operations Command

FORCES BY ROLE

1 Special Operations HQ

SF	1 regt (SAS)
Cdo	2 bn (1 reserve)
Incident Response	1 unit

Training Command 3,160

Reserve Organisations

Land Command 17,200 reservists

FORCES BY ROLE

1 div HQ, 6 bde HQ

Recce	2 regt; 1 sqn
Inf	13 bn
APC	1 regt
Cdo	1 regt
Fd arty	3 regt; 3 indep bty
Cbt engr	3 regt
Engr construction	2 regt
Fd Engr	3 (fd) sqn

EQUIPMENT BY TYPE

TK • MBT • LEOPARD 1 101: 71 1A3 (excl variants); 30 in store

APC 619

   APC (T) 364: 245 M-113 (to be upgraded); 119 in store (to be upgraded)

   APC (W) • ASLAV 255: 255 ASLAV-25 (being delivered)

ARTY 566

   TOWED 270

      105mm 234: 109 L-118 Light Gun; 125 L-5/M-2A2

      155mm 36: 36 M-198

   MOR 296: 296 81mm

AT • RCL 651

   106mm • M-40 74: 74 M-40A1

   84mm 577: 577 *Carl Gustav*

AIRCRAFT • TPT 6: 3 Beech 200 *Super King Air* (on lease); 1 Beech 350 *Super King Air* (on lease); 2 DHC-6 *Twin Otter* (on lease)

HELICOPTERS

   ATK 22: 22 AS-665 *Tiger* (delivery from July 2004)

   SPT 40

      CH-47 6: 6 CH-47D *Chinook*

      S-70 34: 34 S-70 A-9 (S-70A) *Black Hawk*

   UTL 55

      BELL 206 • BELL 206B 38: 38 Bell 206B-1 *Kiowa* (to be upgraded)

      UH-1 17: 17 UH-1H *Iroquois*

AD • SAM 48

   TOWED 18: 18 *Rapier* B1M

   MANPAD 30: 30 RBS-70

RADAR • LAND 21: 7 AN/TPQ-36 *Firefinder* (arty, mor);

14 RASIT (veh, arty)
AMPHIBIOUS • CRAFT 15: 15 LCM

Navy 13,167; 1,600 reservists (total 14,767)
EQUIPMENT BY TYPE
SUBMARINES • TACTICAL • SSK 6:
6 *Collins* each with UGM-84C *Harpoon* tactical USGW, 6 single 533mm TT each with 1 Mk48 *Sea Arrow* HWT
PRINCIPAL SURFACE COMBATANTS • FRIGATES 10
FFG 6:
6 *Adelaide* (capacity either 2 AS-350 *Ecureuil* spt hel/S-70B *Seahawk* ASW hel) each with 2 S-70B *Seahawk* ASW hel, 2 Mk32 triple 324mm each with Mk 32/Mk 46, 1 Mk 13 GMLS with SM-1 MR SAM, RGM-84C *Harpoon* tactical SSM, 1 76mm gun
FF 4:
4 *Anzac* each with 1 S-70B-2 *Seahawk* ASW hel (being replaced by SH-2GA *Super Seasprite*), 2 triple 324mm ASTT (6 eff.) each with Mk 32/Mk 46, 1 32 cell Mk 41 VLS (32 eff.) with up to 32 RIM-7NP *Sea Sparrow* SAM, 1 127mm gun
PATROL AND COASTAL COMBATANTS • PCO 15: 15 *Fremantle*
MINE WARFARE • MINE COUNTERMEASURES 9
MHC 6: 6 *Huon*
MSA 3: 2 *Bandicoot*; 1 *Brolga*
AMPHIBIOUS
PRINCIPAL AMPHIBIOUS SHIPS • LPH 2:
2 *Kanimbla* (capacity 450 troops; 2 LCM; either 4 UH-60 *Black Hawk* utl hel or 3 SH-3H *Sea King* utl hel))
LS • LST 1:
1 *Tobruk* (capacity 500 troops; 2 LCM; 2 LCVP)
CRAFT 20: 14 LCM
LCH 6: 6 *Balikpapan*
LOGISTICS AND SUPPORT 18
AGHS (SVY) 2: 2 *Leuwin*
AO 2: 1 *Success*; 1 *Westralia*
AT 5
Craft 5
TRV 3
TRG 1: 1 AXS
FACILITIES
Base 1 located at Sydney, 1 located at Darwin, 1 located at Cairns, 1 located at Stirling, 1 located at Jervis Bay, 1 located at Noura, 1 located at Flinders

COMFLOT
Navy 1 HQ

Maritime Comd
Navy 1 HQ located at Stirling

Naval Aviation 990
HELICOPTERS
ASW 23
S-70B 16: 16 S-70B-2
Sea King **MK50** 7
SPT • AS-350 12: 12 AS-350BA *Ecureuil*

Naval Systems Comd
Navy 1 HQ

Air Force 13,670; 2,000 reservists (total 15,670)
2 comds – air,trg
Flying hours 175 hrs/year on F/A-18 *Hornet* FGA ac; 200 hrs/year on F-111 *Aardvark* bbr ac

FORCES BY ROLE
Air cbt 1 gp (1 ftr/tac wg (1 OCU, 3 ftr sqn with 55 F/A-18A *Hornet*; 16 F/A-18B *Hornet*), 1 recce/strike wg (2 FGA/recce sqn with 17 F-111C *Aardvark*; 4 RF-111 *Aardvark*; 1 EC-130H *Compass Call*; 2 EP-3C *Orion*), 1 tac trg wg (1 FAC flt with 4 PC-9A, 2 trg sqn with 33 *Hawk* MK127))
MP 1 gp (3 MP sqn (incl OCU) with 19 AP-3C *Orion*/ P-3C *Orion**; 3 TAP-3B *Orion*)
SAR S-76 (civil contract) at 4 air bases
Airlift 1 gp (1 Tkr/Tpt sqn with 4 B-707 (tkr/tpt), 1 Tpt sqn with 7 Beech 300 *Super King Air* (navigation trg), 1 (VIP) Tpt sqn with 2 B-737 BBJ; 3 CL-604 *Challenger*, 2 Tpt sqn with 14 DHC-4 *Caribou*, 2 Tkr/Tpt sqn with 1 EC-130H *Compass Call*; 11 C-130H *Hercules*; 12 C-130J *Hercules*)
Trg Flg trg schl with 58 PC-9A
AD 1 airfield def wg (3 air sqn); 1 surveillance and response gp with 3 tactical radar and with radar coord centre located at Edinburgh (S. Australia) with 1 *Jindalee* OTH-B AD radar located at Alice Springs; 1 at Laverton (W.Australia); 1 at Longreach (N. Queensland)

EQUIPMENT BY TYPE
AIRCRAFT 140 combat capable
BBR • F-111 22: 17 F-111C *Aardvark*; 5 F-111G *Aardvark* in store
FGA 104
F/A-18 71: 55 F/A-18A *Hornet*; 16 F/A-18B *Hornet*
Hawk **MK127** 33
RECCE 4: 4 RF-111C *Aardvark*
MP 19: 19 AP-3C *Orion*/P-3C *Orion**
EW 4
EC-130 2: 2 EC-130H *Compass Call*
ELINT • EP-3 2: 2 EP-3C *Orion*
TPT 53:
B-707 4 (tkr)
B-737 2: 2 B-737 BBJ
Beech 300 *Super King Air* 7 (navigation trg)
C-130 23: 11 C-130H *Hercules*; 12 C-130J *Hercules*
CL-604 *Challenger* 3 **DHC-4** *Caribou* 14
TRG 65: 62 PC-9A; 3 TAP-3 *Orion*
HELICOPTERS • UTL: some S-76 (civil contract)
RADAR • AD RADAR 6
OTH-B 3: 3 *Jindalee* located at Alice Springs
Tactical 3
MSL • TACTICAL •
ASM: some AGM-142 *Popeye*; some AGM-84A *Harpoon*
AAM: some AIM-120 AMRAAM; some AIM-9M *Sidewinder*; some ASRAAM

Paramilitary

Australian Customs Service

ε6 naval vessels

AIRCRAFT
TPT 9
BN-2 ISLANDER 6: 6 BN-2B *Islander*
DHC-8 *Dash 8* 3
UTL 3: 3 F406 *Caravan II*
HELICOPTERS • UTL • BELL 206 1: 1 Bell 206L *LongRanger*

DEPLOYMENT

AFGHANISTAN
UN • UNAMA 1 obs

CYPRUS
UN • UNFICYP 15 civ police

EAST TIMOR
UN • UNOTIL 2 obs

EGYPT
MFO 25 staff

IRAQ
Army 850 (Peace Support)
Air force
AIRCRAFT • MP • P-3 1: 1 P-3C *Orion*

MALAYSIA
Army 115
1 inf coy (on 3-month rotational tours)
Air force 12

MIDDLE EAST
UN • UNTSO 12 obs

PAPUA NEW GUINEA
Army 38 1 Trg unit

SOLOMON ISLANDS
RAMSI 530+ (*Op Anode*) police/
AIRCRAFT • TPT 2: 2 DHC-4 *Caribou*

SUDAN
UN • UNMIS 3, 6 obs

FOREIGN FORCES

New Zealand Army: 9 (navigation) trg
Singapore Air Force: School with 27 S-211 trg ac (flying trg) located at Pearce; School with 12 AS-332 *Super Puma* Spt/AS-532 *Cougar* utl (flying trg) located at Oakey; 230 air
United States USPACOM: SEWS located at Pine Gap; comms facility located at NW Cape; SIGINT stn located at Pine Gap; 59; 31

Brunei Bru

Brunei Dollar B$		2003	2004	2005
GDP	B$	8.79bn	8.89bn	
	US$	5.1bn	5.2bn	
per capita	US$	14,123	14,249	
Growth	%	3.1	1.1	
Inflation	%	0.3	0.9	
Def bdgt	B$	474m	502m	592m
	US$	272m	294m	357m
US$1=B$		1.74	1.71	1.66

Population   372,361

Ethnic groups: Muslim 71%; Malay 67%; Chinese 16%; non-Malay indigenous 6%

Age	0–14	15–19	20–24	25–29	30–64	65 plus
Male	15%	5%	4%	5%	22%	1%
Female	14%	4%	4%	4%	19%	2%

Capabilities

ACTIVE 7,000 (Army 4,900 Navy 1,000 Air 1,100)
Paramilitary 7,500

RESERVE 700 (Army 700)

ORGANISATIONS BY SERVICE

Army 4,900; 700 reservists (total 5,600)

FORCES BY ROLE
Inf   3 bn
Spt   1 bn (1 armd recce sqn, 1 engr sqn)
Reserves   1 bn

EQUIPMENT BY TYPE
TK • LT TK 20: 20 *Scorpion* (16 to be upgraded)
APC • APC (W) 39: 39 VAB
ARTY • MOR 24: **81mm** 24
AT • RL • **67mm**: some *Armbrust*

Navy 1,000

FORCES BY ROLE
SF 1 sqn

EQUIPMENT BY TYPE
PATROL AND COASTAL COMBATANTS 6+
  MISC BOATS/CRAFT: some boats
  PFI 3: 3 *Perwira*† (sid)
  PFM 3: 3 *Waspada* each with 2 MM-38 *Exocet* tactical SSM
AMPHIBIOUS • CRAFT 4: 4 LCU

Air Force 1,100

FORCES BY ROLE
Tpt 1 sqn with 1 CN-235M
Trg 1 sqn with 4 PC-7 *Turbo Trainer*; 2 SF-260W *Warrior*; 2 Bell 206B *JetRanger II*

Hel 1 sqn with 5 BO-105 (armed, 81mm rockets); 1 sqn with 4 S-70A *Black Hawk*; 1 S-70C *Black Hawk* (VIP); 10 Bell 212; 1 Bell 214 (SAR)

AD 2 sqn with 12 *Rapier* each with *Blindfire* land; 16 *Mistral*

EQUIPMENT BY TYPE
AIRCRAFT
TPT • CN-235 1: 1 CN-235M
TRG 6: 4 PC-7 *Turbo Trainer*; 2 SF-260W *Warrior*
HELICOPTERS
SPT • S-70 5: 4 S-70A *Black Hawk*; 1 S-70C *Black Hawk* (VIP)
UTL 18: 5 BO-105 (armed, 81mm rockets); 2 Bell 206B *JetRanger II*; 10 Bell 212; 1 Bell 214 (SAR)
AD • SAM 28: 12 *Rapier* each with *Blindfire*; 16 *Mistral*

Paramilitary ε3,750

Gurkha Reserve Unit ε2,000+
Army 2 bn

Royal Brunei Police 1,750
PATROL AND COASTAL COMBATANTS 7: 7 PCI less than 100 tonnes

FOREIGN FORCES
Singapore Armed Forces: 500; 1 hel det with 5 UH-1H *Iroquois*
United Kingdom Army: 1 Gurkha bn; 1 hel flt with 3 hel; ε1,120

Cambodia Cam

Cambodian Riel r		2003	2004	2005
GDP	r	16.4tr	18.0tr	
	US$	4.14bn	4.51bn	
per capita	US$	315	337	
Growth	%	5.2	4.3	
Inflation	%	1.2	2.0	
Debt	US$	3.13bn		
Def bdgt	r	268bn	277bn	ε300bn
	US$	67.7m	69.6m	73.8m
US$1=r		3,973	3.99k	4,065

Population 13,636,398
Ethnic groups: Khmer 90%; Vietnamese 5%; Chinese 1%

Age	0–14	15–19	20–24	25–29	30–64	65 plus
Male	18%	7%	6%	3%	14%	1%
Female	18%	6%	5%	3%	16%	2%

Capabilities

ACTIVE 124,300 (Army 75,000 Navy 2,800 Air 1,500 Provincial Forces 45,000) Paramilitary 67,000
Terms of service conscription authorised but not implemented since 1993

ORGANISATIONS BY SERVICE

Army ε75,000
FORCES BY ROLE
6 Military Regions (incl 1 special zone for capital)

Armd	3 bn
Recce	some indep bn
Inf	22 div (established str 3500; actual str <1500); 3 indep bde; 9 indep regt
AB / SF	1 regt
Arty	some bn
Protection	1 bde (4 bn)
Engr Construction	1 regt
Fd Engr	3 regt
AD	some bn

EQUIPMENT BY TYPE
TK 170+
  MBT 150+: 50 Type-59; 100+ T-54/T-55
  LT TK 20+: some Type-62; 20 Type-63
RECCE • BRDM: some BRDM-2
AIFV • BMP 70: 70 BMP-1
APC 190+
  APC (T): some M-113
  APC (W) 190
    BTR 160: 160 BTR-152/BTR-60
    OT 30: 30 OT-64
ARTY 428+
  TOWED some 400+: D-30 122mm/M-30 *M-1938* 122mm/ Type-59-I 130mm/ZIS-3 *M-1942* 76mm
  MRL 28+
    107mm: some Type-63
    122mm 8: 8 BM-21
    132mm: some BM-13-16 (BM-13)
    140mm 20: 20 BM-14-16 (BM-14)
  MOR
    82mm: some M-37
    120mm: some M-43
    160mm: some M-160
AT • RCL
  107mm: some B-11
  82mm: some B-10
AD • GUNS
  14.5mm • TOWED • ZPU: some ZPU-1/ZPU-2/ZPU-4
  37mm • TOWED: some M-1939
  57mm • TOWED: some S-60

Navy ε2,800 (incl. 1,500 Naval Infantry)
EQUIPMENT BY TYPE
PATROL AND COASTAL COMBATANTS 10
  MISC BOATS/CRAFT 6: 6 assault craft
  PCR 2: 2 *Kaoh Chhlam*
  PFC 2: 2 *Stenka*
FACILITIES
Base 1 (river) located at Prek Ta Ten, 1 (maritime) located at Ream

Naval Infantry 1,500
Inf 7 bn
Arty 1 bn

Air Force 1,500
FORCES BY ROLE

Ftr   1 sqn with 14 MiG-21bis *Fishbed L & N*†;
5 MiG-21UM *Mongol B*† (up to 9 to be
upgraded by IAI: 2 returned but status
unclear)

Recce / trg   some sqn with 5 P-92 *Echo* (pilot trg/recce);
5 L-39 *Albatros** (lead-in trg)

Tpt   1 (VIP (reporting to Council of Ministry))
sqn with 2 An-24RV *Coke*; 1 AS-350 *Ecureuil*;
1 AS-365 *Dauphin 2*; 1 sqn with 1 BN-2
Islander; 1 Cessna 421; 2 Y-12

Hel   1 sqn with 1 Mi-8P *Hip K* (VIP); 2 Mi-26
Halo; 13 MI-17 (Mi-8MT) *Hip H/Mi-8 Hip*

EQUIPMENT BY TYPE
AIRCRAFT 24 combat capable
  FTR • MiG-21 14: 14 MiG-21bis *Fishbed L & N*†
  TPT 6
    An-24 2: 2 An-24RV *Coke*
    BN-2 *Islander* 1
    Cessna 421 1
    Y-12 2
  UTL 5: 5 P-92 *Echo* (pilot trg/recce)
  TRG 10: 5 L-39 *Albatros** (lead-in trg)
    MiG-21U 5: 5 MiG-21UM *Mongol B**†
HELICOPTERS
  ELINT 1: 1 Mi-8P *Hip K* (VIP)
  SPT 16: 1 AS-350 *Ecureuil*; 2 Mi-26 *Halo*; 13 MI-17 (Mi-8MT) *Hip H/Mi-8 Hip* Spt
  UTL 1: 1 AS-365 *Dauphin 2*

Provincial Forces 45,000+
Reports of at least 1 inf regt per province, with varying
numbers of inf bn with lt wpn

Paramilitary

Police 67,000 (including gendarmerie)

NON-STATE ARMED GROUPS
see Part II

DEPLOYMENT

SUDAN
UN • UNMIS 5 obs

China, Peoples Republic of PRC

Chinese Yuan Renminbi Y		2003	2004	2005
GDP	Y	11.7tr	13.9tr	
	US$	1.41tr	1.68tr	
per capita	US$	1,093	1,293	
Growth	%	9.3	9.5	
Inflation	%	1.2	3.9	
Debt	US$	193bn		
Def exp[a]	US$	ε55.9bn	ε62.5bn	
Def bdgt[b]	Y	185bn	207bn	244bn
	US$	22.3bn	25bn	29.5bn
US$1=Y		8.28	8.28	8.28

[a] estimate including extra-budgetary military expenditure
[a] official budget at market exchange rates

Population   1,306,313,812

Ethnic groups: Tibetan, Uighur and other non-Han 8%; Xinjiang Muslim ε60%; of which Uighur ε44% Tibet Chinese ε60%; Tibetan ε40%

Age	0–14	15–19	20–24	25–29	30–64	65 plus
Male	11%	5%	4%	4%	24%	4%
Female	10%	5%	4%	4%	23%	4%

Capabilities

ACTIVE 2,255,000 (Army 1,600,000 Navy 255,000 Air 400,000) **Paramilitary 3,969,000**
Terms of service selective conscription; all services 2 years

RESERVE some 800,000

ORGANISATIONS BY SERVICE

Strategic Missile Forces (100,000+)

Offensive
Org as 20 launch bdes within 6 msl armies; org varies by msl type; one testing and one trg base
MSL • STRATEGIC 806
  ICBM 46: circa 6 DF-31 (CSS-9) (1 bde); circa 20 DF-4 (CSS-3) (2 bde); 20 DF-5A (CSS-4 Mod 2) (4 bdes)
  IRBM 35: circa 33 DF-21 (CSS-5) (4 Bde); circa 2 DF-3A (CSS-2 Mod) (1 bde)
  SRBM 725
    DF-11/M-11 (CSS-7) 500: 500 DF-11A/M-11A (CSS-7 Mod 2) (4 bdes)
    DF-15/M-9 (CSS-6) 225 (2 bdes)

Navy
SUBMARINES • STRATEGIC • SSBN 1: 1 *Xia* (capacity 12 JL-1 (CSS-N-3) strategic SLBM)

Defensive
RADAR • STRATEGIC: some phased array radar; some detection and tracking radars (cover Central Asia and Shanxi (northern border)) located at Xinjiang

People's Liberation Army ε800,000; ε800,000 conscript (reductions continue) (total 1,600,000)

FORCES BY ROLE

Group army: strength from 30–65000, org varies, normally with 2–3 mech/mot inf div/bde, 1 armd div/bde, 1 arty div/bde, 1 SAM/AAA or AAA bde, cbt readiness category varies with 10 GA at category A and 8 at category B (reorg to bde structure in progress)

Army	18 (Group) Armies (*total:* 1 mech inf bde, 1 AT bde, 12 armd bde, 12 ADA bde, 14 arty bde, 15 inf div, 2 amph aslt div, 22 mot inf bde, 24 mot inf div, 3 mech inf div, 4 AT regt, 7 arty div, 9 armd div, 9 (SAM/AAA) AD bde)
Arty / air	(coastal defence) air forces
Mil region	7 comd
Provincial mil	28 district
Inf	5 (border) indep regt
Mot inf	1 indep bde; 1 indep regt
Mtn inf	2 (indep) bde
AB	1 ((manned by AF)) corps (3 AB div, 35,000 AB)
Arty	1 indep regt
SSM	1 indep bde; 9 (coastal defence) regt
ADA	1 indep regt
Engr	1 indep bde; 50 regt
Sigs	50 regt
Avn	2 (indep) regt (trg); 8 indep regt
Gd	4 (garrison) comd (with 1 mtn inf bde, 12 inf div, 4 inf bde, 87 (bn) inf regt)
AD	8 (coastal defence) regt

Reserves

some 30 inf div (each 3 inf, 1 arty regt); 12 AD div; 7 log spt bde

EQUIPMENT BY TYPE

TK 8,580+
  MBT 7,580+: 1,200 Type-96; 1,000 Type-88A/Type-88B; 80 Type-98A; 300 Type-79; 5,000+ Type-59-II/Type-59-I
  LT TK 1,000
    TYPE-62 400: 400 Type-62 Lt Tk Tk/Type-62-I
    TYPE-63 600: 200 **Type-63A** 400
AIFV 1,000: 1,000 Type-86A *WZ-501*
APC 3,500+
  APC (T) 2,600
    TYPE-63 2,300: 2,300 Type-63-II/Type-63-I/Type-63A/Type-63C
    TYPE-89-I 300
  APC (W) 900+
    TYPE-77 200: 200 Type-77-II
    TYPE-92 600+
    WZ-523 100
ARTY 17,700+
  TOWED 14,000: 13,850 Type-54 (D-1) 152mm/Type-54-1 (M-30) *M-1938* 122mm/Type-59 (M-1944) 100mm/Type-59 (M-46) 130mm/Type-59-I 130mm/Type-60 (D-74) 122mm/Type-66 (D-20) 152mm/Type-83 122mm; 150

Type 88 WAC-21 155mm
  SP 1,200
    122mm 700: ε200 Type-70-I; ε500 Type-89
    152mm 500: ε500 Type-83
  GUN/MOR • 120mm 100: 100 2S23 *NONA-SVK*
  MRL 2,400+: 2,400+ Type-70 SP 130mm/Type-81 122mm/Type-82 130mm/Type-83 273mm/Type-89 SP 122mm/Type-96 (WS-1) 320mm
  MOR
    81mm: some Type-W87
    82mm: some Type-53 (M-37)/Type-67/Type-82 SP/Type-82
    100mm: some Type-71 (reported)
    120mm: some Type-55 (incl SP)
    160mm: some Type-56 (M-160)
AT
  MSL 7200: 7,176 HJ-73A/HJ-73B/HJ-73C/HJ-8A/HJ-8C/HJ-8E; 24 HJ-9 *Red Arrow 9*
  RCL
    105mm: some Type-75
    75mm: some Type-56
    82mm: some Type-65 (B-10)/Type-78
  RL • 62mm: some Type-70-1
  GUNS 300+
    100mm: some Type-73 (T-12)/Type-86
    120mm 300+: 300+ Type-89 SP
HELICOPTERS
  SAR 7: 7 SA-321 *Super Frelon*
  ATK 31: 31 WZ-9
  ASLT 8: 8 SA-342 *Gazelle* (with HOT)
  SPT 260:
    AS-350 *Ecureuil* 53
    MI-171 95: 45; 50 Mi-171V5
    Mi-6 *Hook* 3
    S-70 19: 19 S-70C2 (S-70C) *Black Hawk*
    MI-8 90: 40 MI-17 (Mi-8MT) *Hip H*; 50 Mi-8T *Hip*
  UTL 69+
    AS-365 61: 61 AS-365 *Dauphin 2* utl hel/Z-9 (AS-365N) *Dauphin 2*
    SA-316 *Alouette III* 8
    Z-10 some
UAV: some ASN-104/ASN-105/ASN-206/W-50
AD
  SAM 284+
    HQ-61 (CSA-N-2) 24: 24 HQ-61A *Red Leader*
    SP 260
      HQ-7 200: 200 HQ-7A
      SA-15 *Gauntlet* 60 (Tor-M1)
    MANPAD
      HN-5: some HN-5A/HN-5B *Hong Nu*
      FN-6/QW-1/QW-2 some
  GUNS 7,700+: 50+ Type-90 (GDF-002) towed 35mm; 7,650 Type-55 (M-1939) towed 37mm/Type-56 (M-1939) *KS-12* towed 85mm/Type-59 (KS-19) towed 100mm/Type-59 (S-60) towed 57mm/Type-65 towed 37mm/Type-74 towed 37mm/Type-80 (ZU-23-2) towed 23mm/Type-80 SP SP 57mm/Type-85 towed 25mm/Type-88 SP SP 37mm
RADAR • LAND: some *Cheetah* (arty); some RASIT (veh, arty); some Type-378 (veh)
MSL • TACTICAL • SSM: some HY-2 (CSS-C-3) *Seerseeker*; some HY-4 (CSS-C-7) *Sadsack*

North East–Shenyang MR ε250,000

Army 3 gp ((Heilongjiang, Jilin, Liaoning MD): 2 armd, 1 mech, 4 mot, 1 arty div; 2 armd, 5 mot, 3 arty, 1 SAM/ AAA, 3 AAA, 1 ATK bde)

North–Beijing MR ε300,000

Army 3 gp ((Beijing, Tianjin Garrison, Inner Mongolia, Hebei, Shanxi MD): 2 armd, 1 mech, 5 mot, 1 arty div; 3 armd, 7 mot inf, 4 arty, 2 SAM/AAA, 3 AAA bde; 1 ATK regt)

West–Lanzhou MR ε220,000

Army 2 gp ((incl Ningxia, Shaanxi, Gansu, Qing-hai, Xinjiang, South Xinjiang MD): 1 armd, 2 mot inf, 1 arty div; 1 armd, 2 mot inf, 1 arty, 1 AAA bde; 1 ATK regt)

South-West–Chengdu–MR ε180,000

Army 2 gp ((incl Chongqing Garrison, Sichuan, Guizhou, Yunnan, Tibet MD): 4 mot inf, 1 arty div; 2 armd, 1 arty, 2 AAA bde)

South–Guangzhou MR ε180,000

Army 2 gp ((Hubei, Hunan, Guangdong, Guangxi, Hainan MD): 1 mech, 3 mot inf, 1 arty div; 2 armd, 1 arty, 1 SAM/AAA, 1 AAA bde. Hong Kong: ε7,000 with 1 inf bde (3 inf, 1 mech inf, 1 arty regt, 1 engr bn), 1 hel unit)

Centre–Jinan MR ε190,000

Army 3 gp ((Shandong, Henan MD): 2 armd, 1 mech inf, 3 mot inf, 1 arty div; 1 armd, 1 mech inf, 4 mot inf, 2 arty, 2 SAM/AAA, 1 AAA bde, 1 ATK regt)

East–Nanjing MR ε250,000

Army 3 gp ((Shanghai Garrison, Jiangsu, Zhejiang, Fujian, Jiangxi, Anhui MD): 2 armd, 1 mech inf, 3 mot inf, 1 arty div; 1 armd, 4 mot inf, 2 arty, 2 SAM/AAA, 1 AAA bde; 1 ATK regt)

Navy ε215,000; 40,000 conscript (total 255,000)
SUBMARINES 69
STRATEGIC • SSBN 1:
  1 *Xia* (capacity 12 JL-1 (CSS-N-3) strategic SLBM) opcon offensive
TACTICAL 68
  SSN 5:
    5 *Han* (Type 091) each with YJ-82 tactical SSM, 6 single 533mm TT
  SSG 1:
    1 mod *Romeo* (Type S5G) with 6 YJ-1 (CSS-N-4) *Sardine* tactical SSM, 8 single 533mm TT (test platform)
  SSK 61:
    2 *Kilo* (RF Type EKM 636) each with 6 single 533mm TT
    2 *Kilo* (RF Type EKM 877) each with 6 single 533mm TT
    3 *Ming* (Type ES5C/D) each with single 533mm TT
    35 *Romeo*† (Type ES3B) each with 8 533mm TT
    3 *Song* each with YJ-2 (CSS-N-8) *Saccade* tactical SSM,

6 single 533mm TT
    16 imp *Ming* (imp, Type ES5E) each with 8 single 533mm TT
  SS 1: 1 *Golf* (SLBM trials)
PRINCIPAL SURFACE COMBATANTS 63
  DESTROYERS • DDG 21:
    2 *Hangzhou* (capacity either 1 Z-9C (AS-565SA) *Panther* ASW hel or 1 KA-28 ASW hel) (RF *Sovremeny*) each with 2 SA-N-7 SAM, 2 Twin 533mm ASTT (4 eff.), 2 quad (8 eff.) each with SS-N-22 *Sunburn* tactical SSM, 2 RBU 1000 *Smerch 3*, 2 twin 130mm gun (4 eff.)
    1 *Luda* III with 2 triple 324mm ASTT (6 eff.), 4 Twin (8 eff.) each with 2 YJ-1 (CSS-N-4) *Sardine* tactical SSM, 2 twin 130mm gun (4 eff.)
    11 *Luda* Type-051 each with 2 triple 324mm ASTT (6 eff.), 2 triple (6 eff.) each with HY-2 (CSS-N-2) *Silkworm*/YJ-1 (CSS-N-4) *Sardine*, 2 FQF 2500 (24 eff.), 2 twin 130mm gun (4 eff.)
    1 *Luhai* (capacity either 2 Z-9C (AS-565SA) *Panther* ASW hel or 2 KA-28 ASW hel) with 2 triple 324mm ASTT (6 eff.), 1 octuple (8 eff.) with 8 *Crotale* SAM, 4 quad (16 eff.) each with YJ-1 (CSS-N-4) *Sardine* tactical SSM, 1 twin 100mm gun (2 eff.)
    2 *Luhu* (capacity 2 Z-9C (AS-565SA) *Panther* ASW hel) (Type 052A) each with 2 triple 324mm ASTT (6 eff.), 1 octuple (8 eff.) with *Crotale* SAM, 4 quad (16 eff.) each with YJ-1 (CSS-N-4) *Sardine* tactical SSM, 2 FQF 2500 (24 eff.), 1 twin 100mm gun (2 eff.)
    2 mod *Luda* (capacity 2 Z-9C (AS-565SA) *Panther* ASW hel) each with 2 triple 324mm ASTT (6 eff.), 2 triple (6 eff.) each with HY-2 (CSS-N-2) *Silkworm* tactical SSM, 1 twin 130mm gun (2 eff.), mine (capability)
    2 mod *Luda* Type-051DT each with 1 octuple (8 eff.) with *Crotale* SAM, 2 quad (8 eff.) each with YJ-1 (CSS-N-4) *Sardine* tactical SSM, 2 FQF 2500 (24 eff.), 2 twin 130mm gun (4 eff.), mine (capability)
  FRIGATES • FFG 42:
    ε26 *Jianghu* Type I each with ε2 Twin (4 eff.) each with ε2 SY-1 (CSS-N-1) *Scrubbrush* tactical SSM, ε4 RBU 1200 (20 eff.), ε2 100mm gun
    ε1 *Jianghu* Type II (capacity 1 Z-9C (AS-565SA) *Panther* ASW hel) with ε1 twin (2 eff.) with εSY-1 (CSS-N-1) *Scrubbrush* tactical SSM, ε2 RBU 1200 (10 eff.), ε1 twin 100mm gun (2 eff.)
    ε3 *Jianghu* Type III each with ε8 YJ-1 (CSS-N-4) *Sardine* tactical SSM, ε4 RBU 1200 (20 eff.), ε2 twin 100mm gun (4 eff.)
    4 *Jiangwei* I (capacity 2 Z-9C (AS-565SA) *Panther* ASW hel) each with 1 HQ-61 (CSA-N-2) SAM, 2 triple (6 eff.) each with 3 YJ-1 (CSS-N-4) *Sardine* tactical SSM, 2 RBU 1200 (10 eff.), 1 twin 100mm gun (2 eff.)
    8 *Jiangwei* II (capacity 2 Z-9C (AS-565SA) *Panther* ASW hel) each with YJ-1 (CSS-N-4) *Sardine* tactical SSM, 1 octuple (8 eff.) with 1 *Crotale* SAM, 2 RBU 1200 (10 eff.), 2 100mm gun
PATROL AND COASTAL COMBATANTS 331
  PCC 21:
    2 *Haijui* each with 4 RBU 1200 (20 eff.)
    19 *Haiqing* each with 2 Type-87 (12 eff.)
  PCI 87: 8 *Haizui* less than 100 tonnes; 79 *Shanghai* less than 100 tonnes
  PCR ε30 less than 100 tonnes
  PFC 88: ε88 *Hainan* each with ε4 RBU 1200 (20 eff.)

PFM 96:

31 *Houku* (Komar-Type) each with 2 SY-1 (CSS-N-1) *Scrubbrush* tactical SSM

22 *Houxin* each with 4 YJ-1 (CSS-N-4) *Sardine* tactical SSM

5 *Huang* each with 6 YJ-1 (CSS-N-4) *Sardine* tactical SSM

ε38 *Huangfeng/Hola* (FSU *Osa* I-Type) each with ε4 SY-1 (CSS-N-1) *Scrubbrush* tactical SSM

PHT 9: 9 *Huchuan*

MINE WARFARE 130

MINE COUNTERMEASURES 129

MSC 55: 50 *Lienyun* aux; 5 *Wosao*

MSD • MSD INSHORE 46: 4 drone; 42 in reserve

MSI 4: 1 *Shanghai* II; 3 *Wochang*

MSO 24: 24 T-43

MINELAYERS • ML 1: 1 *Wolei*

AMPHIBIOUS

LS 50

LSM 31:

1 *Yudao*

1 *Yudeng* (capacity 9 tanks; 500 troops)

12 *Yuhai* (capacity 2 tanks; 250 troops)

17 *Yuliang* (capacity 3 tanks; 100 troops)

LST 19:

3 *Shan* (capacity 16 tanks; 165 troops) (US LST-1)

7 *Yukan* (capacity 10 tanks; 200 troops)

9 *Yuting* (capacity 10 tanks; 250 troops) each with 2 hel

CRAFT 285+: 45 LCU; 230+ in reserve; 10 ACV utl

LOGISTICS AND SUPPORT 163:

AF 14

AGB 4

AGOR 33

AH (MED) 6: 6 *Qiongsha*

AO 3: 2 *Fuqing*; 1 *Nanchang*

AOT 33

AR 2

AS 10

ASR 1

ATF 25

Tpt 30

Trg 2 (one hel trg)

Merchant Fleet

LOGISTICS AND SUPPORT 1957: 913 (other)**AOT** 298 **container** 191 **dry bulk** 555

Naval Aviation 26,000

AIRCRAFT 436 combat capable

BBR 68:

ε50 H-5,F-5,F-5B (Il-28) *Beagle* (torpedo-carrying lt bbr)

18 H-6D each with YJ-6 (CAS-1) *Kraken* ALCM ASM

FTR 74

J-8 36: 24 J-8 *Finback* ftr ac/J-8A *Finback*; 6 J-8B *Finback*; 6 J-8D *Finback*

J-8IIA *Finback* 12

MiG-21 26: 26 J-7 (MiG-21F) *Fishbed C*

FGA 274: 20 JH-7; ε30 Q-5 *Fantan*; 24 Su-30Mk2; ε200 J-6 (MiG-19S) *Farmer B*

ASW 4: 4 PS-5 (SH-5)

RECCE 7: 7 HZ-5 (Il-28R) *Beagle*

MP 4: 4 Y-8X

TKR 3: 3 HY-6

TPT 66

An-12 4: 4 Y-8 (An-12BP) *Cub A*

Y-5 (An-2) *Colt* 50

Y-7 (An-24) *Coke* 4

Y-7H (An-26) *Curl* 6

Yak-42 2

TRG 73: 16 JJ-6 (MiG-19UTI) *Farmer**; 4 JJ-7 *Mongol A**; 53 PT-6 (CJ-6)

HELICOPTERS

SAR 27: 15 SA-321; 12 Z-8,Z-8A (SA-321Ja) *Super Frelon*

ASW • KA-27 8: 8 Ka-28 (Ka-27PL) *Helix A*

ASLT 8: 8 AS-565

SPT 8: 8 Mi-8 *Hip*

MSL • TACTICAL • ASM • ALCM:

YJ-6 (CAS-1): some; some YJ-61 (CAS-1 (improved)) *Kraken*

YJ-8K (CSS-N-4) *Sardine* some

Marines ε10,000

FORCES BY ROLE

Army   3 ((also have amph role)) div

marine inf 2 bde (*each*: 1 inf bn, 1 AD bn, 1 (armd) mech inf bn, 2 amph recce bn, 2 arty bn, 2 tk bn)

EQUIPMENT BY TYPE

TK • LT TK • TYPE-63 150: 150 Type-63A

APC • APC (T) 60: 60 Type-63

APC (W): some Type-92

ARTY • TOWED • 122mm: some Type-83

MRL • 107mm: some Type-63

AT • MSL: some HJ-73; some HJ-8

AD • SAM • MANPAD: some HN-5 *Hong Nu/Red Cherry*

North Sea Fleet

coastal defence from DPRK border (Yalu River) to south of Lianyungang (approx 35°10′N); equates to Shenyang, Beijing and Jinan MR, and to seaward; 9 coastal defence districts

FORCES BY ROLE

under review

Navy 1 HQ located at Qingdao

FACILITIES

Support base 1 (HQ) located at Qingdao, 1 located at Lushun

East Sea Fleet

coastal defence from south of Lianyungang to Dongshan (approx 35°10′N to 23°30′N); equates to Nanjing Military Region, and to seaward; 7 coastal defence districts

FORCES BY ROLE

Navy 1 HQ located at Dongqian Lake (Ninsbo)

FACILITIES

Base 1 located at Fujian, 1 located at Zhousnan, 1 located at Dongqian Lake (Ninsbo)

East Asia and Australasia

South Sea Fleet

coastal defence from Dongshan (approx 23°30′N) to Vn border; equates to Guangzhou MR, and to seaward (including Paracel and Spratly Islands)

FORCES BY ROLE

Navy 1 comd HQ located at Guangzhou

FACILITIES

Base 1 located at Yulin, 1 located at Guangzhou, 1 located at Zuanjiang

Air Force 210,000 (AD); 40,000 (strategic forces); 150,000 conscript (total 400,000)

32 air divs (22 ftr,3 bbr,5 attack,2 tpt). Up to 4 sqn,each with 10–15 ac,1 maint unit,some tpt and trg ac,make up an air regt; 3 air regt form an air div. Varying numbers of air divs in the Mil regions – many in the south-east.

Flying hours 130 hrs/year on J-8 *Finback* ftr ac; 180 hrs/year on Su-27 *Flanker*/Su-30 *Flanker*; 80 hrs/year on H-6 (Tu-16) *Badger* bbr ac; 130 hrs/year on J-7 (MiG-21F) *Fishbed* C MiG-21 ftr

FORCES BY ROLE

Bbr 5 regt with up to 50 H-6E/H-6F/H-6H; 8 regt with 94 H-5,F-5,F-5B (Il-28) *Beagle*; 1 (nuclear ready) regt with up to 20 H-6 (Tu-16) *Badger*; 3 regt with 46 H-6H (possibly with YJ-63 cruise missile)

Ftr 3 regt with 28 J-8 IIB *Finback*; 3 regt with 62 J-8D *Finback*; 16 regt with 400 J-7II *Fishbed*/J-7IIA; 1 regt with 11 J-8F *Finback*; 9 regt with 116 J-11 (Su-27SK) *Flanker*; 12 regt with 296 J-7E *Fishbed*; 5 regt with 32 Su-27UBK *Flanker*; 2 regt with 36 J-7C *Fishbed*; 1 regt with 24 J-7G *Fishbed*; 4 regt with 80 J-8 *Finback*; 1 regt with 24 J-8 IID *Finback*; 2 regt with 40 J-8III *Finback*

FGA 12 regt with 408 Q-5C *Fantan*/Q-5D *Fantan*; 2 regt each with 31 J-10; 25 regt with 722 MiG-19 *Farmer*; 4 regt with 73 Su-30MKK *Flanker*; 2 regt each with 13 JH-7A

ELINT / Recce 2 regt with 45 JZ-6 (MiG-19R); some regt with ε126 Aircraft; JZ-7 (MiG-21R) *Fishbed* H; 1 Tu-154M *Careless*; 1 regt with 8+ JZ-8 *Finback*

AEW / AWACS some regt with A-50 *Mainstay*; 4 Y-8

Tpt 1 regt with 16+ Tu-154M *Careless*; 3 regt with 13 Il-76MD *Candid* B; 3 regt with ε4 tpt; 1 An-12 *Cub*; 170 Y-5 (An-2) *Colt*; 41 Y-7 (An-24) *Coke*/Y-7H (An-26) *Curl*; 15 B-737-200 (VIP); 5 CL-601 *Challenger*; 2 Il-18 *Coot*; 20 Y-11; 8 Y-12

Tkr 1 regt with 10 HY-6

ADA / SAM 1 div located at North

ADA 1 bde located at Centre; 1 bde located at East; 1 bde located at North-East

Trg 1 regt with 12 H-6H; some regt with ε142 Trg; PT-6 (CJ-6); 179+ JJ-7 *Mongol A*; 140+ JL-8 (K-8); JJ-6 (MiG-19UTI) *Farmer*

Hel some regt with ε30–40 hel; 6 AS-332 *Super Puma* (VIP); 50 Mi-8 *Hip*; 20 Z-9 (AS-365N) *Dauphin 2*; 4 Bell 214

SAM 3 div located at North; 2 bde located at South; 1 bde located at North-East; 2 bde located at East; 1 bde located at South West; 100+ unit with 60+ HQ-7; 24 HQ-9; 144 S-300PMU2 (SA-10C) *Grumble*/SA-10D *Grumble*; 500+ HQ-2 (SA-2) *Guideline*/HQ-2A/HQ-2B(A); 160 (Strategic Air Defence) unit with 850 S-300PMU1 (SA-10B) *Grumble*/S-300PMU2 (SA-10C) *Grumble*

EQUIPMENT BY TYPE

AIRCRAFT 2,643 combat capable

BBR up to 222: 94 H-5,F-5,F-5B (Il-28) *Beagle*; up to 20 H-6 (Tu-16) *Badger*; up to 50 H-6E/H-6F/H-6H; 12 H-6H; 46 (possibly with YJ-63 cruise missile)

FTR 1,252

J-7II 400: 400 J-7II *Fishbed* ftr Aircraft/J-7IIA

J-7C *Fishbed* 36

J-7E *Fishbed* 296

J-7G *Fishbed* 24

J-8 153: 80; 62 J-8D *Finback*; 11 J-8F *Finback*

J-8IIA 52: 28 J-8 IIB *Finback*; 24 J-8 IID *Finback*

J-8III *Finback* 40

J-10 62

Su-30 73: 73 Su-30MKK *Flanker*

Su-27 116: 116 J-11 (Su-27SK) *Flanker*

FGA 1,169:

JH-7 39: 13; 26 JH-7A

Q-5 408: 408 Q-5C *Fantan*/Q-5D *Fantan*

MiG-19 *Farmer* 722

RECCE 53+: 45 JZ-6 (MiG-19R); some JZ-7 (MiG-21R) *Fishbed* H; 8+ JZ-8 *Finback*

AEW 4+: some A-50 *Mainstay*; 4 Y-8

TKR 10: 10 HY-6

TPT 296+: ε4 An-12 *Cub* 1

B-737 15: 15 B-737-200 (VIP)

CL-601 *Challenger* 5 Il-18 *Coot* 2

Il-76 13: 13 Il-76MD *Candid* B

Tu-154 17+: 17+ Tu-154M *Careless*

Y-11 20 Y-12 8 Y-5 (An-2) *Colt* 170 Y-7 (An-24) *Coke*/Y-7H (An-26) *Curl* 41

TRG 493+: ε142 JJ-6 (MiG-19UTI) *Farmer* some JJ-7 *Mongol A* 179+ JL-8 (K-8) 140+ PT-6 (CJ-6) some Su-27UB 32: 32 Su-27UBK *Flanker*

HELICOPTERS

SPT 56: 6 AS-332 *Super Puma* (VIP); 50 Mi-8 *Hip*

UTL 24

AS-365 20: 20 Z-9 (AS-365N) *Dauphin 2*

Bell 214 4

UAV: some *Chang Hong* 1

AD

SAM 1,578+

SP 1,078+: 60+ HQ-7; 24 HQ-9

S-300PMU (SA-10) 994: 850 S-300PMU1 (SA-10B) *Grumble*/S-300PMU2 (SA-10C) *Grumble*; 144 S-300PMU2 (SA-10C) *Grumble*/SA-10D *Grumble*

HQ-2 (SA-2) *Guideline* Towed/HQ-2A/HQ-2B(A) 500+

GUNS 16,000: 16,000 100mm/85mm

MSL • TACTICAL 4,500+

ASM: some AS-14 *Kedge*; some AS-17 *Krypton*; some AS-18 *Kazoo*; some YJ-63 (expected)

AAM 4,500+: 100 AA-12 *Adder*; 1,200 P-27 (AA-10) *Alamo*; 3,200 P37 (AA-11) *Archer*; some PL-12; some PL-2B; some PL-5B; some PL-8

Paramilitary ε1,500,000 active

People's Armed Police ε1,500,000

Ministry of Public Security

Police 45 div (14 each with 4 regt, remainder no standard organisation; 1–2 div per province)

Border Defence 100,000+

Comms 69,000+

Internal Security ε800,000

NON-STATE ARMED GROUPS

see Part II

DEPLOYMENT

BURUNDI
UN • ONUB 3 obs

CÔTE D'IVOIRE
UN • UNOCI 7 obs

DEMOCRATIC REPUBLIC OF CONGO
UN • MONUC 1 (bn) inf gp; 10 obs; 220

ETHIOPIA/ERITREA
UN • UNMEE 6 obs

LIBERIA
UN • UNMIL 5 obs; 567; 25 civ police

MIDDLE EAST
UN • UNTSO 4 obs

SERBIA AND MONTENEGRO
UN • UNMIK 1 obs

SIERRA LEONE
UN • UNAMSIL 2 obs

SUDAN
UN • UNMIS 8 civ police

WESTERN SAHARA
UN • MINURSO 19 obs

East Timor TL

Timorian Escudo TPE		2003	2004	2005
per capita	US$	244bn	244bn	244bn

Population 1,040,880

Age	0–14	15–19	20–24	25–29	30–64	65 plus
Male	19%	6%	5%	3%	16%	1%
Female	18%	6%	5%	3%	16%	2%

Capabilities

ACTIVE 1,250 (Army 1,250 Naval Element 36)

ORGANISATIONS BY SERVICE

Army 1,250 (including 30 women)

Training began in Jan 2001 with the aim of deploying 1,500 full time personnel and 1,500 reservists
Inf 2 bn

Naval Element 36

FOREIGN FORCES

Australia 3 obs (UNOTIL); about 30
Brazil 2 obs
Fiji 138 Navy: base located at Walu Bay; base (trg) located at Viti
Jordan 1 obs
Malaysia 3 obs
New Zealand 1 obs
Pakistan 1 obs
Philippines 2 obs
Portugal 3 obs

Fiji Fji

Fijian Dollar F$		2003	2004	2005
GDP	F$	4.09bn	4.29bn	
	US$	2.16bn	2.42bn	
per capita	US$	2,497	2,757	
Growth	%	4.8	4.7	
Inflation	%	4.2	2.4	
Debt	US$	263m		
Def bdgt	F$	62.9m	70.0m	65.8m
	US$	33.3m	39.6m	39.2m
US$1=F$		1.89	1.77	1.68

Population 893,354

Ethnic groups: Fijian 51%; Indian 44%; European/Others 5%

Age	0–14	15–19	20–24	25–29	30–64	65 plus
Male	16%	5%	5%	4%	18%	2%
Female	15%	5%	5%	4%	18%	2%

Capabilities

ACTIVE 3,500 (Army 3,200 Navy 300)

East Asia and Australasia

RESERVE some 6,000
(to age 45)

ORGANISATIONS BY SERVICE

Army 3,200 (incl 300 recalled reserves)

FORCES BY ROLE

Inf   7 bn (incl 4 cadre)
Spec Ops 1 coy
Arty   1 bty
Engr   1 bn

EQUIPMENT BY TYPE

ARTY 16
    TOWED • 85mm 4: 4 25-pdr (ceremonial)
    MOR 12: 12 81mm
HELICOPTERS
    SPT 1: 1 AS-355 *Ecureuil*
    UTL 1: 1 AS-365 *Dauphin 2*

Navy 300

EQUIPMENT BY TYPE

PATROL AND COASTAL COMBATANTS 9
    PCC 3: 3 *Kula*
    PCI 6: 2 *Levuka*; 4 *Vai*
LOGISTICS AND SUPPORT 2
    AGHS (SVY) 1: 1 *Tovutu*
    TRG 1: 1 *Cagi Donu* (Presidential Yacht)

FACILITIES

Base 1 (trg) located at Viti, TL, 1 located at Walu Bay, TL

DEPLOYMENT

EAST TIMOR
Navy
Base 1 located at Walu Bay, TL, trg base located at Viti, TL

EGYPT
MFO 1 inf bn; 338

SOLOMON ISLANDS
RAMSI 1 inf coy; ε120

SUDAN
UN • UNMIS 2 obs

Indonesia Indo

Indonesian Rupiah Rp		2003	2004	2005
GDP	Rp	2,086tr	2,303tr	
	US$	243bn	251bn	
per capita	US$	1,035	1,055	
Growth	%	4.9	5.1	
Inflation	%	6.8	6.1	
Debt	US$	134bn		
Def exp[a]	US$	ε7.29bn	ε7.55bn	
Def bdgt	Rp	18.2tr	21.4tr	23.9tr
	US$	2.12bn	2.34bn	2.53bn
FMA (US)	US$			1.59m
US$1=Rp		8,577	9,147	9,451

[a] including extra-budgetary funding

Population   241,973,879

Ethnic groups: Muslim 87%; Javanese 45%; Sundanese 14%; Maduerse 8%; Malay 8%; Chinese 3%; other 22%

Age	0–14	15–19	20–24	25–29	30–64	65 plus
Male	15%	5%	5%	5%	19%	2%
Female	14%	4%	5%	5%	19%	3%

Capabilities

ACTIVE 302,000 (Army 233,000 Navy 45,000 Air 24,000) **Paramilitary 280,000**
Terms of service 2 years selective conscription authorised

RESERVE 400,000
Army cadre units; numbers str n.k., obligation to age 45 for officers

ORGANISATIONS BY SERVICE

Army ε233,000

11 Mil Area Command 150,000
Provincial (KOREM) and District (KODIM) Comd

Avn / composite   1 sqn
Cav   8 bn
Inf   2 bde (6 bn); 60 bn
AB   5 bn
Fd arty   10 bn
Engr   7 bn
Hel   1 sqn
AD   7 bn

Special Forces Command (KOPASSUS) ε5,300
SF 3 gp (*total:* 1 trg unit, 1 (int) SF unit, 2 cdo/para unit, 8 counter-terrorist unit)

Strategic Reserve Command (KOSTRAD) 30,000

Armd   2 bn
Inf   2 div HQ; 3 bde (9 bn)
AB   2 bde

Fd arty   2 regt (6 bn)
ADA   1 regt (2 bn)
Engr   2 bn

EQUIPMENT BY TYPE

TK • LT TK 350: 275 AMX-13 (to be upgraded); 15 PT-76; 60 *Scorpion* 90

RECCE 142: 55 *Ferret* (13 upgraded); 69 *Saladin* (16 upgraded); 18 VBL

AIFV • BMP 11: 11 BMP-2

APC 356

  APC (T) 115: 75 AMX-VCI; 40 FV4333 *Stormer*

  APC (W) 241

    BTR 114: 80 BTR-40; 34 BTR-50PK

    Commando Ranger 22

    FV603 *Saracen* 45 (14 upgraded)

    LAV 60: 60 LAV-150 *Commando*

ARTY 1060

  TOWED 185

    76mm 50: 50 M-48 *M-1948*

    105mm 130: 120 M-101; 10 M-56

    155mm 5: 5 FH-2000

  MOR 875:

    81mm 800

    120mm 75: 75 Brandt

AT

  RCL 135

    106mm • M-40 45: 45 M-40A1

    90mm 90: 90 M-67

  RL • 89mm 700: 700 LRAC

AIRCRAFT • TPT 11: 3 DHC-5 *Buffalo*; 6 NC-212 (CASA 212) *Aviocar*; 2 Rockwell *Turbo Commander* 680

HELICOPTERS

  ATK 2: 2 Mi-35 *Hind*

  UTL 37

    BELL 205 8: 8 Bell 205A

    NB-412 (Bell 412) *Twin Huey* 12

    NBO-105 (BO-105) 17

  TRG • HUGHES 300 12: 12 Hughes 300C

AD

  SAM 68: 51 *Rapier*; 17 RBS-70

  GUNS • TOWED 413

    20mm 121: 121 Rh 202

    40mm 36: 36 L/70

    57mm 256: 256 S-60

Navy ε29,000

EQUIPMENT BY TYPE

SUBMARINES • TACTICAL • SSK 2:

  2 *Cakra* each with 8 single 533mm TT with 14 SUT HWT

PRINCIPAL SURFACE COMBATANTS 29

  FRIGATES 13

    FFG 10:

      6 *Ahmad Yani* (capacity either 1 HAS-1 *Wasp* ASW hel or 1 NBO-105 (BO-105) utl hel) each with 2 triple 324mm ASTT (6 eff.) each with Mk 46 LWT, 2 SIMBAD x2 manual each with *Mistral* SAM, 2 Mk 141 *Harpoon* quad (8 eff.) each with 1 RGM-84A *Harpoon* tactical SSM, 1 76mm gun

      3 *Fatahillah* each with 2 B515 *ILAS-3*/triple 324mm ASTT (2-6 eff.) (not on Nala) with 12 A244/Mk 46, 2 twin (4 eff.) each with 1 MM-38 *Exocet* tactical SSM, 1 2 tube *Bofors* 375mm (2 eff.), 1 120mm gun

1 *Hajar Dewantara* (capacity 1 NBO-105 (BO-105) utl hel) (trg) with 2 x1 533mm ASTT each with SUT HWT, 2 twin (4 eff.) each with 1 MM-38 *Exocet* tactical SSM, 1 single

  FF 3:

    3 *Samadikun* each with 2 triple 324mm ASTT (6 eff.) each with Mk 46 LWT, 1 76mm gun

CORVETTES • FS 16:

  16 *Kapitan Patimura* each with 4 x1 400mm ASTT, Twin each with SA-N-5 *Grail* SAM, 2 RBU 6000 *Smerch 2* (24 eff.), 1 57mm gun

PATROL AND COASTAL COMBATANTS 23

  PCC 11:

    3 KAL-35 each with 2 20mm gun

    8 *Sibarau*

  PFM 4:

    4 *Mandau* each with 4 MM-38 *Exocet* tactical SSM

  PCT 4:

    4 *Singa* each with 2 Single 533mm TT

  PCO 4: 4 *Kakap*

MINE WARFARE • MINE COUNTERMEASURES 11

  MCC 3: 1 *Pulau Rani*; 2 *Pulau Rengat*

  MSC 8: 8 *Palau Rote* mostly non-operational

AMPHIBIOUS

  LS • LST 26: 1 *Teluk Amboina* (capacity 16 tanks; 200 troops); 12 *Teluk Gilimanuk*; 7 *Teluk Langsa* (capacity 16 tanks; 200 troops); 6 *Teluk Semangka* (capacity 17 tanks; 200 troops)

  CRAFT 65: 65 LCM/LCVP

LOGISTICS AND SUPPORT 15:

  AGOR 6

  AO 2: 1 *Arun*; 1 *Sorong*

  AOT 2: 2 *Khobi*

  AR 1

  ATF 2

  RY 1 (Presidential Yacht)

  Spt 1

FACILITIES

Base 1 located at Belawan, 1 located at Vayapura, 1 located at Ujung Pandang

Marines 15,000

FORCES BY ROLE

SF   1 bn under strength

Marine   2 (corps) gp (*each*: 1 indep marine inf bde (3 marine inf bn), 3 marine inf bn)

Cbt Sp   1 regt (arty, AD)

EQUIPMENT BY TYPE

TK • LT TK 55: 55 PT-76†

RECCE 21: 21 BRDM

AIFV 34: 24 AMX-10P; 10 AMX-10 PAC 90

APC • APC (W) • BTR • BTR-50 100: 100 BTR-50P

ARTY 62+

  TOWED 50+

    105mm • LG1 22: 22 LG1 MK II

    122mm 28+: 28+ M-38 *M-1938*

  MRL • 140mm 12: 12 BM-14

  MOR: some 81mm

AD: 150+ guns incl. 5 L/60/L/70 40mm, S-60 towed 57mm

Naval Aviation ε1,000

AIRCRAFT

MP 27: 2 CASA 235 MPA; 15 GAF N-22B *Searchmaster B*; 10 GAF N-22SL *Searchmaster L*
TPT 15
   CN-235 1: 1 CN-235M
   DHC-5 *Buffalo* 2
   NC-212 (CASA 212) 4: 4 CASA 212-200 *Aviocar*
   PA-34 *Seneca* 4
   Rockwell *Commander* 100 4
  TRG 6: 6 PA-38 *Tomahawk*
HELICOPTERS
  ASW 9: 9 HAS-1 *Wasp*
  SPT • **AS-332** 6: 6 NAS-322L (AS-332L) *Super Puma*
  UTL 22
   EC-120 3: 3 EC-120B *Colibri* (+6 on order)
   NB-412 (Bell 412) *Twin Huey* 2
   ***NBO-105 (BO-105)** 17

Eastern Command

FORCES BY ROLE
Navy 1 HQ located at Surabaya

FACILITIES
13 Minor bases

Western Command

FORCES BY ROLE
Navy 1 HQ located at Teluk Ratai (Jakarta)

FACILITIES
10 Minor bases
Minor Base 1 (10) located at Teluk Ratai (Jakarta)

Air Force 24,000
2 operational cmds (East and West Indo) plus trg cmd. Only 45% of ac op

FORCES BY ROLE
Ftr   1 sqn with 8 F-5E *Tiger II*; 4 F-5F *Tiger II*

FGA   1 sqn with 2 Su-30 MKI *Flanker* (multirole); 2 Su-27SK *Flanker* (AD); 1 sqn with 7 F-16A *Fighting Falcon*; 3 F-16B *Fighting Falcon*; 1 sqn with 11 A-4E *Skyhawk*; 1 TA-4H *Skyhawk*; 2 TA-4J *Skyhawk*; 2 sqn with 7 *Hawk* MK109; 28 *Hawk* MK209 (FGA/ftr)

Recce 1 flt with 12 OV-10F *Bronco** mostly non-operational

MR   1 sqn with 3 B-737-200

Tpt   5 sqn with 1 B-707; 8 C-130B *Hercules*; 4 C-130H *Hercules*; 6 C-130H-30 *Hercules*; 10 NC-212 (CASA 212) *Aviocar*; 10 CN-235-110; 5 Cessna 401; 2 Cessna 402; 6 F-27-400M *Troopship*; 1 F-28-1000; 2 F-28-3000; 3 L-100-30; 1 SC.7 3M *Skyvan* (survey); 4 Cessna 207 *Stationair*

Tkr   some sqn with 2 KC-130B *Hercules*

Trg   3 sqn with 2 Cessna 172; 39 AS-202 *Bravo*; 7 *Hawk* MK53*; 7 KT-1B; 19 SF-260M/SF-260W *Warrior*; 20 T-34C *Turbo Mentor*; 6 T-41D *Mescalero*

Hel   3 sqn with 10 S-58T; 5 NAS-322L (AS-332L) *Super Puma* (VIP/CSAR); 11 NAS-330 (SA-330) *Puma* (1 NAS-330SM VIP); 12 EC-120B *Colibri*

EQUIPMENT BY TYPE
AIRCRAFT 94 combat capable
FTR 26
  F-5 12: 8 F-5E *Tiger II*; 4 F-5F *Tiger II*
  Su-30 2: 2 Su-30 MKI *Flanker* (multirole)
  F-16 10: 7 F-16A *Fighting Falcon*; 3 F-16B *Fighting Falcon*
  Su-27 2: 2 Su-27SK *Flanker* (AD)
FGA 18
  A-4 11: 11 A-4E *Skyhawk*
  Hawk **MK109** 7; *Hawk* **MK209 (FGA/ftr)** 28
FAC • **OV-10** 12: 12 OV-10F *Bronco** mostly non-operational
TKR • **KC-130** 2: 2 KC-130B *Hercules*
TPT 62:
  B-707 1
  B-737 3: 3 B-737-200
  C-130 18: 8 C-130B *Hercules*; 4 C-130H Hercules; 6 C-130H-30 *Hercules*
  CN-235 10: 10 CN-235-110
  Cessna 401 5
  Cessna 402 2
  F-27 6: 6 F-27-400M *Troopship*
  F-28 3: 1 F-28-1000; 2 F-28-3000
  L-100 3: 3 L-100-30
  NC-212 (CASA 212) *Aviocar:* 10
  SC.7 3M *Skyvan:* 1 (survey)
UTL 6: 2 Cessna 172; 4 Cessna 207 *Stationair*
TRG 129:
  AS-202 Bravo 39
  Hawk **MK53*** 7
  KT-1 7: 7 KT-1B
  SF-260 19: 19 SF-260M/SF-260W *Warrior*
  T-34 20: 20 T-34C *Turbo Mentor*
  T-41 6: 6 T-41D *Mescalero*
  TA-4 3: 1 TA-4H *Skyhawk**; 2 TA-4J *Skyhawk**
HELICOPTERS
  SAR 10: 10 S-58T
  SPT 16
   AS-332 5: 5 NAS-322L (AS-332L) *Super Puma* (VIP/CSAR)
   NAS-330 (SA-330) *Puma* 11 (1 NAS-330SM VIP)
  UTL • **EC-120** 12: 12 EC-120B *Colibri*
MSL • **TACTICAL**
  ASM • **AGM-65**: some AGM-65G *Maverick*
  AAM • **AIM-9**: some AIM-9P *Sidewinder*

Special Forces (Paskhasan)
Special Ops 3 ((PASKHASAN)) wg (*total:* 6 Special Ops sqn); 4 indep coy

Paramilitary ε280,000 active

Customs
PATROL AND COASTAL COMBATANTS 72: 72 PFI

Marine Police
PATROL AND COASTAL COMBATANTS 25: 10 PCC; 6 PCI (small); 9 more

Police ε280,000 (including 14,000 police 'mobile bde' (BRIMOB) org in 56 coy, incl CT unit (Gegana))
APC • **APC (W)** 34: 34 *Tactica*

AIRCRAFT • TPT 5: 2 Beech 18; 2 NC-212 (CASA 212) *Aviocar*; 1 Rockwell *Turbo Commander* 680
HELICOPTERS • UTL 22: 3 Bell 206 *JetRanger*; 19 NBO-105 (BO-105)

Sea Commuications Agency
Responsible to Dept. of Communications
PATROL AND COASTAL COMBATANTS • PCI 9: 4 *Golok* (SAR); 5 *Kujang*

Reserve Organisations

Kamra ε40,000 (report for 3 weeks' basic training each year; part time police auxiliary)
People's Security

NON-STATE ARMED GROUPS

see Part II

DEPLOYMENT

DEMOCRATIC REPUBLIC OF CONGO
UN • MONUC 9 obs; 179

GEORGIA
UN • UNOMIG 4 obs

LIBERIA
UN • UNMIL 3 obs

SIERRA LEONE
UN • UNAMSIL 6 obs

SUDAN
UN • UNMIS 4 obs

Japan J

Japanese Yen ¥		2003	2004	2005
GDP	¥	497tr	503tr	
	US$	4.32tr	4.66tr	
per capita	US$	34,028	36,598	
Growth	%	1.4	2.6	
Inflation	%	-0.3	0.0	
Public Debt	%	154	157	
Def bdgt	¥	4.92tr	4.87tr	4.83tr
	US$	42.8bn	45.1bn	44.7bn
US$1=¥		115	108	108

Population 127,417,244

Ethnic groups: Korean <1%

Age	0–14	15–19	20–24	25–29	30–64	65 plus
Male	7%	3%	3%	3%	24%	8%
Female	7%	3%	3%	3%	24%	10%

Capabilities

ACTIVE 239,900 (Air 45,600 Maritime Self-Defense Force 34,600 Naval Aviation 9,800 Ground Self-Defense Force 148,200 Naval Aviation 9,800) Paramilitary 12,250

RESERVE some **44,395**

ORGANISATIONS BY SERVICE

Ground Self-Defense Force some 148,200

FORCES BY ROLE
5 Army HQ (regional comds)
Composite 2 bde
Army 9 div
Armd 1 div
Inf 3 bde
Spec Ops 1 unit
AB 1 bde
Arty 1 bde; 1 unit
Engr 5 bde
Hel 1 bde
Trg 3 bde; 1 regt
AD 2 bde; 3 gp

EQUIPMENT BY TYPE
TK • MBT 980: 700 Type-74; 280 Type-90
RECCE 100: 100 Type-87
AIFV 70: 70 Type-89
APC 730
  APC (T) 370: 30 Type-60; 340 Type-73
  APC (W) 360: 200 Type-82; 160 Type-96
ARTY 1,980
  TOWED • 155mm 480: 480 FH-70
  SP 250
    155mm 160: 140 Type-75; 20 Type-99
    203mm 90: 90 M-110A2
  MRL 110
    130mm 20: 20 Type-75 SP
    227mm 90: 90 MLRS
  MOR 1,140: 670 81mm; 90 107mm; 380 120mm (20 SP)
AT
  MSL 690: 60 Type-64 *Chu-MAT*; 220 Type-79; 410 Type-87 *Jyu-MAT*
  RCL 2,820
    106mm 100: 100 Type-60 SP
    84mm 2,720: 2,720 *Carl Gustav*
  RL 910: 910 89mm
AIRCRAFT
  TPT 10: 10 LR-2 (Beech 350) *Super King Air*
  UTL 10: 10 LR-1 (MU-2)
HELICOPTERS
  ATK • AH-1 90: 90 AH-1S *Cobra*
  SPT 53
    AS-332 3: 3 AS-332L *Super Puma* (VIP)
    CH-47 50: 50 CH-47J (CH-47D) *Chinook*/CH-47JA *Chinook*
  UTL 300: 120 MD-500
    UH-1 150: 150 UH-1J (UH-1H) *Iroquois*
    UH-60 30: 30 UH-60JA (UH-60L) *Black Hawk*
AD
  SAM 640: 60 Type-81 *Tan-SAM*
    SP 90: 90 Type-93 *Kin-SAM*
    TOWED • MIM-23 200: 200 I-HAWK MIM-23B
    MANPAD 290: 80 FIM-92A *Stinger*; 210 Type-91 *Kin-SAM*

East Asia and Australasia

GUNS • **35mm** 60: 10 (twin); 50 Type-87 SP MAT
MSL • TACTICAL • SSM 100: 100 Type-88 (coastal)

Maritime Self-Defense Force ε44,400

Surface units org into 4 escort flotillas of 8 DD/FF each. Bases Yokosuka, Kure, Sasebo, Maizuru SS org into 2 flotillas. Bases Kure, Yokosuka. Remainder assigned to 5 regional districts.

EQUIPMENT BY TYPE
SUBMARINES • TACTICAL • SSK 16:

7 *Harushio* each with 6 single 533mm TT each with T-89 HWT/UGM-84C *Harpoon* tactical USGW

6 *Oyashio* each with 6 single 533mm TT each with UGM-84C *Harpoon* tactical USGW

3 *Yuushio* each with 6 single 533mm TT each with T-89 HWT/UGM-84C *Harpoon* tactical USGW

PRINCIPAL SURFACE COMBATANTS 53
DESTROYERS 44
DDG 39:

6 *Asagiri* (capacity 1 SH-60J *Seahawk* ASW hel) each with 2 triple 324mm ASTT (6 eff.) each with Mk 46 LWT, 1 Mk 112 octuple (8 eff.) with tactical ASROC, 1 Mk 29 *Sea Sparrow* octuple with 20+ *Sea Sparrow* SAM, 2 Mk 141 *Harpoon* quad (8 eff.) each with 1 RGM-84C *Harpoon* tactical SSM, 1 76mm gun

2 *Hatakaze* each with 2 triple 324mm ASTT (6 eff.), 1 Mk 13 GMLS with 40 SM-1 MR SAM, 1 Mk 112 octuple (8 eff.), 2 Mk 141 *Harpoon* quad (8 eff.) each with 1 RGM-84C *Harpoon* tactical SSM, 2 127mm gun, 1 hel landing platform

11 *Hatsuyuki* (capacity 1 SH-60J *Seahawk* ASW hel) each with 2 triple 324mm ASTT (6 eff.) each with Mk 46 LWT, 1 Mk 112 octuple (8 eff.) with tactical ASROC, 1+ Mk 29 *Sea Sparrow* octuple with 20+ RIM-7F/M *Sea Sparrow* SAM, 2 Mk 141 *Harpoon* quad (8 eff.) each with 1 RGM-84C *Harpoon* tactical SSM, 1 76mm gun

4 *Kongou* (with hel deck) each with 2 triple 324mm ASTT (6 eff.), 2 Mk 141 *Harpoon* quad (8 eff.) each with 1 RGM-84C *Harpoon* tactical SSM, 1 29 cell Mk 41 VLS (29 eff.) with SM-2 MR SAM, tactical ASROC, 1 61 cell Mk 41 VLS (61 eff.) with SM-2 MR SAM, tactical ASROC, 1 127mm gun, 1 hel landing platform; *Aegis* Baseline 4 C2

9 *Murasame* (capacity 1 SH-60J *Seahawk* ASW hel) each with 2 quad (8 eff.) each with tactical SSM-1B, 2 triple 324mm TT (6 eff.) each with Mk 46 LWT, 1 16 cells Mk 41 VLS with up to 29 tactical ASROC, 1 16 cell Mk 48 VLS with RIM-7M *Sea Sparrow* SAM, 2 76mm gun

3 *Tachikaze* each with 2 triple 324mm ASTT (6 eff.) each with Mk 46 LWT, 1 Mk 13 GMLS with 32 SM-1 MR SAM, 8+ RGM-84C *Harpoon* tactical SSM, 1 Mk 112 octuple (8 eff.) with up to 8 tactical ASROC, 1 127mm gun

4 *Takanami* (capacity 1 SH-60J *Seahawk* ASW hel) (*Improved Murasame*) each with 1 SH-60J *Seahawk* ASW hel, 2 quad (8 eff.) each with tactical SSM-1B, 2 triple 324mm TT (6 eff.) each with Mk 46 LWT, 1 32 cell Mk 41 VLS (32 eff.) with tactical ASROC/RIM-7P *Sea Sparrow* SAM, 1 *Otobreda* 127mm gun

DD 5:

2 *Haruna* each with 3 SH-60J *Seahawk* ASW hel, 2 triple ASTT (6 eff.) each with Mk 46 LWT, 1 Mk 112 octuple (8 eff.) with tactical ASROC, 1 Mk 29 *Sea Sparrow* octuple with RIM-7F/M *Sea Sparrow* SAM, 2 127mm gun

2 *Shirane* each with 3 SH-60J *Seahawk* ASW hel, 2 triple ASTT (6 eff.) each with Mk 46 LWT, 1 Mk 112 octuple (8 eff.) with tactical ASROC, 1+ Mk 29 *Sea Sparrow* octuple with 24+ RIM-162A *Sea Sparrow* SAM, 2 127mm gun

1 *Yamagumo* with 2 triple ASTT (6 eff.) each with Mk 46 LWT, 1 Mk 112 octuple (8 eff.) with tactical ASROC, 1 Type 71/ 4 tube *Mitsubshi* 375mm *Bofors* (4 eff.), 2 76mm twin gun

FRIGATES • FFG 9:

6 *Abukuma* each with 2 triple ASTT (6 eff.) each with Mk 46 LWT, 1 Mk 112 octuple (8 eff.) with tactical ASROC, 2 Mk 141 *Harpoon* quad (8 eff.) each with 1 RGM-84C *Harpoon* tactical SSM, 1 76mm gun

1 *Ishikari* with 2 triple ASTT (6 eff.) each with Mk 46 LWT, 2 Mk 141 *Harpoon* quad (8 eff.) each with 1 RGM-84C *Harpoon* tactical SSM, 1 Type 71/ 4 tube *Mitsubshi* 375mm *Bofors* (4 eff.), 1 76mm gun

2 *Yubari* each with 2 triple ASTT (6 eff.), 2 Mk 141 *Harpoon* quad (8 eff.) each with 1 RGM-84C *Harpoon* tactical SSM, 1 Type 71/ 4 tube *Mitsubshi* 375mm *Bofors* (4 eff.), 1 76mm gun

PATROL AND COASTAL COMBATANTS 9
PFM 6:

6 *Hayabusa* each with 4 tactical SSM-1B

PHM 3:

3 *Ichi-Go* each with 4 tactical SSM-1B

MINE WARFARE • MINE COUNTERMEASURES 31
MCM SPT 4:

2 *Nijma*

2 *Uraga* each with 1 hel landing platform (for MH-53E)

MSC 24: 5 *Hatsushima*; 10 *Sugashima*; 9 *Uwajima*
MSO 3: 3 *Yaeyama*
AMPHIBIOUS
LS • LST 4:

1 *Atsumi* (capacity 5 Type-74 MBTs; 130 troops; 2 LCVP)

3 *Osumi* (capacity 10 tanks; 330 troops; 10 Type-90 MBTs; 330 troops; 2 LCAC(L) ACV) each with 1 hel landing platform (for 2 x CH-47)

CRAFT 23
LCU 4: 2 *Ichi-Go*; 2 *Yuru* (capacity 70 troops)
LCM 13
ACV 6: 6 LCAC(L) (capacity either 1 MBT or 60 troops)

LOGISTICS AND SUPPORT 28:
AG 10
AGB 1
AGS 4
AOE 5: 2 *Mashu*; 3 *Towada* each with 1 hel landing platform (for up to SH-3)
ARC 1
AS 2
Spt 2

TRG 3: 1 *Kashima*; 1 *Shimayuki*; 1 *Yamagumo* TV35 with 2 triple ASTT (6 eff.) each with Mk 46 LWT, 1 Mk 112 octuple (8 eff.) with tactical ASROC, 1 Type 71/ 4 tube *Mitsubshi* 375mm *Bofors* (4 eff.), 4 76mm gun

FACILITIES

Base 1 located at Kure, 1 located at Sasebo, 1 located at Yokosuka, 1 located at Maizuru, 1 located at Ominato

Naval Aviation ε9,800

FORCES BY ROLE

7 Air Groups

ASW 5 (land based, 1 trg) sqn with SH-60J *Seahawk*; 4 (shipboard) sqn with SH-60J *Seahawk*

MR 9 (1 trg) sqn with P-3C *Orion*

EW 1 sqn with EP-3 *Orion*

MCM 1 sqn with MH-53E *Sea Dragon*

SAR 7 sqn with UH-60J *Black Hawk*; 1 sqn with Shin Meiwa US-1A

Tpt 1 sqn with YS-11M

Trg 1 sqn with OH-6D (MD-500MD); OH-6DA (MD-500ME); 4 sqn with T-5; TC-90; YS-11T

EQUIPMENT BY TYPE

AIRCRAFT 80 combat capable

MP • P-3 80: 80 P-3C *Orion*

SAR • SHIN MEIWA US-1 7: 7 *Shin Meiwa* US-1A

TPT • YS-11 4: 4 YS-11M

TRG 66: 35 T-5; 25 TC-90; 6 YS-11T

HELICOPTERS

MCM 10: 10 MH-53E *Sea Dragon*

SAR 18: 18 UH-60J *Black Hawk*

ASW 88: 3 S-61 *Sea King*; 85 SH-60J *Seahawk*

UTL • MD-500 • MD-500M 12: 7 OH-6D (MD-500MD); 5 OH-6DA (MD-500ME)

TRG 15: 15 H-60K *Black Hawk*

Air Self-Defense Force up to 45,600

Flying hours 150 hrs/year on Aircraft

FORCES BY ROLE

7 cbt wings

Ftr 2 sqn with 50 F-4EJ (F-4E) *Phantom II*; 7 sqn with 130 F-15 *Eagle*

FGA 1 sqn with 20 Mitsubishi F-1; 1 sqn with 20 F-4EJ (F-4E) *Phantom II*; 1 sqn with 40 Mitsubishi F-2

Recce 1 sqn with 20 RF-EJ (RF-4E) *Phantom II**

EW 2 sqn with 1 Kawasaki EC-1; 10 YS-11E

AEW 1 sqn with 10 E-2C *Hawkeye*; E-767 (AWACS)

SAR 1 wg with 20 U-125A *Peace Krypton*; LR-1 (MU-2); 20 UH-60J *Black Hawk*; 10 KV-107 (Boeing Vertol 107) (10 SAR det)

Tpt 3 sqn with 20 C-1; 10 C-130H *Hercules*; YS-11; 1 sqn with B-747-400 (VIP); 4 (hy-lift) flt with 10 CH-47 *Chinook*

Liaison some sqn with U-4; 90+ T-4

CAL 1 sqn with U-125-800 *Peace Krypton*; YS-11

Test 1 wg with F-15 *Eagle*/F-15D *Eagle*; 10 Kawasaki T-4

Trg 5 wg; 12 sqn with 20 F-15 *Eagle*/F-15D *Eagle** training; 20 Mitsubishi F-2B; 40 T-3; 80 T-4; 10 T-400

EQUIPMENT BY TYPE

AIRCRAFT 300 combat capable

FTR 150: 130 F-15 *Eagle*; 20 F-15 *Eagle* ftr ac/F-15D *Eagle** trg

FGA 130: 40 Mitsubishi F-2; 20 Mitsubishi F-1; 70 F-4EJ (F-4E) *Phantom II*

RECCE • RF-4 20: 20 RF-EJ (RF-4E) *Phantom II**

EW 1: 1 Kawasaki EC-1

AEW • E-2 10: 10 E-2C *Hawkeye*

SAR • U-125 20: 20 U-125A *Peace Krypton*

TPT 30: 20 C-1; 10 C-130H *Hercules*

TRG 260+: 10 Kawasaki T-4; 20 Mitsubishi F-2B; 40 T-3; 170+ T-4; 10 T-400; 10 YS-11E

HELICOPTERS

SAR 20: 20 UH-60J *Black Hawk*

SPT 20: 10 CH-47 *Chinook*; 10 KV-107 (Boeing Vertol 107)

Air Defence

FORCES BY ROLE

ac control and warning

AD 4 wg; 28 radar sites; 1 (Air Base Defence) gp with Type-81 *Tan-SAM*; FIM-92A *Stinger*; Type-91 *Kin-SAM*; M-167 *Vulcan*

SAM 6 gp each with 120+ MIM-104 *Patriot* (total: 24 SAM sqn)

EQUIPMENT BY TYPE

AD

SAM 720+: some Type-81 *Tan-SAM*

TOWED 720+: 720+ MIM-104 *Patriot*

MANPAD: some FIM-92A *Stinger*; some Type-91 *Kin-SAM*

GUNS • 20mm • TOWED: some M-167 *Vulcan*

MSL • TACTICAL

ASM: some ASM-1Type-80; some ASM-2 Type-93

AAM: some AAM-4 (Type-99); some AIM-7 *Sparrow*; some AIM-9 *Sidewinder*; some Type-90 (AAM-3)

FACILITIES

Radar stn 28 (ac control and warning)

Paramilitary 12,250

Coast Guard

Ministry of Transport, no cbt role

PATROL AND COASTAL COMBATANTS 419

MISC BOATS/CRAFT 86: 86 boats

PCC 66 (under 1000 tons)

PCI 225

PSO 28: 28 *Shiretok* (over 1,000)

PSOH 14:

2 *Izu* (over 1,000)

1 *Kojima* (over 1,000, trg)

2 *Mizuho* (over 1,000) each with 2 Bell 212 utl hel

1 *Shikishima* (over 1,000) with 2 AS-332 *Super Puma* spt hel

8 *Soya* (over 1,000) each with 1 Bell 212 utl hel

LOGISTICS AND SUPPORT 74: 4 ABU; 13 AGHS; 54 small tenders; 3 Trg
AIRCRAFT
  AEW 2: 2 SAAB 340 *Erieye*
  TPT • BEECH 90 19: 19 Beech C90 *King Air*
  UTL 6
    CESSNA 206 • CESSNA U-206 1: 1 Cessna U-206G *Stationair*
    YS-11 5: 5 YS-11A
HELICOPTERS
  SPT 4: 4 AS-332 *Super Puma*
  UTL 40
    BELL 206 4: 4 Bell 206B *JetRanger II*
    Bell 212 26 Bell 412 *Twin Huey* 6
    S-76 4: 4 S-76C

DEPLOYMENT

IRAQ
Ground Self-Defense Force ε560 (Peace Support)
Maritime Self- Defense Force ε300 (Peace Support)
Air Self-Defense Force 200 (Peace Support – in Kuwait)

SYRIA/ISRAEL
UN • UNDOF 30

NON-STATE ARMED GROUPS

see Part II

FOREIGN FORCES

United States Navy: base located at Sasebo; base located at Yokosuka USAF: 14,700 USPACOM: 9 principal surface combatants located at Yokosuka; 1 aircraft carrier located at Yokosuka; 1 *Blue Ridge* LCC (capacity 3 LCPL; 2 LCVP; 700 troops; 1 SH-3H *Sea King* utl hel) located at Yokosuka; 4 amphibious vessels located at Sasebo; 1 HQ (7th Fleet) located at Yokosuka; 1 5th Air Force HQ located at Okinawa–Kadena AB; 1 HQ (9th Theater Army Area Command) located at Zama (HQ USARPAC)); Elems MEF div; 1 ftr wg located at Okinawa–Kadena AB (2 ftr sqn each with 18 F-16 *Fighting Falcon* located at Misawa AB); 1 ftr wg located at Okinawa–Kadena AB (1 SAR sqn with 8 HH-60G *Pave Hawk*, 1 AEW sqn with 2 E-3B *Sentry*, 2 ftr sqn each with 24 F-15C *Eagle*/F-15D *Eagle*); 1 MCM sqn located at Sasebo; 1 Special Ops gp located at Okinawa–Kadena AB; 1 airlift wg located at Yokota AB with 10 C-130E *Hercules*; 4 C-21 *Learjet*; 4 C-9 *Nightingale*

Korea, Democratic Peoples Republic of DPRK

North Korean Won		2003	2004	2005
GDP	US$	ε22bn	ε22bn	
per capita	US$	979	969	
Def exp	US$	ε5.5bn	ε5.5bn	
Def bdgt	won	3.62bn	3.93bn	ε4.19bn
	US$	1.64bn	1.79bn	1.9bn
US$1=won		2.2	2.2	2.2

Population		22,912,177				

Age	0–14	15–19	20–24	25–29	30–64	65 plus
Male	12%	4%	4%	3%	22%	3%
Female	12%	4%	4%	3%	23%	5%

Capabilities

ACTIVE 1,106,000 (Army 950,000 Navy 46,000 Air 110,000) Paramilitary 189,000
Terms of service Army 5–12 years Navy 5–10 years Air Force 3–4 years, followed by compulsory parttime service to age 40. Thereafter service in the Worker/Peasant Red Guard to age 60.

RESERVE 4,700,000 (Army 600,000, Navy 65,000), Paramilitary 3,500,000
Reservists are assigned to units (see also Paramilitary)

ORGANISATIONS BY SERVICE

Army ε950,000

FORCES BY ROLE

Army	corps tps: 14 arty bde (incl 122mm, 152mm, SP, MRL); 1 tps (1 (FROG) SSM regt, 1 *Scud*) SSM bde, 6 hy arty bde (incl MRL))
Armd	1 corps; 15 bde
Mech	4 corps
Inf	12 corps; 27 div; 14 bde
Arty	2 corps; 21 bde
MRL	9 bde
Capital Defence	1 corps

Special Purpose Forces Command 88,000

Army	6 (sniper) bde
Recce	17 bn
Amph	2 (sniper) bde
SF	8 (Bureau of Reconnaissance) bn
Lt inf	9 bde
AB	2 (sniper) bde; 3 bde; 1 bn

Reserves 600,000

Inf 40 div; 18 bde

EQUIPMENT BY TYPE
TK 4,060+

MBT 3,500+: 3,500+ T-34/T-54/T-55/T-62/Type-59

LT TK 560+: some M-1985; 560 PT-76

AIFV: some BTR-80A

APC 2,500+

  APC (T): some Type-531 (Type-63); some VTT-323

  APC (W) • **BTR** 2500: 2,500 BTR-152/BTR-40/BTR-50/BTR-60

ARTY 17,900+

  TOWED 3,500: 3,500 D-30 122mm/D-74 122mm/M-1931/37 122mm/M-1937 152mm/M-1938 152mm/M-1943 152mm/M-46 130mm

  SP 4,400: 4,400 M-1974 152mm/M-1975 130mm/M-1977 122mm/M-1977 152mm/M-1978 170mm/M-1981 122mm/M-1981 130mm/M-1985 122mm/M-1989 170mm/M-1991 122mm/M-1991 130mm

  GUN/MOR: some 120mm (reported)

  MRL 2,500: 2,500 BM-11 122mm/M-1977 (BM-21) 122mm/M-1985 122mm/M-1985 240mm/M-1989 240mm/M-1991 240mm/M-1992 122mm/M-1993 122mm/Type-63 107mm

  MOR 7,500: 7,500 M-37 82mm/M-43 120mm/M-43 160mm

AT

  MSL: some AT-1 *Snapper*; some AT-3 *Sagger* (some SP); some AT-4 *Spigot*; some AT-5 *Spandrel*

  RCL • **82mm** 1700: 1,700 B-10

AD

  SAM • **MANPAD** 10,000+: ε10,000+ SA-16 *Gimlet*/SA-7 *Grail*

  GUNS 11,000: 11,000 KS-19 towed 100mm/M-1939 *KS-12* towed 85mm/M-1939 towed 37mm/M-1984 SP SP 14.5mm/M-1985 SP SP 57mm/M-1992 SP 37mm/M-1992 SP SP 23mm/S-60 towed 57mm/ZPU-1 towed 14.5mm/ZPU-2 towed 14.5mm/ZPU-4 towed 14.5mm/ZU-23 towed 23mm

MSL • **TACTICAL** • **SSM** 64+: 24 FROG-3/FROG-5/FROG-7; ε10 *No-dong* (est. 90+ msl); 30+ *Scud*-B/*Scud*-C (200+ msl)

Navy ε46,000

FORCES BY ROLE

Navy 2 (Fleet) HQ located at Tasa-ri; 1 HQ located at Nampo; 1 HQ located at Toejo Dong

EQUIPMENT BY TYPE

SUBMARINES • **TACTICAL** 88

  SSK 22: 22 PRC Type-031/FSU *Romeo* each with 8 single 533mm TT with 14 SAET-60 HWT

  SSC 21: 21 *Sang-O†* each with 2 single 533mm TT (in some) each with Russian 53–65 ASW

  SSI 45†

PRINCIPAL SURFACE COMBATANTS 9

  FRIGATES • **FF** 3:

    2 *Najin* each with 2 single each with 1 SS-N-2 tactical SSM, 2 RBU 1200 (10 eff.), 2 100mm sun

    1 *Soho* with 4 single each with 1 SS-N-2 tactical SSM, 2 RBU 1200 (10 eff.), 1 100mm gun, 1 hel landing platform (for med hel)

  CORVETTES • **FS** 6:

    4 *Sariwon* each with 1 85mm gun

    2 *Tral* each with 1 85mm gun

PATROL AND COASTAL COMBATANTS 301

  PC 6:

    6 *Chong-Ju* each with 2 RBU 1200 (10 eff.), 1 85mm gun

  PCI 121: 100 (small); 3 *Chodo*; 18 FSU SO-1

  PFC 19:

    6 *Hainan* each with 4 RBU 1200 (20 eff.)

    13 *Taechong* each with 2 RBU 1200 (10 eff.)

  PFI 12: 12 *Shanghai* II

  PTG 21:

    6 *Sohung*

    15 *Sojo* each with 4 single each with 1 SS-N-2 tactical SSM

  PFM 22:

    4 *Huangfen* each with 4 single each with 1 SS-N-2 tactical SSM

    10 *Komar* each with 2 single each with 1 SS-N-2 tactical SSM

    8 *Osa* II each with 2 single each with 1 SS-N-2 tactical SSM

  PHT 100: 60 *Ku Song*; 40 *Sin Hung*

MINE WARFARE • **MINE COUNTERMEASURES** 23: circa 23 MSI

AMPHIBIOUS

  LS • **LSM** 10: 10 *Hantae* (capacity 3 tanks; 350 troops)

  CRAFT 260: 15 LCU

    LCVP 100: ε100 *Nampo* (capacity 35 troops)

    LCM 15

    ACV ε130

LOGISTICS AND SUPPORT 7: 3 AGHS (inshore); 1 (Ocean); 1 AS; 2 ATF

FACILITIES

Base 1 (West Coast) located at Tasa-ri, 1 (West Coast) located at Koampo, 1 (East Coast) located at Puam-Dong, 1 (West Coast) located at Chodo-ri, 1 (West Coast) located at Sagon-ni, 1 (West Coast) located at Pipa Got, 1 (West Coast) located at Nampo, 1 (East Coast) located at Toejo Dong, 1 (East Coast) located at Chaho Nodongjagu, 1 (East Coast) located at Mayang-do, 1 (East Coast) located at Mugye-po, 1 (East Coast) located at Najin, 1 (East Coast) located at Songjon-pardo, 1 (East Coast) located at Changjon, 1 (East Coast) located at Munchon

Coastal Defence

FORCES BY ROLE

SSM 2 (*Silkworm* in 6 sites, and probably some mobile launchers) regt

EQUIPMENT BY TYPE

ARTY •

  TOWED

    122mm: some M-1931/37

    152mm: some M-1937

  COASTAL • **130mm**: some M-1992; some SM-4-1

Air Force 110,000

4 air divs. 1st, 2nd and 3rd Air Divs (cbt) responsible for N, E and S air defence sectors respectively. 8th Air Div (trg) responsible for NE sector. 33 regts (11 ftr/fga, 2 bbr, 7 hel, 7 pt, 6 trg) plus 3 indep air bns (recce/EW, test and evaluation, naval spt). The AF controls the national airline. Approx 70 full time/contingency air bases.

Flying hours 20 hrs/year on ac

FORCES BY ROLE

Bbr   3 (lt) regt with 80 H-5 (Il-28) *Beagle*

Ftr / FGA   1 regt with 20 MiG-29 *Fulcrum*; 1 regt with 18 Su-7 *Fitter*; 6 regt with 107 J-5 (MiG-17F) *Fresco C*; 5 regt with 120 J-7 (MiG-21F) *Fishbed C*; 4 regt with 159 J-6 (MiG-19S) *Farmer B*; 1 regt with 46 MiG-23 *Flogger*; 1 regt with 34 Su-25 *Frogfoot*

Tpt   some regt with ε300 Y-5 (An-2) *Colt* (to infiltrate 2 air force sniper brigades deep into ROK rear areas); 6 An-24 *Coke*; 2 Il-18 *Coot*; 4 Il-62M *Classic*; 2 Tu-134 *Crusty*; 4 Tu-154 *Careless*

Aslt hel   some regt with 24 Mi-24 *Hind*

Trg   some regt with 6 MiG-21 *Fishbed*; 7 CJ-6; 35 FT-2 (MiG-15UTI) *Midget*; 10 CJ-5,CJ-6 (Yak-18) *Max*; 170 more

Hel   some regt with 48 Z-5 (Mi-4) *Hound*; 15 Mi-17 (Mi-8MT) *Hip H*/Mi-8 *Hip*; 139 PZL Mi-2 *Hoplite*; 80 Hughes 500D (Tpt)

SAM   19 bde each with 3,400 SAM; 7 SA-3 *Goa*; 40+ SA-2 *Guideline*; 2 SA-5 *Gammon*; + SA-14 *Gremlin*/SA-16 *Gimlet*/SA-7 *Grail* (Possible W systems, reverse-engineered *Stinger*)

EQUIPMENT BY TYPE

AIRCRAFT 590 combat capable
 BBR 80: 80 H-5 (Il-28) *Beagle*
 FTR 299: 20 MiG-29 *Fulcrum*; 46 MiG-23 *Flogger*; 6 MiG-21; 120 J-7 (MiG-21F) *Fishbed C*; 107 J-5 (MiG-17F) *Fresco C*
 FGA 211: 34 Su-25 *Frogfoot*; 18 Su-7 *Fitter*; 159 J-6 (MiG-19S) *Farmer B*
 TPT 318: 6 An-24 *Coke*; 2 Il-18 *Coot*; 4 Il-62M *Classic*; 2 Tu-134 *Crusty*; 4 Tu-154 *Careless*; ε300 Y-5 (An-2) *Colt* (to infiltrate 2 air force sniper brigades deep into ROK rear areas)
 TRG 222: 180 CJ-5, CJ-6 (Yak-18) *Max*; 7 CJ-6; 35 FT-2 (MiG-15UTI) *Midget*

HELICOPTERS
 ATK 24: 24 Mi-24 *Hind*
 SPT 202: 48 Z-5 (Mi-4) *Hound*; 15 MI-17 (Mi-8MT) *Hip H*/Mi-8 *Hip* Spt; 139 PZL MI-2 *Hoplite*
 UTL • HUGHES 500 80: 80 Hughes 500D (Tpt)
UAV: some *Shmel*
AD:
 SAM 65,531+: 64,600; 133 SA-3 *Goa*
  TOWED 760+: 760+ SA-2 *Guideline*
  STATIC 38: 38 SA-5 *Gammon*
  MANPAD: some+ SA-14 *Gremlin*/SA-16 *Gimlet*/SA-7 *Grail* (Possible W systems, reverse-engineered *Stinger*)
MSL • TACTICAL • AAM: some AA-10 *Alamo*; some AA-11 *Archer*; some AA-2 *Atoll*; some AA-7 *Apex*; some AA-8 *Aphid*; some PL-5; some PL-7

Paramilitary 189,000 active

Security Troops 189,000 (incl border guards, public safety personnel)
Ministry of Public Security

Worker/Peasant Red Guard 3,500,000+ reservists
Org on a provincial/town/village basis; comd structure is bde–bn–coy–pl; small arms with some mor and AD guns (but many units unarmed)

DEPLOYMENT

SUB-SAHARAN AFRICA
Army (Advisers in some 12 African countries)

Korea, Republic of ROK

South Korean Won		2003	2004	2005
GDP	won	724tr	778tr	
	US$	608bn	673bn	
per capita	US$	12,666	13,973	
Growth	%	3.1	4.6	
Inflation	%	3.5	3.6	
Public Debt	%	19.2	21.7	
Def bdgt	won	17.4tr	18.9tr	20.8tr
	US$	14.6bn	16.3bn	20.7bn
US$1=won		1,191	1,155	1,004

Population	48,640,671

Age	0–14	15–19	20–24	25–29	30–64	65 plus
Male	10%	3%	4%	4%	25%	4%
Female	9%	3%	4%	4%	25%	5%

Capabilities

ACTIVE 687,700 (Army 560,000 Navy 63,000 Air 64,700) Paramilitary 4,500
Terms of service conscription Army 26 months Navy and Air Force 30 months; First Combat Forces (Mobilisation Reserve Forces) or Regional Combat Forces (Homeland Defence Forces) to age 33

RESERVE 4,500,000 Paramilitary 3,500,000
Being re-organised

ORGANISATIONS BY SERVICE

Army 420,000; 140,000 conscript (total 560,000)

FORCES BY ROLE
Commands: 3 Fd Army, 1 Special Warfare, 1 Capital Defence, 1 Army Avn

Army	10 corps
Mech inf	3 div (*total*: 1 recce bde, 1 fd arty bde, 1 engr bde, 3 tk bde, 3 mech inf bde)
Inf	19 div (*each*: 1 arty regt (4 arty bn), 1 recce bn, 1 engr bn, 1 tk bn, 3 inf regt); 2 indep bde
SF	7 bde
Air aslt	1 bde
Counter-infiltration	3 bde
SSM	3 bn
ADA	3 bde
SAM	2 (*Nike Hercules*) bn (10 sites); 3 (I HAWK) bn (24 sites)

Reserves

1 army HQ

Inf 23 div

EQUIPMENT BY TYPE

TK • MBT 2,330: 1,000 Type-88 *K1*

T-80 80: 80 T-80U

M-47 400 **M-48** 850

AIFV • BMP 40: 40 BMP-3

APC 2,480

APC (T) 2,260: 1,700 KIFV; 420 M-113; 140 M-577

APC (W) 220

BTR 20: 20 BTR-80

KM-900/-901 (Fiat 6614) 200

ARTY 10,774+

TOWED 3,500+

105mm 1700: 1,700 M-101

KH-178 105mm/KH-179 155mm/M-114 155mm/M-115 203mm/M-53 155mm 1,800+

SP 1,089+

155mm 1076: ε36 K-9 *Thunder*; 1,040 M-109A2

175mm: some M-107

203mm 13: 13 M-110

MRL 185

130mm 156: 156 Kooryong

227mm 29: 29 MLRS (all ATACMS capable)

MOR 6,000: 6,000 KM-29 (M-29) 81mm/M-30 107mm

AT

MSL: some AT-7 *Saxhorn*/TOW-2A

RCL: some 57mm/75mm/M-40A2 106mm/M-67 90mm

RL • 67mm: some PZF 44 *Panzerfaust*

GUNS 58

76mm 8: 8 M-18 *Hellcat* (AT gun)

90mm 50: 50 M-36 SP

HELICOPTERS

ATK • AH-1 60: 60 AH-1F *Cobra*/AH-1J *Cobra*

SPEC OP 6: 6 MH-47 *Chinook*

SPT 21

AS-332 3: 3 AS-332L *Super Puma*

CH-47 18: 18 CH-47D *Chinook*

UTL 337:

BO-105 12

HUGHES 500 130: 130 Hughes 500D

MD-500 45

UH-1 20: 20 UH-1H *Iroquois*

UH-60 130: 130 UH-60P *Black Hawk*

AD

SAM 1,090+

SP: some *Chun Ma Pegasus* (reported)

TOWED • MIM-23 110: 110 I-HAWK MIM-23B

STATIC 200: 200 MIM-14 *Nike Hercules*

MANPAD 780+: 60 FIM-43 *Redeye*; ε200 FIM-92A *Stinger*; 350 *Javelin*; 170 *Mistral*; some SA-16 *Gimlet*

GUNS 600

SP

30mm 20: 20 BIHO SP *Flying Tiger*

TOWED

20mm 60: 60 M-167 *Vulcan*

35mm 20: 20 GDF-003

40mm 80: 80 L/60/L/70, M1

KIFV SPAAG SP 20mm/M-1 towed 40mm 420

RADAR • LAND: some AN/TPQ-36 *Firefinder* (arty, mor); some AN/TPQ-37 *Firefinder* (arty); some RASIT (veh, arty)

MSL • TACTICAL • SSM 12: 12 NHK-I/-II *Hyonmu*

Navy 44,000; ε19,000 conscript (total 63,000)

EQUIPMENT BY TYPE

SUBMARINES • TACTICAL 20

SSK 9:

9 *Chang Bogo* each with 8 single 533mm TT each with SUT HWT

SSI 11:

8 *Dolphin* each with 2 533mm TT

3 KSS-1 *Dolgorae* each with 2 single 406mm TT

PRINCIPAL SURFACE COMBATANTS 43

DESTROYERS • DDG 6:

3 *King Kwanggaeto* (capacity 1 *Super Lynx* utl hel) each with 2 Mk 141 *Harpoon* quad (8 eff.) each with AGM-84 *Harpoon* tactical ASM, 1 16 cell Mk 48 VLS with *Sea Sparrow* SAM, 1 127mm gun

3 *Kwang Ju* (capacity either 1 SA-316B *Alouette III* IAR-316 (SA-316) utl or 1 *Super Lynx* utl hel) each with 2 triple ASTT (6 eff.) each with Mk 46 LWT, 1 Mk 112 octuple (8 eff.) with tactical ASROC, 2 Mk 141 *Harpoon* quad (8 eff.) each with 1 RGM-84C *Harpoon* tactical SSM, 2 twin 127mm gun (4 eff.)

FRIGATES • FFG 9:

9 *Ulsan* each with 2 triple ASTT (6 eff.) each with Mk 46 LWT, 2 Mk 141 *Harpoon* quad (8 eff.) each with 1 RGM-84C *Harpoon* tactical SSM, 2 76mm gun

CORVETTES • FS 28:

4 *Dong Hae* each with 2 triple ASTT (6 eff.) each with Mk 46 LWT

24 *Po Hang* each with 2 MM-38 *Exocet* tactical SSM (on some vessels), 2 triple ASTT (6 eff.) each with Mk 46 LWT

PATROL AND COASTAL COMBATANTS 80

SEA DOLPHIN (PFI) 75: 75 *Sea Dolphin* (*Kilurki*-11)

PFM 5:

5 Pae-Ku-52 each with 2 Mk-141 *Harpoon* twin each with 1 RGM-84C *Harpoon* tactical SSM, 2 76mm gun

MINE WARFARE 15

MINE COUNTERMEASURES 14

MHC 6: 6 *Kan Keong*

MSC 8: 8 *Kum San*

MINELAYERS • ML 1: 1 *Won San*

AMPHIBIOUS

LS 12

LSM 2: 2 *Ko Mun* (capacity 4 tanks; 50 troops)

LST 10: 4 *Alligator* (capacity 20 tanks; 300 troops); 6 *Un Bong* (capacity 16 tanks; 200 troops)

CRAFT 36: 6 LCT; 20 LCVP; 10 LCM

LOGISTICS AND SUPPORT 14: 4 AGHS (civil manned, funded by the Min. of Transport); 2 AK; 3 AOE; 1 ASR; 2 ATF; 2 diving tender/spt

FACILITIES

Base 1 located at Pusan, 1 located at Mukho, 1 located at Cheju, 1 located at Pohang, 1 located at Mokpo

Naval Aviation

AIRCRAFT 16 combat capable

ASW • S-2 8: 8 S-2E *Tracker**

MP • **P-3** 8: 8 P-3C *Orion**
UTL 5: 5 F406 *Caravan II*
HELICOPTERS
ASW 11: 11 *Lynx* MK99
UTL 34
  BELL 206 2: 2 Bell 206B *JetRanger II*
  IAR-316 (SA-316) *Alouette III* 10
  MD-500 • **MD-500M** 22: 22 MD-500MD

Marines 28,000
FORCES BY ROLE
Spt   some unit
Marine 2 div; 1 bde

EQUIPMENT BY TYPE
TK • **MBT** 60: 60 M-47
AAV 102
  AAV-7 42: 42 AAV-7A1
  LVTP-7 60
ARTY • **TOWED**: some 105mm; some 155mm
LNCHR: some single (truck mounted) each with RGM-84A *Harpoon* tactical SSM

Air Force 64,000
FORCES BY ROLE
4 Cmds (Ops, Southern Combat Logs, Trg), Tac Airlift Wg and Composite Wg are all responsible to ROK Air Force HQ.
Ftr   2 wg with 104 KF-16C *Fighting Falcon*; 49 KF-16D *Fighting Falcon*
FGA   2 wg with 60 F-4D *Phantom II*; 70 F-4E *Phantom II*; 3 wg with 150 F-5E *Tiger II*; 35 F-5F *Tiger II*. First 2 of 40 F-15K delivered
FAC   1 wg with 10 O-2A *Skymaster*; 20 Cessna O-1A *Bird Dog*
ELINT   some (SIGINT) sqn with 4 *Hawker* 800XP
Recce   1 gp with 4 *Hawker* 800RA; 18 RF-4C *Phantom II**; 5 RF-5A *Tiger II**
SAR   1 sqn with 4 Bell 212; 5 UH-1H *Iroquois*
CCT   1 wg with 22 A-37B *Dragonfly*
Airlift   some wg with 1 B-737-300 (VIP); 2 BAe-748 (VIP); 1 C-118 *Liftmaster*; 10 C-130H *Hercules*; 20 CN-235-220/CN-235M; 3 AS-332 *Super Puma*; 6 CH-47 *Chinook*; 7 KA-32 *Helix C* (SAR); 3 VH-60 *White Knight*
Trg   some sqn with 25 F-5B *Freedom Fighter**; 17 *Hawk* MK67; 55 KT-1; 50 T-37 *Tweet*; 30 T-38 *Talon*; 25 T-41B *Mescalero*. First T-50 delivered. 5 Il-103 (15 more to be delivered)

EQUIPMENT BY TYPE
AIRCRAFT 540 combat capable
  FTR • **F-5** 210: 25 F-5B *Freedom Fighter**; 150 F-5E *Tiger II*; 35 F-5F *Tiger II*
  FGA 283: 104 KF-16C *Fighting Falcon*; 49 KF-16D *Fighting Falcon*; 2 F-15K
  F-4 130: 60 F-4D *Phantom II*; 70 F-4E *Phantom II*
  RECCE 57: 4 *Hawker* 800RA
  O-2 10: 10 O-2A *Skymaster*
  OBS 20: 20 Cessna O-1A *Bird Dog*
  RF-4 18: 18 RF-4C *Phantom II**

  RF-5A *Tiger II* 5*
EW • **ELINT** 4: 4 *Hawker* 800XP
TPT 34
  B-737 1: 1 B-737-300 (VIP)
  BAe-748 2 (VIP)
  C-118 *Liftmaster* 1
  C-130 10: 10 C-130H *Hercules*
  CN-235 20: 20 CN-235-220/CN-235M
  TRG 183: 17 *Hawk* MK67; 55 KT-1; 50 T-37 *Tweet*; 30 T-38 *Talon*; 25 T-41B *Mescalero*; 5 Il-103; 1 T-50
HELICOPTERS
  SPT 9: 3 AS-332 *Super Puma*; 6 CH-47 *Chinook*
  UTL 19: 4 Bell 212; 7 KA-32 *Helix C* (SAR); 5 UH-1H *Iroquois*; 3 VH-60 *White Knight*
UAV • **RECCE** • **TAC** 103: 100 *Harpy*; 3 *Searcher*
MSL • **TACTICAL**
  ASM: some AGM-130; some AGM-142 *Popeye*
  AGM-65: some AGM-65A *Maverick*
  AGM-84: some AGM-84 *Harpoon*
  ARM: some AGM-88 *HARM*
  AAM
    AIM-120: some AIM-120B *AMRAAM*/AIM-120C5 *AMRAAM*
    AIM-7 *Sparrow* some **AIM-9** *Sidewinder* some

Paramilitary ε4,500 active

Civilian Defence Corps 3,500,000 reservists (to age 50)

Maritime Police ε4,500
PATROL AND COASTAL COMBATANTS 81+:
  PBI 18+: some; 18 *Seagull*
  PCC 33: 4 *Bukhansan*; 7 Hyundai Type; 22 *Sea Wolf/Shark*
  PCI circa 20
  PCO 10: 1 *Han Kang*; 3 *Mazinger*; 6 *Sea Dragon/Whale*
LOGISTICS AND SUPPORT 3: 3 ARS
HELICOPTERS • **UTL** 9: 9 Hughes 500

DEPLOYMENT

AFGHANISTAN
UN • **UNAMA** 1 obs

BURUNDI
UN • **ONUB** 2 obs

GEORGIA
UN • **UNOMIG** 7 obs

INDIA/PAKISTAN
UN • **UNMOGIP** 9 obs

KAZAKHSTAN
Army 205 engr/medical (*Op Enduring Freedom*)

LIBERIA
UN • **UNMIL** 1; 1 obs

WESTERN SAHARA
UN • **MINURSO** 19

FOREIGN FORCES

United States USPACOM: 116 M-1 *Abrams* MBT; 126 M-2 *Bradley* AIFV each with 2 TOW Msl, 1 30mm gun; 111 APC (T); 45 mor/MRL/SP; 1 HQ 7th Air Force HQ (AF) HQ (HQ 7th Air Force) located at Osan AB; 1 (UN Comd) HQ Eighth Army HQ located at Seoul; 1 ftr wg located at Kusan AB (2 ftr sqn with 20 F-16C *Fighting Falcon*/F-16D *Fighting Falcon*); 1 ftr wg located at Osan AB (1 ftr sqn with 20 F-16C *Fighting Falcon*/F-16D *Fighting Falcon*, 1 ftr sqn with 24 A-10 *Thunderbolt II*/OA-10 *Thunderbolt II* (12 of each type) located at Osan AB); 1 elems HQ 2ID armd inf HQ located at Tongduchon (1 avn bde (1 aslt hel bn, 1 atk hel bn), 1 armd bde (1 armd inf bn, 2 tk bn), 1 air cav bde (2 atk hel bn), 2 SP arty bn, 2 fd arty bn with MLRS); 1 Special Ops sqn; 1 SAM bn located at Uijongbu with MIM-104 *Patriot*; 8,900 (AF); 25,000 (Army); 20,180 Navy); 40,360 (Navy); 180 (USMC)

Laos Lao

New Lao Kip		2003	2004	2005
GDP	kip	20.3tr	24.6tr	
	US$	1.92bn	3.12bn	
per capita	US$	324	515	
Growth	%	5.3	6.0	
Inflation	%	15.5	11.2	
Debt	US$	2.84bn		
Def bdgt	kip	399bn	n.a.	n.a.
	US$	37.8m	n.a.	n.a.
US$1=kip		10,569	7,882	10,210

Population　6,217,141

Ethnic groups: lowland Lao Loum 68%; upland Lao Theung 22%; highland Lao Soung incl Hmong and Yao 9%; Chinese and Vietnamese 1%

Age	0–14	15–19	20–24	25–29	30–64	65 plus
Male	21%	6%	5%	4%	13%	1%
Female	21%	5%	5%	4%	14%	2%

Capabilities

ACTIVE 29,100 (Army 25,600 Air 3,500) Paramilitary 100,000
Terms of service conscription, 18 month minimum

ORGANISATIONS BY SERVICE

Army 25,600

FORCES BY ROLE
4 Mil Regions
Armd	1 bn
Inf	5 div; 7 indep regt; 65 indep coy
Arty	5 bn
ADA	9 bn
Engr	1 regt
Avn	1 (liason) light flt

Engr construction　2 regt

EQUIPMENT BY TYPE
TK 35
　MBT 25: 15 T-54/T-55; 10 T-34/85
　LT TK 10: 10 PT-76
APC • APC (W) • BTR 50: 20 BTR-152; 30 BTR-40/BTR-60
ARTY
　TOWED 82
　　75mm 20: 20 M-116 pack
　　105mm 20: 20 M-101
　　122mm 20: 20 D-30/M-30 *M-1938*
　　130mm 10: 10 M-46
　　155mm 12: 12 M-114
　MOR
　　81mm/82mm: some
　　107mm: some M-1938/M-2A1
　　120mm: some M-43
AT • RCL • 106mm: some M-40
　107mm: some B-11
　57mm • M-18: some M-18/A1
　75mm: some M-20
　RL • 73mm: some RPG-7 *Knout*
AD
　SAM • MANPAD: some SA-7 *Grail*
　GUNS
　　14.5mm: some ZPU-1/ZPU-4 towed
　　23mm: some ZSU-23-4 SP/ZU-23 towed
　　37mm: some M-1939 towed
　　57mm: some S-60 towed

Army Marine Section ε600

PATROL AND COASTAL COMBATANTS 52: circa 40 PBR; 12 PCR less than 100 tonnes
AMPHIBIOUS • CRAFT 4: 4 LCM

Air Force 3,500

FORCES BY ROLE
FGA　2 sqn with up to 22 MiG-21bis *Fishbed L* & N†; up to 2 MiG-21UM *Mongol B*†

Tpt　1 sqn with 4 An-2 *Colt*; 5 Y-7 (An-24) *Coke*; 3 An-26 *Curl*; 1 An-74 *Coaler*; 1 Y-12; 1 Yak-40 *Codling* (VIP)

Trg　some sqn with 8 Yak-18 *Max*

Hel　1 sqn with 3 SA-360 *Dauphin*; 1 KA-32T *Helix C* ((5 more on order)); 1 Mi-26 *Halo*; 1 Mi-6 *Hook*; 9 Mi-8 *Hip*; 12 MI-17 (Mi-8MT) *Hip H*

EQUIPMENT BY TYPE
AIRCRAFT 22† combat capable
　FTR • MiG-21 up to 22: up to 22 MiG-21bis *Fishbed L* & N†
　TPT 15: 4 An-2 *Colt*; 3 An-26 *Curl*; 1 An-74 *Coaler*; 1 Y-12; 5 Y-7 (An-24) *Coke*; 1 Yak-40 *Codling* (VIP)
　TRG up to 10
　　MiG-21U up to 2: up to 2 MiG-21UM *Mongol B*†
　　Yak-18 *Max* 8
HELICOPTERS
　SAR 3: 3 SA-360 *Dauphin*
　SPT 24: 1 KA-32T *Helix C* (5 more on order); 1 Mi-26 *Halo*; 1 Mi-6 *Hook*; 9 Mi-8; 12 MI-17 (Mi-8MT) *Hip H*
MSL • TACTICAL • AAM: some AA-2 *Atoll*†

East Asia and Australasia

Paramilitary

Militia Self-Defence Forces 100,000+
Village 'home guard' or for local defence

Malaysia Mal

Malaysian Ringgit RM		2003	2004	2005
GDP	RM	393bn	446bn	
	US$	103bn	117bn	
per capita	US$	4,489	5,000	
Growth	%	5.3	7.1	
Inflation	%	1.1	1.4	
Debt	US$	49bn		
Def bdgt[a]	RM	9.16bn	8.57bn	9.39bn
	US$	2.41bn	2.25bn	2.47bn
US$1=RM		3.8	3.8	3.8

[a] excluding procurement and extra-budgetary funding

Population   23,953,136

Ethnic groups: Muslim 54%; Malay and other indigenous 64%; Chinese 27%; Indian 9%; Sabah and Sarawak non-Muslim Bumiputras form the majority of the population; 1m+ Indo and Pi illegal immigrants in 1997

Age	0–14	15–19	20–24	25–29	30–64	65 plus
Male	17%	5%	5%	4%	18%	2%
Female	16%	5%	4%	4%	18%	3%

Capabilities

ACTIVE 110,000 (Army 80,000 Navy 15,000 Air 15,000) Paramilitary 20,100

RESERVE 51,600 (Army 50,000, Navy 1,000 Air Force 600) Paramilitary 244,700

ORGANISATIONS BY SERVICE

Army 80,000 (to be 60–70000)

FORCES BY ROLE

2 Mil Regions, 1 HQ Fd Comd, 4 Area Comd (div)

Armd	5 regt
Mech inf	1 bde; 3 bn
Inf	11 bde; 28 bn
SF	1 regt (3 SF bn)
AB	1 (Rapid Deployment Force) bde (1 lt tk sqn, 1 light arty regt, 3 AB bn)
Arty	2 (med) regt
Fd arty	7 regt
MRL	1 regt
ADA	3 regt
Engr	5 regt
Hel	1 sqn
arty loc	1 regt

Reserves

Territorial Army

Police	5 (highway sy) bn
Inf	16 regt

EQUIPMENT BY TYPE

TK • LT TK • 26 *Scorpion* 90

RECCE 418
  AML 140: 140 AML-60/AML-90
  FERRET 92 (60 mod)
  SIBMAS 186

APC 1020
  APC (T) 347: 211 *Adnan* (incl variants); 25 FV4333 *Stormer*; 111 KIFV (incl variants)
  APC (W) 673: 452 *Condor* (150 upgraded); 37 M-3 *Panhard*; 184 LAV-150 *Commando*/V-100 *Commando*

ARTY 414
  TOWED 164
    105mm 130: 130 Model 56 pack howitzer
    155mm 34: 12 FH-70; 22 G-5
  MRL 18: 18 ASTROS II (equipped with 127mm SS-30)
  MOR 232: 232 81mm

AT
  MSL 60: 18 AT-7 *Saxhorn*; 24 *Eryx*; 18 HJ-8
  RCL 260
    106mm 24: 24 M-40
    84mm 236: 236 *Carl Gustav*
  RL • 73mm 584: 584 RPG-7 *Knout*

AMPHIBIOUS • CRAFT • LCA 165:
  165 *Damen* assault craft 540 (capacity 10 troops)

HELICOPTERS • UTL • SA-316 9: 9 SA-316B *Alouette III*

AD
  SAM • MANPAD 48+: some *Anza*; some SA-18 *Grouse (Igla)*; 48 Starburst
  GUNS 60
    35mm: 24 GDF-005 towed
    40mm: 36 L40/70 towed

Navy 15,000

PRINCIPAL SURFACE COMBATANTS 10
  FRIGATES 4
    FFG 2:
      2 *Lekiu* (capacity 1 *Super Lynx* utl hel) each with 2 B515 ILAS-3 triple 324mm each with 1 *Sting Ray* LWT, 2 quad (8 eff.) each with 1 MM-40 *Exocet* tactical SSM, 1 *Sea Wolf* VLS with 16 *Sea Wolf* SAM
    FF 2:
      1 *Hang Tuah* trg with 3 *Limbo* non-operational, 1 57mm gun, 1 hel landing platform (for *Wasp* or *Super Lynx*)
      1 *Rahmat* with 3 *Limbo*, 1 114mm gun, 1 hel landing platform
  CORVETTES 6
    FSG 4:
      4 *Laksamana* each with 2 B515 ILAS-3 triple 324mm each with A244 LWT, 1 quad (4 eff.) with 12 *Aspide* SAM, 3 twin (6 eff.) each with 1 Mk 2 *Otomat* SSM, 1 76mm gun
    FS 2:
      2 *Kasturi* each with 2 twin (4 eff.) each with 1 MM-38 *Exocet* tactical SSM, 1 Mle 54 *Creusot-Loire* 375mm *Bofors* (6 eff.), 1 100mm gun, 1 hel landing platform (For 1 Westland *Wasp* HAS Mk 1)

PATROL AND COASTAL COMBATANTS 35

PCC 18: 14 *Kris*; 4 *Sabah*

PCI 1: 1 *Kedah*

PFC 6: 6 *Jerong*

PFM 8:

4 *Handalan* each with 2 twin (4 eff.) each with 1 MM-38 *Exocet* tactical SSM, 1 57mm gun

4 *Perdana* each with 2 single each with 1 MM-38 *Exocet* tactical SSM, 1 57mm gun

PCO 2:

2 *Musytari* each with 1 100mm gun, 1 hel landing platform

MINE WARFARE • MINE COUNTERMEASURES • MCO 4: 4 *Mahamiru*

AMPHIBIOUS

LS • LST 1: 1 *Sri Inderapura* (capacity 10 tanks; 400 troops)

AGHS (Svy) /AGOS 2

AMPHIBIOUS

CRAFT 115: 115 LCM/LCU

LOGISTICS AND SUPPORT 3: 1 diving tender/spt; 2 Spt

Naval Aviation 160

HELICOPTERS • ASW 6: 6 *Wasp* (all non-op)

Special Forces

Naval commandos   1 unit

Air Force 15,000

1 Air Op HQ, 2 Air Div, 1 trg and Log Cmd, 1 Intergrated Area Def Systems HQ

Flying hours   60 hrs/year

FORCES BY ROLE

Ftr	2 sqn with 15 MiG-29N (MiG-29) *Fulcrum*; 2 MiG-29U *Fulcrum*
FGA	1 sqn with 8 F/A-18D *Hornet*; 2 sqn with 8 *Hawk* MK108; 17 *Hawk* MK208
FGA / Recce	1 sqn with 13 F-5E *Tiger II*/F-5F *Tiger II*; 2 RF-5E *Tigereye*
MR	1 sqn with 4 Beech 200T *Maritime Patrol*
SF	1 (Air Force Commando) unit (air field defence)
Tpt	2 sqn with 4 KC-130H *Hercules* (tkr); 4 C-130H *Hercules*; 8 C-130H-30 *Hercules*; 9 Cessna 402B (2 modified for aerial survey); 1 (VIP) sqn with 1 B-737-700 BBJ; 1 BD700 *Global Express*; 1 F-28 *Fellowship*; 1 *Falcon* 900; 2 S-61N; 2 S-70A *Black Hawk*; 1 A-109; 1 sqn with 6 CN-235
Trg	some sqn with 8 MB-339A; 20 MD3-160; 45 PC-7 MK II *Turbo Trainer*; 13 SA-316 *Alouette III*
Hel	4 (tpt/SAR) sqn with 31 S-61A-4 *Nuri*; 2 S-61N; 2 S-70A *Black Hawk*
SAM	1 sqn with *Starburst*

EQUIPMENT BY TYPE

AIRCRAFT 63 combat capable

FTR 28

F-5 13: 13 F-5E *Tiger II*/F-5F *Tiger II*

MiG-29N (MiG-29) *Fulcrum* 15

FGA 16

F/A-18 8: 8 F/A-18D *Hornet*

Hawk **MK108** 8

RECCE 2: 2 RF-5E *Tigereye*

MP 4: 4 Beech 200T *Maritime Patrol*

TKR • KC-130 4: 4 KC-130H *Hercules* (tkr)

TPT 31

B-737 1: 1 B-737-700 BBJ

BD700 *Global Express* 1

C-130 12: 4 C-130H *Hercules*; 8 C-130H-30 *Hercules*

CN-235 6

CESSNA 402 9: 9 Cessna 402B (2 modified for aerial survey)

F-28 *Fellowship* 1

Falcon **900** 1

TRG 92

Hawk **MK208** 17*

MB-339 8: 8 MB-339AB

MD3-160 20

MiG-29U *Fulcrum* 2*

PC-7 45: 45 PC-7 MK II *Turbo Trainer*

HELICOPTERS

ASW • S-61 • S-61A 31: 31 S-61A-4 *Nuri*

SPT 8: 4 S-61N; 4 S-70A *Black Hawk*

UTL 14: 1 A-109; 13 SA-316 *Alouette III*

UAV • RECCE • TAC 3: 3 *Eagle* 150

AD • SAM • MANPAD: some *Starburst*

MSL • TACTICAL

ASM: AGM-65 *Maverick*; AGM-84D *Harpoon*

AAM: some AA-10 *Alamo*; AA-11 *Archer*; some AIM-7 *Sparrow*; some AIM-9 *Sidewinder*

Paramilitary ε20,100

Police-General Ops Force 18,000

FORCES BY ROLE

Police	5 bde HQ; 2 (Aboriginal) bn; 19 bn; 4 indep coy
Spec Ops	1 bn

EQUIPMENT BY TYPE

RECCE 100: ε100 S52 *Shorland*

APC • APC (W) 170: 140 AT105 *Saxon*; ε30 SB-301

Marine Police

EQUIPMENT BY TYPE

PATROL AND COASTAL COMBATANTS 150: 120 PBI

PFI 30: 9 *Imp* PX; 15 *Lang Hitam*; 6 *Sangitan*

LOGISTICS AND SUPPORT 8: 2 AT; 6 tpt

FACILITIES

Base 1 located at Kuala Kemaman, 1 located at Penang, 1 located at Tampoi, 1 located at Sandakan

Police Air Unit

AIRCRAFT

TPT 7: 7 PC-6 *Turbo-Porter*

UTL 10: 4 Cessna 206; 6 Cessna 208 *Caravan I*

HELICOPTERS

SPT • AS-355 2: 2 AS-355F *Ecureuil II*

UTL • BELL 206 1: 1 Bell 206L *LongRanger*

Area Security Units (R) 3,500

aux General Ops Force

Paramilitary 89 unit

Border Scouts (R) 1,200

in Sabah, Sarawak

People's Volunteer Corps 240,000 reservists (some 17500 armed)

RELA

NON-STATE ARMED GROUPS

see Part II

DEPLOYMENT

BURUNDI
UN • ONUB 3 obs

DEMOCRATIC REPUBLIC OF CONGO
UN • MONUC 5 obs; 12

EAST TIMOR
UN • UNOTIL 3 obs

ETHIOPIA/ERITREA
UN • UNMEE 7 obs; 4

HAITI
UN • MINUSTAH 1

LIBERIA
UN • UNMIL 10 obs

SERBIA AND MONTENEGRO
UN • UNMIK 1 obs

SIERRA LEONE
UN • UNAMSIL 3 obs

SUDAN
UN • UNMIS 2

WESTERN SAHARA
UN • MINURSO 14 obs

FOREIGN FORCES

Australia Air Force: 12 Army: 1 inf coy (on 3-month rotational tours); 115

Mongolia Mgl

Mongolian Tugrik t		2003	2004	2005
GDP	t	1.36tr	1.44tr	
	US$	1.18bn	1.23bn	
per capita	US$	438	448	
Growth	%	5.3	6.0	
Inflation	%	0.9	5.0	
Debt	US$	1.47bn		
Def bdgt	t	17.6bn	20.7bn	21.0bn
	US$	15.4m	17.6m	17.6m
FMA (US)	US$	1.75m	1.86m	1.84m
US$1=t		1,146	1,174	1,188

Population   2,791,272

Ethnic groups: Kazak 4%; Russian 2%; Chinese 2%

Age	0–14	15–19	20–24	25–29	30–64	65 plus
Male	15%	6%	5%	5%	17%	2%
Female	14%	6%	5%	5%	18%	2%

Capabilities

ACTIVE 8,600 (Army 7,500 Air 800 Construction Troops 300) **Paramilitary 14,400**

Terms of service conscription: males 18–25 years, 1 year

RESERVE 137,000 (Army 137,000)

ORGANISATIONS BY SERVICE

Army 4,200; 3,300 conscript (total 7,500)

FORCES BY ROLE

MRR   6 (under strength) regt

Lt inf   1 bn (rapid deployment – 2nd bn to form)

AB   1 bn

Arty   1 regt

EQUIPMENT BY TYPE

TK • **MBT** 370: 370 T-54/T-55

RECCE • **BRDM** 120: 120 BRDM-2

AIFV • **BMP** 310: 310 BMP-1

APC • APC (W) • **BTR** 150: 150 BTR-60

ARTY 570

TOWED 300: ε300 D-30 122mm/M-30 *M-1938* 122mm/M-46 130mm/ML-20 *M-1937* 152mm

MRL • **122mm** 130: 130 BM-21

MOR 140: 140 120mm/160mm/82mm

AT • **GUNS** 200: 200 D-44 85mm/D-48 85mm/M-1944 100mm/MT-12 100mm

Air Forces 800

FORCES BY ROLE

Tpt   some sqn with 1 A-310-300; 6 An-2 *Colt*; 1 An-26 *Curl*; 1 B-737

Atk hel   some sqn with 11 Mi-24 *Hind*; 2 Mi-8 *Hip*

AD   2 regt with 150 S-60/ZPU-4/ZU-23

EQUIPMENT BY TYPE

AIRCRAFT

TPT 9

A-310 1: 1 A-310-300

An-2 *Colt* 6

An-26 *Curl* 1

B-737 1

HELICOPTERS

ATK 11: 11 Mi-24 *Hind*

SPT 2: 2 Mi-8 *Hip*

AD • **GUNS** 150: 150 S-60 towed 57mm/ZPU-4 towed 14.5mm/ZU-23 towed 23mm

Paramilitary 7,200 active

Border Guard 1,300; 4,700 conscript (total 6,000)

Internal Security Troops 400; 800 conscript (total 1,200)

Gd 4 unit

DEPLOYMENT

AFGHANISTAN
Army 21 Army (instructors)

DEMOCRATIC REPUBLIC OF CONGO
UN • **MONUC** 2 obs

IRAQ
Army 130 (Peace Support)

SUDAN
UN • **UNMIS** 2 obs

WESTERN SAHARA
UN • **MINURSO** 3 obs

Myanmar My

Myanmar Kyat K		2003	2004	2005
GDP	K	7.7tr	8.2tr	
	US$a	65bn	69bn	
per capita	US$a	1,412	1,483	
Growth	%	13.8	5.0	
Inflation	%	24.9	9.0	
Debt	US$	7.31bn		
Def bdgt	Kb	ε37.9bn	ε39.9bn	ε43.9bn
	US$	6.26bn	6.23bn	6.85bn
US$1=K		6.07	6.42	6.42

a PPP estimate
a defence budget at market exchange rates

Population   49,362,000

Ethnic groups: Burmese 68%; Shan 9%; Karen 7%; Rakhine 4%; Chinese 3+%; Other Chin, Kachin, Kayan, Lahu, Mon, Palaung, Pao, Wa, 9%

Age	0–14	15–19	20–24	25–29	30–64	65 plus
Male	13%	5%	5%	5%	18%	2%
Female	13%	5%	5%	5%	19%	3%

Capabilities

ACTIVE 428,000 (Army 350,000 Navy 13,000 Air 12,000 Naval Infantry 800) **Paramilitary 107,250**

ORGANISATIONS BY SERVICE

Army 350,000

FORCES BY ROLE
12 Regional Comd, 4 Regional Op Comd, 14 Military Op Comd, 34 Tactical Op Comd (TDC)
Armd   10 bn
Inf   100 bn; 337 bn (regional comd)
Lt inf   10 div
Arty   7 bn; 37 indep coy
AD   7 bn

EQUIPMENT BY TYPE
TK 255
  MBT 150: 50 T-72; 100 Type-69-II
  LT TK 105: 105 Type-63 (est. 60 serviceable)
RECCE 115: 45 *Ferret*; 40 Humber *Pig*; 30 Mazda

APC 325
  APC (T) 305: 250 Type-85; 55 Type-90
  APC (W) 20: 20 *Hino*
ARTY 388+
  TOWED 278+
    76mm 100: 100 M-48 *M-1948*
    88mm 50: 50 25-pdr
    105mm 96: 96 M-101
    122mm some
    130mm 16: 16 M-46
    140mm some
    155mm 16: 16 *Soltam*
  MRL
    107mm 30: 30 Type-63
    122mm: some BM-21 (reported)
  MOR 80+
    81mm: some
    82mm: some Type-53 (M-37)
    120mm 80+: 80 Soltam; some Type-53 (M-1943)
AT
  RCL 1000+
    106mm • **M-40**: some M-40A1
    84mm 1000: ε1,000 *Carl Gustav*
  RL • **73mm**: RPG-7 *Knout*
  GUNS 60: 60 17-pdr 76.2mm/6-pdr 57mm
AD
  SAM • **MANPAD**: some HN-5 *Hong Nu/Red Cherry* (reported); some SA-16 *Gimlet*
  GUNS 46
    TOWED
      37mm 24: 24 Type-74
      40mm 10: 10 M-1
    SP
      57mm 12: 12 Type-80 SP

Navy ε13,000

EQUIPMENT BY TYPE
PRINCIPAL SURFACE COMBATANTS • **CORVETTES**
• **FS** 4:
  2 *Yan Gyi Aung* each with 1 76mm gun
  2 *Yan Taing Aung* each with 1 76mm gun
PATROL AND COASTAL COMBATANTS 71
  PCC 10: 10 *Yan Sit Aung*
  PCI 15: 12 PGM 401; 3 *Swift*
  PCR 29: 15 (small)
  Nawarat 2
  Y-301 10
  Imp Y-301 2
  PFI 3: 3 PB-90
  PFM 11: 5; 6 *Houxin* each with 2 twin (4 eff.) each with 4 C-801 (CSS-N-4) *Sardine* tactical SSM
  PCO 3: 3 *In Daw*
AMPHIBIOUS • **CRAFT** 11: 1 LCU; 10 LCM
LOGISTICS AND SUPPORT 15: 1 ABU; 1 AOT; 1 diving tender/spt; 6 Spt; 6 Tpt (coastal)

FACILITIES
Base 1 located at Bassein, 1 located at Mergui, 1 located at Moulmein, 1 located at Seikyi, 1 located at Yangon (Monkey Point), 1 located at Sittwe

Naval Infantry 800

Navy 1 bn

East Asia and Australasia

Air Force 12,000

FORCES BY ROLE

Ftr	3 sqn with 8 MiG-29B *Fulcrum*; 50 F-7 (MiG-21F) *Fishbed C*; 10 FT-7 (JJ-7) *Mongol A**; 2 MiG-29UB *Fulcrum**
FGA	2 sqn with 22 A-5M (Q-5II) *Fantan*
CCT	2 sqn with 12 G-4 *Super Galeb**; 12 PC-7 *Turbo Trainer**; 9 PC-9*
Tpt	1 sqn with 2 An-12 *Cub*; 3 F-27 *Friendship*; 4 FH-227; 5 PC-6A *Turbo Porter*/PC-6B *Turbo Porter*
Trg / liaison	some sqn with 1 CE-550 *Citation II*; 4 Cessna 180 *Skywagon*; 12 K-8
Hel	4 sqn with 10 PZL W-3 *Sokol*; 11 Mi-17 (Mi-8MT) *Hip H**; 18 PZL Mi-2 *Hoplite**; 12 Bell 205; 6 Bell 206 *JetRanger*; 9 SA-316 *Alouette III*

EQUIPMENT BY TYPE

AIRCRAFT 125 combat capable
  FTR 58
    MiG-29 8: 8 MiG-29B *Fulcrum*
    MiG-21 50: 50 F-7 (MiG-21F) *Fishbed C*
  FGA 22: 22 A-5M (Q-5II) *Fantan*
  TPT 15: 2 An-12 *Cub*; 1 CE-550 *Citation II*; 3 F-27 *Friendship*; 4 FH-227; 5 PC-6A *Turbo Porter*/PC-6B *Turbo Porter*
  UTL 4: 4 Cessna 180 *Skywagon*
  TRG 57: 10 FT-7 (JJ-7) *Mongol A**; 12 G-4 *Super Galeb**; 12 K-8; 2 MiG-29UB *Fulcrum**; 12 PC-7 *Turbo Trainer**; 9 PC-9*
HELICOPTERS
  SPT 39: 10 PZL W-3 *Sokol*; 11 Mi-17 (Mi-8MT) *Hip H**; 18 PZL MI-2 *Hoplite**
  UTL 27: 12 Bell 205; 6 Bell 206 *JetRanger*; 9 SA-316 *Alouette III*

Paramilitary

People's Police Force 72,000

People's Militia 35,000

People's Pearl and Fishery Ministry ε250

PATROL AND COASTAL COMBATANTS 11
  PCC 3: 3 *Indaw*
  PCI 8: 5 *Carpentaria*; 3 *Swift*

NON-STATE ARMED GROUPS

see Part II

New Zealand NZ

New Zealand Dollar NZ$		2003	2004	2005
GDP	NZ$	133bn	145bn	
	US$	77.5bn	94.8bn	
per capita	US$	19,613	23,737	
Growth	%	3.4	5.0	
Inflation	%	1.8	2.3	
Public Debt	%	20.5	17.8	
Def bdgt	NZ$	2.01bn	1.73bn	2.01bn
	US$	1.17bn	1.12bn	1.42bn
US$1=NZ$		1.72	1.54	1.41

Population   4,035,461

Ethnic groups: Maori 15%; Pacific Islander 6%

Age	0–14	15–19	20–24	25–29	30–64	65 plus
Male	11%	4%	4%	4%	22%	5%
Female	10%	3%	3%	4%	22%	7%

Capabilities

ACTIVE 8,660 (Army 4,430 Navy 1,980 Air 2,250)

RESERVE 10,800 (Regular some 8,600 (Army 4,420 Navy 1,980 Air Force 2,200) Territorial 2,660 (Army 2,070 Navy 370)

ORGANISATIONS BY SERVICE

Army 4,430

FORCES BY ROLE
1 Land Force Comd HQ, 2 Land Force Gp HQ

Recce / APC	1 sqn
Inf	2 bn
SF	1 sqn; 1 sqn
Arty	1 regt (1 AD tps, 2 fd arty bty)
Engr	1 regt under strength

Reserves

Territorial Force 2,070 reservists
responsible for providing trained individuals for top-up and round-out of deployed forces
Trg 6 (territorial force regional) regt

EQUIPMENT BY TYPE
APC • APC (W) 105: 105 NZLAV
ARTY 74
  TOWED • 105mm 24: 24 L-118 Light Gun
  MOR 50: 50 81mm
AT
  MSL 24: 24 *Javelin*
  RCL • 84mm 42: 42 *Carl Gustav*
AD • SAM • MANPAD 12: 12 *Mistral*

Navy 1,980

FORCES BY ROLE
Navy 1 (Fleet) HQ located at Auckland

EQUIPMENT BY TYPE
PRINCIPAL SURFACE COMBATANTS • FRIGATES •
FF 2:

2 *Anzac* each with 1 SH-2G *Super Seasprite* ASW hel, 1 MK 15 *Phalanx* CIWS guns, 2 triple 324mm TT (6 eff.), 1 octuple Mk41 *Sea Sparrow* (8 eff.) with 1 RIM-7M *Sea Sparrow* SAM, 1 127mm gun

PATROL AND COASTAL COMBATANTS • PCI 4: 4 *Moa* (Due for replacement in 2007 with 4 PCI and 2 PCO (SH-2G capable))

LOGISTICS AND SUPPORT 5
AGHS (SVY) 1: 1 *Resolution*
AGS 1 (Due for replacement in 2007 with multi-role vessel (sealift))
AO 1: 1 *Endeavour*
Diving tender/spt 1
Trg 1

FACILITIES
Base 1 located at Auckland

Naval Aviation

HELICOPTERS • ASW • SH-2G 5: 5 SH-2G(G) *Super Seasprite* (maintained by Air Force)

Air Force 2,250

Flying hours   190

FORCES BY ROLE
MR 1 sqn with 6 P-3K *Orion**

Tpt 1 sqn with 14 UH-1H *Iroquois*; 1 sqn with 2 B-757-200; 5 C-130H *Hercules*

Trg 2 sqn with 5 Beech 100 *King Air* (leased); 13 CT-4E; 5 Bell 47G

EQUIPMENT BY TYPE
AIRCRAFT 6 combat capable
  MP • P-3 6: 6 P-3K *Orion**
  TPT 12
    B-757 2: 2 B-757-200
    Beech 100 *King Air* 5 (leased)
    C-130 5: 5 C-130H *Hercules*
  TRG • CT-4 13: 13 CT-4E
HELICOPTERS
  UTL • UH-1 14: 14 UH-1H *Iroquois*
  TRG 5: 5 Bell 47G
  MSL • TACTICAL • ASM • AGM-65: some AGM-65B *Maverick*/AGM-65G *Maverick*

DEPLOYMENT

AFGHANISTAN
NATO • ISAF ε50 SF; 131 (for Provincial Reconstruction Team and various ISAF posts)
UN • UNAMA 1 obs

AUSTRALIA
Army 9 (navigation) trg

BOSNIA-HERZEGOVINA
EU • EUFOR II 12

EAST TIMOR
UN • UNOTIL 1 obs

EGYPT
MFO 26

GULF OF OMAN
New Zealand Armed Forces some Navy (OP ENDURING FREEDOM)

IRAQ
Army 61 (Peace Support)

MIDDLE EAST
UN • UNTSO 8 obs

SERBIA AND MONTENEGRO
UN • UNMIK 1 obs

SINGAPORE
Army 11 1 spt unit

SOLOMON ISLANDS
RAMSI some Police

Papua New Guinea PNG

Papua New Guinea Kina K		2003	2004	2005
GDP	K	13.5bn	13.9bn	
	US$	3.8bn	4.4bn	
per capita	US$	719	817	
Growth	%	2.7	2.5	
Inflation	%	14.7	7.4	
Debt	US$	2.46bn		
Def bdgt	K	67.9m	77.9m	81.8m
	US$	19m	24.6m	26.7m
US$1=K		3.57	3.16	3.06

Population	5,545,268					
Age	0–14	15–19	20–24	25–29	30–64	65 plus
Male	19%	5%	5%	5%	16%	2%
Female	19%	5%	4%	4%	15%	2%

Capabilities

ACTIVE 3,100 (Army 2,500 Air 200 Maritime Element 400)

ORGANISATIONS BY SERVICE

Army ε2,500

FORCES BY ROLE
Inf   2 bn
Engr 1 bn

EQUIPMENT BY TYPE
ARTY • MOR 3+: some 81mm; 3 120mm

Maritime Element 400

FORCES BY ROLE
Navy   1 HQ located at Port Moresby
Maritime some sqn located at Lombrun (Manus Island) with Patrol and Coastal Combatants

East Asia and Australasia

EQUIPMENT BY TYPE

PATROL AND COASTAL COMBATANTS 4+: some
  PCC 4: 4 *Tarangau*
AMPHIBIOUS:
  CRAFT 6: 4 (civil manned)
    LCH 2: 2 *Salamaua*
FACILITIES

Base 1 (forward) located at Alotau, 1 (forward) located at Kieta, 1 located at Lombrun (Manus Island), 1 located at Port Moresby

Air Force 200

FORCES BY ROLE

Tpt some sqn with 1 CASA 212 *Aviocar*; 2 CN-235; 3 IAI-201 *Arava*

Hel some sqn with 4 UH-1H *Iroquois*†

EQUIPMENT BY TYPE

AIRCRAFT • TPT 6: 1 CASA 212 *Aviocar*; 2 CN-235; 3 IAI-201 *Arava*
HELICOPTERS • UTL • UH-1 4: 4 UH-1H *Iroquois*†

DEPLOYMENT

SOLOMON ISLANDS
RAMSI some

FOREIGN FORCES

Australia Army: 1 trg unit; 38

Philippines Pi

Philippine Peso P		2003	2004	2005
GDP	P	4.29tr	4.84tr	
	US$	79.3bn	86.5bn	
per capita	US$	937	1,003	
Growth	%	4.7	6.1	
Inflation	%	3 0	5.5	
Debt	US$	62.6bn		
Def bdgt	P	45.5bn	46.1bn	46.0bn
	US$	840m	824m	844m
FMA (US)	US$	52.2m	22.5m	32.7m
US$1=P		54.2	55.97	54.5

Population   87,857,473

Ethnic groups: Muslim 5–8%; Mindanao provinces Muslim 40–90%; Chinese 2%

Age	0–14	15–19	20–24	25–29	30–64	65 plus
Male	18%	5%	5%	4%	16%	2%
Female	17%	5%	5%	4%	16%	2%

Capabilities

ACTIVE 106,000 (Army 66,000 Navy 24,000 Air 16,000) **Paramilitary 40,500**

RESERVE 131,000 (Army 100,000 Navy 15,000 Air 16,000) **Paramilitary 40,000 (to age 49)**

ORGANISATIONS BY SERVICE

Army 66,000

FORCES BY ROLE

5 Area Unified Comd (joint service), 1 National Capital Region Comd

Lt reaction	3 coy
Lt inf	8 div (*each:* 1 arty bn, 3 inf bde)
Spec Ops	1 comd (1 Scout Ranger regt, 1 SF regt, 1 lt armd bde (regt))
Arty	1 regt HQ
Engr	5 bn
Presidential Guard	1 gp

EQUIPMENT BY TYPE

TK • LT TK 65: 65 *Scorpion*
AIFV 85: 85 YPR-765
APC 370
  APC (T) 100: 100 M-113
  APC (W) 270
    LAV 100: 100 LAV-150 *Commando*
    Simba 150
    V-200 *Chaimite* 20
ARTY 282+
  TOWED 242
    105mm 230: 230 M-101/M-102/M-26/M-56
    155mm 12: 12 M-114/M-68
  MOR 40+
    81mm: some M-29
    107mm 40: 40 M-30
AT • RCL
  106mm • M-40: some M-40A1
  75mm: some M-20
  90mm: some M-67
AIRCRAFT
  TPT 3: 1 Beech 80 *Queen Air*; 1 Cessna 170; 1 P-206A
  UTL 1: 1 Cessna 172

Navy ε24,000; 15,000 reservists (total 39,000)

EQUIPMENT BY TYPE

PRINCIPAL SURFACE COMBATANTS • FRIGATES • FF 1:
  1 *Rajah Humabon* with single, 3 76mm gun
PATROL AND COASTAL COMBATANTS 58
  PCC 11: 3 *Aguinaldo*; 3 *Kagitingan*; 5 *Thomas Batilo*
  PCI 34: 22 *Jose Andrada*; 12 other
  PCO 13:
    3 *Emilio Jacinto* each with 1 76mm gun
    8 *Miguel Malvar* each with 1 76mm gun
    2 *Rizal* each with 3 Twin ASTT (6 eff.)†, 2 76mm gun, 1 hel landing platform
AMPHIBIOUS
  LS • LST 7:
    2 US F.S. *Besson*-class (capacity 32 tanks; 150 troops) each with 1 hel landing platform
    5 *Zamboanga del Sur* (capacity 16 tanks; 200 troops)
  CRAFT 39: 3 LCU; 6 LCVP; 30 LCM
LOGISTICS AND SUPPORT 11: 3 AGOR/AGOS; 2 AOT (small); 1 AR; 2 AWT; 3 spt
FACILITIES

Base 1 located at Sangley Point/Cavite, 1 located at Zamboanga, 1 located at Cebu

Naval Aviation
AIRCRAFT • TPT 6
4 BN-2A *Defender*
2 CESSNA 177 *Cardinal*
HELICOPTERS • UTL 4: 4 BO-105

Marines 7,500
FORCES BY ROLE
structure re-org; to be 2 bde (6 bn)
Marine 3 bde (*total:* 10 Marine bn)

EQUIPMENT BY TYPE
APC • APC (W) • LAV 24: 24 LAV-300
AAV 85: 30 LVTP-5; 55 LVTP-7
ARTY • TOWED • 105mm 150: 150 M-101
  MOR • 107mm: some M-30

Air Force ε16,000; 16,000 reservists (total 32,000)
FORCES BY ROLE
PAF HQ, 5 Cmds (AD, tac ops, air ed and trg, air log and supp, air res)

Ftr	3 sqn with 11 F-5A *Freedom Fighter*/F-5B *Freedom Fighter*; 10 S-211
RECCE	some sqn with 1 Rockwell *Turbo Commander* 690A
MP	1 sqn with 1 F-27 MK 200MPA; 1 GAF N-22SL *Nomad*
SAR / Comms	4 sqn with AB-412SP *Griffon*; total of 27 UH-1M *Iroquois*
Tpt	1 sqn with 2 C-130B *Hercules*; 2 C-130H *Hercules*; 4 C-130K *Hercules*; 1 sqn with 2 Cessna 210 *Centurion*; 1 GAF N-22B *Nomad*; 1 sqn with 1 F-27-200 *Friendship*
COIN	1 sqn with 15 OV-10 *Bronco*
Trg	1 sqn with 28 SF-260TP; 1 sqn with 14 T-41D *Mescalero*
Hel	2 sqn with 20 UH-1H *Iroquois*; 1 (VIP) sqn with 1 S-70 A-5 (S-70A) *Black Hawk*; 1 SA-330L *Puma*; 6 Bell 412EP *Twin Huey*/Bell 412SP *Twin Huey*; 2 sqn with 5 AUH-76; 20 MD-520MG

EQUIPMENT BY TYPE
21 combat capable
AIRCRAFT
 FTR • F-5 11: 11 F-5A *Freedom Fighter*/F-5B *Freedom Fighter*
 FAC 15: 15 OV-10 *Bronco*
 MP 1: 1 F-27 MK 200MPA
 TPT 17
  C-130 14: 2 C-130B *Hercules*; 6 in store; 2 C-130H *Hercules*; 4 C-130K *Hercules*
  F-27 1: 1 F-27-200 *Friendship*
  L-100 1: 1 L-100-20 in store
  ROCKWELL TURBO COMMANDER 690 1: 1 Rockwell *Turbo Commander* 690A
 UTL 9: 2 Cessna 210 *Centurion*; 7 GAF N-22B 7; 1 GAF N-22SL *Nomad*; 5 in store
 TRG 52:

S-211 10*
SF-260 28: 28 SF-260TP
T-41 14: 14 T-41D *Mescalero*
HELICOPTERS
 ASLT 25: 5 AUH-76; 20 MD-520MG
 SPT 2
  S-70 1: 1 S-70 A-5 (S-70A) *Black Hawk*
  SA-330 1: 1 SA-330L *Puma*
 UTL 53+: some AB-412SP *Griffon*
  BELL 412 6: 6 Bell 412EP *Twin Huey*/Bell 412SP *Twin Huey*
  UH-1 47: 20 UH-1H *Iroquois*; 27 UH-1M *Iroquois*
UAV 2: 2 *Blue Horizon* II
MSL • TACTICAL • AAM • AIM-9: some AIM-9B *Sidewinder*

Paramilitary

Philippine National Police 40,500
Deptartment of Interior and Local Government
FORCES BY ROLE

Aux	62,000
Provincial	73 comd
Regional	15 comd

EQUIPMENT BY TYPE
AIRCRAFT
 TPT 2: 2 BN-2 *Islander*
 TRG 3: 3 Lancair 320

Coast Guard
PATROL AND COASTAL COMBATANTS 43
 PCI 42: 4 *Basilan*; 3 *De Haviland*; 35 *Swift*
 PCO 1: 1 *San Juan*
HELICOPTERS: 3 SAR

Citizen Armed Force Geographical Units 40,000 reservists
CAFGU
Militia 56 bn (part-time units which can be called up for extended periods)

NON-STATE ARMED GROUPS
see Part II

DEPLOYMENT

BURUNDI
UN • ONUB 3 obs

CÔTE D'IVOIRE
UN • UNOCI 4 obs; 1

EAST TIMOR
UN • UNOTIL 2 obs

HAITI
UN • MINUSTAH 157

LIBERIA
UN • UNMIL 3 obs; 172

East Asia and Australasia

Singapore Sgp

Singapore Dollar S$		2003	2004	2005
GDP	S$	159bn	179bn	
	US$	91.4bn	105bn	
per capita	US$	21,379	24,176	
Growth	%	1.4	8.4	
Inflation	%	0.5	1.6	
Debt	US$	23.7bn		
Def bdgt	S$	8.24bn	8.62bn	9.25bn
	US$	4.74bn	5.04bn	5.57bn
US$1=S$		1.74	1.71	1.66

Population 4,425,720

Ethnic groups: Chinese 76%; Malay 15%; Indian 6%

Age	0–14	15–19	20–24	25–29	30–64	65 plus
Male	8%	3%	3%	4%	27%	3%
Female	8%	3%	3%	4%	29%	4%

Capabilities

ACTIVE 72,500 (Army 50,000 Navy 9,000 Air 13,500)
Paramilitary 93,800
Terms of service conscription 24 months

RESERVE 312,500 (Army 300,000 Navy 5,000 Air 7,500) **Paramilitary 44,000**
Annual trg to age of 40 for army other ranks, 50 for officers

ORGANISATIONS BY SERVICE

Army 15,000; 35,000 conscripts (total 50,000)

1 Rapid Deployment div (1 inf bde, 1 amph bde (3 amph bn), 1 air mob bde); 3 (mixed active/reserve formations) combined arms div (each: 2 inf bde (each: 3 inf bn), 1 armd bde, 1 recce bn, 2 arty bn, 1 AD bn, 1 engr bn)

FORCES BY ROLE

Recce / lt armd	4 bn
Mech	1 bde
Inf	9 bn
Cdo	1 bn
Arty	4 bn
Engr	4 bn

Reserves

9 inf bde incl in mixed active/inactive reserve formations listed above; 1 op reserve div with additional inf bde; 2 People's Defence Force Comd with 12 inf bn

Recce / lt armd	ε8 bn
Inf	ε60 bn
Cdo	ε1 bn
Arty	ε12 bn
Engr	ε8 bn

EQUIPMENT BY TYPE

TK 450
  MBT 100: 80–100 *Centurion*

LT TK • AMX-13 350: ε350 AMX-13 SM1
AIFV 294:
  AMX-10P 44: 22; 22 AMX-10 PAC 90 (recce)
  IFV-25 250
APC 1,280+
  APC (T) 1,000+: some ATTC *Bronco*; 250 IFV-40/50
    M-113 750+: 750+ M-113A1/M-113A2 (some with 40mm AGL, some with 25mm gun)
  APC (W) 280: 250 LAV-150 *Commando*/V-200 *Commando*; 30 V-100 *Commando*
ARTY 286+
  TOWED 206
    105mm 37: 37 LG1
    155mm 169: 18 FH-2000; 52 FH-88; 16 M-114A1 some in store; 45 M-68 some in store; 38 M-71S
  SP • 155mm 18: ε18 SSPH-1 *Primus*
  MOR 62+:
    81mm: some, some SP
    120mm: 50, some SP in M-113
    160mm 12: 12 M-58 Tampella
AT
  MSL 30+: 30+ *Gil/Spike Spike/Milan*
  RCL 290
    106mm • M-40 90: 90 M-40A1 in store
    84mm 200: ε200 *Carl Gustav*
  RL
    67mm: some *Armbrust*
    89mm: some M-20
AD
  SAM • MANPAD 75+: 75+ *Mistral/RBS-70/SA-18 Grouse (Igla)* (some SP as V-200; air force)
  GUNS • 20mm • TOWED 30: 30 GAI-C01 (some SP)
RADAR • LAND: some AN/TPQ-36 *Firefinder*/AN/TPQ-37 *Firefinder* (arty, mor)
FACILITIES

Training camp	3 (incl inf, arty and armd) located in Taiwan (Republic of China), 1 (arty, cbt engr) located in Thailand

Navy 2,200; 1,800 conscript; ε5,000 active reservists (total 9,000)

EQUIPMENT BY TYPE

SUBMARINES • TACTICAL • SSK 3:
  3 *Challenger* each with 4 single 533mm TT
PRINCIPAL SURFACE COMBATANTS • CORVETTES • FSG 6:
  6 *Victory* each with 2 triple ASTT (6 eff.), 2 octuple (16 eff.) each with 1 *Barak* SAM, 2+ Mk 140 *Harpoon* quad (8 eff.) each with 1 RGM-84C *Harpoon* tactical SSM, 1 76mm gun
PATROL AND COASTAL COMBATANTS 17
  PFM 6:
    6 *Sea Wolf* each with 2 Mk 140 *Harpoon* quad (8 eff.) each with RGM-84C *Harpoon* tactical SSM, 1 twin (2 eff.) (manually operated) with *Mistral* SAM, 4 (8 eff.) each with GI *Gabriel I* tactical SSM, 1 57mm gun
  PCO 11:
    6 *Fearless* each with 2 *Sadral* sextuple each with *Mistral* SAM
    5 *Fearless* each with 2 *Sadral* sextuple each with *Mistral* SAM, 1 76mm gun

MINE WARFARE • MINE COUNTERMEASURES •
MHC 4: 4 *Bedok*
AMPHIBIOUS
  LS • LST 4:
    4 *Endurance* (capacity 350 troops; 18 MBTs; 4 LCVP; 2
    hel) (with hel deck) each with 2 Twin (4 eff.) each with
    Mistral SAM, 1 76mm gun
  CRAFT 36: 30 LCU; 6 LCM
LOGISTICS AND SUPPORT 2
  AS 1: 1 *Kendrick*
  Trg 1
LNCHR • TT • 324mm 6: 6 x1
GUN • GUN 1: 1 76mm

FACILITIES
Base 1 located at Changi, 1 located at Tuas (Jurong)

Air Force 10,500; 3,000 conscript; 7,500 reservists (total 21,000)

FORCES BY ROLE
(incl 3,000 conscripts, plus 7,500)

FGA	2 sqn with 28 F-5S *Tiger II*; 9 F-5T *Tiger II* (secondary GA role); 2 (in US) sqn each with 24 F-16C *Fighting Falcon*/F-16D *Fighting Falcon*; 3 sqn with 6 F-16A *Fighting Falcon*/F-16B *Fighting Falcon*; 38 F-16C *Fighting Falcon*/F-16D *Fighting Falcon*
Recce	1 sqn with 8 RF-5S *Tiger*
Recce / tkr / tpt	1 sqn with 4 KC-130B *Hercules* (trk/tpt); 1 KC-130H *Hercules*; 5 C-130 *Hercules* (2 Elint); 1 sqn with 9 F-50 *Maritime Enforcer* (4 tpt, 5 MR)
AEW	1 sqn with 4 E-2C *Hawkeye*
Tkr	1 sqn with 4 KC-135R *Stratotanker*
Trg	det with 12 F-16C *Fighting Falcon*/F-16D *Fighting Falcon* on lease located at Cannon AFB, (NM), US; 12 on lease located at Luke AFB, (AZ), US; AH-64D *Apache* located at Marana, (AZ), US; 6+ CH-47D *Chinook* located at Grand Prairie, (TX), US; 1 sqn with 12 AS-550 *Fennec*; 1 sqn with 4 A-4SU *Super Skyhawk*; 10 TA-4SU *Super Skyhawk*; 1 sqn with 27 S-211
Hel	1 sqn with 6 AB-205A (Bell 205A); 19 UH-1H *Iroquois*; 1 sqn with 10 CH-47SD *Super D Chinook*; 2 sqn with 18 AS-332M *Super Puma* (incl 5 SAR); 12 AS-532UL *Cougar*; 2 sqn with 8 AH-64D *Apache*; 20 AS-550A2 *Fennec*/AS-550C2 *Fennec*
UAV	1 sqn with *Blue Horizon*; 24 *Chukar* III; 40 *Searcher* MK II .

EQUIPMENT BY TYPE
AIRCRAFT 111 combat capable
  FTR 43
    F-5 37: 28 F-5S *Tiger II*; 9 F-5T *Tiger II* (secondary GA role)
    F-16 6: 6 F-16A *Fighting Falcon*/F-16B *Fighting Falcon*
  FGA 44
    A-4 6: 6 A-4SU *Super Skyhawk*
    F-16C *Fighting Falcon*/**F-16D** *Fighting Falcon* 38
  RECCE 8: 8 RF-5S *Tiger*
  MP 9: 9 F-50 *Maritime Enforcer* (4 tpt, 5 MR)
  AEW • E-2 4: 4 E-2C *Hawkeye*

TKR 9
  KC-130 5: 4 KC-130B *Hercules* (trk/tpt); 1 KC-130H *Hercules*
  KC-135 4: 4 KC-135R *Stratotanker*
TPT • C-130 5: 5 C-130H *Hercules* (2 Elint)
TRG 47: 27 S-211
  TA-4 10: 10 TA-4SU *Super Skyhawk*
HELICOPTERS
  ATK 28
    AH-64 8: 8 AH-64D *Apache*
    AS-550A2 *Fennec*/**AS-550C2** *Fennec* 20
  SPT 28
    AS-332 18: 18 AS-332M *Super Puma* (incl 5 SAR)
    CH-47 10: 10 CH-47SD *Super D Chinook*
  UTL 54
    AS-532 12: 12 AS-532UL *Cougar*
    AS-550 *Fennec* 12
    BELL 205 6: 6 AB-205A (Bell 205A)
    UH-1 24: 24 UH-1H *Iroquois*
UAV 64+: some *Blue Horizon*; 24 *Chukar* III; 40 *Searcher* MK II .

FACILITIES
School 1 (trg) located in Brunei, 1 with 27 S-211 (flying trg) located at Pearce, Aus, 1 with 12 AS-332 *Super Puma* Spt/AS-532 *Cougar* Utl (flying trg) located at Oakey, Aus

Air Defence Systems Divison

FORCES BY ROLE
Air 4 (field def) sqn

EQUIPMENT BY TYPE
MSL • TACTICAL
  ASM: some AGM-45 *Shrike*
    AGM-65: some AGM-65B *Maverick*; some AGM-65G *Maverick*
    AGM-84 *Harpoon* some
  AAM
    AIM-120: some AIM-120C *AMRAAM* in store (US)
    AIM-7: some AIM-7P *Sparrow*
    AIM-9: some AIM-9N *Sidewinder*/AIM-9P *Sidewinder*

Air Defence Bde

FORCES BY ROLE
Air some bde (*total:* 1 AD sqn with Oerlikon, 1 AD sqn with 18+ MIM-23 *HAWK*, 1 AD sqn with *Rapier-Blindfire*)

EQUIPMENT BY TYPE
RADAR • LAND: some *Blindfire*

Air Force Systems Bde

Air some bde (*total:* 1 AD sqn with radar (mobile), 1 AD sqn with LORADS)

Divisional Air Def Arty Bde

attached to army divs
FORCES BY ROLE
AD some bde (*total:* 1 AD bn with 36 *Mistral*, 1 AD bn with SA-18 *Grouse (Igla)*, 3 AD bn with RBS-70)

EQUIPMENT BY TYPE
AD
  SAM 36+: 36 *Mistral*; some RBS-70

MANPAD: some SA-18 *Grouse (Igla)*

Paramilitary 93,800 active

Civil Defence Force 81,800 incl. 1,600 regulars, 3,200 conscripts, 23,000 reservists; 54,000+ volunteers; 1 construction bde (2,500 conscripts)

Singapore Police Force 8,500; 3,500 conscript; 21,000 reservists (total 33,000)

Singapore Gurkha Contingent 1,500

6 coy

DEPLOYMENT

AUSTRALIA
Air Force
FORCES BY ROLE
230 air
EQUIPMENT BY TYPE
AIRCRAFT • TRG 27: 27 S-211
HELICOPTERS: 12 AS-332 *Super Puma* Spt/AS-532 *Cougar* Utl
FACILITIES
School 1 with 12 AS-332 *Super Puma* Spt/AS-532 *Cougar* utl (flying trg) located at Oakey, Aus, 1 with 27 S-211 trg ac (flying trg) located at Pearce, Aus

BRUNEI
Air Force
FORCES BY ROLE
500 air; 1 hel det with 5 UH-1H *Iroquois*
FACILITIES
School 1 (trg) located in Brunei

FRANCE
Air Force
200 air; some trg sqn with 6 A-4SU *Super Skyhawk*; 10 TA-4SU *Super Skyhawk*

TAIWAN (REPUBLIC OF CHINA)
Army
Training camp   3 (incl inf, arty and armd) located in Taiwan (Republic of China)

THAILAND
Army
Training camp   1 (arty, cbt engr) located in Thailand

UNITED STATES
Air Force
AIRCRAFT • FGA 24: 12 F-16C *Fighting Falcon*/F-16D *Fighting Falcon* on lease located at Cannon AFB, (NM), US; 12 on lease located at Luke AFB, (AZ), US
HELICOPTERS
 ATK • AH-64: some AH-64D *Apache* located at Marana, (AZ), US
 SPT • CH-47 6+: 6+ CH-47D *Chinook* located at Grand Prairie, (TX), US

FOREIGN FORCES
New Zealand Army: 1 spt unit; 11
United States Navy: support facility located at Singapore
USPACOM: 1 log spt sqn located at Singapore; 50; 39

Taiwan (Republic of China) ROC

New Taiwan Dollar NT$		2003	2004	2005
GDP	NT$	9.8tr	10.2tr	
	US$	280bn	304bn	
per capita	US$	12,422	13,390	
Growth	%	3.3	5.7	
Inflation	%	-0.3	1.6	
Debt	US$	63bn		
Def bdgt[a]	NT$	230bn	251bn	260bn
	US$	6.63bn	7.51bn	8.32bn
US$1=NT$		34.8	33.5	31.3

[a] excluding special procurement funds

Population   22,894,384

Ethnic groups: Taiwanese 84%; mainland Chinese 14%

Age	0–14	15–19	20–24	25–29	30–64	65 plus
Male	10%	4%	4%	4%	24%	5%
Female	9%	3%	4%	4%	23%	5%

Capabilities

ACTIVE 290,000 (Army 200,000 Navy 45,000 Air 45,000) **Paramilitary 26,650**

Terms of service 20 months

Paramilitary 22,000

RESERVE 1,653,500 (Army 1,500,000 Navy 32,000 Air Force 90,000)
Army reservists have some obligation to age 30

ORGANISATIONS BY SERVICE

Army ε200,000 (incl mil police)
FORCES BY ROLE
Comd	4 (defence) HQ
Army	3 corps
Armd	5 bde
Armd inf	1 bde
Inf	28 bde
Avn / SF	1 comd (1 spec war bde, 3 avn bde)
Mot inf	3 bde
SSM	1 (coastal def) bn

Missile Command
AD 1 (AD msl) comd (2 AD/SAM gp (*each:* 2 SAM bn each with 40 MIM-14 *Nike Hercules* (to be retired), 4 SAM bn each with 100 MIM-23 HAWK))

Reserves

Lt inf 7 div

EQUIPMENT BY TYPE

TK 1,831+
  MBT 926+
    M-60 376: 376 M-60A3
    M-48 550+: 100 M-48A5; 450+ M-48H *Brave Tiger*
  LT TK 905: 230 M-24 *Chaffee* (90mm gun); 675 M-41/
    Type-64
AIFV 225: 225 CM-25 *AIFV* (M-113 with 20-30mm cannon)
APC 950
  APC (T) 650: 650 M-113
  APC (W) • LAV 300: 300 LAV-150 *Commando*
ARTY 1,815+
  TOWED 1,060+
    105mm 650: 650 T-64 (M-101)
    155mm 340+: some M-44; 90 M-59; 250 T-65 (M-114)
    203mm 70: 70 M-115
  SP 405
    105mm 100: 100 M-108
    155mm 245
      M-109 225: 225 M-109A2/M-109A5
      T-69 20
    203mm 60: 60 M-110
  COASTAL • 127mm 50: ε50 US Mk 32 (reported)
  MRL 300+: 300+ *Kung Feng* III 126mm/*Kung Feng* IV
    126mm/*Kung Feng* VI 117mm/RT 2000 *Thunder* (KF
    towed and SP)
  MOR
    81mm: some M-29 (some SP)
    107mm some
AT
  MSL 1,000: 1,000 TOW (some SP)
  RCL
    106mm • M-40 500: 500 M-40A1
    Type-51 some
    90mm: some M-67
HELICOPTERS
  ATK 101
    AH-1 62: 62 AH-1W *Cobra*
    OH-58D *Warrior* 39
  SPT • CH-47 9: 9 CH-47SD *Super D Chinook*
  UTL • UH-1 80: 80 UH-1H *Iroquois*
  TRG 30: 30 TH-67 *Creek*
UAV: some *Mastiff* III
AD
  SAM 581+: some *Tien Kung* II/*Tien Kung* I
    SP 76: 74 FIM-92A *Avenger*; 2 M-48 *Chaparral*
    TOWED 425: 25 MIM-104 *Patriot*; 400 MIM-23 HAWK
    STATIC 80: 80 MIM-14 *Nike Hercules* (to be retired)
    MANPAD: some FIM-92A *Stinger*
  GUNS • 40mm 400: 400 L/70 towed/M-42 SP
MSL • TACTICAL • SSM: some *Ching Feng*

Navy 45,000; circa 67,000 reservists (total 112,000)

FORCES BY ROLE

Navy 3 district; 1 (ASW) HQ located at Hualein; 1 HQ
  located at Tsoying; 1 New East Coast Fleet

EQUIPMENT BY TYPE

SUBMARINES • TACTICAL • SSK 4:

2 *Hai Lung* each with 6+ single 533mm TT each with 20+
  SUT HWT
2 *Hai Shih* (trg only) each with 4 Single 533mm TT (aft)
  each with SUT HWT, 6 (fwd) each with SUT HWT

PRINCIPAL SURFACE COMBATANTS 32
  DESTROYERS • DDG 11:
    7 *Chien Yang* (capacity 1 Hughes 500MD *Scout Defender*
    aslt hel) (US *Gearing Wu Chin* III conversion) each with
    2 triple ASTT (6 eff.) each with Mk 46 LWT, 1 Mk 112
    octuple (8 eff.) with tactical ASROC, 1 quad (4 eff.)
    with 4 *Hsiung Feng* tactical SSM, 2 triple (6 eff.) each
    with SM-1 MR SAM, 2 twin (4 eff.) each with SM-1 MR
    SAM
    2 *Fu Yang* (capacity 1 Hughes 500MD *Scout Defender*
    aslt hel) each with 2 triple ASTT (6 eff.) each with Mk
    46 LWT, 1 quad (4 eff.) with *Sea Chaparral* SAM, 2 single
    each with GII *Gabriel II/Hsiung Feng*, 1 triple (3 eff.)
    with GII *Gabriel II/Hsiung Feng*, up to 2 127mm gun
    1 *Fu Yang* (capacity 1 Hughes 500MD *Scout Defender* aslt
    hel) (*Shei Yang*) with 2 triple ASTT (6 eff.) each with Mk
    46 LWT, 1 Mk 112 octuple (8 eff.) with tactical ASROC,
    1 GWS 25 *Seawolf* quad (4 eff.) with *Sea Chaparral* SAM,
    2 single each with GII *Gabriel II/Hsiung Feng*, 1 triple
    (3 eff.) with GII *Gabriel II/Hsiung Feng*, up to 2 127mm
    gun
    1 *Po Yang* (capacity 1 Hughes 500MD *Scout Defender*
    aslt hel)† with *Hsiung Feng* tactical SSM, 2 triple ASTT
    (6 eff.) each with Mk 46 LWT, up to 2 127mm gun
  FRIGATES • FFG 21:
    7 *Cheng Kung* (capacity 2 S-70C *Defender* ASW hel) each
    with 2 triple ASTT (6 eff.) each with Mk 46 LWT, 1 Mk
    13 GMLS with 40+ SM-1 MR SAM, 2 quad (8 eff.) each
    with *Hsiung Feng* tactical SSM, 1 76mm gun
    8 *Chin Yang* (capacity 1 MD-500 utl hel) each with 2
    Twin 324mm ASTT (4 eff.) each with Mk 46 LWT, 1
    Mk16 Mk 112 octuple with ASROC/RGM-84C *Harpoon*
    SSM, 1 127mm gun
    6 *Kang Ding* (capacity 1 S-70C *Defender* ASW hel) each
    with 2 triple 324mm ASTT (6 eff.) each with Mk 46 LWT,
    1 quad (4 eff.) with *Sea Chaparral* SAM, 2 (8 eff.) each
    with *Hsiung Feng* tactical SSM, 1 76mm gun

PATROL AND COASTAL COMBATANTS • PFM 59:
  48 *Hai Ou* each with 2 single each with 2 *Hsiung Feng*
  tactical SSM
  9 *Jinn Chiang* each with 1 quad (4 eff.) with 4 *Hsiung Feng*
  tactical SSM
  2 *Lung Chiang* each with 4 single each with 4 *Hsiung Feng*
  tactical SSM

MINE WARFARE • MINE COUNTERMEASURES 12
  MSC 8: 4 *Yung Chou*; 4 *Yung Feng*
  MSO 4: 4 *Aggressive* (Ex US)
COMMAND SHIPS • LCC 1: 1 *Kao Hsiung*
AMPHIBIOUS
  PRINCIPAL AMPHIBIOUS SHIPS • LSD 1:
    1 *Shiu Hai* (capacity 360 troops; either 2 LCU or 18
    LCM) with 1 hel landing platform
  LS 17
    LSM 4: 4 *Mei Lo* (capacity 4 tanks)
    LST 13:
      11 *Chung Hai* (capacity 16 tanks; 200 troops)
      2 *Chung Ho* (capacity 400 troops; 3 LCVP; 1 LCPA)
      each with 1 hel landing platform

CRAFT 325: 20 LCU; 100 LCVP; 205 LCM
LOGISTICS AND SUPPORT 20
  AGOR 1: 1 *Te Kuan*
  AO 3
  AR 2
  ATF 7
  SPT 1: 1 *Wu Yi* with 1 hel landing platform
  TPT 6: 2; 2 *Wu Kang* each with 1 hel landing platform; 2 *Yuen Feng*

FACILITIES
Base 1 located at Makung (Pescadores), 1 located at Keelung, 1 located at Tsoying, 1 located at Hualein, 1 located at Suo

Marines 15,000

FORCES BY ROLE

Marine 2 bde

Spt some elm

EQUIPMENT BY TYPE

AAV • LVTP-5 150: 150 LVTP-5A1
ARTY • TOWED: some 105mm; some 155mm
AT • RCL: some 106mm

Naval Aviation

FORCES BY ROLE

ASW some sqn with 20 S-70C *Defender**
MR some sqn with 24 S-2E *Tracker*; 8 S-2G *Tracker*

EQUIPMENT BY TYPE

AIRCRAFT 32 combat capable
  ASW • S-2 32: 24 S-2E *Tracker**; 8 S-2G *Tracker**
HELICOPTERS
  ASW 20: 20 S-70C *Defender**

Air Force 45,000

Flying hours   180 hrs/year

FORCES BY ROLE

Ftr 3 sqn with 10 *Mirage* 2000-5DI (M-2000-5D); 47 *Mirage* 2000-5EI (M-2000-5E)

Ftr / FGA 1 sqn with 22 AT-3 *Tzu-Chung*; 6 sqn with 90 F-5E *Tiger II*/F-5F *Tiger II* some in store; 6 sqn with 128 *Ching Kuo*; 6 sqn with 136 F-16A *Fighting Falcon*/F-16B *Fighting Falcon*

Recce 1 sqn with 10 F-16A *Fighting Falcon*/F-16B *Fighting Falcon* (recce role); 1 sqn with 8 RF-5E *Tigereye*

EW 1 sqn with 2 C-130HE *Tien Gian*; 2 CC-47 (C-47) *Skytrain*

AEW some sqn with 4 E-2T (E-2) *Hawkeye*

SAR 1 sqn with 17 S-70C *Black Hawk*

Tpt 2 sqn with 19 C-130H *Hercules* (1 EW); 1 (VIP) sqn with 4 B-727-100; 1 B-737-800; 10 Beech 1900; 3 Fokker 50

Trg some sqn with 42 T-34C *Turbo Mentor*

Hel some sqn with 3 CH-47 *Chinook*; 14 S-70 *Black Hawk*; 1 S-62A (VIP)

EQUIPMENT BY TYPE

AIRCRAFT 479 combat capable
  FTR 293

F-5 90: 90 F-5E *Tiger II*/F-5F *Tiger II* some in store
F-16 146: 10 F-16A *Fighting Falcon*/F-16B *Fighting Falcon* (recce role); 136 more
M-2000-5 57: 10 *Mirage* 2000-5DI (M-2000-5D); 47 *Mirage* 2000-5EI (M-2000-5E)
FGA 128: 128 *Ching Kuo*
RECCE 8: 8 RF-5E *Tigereye*
EW 2: 2 C-130HE *Tien Gian*
AEW 4: 4 E-2T (E-2) *Hawkeye*
TPT 39
  B-727 4: 4 B-727-100
  B-737 1: 1 B-737-800
  Beech 1900 10
  C-130 19: 19 C-130H *Hercules* (1 EW)
  CC-47 (C-47) *Skytrain* 2 **Fokker 50** 3
TRG 100
  AT-3 58: 22; 36 AT-3A *Tzu-Chung*/AT-3B *Tzu-Chung**
  T-34 42: 42 T-34C *Turbo Mentor*
HELICOPTERS
  SPT 34:
    CH-47 Chinook 3
    S-70 31: 14; 17 S-70C *Black Hawk*
  UTL 1: 1 S-62A (VIP)
MSL • TACTICAL
  ASM • AGM-65: some AGM-65A *Maverick*; AGM-84 *Harpoon*
  ARM: some *Sky Sword* IIA
  AAM •
    AIM-120: some AIM-120C *AMRAAM*
    AIM-4D *Falcon* some
    AIM-9: some AIM-9J *Sidewinder*/AIM-9P *Sidewinder*
    MICA some
    R-550: some R-550 *Magic 2*
    Shafrir some *Sky Sword* I some *Sky Sword* II some

Paramilitary ε26,500

Security Groups 25,000

Coast Guard Administration 22,000 (civilian)

responsible for guarding the Spratly and Pratas island groups, and enforcing law and order at sea.

Customs Service 650

Ministry of Finance
PATROL AND COASTAL COMBATANTS 13: 2 PCC; 1 PCI; 5 less than 100 tonnes; 5 PCO

Maritime Police ε1,000

PATROL AND COASTAL COMBATANTS 38: ε38 PB (armed)

Thailand Th

Thai Baht b		2003	2004	2005
GDP	b	5.92tr	6.57tr	
	US$	143bn	161bn	
per capita	US$	2,228	2,497	
Growth	%	6.9	6.1	
Inflation	%	1.8	2.7	
Debt	US$	51.7bn		
Def bdgt	b	79.9bn	78.5bn	78.0bn
	US$	1.93bn	1.93bn	1.95bn
FMA (US)	US$	3.75m	3.45m	3.98m
US$1=b		41.4	40.6	40

Population   64,185,502

Ethnic groups: Thai 75%; Chinese 14%; Muslim 4%

Age	0–14	15–19	20–24	25–29	30–64	65 plus
Male	11%	4%	4%	5%	22%	4%
Female	11%	4%	4%	4%	23%	4%

Capabilities

ACTIVE 306,600 (Army 190,000 Navy 70,600 Air 46,000) **Paramilitary 113,700**

Terms of service 2 years

RESERVE 200,000 Paramilitary 45,000

ORGANISATIONS BY SERVICE

Army 120,000; ε70,000 conscript (total 190,000)

4 Regional Army HQ, 2 Corps HQ

FORCES BY ROLE

Armd air cav	1 regt (3 air mob coy)
Rapid reaction	1 force (1 bn per region forming)
Cav	2 div; 1 indep regt
Recce	4 coy
Mech inf	2 div
Armd inf	3 div
Inf	8 indep bn
SF	2 div
Lt inf	1 div
Arty	1 div
ADA	1 div (6 ADA bn)
Engr	1 div
Hel	some flt
Economic development	4 div

Reserves

Inf 4 div HQ

EQUIPMENT BY TYPE

TK 848
  MBT 333
    M-60 178: 53 M-60A1; 125 M-60A3
    Type-69 50 training in store

M-48 105: 105 M-48A5
LT TK 515: 255 M-41; 104 *Scorpion*; 50 in store; 106 *Stingray*
RECCE 32+: some M1114 *HMMWV*
  S52 32: 32 S52 Mk 3
APC 950
  APC (T) 790
    M-113 340: 340 M-113A1/M-113A3
    Type-85 450
  APC (W) 160: 18 *Condor*
    LAV 142: 142 LAV-150 *Commando*
ARTY 2473+
  TOWED 553
    105mm 353
      LG1 24: 24 LG1 MK II
      M-101 285: 285 M-101 -Mod/M-101 105mm Towed
      M-102 12
      M-618A2 32
    130mm 15: 15 Type-59-I
    155mm 185
      GHN-45 42: 42 GHN-45 A1
      M-114 50
      M-198 61
      M-71 32
  SP • 155mm • M-109 20: 20 M-109A2
  MRL • 130mm: some Type-85 (reported)
  MOR 1,900: 1,867 81mm/M-106A1 107mm
    81mm • M-125 21: 21 M-125A3 (SP)
    120mm 12: 12 M-1064A3 (SP)
AT
  MSL 318+: 300 M47 *Dragon*
    TOW 18+: some
      M-901 18: 18 M-901A5
  RCL 180
    106mm 150: 150 M-40
    75mm 30: 30 M-20
  RL • 66mm: some M-72 *LAW*
AIRCRAFT
  RECCE • OBS 40: 40 Cessna O-1A *Bird Dog*
  TPT 10
    BEECH 1900 2: 2 Beech 1900C
    Beech 200 *Super King Air* 2 **CASA 212** *Aviocar* 2 *Jetstream* **41** 2 **Short 330UTT** 2
  UTL • U-17 10: 10 U-17B
  TRG 33
    MX-7 18: 18 MX-7-235 *Star Rocket*
    T-41 15: 15 T-41B *Mescalero*
HELICOPTERS
  ATK • AH-1 5: 5 AH-1F *Cobra*
  SPT • CH-47 6: 6 CH-47D *Chinook*
  UTL 159: 65 AB-212 (Bell 212)/Bell 206 *JetRanger*/Bell 214/ Bell 412 *Twin Huey*; 92 UH-1H *Iroquois*; 2 UH-60L *Black Hawk*
  TRG • HUGHES 300 42: 42 Hughes 300C
UAV • RECCE • TAC: some *Searcher*
AD
  SAM • STATIC: some *Aspide*
    MANPAD: some FIM-43 *Redeye*
      HN-5: some HN-5A
  GUNS 202
    20mm 48

SP 24: 24 M-163 *Vulcan*
TOWED 24: 24 M-167 *Vulcan*
37mm 52: 52 Type-74 towed
40mm 78: 30 M-1 towed/M-42 SP; 48 L/70 towed
57mm 24+: ε6 Type-59 (S-60) towed; 18+ non-operational towed
RADAR • LAND: some AN/TPQ-36 *Firefinder* (arty, mor); some RASIT (veh, arty)

Navy 44,751 (incl Naval Aviation, Marines, Coastal Defence); 25,849 conscript (total 70,600)

FORCES BY ROLE
Air wing 1 div
Navy 1 (Fleet) HQ located at Sattahip; 1 ((Mekong River Operating Unit)) HQ located at Nakhon Phanom

EQUIPMENT BY TYPE
PRINCIPAL SURFACE COMBATANTS 18
  AIRCRAFT CARRIERS • CVH 1:
    1 *Chakri Naruebet* (capacity 9 AV-8A *Harrier* FGA ac; 6 S-70B *Seahawk* ASW hel)
  FRIGATES 12
    FFG 8:
      2 *Chao Phraya* each with 4 twin (8 eff.) each with 1 CSS-N-4 *Sardine* tactical SSM, 2 (4 eff.) non-operational each with 1 HQ-61 (CSA-N-2) SAM non-operational, 2 RBU 1200 (10 eff.), 2 twin 100mm gun (4 eff.), 2 twin 37mm gun (4 eff.), 1 hel landing platform
      2 *Kraburi* (capacity 1 AB-212 (Bell 212) utl hel) each with 2 twin (4 eff.) each with 1 HQ-61 (CSA-N-2) SAM, 4 (8 eff.) each with 1 CSS-N-4 *Sardine* tactical SSM, 2 RBU 1200 (10 eff.), 1 twin 100mm gun (2 eff.), 2 twin 37mm gun (4 eff.)
      2 *Naresuan* (capacity either 1 S-70B-2 *Seahawk* ASW hel or 1 *Super Lynx* utl hel) each with 2 Mk 141 *Harpoon* quad (8 eff.) each with 1 RGM-84A *Harpoon* tactical SSM, 2 triple 324mm TT (6 eff.), 1 8 cell Mk 41 VLS with 1 RIM-7M *Sea Sparrow* SAM, 1 127mm gun
      2 *Phuttha Yotfa Chulalok* (capacity 1 AB-212 (Bell 212) utl hel) (leased from US) each with 2 Twin ASTT (4 eff.) with 22 Mk 46 LWT, 1 Mk16 Mk 112 octuple with 1 RGM-84C *Harpoon* tactical SSM, tactical ASROC, 1 127mm gun
    FF 4:
      1 *Makut Rajakumarn* with 2 triple ASTT (6 eff.), 2 114mm gun
      1 *Pin Klao* with 6 x1 324mm ASTT, 3 76mm gun
      2 *Tapi* each with 6 x1 324mm ASTT each with Mk 46 LWT, 1 76mm gun
  CORVETTES 5
    FSG 2:
      2 *Rattanakosin* each with 2 triple ASTT (6 eff.), 1 *Albatros* octuple with 1 *Aspide* SAM, 2 Mk 140 *Harpoon* quad (8 eff.) each with 1 RGM-84A *Harpoon* tactical SSM, 1 76mm gun
    FS 3:
      3 *Khamronsin* each with 2 triple ASTT (6 eff.), 1 76mm gun
PATROL AND COASTAL COMBATANTS 110
  PBR 35

PC 6: 6 *Sattahip* each with 1 40mm gun, 1 76mm gun
PCC 3 each with 1 40mm gun, 1 76mm gun
PCI 49: 12 *Swift*; 10 T-11; 15 T-213; 3 T-81; 9 T-91
PCR 6
PFC 3: 3 *Chon Buri* each with 2 76mm gun
PFM 6:
  3 *Prabparapak* each with 2 single each with 1 GI *Gabriel I* tactical SSM, 1 triple (3 eff.) with 1 GI *Gabriel I* tactical SSM, 1 40mm gun, 1 57mm gun
  3 *Ratcharit* each with 2 twin (4 eff.) each with 1 MM-38 *Exocet* tactical SSM, 1 76mm gun
PCO 2: 2 *Hua Hin* each with 2 20mm gun, 1 76mm gun
MINE WARFARE • MINE COUNTERMEASURES 20
  MCC 2: 2 *Bang Rachan*
  MCM SPT 1: 1 *Thalang*
  MCMV 2: 2 *Lat Ya*
  MS ε12
  MSC 3: 3 *Bangkeo*
AMPHIBIOUS:
  LS 9: 2
    LSM 1: 1 *Kut* (capacity 4 tanks)
    LST 6:
      4 *Angthong* (capacity 16 tanks; 200 troops) each with 6 40mm gun
      2 *Srichang* (capacity 14 tanks; 300 troops) training each with 2 40mm gun, 1 hel landing platform
  CRAFT 53: 1; ε13 LCU; 12 LCVP; 24 LCM; 3 ACV
LOGISTICS AND SUPPORT 18:
  AG 5
  AOR 2: 1 *Chula*; 1 *Similan* (1 hel)
  AOT 5: 4 *Prong*; 1 *Samui*
  YTL 2
  YTM 4

FACILITIES
Base 1 located at Bangkok, 1 located at Sattahip, 1 located at Songkhla, 1 located at Phang Nga, 1 located at Nakhon Phanom

Naval Aviation 1,940

AIRCRAFT 18 combat capable
  FGA • AV-8 7: 7 AV-8A *Harrier*
  RECCE • OBS 9: 9 *Sentry* 02-337
  MP 9: 5 DO-228-212*; 2 F-27 MK 200MPA*; 2 P-3T (P-3A) *Orion**
  TPT • F-27 2: 2 F-27-400M *Troopship*
  UTL 7: 2 CL-215-III; 4 GAF N-24A *Search Master*; 1 UP-3T (UP-3A) *Orion*
  TRG 20:
    TA-7 18: 14; 4 TA-7C *Corsair II*
    TAV-8 2: 2 TAV-8A *Harrier**
HELICOPTERS
  ASW 6: 6 S-70B *Seahawk*
  UTL 17:
    AB-212 (Bell 212) 5
    BELL 214 5: 5 AB-214ST
    S-76 5: 5 S-76B
    SUPER LYNX 2
MSL • TACTICAL • ASM: some AGM-84 *Harpoon*

Marines 23,000

FORCES BY ROLE

Recce   1 bn
Amph aslt 1 bn
Inf   2 regt
Arty   1 regt (1 ADA bn, 3 fd arty bn)
Marine   1 div HQ

EQUIPMENT BY TYPE
APC • APC (W) • LAV 24: 24 LAV-150 *Commando*
AAV 33: 33 LVTP-7
ARTY • TOWED 48: 36 105mm (reported); 12 GC-45 155mm
AT • MSL 24+: some M47 *Dragon*
   TOW 24+: some; 24 HMMWV
AD • GUNS 14: 14 12.7mm

Air Force ε46,000
4 air divs, one flying trg school
Flying hours   100 hrs/year

FORCES BY ROLE
FTR/ FGA   2 sqn with 34 L-39ZA/MP *Albatros*; 1 sqn with 20 *Alpha Jet*; 3 (1 aggressor) sqn with 35 F-5E *Tiger II*/F-5F *Tiger II* (32 being upgraded), 2 F-5B; 3 sqn with 41 F-16A *Fighting Falcon*; 9 F-16B *Fighting Falcon*
Recce/ ELINT 1 sqn with 3 IAI-201 *Arava*, 2 Learjet 35A
Tpt   1 sqn with 9 Basler *Turbo-67*; 15 GAF N-22B *Nomad*; 1 sqn with 4 BAe-748; 3 G-222; 1 sqn with 7 C-130H *Hercules*; 5 C-130H-30 *Hercules*
VIP   1 (Royal Flight) sqn with 1 A-310-324; 1 Airbus A319CJ; 1 B-737-200; 2 BAe-748; 2 737-400; 2 Beech 200 *Super King Air*; 3 SA-226AT *Merlin IV/IVA*; 3 AS-532A2 *Cougar MKII*; 3 AS-332L *Super Puma*; 2 Bell 412 *Twin Huey*
Utl   1 sqn with 22 AU-23A *Peacemaker**, 1 sqn with 12 L-392A*, 1 with 10 *Alpha Jet**
Liaison some sqn with 2 Beech 65 *Queen Air*; 1 Beech E90 *King Air*; 3 Rockwell *Commander* 500; 3 Cessna 150; 12 T-41D *Mescalero*
Survey some sqn with 3 SA-226AT *Merlin IV/IVA*; 3 GAF N-22B *Nomad*
Trg   some sqn with 29 CT-4B/E *Airtrainer*; 23 PC-9; 6 Bell 206B *JetRanger II*
Hel   1 sqn with 20 UH-1H *Iroquois*; 1 sqn with 13 Bell 412

EQUIPMENT BY TYPE
AIRCRAFT 165 combat capable
FTR/FGA 87
   F-5 49: 35 F-5E *Tiger II*/F-5F *Tiger II* (32 being upgraded), 2 F-5B
   F-16 50: 41 F-16A *Fighting Falcon*; 9 F-16B *Fighting Falcon*
TPT 47
   A-310 1: 1 A-310-324
   A-319CJ 1
   B-737 3: 1 B-737-200; 2 B737-400
   BAe-748 6
   Basler Turbo-67 9
   Beech 200 *Super King Air* 2
   Beech 65 *Queen Air* 2

Beech 90 1: 1 Beech E90 *King Air*
C-130 12: 7 C-130H *Hercules*; 5 C-130H-30 *Hercules*
G-222 3
IAI-201 *Arava* 3
LEARJET 35 2: 2 *Learjet* 35A
Rockwell *Commander* 500 3
SA-226 6: 6 SA-226AT *Merlin IV/IVA*
UTL 37: 22 AU-23A *Peacemaker**; 15 GAF N-22B *Nomad*
TRG 123: 10 Alpha Jet*; 29 CT-4B/E *Airtrainer*; 3 Cessna 150
   L-39 46: 46 L-39ZA/MP *Albatros**
   PC-9 23
   T-41 12: 12 T-41D *Mescalero*
HELICOPTERS
   SPT 19: 3 AS-332L *Super Puma*; 3 AS-532A2 *Cougar MKII*; 13 Bell 212
   UTL 28
      BELL 206 6: 6 Bell 206B *JetRanger II*
      Bell 412 *Twin Huey* 2
      UH-1 20: 20 UH-1H *Iroquois*
MSL • TACTICAL • AAM: some AIM-120 *AMRAAM*
   AIM-9: some AIM-9B *Sidewinder*/AIM-9J *Sidewinder*
   Python III some
   ASM: some AGM-65 *Maverick*

Paramilitary ε113,700 active

Border Patrol Police 41,000

Marine Police 2,200
PATROL AND COASTAL COMBATANTS 124+: 3 PCC; 110+ PCI; 8 PFI; 3 PCO

National Security Volunteer Corps 45,000

Police Aviation 500
AIRCRAFT
   TPT 16: 2 CN-235; 1 Fokker 50; 8 PC-6 *Turbo-Porter*; 3 SC.7 3M *Skyvan*; 2 Short 330UTT
   UTL 6: 6 AU-23A *Peacemaker*
HELICOPTERS • UTL 67
   AB-212 (Bell 212) 20
   BELL 205 27: 27 Bell 205A
   Bell 206 *JetRanger* 14 **Bell 412** *Twin Huey* 6

Provincial Police 50,000 (incl est. 500 Special Action Force)

Thahan Phran (Hunter Soldiers) ε20,000
Volunteer irregular force
Paramilitary 13 regt (*each*: 107 Paramilitary coy)

NON-STATE ARMED GROUPS
see Part II

DEPLOYMENT

BURUNDI
UN • ONUB 177; 3 obs

SIERRA LEONE
UN • UNAMSIL 3 obs

FOREIGN FORCES

United States USPACOM: 10; 30; 29

Vietnam Vn

Vietnamese Dong d		2003	2004	2005
GDP	d	613tr	715tr	
	US$	39.5bn	45.4bn	
per capita	US$	483	550	
Growth	%	7.3	7.7	
Inflation	%	3.2	7.7	
Debt	US$	15.8bn		
Def bdgt	d	45tr	ε50tr	ε55tr
	US$	2.9bn	3.17bn	3.47bn
US$1=d		15,510	15,734	15,844

Population 83,535,576

Ethnic groups: Chinese 3%

Age	0–14	15–19	20–24	25–29	30–64	65 plus
Male	14%	6%	5%	5%	17%	2%
Female	13%	5%	5%	4%	19%	3%

Capabilities

ACTIVE 484,000 (Army 412,000 Navy 42,000 Air 30,000) **Paramilitary 5,080,000**

Terms of service 2 years Army and Air Defence, 3 years Air Force and Navy, specialists 3 years, some ethnic minorities 2 years

RESERVES 3–4,000,000

ORGANISATIONS BY SERVICE

Army ε412,000

9 Mil Regions (incl capital), 14 Corps HQ

FORCES BY ROLE

Armd	10 bde
Mech inf	3 div
Inf	58 div (div str varies from 5000 to 12,500); 15 indep regt
SF	1 bde (1 AB bde, 1 demolition engr regt)
Fd arty	10+ bde
Engr	8 div; 20 indep bde
Economic construction	10-16 div

EQUIPMENT BY TYPE

TK 1,935

  MBT 1,315: 70 T-62; 350 Type-59; 850 T-54/T-55; 45 T-34

  LT TK 620: 300 PT-76; 320 Type-62/Type-63

RECCE • BRDM 100: 100 BRDM-1/BRDM-2

AIFV • BMP 300: 300 BMP-1/BMP-2

APC 1380

  APC (T) 280: 200 M-113 (to be upgraded); 80 Type-63

  APC (W) • BTR 1100: 1,100 BTR-152/BTR-40/BTR-50/BTR-60

ARTY 3,040+

  TOWED 2,300: 2,300 76mm/85mm/D-20 152mm/D-30 122mm/M-101 105mm/M-102 105mm/M-114 155mm/M-1944 100mm/M-46 130mm/Type-54 (M-30) *M-1938* 122mm/Type-60 (D-74) 122mm

  SP

    152mm 30: 30 2S3

    175mm: some M-107

  GUN/MOR • 120mm: some 2S9 *NONA* (reported)

  MRL 710+

    107mm 360: 360 Type-63

    122mm 350: 350 BM-21

    140mm: some BM-14

  MOR:

    82mm: some

    120mm: some M-43

    160mm: some M-43

AT

  MSL: some AT-3 *Sagger*

  RCL

    75mm: some Type-56

    82mm: some Type-65 (B-10)

    87mm: some Type-51

  GUNS

    100mm: some Su-100 SP; some T-12 (arty)

    122mm: some Su-122 SP

AD

  SAM • MANPAD: some SA-16 *Gimlet*/SA-18 *Grouse (Igla)*/SA-7 *Grail*

  GUNS 12,000: 12,000 100mm/14.5mm/30mm/37mm/57mm/85mm/ZSU-23-4 SP 23mm

MSL • TACTICAL • SSM • SCUD: some *Scud*-B/*Scud*-C (reported)

Navy ε15,000

FORCES BY ROLE

Navy 1 HQ located at Haiphong

EQUIPMENT BY TYPE

SUBMARINES • TACTICAL • SSI 2: 2 DPRK *Yugo*

PRINCIPAL SURFACE COMBATANTS 11

  FRIGATES • FF 6:

    1 *Barnegat* with 1 127mm gun

    3 FSU *Petya* II each with 2 x5 406mm ASTT (10 eff.), 4 RBU 6000 *Smerch 2* (48 eff.), 4 76mm gun

    2 FSU *Petya* III each with 1 triple 533mm ASTT (3 eff.), 4 RBU 2500 *Smerch 1* (64 eff.), 4 76mm gun

  CORVETTES • FSG 5:

    4 FSU *Tarantul* each with 2 twin (4 eff.) each with 1 SS-N-2D *Styx* tactical SSM

    1 HO-A with SA-N-5 *Grail* SAM (manually operated), 2 quad (8 eff.) each with SS-N-25 *Switchblade* tactical SSM non-operational

PATROL AND COASTAL COMBATANTS 37

  PCI 19: 2 FSU *Poluchat*; 4 FSU SO-1; 3 PGM-59/PGM-71; 10 *Zhuk*

  PFM 8:

    8 *Osa* II each with 4 single each with 1 SS-N-2 tactical SSM

PFT 5:

5 FSU *Shershen* each with 4 single 533mm TT

PHT 5:

2 *Turya*

3 *Turya* each with 4 single 533mm TT

MINE WARFARE • MINE COUNTERMEASURES 15

MCMV 5: 5 K-8

MSC 8: 2 PRC *Lienyun*; 3 *Sonya*; 1 *Vanya*; 2 *Yurka*

MSI 2: 2 *Yevgenya*

AMPHIBIOUS

LS 6

LSM 3:

1 *Polnochny* A (capacity 6 MBT; 180 troops)

2 *Polnochny* B (capacity 180 troops; 6 MBT)

LST 3: 3 US LST-510-511 (capacity 16 tanks; 200 troops)

CRAFT 30: 18 LCU; 12 LCM

LOGISTICS AND SUPPORT 18: 1 AGS; 4 AO; ε12 tpt (small); 1 trg

NAVAL SHIP ASSET 2: 2 floating dock

FACILITIES

Base 1 located at Hanoi, 1 located at Ho Chi Minh City, 1 located at Da Nang, 1 located at Cam Ranh Bay, 1 located at Ha Tou, 1 located at Haiphong, 1 located at Can Tho

Naval Infantry 27,000

Amphib	some
Naval commandos	some

People's Air Force 30,000

3 air divs (each with 3 regts), a tpt bde

FORCES BY ROLE

Ftr	7 regt withsome 140 MiG-21bis *Fishbed L*
FGA	2 regt with 4 Su-30MKK *Flanker*; 7 Su-27SK *Flanker*; 53 Su-22M-3 (Su-17M-3) *Fitter J*/Su-22M-4 (Su-17M-4) *Fitter K*/Su-22MR (Su-17R) *Fitter C*; 2 Su-17UM-3 *Fitter G*; 5 Su-27UBK *Flanker*
ASW	some (The PAF also maintains Vn naval air arm) sqn with 3 Ka-25 *Hormone*; 10 Ka-28 (Ka-27PL) *Helix A*; 2 KA-32 *Helix C*
MR	some sqn with 4 Be-12 *Mail*
Tpt	3 regt with 12 An-2 *Colt*; 12 An-26 *Curl*; 4 Yak-40 *Codling* (VIP); 4 Mi-6 *Hook*; 30 MI-17 (Mi-8MT) *Hip H*/Mi-8 *Hip*
Atk hel	some sqn with 26 Mi-24 *Hind*
Trg	some regt with 10 BT-6; 18 L-39 *Albatros*; 10 MiG-21UM *Mongol B*; 10 BT-6 (Yak-18) *Max*

AD	4 bde with 100mm; 130mm; 37mm; 57mm; 85mm; some (People's Regional) force (*total:* ε1,000 AD unit, 6 radar bde with 100 radar stn)

EQUIPMENT BY TYPE

AIRCRAFT 221 combat capable

FTR 204

Su-30 4: 4 Su-30MKK *Flanker*

Su-27 7: 7 Su-27SK *Flanker*

MiG-21 140: 140 MiG-21bis *Fishbed L & N*

Su-22M-3 (Su-17M-3) *Fitter J* **Su-17M** *Fitter C* FGA/**Su-22M-4 (Su-17M-4)** *Fitter K* **Su-17M** *Fitter C* FGA/**Su-22MR (Su-17R)** *Fitter C* RECCE 53

ASW 4: 4 Be-12 *Mail*

TPT 28: 12 An-2 *Colt*; 12 An-26 *Curl*; 4 Yak-40 *Codling* (VIP)

TRG 45+: 10 BT-6; 10 BT-6 (Yak-18) *Max*; 18 L-39 *Albatros*

MiG-21U: 10 MiG-21UM *Mongol B**

Su-17U 2: 2 Su-17UM-3 *Fitter G**

Su-27UB 5: 5 Su-27UBK *Flanker**

HELICOPTERS

ATK 26: 26 Mi-24 *Hind*

ASW 13: 3 Ka-25 *Hormone**; 10 Ka-28* (Ka-27PL) *Helix A*

SPT 36: 2 KA-32s *Helix C*; 4 Mi-6 *Hook*; 30 MI-17 (Mi-8MT) *Hip H*/Mi-8 *Hip* Spt

AD

SAM: some SA-16 *Gimlet* MANPAD/SA-2 *Guideline* Towed/SA-3 *Goa*/SA-6 *Gainful* SP/SA-7 *Grail* MANPAD

GUNS: some 100mm; some 130mm; some 37mm; some 57mm; some 85mm

MSL • TACTICAL

ASM: some AS-14 *Kedge*; some AS-17 *Krypton*; some AS-18 *Kazoo*; some AS-9 *Kyle*

AAM: some AA-10 *Alamo*; some AA-12 *Adder*; some AA-2 *Atoll*; some AA-8 *Aphid*

FACILITIES

SAM site	66 with SA-16 *Gimlet* MANPAD/SA-2 *Guideline* Towed/SA-3 *Goa*/SA-6 *Gainful* SP/SA-7 *Grail* MANPAD

Paramilitary 40,000 active

Border Defence Corps ε40,000

Coast Guard

came into effect on 1 Sep 1998

Local Forces up to 5,000,000+

incl People's Self-Defence Force (urban units), People's Militia (rural units); comprises of static and mobile cbt units, log spt and village protection pl; some arty, mor and AD guns; acts as reserve.

ARTY: some; some mor

AD: some guns

EAST ASIA AND AUSTRALASIA – DEFENCE ECONOMICS

The economies of East Asia and Australasia carried the positive economic momentum of the recovery that began in 2003 into the first half of 2004, before a global slowdown, coupled with reduced demand for semiconductors and higher oil prices, reduced growth to more sustainable levels. Once again, the main exception to this trend was China, where growth in 2004 actually rose to 9.5% and is forecast to moderate only slightly in 2005. Despite a weaker end to the year, regional GDP growth in 2004 was the highest since the 1997–98 financial crisis, supported by strong external demand, improving domestic demand and rising business investment, which had been lagging since the financial crisis.

Continuing to underpin the entire region was the strength of the Chinese economy, which showed few signs of a slowdown despite measures to prevent the possibility of overheating, and its corresponding impact on intra-regional trade, which grew by 25% in 2004. The Asian Development Bank has concluded that the region has a 'confident baseline outlook' over the next three years, highlighting the growing importance of domestic demand in supporting overall growth. Robust income growth across the region has boosted consumer confidence and spending while investor sentiment has also improved, leading to rising foreign and domestic investment. The continued integration of China and India with the rest of developing Asia will provide further support via the continued expansion of intra-regional trade.

The **Australian** economy continued to benefit from buoyant exports and positive domestic factors, including a strong housing market. With unemployment at historic lows, the government enjoyed a significant boost to tax receipts that will once again lead to a 2005-06 federal budget surplus. The healthy budget position resulted in a 7.4% increase in defence spending, which rose to A\$17.4bn (A\$20.0bn including military pensions and housing subsidies) in 2005 from A\$16.3bn (A\$ 18.7bn) in 2004 and maintains defence spending at 1.9% of GDP. The 2005 budget includes A\$4.57bn for capital investments, an increase of A\$510m over 2004, and is the minimum required to keep the ambitious Defence Capability Plan (DCP) on target. The DCP, revised in 2004, covers a ten-year period to 2010 and allocates A\$50bn for the acquisition of new capabilities and technologies during that period. To date around 140 major projects have been approved with an all-up cost of around A\$22bn. In 2005–06 new projects to be considered include:

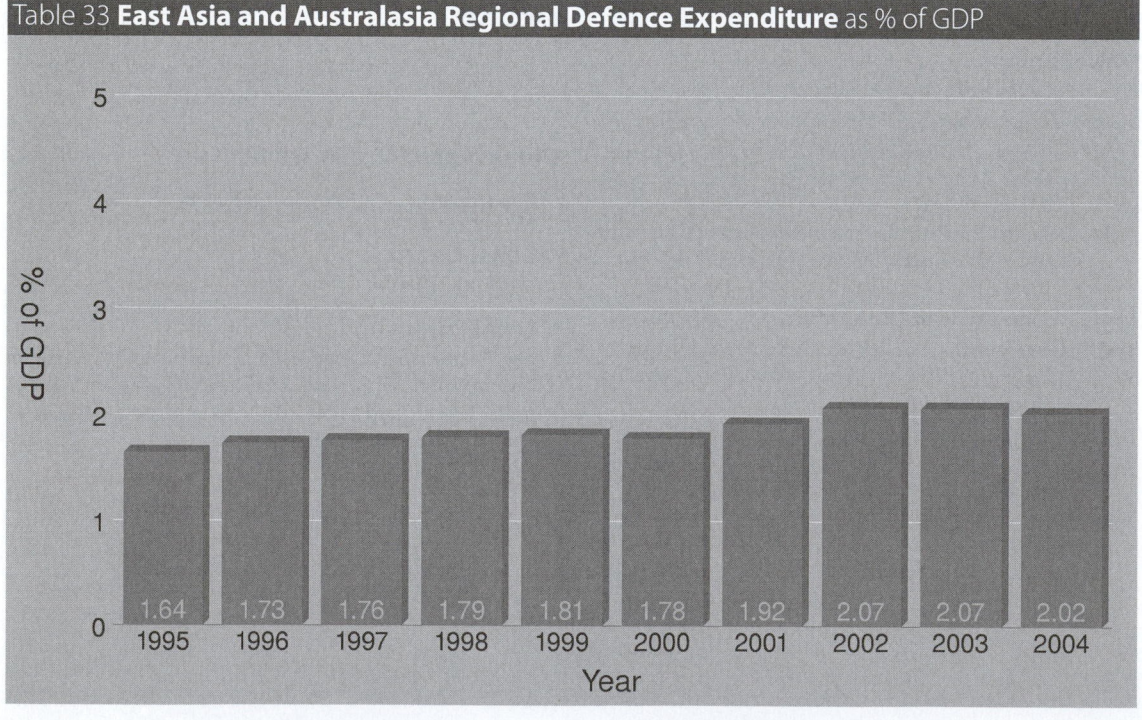

Table 33 **East Asia and Australasia Regional Defence Expenditure** as % of GDP

Year	% of GDP
1995	1.64
1996	1.73
1997	1.76
1998	1.79
1999	1.81
2000	1.78
2001	1.92
2002	2.07
2003	2.07
2004	2.02

- Follow-On Stand-off Weapon Capability
- Electronic Warfare capability for F/A-18 aircarft
- Airborne surveillance for land operations
- Amphibious Deployment and Sustainment
- Joint Coalition Training Capability
- Improved Logistics Information Systems

In addition to these scheduled programmes, Defence Minister Robert Hill also announced a major investment in technologies specifically targeted towards Australia's Special Forces. Known as Project Redfin, some A$450m will be made available to investigate and procure specialist equipment, for use in reconnaissance, offensive operations, special recovery, counter-terrorism and response to chemical, biological and radiation incidents. Other procurement decisions finalised during the past year include the selection of 12 NH-90 hel over a rival offer of UH-60 *Black Hawk* aircraft from Sikorsky. The A$1bn deal is likely to be the first part of a programme that will see the army acquire 40 aircraft to replace its current fleet of 35 S-70 hel. In a change to naval priorities, the government indicated that it had delayed the delivery of two landing helicopter dock ships by at least 12 months, in order to fast-track construction of the navy's new 8,000-ton Air Warfare Defence Destroyers. The AWDs, to be built in Australia at a cost of around A$6bn, will be equipped with *Aegis* radar systems and are due to enter service in 2013.

New Zealand recorded GDP growth of 5% in 2004, the strongest for a decade, and announced several significant defence-related developments during the year. In May 2005, the government published plans to boost defence spending by NZ$4.6bn over the following 10 years. The majority of the additional funds, NZ$4.4bn, will be directed into the New Zealand Defence Force's operational budget and will be used to increase salaries, enhance training, and improve maintenance and development of infrastructure. The remaining NZ$200m is earmarked for capital expenditure and, as such, will be rolled into the 2001 Defence Long Term Development Plan, a ten-year initiative to address the NZDF's major capability shortfalls. The new funds were made available as a result of findings uncovered by a Defence Capability and Resourcing Review, which highlighted a long-term decline in personnel strength, insufficient training and a lack of contingency reserve stocks of key items at a time when the armed forces operational commitments and tempo have markedly increased. Concerning procurement matters, the navy announced a NZ$500m contract with local shipbuilder Tenix for the construction of seven new vessels comprising four 340-ton inshore patrol vessels, two 1,600-ton offshore patrol vessels and an 8,800-ton multi-role vessel. The air force announced plans to convert two Boeing 757 aircraft into strategic transporters, extend the life of its C-130H aircraft, and upgrade the mission systems and communications and navigations systems of six P-3K maritime patrol aircraft. Another capability gap was filled with the selection of the NH90 multi-role medium helicopter to replace the air force's existing fleet of 14 UH-1H *Iroquois* aircraft. No decision on a final number will be made until a parallel programme to replace the Bell *Sioux* training helicopter matures, although no more than 12 platforms are likely to be bought to the replace the *Iroquois*.

Following the SARS-induced problems of 2003, **Taiwan's** economy rebounded in 2004 thanks largely to a pick up in external demand for IT products, the mainstay of the Taiwanese economy. However, despite real GDP growth of 5.7%, the defence budget increased by only around 1.5%, once inflation is taken into account. The government's plan to go ahead with the acquisition of eight diesel submarines, 12 P-3C anti-submarine marine warfare aircraft and six *Patriot* anti-missile systems continued to provoke intense reaction from the public and opposition parties. Under an original proposal, the government intended to fund the NT$610.8bn procurement package by selling Ministry of National Defence land, privatising state industry and issuing special bonds. However, in late 2004, and following large public rallies, the Taiwan parliament rejected the package as too expensive. A revised deal was announced in 2005, dropping a demand that the submarines be built in Taiwan and allocating regular budget funds to the construction of new submarine docks, which reduces the cost to NT$410. However, due to delaying tactics by the pro-unification Chinese Nationalist Party (KMT), the new proposal has so far not been ratified. The United Sates, which proposed the deal in 2001, has indicated that during the subsequent political impasse its stock of available P-3 aircraft has fallen and that time is running out for a successful conclusion to the initiative.

The MND had somewhat more success in implementing its modernisation programme, with the navy taking delivery of two more E-2C *Hawkeye* airborne early warning and control aircraft and the decision to go ahead with a $750m contract to provide Taiwan with a ground-based early warning radar system, designed to counter the threat of Chinese ballistic missiles. However, the army's 30-strong attack helicopter competition fell victim to budget pressures and has been delayed by at least another year. Budget pressures are also likely to result in the mothballing of a number of the air force's *Mirage* 2000-5 and Indigenous Defence Fighters (IDF), while the air force is apparently considering the suitability of the Joint Strike Fighter (JSF) as its next fighter aircraft platform.

As previously noted, **China** enjoyed another year of solid economic activity with real GDP growth accelerating to 9.5% in 2004, despite measures by the government to engineer a controlled economic slowdown. In the face of strong domestic demand, buoyant foreign trade and public sector investment, and signs of overheating in certain sectors such as steel, aluminium and cement, the authorities introduced a series of measures, including higher interest rates, that succeeded in curbing inflationary pressures but failed to moderate growth. The failure to achieve a soft landing now is thought to have increased the chance that the Chinese economy will suffer a more dramatic slowdown sometime in the future.

Despite previous announcements that the People's Liberation Army is to be radically restructured, including the loss of some 200,000 personnel, there is little evidence that the plan is being implemented. Even so, official defence expenditure was again substantially increased, rising to Y244bn in 2005. The majority of additional funds will be used to increase salaries and social security guarantees for serving personnel as well as make provision for those officers and soldiers who will be discharged as part of the downsizing programme. In 2006, the PLA will begin its 11th Five-Year Defence Plan, and although no details of the programme have been revealed it is thought that the programme will outline certain priorities for the defence industrial base. In particular, the plan is likely to encourage the pursuit of a 'leapfrog' approach to technological development, whereby certain stages of the modernisation process are ignored in favour of directing investment to next-generation information technology-related capabilities rather than conventional mechanised systems. In addition to the development of information systems, the latest Defence White Paper, issued in December 2004, admitted that the tri-service strategic missile forces were at the forefront of PLA transformation priorities and as such will enjoy a greater share of funding.

As *The Military Balance* has previously noted, the publicly reported defence budget only represents part of actual military expenditure: proceeds from defence sales are not included, and procurement,

research and development (R&D) and most pensions for retired personnel are funded from elsewhere within the state budget.

Following the 2003 slump created by a widespread household debt crisis, the economy of **South Korea** improved in 2004, driven largely by a substantial jump in merchandise exports. Private consumption and business investment remain weak, however, and the government will need to initiate structural reforms for the recovery to gain traction. Despite the uncertain economic background, the government responded to the changing security environment and increased defence spending by 9.8% to SWon20.8tr ($8.3bn) in 2005, up from SWon18.9tr ($7.5bn) in 2004. The budget was lower than that originally proposed by the Ministry of National Defence, which had requested a 13.7% increase in defence funds for the year. The 9.8% increase in the 2005 defence budget comes on top of a similar 8.6% increase in the 2004 defence budget as South Korea attempts to compensate for the planned reduction of US troops on the peninsula and become more self-sufficient in its defence. The US currently has about 32,000 troops in South Korea, which is scheduled to fall to 25,000 by 2008. President Roh Moo-hyun has regularly stated that it is unacceptable for the world's twelfth-largest economy not to be able to 'assume the role of main actor' in its own defence matters and has indicated that the defence budget will increase by around 10% a year for the next five years. In addition to increasing funding, the MND is also trying to improve efficiency with a planned reduction in the strength of the armed forces of 6.5%, around 45,000 personnel, by 2008. A core element of South Korea's self sufficiency drive is the intention to increase military research and development by an annual rate of 18%, the highest among defence budget items, in order to produce more advanced weapons indigenously.

As part of the government's plans to reform various ministries, the MND has outlined plans to establish a new defence acquisition agency, in order to increase the efficiency and competitiveness of the domestic defence industry. The new agency is due to begin operations in January 2006 and will consolidate nine existing organisations into one department within the MND. At the same time, the MND has revealed plans to address a perceived deficiency of qualified personnel with the introduction of a defence acquisition college within the Korea National Defence University.

Little progress has been made in the past year on two key procurement programmes: the Korea

Helicopter Programme (KHP) and the E-X airborne early warning programme. The KHP was formally launched in 2004 (when it was known as the Korean Multirole Helicopter KMH programme) to develop up to 300 utility hel and 170 attack variants to begin service in 2010. In April 2005, the KMH programme was scrapped and the much less ambitious KHP project was launched, covering the development and production of 280 utility hel only. Korea Aerospace Industries will lead the development programme in conjunction with a foreign company, to be chosen after consideration is given to submitted bids. The other stalled project, to acquire an airborne early warning and control platform, is intended to reduce South Korea's reliance on three USAF E-3 AWACS. The E-X airborne early warning programme was originally launched in 2000, then suspended in 2002 due to budget constraints and formally re-launched in the summer of 2005. Although there is no conformation as to the scope of the requirement, it is thought likely that the MND would like a fleet of four aircraft to be delivered between 2009 and 2011. In a separate development, the air force is thought to be considering the possible acquisition timetable of a further 40 F-15K aircraft, following the purchase of a similar number of platforms from Boeing in 2002. The first batch of aircraft will be delivered between 2005 and 2008, and Boeing has indicated that if South Korea wants a second batch then a contract must be signed in 2006 to avoid a potential gap in the production line, which would significantly increase the cost of each plane.

In line with other countries that suffered an economic slowdown as a result of the SARS virus in the first half of 2003, **Singapore** enjoyed stronger than expected growth in 2004, reflecting a broad recovery in both domestic and external demand. The 2005 defence budget continued the trend of recent years, increasing 7.4% to S$9.25bn ($5.57bn). In July 2004, the Singaporean navy took delivery of its second new *Formidable*-class multi-mission frigate, based on the French *Lafayette* design, but built locally by Singapore Technologies Marine. Earlier in the year, the Ministry of Defence selected the Sikorsky S-70B *Seahawk* as the ship-borne naval combat helicopter for its fleet of six *Formidable* frigates. The six hel will be equipped for anti-surface and anti-submarine warfare roles, and are scheduled for delivery between 2008 and 2010. The Singaporean air force moved a step closer to choosing its next-generation fighter aircraft, which will eventually replace the current fleets of upgraded A-4SU *Skyhawk* and F-5s. In a surprise decision, it was announced that the Eurofighter *Typhoon* had been dropped from the competition due to problems with capabilities and delivery schedules, leaving Boeing's F-15T and Dassualt's *Rafale* in the running for an initial order of eight to 12 aircraft out of a total of 20.

The exceptional growth exhibited by the **Japanese** economy between the second quarter of 2003 and the first quarter of 2004 failed to last, as exports – the major engine of growth – came under pressure with the emergence of a global slowdown and higher oil prices. Most sectors of the economy suffered: business investment slowed, the tentative recovery in domestic demand came to an abrupt halt as confidence fell, and industrial production dropped. The near-term outlook is bleak, with growth of just 1.1% forecast for 2005, while in the medium-term, an unfavourable demographic profile and associated high pensions burden suggest that weakness, particularly in the domestic sector, will persist.

In December 2004, the Japanese government released its third National Defence Programme Guidelines (NDPG, previously know as the National Defence Programme Outline) which referred to 'opaque and uncertain elements relating to problems over the Taiwan Strait and Korean Peninsula', and specifically named China and North Korea for the first time as the main potential threats to Japanese security.

The development of operational capabilities for the period 2005–09 was outlined in a Mid-Term Defence Programme (MDTP), which was released at the same time as the new NDPG. The MDTP allocates ¥24.4tr (in real terms) to equipment programmes over the five-year period, although this is reduction of ¥770bn from the previous five-year MDTP. In addition to new procurement programmes, the plan also outlines major reductions in the existing inventory. The JGSDF will retire up to a third of its Main Battle Tanks and artillery pieces, reducing those in service from 900 to 600 (suggesting that production of the Type 90 MBT will end in 2–3 years). The JASDF's troubled F-2 programme will continue, but the number of planes to be procured will halve to just four a year, suggesting that the original target of 130 aircraft will not be reached before the programme is prematurely halted. The JMSDF will reduce the number of surface combat ships by three to 47, although there will be no reduction in the number of submarines. Highlights of the new procurement plan include the allocation of ¥500bn for missile defence, new air refuelling tankers, next-generation maritime patrol aircraft, F-X aircraft and transporters.

Table 34 Arms orders and deliveries, East Asia and Australasia

	Country Supplier	Classification	Designation	Quantity	Order date	Delivery date	Comment
Australia (Aus)	US	hel	SH-2G (*Super Seasprite*)	11	1997	2000	Deliveries to 2002. Penguin ASSM (No)
	UK	FGA	F/A-18 (*Hornet*)	71	1998	2005	Upgrade. AMRAAM (US), ASRAAM (UK)
	No	ASSM	AGM-119 (*Penguin*)		1999	2003	
	dom	LACV	*Bushmaster*	299	1999	2006	Reduced from 370
	US	hel	S-70B-2	16	2000		Upgrade
	US	AAM	AIM-120 (AMRAAM)		2000	2003	
	US	AEWAC	B-737	6	2000	2006	Increased from 4 to 6 in 2004
	Sp	hel	AS-665 (*Tiger*)	22	2001	2004	Being delivered
	US	ASSM	*Enhanced Sea Sparrow*	225	2002	2002	To equip Anzac FFs
	US	ASSM	RGM-84 Block 2 (*Harpoon 2*)	64	2003		To equip Anzac FFs
	US	ATGW	*Javelin*	92	2003	2005	666 missiles
	dom		*Armidale*	12	2003	2005	($410m) 1st launched Feb 2005, 2nd and 3rd boats due for launch mid 2005.
	Swe	SHORAD	RBS-70	15	2003	2006	
	US	MBT	M1-A1 (*Abrams*)	59	2004	2007	
	US	tkr	A-330-200	5	2004	2007	
	dom	EWSP	*Soothsayer*		2005		revived EWSP (electronic warfare self protection) fit to C-130H, CH-47 and S-70A-9s with MILDS (missile launch and detection system)
	dom	hel	NH-90	12	2005	2007	($1bn) 1st four coming direct from NH Industries 8 from Australian Aerospace. Final delivery 2009.
	dom	FFG	*Anzac*		2005	2009	($260m) Class upgrade to be complete by 2012
Brunei (Bru)	UK	FSG	*Brunei*	3	1995	2001	First delivered 2001
	UK	FAC	*Waspada*	3	1997	1998	Upgrade
Cambodia (Cam)	Il	trg	L-39 (*Albatros*)	5	1994	1996	Second-hand
China, Peoples Republic of (PRC)	dom	ICBM	CSS-X-10		1985	2005	Dev; DF-41 range 12,000km
	dom	IRBM	CSS-9		1985	2005	Dev; DF-31 range 8,000km. Tested Aug 1999
	dom	SSGN	Type 093	1	1985	2006	Similar to RF Victor 3.
	dom	ICBM	CSS-NX-5		1985	2008	Dev; range 8,000km
	dom	SSBN	Type 094	4	1985	2009	Dev programme
	Fr	hel	AS-365 (*Dauphin 2*)	50	1986	1989	Local production continues
	dom	FGA	JH-7	20	1988	1993	Upgrade to FBC-2 standard has begun
	RF	SAM	SA-10 (*Grumble* (quad))	30	1990	1992	
	dom	hel	EC-120 (*Colibri*)		1990	2005	With Pak (150 units). 1st flight in 2000
	dom	FGA	J-10		1993		Dev continues
	dom	SSK	*Song*	4	1994	2002	2 Song under construction at continuing
	RF	FGA	Su-27 (*Flanker*)	200	1996	1998	15 units for production 1998-2000
	RF	DDG	*Sovremenny*	2	1996	2000	Both delivered 2000

Table 34 Arms orders and deliveries, East Asia and Australasia

	Country Supplier	Classification	Designation	Quantity	Order date	Delivery date	Comment
	Il	SSM	CSS-N-4 (*Sardine*)	4	1997	2002	Under development
	RF	SSM	SSN-24	24	1998	2000	For Sovremenny
	RF	SAM	FT-2000	12	1998	2000	For DDG operation
	dom	IRBM	DF-21X		1999		Modernised DF-15
	RF	FGA	Su-30MKK (*Flanker*)	38	1999	2000	
	RF	AEW	A-50 (*Mainstay*)	6	2000		Part of debt settlement
	RF	FGA	Su-27UBK (*Flanker*)	28	2000	2001	Trainers
	RF	ASM	AS-13 (*Kingbolt*)		2001		To equip Su-30MKK
	RF	DDG	*Sovremenny*	2	2002	2005	(further 2 hulls expected 2005-06)
	RF	SSK	*Kilo*	8	2002	2007	
	RF	FGA	Su-30MKK (*Flanker*)	28	2003	2004	Option to increase to 50
Indonesia (Indo)	RF	hel	Mi-8 (Hip)	2	1997	2000	
	RF	hel	PZL MI-2 (*Hoplite*)	8	2001		
	ROK	trg	KT-1	7	2001	2003	
	Sgp	trg	SF-260	19	2002	2002	
	Nl	PCO	*Sigma*	2	2003		
	RF	hel	Mi-35 (*Hind*)	2	2003	2003	Delivered 2004
	RF	hel	Mi-35 (*Hind*)	2	2003	2003	
	ROK	SSK	SSK	4	2003	2008	Order not yet confirmed
	Pl	hel	M-28 (*Skytruck*)	11	2004		
	RF	hel	Mi-8 (*Hip*)	8	2004		
	RF	FGA	Su-27 (*Flanker*)	4	2004		2 Delivered 2004
	RF	hel	Mi-35 (*Hind*)	3	2004		
	RF	FGA	Su-30 (*Flanker*)	2	2004		Delivered 2004
Japan (J)	dom	SSK	*Oyashio*	8	1993	2000	5 delivered by 2002
	dom	LST	*Osumi*	3	1994	1997	All delivered by 2003
	dom	AAM	XAAM-5		1994	2001	Dev
	dom	BMD	TMD		1997		Joint dev with US from late 1998
	dom	recce	Satellites	4	1998	2002	Dev Prog. 2 optical, 2 radar
	dom	arty	MLRS		1999		90 delivered by 2004
	dom	arty	MLRS		1999		10 delivered by 2004
	dom	FGA	*Mitsubishi F-2*	130	1999	2000	18 to be delivered by 2001
	dom	mor	L16	42	1999	2000	
	dom	mor	120mm	27	1999	2000	
	dom	hel	SH-60J (*Seahawk*)	9	1999	2000	37 req under 1996-2000 MTDP
	dom	PCC	*Hayabusa*	6	1999	2000	All delivered by 2004
	dom	ASSM	Type-88	4	1999	2000	24 req under 1996-2000 MTDP
	dom	hel	OH-1	3	1999	2000	Cost $66m
	dom	SAR	U-125A (*Peace Krypton*)	2	1999	2000	Cost $76m
	dom	tpt	Beech 350 (*Super King Air*)	1	1999	2000	Cost $24m
	dom	trg	U-4		1999	2000	
	dom	recce	Type-87		1999	2000	100 delivered by 2004
	dom	MCMV	*Sugashima*	12	1999	2007	5 delivered by 2002
	dom	trg	T-X	50	2000		Dev Prog. Replacing Fuji T-3s. Delayed

Table 34 Arms orders and deliveries, East Asia and Australasia

Country Supplier	Classification	Designation	Quantity	Order date	Delivery date	Comment
US	ASM	AGM-78 (Standard)	16	2000		Block III
dom	tpt	C-X		2000		Replacement for P3
dom	hel	AH-64D (Apache)	10	2001	2003	Up to 50 required
US	tpt	B-767		2002	2007	
UK	hel	EH-101 (Merlin)	14	2003	2004	
dom	DDH	16 DDH	2	2003	2009	
US	SAM	SM-3	9	2004		
US	MPA	PAC-3 (Patriot)	16	2005	2006	part of US Army order of 536 msl ($512m Lot 6) 48 of which are going to foreign customers.
Korea, Democratic Peoples Republic of (DPRK) dom	MRBM	Taepo-dong 1				Tested October 1998
RF	hel	Mi-8 (Hip)	5	1998	1998	
Kaz	FGA	MiG-21	30	1999	1999	Also spare parts for existing fleet
RF	FGA	MiG-21	10	1999	2000	
Korea, Republic of (ROK) dom	SSK	Chang Bogo	9	1987	2001	9th delivered in 2001
dom	MBT	Type-88 (K1)		1995	1996	Upgrade programme began in 1996
Il	AAM	AGM-142 (Popeye)	100	1996	2000	Deliveries 2000-02
dom	SAM	Chun Ma (Pegasus)		1997	1999	Being delivered
Il	UAV	Harpy	100	1997	2001	
RF	tpt	BE-200	1	1998	2000	
dom	DDG	KDX-2	3	1998	2003	
dom	SAM	Type-91 (Kin-SAM)		1998	2003	Dev
US	AAV	AAV-7A1	57	1998	2006	Licence. Following delivery of 103 from US
dom	SAM	MSAM		1998	2008	Dev
US	SAM	RIM-116 (RAM)	64	1999		Block I
dom	SSM	Nazeat		1999		300km and 500km variants
RF	hel	KA-32 (Helix C)	31	1999	2000	Upgrades
RF	hel	KA-32T (Helix C)	3	1999	2000	Follow on order expected
US	FGA	F-16C (Fighting Falcon)	20	1999	2003	Follow on order after orders for 120
US	ASM	AGM-78 (Standard)	110	2000		
US	ASM	Harpoon	96	2000		
Ge	SSK	Type 214	3	2000	2007	
dom	SAM	SM-2	3	2000	2008	To be equipped with USN Aegis
RF	trg	IL-103	15	2002		Part of debt settlement
RF	AAM	AIM-9X (Sidewinder)	10	2002		Part of debt settlement
US	FGA	F-15K (Eagle)	40	2002	2005	
dom	trg	T-50 (Golden Eagle)	25	2003	2005	Total of 100 approved
Malaysia (Mal) RF	FGA	MiG-29 (Fulcrum)	18	1997	1999	Upgrade
Ge	FFG	MEKO A100	6	1997	2004	Licence built. Req for 27 over 20 yrs
UK	hel	Super Lynx	6	1999	2001	
Sp	hel	AS-555 (Fennec)	6	2001	2003	
It	SAM	Rapier		2002	2005	

Table 34 Arms orders and deliveries, East Asia and Australasia

Country	Country Supplier	Classification	Designation	Quantity	Order date	Delivery date	Comment
	Fr	SSK	*Scorpene*	2	2002	2008	
	NZ	trg	MB-339	17	2003		Second-hand
	SF	hel	A-109	11	2003		
	RF	hel	Mi-8 (*Hip*)	10	2003	2004	
	PI	MBT	PT-91M (*Twardy*)	48	2003	2005	
	RF	FGA	Su-30MKM (*Flanker*)	18	2003	2005	To be delivered by 2008
Myanmar (My)	PRC	trg	K-8	4	1998	2000	
	RF	FGA	MiG-29 (*Fulcrum*)	10	2001		
	RF	FGA	MiG-29UB (*Fulcrum*)	2	2001		
New Zealand (NZ)	Fr	hel	NH-90	8-12			($392m) replacement for Iroquois
	US	MPA	P-3K (*Orion*)	6	1995	1998	Upgrade. 1 delivered. Project abandoned in 2000
	US	trg	CT-4E	13	1997	1998	11 delivered. Lease programme
	US	hel	SH-2G (*Super Seasprite*)	5	1997	2000	
	US	tpt	C-130J (*Hercules*)	5	1999		Lease of 5 to 7. Delayed
	Ca	APC	LAV-III	105	2000	2002	Deliveries 2002-04. 50 delivered
	US	ATGW	*Javelin*	24	2000	2004	Being delivered
	UK	lt veh	*Pinzgauer*	321	2003	2004	
Papua New Guinea (PNG)	Fr	hel	BO-105	1	1998	1999	
Philippines (Pi)	ROC	FGA	F-5E (*Tiger II*)	40	1999		
	US	hel	UH-1H (*Iroquois*)	8	2000	2001	Excess Defence Article stock
	US	tpt	C-130B (*Hercules*)	1	2000	2001	Excess Defence Article stock
	Aus	MPA	PCC (Patrol craft coastal)	6	2001		For Coast Guard
Singapore (Sgp)	US	FGA	F-16C (*Fighting Falcon*)	42	1995	1998	First order for 18, follow-on for 24
	Swe	SSK	*Sjoormen*	4	1995	2000	2nd delivered 2001
	US	hel	CH-47D (*Chinook*)	8	1997	2000	Follow-on order after 1994 order for 6
	US	tkr	KC-135 (*Stratotanker*)	4	1997	2000	
	US	AAM	AIM-120 (AMRAAM)	100	2000		Only to be delivered if under military threat
	Fr	SSM	MM-40 (*Exocet*)		2000		Exocet
	US	FGA	F-16 (*Fighting Falcon*)	20	2000	2003	
	US	atk hel	AH-64D (*Apache*)	12	2000	2003	
	Fr	FFG	*La Fayette*	6	2000	2005	mod Lafayette. 1st to be built in Fr. Final delivery 2009. 1st delivered Jul 2005. Singapore Formidable Class 2nd and 3rd launched Jul 2004 and Jan 2005 in Singapore.
Taiwan (Republic of China) (ROC)	dom	PFM	*Jinn Chiang*	12	1992	1994	8 delivered
	US	tpt	C-130 (*Hercules*)	12	1993	1995	Deliveries continue
	Sgp	MPA	P-3 (*Orion*)	7	1996	1998	
	dom	trg	AT-3 (*Tzu-Chung*)	40	1997		Order rescheduled
	US	ASW hel	S-70C (*Defender*)	11	1997	2000	
	US	ASSM	RGM-84 (*Harpoon*)	58	1998		

Table 34 Arms orders and deliveries, East Asia and Australasia

Country Supplier	Classification	Designation	Quantity	Order date	Delivery date	Comment
US	hel	OH-58D (*Warrior*)	13	1998	2001	Following deliveries of 26 1994-95
US	LSD	*Anchorage*	1	1999	2000	USS Pensacola to replace existing 2 LSDs
US	hel	CH-47SD (*Super D Chinook*)	9	1999	2002	Following deliveries of 7 1993-97
US	AEW	E-2 (*Hawkeye*)	4	1999	2002	E-2T Following delivery of 4 in 1995. 2 delivered 2005
US	radar	PAVE PAWS		1999	2002	
dom	FFG	*Cheng Kung*	8	1999	2003	Based on US Oliver Hazard Perry; all operational by 2004
US	hel	CH-47SD (*Super D Chinook*)	9	2000		3 plus long lead time for further 6
Thailand (Th) PRC		WMZ 551	97			($51.3m) barter deal MOU signed. Deal to finalised
Vietnam (Vn) Pl	hel	M-28 (*Bryza TD*)	10	2005		Part of Polish contract
Pl	MBT	T-72	150	2005	2005	Part of ($150m) large contract to supply ac electronics and equipment Part of Polish contractsupport
Pl	FGA	Su-22K (*Fitter*)	40	2005	2005	Part of Polish contract

Chapter Seven
Caribbean and Latin America

Eighteen months after President Jean-Bertrand Aristide went into exile, unrest in **Haiti** continues. Pro-Aristide militias incite violence through kidnapping and crime, targeting both civilians and the UN peacekeepers who are mandated to maintain order. The problem is exacerbated by Haiti's inability to build a police force of sufficient size for the task of establishing the rule of law – the present force totals 4,000 officers for a population of 8 million. Therefore, in an attempt to overcome this problem, on 21 June 2005 the UN extended the United Nations Stabilisation Mission in Haiti (MINUSTAH) mandate for another eight months and deployed an additional 1,000 peacekeepers to the country. The extra troops will join the 7,600 personnel who already comprise the peacekeeping element of MINUSTAH, and will be permitted to use force against the rebels and criminal gangs in an attempt to restore order.

The ongoing crisis in Haiti is increasing tension with the **Dominican Republic** as a growing number of Haitian refugees cross the border to escape the violence. Many Haitians living in the Dominican Republic are legal immigrants and are an important labour resource in the republic's economy. However, violence against immigrants and forced expulsions have increased in recent months with a growing number of attacks on Haitian schools by the Dominican authorities. In May and June 2005 three Haitians were killed and 2,500 immigrants – including some Haitian residents of the Dominican Republic – were forcibly deported.

Cuba carried out a nationwide military exercise, *Bastion 2004*, between 13 and 19 December 2004. The *Bastion* exercises are run annually, but this year's event was one of the largest of its kind, with an estimated 100,000 soldiers and 400,000 reservists as well as a number of civilian participants. The exercise practiced guerrilla warfare in defence of the country with the perceived threat being from the US, which Havana regards as the main danger to its security.

MILITARY ASSISTANCE

Meanwhile, **Cuba** and **Venezuela** maintain a close relationship. In addition to the $1 billion in oil assistance Cuba receives from Caracas, the countries are believed to have jointly purchased military equipment – mostly infantry weapons and vehicles – from the Ukraine, delivered in October 2004.

In June 2005, **Cuba** ratified agreements with Russia and China for the delivery of spare parts and for a programme of upgrading for aircraft, tanks, anti-air missiles and naval vessels. And **Mexico** and Russia discussed military-technical cooperation in their Commission for Economic, Trade, and Science-Technical Cooperation on 8 June 2005.

Following the diplomatic row which resulted in the withdrawal of their respective ambassadors in May 2004, **Cuba**'s relationship with **Mexico** remains strained. Although diplomatic contacts between the two countries were re-established on 26 July 2004, the Mexican government continues to complain about Cuban interference in its internal politics. In 2004, Mexico accused Cuba of assisting the communist Democratic Revolution Party (PRD) in its campaign for the 2006 presidential elections. In April 2005, Fidel Castro again received censure from the three major parties in Mexico after he publicly demanded President Vicente Fox's resignation.

An armed criminal group, Zetas, which is seeking to control drug trafficking from the southern border of **Mexico** to the US is believed to be responsible for hundreds of deaths in the country. Initially the Zetas were trained by the US to interdict other gangs trafficking illicit drugs before they reached the US border. Moreover, contrary to the findings of a presidential report published on 20 July 2005, *Mexico Seguro*, the counter-narcotics offensive in the states of Tamaulipas, Sinaloa and Baja California, which was launched on 11 June 2005, has so far had little impact on drug-trafficking and violent crime; particularly in areas like Nuevo Laredo, the Zetas's stronghold. However, the anti-narcotics programme may be extended to Mexico City.

Meanwhile, the Mexican government has softened its position towards the Zapatista (EZLN) movement. EZLN leaders released a statement in June 2005 stating the group's intention to engage in protest through political action and not through armed resistance. In response, government offi-

Caribbean and Latin America

cials said that past EZLN violent actions would not prevent it becoming a political party.

In **Nicaragua,** Sandanista leader and former president Daniel Ortega aspires to force current President, Enrique Bolanos, to resign and to reclaim the presidency. Ortega and the Sandinista National Liberation Front (FSLN) have formed an alliance with Arnoldo Aleman, another former president and member of the Liberal Constitutionalist Party (PLC), in order to make up a majority in the Congress which would enable them to pass legislation denying Bolanos his executive powers. At the same time, Sandinista members are mounting a campaign of public protest against the government which carries a risk of violent confrontation with the police.

LATIN AMERICA

International military assistance

Under an agreement signed in March 2005, **Venezuela** announced its intention to purchase a number of Mi-26 helicopters from Russia. The helicopters are probably intended for deployment along the state's western border with Colombia. Caracas is also negotiating the purchase of some 100,000 AK-47 assault rifles from Russia. Meanwhile, on 30 March 2005, Spain agreed to sell Venezuela ten C-295 military transport planes, two CN-235 naval patrol planes, and some 8–10 coastal patrol vessels. The two states also signed seven bilateral agreements, some of which pertained to military and defence cooperation. Despite assurances that the purchases are intended for defensive patrolling, counterterrorism and counter-trafficking, the US and other countries, particularly Colombia, are concerned that some weapons will be supplied to the Fuerzas Armadas Revolucionarias de Colombia (FARC) and could increase instability in the region. Meanwhile, Spain has agreed to lease three C-212 planes and some helicopters to **Colombia**.

The relationship between the US and **Venezuela** worsened with the ending of a 35-year-old bilateral agreement that provided for training of Venezuelan troops. In April 2005 Venezuela expelled four US military instructors and one student without explanation.

Meanwhile, the US has maintained its support to **Colombia** through *Plan Colombia*, which is due to expire at the end of 2005. However, on 3 August 2005, President Uribe visited the US to request more military and financial aid, indicating that the assistance programme could be extended or another programme of assistance could be instituted, as suggested by the granting of a $70 million aid package announced on 1 August 2005 which had been delayed pending the granting of human rights certification for Colombia. Furthermore, in October 2004, the US Congress increased support to Bogota by raising the number of US troops in the country to 800 and approving a 50% increase, to 600, in the number of civilian contractors stationed there.

The counter-insurgency and counter trafficking strategy of President Uribe, *Plan Patriota,* targets some 12,000 armed guerrillas – mainly (FARC) and the National Liberation Army (ELN) – in the rural regions of the country. The strategy has led to several disputes with the left wing government of Venezuela due to cross-border operations carried out by Colombian forces of the 10th brigade. Colombia believes Venezuela provides 'safe-havens' for FARC rebels along the Venezuela–Colombia border. In one incident in January 2005, the Colombian authorities admitted to the kidnapping of FARC member Rodrigo Granda from within Venezuela, and refused to offer an apology for what Venezuela claimed was a violation of its sovereignty. However, relations between the two countries improved in February when Bogota agreed to review its policy on cross-border operations and Caracas pledged to hand over another FARC member it had detained.

President Uribe has proposed a new initiative, the 'Justice and Peace Law', offering members of the right-wing paramilitary group the United Self-Defence Forces (AUC) amnesty in exchange for disarmament. Moreover, more lenient sentences for murder and drug trafficking are promised to those who accept the arrangement, as well as protection against extradition to the US. On 27 May, Diego Murillo, an AUC commander, was one of the first to accept the arrangement and surrendered himself to Colombian authorities. As of 3 August, some 8,500 AUC fighters had disarmed. A similar compromise has not been offered to the FARC or ELN, who do not enjoy the same domestic political support as the AUC. However, as the government modifies its approach to the AUC, there is concern about the degree of AUC influence in the Colombian government.

Elsewhere in Latin America, and supplementing training at its base in **Ecuador**, the United States is offering some military assistance to **Paraguay**. Paraguay's Senate authorised for US troops to enter the country on 28 June 2005, and the first deployment of seven soldiers arrived on 3 July. Two hundred and four soldiers will rotate through Paraguay in groups of 10–32 through December 2006, assisting in counterinsurgency and anti-trafficking operations and training.

On 15 July 2005, **Brazil** signed an agreement with France to purchase 12 *Mirage* 2000-C fighters, which are to be delivered in 2006. The planes are equipped with advanced fire-control and targeting systems, and will replace the 30-year-old *Mirage* III ERs with which the Brazilian Air Force is currently equipped.

On 24 June 2005, following lengthy negotiations, **Chile** announced that it will purchase three second-hand Type 23 destroyers from the **UK**. Santiago initially planned to purchase four second-hand frigates from the Royal Netherlands Navy (see *The Military Balance* 2004–05), but cancelled the arrangement in favour of the Type 23s. However, in March 2005, procurement proceedings were frozen, only to be re-instituted in June, and the vessels, which are to replace the *Leander* class *Zenteno* in Chile's navy, are expected to be delivered between September 2006 and January 2008, The Type 23s will complete Chile's objective of having eight capital ships in its fleet which will not need replacement for some 20 years. As a consequence of this issue being successfully resolved without criticism from neighbouring countries, there is speculation the government may proceed with plans to purchase used F-16 aircraft from the Netherlands.

Meanwhile, on 21 July 2005, **Chile** began de-mining its border with Bolivia as part of its commitments under the Ottawa Convention 1997. By 2012, Chile must destroy the 118,377 anti-personnel mines that it has declared along its borders; with reports estimating that 3,300 anti-personnel and 1,100 anti-tank devices will be cleared from the Bolivian border alone.

POLITICAL UNREST

In **Bolivia,** following countrywide protests by the Aymara Indian majority which began on 6 June 2005 and came to a head when a protesting miner – a leader of a local union – was shot and killed by Bolivian troops, President Carlos Mesa resigned. On 10 June 2005 Eduardo Rodriguez was chosen as the new president by the Congress and immediately announced that new elections, nationalisation of the energy sector and a new draft constitution (which would give more rights to the Aymara) would follow. Presidential and parliamentary elections are scheduled for December 2005; meanwhile, opposition leader Evo Morales said that the new president would be given time to institute reforms, but other Aymara groups pledged to continue the protest movement, and leaders in the eastern and southern provinces are demanding a referendum on greater autonomy.

Ecuador also faced political upheaval as President Lucio Gutierrez was removed from office to be replaced by Vice President Alfredo Palacio on 20 April 2005. His impeachment resulted from his December 2004 attempt to remove 27 of the 31 Supreme Court justices from office, and to unilaterally select their successors. Congress' unanimous decision to remove Guiterrez followed escalating public demonstrations and fears of imminent violence without a change in authority. Gutierrez was granted asylum in Brazil after the new Palacio government ordered his arrest for his repressive actions against civil protest.

Antigua and Barbuda AB

East Caribbean Dollar EC$		2003	2004	2005
GDP	EC$	1.9bn	2.0bn	
	US$	703m	740m	
per capita	US$	10,364	10,842	
Growth	%	4.9	4.1	
Inflation	%	1.0	-1.3	
Debt	US$	350m		
Def bdgt	EC$	11.9m	11.9m	12.9m
	US$	4.44m	4.44m	4.81m
US$1=EC$		2.7	2.7	2.7

Population (2004)   68,722

Age	0 - 14	15 - 19	20 - 24	25 - 29	30 - 64	65 plus
Male	14%	4%	4%	4%	23%	2%
Female	14%	4%	4%	4%	23%	3%

Capabilities

ACTIVE 170 (Army 125 Navy 45)
(all services form combined Antigua and Barbuda Defence Force)

RESERVE 75 (Joint 75)

ORGANISATIONS BY SERVICE

Army 125

Navy 45
EQUIPMENT BY TYPE
PATROL AND COASTAL COMBATANTS • PCI 3: 1 *Dauntless* less than 100 tonnes; 1 Point less than 100 tonnes; 1 *Swift* less than 100 tonnes
FACILITIES
Base 1 located at St Johns

FOREIGN FORCES

United States US STRATCOM: 1 DETECTION AND TRACKING RADARS Strategic located at Antigua

Argentina Arg

Argentine Peso P		2003	2004	2005
GDP	P	375bn	446bn	
	US$	129bn	152bn	
per capita	US$	3,346	3,884	
Growth	%	8.8	9.0	
Inflation	%	13.4	4.4	
Debt	US$	166bn		
Def exp	P	5.88bn	4.70bn	
	US$	2.02bn	1.59bn	
Def bdgt	P	4.48bn	4.75bn	5.04bn
	US$	1.54bn	1.61bn	1.75bn
FMA	US$	3.0m	1.1m	1.8m
US$1=P		2.90	2.94	2.88

Population (2004)   39,537,943

Age	0 - 14	15 - 19	20 - 24	25 - 29	30 - 64	65 plus
Male	13%	4%	4%	4%	19%	4%
Female	12%	4%	4%	4%	19%	6%

Capabilities

ACTIVE 71,400 (Army 41,400 Navy 17,500 Air 12,500) Paramilitary 31,240

RESERVE none formally established or trained

ORGANISATIONS BY SERVICE

Army 41,400
FORCES BY ROLE
Comd   3 Corps HQ
Army   1 corps (1 AB bde, 1 mech inf bde, 1 mtn inf bde);
       1 corps (1 mtn inf bde, 1 armd bde,
       3 Mech inf bde);
       1 corps (1 jungle bde, 1 armd bde, 1 trg bde)
Mot cav 1 regt (Presidential Escort)
Mot inf 1 bn (army HQ Escort Regt)
Arty   1 gp
ADA   2 gp
Engr   1 bn
Avn   3 bn

Strategic Reserve
Rapid Reaction   1 (Rapid Deployment) force with
                 1 armd cav sqn, 1 AB bn, 2 SF coy

EQUIPMENT BY TYPE
TK 350
   MBT 200: 200 TAM
   LT TK 150: 50 AMX-13; 100 SK-105 *Kuerassier*
RECCE 74
   AML 40: 40 AML-90
   34 **M1114** *HMMWV*
AIFV 105: 105 VCTP (incl variants)
APC • APC (T) 422: 317 M-113; 105 M-5 (half track)
ARTY 1,701

TOWED 200

105mm 100: 100 M-56 (Oto Melara)

155mm 100: 100 Model 77 *CITEFA*/Model 81 *CITEFA*

SP • 155mm 35: 20 Mk F3; 15 VCA 155 *Palmaria*

MRL 6

105mm 4: 4 SLAM *Pampero*

127mm 2: 2 SLAM SAPBA-1

MOR 1,460

81mm: 1,100

120mm 360: 360 Brandt (37 SP in VCTM AIFV)

AT

MSL 600+: 600 SS-11/SS-12; some *Cobra* (*Mamba*)

RCL 1,105

75mm 75: 75 M-20

90mm 100: 100 M-67

105mm 930: 930 M-1968

RL • 66mm: some M-72 *LAW*

AIRCRAFT

PTRL/SURV • OV-1 21: 10 OV-1D *Mohawk*; 11 non-operational

TPT 15: 1 *Beech* 80 *Queen Air*

CASA 212 1: 1 CASA 212-200 *Aviocar*

Cessna **500** ***Citation I*** 1; 2 DHC-6 *twin Otter*; 3 G-222; 1 *Gaviao* 75A

SA-226 6: 3 SA-226 *Merlin IIIA*; 3 SA-226AT *Merlin IV/IVA*

UTL 3: 3 *Cessna* 207 *Stationair*

TRG 5: 5 T-41 *Mescalero*

HELICOPTERS

SPT • AS-332 3: 3 AS-332B *Super Puma*

UTL 48: 4 A-109; 1 Bell 212; 4 FH-1100

SA-315 2: 2 SA-315B *Lama*

UH-1 37: 37 UH-1H *Iroquois*

TRG 8: 8 UH-12

AD

SAM 48: 44 *Tigercat*

MANPAD 4: 4 *Blowpipe*

GUNS 226

30mm: 150

40mm • TOWED 76: 76 L/60/L/70

RADAR • LAND: some M-113 A1GE *Green Archer* (mor); some RASIT; some RATRAS (veh, arty); some *Skyguard*

Navy 17,500

Commands: Surface Fleet, Submarines, Naval Avn, Marines

FORCES BY ROLE

Navy 1 (SS and HQ Atlantic) HQ located at Mar del Plata; 1 (HQ South) HQ located at Ushuaio; 1 (HQ Centre) HQ located at Puerto Belgrano

EQUIPMENT BY TYPE

SUBMARINES • TACTICAL • SSK 3:

1 *Salta* (Ge T-209/1200) with 8 single 533mm TT with 14 Mk 37/SST-4

2 *Santa Cruz* (Ge TR-1700) each with 6 single 533mm TT with 22 SST-4 HWT

PRINCIPAL SURFACE COMBATANTS 13

DESTROYERS • DDG 5:

4 *Almirante Brown* (capacity 1 AS-555 *Fennec* utl hels) (Ge MEKO 360) each with 1 AS-555 *Fennec* utl hels, 2 B515 *ILAS-3* triple 324mm with 24 A244 LWT, 2 quad (8 eff.) each with 1 MM-40 *Exocet* tactical SSM, 1 127mm gun

1 *Hercules* (capacity 1 SH-3H *Sea King* utl hels) (UK Type 42) with 1 ASH-3H *Sea King* ASW/ASUW hels, 4 MM-

38 *Exocet* tactical SSM, 2 B515 *ILAS-3* triple 324mm each with A244 LWT, 1 114mm gun

FRIGATES • FFG 8:

3 *Drummond* (Fr A-69) each with 2 Mk32 triple 324mm each with A244 LWT, 2 twin (4 eff.) each with 1 MM-38 *Exocet* tactical SSM, 1 100mm gun

5 *Espora* (capacity either 1 SA-319 *Alouette III* utl hel or 1 AS-555 *Fennec* utl hels) (Ge MEKO 140) each with 1 SA-319B *Alouette III* ASW hels, 2 B515 *ILAS-3* triple 324mm each with A244 LWT, 2 twin (4 eff.) each with 1 MM-38 *Exocet* tactical SSM, 1 76mm gun

PATROL AND COASTAL COMBATANTS 14

PCI 5: 4 Baradero less than 100 tonnes (Dabur); 1 Point less than 100 tonnes

PFT 2:

1 Interpida (Ge Lurssen 45m) with 2 single 533mm TT each with SST-4 HWT

1 Interpida (Ge Lurssen 45m) with 2 single each with 1 MM-38 *Exocet* tactical SSM, 2 single 533mm TT each with SST-4 HWT

PCO 7:

3 *Irigoyen* (US *Cherokee* AT)

2 *King* (trg) each with 3 105mm gun

1 *Sobral* (US *Sotoyomo* AT)

1 *Teniente Olivieri* (ex-US oilfield tug)

MINE WARFARE • MINE COUNTERMEASURES • MHC: Chaco (Withdrawn from service 2002)

AMPHIBIOUS • CRAFT 20: 16 LCVP; 4 LCM

LOGISTICS AND SUPPORT 14

ABU 3: 3 Red

AGB *Icebreaker* 1; 1 AGHS (Svy) *Svy Vsl*; 1 AGOR *Research Vsl*

AO 1:

1 *Durance* with 1 SA-316 *Alouette III* utl hels

Craft 2; 1 Diving tender/spt

TPT 4: 1 *Bahia san Blas*; 3 *Costa*

FACILITIES

Base	1 (HQ Centre) located at Ushuaio, 1 (SS and HQ Atlantic) located at Mar del Plata, 1 located at Buenos Aires, 1 (HQ Centre) located at Puerto Belgrano, 1 (river craft) located at Zarate
Naval airbase	1 (naval avn) located at Trelew, 1 (naval avn) located at Punta Indio
Construction and Repair Yard	1 (shipbuilding) located at Rio Santiago

Naval Aviation 2,000

AIRCRAFT 11 combat capable

STRIKE/FGA 6: 6 *Super Etendard*

ASW • S-2 5: 5 S-2T *Tracker**

MP • P-3 4: 4 P-3B *Orion*

TPT 5

BEECH 200 2: 2 *Beech* 200F *Super King Air*

F-28 *Fellowship* 3

UTL • BE-200 5: 5 BE-200G/BE-200M

TRG 21: 11 EMB-326 *Xavante*

T-34 10: 10 T-34C *Turbo Mentor*

HELICOPTERS

ASW/ASUW 7: 7 ASH-3H *Sea King*

RECCE • PL-6 2: 2 PL-6A

UTL 16: 4 AS-555 *Fennec*

SA-316 5: 5 SA-316B *Alouette III*
UH-1 7: 7 UH-1H *Iroquois*
MSL • TACTICAL • ASM: some AM-39 *Exocet*; some AS-12 *Kegler*; some CITEFA *Martin Pescador*
AAM: some R-550 *Magic*

Marines 2,500

FORCES BY ROLE

Spt / Amph   1 force (1 marine inf bn)
Marine   1 (Fleet) force (1 arty bn, 1 AAV bn, 1 cdo gp, 1 ADA bn, 1 marine inf bn); 1 (Fleet) force (2 marine inf bn, 2 Navy det)

EQUIPMENT BY TYPE

RECCE 12+: 12 ERC-90F *Sagaie*; some M1114 *HMMWV*
APC • APC (W) 42: 6 *Grenadier*; 36 M-3 *Panhard*
AAV 25: 15 LARC-5; 10 LVTP-7
ARTY 100
  TOWED • 105mm 18: 6 M-101; 12 Model 56 pack howitzer
  MOR 82: 70 81mm; 12 120mm
AT
  MSL 50: 50 *Cobra*/RB-53 *Bantam*
  RCL • 105mm 30: 30 M-1974 FMK-1
  RL • 89mm 60: 60 M-20
AD
  SAM • MANPAD 6: 6 RBS-70
  GUNS • 30mm • TOWED 10: 10 HS-816
  35mm • TOWED • GDF: some GDF-001

Air Force 12,500

4 Major Comds - Air Operations, Personnel, Air regions, Logistics

Air Operations Command

FORCES BY ROLE

Surv and Control   1 gp
Air   8 bde
Ftr   1 (Airspace Defence) sqn with 13 *Mirage* III/EA (*Mirage* III/E)
FGA   2 (Strategic Air) sqn with 36 A-4AR *Skyhawk*; 2 (Strategic Air) sqn with 19 Nesher; 1 (Strategic Air) sqn with 7 *Mirage* 5; 2 (Tac Air) sqn with 29 IA-58 *Pucara*
RECCE / Survey   1 sqn with 2 IA-50 *Guarani*; 1 B-707; 5 *Learjet* 35A
EW   1 gp
SAR   some sqn with 6 Bell 212; 15 *Hughes* 369*; 4 MD-500*; 2 SA-315B *Lama*; 9 UH-1H *Iroquois* *
Tkr / Tpt   1 sqn with 4 B-707; 1 sqn with 7 F-27 *Friendship*; 1 sqn with 3 IA-50 *Guarani* (for misc comms); 6 DHC-6 *twin Otter*; 2 sqn with 2 KC-130H *Hercules*; 3 C-130B *Hercules*; 5 C-130H *Hercules*; 1 L-100-30; 1 (Pres) flt with 1 B-757-23ER; 2 F-28 *Fellowship*; 1 S-70 *Black Hawk*; 1 sqn with 4 F-28 *Fellowship*

EQUIPMENT BY TYPE

AIRCRAFT 104 combat capable
FTR 13: 13 *Mirage* III/EA (*Mirage* IIIE)
FGA 91
  A-4 36: 36 A-4AR *Skyhawk*
  Nesher 19; 7 *Mirage* 5; 29 IA-58 *Pucara*
  RECCE 5: 3 IA-50 *Guarani* (for misc comms); 2 more
TKR • KC-130 2: 2 KC-130H *Hercules*
TPT 39: 5 B-707
  B-757 • B-757-23 1: 1 B-757-23ER
  C-130 8: 3 C-130B *Hercules*; 5 C-130H *Hercules*
  DHC-6 *twin Otter* 6; 7 F-27 *Friendship*; 6 F-28 *Fellowship*
  L-100 1: 1 L-100-30
  LEARJET 35 5: 5 *Learjet* 35A
HELICOPTERS
  SPT 1: 1 S-70 *Black Hawk*
  UTL 36: 6 Bell 212; 15 *Hughes* 369*; 4 MD-500*
  SA-315 2: 2 SA-315B *Lama*
  UH-1 9: 9 UH-1H *Iroquois**
AD
  SAM • SP 3: 3 *Roland* (Airspace Defence)
  GUNS 87: 86 200mm (Airspace Defence); 1 35mm (Airspace Defence)
RADAR 3: 3 AD Radar (Airspace Defence)
FACILITIES
Air base 2

Personnel Command

FORCES BY ROLE

Trg some sqn with 29 B-45 *Mentor* (basic); 27 EMB-312 *Tucano* (primary); 13 IA-63 *Pampa**; 8 SU-29AR; 3 MD-500

EQUIPMENT BY TYPE

AIRCRAFT • TRG 88: 29 B-45 *Mentor* (basic); 27 EMB-312 *Tucano* (primary); 13 IA-63 *Pampa**; 11 MS-760 *Paris** (Advanced)
  SU-29 8: 8 SU-29AR
HELICOPTERS • UTL 3: 3 MD-500
MSL • TACTICAL • ASM: some *Martin Pescador* (ASM-2 Type-93)
  AAM: some R-550 *Magic* ; some R530; some *Shafrir*

Paramilitary 31,240

Gendarmerie 18,000

Ministry of Interior

FORCES BY ROLE

Region   5 comd
Paramilitary 16 bn

EQUIPMENT BY TYPE

RECCE: some S52 *Shorland*
APC • APC (W) 87: 47 *Grenadier*; 40 UR-416
ARTY • MOR: some 81mm
AIRCRAFT
  TPT 6: 3 PA-28-236 *Dakota*/PA-31P *Pressurized Navajo*; 3 PC-6 *Turbo-Porter*
  UTL 1: 1 *Cessna* 206
HELICOPTERS
  SPT 3: 3 AS-350 *Ecureuil*
  UTL • MD-500 3: 3 MD-500C/MD-500D

Prefectura Naval (Coast Guard) 13,240

PATROL AND COASTAL COMBATANTS 32+
  MISC BOATS/CRAFT: some boats
  PCI *Patrol craft inshore* 4; 21 PCI *Patrol craft inshore* less than 100 tonnes
  PCR 1: 1 Delfin
  PCO 6: 1 *Mandubi*; 5 *Mantilla*
AIRCRAFT • TPT 5: 5 CASA 212 *Aviocar*
HELICOPTERS
  SAR 1: 1 AS-565MA
  SPT • SA-330 1: 1 AS-330L (SA-330L) Puma
  UTL 2: 2 AS-365 *Dauphin 2*
  TRG • SCHWEIZER 300 2: 2 Schweizer 300C

Armed Forces some reservists (none formally established or trained)

Inf	1 bn opcon UNFICYP
Peacekeeping	3 obs opcon UNTSO; 403 opcon UNFICYP; 113 opcon KFOR I; 1 opcon MINUSTAH; 1 obs opcon MINURSO; 1 obs opcon UNMIK

DEPLOYMENT

CYPRUS
UN • UNFICYP 1 inf bn; 298

HAITI
UN • MINUSTAH 558

MIDDLE EAST
UN • UNTSO 3 obs

SERBIA AND MONTENEGRO
NATO • KFOR I 113
UN • UNMIK 130 civ police; 1 obs

WESTERN SAHARA
UN • MINURSO 1 obs

Bahamas Bs

Bahamian Dollar B$		2003	2004	2005
GDP	B$	5.3bn	5.5bn	
	US$	5.3bn	5.5bn	
per capita	US$	17,816	18,351	
Growth	%	1.9	3.3	
Inflation	%	2.8	1.5	
Debt	US$	545m		
Def bdgt	B$	29m	e 30m	e 32m
	US$	29m	30m	32m
US$1=B$		1	1	1

Population (2004)   301,790.79

Age	0 - 14	15 - 19	20 - 24	25 - 29	30 - 64	65 plus
Male	14%	5%	4%	4%	19%	3%
Female	14%	5%	4%	4%	21%	4%

Capabilities

ACTIVE 860 (Other 860)

ORGANISATIONS BY SERVICE

Royal Bahamian Defence Force 860 (incl 70 women)

FORCES BY ROLE
Marine 1 (Military Operations; b.epsi120) pl (Marines with internal and base sy duties)

EQUIPMENT BY TYPE
PATROL AND COASTAL COMBATANTS 7
  PCI 2: 1 Cape less than 100 tonnes; 1 Keith Nelson less than 100 tonnes
  PFC 3: 3 Protector
  PCO 2: 2 Bahamas
LOGISTICS AND SUPPORT 7
  AG 3: 2 Dauntless less than 100 tonnes; 1 Fort Montague less than 100 tonnes
  SPT 4: 4 Boston Whaler less than 100 tonnes
AIRCRAFT • TPT 4: 2 C-26 *Metro*; 1 *Cessna* 404 *Titan*; 1 *Cessna* 421
FACILITIES
Base 1 located at Coral Harbour, 1 located at New Providence Island

FOREIGN FORCES

Bolivia Navy: Base located at Coral Harbour
Guyana Navy: Base located at New Providence Island

Barbados Bds

Barbados Dollar B$		2003	2004	2005
GDP	B$	5.4bn	5.6bn	
	US$	2.7bn	2.8bn	
per capita	US$	9,738	10,061	
Growth	%	2.2	3.0	
Inflation	%	1.5	1.5	
Debt	US$	721m		
Def bdgt	B$	26m	e 26m	e 28m
	US$	13m	13m	14m
US$1=B$		2	2	2

Population (2004)   278,870.87

Age	0 - 14	15 - 19	20 - 24	25 - 29	30 - 64	65 plus
Male	10%	4%	4%	4%	23%	3%
Female	10%	4%	4%	4%	25%	5%

Capabilities

ACTIVE 610 (Army 500 Navy 110)

RESERVE 430 (Joint 430)

ORGANISATIONS BY SERVICE

Armed Forces 430 reservists

Army 500
Inf 1 bn (cadre)

Navy 110

FORCES BY ROLE

Navy 1 HQ located at St Ann's Fort

EQUIPMENT BY TYPE

PATROL AND COASTAL COMBATANTS 5+

MISC BOATS/CRAFT: some boats

PCC 1: 1 Kebir

PCI 4: 1 Dauntless less than 100 tonnes; 3 Guardian less than 100 tonnes

FACILITIES

Base 1 located at St Ann's Fort, 1 located at Bridgetown

Belize Bze

Belize Dollar BZ$		2003	2004	2005
GDP	BZ$	2.1bn	2.2bn	
	US$	1.0bn	1.1bn	
per capita	US$	3,940	4,030	
Growth	%	9.4	3.0	
Inflation	%	2.5	2.7	
Debt	US$	1.05bn		
Def bdgt	BZ$	30m	e 32m	e 32m
	US$	15m	16m	16m
US$1=BZ$		2	2	2

Population (2004)   281,084

Age	0 - 14	15 - 19	20 - 24	25 - 29	30 - 64	65 plus
Male	20%	6%	5%	4%	14%	2%
Female	20%	6%	5%	4%	14%	2%

Capabilities

ACTIVE ε1,050 (Army ε1,050)

RESERVE 700 (Joint 700)

ORGANISATIONS BY SERVICE

Armed Forces 700 reservists

Army ε1,050

FORCES BY ROLE

Army 3 (Reserve) coy

Inf   3 bn (*each*: 3 inf coy)

Spt   1 gp

EQUIPMENT BY TYPE

ARTY • MOR 6: 6 81mm

AT • RCL • 84mm 8: 8 Carl Gustav

Maritime Wing

PATROL AND COASTAL COMBATANTS • MISC BOATS/CRAFT up to 14: up to 14 armed boats

Air Wing

FORCES BY ROLE

MR / Tpt some sqn with 1 BN-2A *Defender*; 1 BN-2B *Defender*

Trg   some sqn with 1 *Cessna* 182 *Skylane*; 1 T67-200 *Firefly*

EQUIPMENT BY TYPE

AIRCRAFT

TPT • BN-2 DEFENDER 2: 1 BN-2A *Defender*; 1 BN-2B *Defender*

TRG 2: 1 *Cessna* 182 *Skylane*

T67 1: 1 T67-200 *Firefly*

FOREIGN FORCES

United Kingdom Army: 30

Bolivia Bol

Bolivian Boliviano B		2003	2004	2005
GDP	B	61.9bn	68.9bn	
	US$	8.1bn	8.7bn	
per capita	US$	943	997	
Growth	%	2.5	3.8	
Inflation	%	3.3	4.4	
Debt	US$	5.68bn		
Def bdgt	B	1.15bn	e 1.14bn	1.18bn
	US$	151m	145m	146m
FMA	US$	2.8m	4.5m	2.8m
US$1=B		7.65	7.93	8.09

Population (2004)   8,857,870.87

Age	0 - 14	15 - 19	20 - 24	25 - 29	30 - 64	65 plus
Male	18%	6%	5%	4%	14%	2%
Female	18%	6%	5%	4%	16%	3%

Capabilities

ACTIVE 31,500 (Army 25,000 Navy 3,500 Air 3,000) **Paramilitary 37,100**

Active strength to be 35,000. Incl some 20,000 conscripts. *Terms of service* 12 months, selective

ORGANISATIONS BY SERVICE

Army 7,000; 18,000+ conscript (total 25,000)

FORCES BY ROLE

HQ: 6 Military Regions

Army	10 (org, composition varies) div (*total*: 1 (aslt) cav gp, 1 (mot) cav gp, 2 AB regt (bn), 2 mech inf regt, 21 inf bn, 3 mot inf regt, 5 (horsed) cav gp, 6 arty regt (bn), 6 engr bn)
Armd	1 bn
Mech	1 (cav) regt
Inf / Presidential Guard	1 regt

SF	3 regt
ADA	1 regt
Avn	2 coy

EQUIPMENT BY TYPE

TK • LT TK 36: 36 SK-105 *Kuerassier*
RECCE 24: 24 EE-9 *Cascavel*
APC 77
  APC (T) 18: 18 M-113
  APC (W) 59: 24 EE-11 *Urutu*; 20 MOWAG *Roland*; 15 V-100 *Commando*
ARTY 168+
  TOWED 118
    75mm 70: 60 M-116 pack; ε10 M-1935
    105mm 30: 30 FH-18/M-101
    122mm 18: 18 M-30 *M-1938*
  MOR 50+: 50 81mm
    107mm: some M-30
AIRCRAFT
  TPT 3: 1 *Beech* 200 *Super King Air*; 1 *Beech* 90 *King Air*; 1 CASA 212 *Aviocar*
  UTL 1: 1 *Cessna* 210 *Centurion*

Navy 3,500

FORCES BY ROLE

Navy 1 HQ located at Puerto Guayaramerín; 1 HQ located at Riberalta; 1 HQ (exercise) located at Trinidad; 1 HQ located at Puerto Suárez; 1 HQ located at Tiquina; 1 HQ located at Corbija; 1 HQ located at Santa Cruz; 1 HQ located at Bermejo; 1 HQ located at Cochabamba

EQUIPMENT BY TYPE

PATROL AND COASTAL COMBATANTS 60: 60 PCR
Patrol Craft Riverine less than 100 tonnes
LOGISTICS AND SUPPORT 18: 18 Spt
FACILITIES

Base 1 located at Riberalta, 1 located at Tiquina, 1 located at Puerto Busch, 1 located at Puerto Guayaramerín, 1 located at Puerto Villarroel, 1 located at Trinidad, 1 located at Puerto Suárez, 1 located at Coral Harbour, Bs, 1 located at Santa Cruz, 1 located at Bermejo, 1 located at Cochabamba, 1 located at Puerto Villeroel

Marines 1,700

Marine 6 bn (1 in each Naval District)

Air Force 1,000; ε2,000 conscript (total 3,000)

FORCES BY ROLE

FGA	2 sqn with 18 AT-33AN *Shooting Star*
SAR / COMMS	1 sqn with 4 HB-315B *Gaviao*; 2 SA-315B *Lama*
Tpt	3 sqn with 3 *Beech* 90 *King Air*; 9 C-130A *Hercules*/C-130B *Hercules*/C-130H *Hercules*; 2 C-47 *Skytrain*; 1 CASA 212 *Aviocar*; 3 CV-580; 3 F-27-400 *Friendship*; 1 IAI-201 *Arava*; 1 *Gaviao* 60
Trg / COIN	some sqn with 19 PC-7 *Turbo Trainer*
Liaison	some sqn with 1 *Beech* 55 *Baron*; 9 *Cessna* 152; 1 *Cessna* 185; 2 *Cessna* 402; 1 PA-32 *Saratoga*; 3 PA-34 *Seneca*; 13 *Cessna* 206; 1 *Cessna* 208 *Caravan I*; 1 *Beech* F-33 *Bonanza*
Survey	1 sqn with 1 *Cessna* 402; 2 *Learjet* 25A/*Learjet* 25D (secondary VIP role); 5 *Cessna* 206; 1 *Cessna* 210 *Centurion*
Trg	some sqn with 1 *Cessna* 152; 2 *Cessna* 172; 1 *Lancair* 320; 4 SF-260W *Warrior*; 6 T-23; 10 T-34A *Beech Turbo Mentor*
Hel	some sqn with 12 UH-1H *Iroquois* ; 1 sqn (anti-drug) with 16 *Hughes* 500M; 2 (VIP)
AD	1 regt† with *Oerlikon*; 18 Type-65

EQUIPMENT BY TYPE

AIRCRAFT 37 combat capable
  FGA • AT-33 18: 18 AT-33AN *Shooting Star*
  TPT 45: 1 *Beech* 55 *Baron*; 3 *Beech* 90 *King Air*
    C-130 9: 9 C-130A *Hercules*/C-130B *Hercules*/C-130H *Hercules*
    C-47 *Skytrain* 2; 1 CASA 212 *Aviocar*; 3 CV-580; 10 *Cessna* 152; 1 *Cessna* 185; 3 *Cessna* 402
    F-27 3: 3 F-27-400 *Friendship*
    IAI-201 *Arava* 1; 1 L-188 *Electra* in store
    LEARJET 25 2: 2 *Learjet* 25A/*Learjet* 25D (secondary VIP role)
    PA-32 *Saratoga* 1; 3 PA-34 *Seneca*; 1 *Gaviao* 60
  UTL 22: 2 *Cessna* 172; 18 *Cessna* 206; 1 *Cessna* 208 *Caravan I*; 1 *Cessna* 210 *Centurion*
  TRG 41: 1 *Beech* F-33 *Bonanza*; 1 *Lancair* 320; 19 PC-7 *Turbo Trainer**
    SF-260CB (SF-260) 4: 4 SF-260W *Warrior*
    T-23 6
    T-34 10: 10 T-34A *Beech Turbo Mentor*
HELICOPTERS
  UTL 36: 4 HB-315B *Gaviao*
    HUGHES 500 18: 16 *Hughes* 500M; 2 (VIP)
    SA-315 2: 2 SA-315B *Lama*
    UH-1 12: 12 UH-1H *Iroquois*
AD • GUNS 18+
  20mm • TOWED: some *Oerlikon*
  37mm • TOWED 18: 18 Type-65

Paramilitary 37,100

National Police 31,100+

Frontier	27 unit
Paramilitary	9 bde; 2 (rapid action) regt

Narcotics Police 6,000+

DEPLOYMENT

BAHAMAS
Navy
Base 1 located at Coral Harbour, Bs

BURUNDI
UN • ONUB 4 obs

CÔTE D'IVOIRE
UN • UNOCI 3 obs

DEMOCRATIC REPUBLIC OF CONGO
UN • MONUC 4 obs; 221

HAITI
UN • MINUSTAH 4

LIBERIA
UN • UNMIL 1; 2 obs

SERBIA AND MONTENEGRO
UN • UNMIK 1 obs

SIERRA LEONE
UN • UNAMSIL 3 obs

Brazil Br

Brazilian Real R		2003	2004	2005
GDP	R	1.55tr	1.76tr	
	US$	506bn	581bn	
per capita	US$	2,784	3,160	
Growth	%	0.5	5.2	
Inflation	%	14.8	6.6	
Debt	US$	235bn		
Def exp[a]	R	28bn	28bn	
	US$	9.14bn	9.23bn	
Def bdgt	R	28bn	28bn	32bn
	US$	9.14bn	9.23bn	13.08bn
US$1=R		3.07	3.04	2.45

Population (2004)   186,112,794

Age	0 - 14	15 - 19	20 - 24	25 - 29	30 - 64	65 plus
Male	13%	5%	5%	5%	20%	2%
Female	13%	5%	5%	5%	20%	4%

Capabilities

ACTIVE 302,909 (Army 189,000 Navy 48,600 Air 65,309) **Paramilitary 385,600**

RESERVE 1,340,000 (Joint 1,340,000) **Paramilitary 385,600**

Terms of service 12 months (can be extended to 18)

ORGANISATIONS BY SERVICE

Army 149,000; 40,000 conscript (total 189,000)
FORCES BY ROLE
HQ: 7 Military Command, 12 Military Regions; 8 div (3 with Regional HQ)

Army	1 (frontier) bde (6 army bn); 4 (jungle) bde; 3 (armd inf) bde (*each:* 1 armd cav bn, 1 arty bn, 2 (armd inf) army bn)
Armd cav	1 bde (1 arty bn, 1 armd bn, 2 armd cav bn)
Mech cav	4 bde (*each:* 1 armd cav bn, 1 arty bn, 2 Mech cav bn)
SF	1 bde (1 SF bn, 1 Cdo bn) with Training Centre (SF)
Mot Inf	10 bde (*total:* 26 mot inf bn)
Lt inf	1 bde (3 Lt inf bn)
AB	1 bde (1 arty bn, 3 AB bn)
Arty	6 (med) gp
SP Arty	4 gp
ADA	1 (and coast) bde (3 AD gp, 8 army bn)
Engr	2 (railway) bn; 2 gp (*total:* 9 engr bn); 8 bn
Hel	1 bde (2 hel bn (*each:* 2 hel sqn))
Gd	3 (cav) regt

EQUIPMENT BY TYPE
TK 464
  MBT 178: 87 *Leopard* 1
    M-60 91: 91 M-60A3
  LT TK • **M-41** 286: 286 M-41B/M-41C
RECCE 409: 409 EE-9 *Cascavel*
APC 803
  APC (T) 584: 584 M-113
  APC (W) 219: 219 EE-11 *Urutu*
ARTY 1,554+
  TOWED 408+
    105mm 316+: 280 M-101/M-102; 36 L-118 *Light gun*; some Model 56 pack howitzer
    155mm 92: 92 M-114
  SP 110
    105mm 72: 72 M-108/M-7
    155mm • **M-109** 38: 38 M-109A3
  MRL 16+
    70mm: some SBAT-70
    ASTROS II 16
  MOR 1,020: 707 81mm
    107mm 236: 236 M-30
    120mm 77: 77 K6A3
AT
  MSL 32: 20 Eryx; 12 Milan
  RCL 290
    106mm • **M-40** 163: 163 M-40A1
    84mm 127: 127 Carl Gustav
  RL • **84mm** 540: 540 AT-4
HELICOPTERS
  SPT 19: 15 AS-355 *Ecureuil* (armed)
    S-70 4: 4 S-70A *Black Hawk*
  UTL 56: 33 AS-365 *Dauphin 2*; 8 AS-532 *Cougar*; 15 AS-550 *Fennec*
AD
  SAM 54
    SP • **ROLAND** 4: 4 *Roland* II
    MANPAD 50: 50 SA-18 *Grouse (Igla)*
  GUNS 134: 134 GDF-001 towed 35mm/L/60 towed 40mm/L/70 towed 40mm (some L-60/-70 with BOFI)

Paramilitary 385,600+ reservists

Navy 29,650; 3,200 conscript (total 32,850)
FORCES BY ROLE

Navy 1 (HQ IV Naval District) HQ located at Belém; 1 (HQ V Naval District) HQ located at Floriancholis; 1 (HQ VI Naval District) HQ located at Sao Paolo; 1 (HQ I Naval District) HQ (exercise) located at Rio de Janeiro; 1 (HQ II Naval District) HQ located at Salvador; 1 (HQ III Naval District) HQ located at Recife

EQUIPMENT BY TYPE
SUBMARINES • TACTICAL • SSK 4:
4 Tupi (Ge T-209/1400) each with 8 single 533mm TT each with Tigerfish HWT
PRINCIPAL SURFACE COMBATANTS 19
AIRCRAFT CARRIERS • CV 1:
1 Sao Paolo (capacity 15-18 A-4 *Skyhawk* FGA ac; 4-6 SH-3D *Sea King* ASW hels/SH-3A *Sea King* ASW hels; 3 AS-355F *Ecureuil II* spt hels/AS-350BA *Ecureuil* spt hels; 2 AS-532 *Cougar* utl hels) (Fr Clemenceau)
FRIGATES 14
FFG 10:
4 Constitucao
4 Greenhaigh (ex-UK Broadsword) each with 1 *Lynx* MK21A (Super *Lynx*) utl hels, 6 x1 324mm ASTT each with Mk 46 LWT, 4 single each with 1 MM-38 *Exocet* tactical SSM, 2+ sextuple (12 eff.) with 32 Sea Wolf SAM
2 Niteroi each with 1 *Lynx* MK21A (Super *Lynx*) utl hels, 4 MM-40 *Exocet* tactical SSM, 2 triple 324mm ASTT (6 eff.) each with Mk 46 LWT, 1 Albatros Octuple with 24 Aspide SAM, 1 2 tube *Bofors* 375mm (2 eff.), 1 115mm gun
FF 4:
4 Para (US *Garcia*) each with 1 *Lynx* MK21A (Super *Lynx*) utl hels, 2 triple ASTT (6 eff.) each with Mk 46 LWT, 1 Mk16 Mk 112 Octuple with tactical ASROC, 2 127mm gun
CORVETTES • FSG 4:
4 Inhauma each with 1 *Lynx* MK21A (Super *Lynx*) utl hels, 2 triple ASTT (6 eff.) each with Mk 46 LWT, 1 single with 1 MM-40 *Exocet* tactical SSM, 1 114mm gun
PATROL AND COASTAL COMBATANTS 50
PCC 10: 4 Bracui (UK *River*); 6 Piratini (US PGM)
PCI 16: 16 Tracker
PCR 5: 2 Pedro Teixeira; 3 Roraima
PCO 19:
10 Grajau
9 Imperial Marinheiro each with 1 76mm gun
MINE WARFARE • MINE COUNTERMEASURES •
MSC 6: 6 Aratu (Ge Schutze)
AMPHIBIOUS
PRINCIPAL AMPHIBIOUS SHIPS • LSD 2:
2 Ceara (capacity 345 troops; either 21 LCM or 9 LCM/LCU Craft *Landing Craft* Amphibious) (US Thomaston)
LS • LST 1:
1 Mattoso Maia (capacity 400 troops; 3 LCVP Craft *Landing Craft* Amphibious; 1 LCPL Craft *Landing Craft* Amphibious) (US Newport)
CRAFT 48: 3 LCU; 35 LCVP; 10 LCM
LOGISTICS AND SUPPORT 31: 1 AF *Stores ship RAS* (river gp); 4 AG *Aux Misc*; 1 AGHS (Svy) *Svy Vsl*; 2 AGOR

Research Vsl
AGOR 4: 2 Polar
AH (med) *Hospital ship* 2; 1 AK *Cargo Ship*; 1 (river gp); 1 AO; 1 AOT *Tkr* (river gp); 1 ASR *Sub Rescue Craft*; 5 ATF *Ocean Tug*; 6 Craft; 3 Tpt (trp)

Naval Aviation 1,150
FORCES BY ROLE
FGA some sqn with 23 A-4 *Skyhawk*/A-4MB *Skyhawk*/TA-4 *Skyhawk*; 3 TA-4MB *Skyhawk*
ASW some regt with 6 SH-3G *Sea King*/SH-3H *Sea King*; 6 SH-3B *Sea King*; 7 SH-3D *Sea King*
Utl some sqn with 5 AS-332 *Super Puma*; 12 AS-350 *Ecureuil* (armed); 9 AS-355 *Ecureuil* (armed)
Atk Hel some sqn with 13 Mk21A *Lynx*
Trg some sqn with 13 TH-57 *Sea Ranger*

EQUIPMENT BY TYPE
AIRCRAFT 26 combat capable
23 A-4 *Skyhawk* FGA/A-4MB *Skyhawk* FGA/TA-4 *Skyhawk* Trg*
TRG • TA-4 3: 3 TA-4MB *Skyhawk**
HELICOPTERS
6 SH-3G *Sea King* spt/SH-3H *Sea King* Utl
ASW 26: 13 Mk21A *Lynx*
SH-3 13: 6 SH-3B *Sea King*; 7 SH-3D *Sea King*
SPT 26: 5 AS-332 *Super Puma*; 12 AS-350 *Ecureuil* (armed); 9 AS-355 *Ecureuil* (armed)
TRG 13: 13 TH-57 *Sea Ranger*
MSL • TACTICAL • ASM: some AS-11 *Kilter*; some AS-12 *Kegler*; some Sea Skua

Marines 14,600
FORCES BY ROLE
Amph 1 (Fleet Force) div (1 Comd bn, 1 arty gp, 3 inf bn)
SF 1 bn
Marine 8+ (Regional) gp; 3 bn
Engr 1 bn

EQUIPMENT BY TYPE
TK • LT TK 17: 17 SK-105 *Kuerassier*
RECCE 6: 6 EE-9 *Cascavel*
APC 45
APC (T) 40: 40 M-113
APC (W) 5: 5 EE-11 *Urutu*
AAV 25
AAV-7 13: 13 AAV-7A1
LVTP-7 12
ARTY 49+
TOWED 41
105mm 33: 18 L-118 *Light gun*; 15 M-101
155mm 8: 8 M-114
MOR 8+: some 81mm
120mm 8: 8 K6A3
AT
MSL: some RB-56 *Bill*
RCL • 106mm • M-40 8: 8 M-40A1
RL • 89mm: some M-20
AD • GUNS • 40mm • TOWED 6: 6 L/70 (with BOFI)

Air Force 62,802; 2,507 conscript (total 65,309)

Four cmds- COMGAR (operations), COMDABRA (aerospace defence), COMGAP (logistics), COMGEP (personnel). Seven air regions. COMGAR assets divided among three air forces.

MSL • TACTICAL • AAM • AIM-9: some AIM-9B *Sidewinder*

MAA-1 *Piranha* some
R-550: some R-550 *Magic 2*
R530 some

Second Air Force

FORCES BY ROLE

ASW / MP	4 gp with 21 P-95A *Bandeirante*/P-95B *Bandeirante*; 9 P-3A *Orion* /P-3B *Orion*
SAR	1 gp with 4 SC-95B; 2 UH-1H *Iroquois*
SAR / Utl	up to 5 gp with 7 L-42 *Regente*; 14 U-7 (PA-34) *Seneca*; T-25C *Universal*; total of 35 UH-50 (AS-350B) *Ecureuil*; 3 CH-34 (AS-532UL) *Cougar*; 53 UH-1H *Iroquois*
Trg	1 gp with 10 T-25C *Universal*; UH-50 (AS-350B) *Ecureuil*

EQUIPMENT BY TYPE

AIRCRAFT 9 combat capable
  RECCE 7: 7 L-42 *Regente*
  MP 30: 21 P-95A *Bandeirante*/P-95B *Bandeirante*
    P-3 9: 9 P-3A *Orion* /P-3B *Orion* *
  SAR 4: 4 SC-95B
  TPT 14: 14 U-7 (PA-34) *Seneca*
  TRG • T-25 10+: 10+ T-25C *Universal*
HELICOPTERS
  SPT • AS-350 35+: 35 UH-50 (AS-350B) *Ecureuil*; some more
  UTL 58
    AS-532 3: 3 CH-34 (AS-532UL) *Cougar*
    UH-1 55: 2 UH-1H *Iroquois* ; 53 more

Third Air Force

FORCES BY ROLE

AD / FGA	3 gp with 45 F-5E *Tiger II*/F-5F *Tiger II* (being upgraded to F-5BR); 12 F-103E (*Mirage* IIIE); 41 AT-27 *Tucano*; 3 *Mirage* IIID
FGA / RECCE / Trg	3 gp with 33 AMX A1-A
FGA / COIN	3 gp with 68 AT-26 *Xavante*; 42 AT-27 *Tucano*; 76 AT-29 *Super Tucano* (being delivered)
AEW / RECCE / Survey	up to 5 gp with 7 L-42 *Regente*; 4 RC-95 *Bandeirante*; 3 R-99B (EMB-145RS) (Remote Sensing); 4 Hawker 800XP (Amazon inspection/calibration); 5 R-99A (EMB-145SA) *Erieye*; 4 CH-34 (AS-532UL) *Cougar*

EQUIPMENT BY TYPE

AIRCRAFT 320 combat capable
  FTR 57: 12 F-103E (*Mirage* IIIE)
    F-5 45: 45 F-5E *Tiger II*/F-5F *Tiger II* (being upgraded to F-5BR)

FGA • AMX 33: 33 AMX A1-A
RECCE 11: 7 L-42 *Regente*; 4 RC-95 *Bandeirante*
EW • ELINT 7: 4 Hawker 800XP (Amazon inspection/calibration); 3 R-99B (EMB-145RS) (Remote Sensing)
AEW • EMB-145 5: 5 R-99A (EMB-145SA) *Erieye*
TRG 230: 68 AT-26 *Xavante**; 83 AT-27 *Tucano**; 76 AT-29 *Super Tucano** (being delivered); 3 *Mirage* IIID*
HELICOPTERS • UTL • AS-532 4: 4 CH-34 (AS-532UL) *Cougar*

Fifth Air Force

FORCES BY ROLE

Tkr / Tpt	1 gp with 2 SC-130E *Hercules*; 2 KC-130H *Hercules*; 10 C-130H *Hercules*; 1 gp with 4 KC-137 (B-707-320C)
Tpt	1 gp; 2 gp with 17 C-115 (DHC-5) *Buffalo*; 1 gp with 5 C-130H *Hercules*; 1 gp with 2 B-737-200 (Presidental); 8 VU-93 (BAe-125) (VIP); 1 C-95B
COMMS	7 sqn with 59 C-95; 7 C-115 (DHC-5) *Buffalo*; 5 VC-97 *Brasilia*; 5 VU-9 *Xingu*; 3 C-98 (*Cessna 208*) *Caravan I*

EQUIPMENT BY TYPE

AIRCRAFT
  SAR • SC-130 2: 2 SC-130E *Hercules*
  TKR 6
    KC-130 2: 2 KC-130H *Hercules*
    KC-137 (B-707-320C) 4
  TPT 131
    B-737 2: 2 B-737-200 (Presidental)
    C-115 (DHC-5) *Buffalo* 24
    C-130 15: 15 C-130H *Hercules*
    C-91 (BAe-748) 12 (being replaced by 10 ERJ-145); 59 C-95
    C-95 60: 1 C-95B
    VC-97 *Brasilia* 5; 5 VU-9 *Xingu*; 8 VU-93 (BAe-125) (VIP)
    UTL 3: 3 C-98 (*Cessna 208*) *Caravan I*

Training

AIRCRAFT • TRG 133: 10 AMX-T *Ghibli**
  T-25 62: 62 T-25A *Universal*/T-25C *Universal* (basic)
  T-27 *Tucano* 61 (advanced)
HELICOPTERS • SPT • AS-350: some UH-50 (AS-350B) *Ecureuil*

Paramilitary 385,600+ reservists opcon Army

Public Security Forces 385,600+

in state mil pol org (state militias) under army control and considered army reserve

Armed Forces 225,000 reservists (Second-line); 1,115,000 reservists (Trained first-line; 400,000 subject to immediate recall) (total 1,340,000)

DEPLOYMENT

CÔTE D'IVOIRE
UN • ONUCI 3; 4 obs

EAST TIMOR
UN • UNOTIL 2 obs

HAITI
UN • MINUSTAH 1,213

LIBERIA
UN • UNMIL 1

SUDAN
UN • UNMIS 7 obs

Chile Chl

Chilean Peso pCh		2003	2004	2005
GDP	pCh	50.7tr	67.4tr	
	US$	68.1bn	86.9bn	
per capita	US$	4,347	5,491	
Growth	%	3.3	6.0	
Inflation	%	2.8	1.1	
Debt	US$	43.2bn		
Def exp[a]	pCh	1.88tr	2.08tr	
	US$	2.53bn	3.15bn	
Def bdgt	pCh	830bn	947bn	1.01tr
	US$	1.11bn	1.43bn	1.66bn
FMA	US$	–	–	1.1m
US$1=pCh		745	660	608

Population (2004) 15,980,912

Age	0 - 14	15 - 19	20 - 24	25 - 29	30 - 64	65 plus
Male	13%	4%	4%	4%	21%	3%
Female	12%	4%	4%	4%	21%	5%

Capabilities

ACTIVE 78,098 (Army 47,700 Navy 19,398 Air 11,000) Paramilitary 38,000

Incl some 22,400 conscripts
Terms of service Army 1 year Navy and Air Force 22 months. To be voluntary from 2005

RESERVE 50,000 (Army 50,000)

ORGANISATIONS BY SERVICE

Army 27,000; 20,700 conscript (total 47,700)
FORCES BY ROLE
6 Military Regions, 3 Theatre of Ops (North, Centre, South)
Army 6 div (org, composition varies) (*total:* 10 armd cav regt, 25 (incl 10 reinforced) inf regt (*total:* 1 Mech inf regt, 11 Mtn inf regt, 13 mot inf regt), 7 engr regt, 7 arty regt)
AB 1 regt (1 SF bn, 1 AB bn)
Engr 1 regt
Avn 1 bde

EQUIPMENT BY TYPE
TK • MBT 260: 60 AMX-30; 200 *Leopard* 1

RECCE 157: 157 EE-9 *Cascavel*
AIFV 20: 20 MOWAG Piranha (with 90mm gun)
APC 1066
  APC (T) • M-113 658: 158 M-113C/M-113R
    M-113 500
  APC (W) 408: ε290 EE-11 *Urutu*; 118 Piranha
ARTY 615+
  TOWED 163
    105mm 120: 66 M-101; 54 Model 56 pack howitzer
    155mm 43: 24 G-4; 11 M-68; 8 M-71
  SP • 155mm 12: 12 Mk F3
  MRL • 160mm: some LAR-160
  MOR 440
    81mm 300: 300 M-29
    107mm 15: 15 M-30
    120mm 125: 125 FAMAE (incl 50 SP)
AT • MSL: some *Mamba*/Milan; some MAPATS
  RCL • 106mm • M-40: some M-40A1
    57mm: some M-18
  RL • 89mm: some M-20 (3.5in)
AIRCRAFT
  TPT 12: 1 *Beech* 100 *King Air*; 1 *Beech* 58 *Baron*; 6 CASA 212 *Aviocar*; 3 CN-235; 1 *Cessna* 500 *Citation I* (VIP)
  UTL 8: 8 *Cessna* 208 *Caravan I*
  TRG 10: 10 *Cessna* R172K *Hawk XP*
HELICOPTERS
  SPT 18: 2 AS-332 *Super Puma*
    AS-350 6: 6 AS-350B3 *Ecureuil*
    SA-330 *Puma* 10
  UTL • MD-530 20: 20 MD-530F *Lifter* (armed)
  TRG 12: 12 Enstrom 280FX
AD
  SAM 67+
    SP 5: 5 Crotale
    MANPAD 62+: 50 *Blowpipe*; some Javelin; 12 Mistral
  GUNS 60: 60 20mm (incl some SP (Cardoen/MOWAG))

Navy 17,738; 1,660 conscript (total 19,398)
FORCES BY ROLE
Main Command: Fleet (includes DD and FF), SS flotilla, tpt.
Navy 1 (Puerto Montt 3rd Naval Zone 43S to Antarctica) HQ located at Punta Arenas; 1 (Puerto Williams 4th Naval Zone north of 26S approx) HQ located at Iquique; 1 (1st Naval Zone: 26S-36S approx) HQ located at Valparaiso; 1 (2nd Naval Zone: 36S-43S approx) HQ located at Talcahuano

EQUIPMENT BY TYPE
SUBMARINES • TACTICAL • SSK 4:
  2 O'Higgins (Scorpene) (being delivered) each with 6 single 533mm TT with 18 A-184 *Black Shark* HWT
  2 Thompson (Ge T-209/1300) each with 8 single 533mm TT with 14 SUT HWT
PRINCIPAL SURFACE COMBATANTS 6
  DESTROYERS • DDG 2:
    2 UK Country Class each with 2 AS-332F *Super Puma* spt hels, 2 triple ASTT (6 eff.) each with Mk 46 LWT, 4 single each with 1 MM-38 *Exocet* tactical SSM, 2 octuple VLS with 16 Barak SAM, 2 114mm gun
  FRIGATES • FFG 4:
    1 Condell (capacity 500 trucks; 400 troops)/Zenteno

(capacity 500 trucks; 400 troops) (mod UK Leander) with 1 AS-332 *Super Puma* spt hels, 2 triple ASTT (6 eff.) each with Mk 46 LWT, 4 single each with 1 MM-38 *Exocet* tactical SSM, 2 114mm gun

2 Condell (capacity 500 trucks; 400 troops) (mod UK Leander) each with 1 AS-332F *Super Puma* spt hels, 2 triple ASTT (6 eff.) each with Mk 46 LWT, 4 single each with 1 MM-40 *Exocet* tactical SSM, 2 114mm gun

1 Williams (ex-UK T22)

PATROL AND COASTAL COMBATANTS 25
  PCC 3: 2 Guacolda (Ge Lurssen 36m); 1 Yagan
  PCI 10: 10 Grumete Diaz less than 100 tonnes (Il Dabur)
  PFM 7:
    3 Casma (Il Sa'ar 4) each with 8 GI *Gabriel I* tactical SSM, 2 76mm gun
    4 Tiger (Ge Type 148) each with 4 single each with 1 MM-40 *Exocet* tactical SSM, 1 6mm gun
  PCO 5: 5 Micalvi
AMPHIBIOUS • LS 5
  LSM 2: 2 Elicura
  LST 3: 2 Maipo (capacity 7 tanks; 140 troops) (Fr Batral); 1 Valdivia (capacity 400 troops) (US Newport)
LOGISTICS AND SUPPORT 12: 2 AG *Aux Misc*; 1 AGB *Icebreaker*; 1 AGHS (Svy) *Svy Vsl*; 1 AGOR *Research Vsl*; 1 AK *Cargo Ship*
  AO 1: 1 Araucano
  ATF *Ocean Tug* 3; 1 Tpt; 1 Trg
MSL • TACTICAL • SSM: some Excalibur each with 4 MM-38 *Exocet* tactical SSM

FACILITIES
Base 1 located at Valparaiso, 1 located at Talcahuano, 1 located at Puerto Montt, 1 located at Puerto Williams, 1 located at Iquique, 1 located at Punta Arenas

Naval Aviation 600
AIRCRAFT 6 combat capable
  MP • P-3 3: 3 P-3A *Orion*
  TPT 17
    CASA 212 5: 5 CASA 212A *Aviocar*
    Cessna 337 Skymaster 8; 4 EMB-110 *Bandeirante*
  TRG 6: 6 PC-7 *Turbo Trainer**
HELICOPTERS
UTL 17: 6 AS-532 *Cougar**; 5 BO-105; 6 Bell 206 *JetRanger*

MSL • TACTICAL • ASM: some AM-39 *Exocet*

Marines 3,500
Excalibur Coast Defence System, this weapons system is composed of a trailer mounted command post, complete with controls and surveillance radar, and two trailers carrying two *Exocet* MM38 missiles. Ex-UK Navy, modernised in France before delivery.

FORCES BY ROLE
Amph   1 bn
Marine 4 gp (*total*: 1 SSM bty, 2 Trg bn, 4 inf bn, 4 ADA bty, 4 fd arty bty)

EQUIPMENT BY TYPE
TK • LT TK 12: 12 Scorpion
APC • APC (W) 25: 25 MOWAG *Roland*

ARTY 94
  TOWED 44
    105mm 16: 16 KH-178
    155mm 28: 28 G-5
  MOR 50: 50 81mm
AT • RCL • 106mm • M-40 30: ε30 M-40A1
AD • SAM • MANPAD: some *Blowpipe*

Coast Guard
integral part of the Navy
PATROL AND COASTAL COMBATANTS 53
  MISC BOATS/CRAFT 30: 30 boats
  PCC 2: 2 Alacalufe
  PCI 21: 6; 15 *Rodman*

Air Force 10,300; 700 conscript (total 11,000)
Flying hours   100 hrs/year

FORCES BY ROLE
5 Air Bde, 5 wg, 13 sqns

Ftr	1 sqn with 15 F-5E *Tiger II*; 3 F-5F *Tiger II*
Ftr / RECCE	1 sqn with 1 *Mirage* 5; 15 *Mirage* 5MA *Elkan*; 2 *Mirage* 5BR (*Mirage* 5R); 5 *Mirage* 5MD *Elkan*
FGA	some sqn with 6 F-16C Block 50 (to be delivered 2006); 4 F-16D Block 50 (to be delivered 2006); 1 sqn with 12 *Mirage* 50DCM *Pantera*; 1 *Mirage* 50M *Pantera*; 1 *Mirage* IIIBE
RECCE	1 (photo) unit with 1 *Beech* A-100 *King Air*; 3 DHC-6-100 *twin Otter*; 2 *Learjet* 35A
AEW	some sqn with 1 IAI-707 *Phalcon*; 1 B-737-300
CCT	2 sqn with 18 A-37B *Dragonfly*; 12 A-36 *Bonanza*
Tpt	some sqn with 2 B-707 (1 tpt, 1 tkr); 1 B-737-500 (VIP); 6 *Beech* 99 *Petrel Beta* (ELINT, tpt, trg); 3 C-130B *Hercules*; 2 C-30H *Hercules*; 4 CASA 212 *Aviocar*; 5 *Cessna* 525 *Citation CJ-1*; 5 DHC-6-100 *twin Otter*; 10 DHC-6-300 *twin Otter*; 1 *Gulfstream IV* (VIP); 2 *Learjet* 35A; 15 PA-28-140 *Cherokee*
Trg	1 wg with 5 Extra 300; 38 T-35A *Pillan*/T-35B *Pillan*; 23 T-36 *Halcon*; 2 Bell 206A *JetRanger*
Hel	some sqn with 1 BO-105; 4 Bell 412 *twin Huey* (first of 10-12 planned to replace UH-1H); 6 UH-1H *Iroquois* ; 1 UH-60 *Black Hawk*
AD	1 regt with Mygale; Mistral; M-163 *Vulcan*/M-167 *Vulcan*; GDF-005; *Oerlikon* (5 AD gp)

EQUIPMENT BY TYPE
AIRCRAFT 87 combat capable
FTR • F-5 18: 15 F-5E *Tiger II*; 3 F-5F *Tiger II*
FGA 69
  A-37 18: 18 A-37B *Dragonfly*
  F-16C 6: 6 F-16C Block 50 (to be delivered 2006)
  F-16D 4: 4 F-16D Block 50 (to be delivered 2006)
  Halcon (CASA C-11CC) Aviojet 12: 12
  MIRAGE 50 13: 12 *Mirage* 50DCM *Pantera*; 1 *Mirage* 50M *Pantera*

MIRAGE 5 16: 1
   MIRAGE 5M 15: 15 *Mirage 5MA Elkan*
RECCE 2: 2 *Mirage 5BR* (*Mirage 5R*)
AEW 1: 1 IAI-707 *Phalcon*
TPT 63: 2 B-707 (1 tpt, 1 tkr)
  B-737 2: 1 B-737-300; 1 B-737-500 (VIP)
  Beech **99** *Petrel Beta* 6 (ELINT, tpt, trg); 1 *Beech* A-100 *King Air*
  C-130 5: 3 C-130B *Hercules*; 2 C-130H *Hercules*
  CASA 212 *Aviocar* 4; 5 *Cessna 525 Citation CJ-1*
  DHC-6 18: 8 DHC-6-100 *twin Otter*; 10 DHC-6-300 *twin Otter*
  Gulfstream IV 1 (VIP)
  LEARJET 35 4: 4 *Learjet 35A*
  PA-28-140 *Cherokee* 15
TRG 84: 12 A-36 *Bonanza*; 5 Extra 300; 5 *Mirage 5MD Elkan*
  MIRAGE IIIB 1: 1 *Mirage IIIBE*
  T-35 38: 38 T-35A *Pillan*/T-35B *Pillan*
  T-36 *Halcon* 23
HELICOPTERS
  UTL 14: 1 BO-105
  BELL 206 2: 2 Bell 206A *JetRanger*
  Bell 412 *twin Huey* 4 (first of 10-12 planned to replace UH-1H)
  UH-1 6: 6 UH-1H *Iroquois*
  UH-60 *Black Hawk* 1
AD • SYSTEMS: some Mygale
  SAM: some Mistral
  GUNS • 20mm: some M-163 *Vulcan* SP/M-167 *Vulcan* towed
  35mm • TOWED • GDF: some GDF-005 *Oerlikon* some
MSL • TACTICAL • AAM • AIM-9: some AIM-9B *Sidewinder*/AIM-9J *Sidewinder*
  Python III some; some *Shafrir*
FACILITIES
School 3 with 5 Extra 300 Trg ac; 38 T-35A *Pillan*/T-35B *Pillan*; 23 T-36 *Halcon* Trg ac; 2 Bell 206A *JetRanger* utl hels (flying)

Paramilitary 38,000

Carabineros 38,000
Ministry of Defence
FORCES BY ROLE
13 Zones
Paramilitary 39 district; 174 comisaria
EQUIPMENT BY TYPE
APC • APC (W) 20: 20 MOWAG *Roland*
ARTY • MOR: some 60mm; some 81mm
AIRCRAFT: some *Cessna 182 Skylane* Tpt/*Cessna 206* Utl/*Cessna 210 Centurion* Utl
  TPT 1+: some *Cessna 500 Citation I*; 1 PA-31 *Navajo*
  PA-31 1+: some PA-31T *Navajo*/*Cheyenne II*
HELICOPTERS • UTL 12+: some BK-117; 8+ BO-105; 2 Bell 206 *JetRanger*; 2 EC-135

NON-STATE ARMED GROUPS
see Part II

DEPLOYMENT

HAITI
UN • MINUSTAH 542

INDIA/PAKISTAN
UN • UNMOGIP 2 obs

MIDDLE EAST
UN • UNTSO 3 obs

Colombia Co

Colombian Peso pC		2003	2004	2005
GDP	pC	230tr	255tr	
	US$	79.9bn	95.6bn	
per capita	US$	1,919	2,261	
Growth	%	4.0	4.0	
Inflation	%	7.1	5.9	
Debt	US$	32.9bn		
Def exp	pC	9.3tr	10.4tr	
	US$	3.23bn	3.9bn	
Def bdgt	pC	6.7tr	7.4tr	8.2tr
	US$	2.31bn	2.76bn	3.5bn
FMA[a]	US$	18.2	100.1	100.9
US$1=pC		2,877	2,675	2,337

Population (2004) 42,954,279

Age	0 - 14	15 - 19	20 - 24	25 - 29	30 - 64	65 plus
Male	16%	5%	4%	4%	19%	2%
Female	15%	5%	4%	4%	20%	3%

Capabilities

ACTIVE 207,000 (Army 178,000 Navy 22,000 Air 7,000) Paramilitary 129,000
Terms of service 24 months

RESERVE 60,700 (Army 54,700 Navy 4,800 Air 1,200) incl 2000 first-line

ORGANISATIONS BY SERVICE

Army ε114,200; 63,800 conscript; 54,700 reservists **(total** 232,700**)**
FORCES BY ROLE
6 div HQ

Army	1 (anti-terrorism) unit; 1 (counter-narcotics) bde (3 army bn); 9 Mobile Counter Guerrilla Force bde (*each:* 1 Cdo unit, 4 army bn)
Mech	6 bde (*each:* 1 engr bn, 1 arty bn, 1 Mech cav bn, 3 inf bn)
Air Mob	2 (air-portable) bde (*each:* 2 inf bn)
Inf	8 bde (*each:* 2 inf bn); 1 bde (4 inf bn)
SF	1 bde (4 SF bn)

Mtn Inf	4 (high) bn
Arty	2 bn
ADA	1 bn
Avn	1 bde (1 hel bn, 1 avn bn)
Border Guard	1 bde (Forming - to be 4 bn with 43 AMX-30 (to be delivered)) (1 SF gp)
Trg	1 bde

EQUIPMENT BY TYPE
TK • LT TK 12: 12 M-3A1 *Stuart* (in store)
RECCE 135: 130 EE-9 *Cascavel*; 5 M-8
APC 192+
  APC (T) 88: 88 M-113
  APC (W) 104+: 100+ EE-11 *Urutu*; 4 RG-31 *Nyala*
ARTY 639
  TOWED 156
    75mm 70: 70 M-116 pack
    105mm 86: 86 M-101
  MOR 483
    81mm 125: 125 M-1
    107mm 148: 148 M-2
    120mm 210: 210 Brandt
AT
  MSL 20: 20 TOW (incl 8 SP)
  RCL • 106mm • M-40 63: 63 M-40A1
  RL 15+
    66mm: some M-72 *LAW*
    89mm 15: 15 M-20
HELICOPTERS
  OBS • OH-6 6: 6 OH-6A *Cayuse*
  SPT • MI-8 12: 12 MI-17 (Mi-8MT) *Hip H*
  UTL 23: 23 UH-60 *Black Hawk*
    57 Bell 205 Utl/Bell 206 *JetRanger* Utl/Bell 212 Utl/Bell 412 *twin Huey* Utl/Hughes 300 Trg/Hughes 500 Utl/MD-500 Utl/MD-530 *Lifter* Utl/UH-1B *Iroquois* Utl
AD • GUNS • 40mm • TOWED • M-1 30: 30 M-1A1

Navy 15,000; 7,000 conscript; 4,800 reservists (total 26,800)

FORCES BY ROLE
Navy 1 HQ (tri-Service Unified Eastern Command HQ) located at Puerto Carreño

EQUIPMENT BY TYPE
SUBMARINES • TACTICAL 4
  SSK 2:
    2 *Pijao* (Ge T-209/1200) each with 8 single 533mm TT with 14 SUT HWT
  SSI 2: 2 *Intrepido* (It SX-506, SF delivery)
PRINCIPAL SURFACE COMBATANTS • CORVETTES • FSG 4:
  4 *Almirante Padilla* each with 1 BO-105 utl hel, 2 B515 *ILAS-3* triple 324mm each with A244 LWT, 2 quad (8 eff.) each with 1 MM-40 *Exocet* tactical SSM, 1 76mm gun
PATROL AND COASTAL COMBATANTS 179
  PCC 4: 2 *Castillo Y Rada*; 2 *Jose Gaarcia*
  PCI 4: 2 *Jaime Gomez*; 2 *Jose Palas*
  PCR 165: 76; 3 *Arauca*; 20 *Delfin*; 10 *Diligente*; 42 *Pirana*; 5 *Rio Magdalena*; 9 *Tenerife*
  PFC 1:
    1 *Quito Sueno* (US Asheville) with 1 76mm gun

PCO 4:
  2 *Lazags*
  2 *Pedro de Heredia* (ex-US tugs) each with 1 76mm gun
PFO 1: 1 *Esperanta* (Sp *Cormoran*)
LOGISTICS AND SUPPORT 7: 2 AGHS (Svy) *Svy Vsl*; 2 AGOR *Research Vsl*; 1 AH (med) *Hospital ship*; 1 Tpt; 1 Trg (sail)

FACILITIES
Base 1 located at Puerto Leguízamo, 1 located at Buenaventura, 1 (Pacific) located at Málaga, 1 (Main) located at Catagena, 1 located at Barrancabermeja, 1 located at Puerto Carreño, 1 located at Leticia, 1 located at Puerto Orocue, 1 located at Puerto Inirida

Naval Aviation 100

AIRCRAFT
  TPT 7: 3 PA-28-140 *Cherokee*; 2 PA-31 *Navajo*; 2 Rockwell Commander 500
  UTL 2: 2 *Cessna* 206
HELICOPTERS
  ASW 1: 1 AS-555SN *Fennec*
  UTL 2: 2 BO-105

Marines 14,000

Sy	1 bn
Amph aslt	1 op
SF	1 bn
Marine	2 bde (*each*: 2 Marine bn); 1 (*River*) op (15 Amph aslt unit (Patrol))

Air Force 3,100; 3,900+ conscript; 1,200 reservists (total 8,200)

MSL • TACTICAL • AAM: some Python III; some R530

Air Combat Command

FORCES BY ROLE
FGA 1 sqn with 11 Kfir C-7; 1 Kfir TC-7; 1 sqn with 10 *Mirage* 5

EQUIPMENT BY TYPE
AIRCRAFT 22 combat capable
  FGA 21: 11 Kfir C-7; 10 *Mirage* 5
  TRG 1: 1 Kfir TC-7*

Tactical Air Support Command

FORCES BY ROLE

FGA / FAC / Special Ops	some sqn with 14 A-37B *Dragonfly*; 3 IA-58A *Pucara*; 13 OV-10A *Bronco*; 2 AC-47; 3 AC-47T *Fantasma*
RECCE	some sqn with 5 SA-2-37A/SA-2-37B; 3 C-26 *Metro*
Hel	some sqn with 5 Bell 205; 14 Bell 212; 2 Bell 412 *twin Huey*; 2 MD-500D*; 11 MD-500ME*; 3 MD-530F *Lifter**; 12 UH-60A *Black Hawk*; 5 UH-60L *Black Hawk*; 7*

EQUIPMENT BY TYPE
AIRCRAFT 30 combat capable
  FGA 17

A-37 14: 14 A-37B *Dragonfly*
IA-58 3: 3 IA-58A *Pucara*
FAC • OV-10 13: 13 OV-10A *Bronco*
RECCE • SA-2-37 5: 5 SA-2-37A/SA-2-37B
SPEC OPS 5: 2 AC-47
   AC-47 5: 3 AC-47T *Fantasma*
TPT 3: 3 C-26 *Metro*
HELICOPTERS
UTL 61: 5 Bell 205; 14 Bell 212; 2 Bell 412 *twin Huey*
MD-500 13: 2 MD-500D*
   MD-500M 11: 11 MD-500ME*
MD-530 3: 3 MD-530F *Lifter**
UH-60 24: 12 UH-60A *Black Hawk*; 12 UH-60L *Black Hawk (7*)*

Military Air Transport Command
AIRCRAFT
TPT 24: 1 B-707; 2 B-727
   B-737 1: 1 B-737-74V (VIP)
   C-117 1
   C-130 9: 7 C-130B *Hercules*; 2 C-130H *Hercules*
   C-47 *Skytrain* 2; 2 CASA 212 *Aviocar*; 3 CN-235; 2 EMB-110 *Bandeirante*; 1 F-28 *Fellowship*
HELICOPTERS
SPT • MI-8 6: 6 MI-17 (Mi-8MT) *Hip H*
UTL • UH-1 17: 17 UH-1H *Iroquois*

Air Training Command
AIRCRAFT
TRG 41: 12 T-27 *Tucano*
   T-34 9: 9 T-34M *Turbo Mentor*
   T-37 *Tweet* 12; 8 T-41 *Mescalero*
HELICOPTERS
UTL • UH-1 6: 2 UH-1B *Iroquois* ; 4 UH-1H *Iroquois*
TRG • ENSTROM F-28 12: 12 Enstrom F-28F

Paramilitary 129,000

National Police Force 121,000
AIRCRAFT
FAC • OV-10 5: 5 OV-10A *Bronco*
TPT 11: 11 Basler Turbo-67
UTL 12: 12 Gavilán 358 *Gavilan*
HELICOPTERS
UTL 145
BELL 206 10: 10 Bell 206L *LongRanger*
Bell 212 37
HUGHES 500 2: 2 *Hughes* 500D
UH-1 85: 60 UH-1H *Iroquois* /UH-1H-II *Huey II*; 25 UH-1N *Iroquois*
UH-60 11: 11 UH-60L *Black Hawk*

Rural Militia 8,000

NON-STATE ARMED GROUPS
see Part II

DEPLOYMENT

EGYPT
MFO 1 Inf bn; 358

Costa Rica CR

Costa Rican Colon C		2003	2004	2005
GDP	C	6.94tr	8.09tr	
	US$	17.4bn	18.4bn	
per capita	US$	4,480	4,674	
Growth	%	6.5	4.2	
Inflation	%	9.4	12.3	
Debt	US$	5.42bn		
Sy Bdgt[a]	C	37.5bn	46.0bn	47.7bn
	US$	94m	105m	101m
US$1=C		398	438	473

Population (2004)   4,016,173

Age	0 - 14	15 - 19	20 - 24	25 - 29	30 - 64	65 plus
Male	15%	5%	5%	4%	19%	3%
Female	14%	5%	5%	4%	19%	3%

Capabilities

ACTIVE 0 Paramilitary 8,400

ORGANISATIONS BY SERVICE

Paramilitary 8,400

Civil Guard 4,400
Police	1 (tac) *comisaria*
Provincial	6 *comisaria*
Spec Ops	1 unit
Paramilitary	7 (Urban) *comisaria* (reinforced coy)

Border Security Police 2,000
Sy 2 (Border) comd (8 *comisaria*)

Maritime Surveillance Unit 300
EQUIPMENT BY TYPE
PATROL AND COASTAL COMBATANTS 18
  MISC BOATS/CRAFT 10: circa 10 boats
  PCC 1: 1 *Astronauta* (US Cape)
  PCI 6: 4 less than 100 tonnes; 2 Point less than 100 tonnes
  PFC 1: 1 *Isla del Coco* (US *Swift* 32m)
FACILITIES
Base 1 located at Golfito, 1 located at Punta Arenas, 1 located at Cuajiniquil, 1 located at Quepos, 1 located at Limbe, Crn, 1 located at Moin

Air Surveillance Unit 300
AIRCRAFT
RECCE • OBS 1: 1 *Cessna O-1A Bird Dog*
TPT 3: 1 DHC-4 *Caribou*; 1 PA-31 *Navajo*; 1 PA-34 *Seneca*
UTL • CESSNA 206 • CESSNA U-206 4: 4 *Cessna U-206G Stationair*
HELICOPTERS
SPT • MI-8 1: 1 MI-17 (Mi-8MT) *Hip H*
UTL • MD-500 2: 2 MD-500E

Rural Guard 2,000

Ministry of Government and Police.
small arms only
Paramilitary 8 comd

DEPLOYMENT

CAMEROON

Paramilitary • Border Security Police • Maritime Surveillance Unit
Base 1 located at Limbe, Crn

Cuba C

Cuban Convertible Peso P		2003	2004	2005
GDP	P	634bn	680bn	
	US$	30.2bn	32.4bn	
per capita	US$	2,679	2,865	
Growth	%	2.9	3.9	
Inflation	%	0.6	1.0	
Debt	US$	12.7bn		
Def exp	US$	e 1.2bn	e 1.3bn	
US$1=P		21	21	21

Population   11,346,670.67

Age	0 - 14	15 - 19	20 - 24	25 - 29	30 - 64	65 plus
Male	10%	4%	3%	3%	25%	5%
Female	10%	4%	3%	3%	25%	6%

Capabilities

ACTIVE 49,000 (Army 38,000 Navy 3,000 Air 8,000)
Paramilitary 26,500 Inactive Other 120,000
Terms of service 2 years

RESERVE 39,000 (Army 39,000) **Paramilitary 1,000,000**
Ready Reserves (serve 45 days per year) to fill out Active and Resrve units; see also Paramilitary.

ORGANISATIONS BY SERVICE

Army ε38,000; 39,000 reservists (total 77,000)

FORCES BY ROLE
3 Regional comd HQ, 3 army comd HQ
Army   1 (frontier) bde; 14 (reserve) bde
Armd   up to 5 bde
Mech Inf   9 bde (*each:* 1 armd regt, 1 arty regt, 1 ADA regt, 3 Mech inf regt)
AB   1 bde
ADA   1 regt
SAM   1 bde

EQUIPMENT BY TYPE
TK • MBT 900: ε900 T-34/T-54/T-55/T-62
   LT TK: some PT-76

RECCE • BRDM: some BRDM-1/BRDM-2
AIFV • BMP: some BMP-1
APC • APC (W) • BTR 700: ε700 BTR-152/BTR-40/BTR-50/BTR-60
ARTY 1715+
   TOWED 500: 500 D-1 152mm/D-30 122mm/M-1937 152mm/M-30 *M-1938* 122mm/M-46 130mm/ZIS-3 *M-1942* 76mm
   SP 40: 40 2S1 *Carnation* 122mm/2S3 152mm
   MRL 175: 175 BM-14 140mm/BM-21 122mm
   MOR 1,000: 1,000 M-38 120mm/M-41 82mm/M-43 120mm/M-43 82mm
   STATIC • 122mm: some JS-2 (hy tk)
      85mm: some T-34
AT • MSL: some AT-1 *Snapper*; some AT-3 *Sagger*
   GUNS • 100mm: some Su-100 SP; some T-12
      85mm: some D-44
AD
   SAM 300: 300 SA-13 *Gopher* SP/SA-14 *Gremlin* MANPAD/SA-16 *Gimlet* MANPAD/SA-6 *Gainful* SP/SA-7 *Grail* MANPAD/SA-8 *Gecko* SP/SA-9 *Gaskin* SP (300-1800 eff.)
   GUNS 400: 400 BTR-60P SP 30mm/KS-19 towed 100mm/M-1939 *KS-12* towed 85mm/M-1939 towed 37mm/M-53 towed 30mm/S-60 towed 57mm/ZSU-23-4 SP 23mm/ZSU-57-2 SP 57mm/ZU-23 towed 23mm

Navy ε3,000

FORCES BY ROLE
Navy 1 (HQ Western Comd) HQ located at Cabanas; 1 (HQ Eastern Comd) HQ located at Holquin

EQUIPMENT BY TYPE
PATROL AND COASTAL COMBATANTS 5
   PFC 1:
      1 Pauk II† (FSU) with 4 single ASTT, 1 x4 Manual with SA-N-5 *Grail* SAM, 2 RBU 1200 (10 eff.), 1 76mm gun
   PFM 4:
      4 Osa II† (FSU) each with 4 single each with 1 SS-N-2B *Styx* tactical SSM (missiles removed to coastal defence units)
MINE WARFARE • MINE COUNTERMEASURES 6
   MHC 4: 4 *Yevgenya*† (FSU)
   MSC 2: 2 *Sonya*† (FSU)
LOGISTICS AND SUPPORT 1: 1 AGHS (Svy) *Svy Vsl*†
FACILITIES
Base 1 located at Cabanas, 1 located at Havana, 1 located at Cienfuegos, 1 located at Holquin, 1 located at Nicaro, 1 located at Punta Movida, 1 located at Mariel

Coastal Defence

ARTY • TOWED • 122mm: some M-1931/37
   130mm: some M-46
   152mm: some M-1937
MSL • TACTICAL • SSM 2+: some Bandera IV (reported); 2 SS-C-3 *Styx*

Naval Infantry 550+

Amph aslt 2 bn

Air Force ε8,000

incl AD and conscripts
Flying hours 50 hrs/year

FORCES BY ROLE

Ftr	2 sqn with up to 3 MIG-21F *Fishbed C*; up to 27 non-operational; 1 sqn with 5 MIG-21bis *Fishbed L & N*; up to 45 non-operational; 1 sqn with up to 3 MiG-29 *Fulcrum*; 10 MiG-23 *Flogger*; up to 10 MiG-23MF *Flogger E* non-operational
FGA	2 sqn with 10 MIG-23BN *Flogger H*
ASW	some sqn with 5 Mi-14 *Haze*
Tpt	4 sqn with 8 AN-2 *Colt*; 1 AN-24 *Coke*; 15 AN-26 *Curl*; 1 AN-30 *Clank*; 2 AN-32 *Cline*; 2 IL-76 *Candid* (Air Force ac in civilian markings); 4 yak-40 *Codling*
Civilian Fleet	some sqn with 1 AN-30 *Clank* (tp); 10 IL-62 *Classic*; 7 TU-154 *Careless*; 12 Yak-42
Atk Hel	some sqn with Mi-25 *Hind D*/Mi-35 *Hind*; 45 MI-17 (Mi-8MT) *Hip H*/Mi-8 *Hip*
Trg	some sqn with 25 L-39 *Albatros*; 8 MIG-21U *Mongol A**; 4 MIG-23U *Flogger**; 2 MIG-29UB *Fulcrum**; 20 Z-326 *Trener Master*
Hel	some sqn with 40 Mi-8 *Hip*

EQUIPMENT BY TYPE

AIRCRAFT 127 combat capable (of which 25 are operational)
  FTR up to 103: up to 3 MiG-29 *Fulcrum*; 10 MiG-23 *Flogger*
    MIG-23 up to 20: up to 10 MiG-23MF *Flogger E* non-operational
    MIG-21 up to 80: up to 3 MIG-21F *Fishbed C*; up to 27 non-operational; 5 MIG-21bis *Fishbed L & N*; up to 45 non-operational
  FGA • MIG-23B 10: 10 MIG-23BN *Flogger H*
  TPT 63: 8 AN-2 *Colt*; 1 AN-24 *Coke*; 15 AN-26 *Curl*; 1 AN-30 *Clank* (tp); 1 more; 2 AN-32 *Cline*; 10 IL-62 *Classic*; 2 IL-76 *Candid* (Air Force ac in civilian markings); 7 TU-154 *Careless*; 4 yak-40 *Codling*; 12 Yak-42
  TRG 59: 25 L-39 *Albatros*; 8 MIG-21U *Mongol A**; 4 MIG-23U *Flogger**
    MIG-29U 2: 2 MIG-29UB *Fulcrum**
    Z-326 *Trener Master* 20
HELICOPTERS
  ATK: some 40 Mi-25 *Hind D*/Mi-35 *Hind*
  ASW 5: 5 Mi-14 *Haze*
  SPT 85: 40 Mi-8 *Hip*
    MI-8 85: 45 MI-17 (Mi-8MT) *Hip H*/Mi-8 *Hip* spt hels
AD • SAM: some SA-3 *Goa*
  TOWED: some SA-2 *Guideline*
MSL • TACTICAL • ASM: some AS-7 *Kerry*
  AAM: some AA-10 *Alamo*; some AA-11 *Archer*; some AA-2 *Atoll*; some AA-7 *Apex*; some AA-8 *Aphid*

FACILITIES

Surface To Air Missile Site	13 with SA-3 *Goa* SAM; SA-2 *Guideline* Towed SAM (active)

Paramilitary 26,500 active

State Security 20,000
Ministry of Interior

Border Guards 6,500
Ministry of Interior
PATROL AND COASTAL COMBATANTS 23+
  MISC BOATS/CRAFT: some boats

PFI 23: 3 Stenka less than 100 tonnes (FSU); 20 Zhuk (FSU)

Youth Labour Army 70,000

Civil Defence Force 50,000

Territorial Militia ε1,000,000 reservists

Dominican Republic DR

Dominican Peso pRD		2003	2004	2005
GDP	pRD	508bn	795bn	
	US$	16.5bn	17.6bn	
per capita	US$	1,896	2,002	
Growth	%	-1.6	2.0	
Inflation	%	27.4	51.5	
Debt	US$	6.29bn		
Def bdgt	pRD	4.78bn	5.36bn	5.49bn
	US$	155m	119m	190m
FMA	US$	–	3.0m	2.1m
US$1=pRD		30.8	45.0	28.8

Population (2004) 9,049,595

Age	0 - 14	15 - 19	20 - 24	25 - 29	30 - 64	65 plus
Male	17%	5%	5%	4%	18%	3%
Female	16%	5%	4%	4%	17%	3%

Capabilities

ACTIVE 24,500 (Army 15,000 Navy 4,000 Air 5,500)
Paramilitary 15,000

ORGANISATIONS BY SERVICE

Army 15,000

FORCES BY ROLE
3 Defence Zones

Armd	1 bn
Inf	6 bde (*total*: 15 inf bn)
SF	1 bn
Mtn Inf	1 bn
Arty	1 bn
Engr	1 bn
Presidential Guard	1 bn

EQUIPMENT BY TYPE
TK • LT TK • M-41 12: 12 M-41A1 (76mm)
APC 28
  APC (T) 20: 20 M-2/M-3 (half-track)
  APC (W) • LAV 8: 8 LAV-150 *Commando*
ARTY 56+
  TOWED • 105mm 28: 28 M-101
  MOR 28+
    81mm: some M-1
    107mm 4: 4 M-30
    120mm 24: 24 ECIA

AT

RCL • 105mm 14: 14 m/45
GUNS • 37mm 20: 20 M3

Navy 4,000

FORCES BY ROLE

Marine Sy 1 unit

Navy 1 HQ located at Santo Domingo

SEAL 1 unit

EQUIPMENT BY TYPE

PATROL AND COASTAL COMBATANTS 15

PCC 1: 1 *Betelgeuse* (US PGM-71)

PCI 9: 7 less than 100 tonnes; 2 Canopus less than 100 tonnes

PCO 5:

1 *Balsam*

2 *Cohoes* each with 2 76mm gun

1 *Prestol* (US *Admirable*) with 1 76mm gun

1 *Sotoyoma* with 1 76mm gun

LOGISTICS AND SUPPORT 4: 1 AOT (small harbour); 3 AT

FACILITIES

Base 1 located at Santo Domingo, 1 located at Las Calderas

Air Force 5,500

Flying hours 60 hrs/year

FORCES BY ROLE

SAR / MP	1 sqn
SF	1 (AB) bn
SAR / Medivac / Hel / Liaison	1 sqn with 9 OH-58 *Kiowa*; 1 OH-6A *Cayuse*; 1 AS-365N *Dauphin 2* (VIP); 2 R-22; 1 SE 3130 *Alouette II*; 4 Schweizer 333; 10 UH-1H *Iroquois*
CCT	1 sqn with 6 A-37B *Dragonfly*
Tpt	1 sqn with 3 CASA 212-400 *Aviocar*; 1 PA-31 *Navajo*; 1 Cessna 207 *Stationair*
Trg	some sqn with 10 EMB-314 *Super Tucano* (to be delivered); 8 T-35B *Pillan*; 1 T-41D *Mescalero*
AD	1 bn with 4 20mm

EQUIPMENT BY TYPE

AIRCRAFT 6 combat capable

FGA • A-37 6: 6 A-37B *Dragonfly*

MP 3: 3 CASA 212-400 *Aviocar*

TPT 1: 1 PA-31 *Navajo*

UTL 1: 1 Cessna 207 *Stationair*

TRG 19: 10 EMB-314 *Super Tucano* (to be delivered)

T-35 8: 8 T-35B *Pillan*

T-41 1: 1 T-41D *Mescalero*

HELICOPTERS

OBS 10: 9 OH-58 *Kiowa*

OH-6 1: 1 OH-6A *Cayuse*

UTL 18

AS-365 1: 1 AS-365N *Dauphin 2* (VIP)

R-22 2; 1 SE 3130 *Alouette II*; 4 Schweizer 333

UH-1 10: 10 UH-1H *Iroquois*

AD • GUNS 4: 4 20mm

Paramilitary 15,000

National Police 15,000

DEPLOYMENT

CÔTE D'IVOIRE

UN • ONUCI 4 obs

Ecuador Ec

Ecuadorian Sucre ES		2003	2004	2005
GDP	ES	677tr	757tr	
	US$	27.1bn	30.2bn	
per capita	US$	2,071	2,291	
Growth	%	2.7	6.6	
Inflation	%	7.9	2.7	
Debt	US$	16.8bn		
Def bdgt	ES	16.0tr	14.7tr	14.8tr
	US$	640m	588m	593m
FMA	US$	1.6m	–	1.3m
US$1=ES		25k	25k	25k

Population (2004) 13,363,593

Age	0 - 14	15 - 19	20 - 24	25 - 29	30 - 64	65 plus
Male	17%	5%	5%	4%	16%	2%
Female	16%	5%	5%	4%	17%	3%

Capabilities

ACTIVE 46,500 (Army 37,000 Navy 5,500 Air 4,000)

Paramilitary 270

Terms of Service conscription 1 year, selective

RESERVE 118,000 (Joint 118,000)

Ages 18–55

ORGANISATIONS BY SERVICE

Army 37,000

FORCES BY ROLE

Army	3 (hy mor) coy; 4 (org, composition varies) div (total: 1 engr bde, 1 Avn bde, 1 armd bde, 1 SF bde, 1 arty bde, 3 (jungle) army bde, 5 inf bde)
Armd cav	8 gp
Armd Recce	3 sqn
Mech Inf	2 bn
Inf	13 bn; 10 (jungle) bn
AB / SF	6 bn
Arty	6 gp
SP Arty	1 gp
MRL	1 gp
ADA	1 gp
Engr	3 bn

Avn   5 bn

EQUIPMENT BY TYPE
TK 180+
  MBT 30+: 30+ T-55†
  LT TK 150: 150 AMX-13
RECCE 90+
  AML 50+: 50+ AML-60/AML-90
  EE-3 *Jararaca* 10; 30 EE-9 *Cascavel*
APC 130
  APC (T) 100: 80 AMX-VCI; 20 M-113
  APC (W) 30: 30 EE-11 *Urutu*
ARTY 156+
  TOWED 128
    105mm 104: 30 M-101
    M-2 50: 50 M-2A2
    Model 56 pack howitzer 24
    155mm 24: 12 M-114; 12 M-198
  SP • 155mm 10: 10 Mk F3
  MRL • 122mm 6: 6 RM-70 *Dana*
  MOR 12+
    81mm: some M-29
    107mm: some M-30 (4.2in)
    160mm 12: 12 M-66 *Soltam*
AT • RCL 404
  106mm • M-40 24: 24 M-40A1
  90mm 380: 380 M-67
AIRCRAFT • TPT 11: 1 *Beech* 100 *King Air*; 1 *Beech* 200
Super King Air; 1 CN-235; 1 *Cessna* 500 *Citation I*
  DHC-5 1: 1 DHC-5D *Buffalo*
  IAI-201 *Arava* 5; 1 PC-6 *Turbo-Porter*
HELICOPTERS
  ATK 20: 20 SA-342 *Gazelle*
  SPT 10: 4 AS-332 *Super Puma*; 1 AS-350 *Ecureuil*
  MI-8 5: 5 Mi-8MT *Hip H*
  UTL • SA-315 2: 2 SA-315B *Lama*
AD
  SAM 165+
    SP: some SA-8 *Gecko*
    MANPAD 165+: 75 *Blowpipe*; some Chaparral; some
    SA-16 *Gimlet*; 90 SA-18 *Grouse (Igla)* (reported); some
    SA-7 *Grail*
  GUNS 260
    14.5mm • TOWED • ZPU 128: 128 ZPU-1/ZPU-2
    20mm • TOWED 20: 20 M-1935
    23mm • TOWED 34: 34 ZU-23
    35mm • TOWED • GDF 30: 30 GDF-002 (twin)
    37mm • TOWED 18: 18 Ch
    40mm • TOWED 30: 30 L/70

Navy 5,500

EQUIPMENT BY TYPE
SUBMARINES • TACTICAL • SSK 2:
  2 Shyri (Ge T-209/1300) each with 8 single 533mm TT
  with 14 SUT HWT
PRINCIPAL SURFACE COMBATANTS 8
  FRIGATES • FFG 2:
    2 Presidente Eloy Alfaro (ex UK Leander batch II) each
    with 1 Bell 206B *JetRanger II* utl hels, 4 single each with
    1 MM-38 *Exocet* tactical SSM, 3 twin (6 eff.) each with
    Mistral SAM
  CORVETTES • FSG 6:

6 Esmeraldas each with 2 B515 *ILAS-3* triple 324mm
each with A244 LWT, 1 Quad (4 eff.) with 1 Aspide
SAM, 2 triple (6 eff.) each with 1 MM-40 *Exocet* tactical
SSM, 1 76mm gun, 1 hel Landing Platform
PATROL AND COASTAL COMBATANTS • PFM 5:
  2 Manta† (Ge Lurssen 36m) each with 4 single each with
  1 GII *Gabriel II* tactical SSM
  3 Quito (Ge Lurssen 45m) each with 4 single each with 1
  MM-38 *Exocet* tactical SSM, 1 76mm gun
AMPHIBIOUS • LS • LST 1:
  1 Hualcopo (capacity 150 troops) (US LST-512-1152)
LOGISTICS AND SUPPORT 7: 1 AE (Ammo) *Aux Ammo*;
1 AGOR *Research Vsl*; 2 AOT *Tkr* (small); 2 ATF *Ocean Tug*;
1 Trg (sail)

FACILITIES
Base   1 (main base) located at Guayaquil,
              1 located at Galápagos Islands
Naval airbase 1 located at Jaramijo

Naval Aviation 250

AIRCRAFT
  TPT 5: 3 *Beech* 200 *Super King Air*; 1 *Beech* 300 *Super
  King Air*; 1 CN-235
  TRG • T-34 3: 3 T-34C *Turbo Mentor*
HELICOPTERS
  UTL 6: 4 Bell 206 *JetRanger*
    BELL 412 2: 2 Bell 412EP *twin Huey*
  TRG 4: 4 TH-57 *Sea Ranger*

Marines 1,700

Cdo   1 bn (no hy wpn/veh)
Marine 2 bn (on garrison duties)

Air Force 4,000

FORCES BY ROLE
AB 1 sqn

EQUIPMENT BY TYPE
MSL • TACTICAL • AAM: some Python III; some Python
IV; some R-550 *Magic*
  R530: some Super 530
  Shafrir some

Military Air Transport Group

FORCES BY ROLE
SAR / Liaison some sqn with 2 AS-332 *Super Puma*; 1
               SA-330 *Puma*; 6 Bell 206B *JetRanger II*;
               1 Bell 212; 5 SA-316B *Alouette III*
Tpt   1 TAME sqn with 3 B-727; 5 C-130B
               Hercules/C-130H *Hercules*; 3 DHC-6 *twin
               Otter*; 1 F-28 *Fellowship*; 1 L-100-30
Liaison   some sqn with 1 *Beech* E90 *King Air*; 1
               Gaviao 60
Civilian Fleet 1 ECUATORIANA sqn with 2 A-310; 3
               B-707-320; 1 DC-10-30
Trg   some sqn with 22 AT-33 *Shooting Star**; 5
               Cessna 172; 20 *Cessna* 150; 17 T-34C *Turbo
               Mentor*; 1 T-41 *Mescalero*

EQUIPMENT BY TYPE
AIRCRAFT 22 combat capable

FGA 22: 22 AT-33 *Shooting Star**
TPT 26: 2 A-310
    B-707 3: 3 B-707-320
    B-727 3; 5 BAe-748
    BEECH 90 1: 1 *Beech E90 King Air*
    C-130 5: 5 C-130B *Hercules*/C-130H *Hercules*
    DC-10 1: 1 DC-10-30
    DHC-6 *twin Otter* 3; 1 F-28 *Fellowship*
    L-100 1: 1 L-100-30
    Gaviao **60** 1
    UTL 5: 5 *Cessna* 172
    TRG 38: 20 *Cessna* 150
    T-34 17: 17 T-34C *Turbo Mentor*
    T-41 *Mescalero* 1
HELICOPTERS
    SPT 3: 2 AS-332 *Super Puma*; 1 SA-330 *Puma*
    UTL 12
    BELL 206 6: 6 Bell 206B *JetRanger II*
    Bell 212 1
    SA-316 5: 5 SA-316B *Alouette III*

Operational Command

FORCES BY ROLE
Air   2 wg
Ftr   1 sqn with 13 *Mirage* F-1JE (F-1E); 1 *Mirage* F-1JB (F-1B)
FGA 1 sqn with 26 A-37B *Dragonfly*; 1 sqn with 11 Kfir C-2; 3 Kfir TC-2; 1 sqn with 6 Jaguar S(E) (Jaguar S International)†; 2 Jaguar B(E) (SEPECAT Jaguar International B)†
CCT some sqn with 8 BAC-167 MK 89A *Strikemaster*

EQUIPMENT BY TYPE
AIRCRAFT 56 combat capable
  FTR • **F-1** 13: 13 *Mirage* F-1JE (F-1E)
  FGA 43
    A-37 26: 26 A-37B *Dragonfly*
    Kfir C-2 11; 6 Jaguar S(E) (Jaguar S International)†
  TRG 14
    BAC-167 • **BAC-167 MK 89** 8: 8 BAC-167 MK 89A *Strikemaster*
    Jaguar B(E) (SEPECAT Jaguar International B) 2†; 3 Kfir TC-2; 1 *Mirage* F-1JB (F-1B)

Paramilitary • Coast Guard 270

PATROL AND COASTAL COMBATANTS up to 12
  MISC BOATS/CRAFT up to 8: up to 8 boats
  PCC 2: 2 5 de Agosto
  PCI 2: 1 PGM-71; 1 Point

Armed Forces 118,000 reservists (Ages 18-55)

DEPLOYMENT

CÔTE D'IVOIRE
UN • ONUCI 2 obs

HAITI
UN • MINUSTAH 67

LIBERIA
UN • UNMIL 3 obs; 1

El Salvador EIS

El Salvador Colon C		2003	2004	2005
GDP	C	129bn	137bn	
	US$	14.8bn	15.7bn	
per capita	US$	2,296	2,394	
Growth	%	1.8	1.5	
Inflation	%	2.5	4.5	
Debt	US$	7.08bn		
Def bdgt	C	927m	926m	929m
	US$	106m	105m	106m
FMA	US$	3.6m	6.5m	3.1m
US$1=C		8.75	8.75	8.75

Population (2004) 6,704,932

Age	0 - 14	15 - 19	20 - 24	25 - 29	30 - 64	65 plus
Male	19%	5%	5%	4%	14%	2%
Female	18%	5%	5%	4%	16%	3%

Capabilities

ACTIVE 15,500 (Army 13,850 Navy 700 Air 950)
Terms of Service conscription 1 year, selective

RESERVE 9,900 (Joint 9,900)

ORGANISATIONS BY SERVICE

Army 9,850; 4,000 conscript (total 13,850)

FORCES BY ROLE
6 Military Zones
Army   1 (special sy) bde (2 Border Guard bn, 2 MP bn)
Armd cav 1 regt (2 armd cav bn)
Inf   6 bde (*each*: 1 inf bn); 8 (bn) det
Spec Ops 1 gp (1 SF coy, 1 Para bn, 1 (naval inf) army coy)
Arty   1 bde (1 AD bn, 2 fd arty bn)
Engr   1 comd (2 engr bn)

EQUIPMENT BY TYPE
RECCE • **AML** 10: 10 AML-90 (2 in store)
APC • **APC (W)** 51: 41 M-37B1 *Cashuat* (mod); 10 UR-416
ARTY 600+
  TOWED • **105mm** 50: 8 M-101 in store; 24 M-102; 18 M-56
  MOR 550+
    60mm 306: 306 M-19
    81mm 151+: some; 151 M-29
    120mm 93+: some M-74 in store; 93 UBM 52
AT
  RCL 399
    106mm • **M-40** 20: 20 M-40A1 (incl 16 SP)
    90mm 379: 379 M-67
  RL • **94mm** 791: 791 LAW
AD • **GUNS** • **20mm** • **TOWED** 35: 31 M-55; 4 TCM-20

Air Force ε750; ε200 conscript (total 950)

Flying hours 90 hrs/year on A-37 *Dragonfly* FGA ac

FORCES BY ROLE

incl AD

FGA / RECCE	some sqn with 5 A-37B *Dragonfly*; 10 O-2A *Skymaster*/O-2B *Skymaster*; 4 OA-37B *Dragonfly*; 2 CM-170 *Magister*
Tpt	1 sqn with 1 Bell 407; 4 Bell 412 *twin Huey*; 7 MD-500; 22 UH-1H *Iroquois* (incl 4 SAR); 1+ sqn with 3 Basler Turbo-67; 2 C-47R *Skytrain*; 1 Cessna 337G *Skymaster*; 1 SA-226T *Merlin IIIB*; 2 Cessna 210 *Centurion*
Trg	some sqn with 5 Rallye 235GT; 5 T-35 *Pillan*; 1 T-41D *Mescalero*; 6 TH-300
Hel	some (armed) sqn with 5 UH-1M *Iroquois*

EQUIPMENT BY TYPE

AIRCRAFT 21 combat capable

FGA • A-37 5: 5 A-37B *Dragonfly*

RECCE 14

O-2 10: 10 O-2A *Skymaster*/O-2B *Skymaster**

OBS • OA-37 4: 4 OA-37B *Dragonfly**

TPT 7: 3 Basler Turbo-67

C-47 2: 2 C-47R *Skytrain*

CESSNA 337 1: 1 Cessna 337G *Skymaster*

SA-226 1: 1 SA-226T *Merlin IIIB*

UTL 2: 2 Cessna 210 *Centurion*

TRG 13: 2 CM-170 *Magister*

RALLYE 235 5: 5 Rallye 235GT

T-35 *Pillan* 5

T-41 1: 1 T-41D *Mescalero*

HELICOPTERS

UTL 39: 1 Bell 407; 4 Bell 412 *twin Huey*; 7 MD-500

UH-1 27: 22 UH-1H *Iroquois* (incl 4 SAR); 5 UH-1M *Iroquois **

TRG 6: 6 TH-300

MSL • TACTICAL • AAM: some *Shafrir*

Navy 700 (incl some 90 Naval Inf and spt forces)

EQUIPMENT BY TYPE

PATROL AND COASTAL COMBATANTS 38

MISC BOATS/CRAFT 33: 33 river boats

PCC 3: 3 Camcraft (30m)

PCI *Patrol craft inshore* 2 less than 100 tonnes

FACILITIES

Base	1 located at La Unión
Minor Base	1 located at La Libertad, 1 located at Acajutla, 1 located at El Triunfo, 1 located at Guija Lake

Naval Infantry 90+

Sy 1 coy

Paramilitary 12,000

National Civilian Police 12,000+

Ministry of Public Security

small arms

PATROL AND COASTAL COMBATANTS • MISC BOATS/CRAFT 10: 10 river boats

AIRCRAFT • RECCE • O-2 1: 1 O-2A *Skymaster*

HELICOPTERS • UTL 3

MD-500 1: 1 MD-500D

MD-520 1: 1 MD-520N

UH-1 1: 1 UH-1H *Iroquois*

Armed Forces 9,900+ reservists (registered)

DEPLOYMENT

IRAQ

Army 360 (Peace Support)

CÔTE D'IVOIRE

UN • UNOCI 3 obs

LIBERIA

UN • UNMIL 3 obs

SUDAN

UN • UNMIS 5 obs

WESTERN SAHARA

UN • MINURSO 5 obs

Guatemala Gua

Guatemalan Quetzal q		2003	2004	2005
GDP	q	195bn	212bn	
	US$	24.7bn	27.0bn	
per capita	US$	1,776	1,892	
Growth	%	2.2	2.6	
Inflation	%	5.9	7.0	
Debt	US$	4.98bn		
Def bdgt	q	1.41bn	879m	767m
	US$	178m	111m	101m
US$1=q		7.93	7.88	7.6

Population (2004)   12,013,907

Age	0 - 14	15 - 19	20 - 24	25 - 29	30 - 64	65 plus
Male	21%	6%	5%	4%	13%	2%
Female	20%	6%	5%	4%	14%	2%

Capabilities

ACTIVE 29,200 (Army 27,000 Navy 1,500 Air 700)
Paramilitary 19,000 Inactive Other 2,500
Terms of Service conscription 30 months, selective

RESERVE 35,200 (Army 35,000 Navy some Air 200)
(National Armed Forces are combined; the Army provides log spt for navy and Air Force)

ORGANISATIONS BY SERVICE

Army ε4,000; ε23,000 conscript (total 27,000)

FORCES BY ROLE

15 Military Zones

Army	1 (frontier) det; 2 (strategic) bde (*total:* 1 Recce sqn, 1 (lt) armd bn, 2 arty bty, 4 inf bn)
Armd	6 sqn
Inf	22 bn; 5 (bn) gp (*each:* 1 arty bty, 1 Recce sqn, 1 inf bn)
SF	1 gp (1 Trg coy, 2 SF coy)

AB   2 bn
Engr   1 bn
Presidential Guard   1 bn (to be disbanded)
Trg   1 bn

EQUIPMENT BY TYPE
RECCE 16: 7 M-8 in store; 9 RBY-1 *RAMTA*
APC 52
  APC (T) 15: 10 M-113; 5 in store
  APC (W) 37: 30 Armadillo; 7 V-100 *Commando*
ARTY 161
  TOWED • 105mm 76: 12 M-101; 8 M-102; 56 M-56
  MOR 85
    81mm 55: 55 M-1
    107mm 12: 12 M-30 in store
    120mm 18: 18 ECIA
AT • RCL 120+
  105mm 64: 64 M-1974 FMK-1 (Arg)
  106mm • M-40 56: 56 M-40A1
  75mm: some M-20
  RL • 89mm: some M-20 in store (3.5in)
AD • GUNS • 20mm • TOWED 32: 16 GAI-D01; 16 M-55

Reserves ε35,000 reservists (trained)
inf ε19 bn

Navy ε1,500
EQUIPMENT BY TYPE
PATROL AND COASTAL COMBATANTS 35
  PBI 6: 6 Vigilante
  PCI 9: 6 Cutlas less than 100 tonnes; 1 Kukulkan less than 100 tonnes (US Broadsword 32m); 2 Stewart less than 100 tonnes
  PCR *Patrol Craft Riverine* 20
FACILITIES
Base 1 located at Santo Tomás de Castilla, 1 located at Puerto Quetzal

Marines ε650; some reservists (total 650)
Marine 2 bn under strength

Air Force 700; 200 reservists (total 900)
FORCES BY ROLE
Serviceability of ac is less than 50%
FGA /Trg   1 sqn with 4 A-37B *Dragonfly*; 1 sqn with 6 PC-7 *Turbo Trainer*
Tpt   1 sqn with 4 Basler Turbo-67; 1 *Beech* 100 *King Air*; 1 *Beech* 90 *King Air*; 2 F-27 *Friendship*; 4 IAI-201 *Arava*; 1 PA-31 *Navajo*
Liaison   1 sqn with 1 *Cessna* 310; 2 *Cessna* 206
Trg   some sqn with 5 *Cessna* R172K *Hawk XP*; 5 T-35B *Pillan*; 6 T-41 *Mescalero*
Hel   1 sqn with 9 Bell 206 *JetRanger*; 9 Bell 212 (armed); 3 Bell 412 *twin Huey* (armed); 3 S-76; 3 UH-1H *Iroquois*

EQUIPMENT BY TYPE
AIRCRAFT 10 combat capable
  FGA • A-37 4: 4 A-37B *Dragonfly*
  TPT 14: 4 Basler Turbo-67; 1 *Beech* 100 *King Air*; 1 *Beech* 90 *King Air*; 1 *Cessna* 310; 2 F-27 *Friendship*; 4 IAI-201 *Arava*;

1 PA-31 *Navajo*
  UTL 2: 2 *Cessna* 206
  TRG 22: 5 *Cessna* R172K *Hawk XP*; 6 PC-7 *Turbo Trainer*
    T-35 5: 5 T-35B *Pillan*
    T-41 *Mescalero* 6
HELICOPTERS
  UTL 27: 9 Bell 206 *JetRanger*; 9 Bell 212 (armed); 3 Bell 412* *twin Huey** (armed); 3 S-76
  UH-1 3: 3 UH-1H *Iroquois*

Tactical Security Group
Air Military Police
Armd   1 sqn
CCT   3 coy
AD   1 bty (army units for air-base sy)

Paramilitary 19,000 active

National Police 19,000
Army   1 (integrated task force) unit (incl mil and treasury police)
SF   1 bn
Paramilitary   21 (departments) region

Treasury Police 2,500

DEPLOYMENT

BURUNDI
UN • ONUB 1; 4 obs

CÔTE D'IVOIRE
UN • UNOCI 5 obs

DEMOCRATIC REPUBLIC OF CONGO
UN • MONUC 4 obs; 107

HAITI
UN • MINUSTAH 83

SUDAN
UN • UNMIS 6 obs

Guyana Guy

Guyanese Dollar G$		2003	2004	2005
GDP	G$	149bn	155bn	
	US$	777m	865m	
per capita	US$	1,021	1,134	
Growth	%	-0.7	1.6	
Inflation	%	6.0	4.7	
Debt	US$	1.44bn		
Def bdgt	G$	e 1.03bn	e 1.03bn	e 1.05bn
	US$	5.38m	5.81m	5.92m
US$1=G$		193	179	179

Population (2004)   765,283

Age	0 - 14	15 - 19	20 - 24	25 - 29	30 - 64	65 plus
Male	13%	5%	5%	5%	19%	2%
Female	13%	5%	5%	5%	20%	3%

Capabilities

ACTIVE 1,100 (Army 900 Navy 100 Air 100)
Paramilitary 1,500
Active numbers combined Guyana Defence Force

RESERVE 670 (Army 500 Navy 170)

ORGANISATIONS BY SERVICE

Army 900; 500 reservists (total 1,400)

FORCES BY ROLE

Inf	1 bn
SF	1 coy
Engr	1 coy
Spt	1 (spt wpn) coy
Presidential Guard	1 bn

EQUIPMENT BY TYPE
RECCE 9: 6 EE-9 *Cascavel* (reported); 3 S52 *Shorland*
ARTY 54
   TOWED • 130mm 6: 6 M-46†
   MOR 48
     81mm 12: 12 L16A1
     82mm 18: 18 M-43
     120mm 18: 18 M-43

Navy 100; 170 reservists (total 270)

EQUIPMENT BY TYPE
PATROL AND COASTAL COMBATANTS 3
  MISC BOATS/CRAFT 2: 2 boats
  PCC 1: 1 Orwell
FACILITIES
Base 1 located at Georgetown, 1 located at New
   Providence Island, Bs

Air Force 100

FORCES BY ROLE
Tpt some sqn with 2 SC.7 3M *Skyvan*; 1 Y-12; 1 Bell 206
   JetRanger; 1 Bell 412 *twin Huey*

EQUIPMENT BY TYPE
AIRCRAFT • TPT 3: 2 SC.7 3M *Skyvan*; 1 Y-12
HELICOPTERS • UTL 2: 1 Bell 206 *JetRanger*; 1 Bell 412
twin Huey

Paramilitary 1,500+

Guyana People's Militia 1,500+

DEPLOYMENT

BAHAMAS
Navy
Base 1 located at New Providence Island, Bs

Haiti RH

Haitian Gourde G		2003	2004	2005
GDP	G	118bn	138bn	
	US$	2.81bn	4.27bn	
per capita	US$	362	538	
Growth	%	0.4	-3.5	
Inflation	%	32.5	27.1	
Debt	US$	1.3bn		
US$1=G		42.3	32.5	38

Population   8,121,622

Age	0 - 14	15 - 19	20 - 24	25 - 29	30 - 64	65 plus
Male	21%	6%	5%	4%	11%	2%
Female	21%	6%	5%	4%	12%	2%

Capabilities

No active armed forces. On June 1st 2004 following a period of armed conflict the United Nations established a multi national stabilisation mission in Haiti (MINUSTAH). The mission has an authorised strength of up to 6700 military personnel and 1622 civilian police. A National Police Force of some 2000 pers remains operational.

FOREIGN FORCES

Argentina 558	**Jordan** 755
Bolivia 4	**Morocco** 167
Brazil 1,213	**Nepal** 758
Canada 3	**Paraguay** 3
Chile 542	**Peru** 210
Croatia 1	**Philippines** 157
Ecuador 67	**Spain** 202
France 3	**Sri Lanka** 754
Guatemala 83	**Uruguay** 779

Honduras Hr

Honduran Lempira L		2003	2004	2005
GDP	L	119bn	136bn	
	US$	6.93bn	7.52bn	
per capita	US$	1,039	1,102	
Growth	%	3.5	4.2	
Inflation	%	7.7	8.1	
Debt	US$	5.64bn		
Def bdgt	L	917m	949m	988m
	US$	53m	52.1m	52.4m
FMA	US$	1.6m	3.7m	2.1m
US$1=L		17.3	18.21	18.85

Population (2004)   7,167902

Age	0 - 14	15 - 19	20 - 24	25 - 29	30 - 64	65 plus
Male	21%	6%	5%	4%	13%	2%
Female	20%	6%	5%	4%	14%	2%

Capabilities

ACTIVE 12,000 (Army 8,300 Navy 1,400 Air 2,300)
Paramilitary 8,000

RESERVE 60,000 (Joint 60,000)

ORGANISATIONS BY SERVICE

Army 8,300

FORCES BY ROLE

6 Military Zones

Armd cav	1 regt (1 Lt tk sqn, 1 ADA bty, 1 arty bty, 1 Recce sqn, 2 Mech bn)
Inf	1 bde (3 inf bn); 3 bde (each: 1 arty bn, 3 inf bn)
Spec Ops	1 (special tac) gp (1 SF bn, 1 (inf) AB bn)
Engr	1 bn
Presidential Guard	1 coy

EQUIPMENT BY TYPE
TK • LT TK 12: 12 Scorpion
RECCE 57: 13 RBY-1 *RAMTA*; 40 Saladin; 3 Scimitar; 1 Sultan
ARTY 118+
   TOWED 28
      105mm 24: 24 M-102
      155mm 4: 4 M-198
   MOR 90+: some 60mm; some 81mm
      120mm 60: 60 FMK-2
      160mm 30: 30 M-66 *Soltam*
AT • RCL 170
   106mm • M-40 50: 50 M-40A1
   84mm 120: 120 Carl Gustav
AD • GUNS • 20mm • TOWED 48
   M-55 24: 24 M-55A2
   TCM-20 24

Reserves
Inf 1 bde

Navy 1,400

EQUIPMENT BY TYPE
PATROL AND COASTAL COMBATANTS 31
   MISC BOATS/CRAFT 15: 15 river boats
   PBR *Patrol boat riverine* 5 less than 100 tonnes
   PC 7: 6 *Swift* 21m; 1 *Swift* 26m
   PFC 3: 3 Guaymuras (US Swiftship 31m)
   PFI 1: 1 Copan less than 100 tonnes (US Guardian 32m)
AMPHIBIOUS • CRAFT • LCT 1: 1 Punta Caxinas

FACILITIES
Base 1 located at Puerto Cortés, 1 located at Puerto
   Castilla, 1 located at Amapala

Marines 830
Marine 3 indep coy under strength

Air Force 2,300

FORCES BY ROLE

FGA	1 sqn with 8 A-37B *Dragonfly*; 1 sqn with 8 F-5E *Tiger II*
Tpt	some sqn with 1 C-130A *Hercules*; 2 C-47 *Skytrain*; 1 L-188 *Electra*
Trg / COIN	some sqn with 2 CASA C-101CC *Aviojet**; 2 *Cessna* 182 *Skylane*
Liaison	some sqn with 4 *Cessna* 185; 1 *Cessna* 401; 1 PA-31 *Navajo*; 1 PA-32T *Saratoga*; 1 Rockwell Commander 114
Hel	some sqn with 1 A-109 (VIP); 5 Bell 412SP *twin Huey*; 2 Hughes 500; 2 UH-1H *Iroquois*

EQUIPMENT BY TYPE
AIRCRAFT 18 combat capable
   FTR • F-5 8: 8 F-5E *Tiger II*
   FGA 15
      A-37 8: 8 A-37B *Dragonfly*
      B2 *Super Mystére* 5 in store; 2 CASA C-101CC *Aviojet**
   TPT 13
      C-130 1: 1 C-130A *Hercules*
      C-47 *Skytrain* 2; 2 *Cessna* 182 *Skylane*; 4 *Cessna* 185; 1 *Cessna* 401; 1 L-188 *Electra*; 1 PA-31 *Navajo*
      PA-32 1: 1 PA-32T *Saratoga*
   UTL 1: 1 Rockwell Commander 114
HELICOPTERS
   UTL 10: 1 A-109 (VIP)
   BELL 412 5: 5 Bell 412SP *twin Huey*
   Hughes **500** 2
   UH-1 2: 2 UH-1H *Iroquois*
MSL • TACTICAL • AAM: some *Shafrir*

Paramilitary 8,000

Public Security Forces 8,000
Ministry of Public Security and Defence
Region 11 comd

Armed Forces 60,000 reservists (Ex-servicemen registered)

DEPLOYMENT

WESTERN SAHARA
UN • MINURSO 12 obs

Jamaica Ja

Jamaican Dollar J$		2003	2004	2005
GDP	J$	469bn	540bn	
	US$	8.14bn	8.91bn	
per capita	US$	3,021	3,285	
Growth	%	2.0	2.5	
Inflation	%	12.9	11.5	
Debt	US$	5.58bn		
Def bdgt	J$	2.98bn	3.23bn	3.51bn
	US$	51.8m	53.2m	57.5m
FMA	US$	1.3m	1.3m	1.3m
US$1=J$		57.7	60.7	61

Population (2004)   2,735,520.52

Age	0 - 14	15 - 19	20 - 24	25 - 29	30 - 64	65 plus
Male	17%	5%	5%	4%	15%	3%
Female	17%	5%	5%	4%	15%	4%

Capabilities

ACTIVE 2,830 (Army 2,500 Navy 190 Air 140)
(combined Jamaican Defence Force)

RESERVE 953 (Army 877 Navy 60 Air 16)

ORGANISATIONS BY SERVICE

Army 2,500; 877 reservists (total 3,377)

FORCES BY ROLE
Inf   2 bn
Engr   1 regt (4 engr sqn)
Spt   1 bn

EQUIPMENT BY TYPE
APC • APC (W) • LAV 4: 4 LAV-150 *Commando*
ARTY • MOR • 81mm 12: 12 L16A1

Reserves
Inf 1 bn

Coast Guard 190; 60 reservists (total 250)

EQUIPMENT BY TYPE
PATROL AND COASTAL COMBATANTS 9
    PCI 6: 4 Dauntless; 2 Point less than 100 tonnes
    PFC 1: 1 Fort Charles (US 34m)
    PFI 2: 1 Holland Bay less than 100 tonnes; 1 Paul Bogle
    less than 100 tonnes (US-31m)
FACILITIES
Base   1 located at Port Royal, 1 located at Pedro Cays
Minor Base 1 located at Discovery Bay

Air Wing 140; 16 reservists (total 156)
plus National Reserve

FORCES BY ROLE
Tpt / MP   1 flt with 1 BN-2A *Defender* non-operational; 1
           Beech 90 *King Air* non-operational; 1 *Cessna* 210
           Centurion non-operational
SAR / Tpt 2 flt with 4 AS-355 *Ecureuil*; 4 Bell 206 *JetRanger*
           non-operational; 3 Bell 412 *twin Huey*

EQUIPMENT BY TYPE
All apart from 4 AS-355 and 3 Bell 412 reported as
grounded.
AIRCRAFT
   TPT 2
      BN-2 DEFENDER 1: 1 BN-2A *Defender* non-
      operational
      Beech 90 *King Air* 1 non-operational
   UTL 1: 1 *Cessna* 210 *Centurion* non-operational
HELICOPTERS
   SPT 4: 4 AS-355 *Ecureuil*
   UTL 7: 4 Bell 206 *JetRanger* non-operational; 3 Bell 412
   twin Huey

Mexico Mex

Mexican Peso NP		2003	2004	2005
GDP	NP	6.89tr	7.63tr	
	US$	638bn	664bn	
per capita	US$	6,151	6,335	
Growth	%	1.6	4.4	
Inflation	%	4.5	4.7	
Debt	US$	140bn		
Def bdgtᵃ	NP	31.7bn	31.8bn	33.7bn
	US$	2.93bn	2.77bn	3.09bn
FMA	US$	–	1.3m	1.2m
US$1=NP		10.8	11.48	10.9

Population (2004)   106,202,903

Age	0 - 14	15 - 19	20 - 24	25 - 29	30 - 64	65 plus
Male	16%	5%	4%	4%	17%	2%
Female	15%	5%	5%	4%	19%	3%

Capabilities

ACTIVE 192,770 (Army 144,000 Navy 37,000 Air
11,770) **Paramilitary 11,000**
Terms of service 1 year conscripts (4 hours per week) by
lottery

RESERVE 300,000 (Joint 300,000) **Paramilitary
14,000**

ORGANISATIONS BY SERVICE

Army 84,000; ε60,000 conscript (total 144,000)

FORCES BY ROLE
12 Military Regions
Army 3 corps HQ (*each:* 3 inf bde)
Mil   44 (garrisons) zone (*total:* 1 mech inf bn, 19 (mot)
      cav regt, 3 arty regt, 44 (air-mobile) SF unit, 80 inf
      bn)

EQUIPMENT BY TYPE
RECCE 264: 25 (MOWAG); 119 ERC-90F *Sagaie*; 40 M-8; 40
MAC-1; 40 VBL
APC 862+
   APC (T) 567: 495 AMX-VCI; 40 HWK-11
      M-2 32: 32 M-2A1 *Half-track*
   APC (W) 295+: 95 BDX
      BTR: some BTR-60 (reported)
      DN 134: 24 DN-3 *Sedena 1000*; 40 DN-4 *Cabello*; 70 DN-
      5 *Toro*
      LAV 26: 26 LAV-150 ST
      VCR/TT 40
ARTY 1774
   TOWED 194
      75mm 18: 18 M-116 pack
      105mm 176: 16 M-2A1/M-3; 80 M-101; 80 M-56
   SP • 75mm 5: 5 DN-5 *Bufalo*
   MOR 1575: 1,500 81mm
      120mm 75: 75 Brandt

AT

MSL: some Milan (incl 8 VBL)
RL • 82mm: some B-300
GUNS • 37mm 30: 30 M3

AD

SAM • MANPAD: some RBS-70
GUNS 80
    12.7mm • TOWED 40: 40 M-55
    20mm • TOWED 40: 40 GAI-B01

Strategic Reserve

Armd   4 bde (*each:* 1 mech inf bn, 1 arty regt, 1 AT gp, 2 armd Recce regt)

AB   1 bde (3 AB bn)

Engr   1 bde

MP   1 bde (1 armd cav regt, 3 MP bn)

Navy 37,000

COMMANDS: Gulf (6 zones), Pacific (11 zones)

FORCES BY ROLE

Navy 1 HQ located at Acapulco; 1 HQ (exercise) located at Vera Cruz

EQUIPMENT BY TYPE

PRINCIPAL SURFACE COMBATANTS 11
  DESTROYERS • DD 1:
    1 Ilhuicamina (ex Quetzacoatl, US Gearing) with 1 BO-105 utl hels, 2 twin 127mm gun (4 eff.)
  FRIGATES • FF 10:
    1 Comodoro Manuel Azueta (US Edsall, trg) with 2 76mm gun
    2 H Galeana (US Bronstein) each with 2 triple ASTT (6 eff.) each with Mk 46 LWT, 1 Mk 112 Octuple (8 eff.) with tactical ASROC, 1 hel Landing Platform
    3 Hindalgo each with 1 127mm gun
    4 Knox each with 1 BO-105 utl hels, 1 Mk 29 GMLS with Sea Sparrow SAM, 1 Mk16 Mk 112 Octuple with ASROC/RGM-84C Harpoon SSM, 2 twin TT (4 eff.) each with Mk 46 LWT, 1 127mm gun
PATROL AND COASTAL COMBATANTS 109
  PCC 41: 31 Azteca; 3 Cabo (US Cape Higgon); 7 Tamiahua (US Polimar)
  PCI 6: 4 Isla less than 100 tonnes (US Halter); 2 Punta less than 100 tonnes (US Point)
  PCR *Patrol Craft Riverine* 18 less than 100 tonnes
  PCO 44:
    1 Centenario
    1 Guanajuato with 2 102mm gun
    4 Holzinger 2000 each with 1 MD-902 *Explorer* MR RECCE
    17 Leandro Valle (US Auk MSF)
    11 Negrete each with 1 BO-105 utl hels
    4 S J Holzinger (ex-Uxmal, imp Uribe) each with 1 BO-105 utl hels
    6 Uribe (Sp 'Halcon') each with 1 BO-105 utl hels
AMPHIBIOUS • LS • LST 3: 1 Grijalva (US-511); 2 Panuco (US-511)
LOGISTICS AND SUPPORT 19: 2 AGHS (Svy) *Svy Vsl*; 3 AGOR *Research Vsl*; 4 AK *Cargo Ship*; 1 AOT *Tkr*; 6 ATF *Ocean Tug*; 2 spt (log spt); 1 Trg (sail)

FACILITIES

Base 1 located at Vera Cruz, 1 located at Tampico, 1 located at Chetumal, 1 located at Ciudad del Carmen, 1 located at Yukalpetén, 1 located at Lerna, 1 located at Frontera, 1 located at Coatzacoalcos, 1 located at Isla Mujéres, 1 located at Acapulco, 1 located at Ensenada, 1 located at La Paz, 1 located at Guaymas, 1 located at Mayport (FL), US, 1 located at Salina Cruz, 1 located at Puerto Madero, 1 located at Lazaro Cádenas, 1 located at Puerto Vallarta, 1 located at Puerto Vallarta

Naval Aviation 1,100

FORCES BY ROLE

MR some sqn with 10 MD-902 *Explorer*; 12 BO-105 (8 afloat); 1 sqn with 8 CASA 212-200M *Aviocar**

Tpt some sqn with 5 AN-32 *Cline*; 1 Beech 90 King Air; 1 CASA 212 *Aviocar*; 3 Cessna 310; 2 Cessna 337 *Skymaster*; 2 Cessna 402; 1 DHC-5 *Buffalo*; 1 FH-227; 1 *Learjet* 24; 1 Rockwell Turbo Commander 1000; 2 Cessna 180 *Skywagon*; 1 MU-2F tpt/SAR

Utl some sqn with 20 MI-17 (Mi-8MT) *Hip H*/Mi-8 *Hip*; 4 AS-555 *Fennec*; 2 R-22 *Mariner*; 1 R-44; 4 SA-319 *Alouette III*

Trg some sqn with 10 Beech F-33C *Bonanza*; 10 L-90 *Redigo*; 12 MX-7 *Star Rocket*; some sqn with 4 MD-500E

EQUIPMENT BY TYPE

AIRCRAFT 8 combat capable
  RECCE • MR 8: 8 CASA 212-200M *Aviocar**
  TPT 18: 5 AN-32 *Cline*; 1 Beech 90 King Air; 1 CASA 212 *Aviocar*; 3 Cessna 310; 2 Cessna 337 *Skymaster*; 2 Cessna 402; 1 DHC-5 *Buffalo*; 1 FH-227; 1 *Learjet* 24; 1 Rockwell Turbo Commander 1000
  UTL 3: 2 Cessna 180 *Skywagon*
    MU-2 1: 1 MU-2F tpt/SAR
  TRG 32
    BEECH F-33 10: 10 Beech F-33C *Bonanza*
    L-90 *Redigo* 10: 12 MX-7 *Star Rocket*
HELICOPTERS
  RECCE • MR 10: 10 MD-902 *Explorer*
  SPT 23: 3 Bell 47
    MI-8 20: 20 MI-17 (Mi-8MT) *Hip H*/Mi-8 *Hip* spt hels
  UTL 27: 4 AS-555 *Fennec*; 12 BO-105 (8 afloat)
    MD-500 4: 4 MD-500E
    R-22 Mariner 2; 1 R-44; 4 SA-319 *Alouette III*

Marines 8,700

FORCES BY ROLE

Regional	11 bn
Sy	1 (indep) coy
AB	1 regt (2 AB bn)
Marine	1 (coast def) gp (2 (coast) arty bn); 3 bde (*each:* 3 Marine bn)
Presidential Guard	1 bn

EQUIPMENT BY TYPE

AAV 25: 25 Pegaso VAP-3550
ARTY 122

TOWED • **105mm** 16: 16 M-56
MRL • **122mm** 6: 6 Firos-25
MOR 100: 100 60mm/81mm
AT • RCL • **106mm** • **M-40**: some M-40A1
PATROL AND COASTAL COMBATANTS • MISC
BOATS/CRAFT 60: 60 assault craft (Swe)
AD • GUNS • **20mm** • **TOWED**: some *Bofors* LAAG
GUN • GUN • **25MM**: some MK 38

Air Force 11,770

FORCES BY ROLE

Ftr	1 sqn with 8 F-5E *Tiger II*; 2 F-5F *Tiger II*
RECCE	1 (photo) sqn with 2 SA-2-37A; 4 C-26 *Metro*; 10 Rockwell Commander 500S*
AEW / MP	some sqn with 3 EMB-145MP *Erieye* (incl 1 AEW version)
CCT	7 sqn with 70 PC-7 *Turbo Trainer*; 2 sqn with 17 AT-33 *Shooting Star* (being replaced by 14 F-5E Tiger II)
Tpt	5 sqn with 1 C-118 *Liftmaster*; 7 C-130A *Hercules*; 1 CV-580; 1 *Cessna* 500 *Citation I*; 1 Jetstar; 1 L-100 *Hercules*; 10 Rockwell Commander 500S; 1 sqn with 9 IAI-201 *Arava* (tpt/SAR); some (Presidential) sqn with 3 B-727-100; 1 B-757
Liaison / Utl	some sqn with 1 *Beech 300 Super King Air*; 1 *Beech* A90 *King Air*; 3 *Beech* C90 *King Air*; 9 IAI-201 *Arava*; 4 PC-6 *Turbo-Porter*; 6 Rockwell Turbo Commander 680; 11 *Cessna* 206; 11 *Cessna* 210 *Centurion*; 1 B-23 *Musketeer*; 29 *Beech* F-33C *Bonanza*; 73 *Cessna* 182S *Skylane*
Trg	some sqn with 6 MX-7 *Star Rocket*; 21 MXT-7-180 *Star Rocket*; 12 PT-17 *Kaydet*; 30 SF-260; 24 MD-530F *Lifter** (SAR/paramilitary/trg)
Hel	some sqn with 1 Mi-26T *Halo*; 6 S-70A *Black Hawk*; 11 Mi-8 *Hip*; 24 MI-17 (Mi-8MT) *Hip H*; 1 PZL MI-2 *Hoplite*; 1 sqn with 1 Bell 205A; 15 Bell 206B *JetRanger II*; 7 Bell 206L-3 *LongRanger III*; 24 Bell 212

EQUIPMENT BY TYPE
AIRCRAFT 107 combat capable
 FTR • F-5 10: 8 F-5E *Tiger II*; 2 F-5F *Tiger II*
 FGA 17: 17 AT-33 *Shooting Star* (being replaced by 14 F-5E Tiger II)
 RECCE • SA-2-37 2: 2 SA-2-37A
 AEW • EMB-145 3: 3 EMB-145MP *Erieye* (incl 1 AEW version)
 TPT 73
  B-727 3: 3 B-727-100
  B-757 1; 1 *Beech 300 Super King Air*
  BEECH 90 4: 1 *Beech* A90 *King Air*; 3 *Beech* C90 *King Air*
  C-118 *Liftmaster* 1
  C-130 7: 7 C-130A *Hercules*
  C-26 *Metro* 4; 1 CV-580; 1 *Cessna* 500 *Citation I*; 9 IAI-201 *Arava*; 9 (tpt/SAR); 1 Jetstar; 1 L-100 *Hercules*; 4 PC-6 *Turbo-Porter*
  ROCKWELL COMMANDER 500 20: 10 Rockwell Commander 500S; 10*
  Rockwell Turbo Commander 680 6

UTL 22: 11 *Cessna* 206; 11 *Cessna* 210 *Centurion*
TRG 242: 1 B-23 *Musketeer*
 BEECH F-33 29: 29 Beech F-33C *Bonanza*
 CESSNA 182 73: 73 *Cessna* 182S *Skylane*
 MX-7 27: 6; 21 MXT-7-180 *Star Rocket*
 PC-7 *Turbo Trainer* 70*; 12 PT-17 *Kaydet*; 30 SF-260
HELICOPTERS
 SPT 43
  MI-26 1: 1 Mi-26T *Halo*
  S-70 6: 6 S-70A *Black Hawk*
  MI-8 35: 11; 24 MI-17 (Mi-8MT) *Hip H*
  PZL MI-2 *Hoplite* 1
 UTL 71
  BELL 205 1: 1 Bell 205A
  BELL 206 22: 15 Bell 206B *JetRanger II*
   BELL 206L 7: 7 Bell 206L-3 *LongRanger III*
  Bell 212 24
  MD-530 24: 24 MD-530F *Lifter** (SAR/paramilitary/trg)
MSL • TACTICAL • AAM • **AIM-9**: some AIM-9J *Sidewinder*

Paramilitary ε11,000

Federal Representative Police ε11,000
Ministry of Interior

Rural Defence Militia (R) 14,000 reservists

Coast Guard
PATROL AND COASTAL COMBATANTS • PCI 4: 4 *Mako* less than 100 tonnes (295)

Armed Forces 300,000 reservists

DEPLOYMENT

UNITED STATES
Navy
Base 1 located at Mayport (FL), US

Nicaragua Nic

Nicaraguan Gold Cordoba Co		2003	2004	2005
GDP	Co	62.3bn	70.3bn	
	US$	4.13bn	4.45bn	
per capita	US$	786	831	
Growth	%	2.3	4.0	
Inflation	%	5.3	8.2	
Debt	US$	6.91bn		
Def bdgt	Co	470m	503m	565m
	US$	31.1m	31.8m	34.7m
FMA	US$	–	1.7m	1.1m
US$1=Co		15.1	15.8	16.3

Population (2004)   5,465,100.1

Age	0 - 14	15 - 19	20 - 24	25 - 29	30 - 64	65 plus
Male	19%	6%	5%	4%	14%	1%
Female	18%	6%	5%	4%	15%	2%

Capabilities

ACTIVE 14,000 (Army 12,000 Navy 800 Air 1,200)
Terms of service voluntary, 18-36 months

ORGANISATIONS BY SERVICE

Army ε12,000
FORCES BY ROLE
Region 6 comd (*total*: 1 tk coy, 11 inf coy)
Comd 1 regt (1 inf bn, 1 (sy) army bn)
Mil 2 det (*total*: 2 inf bn)
Mech 1 (lt) bde (1 tk bn, 1 mech inf bn, 1 Recce bn, 1 AT gp, 1 fd arty gp (2 fd arty bn))
SF 1 bde (3 SF bn)
Engr 1 bn
Tpt 1 regt (1 (APC) army bn)
EQUIPMENT BY TYPE
TK 137+
 MBT 127+: 127+ T-55 (62 op remainder in store)
 LT TK 10: 10 PT-76 in store
RECCE • BRDM 20: 20 BRDM-2
APC • APC (W) • BTR 166: 102 BTR-152 in store; 64 BTR-60
ARTY 800
 TOWED 42
  122mm 12: 12 D-30
  152mm 30: 30 D-20 in store
 MRL 151
  107mm 33: 33 Type-63
  122mm 118: 18 BM-21; 100 GRAD 1P (BM-21P) (single-tube rocket launcher)
 MOR 607: 579 82mm
  120mm 24: 24 M-43
  160mm 4: 4 M-160 in store
AT
 MSL: some AT-3 *Sagger* (12 on BRDM-2)
 RCL • 82mm: some B-10
 RL • 73mm: some RPG-16/RPG-7 *Knout*
 GUNS 461
  100mm 24: 24 M-1944
  57mm 354: 354 ZIS-2 *M-1943* (90 in store)
  76mm 83: 83 ZIS-3
AD • SAM • MANPAD 200+: 200+ SA-14 *Gremlin*/SA-16 *Gimlet*/SA-7 *Grail*

Navy ε800
EQUIPMENT BY TYPE
PATROL AND COASTAL COMBATANTS 5+
 MISC BOATS/CRAFT: some boats
 PFI 5: 3 Dabur less than 100 tonnes; 2 Zhuk less than 100 tonnes (FSU)
MINE WARFARE • MINE COUNTERMEASURES • MHI 2: 2 Yevgenya
FACILITIES
Base 1 located at Corinto, 1 located at Puerto Cabezzas, 1 located at El Bluff

Air Force 1,200
FORCES BY ROLE
Tpt some sqn with 1 AN-2 *Colt*; 4 AN-26 *Curl*; 1 *Cessna* 404 *Titan* (VIP)
Trg / Utl some sqn with 1 T-41D *Mescalero*
ADA 1 gp with 18 ZU-23; 18 C3-Morigla M1
Hel some sqn with 1 MI-17 (Mi-8MT) *Hip H* (VIP); 3 (tpt/armed); 12† (tpt/armed)
EQUIPMENT BY TYPE
AIRCRAFT
 TPT 6: 1 AN-2 *Colt*; 4 AN-26 *Curl*; 1 *Cessna* 404 *Titan* (VIP)
 TRG • T-41 1: 1 T-41D *Mescalero*
HELICOPTERS
SPT • MI-8 16: 1 MI-17 (Mi-8MT) *Hip H* (VIP); 3 (tpt/armed); 12† (tpt/armed)
AD • GUNS 36
 23mm • TOWED 18: 18 ZU-23
 C3-Morigla M1 18
MSL • TACTICAL • ASM: some AT-2 *Swatter*

Panama Pan

Panamanian Balboa B		2003	2004	2005
GDP	B	12.8bn	13.4bn	
	US$	12.8bn	13.4bn	
per capita	US$	4,323	4,465	
Growth	%	4.3	6.0	
Inflation	%	1	0.5	
Debt	US$	8.77bn		
Def bdgt	B	e 130m	e 140m	158m
	US$	130m	140m	158m
FMA	US$	1.2m	2.5m	1.6m
US$1=B		1	1	1

Population (2004) 3,140,232

Age	0 - 14	15 - 19	20 - 24	25 - 29	30 - 64	65 plus
Male	16%	5%	4%	4%	19%	3%
Female	15%	5%	4%	4%	18%	3%

Capabilities

ACTIVE 0 Paramilitary 11,800

ORGANISATIONS BY SERVICE

Paramilitary ε11,800

National Police Force 11,000
no hy mil eqpt, small arms only
Police	18 coy
SF	1 unit (reported)
Paramilitary	8 coy
Presidential Guard	1 bn under strength
MP	1 bn

National Maritime Service ε400

FORCES BY ROLE
Air Wing 1 HQ located at Amador

EQUIPMENT BY TYPE
PATROL AND COASTAL COMBATANTS 39
MISC BOATS/CRAFT 25: 25 boats
PCC 5: 3; 2 Panquiaco (UK Vosper 31.5m)
PCI 9: 3 less than 100 tonnes (ex-US); 1 Negrita less than 100 tonnes; 1 Swiftships less than 100 tonnes (65ft); 3 Tres De Noviembre less than 100 tonnes (ex-US Point); 1 US MSB Class (MSB 5)

FACILITIES
Base 1 located at Amador, 1 located at Balboa, 1 located at Colón

National Air Service 400

FORCES BY ROLE
Tpt some sqn with 1 BN-2B Islander; 3 CASA 212M Aviocar; 1 CN-235-2A; 1 PA-34 Seneca
Trg some sqn with 6 T-35D Pillan
Hel some sqn with 2 Bell 205; 6 Bell 212; 13 UH-1H Iroquois

EQUIPMENT BY TYPE
AIRCRAFT
TPT 6
BN-2 ISLANDER 1: 1 BN-2B Islander
CASA 212 3: 3 CASA 212M Aviocar
CN-235 1: 1 CN-235-2A
PA-34 Seneca 1
TRG • T-35 6: 6 T-35D Pillan
HELICOPTERS
UTL 21: 2 Bell 205; 6 Bell 212
UH-1 13: 13 UH-1H Iroquois

Paraguay Py

Paraguayan Guarani Pg		2003	2004	2005
GDP	Pg	38.8tr	39.0tr	
	US$	6.04bn	6.58bn	
per capita	US$	1,000	1,064	
Growth	%	2.6	2.1	
Inflation	%	14.2	5.2	
Debt	US$	3.21bn		
Def bdgt	Pg	285bn	309bn	359bn
	US$	44.4m	52.2m	57.6m
US$1=Pg		6,424	5,920	6,245

Population (2004) 6,347,884

Age	0 - 14	15 - 19	20 - 24	25 - 29	30 - 64	65 plus
Male	19%	5%	4%	4%	16%	2%
Female	19%	5%	4%	4%	15%	3%

Capabilities

ACTIVE 10,300 (Army 7,600 Navy 1,600 Air 1,100)
Paramilitary 14,800

Terms of service 12 months Navy 2 years

RESERVE 164,500 (Joint 164,500)

ORGANISATIONS BY SERVICE

Army 6,100; 1,500 conscript (total 7,600)

FORCES BY ROLE
6 Military Region, 3 corps HQ

Army	20 (frontier) det
Armd cav	3 regt
cav	3 (horse) regt; 3 div HQ
Inf	9 (bn) regt; 6 div HQ
Arty	3 gp (bn)
ADA	1 gp
Engr	6 bn
Presidential Guard	1 unit (1 arty bty, 1 inf bn, 1 MP bn, 1 (lt) armd sqn)

EQUIPMENT BY TYPE
TK 17
MBT 12: 12 M4A3 Sherman
LT TK 5: 5 M-3A1 Stuart
RECCE 38: 30 EE-9 Cascavel; 8 M-8
APC • APC (W) 10: 10 EE-11 Urutu
ARTY 121
TOWED 35
75mm 20: 20 Model 1927/1934
105mm 15: 15 M-101
COASTAL • 152mm 6: 6 Mk5 Vickers 6in
MOR 80: 80 81mm
AT • RCL • 75mm: some M-20
RL • 66mm: some M-72 LAW
AD • GUNS 30
20mm • TOWED 20: 20 Bofors LAAG
40mm • TOWED • M-1 10: 10 M-1A1

Reserves
cav 4 regt
Inf 14 regt

Navy 1,100; 300 conscript (total 1,400)

EQUIPMENT BY TYPE
PATROL AND COASTAL COMBATANTS 28
MISC BOATS/CRAFT 20: 20 craft
PCR 8: 2 (ROC); 1 Capitan Cabral; 2 Capitan Ortiz less than 100 tonnes (ROC Hai Ou); 1 Itapu; 2 Nanawa (may be non-op)
AMPHIBIOUS • CRAFT 2: 2 LCT
LOGISTICS AND SUPPORT 3: 1 AGHS (Svy) Svy Vsl less than 100 tonnes; 1 tpt; 1 Trg (also tpt)

FACILITIES
Base 1 located at Asunción (Puerto Sajonia), 1 located at Bahía Negra, 1 located at Cuidad Del Este

Naval Aviation 100

FORCES BY ROLE
Utl some sqn with 2 HB-350 Esquilo; 1 OH-13 Sioux

Caribbean and Latin America

Liaison some sqn with 2 *Cessna* 206; 1 *Cessna* 210 *Centurion*; 2 *Cessna* 150

EQUIPMENT BY TYPE
AIRCRAFT
UTL 3: 2 *Cessna* 206; 1 *Cessna* 210 *Centurion*
TRG 2: 2 *Cessna* 150
HELICOPTERS
SPT 2: 2 HB-350 *Esquilo*
UTL 1: 1 OH-13 *Sioux*

Marines 700; 200 conscript (total 900)

Marine 4 bn under strength

Air Force 900; 200 conscript (total 1,100)

FORCES BY ROLE
Tac — some sqn with 2 AT-33A *Shooting Star*; 3 EMB-312 *Tucano*; 5 EMB-326 *Xavante*

SAR / Liaison — some sqn with 2 *Cessna* 402B; 1 PA-32R *Saratoga*; 3 *Cessna* U-206 *Stationair*; 2 PZL-104 *Wilga 80*

Tpt — some sqn with 1 C-47 *Skytrain*; 4 CASA 212 *Aviocar*; some (Presidential) flt with 1 B-707; 1 DHC-6 *twin Otter*

Trg — some sqn with 8 T-35A *Pillan*; 4 T-35B *Pillan*

Hel — some sqn with 3 HB-350 *Esquilo*; 7 UH-1H *Iroquois* ; 1 *Hughes* 300

EQUIPMENT BY TYPE
AIRCRAFT 10 combat capable
FGA • AT-33 4: 2 AT-33A *Shooting Star*; 2 in store
TPT 12: 1 B-707; 1 *Beech* 55 *Baron* (Army Co-op); 1 C-47 *Skytrain*; 4 CASA 212 *Aviocar*; 1 *Cessna* 310 (Army Co-op)
  CESSNA 402 2: 2 *Cessna* 402B
  DHC-6 *twin Otter* 1
  PA-32 1: 1 PA-32R *Saratoga*
UTL 6: 1 *Cessna* 206 (Army Co-op)
  CESSNA 206 4: 3 *Cessna* U-206 *Stationair*
  PZL-104 *Wilga 80* 2
TRG 20: 3 EMB-312 *Tucano**; 5 EMB-326 *Xavante* *
  T-35 12: 8 T-35A *Pillan*; 4 T-35B *Pillan*
HELICOPTERS
SPT 3: 3 HB-350 *Esquilo*
UTL • UH-1 7: 7 UH-1H *Iroquois*
TRG 1: 1 *Hughes* 300

Paramilitary 14,800

Special Police Service 10,800; 4,000 conscript (total 14,800)

Armed Forces 164,500+ reservists

DEPLOYMENT

BURUNDI
UN • ONUB 3 obs

CÔTE D'IVOIRE
UN • UNOCI 2; 9 obs

DEMOCRATIC REPUBLIC OF CONGO
UN • MONUC 17 obs

ETHIOPIA/ERITREA
UN • UNMEE 3 obs

HAITI
UN • MINUSTAH 63

LIBERIA
UN • UNMIL 1; 3 obs

SUDAN
UN • UNMIS 6 obs

Peru Pe

Peruvian Nuevo Sol NS		2003	2004	2005
GDP	NS	209bn	232bn	
	US$	60.5bn	66.5bn	
per capita	US$	2,228	2,416	
Growth	%	3.8	5.1	
Inflation	%	2.3	3.7	
Debt	US$	29.8bn		
Def bdgt	NS	3.06bn	3.14bn	3.6bn
	US$	883m	899m	1.08bn
FMA	US$	1.6m	–	1.3m
US$1=NS		3.47	3.5	3.32

Population (2004) 27,925,628

Age	0 - 14	15 - 19	20 - 24	25 - 29	30 - 64	65 plus
Male	16%	5%	4%	4%	18%	2%
Female	15%	5%	4%	4%	18%	3%

Capabilities

ACTIVE 80,000 (Army 40,000 Navy 25,000 Air 15,000) **Paramilitary 77,000 Inactive Other 7,000**

RESERVE 188,000 (Army 188,000)

ORGANISATIONS BY SERVICE

Army 40,000

FORCES BY ROLE
4 Military Regions
Region 1 (regional comd) tps (1 mot inf bn, 1 engr gp, 1 inf bn, 1 (Presidential Escort) army regt, 1 (mech cav) army regt, 3 fd arty gp, 3 engr bn, 3 ADA gp); 1 (regional) tps (1 SF bde, 1 (armd) Trg bde, 2 mot inf bde, 2 Mtn inf bde, 2 armd bde, 2 (mech cav) army bde, 5 inf bde)

Army 1 tps (1 avn bde (1 avn sqn, 1 avn bn, 2 hel bn))

EQUIPMENT BY TYPE
TK 385
  MBT 275: 275 T-54/T-55 (est. 200 serviceable)
  LT TK 110: 110 AMX-13 (est. 90 are serviceable)
RECCE 105
  BRDM 30: 30 BRDM-2
  Fiat 6616 15; 10 M-3A1; 50 M-9A1
APC 276+

APC (T) 130: 130 M-113
APC (W) 146+
  BTR 12: 12 BTR-60
  Casspir some; some Fiat 6614; 4 Repontec; 130 UR-416
ARTY 1002
  TOWED 264
    105mm 150: 130 M-101; 20 Model 56 pack howitzer
    122mm 42: 42 D-30
    130mm 36: 36 M-46
    155mm 36: 36 M-114
  SP • 155mm 24
    M-109 12: 12 M-109A2
    Mk F3 12
  MRL • 122mm 14: 14 BM-21
  MOR 700: 400 107mm/81mm/ECIA 120mm (incl some SP)
    120mm 300: 300 Brandt
  AT • MSL 300: 300 SS-11
  RCL • 106mm • M-40: some M-40A1
AIRCRAFT
  TPT 12: 2 AN-28 *Cash*
    AN-32 4: 4 AN-32B *Cline*
    Beech **80 Queen Air** 1
    BEECH 90 1: 1 *Beech* C90 *King Air*
    L-410 1: 1 L-410UVP *Turbolet*
    PA-31 2: 2 PA-31T *Navajo/Cheyenne II*
    PA-34 *Seneca* 1
  UTL 10
    CESSNA 206 5: 5 *Cessna* U-206 *Stationair*
    Cessna **208 Caravan I** 1; 4 IL-103
HELICOPTERS
  SPT 47: 2 Mi-26 *Halo*; 20 Mi-8 *Hip*
    MI-8 35: 15 MI-17 (Mi-8MT) *Hip H*
    PZL MI-2 *Hoplite* 10
  UTL 4
    A-109 2: 2 A-109K2
    SA-318 2: 2 SA-318C *Alouette II*
  TRG • ENSTROM F-28 3: 3 Enstrom F-28F
AD
  SAM • MANPAD 450+: 450+ Javelin/SA-16 *Gimlet*/SA-18 *Grouse* (Igla)/SA-7 *Grail*
  GUNS 262
    23mm 127
      SP 47: 47 ZSU-23-4
      TOWED 80: 80 ZU-23-2
    30mm • SP 10: 10 2S6
    40mm • TOWED 125: 80 L/60/L/70; 45 M-1

Reserves 188,000 reservists

Navy 25,000 (incl 1,000 Coast Guard)

Commands: Pacific, Lake Titicaca, Amazon *River*
EQUIPMENT BY TYPE
SUBMARINES • TACTICAL • SSK 6:
  4 *Casma* (Ge T-209/1200) each with 6 single 533mm TT each with A-185 HWT
  2 *Casma* in refit (Ge T-209/1200) each with 6 single 533mm TT each with A-185 HWT
PRINCIPAL SURFACE COMBATANTS 5
  CRUISERS • CG 1:
    1 *Almirante Grau* (Nl *De Ruyter*) with 8 single each with 1 Mk 2 Otomat SSM, 4 twin 152mm gun (8 eff.)

FRIGATES • FFG 4:
  4 *Carvajal* (mod It Lupo) each with 1 AB-212 (Bell 212) Utl/SH-3D *Sea King* ASW, 2 triple ASTT (6 eff.) each with A244 LWT, 1+ *Albatros* octuple with *Aspide* SAM, 8 single each with 1 Mk 2 Otomat SSM, 1 127mm gun
PATROL AND COASTAL COMBATANTS 13
  MISC BOATS/CRAFT 3: 3 craft (for lake patrol)
  PCR 4:
    2 *Amazonas* each with 1 76mm gun
    2 *Maranon* each with 2 76mm gun
  PFM 6:
    6 *Velarde* (Fr PR-72 64m) each with 4 single each with 1 MM-38 *Exocet* tactical SSM, 1 76mm gun
AMPHIBIOUS • LS • LST 3: 3 *Paita* (capacity 395 troops) (US Terrebonne Parish)
LOGISTICS AND SUPPORT 9: 2 AGHS (Svy) *Svy Vsl*; 1 AGOR *Research Vsl*; 3 AO; 1 AOT *Tkr*; 1 ATF *Ocean Tug* (SAR); 1 tpt
FACILITIES
Base 1 (Ocean) located at Callao, 1 (*River*) located at Puerto Maldonaldo, 1 (*River*) located at Iquitos, 1 (Ocean) located at Talara, 1 (Lake) located at Puno, 1 (Ocean) located at Paita, 1 (Ocean) located at San Lorenzo Island

Naval Aviation 800+

FORCES BY ROLE

ASW / MR	some sqn with 1 F-27 *Maritime Enforcer*; 5 Beech 200T *Maritime Patrol*; 3 SH-3D *Sea King*; 6 AB-212 (Bell 212)
Tpt	some sqn with 2 AN-32B *Cline*
Liaison	some sqn with 4 Mi-8 *Hip*; 5 Bell 206B *JetRanger II*
Trg	some sqn with 5 T-34C *Turbo Mentor*

EQUIPMENT BY TYPE
AIRCRAFT 1 combat capable
  ASW 1: 1 F-27 *Maritime Enforcer**
  MP 5: 5 *Beech* 200T *Maritime Patrol*
  TPT • AN-32 2: 2 AN-32B *Cline*
  TRG • T-34 5: 5 T-34C *Turbo Mentor*
HELICOPTERS
  ASW • SH-3 3: 3 SH-3D *Sea King*
  SPT 4: 4 Mi-8 *Hip*
  UTL 11: 6 AB-212 (Bell 212)
    BELL 206 5: 5 Bell 206B *JetRanger II*
MSL • TACTICAL • ASM: some AM-39 *Exocet*

Marines 4,000

FORCES BY ROLE

Inf	1 (jungle) bn; 2 (indep) bn; 1 gp
Cdo	1 gp
Marine	1 bde (1 arty gp, 1 Spec Ops gp, 1 Recce bn, 1 (Amph veh) Amph bn, 2 inf bn)

EQUIPMENT BY TYPE
APC • APC (W) 35+: 20 BMR-600; some V-100 *Commando*; 15 V-200 *Chaimite*
ARTY 18+
  TOWED • 122mm: some D-30
  MOR 18+: some 81mm; ε18 120mm

AT • RCL • 106mm • M-40: some M-40A1
84mm: some Carl Gustav
AD • GUNS • 20mm: some SP (twin)

Air Force 15,000

FORCES BY ROLE

Air Force divided into five regions - North, Lima, South, Central, Amazon.

Bbr	some sqn with 5 B(I) MK 58 *Canberra*
Air	1 (Presidential) flt with 1 F-28 *Fellowship*; 1 Falcon 20F
Ftr	2 sqn with 9 *Mirage* 5P (*Mirage* 5); 2 *Mirage* 5DP30; 1 sqn with 15 MIG-29C *Fulcrum*; 3 MIG-29SE *Fulcrum*; 2 MIG-29UB *Fulcrum*
FGA	1 sqn with 10 M-2000P (M-2000E) *Mirage*; 2 M-2000DP (M-2000ED) *Mirage*; 1 sqn with 12 A-37B *Dragonfly*; 3 sqn with 10 SU-25A *Frogfoot A†*; 12 SU-22 (SU-17M-2) *Fitter D†*; 3 SU-22U (SU-17UM-2D) *Fitter E†**; 8 SU-25UB *Frogfoot B†**
RECCE	some sqn with 3 MIG-25RB *Foxbat B*; 1 (photo-survey) unit with 2 *Learjet* 25B; 2 *Learjet* 36A
Tpt	3 gp; 7 sqn with 7 AN-32 *Cline*; 3 AN-72 *Coaler*; 1 B-737; 1 C-130A *Hercules*; 6 C-130D *Hercules*; 2 DC-8-62F; 12 DHC-5 *Buffalo*; 5 DHC-6 *twin Otter*; 1 FH-227; 5 L-100-20; 9 PC-6 *Turbo-Porter*; 6 Y-12(II)
Tkr	some sqn with 1 KC-707-323C
Liaison	some sqn with 15 *Beech* 80 *Queen Air*; 3 *Beech* 90 *King Air*; 2 *Beech* 99 *Petrel Beta*; 3 *Cessna* 185; 1 *Cessna* 320; 1 PA-31T *Navajo/Cheyenne II*; 8 UH-1D *Iroquois*
Atk Hel / Aslt Hel	1 sqn with 16 Mi-24 *Hind*/Mi-25 *Hind D*; 8 Mi-17TM *Hip H*; 1 Bell 214
Spt Hel	3 sqn with 5 Mi-8 *Hip*; 10 MI-17 (Mi-8MT) *Hip H*; 10 BO-105C; 8 Bell 206 *JetRanger*; 14 AB-212 (Bell 212); 5 Bell 214; 1 Bell 412 *twin Huey*; 5 SA-316 *Alouette III*; 6 Schweizer 300C
Trg	some (Drug Interdiction) sqn with 6 IL-103; 19 EMB-312 *Tucano*; 13 MB-339A; 6 T-41A *Mescalero*/T-41D *Mescalero*; 15 Z-242; 12 Bell 47G
AD	3 bn with SA-2 *Guideline*; 6 bn with SA-3 *Goa*

EQUIPMENT BY TYPE

AIRCRAFT 89 combat capable
FTR • MIG-29 18: 15 MIG-29C *Fulcrum*; 3 MIG-29SE *Fulcrum*
STRIKE/FGA 5: 5 B(I) MK 58 *Canberra*
FGA 73+
  A-37 12: 12 A-37B *Dragonfly*
  M-2000 12: 2 M-2000DP (M-2000ED) *Mirage*; 10 M-2000P (M-2000E) *Mirage*
  Mirage **5P (*Mirage* 5)** 9
  SU-25 10: 10 SU-25A *Frogfoot A†*
  SU-17 • SU-17M 30+: 18+ SU-22 (SU-17M-2) *Fitter D* in store; 12†
RECCE 3: 3 MIG-25RB *Foxbat B*
TKR • B-707-323 1: 1 KC-707-323C

TPT 89: 7 AN-32 *Cline*; 3 AN-72 *Coaler*; 1 B-737; 15 *Beech* 80 *Queen Air*; 3 *Beech* 90 *King Air*; 2 *Beech* 99 *Petrel Beta*
  C-130 7: 1 C-130A *Hercules*; 6 C-130D *Hercules*
  Cessna **185** 3; 1 *Cessna* 320
  DC-8 • DC-8-62 2: 2 DC-8-62F
  DHC-5 *Buffalo* 12; 5 DHC-6 *twin Otter*; 1 F-28 *Fellowship*; 1 FH-227
  FALCON 20 1: 1 Falcon 20F
  L-100 5: 5 L-100-20
  LEARJET 25 2: 2 Learjet 25B
  LEARJET 36 2: 2 Learjet 36A
  PA-31 1: 1 PA-31T *Navajo/Cheyenne II*
  PC-6 *Turbo-Porter* 9
  Y-12 6: 6 Y-12(II)
UTL 6: 6 IL-103
TRG 68: 19 EMB-312 *Tucano*
  MB-339 13: 13 MB-339A
  MIG-29U 2: 2 MIG-29UB *Fulcrum*
  MIRAGE 5DP (MIRAGE 5D) 2: 2 *Mirage* 5DP30
  SU-17U 3: 3 SU-22U (SU-17UM-2D) *Fitter E†**
  T-41 6: 6 T-41A *Mescalero*/T-41D *Mescalero*
  Z-242 15; 8 SU-25UB *Frogfoot B†**
HELICOPTERS
  ATK 16: 16 Mi-24 *Hind*/Mi-25 *Hind D*
  SPT 23
    MI-17T 8: 8 Mi-17TM *Hip H*
    MI-8 15: 5; 10 MI-17 (Mi-8MT) *Hip H*
  UTL 52: 14 AB-212 (Bell 212)
    BO-105 10: 10 BO-105C
    Bell 206 *JetRanger* 8; 1 Bell 214; 5 more; 1 Bell 412 *twin Huey*; 5 SA-316 *Alouette III*
    UH-1 8: 8 UH-1D *Iroquois*
  TRG 18: 12 Bell 47G
    SCHWEIZER 300 6: 6 Schweizer 300C
AD • SAM: some SA-3 *Goa*
  TOWED: some SA-2 *Guideline*
MSL • TACTICAL • ASM: some AS-30
  AAM: some AA-10 *Alamo*; some AA-12 *Adder*; some AA-2 *Atoll*; some AA-8 *Aphid*; some R-550 *Magic*

Paramilitary • National Police 77,000 (100,000 reported)

APC • APC (W) 100: 100 MOWAG *Roland*

General Police 43,000

Security Police 21,000

Technical Police 13,000

Coast Guard 1,000

personnel part of Navy
PATROL AND COASTAL COMBATANTS 21
  PCC 5: 5 Rio Nepena
  PCI 16: 3
  10 less than 100 tonnes (riverine)
  PCI 16: 3 Dauntless less than 100 tonnes

Rondas Campesinas ε7,000 gp

peasant self-defence force. Perhaps 7,000 rondas 'gp', up to pl strength, some with small arms. Deployed mainly in emergency zone.

Armed Forces

Peacekeeping 2 opcon MINUSTAH

NON-STATE ARMED GROUPS

see Part II

DEPLOYMENT

BURUNDI
UN • ONUB 3 obs

CÔTE D'IVOIRE
UN • UNOCI 3 obs

DEMOCRATIC REPUBLIC OF CONGO
UN • MONUC 4 obs

ETHIOPIA/ERITREA
UN • UNMEE 3 obs

HAITI
UN • MINUSTAH 210

LIBERIA
UN • UNMIL 3; 2 obs

SUDAN
UN • UNMIS 8 obs

Suriname Sme

Suriname Dollar gld		2003	2004	2005
GDP	gld	2.24tr	3.02tr	
	US$	863m	1.1bn	
per capita	US$	1,982	2,530	
Growth	%	5.3	4.6	
Inflation	%	23.1	9.0	
Def exp	gld	e 21bn	e 21bn	21bn
	US$	8.1m	7.7m	7.7m
US$1=gld		2.600	2,735	2,710

Population (2004) 438,144

Age	0 - 14	15 - 19	20 - 24	25 - 29	30 - 64	65 plus
Male	15%	5%	5%	4%	19%	3%
Female	14%	5%	4%	4%	19%	3%

Capabilities

ACTIVE 1,840 (Army 1,400 Navy 240 Air 200)
(all services form part of the army)

ORGANISATIONS BY SERVICE

Army 1,400

FORCES BY ROLE
Army 1 (mech cav) sqn
Inf 1 bn (4 inf coy)
MP 1 (coy) bn

EQUIPMENT BY TYPE
RECCE 6: 6 EE-9 *Cascavel*
APC • APC (W) 15: 15 EE-11 *Urutu*
ARTY • MOR 6: 6 81mm
AT • RCL • 106mm • M-40: some M-40A1

Navy 240

EQUIPMENT BY TYPE
PATROL AND COASTAL COMBATANTS 8
   MISC BOATS/CRAFT 5: 5 boats
   PCI 3: 3 Rodman less than 100 tonnes (100)
FACILITIES
Base 1 located at Paramaribo

Air Force ε200

FORCES BY ROLE
MP   some sqn with 2 CASA 212-400 *Aviocar**
Trg / Tpt some sqn with 4 BN-2 Defender*; 1 PC-7 *Turbo Trainer**
Liaison   some sqn with 1 *Cessna* U-206 *Stationair*
Hel   some sqn with 1 AB-205 (Bell 205); 2 SA-316 *Alouette III*

EQUIPMENT BY TYPE
AIRCRAFT 7 combat capable
   MP 2: 2 CASA 212-400 *Aviocar**
   TPT 4: 4 BN-2 Defender*
   UTL • CESSNA 206 1: 1 *Cessna* U-206 *Stationair*
   TRG 1: 1 PC-7 *Turbo Trainer**
HELICOPTERS • UTL 3: 1 AB-205 (Bell 205); 2 SA-316 *Alouette III*

Trinidad and Tobago TT

Trinidad and Tobago Dollar TT$		2003	2004	2005
GDP	TT$	67.8bn	74.0bn	
	US$	10.7bn	12.0bn	
per capita	US$	9,776	10,969	
Growth	%	13.2	6.2	
Inflation	%	3.8	3.9	
Debt	US$	2.75bn		
Def bdgt	TT$	179m	197m	200m
	US$	28.6m	32.1m	32.0m
US$1=TT$		6.29	6.16	6.25

Population (2004) 1,075,066

Age	0 - 14	15 - 19	20 - 24	25 - 29	30 - 64	65 plus
Male	11%	5%	6%	4%	22%	4%
Female	10%	5%	5%	4%	20%	5%

Capabilities

ACTIVE 2,700 (Army 2,000 Navy 700)
(all services form part of the **Trinidad and Tobago Defence Force**)

ORGANISATIONS BY SERVICE

Army ε2,000
FORCES BY ROLE
Inf 2 bn
SF 1 unit
Spt 1 bn

EQUIPMENT BY TYPE
ARTY • MOR 46: ε40 60mm
  81mm 6: 6 L16A1
AT
  RCL • **84mm** 24: ε24 Carl Gustav
  RL • **82mm** 13: 13 B-300

Coast Guard 700
FORCES BY ROLE
Marine 1 HQ located at Staubles Bay

EQUIPMENT BY TYPE
PATROL AND COASTAL COMBATANTS 24
  MISC BOATS/CRAFT 12: 2 aux vessels; 10 boats
  PCI 9: 4 Plymouth less than 100 tonnes; 3 Point less than 100 tonnes; 2 Wasp less than 100 tonnes
  PFC 2: 2 Barracuda (Sw Karlskrona 40m, non op)
  PCO 1: 1 Nelson (UK Island)

FACILITIES
Base 1 located at Staubles Bay, 1 located at Hart's Cut, 1 located at Point Fortin, 1 located at Tobago, 1 located at Galeota

Air Wing 50
AIRCRAFT
  TPT 6: 2 C-26 *Metro*; 1 *Cessna* 310; 1 *Cessna* 402; 2 PA-31 *Navajo*
  UTL 1: 1 *Cessna* 172

Uruguay Ury

Uruguayan Peso pU		2003	2004	2005
GDP	pU	313bn	378bn	
	US$	11.1bn	12.8bn	
per capita	US$	3,292	3,766	
Growth	%	2.5	12.0	
Inflation	%	19.4	9.2	
Debt	US$	11.7bn		
Def bdgt	pU	3.5bn	e 4.0bn	e 4.0bn
	US$	125m	135m	163m
FMA	US$	1.4m	–	–
US$1=pU		28.2	29.6	24.4

Population (2004)   3,415,920.92

Age	0 - 14	15 - 19	20 - 24	25 - 29	30 - 64	65 plus
Male	12%	4%	4%	4%	20%	5%
Female	11%	4%	4%	4%	21%	8%

Capabilities

ACTIVE 24,000 (Army 15,200 Navy 5,700 Air 3,100)
Paramilitary 920

ORGANISATIONS BY SERVICE

Army 15,200
FORCES BY ROLE
4 Military Regions/div HQ
cav   3 bde (*each:* 1 armd cav bn, 2 (mot) cav bn, 3 (mech cav) army bn, 4 (horse) cav bn)
Inf   1 bde (1 mot inf bn, 1 mech inf bn, 1 Para bn); 4 bde (*each:* 3 inf bn)
Arty   3 bn; 1 bde (1 ADA bn, 2 arty bn)
Engr   1 bde (3 engr bn)
Cbt engr   4 bn

EQUIPMENT BY TYPE
TK 83
  MBT 15: 15 T-55
  LT TK 68: 17 M-24 *Chaffee*; 29 M-3A1 *Stuart*
    M-41 22: 22 M-41A1
  RECCE 31: 16 EE-3 *Jararaca*; 15 EE-9 *Cascavel*
  AIFV • BMP 15: 15 BMP-1
  APC 134
    APC (T) 47: 15 M-113; 32 M-93 (MT-LB)
    APC (W) 87: 44 Condor
      OT 43: 43 OT-64 SKOT (OT-64)
  ARTY 207
    TOWED 66
      75mm 10: 10 M-1902 (BOFORS)
      105mm 48: 48 M-101A1/M-102
      155mm • M-114 8: 8 M-114A1
    SP • 122mm 2: 2 2S1 *Carnation*
    MRL • 122mm 3: 3 RM-70 *Dana*
    MOR 136: 93 81mm
      107mm 9: 9 M-30
      120mm 34
  AT
    MSL 5: 5 Milan
    RCL 100
      106mm • M-40 30: 30 M-40A1
      57mm 67: 67 M-18
      75mm 3
  AD • GUNS 23
    20mm • TOWED 15: 6 M-167 *Vulcan*; 9 TCM-20
    40mm • TOWED 8: 8 L/60

Navy 5,700 (incl 1,950 Prefectura Naval (Coast Guard))
FORCES BY ROLE
Navy 1 HQ located at Montevideo

EQUIPMENT BY TYPE
PRINCIPAL SURFACE COMBATANTS • FRIGATES • FFG 3:
  3 General Artigas (Fr Cdt Riviere) each with 2 triple 550mm ASTT (6 eff.)(may be non op) each with L3 HWT, 2 single, 2 100mm gun

PATROL AND COASTAL COMBATANTS 18
  MISC BOATS/CRAFT 9: 9 craft
  PCC 3: 3 15 de Noviembre (Fr Vigilante 42m)
  PCI 5: 2 less than 100 tonnes; 2 Colonia less than 100 tonnes (US Cape); 1 Paysandu less than 100 tonnes
  PCO 1: 1 Campbell (US Auk MSF, Antarctic patrol/research)
MINE WARFARE • MINE COUNTERMEASURES • MSC 3: 3 Temerario (Ge Kondor II)
AMPHIBIOUS • CRAFT 4: 2 LCVP; 2 LCM
LOGISTICS AND SUPPORT 5: 1 AGHS (Svy) Svy Vsl; 1 AGOR Research Vsl
  ARS 1: 1 Vanguardia
  AT Tug 1 (ex-GDR Elbe-Class); 1 Trg

FACILITIES

| Base | 1 located at Montevideo, 1 (river) located at Paysando |
| Naval airbase | 1 located at La Paloma, 1 located at Laguna del Sauce |

Naval Aviation 300

FORCES BY ROLE

ASW	some sqn with 1 Beech 200T Maritime Patrol*
Utl	some sqn with 4 Wessex HC2; 1 Wessex MK60
Trg / Liaison	some sqn with 3 S-2G Tracker*; 1 Jetstream T MK2; 2 T-34C Turbo Mentor

EQUIPMENT BY TYPE
AIRCRAFT 4 combat capable
  ASW • S-2 3: 3 S-2G Tracker*
  MP 1: 1 Beech 200T Maritime Patrol*
  TRG 3: 1 Jetstream T MK2
  T-34 2: 2 T-34C Turbo Mentor
HELICOPTERS
  UTL 5: 4 Wessex HC2; 1 Wessex MK60
  TRG 1: 1 Bell 47G

Naval Infantry 450

Marine 1 bn

Air Force 3,100

Flying hours   120 hrs/year

FORCES BY ROLE

FGA	1 sqn with 12 A-37B Dragonfly; 1 sqn with 6 IA-58B Pucara
Tpt	1 sqn with 2 UB-58 (Beech 58) Baron; 3 C-130B Hercules; 1 Cessna 310 (VIP); 3 EMB-110C Bandeirante; 2 U-8F Seminole
Liaison	some sqn with 2 Cessna 182 Skylane; 11 Cessna 206H
Survey	some sqn with 3 CASA 212 Aviocar (tpt/SAR); 1 EMB-110B1 Bandeirante
Trg	some sqn with 6 PC-7U Turbo Trainer; 13 SF-260EU (SF-260E)*; 5 T-41D Mescalero
Hel	1 sqn with 2 AS-365 Dauphin 2; 2 Bell 212; 6 UH-1H Iroquois ; 6 Wessex HC2

EQUIPMENT BY TYPE
AIRCRAFT 31 combat capable
  FGA 18
    A-37 12: 12 A-37B Dragonfly
    IA-58 6: 6 IA-58B Pucara
  TPT 17
    C-130 3: 3 C-130B Hercules
    CASA 212 Aviocar 3 (tpt/SAR); 2 Cessna 182 Skylane; 1 Cessna 310 (VIP)
    EMB-110 4: 1 EMB-110B1 Bandeirante; 3 EMB-110C Bandeirante
    U-8 2: 2 U-8F Seminole
    UB-58 (Beech 58) **Baron** 2
  UTL • CESSNA 206 11: 11 Cessna 206H
  TRG 24
    PC-7 6: 6 PC-7U Turbo Trainer
    SF-260 13: 13 SF-260EU (SF-260E)*
    T-41 5: 5 T-41D Mescalero
HELICOPTERS • UTL 16: 2 AS-365 Dauphin 2; 2 Bell 212
  UH-1 6: 6 UH-1H Iroquois
  Wessex HC2 6

Paramilitary 920

Guardia de Coraceros 470

Guardia de Granaderos 450

Coast Guard 1,950

Prefectura Naval (PNN) is part of the Navy
PATROL AND COASTAL COMBATANTS 12
  MISC BOATS/CRAFT 9: 9 boats
  PCC Patrol craft coastal 3
AMPHIBIOUS • CRAFT 2: 2 LCM

DEPLOYMENT

AFGHANISTAN
UN • UNAMA 1 obs

BURUNDI
UN • ONUB 3 obs

CÔTE D'IVOIRE
UN • ONUCI 1; 1 obs

CYPRUS
UN • UNFICYP 1

DEMOCRATIC REPUBLIC OF CONGO
UN • MONUC 27 obs; 1,543

EGYPT
MFO 60

ETHIOPIA/ERITREA
UN • UNMEE 36; 4 obs

GEORGIA
UN • UNOMIG 3 obs

HAITI
UN • MINUSTAH 779

INDIA/PAKISTAN
UN • UNMOGIP 1 obs

SIERRA LEONE
UN • UNAMSIL 5 obs

WESTERN SAHARA
UN • MINURSO 8 obs

Venezuela Ve

Venezuelan Bolivar Bs		2003	2004	2005
GDP	Bs	137tr	206tr	
	US$	85.3bn	80.7bn	
per capita	US$	3,459	3,229	
Growth	%	-7.7	17.3	
Inflation	%	31.1	21.7	
Debt	US$	34.8bn		
Def exp	Bs	2.06tr	2.68tr	
	US$	1.28bn	1.05bn	
Def bdgt	Bs	1.81tr	2.43tr	n.a.
	US$	1.12bn	953m	n.a.
US$1=Bs		1,606	2,550	2,611

Population			25,375,281			
Age	0 - 14	15 - 19	20 - 24	25 - 29	30 - 64	65 plus
Male	15%	5%	5%	5%	18%	2%
Female	14%	5%	5%	4%	19%	3%

Capabilities

ACTIVE 82,300 (Army 34,000 Navy 18,300 Air 7,000 Other 23,000)

Terms of service 30 months selective, varies by region for all services

RESERVE 8,000 (Army 8,000)

ORGANISATIONS BY SERVICE

Army 7,000; 27,000 conscript (total 34,000)

FORCES BY ROLE
Army   1 (mobile counter guerrilla) bde (1 mot inf bn, 1 (Civil Affairs) army bn, 2 SF bn)

Armd   1 (lt) bde; 1 bde

cav   1 bde

Inf   6 div HQ; 7 bde (total: 1 mech inf bn, 18 inf bn, 4 fd arty bn)

Ranger   1 bde (4 Ranger bn); 1 bde (2 Ranger bn)

AB   1 bde

Engr   2 regt

Avn   1 regt

MP   1 bde

EQUIPMENT BY TYPE
TK 197
  MBT 81: 81 AMX-30
  LT TK 116: 36 AMX-13
    SCORPION 80: 80 Scorpion 90

RECCE 30: 30 M-8
APC 290
  APC (T) 25: 25 AMX-VCI
  APC (W) 265: 100 Dragoon (some with 90mm gun); 35 EE-11 *Urutu*
    LAV 30: 30 LAV-150 *Commando*
    V-100 *Commando* 100
ARTY 347
  TOWED 92
    105mm 80: 40 M-101; 40 Model 56 pack howitzer
    155mm 12: 12 M-114
  SP • 155mm 10: 10 Mk F3
  MRL • 160mm 20: 20 LAR SP (LAR-160)
  MOR 225: 165 81mm
    120mm 60: 60 Brandt
AT
  MSL 24: 24 MAPATS
  RCL • 106mm • M-40 175: 175 M-40A1
    84mm: some Carl Gustav
  RL • 84mm: some AT-4
  GUNS • 76mm 75: 75 M-18 *Hellcat*
AIRCRAFT
  TPT 7: 2 *Cessna 182 Skylane*; 5 IAI-202 *Arava*
  UTL 5: 2 *Cessna 206*; 1 *Cessna 207 Stationair*; 2 M-28 *Skytruck*
HELICOPTERS • UTL 26: 7 A-109 (ATK)
  AS-61 8: 4 AS-61A (tpt); 4 AS-61D (spt)
  Bell 204 3 (tpt); 2 Bell 206 *JetRanger* (Spt); 2 Bell 412 *twin Huey* (tpt)
  UH-1 4: 4 UH-1H *Iroquois* (tpt)
RADAR • LAND: some RASIT (veh, arty)
MSL • TACTICAL • ASM: some AS-11 *Kilter*

Reserve Organisations

Reserves 8,000 reservists
Armd   1 bn
Inf   4 bn
Ranger   1 bn
Arty   1 bn
Engr   2 regt

Navy ε14,300; ε4,000 conscript (total 18,300)
Naval Commands: Fleet, Marines, Naval Avn, Coast Guard, Fluvial (*River* Forces)

FORCES BY ROLE
Navy   1 HQ (HQ *Arauca River*) located at El Amparo; 1 HQ (HQ Fluvial Forces) located at Ciudad Bolivar; 1 HQ located at Caracas

EQUIPMENT BY TYPE
SUBMARINES • TACTICAL • SSK 2:
  2 Sabalo (Ge T-209/1300) each with 8 single 533mm TT each with 14 SST-4 HWT
PRINCIPAL SURFACE COMBATANTS • FRIGATES • FFG 6:
  6 Mariscal Sucre (It mod Lupo) each with 1 AB-212 (Bell 212) utl hels, 2 triple ASTT (6 eff.) each with A244 LWT, 1 Albatros Octuple with 8 Aspide SAM, 8 single each with 1 Mk 2 Otomat SSM, 1 127mm gun

PATROL AND COASTAL COMBATANTS 6

PFM 3:

3 Constitucion (UK Vosper 57m) each with 2 single each with 1 Mk 2 Otomat SSM

PCO 3:

3 Constitucion (UK Vosper 37m) each with 1 76mm gun

AMPHIBIOUS

LS • LST 4: 4 Capana (capacity 12 tanks; 200 troops) (FSU Alligator)

CRAFT 14: 2 LCU (river comd); 12 LCVP

LOGISTICS AND SUPPORT 6: 2 AGHS (Svy) *Svy Vsl*

AGOR 1: 1 Punta Brava

AO 1; 1 Spt (log spt); 1 Trg (sail)

FACILITIES

Base	1 (SS, FF, amph and service sqn) located at Puerto Caballo, 1 located at Caracas, 1 (patrol sqn) located at Punto Fijo
Minor Base	1 (Coast Guard) located at Maracaibo, 1 located at Ciudad Bolivar, 1 located at El Amparo, 1 (Coast Guard) located at La Guaira
Naval airbase	1 located at Turiamo, 1 located at Puerto Hierro, 1 located at La Orchila

Naval Aviation 500

FORCES BY ROLE

ASW	1 sqn with 9 AB-212 (Bell 212)
MP	some sqn with 3 CASA 212-200 MPA
Spt	some sqn with 4 Bell 412EP *twin Huey*
Tpt	some sqn with 1 *Beech* 200 *Super King Air*; 5 CASA 212 *Aviocar*; 1 DHC-7 *Dash 7*; 1 Rockwell Turbo Commander 980C
Trg	some sqn with 2 *Cessna* 310Q; 2 *Cessna* 402; 1 *Cessna* 210 *Centurion*

EQUIPMENT BY TYPE

AIRCRAFT 3 combat capable

MP 3: 3 CASA 212-200 MPA*

TPT 12: 1 *Beech* 200 *Super King Air*; 5 CASA 212 *Aviocar*

CESSNA 310 2: 2 *Cessna* 310Q

Cessna 402 2; 1 DHC-7 *Dash 7*

ROCKWELL TURBO COMMANDER 980 1: 1 Rockwell Turbo Commander 980C

UTL 1: 1 *Cessna* 210 *Centurion*

HELICOPTERS

UTL 14: 9 AB-212 (Bell 212)*

BELL 206 1: 1 Bell 206B *JetRanger II* (trg)

BELL 412 4: 4 Bell 412EP *twin Huey*

Marines ε7,800

FORCES BY ROLE

HQ	1 div HQ
Amph	1 (amph veh) bn
Inf	2 (river) bn; 6 bn
Arty	1 bn (1 AD bn, 3 fd arty bty)
Marine	1 (river) bde; 2 (landing) bde
Engr	1 BCT; 4 bn

EQUIPMENT BY TYPE

APC • APC (W) 35: 25 EE-11 *Urutu*; 10 TPz-1 *Fuchs*

AAV 11: 11 LVTP-7 (to be mod to -7A1)

ARTY • TOWED • 105mm 18: 18 M-56

AD • GUNS • 40mm • SP 6: 6 M-42

Coast Guard 1,000

EQUIPMENT BY TYPE

PRINCIPAL SURFACE COMBATANTS • CORVETTES • FS 2:

2 Almirante Clemente each with 2 triple ASTT (6 eff.), 2 76mm gun

PATROL AND COASTAL COMBATANTS 43

PCI 16: 12 Gairon less than 100 tonnes; 4 Petrel (USCG Point class)

PCR *Patrol Craft Riverine* 27

LOGISTICS AND SUPPORT 1: 1 Spt

FACILITIES

Minor Base	1 (operates under Naval Comd and Control, but organisationally separate) located at La Guaira

Air Force 7,000

some conscripts

Flying hours   155 hrs/year

FORCES BY ROLE

Ftr / FGA	1 gp with 16 *Mirage* 50DV *Pantera/Mirage* 50EV *Pantera*; 1 gp with 12 CF-5A *Freedom Fighter*; 4 CF-5B *Freedom Fighter*; 7 NF-5A *Tiger/NF-5B Tiger*; 2 gp with 18 F-16A *Fighting Falcon*; 4 F-16B *Fighting Falcon*; 2 gp with 20 EMB-312 *Tucano*
RECCE	some gp with 15 OV-10A *Bronco**
ECM	some gp with 3 Falcon 20DC
Tpt	some gp with 2 B-707 (tkr); 7 C-123 *Provider*; 5 C-130H *Hercules*; 8 G-222; 2 HS-748; 7 AS-332B *Super Puma*; 18 MI-17 (Mi-8MT) *Hip H/Mi-8 Hip*; 2 Bell 214; 4 Bell 412 *twin Huey*; 2 UH-1N *Iroquois* ; some (Presidential) flt with 1 A-319CJ; 1 B-707; 1 Gulfstream III; 1 Gulfstream IV; 1 Learjet 24D; 1 Bell 412 *twin Huey*
Liaison	some gp with 5 *Beech* 200 *Super King Air*; 2 *Beech* 65 *Queen Air*; 5 *Beech* 80 *Queen Air*; 1 CE-550 *Citation II*; 9 *Cessna* 182 *Skylane*; 1 *Cessna* 500 *Citation I*; 9 SA-316B *Alouette III*
Trg	1 gp with 12 EMB-312 *Tucano**; 12 SF-260E; 17 T-2D *Buckeye**; 20 T-34 *Turbo Mentor*
Hel	1 (Armed) gp with 4 AS-532 *Cougar*; 10 SA-316 *Alouette III*; 12 UH-1D *Iroquois* ; 5 UH-1H *Iroquois*

EQUIPMENT BY TYPE

AIRCRAFT 125 combat capable

FTR 38

CF-5 16: 12 CF-5A *Freedom Fighter*; 4 CF-5B *Freedom Fighter*

F-16 22: 18 F-16A *Fighting Falcon*; 4 F-16B *Fighting Falcon*

FGA • MIRAGE 50 16: 16 *Mirage* 50DV *Pantera/Mirage* 50EV *Pantera*

FAC • OV-10 15: 15 OV-10A *Bronco**

Caribbean and Latin America (side tab)

TPT 55

  A-319 1: 1 A-319CJ

  B-707 1; 2 B-707 (tkr); 5 Beech 200 Super King Air; 2 Beech 65 Queen Air; 5 Beech 80 Queen Air; 7 C-123 Provider

  C-130 5: 5 C-130H Hercules

  CE-550 Citation II 1; 9 Cessna 182 Skylane; 1 Cessna 500 Citation I

  FALCON 20 3: 3 Falcon 20DC

  G-222 8; 1 Gulfstream III; 1 Gulfstream IV; 2 HS-748

  LEARJET 24 1: 1 Learjet 24D

TRG 81: 20 EMB-312 Tucano; 12*

  SF-260 12: 12 SF-260E

  T-2 17: 17 T-2D Buckeye*

  T-34 Turbo Mentor 20

  TRIALS AND TEST • NF-5 7: 7 NF-5A Tiger/NF-5B Tiger

HELICOPTERS

  SPT 25

    AS-332 7: 7 AS-332B Super Puma

    MI-8 18: 18 MI-17 (Mi-8MT) Hip H/Mi-8 Hip spt hels

  UTL 49: 4 AS-532 Cougar*; 2 Bell 214; 5 Bell 412 twin Huey; 10 SA-316 Alouette III *

    SA-316 19: 9 SA-316B Alouette III

    UH-1 19: 12 UH-1D Iroquois *; 5 UH-1H Iroquois *; 2 UH-1N Iroquois

AD

  SAM • SP 10: 10 Roland

    MANPAD: some RBS-70

GUNS 228+: 114

  20mm • TOWED: some TCM-20

  35mm some

  40mm • TOWED 114: 114 L/70

MSL • TACTICAL • ASM: some AM-39 Exocet

  AAM • AIM-9: some AIM-9L Sidewinder; some AIM-9P Sidewinder

  R530 some

National Guard (Fuerzas Armadas de Cooperacion) 23,000

(internal sy, customs) 8 regional comd

APC • APC (W) 44: 24 Fiat 6614; 20 UR-416

ARTY • MOR 150: 100 60mm; 50 81mm

PATROL AND COASTAL COMBATANTS • MISC BOATS/CRAFT 52: 52 boats/craft

AIRCRAFT

  TPT 12

    BN-2 ISLANDER 1: 1 BN-2A Islander

    BEECH 200 1: 1 Beech 200C Super King Air

    Beech **55 Baron** 1; 2 Beech 80 Queen Air; 1 Beech 90 King Air; 2 Cessna 185; 4 IAI-201 Arava

  UTL 11

    CESSNA 206 5: 5 Cessna U-206 Stationair

    M-28 Skytruck 6

HELICOPTERS • UTL 26: 4 A-109; 2 AB-212 (Bell 212); 20 Bell 206 JetRanger

CARIBBEAN AND LATIN AMERICA – DEFENCE ECONOMICS

The economies of Latin America continued their impressive recovery from the deep recession of 2001–02, recording GDP growth in 2004 of 5.7%, the highest for the region since 1980. Although growth was widespread throughout the region, Uruguay and Venezuela showed the most significant improvements as they bounced back from recession, while Brazil and Chile continued to benefit from sound macroeconomic policies and structural reforms. In contrast to other periods of recovery in Latin America, many countries have used the favourable economic developments to strengthen their fiscal and debt positions rather than boosting public spending, notable exceptions being Ecuador, Mexico and Venezuela, where revenue gains resulting from high oil prices appear to have fed into primary government expenditures. The IMF has welcomed the general improvement in public debt in the region, but cautioned that debt levels still remain high and are consequently a significant source of vulnerability should economic conditions worsen.

Although prospects for 2005–06 look encouraging, with growth forecast, to ease to a more sustainable level of 4.1%, Latin American countries remain vulnerable to a weakening in the global economy and the volatility of oil prices. In its April 2005 World Economic Outlook, the IMF urges governments in the region to take advantage of the current healthy economic to continue with structural measures to improve future growth opportunities, and suggests that oil-exporting nations in particular use this opportunity to improve fiscal positions. In past attempts to address budget deficits, several countries have made the mistake of implementing unrealistic spending cuts or distorting taxes that actually undermine the economy and lead to social unrest. With ever vigilant financial markets increasing their trading activities in Latin American assets, governments will find it increasingly difficult to adopt such unrealistic practices and as such, the current trend towards structural reform programmes is likely to continue.

The strong recovery in **Argentina** continued in 2004 with GDP growth reaching 9%, although debt remains a significant problem. Given the government's declared policy, following the serious economic crisis in 2001, of reducing debt and unemployment, a sustained period of prudent fiscal policy will be required. Although the military received its first full funding for several years in 2003, the government's budget plan for the period 2003–06, formulated under guidance from the IMF, suggests that defence spending will gradually fall to around 1% of GDP. With personnel costs and military pensions consuming the vast majority of the defence budget, there is little money available for equipment purchases and the armed forces will have to concentrate on effective upgrades to their existing inventory, together with the purchase of second-hand equipment. Should the resources for new equipment be found, then the top priority appears to be the acquisition of a new class of offshore patrol vessel. Under the much delayed Patrulleros de Alta Mar (PAM) programme, the navy is looking to procure five 1,800-ton vessels from a foreign shipbuilder, to be constructed under licence at a domestic shipyard. The programme has acquired additional traction of late as part of a government plan to revitalise the local shipbuilding industry and it is hoped that

if successful, additional PAMs could be exported to neighbouring countries.

In **Brazil**, the government's adherence to sound macroeconomic policies and its pursuit of structural reforms has led to robust investment and strong exports that boosted GDP by 5.2%. In addition, the authorities have been successful in maintaining a tight fiscal policy, which is expected to continue in an effort to reduce Brazil's colossal foreign debt. Under the budget guidelines imposed by the IMF, the defence budget increased by 7% in 2005, to R32.1bn ($13.1bn), having been unchanged for the previous three years. However, despite the increase in funding the structure of Brazil's defence budget is still seriously unbalanced, with very little money available for much needed modernisation. Of the total defence budget, around 75% is allocated to personnel costs and a further 20% goes towards other operational expenditures such as fuel, training and maintenance leaving just 5%, or around $500m for the procurement of equipment. Financial shortfalls forced the Brazilian Air Force finally to cancel the much delayed next-generation F-X fighter aircraft programme. The original plan was launched in 1999 to cover the $700m purchase of 12–24 new fighter aircraft to replace the aging fleet of Mirage IIIEBr's. In cancelling the programme, officials indicated that

Table 35 **Caribbean and Latin America Regional Defence Expenditure** as % of GDP

Year	1995	1996	1997	1998	1999	2000	2001	2002	2003	2004
% of GDP	1.77	1.68	1.65	1.61	1.55	1.49	1.57	1.47	1.41	1.3

Caribbean and Latin America

they would be willing to wait a few years to see what new technologies emerge and thus avoid the risk of buying now what may quickly become viewed as obsolete technology. As an interim measure, the Brazilian Air Force is considering a French offer to lease 12 *Mirage* 2000C aircraft for an annual cost equivalent to that required to keep the current older *Mirages* in service.

A more positive outcome was revealed covering the purchase of transport aircraft and improvements to the maritime patrol fleet. As the result of a $721m loan from a consortium of banks, Brazil will take delivery of 12 C-295 twin turbo-prop transport aircraft and will upgrade eight ex-US Navy P-3A Orion maritime patrol aircraft to P-3BR standard. Brazil originally acquired 12 P-3As from US Navy stocks for a nominal sum of $10m and will spend around $400m on upgrading eight while keeping the remaining four for training missions and spare parts.

The continuing high demand for copper, particularly from China and India, helped **Chile** record another year of robust economic growth, and with demand and prices likely to stay high, the outlook for the economy remains favourable. The government's healthy financial position led to a 7% increase in the defence budget, from P947 in 2004 to P1012bn in 2005. However, total national defence-related funding in Chile is composed of several other elements in addition to the official budget, including a proportion of the Social Security budget that funds military pensions, revenue generated by the military's own business interests and money received from a proportion of the country's annual copper exports. In general, the defence budget has been used to finance normal operational expenses while the cash diverted from the state mining company CODELCO is used for equipment procurement. When all these additional sources of funding are considered, total defence expenditure in Chile was some P2,084bn in 2004. Over the past few years, the Copper Law has provided an average of around $200–250m a year for military procurement; however, with high prices and increased production it is thought that the military's share of the country's copper exports may reach over $500m in 2005.

In light of the economic windfall, Chile has been able to kick-start the extensive process of restructuring and modernisation that was outlined in the National Defence White Paper 2003. At present there are procurement programmes under consideration in all three services. The army is in advanced negoti-

ations to buy up to 90 used *Leopard* main battle tanks and would also like to acquire used M-113 armoured personnel carriers. In terms of air mobility, the army is in negotiation to buy a batch of 12 Mi-17 hel and in the longer term is looking to acquire 36 rotary wing aircraft to replace its current inventory of *Puma* and *Lama* hel. Following the cancellation of the much delayed *Fregata* frigate programme in January 2004, the navy was also forced to embark on a programme to buy second-hand rather than newly built ships. In 2003 a second-hand Type 22 frigate was purchased from the UK, followed in 2004 by the purchase from the Netherlands of two *Jacob van Heemskerck*-class air defence L frigates and two *Karel Doorman* M frigates. The fleet renewal programme was concluded in June 2005 with the agreement by the navy to purchase three ex-UK Type 23 frigates for around $350m. However, with the increased revenue from CODELCO now becoming available, the navy has been able to proceed with plans to procuring two newly-built Offshore Patrol vessels under the Danubio IV programme. The ships will be designed by the German company Fassmer and built under licence in Chile. The main outstanding requirement for the air force is a replacement for its aging fleet of *Mirage*-5 and *Mirage*-50 aircraft, and negotiations are under way with the Netherlands for the purchase of up to 28 surplus Dutch F-16s. Given that Chile will soon receive 10 newly-built F-16s, which it purchased in 2001, the acquisition of additional similar aircraft would increase commonality in the combat aircraft inventory and help streamline maintenance programmes. The impact of additional procurement funds enabled the air force to complete a surprising deal under which it will replace its current fleet of six C-130s with the Airbus A400M strategic transport aircraft. The $250m contract covers the purchase of three aircraft and includes an option for a further three at a later date.

In the Andean region, growth jumped from 1.4% in 2003 to 7.3% in 2004, largely as a result of the remarkable economic turnaround in **Venezuela**. A disastrous two-month national oil strike in 2002–03 had temporarily halted economic activity and led to two years of severe recession, finally reversed in 2004 as the economy grew by 17.3%. With the economy improving and foreign reserves boosted by improved oil production, Venezuela has indicated that it intends to seize the opportunity provided by high oil prices to initiate selected procurement programmes with equipment from Russia and Spain.

During a two-day visit to Russia in November 2004, Venezuelan President Hugo Chavez announced that he had agreed terms for the purchase of 100,000 machine guns and up to 40 hel for troop transport and close-air support missions. It is also thought that talks took place concerning the replacement of Venezuela's fleet of F-16 aircraft with MiG-29s. Venezuela's other major arms deal during the year was made following government-level meetings with Spanish ministers and resulted in contracts for the purchase of eight patrol ships and 12 military aircraft. The aircraft order comprises 10 CN-295 transports and two CN-235 maritime surveillance aircraft, described as assets that will be used to contribute to the fight against drug trafficking and terrorism. The patrol vessels are likely to be of two different sizes: four smaller coastal patrol ships of around 1,200 tons and four corvette-style, ocean-going patrol vessels of approximately 1,700 tons. Both Colombia and the US expressed their concern over Venezuela's military acquisition plans, known as the Strategic Plan for Consolidation of Defence, and are keeping a close eye on further procurement initiatives that could see the air force acquire additional AMX fighter jets and Embraer Super Tucano light strike/counter insurgency aircraft from Brazil.

Continued improvement in the security situation helped **Colombia** to maintain its recent economic progress. As a result, and with US encouragement, Colombia has steadily increased national defence spending in recent years and at over 4% of GDP it is now the highest in Latin America. In addition to the country's armed forces, the National Police have taken on an increasingly important security role and are now well equipped with hel and patrol craft. Traditionally, the armed forces focused on leftist insurgents, while the National Police concentrated on anti-drug activities; however, the distinction between these two activities is becoming more blurred. In addition to increased budget allocations, the military and police have also benefited from the imposition of a one-off 'wealth tax', which raised over $800m for the security forces, as well as annual aid from the US, in the form of Foreign Military Financing and counter-drug initiatives. In 2005, US government assistance will amount to $562.7m, including $100.7m for military training and equipment purchases and $462m under the Andean Drug Programme. The military is also known to benefit from additional funding derived from departmental or municipal governments as well as revenues from the armed forces' own security-related business. In recent years, the vast majority of this additional spending has been allocated to force expansion, training programmes, small-arms purchases and ammunition, with very little going to expensive non-domestic procurements. However, the Colombian air force is currently examining proposals for at least 22 jet-powered or turbo-prop light strike aircraft that would replace the current fleet of Cessna A-37s and Rockwell OV-10As.

Peru also benefited from buoyant economic activity within the Andean region, and the government used the opportunity to increase the 2005 defence budget by 14% while announcing its intention to modernise defence forces via a Defence and National Security Fund additional to the defence budget. The fund will be partly financed by a tax on the countries mining and natural gas industries and partly by various business enterprises run by the military and is hoped to reach $150–200m a year by 2009. As part of its commitment to the modernisation process, the government concluded three separate defence cooperation agreements with primary weapons suppliers. In a deal with Russia, Peru has been offered a $250m credit facility that is likely to be used initially for the upgrade of Russian-built hel and Antonov transport aircraft, but at a later date could also cover the major upgrade of MiG-29 and Su-25 fighter aircraft that would keep them in service until 2020. A major contract with Italy covers the purchase of two *Lupo*-class frigates, currently undergoing refit, and it is thought that a further two ships will eventually be purchased. In an agreement with France, the French air force will continue to train Peruvian air force pilots, and France will undertake the future overhaul and upgrade of the services fleet of *Mirage* 2000 aircraft.

Table 36 Arms orders and deliveries, Caribbean and Latin America

Country Supplier	Classification	Designation	Quantity	Order date	Delivery date	Comment
Brazil (Br) Fr	FGA	M-2000C (*Mirage*)	12	2005		Second-hand
Sp	tpt	CASA C-295	12	2005	2006	($298m)
Sp	MPA	P-3A (*Orion*)	8	2005	2007	($401m) upgrade from P-3A to P-3BR incl Link 11 FLIR, ESM and new radar by EADS-CASSA
Chile (Chl) Nl	FFG	*Karel Doorman*	2	2004	2005	Second-hand
Nl	FFG	*Van Heemskerck*	2	2004	2005	Second-hand
UK	FFG	Frigates	3	2005	2006	($350) Ex UK RN HMS Norfolk, Marborough and Grafton Definitive contract to be signed Sept 05. Last delivery 2008
Colombia (Co) Sp	tpt	CN-235	3	1996	1998	
Sp	MBT	AMX-30	46	2004		
Sp	arty	M-114A2	20	2004		
Sp	tpt	CASA 212 (*Aviocar*)	2	2004		
Dominican Republic (DR) Br	trg	EMB-314 (*Super Tucano*)	10	2001		
Ecuador (Ec) Il	FGA	Kfir C-2	2	1998	1999	Ex-IAF; also upgrade of 11
Sp	OPV	OPV (Off-shore Patrol Vsl)	3	2004		Depends on funding
El Salvador (ElS) US	hel	MD-520N	2	1997	1998	
Guatemala (Gua) Chl	trg	T-35B (*Pillan*)	10	1997	1998	Ex-Chl Air Force
Mexico (Mex) RF	hel	Mi-26 (*Halo*)	1	2000	2000	
Br	MPA/AEW	EMB-145 (*Erieye*)	3	2001		Including 1 AEW&C
Sp	hel	AS-565	2	2003	2005	Option for a further 8
Il	AEW	E-2C (*Hawkeye*)	3	2004		Ex Israeli inventory
Il	FAC	Aliya	2	2004	2004	
Peru (Pe) RF	hel	Mi-8 (*Hip*)	36	2003		Upgrade
RF	tpt	AN-32 (*Cline*)	22	2003		Upgrade
It	FFG	*Lupo*	2	2004	2004	
Uruguay (Ury) Ge	AG	AG (*Aux Misc*)	1	2005		Ex German Navy Luneberg class (Freiburg) hel AS-355 may also be procured from Brazil
Venezuela (Ve) Br	trg	AT-29 (*Super Tucano*)	2005-20			
Fr	hel	AS-532 (*Cougar*)	6	1997	2000	
It	trg	MB-339FD	10	1998	2000	Req for up to 24. Deliveries to 2001
It	FGA	AMX (*Ghibli*)	8	1998	2001	In cooperation with Br. Up to 24 req
Il	SAM	*Barak*	6	1999	2000	Part of Guardian Air Defence modernisation
Fr	radar	*Flycatcher*	3	1999	2000	Deliveries to early 2002. Part of Guardian
Sp	tpt	CASA C-295M	10	2005		

Chapter Eight
Sub-Saharan Africa

REGIONAL TRENDS

In a year when the G8, under the presidency of the UK, put Africa at the top of its agenda, the region continues to be afflicted by disease, famine, weak governance, and conflict. However, there are indications of greater cooperation on security issues and a growing number of national forces are being deployed on regional and continental peace support operations. At its July 2005 summit, the G8 pledged that aid to Africa would be increased by $25 billion a year by 2010, while it restated its 'Sea Island commitment to train and equip, some 75,000 troops by 2010 to take part in peace support operations worldwide, with a sustained focus on Africa'.

DISEASE AND FAMINE

Nevertheless, the ability of African nations to deploy troops is hampered by a lack of strategic airlift capabilities, as well as by the continuing high prevalence of HIV/AIDS within armed forces. This particularly impacts South Africa which, despite having the most modern forces on the continent, suffers from an acute HIV/AIDS problem. For instance, at least two South African battalions are believed to be 83% HIV positive. However, the disease is a prolific problem shared by other militaries: an estimated 43% of the Nigerian armed forces are thought infected. There is some concern that deployed personnel may contribute to spreading the disease. In one such case, after Nigerian peacekeepers arrived in Liberia, the rate of HIV infection rose from 3% to 7%.

Meanwhile, low crop yields resulting from drought have led to famine in Niger, where the UN World Food Programme (UNWFP) believes some 3 million people, including 800,000 children, are starving and in February 2005, UNWFP launched an emergency operation to assist some 400,000 of those starving and suffering from malnutrition. But by July, following an appeal for $30 million worth of food aid, only $10 million had been received, with the EU – a major potential donor – stating that poor infrastructure and the lack of a significant NGO presence in the region made mobilisation and delivery problem-atic. Meanwhile, in Ethiopia, some 3.8 million people are suffering from the repercussions of drought and famine, and in May the government requested $50 million from the international community to feed the population.

POLITICAL UNREST

Political discord in Ethiopia between President Zenawi's People's Revolutionary Democratic Front (EPRDF) and opposition groups continued during the country's first multi-party parliamentary elections which took place on 15 May 2005. Although on 16 May the EPRDF conceded that the Coalition for Unity and Democracy (CUD) had won a majority in Addis Ababa, the National Electoral Board of Ethiopia (NEBE) carried out wide-ranging investigations into voter fraud and other irregularities, delaying countrywide results until 9 August 2005. In the event, the EPRDF won 56% of the vote, enabling it to form a government. The delay and fraud accusations prompted demonstrations on 8 June, in which 36 people were killed and some 100 were injured, with an estimated 3,600 people arrested by Ethiopian security forces.

Meanwhile, hostilities between the Oromo Liberation Front (OLF), the Ogaden National Liberation Front (ONLF) and the government continue. The groups carry out attacks on government forces and ethnic groups with government affiliations. In one instance in April 2005, some 400 people were killed in a clash between the Oromo Guji people and the Geberas, an ethnic group believed to have ties to the government. Moreover, in April 2005, the ONLF began *Operation Mandad*, an offensive targeting government troops throughout southeast Ethiopia. In total, the ONLF has claimed to have killed 350 Ethiopian soldiers, whilst the OLF claimed to have killed 50. Meanwhile, an October 2004 referendum failed to settle a border dispute between the Oromiya and Somali regions, where some 21,000 people were displaced and an additional 48,000 refugees – believed to be ethnic Anuaks repatriated from Sudan – are living in camps along the Sudanese border.

In Zimbabwe, government actions continue to hit hard the lower urban class, particularly in Harare and Bulawayo, with police raids on markets, workshops and housing settlements. The seizure and destruction of homes and possessions, evictions and arrests are widespread. On 25 May, the government began *Operation Murambatsvina*, which led to the destruction of some 700,000 homes. The operation was thought to be to be aimed at pre-empting riots in Harare which might have followed price increases in maize meal and bread. However, the official reason given by the government was that it was to purge 'economic saboteurs' and 'illegal structures' subverting Zimbabwe's economy. The operation, which the UN declared was in violation of international law, ended in July.

By June 2005, Zimbabwe's unemployment rate was 70%, with a 129% inflation rate. Zimbabwe cannot afford to repay World Bank or International Monetary Fund (IMF) loans. In July, having failed to secure sufficient financial support from China, President Mugabe requested a $1 billion loan from South Africa to manage debt and to prevent possible expulsion from the IMF in September. However, South Africa has predicated its willingness to give the loan on changes in Zimbabwe's economic and political policies and no agreement has been reached. Meanwhile, the charge of treason against Morgan Tsvangirai, leader of the opposition Movement for Democratic Change, was dropped in August 2005.

On 3 August 2005 a group of **Mauritanian** army officers overthrew President Maaouiya Ould Sid Ahmed Taya in a bloodless coup and announced the formation of a 17-member Council for Justice and Democracy. The council, headed by Colonel Ely Ould Mohammed Vall, will govern the country for the next two years before returning the country to democratic rule.

CONFLICT

Sudan (see map, back cover) remains a country with two separate conflicts connected by one common factor, the divide between the ethnic-Arab-dominated government and the ethnic-African populations of the south and west. In the southern conflict with the Sudan People's Liberation Movement/Army (SPLM/A), the Comprehensive Peace Agreement, signed on 9 January 2005, has held, bringing an end to 21 years of civil war. In addition to the ceasefire, compromises on government power-sharing, resource-sharing and an option for the south to secede after a six-year interim period were key tenets of the arrangement.

However, following the sudden death of SPLM/A leader and newly appointed Sudanese Vice-President John Garang in a helicopter crash on 30 July 2005, the cease fire was threatened by rioting in Khartoum. This led to some 100 deaths and heightened tension between the government and the southern rebel movement. However, further violence was avoided with the appointment of Salva Kiir Mayardit as Garang's successor. Mayardit was quick to voice his support for the cease fire. Meanwhile, the African Union (AU) and the United Nations (UN) intensified their efforts to maintain the cease fire.

The AU announced on 11 May that its ceasefire monitors under the African Union Mission in Sudan (AMIS II) could now protect civilians. It also oversaw the signing of a Declaration of Principles in Abuja, Nigeria on 5 July, which established a framework for further discussions that are intended to incorporate other actors and groups not yet party to the talks. Additionally, on 24 March 2005, the UN approved the United Nations Mission in Sudan (UNMIS), a force of 10,000 peacekeepers and 700 police, to assist with the implementation of the peace agreement, specifically focusing on disarmament, demobilisation and rehabilitation (DDR) of combatants. As of 31 July 2005, a total of 1,419 uniformed personnel were in theatre.

Meanwhile, the AU continues to spearhead the Darfur Integrated Task Force (DITF), the strategic component of AMIS II in Darfur, in an attempt to manage the humanitarian crisis plaguing the region. DITF has contributed to the political element of crisis-management, negotiating the signing of Humanitarian and Security protocols between the government, the SLM/A, and the Justice and Equality Movement (JEM) in November 2004. As at April 2005, the AU had some 2,372 personnel stationed in Sudan with plans to double forces to some 7,731 by the end of September 2005 and, ultimately, to reach a deployment of some 12,000–15,000 troops by 2006. The first battalion, comprising some 680 Nigerian personnel, deployed on 13 July 2005. In a significant move, NATO agreed on 8 June 2005 to support the AU's efforts in Darfur by assisting with intelligence, strategic airlift and command and control training. Although NATO has stipulated it will not provide any peacekeepers, its involvement in Africa is the first of its kind and adds to assistance from the European Union (EU), which has also agreed to help the AU in a logistical capacity. The UN, in turn, has targeted accountability measures as its contribution. On 31 January, the UN published a report refuting the term 'genocide' in the context of the crisis in Darfur. Nevertheless, on 29 March, the UN Security Council (UNSC) voted to impose sanctions on parties to the conflict found guilty of human-rights abuses or, in the case of the north–south conflict, ceasefire violations. On 31 March, the UNSC passed Resolution 1593, referring all cases of crimes against humanity since July 2002 to the International Criminal Court (ICC). However, Sudan is not a signatory to the ICC and has previously refused to submit its citizens to trial outside the domestic internal system established to handle such actions: on 18 June, Sudanese courts began hearing the first of 160 cases.

It is estimated that some 300,000 civilians and soldiers have died in Darfur since February 2003. Furthermore, there are some 1.8–4.2m internally displaced persons (IDPs), with another estimated 200,000 Sudanese refugees living in 12 refugee camps in neighbouring Chad. The UN criticised the Sudanese government for breaching international law when it tried to destroy various shelters and forcibly move IDPs in November 2004. In February 2005, the AU began stationing police at the camps as IDPs and humanitarian workers increasingly became the targets of the Janjaweed militias. Two UN World Food Programme employees, two independent NGO workers, and three UNHCR workers in Chad were killed in 2005.

Violence extends beyond the camps where continued attacks have prompted a cycle of violence involving rebel and government-loyalist groups; this has hindered peace talks. One such incident took place on 7 April when some 350 armed Nigeaga fighters, loyal to the government, destroyed the town of Khor Abeche in southern Darfur. Moreover, despite signing the November 2004 Humanitarian and Security protocols, the JEM and the SLA continue to fight against militias and the Sudanese government. In June 2005, the JEM was implicated in an offensive along the Eritrean border with the Eastern Front, a new rebel group formed by the Free Lions and the Beja Congress in February 2005. (For details see the List of Non-State Armed Groups, p. 422) Moreover, the SLM refused to attend a new round of peace negotiations sponsored by the AU on 10 June, and has rejected discussions of demobilisation.

Despite progress in establishing democratic institutions, latent instability remains in the **Democratic Republic of the Congo** (DRC). The United Nations Mission in the DRC (MONUC) supervised disarmament between March and April 2005, and around 11,500 combatants voluntarily disarmed. However, some 3,000–5,000 militants are still thought to be armed and operating in the country. The DDR programme was hampered, not only by a lack of participation (the Union of Congolese Patriots-Lunbanga (UPC-L) and the Armed Forces of the Congolese People (FAPC) in the Ituri region boycotted the programme and missed the initial 31 March deadline), but also by disingenuous participation and continued arms smuggling. MONUC monitors believe that some combatants turned in faulty and surplus weapons in order to receive financial compensation whilst continuing to fight with their groups. Moreover, in June 2005, MONUC learned that weapons from Uganda and Sudan were being transported through the DRC border across Lake Albert, largely for use in the Ituri region. MONUC has now stated that it will forcibly disarm those that do not relinquish their weapons and will consider them war criminals. Meanwhile, war-crimes trials began on 15 March, under the auspices of the International Criminal Court.

An extended mandate for MONUC permits its 16,270 personnel to remain in the DRC until 1 October 2005. However, UN peacekeepers are being increasingly targeted: the worst instance occurred on 25 February in Ituri when nine Bengali peacekeepers were killed and 11 were wounded (Nationalist and Integrationist Front (FNI) involvement was suspected). However, the UN's decision to extend the mandate also comes with more heightened scrutiny of troop conduct. A MONUC operation on 1 March 2005, targeting FNI strongholds, was the largest offensive of its kind in terms of the number of victims. 50 militiamen and civilians, including ten children, were killed. Despite allegations of abuse, the 90 MONUC troops involved denied firing on civilians. There were also reports of UN troops committing sexual abuse and other human-rights violations in the Congo, prompting the UN Security Council, on 31 May, to hold its first ever meeting on the issue of troop behaviour and accountability. The UN Security Council urged more stringent disciplinary action and encouraged troop contributing countries to prosecute soldiers suspected of abuse.

Closer coordination has also been seen between MONUC and the Forces Armées de la République Démocratique du Congo (FARDC). FARDC, in accordance with the reintegration programmes, incorporates former militia and rebel combatants into the armed services. MONUC set up the first combined brigade containing ex-army and ex-militia forces in

May 2005. This brigade subsequently joined MONUC operations in the eastern DRC. However, FARDC troops suffer from insufficient funding for food, salaries and equipment. On 17 June 2005, the DRC signed a convention with France in which France offered to fund and assist FARDC modernisation. Furthermore, factional tensions within FARDC persist in undermining its cohesion, while the group's credibility is further subverted by allegations of human-rights abuses. Despite releasing some 2,500 children from the armed services, children were still found among FARDC's ranks in May 2005.

The government wants to replace MONUC troops guarding Internationally Displaced Persons (IDPs) camps with FARDC forces. However, many IDPs are fearful of FARDC protection and, in April 2005, many began leaving the camps. In Kafe camp, which houses 25,000 IDPs near Bunia, this migration contributed to a cholera outbreak. Originally detected on 27 March, there were 800 reported cases of the disease, and 23 deaths by 14 April. Subsequently, UNHCR, MONUC and the transitional government have started a repatriation campaign, which began in May 2005 for some 350,000 Congolese refugees and some 67,000 IDPs. However, in April 2005, fighting between FARDC factions displaced over 3,000 families in Nord-Kivu, while 100,000 people – predominantly Hema – have been displaced in the Ituri region since the beginning of 2005.

The repatriation of former armed groups to their countries of origin is proving problematic. Some 11,410 foreign fighters had returned to Uganda, Rwanda and Burundi by early 2005. However, there are still an estimated 700 Ugandan fighters and 15,000 fighters of the Democratic Forces for the Liberation of Rwanda (FDLR) in the eastern DRC. On 31 March, the FDLR announced its intention to disarm and return to Rwanda. Their departure was planned to begin on 5 May, but the deadline passed after failure to reach agreement with the Rwandan government on the terms of repatriation. The FDLR requested an international monitoring committee, a request rejected by the Rwandan government which stated that it would not offer amnesty to FDLR combatants who participated in the 1994 genocide. A stalemate resulted when the FDLR admitted it could not control its militias, and one splinter group, the Rasta Movement, intensified attacks on Congolese civilians, Rwandan Hutu refugees, and FDLR fighters in May. In response, on 29 June, MONUC deployed 3,700 peacekeepers to the Nindja district in Sud-Kivu to protect civilians, and

also to sever economic funding for rebel militias by blocking local gold mines. In June, the AU pledged to assist MONUC peacekeepers by sending some 45,000 troops to forcibly disarm the FDLR militias, though there is some doubt over the AU's ability to deploy personnel in such numbers.

FDLR repatriation similarly posed obstacles for Rwanda, not only because of the renewed violence that ensued after negotiations failed, but also because some government officials suspect the group of assisting Rwandan Hutus to cross into the DRC, in order to evade prosecution in the Gacaca courts which were re-instituted on 10 March. These traditional, community-based courts were re-opened to reduce the backlog of 120,000 cases of genocide still awaiting trial, although since their inception, they have been undermined by witness intimidation. In April 2005, some 8,000 Hutus fled to Burundi to avoid the courts, but were subsequently returned as neither Burundi nor Rwanda would give them refugee status.

Demobilisation continues to be a priority. The Rwandan Demobilisation and Reintegration Commission (RDRC) reported in August 2004 that some 78,692 combatants had been disarmed and demobilised since 1997. In April 2005, the Rwandan government destroyed 6,000 small arms. These weapons, however, represent only 5% of the 120,000 arms still believed to exist in the country.

Border security is another fundamental issue for the Rwandan government. The Armée de Liberation du Rwanda (ALIR) – made up of the Forces Armées Rwandaises (FAR) and the Interahamwe civilian militia – although based in the DRC, has two branches that continue to instigate cross-border attacks, mostly on ethnic Tutsis, in northwest and southwest Rwanda. On 27 October 2004, Rwanda signed a regional security accord with Uganda and the DRC to strengthen security and border control. And in February 2005, Rwanda and the DRC implemented a joint verification mechanism, originally proposed in 2002, to investigate and ultimately stem the movement of fighters and weapons across their border.

Meanwhile, repatriation also concerns the government. In October 2004, several hundred Burundian Tutsi refugees crossed into Rwanda, fearing that Burundi's transition process and elections (see *The Military Balance* 2004–05) would fail. At that time, it was reported that some 180,000 IDPs remained inside Rwanda. Conversely, Rwanda also experienced refugee movements as 500 Rwandans returned from Uganda in February 2005, bringing the total to some 2,500 Rwandans repatriated from Uganda since the signing of the tripartite agreement (by Rwanda, Uganda and the UNHCR) in 2003.

Negotiations between the Ugandan government and the Lord's Resistance Army (LRA) continued, but there was little progress towards a lasting peace agreement. A ceasefire between the two parties, announced on 14 November 2004, was broken intermittently, leading to a second ceasefire declaration on 4 February 2005. Although the first was extended several times until the end of December as negotiations and meetings progressed, the latter expired on 22 February with talks finally breaking down on 5 March. The LRA then intensified its campaign against the Uganda People's Defence Forces (UPDF) whilst continuing to kidnap civilians – some from IDP camps. As a result of the violence some 1.4m people had been displaced in northern Uganda by June 2005.

To enable more effective operations, in April 2005, Uganda renewed a 2001 agreement with Sudan (extant until 30 June 2005) which allowed Ugandan troops to cross into southern Sudan in pursuit of LRA fighters. A UN mandate permitting such operations is now being considered. Meanwhile, President Museveni has continued his army modernisation initiative. The military budget was increased by some $1.1m in early April 2005, highlighting computerisation, air force training and assaults on LRA positions as the key projects to benefit from the increase.

Ethnic and religious violence continue to bring instability to **Nigeria**. Violence flared up with the end of the three-year peace between communities in Benue and Taraba states where, on 10 April 2005, Fulani nomads killed 14 people. A cycle of revenge attacks ensued between mainly Muslim cattle herders and Christian farmers. There has also been a pattern of arbitrary and extrajudicial killings by the police following outbreaks of communal violence in Plateau, Kaduna and Bauchi states. The total number of IDPs in the country is estimated to be some 200,000.

Meanwhile, fighting between the Niger Delta People's Volunteer Force (NDPVF) and the Niger Delta Vigilante (NDV) continued in the oil-rich Delta region. Although the two groups agreed to an immediate ceasefire on 1 October 2004, fighting over oil proceeds continued. Oil companies pay fighters to guard their assets while illegal oil bunkering is widespread. The Nigerian navy is deployed on anti-piracy and anti-bunkering duties.

Resolution of the conflict in Côte d'Ivoire has been impeded due to tension between France and the government of Laurent Gbagbo, with attacks on UN peacekeepers and a growing mistrust between some parties to the conflict and the South African President Thabo Mbeki, who is acting as mediator. The UN extended the mandate of the UN operation in Côte d'Ivoire (UNOCI), passing Resolution 1609 on 24 June 2005. The mandate authorises the 6,548-strong mission – including some 6,000 French troops – to stay for an additional seven months, until 24 January 2006. Militia disarmament, security and humanitarian needs are central to the resolution.

Fighting escalated on 6 November 2004, when the government launched air strikes on rebel-controlled Bouaké. Nine French peacekeepers were killed in the attack and France responded by destroying the Ivoirian air force. On 16 November 2004, an arms embargo was authorised by UN Resolution 1572. Meanwhile, on 28 February 2005, 100 armed individuals, allegedly belonging to the Mouvement Ivorien de Liberation de l'Ouest de la Côte d'Ivoire (MILOCI), attacked a Forces Nouvelles checkpoint in Logoualé, north of Bangolo in the zone of confidence. UNOCI troops deployed to the area and, in an operation in which a Bangladeshi soldier was seriously injured, regained control of the town. The attack, which was not condemned by President Gbagbo, led to a significant increase in tension, with the Forces Nouvelles reinforcing their positions. There were also fresh outbursts of ethnic violence in Duékoué between ethnic Guere and non-native Dioula.

In February 2005, the Forces Nouvelles reorganised the areas under their control, creating five new territorial entities. At the same time, Guillaume Soro, secretary-general of the Forces Nouvelles, announced the opening of a new police and customs academy, as well as a new bank in Bouaké. On 6 April, South African President Mbeki and five rebel government leaders signed the Pretoria Peace Agreement, which allows for an immediate ceasefire, a disarmament process supervised by the UN, and presidential elections planned for 30 October 2005. All signatories to the 2003 Linas–Marcoussis Peace Accord are allowed to run in the elections, including opposition leader Alassane Dramane Ouattara who was previously excluded from running in elections because he is not Ivorian. As part of a plan laid out in Pretoria in June to end Côte d'Ivoire's three-year crisis, Gbagbo used special constitutional powers to pass a series of laws dealing with nationality, citizenship rights and the composition of the Independent Electoral Commission.

However, the UN plan for disarming rebels, due to come into force between 26 September and 3 October, suffered a setback when rebels failed to report to designated cantonment sites on 31 July, as agreed. This non-compliance was reportedly due to alleged favouritism by President Mbeki towards the government which upset the 'northern' parties. Thus by August 2005, the plan had largely stalled; there were no Forces Nouvelles ministers in the Government of National Reconciliation and the military dialogue had been interrupted. All this delayed the disarmament, demobilisation and reintegration process, and threw into doubt the feasibility of holding presidential elections on 30 October 2005.

MILITARY DEVELOPMENTS

(see pp. 14, 46)

The AU announced on 20 June 2005 that it would host several joint exercises with the EU, the US and Canada in the fifth cycle of Reinforcement of the African Capacities of Maintenance of Peace (RECAMP) exercises. Cameroon will play host, and Angola, Burundi, the Central African Republic, Chad, Congo Brazzaville, the DRC, Equatorial Guinea, Gabon, Rwanda and São Tomé will participate. The exercises are designed to enhance the organisational and defensive capabilities of AU-constituent armies, ultimately strengthening coordination and interoperability of the African Standby Force (ASF), the armed branch of the AU's Peace and Security Council (see *The Military Balance* 2004–05).

ASF preparations and training continued, and the first stage is planned for completion in 2006. In January 2005, African foreign ministers of AU participating countries met in Addis Ababa and signed the Draft Framework for a Common African Defence and Security Policy. Later, on 31 January, AU participants signed a Non-Aggression and Common Defence Pact, reaffirming their commitment to military integration and preparations. Meanwhile, in April 2005, AU officials also announced that the East African Standby Brigade (EASBRIG) will be operational by the end of 2005. One of five regional units comprising the ASF, EASBRIG is planned to comprise a minimum of 5,500 troops from 11 African countries; these will operate initially under an Ethiopian commander. Meanwhile, the Southern African Development Community (SADC) is beginning preparations to contribute to the ASF. Meanwhile, the organisation continues to engage in peacekeeping operations throughout the continent, most recently being asked to assist in the DRC in July 2005.

Mali is one focus of the US regional effort in its campaign against extremism. A US military training team deployed to Kidal near the Algerian border, believed to be used by the terrorist group, Groupe Salafiste pour la Predication et le Combat (GSPC) which is responsible for terrorist attacks in Algeria. There are also some 2,000 Malian troops stationed in Kidal, which suffers widespread unemployment amongst its largely Sufi Muslim population, and where illegal trade is both traditional and serves to offset the poor economic conditions. The US and Malian government effort, which aims to 'deny sanctuary, mobility, and support' to the GSPC, has been criticised for failing to create better economic conditions for locals, which some analysts assert may mitigate moves towards criminality and radical Islamist sentiment.

Angola Ang

New Angolan Kwanza AOA		2003	2004	2005
GDP	AOA	97.5bn	1.44tr	
	US$	13.1bn	17.3bn	
per capita	US$	1,215	1,581	
Growth	%	3.4	11.2	
Inflation	%	98.3	43.6	
Debt	US$	9.7bn		
Def exp	US$	ε750m	ε1.0bn	
Def bdgt	AOA	27bn	80bn	103bn
	US$	365m	958m	1.16bn
USD1=AOA		74.6	83.5	88.9

Population (2004)   11,827,315

Ethnic Groups: Ovimbundu 37%; Kimbundu 25%; Bakongo 13%

Age	0 – 14	15 – 19	20 – 24	25 – 29	30 – 64	65 plus
Male	22%	5%	4%	4%	14%	1%
Female	22%	5%	4%	4%	13%	2%

Capabilities

ACTIVE 108,400 (Army 100,000 Navy 2,400 Air 6,000) **Paramilitary 10,000**

ORGANISATIONS BY SERVICE

Army 100,000

FORCES BY ROLE
Armd / inf   42 regt (dets/gps – strength varies)
Inf   16 indep bde

EQUIPMENT BY TYPE†
TK • MBT 300+: ε200 T-54/T-55; some T-80/T-84 (reported); 50 T-62; 50 T-72
RECCE • BRDM 600: 600 BRDM-2
AIFV 250+
  BMD: some BMD-3
  BMP 250: 250 BMP-1/BMP-2
APC • APC (W) • BTR 170: ε170 BTR-152/BTR-60/BTR-80
ARTY 1,396+
  TOWED 552
    122mm 500: 500 D-30
    130mm 48: 48 M-46
    152mm 4: 4 D-20
  SP 4+
    122mm: some 2S1 Carnation
    152mm 4: 4 2S3
    203mm: some 2S7
  MRL • 122mm 90: 50 BM-21; 40 RM-70 Dana
    240mm: some BM-24
  MOR 750: 250 82mm; 500 120mm
AT
  MSL: some AT-3 Sagger
  RCL 500: 400 B-10 82mm/B-11 107mm†; 100 106mm†
  RL • 73mm: some RPG-7 Knout†
  GUNS • 100mm: some SU-100 SP†

AD
  SAM • MANPAD 500: 500 SA-14 Gremlin/SA-16 Gimlet/SA-7 Grail TOWED
  GUNS 450+
  TOWED
    14.5mm: ZPU-4
    23mm: ZU-23-2
  SP
    37mm: M-1939
    57mm: S-60

Navy ε2,400

FORCES BY ROLE
Navy 1 HQ located at Luanda

EQUIPMENT BY TYPE
Amphibious/Spt Logistics and Support 1
PATROL AND COASTAL COMBATANTS • PCI 9: 4 Mandume (all non-op); 2 Namacurra; 3 Patrulheiro (all non-op)
FACILITIES
Base 1 located at Luanda

Coastal Defence
MSL • TACTICAL • SSM: some SS-C-1B Sepal (at Luanda base)

Air Force/Air Defence 6,000

FORCES BY ROLE

Ftr	some sqn with 20 MIG-21bis Fishbed L & N/MIG-21MF Fishbed J
FGA	some sqn with 2 SU-27 Flanker; 30 MiG-23 Flogger; 10 SU-25 Frogfoot; 4 SU-24 Fencer; 15 SU-22 (SU-17M-2) Fitter D
RECCE / CCT	some sqn with 9 PC-7 Turbo Trainer/PC-9*
MR	some sqn with 1 F-27 MK 200MPA; 7 CASA 212 Aviocar
Tpt	some sqn with 8 AN-12 Cub; 4 AN-26 Curl; 2 AN-32 Cline; 2 C-130 Hercules; 2 CASA 212 Aviocar; 1 IL-62 Classic; 1 IL-76 Candid; 4 PC-6B Turbo Porter
Atk hel	some sqn with 14 Mi-24 Hind/Mi-35 Hind; 2 SA-342M Gazelle (HOT)
Trg	some sqn with 6 EMB-312 Tucano; 6 L-29 Delfin
Hel	some sqn with 8 AS-565; 25 MI-17 (Mi-8MT) Hip H/Mi-8 Hip; 2 Bell 212; 10 IAR-316 (SA-316) Alouette III (incl trg)
SAM	5 bn; 10 bty each with 12 SA-3 Goa; 10 SA-13 Gopher (40 eff.)†; 25 SA-6 Gainful (75 eff.); 15 SA-8 Gecko (90 eff.); 20 SA-9 Gaskin (80 eff.); 40 SA-2 Guideline

EQUIPMENT BY TYPE
AIRCRAFT 90 combat capable
  FTR 22: 2 SU-27 Flanker; MIG-21 20: 20 MIG-21bis Fishbed L & N/MIG-21MF Fishbed J
  FGA 59: 10 SU-25 Frogfoot; 4 SU-24 Fencer; 30 MiG-23 Flogger
    SU-17 • SU-17M 15: 15 SU-22 (SU-17M-2) Fitter D

MP 8: 1 F-27 MK 200MPA; 7 CASA 212 *Aviocar*

TPT 24: 8 AN-12 *Cub*; 4 AN-26 *Curl*; 2 AN-32 *Cline*; 2 C-130 *Hercules*; 2 CASA 212 *Aviocar*; 1 IL-62 *Classic*; 1 IL-76 *Candid*; 4 PC-6B *Turbo Porter*

TRG 21: 9 PC-7 *Turbo Trainer*/PC-9*; 6 EMB-312 *Tucano*; 6 L-29 *Delfin*

HELICOPTERS

ATK 16: 14 Mi-24 *Hind*/Mi-35 *Hind*; 2 SA-342M *Gazelle* (HOT)

ASLT 10: 8 AS-565

SPT • MI-8 25: 25 MI-17 (Mi-8MT) *Hip H*/Mi-8 *Hip* spt hel

UTL 12: 2 Bell 212; 10 IAR-316 (SA-316) *Alouette III* (incl trg)

AD • SAM 1,220: 120 SA-3 *Goa*

SP 700: 100 SA-13 *Gopher†*; 250 SA-6 *Gainful*; 150 SA-8 *Gecko*; 200 SA-9 *Gaskin*

TOWED 400: 400 SA-2 *Guideline*

MSL • TACTICAL • ASM: some AS-9 *Kyle*; some AT-2 *Swatter*; some HOT

AAM: some AA-2 *Atoll*; some AA-6 *Acrid*; some AA-7 *Apex*; some AA-8 *Aphid*

Paramilitary 10,000

Rapid-Reaction Police 10,000

NON-STATE ARMED GROUPS

see Part II

Benin Bn

CFA Franc BCEAO fr		2003	2004	2005
GDP	fr	2.09tr	2.13tr	
	US$	3.6bn	4.1bn	
per capita	US$	505	551	
Growth	%	4.8	3.0	
Inflation	%	1.5	2.6	
Debt	US$	1.8bn		
Def bdgt	fr	ε35bn	ε36bn	ε37bn
	US$	60.2m	67.5m	70.8m
US$1=fr		581	533	522

Population (2004)   7,649,360

Age	0 – 14	15 – 19	20 – 24	25 – 29	30 – 64	65 plus
Male	24%	6%	5%	4%	11%	1%
Female	23%	5%	5%	4%	12%	1%

Capabilities

ACTIVE 4,550 (Army 4,300 Navy 100 Air 150)
Paramilitary 2,500
Terms of service conscription (selective), 18 months

ORGANISATIONS BY SERVICE

Army 4,300

FORCES BY ROLE

Armd	1 sqn
Inf	3 bn
Cdo / AB	1 bn
Arty	1 bty
Engr	1 bn

EQUIPMENT BY TYPE

TK • LT TK 18: 18 PT-76 (op status uncertain)

RECCE 31

BRDM 14: 14 BRDM-2

7 M-8; 10 VBL

ARTY • TOWED • 105mm 16: 12 L-118 *Light* gun; 4 M-101

MOR: some 81mm

AT • RL • 73mm: some RPG-7 *Knout*

89mm: some LRAC

Navy ε100†

EQUIPMENT BY TYPE

PATROL AND COASTAL COMBATANTS • PFI 1: 1 *Patriote* less than 100 tonnes ((Fr 38m))

FACILITIES

Naval airbase   1 located at Cotonou

Air Force 150†

no cbt ac

AIRCRAFT • TPT 13: 2 AN-26 *Curl†*

B-707 1: 1 B-707-320† (VIP)

C-47 *Skytrain* 2†; 1 DHC-6 twin *Otter†*; 2 DO-128 *Skyservant†*; 1 F-28 *Fellowship†* (VIP); 3 HS-748†

ROCKWELL COMMANDER 500 1: 1 Rockwell Commander 500B†

HELICOPTERS

SPT • AS-350 2: 2 AS-350B *Ecureuil†*

UTL 1: 1 SE 3130 *Alouette II†*

Paramilitary 2,500

Gendarmerie 2,500

4 (mobile) coy

DEPLOYMENT

BURUNDI

UN • **ONUB** 2 obs

CÔTE D'IVOIRE

UN • **ONUCI** 8 obs; 309

DEMOCRATIC REPUBLIC OF CONGO

UN • **MONUC** 18 obs

LIBERIA

UN • **UNMIL** 2 obs

SUDAN

UN • **UNMIS** 4 obs

Botswana Btwa

Botswana Pula P		2003	2004	2005
GDP	P	36.5bn	39.9bn	
	US$	7.4bn	8.7bn	
per capita	US$	4,540	5,302	
Growth	%	6.6	5.2	
Inflation	%	8.7	6.3	
Debt	US$	513m		
Def bdgt	P	1.5bn	1.6bn	ε1.7bn
	US$	304m	348m	359m
FMA (US)	US$		1.4m	1.2m
US$1=P		4.94	4.59	4.73

Population (2004) 1,640,115

Age	0 – 14	15 – 19	20 – 24	25 – 29	30 – 64	65 plus
Male	20%	7%	6%	4%	11%	1%
Female	19%	7%	6%	5%	12%	2%

Capabilities

ACTIVE 9,000 (Army 8,500 Air 500) Paramilitary 1,500

ORGANISATIONS BY SERVICE

Army 8,500

FORCES BY ROLE

Armd 1 bde (under strength)

Inf 2 bde (total: 1 cdo unit, 1 armd recce regt, 1 engr regt, 2 ADA regt, 4 inf bn)

Arty 1 bde

AD 1 bde (under strength)

EQUIPMENT BY TYPE

TK • LT TK 60: ε30 SK-105 *Kuerassier*; 30 Scorpion (incl variants)

RECCE: some RAM-V

APC 53

  APC (T) 6: 6 FV 103 *Spartan*

  APC (W) 47

    20 BTR-60; ε8 RAM-V-2

    LAV 19: 12 LAV-150 *Commando* (some with 90mm gun); 7 *Piranha* III

ARTY 46

  TOWED 30

    105mm 18: 12 L-118 *Light* gun; 6 Model 56 pack howitzer

    155mm 12: 12 Soltam

  MOR 16: **81mm**: 10

    120mm 6: 6 M-43

AT

  MSL 6: 6 TOW (some SP on V-150)

  RCL • 84mm 30: 30 *Carl Gustav*

  RL • 73mm: some RPG-7 *Knout*

AD

  SAM • MANPAD 27: 5 Javelin; 10 SA-16 *Gimlet*; 12 SA-7 *Grail*

  GUNS • 20mm • TOWED 7: 7 M-167 *Vulcan*

Air Wing 500

FORCES BY ROLE

Ftr / FGA 1 sqn with 10 F-5A *Freedom Fighter*; 5 F-5D *Tiger II*

Tpt 2 sqn with 5 O-2 *Skymaster*; 10 BN-2 *Defender**; 1 Beech 200 *Super King Air* (VIP); 3 C-130B *Hercules*; 2 CASA 212 *Aviocar*; 2 CN-235; 1 *Gulfstream* IV

Trg 1 sqn with 6 PC-7 *Turbo Trainer**

Hel 1 sqn with 8 AS-350B *Ecureuil*; 1 Bell 412 twin *Huey*; 1 Bell 412EP twin *Huey* (VIP); 5 Bell 412SP twin *Huey*

EQUIPMENT BY TYPE

AIRCRAFT 31 combat capable

  FTR • F-5 15: 10 F-5A *Freedom Fighter*; 5 F-5D *Tiger II*

  RECCE 5: 5 O-2 *Skymaster*

  TPT 19: 10 BN-2 *Defender**; 1 Beech 200 *Super King Air* (VIP)

    C-130 3: 3 C-130B *Hercules*

    CASA 212 *Aviocar* 2; 2 CN-235; 1 *Gulfstream* IV

  TRG 6: 6 PC-7 *Turbo Trainer**

HELICOPTERS

  SPT • AS-350 8: 8 AS-350B *Ecureuil*

  UTL 7: 1 Bell 412 twin *Huey*

    BELL 412 7: 1 Bell 412EP twin *Huey* (VIP); 5 Bell 412SP twin *Huey*

Paramilitary 1,500

Police Mobile Unit 1,500 (org in territorial coy)

Burkino Faso BF

CFA Franc BCEAO fr		2003	2004	2005
GDP	fr	2.5tr	2.7tr	
	US$	4.2bn	5.0bn	
per capita	US$	320	369	
Growth	%	8.0	4.8	
Inflation	%	2.0	-0.4	
Debt	US$	1.8bn		
Def bdgt	fr	ε32bn	ε33bn	ε38bn
	US$	55.0m	61.9m	72.7m
US$1=fr		581	533	522

Population (2004) 13,491,736

Age	0 – 14	15 – 19	20 – 24	25 – 29	30 – 64	65 plus
Male	24%	6%	5%	4%	11%	1%
Female	23%	5%	5%	4%	12%	1%

Capabilities

ACTIVE 10,800 (Army 6,400 Air 200 Gendarmerie 4,200) Paramilitary 250

ORGANISATIONS BY SERVICE

Army 6,400

FORCES BY ROLE

3 Mil Regions

Tk   1 bn (2 tk pl)

Inf   5 regt HQ [*each:* 3 inf bn (*each:* 1 inf coy (5 inf pl)]

AB   1 regt HQ (1 AB bn, 2 AB coy)

Arty   1 bn (2 arty tps)

Engr   1 bn

EQUIPMENT BY TYPE

RECCE 79
   15 AML-60/AML-90
   24 EE-9 *Cascavel*; 30 *Ferret*; 2 M-20; 8 M-8

APC • APC (W) 13: 13 M-3 *Panhard*

ARTY 18+
   TOWED 14
      105mm 8: 8 M-101
      122mm 6
   MRL • 107mm 4: ε4 Type-63
   MOR • 81mm: some Brandt

AT • RCL • 75mm: some Type-52 (M-20)
   84mm: some *Carl Gustav*
   RL • 89mm: some LRAC; some M-20

AD
   SAM • MANPAD: some SA-7 *Grail*
   GUNS 42
      14.5mm • TOWED 30: 30 ZPU
      20mm • TOWED 12: 12 TCM-20

Air Force 200

FORCES BY ROLE

Tpt   some sqn with 1 B-727 (VIP); 1 Beech 200 *Super King Air*; 1 HS-748; 1 N-262 *Fregate*; 1 Rockwell Commander 500B

Liaison some sqn with 2 Cessna 150/Cessna 172; 1 AS-350 *Ecureuil*; 3 MI-17 (Mi-8MT) *Hip H*/Mi-8 *Hip*; 1 SA-316B *Alouette III*

Trg   some sqn with 5 SF-260W *Warrior*/SF-260WL *Warrior**

EQUIPMENT BY TYPE

AIRCRAFT 5 combat capable
   TPT 5: 1 B-727 (VIP); 1 Beech 200 *Super King Air*; 1 HS-748; 1 N-262 *Fregate*
      ROCKWELL COMMANDER 500 3: 1 Rockwell Commander 500B, 2 Cessna 150 Trg/Cessna 172 utl
   TRG • SF-260 • SF-260W 5: 5 SF-260W *Warrior* Trg ac/SF-260WL *Warrior**

HELICOPTERS
   SPT 4: 1 AS-350 *Ecureuil*
      MI-8 3: 3 MI-17 (Mi-8MT) *Hip H*/Mi-8 *Hip* spt hel
   UTL • SA-316 1: 1 SA-316B *Alouette III*

Paramilitary

Gendarmerie 4,200

People's Militia (R) 45,000 reservists (trained)

Security Company 250

DEPLOYMENT

BURUNDI
UN • ONUB 13 obs, 2

DEMOCRATIC REPUBLIC OF CONGO
UN • MONUC 12 obs

HAITI
UN • MINUSTAH 50 civ police

Burundi Bu

Burundi Franc fr		2003	2004	2005
GDP	fr	650bn	737bn	
	US$	601m	696m	
per capita	US$	98	111	
Growth	%	-1.2	5.5	
Inflation	%	10.7	7.9	
Debt	US$	1.3bn		
Def bdgt	fr	45.5bn	47.7bn	ε50.0bn
	US$	42.1m	45.0m	46.1m
US$1=fr		1,082	1,060	1,084

Population (2004) 7,795,426

Ethnic Groups: Hutu 85%; Tutsi 14%

Age	0 – 14	15 – 19	20 – 24	25 – 29	30 – 64	65 plus
Male	23%	6%	5%	4%	10%	1%
Female	23%	6%	5%	3%	11%	2%

Capabilities

ACTIVE 50,500 (Army 45,000 Gendarmerie 5,500)
Paramilitary 31,000

(Active Forces to be reduced by 14,000). In line with the Pretoria Peace Accord signed in October 2003 rebels from the FDD and government forces are now being integrated into a new National Defence Force.

ORGANISATIONS BY SERVICE

Army 45,000

FORCES BY ROLE

Lt armd 2 bn (sqn)

Inf   7 bn; some indep coy

Arty   1 bn

Engr   1 bn

AD   1 bn

EQUIPMENT BY TYPE

RECCE 85 incl
   AML 18: 6 AML-60; 12 AML-90
   BRDM 30: 30 BRDM-2
   7 S52 *Shorland*

APC • APC (W) 47
   BTR 20: 20 BTR-40
   9 M-3 *Panhard*; 12 RG-31 *Nyala*; 6 *Walid*

ARTY 120

TOWED • **122mm** 18: 18 D-30
MRL • **122mm** 12: 12 BM-21
MOR 90
    82mm 15: 15 M-43
    120mm: ε75
AT
MSL: some Milan (reported)
RCL • **75mm** 60: 60 Type-52 (M-20)
RL • **83mm**: some RL-83 *Blindicide*
AD
SAM • **MANPAD** 30: ε30 SA-7 *Grail*
GUNS 150+: 135+ Type-55 (M-1939) towed 37mm/ZU-23 towed 23mm
    14.5mm • **TOWED** • **ZPU** 15: 15 ZPU-4

Reserves

Army 10 (reported) bn

Air Wing 200
AIRCRAFT 2 combat capable
    TPT 2: 2 DC-3
    TRG • **SF-260** 2: 2 SF-260TP/SF-260W *Warrior**
HELICOPTERS
    ATK 2: 2 Mi-24 *Hind**
    SPT 2: 2 Mi-8 *Hip*
    UTL • **SA-316** 3: 3 SA-316B *Alouette III*

Paramilitary

Gendarmerie ε5,500 (incl estimated 50 Marine Police)
16 territorial districts
PATROL AND COASTAL COMBATANTS 7: 4 Misc Boats/Craft
    PHT 3: 3 Huchuan†
AMPHIBIOUS • **CRAFT** 1: 1 LCT
LOGISTICS AND SUPPORT 1: 1 spt

General Administration of State Security ε1,000

Local Defence Militia ε30,000

NON-STATE ARMED GROUPS
see Part II

FOREIGN FORCES
(all ONUB)
Algeria 2; 1 obs
Bangladesh 2 obs
Belgium 2 obs
Benin 2 obs
Bolivia 3 obs
Burkina Faso 2; 13 obs
Chad 1 obs
China 3 obs
Egypt 2 obs
Ethiopia 855; 7 obs
Gabon 5 obs
Gambia 2 obs
Ghana 2 obs

Guatemala 1; 4 obs
Guinea 2 obs
India 2; 7 obs
Jordan 62; 5 obs
Kenya 1,007; 2 obs
Kyrgyzstan 1 obs
Malawi 1 obs
Malaysia 3 obs
Mali 2; 17 obs
Mozambique 183; 3 obs
Namibia 3 obs
Nepal 937; 6 obs
Netherlands 1
Niger 2 obs
Nigeria 1; 2 obs
Pakistan 1,190; 5 obs
Paraguay 3 obs
Peru 3 obs
Philippines 3 obs
Portugal 2 obs
Republic of Korea 2 obs
Romania 3 obs
Russia 1; 7 obs
Senegal 5; 6 obs
Serbia and Montenegro 1
South Africa 913, 5 obs
Sri Lanka 1 obs
Thailand 177; 3 obs
Togo 3; 10 obs
Tunisia 3; 12 obs
Uruguay 3 obs
Yemen 5 obs
Zambia 2 obs

Cameroon Crn

CFA Franc BEAC fr		2003	2004	2005
GDP	fr	7.0tr	7.2tr	
	US$	12.1bn	13.5bn	
per capita	US$	766	846	
Growth	%	4.5	4.3	
Inflation	%	0.6	0.3	
Debt	US$	9.2bn		
Def bdgt	fr	150bn	151bn	ε160bn
	US$	258m	283m	306m
US$1=fr		581	533	522

Population (2004) 16,988,132

Age	0 – 14	15 – 19	20 – 24	25 – 29	30 – 64	65 plus
Male	21%	6%	5%	4%	13%	1%
Female	21%	6%	5%	4%	13%	2%

Capabilities

ACTIVE 23,100 (Army 12,500 Navy 1,300 Air 300 Gendarmerie 9,000)

ORGANISATIONS BY SERVICE

Army 12,500

FORCES BY ROLE
3 Mil Regions
Armd recce	1 bn
Inf	3 bn (under comd of Mil Regions); 5 bn; 1 bn (trg)
Cdo / AB	1 bn
Arty	1 bn (5 arty bty)
Engr	1 bn
Presidential Guard	1 bn
AD	1 bn (6 AD bty)

EQUIPMENT BY TYPE
RECCE 65
  AML 31: 31 AML-90
  AMX-10RC 6; 15 *Ferret*; 8 M-8; 5 VBL
APC 55
  APC (T) 12: 12 M-3
  APC (W) • **LAV** 43: 43 LAV-150 *Commando* incl 8 with 20mm gun; 14 with 90mm gun
ARTY 94+
  TOWED 58
    75mm 6: 6 M-116 pack
    105mm 20: 20 M-101
    130mm 24: 12 Model 1982 gun *82* (reported); 12 Type-59 (M-46)
    155mm 8: 8 I1
  MRL • **122mm** 20: 20 BM-21
  MOR 16+: some 81mm (some SP)
    120mm 16: 16 Brandt
AT
  MSL 49: 25 Milan; 24 TOW (on jeeps)
  RCL 53
    106mm • **M-40** 40: 40 M-40A2
    75mm 13: 13 Type-52 (M-20)
  RL • **89mm**: some LRAC
AD • GUNS 54
  14.5mm • **TOWED** • **ZPU** 18: 18 Type-58 (ZPU-2)
  35mm • **TOWED** • **GDF** 18: 18 GDF-002
  37mm • **TOWED** 18: 18 Type-63

Navy ε1,300

FORCES BY ROLE
Navy 1 HQ located at Douala

EQUIPMENT BY TYPE
PATROL AND COASTAL COMBATANTS 21
  PB 6: 2 Rodman 101; 4 Rodman 46
  PCC 2: 1 Bakassi (Fr P-48); 1 L'Audacieux (Fr P-48)
  PCI 1: 1 *Quartier*
  PCR 12: 6 *Simonneau* (sid); 6 *Swift*-38 (only 2 swift vessels are op, sid)
AMPHIBIOUS • CRAFT 2: 2 LC (30 ft)

FACILITIES
Base 1 located at Douala, 1 located at Limbe, 1 located at Kribi

Air Force 300

FORCES BY ROLE

Air	1 composite sqn; 1 Presidential Fleet
FGA	some sqn with 6 MB-326K; 4 Alpha Jet†; 5 CM-170 *Magister*
MR	some sqn with 2 DO-128D-6 *Turbo SkyServant*
Tpt	some sqn with 1 B-707; 3 C-130H-30 *Hercules*; 1 DHC-4 *Caribou*; 4 DHC-5D *Buffalo*; 1 DO-128 *Skyservant*; 1 *Gulfstream* III; 1 IAI-201 *Arava*; 2 PA-23 *Aztec*
Atk hel	some sqn with 3 Mi-24 *Hind*; 4 SA-342 *Gazelle* (with HOT)
Spt hel	some sqn with 1 AS-332 *Super Puma*; 1 AS-365 *Dauphin* 2; 3 Bell 206 *JetRanger*; 1 SA-318 *Alouette II*; 3 SA-319 *Alouette III*; 3 SE 3130 *Alouette II*

EQUIPMENT BY TYPE
AIRCRAFT 15 comabat capable
  FGA 15: 6 MB-326K; 4 Alpha Jet†; 5 CM-170 *Magister*
  TPT 14: 1 B-707
    C-130 • **C-130H** 3: 3 C-130H-30 *Hercules*
    DHC-4 *Caribou* 1
    DHC-5 4: 4 DHC-5D *Buffalo*
    DO-128 3: 1; 2 DO-128D-6 *Turbo SkyServant*
    Gulfstream III 1; 1 IAI-201 *Arava*
    UTL 2: 2 PA-23 *Aztec*
HELICOPTERS
  ATK 3: 3 Mi-24 *Hind*; 4 SA-342 *Gazelle* (with HOT)
  SPT 1: 1 AS-332 *Super Puma*
  UTL 11: 1 AS-365 *Dauphin* 2; 3 Bell 206 *JetRanger*; 1 SA-318 *Alouette II*; 3 SA-319 *Alouette III*; 3 SE 3130 *Alouette II*

Paramilitary

Gendarmerie 9,000
Regional Spt 3 gp

DEPLOYMENT

DEMOCRATIC REPUBLIC OF CONGO
UN • MONUC 3 obs

Cape Verde CV

Cape Verde Escudo E		2003	2004	2005
GDP	E	79.5bn	83.9bn	
	US$	824m	777m	
per capita	US$	2,001	1,872	
Growth	%	5.3	4.0	
Inflation	%	1.2	-1.9	
Debt	US$	480m		
Def bdgt	E	ε553m	ε600m	ε600m
	US$	5.7m	5.6m	6.8m
US$1=E		97	108	87.6

Population (2004) 418,224

Age	0 – 14	15 – 19	20 – 24	25 – 29	30 – 64	65 plus
Male	20%	6%	5%	3%	12%	3%
Female	19%	6%	5%	3%	14%	4%

Capabilities

ACTIVE 1,200 (Army 1,000 Coast Guard 100 Air 100)

Terms of service conscription (selective)

ORGANISATIONS BY SERVICE

Army 1,000

FORCES BY ROLE
Inf 2 bn (gp)

EQUIPMENT BY TYPE
RECCE • BRDM 10: 10 BRDM-2
ARTY 42
   TOWED 24: 12 75mm; 12 76mm
   MOR 18: 12 82mm
     120mm 6: 6 M-1943
AT • RL • 73mm: some RPG-7 *Knout*
   89mm some (3.5in)
AD
   SAM • MANPAD 50: 50 SA-7 *Grail*
   GUNS 30
     14.5mm • TOWED • ZPU 18: 18 ZPU-1
     23mm • TOWED 12: 12 ZU-23

Coast Guard ε100

PATROL AND COASTAL COMBATANTS 3
   PCC 1: 1 Kondor I
   PCI 2: 1 Espadarte less than 100 tonnes; 1 Zhuk† less than 100 tonnes

Air Force up to 100

FORCES BY ROLE
MR 1 DO-228

EQUIPMENT BY TYPE
AIRCRAFT • TPT 1: 1 DO-228

Central African Republic CAR

CFA Franc BEAC fr		2003	2004	2005
GDP	fr	746bn	695bn	
	US$	1.3bn	1.3bn	
per capita	US$	312	313	
Growth	%	-7.0	0.9	
Inflation	%	4.0	-2.2	
Debt	US$	1.3bn		
Def bdgt	fr	7.8bn	ε8.0bn	ε8.0bn
	US$	13m	15m	15m
US$1=fr		581	533	522

Population		4,237,703				

Age	0 – 14	15 – 19	20 – 24	25 – 29	30 – 64	65 plus
Male	21%	6%	5%	4%	12%	2%
Female	21%	6%	5%	4%	13%	2%

Capabilities

ACTIVE 2,550 (Army 1,400 Air 150 Gendarmerie 1,000)

Terms of service conscription (selective), 2 years; reserve obligation thereafter, term n.k.

ORGANISATIONS BY SERVICE

Army ε1,400

FORCES BY ROLE
Territorial Def 1 regt (bn)
HQ / Spt 1 regt
Army 1 (combined arms) regt (1 mech bn, 1 inf bn)

EQUIPMENT BY TYPE
TK • MBT 3: 3 T-55†
RECCE 8: 8 *Ferret*†
APC • APC (W) 39+
   BTR 4: 4 BTR-152†
   TPK 4.20 VSC *ACMAT* 25+†; 10+ VAB†
ARTY • MOR 12+: some 81mm†
   120mm 12: 12 M-1943†
AT • RCL • 106mm 14: 14 M-40†
   RL • 73mm: some RPG-7 *Knout*†
     89mm: some LRAC†
PATROL AND COASTAL COMBATANTS 9: 9 PCR *Patrol Craft Riverine*† less than 100 tonnes

Air Force 150

FORCES BY ROLE
no cbt ac, no armed hel
Tpt some sqn with 1 Caravelle; 1 Cessna 337 *Skymaster*; 1 Mystere 20 (*Falcon* 20)
Liaison some sqn with 6 AL-60; 6 MH-1521 *M Broussard*
Hel some sqn with 1 AS-350 *Ecureuil*; 1 SE 3130 *Alouette II*

EQUIPMENT BY TYPE
AIRCRAFT • TPT 15: 6 AL-60; 1 Caravelle; 1 Cessna 337 *Skymaster*; 6 MH-1521 *M Broussard*; 1 Mystere 20 (*Falcon* 20)
HELICOPTERS
   SPT 1: 1 AS-350 *Ecureuil*
   UTL 1: 1 SE 3130 *Alouette II*

Paramilitary

Gendarmerie ε1,000
3 Regional legions, 8 bde

FOREIGN FORCES

Chad 120 opcon CEMAC
Congo 120 opcon CEMAC
France 200
Gabon 140 opcon CEMAC

Chad Cha

CFA Franc BEAC fr		2003	2004	2005
GDP	fr	1.5tr	2.6tr	
	US$	2.7bn	4.8bn	
per capita	US$	287	501	
Growth	%	11.3	30.5	
Inflation	%	-1.8	-4.8	
Debt	US$	1.5bn		
Def bdgt	fr	25bn	ε25bn	ε30bn
	US$	43m	46.9m	57.4m
US$1=fr		581	533	522

Population (2004)   9,657,069

Age	0 – 14	15 – 19	20 – 24	25 – 29	30 – 64	65 plus
Male	24%	5%	4%	4%	10%	1%
Female	24%	5%	4%	4%	12%	2%

Capabilities

ACTIVE 30,350 (Army 25,000 Air 350 Republican Guard 5,000) **Paramilitary 4,500**

Terms of service conscription authorised

ORGANISATIONS BY SERVICE

Army ε25,000 (being re-organised)

Being reorganised

FORCES BY ROLE
7 Mil Regions
Armd   1 bn
Inf   7 bn
Arty   1 bn
Engr   1 bn

EQUIPMENT BY TYPE
TK • MBT 60: 60 T-55
RECCE 174+
  AML 50+: 50+ AML-60/AML-90
  BRDM 100: ε100 BRDM-2
  20 **EE-9** *Cascavel*; 4 ERC-90F *Sagaie*
APC • APC (W) 29
  BTR 20: ε20 BTR-60
  LAV 9: 9 LAV-150 *Commando* (with 90mm)
ARTY • TOWED • 105mm 5: 5 M-2
  MOR
    81mm: some
    120mm: some AM-50
AT • MSL: some Eryx; some Milan
  RCL • 106mm • M-40: some M-40A1
  RL • 112mm: some APILAS
    73mm: some RPG-7 *Knout*
    89mm: some LRAC
AD • GUNS • 14.5mm • TOWED • ZPU: some ZPU-1/ZPU-2/ZPU-4
  23mm • TOWED: some ZU-23

Air Force 350

FORCES BY ROLE
Tpt   some sqn with 1 AN-26 *Curl*; 2 C-130 *Hercules*; 2 MI-17 (Mi-8MT) *Hip H*; 2 SA-316 *Alouette III**
Liaison some sqn with 5 FTB-337 *Milirole*; 2 PC-6B *Turbo Porter*
Hel   some (Armed) sqn with 2 Mi-25V *Hind E*

EQUIPMENT BY TYPE
AIRCRAFT 2 combat capable
  RECCE 5: 5 FTB-337 *Milirole*
  TPT 5: 1 AN-26 *Curl*; 2 C-130 *Hercules*
    PC-6 2: 2 PC-6B *Turbo Porter*
  TRG 2: 2 PC-7 *Turbo Trainer**
HELICOPTERS
  ATK • MI-25 2: 2 Mi-25V *Hind E*
  SPT • MI-8 2: 2 MI-17 (Mi-8MT) *Hip H*
  UTL 2: 2 SA-316 *Alouette III**

Paramilitary 4,500 active

Republican Guard 5,000

Gendarmerie 4,500

NON-STATE ARMED GROUPS

see Part II

DEPLOYMENT

BURUNDI
UN • ONUB 1 obs

CENTRAL AFRICAN REPUBLIC
CEMAC 120

CÔTE D'IVOIRE
UN • ONUCI 3 obs

FOREIGN FORCES

France 950 Army: 1 recce sqn with ERC-90F *Sagaie*; 2 inf coy Air Force: 6 F-1CR *Mirage* RECCE/F-1CT *Mirage* Strike/FGA; 1 C-135 *Stratolifter* Tpt ac; 3 C-160 *Transall* Tpt ac; 3 SA-330 *Puma* spt hel Navy: 400

Congo RC

CFA Franc BEAC fr		2003	2004	2005
GDP	fr	3.3tr	2.4tr	
	US$	5.6bn	4.5bn	
per capita	US$	1,044	1,203	
Growth	%	5.7	6.8	
Inflation	%	12.8	3.9	
Debt	US$	11.1bn		
Def bdgt	fr	28.3bn	ε30.0bn	ε30.0bn
	US$	48.8m	56.2m	57.4m
US$1=fr		581	533	522

Capabilities

ACTIVE 10,000 (Army 8,000 Navy 800 Air 1,200)
Paramilitary 2,000

ORGANISATIONS BY SERVICE

Army 8,000

FORCES BY ROLE

Armd 2 bn
Inf 1 bn; 2 bn (gp) (each: 1 lt tk tp, 1 (76mm gun) arty bty)
Cdo / AB 1 bn
Arty 1 gp (how, MRL)
Engr 1 bn

EQUIPMENT BY TYPE†
TK 53+
  MBT 40+: 25 T-54/T-55; 15 Type-59; some T-34 in store
  LT TK 13: 3 PT-76; 10 Type-62
RECCE • BRDM 25: 25 BRDM-1/BRDM-2
APC • APC (W) 68+
  BTR 50: 20 BTR-152; 30 BTR-60
  M-3 *Panhard* some; 18 *Mamba*
ARTY 66+
  TOWED 25+
    76mm: some ZIS-3 *M-1942*
    100mm 10: 10 M-1944
    122mm 10: 10 D-30
    130mm 5: 5 M-46
    152mm: some D-20
  SP • 122mm 3: 3 2S1 *Carnation*
  MRL 10+: some BM-14 140mm/BM-16 122mm
    122mm 10: 10 BM-21
  MOR 28+: some 82mm
    120mm 28: 28 M-43
AT
  RCL • 57mm: some M-18
  RL • 73mm: some RPG-7 *Knout*
  GUNS • 57mm 5: 5 ZIS-2 *M-1943*
AD • GUNS 28+
  100mm • TOWED: some KS-19
  14.5mm • TOWED • ZPU: some ZPU-2/ZPU-4
  23mm • SP: some ZSU-23-4
  37mm • TOWED 28: 28 M-1939
  57mm • TOWED: some S-60

Navy ε800

EQUIPMENT BY TYPE
PATROL AND COASTAL COMBATANTS 3+
  MISC BOATS/CRAFT: some river boats†
  PFI 3: 3 Zhuk non-operational
FACILITIES
Base 1 located at Pointe Noire

Air Force 1,200†

FORCES BY ROLE
FGA some sqn with 12 MiG-21 *Fishbed*

Tpt some sqn with 5 AN-24 *Coke*; 1 AN-26 *Curl*; 1 B-727; 1 N-2501 *Noratlas*
Trg some sqn with 4 L-39 *Albatros*
Hel some sqn with 2 Mi-8 *Hip*; 1 AS-365 *Dauphin 2*; 2 SA-316 *Alouette III*; 2 SA-318 *Alouette II*

EQUIPMENT BY TYPE†
AIRCRAFT 12 combat capable
  FTR 12: 12 MiG-21 *Fishbed*
  TPT 8: 5 AN-24 *Coke*; 1 AN-26 *Curl*; 1 B-727; 1 N-2501 *Noratlas*
  TRG 4: 4 L-39 *Albatros*
HELICOPTERS
  SPT 2: 2 Mi-8 *Hip*
  UTL 5: 1 AS-365 *Dauphin 2*; 2 SA-316 *Alouette III*; 2 SA-318 *Alouette II*
MSL • TACTICAL • AAM: some AA-2 *Atoll*

Paramilitary 2,000 active

Gendarmerie 2,000
Paramilitary 20 coy

Presidential Guard some
Paramilitary 1 bn

DEPLOYMENT

CENTRAL AFRICAN REPUBLIC
CEMAC 120

CÔTE D'IVOIRE
UN • ONUCI 5 obs

Côte D'Ivoire CI

CFA Franc BCEAO fr		2003	2004	2005
GDP	fr	8.1tr	8.0tr	
	US$	14bn	15bn	
per capita	US$	846	886	
Growth	%	-1.6	-0.9	
Inflation	%	3.3	1.5	
Debt	US$	12.1bn		
Def bdgt	fr	123bn	ε100bn	ε100bn
	US$	213m	187m	191m
US$1=fr		581	533	522

Population (2004) 17,298,040

Age	0 – 14	15 – 19	20 – 24	25 – 29	30 – 64	65 plus
Male	20%	6%	5%	4%	14%	1%
Female	21%	6%	5%	4%	13%	1%

Capabilities

ACTIVE 17,050 (Army 6,500 Navy 900 Air 700
Presidential Guard 1,350 Gendarmerie 7,600)
Paramilitary 1,500

RESERVE 10,000 (Joint 10,000)

ORGANISATIONS BY SERVICE

Army 6,500

FORCES BY ROLE
4 Mil Regions
Armd 1 bn
Inf 3 bn
AB 1 gp
Arty 1 bn
ADA 1 coy
Engr 1 coy

EQUIPMENT BY TYPE
TK 15
 MBT 10: 10 T-55
 LT TK 5: 5 AMX-13
RECCE 21
 AML 15: 15 AML-60/AML-90
 6 **ERC-90F4** *Sagaie*
AIFV • BMP 10: 10 BMP-1/BMP-2
APC • APC (W) 35: 12 M-3 *Panhard*; 10 *Mamba*; 13 VAB
ARTY 20+
 TOWED • 105mm 4: 4 M-1950
 122mm: some (reported)
 MOR 16+
 81mm: some
 120mm 16: 16 AM-50
AT
 MSL: some AT-14 *Kornet* (reported); some AT-5 *Spandrel* (reported)
 RCL • 106mm • M-40 12: ε12 M-40A1
 RL • 73mm: some RPG-7 *Knout*
 89mm: some LRAC
AD
 SAM • MANPAD: some SA-7 *Grail* (reported)
 GUNS 21+
 20mm: 16 incl
 SP 6: 6 M3 VDAA
 23mm • TOWED: some ZU-23-2
 40mm • TOWED 5: 5 L/60

Navy ε900

EQUIPMENT BY TYPE
PATROL AND COASTAL COMBATANTS • PCC 2: 2 *L'Ardent*† (Fr Patra)
AMPHIBIOUS • LS • LST 1: 1 *L'Elephant* (capacity 8 PB; 140 troops; 7 tks)† (Fr Batral) with 1 helicopter landing platform†

FACILITIES
Base 1 located at Locodjo (Abidjan)

Air Force 700

FORCES BY ROLE
Air some (Presidential) flt with 1 F-28 *Fellowship*; 3 Fokker 100; 1 *Gulfstream* IV; 2 IAR-330L (SA-330L) *Puma*
Ftr some sqn with 2 MIG-23MLD *Flogger K*
FGA some sqn with 5 Alpha Jet†; 2 BAC-167 *Strikemaster*
Tpt 1 sqn with 1 SA-330 *Puma*; 2 AS-365C *Dauphin II*; 1 SA-319 *Alouette III*
Liaison some sqn with 1 Beech 200 *Super King Air*; 1 Cessna 421
Trg some sqn with 2 Reims Cessna 150H; 4 Beech F-33C *Bonanza*
Hel some (Armed) sqn with 3 Mi-24 *Hind*; 5 PZL MI-2 *Hoplite*

EQUIPMENT BY TYPE
Inventory and serviceability uncertain following French attack on 6 Nov 04.
AIRCRAFT 9 combat capable†
 FTR • MIG-23 2: 2 MIG-23MLD *Flogger K*
 TPT 9: 1 Beech 200 *Super King Air*; 1 Cessna 421; 1 F-28 *Fellowship*; 3 Fokker 100; 1 *Gulfstream* IV; 2 Reims Cessna 150H
 TRG 11: 5 Alpha Jet†*; 2 BAC-167 *Strikemaster**; 4 Beech F-33C *Bonanza*
HELICOPTERS
 ATK 3: 3 Mi-24 *Hind*
 SPT 8: 1 SA-330 *Puma*
 SA-330 3: 2 IAR-330L (SA-330L) *Puma*
 PZL MI-2 *Hoplite* 5
 UTL 3
 AS-365 2: 2 AS-365C *Dauphin II*
 SA-319 *Alouette III* 1

Paramilitary

Presidential Guard 1,350

Gendarmerie 7,600
APC • APC (W): some VAB
PATROL AND COASTAL COMBATANTS 4: 4 PB *Patrol boat*

Militia 1,500

Armed Forces 10,000 reservists

NON-STATE ARMED GROUPS
see Part II

FOREIGN FORCES
(all ONUCI)
Bangladesh 3,025; 10 obs
Benin 8 obs; 309
Bolivia 3 obs
Brazil 3; 4 obs
Chad 3 obs
China, Peoples Republic of 7 obs
Congo 5 obs
Croatia 3 obs
Dominican Republic 4 obs
Ecuador 2 obs
El Salvador 3 obs

France 186; 2 obs
Gambia 5 obs; 1
Ghana 6 obs; 402
Guatemala 5 obs
Guinea 3 obs
India 7 obs
Ireland 1 obs
Jordan 210; 7 obs
Kenya 4; 5 obs
Moldova 4 obs
Morocco 1 obs; 734
Namibia 3 obs
Nepal 3 obs
Niger 5 obs; 367
Nigeria 5 obs
Pakistan 374; 10 obs
Paraguay 9 obs; 2
Peru 3 obs
Philippines 1; 4 obs
Poland 2 obs
Romania 6 obs; 2
Russia 11 obs
Senegal 323; 8 obs
Serbia and Montenegro 3 obs
Togo 6 obs; 296
Tunisia 2 obs; 1
Uganda 2; 2 obs
Uruguay 1; 1 obs
Yemen 5 obs
Zambia 2 obs

Democratic Republic of Congo
DROC

Congolese Franc fr		2003	2004	2005
GDP	fr	2.2tr	2.7tr	
	US$	5.6bn	4.5bn	
per capita	US$	98	97	
Growth	%	5.7	6.8	
Inflation	%	12.8	3.9	
Debt	US$	11.1bn		
Def bdgt	fr	na	na	na
US$1=fr		405	593	511

Capabilities

ACTIVE 64,800 (Army 60,000 Navy 1,800 Air 3,000)

ORGANISATIONS BY SERVICE

Army ε60,000
FORCES BY ROLE
Mech inf   1 bde
Inf   30+ bde

Cdo   1 bde (reported)
Presidential Guard   1 bde

EQUIPMENT BY TYPE†
TK 70+
  MBT 30: 30 Type-59 (being refurbished)
  LT TK 40+: 40+ Type-62
RECCE • AML 40+: 40+ AML-60/AML-90
APC • APC (T): some M-113; some Type-63
  APC (W): some *Casspir*; some M-3 *Panhard*; some TH 390 *Fahd*; some Wolf Turbo 2
ARTY 130+
  TOWED 100+:
    75mm: M-116 pack
    122mm: *M-1938*/D-30; Type-60
    130mm: Type-59
  MRL 30
    107mm: Type-63
    122mm: ε30 BM-21
  MOR
    81mm: some
    107mm: some M-30
    120mm: some Brandt
AT • RCL • 106mm • M-40: some M-40A1
  57mm: some M-18
  75mm: some M-20
  GUNS • 85mm: some Type-56 (D-44)
AD
  SAM • MANPAD: some SA-7 *Grail*
  GUNS 50
    14.5mm: ZPU-4 towed
    37mm: M-1939 towed
    40mm: ε50 L/60 towed

Navy ε1,800
EQUIPMENT BY TYPE
PATROL AND COASTAL COMBATANTS 8: 6 PB *Patrol boat* mostly non-operational (armed)
  PCI 2: 2 *Swiftships* mostly non-operational
FACILITIES
Base 1 (*River*) located at Kinshasa, 1 (*River*) located at Boma, 1 (3 boats) located at Lake Tanganyika, 1 (*Coastal*) located at Matadi

Air Force ε3,000
AIRCRAFT 6 combat capable
  FTR 2: 2 MiG-23 *Flogger*
  FGA 4: 4 SU-25 *Frogfoot*
HELICOPTERS
  ATK 6: 6 Mi-24 *Hind*
  SPT 1+: 1 Mi-26 *Halo*; some Mi-8 *Hip*

Paramilitary • National Police Force some
incl Rapid Intervention Police (National and Provincial forces)

People's Defence Force some

NON-STATE ARMED GROUPS

see Part II

FOREIGN FORCES

(all MONUC)

Algeria 8 obs
Bangladesh 1,301; 15 obs
Belgium 8
Benin 18 obs
Bolivia 221; 4 obs
Bosnia and Herzegovina 5 obs
Burkina Faso 12 obs
Cameroon 1; 3 obs
Canada 8
China 220; 10 obs
Czech Republic 1 obs
Denmark 1; 1 obs
Egypt 15; 8 obs
France 8; 1obs
Ghana 464; 23 obs
Guatemala 107; 4 obs
India 3,514; 36 obs
Indonesia 179; 9 obs
Ireland 1; 2 obs
Jordan 6; 20 obs
Kenya 12; 28 obs
Malawi 27 obs
Malaysia 12; 5 obs
Mali 24 obs
Mongolia 2 obs
Morocco 804; 1 obs
Mozambique 1 obs
Nepal 1,126; 19 obs
Netherlands 1
Niger 2; 18 obs
Nigeria 1; 25 obs
Pakistan 3,770; 25 obs
Paraguay 17 obs
Peru 4 obs
Poland 2 obs
Romania 22; 1 obs
Russia 1; 22 obs
Senegal 473; 9 obs
Serbia and Montenegro 6
South Africa 1,394; 3 obs
Spain 2 obs
Sri Lanka 2 obs
Sweden 5 obs
Switzerland 2
Tunisia 168; 22 obs
Ukraine 1; 12 obs
United Kingdom 6
Uruguay 1,543; 27 obs
Zambia 4; 18 obs

Djibouti Dj

Djiboutian Franc fr		2003	2004	2005
GDP	fr	108bn	110bn	
	US$	610m	624m	
per capita	US$	1,341	1,338	
Growth	%	3.5	3.0	
Inflation	%	2.0	3.0	
Debt	US$	396m		
Def bdgt	fr	4.3bn	ε4.5bn	ε4.6bn
	US$	23.9m	25.3m	25.8m
FMA (US)	US$	13.3m	6.8m	
US$1=fr		178	178	178

Population (2004)   476,703

Ethnic Groups: Somali 60%; Afar 35%

Age	0 – 14	15 – 19	20 – 24	25 – 29	30 – 64	65 plus
Male	22%	5%	5%	4%	14%	2%
Female	22%	5%	5%	4%	12%	2%

Capabilities

ACTIVE 9,850 (Army 8,000 Navy 200 Air 250
Gendarmerie 1,400) **Paramilitary 2,500**

ORGANISATIONS BY SERVICE

Army ε8,000

FORCES BY ROLE
3 Comd (North, Central and South)
Armd   1 sqn
Inf   1 bn (1 AT pl, 1 mor pl)
Cdo   2 (border) bn
AB   1 coy
Arty   1 bty
Spt   1 bn

EQUIPMENT BY TYPE
RECCE 19
   AML 4: 4 AML-60†
   VBL 15
APC • APC (W) • BTR 12: 12 BTR-60 (op status
uncertain)
ARTY 51
   TOWED • 122mm 6: 6 D-30
   MOR 45
      81mm: 25
      120mm 20: 20 Brandt
AT • RCL • 106mm • M-40 16: 16 M-40A1
   RL • 73mm: some RPG-7 *Knout*
      89mm: some LRAC
AD • GUNS 15
   20mm • TOWED 5: 5 M-693 (SP)
   23mm • TOWED 5: 5 ZU-23
   40mm • TOWED 5: 5 L/70

Navy ε200

EQUIPMENT BY TYPE

PATROL AND COASTAL COMBATANTS 7+: some PB

Patrol boat

  PCI 7: 2 *Moussa Ali* less than 100 tonnes; 5 *Sawari* less than 100 tonnes

FACILITIES

Base 1 located at Djibouti

Air Force 250

FORCES BY ROLE

Tpt some sqn with 1 AN-28 *Cash*; 2 L-410UVP *Turbolet*; 1 Cessna U-206G *Stationair*; 1 Cessna 208 *Caravan I*

Hel some sqn with 1 AS-355F *Ecureuil II*; 1 MI-17 (Mi-8MT) *Hip H*

EQUIPMENT BY TYPE

AIRCRAFT

  TPT 4: 1 AN-28 *Cash*; 1 Cessna 402 in store

  L-410 2: 2 L-410UVP *Turbolet*

  UTL 2

    CESSNA 206 • CESSNA U-206 1: 1 Cessna U-206G *Stationair*

    Cessna 208 *Caravan I* 1

  HELICOPTERS • SPT 4

    AS-355 2: 1 AS-355F *Ecureuil II*; 1 in store

    MI-8 2: 1 in store; 1 MI-17 (Mi-8MT) *Hip H*

Paramilitary ε2,500 active

Gendarmerie 1,400

Ministry of Defence

FORCES BY ROLE

1 bn

EQUIPMENT BY TYPE

PATROL AND COASTAL COMBATANTS 1: 1 PB

Patrol boat

National Security Force ε2,500

Ministry of Interior

FOREIGN FORCES

France 2,850 Army: 2 (combined) army regt (*total:* 1 engr coy, 1 arty bty, 2 recce sqn, 2 inf coy) Air Force: 1 Air sqn with 10 M-2000 *Mirage*; 1 C-160 *Transall*; 3 SA-342 *Gazelle*; 7 SA-330 *Puma*; 1 AS-555 *Fennec*; 1 SA-319 *Alouette III*
Germany 3 Tornado ECR SEAD ac opcon EUFOR II/ KFOR; 2 *Sea King* MK41 SAR hel; 2 UH-1D *Iroquois* utl hel

Equatorial Guinea EG

CFA Franc BEAC fr		2003	2004	2005
GDP	fr	1.5tr	2.9tr	
	US$	2.6bn	5.5bn	
per capita	US$	5,081	10,420	
Growth	%	18.3	34.2	
Inflation	%	7.0	8.0	
Debt	US$	319m		
Def bdgt	fr	ε3.4bn	ε3.6bn	ε3.8bn
	US$	5.9m	6.8m	7.3m
US$1=fr		581	533	522

Population (2004)   529,034

Age	0 – 14	15 – 19	20 – 24	25 – 29	30 – 64	65 plus
Male	21%	5%	5%	4%	12%	2%
Female	21%	5%	5%	4%	14%	2%

Capabilities

ACTIVE 1,320 (Army 1,100 Navy 120 Air 100)

ORGANISATIONS BY SERVICE

Army 1,100

FORCES BY ROLE

Inf 3 bn

EQUIPMENT BY TYPE

RECCE • BRDM 6: 6 BRDM-2

APC • APC (W) • BTR 10: 10 BTR-152

Navy 120

EQUIPMENT BY TYPE†

PATROL AND COASTAL COMBATANTS 2: 2 PCI† less than 100 tonnes

FACILITIES

Base 1 located at Bata, 1 located at Malabo (Santa Isabel)

Air Force 100

FORCES BY ROLE

Tpt some sqn with 3 CASA 212 *Aviocar*; 1 Cessna 337 *Skymaster*; 1 YAK-40 *Codling*; 2 SA-316 *Alouette III*

EQUIPMENT BY TYPE

AIRCRAFT • TPT 5: 3 CASA 212 *Aviocar*; 1 Cessna 337 *Skymaster*; 1 YAK-40 *Codling*

HELICOPTERS • UTL 2: 2 SA-316 *Alouette III*

Paramilitary

Guardia Civil some

2 coy

Coast Guard

PATROL AND COASTAL COMBATANTS 1: 1 PCI†

Eritrea Er

Eritrean Nakfa ERN		2003	2004	2005
GDP	ERN	10.8bn	11.1bn	
	US$	791m	822m	
per capita	US$	181	184	
Growth	%	3.0	1.8	
Inflation	%	22.7	21.4	
Debt	US$	634m		
Def bdgt	ERN	2.0bn	ε1.0bn	ε1.0bn
	US$	146m	74m	74m
USD1=ERN		13.8	13.5	13.5

Population (2004)   4,669,638

Ethnic Groups: Tigrinya 50%; Tigre and Kunama 40%; Afar; Saho 3%

Age	0 – 14	15 – 19	20 – 24	25 – 29	30 – 64	65 plus
Male	22%	5%	5%	4%	12%	2%
Female	22%	5%	5%	4%	12%	2%

Capabilities

ACTIVE 201,750 (Army 200,000 Navy 1,400 Air 350)
Terms of service 16 months (4 month mil trg)

RESERVE 120,000 (Army ε120,000)

ORGANISATIONS BY SERVICE

Army ε200,000; ε120,000 reservists ((reported) Total Holdings of army assets n.k.) **(total** 320,000)

FORCES BY ROLE

Army   4 corps
Mech   1 bde
Inf   1 div; 19 div
Cdo   1 div

EQUIPMENT BY TYPE

TK • **MBT** 150: 150 T-54/T-55
RECCE • **BRDM** 40: 40 BRDM-1/BRDM-2
AIFV/APC 40: 40 **BMP-1; BTR-60 APC (W)**
ARTY 170+
   TOWED 10+
      122mm: some D-30
      130mm 10: 10 M-46
   SP 25
      122mm 12: 12 2S1 *Carnation*
      152mm 13: 13 2S5
   MRL • **122mm** 35: 35 BM-21
   MOR 100+: 100+ 120mm/160mm
AT • **MSL** 200: 200 AT-3 *Sagger*/AT-5 *Spandrel*
   RL • **73mm**: some RPG-7 *Knout*
   GUNS • **85mm**: some D-44
AD
   SAM • **MANPAD**: some SA-7 *Grail*
   GUNS • **23mm** 70+: 70+ ZSU-23-4 SP/ZU-23 towed

Navy 1,400

FORCES BY ROLE

Navy 1 HQ located at Massawa

EQUIPMENT BY TYPE

PATROL AND COASTAL COMBATANTS 8
   PCI 3: 3 *Swiftships*
   PFI 4: 4 super Dvora less than 100 tonnes
   PFM 1:
      1 Osa II non-operational with 4 Single each with 1 SS-N-2B *Styx* tactical SSM
AMPHIBIOUS
   LS • LST 1: 1 Chamo (Ministry of Transport)
   CRAFT • LCU 2: 2 Soviet†
FACILITIES
   Base 1 located at Massawa, 1 located at Assab, 1 located at Dahlak

Air Force ε350

FORCES BY ROLE

Ftr / FGA   some sqn with 5 MiG-29 *Fulcrum*; 1 SU-27 *Flanker*; 4 MiG-23 *Flogger*†; 3 MiG-21 *Fishbed*†; 1 MIG-29UB *Fulcrum*
Tpt   some sqn with 1 IAI-1125 *Astra*; 3 Y-12(II)
Trg   some sqn with 6 L-90 *Redigo*; 4 MB-339CE*
Hel   some sqn with 1 Mi-24-4 *Hind*; 4 MI-17 (Mi-8MT) *Hip H*/Mi-8 *Hip*

EQUIPMENT BY TYPE

AIRCRAFT 17 combat capable
   FTR 13: 5 MiG-29 *Fulcrum*; 1 SU-27 *Flanker*; 4 MiG-23 *Flogger*†; 3 MiG-21 *Fishbed*†
   TPT 4: 1 IAI-1125 *Astra*
      Y-12 3: 3 Y-12(II)
   TRG 11: 6 L-90 *Redigo*
      MB-339 4: 4 MB-339CE*
      MIG-29U 1: 1 MIG-29UB *Fulcrum*
HELICOPTERS
   ATK • MI-24 1: 1 Mi-24-4 *Hind*
   SPT • MI-8 4: 4 MI-17 (Mi-8MT) *Hip H*/Mi-8 *Hip* spt hel

NON-STATE ARMED GROUPS

see Part II

Ethiopia Eth

Ethiopian Birr EB		2003	2004	2005
GDP	EB	56.6bn	63.6bn	
	US$	6.6bn	7.4bn	
per capita	US$	95	104	
Growth	%	-3.9	11.6	
Inflation	%	15.1	9.0	
Debt	US$	7.15bn		
Def bdgt	EB	2.6bn	ε2.5bn	ε2.0bn
	US$	298m	290m	229m
FMA (US)	US$	4.2m	3.0m	2.6m
US$1=EB		8.6	8.6	8.7

Population (2004) 73,053,286

Ethnic Groups: Oromo 40%; Amhara and Tigrean 32%; Sidamo 9%; Shankella 6%; Somali 6%; Afar 4%

Age	0 – 14	15 – 19	20 – 24	25 – 29	30 – 64	65 plus
Male	22%	6%	5%	4%	13%	1%
Female	22%	6%	5%	4%	13%	1%

Capabilities

ACTIVE 182,500 (Army 180,000 Air 2,500)

ORGANISATIONS BY SERVICE

Army 180,000

FORCES BY ROLE

Reorg to consist of 3 Mil Regions each with corps HQ; strategic reserve div of 6 bde will be located at Addis Ababa.

Army 3 corps HQ (*each*: 1 (reinforced) mech bde, 2 army div)

EQUIPMENT BY TYPE

TK • MBT 250+: 250+ T-54/T-55/T-62

RECCE/AIFV/APC (W) ε400: BRDM, BMP, BTR-152, BTR-60

ARTY 460+

　TOWED 400

　76mm: ZIS-3 *M-1942*

　122mm: ε400 D-30/M-30 *M-1938*

　130mm: M-46

　SP 10+

　　122mm: some 2S1 *Carnation*

　　152mm 10: 10 2S19 *Farm*

　MRL • **122mm** 50: ε50 BM-21

　MOR • **81mm:** some M-1/M-29

　　82mm: some M-1937

　　120mm: some M-1944

AT • MSL: some AT-3 *Sagger*

　RCL • **82mm:** some B-10

　　107mm: some B-11

　GUNS • **85mm:** εD-44

AD • SAM 370: ε370 SA-2 *Guideline* Towed/SA-3 *Goa*/SA-7 *Grail* MANPAD

　GUNS • **23mm** • SP: some ZSU-23-4

　TOWED: some ZU-23

　37mm • TOWED: some M-1939

　57mm • TOWED: some S-60

Air Force ε2,500

FORCES BY ROLE

FGA　some sqn with 6 SU-27 *Flanker*; 25 MIG-21MF *Fishbed J*; 2 SU-25T *Frogfoot*; 13 MIG-23BN *Flogger H*; 2 SU-25UB *Frogfoot B*

Tpt　some sqn with 10 AN-12 *Cub*; 4 C-130B *Hercules*; 6 DHC-6 twin *Otter*; 2 Y-12; 1 YAK-40 *Codling* (VIP)

Atk hel　some sqn with 25 Mi-24 *Hind*

Spt hel　some sqn with 12 MI-17 (Mi-8MT) *Hip H*/Mi-8 *Hip*

Trg　some sqn with 12 L-39 *Albatros*; 4 SF-260

EQUIPMENT BY TYPE

AIRCRAFT 48 combat capable

　FTR 31: 6 SU-27 *Flanker*

　　MIG-21 • MIG-21M 25: 25 MIG-21MF *Fishbed J*

　FGA 15

　　SU-25 2: 2 SU-25T *Frogfoot*

　　MIG-23B 13: 13 MIG-23BN *Flogger H*

　TPT 23: 10 AN-12 *Cub*

　　C-130 4: 4 C-130B *Hercules*

　　DHC-6 twin *Otter* 6; 2 Y-12; 1 YAK-40 *Codling* (VIP)

　TRG 18: 12 L-39 *Albatros*; 4 SF-260; 2 SU-25UB *Frogfoot B**

HELICOPTERS

　ATK 25: 25 Mi-24 *Hind*

　SPT • MI-8 12: 12 MI-17 (Mi-8MT) *Hip H*/Mi-8 *Hip* spt hel

Armed Forces

Peacekeeping　855 opcon ONUB; 1,703 opcon UNMIL; 17 obs opcon UNMIL

NON-STATE ARMED GROUPS

see Part II

DEPLOYMENT

BURUNDI

UN • ONUB 855; 7 obs

LIBERIA

UN • UNMIL 2,547; 17 obs

Gabon Gbn

CFA Franc BEAC fr		2003	2004	2005
GDP	fr	4.5tr	4.8tr	
	US$	7.7bn	9.0bn	
per capita	US$	5,860	6,645	
Growth	%	2.6	1.9	
Inflation	%	2.1	1.0	
Debt	US$	3.8bn		
Def bdgt	fr	ε9.0bn	ε9.0bn	ε10.0bn
	US$	15.4m	16.8m	19.1m
US$1=fr		581	533	522

Population (2004)   1,394,307

Age	0 – 14	15 – 19	20 – 24	25 – 29	30 – 64	65 plus
Male	21%	6%	4%	3%	13%	2%
Female	21%	6%	4%	4%	13%	2%

Capabilities

ACTIVE 4,700 (Army 3,200 Navy 500 Air 1,000)
Paramilitary 2,000

ORGANISATIONS BY SERVICE

Army 3,200

FORCES BY ROLE
Inf	8 coy
Cdo / AB	1 coy
Engr	1 coy
Presidential Guard	1 (bn) gp (under direct presidential control) (1 ADA bty, 1 arty bty, 1 armd/recce coy, 3 inf coy)

EQUIPMENT BY TYPE
RECCE 70
   AML 24: 24 AML-60/AML-90
   12 **EE-3** *Jararaca*; 14 EE-9 *Cascavel*; 6 ERC-90F4 *Sagaie*; 14 VBL
APC • APC (W) 33+: 12 EE-11 *Urutu* (with 20mm gun)
   LAV 9: 9 LAV-150 *Commando*
   some **M-3** *Panhard*; 12 VXB-170
ARTY 51
   TOWED • 105mm 4: 4 M-101
   MRL • 140mm 8: 8 Teruel
   MOR 39
      81mm: 35
      120mm 4: 4 Brandt
AT • MSL 4: 4 Milan
   RCL • 106mm • M-40: some M-40A1
   RL • 89mm: some LRAC
AD • GUNS 41
   20mm • SP 4: 4 ERC-20
   23mm • TOWED 24: 24 ZU-23-2
   37mm • TOWED 10: 10 M-1939
   40mm • TOWED 3: 3 L/70

Navy ε500

FORCES BY ROLE
Navy 1 HQ located at Port Gentil

EQUIPMENT BY TYPE
PATROL AND COASTAL COMBATANTS • PCC 2: 2 General Ba'Oumar (Fr P-400)
AMPHIBIOUS
   LS • LST 1:
      1 President Omar Bongo (capacity 140 troops; 7 Tks) (Fr Batral)
   CRAFT 1: 1 LCM
FACILITIES
Base 1 located at Port Gentil

Air Force 1,000

FORCES BY ROLE
FGA	some sqn with 2 *Mirage* 5G (*Mirage* 5); 4 *Mirage* 5E2; 3 *Mirage* 5DG (*Mirage* 5D)
MR	some sqn with 1 EMB-111*
CCT	some (Presidential Guard) sqn with 4 CM-170 *Magister*; 3 T-34 *Turbo Mentor*
Tpt	some (Presidential Guard) sqn with 1 ATR-42F; 1 EMB-110 *Bandeirante*; 1 *Falcon* 900; 1 AS-332 *Super Puma*; some sqn with 1 C-130H *Hercules*; 1 CN-235; 1 EMB-110 *Bandeirante*; 3 L-100-30; 2 YS-11A
Hel	some sqn with 5 SA-342 *Gazelle**; 3 SA-330C *Puma*/SA-330H *Puma*; 3 SA-316 *Alouette III*/SA-319 *Alouette III*; 2 AB-412 (Bell 412) twin *Huey*

EQUIPMENT BY TYPE
AIRCRAFT 10 combat capable
   FGA 6: 2 *Mirage* 5G (*Mirage* 5); 4 *Mirage* 5E2
   RECCE • MR 1: 1 EMB-111*
   TPT 9: 1 ATR-42F
      C-130 1: 1 C-130H *Hercules*
      CN-235 1; 2 EMB-110 *Bandeirante*; 1 *Falcon* 900
      L-100 3: 3 L-100-30
   UTL • YS-11 2: 2 YS-11A
   TRG 10: 4 CM-170 *Magister*; 3 *Mirage* 5DG (*Mirage* 5D)*; 3 T-34 *Turbo Mentor*
HELICOPTERS
   ATK 5: 5 SA-342 *Gazelle**
   SPT 4: 1 AS-332 *Super Puma*
      SA-330 3: 3 SA-330C *Puma*/SA-330H *Puma*
   UTL 5: 3 SA-316 *Alouette III*/SA-319 *Alouette III*; 2 AB-412 (Bell 412) twin *Huey*

Paramilitary 2,000

Gendarmerie 2,000
FORCES BY ROLE
Armd	2 sqn
Paramilitary	3 bde; 11 coy
Avn	1 unit with 2 AS-350 *Ecureuil*; 1 AS-355 *Ecureuil*

EQUIPMENT BY TYPE
HELICOPTERS • SPT 3: 2 AS-350 *Ecureuil*; 1 AS-355 *Ecureuil*

DEPLOYMENT

BURUNDI
UN • ONUB 5 obs

CENTRAL AFRICAN REPUBLIC
CEMAC 140

FOREIGN FORCES

France 1,560: Army: 1 recce pl with ERC-90F *Sagaie*; 1 marine inf bn; 4 AS-532 *Horizon* RECCE hel Air Force: 2 C-160 *Transall* Tpt ac; 1 AS-555 *Fennec* utl hel

The Gambia Gam

Gambian Dalasi D		2003	2004	2005
GDP	D	9.0bn	10.4bn	
	US$	330m	353m	
per capita	US$	220	228	
Growth	%	6.7	7.7	
Inflation	%	17.0	14.6	
Debt	US$	628m		
Def bdgt	D	64m	ε65m	ε65m
	US$	2.4m	2.2m	2.3m
US$1=D		27.2	29.7	28.3

Population (2004) 1,595,086

Age	0 – 14	15 – 19	20 – 24	25 – 29	30 – 64	65 plus
Male	22%	5%	4%	4%	13%	1%
Female	22%	5%	4%	4%	13%	1%

Capabilities

ACTIVE 800 (Army 800)

ORGANISATIONS BY SERVICE

Gambian National Army 800
Inf	2 bn
Engr	1 sqn
Presidential Guard	1 coy

Marine Unit circa 70
EQUIPMENT BY TYPE
PATROL AND COASTAL COMBATANTS 3: 3 PCI less than 100 tonnes
FACILITIES
Base 1 located at Banjul

DEPLOYMENT

BURUNDI
UN • ONUB 2 obs

CÔTE D'IVOIRE
UN • ONUCI 1; 5 obs

ETHIOPIA/ERITREA
UN • UNMEE 2; 4 obs

LIBERIA
UN • UNMIL 5 obs

SIERRA LEONE
UN • UNAMSIL 8 obs

Ghana Gha

Ghanaian Cedi C		2003	2004	2005
GDP	C	6.4tr	7.7tr	
	US$	7.4bn	8.5tr	
per capita	US$	360	408	
Growth	%	5.2	5.5	
Inflation	%	26.7	12.6	
Debt	US$	8bn		
Def bdgt	C	439bn	ε450bn	ε450bn
	US$	50.6m	49.6m	49.5m
FMA (US)	US$	1.0m	1.7m	1.1m
US$1=C		8,677	9,055	9,080

Population (2004) 21,946,247

Age	0 – 14	15 – 19	20 – 24	25 – 29	30 – 64	65 plus
Male	20%	6%	5%	4%	14%	2%
Female	19%	6%	5%	4%	14%	2%

Capabilities

ACTIVE 7,000 (Army 5,000 Navy 1,000 Air 1,000)

ORGANISATIONS BY SERVICE

Army 5,000
FORCES BY ROLE
2 Comd HQ
Army	2 bde (*total:* 1 spt unit, 1 (ECOMOG) inf bn, 1 (UNIFIL) inf bn, 4 inf bn)
Recce	1 regt (3 recce sqn)
AB / SF	2 coy
Arty	1 regt (1 arty bty, 2 mor bty)
Presidential Guard	1 bn
Fd engr	1 regt (bn)
Trg	1 bn

EQUIPMENT BY TYPE
RECCE 3: 3 EE-9 *Cascavel*
APC • APC (W) 50: 50 Piranha
ARTY 84
  TOWED • 122mm 6: 6 D-30
  MOR 78
    81mm: 50
    120mm 28: 28 Tampella
AT • RCL • 84mm 50: 50 *Carl Gustav*
AD
  SAM • MANPAD: some SA-7 *Grail*
  GUNS 8+
    14.5mm • TOWED • ZPU 4+: 4 ZPU-2; some ZPU-4
    23mm • TOWED 4: 4 ZU-23-2

Navy 1,000

FORCES BY ROLE
Navy 1 (Western) HQ located at Sekondi; 1 (Eastern) HQ located at Tema

EQUIPMENT BY TYPE
PATROL AND COASTAL COMBATANTS 6
  PCC 4: 2 Anzole (US); 2 Dzata (Ge Lurssen 45m)
  PFC 2: 2 Achimota (Ge Lurssen 57m)

FACILITIES
Base 1 located at Sekondi, 1 located at Tema

Air Force 1,000

FORCES BY ROLE
Tpt some sqn with 1 CASA 212 *Aviocar*; 4 F-27 *Friendship*; 1 F-28 *Fellowship* (VIP); 1 *Gulfstream* III; 6 SC.7 3M *Skyvan*

Trg some sqn with 3 MB-326K*; 12 L-29 *Delfin**; 2 L-39 *Albatros**; 2 MB-339F*

Hel some sqn with 2 PZL MI-2 *Hoplite*; 4 AB-212 (Bell 212) (1 VIP, 3 utl); 4 SA-319 *Alouette III*

EQUIPMENT BY TYPE
AIRCRAFT 19 combat capable
  FGA 3: 3 MB-326K*
  TPT 13: 1 CASA 212 *Aviocar*; 4 F-27 *Friendship*; 1 F-28 *Fellowship* (VIP); 1 *Gulfstream* III; 6 SC.7 3M *Skyvan*
  TRG 16: 12 L-29 *Delfin**; 2 L-39 *Albatros**
    MB-339 2: 2 MB-339F*
HELICOPTERS
  SPT 2: 2 PZL MI-2 *Hoplite*
  UTL 8: 4 AB-212 (Bell 212) (1 VIP, 3 utl); 4 SA-319 *Alouette III*

DEPLOYMENT

BURUNDI
UN • **ONUB** 2 obs

CÔTE D'IVOIRE
UN • **ONUCI** 402; 6 obs

DEMOCRATIC REPUBLIC OF CONGO
UN • **MONUC** 464; 23 obs

ETHIOPIA/ERITREA
UN • **UNMEE** 4; 12 obs

LEBANON
UN • **UNIFIL** 1 inf bn; 652

LIBERIA
UN • **UNMIL** 859; 11 obs

SIERRA LEONE
UN • **UNAMSIL** 762; 4 obs

WESTERN SAHARA
UN • **MINURSO** 7; 10 obs

Guinea Gui

Guinean Franc fr		2003	2004	2005
GDP	fr	7.5tr	9.2tr	
	US$	3.8bn	4.5bn	
per capita	US$	419	484	
Growth	%	2.1	2.5	
Inflation	%	12.9	17.5	
Debt	US$	3.5bn		
Def bdgt	fr	ε200bn	ε220bn	εε250bn
	US$	100m	107m	72m
US$1=fr		1,984	2,055	3,470

Population (2004) 9,452,670

Age	0 – 14	15 – 19	20 – 24	25 – 29	30 – 64	65 plus
Male	22%	5%	4%	4%	13%	1%
Female	22%	5%	4%	4%	13%	2%

Capabilities

ACTIVE 9,700 (Army 8,500 Navy 400 Air 800)
Paramilitary 2,600 Inactive Other 7,000
Terms of service conscription, 2 years

ORGANISATIONS BY SERVICE

Army 8,500

FORCES BY ROLE
Armd 1 bn
Inf 5 bn
SF 1 bn
Ranger 1 bn
Cdo 1 bn
Arty 1 bn
Engr 1 bn
AD 1 bn

EQUIPMENT BY TYPE†
TK 53
  MBT 38: 8 T-54 ; 30 T-34
  LT TK 15: 15 PT-76
RECCE 27
  AML 2: 2 AML-90
  BRDM 25: 25 BRDM-1/BRDM-2
APC • **APC (W)** • **BTR** 40: 6 BTR-152; 16 BTR-40; 10 BTR-50; 8 BTR-60
ARTY 40+
  TOWED 20
    76mm 8: 8 ZIS-3 *M-1942*
    122mm 12: 12 M-1931/37
  MOR 20+
    82mm: some M-43
    120mm 20: 20 M-1943/M-38
AT
  MSL: some AT-3 *Sagger*
  RCL • **82mm**: some B-10
  RL • **73mm**: some RPG-7 *Knout*
  GUNS 6+

57mm: some ZIS-2 *M-1943*
85mm 6: 6 D-44

AD
SAM • MANPAD: some SA-7 *Grail*
GUNS 24+
30mm • TOWED: some M-53 (twin)
37mm • TOWED 8: 8 M-1939
57mm • TOWED 12: 12 Type-59 (S-60)
100mm • TOWED 4: 4 KS-19

Navy 400

EQUIPMENT BY TYPE†
PATROL AND COASTAL COMBATANTS • PCI 2: 2
Swiftships† less than 100 tonnes

FACILITIES
Base 1 located at Conakry, 1 located at Kakanda

Air Force 800

FORCES BY ROLE
FGA   some sqn with 4 MiG-21 *Fishbed*; 4 MIG-17F *Fresco C*
Tpt   some sqn with 1 AN-24 *Coke*; 4 AN-14
Trg   some sqn with 2 MIG-15UTI *Midget*
Hel   some sqn with 1 SA-342K *Gazelle*; 1 SA-330
       Puma; 1† (IAR); 1 Mi-8 *Hip*; 1 SA-316B *Alouette III*

EQUIPMENT BY TYPE†
AIRCRAFT 8 combat capable
FTR 8: 4 MiG-21 *Fishbed*
   MIG-17 4: 4 MIG-17F *Fresco C*
TPT 1: 1 AN-24 *Coke*
UTL 4: 4 AN-14
TRG 2: 2 MIG-15UTI *Midget*
HELICOPTERS
ATK • SA-342 1: 1 SA-342K *Gazelle*
SPT 3: 1 SA-330 *Puma*; 1 (IAR); 1 Mi-8 *Hip*
UTL • SA-316 1: 1 SA-316B *Alouette III*
MSL • TACTICAL • AAM: some AA-2 *Atoll*

Paramilitary 2,600 active

Gendarmerie 1,000

Republican Guard 1,600

People's Militia 7,000

NON-STATE ARMED GROUPS

see Part II

DEPLOYMENT

BURUNDI
UN • ONUB 2 obs

CÔTE D'IVOIRE
UN • ONUCI 3 obs

DEMOCRATIC REPUBLIC OF CONGO
UN • MONUC 107; 4 obs

SIERRA LEONE
UN • UNAMSIL 5 obs

WESTERN SAHARA
UN • MINURSO 3 obs

Guinea Bissau GuB

CFA Franc BCEAO fr		2003	2004	2005
GDP	fr	137bn	144bn	
	US$	237m	272m	
per capita	US$	174	195	
Growth	%	0.6	4.3	
Inflation	%	3.0	3.0	
Debt	US$	745		
Def exp	fr	4.4bn	ε4.5bn	ε4.5bn
	US$	7.5m	8.4m	8.6m
US$1=fr		581	533	522

Population (2004)   1,413,446

Age	0 – 14	15 – 19	20 – 24	25 – 29	30 – 64	65 plus
Male	21%	5%	5%	4%	13%	1%
Female	21%	5%	5%	4%	13%	2%

Capabilities

ACTIVE 9,250 (Army 6,800 Navy 350 Air 100
Gendarmerie 2,000)
Terms of service conscription (selective).
As a result of the 1998 revolt by dissident army tps,
manpower and eqpt totals should be treated with caution.

ORGANISATIONS BY SERVICE

Army 6,800

FORCES BY ROLE
Armd   1 bn (sqn)
Recce   1 coy
Inf   5 bn
Arty   1 bn
Engr   1 coy

EQUIPMENT BY TYPE
TK 25
   MBT 10: 10 T-34
   LT TK 15: 15 PT-76
RECCE • BRDM 10: 10 BRDM-2
APC • APC (W) • BTR 55: 35 BTR-40/BTR-60/Type-56
(BTR-152); 20 Type-56 (BTR-152)
ARTY 26+
   TOWED • 122mm 18: 18 D-30/*M-1938*
   MOR 8+
      82mm: some M-43
      120mm 8: 8 M-1943
AT
   RCL • 75mm: some Type-52 (M-20)
      82mm: some B-10
   RL • 89mm: some M-20
   GUNS • 85mm 8: 8 D-44
AD
   SAM • MANPAD: some SA-7 *Grail*
   GUNS 34
      23mm • TOWED 18: 18 ZU-23
      37mm • TOWED 6: 6 M-1939
      57mm • TOWED 10: 10 S-60

Navy ε350

EQUIPMENT BY TYPE
PATROL AND COASTAL COMBATANTS 3: 1 PCI
  PCI 3: 2 Alfeite
FACILITIES
Base 1 located at Bissau

Air Force 100

FORCES BY ROLE
Ftr / FGA some sqn with 3 MiG-17 *Fresco*
Hel   some sqn with 1 SA-318 *Alouette II*;
           2 SA-319 *Alouette III*

EQUIPMENT BY TYPE
AIRCRAFT 3 combat capable
FTR 3: 3 MiG-17 *Fresco*
HELICOPTERS • UTL 3: 1 SA-318 *Alouette II*; 2 SA-319 *Alouette III*

Paramilitary

Gendarmerie 2,000

Kenya Kya

Kenyan Shilling sh		2003	2004	2005
GDP	sh	1.1tr	1.1tr	
	US$	14.3bn	13.9bn	
per capita	US$	446	422	
Growth	%	1.6	3.1	
Inflation	%	9.8	11.5	
Debt	US$	6.8bn		
Def bdgt	sh	18.7bn	ε20.0bn	ε22.0bn
	US$	246m	251m	288m
FMA (US)	US$	1.6m	7.2m	7.6m
US$1=sh		75.9	79.4	76.4

Population (2004) 32,982,109

Ethnic Groups: Kikuyu ε22–32%

Age	0 – 14	15 – 19	20 – 24	25 – 29	30 – 64	65 plus
Male	21%	6%	6%	5%	12%	1%
Female	21%	6%	5%	4%	12%	1%

Capabilities

ACTIVE 24,120 (Army 20,000 Navy 1,620 Air 2,500)
Paramilitary 5,000
(incl HQ staff)

ORGANISATIONS BY SERVICE

Army 20,000

FORCES BY ROLE
Armd   1 bde (3 armd bn)
Air Cav 1 indep bn
Inf   1 bde (2 inf bn); 1 bde (3 inf bn); 1 indep bn

AB   1 bn
Arty   1 bde (2 arty bn)
ADA   1 bn
Engr   1 bde (2 engr bn)

EQUIPMENT BY TYPE
TK • MBT 78: 78 Vickers Mk 3
RECCE 92
  AML 72: 72 AML-60/AML-90
  12 *Ferret*; 8 S52 *Shorland*
APC • APC (W) 62: 10 M-3 *Panhard* (in store); 52 UR-416
ARTY 110
  TOWED • 105mm 48: 8 Model 56 pack howitzer; 40 lt
  MOR 62
    81mm: 50
    120mm 12: 12 Brandt
AT
  MSL 54: 40 Milan; 14 Swingfire
  RCL • 84mm 80: 80 *Carl Gustav*
AD • GUNS 94
  20mm • TOWED 81: 11 Oerlikon; ε70 TCM-20
  40mm • TOWED 13: 13 L/70

Navy 1,620 (incl 120 marines)

EQUIPMENT BY TYPE
PATROL AND COASTAL COMBATANTS 4
  PFM 2:
    2 Nyayo (UK Vosper 57m) each with 2 twin (4 eff.) each with 1 Otomat tactical SSM, 1 76mm gun
  PCO 2:
    2 Shujaa each with 1 76mm gun
AMPHIBIOUS • CRAFT • LCM 2: 2 Galana
LOGISTICS AND SUPPORT 1: 1 AT *Tug*
FACILITIES
Base 1 located at Mombasa

Air Force 2,500

FORCES BY ROLE
FGA   some sqn with 9 F-5E *Tiger II*/F-5F *Tiger II*†
Tpt   some sqn with 7 DHC-5D *Buffalo*†; 3 DHC-8 *Dash 8*†; 1 Fokker 70† (VIP); 1 PA-31 *Navajo*†; 12 Y-12(II)†
Atk hel some sqn with 11 Hughes 500MD *Scout Defender*† (with TOW); 8 Hughes 500ME†; 15 Hughes 500M†
Spt hel some sqn with 3 SA-330 *Puma*†; 9†; 5 MI-17 (Mi-8MT) *Hip H*†
Trg   some sqn with up to 5 Bulldog 103/Bulldog 127†; 12 EMB-312 *Tucano*†*; 8 *Hawk* MK52†*; 2 Hughes 500D†

EQUIPMENT BY TYPE†
AIRCRAFT 29 combat capable
  FTR • F-5 9: 9 F-5E *Tiger II*/F-5F *Tiger II*†
  TPT 30
    DHC-5 7: 7 DHC-5D *Buffalo*†
    DHC-8 *Dash 8* 3†
    DO-28 • DO-28D 6: 6 DO-28D-2† in store
    Fokker 70 1† (VIP); 1 PA-31 *Navajo*†
    Y-12 12: 12 Y-12(II)†
  TRG up to 25: up to 5 Bulldog 103/Bulldog 127†;

12 EMB-312 *Tucano*†*; 8 *Hawk* MK52†*

HELICOPTERS
ATK: 11 Hughes 500MD *Scout Defender*† (with TOW);
ASLT: 8 Hughes 500ME†
SPT 17: 12 SA-330 *Puma*† MI-8 5: 5 MI-17 (Mi-8MT) *Hip H*†
UTL • HUGHES 500 17: 2 Hughes 500D†; 15 Hughes 500M†

MSL • TACTICAL • ASM: some AGM-65 *Maverick* (TOW)
AAM: some AIM-9 *Sidewinder*

Paramilitary 5,000

Police General Service Unit 5,000
PATROL AND COASTAL COMBATANTS 17
MISC BOATS/CRAFT 12: 12 boats
PCI 5 less than 100 tonnes (2 Lake Victoria)

Air Wing
AIRCRAFT: 7 tpt (Cessna)
HELICOPTERS
UTL • BELL 206 1: 1 Bell 206L *LongRanger*
TRG 2: 2 Bell 47G

DEPLOYMENT

BURUNDI
UN • **ONUB** 2 obs; 1,007

CÔTE D'IVOIRE
UN • **ONUCI** 5 obs; 4

DEMOCRATIC REPUBLIC OF CONGO
UN • **MONUC** 12; 29 obs

ETHIOPIA/ERITREA
UN • **UNMEE** 11 obs; 325

LIBERIA
UN • **UNMIL** 4; 3 obs

SERBIA AND MONTENEGRO
UN • **UNMIK** 1 obs

SIERRA LEONE
UN • **UNAMSIL** 6 obs

SUDAN
UN • **UNMIS** 3 obs

WESTERN SAHARA
UN • **MINURSO** 10 obs

FOREIGN FORCES

United Kingdom Army: 20

Lesotho Ls

Lesotho Loti M		2003	2004	2005
GDP	M	8.6bn	10.2bn	
	US$	1.1bn	1.7bn	
per capita	US$	610	903	
Growth	%	5.2	2.3	
Inflation	%	7.6	5.5	
Debt	US$	706m		
Def bdgt	M	ε200m	ε200m	ε210m
	US$	26.4m	32.7m	32.3m
US$1=M		7.6	6.1	6.5

Population (2004)   2,031,348

Age	0 – 14	15 – 19	20 – 24	25 – 29	30 – 64	65 plus
Male	19%	6%	5%	4%	12%	2%
Female	18%	6%	5%	4%	14%	3%

Capabilities

ACTIVE 2,000 (Army 2,000)

ORGANISATIONS BY SERVICE

Army ε2,000
FORCES BY ROLE
Recce   1 coy
Inf   7 coy
Arty   1 bty under strength
Avn   1 sqn
Spt   1 coy (with 81mm mor)

EQUIPMENT BY TYPE
RECCE 22
AML 4: 4 AML-90
10 RBY-1 *RAMTA*; 8 S52 *Shorland*
ARTY 12
TOWED 2
105mm: 2
MOR 10
81mm: 10
AT • RCL • 106mm 6: 6 M-40

Air Wing 110
AIRCRAFT
MP 1: 1 CASA 212-400 *Aviocar* (tpt, VIP tpt, casevac)
TPT 3
CASA 212 2: 2 CASA 212-300 *Aviocar*
GA-8 *Airvan* 1
HELICOPTERS
UTL 4
BO-105 • BO-105LSA 1: 1 BO-105LSA-3 (tpt, trg)
BELL 412 3: 2 (SP); 1 Bell 412EP twin *Huey* (tpt, VIP tpt, SAR)

Liberia Lb

Liberian Dollar L$		2003	2004	2005
GDP	L$	23.4bn	24.5bn	
	US$	396m	490m	
per capita	US$	119	144	
Growth	%	-31.3	2.4	
Inflation	%	10.3	7.8	
Debt	US$	ε2.56 bn		
Def exp	L$	ε45m	ε50m	ε50m
	US$	0.8m	0.9m	1.0m
FMA (US)	US$			3m
US$1=L$		59.3	50.0	50.0

Population (2004)   2,900,269

Ethnic Groups: Americo-Liberians 5%

Age	0 – 14	15 – 19	20 – 24	25 – 29	30 – 64	65 plus
Male	21%	6%	5%	4%	13%	1%
Female	21%	6%	5%	4%	13%	1%

Capabilities

ACTIVE 15,000 (Joint 15,000)

ORGANISATIONS BY SERVICE

Armed FORCES BY ROLE ε11,000–15,000 on mobilisation

Total includes militias supporting govt forces. No further details.

NON-STATE ARMED GROUPS

see Part II

FOREIGN FORCES

(all UNMIL)

Bangladesh 3,199; 17 obs
Benin 2 obs; 1
Bolivia 1; 3 obs
Brazil 1
Bulgaria 2 obs
China, Peoples Republic of 567; 5 obs
Croatia 3
Czech Republic 3 obs
Denmark 1 obs
Ecuador 1; 3 obs
Egypt 8 obs
El Salvador 3 obs
Ethiopia 2,549; 17 obs
Finland 2
France 1
Germany 15
Ghana 11 obs; 859
Indonesia 3 obs

Ireland 426
Jordan 124; 7 obs
Kenya 4; 3 obs
Kyrgyzstan 3 obs
Malawi 2
Malaysia 10 obs
Mali 4 obs; 2
Moldova 1 (staff officer); 3 obs
Namibia 864; 3 obs
Nepal 42; 3 obs
Niger 3 obs
Nigeria 1,967; 19 obs
Pakistan 16 obs; 2,749
Paraguay 3 obs; 1
Peru 2; 3 obs
Philippines 172; 3 obs
Poland 2 obs
Republic of Korea 1; 1 obs
Romania 3 obs
Russia 6 obs
Senegal 3 obs; 603
Serbia and Montenegro 6 obs
Sweden 233
The Gambia 5 obs
Togo 2 obs; 1
Ukraine 300; 3 obs
United Kingdom 3
United States 7 obs; 6
Zambia 3 obs

Madagascar Mdg

Malagsy Ariary fr		2003	2004	2005
GDP	fr	33.9tr	36.0tr	
	US$	5.5bn	3.9bn	
per capita	US$	322	221	
Growth	%	9.8	5.3	
Inflation	%	-1.1	13.8	
Debt	US$	5bn		
Def bdgt	fr	400bn	468bn	538bn
	US$	64.7m	50.4m	275m
US$1=fr		6,191	9,305	1,954

Population (2004)   18,040,341

Age	0 – 14	15 – 19	20 – 24	25 – 29	30 – 64	65 plus
Male	22%	5%	4%	4%	12%	1%
Female	22%	5%	4%	4%	13%	2%

Capabilities

ACTIVE 13,500 (Army 12,500 Navy 500 Air 500)
Paramilitary 8,100
Terms of service conscription (incl for civil purposes) 18 months

ORGANISATIONS BY SERVICE

Army 12,500+

FORCES BY ROLE

Army 2 (gp) bn

Engr 1 regt

EQUIPMENT BY TYPE

TK • LT TK 12: 12 PT-76

RECCE 73

   BRDM 35: ε35 BRDM-2

   10 *Ferret*; ε20 M-3A1; 8 M-8

APC • APC (T) 30: ε30 M-3A1 half-track;

ARTY 37+

   TOWED 29

     76mm 12: 12 ZIS-3

     105mm 5: 5 M-101

     122mm 12: 12 D-30

   MOR 8+

     82mm: some M-37

     120mm 8: 8 M-43

AT • RCL • 106mm • M-40: some M-40A1

RL • 89mm: some LRAC

AD • GUNS 70

   14.5mm • TOWED • ZPU 50: 50 ZPU-4

   37mm • TOWED 20: 20 Type-55 (M-1939)

Navy 500 (incl some 100 Marines)

EQUIPMENT BY TYPE

AMPHIBIOUS • CRAFT 1: 1 LCT† (Fr Edic)

LOGISTICS AND SUPPORT 1: 1 tpt/trg†

FACILITIES

Base 1 located at Diégo Suarez, 1 located at Tamatave, 1 located at Fort Dauphin, 1 located at Tuléar, 1 located at Majunga

Air Force 500

FORCES BY ROLE

Tpt   some sqn with 1 AN-26 *Curl*; 3†; 1 BN-2 Islander; 2 CASA 212 *Aviocar*; 2 YAK-40 *Codling* (VIP)

Liaison some sqn with 1 Cessna 310; 2 Cessna 337 *Skymaster*; 1 PA-23 *Aztec*

Trg   some sqn with 4 Cessna 172

Hel   1 sqn with 6 Mi-8 *Hip*

EQUIPMENT BY TYPE

AIRCRAFT

   TPT 14: 1 AN-26 *Curl*; 3†; 1 BN-2 Islander; 2 CASA 212 *Aviocar*; 1 Cessna 310; 2 Cessna 337 *Skymaster*; 4 YAK-40 *Codling* (VIP)

   UTL 5: 4 Cessna 172; 1 PA-23 *Aztec*

HELICOPTERS • SPT 6: 6 Mi-8 *Hip*

Paramilitary 8,100

Gendarmerie 8,100

PATROL AND COASTAL COMBATANTS 5: 5 PCI less than 100 tonnes

Malawi Miw

Malawian Kwacha K		2003	2004	2005
GDP	K	153bn	168bn	
	US$	1.6bn	1.6bn	
per capita	US$	135	131	
Growth	%	3.9	4.3	
Inflation	%	9.6	11.6	
Debt	US$	3.1bn		
Def bdgt	K	1.3bn	ε1.4bn	ε1.5bn
	US$	13.4m	12.9m	12.8m
US$1=K		97.4	108	117

Population (2004) 12,707,464

Age	0 – 14	15 – 19	20 – 24	25 – 29	30 – 64	65 plus
Male	23%	6%	5%	4%	11%	1%
Female	23%	6%	5%	4%	11%	2%

Capabilities

ACTIVE 5,300 (Army 5,300) **Paramilitary 1,500**

ORGANISATIONS BY SERVICE

Army 5,300

FORCES BY ROLE

Inf   3 bn

Para 1 indep bn

Marine 1+ coy

Spt   1 (general) bn (1 armd recce sqn, 1 engr unit, 2 lt arty bty)

EQUIPMENT BY TYPE

Less than 20% serviceability

RECCE 41: 13 Eland; 20 FV721 *Fox*; 8 Ferret

ARTY 17

   TOWED • 105mm 9: 9 lt

   MOR • 81mm 8: 8 L16

AD

   SAM • MANPAD 15: 15 Blowpipe

   GUNS • 14.5mm • TOWED • ZPU 40: 40 ZPU-4

Maritime Wing 220

EQUIPMENT BY TYPE

PATROL AND COASTAL COMBATANTS 14

   MISC BOATS/CRAFT 12: 12 boats non-operational

   PCI 2: 1 Kasungu† less than 100 tonnes (may be op); 1 Namacurra non-operational less than 100 tonnes

AMPHIBIOUS • CRAFT 1: 1 LCU

FACILITIES

Base 1 located at Monkey Bay (Lake Nyasa)

Air Wing 200

FORCES BY ROLE

Tpt   1 sqn with 2 Basler Turbo-67; 4 DO-228; 1 Hawker 800

Sub-Saharan Africa

Tpt hel   some sqn with 1 AS-332 *Super Puma* (VIP);
3 AS-350L *Ecureuil*; 1 SA-330F *Puma*

EQUIPMENT BY TYPE
AIRCRAFT • TPT 7: 2 Basler Turbo-67; 4 DO-228;
1 Hawker 800
HELICOPTERS • SPT 5: 1 AS-332 *Super Puma* (VIP)
    AS-350 3: 3 AS-350L *Ecureuil*
    SA-330 1: 1 SA-330F *Puma*

Paramilitary 1,500

Mobile Police Force 1,500
RECCE 8: 8 S52 *Shorland*
AIRCRAFT: 4 (Cessna)
    MP 3: 3 BN-2T *Defender* (border patrol)
    TPT 1: 1 SC.7 3M *Skyvan*
HELICOPTERS • UTL 2: 2 AS-365 *Dauphin 2*

DEPLOYMENT

BURUNDI
UN • ONUB 1 obs

DEMOCRATIC REPUBLIC OF CONGO
UN • MONUC 27 obs

LIBERIA
UN • UNMIL 2

SERBIA AND MONTENEGRO
UN • UNMIK 1 obs

SUDAN
UN • UNMIS 7 obs

Mali RMM

CFA Franc BCEAO fr		2003	2004	2005
GDP	fr	2.5tr	2.6tr	
	US$	4.3bn	4.9bn	
per capita	US$	369	407	
Growth	%	7.4	2.2	
Inflation	%	-1.3	-3.1	
Debt	US$	3.1bn		
Def bdgt	fr	ε47bn	ε50bn	ε53bn
	US$	80.8m	93.8m	101m
US$1=fr		581	533	522

Population (2004)   11,415,261

Ethnic Groups: Tuareg 6-10%

Age	0 – 14	15 – 19	20 – 24	25 – 29	30 – 64	65 plus
Male	24%	6%	5%	4%	9%	1%
Female	24%	5%	4%	4%	12%	2%

Capabilities

ACTIVE 7,350 (Army 7,350) **Paramilitary 4,800**
Inactive Militia 3,000
Terms of service conscription (incl for civil purposes), 2 years
(selective)

ORGANISATIONS BY SERVICE

Army circa 7,350
FORCES BY ROLE
Tk   2 bn
Inf   4 bn
SF   1 bn
AB   1 bn
Arty   2 bn
Engr   1 bn
AD   2 bty
SAM   1 bty

EQUIPMENT BY TYPE†
TK 51
    MBT 33: 12 T-54/T-55; 21 T-34
    LT TK 18: 18 Type-62
RECCE • BRDM 20: 20 BRDM-2
APC • APC (W) • BTR 50: 10 BTR-152; 30 BTR-40; 10 BTR-60
ARTY 46+
    TOWED 14+
        100mm 6: 6 M-1944
        122mm 8: 8 D-30
        130mm: some M-46 (reported)
    MRL • 122mm 2: 2 BM-21
    MOR 30+
        82mm: some M-43
        120mm 30: 30 M-43
AT
    MSL: some AT-3 *Sagger*
    RL • 73mm: some RPG-7 *Knout*
    GUNS • 85mm 6: 6 D-44
AD
    SAM 12+: 12 SA-3 *Goa*
        MANPAD: some SA-7 *Grail*
    GUNS 12
        37mm • TOWED 6: 6 M-1939
        57mm • TOWED 6: 6 S-60

Navy circa 50
EQUIPMENT BY TYPE
PATROL AND COASTAL COMBATANTS 3: 3 PCR
Patrol Craft Riverine† less than 100 tonnes
FACILITIES
Base 1 located at Bamako, 1 located at Mopti, 1 located
    at Segou, 1 located at Timbuktu

Air Force 400
FORCES BY ROLE
Ftr   some sqn with 11 MiG-21 *Fishbed*
FGA   some sqn with 5 MIG-17F *Fresco C*
Tpt   some regt with 2 AN-24 *Coke*; 1 AN-26 *Curl*
Trg   some sqn with 6 L-29 *Delfin*; 1 MIG-15UTI *Midget*;
       4 YAK-11 *Moose*; 2 YAK-18 *Max*
Hel   some sqn with 1 AS-350 *Ecureuil*; 1 Mi-8 *Hip*;
       2 Z-9 (AS-365N) *Dauphin 2*

EQUIPMENT BY TYPE
AIRCRAFT 16 combat capable
  FTR 16: 11 MiG-21 *Fishbed*
    MIG-17 5: 5 MIG-17F *Fresco C*
  TPT 3: 2 AN-24 *Coke*; 1 AN-26 *Curl*
  TRG 13: 6 L-29 *Delfin*; 1 MIG-15UTI *Midget*; 4 YAK-11 *Moose*; 2 YAK-18 *Max*
  HELICOPTERS
    SPT 2: 1 AS-350 *Ecureuil*; 1 Mi-8 *Hip*
    UTL • AS-365 2: 2 Z-9 (AS-365N) *Dauphin 2*

Paramilitary 4,800 active

Gendarmerie 1,800
Paramilitary 8 coy

Republican Guard 2,000

National Police 1,000

Militia 3,000

NON-STATE ARMED GROUPS
see Part II

DEPLOYMENT

BURUNDI
UN • ONUB 2; 17 obs

DEMOCRATIC REPUBLIC OF CONGO
UN • MONUC 24 obs;

LIBERIA
UN • UNMIL 2; 4 obs

Mauritius Ms

Mauritian Rupee R		2003	2004	2005
GDP	R	156bn	172bn	
	US$	5.6bn	6.1bn	
per capita	US$	4,648	5,026	
Growth	%	3.0	4.4	
Inflation	%	5.2	4.4	
Debt	US$	2.6bn		
Def bdgt	R	328m	544m	622m
	US$	11.7m	19.3m	21.4m
US$1=R		27.9	28.2	29.0

Population (2004)   1,230,602

Age	0–14	15–19	20–24	25–29	30–64	65 plus
Male	12%	4%	4%	4%	22%	3%
Female	12%	4%	4%	4%	22%	4%

Capabilities
ACTIVE NIL Paramilitary 2,000

ORGANISATIONS BY SERVICE

Paramilitary 2,000

Special Mobile Force ε1,500
FORCES BY ROLE
Rifle   6 coy
Paramilitary 2 (mob) coy
Engr   1 coy
Spt   1 tps

EQUIPMENT BY TYPE
RECCE • BRDM: some BRDM-2
  some *Ferret*
APC • APC (W) 18: 7 Tactica; 11 VAB (2 with 20mm)
ARTY • MOR 2: 81mm: 2
AT • RL • 89mm 4: 4 LRAC

Coast Guard ε500
PATROL AND COASTAL COMBATANTS 8
  PCC 1: 1 Guardian
  PCI 6: 4 Mandovi; 2 Zhuk less than 100 tonnes (FSU)
  PCO 1
    1 Vigilant (capacity 1 hel) (Ca Guardian design)
AIRCRAFT • MP 3: 1 BN-2T *Defender*; 2 DO-228-101

Police Air Wing
HELICOPTERS • UTL 2: 2 SA-316 *Alouette III*

Mozambique Moz

Mozambique Metical M		2003	2004	2005
GDP	M	117tr	137tr	
	US$	4.9bn	6.1bn	
per capita	US$	263	318	
Growth	%	7.1	7.8	
Inflation	%	13.5	12.6	
Debt	US$	4.9bn		
Def bdgt	M	2.5tr	ε2.5tr	ε2.7tr
	US$	105m	110m	116m
US$1=M		23,782	22,628	23,697

Population (2004)   19,406,703

Age	0–14	15–19	20–24	25–29	30–64	65 plus
Male	22%	5%	4%	4%	13%	1%
Female	21%	5%	4%	4%	14%	2%

Capabilities
ACTIVE 11,200 (Army 10,000 Navy 200 Air 1,000)
Terms of service conscription, 2 years

ORGANISATIONS BY SERVICE

Army ε9,000–10,000
FORCES BY ROLE
Inf   7 bn

SF   3 bn
Arty 2-3 bty
Engr 2 bn
Log   1 bn

EQUIPMENT BY TYPE†
Equipment at est 10% or less serviceability
TK • MBT 60+: 60+ T-54
RECCE • BRDM 30: 30 BRDM-1/BRDM-2
AIFV • BMP 40: 40 BMP-1
APC • APC (W) • BTR 260: 100 BTR-152; 160 BTR-60
   some *Casspir*
ARTY 166
   TOWED 102
      76mm 40: 40 ZIS-3 *M-1942*
      100mm 20: 20 M-1944
      105mm 12: 12 M-101
      122mm 12: 12 D-30
      130mm 6: 6 M-46
      152mm 12: 12 D-1
   MRL • 122mm 12: 12 BM-21
   MOR 52
      82mm 40: 40 M-43
      120mm 12: 12 M-43
AT
   MSL: some AT-3 *Sagger*; some AT-4 *Spigot*
   RCL • 107mm: some B-11
      75mm: some
      82mm: some B-10
   GUNS • 85mm 18: 6 D-48; 12 Type-56 (D-44)
AD • SAM • MANPAD: some SA-7 *Grail*
   GUNS • 20mm • TOWED: some M-55
      23mm • TOWED: some ZU-23-2
      37mm • TOWED: some M-1939
      57mm • SP: some ZSU-57-2
         TOWED: some S-60

Navy 200
Base 1 located at Pemba, 1 (Inventory consists of some boats on Lake Malawi) located at Metangula (Lake Malawi), 1 located at Nacala, 1 located at Beira, 1 located at Maputo

Air Force 1,000

FORCES BY ROLE
(incl AD units)
FGA some sqn with MIG-21bis *Fishbed L & N* non-operational
Tpt 1 sqn with 5 AN-26 *Curl*; 2 CASA 212 *Aviocar*; 4 PA-32 *Cherokee* non-operational
Trg some sqn with 1 Cessna 182 *Skylane*; 7 Z-326 *Trener Master*
Hel some sqn with 4 Mi-24 *Hind*†*; 5 Mi-8 *Hip* non-operational
SAM some bty with 10 SA-3 *Goa* non-operational; SA-2 *Guideline*†

EQUIPMENT BY TYPE
AIRCRAFT
   FTR • MIG-21: some MIG-21bis *Fishbed L & N* non-operational

TPT 8: 5 AN-26 *Curl*; 2 CASA 212 *Aviocar*; 1 Cessna 182 *Skylane*
TRG 11: 4 PA-32 *Cherokee* non-operational; 7 Z-326 *Trener Master*
HELICOPTERS
   ATK 4: 4 Mi-24 *Hind*†*
   SPT 5: 5 Mi-8 *Hip* non-operational
AD • SAM 10+: 10 SA-3 *Goa* non-operational
   TOWED: some SA-2 *Guideline*†

DEPLOYMENT

BURUNDI
UN • ONUB 183; 3 obs

DEMOCRATIC REPUBLIC OF CONGO
UN • MONUC 1 obs

SUDAN
UN • UNMIS 1 obs

Namibia Nba

Namibian Dollar N$		2003	2004	2005
GDP	N$	32.2bn	35.6bn	
	US$	4.3bn	5.8bn	
per capita	US$	2,143	2,901	
Growth	%	3.7	4.4	
Inflation	%	7.2	5.5	
Debt	US$	1bn		
Def bdgt	N$	992m	1.1bn	1.1bn
	US$	131m	177m	160m
US$1=N$		7.6	6.1	6.6

Population (2004)   2,030,692

Age	0 – 14	15 – 19	20 – 24	25 – 29	30 – 64	65 plus
Male	20%	6%	5%	4%	13%	2%
Female	19%	6%	5%	4%	14%	2%

Capabilities

ACTIVE 9,200 (Army 9,000 Navy 200) **Paramilitary 6,000**

ORGANISATIONS BY SERVICE

Army 9,000
FORCES BY ROLE
Inf	6 bn
AT	1 regt
Cbt Sp	1 bde (1 arty regt)
Presidential Guard	1 bn
AD	1 regt

EQUIPMENT BY TYPE
TK • MBT: some T-54/T-55†; some T-34†
RECCE • BRDM 12: 12 BRDM-2

APC • APC (W) 60
  BTR 10: 10 BTR-60
  20 *Casspir*; 30 Wolf Turbo 2
ARTY 81
  TOWED 36
    76mm 12: 12 ZIS-3
    140mm 24: 24 G2
  MRL • 122mm 5: 5 BM-21
  MOR 40: 40 81mm/82mm
AT
  RCL • 82mm: some B-10
  GUNS 12+
    57mm: some
    76mm 12: 12 ZIS-3
AD
  SAM • MANPAD 74: 74 SA-7 *Grail*
  GUNS 65
    14.5mm • TOWED • ZPU 50: 50 ZPU-4
    23mm • SP 15: 15 *Zumlac*

Navy ε200

fishery protection, part of the Ministry of Fisheries

EQUIPMENT BY TYPE
PATROL AND COASTAL COMBATANTS 2
  PCC 1: 1 *Oryx*
  PCO 1: 1 Osprey
AIRCRAFT • UTL 1: 1 F406 *Caravan II*
hel 1

FACILITIES
Base 1 located at Walvis Bay

Paramilitary 6,000

Police Force • Special Field Force 6,000 (incl Border Guard and Special Reserve Force)

Air Force

FORCES BY ROLE
FGA some sqn with 2 MiG-23 *Flogger* (reported)
Surv some sqn with 5 Cessna 337 *Skymaster*/O-2A *Skymaster*
Tpt some sqn with 2 AN-26 *Curl*; 1 *Falcon* 900; 1 Learjet 36; 2 Y-12
Trg some sqn with 4 K-8
Hel some sqn with 2 Mi-25 *Hind D*; 2 MI-17 (Mi-8MT) *Hip H*; 2 SA-319 *Alouette III*

EQUIPMENT BY TYPE
AIRCRAFT 2 combat capable
  FTR 2: 2 MiG-23 *Flogger* (reported)
  TPT 11: 2 AN-26 *Curl*; 1 *Falcon* 900; 1 Learjet 36; 2 Y-12, 5 Cessna 337 *Skymaster* tpt/O-2A *Skymaster* RECCE
  TRG 4: 4 K-8
HELICOPTERS
  ATK 2: 2 Mi-25 *Hind D*
  SPT • MI-8 2: 2 MI-17 (Mi-8MT) *Hip H*
  UTL 2: 2 SA-319 *Alouette III*

DEPLOYMENT

BURUNDI
UN • ONUB 3 obs

CÔTE D'IVOIRE
UN • ONUCI 3 obs

ETHIOPIA/ERITREA
UN • UNMEE 2; 4 obs

LIBERIA
UN • UNMIL 864; 3 obs

SUDAN
UN • UNMIS 2 obs

Niger Ngr

CFA Franc BCEAO fr		2003	2004	2005
GDP	fr	1.4tr	1.6tr	
	US$	2.4bn	3.1bn	
per capita	US$	218	268	
Growth	%	5.3	0.9	
Inflation	%	-1.8	0.4	
Debt	US$	2.1bn		
Def bdgt	fr	14.2bn	ε15.0bn	ε16.0bn
	US$	24.6m	28.1m	30.6m
US$1=fr		581	533	522

Population (2004) 12,162,856

Ethnic Groups: Tuareg 8-10%

Age	0 – 14	15 – 19	20 – 24	25 – 29	30 – 64	65 plus
Male	24%	6%	4%	4%	11%	1%
Female	23%	5%	4%	4%	13%	1%

Capabilities

ACTIVE 5,300 (Army 5,200 Air 100) **Paramilitary 5,400**
Terms of service selective conscription (2 year)

ORGANISATIONS BY SERVICE

Army 5,200

FORCES BY ROLE
3 Mil Districts
Armd recce 4 sqn
Inf 7 coy
AB 2 coy
Engr 1 coy
AD 1 coy

EQUIPMENT BY TYPE
RECCE 132
  AML 125: 35 AML-20/AML-60; 90 AML-90
  7 VBL
APC • APC (W) 22: 22 M-3 *Panhard*

ARTY • MOR 40
  81mm 19: 19 Brandt
  82mm: 17
  120mm 4: 4 Brandt
AT
  RCL 14
    106mm 8: 8 M-40
    75mm 6: 6 M-20
  RL • 89mm 36: 36 LRAC
AD • GUNS 39
  20mm: 29
  SP 10: 10 M3 VDAA

Air Force 100

FORCES BY ROLE

Tpt   some sqn with 1 AN-26 *Curl*; 1 B-737-200 (VIP); 1
         C-130H *Hercules*; 1 DO-228; 1 DO-28

Liaison some sqn with 2 Cessna 337D *Skymaster*

EQUIPMENT BY TYPE
AIRCRAFT
  TPT 7: 1 AN-26 *Curl*
  B-737 1: 1 B-737-200 (VIP)
  C-130 1: 1 C-130H *Hercules*
  CESSNA 337 2: 2 Cessna 337D *Skymaster*
  DO-228 1; 1 DO-28

Paramilitary 5,400

Gendarmerie 1,400

Republican Guard 2,500

National Police 1,500

DEPLOYMENT

BURUNDI
UN • ONUB 2 obs

CÔTE D'IVOIRE
UN • ONUCI 5 obs; 367

DEMOCRATIC REPUBLIC OF CONGO
UN • MONUC 2; 18 obs

LIBERIA
UN • UNMIL 3 obs

Nigeria Nga

Nigerian Naira N		2003	2004	2005
GDP	N	7.2tr	8.6tr	
	US$	55.7bn	64.3bn	
per capita	US$	453	511	
Growth	%	10.7	3.5	
Inflation	%	14.0	15.0	
Debt	US$	34.9bn		
Def exp	N	ε109bn	ε109bn	
	US$	852m	827m	
Def bdgt	N	76.8bn	76bn	111bn
	US$	596m	571m	841m
FMA (US)	US$			1.3m
US$1=N		129	133	133

Population (2004)   128,765,768

Ethnic Groups: North Hausa and Fulani South-west Yoruba
South-east Ibo; these tribes make up ε65% of population

Age	0 – 14	15 – 19	20 – 24	25 – 29	30 – 64	65 plus
Male	21%	5%	5%	4%	14%	1%
Female	21%	5%	5%	4%	13%	2%

Capabilities

ACTIVE 78,500 (Army 62,000 Navy 7,000 Air 9,500)
Paramilitary 82,000
Reserves planned, none org

ORGANISATIONS BY SERVICE

Army 62,000
FORCES BY ROLE
Army   1 (comp) div (1 mot inf bde, 1 AB bn,
                      1 amph bde, 1 engr bde, 1 arty bde, 1
                      recce bn)
Armd   1 div (1 recce bn, 1 engr bde, 1 arty
                      bde, 2 armd bde)
Mech   2 div (*each*: 1 engr bde, 1 mot inf bde,
                      1 mech bde, 1 recce bn, 1 arty bde)
Presidential Guard   1 bde (2 Gd bn)
AD   1 bde

EQUIPMENT BY TYPE
TK 350
  MBT 250: 150 Vickers Mk 3; 100 T-55†
  LT TK 100: 100 Scorpion
RECCE 342
  AML 130: 90 AML-60; 40 AML-90
  70 EE-9 *Cascavel*; 50 FV721 *Fox*
  SALADIN 20: 20 Saladin Mk2
  72 VBL (reported)
APC 397+
  APC (T) 317: 250 4K-7FA *Steyr*; 67 MT-LB
  APC (W) 80+: some EE-11 *Urutu* (reported); 10 FV603
  Saracen; 70 Piranha
ARTY 813+

TOWED 431
105mm 200: 200 M-56
122mm 200: 200 D-30/D-74
130mm 7: 7 M-46
155mm • **FH-77** 24: 24 FH-77B in store
SP • **155mm** 27: 27 VCA 155 *Palmaria*
MRL • **122mm** 25: 25 APR-21
MOR 330+
81mm: 200
82mm: 100
120mm: 30+
AT • **MSL**: some Swingfire
RCL • **106mm** • **M-40**: some M-40A1
84mm: some *Carl Gustav*
AD
SAM 164
SP 16: 16 Roland
MANPAD 148: 48 Blowpipe; ε100 SA-7 *Grail*
GUNS 90+:
20mm: 60+
23mm • **TOWED**: some ZU-23
SP 30: 30 ZSU-23-4
40mm • **TOWED**: some L/60
RADAR • **LAND**: some RASIT (veh, arty)

Navy 7,000 (incl Coast Guard)

FORCES BY ROLE
Navy 1 (Western Comd) HQ located at Apapa; 1 (Eastern Comd) HQ located at Calabar

EQUIPMENT BY TYPE
PRINCIPAL SURFACE COMBATANTS 3
FRIGATES • **FFG** 1:
1 *Aradu* (capacity 1 *Lynx* MK 89 SAR hel)† (Ge MEKO 360) with 2 STWS 1B triple 324mm with 18 A244 LWT, 1 Albatros octuple with 24 Aspide SAM, 8 single each with 1 Otomat tactical SSM, 1 127mm gun
CORVETTES • **FS** 2:
2 *Erinomi* non-operational (UK Vosper Mk 9) each with 1 x3 Seacat Systems (3 eff.) with Seacat SAM, 1 2 tube *Bofors* 375mm (2 eff.), 1 TAK-76 76mm gun
PATROL AND COASTAL COMBATANTS 6
PCC 1:
1 *Ekpe* (Ge Lurssen 57m (further 2 believed to be non-op)) with 1 76mm gun
PFM 3:
3 *Ayam*† (Fr Combattante, sid) each with 2 twin (4 eff.) each with 1 MM-38 *Exocet* tactical SSM, 1 76mm gun
PCO 2: 2 *Balsam*† (buoy tenders (ex-US))
MINE WARFARE • **MINE COUNTERMEASURES** • **MCC** 2: 2 Ohue† non-operational (mod It Lerici)
AMPHIBIOUS • **LS** • **LST** 1: 1 Ambe (capacity 5 tanks; 220 troops) (Ge)
LOGISTICS AND SUPPORT 5: 1 AGHS (Svy) *Svy Vsl*; 3 AT *Tug*; 1 Trg
FACILITIES
Base 1 located at Lagos, 1 located at Apapa, 1 located at Calabar

Naval Aviation

HELICOPTERS
SAR 2: 2 *Lynx* MK 89† non-operational
UTL • **A-109** 2: 2 A-109E *Power*†

Air Force 9,500

FORCES BY ROLE†
Ftr / FGA   1 sqn with 12 Jaguar S(N) (Jaguar S International)† non-operational; 3 Jaguar B(N) (SEPECAT Jaguar International B)† non-operational; 1 sqn with 6 Alpha Jet (FGA/trg); 9 non-operational (FGA/trg); 1 sqn with 12 MIG-21bis *Fishbed* L & N/MIG-21FR *Fishbed*†; 5 MIG-21MF *Fishbed* J†; 1 MIG-21U *Mongol* A†
Tpt   2 sqn with 5 C-130H *Hercules*; 3 C-130H-30 *Hercules*; 17 DO-128D-6 *Turbo SkyServant*; 16 DO-228-200 (incl 2 VIP); 5 G-222 non-operational; 7 AS-332 *Super Puma*; 2 SA-330 *Puma*; 5 Mi-34 *Hermit* non-operational; some (Presidential) flt with 2 Gulfstream II/*Gulfstream* IV; 1 B-727; 1 BAe-125-1000; 2 *Falcon* 900
Trg   some sqn with 24 L-39MS *Albatros*†*; 58 Air Beetle† (up to 20 awaiting repair); 12 MB-339AN (MB-339A)†* (all awaiting repair); 13 Hughes 300
Hel   some (Armed) sqn with 2 Mi-35 *Hind*; 3 non-operational; 5 BO-105D†

EQUIPMENT BY TYPE
AIRCRAFT 84 combat capable
FTR • **MIG-21** • **MIG-21M** 17: 5 MIG-21MF *Fishbed* J†; 12 MiG-21bis *Fishbed* L & N MiG-21 FTR/MIG-21FR *Fishbed* RECCE†
FGA 36: 24 L-39MS *Albatros*†*; 12 Jaguar S(N) (Jaguar S International)† non-operational
TPT 52: 2 Gulfstream II/*Gulfstream* IV; 1 B-727
BAE-125 1: 1 BAe-125-1000
C-130 8: 5 C-130H *Hercules*
C-130H 8: 3 C-130H-30 *Hercules*
DO-128 17: 17 DO-128D-6 *Turbo SkyServant*
DO-228 16: 16 DO-228-200 (incl 2 VIP)
Falcon **900** 2; 5 G-222 non-operational
TRG 89: 58 Air Beetle† (up to 20 awaiting repair); 6 Alpha Jet (FGA/trg); 9 non-operational (FGA/trg); 3 Jaguar B(N) (SEPECAT Jaguar International B)† non-operational
MB-339 12: 12 MB-339AN (MB-339A)†* (all awaiting repair)
MIG-21U *Mongol* A 1†
HELICOPTERS
ATK 5: 2 Mi-35 *Hind*; 3 non-operational
SPT 9: 7 AS-332 *Super Puma*; 2 SA-330 *Puma*
UTL 10
BO-105 5: 5 BO–105D†
Mi-34 *Hermit* 5 non-operational
TRG 13: 13 Hughes 300
MSL • **TACTICAL** • **AAM**: some AA-2 *Atoll*

Paramilitary ε82,000

Coast Guard some

Port Security Police ε2,000

PATROL AND COASTAL COMBATANTS • MISC
BOATS/CRAFT 60+: 60+ boats
AMPHIBIOUS • CRAFT 5+: 5+ ACV

Security and Civil Defence Corps • Police 80,000

APC • APC (W) 70+: 70 AT105 Saxon†; some UR-416
AIRCRAFT • TPT 4: 1 Cessna 500 Citation I; 2 PA-31 Navajo
   PA-31 3: 1 PA-31-350 Navajo Chieftain
HELICOPTERS • UTL 4: 2 AB-212 (Bell 212); 2 AB-222 (Bell 222)

NON-STATE ARMED GROUPS

see Part II

DEPLOYMENT

BURUNDI
UN • ONUB 1; 2 obs

CÔTE D'IVOIRE
UN • ONUCI 5 obs

DEMOCRATIC REPUBLIC OF CONGO
UN • MONUC 1; 29 obs

ETHIOPIA/ERITREA
UN • UNMEE 4; 7 obs

LIBERIA
UN • UNMIL 1,967; 19 obs

SIERRA LEONE
UN • UNAMSIL 7 obs; 751

SUDAN
UN • UNMIS 9 obs

WESTERN SAHARA
UN • MINURSO 6 obs

Rwanda Rwa

Rwandan Franc fr		2003	2004	2005
GDP	fr	949bn	996bn	
	US$	1.8bn	1.8bn	
per capita	US$	219	215	
Growth	%	0.9	4.0	
Inflation	%	7.4	12	
Debt	US$	1.5bn		
Def bdgt	fr	36.7bn	25.8bn	31.1bn
	US$	68.5m	46.0m	56.8m
US$1=fr		537	562	547

Population (2004) 8,440,820

Ethnic Groups: Hutu 80%; Tutsi 19%

Age	0 – 14	15 – 19	20 – 24	25 – 29	30 – 64	65 plus
Male	21%	6%	5%	4%	12%	1%
Female	21%	6%	5%	4%	13%	2%

Capabilities

ACTIVE 51,000 (Army 40,000 Air 1,000 National Police 10,000) **Paramilitary 2,000**

ORGANISATIONS BY SERVICE

Army 40,000

FORCES BY ROLE
Army 4 div (each: 3 Army bde)

EQUIPMENT BY TYPE
TK • MBT 24: 24 T-54/T-55
RECCE 106
   AML 90: ε90 AML-245/AML-60/AML-90
   VBL 16
AIFV: some BMP
APC • APC (W) 16+: some BTR; some Buffalo (Panhard); 16 RG-31 Nyala
ARTY 155
   TOWED 35: 29 105mm/Type-54 (D-1) 152mm†
      122mm 6: 6 D-30
   MRL • 122mm 5: 5 RM-70 Dana
   MOR 115: 115 120mm/81mm/82mm
AD
   SAM • MANPAD: some SA-7 Grail
   GUNS 150: ε150 14.5mm/23mm/37mm

Air Force ε1,000

FORCES BY ROLE
Tpt   some sqn with AN-2 Colt; 2-3 AN-8 Camp; 1 B-707; 1 BN-2A Islander
Trg   some sqn with L-39 Albatros
Hel   some sqn with 5-7 Mi-24V Hind E; 8-12 MI-17MD (Mi-8MTV5) Hip H

EQUIPMENT BY TYPE
AIRCRAFT
   TPT 5+: some AN-2 Colt; 2-3 AN-8 Camp; 1 B-707
   BN-2 ISLANDER 1: 1 BN-2A Islander
   TRG: some L-39 Albatros
HELICOPTERS
   ATK • MI-24 7: 5-7 Mi-24V Hind E
   SPT • MI-8 • MI-8MTV 12: 8-12 MI-17MD (Mi-8MTV5) Hip H

Paramilitary

Local Defence Forces ε2,000

National Police up to 10,000 (reported)

NON-STATE ARMED GROUPS

see Part II

DEPLOYMENT

SUDAN
UN • UNMIS 6 obs

Senegal Sen

CFA Franc BCEAO fr		2003	2004	2005
GDP	fr	3.7tr	3.9tr	
	US$	6.4bn	7.3bn	
per capita	US$	605	672	
Growth	%	6.5	6.0	
Inflation	%	0.1	0.5	
Debt	US$	4.4bn		
Def bdgt	fr	48.3bn	ε50.0bn	ε52.0bn
	US$	83.1m	93.8m	99.6m
FMA (US)	US$	1.5m	1.9m	1.6m
US$1=fr		581	533	522

Population (2004) 11,706,498

Ethnic Groups: Wolof 36%; Fulani 17%; Serer 17%; Toucouleur 9%; Man-dingo 9%; Diola 9% (of which 30-60% in Casamance)

Age	0 – 14	15 – 19	20 – 24	25 – 29	30 – 64	65 plus
Male	21%	6%	5%	4%	13%	1%
Female	20%	6%	5%	4%	14%	2%

Capabilities

ACTIVE 13,620 (Army 11,900 Navy 950 Air 770)
Paramilitary 5,000
Terms of service conscription, 2 years selective

ORGANISATIONS BY SERVICE

Army 11,900 (incl conscripts)

FORCES BY ROLE
4 Mil Zone HQ

Armd	3 bn
Inf	6 bn
Cdo / AB	1 bn
Arty	1 bn
Engr	1 bn
Presidential Guard	1 bn (horsed)
Construction	3 coy

EQUIPMENT BY TYPE
RECCE 71
  AML 57: 30 AML-60; 27 AML-90
  4 **M-20**; 10 M-8
APC 28+
  APC (T) 12: 12 M-3
  APC (W) 16+: 16+ M-3 *Panhard*
ARTY 34
  TOWED 18
    75mm 6: 6 M-116 pack
    105mm 6: 6 HM-2/M-101
    155mm 6: ε6 Model-50
  MOR 16
    81mm 8: 8 Brandt
    120mm 8: 8 Brandt
AT
  MSL 4: 4 Milan

RL • **89mm** 31: 31 LRAC
AD • GUNS 33
  20mm • **TOWED** 21: 21 M-693
  40mm • **TOWED** 12: 12 L/60

Navy 950

EQUIPMENT BY TYPE
PATROL AND COASTAL COMBATANTS 10
  PCC 5: 1 *Fouta* (Dk Osprey); 1 *Njambour* (Fr SFCN 59m); 3 *Saint Louis* (Fr 48m)
  PCI 2: 2 *Alioune Samb*
  PFI 3: 3 *Senegal* II
AMPHIBIOUS • CRAFT • LCT • EDIC 2: 2 *Edic* 700
FACILITIES
Base 1 located at Dakar, 1 located at Casamance

Air Force 770

FORCES BY ROLE

MR / SAR	some sqn with 1 EMB-111
Tpt	1 sqn with 1 B-727-200 (VIP); 1 DHC-6 twin *Otter*; 6 F-27-400M *Troopship*
Trg	some sqn with 4 CM-170 *Magister**; 2 *Rallye* 160; 4 *Rallye* 235 *Guerrier**; 2 *Rallye* 235A
Hel	some sqn with 2 SA-330 *Puma*; 1 SA-341H *Gazelle*; 2 SA-318C *Alouette* II

EQUIPMENT BY TYPE
AIRCRAFT
  RECCE • **MR** 1: 1 EMB-111
  TPT 8
    B-727 1: 1 B-727-200 (VIP)
    DHC-6 twin *Otter* 1
    F-27 6: 6 F-27-400M *Troopship*
  TRG 12: 4 CM-170 *Magister**; 2 *Rallye* 160; 4 *Rallye* 235 *Guerrier**
    RALLYE 235 6: 2 *Rallye* 235A
HELICOPTERS
  SPT 3: 2 SA-330 *Puma*
    SA-341 1: 1 SA-341H *Gazelle*
  UTL • **SA-318** 2: 2 SA-318C *Alouette* II

Paramilitary 5,000

Gendarmerie 5,000
APC • **APC (W)** 12: 12 VXB-170

Customs
PATROL AND COASTAL COMBATANTS 2: 2 PCI less than 100 tonnes

NON-STATE ARMED GROUPS

see Part II

DEPLOYMENT

BURUNDI
UN • ONUB 5; 6 obs

CÔTE D'IVOIRE
UN • ONUCI 323; 8 obs

DEMOCRATIC REPUBLIC OF CONGO
UN • MONUC 9 obs; 473

LIBERIA
UN • UNMIL 603; 3 obs

FOREIGN FORCES

France ε1,100 Army 610: 1 marine inf bn (1 recce sqn with ERC-90F *Sagaie*) Air Force: 1 C-160 *Transall* tpt ac; 1 AS-555 *Fennec* utl hel Navy 230: 1 Atlantic MP ac

Seychelles Sey

Seychelles Rupee SR		2003	2004	2005
GDP	SR	3.9bn	4.0bn	
	US$	722m	724m	
per capita	US$	8,975	8,964	
Growth	%	-6.3	-2.0	
Inflation	%	3.2	4.0	
Debt	US$	547m		
Def bdgt	SR	64m	ε70m	ε70m
	US$	11.8m	12.6m	12.6m
US$1=SR		5.4	5.5	5.5

Population (2004) 81,188

Age	0 – 14	15 – 19	20 – 24	25 – 29	30 – 64	65 plus
Male	13%	5%	5%	4%	19%	2%
Female	13%	5%	5%	5%	21%	4%

Capabilities

ACTIVE 450 (Army 200 National Guard 250)

ORGANISATIONS BY SERVICE

Army 200

FORCES BY ROLE
Sy 1 unit
Inf 1 coy

EQUIPMENT BY TYPE
Equipment†
RECCE • BRDM 6: 6 BRDM-2†
ARTY • MOR • 82mm 6: 6 M-43†
AT • RL • 73mm: some RPG-7 *Knout*†
AD • SAM • MANPAD 10: 10 SA-7 *Grail*†
  GUNS
  14.5mm • TOWED • ZPU: some ZPU-2/ZPU-4†
  37mm • TOWED: some M-1939†

Paramilitary

National Guard 250

Air Wing 20
AIRCRAFT
  TPT 2: 1 BN-2 Islander; 1 Cessna 152
  UTL 1: 1 F406 *Caravan II*

Coast Guard 200 (incl 80 Marines)
EQUIPMENT BY TYPE
PATROL AND COASTAL COMBATANTS 5
  PCC 1: 1 *Andromache* (It *Pichiotti* 42m)
  PCI 4: 3 less than 100 tonnes; 1 *Zhuk* less than 100 tonnes
  AMPHIBIOUS • CRAFT • LCT 1: 1 *Cinq Juin* (govt owned but civilian op)
FACILITIES
Base 1 located at Port Victoria

Sierra Leone SL

Sierra Leonean Leone L		2003	2004	2005
GDP	L	2.5tr	3.0tr	
	US$	1.1bn	1.2bn	
per capita	US$	187	209	
Growth	%	8.6	7.4	
Inflation	%	8.2	13.7	
Debt	US$	1.6bn		
Def bdgt	L	67bn	ε70bn	ε75bn
	US$	28.4m	28.5m	26.1m
US$1=L		2,347	2,455	2,870

Population (2004) 5,867,426

Age	0 – 14	15 – 19	20 – 24	25 – 29	30 – 64	65 plus
Male	22%	5%	4%	4%	12%	2%
Female	23%	5%	4%	4%	13%	2%

Capabilities

ACTIVE 12–13,000 (Joint 13,000)

ORGANISATIONS BY SERVICE

Total Armed Forces ε12,000-13,000

The process of disarming the various factions was completed in Jan 2002, with over 45,000 combatants registering. A new, UK-trained, national army has formed, which has an initial strength of 13-14,000. This initial strength is set to reduce to some 10,000 over a ten year period.

ARTY • MOR 31
  81mm: ε27
  82mm: 2
  120mm: 2
AT • RCL • 84mm: some *Carl Gustav*
HELICOPTERS
  ATK 1: 1 Mi-24 *Hind*
  SPT • MI-8 2: 2 MI-17 (Mi-8MT) *Hip H*/Mi-8 *Hip* spt hel† (contract flown and maintained)
AD • GUNS 7: 4 12.7mm; 3 14.5mm

Navy ε200†

EQUIPMENT BY TYPE
PATROL AND COASTAL COMBATANTS 5: 2 PCI† less than 100 tonnes

PCI 4: 1 *Swiftships* non-operational less than 100 tonnes (32m); 1 *Tracker*† less than 100 tonnes
PFI 1: 1 *Shanghai* II non-operational less than 100 tonnes (PRC)

FACILITIES
Base 1 located at Freetown

NON-STATE ARMED GROUPS
see Part II

FOREIGN FORCES
(all UNAMSIL)
Bangladesh 240; 8 obs
Bolivia 3 obs
China, Peoples Republic of 2 obs
Croatia 6 obs
Czech Republic 2 obs
Egypt 5 obs
Germany 8
Ghana 762; 4 obs
Guinea 5 obs
Indonesia 6 obs
Jordan 72; 3 obs
Kenya 6 obs; 7
Kyrgyzstan 4 obs
Malaysia 3 obs
Nepal 2; 5 obs
Nigeria 7 obs; 751
Pakistan 1,264; 8 obs
Russia 109; 7 obs; 4 Mi-24 *Hind* atk hel
Slovakia 1 obs
Sweden 1 obs; 1
Tanzania 5 obs
Thailand 3 obs
The Gambia 8 obs
Ukraine 3 obs
United Kingdom 5; 8 obs Army: ε100 (incl Trg Team, Tri-service HQ and spt)
Uruguay 5 obs
Zambia 1; 3 obs

Somali Republic SR

Somali Shilling sh		2003	2004	2005
GDP	US$	ε1bn	ε1bn	
per capita	US$	124	120	
Debt	US$	2.68bn		

Population		8,591,629				

Age	0 – 14	15 – 19	20 – 24	25 – 29	30 – 64	65 plus
Male	22%	5%	4%	3%	14%	1%
Female	22%	5%	4%	4%	13%	2%

Capabilities
Following the 1991 revolution, national armed forces have yet to be formed. A Transitional National Government (TNG) has however formed with an estimated 5,000 tps but only has controls northern Mogadishu. The Somali National Movement has declared northern Somalia the independent 'Republic of Somaliland', and the northeast has seen the self-proclaimed regional adminstration in Puntland remain autonomous, while various groups compete for local supremacy in the south. Hy mil eqpt is in poor repair or inoperable.

NON-STATE ARMED GROUPS
see Part II

South Africa RSA

South African Rand R		2003	2004	2005
GDP	R	1.3tr	1.4tr	
	US$	165bn	224bn	
per capita	US$	3,720	5,059	
Growth	%	2.8	3.7	
Inflation	%	5.8	1.4	
Debt	US$	27.8bn		
Def exp	R	19.8bn	19.4bn	
	US$	2.6bn	3.2bn	
Def bdgt	R	20.0bn	20.4bn	22.4bn
	US$	2.7bn	3.4bn	3.4bn
FMA (US)	US$	7.2m		
US$1=R		7.6	6.1	6.6

Population (2004)   44,448,470

Age	0 – 14	15 – 19	20 – 24	25 – 29	30 – 64	65 plus
Male	15%	6%	5%	4%	16%	2%
Female	15%	6%	5%	4%	18%	3%

Capabilities

ACTIVE 55,750 (Army 36,000 Navy 4,500 Air 9,250 South African Military Health Service (SAMHS) 6,000)

CIVILIAN 2,000 (Navy 2,000)

RESERVE 60,000 (Army 57,500 Navy 1,300 Air 500 SAMHS 700)

ORGANISATIONS BY SERVICE

Army ε36,000
FORCES BY ROLE
Formations under direct command and control of SANDF Chief of Joint Operations: 9 Joint Operational Tactical HQs, tps are provided when necessary by permanent and reserve force units from all services and SF Bde). 8 type formations.

HQ	2 bde
Tk	1 bn
Armd recce	1 bn
Mech inf	2 bn
SF	1 bde under strength (2 SF bn under strength)
Mot inf	3 bn
Lt inf	10 bn
AB	1 bn
Arty	1 bn
ADA	1 bn
Engr	5 bn

EQUIPMENT BY TYPE
TK • MBT • OLIFANT 167+: 42+ 1A/1B; 125 in store
RECCE 176: 82 *Rooikat*-76; 94 in store
AIFV • FSV 90 1,200: 534 Mk III-60/*Ratel*-20 Mk III-20/Ratel-90 Mk III-90; 666 in store
APC • APC (W) 810: 370 *Casspir*; 440 *Mamba*
ARTY 1,467
  TOWED 147
    140mm 75: 75 G2 in store
    155mm 72: 21 G-5; 51 in store
  SP • 155mm 43: 12 G-6; 31 in store
  MRL • 127mm 51: 26 *Valkiri* Mk I in store (24 tube); 21 *Valkiri* Mk II MARS *Bataleur* (40 tube); 4 in store (40 tube)
  MOR 1,226
    81mm: 1,190 (incl some SP)
    120mm: 36
AT
  MSL 52: 16 ZT-3 *Swift*; 36 in store
  RCL • 106mm • M-40 100: 100 M-40A1 (some SP)
  RL • 92mm: some FT-5
AD • GUNS 76
  23mm • SP 36: 36 *Zumlac*
  35mm • TOWED 40: 40 GDF
RADAR • LAND: some *Cymberline* (mor); some M-113 A1GE *Green Archer* (mor)

Reserve Organisations

Regular ε10,500 reservists
cadre units

Armd	8 bn
Inf	26 bn
AB	1 bn
Arty	7 bn
Engr	4 bn
AD	5 bn

Territorial ε47,000 reservists

Home Def	128+ ('Cdo') bn (all to be demobilised by 2009)

Navy ε4,500; 2,000 (civilian); ε1,300 reservists (total 5,800 plus 2,000 civilians)
FORCES BY ROLE

SS	some flotilla
Strike	some flotilla
Navy	1 Fleet HQ HQ located at Simon's Town; 1 Naval HQ HQ located at Pretoria
MCM	some flotilla

EQUIPMENT BY TYPE
SUBMARINES • TACTICAL • SSK 3: 3 209 Type 1400 (under construction in Germany. ISD: 1 per year from 2005)
PRINCIPAL SURFACE COMBATANTS • CORVETTES • FSG • VALOUR 4: 4 MEKO A200 (German built; all now delivered to Simonstown for fitting out. First of class due to become operational in late 2005)
PATROL AND COASTAL COMBATANTS 34: 26 PCI less than 100 tonnes (Harbour Patrol)
  PCI 29: 3 T craft less than 100 tonnes
  PFM 5:
    5 *Warrior* (Il Reshef) each with 6 *Skerpioen* tactical SSM (Il Gabriel)
MINE WARFARE • MINE COUNTERMEASURES 9
  MHC 4: 2 *River* (Ge *Navors*); 1 in reserve; 1 in refit
  MSC 5: 2 *City* (Ge *Lindau*); 3 in reserve
AMPHIBIOUS • CRAFT 6: 6 LCU
LOGISTICS AND SUPPORT 6: 1 AGHS (Svy) *Svy Vsl* (UK Hecla)
  AO 1:
    1 Drakensburg (capacity 60 troops; 2 LCU) (extempore amph capability) with 2 hel (Outeniqua paid off/for sale)
  AT *Tug* 3; 1 tpt (operated by private co. for Dept of Environment)

FACILITIES
Base 1 (Naval Station) located at Durban Salisbury Island, 1 located at Pretoria, 1 located at Simon's Town

Air Force 9,250; ε500 reservists (total 9,750)
Air Force office, Pretoria, and 4 op gps

FORCES BY ROLE

Ftr / FGA	1 (Lead-in Ftr Trg) sqn with 12 Impala MKII (MB-326KC) (first of 24 *Hawk* Mk120 del by June 06); 12 Impala MKI (MB-326M); 1 sqn with 16 *Cheetah* C; 10 *Cheetah* D
Tkr / EW / tpt	1 sqn with 3 B-707-320 (only 1/2 op)
Tpt	1 (VIP) sqn with 1 B-737 BBJ; 2 CE-550 *Citation II*; 2 *Falcon* 50; 1 *Falcon* 900; 1 sqn with 11 C-47TP (Basler Turbo-67) (6 maritime, 4 tpt, 1 PR/EW trg); 1 sqn with 3 Beech 200 *Super King Air*; 1 Beech 300 *Super King Air*; 11 Cessna 208 *Caravan I*; 1 PC-12; 1 sqn with 4 CASA 212 *Aviocar*; 1 CN-235; 13 Cessna 185; 1 sqn with 9 C-130BZ *Hercules* (only 1/2 op)
Tpt hel	4 sqn with 40 *Oryx* (AS-332B) *Super Puma*; 8 BK-117; 14 SA-319 *Alouette III* (being replaced by 30 A109UH between 2004-7)
Hel	1 (cbt spt) sqn with 12 CSH-1 *Rooivalk**
Reserves	9 sqn with ε130 ac (private ac)

Trg 1 with 9 *Oryx* (AS-332B) *Super Puma* AS-332 spt; 12 SA-319 *Alouette III* utl hel (Flying trg), 1 with 55 PC-7 *Turbo Trainer* Trg ac (some 30 in store) (Flying trg)

EQUIPMENT BY TYPE
AIRCRAFT: ε130 (private ac), 50 combat capable
 FTR 26: 16 *Cheetah* C; 10 *Cheetah* D
 FGA • MB-326K 12: 12 Impala MKII (MB-326KC) (first of 24 *Hawk* Mk120 del by June 06)
 TPT 51
  B-707 3: 3 B-707-320 (only 1/2 op)
  B-737 1: 1 B-737 BBJ
  Beech 200 *Super King Air* 3; 1 Beech 300 *Super King Air*
  C-130 • C-130B 9: 9 C-130BZ *Hercules* (only 1/2 op)
  C-47TP (Basler Turbo-67) 11 (6 maritime, 4 tpt, 1 PR/EW trg); 4 CASA 212 *Aviocar*; 2 CE-550 *Citation II*; 1 CN-235; 13 Cessna 185; 2 *Falcon* 50; 1 *Falcon* 900
 UTL 12: 11 Cessna 208 *Caravan I*; 1 PC-12
 TRG 67: 12 Impala MKI (MB-326M)*; 55 PC-7 *Turbo Trainer* (some 30 in store)
HELICOPTERS
 ASLT 12: 12 CSH-1 *Rooivalk**
 SPT • AS-332 49: 9 *Oryx* (AS-332B) *Super Puma*; 40 more
 UTL 34: 8 BK-117; 12 SA-319 *Alouette III*; 14 (being replaced by 30 A109UH between 2004-7)
AD: some SAM (Capability closed down)
MSL • TACTICAL • ASM: some ZT-3 *Raptor*; some ZT-6 *Mokopa*
 AAM: some V3C *Darter*; some V4 *R-Darter*

Ground Defence
FORCES BY ROLE
Air some SAAF regt (*total:* 12 (security) Air sqn)

EQUIPMENT BY TYPE
2 Radar (static) located at Ellisras and Mariepskop; 2 (mobile long-range); 4 (tactical mobile)

FACILITIES
Radar air control sectors 1 located at Pretoria, 1 located at Hoedspruit

South African Military Health Service 6,000; ε700 reservists **(total** 6,700**)**
A seperate service within the SANDF

NON-STATE ARMED GROUPS
see Part II

DEPLOYMENT

BURUNDI
UN • ONUB 913; 5 obs

DEMOCRATIC REPUBLIC OF CONGO
UN • MONUC 1,394
1 (bn) inf gp; 1 engr coy; 3 obs; 1,394 (Op.'Mistral')
Armed Forces
78 Advisory (Op. 'Teutonic' – Assist DROC Military)

ETHIOPIA/ERITREA
UN • UNMEE 4 obs

Sudan Sdn

Sudanese Dinar d		2003	2004	2005
GDP	d	4.2tr	5.0tr	
	US$	16.1bn	19.4bn	
per capita	US$	421	496	
Growth	%	6.0	7.3	
Inflation	%	7.7	8.4	
Debt	US$	17.4bn		
Def bdgt	d	101bn	ε110bn	ε120bn
	US$	392m	426m	483m
US$1=d		260	258	248

Population (2004) 40,187,486

Ethnic Groups: Muslim 70% mainly in North; Christian10% mainly in South African; 52% mainly in South; Arab 39% mainly in North

Age	0 – 14	15 – 19	20 – 24	25 – 29	30 – 64	65 plus
Male	22%	6%	5%	4%	13%	1%
Female	21%	5%	5%	4%	13%	1%

Capabilities

ACTIVE 104,800 (Army 100,000 Navy 1,800 Air 3,000) Paramilitary 17,500
Terms of service conscription (males 18-30), 2 years

RESERVE NIL Paramilitary 85,000

ORGANISATIONS BY SERVICE

Army ε80,000; ε20,000 conscript **(total 100,000)**
FORCES BY ROLE
Armd 1 div
Mech inf 1 div; 1 indep bde
Inf 6 div; 7 indep bde
SF 5 coy
AB 1 div
Engr 1 div
Border Guard 1 bde

EQUIPMENT BY TYPE
TK 270
 MBT 200: 200 T-54/T-55
 LT TK 70: 70 Type-62
RECCE 218
 AML 6: 6 AML-90
 BRDM 60: 60 BRDM-1/BRDM-2
 Ferret 80; 42 M1114 *HMMWV*; 30 Saladin
AIFV • BMP 75: 75 BMP-1/BMP-2
APC 241
 APC (T) 42: 42 M-113
 APC (W) 199: 19 LAV-150 *Commando*/V-100 *Commando*
  BTR 40: 40 BTR-152/BTR-50
  OT 20: 20 OT-62/OT-64
  120 *Walid*
ARTY 1,105+

TOWED 450 incl
105mm: M-101
122mm: D-30; D-74; M-30
130mm: M-46/Type-59-I
SP • 155mm 20+: 20 M-114A1; some Mk F3
MRL 635
107mm: Type-63
122mm: BM-21; Type-81
MOR: some 81mm; some 82mm
120mm: some AM-49; some M-43
AT
MSL 4: 4 Swingfire
RCL • 106mm • M-40 40: 40 M-40A1
RL • 73mm: some RPG-7 *Knout*
GUNS 40+
76mm: ZIS-3
85mm: some D-44
100mm: M-1944
AD
SAM • MANPAD 54: 54 SA-7 *Grail*
GUNS 1,000+
TOWED
14.5mm: ZPU-2; ZPU-4
23mm: ZU-23-2
37mm: M-1939; Type-63
57mm: S-60
85mm: M-1944
RADAR • LAND: some RASIT (veh, arty)

Sudanese Navy ε1,800

FORCES BY ROLE
Navy 1 HQ located at Port Sudan

EQUIPMENT BY TYPE
PATROL AND COASTAL COMBATANTS 18
MISC BOATS/CRAFT 12: circa 12 armed boats
PCI 2: 2 Kadir
PCR *Patrol Craft Riverine* 4
AMPHIBIOUS • CRAFT • LCT 2+: 2+ Sobat
FACILITIES
Base 1 located at Port Sudan, 1 located at Flamingo Bay
(Red Sea), 1 located at Khartoum (Nile)

Air Force 3,000

FORCES BY ROLE
incl Air Defence
BBR some sqn with 3 AN-26 *Curl* (modified as bombers)
FGA some sqn with 5 F-5E *Tiger II*/F-5F *Tiger II*;
10 MIG-29SE *Fulcrum*; 6 MiG-23 *Flogger*; 5 F-7 (MIG-
21F) *Fishbed C*; 8 J-6 (MiG-19S) *Farmer B* (GA/adv
trg); 2 MIG-29UB *Fulcrum*
Tpt some sqn with 3 *Falcon 20*/*Falcon 50*; 2 C-130H
Hercules; 4 DHC-5D *Buffalo*; 2 F-27 *Friendship*
Trg some sqn with 12 PT-6A (CJ-6A)
Hel some sqn with 10 Mi-24V *Hind E**; 2 IAR-330 (SA-
330) *Puma*; 1 Mi-8 *Hip*; 10 non-operational;
4 AB-212 (Bell 212)
AD 5 bty each with 18 SA-2 *Guideline*

EQUIPMENT BY TYPE
AIRCRAFT 34 combat capable

FTR 26
F-5 5: 5 F-5E *Tiger II*/F-5F *Tiger II*
MIG-29 10: 10 MIG-29SE *Fulcrum*
MiG-23 *Flogger* 6
MIG-21 5: 5 F-7 (MIG-21F) *Fishbed C*
FGA • MIG-19 8: 8 J-6 (MiG-19S) *Farmer B* (GA/adv trg)
TPT 14: 3 *Falcon 20*/*Falcon 50*; 3 AN-26 *Curl* (modified as
bombers)
C-130 2: 2 C-130H *Hercules*
DHC-5 4: 4 DHC-5D *Buffalo*
F-27 *Friendship* 2
TRG 14
CJ-6 12: 12 PT-6A (CJ-6A)
MIG-29U 2: 2 MIG-29UB *Fulcrum*
HELICOPTERS
ATK • MI-24 10: 10 Mi-24V *Hind E**
SPT 13: 2 IAR-330 (SA-330) *Puma*; 1 Mi-8 *Hip*; 10 non-
operational
UTL 4: 4 AB-212 (Bell 212)
AD • SAM • TOWED 90: 90 SA-2 *Guideline*

Paramilitary 17,500

Popular Defence Force 17,500 (org in bn
1,000); 85,000 reservists (**total** 102,500)
mil wing of National Islamic Front

NON-STATE ARMED GROUPS
see Part II

FOREIGN FORCES

(all UNMIS, unless otherwise indicated)
Australia 3; 6 obs
Austria 5; 1 opcon UNAMIS II (legal expert); 5 obs
Bangladesh 891; 13 obs
Benin 4 obs
Brazil 7 obs
Cambodia 5 obs
Canada 11
China 7
Croatia 3
Denmark 40
Egypt 98; 2 obs
El Salvador 5 obs
Fiji 2 obs
Finland 3
Germany 5; 2 obs
Greece 2
Guatemala 6 obs
India 332; 5 obs
Indonesia 4 obs
Iran Army: some (mil advisers)
Italy 216
Jordan 4; 3 obs
Kenya 3
Kyryzstan 5 obs
Malawi 7 obs

Malaysia 3
Moldova 1 obs
Mongolia 2 obs
Mozambique 1 obs
Namibia 25 obs AU; 2 obs
Nepal 228
Nigeria 9 obs
Norway 15; 6 obs
Pakistan 9; 8 obs
Paraguay 6 obs
Peru 8 obs
Poland 2
Romania 3
Russia 5 obs
Rwanda 6 obs
South Africa 100 Police (SA Police Service); 1 coy; 248 opcon AU
Spain 3
Sweden 7; 1 obs
Swizerland 1
Turkey 3
Uganda 4 obs
United Kingdom 4
Zambia 6; 9 obs
Zimbabwe 4; 4 obs

Tanzania Tz

Tanzanian Shilling sh		2003	2004	2005
GDP	sh	10.9tr	10.4tr	
	US$	10.5bn	9.5bn	
per capita	US$	298	262	
Growth	%	7.1	6.3	
Inflation	%	4.65	4.6	
Debt	US$	7.5bn		
Def bdgt	sh	311bn	ε400bn	n.a.
	US$	300m	362m	n.a.
US$1=sh		1,038	1,107	1,120

Population   36,766,356

Age	0 – 14	15 – 19	20 – 24	25 – 29	30 – 64	65 plus
Male	22%	6%	5%	4%	11%	1%
Female	22%	6%	5%	4%	12%	1%

Capabilities

ACTIVE 27,000 (Army 23,000 Navy 1,000 Air 3,000)
Paramilitary 1,400
Terms of service incl civil duties, 2 years

RESERVE 80,000 (Joint 80,000)

ORGANISATIONS BY SERVICE

Army ε23,000
FORCES BY ROLE

Tk   1 bde
Inf   5 bde
Arty 6 bn
Mor   2 bn
AT   2 bn
ADA   2 bn
Engr 1 regt (bn)

EQUIPMENT BY TYPE†
TK 100
  MBT 45: 30 T-54/T-55; 15 Type-59
  LT TK 55: 30 Scorpion; 25 Type-62
RECCE • BRDM 10: 10 BRDM-2
APC • APC (W) • BTR 10: ε10 BTR-152/BTR-40
ARTY 378
  TOWED 170
    76mm 40: ε40 ZIS-3
    122mm 100: 20 D-30; 80 Type-54-1 (M-30) *M-1938*
    130mm 30: 30 Type-59-I
  MRL • 122mm 58: 58 BM-21
  MOR 150
    82mm 100: 100 M-43
    120mm 50: 50 M-43
AT
  RCL • 75mm: some Type-52 (M-20)
  RL • 73mm: some RPG-7 *Knout*
  GUNS • 85mm 75: 75 Type-56 (D-44)

Navy ε1,000

EQUIPMENT BY TYPE
PATROL AND COASTAL COMBATANTS 6
  PCC 2: 2 Vosper
  PFC 2: 2 Shanghai II (PRC)
  PHT 2:
    2 Huchuan each with 2 533mm ASTT
AMPHIBIOUS • CRAFT • LCU 2: 2 Yunnan

FACILITIES
Base 1 located at Dar es Salaam, 1 located at Zanzibar, 1 located at Mwanza (Lake Victoria)

Air Defence Command ε1,000; ε2,000 (AD tps) (total 3,000)

FORCES BY ROLE
Ftr   3 sqn with 6 J-7 (MIG-21F) *Fishbed C*; 3 J-5 (MIG-17F) *Fresco C*; 10 J-6 (MiG-19S) *Farmer B*
Tpt   1 sqn with 1 Y-5 (AN-2) *Colt*; 3 DHC-5D *Buffalo*; 2 F-28 *Fellowship*; 1 HS-125-700; 3 HS-748; 2 Y-12(II)
Liaison   some sqn with 5 Cessna 310; 2 Cessna 404 *Titan*; 1 Cessna U-206 *Stationair*; 6 Bell 206B *JetRanger II*
Trg   some sqn with 5 PA-28-140 *Cherokee*; 2 MIG-15UTI *Midget*
Hel   some sqn with 4 AB-205 (Bell 205)

EQUIPMENT BY TYPE
Virtually no air defence assets serviceable.
AIRCRAFT 19 combat capable
  FTR 9
    MIG-21 6: 6 J-7 (MIG-21F) *Fishbed C*
    MIG-17 3: 3 J-5 (MIG-17F) *Fresco C*

FGA • MIG-19 10: 10 J-6 (MiG-19S) *Farmer B*
TPT 24: 5 Cessna 310; 2 Cessna 404 *Titan*
DHC-5 3: 3 DHC-5D *Buffalo*
F-28 *Fellowship* 2; 1 HS-125-700; 3 HS-748; 5 PA-28-140 *Cherokee*
Y-12 2: 2 Y-12(II)
Y-5 (AN-2) *Colt* 1
UTL • CESSNA 206 1: 1 Cessna U-206 *Stationair*
TRG 2: 2 MIG-15UTI *Midget*
HELICOPTERS
UTL 10: 4 AB-205 (Bell 205)
BELL 206 6: 6 Bell 206B *JetRanger II*; 4 SA-316
AD
SAM 160: 20 SA-3 *Goa*†
SP 20: 20 SA-6 *Gainful*†
MANPAD 120: 120 SA-7 *Grail*†
GUNS 200
TOWED
14.5mm • ZPU 40: 40 ZPU-2/ZPU-4†
23mm 40: 40 ZU-23
37mm 120: 120 M-1939

Paramilitary 1,400 active

Police Field Force 1,400
18 sub-units incl Police Marine Unit

Air Wing
AIRCRAFT • UTL • CESSNA 206 1: 1 Cessna U-206 *Stationair*
HELICOPTERS
UTL • BELL 206 4: 2 AB-206A (Bell 206A) *JetRanger*; 2 Bell 206L *LongRanger*
TRG • AB-47G (BELL 47G) 2: 2 AB-47G (Bell 47G) Trg hel/Bell 47G2

Marine Unit 100
PATROL AND COASTAL COMBATANTS • MISC BOATS/CRAFT: some boats

Armed Forces 80,000 reservists

DEPLOYMENT

ETHIOPIA/ERITREA
UN • UNMEE 3; 8 obs

SIERRA LEONE
UN • UNAMSIL 5 obs

Togo Tg

CFA Franc BCEAO fr		2003	•	2004	2005
GDP	fr	1tr		1tr	
	US$	1.8bn		1.9bn	
per capita	US$	330		341	
Growth	%	4.4		2.9	
Inflation	%	-0.9		1.2	
Debt	US$	1.7bn			
Def bdgt	fr	16.7bn		ε18.0bn	ε20.0bn
	US$	28.8m		33.7m	38.3m
US$1=fr		581		533	522

Population (2004)   5,399,991

Age	0 – 14	15 – 19	20 – 24	25 – 29	30 – 64	65 plus
Male	21%	6%	5%	4%	12%	1%
Female	21%	6%	5%	4%	13%	2%

Capabilities

ACTIVE 8,550 (Army 8,100 Navy 200 Air 250)
Paramilitary 750
Terms of service conscription, 2 years (selective)

ORGANISATIONS BY SERVICE

Army 8,100+
FORCES BY ROLE

Inf	1 regt (some spt unit (trg), 2 armd sqn, 3 inf coy)
	1 regt (1 mot inf bn, 1 mech inf bn)
Cdo / Para	1 regt (3 Cdo/Para coy)
Spt	1 regt (1 fd arty bty, 1 engr/log/tpt bn, 2 ADA bty)
Presidential Guard	1 regt (1 Presidential Guard bn, 1 Cdo bn, 2 Presidential Guard coy)

EQUIPMENT BY TYPE
TK 11
MBT 2: 2 T-54/T-55
LT TK 9: 9 Scorpion
RECCE 61
AML 10: 3 AML-60; 7 AML-90
36 **EE-9** *Cascavel*; 3 M-20; 4 M-3A1; 6 M-8; 2 VBL
AIFV • BMP 20: 20 BMP-2
APC • APC (W) 30: 30 UR-416
ARTY 30
TOWED • 105mm 4: 4 HM-2
SP • 122mm: 6
MOR • 82mm 20: 20 M-43
AT
RCL 22
75mm 12: 12 Type-52 (M-20)/Type-56
82mm 10: 10 Type-65 (B-10)
GUNS • 57mm 5: 5 ZIS-2
AD • GUNS 43
14.5mm • TOWED • ZPU 38: 38 ZPU-4
37mm • TOWED 5: 5 M-1939

Navy ε200 (incl Marine Infantry unit)

EQUIPMENT BY TYPE

PATROL AND COASTAL COMBATANTS • PFC 2: 2 Kara (Fr Esterel)

FACILITIES

Base 1 located at Lomé

Air Force 250

FORCES BY ROLE

FGA some sqn with 4 EMB-326G; 5 Alpha Jet

Tpt some sqn with 1 B-707 (VIP); 2 Beech 58 *Baron*; 2 Reims Cessna 337 (Cessna 337) *Skymaster*; 2 DHC-5D *Buffalo*; 1 F-28-1000 (VIP); 1 DO-27

Trg some sqn with 4 CM-170 *Magister**; 3 TB-30 *Epsilon**

Hel some sqn with 1 AS-332 *Super Puma*; 1 SA-330 *Puma*; 2 SA-315 *Lama*; 1 SA-319 *Alouette III*

EQUIPMENT BY TYPE†

AIRCRAFT 16 combat capable

FGA 4: 4 EMB-326G

TPT 8: 1 B-707 (VIP); 2 Beech 58 *Baron*

DHC-5 2: 2 DHC-5D *Buffalo*

F-28 1: 1 F-28-1000 (VIP)

Reims Cessna 337 (Cessna 337) *Skymaster* 2

TRG 13: 5 Alpha Jet*; 4 CM-170 *Magister**; 1 DO-27; 3 TB-30 *Epsilon**

HELICOPTERS

SPT 2: 1 AS-332 *Super Puma*; 1 SA-330 *Puma*

UTL 3: 2 SA-315 *Lama*; 1 SA-319 *Alouette III*

Paramilitary 750

Gendarmerie 750

Ministry of Interior

FORCES BY ROLE

2 reg sections

Paramilitary 1 (mob) sqn

FACILITIES

School 1

DEPLOYMENT

BURUNDI

UN • ONUB 3; 10 obs

CÔTE D'IVOIRE

UN • ONUCI 6 obs; 296

LIBERIA

UN • UNMIL 2 obs

Uganda Uga

Ugandan Shilling Ush		2003	2004	2005
GDP	Ush	12.7tr	13.8tr	
	US$	6.5bn	7.8bn	
per capita	US$	254	296	
Growth	%	4.7	5.9	
Inflation	%	5.1	5.9	
Debt	US$	4.6bn		
Def exp	Ush	310bn	346bn	
	US$	158m	197m	
Def bdgt	Ush	275bn	346bn	348bn
	US$	140m	197m	196m
FMA (	US$		2.4m	2.2m
US$1=Ush		1,963	1,761	1,778

Population (2004) 27,269,482

Age	0 – 14	15 – 19	20 – 24	25 – 29	30 – 64	65 plus
Male	25%	6%	5%	4%	10%	1%
Female	25%	6%	5%	4%	10%	1%

Capabilities

ACTIVE 45,000 Paramilitary 1,800

ORGANISATIONS BY SERVICE

Ugandan People's Defence Force ε40,000-45,000

FORCES BY ROLE

Army 5 div (*each:* up to 5 army bde)

Armd 1 bde

Arty 1 bde

EQUIPMENT BY TYPE†

TK 172

MBT 152: 152 T-54/T-55

LT TK 20: ε20 PT-76

RECCE 46: 40 Eland; 6 *Ferret*

APC • APC (W) 84

BTR 20: 20 BTR-60

20 **Buffel**; 40 *Mamba*

OT 4: 4 OT-64

ARTY 285+

TOWED 225

76mm: ZIS-3

122mm: M-30

130mm: 221

155mm 4: 4 G-5

MRL

107mm (12-tube): some

122mm: some BM-21

MOR 60+

81mm: some L16

82mm: some M-43

120mm 60: 60 Soltam

AD

SAM • MANPAD 200+: some SA-16 *Gimlet*; 200 SA-7 *Grail*

GUNS 20+

  14.5mm • TOWED • ZPU: some ZPU-1/ZPU-2/ZPU-4

  37mm • TOWED 20: 20 M-1939

Air Wing

FORCES BY ROLE

FGA   some sqn with 5 MiG-23 *Flogger*; 6 MiG-21 *Fishbed*

Tpt Hel some sqn with 1 Mi-172 (VIP); 3 MI-17 (Mi-8MT) *Hip H*; 1 non-operational; 3 Bell 206 *JetRanger*; 2 Bell 412 twin *Huey*

Trg   some sqn with 3 L-39 *Albatros*†*; 1 SF-260* non-operational

Hel   some (Armed) sqn with 1 Mi-24 *Hind*; 5 non-operational

EQUIPMENT BY TYPE

AIRCRAFT 15 combat cablable

  FTR 11: 5 MiG-23 *Flogger*; 6 MiG-21 *Fishbed*

  TRG 4: 3 L-39 *Albatros*†*; 1 SF-260* non-operational

HELICOPTERS

  ATK 6: 1 Mi-24 *Hind*; 5 non-operational

  SPT 5: 1 Mi-172 (VIP)

    MI-8 4: 3 MI-17 (Mi-8MT) *Hip H*; 1 non-operational

  UTL 5: 3 Bell 206 *JetRanger*; 2 Bell 412 twin *Huey*

Paramilitary ε1,800 active

Border Defence Unit ε600

small arms

Police Air Wing ε800

HELICOPTERS • UTL 1: 1 Bell 206 *JetRanger*

Marines ε400

PATROL AND COASTAL COMBATANTS 8: 8 PCR *Patrol Craft Riverine* less than 100 tonnes

Local Militia Forces • Amuka Group ε3,000; ε7,000 (reported under trg) (total 10,000)

NON-STATE ARMED GROUPS

see Part II

DEPLOYMENT

CÔTE D'IVOIRE

UN • ONUCI 2; 2 obs

SUDAN

UN • UNMIS 4 obs

Zambia Z

Zambian Kwacha K		2003	2004	2005
GDP	K	23.1tr	28.6tr	
	US$	4.9bn	6.0bn	
per capita	US$	451	540	
Growth	%	5.1	5.0	
Inflation	%	21.5	18 .0	
Debt	US$	6.4bn		
Def bdgt	K	ε128bn	ε190bn	ε223bn
	US$	27.2m	39.7m	48.1m
US$1=K		4,733	4,800	4,655

Population (2004)   11,261,795

Age	0 – 14	15 – 19	20 – 24	25 – 29	30 – 64	65 plus
Male	23%	6%	5%	4%	10%	1%
Female	23%	6%	5%	4%	11%	1%

Capabilities

ACTIVE 15,100 (Army 13,500 Air 1,600) Paramilitary 1,400

RESERVE 3,000 (Army 3,000)

ORGANISATIONS BY SERVICE

Army 13,500; 3,000 reservists (total 16,500)

FORCES BY ROLE

Army 3 bde HQ

Armd 1 regt (1 tk bn, 1 armd recce bn)

Inf   9 bn (incl 3 reserve bn)

Arty 1 regt (1 MRL bn, 2 fd arty bn)

Engr 1 regt

EQUIPMENT BY TYPE

Some equipment†

TK 60

  MBT 30: 20 Type-59; 10 T-55

  LT TK 30: 30 PT-76

RECCE • BRDM 70: 70 BRDM-1/BRDM-2 (est 30 serviceable)

APC • APC (W) • BTR 13: 13 BTR-60

ARTY 217

  TOWED 96

    76mm 35: 35 ZIS-3 *M-1942*

    105mm 18: 18 Model 56 pack howitzer

    122mm 25: 25 D-30

    130mm 18: 18 M-46

  MRL • 122mm 30: 30 BM-21 (est 12 serviceable)

  MOR 91

    81mm: 55

    82mm: 24

    120mm: 12

AT

  MSL: some AT-3 *Sagger*

  RCL • 57mm 12: 12 M-18

    75mm: some M-20

84mm: some *Carl Gustav*
RL • 73mm: some RPG-7 *Knout*
AD
  SAM • MANPAD: some SA-7 *Grail*
  GUNS 136
    TOWED
      20mm 50: 50 M-55 (triple)
      37mm 40: 40 M-1939
      57mm TOWED 30: ε30 S-60
      85mm 16: 16 M-1939 *KS-12*

Air Force 1,600
FORCES BY ROLE
FGA   1 sqn with 12 MiG-19S *Farmer B*; 1 sqn with 12 MIG-21MF *Fishbed J†* (8 undergoing refurbishment)

Tpt   1 sqn with 4 AN-26 *Curl*; 4 DHC-5D *Buffalo*; 4 Y-12(II)

VIP   1 Fleet with 1 HS-748; 2 YAK-40 *Codling*

Liaison some sqn with 5 DO-28

Trg   some sqn with 2 F-5T *Tiger II**; 2 J-1E *Jastreb*; 8 K-8; 2 MIG-21U *Mongol A**; 5 SF-260MZ (SF-260M)*; 5 SF-260TP

Hel   1 sqn with 12 Mi-8 *Hip*; some (Liaison) sqn with 10 Bell 47G

AD   3 bty with SA-3 *Goa*; 1 bn

EQUIPMENT BY TYPE
Very low serviceability.
AIRCRAFT 33 combat capable
  FTR 14
    F-5 2: 2 F-5T *Tiger II**
    MIG-21 • MIG-21M 12: 12 MIG-21MF *Fishbed J†* (8 undergoing refurbishment)
  FGA • MIG-19 12: 12 MiG-19S *Farmer B*
  TPT 20: 4 AN-26 *Curl*
    DHC-5 4: 4 DHC-5D *Buffalo*
    DO-28 5; 1 HS-748
    Y-12 4: 4 Y-12(II)
    YAK-40 *Codling* 2
  TRG 22: 2 J-1E *Jastreb*; 8 K-8; 2 MIG-21U *Mongol A**
    SF-260 10: 5 SF-260MZ (SF-260M)*; 5 SF-260TP
HELICOPTERS
  SPT 12: 12 Mi-8 *Hip*
  TRG 10: 10 Bell 47G
AD • SAM: some SA-3 *Goa*
MSL • TACTICAL • ASM: some AT-3 *Sagger*

Paramilitary 1,400

Police Mobile Unit 700
Police 1 bn (4 Police coy)

Police Paramilitary Unit 700
Paramilitary 1 bn (3 Paramilitary coy)

DEPLOYMENT
BURUNDI
UN • ONUB 2 obs

CÔTE D'IVOIRE
UN • ONUCI 2 obs

DEMOCRATIC REPUBLIC OF CONGO
UN • MONUC 4; 18 obs

ETHIOPIA/ERITREA
UN • UNMEE 3; 10 obs

LIBERIA
UN • UNMIL 3 obs

SERBIA AND MONTENEGRO
UN • UNMIK 1 obs

SIERRA LEONE
UN • UNAMSIL 1; 3 obs

SUDAN
UN • UNMIS 6; 9 obs

Zimbabwe Zw

Zimbabwe Dollar Z$		2003	2004	2005
GDP	Z$	4.5tr	21.4tr	
	US$	18.1bn	4.0bn	
per capita	US$	1,439	316	
Growth	%	-10.0	-4.8	
Inflation	%	431	282	
Debt	US$	4.4bn		
Def bdgt	Z$	76.4bn	1.3tr	2.3tr
	US$	305m	237m	255m
US$1=Z$		250	5,349	9,000

Population (2004)   12,160,782

Age	0 – 14	15 – 19	20 – 24	25 – 29	30 – 64	65 plus
Male	19%	7%	6%	5%	11%	2%
Female	19%	7%	6%	4%	12%	2%

Capabilities
ACTIVE 29,000 (Army 25,000 Air 4,000) Paramilitary 21,800

ORGANISATIONS BY SERVICE

Army ε25,000
FORCES BY ROLE
Armd	1 sqn
Mech	1 bde HQ
Mech inf	1 bn
Inf	5 bde HQ; 15 bn
Cdo	1 bn
Para	1 bn
Arty	1 bde
Fd arty	1 regt
Engr	2 regt

Gd	3 bn
Presidential Guard	1 gp
AD	1 regt

EQUIPMENT BY TYPE

TK • MBT 40: 30 Type-59 mostly non-operational; 10 Type-69 mostly non-operational

RECCE 115: 80 EE-9 *Cascavel* (with 90mm gun); 20 Eland; 15 *Ferret†*

APC 85

  APC (T) 30: 8 Type-63; 22 VTT-323

  APC (W) 55: 55 TPK 4.20 VSC *ACMAT*

ARTY 242

  TOWED • 122mm 20: 4 D-30; 16 Type-60 (D-74)

  MRL 76

    107mm 16: 16 Type-63

    122mm 60: 60 RM-70 *Dana*

  MOR 146: ε140 81mm/82mm

    120mm 6: 6 M-43

AD

  SAM • MANPAD 30: 30 SA-7 *Grail†*

  GUNS 116

    TOWED

      14.5mm • ZPU 36: 36 ZPU-1/ZPU-2/ZPU-4

      23mm 45: 45 ZU-23

      37mm 35: 35 M-1939

Air Force 4,000

Flying hours   100 hrs/year

FORCES BY ROLE

Ftr	1 sqn with 4 F-7N (F-7M) *Airguard†*; 3 F-7II (J-7II) *Fishbed†*; 2 FT-7 (JJ-7) *Mongol A†*
FGA	1 sqn with 3 MiG-23 *Flogger*; 3†; 1 Hawker Hunter; 1 sqn with 5 *Hawk* MK60A/*Hawk* MK60 (being replaced by 6 K-8)
RECCE / Trg / Liaison	1 sqn with 9 SF-260M; 9 SF-260TP*; 6 SF-260W *Warrior*
RECCE / COIN	1 sqn with 14 Cessna 337 *Skymaster*
Tpt	1 sqn with 1 AN-24 *Coke*; 6 BN-2 Islander; 8 CASA 212-200 *Aviocar* (VIP); 1 IL-76 *Candid*

Hel	1 sqn with 4 Mi-35 *Hind*; 2 Mi-35P *Hind* (armed/liaison); 1 SA-319 *Alouette III**; 1 sqn with 2 AS-532UL *Cougar* (VIP); 8 Bell 412 twin *Huey* (incl trg)
AD	1 sqn with 37mm; 57mm

EQUIPMENT BY TYPE

AIRCRAFT 50 combat capable

FTR 13: 4 F-7N (F-7M) *Airguard†*; 3 MiG-23 *Flogger*; 3†; 3 F-7II (J-7II) *Fishbed†*

FGA 1: 1 Hawker Hunter ; 12 Hawker Hunter FGA F80 FGA/Hawker Hunter FGA MK90 FGA/Hawker Hunter T MK81 Trg* (12 in store)

TPT 40: 1 AN-24 *Coke*; 6 BN-2 Islander; 10 C-47 *Skytrain* in store

  CASA 212 8: 8 CASA 212-200 *Aviocar* (VIP)

  Cessna 337 *Skymaster* 14*; 1 IL-76 *Candid*

TRG 31: 2 FT-7 (JJ-7) *Mongol A†*

  HAWK MK60 5: 5 *Hawk* MK60 Trg ac/*Hawk* MK60A (being replaced by 6 K-8)

  SF-260 24: 9 SF-260M; 9 SF-260TP; 6 SF-260W *Warrior*

HELICOPTERS

ATK 6: 4 Mi-35 *Hind**

  MI-35 6: 2 Mi-35P *Hind* (armed/liaison)

UTL 18

  AS-532 2: 2 AS-532UL *Cougar* (VIP)

  Bell 412 *twin Huey* 8 (incl trg); 1 SA-319 *Alouette III**; 7* in store

AD • GUNS: some 100mm (not deployed); some 37mm; some (not deployed); some 57mm; some (not deployed)

FACILITIES

School 1 with 100mm Guns (not deployed); 37mm Guns (not deployed); 57mm Guns (not deployed) (AD)

Paramilitary 21,800

Zimbabwe Republic Police Force 19,500

incl Air Wg

Police Support Unit 2,300

DEPLOYMENT

SUDAN

UN • UNMIS 4 obs

SUB-SAHARAN AFRICA – DEFENCE ECONOMICS

Despite regional variations, pan-African GDP growth accelerated from 4.2% in 2003 to 5.1% in 2004, the highest in almost a decade. The improvement in Sub-Saharan African economic performance is the result of a variety of supportive factors: the strength of the global economy, improved weather conditions, high oil and commodity prices, progress with structural reforms and the end of several protracted armed conflicts. Several countries have also begun to benefit from the reduction of external debt via the Heavily Indebted Poor Countries Initiative (HIPC), which is currently being implemented in 22 African countries who will receive debt relief amounting to US$26.2bn.

At the same time the G8, under the precidency of the UK promised an increase in aid to Africa of $25 billion by 2010.

Prospects for 2005 are also encouraging, with GDP growth expected to measure 5.2%. Those countries that are oil-exporters will enjoy the strongest growth, particularly those that are in a position to expand production, whereas growth in non-oil exporting countries may be less pronounced in light of an expected reduction in certain commodity prices. An important challenge for a number or countries (notably Kenya, Malawi, Madagascar and South Africa) will be adjusting to the elimination of world textile trade quotas, which will increase the competition they face in the US and EU from low cost Asian suppliers.

Despite the acceleration and reduction in volatility of per capita income growth in the past five years, the IMF has suggested that most Sub-Saharan countries are still unlikely to meet the Millennium Development Goals covering poverty reduction and improvements in education, health and gender equality. In their April 2005 World Economic Outlook, the IMF urges countries to deepen their reform programmes, develop an effective strategy to deal with HIV/AIDS, improve infrastructure and strengthen institutions (including better transparency, governance and property rights), whilst also encouraging the international community to support domestic reforms.

Economic activity in **South Africa** was buoyant in 2004, supported by low interest rates and a strong housing market that helped boost domestic demand. Unemployment however remains high and is unlikely to fall without significant action to reduce existing labour market rigidities. The 2005 defence budget was set at R22.45bn, some 15% higher than the eventual outcome in 2004, due largely to annual changes in payments relating to the Strategic Armaments

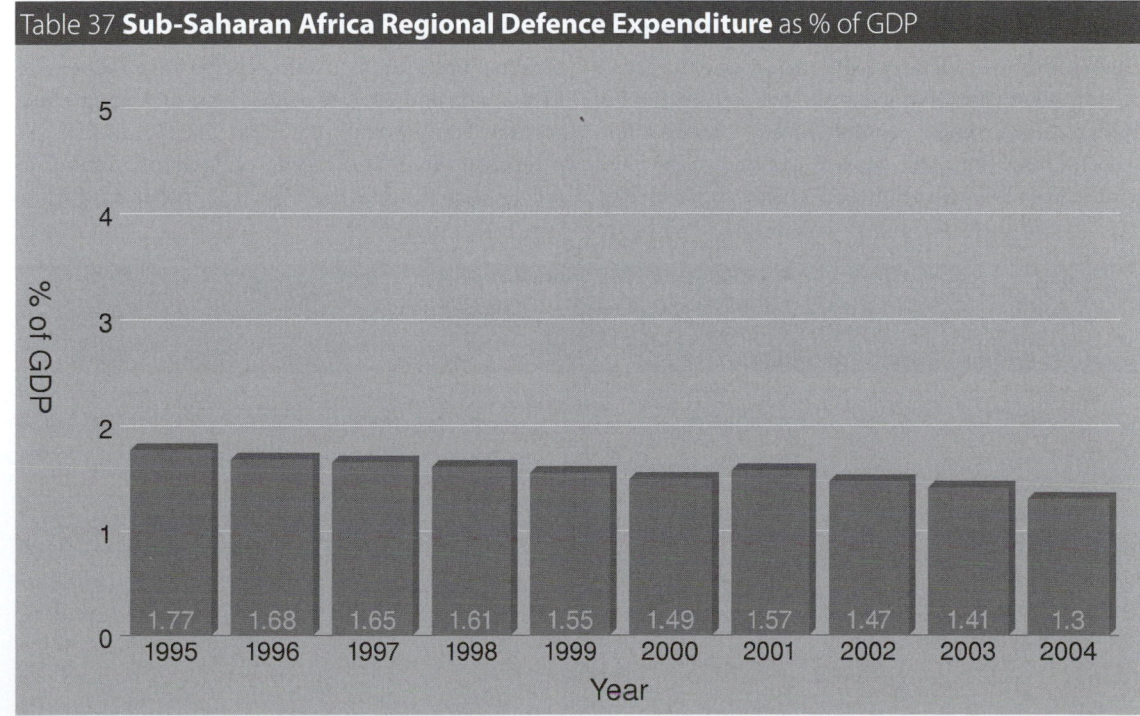

Table 37 **Sub-Saharan Africa Regional Defence Expenditure** as % of GDP

Year	1995	1996	1997	1998	1999	2000	2001	2002	2003	2004
% of GDP	1.77	1.68	1.65	1.61	1.55	1.49	1.57	1.47	1.41	1.3

Procurement (SAP) programme initiated in 2000. The original budget in 2004 had been set at R20.48bn, however due to the strength of the Rand during the year, expenditure on the procurement programme was around R1bn lower than expected. In 2005, the allocation to the Special Defence Account (from where equipment purchases are funded) will increase to R9.10bn from R7.04bn in 2004. The budget plan suggests that defence spending will be marginally higher in 2006 before beginning a slow decline in 2007, as payments for the procurement package start to fall. Once the bulk of the procurement package is paid for, around 2008–09, attention will to financing the future infantry fighting vehicle programme, later phases of the ground-based air-defence system and an armoured personnel carrier and tactical logistics programme. The army has plans to acquire 264 next-generation infantry combat vehicles to replace the *Ratel* family of vehicles, while Project Vistula aims to acquire several hundred 8x8 and 6x6 tactical logistic vehicles to replace the present inventory of Samil trucks.

As noted in *The Military Balance* 2004–05, although there are sufficient funds available to support the payment schedule for the procurement package, this is placing growing pressure on operational and training budgets. In 2005, capital and equipment costs account for 41% of the budget; personnel compensation a further 38%: while operational goods and services account for just 19%. The physical integration of new combat aircraft, helicopters, warships and submarines is adding hidden costs over and above the actual procurement costs. For example, the navy is having to increase its combat capability budget by 20.9% in 2006 to help fund the support contract associated with its four new corvettes and a further 15% in 2007

to fund the operation of three new submarines which will also have begun service by then. Such additional running costs are coming at a time when the SANDF is increasing its regional security role. Although the costs of deployments in the DRC, Burundi and Sudan are estimated to be just R300m a year, this does not include the hidden costs of additional rations, medicines, force preparation and rotation which could at least double the estimated costs.

In the first major procurement decision made since the 2000 SAP, South Africa has committed to buying between eight and 14 A400M transport aircraft, to be delivered between 2010 and 2014, as replacements for the current fleet of upgraded C-130B's. Whilst the actual final number could increase, the cost of an eight aircraft package will be €837m, payable over a 17-year period. Although no details have emerged about the exact payment arrangements, it is thought likely that the government will seek to find a way of funding the procurement from outside the actual defence budget, so that the cost does not impact on other priority programmes. Not only will the A400M increase the operational capability of the SANDF – it can carry a complete *Oryx* or *Rooivalk* helicopter whereas the gearbox must be removed for transportation in a C-130 – but enhanced airlift assets will also fill one of the major gaps identified in the African Standby Force as well as help in disaster and emergency relief operations. The air force is also thought to be considering the A400M as a replacement for its Boeing 707 tankers, which are becoming increasingly expensive to maintain and operate, and as a possible long-range surface-search patrol platform for South Africa's extensive search and rescue obligations. Central to the decision to select the Airbus aircraft is the partici-

Table 38 South African Defence Budget by Programme, 2001–07

Rand m	2001	2002	2003	Revised 2004	Budget 2005	Plan 2006	Plan 2007
Administration	406	467	566	492	681	713	749
Landward Defence	3,288	3,402	3,150	3,422	3,575	3,812	4,084
Air Defence	2,005	2,086	2,176	2,265	2,395	2,505	2,681
Maritime Defence	914	981	1,025	1,108	1,211	1,274	1,357
Military Health Support	1,061	1,235	1,354	1,328	1,577	1,669	1,813
Defence Intelligence	138	132	133	136	148	155	164
Joint Support	1,853	1,975	2,111	2,370	2,490	2,728	3,143
Force Employment	544	746	1,291	1,242	1,363	1,406	1,484
Special Defence Account	5,831	7,807	8,015	7,045	9,105	8,321	6,671
Total	16,044	18,835	19,825	19,411	22,459	22,587	22,152
Total US$m	2,315	1,793	2,622	3,176	3,428	n.a	n.a

pation of South African industry in the wider A400M programme. Under the terms of the contract negotiated by the government, Saouth Africa will be a full partner in the aircraft programme and South African aerospace companies will participate in the 'design, engineering, industrialization, manufacture and in-service support' of the A400M fleet internationally. It is envisaged that the contract to acquire an initial eight aircraft will bring guaranteed work packages worth at least €400m to Denel and Aerosud.

In **Nigeria**, short term economic performance continues to be significantly influenced by developments in the oil and gas sector. Although growth dipped in 2004, GDP expanded by just 3.5% compared to 10.7% in 2003, the opening of a major new oil field and two new liquification streams should see growth pick up to over 7% in 2005. In separate developments international creditors have agreed in principle to write off US$18bn on Nigeria's debt. The deal between Nigeria and the Paris Club was secured after Nigeria agreed to pay back the remainder of its US$31bn bilateral debts to rich countries this year from its soaring oil revenues. Central to the deal is approval from the IMF who must approve Nigeria's economic reforms and establish a continuing monitoring process. In December 2004, the Nigerian government approved a new defence policy for the country, the first since a return to democratic government in 1999. The policy outlines three basic military objectives: vital roles include the defence of Nigeria's territorial borders and the preservation of its unity; strategic roles are defined as protection of the economic, political and diplomatic interests of the country; and peripheral roles cover activities such as the pursuit of terrorists. The new defence policy was accompanied by a 46% increase in the 2005 defence budget, up to N111.9bn (US$841m). New procurement included the delivery of a second batch of four Defender-class fast patrol boats to the navy for patrols in the Niger Delta area. The initial order was for ten of the 7.6m boats, which have been adopted as the US Coast Guard's standard fast response craft, but this has subsequently been increased by a further five. It was also reported that the air force have entered negotiations with Aviation Industries of China for the purchase of a number of F-811M combat jets and have agreed terms with Israel Aircraft Industries to return their grounded MiG-21's to serviceable condition, although no actual upgrading is likely to be done.

In their 2005 Article IV Consultation, the IMF noted that **Uganda's** impressive economic performance based on a first wave of reforms had begun to taper off before conditions that will achieve long-term growth and lasting poverty reduction had been established and urged the authorities to launch a second round of reforms aimed at increasing productivity, reducing poverty, and achieving the Millennium Development Goals (MDGs). As part of a move to strengthen ties between the three members of the East African Cooperation, the finance ministers of Kenya, Tanzania and Uganda all presented their budgets on the same day in June 2005. In 2005/06 Uganda will self finance 60% of its budget compared to 54% the previous year, revenues are projected to increase by 10% and the budget deficit to fall to 9.2% of GDP.

Table 39 Arms orders and deliveries, Sub-Saharan Africa

Country Supplier		Classification	Designation	Quantity	Order date	Delivery date	Comment
Angola (Ang)	Pe	LCA	EMB-312 (*Tucano*)	6	2002	2002	
Eritrea (Er)	SF	trg	L-90 (*Redigo*)	8	1998	1999	
	LAR	hel	Mi-8T (*Hip*)	2	2001	2001	
	Br	PCI	PCI (Patrol craft inshore)	4	2004	2009	
	Br	PCI	PCI (Patrol craft inshore)	1	2004	2009	
South Africa (RSA)	US	tpt	C-130 (*Hercules*)	5	1995	1997	Upgrades for 12 through 2002
	dom	cbt hel	CSH-1 (*Rooivalk*)	12	1996	2004	
	dom	arty	G-6-52		1997	2006	Development complete. Ready for production
	Ge	FSG	MEKO A200	4	1998	2002	Deliveries complete; Last one due to become operational in 2006
	Ge	SSK	Type 209/1400	3	2000	2000	Deliveries 2005–07
	It	hel	A-109	30	2000	2003	Option on further 10
	UK	trg	Hawk MK120	24	2000	2005	
	UK	cbt hel	Lynx Srs 300 (*Super Lynx*)	4	2000	2006	
	Swe	FGA	JAS 39 (*Gripen*)	28	2000	2007	Option on further 19
	dom	MBT	Olifar MK 1B	60	2003	2004	Upgrade to be complete by October 2005
		tpt	A-400M	8	2005	2010	($516m) Long term contract with RSA participation
Sudan (Sdn)	RF	FGA	MiG-29 (*Fulcrum*)	12	2002	2004	
Tanzania (Tz)	RSA	hel	SA-316 (*Alouette III*)	4	1998	1998	Free transfer
Zambia (Z)	PRC	trg	K-8	8	1999	2000	Purchased in kit form
Zimbabwe (Zw)	PRC	FGA	FC-1 (*Xiaolong*)	12	2004		

Chapter Nine
Complex Irregular Warfare: The Face of Contemporary Conflict

OVERVIEW

The 11 September 2001 terrorist attacks ('9/11') presaged several new developments in the global conflict environment. Although the implications of these took some time to become clear, they have begun to force specialists and non-specialists alike, within several advanced Western armed forces, to re-think some basic models and assumptions. This essay explores these new challenges and briefly surveys some of the principal responses to them – responses that are likely to shape the face of twenty-first century conflict, for at least the next few decades.

The RMA – now somewhat doubtful

In the last years of the twentieth century, many Western military forces adopted a style of warfare based on standoff engagement, avoidance of ground combat and reliance on air and maritime strike. This approach was informed by the notion of a Revolution in Military Affairs (RMA) founded on the emerging technologies of stealth, pervasive electronic surveillance and target acquisition, precision engagement, and networked communications. It was epitomised in the US military's 'Transformation' agenda, which sought to replace heavier forces, optimised for intensive ground combat, with medium-weight forces supported by 'reach-back' for precision strike and situational awareness. The assumption was that all-pervasive surveillance, information operations and precision were set to dissipate the 'fog of war', avoiding the need for protracted ground combat, and leading to a new era in warfare. Terms like 'information dominance' and concepts such as 'see first, act first, finish decisively' were seen as central to the future of warfighting.

The conflict environment of the early twenty-first century certainly does represent a new era in warfare: but not the era that Western military planners expected. Instead of pervasive surveillance and information dominance, Western military forces are increasingly being drawn into highly complex and lethal campaigns in urbanised terrain, against irregular enemies invulnerable to many of the advanced technologies central to the RMA approach. Instead of 'network-centric warfare' based upon electronic sensor-to-shooter networks and precision targeting systems, advanced forces are enmeshed in what has been described as 'netwars' based on agile and adaptive human networks. Dealing with this new conflict environment has caused a rethink for many Western forces.

US dominance

Transformation, and the associated RMA agenda, reflected a key feature in the late twentieth-century conflict environment: the overwhelming conventional military dominance of the US. In essence, due to the economic and technological superiority resulting from its status as the sole remaining superpower, the US has achieved unprecedented dominance in conventional military strength. This has rendered US forces virtually invincible in traditional, conventional force-on-force conflict, where this superiority can be brought to bear. Conventional wars therefore tend to be brief, intense and one-sided, resulting in rapid victory for the US, its allies, or the side in a conflict which best approximates US capabilities. This was the conflict environment for which most late twentieth-century militaries planned.

But, perhaps unsurprisingly, America's actual and potential enemies have also taken note of US conventional superiority and acted to dislocate it. Non-state actors like al-Qaeda developed so-called 'asymmetric' approaches that allowed them to sidestep US military power – either by rendering it functionally irrelevant, or by operating in environments where the US cannot bring its conventional superiority to bear.

For example, during the 1990s al-Qaeda operatives moved within the complex human terrain of local indigenous societies, to attack high-tech US installations and platforms – the Khobar Towers facility, the African embassies, the USS *Cole* – while suffering little or no damage in return. On 9/11, al-Qaeda operatives armed only with box-cutters and mobile phones outflanked the US military's high-tech capabilities. The only effective defence on that day was the heroic resistance of unarmed passengers on United Airlines Flight 93 – passengers who, revealingly, had been alerted via private mobile phone calls.

But al-Qaeda was not the only non-state actor to adopt an asymmetric approach. While terrorist and insurgent movements sought to avoid US power via an 'irregular' route, others sought to avoid it by acquiring capabilities that could pose catastrophic threats, such as weapons of mass destruction (WMD), disruptive technologies, or a combination of these measures. Thus, North Korea and Iran sought to deter American conventional power by acquiring nuclear weapons, while Saddam Hussein pursued similar programmes, converted his conventional armed forces into a guerrilla cadre and seemingly developed a range of contacts with regional and transnational terrorist groups. Evidence also suggests that the Iraqi security forces laid careful plans and prepared for a scorched-earth insurgency against potential US invasion. Although the rapid collapse of the resistance organised by the Ba'athist regime put an end to these coordinated 'stay-behind' partisan operations, today's Iraqi insurgents have been the beneficiaries of the detailed planning and preparation undertaken by the regime. All three nations developed links with trans-national terrorism and organised criminal movements, again as a means of balancing and offsetting US conventional superiority.

Consequently, at least for the present, conventional war may have become much less important as the primary arena for military confrontation. US dominance seems to be creating asymmetric 'avoidance behaviour' by its opponents, and rendering victory in the conventional phase of a military campaign much less decisive.

Despite the advantages its enemies gain from asymmetric approaches, the US shows little sign of moving away from a primarily conventional approach to conflict. US planners believe America must maintain its conventional dominance because it needs to consider the potential for longer-term threats from potential peer or near-peer competitors (including, but not limited to China, whose projected rise in influence is difficult for some planners to interpret as a solely peaceful challenge).

Work being carried out on the US Department of Defense's 2005 Quadrennial Defense Review (QDR) has included significant fresh emphasis on 'Irregular Warfare', defined as warfare involving non-state actors or non-traditional methods. Thus, conceptually at least, US planners recognise the need to re-orient from the high technology, state-on-state conflict envisioned in the RMA and Transformation agendas, towards the real-world conflict environment of complex and diffuse irregular threats. Nevertheless, because of the immense inertia of the US military–industrial complex, the influence of Congressional and sectional interests, and the sheer psychological difficulty of moving away from decades of strategic thought, the QDR is likely to produce little real change in expenditure, force allocation, roles and missions or acquisition policy. The bulk of US force structure and defence expenditure will continue to be conventionally focussed.

Enduring irregular challenges

This means that the 'irregular challenges' posed by non-state actors or weaker states who seek to avoid US superiority are likely to be an enduring feature of the conflict environment. Because the US and its Western partners will remain optimised for high-end traditional warfare in the RMA tradition, any smart adversary is likely to use asymmetric means – via WMD, disruptive technologies or irregular warfare – to render Western conventional superiority meaningless. This was highlighted by the US National Intelligence Council in its December 2004 assessment paper, *Mapping the Global Future*, which included the judgement that:

> The key factors that spawned international terrorism show no signs of abating over the next 15 years … The likelihood of great power conflict escalating into total war in the next 15 years is lower than at any time in the past century … Lagging economies, ethnic affiliations, intense religious convictions, and youth bulges will align to create a 'perfect storm', creating conditions likely to spawn internal conflict. The governing capacity of states, however, will determine whether and to what extent conflicts actually occur. Those states unable both to satisfy the expectations of their peoples and to resolve or quell conflicting demands among them are likely to encounter the most severe and most frequent outbreaks of violence.

One implication, noted already, is that victory in conventional battle may no longer be decisive. If an adversary is seeking to confront an advanced military force through means other than conventional conflict, then winning the 'major combat operations' phase of a campaign may not decisively end the war. For example, during the 2003 Iraq war, the conventional phase – lasting only 23 days – was won overwhelmingly by the US-led coalition. But in hindsight the conventional phase is seen as merely a curtain-raiser to the truly decisive phase of the operation – the attempt to replace the Ba'athist regime with a stable, democratic, Western-oriented government: a much more problematic enterprise, in the event.

Another implication is that, because irregular threats are (at least at present) overwhelmingly land based, ground forces (army, marines, special operations forces and elements of air and naval forces that support them) are likely to bear the primary burden of conflict in the next few decades of the twenty-first century. The role of strategic air forces and blue-water navies, although extremely important in shaping the strategic environment, will be less crucial on a day-to-day basis in prosecuting complex irregular conflicts. This is already evident in the demands being placed upon the US defence establishment, where the army and marines are heavily overstretched, suffering battle casualties and personnel wastage and having difficulty meeting recruiting targets. Meanwhile, large portions of the US Navy and air force remain under-utilised, tying up enormous capital and personnel investment but able to make little meaningful contribution to the overall war effort.

There are also consequences for the acquisition of advanced military capability by developed nations. As noted, the RMA was associated with a focus on naval and air platforms with networked information capability to generate precision strike. This has turned out not to be a particularly workable approach for many irregular threats – but the military-industrial complexes of developed nations are often dominated by these air/maritime platforms because they are more expensive than the capabilities needed to oppose irregular threats. In short, there is little money for the defence industry in irregular warfare.

Until this pattern changes, Western military forces in the twenty-first century will be marked by a combination of irrelevance and overstretch. Armies, marines, special forces and their supporting air and maritime elements will be heavily committed, while strategic air forces and navies will remain largely irrelevant to the contemporary conflict environment. This does not mean such forces should be abolished: rather it speaks of a need for re-balancing and for innovative approaches that match the degree of imagination shown by asymmetric adversaries, and allow the full range of capabilities to be brought to bear.

These, then, are the strategic factors that drive the contemporary conflict environment.

The conflict environment

At the tactical level, although some elements in the environment are new, there are continuities between previous forms of warfare and the types of conflict now emerging.

Armed forces today must deal with many adversaries beyond their traditional opponents, the regular armed forces of nation states. These include insurgents, terrorists, organised criminals and many other actual and potential adversaries. This creates a multilateral and ambiguous environment, leading to vastly increased complexity. Instead of a traditional 'bilateral' construct – two opposing sides – armed forces now find themselves in a conflict 'ecosystem' that includes numerous armed or unarmed actors capable of posing a serious threat to mission success, but against whom the application of military force is at best problematic. Thus, while in a previous era of warfare armed forces sought to capture and control territory (a 'terrain-centric approach') or to destroy in battle the main forces of the enemy (an 'enemy-centric approach') they must now seek to dominate the entire environment, including a variety of disparate threat elements, and other challenges which are the result of conflict such as humanitarian and reconstruction tasks.

This might be termed a 'system-centric' approach. The targeting methodologies of the RMA era regarded the enemy as a system and sought to remove the links that allowed it to function. But in the new multilateral threat environment, planners have been forced to recognise that friendly troops, multiple adversaries and neutral populations are all part of a single overall system. For example, in Iraq, actions that target the enemy effectively but alienate the population have proven highly counterproductive, while actions to win over the populace have been stymied by a range of inchoate enemy groups. Thus neither a terrain-centric nor an enemy-centric approach is sufficient as planners have found that they must seek ways to dominate the overall environment and all the actual and potential threat elements within it. Most advanced thinking within Western military establishments is beginning to turn toward this system-centric approach. The 'Systemic Operational Design' model being developed by Israeli theorist Shimon Naveh seeks to generate exactly this type of operational construct.

Further, military forces are increasingly operating within complex groupings of friendly elements including intelligence services, police and law enforcement agencies, aid and development agencies, private enterprise, contractors and allied military forces. Some of these agencies cooperate readily with the military and link easily into command and planning relationships. Many are less easy to coordinate, imposing immense complexity on planners and commanders.

Moreover, globalised communications generate numerous onlookers, neutral elements, commentators and critics. These include local and international media, international non-governmental organisations (NGOs) such as aid agencies, international institutions, neutral or neighbouring population groups and business interests. This creates an audience for every action by any group in a conflict, making the media 'spin' associated with combat action at least as important as the action itself. As troops have learned in Iraq, the insurgents' objective in ambushing a convoy may not be to destroy a few armoured vehicles, but rather to capture global media images of those vehicles burning, in order to influence the global audience.

In addition, the terrain where forces operate is highly complex. Part of the asymmetric 'avoidance' approach by adversaries confronted with RMA-style precision standoff warfare has been to retreat into complex terrain, such as population centres or other cluttered environments that degrade Western target acquisition systems, allowing the enemy to survive 'precision' strikes that often hit uninvolved bystanders. With the increase of urbanisation throughout much of the developing world, such complex terrain is becoming much more commonplace – particularly in the world's littoral zones, those coastal areas where the majority of the global population lives.

This 'complex terrain' includes complex physical terrain, complex human terrain and complex informational terrain:

Complex physical terrain

Examples of complex physical terrain include urbanised areas, littoral regions, crop cultivation, swamps and estuaries, jungles and mountains. Notably, more than 75% of the world's population lives in complex physical terrain. Such terrain typically comprises a mosaic of open spaces (acting as manoeuvre corridors, killing areas or compartments) and patches of restricted terrain that prevent movement and deny observation. This means forces can be drawn into close combat more readily. In open terrain, a force might detect the enemy from standoff distance and avoid it, or engage it only on overwhelmingly favourable terms. In complex terrain the ability to detect the enemy from standoff range is much reduced, meaning that forces can find themselves in close combat without warning.

Complex human terrain

Complex human terrain is where numerous population groups coexist in the same physical space – often a city or other urbanised area. These might include different ethno-linguistic groups, political factions, tribes or clans, religious sects, or ideological movements. These groups may coexist peacefully, ignore each other, or compete (with or without violence). When military forces operate in this terrain, distinguishing between population groups is extremely difficult and requires sophisticated cultural and linguistic understanding. When one or more groups are hostile, extreme difficulty arises in preventing harm to non-combatants or bystanders. Applying physical force in this environment accepts a high risk of counter-productive unintended consequences. Anticipating the second- or third-order effects of using force in complex human terrain is therefore important but difficult – a further complexity inherent in the new irregular forms of warfare that are emerging.

Complex informational terrain

Complex informational terrain is when multiple sources or transmission paths for communications, data or information (including news media) exist in a common operating environment. A force operating in such an environment will be unable to control the information flow in its area of operations. Again, this most often occurs in urbanised terrain, where all sides in a conflict may use the same mobile phone transponders or satellite relays, and gain tactical information from news media operating in the same physical area.

Complex terrain is thus composed of physical, human and informational elements which interact in a mutually reinforcing fashion, leading to extremely high-density operating environments and enormous friction upon military operations. Thus, such operations tend to rapidly become 'bogged down' and stalemated.

Approaches to complexity

Complexity is nothing new. Military operations have always been complex undertakings, and many of the same factors that impact on current operations have existed for a long time. What is new in today's conflict environment is that, because of the ease of international movement and communication inherent in globalisation, an agile adversary can jump between regions and theatres of conflict, using successes at one level to offset defeats at another.

Thus, al-Qaeda bears many similarities to the Nizariya sect of early Islam, the group known in popular culture as the 'Assassins'. Like the Assassins, al-Qaeda is led by a charismatic, elusive figure hiding in a remote mountain fastness. Like the Assassins, al-Qaeda operatives infiltrate open societies and target 'apostate' leaders for destruction. Like the Assassins, their interpretation of Islam differs in significant respects from that of the mainstream Muslim world, but exercises a seductive power over alienated youth and other key groups. But unlike previous fanatical sects, al-Qaeda has access to global communications, financial networks, movement routes and propaganda channels. The 'old man of the mountains' is able to exercise effective global propaganda influence and broad strategic control over a far-flung movement. Thus, enabled by globalisation and its tools, today's Assassins are a vastly more powerful and flexible irregular opponent than their predecessors in the fanatical sects of early Islam.

Similarly, the war on terrorism seems increasingly to comprise three levels. At the global level is a clandestine and counter-clandestine operation against al-Qaeda core leadership, while there is also a series of four regional counterinsurgency campaigns (in North Africa, the Middle East, South/Central Asia and Southeast Asia) and numerous security actions against localised threats in dozens of countries. All of these phenomena have existed separately before – during the Cold War period of 'wars of national liberation', for example. But in today's environment, again enabled by the tools of globalisation, an agile enemy can offset defeats at the regional or local level with global 'armed propaganda', or can offset global defeats by effective media 'spin' on local activities. The simultaneous interaction of multiple types of threat across the global, regional and local levels of the world system creates unprecedented complexity in the new conflict environment.

In the twentieth century, the world wars and the Cold War dominated perceptions, obscuring the more enduring reality of limited conflicts or 'small wars' – the types of conflict that have emerged as central to early twenty-first century warfare. The industrial technology available to twentieth-century nation-states, combined with the severe consequences of defeat, and even of warfare itself, led many states to adopt an industrial approach to the application of force. They focused on combat operations against the armed forces of enemy nation-states, and left the rest of the conflict environment alone. This approach regarded war primarily as an engineering problem rather than a human one.

A more recent approach, advanced by the US Marine Corps General Charles Krulak in 1998, is known as 'Three Block War'. This approach acknowledges the need to conduct many diverse tasks simultaneously, and seeks to manage the complexity by doing these tasks at different times, with different forces or in different places in an overall Area of Operations (AO).

Because of the exponentially increasing complexity described above, the industrial-age approach is inadequate for today's conflict environment. Instead, in an extension of 'three-block war', forces are finding that they must conduct diverse tasks with the same elements, at the same time, in the same place, and with the ability to control their entire environment in a 'system-centric' fashion, while reacting to local, regional and global events. In a sense, the three blocks of the USMC concept have merged into a single block, albeit a much more diverse one. This 'diversity' is the next key element of the tactical environment.

A hundred flowers have bloomed...

The conflict environment has always included terrorists, rural guerrillas, bandits, tribal fighters and mercenaries. But today it also includes drug traffickers, multinational corporations, private military companies, unarmed protesters, environmental groups, computer hackers, rioters, militias, people smugglers, pirates, religious sects, urban guerrillas, media and diplomatic alliances. Many of these groups are not 'threats' in the sense of armed opposition, and applying military force against many of them would be problematic in legal, moral and technical terms. Today's most prominent threat is from transnational terrorists, potentially armed with WMD. But the other threats – including nation-state armed forces – remain and must be addressed simultaneously. Along with the asymmetric 'avoidance behaviour' described earlier, diversity is a major cause of 'asymmetric warfare'.

The globalised environment has also seen a diffusion of conflict, so that it no longer fits into the relatively neat traditional conceptual boundaries of twentieth-century conflict:

Levels of war

Combat has diffused across the strategic, operational and tactical levels of war so that actions at one level have a direct effect at another. This has always been possible, but is now the norm – mirroring the interaction of local, regional and global elements in the conflict environment. The actions of junior leaders in combat, or the demeanour of individual soldiers in humanitarian operations, can be broadcast by international media and affect the course of an operation within minutes. This means that the strategic, operational and tactical levels of war are being compressed. Indeed, the operational level of war may be disappearing, 'squeezed out' by the direct interaction of tactical actions with strategic outcomes.

State/non-state actors

Non-state actors have always been part of warfare. However, the characteristics of state and non-state actors are becoming increasingly similar. Non-state actors now operate sophisticated weapons systems, may control territories and populations, and possess lethality and technological sophistication that was once the preserve of states and their regular armed forces.

Conventional/special operations

Capabilities that once resided exclusively in special operations forces are proliferating to the wider combat forces of advanced militaries. Every soldier in contemporary conflict requires capabilities such as individual initiative, cultural sensitivity, linguistic competence, mastery of sophisticated weapons and sensors, and a capacity for small-group independent operations – characteristics traditionally associated with special forces. Meanwhile, special operations forces are conducting conventional tasks such as screening, defence and large-scale assault, and simultaneously developing more unconventional skills. Special and conventional operations are becoming increasingly integrated, occurring on the same terrain and relying upon intimate cooperation between conventional combat forces, special operations forces and inter-agency elements.

Combatant/non-combatant

The distinction between combatants and non-combatants is eroding. The use of contractors in the battlespace, and the application of the national effects-based approach (NEBA) to warfighting, has meant that civilians who do not directly engage the enemy nevertheless generate critical war-winning effects. The enemies against whom we are currently engaged clearly regard these 'non-combatants' as legitimate targets. In any case, the traditional distinction between combatants and non-combatants is blurring.

Privatisation of conflict

Accelerating this blurring is the increasing privatisation of conflict. Even a decade ago, leading private military companies (PMCs) struggled to achieve legitimacy, being tainted in the public imagination by the stigma which is attached to the concept of mercenaries. Today, PMCs are an essential and increasingly legitimate and accepted element of conflict. Providing VIP protection, logistic support, intelligence support, facilities, advisory and consulting services, such private-enterprise groups have become a fundamental part of the Western way of war. This is a symptom of military forces that, in the post-Cold War era, were subjected to efficiency programmes that effectively removed any spare capacity to fill the types of tasks now being undertaken by contractors. Nevertheless, the employment of PMCs and private security companies (PSC) will continue to be constrained by their comparative lack of accountability when compared to regular forces.

Elements of national power

Traditionally, national strength was defined in terms of political, military, economic, social, informational and industrial power, and the military's job was to provide the 'military' aspect of national power and (in most Western democracies) studiously ignore the rest. This no longer applies to every situation – all elements of national power are being coordinated and integrated by governments into a single national 'whole of government' or 'whole of nation' effort. Military forces no longer 'own' war, rather they are one component in a national response.

Disaggregated battlespace

In complex terrain, in the face of multiple adaptive threats, the traditional notion of 'battlespace' needs refinement. It is more accurate to describe a force's 'mission space' in which 'battle spaces' erupt with little warning. Even against a more conventional enemy, the effect of complex terrain is to create a series of 'mini-battles' between individuals or small semi-autonomous teams. The geographical space between these battlespaces is not empty: it contains non-combatants and uncommitted potential combatants, as well as key infrastructure for population support. This means individual and small team combat capabilities are increasingly important. It is not enough for the overall force to possess key capabilities – it must be able to bring them to bear at the critical place (a small team engagement in complex terrain) and time (a fleeting, unexpected encounter). In a disaggregated battlespace, this factor generates a necessity to proliferate capabilities and control to individuals, smaller teams and sub-units.

Traditionally, defence forces focused on the threat posed by conventional weapons fielded by regular opponents. Today, a vast array of new, highly lethal weapons is proliferating. The most prominent lethality issue remains the threat of global terrorists armed with weapons of mass destruction, but many extremely lethal capabilities have propagated into the hands of individuals. These include thermobaric weapons, long-range heavy calibre sniping systems, advanced explosive and booby-trapping devices, laser eye damage weapons, and an enormous range of other lethal but concealable weapon systems.

Importantly, many of these weapons can be carried, concealed and operated by one person. This means unprecedented levels of lethality are now available to individuals rather than larger organisations. This, in turn, implies that land forces can encounter individuals with extremely high lethality, without warning, in any type of operation. Even planned humanitarian or peace enforcement operations can rapidly turn into a series of highly lethal combat engagements, with little or no warning, as troops encounter irregular adversaries armed with high-lethality systems.

Because individuals with concealable high lethality have little tactical signature and can be encountered in a range of scenarios, predicting the level of lethality likely to be encountered during operations becomes problematic. This has major implications because it means that each individual engagement – even in a supposedly 'low-intensity' operation – can produce a mass-casualty situation with strategic implications.

Increasing lethality has contributed to a reduction in force density on the battlefield. This trend has been apparent since the industrial revolution, but is now accelerating. Lighter, cheaper and more lethal weapons allow smaller, more dispersed teams to generate battlefield effects that once required large numbers of troops. Companies now perform the same tasks, and have equivalent lethality, as the battalions of 50 years ago or the brigades of the early twentieth century. However, the manpower-intensive nature of operations at the low end of the operational spectrum continues to mean that technical solutions leading to manpower reductions are limited – humanitarian, peacekeeping and policing, for example, all require the extensive use of manpower.

Deductions from the environment

In essence, then, the contemporary conflict environment reflects the consequences of globalisation, which has created and empowered a diverse range of enemies of the West; and US conventional dominance, which has caused those adversaries to seek asymmetric arenas and unconventional means with which to confront the West. This renders developed nations less likely to suffer a conventional military attack, but more likely to face ambiguous and asymmetric threats, including terrorism. These factors have produced a complex, diverse, diffuse and lethal environment. There are numerous stakeholders; the terrain (in physical, human and informational terms) is complex; the range of threats is diverse; traditional conceptual distinctions have diffused, and individuals now have the capability to inflict strategic defeat through high-lethality weapons.

Several Western armed forces have drawn similar deductions about the conflict environment. Key deductions have been that:

- land forces must become better at orchestrating effects in an agile, whole-of-government manner across the full range of military operations in complex terrain.
- there is a requirement to raise the strategic defeat threshold for deployed land forces, and become more adaptable and agile in performing, and transitioning between, a wide range of tasks and environments.
- there is a need to improve force protection through instantaneous access to firepower, protection and mobility, improved situational awareness and stealth.
- there is a need to prepare individuals and small teams for a disaggregated, ambiguous, lethal and highly complex battlespace.

Some national responses

Many conventional forces have already responded to the new environment, or are seeking to orient to the increasing complexity of twenty-first-century warfare. However, the three nations that have been most heavily committed to military operations in the new century have been the countries with Anglo-Saxon traditions – Australia, Britain and the US. Each has responded to the new environment in a broadly similar manner, but with key differences of emphasis.

Perhaps due to its tradition of unconventional warfare, or perhaps because of its small size and resultant agility, the Australian Army was one of the first Western forces to adapt to the new conditions. In addition, the Australian experience in late twentieth-century conflicts, particularly in East Timor, appears to have provided an early 'wake-up call' as to the nature of the new environment. As a result, Australia was the first to publish a comprehensive analysis of the new conflict environment and its implications. The doctrine paper Complex Warfighting, first produced in June 2003, argued that land forces needed capabilities to operate in a range of complex terrain environments, in small semi-autonomous teams that could 'swarm' to provide mutual support while seeking to dominate the overall environment by influencing and controlling population groups (including numerous enemy groups). It identified the future threat as coming from increasingly well-armed, networked irregular insurgent and terrorist opponents. Interestingly, the Australian concept envisaged combined arms teams comprising both traditional and non-traditional elements, with protected mobility and a high level of situational awareness, operating within a joint inter-agency setting.

Australian forces operating in Iraq, Afghanistan, the Solomon Islands, East Timor and elsewhere already appear to be applying the concept – adopting integrated combined-arms actions at the small-team level, with evidence of 'swarming' tactics and a highly advanced application of inter-agency teams, particularly in the Solomon Islands operation. More recently, the Australian government announced a programme of 'Hardening and Networking the Army' which seeks to create an army structure optimised for small-team distributed operations in a high-threat environment, in predominantly urbanised environments. In addition, because Australia lacks a marine corps, the Australian Navy and Army have cooperated closely in developing a doctrine for 'manoeuvre operations in the littoral environment' – essentially an advanced form of maritime coastal raiding optimised for expeditionary operations against irregular threats – which seems well suited to the current environment.

In Britain, November 2003 saw the publication of a Future Land Operating Concept (FLOC), which called for smaller, more manoeuvrable units to be known as 'agile mission groups'. Like the earlier Australian concept, the FLOC emphasised the need to control the overall environment in an area of operations, rather than simply target the main forces of a regular enemy. Over time, the FLOC appears to have evolved toward an approach which some have termed 'C-DICT' – Countering Disorder, Insurgency, Criminality and Terrorism. This approach reflects key British experiences in Sierra Leone, Afghanistan and Iraq, as well the experience of domestic crises such as the 2001 foot and mouth disease outbreak, all of which called upon the armed forces to deal effectively with multiple disparate threats simultaneously and in the same area of operations. It also explicitly adopts a 'systems-centric' approach, calling on the land forces to dominate all sources of conflict and threat in the environment.

In practical terms, the British experience of counterinsurgency in Northern Ireland appears to have given British forces an edge in countering the Iraqi insurgency, and in dealing with Afghan irregulars. The British made a much more substantial contribution to both Afghanistan and Iraq than did the Australians, and were able to apply their greater practical experience in counterinsurgency to good effect. Australia subsequently made major increases in its troop commitment to Iraq, and it is reasonable to assume that the close working relationship between British and Australian forces in-theatre will lead to a continuing close alignment in these two nations' approaches to complex irregular warfare.

The American approach has been somewhat more diverse. Both the US Army and the US Marine Corps are heavily committed in Iraq and Afghanistan, and both have produced new conceptual approaches to dealing with the contemporary conflict environment. Because of its size and, arguably, because it took some time for key leaders and planners to recognise the true nature of the irregular challenge in Iraq, the US Army was slower to adapt than either the US Marines or their major coalition partners, the British and Australians.

The US Marines quickly produced an update to their iconic Small Wars Manual, a classic of irregular warfare doctrine first published in 1940. The new update was a well-considered analysis that drew on many of the same observations about the conflict environment, and made some extremely sound recommendations for adapting to it. However, US Marines in Iraq and Afghanistan have often tended to fall back on well-proven concepts from an earlier counterinsurgency era, applying techniques such as combined action platoons in their area of responsibility. These have proved less effective than hoped, because of the increasing complexity and lethality of the conflict environment, and because the enemy was not a single mass movement but a loosely aligned movement of anti-occupation forces.

A second Marine initiative – the concept for Distributed Operations – is currently being developed. Although the details are classified, it appears to involve a similar response to that developed by the British and Australians (with whom the US Marines have long cooperated extremely closely). It envisages a network of small teams, linked to a responsive system for offensive fire support and a pervasive surveillance, reconnaissance and information network, able to respond in an agile manner to changing threats in a rapidly evolving conflict space. The teams could coalesce into larger organisations in the face of large-scale threats, or disperse to cover a wide area with a low-profile presence. The concept dovetails with the Marines' well-developed concepts of Sea Basing, Operational Maneuver from the Sea and Ship-to-Objective Maneuver, which remain some of the most advanced amphibious concepts in existence. Like Sea Basing, Distributed Operations also represents a very sophisticated approach to the current conflict environment. The Marines' well-regarded Center for Emerging Threats and Opportunities has also produced several interesting and useful new approaches to 'cultural intelligence' and the problem of complex human terrain.

The US Army responded to the challenge of irregular conflicts by producing, for the first time since the early 1960s, a new doctrine for counterinsurgency. Issued in October 2004, Field Manual-Interim 3-07.22 Counterinsurgency Operations draws heavily on classical counterinsurgency approaches from the 1960s, but has been updated to reflect some key aspects of twenty-first-century operations. The details are again classified, but in general terms the doctrine appears to be a relatively conservative, evolutionary development rather than the more radical approaches envisaged by the Australians, the British and the US Marines.

The US Army concept for a Modular Army, which envisages smaller, more agile units of action able to work more effectively in an urbanised, populated environment of complex terrain, appears to be a serious attempt to orient the US Army to the demands of the new environment. It is supported by an Army version of Distributed Operations, which envisages larger teams and less small-unit autonomy, but greater combat weight, than the US Marine version of the concept. The US Army also appears to have benefited from its relatively late start in adjusting to complex irregular warfare, by drawing from coalition and joint partners' concepts in developing its own. For example, large portions of the new US future land warfighting concept appear to be have been drawn directly from the Australian Complex Warfighting doctrine, while other passages echo the Marines' Distributed Operations and Small Wars concepts.

A key element of the US Army approach is the innovative use of 'tactical blogs' such as the secure website 'companycommand.com'. These sites allow serving junior commanders to rapidly share lessons learned, operational insights and tactical tips, leading to a much faster – albeit unofficial – adaption cycle in dealing with changing adversary tactics. The army has been highly innovative in supporting this bottom-up initiative and seeking to leverage it into a greater degree of tactical agility. This is perhaps the most impressive army contribution to the current conflict environment.

Thus, while their approaches have differed in detail, the principal Anglo-Saxon nations engaged in the current range of conflicts have all adopted approaches that emphasise small-team, protected, networked operations in complex terrain, against agile irregular enemies, as the basis for future combat. Their approaches to current operations reflect the practical application of these concepts to differing degrees, while acquisition programs also look set to re-orient major military forces toward the new environment.

Beyond the three nations described here in detail, many other defence forces are in a process of re-orientation to the new environment. Notably, the French 'counter-war strategy' adopts a similar approach to dominating the entire conflict environment in order to return it to peaceful conditions, while the notion that ground combat occurs in a 'viscous medium' mirrors the Anglo-Australian emphasis on terrain and population complexity. The German Army is pursuing a similar series of concepts, while seeking to optimise only part of its force for this type of operation, and Scandinavian armies – already well experienced in this form of operation – are adapting quickly along the same lines.

CONCLUSIONS

The conflict environment of the early twenty-first century differs markedly from that envisaged in the late twentieth-century RMA debates, with their emphasis on precision standoff engagement and all-pervasive networked information systems. Instead, the wars that have emerged have been irregular conflicts in which adversaries have deliberately sought to negate Western conventional superiority by retreating into complex terrain and adopting asymmetric approaches to offset technological military power. While air power played an important supporting role in these conflicts, ground forces have increasingly been required to grapple at close quarters, relatively unsupported, with messy and ambiguous conflict situations on the ground.

This is not to say that the precision air and maritime engagement envisaged in the RMA approach, or the notion of network-centric warfare, has been overtaken by events. These remain key elements in the Western way of war and are likely to retain their importance as means to shape the strategic context in which future conflict will be fought. But the day-to-day prosecution of these conflicts will be increasingly irregular, asymmetric and ground based, fought in complex human and physical terrain against a backdrop of vastly increased individual lethality.

As a result, many Western planners – notably in the British and Australian ground and special forces and in the US Marine Corps, which have long traditions of combat in low intensity warfare – have begun a process of evolution toward smaller, more agile mission teams. For the US Army, which has historically concentrated on developing conventional high-intensity capabilities and doctrine, the process may take longer and be less easily accomplished.

Reflected in warfighting concepts, acquisition programmes and actual operations, the trend towards developing smaller mission teams is deliberately optimised for operations in complex, urbanised, populated areas marked by pervasive media presence and globalised communications. However, such evolution is, of course, only likely to spur co-evolution by the various irregular forces opposing Western armies – a process of continuing adaptation that looks set to continue well into the new century, as each actor adapts and seeks to offset the actions of actual or potential adversaries. Moreover, since the US military is likely to remain primarily conventionally focused, even in the wake of the 2005 QDR, most adversaries are likely to continue to seek irregular asymmetric approaches to offset Western conventional superiority.

PART TWO
Non-State Armed Groups

Table 40 **Non State Activity Reference**			
Place	**Activity**	**Group/Trends**	**Reference**
Europe			
UK	International Terrorism, Domestic Terrorism	Suicide in London, IRA disarmament	pp. 49–50
Spain	Domestic Terrorism, Separatism	ETA arrests and bomb attack	p. 50
Turkey	Domestic Terrorism, Suicide	HPG, TAK, PKK	p. 50–51
Moldova	Separatism	Transnistria	p. 47
Georgia	Separatism	Abkhaz, South Ossetian	pp. 48–9
Russia			
Russia – Chechnya	Insurgency, Domestic Terrorism, Separatism, Assassination of Aslan Maskhadov, Crime	Chechen Rebels, Increase in organised crime	p. 156
Russia – Dagestan	Domestic Terrorism, Crime	Jennet, Increase in organised crime	p. 157
Middle East and North Africa			
Iraq	Insurgency	Sunni fundamentalists, Ba'ath Loyalists, Suicide, Increasing use of IEDS	pp. 173–4
Israel/Palestine	Domestic Terrorism, Insurgency	Hamas, PIJ, Al-Aqsa Martyrs Brigades, PLO	pp. 176–7
Lebanon	Assassination	Beirut Car Bomb incident	p. 177–8
Saudi Arabia	Threats to foreign nationals	al-Qaeda arrests	p. 178
Egypt	International Terrorism	Islamic Extremism, Cairo attack. Islamic Extremism, Sharm el-Sheikh attack.	p. 179
Yemen	Terrorist arrests	al-Qaeda	p. 179
Central and South Asia			
Uzbekistan	Local Insurrection	Andijon Incident	p. 223
Afghanistan	Insurgency, Drugs	Taliban and Jihadists	pp. 224–5
Pakistan	Terrorism, Extremism, Sectarianism, Abu Faraj al-Libbi arrested, Domestic, Insurgency	Sunni, Shi'te, al- Qaeda, Baluchistan, BLA	pp. 225–6
India	Terrorism, Separatism, Left Wing Extremism	Naxalites/CPI-Maoist North East, NBFB, ANVM, UPDSA, NSCN-IM	p. 226–7
Sri Lanka	Separatism, Foreign Minister Assassinated	LTTE, Sniper attack	p. 227
Nepal	Insurgency	Maoist rebels	p. 227
Bangladesh	Extremism, Domestic Terrorism	Awani League, Jagrata Muslim Janata, Jamaat-ul-Mujahideen	p. 227
East Asia and Australasia			
Indonesia	Insurgency	GAM	pp. 261–2
Philippines	Domestic Terrorism	MILF, JI, ASG, Moro National Liberation Front	p. 262
Thailand	Separatism	Patani Islamic Warriors Movement	p. 262
Myanmar	Separatism	KNU, SSA, Karenni Shan, SPDC	pp. 262–3
Caribbean, Central and Latin America			
Haiti	Insurgency	Pro-Artiside militias	p. 315
Mexico	Drug Smuggling	Zetas, Zapatista-EZLN	p. 315
Colombia	Drug Smuggling, Insurgency	FARC, ELN, AUC	p. 316
Sub-Saharan Africa			
Sudan	Ethnic Violence	Janjaweed	pp. 360–1
Mali	Domestic Terrorism	GSPC	p. 364
Nigeria	Sectarianism, Insurgency	Benu and Taraba States, Nigerian Fulani nomads, NDPVF, NDV. Oil Delta region	p. 363
Democratic Republic of Congo, Rwanda, Uganda	Insurgency, inter-necine	UPC-L, FAPC, FNI, FARDC, FDLR, ALIR, FAR, LRA	pp. 361–3

Definition

In this table, a 'non-state armed group' is an organized and armed opposition force with a recognized political goal, acting independently from state or government. Groups are only included if they have an effective command structure. The definition covers groups that might be variously described as guerillas, militia forces, paramilitary or self-defence groups and also terrorist groups with political objectives that have caused significant damage and casualties over the years.

The table only includes non-state armed groups that are active or have recently been active and which represent, or have represented, a significant threat to states and governments. Armed groups with solely criminal objectives are excluded.

Notes
A active, C cease-fire, D dormant (inactive for the past 12 months), X defeated

Table 41 **Selected Non-State Armed Groups**

Origin	Organisation * aka	Estb.	Est. Strength	Status	Operates	Aims (Remarks)
NATO AND NON-NATO EUROPE						
Fr	Armata Corsa	1999	30+	A	Corsica, Fr	Self determination for Corsica and fighting FLNC's alleged ties with organised crime
Fr	Accolta Nazinuale Corsa / Resistenza Corsa	2002	n.k.	A	Corsica, Fr	A separate Corsican state
Fr	Clandestini Corsi	2004	n.k.	A	Corsica, Fr	'Rid Corsica of foreigners'
Fr	National Liberation Front of Corsica (FLNC)	1976	600	A	Corsica, France	Leftist group for Corsican independence
SM	Albanian National Army (ANA) / Armaj Kombetare Shiqitare (AKSh)	1999	n.k.	A	Kosovo, FYROM	Insurgent Albanian grp for united Albanian state, most membership from the now disbanded KLA and NLA
SM	Liberation Army of Presevo, Medvedja and Bujanovac (UCPMB)	2000	800	D	Presevo Valley, Serbia, west and north FYROM	Annex Kosovo for ethnic Albanians
Gr	Anarchist Struggle	2000	n.k.	D	Gr	Solidarity with other anarchists; expresses anti-American sentiments
Gr	17 November Revolutionary Organisation	1974	20+	D	Athens	Radical leftist grp, wants to remove US bases from Gr; w/draw Tu troops from Cy; sever Gr ties to NATO and EU
Gr	Revolutionary Nuclei (RN)	1995	100-	A	Athens	Remove US influence, anti-government
Gr	Revolutionary Struggle	2004	n.k.	A	Athens	Anti-capitalist grp
It	Anti-Imperialist Territorial Nuclei (NTA)	1995	20	A	north It	Opposes 'US and NATO imperialism' and condemns Italy's foreign and labour polices.
It	Informal Anarchist Federation / Federazione Anarchia Informale (FAI)	2003	n.k.	A	It	Anarchist grp,opposes current European order
It	New Red Brigades/Communist Combatant Party (BR/ PCC)	1999	30+	A	It	Opposed to Italy's foreign and labour policies and NATO.
It	Proletarian Nuclei for Communism / Nuclei Proletari per Comunismo (NPC) aka Proletarian Combatant Groups	2003	n.k.	A	It	Marxist class-struggle; anarchist anti-state, anti-imperialist grp
It	Revolutionary Front for Communism	1996	n.k.	A	It	Marxist-Leninist grp
It	Revolutionary Proletarian Initiative Nuclei (NIPR)	2000	20+	A	It	Opposes Italy's foreign and labour polices
Mol	Transnistria	1992	7,500	A	Transnistria	Separate state of Transnistria
Sp	Euskadi ta Askatasuna (ETA)	1959	n.k.	A	Basque regions, Sp, Fr	Independent homeland on Marxist principles in Basque autonomous regions
Sw	Global Intifada	2002	n.k.	A	Sw	Leftist grp opposed to 'capitalism, imperialism and current world order'
Tu	Kurdistan Freedom Hawks / Teyrbazen Azadiya Kurdistan (TAK)	2004	n.k.	A	Tu	Separatist grp; targets businesses and government installations

Table 41 Selected Non-State Armed Groups

Origin	Organisation * aka	Estb.	Est. Strength	Status	Operates	Aims (Remarks)
Tu	Great Eastern Islamic Raiders Front (IBDA-C)	1970's	n.k.	A	Turkey	Sunni Salafist group, advocates Islamic rule in Turkey
Tu	Partiya Karkaren Kurdistan (PKK) / People's Congress of Kurdistan (Kongra-Gel)	1978	4,000–5,000	A	Tu, N. Irq, N. Ir, Syr	Marxist-Leninist; in 1999 'peace initiative' claimed halt to use of force. Terminated cease-fire in June 2004; Suicide
Tu	TKP / ML-TIKKO / Turkiye Komunist Partisi / Marksist-Leninist-Turkiye Isci Koylu Kurtulus Ordusu	1972	1000-		Tu	Communist, anti-Western grp
Tu	Revolutionary People's Liberation Party/Front (DHKP/C)	1978	n.k.	A	Tu, Europe, Asia,	Marxist group opposed to the US and to NATO; Suicide
Tu	Turkish Hezbollah	1994	200+	D	Tu	Estb an independent Islamic state
UK	Irish Republican Army (IRA) / Official Irish Republican Army (OIRA)	1922	n.k.	C	UK, Irl, International	Unite N. Ireland with the Republic of Ireland, declared end to 'armed struggle' 28 July 2005
UK	Provisional Irish Republican Army (PIRA)/ Provos	1969	300+	C	UK, international	Remove British forces from N. Ireland, unite N. Ireland with Republic of Ireland
UK	Continuity Irish Republican Army (CIRA) / Continuity Army Council	1994	50+	A	UK, Irl	Reunify Irl' (Armed wing of Republican Sinn Fein. Opposed Sinn Fein's adoption of Jul 1997 cease-fire)
UK	Real Irish Republican Army (RIRA) / True IRA	1997	100+	A	UK, Irl	Oppose Sinn Fein's adoption of Jul 1997 cease-fire (Armed wing of 32 County Sovereignty Committee)
UK	Irish National Liberation Army (INLA) / People's Liberation Army / People's Republican Army / Catholic Reaction Force	1975	150	C	UK, Irl	Remove British forces from N. Ireland and unite it with Irl. Armed wing of Irish Republican Socialist Party
UK	Loyalist Volunteer Force (LVF) / Red Hand Defenders	1996	150+	C	UK, Irl	No political settlement with nationalists in N. Ireland (Faction of UVF)
UK	Orange Volunteers	1970s	20	C	UK, Irl	No political settlement with nationalists in N. Ireland
UK	Ulster Defence Association (UDA) / Ulster Freedom Fighters (UFF)	1971	200+	A	UK, Irl	Protect Loyalist community (Largest loyalist para-military grp in N. Ireland. Backed 1998 Good Friday Agreement. Armed wing of Ulster Democratic Party)
UK	Ulster Volunteer Force (UVF) / Protestant Action Force / Protestant Action Group	1966	150+	C	UK, Irl	Safeguard N. Ireland's constitutional position within U.K. Protect Loyalist community (Armed wing of Progressive Unionist Party)
UK	Secret Organisation Group of al-Qaeda of Jihad Organisation in Europe	2005	n.k.	A	UK	Ideologically opposed to Western culture. Responsible for July 2005 bombings in London; Suicide
FYROM	Kosovo Liberation Army (KLA) / Ushtria Clirimtare e Kosoves (UCK)	1992-3	5–12,000+	D	Kosovo, FYROM	Loose grp desiring autonomy for Kosovars, eventual unification with other Albanians
FYROM	National Liberation Army (NLA) / Ushtria Clirimtare Kombetare (UCK)	1999-2001	no more than 2–3,000	D	FYROM	Greater Albania,overlapping membership with AKSh, KLA, UCPMB, not to be confused with Kosovo's UCK
GEORGIA						
Ga	Abkhazia separatists	early 1990s	1,500+	C	Abkhazia, Ga	Separate, independent Abkhazia, 'protection of Abkhazian culture from Georgian dominance'
Ga	White Legion and Forest Brothers	1997	2–300+	D	Abkhazia, Ga	Georgian group seeking control over Abkhazia and the return of the Georgian and Mingrelian IDPs
Ga	South Ossetia Separatists	early 1990s	n.k.	C	S. Ossetia, Ga	Seek an independent South Ossetia
RUSSIA						
RF	Amanat jama'at	n.k.	n.k.	A	Chechnya, RF	Wahhabi Chechen separatist group

Non-State Armed Groups

Table 41 **Selected Non-State Armed Groups**

Origin	Organisation * aka	Estb.	Est. Strength	Status	Operates	Aims (Remarks)
RF	Black Widows	1999	30+	A	Chechnya, RF	Female suicide bombers for Chechen independence, 'avenge death of relatives in the Chechen struggle'
RF	Chechen Rebels	n.k.	2,000–3,000	A	Chechnya, Dagestan	Independent state (Muslim mercenaries), some demands for an Islamist state; Suicide
RF	Islamic International Peacekeeping Brigade (IIPB) and Special Purpose Islamic Regiment (SPIR)	1996	400	A	Chechnya, Ga, Az, Tu	Withdrawal of Russian forces from Chechnya.
RF	Riyadus-Salikhin Reconnaissance and Sabotage Battalion of Chechen Martyrs (RSRSBCM)	2002	50	A	Chechnya, RF	Withdrawal of Russian forces from Chechnya Suicide
RF	Jama'at of Dagestan 'Shariat' / Shariah Jama'at / Jennet	2004	n.k.	A	Dagestan, RF	Separatists seeking independence for Dagestan
MIDDLE EAST AND NORTH AFRICA						
Ag	Armée Islamique du Salut (AIS)	1992	n.k.	C	Ag	Socialist republic in Ag within framework of Islamic principles. Truce 1997. Armed wing of Front Islamique du Salut (FIS)
Ag	Groupe Islamique Armée (GIA)	1992	100+	A	Ag	Fundamentalist Islamic state in Ag (Refused Jan 2000 peace plan);strength undermined by splinter groups; Suicide
Ag	Groupe Salafiste pour la Prédication et le Combat (GSPC)	1998	500+	A	Ag, Cha, Ngr, RMM	Fundamentalist Islamic state in Ag (Splinter faction of GIA)
Ag	Dhamat Houmet Daawa Salafia	n.k.	n.k.	A	Ag	Splinter group of GIA
Brn	Islamic Front for the Liberation of Bahrain	1981	n.k.	D	Brn, Ir	Anti-monarchy, restore natl parliament, coup attempt 1981
Et	al-Gama'a al-Islamiya / Islamic Group (IG)	1977	<500	A	Afg, Et	Overthrow of the regime of Hosni Mubarak and the estbment of an Islamic state in Egypt
Et	al-Jihad / Egyptian Islamic Jihad / Jihad Group / Islamic Jihad / Vanguards of Conquest	1973	hundreds	A	international	Islamic state in Et. Merged with al-Qaeda in 1998; Suicide
Et	Islamic Brigades of Pride	2005	n.k.	A	Et	"To avenge our brothers, martyrs of injustice, and detainees".
Et	Muslim Brotherhood	1930's	thousands	A	international	Sunni, promote Muslim rights and Islam as a way of life, in Et have been part of political process and have formed pol party but have used violence; in other regions (Ag, Kashmir, Afg) have been involved in armed conflict
Et	Takfir Wal Hijra	early 1970s	300+	A	Et, Sdn, RL, Ag	Amorphous extremist Wahhabi sect, original grp manifestation as Muslim Brotherhood offshoot in Et, resp for Sadat's death, operated as PLO ally RL, now joined with deported Afghan/Pak mujahideen in N Africa "to cleanse society of infidels"
Il	Hilltop Youth	200-2001	5–10+	A	PA	Nascent group of Jewish settlers who want to exclude Palestinians from the OT; suspected in attempted bombing of Palestinian schools and roadside shootings
Il	Kahane Chai / Kach	1990	30+	A	Il, PA	Restore the Biblical state of Israel, excluding Palestinians
Ir	Democratic Party of Iranian Kurdistan (DPKI) / Kurdish Democratic Party of Iran (KDPI)	1995	1,200–1,800	D	Ir	Kurdish autonomy in Ir
Ir	Kurdestan Organisation of the Communist Party of Iran / The Revolutionary Organisation of Working People of Iranian Kurdistan (KOMALA)	1967	200	A	Ir	Communist govt in Ir (Formed Communist Party of Iran in 1983)

Table 41 Selected Non-State Armed Groups

Origin	Organisation * aka	Estb.	Est. Strength	Status	Operates	Aims (Remarks)
Ir	National Liberation Army of Iran (NLA)	1987	6,000–8,000	D	Ir	'Democratic, socialist, Islamic republic in Ir' (Largest and most active armed Ir dissident gp. Armed wing of Mujahideen-e Khalq Organisation)
Irq	Abu Bakr al-Siddiq Fundamentalist Brigades	2004	n.k.	A	Irq	Demands have included the removal of coalition troops from Iraq and the release of female prisoners from U.S. custody
Irq	Al-Faruq Brigades / Jihadist Al Faruq Brigades / Media Commission for the Mujahideen in Iraq	2004	n.k.	A	Irq	Nationalist-Islamist group
Irq	Ansar Al-Jihad / Supporters of Jihad	2004	n.k.	A	Irq	Nationalist-Islamist group
Irq	Army of the Followers of Sunni Islam / Jaish Ansar al-Sunnah	2004	n.k.	A	Irq	Oppose US-led coalition in Iraq
Irq	Ansar al-Sunnah Army	2002-3	n.k.	A	north and west Irq	Collection of small Islamist grps including remnants of Ansar al-Islam; opposes US occupation of Iraq, for Islamic society in Irq
Irq	Al-Dawa (The Call) / Islamic Call Party / Black Brigades	1968	2,000	A	Irq	Shia muslim fundamentalist group, Islamic rule in Iraq; Suicide
Irq	Kurdish Democratic Party (KDP)	1946	15,000	D	Irq	
Irq	Patriotic Union of Kurdestan (PUK)	1975	10,000	A	Irq	'Revitalise resistance and rebuild a democratic Kurdish society' (Evolved into a political movement)
Irq	Ansar al-Islam / Jund al-Islam / Army Supporters of Islam	2001	500, dispersed in Iraq invasion	A	Irq	Opposed to coalition forces, opposes secular Kurdish parties in Irq
Irq	Abu Nidal Organisation (ANO) / Fatah Revolutionary Council / Black September / Arab Revolutionary Brigades / Revolutionary Organisation of Socialist Muslims	1974	300	D	international	'Destroy Il' (Ops in LAR and Et shut down by govts in 1999)
Irq	Divine Wrath Brigades	2004	n.k.	D/A	Irq	Opposes interim Iraqi gov; supports Moqtada al-Sadr
Irq	The Holders of the Black Banners	2004	n.k.	A	Irq	Oppose US presence in Irq, call for release of Irq prisoners from American and Kuwaiti prisons
Irq	Islamic Army in Iraq (IAI) / al-Jaish al-Islami fi al-Iraq	n.k.	n.k.	A	Irq	'Drive coalition- civilian and military forces' out of Irq; Suicide
Irq	Islamic Resistance Brigades	2004	n.k.	A	Irq	'The pullout of foreign entities from Irq'; Suicide
Irq	Islamic Jihad Brigades of Muhammad's Army / Jaish Muhammed	2003	200+	A	Irq	Collection of small Islamist grps, oppose US occupation, kill Iraqi collabourators
Irq	Mahdi Army / Jaish al-Mahdi	2003	6–10,000	A	south Irq	Defend Shia rights and faith from US invasion
Irq	Mafariz al-Intiqam	2003	n.k.	A	Tikrit, Baghdad	Hunt down intel/security personnel from Saddam regime for revenge
Irq	Badr Corps	1982	10,000	A	south Irq	'Oppose Sunni aggression against Ir' Armed wg of Surpreme Council for Islamic Revolution (SCIRI)
Irq	al-Qaeda in Iraq	2003	n.k.	A	North, west and central Irq.	al-Qaeda objectives; suicide; IEDS; leader al-Zarqawi
Irq	Al-Mujahideen Brigades	2004	n.k.	A	Fallujah, Ramadi, Khaldiya	'Oppose US occupation, threaten Iraqis who cooperate'; Suicide
Irq	Iraqi Hezbollah	2003	2–300	A	Irq	Shia group, opposes US occupation of Iraq
Irq	Saddam Fedayeen / Saddam's Men of Sacrifice	1995	30,000	A	Irq	Ba'athist militia created under S. Hussein regime currently resisting American occupation

Table 41 Selected Non-State Armed Groups

Origin	Organisation * aka	Estb.	Est. Strength	Status	Operates	Aims (Remarks)
Irq	Saraya al-Shuhuada al-Jihadiyah fi al-Iraq / Jihadist Martyrs Brigades in Iraq	2004	n.k.	A	Irq	Iraqi Islamist grp; opposes US presence in Irq (probably suicide)
Irq	The Return Party	2003	n.k.	A	Irq	'Return Saddam Hussein to power', oppose the occupation
Irq	Tha'ar Allah / Revenge of Allah	2003	n.k.	A	Basra	Shia group, opposes US occupation of Iraq
Ir	Mujahedin-e Khalq Organisation (MEK or MKO) / National Council of Resistance (NCR) / National Council of Resistance Iran (NCRI)	1960	3,000	A	Ir	Advocate secular Muslim regime
HKJ	Jund al-Shams / the Zarqawi Network / Jama'at al-Tawheed wa'Jihad	n.k.	500–1,000	A	HKJ, Syr, Irq, international	Islamist extremist grp, oppose US invasion of Iraq, anti-monarchy in Jordan; Suicide
RL	Ansar Allah	1994	n.k.	A	RL	
RL	Asbat al-Ansar / League of Partisans	1990's	300	A	RL	Advocates Salafism, opposed to any peace with Israel.
RL	Hezbollah (Party of God) / Islamic Jihad / Revolutionary Justice Organisation / Organisation of the Oppressed on Earth	1982	2,000+	A	Bekaa Valley, Beirut, south RL, South America, esp. Arg, Br, Py	Ir-style Islamic republic in RL; all 'non-Islamic influences removed from area' (Shi'ite; formed to resist Il occupation of south RL with political representation representation in RL Assembly.) Some cells operate internationally; UK has designated this "external security organisation" as a terrorist entity
Lib	Libyan Islamic Fighting Group	1995	300	A	Lib	To overthrow the Gadaffi govt; to 'continue the international jihadist campaign'
Mor	Moroccan Islamic Combatant Group (GICM)	1990's	n.k.	A	W.Eu, Af, Mor	Estb an Islamic state in Morocco supporting al-Qaeda
Mor	Sahrawi People's Liberation Army (SPLA)	1973	3,000–6,000	C	Mor	Independent W. Sahara [Armed wing of the Frente Popular para la Liberacion de Saguia el-Hamra y del Rio de Oro (Polisario Front)]
Mor	Salafya al-Aihadya / Abu Hafs al Masri Brigade / Assirat al-Moustakim	n.k.	200–1000	A	Mor	Loose network of Salafist grps suspected of bombings in Madrid and Casablanca; Suicide
PA	Aa-Aqsa Martyrs Brigades	2000	n.k.	A	PA, Il	Associated, not officially backed, by former Palestinian leadership; Suicide
PA	Al-Saika / Vanguard of the Popular Liberation War	1968	300	A	PA, Il	Mil wing of PA faction of Syr Ba'ath Party (Nominally part of PLO)
PA	Al-Quds Brigades / Jerusalem Battalions / Jerusalem Brigades / al-Quds Battalions	late 1970s	n.k.	A	PA, Il, Syr	Militant wing of Palestinian Islamic Jihad
PA	Arab Liberation Front	1969	500	D	PA, Il	Achieve national goals of PA (Faction of PLO formed by leadership of Irq Ba'ath party)
PA	Democratic Front for the Liberation of Palestine (DFLP)	1969	100+	A	PA, Il	Achieve PA national goals through revolution (Marxist–Leninist; splintered from PFLP)
PA	Hamas (Islamic Resistance Movement) / Izz al-Din al-Qassam Brigades (IDQ)	1987	500+	A	PA, Il	Estb an Islamic Palestinian state in place of Israel; Suicide
PA	Fatah Tanzim	1995	1000+	A	PA, Il	Counter-balance to the military wings of Hamas and Palestinian Islamic Jihad
PA	Palestine Islamic Jihad (PIJ) / Shaqaqi faction / Shalla faction	1970s	500	A	PA, Il	'Destroy Il with holy war and estb Islamic state in PA.'; Suicide
PA	Palestine Liberation Front (PLF)	1977	300–400	D	PA, Il	Armed struggle against Il (Splintered from PFLP); Suicide

Table 41 Selected Non-State Armed Groups

Origin	Organisation * aka	Estb.	Est. Strength	Status	Operates	Aims (Remarks)
PA	Palestinian Resistance Committees (PRC) / Salah al-Din Battalions / Salah al-Din Brigades	late 2000	n.k.	A	PA, Il	Composed of members from PIJ, Hamas, al-Aqsa Martyrs Brigade; claimed resp for roadside bombs; suspected in 2003 attack on US embassy employees
PA	Popular Front for the Liberation of Palestine (PFLP)	1967	1,000	A	PA, Il	Armed struggle against Il (Marxist–Leninist); Suicide
PA	Popular Front for the Liberation of Palestine – General Command (PFLP–GC)	1968	500	D	PA, Il, RL, Syr	Armed struggle against Il (Marxist–Leninist; Split from PFLP to focus on fighting rather than politics); Suicide
Sau	Al-Haramain Brigades	2003	n.k.	A	Sau	Anti-monarchy in Sau, 'implement sharia law, expel the west'; Suicide
Tn	Tunisian Combatant Group / Groupe Combattant Tunisien / Jama'a Combattante Tunisien	2000	n.k.	A	Afg, W Europe	Creation of an Islamic state in Tunisia, anti-US grp
Ye	Islamic Army of Aden (IAA)/ Aden-Abyan Islamic Army (AAIA)	1998	100+	A	South Ye	Overthrow of the Yemeni Government and operations against US and other Western interests in Yemen
Ye	Yemeni Islamic Jihad	1990's	200+	A	Ye	al-Qaeda affiliated Islamist group of ex-Afghan mujahideen
CENTRAL AND SOUTH ASIA						
Afg	al-Qaeda	1988	1,000+	A	international	'Re-establish the Muslim state' worldwide (International network with Osama Bin Laden as a figurehead); Suicide
Afg	Jaish-ul-Muslimin	2004	n.k.	A	Afg	Opposes US govt. and Afghan govt
Afg	United Islamic Front for the Salvation of Afghanistan / Northern Alliance	mid 1980s	15,000	D	Afg	Anti-Taliban grp
Afg	Hizb-e Islami Gulbuddin (HIG)	1977	n.k.	A	Afg, Pak	Force US troops to withdraw from Afghanistan and estb a fundamentalist state. Leader is Gulbuddin Hekmatyar; Suicide
Afg	Saif-ul-Muslimeen / Saif-ul-Muslimeen Lashkar Jihad / Sword of Muslims	2003	n.k.	A	eastern Afg	Anti-Afghan government and Western presence in Afg
Afg	Taleban	mid 1980's	thousands	A	Afg	Re-take power from US backed govt
Bng	Harkat ul-Jihad i-Islami, Bangadesh Cell (HUJI) / Bangladesh Taleban	1992	15,000	A	Bng	Estb by al-Qaeda, goal is to recruit Bangledeshi and Indian Muslims to fight in Kashmir under HuM
Bng/Ind	Borok National Council of Tripura (BNCT)	2000	n.k.	A	Bng, Ind	Splinter of separatist National Liberation Front of Tripura (NLFT)
Bng/Ind	Jama'at ul-Mujahideen (JUM)	late 1980's	n.k.	A	N.E. Ind	Splinter of HUJI, pro-Pak Islamic grp; different from Jama'at ul-Mujahideen, which is splinter from Hizb ul-Mujahideen
Bng	Islami Ch'atra Shibir (ICS)	1941	n.k	A	Bng	Student wing of Jamaat-e-Islami, Bng's third biggest political party. Seeks Taleban-style regime in Bng
Bng	Purba Bangla Communist Party (PBCP)	1968	1,000+	A	Bng	'Capture state power through armed struggle'
Bng/My	Rohingya Solidarity Organisation (RSO)	1882	1–200+	A	My and Bng	Separate state for Rohingya muslims in Arakan region of Myanmar
Bng	Shanti Bahini / Peace Force	1976	3,000	D	Bng	Armed wing of Parbatya Chattagram Jana Sanghati Samity (PCJSS). Fights for autonomy of Chittagong Hill Tracts. Disbanded 1998, though remnants may still exist
Ind	Achik National Volunteers Council (ANVC)	1995	n.k.	A	Meghalaya	Estb Achik homeland in the Garo hills area
Ind	Al-Umar Mujahideen (AUM)	1989	700	A	Kashmir	Merge the state of Jammu and Kashmir with Pakistan
Ind	Arunachel Dragon Force (ADF) / East India Liberation Front (EILF)	1996	60	A	Arunachel Pradesh, Ind	Resist domination of Adi tribe, estb. homeland for tribe of Tai-Khamtis
Ind	Babbar Khalsa International (BKI)	1981	hundreds	A	Punjab/Ind	Estb independent Sikh state called Khalistan; Suicide

Table 41 **Selected Non-State Armed Groups**

Origin	Organisation * aka	Estb.	Est. Strength	Status	Operates	Aims (Remarks)
Ind	National Democratic Front of Bodoland (NDFB)	1988	1,500	A	Assam	Seeks autonomy for Bodoland in areas north of river Brahmaputra
Ind	Bodo Liberation Tigers (BLT) / Bodo Liberation	1996	2600	C	Assam	Autonomy for Bodo inhabited areas, peace accord with govt 2003
Ind	Bru National Liberation Front (BNLF)	1997	100+	C	Mizoram, Assam, Tripura	Protect rights of Reangs in Mizoram, possibly will attempt to negotiate a separate Reang homeland
Ind	All Muslim United Liberation Front of Assam (AMULFA)	mid 1990's	n.k	A	North East Ind	Collection of groups Islamist groups in NE India
Ind	Hynniewtrep National Liberation Council (HNLC)	1992	n.k.	A	Meghalaya	Estb Khasi homeland in Meghalaya, expel Garos and others
Ind	Muslim United Liberation Tigers of Assam (MULTA)	1996	n.k	A	N.E Ind	Islamist state independent of India for Assam's muslims jihad against India's govt
Ind/My	National Socialist Council of Nagaland-Khaplang (NSCN-K)	1988	2,000	A	Ind/My	Estb greater Nagaland in parts of Ind and My
Ind	National Socialist Council of Nagaland-Isaac Muivah (NSCN-IM)	1980	4500	A	Manipur, Nagaland, parts of Assam	Estb a greater socialist Nagaland
Ind	Kanglei Yawol Kanna Lup (KYKL)	1994	n.k	A	Manipur	Rebuild society in Manipur
Ind	Kuki National Army (KNA)	1991	600	A	Ind/My border	Estb indep Kukiland comprising parts of Ind and My
Ind	People's Liberation Army (PLA)	1978	n.k	A	Manipur	Unite Manipur's ethnic groups to liberate Manipur from India
Ind	People's Revolutionary Party of Kangleipak (PREPAK)	1977	200	A	Mizoram, N Tripura	Expel 'outsiders' from Manipur
Ind	United Liberation Front of Assam (ULFA)	1979	n.k	A	Assam	Estb sovereign socialist Assam through armed struggle
Ind	Sanjukta Mukti Fouj (SMF)	1996	1,500	A	Ind, Assam	Estb an autonomous and socialist Assam.
Ind	Indo-Burmese Revolutionary Front (IBRF)	1989	n.k.	A	N.E. Ind	Grp facilitating cooperation among NE India insurgents and foreign groups
Ind	International Sikh Youth Federation (ISYF)	1985	n.k	A	Ind, UK, N. America, Eu	Estb independent Sikh state called Khalistan
Ind	United People's Democratic Solidarity (UPDS)	1999	150	A	Assam	Union of Karbi National Volunteers (KNV)and Karbi Peoples Front (KPF); secession of Karbi 'nation' from N. Assam
Ind	Hmar People's Convention-Democracy (HPC-D)	1986	100–150	A	Mizoram	Independent Hmar state in Hmar areas of Manipur, Mizoram, Assam
Ind	Ranvir Sena	1994	400	A	Ind	Supported by upper caste land owners to eliminate left wing extremist grps in Bihar, esp PWG, MCC
Ind	Students Islamic Movement of India (SIMI)	1977	some 400	A	Ind	Re-establish the Caliphate, sharia based rule, propagate Islam, oppose democracy, secularism, nationalism
Ind	Tamil National Retrieval Troops (TNRT)	late 1980's	30	A	Ind	LTTE sponsored group to estb Tamil homeland in Ind
Ind	United Liberation Front of Barak Valley (ULFBV)	2002	50+	A	Assam	Sep homeland for tribal people of Karimgnj and Hailakandi
Ind	United National Liberation Front (UNLF) / Manipur Peoples' Army (MPA)	1964	n.k.	A	Assam	Independent and socialist Manipur
Ind	Rabha National Security Force (RNSF)	late 1990s	120	A	Assam	Separate homeland for Rabhas
Ind	Kamtapur Liberation Organisation (KLO)	1995	300	A	Assam	Separate Kamtapur state
Ind	Tripura Liberation Organisation Front (TLOF)	1992	n.k.	A	Ind	Secession of Tripura from India

Table 41 Selected Non-State Armed Groups

Origin	Organisation * aka	Estb.	Est. Strength	Status	Operates	Aims (Remarks)
Ind	All Tripura Tiger Force (ATTF)	1990	500–600	A	Ind	Independent Tripura and 'expulsion of Bengali-speaking immigrants from Tripura'
Ind	National Liberation Front of Tripura (NLFT)	1989	800	A	Ind	To estb independence for Tripura through armed struggle
Ind	Maoist Communist Centre (MCC)	1969	1,000+	A	Bihar, Jharkhaad	Seeking people's govt through armed struggle
Ind	The Communist Party of India (CPI-Maoists) / Naxalites / (People's War) / People's War Group (PWG)	1980	1,000	A	Ind	Maoist grp aiming to seize political power through armed struggle
Ind/Pak	Al-Madina	2002	n.k.	A	Kashmir	Believes that India should accept Kashmir as a disputed territory
Ind/Pak	Harkat ul-Mujahideen (HUM) / Harkat ul-Ansar (HUA)	1985	450–500	A	Kashmir	Splinter of Indian/Pakistani HUJI, pro-Pak Islamic grp, want to recruit 5000 fighters; involved in Afg, BiH, My, RF, PI, Tjk; Suicide
Ind/Pak	Harkat ul-Mujahideen al-Almi	2001–2002	n.k.	A	Kashmir	Splinter of HuM, seek unification of Kashmir with Pak, implicated in assassination attempt of Musharraf
Ind/Pak	Hizb ul-Mujahideen (HM)	1989	1500+	A	Kashmir	Pro-Pak Islamic grp, armed wing of Jama'at-e-Islami
Ind/Pak	Tehrik-e-Jihad	1997	n.k.	A	Kashmir	Self-determination for Kashmir; Kashmir to join Pak; Suicide
Ind/Pak	Jaish-e-Mohammed (JeM)	2000	300–400	A	Jammu, Kashmir	Seeks to expel Ind from Jammu and Kashmir; Suicide
Ind/Pak	Jama'at ul-Mujahideen (JuM)	1990's	n.k.	A	Kashmir, Pak	Seeks to expel Ind mil from Jammu and Kashmir splinter grp of HM
Ind/Pak	Al-Badr Mujahideen	1998	40–50	A	Kashmir	Liberate 'Kashmir from Ind forces (Split from Hizb-ul Mujahideen); Suicide
Ind/Pak	Lashkar-e-Jabbar (LeJ) / The Army of the Omnipotent Almighty	n.k.	n.k.	A	Kashmir	'The introduction of strict Sharia'
Ind/Pak	Lashkar-e-Toiba (LT) / Jama'at ud Dawa (JUD)	1989	300	A	Jammu, Kashmir	Create independent Islamic state in Kashmir (Armed wing of Markaz-ud-Dawa-wal-Irshad (MDI)); Suicide
Ind/Pak	Save Kashmir Movement	2002	50-	A	Jammu, Kashmir	Oppose Indian rule in Kashmir
Ind	Manipur People's Liberation Front (MPLF)	1999	n.k.	A	Ind	Estb independent socialist Manipur. A coalition of United National Liberation Front, the Revolutionary People's Front and the People's Revolutionary Party of Kangleipak.
N	Communist Party of Nepal (Maoist) / United People's Front / People's War Group	1995	8–14,000; up to 200,000 sympathisers	A	N	Overthrow N's constitutional monarchy; replace with Maoist republic (Declared 'People's War' in 1996). Headed by 'Prachanda'. Armed wing of Samyukta Jana Morcha (UPF)
Pak	Baluch Liberation Army	2003	n.k.	A	Pak	Separatist/Nationalist grp; fights for the right of the Baluch people
Pak	Baluch People's Liberation Front (BPLF) / Popular Front for Armed Resistance / Baluch Students' Organisation	1963-76	3,000+	A	Pak, Afgh	Independent land for Baluchi Muslims, al-Qaeda associate
Pak	Jama'at ul-Fuqra (JF)	1980	1,000–3,000	A	Pak, N. America	Secretive cult-like group that seeks to purify Islam through violence
Pak	Jund Allah / God's Brigade	2001-2002	20+	A	Pak	Islamist grp, attempted to assassinate Musharraf
Pak	Lashkar e-Jhangvi (LIJ)	1996	300	A	Pak	Estb a Muslim state in Pakistan, al-Qaeda associate
Pak	Lashkar-e-Omar (LeO)	2001-2002	multiple cells 5–15 each	A	Pak	Conglomeration of HUJI, LeJ, JeM members for anti USA attacks in Pakistan region; suspects in Daniel Pearl case; Suicide
Pak	Muttahida Qaumi Movement (MQM) / Muttahida Qaumi Movement-Altaf (MQM-A)	1984	n.k.	A	Pak	Resist Sindh domination of the Punjab

Table 41 Selected Non-State Armed Groups

Origin	Organisation * aka	Estb.	Est. Strength	Status	Operates	Aims (Remarks)
Pak	Haqiqi Muttahida Qaumi Movement (MQM)	1992	n.k.	A	Pak	Splinter faction from MQM-A, engineered by govt to act as counterweight to MQM-A, which it thought more of a threat
Pak	Sipah-e-Muhammad (SMP)	1993	30,000 followers	A	Pak, esp Punjab	Protect Shia community from 'Sunni extremism and terrorism'
Pak	Sipah-e-Sahaba (SSP) / Millat e Islamia Pakistan	1985	3,000–6,000	A	Pak	Sunni state in Pak, oppose Pak/US alliance,operates also as political party
Pak	Tehrik-e-Jaferia	1992	n.k.	A	Pak	'Create Islamic society, protect rights of Shia muslims'
Ska	Liberation Tigers of Tamil Eelam (LTTE) / World Tamil Association / World Tamil Movement	1972	11,000	C	north and east Ska	Independent Tamil state (Began armed conflict in 1983. Cease-fire signed 23 February 2002. Possible al-Qaeda link; Suicide
Uz	Hizb ut-Tahrir	1952	5–10,000	A	Uz	Estb Islamic Caliphate in central Asia, 'jihad against US', its allies, and moderate Muslim regimes-denies use of violence but suspected of spring 2004 bombings.
Uz	Islamic Movement of Uzbekistan (IMU) / Islamic Movement of Turkestan (IMT)	1997	2,000+	A	Uz, Tjk, Ir, Kgz, Afg	Fundamentalist Islamic state in Uz (Coalition of Islamic militants from Uz, other C. Asian states and PRC, also the resurrection of the state of Turkestan, al-Qaeda link
EAST ASIA AND AUSTRALASIA						
Cam	Party of Democratic Kampuchea (Khmer Rouge)	1960	1,000–2,000	D	Cam	Destabilise the Cambodian Government
PRC	East Turkestan Liberation Organisation (ETLO) and East Turkestan Islamic Movement (ETIM)	1990	600	A	north-west PRC, C. Asia	Estb separate E. Turkestan state for Uighur population, with possible links to al-Qaeda and IMT
Indo	Gerakan Aceh Merdeka (GAM) / Free Aceh Movement / Tentara Nasional Aceh (TNA)	1976	2,000	A	Aceh	Independent Islamic state in Aceh; Tentara Nasional Aceh is the armed wing, underground since 1996
Indo	Front Pembela Islam (Islamic Defenders Front) (FPI)	1998	thousands	A	Indo	Implementation of sharia law within current govt framework
Indo	Jemaah Islamiah (JI)	1993-94	500+	A	Indo, Mal, Pi, Th	Estb an independent Islamic state encompassing southern Th, Mal, Indo, and southern Pi, al-Qaeda link; Suicide
Indo	Laskar Jihad	2000	500+	D	Indo, Maluku	Remove Christians from Maluku; Islamic state in Indo, al-Qaeda link
Indo	Organisasi Papua Merdeka (OPM) / Free Papua Movement	1962	150	A	Indo	Independence for W. Papua
J	Aum Supreme Truth / Aum Shinrikyo / Aleph	1987	1,500–2,000	D	J	'Take over J and then the world.' Released Sarin on Tokyo subway in 1995 and other chemical attacks in Japan
J	Chukaku-Ha / Kansai Revolutionary Army (KRA)	1957	3,500	D	J	Protests Japan's imperial system, Western "imperialism"
J	Japanese Red Army / Anti-Imperialist International Brigade (AIIB)	1970	n.k.	D	J	Overthrow the Japanese Government and monarchy and to help foment world revolution.
Lao	United Lao National Liberation Front (ULNLF) / Lao National Liberation Movement (LNLM)	1975	2,000	A	north Lao	Pro-royalist right wing, overthrow current govt.
Mal	Malaysian Mujahideen Group / Kumpulan Mujahideen Malaysia (KMM)	1995	90–100	D	Mal	Estb Muslim state comprising Mal, Indo and southern Pi, allegedly linked to JI and al-Qaeda
My	All Burma Students Democratic Front (ABSDF)	1988	2,000	A	My	'Liberate My from dictatorship, estb democracy and transform into federal union'
My	Chin National Army (CNA) / Chin National Front	1988	n.k.	A	west My, Chin state	Overthrow My govt (Armed wing of Chin National Front)
My	Democratic Karen Buddhist Army (DKBA)	1994	100–500	C	My, Th	Independence for Karen minority (Splinter gp of Karen National Union (KNU). Armed wing of Democratic Karen Buddhist Organisation. Ongoing conflict with KNLA)

Table 41 Selected Non-State Armed Groups

Origin	Organisation * aka	Estb.	Est. Strength	Status	Operates	Aims (Remarks)
My	Kachin Independence Army (KIA)	1961	8,000	C	north My, Khmer range	Promote Buddhism (Armed wing of Kachin Independence Organisation)
My	Karen National Liberation Army (KNLA)	1948	2–4,000	A	Th border	Estb Karen State with right to self-determination (Armed wing of KNU. Ongoing conflict with DKBA)
My	Karenni National Progressive Party (KNPP)	1948	800–2,000	A	north My, Kayah State	Independence of Karenni State (Armed wing of Karenni National Progressive Party)
My	Kayin National Union (KNU) / Karen National Union	1959	5, 000	A	My	Independent homeland for the Karen people
My	Mong Thai Army (MTA)	1964	3,000	C	Th border	Protect Shan population
My	Mon National Liberation Army (MNLA)	1958	1,000	C	Th border	Represent Mon minority (Armed wing of New Mon State Party)
My	Myanmar National Democratic Alliance Army (MNDAA)	1989	1,000	C	east Shan State, PRC–Lao border	Oppose My mil rule (Formerly part of Communist Party of Burma (CPB))
My	Palaung State Liberation Army (PSLA)	1963	700	C	north of Hsipaw	Greater autonomy for Palaung population
My	Shan State Army (SSA) / Shan State Progress Army (SSPA)	1964	3,000	C	south Shan State	Freedom and democracy for Shan State
My	United Wa State Army (UWSA)	1989	15,000	C	Wa Hills	Splinter gp of CPB
My	Vigorous Burmese Student Warriors (VBSW)	1999	n.k.	A	My, Th	anti-govt grp, opposes military regime in Myanmar
Pi	Abu Sayyaf Group (ASG)	1991	450+	A	south Pi	Independent Islamic state in west Mindanao and Sulu split from MNLF;criminal intentions as strong as political ones; linked to al-Qaeda
Pi	Communist Party of the Philippines (CPP) / New People's Army (NPA)	1969	11,500	A	Pi	Overthrow the Philippine government through guerilla warfare, New People's Army is the armed wing
Pi	Revolutionary Proletarian Army – Alex Boncayao Brigade (RPA–ABB)	1997	500+	D	Manila, central Pi	Urban hit squad of Philippines Communist Party
Pi	Moro National Liberation Front (MNLF) / Bangsamoro Army	1972-3	15,000	C	south Pi	Muslim separatist movement – the Bangsamoro army is the armed wing of MNLF)
Pi	Moro Islamic Liberation Front (MILF)	1977	11,000+	C	south Pi	Independent Islamic state in Bangsa Moro and neighbouring islands (Split from MNLF. Signed cease-fire with Pi govt 7 Aug 2001)
Pi	Moro Islamic Reformist Group	1978	900-	A	south Pi	Independent Islamic state in south Pi (Split from MNLF)
Th	United Front for the Independence of Pattani / Bersatu	1989	hundreds	A	Th	Umbrella grp including PULO, New PULO, and BRN wanting to estb an independent Islamic state in S Thailand
Th	Barisan Revolusi Nasional (BRN)	1960	60–80	A	south Th	Muslim separatist movement in Thailand
Th	Pattani United Liberation Organisation (PULO)	1968	100	A	Th	Fighting for the separation of Thailand's mainly Muslim south
Th	Pattani Islamic Mujahideen Movement / Gerakan Mujahideen Islam Pattani (GMIP)	1995	20+	A	south Th	Estb a Muslim state in S. Thailand; al-Qaeda link
CARIBBEAN AND LATIN AMERICA						
Co	Autodefensas Unidas de Colombia (AUC)	1997	12,000	A	north and north-west Co	Coordinating grp for paramilitaries; Right-wing; Co govt grants amnesty
Co	Ejercito de Liberación Nacional (ELN)	1964	4,000	A	north, north-east, south-west Co, Bol	Anti-US 'Maoist–Marxist–Leninist' gp (Peace talks with govt since 1999)
Co	Ejercito Popular de Liberación (EPL)	1967	500-	A	Co	Rid Colombia of 'US imperialism and indigenous oligarchies'; al-Qaeda link

Non-State Armed Groups

Table 41 **Selected Non-State Armed Groups**

Origin	Organisation * aka	Estb.	Est. Strength	Status	Operates	Aims (Remarks)
Co	Ejercito Revolucionario del Pueblo (ERP) / People's Revolutionary Army	1990s	350	A	Co	Faction of ELN, shares communist beliefs
Co	Fuerzas Armadas Revolucionarias de Colombia (FARC)	1964	18,000+	A	Co	'Overthrow govt and ruling classes' (Armed wing of Colombian Communist Party)
Chl	Manuel Rodriguez Patriotic Front (FPMR)	1983	50–100	D	Chl	Anti-American communist group
Ec	People's Fighters Group / Grupos de Combatientes Populares (GCP)	1994	n.k.	A	Ec	Militant branch of Ec Marxist-Leninist Communist Party
Ec	Izquierda Revolucionaria Armada / Armed Revolutionary Left	2004	n.k.	A	Ec	Anti-govt
Ec	People's Revolutionary Militias / Milicias Revolucionarias del Pueblo (MRP)	n.k.	n.k.	A	Ec	Anti-globalisation; insurrection against current Ec gov
RH	National Revolutionary Front for the Liberation of Haiti /Armée Cannibale / Revolutionary Artibonite Resistance Front (RARF)	2003	n.k.	A	RH	Informal alliance of Armée Cannibale, anti govt gangs, and former soldiers of the disbanded Haiti army – anti-Aristide and seek to gain control of Haiti
Mex	Los Zetas	late 1990s	100-	A	Mex	Control drug trade through Mexico
Mex	Comando Jaramillista Morelense 23 Mayo (CJM 23-M)	2004	n.k.	A	Morelos, Mex	Opposes corruption and drug trafficking allowed to continue under Vincente Fox's government
Pe	Movimiento Revolucionario Tupac Amaru (MRTA)	1983	500-	D	Pe, Upper Huallaga river valley	'Estb Marxist regime and seek to rid Pe of imperialist elements' (Less active since Pe govt's 1999 counter-terrorist op)
Pe	Sendero Luminoso (SL) / Shining Path	1960s	600	A	Pe, Upper Huallaga and Ene river valleys	'Estb peasant revolutionary regime in Pe' (Less active since Pe govt's 2000 counter-terrorist op)

SUB-SAHARAN AFRICA

Origin	Organisation * aka	Estb.	Est. Strength	Status	Operates	Aims (Remarks)
Ang	Frente de Libertacao do Enclave de Cabinda – Forcas Armadas de Cabinda (FLEC–FAC)	1980s	300	A	Ang, Cabinda	Independence of Cabinda region (Split from FLEC in the 1980s)
Ang	Frente de Libertacao do Enclave de Cabinda – Renovada (FLEC–Renovada)	1980s	300	A	Ang, Cabinda	Independence of Cabinda region (Split from FLEC in the 1980s)
Ang	União Nacional para a Independencia Total de Angola (UNITA)	1966	5,000	C	Nba, Ang, DRC	Strive for govt proportionally representative of all ethnic gps, clans and classes (Signed peace agreement with govt in April 2002)
Bu	Forces pour la Défense de la Démocratie (FDD)	1994	16–20,000	A	DRC, west Tz, Bu	Restore constitution and institutions set by 1993 elections and form national army (To be disarmed under Lusaka Peace Accord but continues attacks against Bu govt and believed involved in DRC conflict. Armed wing of National Council for the Defence of Democracy)
Bu	Parti pour la Libération du Peuple Hutu (Palipehutu) / Forces for National Liberation	1980	2,000–3,000	A	Bu, Tz borders	Liberate Hutus and estb ethnic quotas based on 1930s Be census (Armed wing of Forces Nationales de Libération)
Cha	Mouvement pour la Démocratie et la Justice au Tchad (MDJT)	1998	n.k.	C	north Cha, Tibesti region	Overthrow Cha govt
CI	Union of Patriots for the Total Liberation of the Ivory Coast (UPLTCI)	2003	thousands	A	w, sw CI; Abidjan	Pro-govt militia, armed wing of the Convention of Patriots for Peace (CPP)
CI	Forces Nouvelles	2003	7,000	C	CI, Lb border	Anti-government merger of MPIGO, MJP, MPCI
DRC	Allied Democratic Forces (ADF)	1995	100+	A	N.E. Congo, Uga	Undermine Uga govt

Non-State Armed Groups 433

Table 41 **Selected Non-State Armed Groups**

Origin	Organisation * aka	Estb.	Est. Strength	Status	Operates	Aims (Remarks)
DRC	Patriotic Resistance Forces in Ituri (FRPI)	n.k.	5,000	C	DRC	Armed wing of Nationalist Integrationist Front (FNI), primarily Lendu
DRC	Union of Congolese Patriots (UPC)	n.k.	n.k.	C	Ituri province	Seek to preserve Hema political advantages over the majority Lendu and want Hema share of resources in Ituri. Now part of transitional government
DRC	Party for Unity and the Safeguard of the Integrity of Congo (PUSIC)	n.k.	2,000–5,000	C	Ituri province	Hema militia supporting Hema against Lendu in DRC's ethnic confict
DRC	Armed Forces of the Congolese People (FAPC)	n.k.	n.k.	C	DRC	Split from UPC, has incorporated the Popular Front for Democracy in Congo (FPDC), elemts frm RCD-ML, APC
DRC	Mouvement de Libération Congolais (MLC)	1998	18,000	C	north DRC	'Fight dictatorship in DRC' (First faction to break from RCD)
DRC	Rassemblement Congolais pour la Démocratie – Mouvement de Libération (RCD–ML)	1999	2,000–3,000	A	DRC	Overthrow DRC govt
DRC	Rassemblement Congolais pour la Démocratie – Goma (RCD–GOMA)	1998	20,000	A	DRC	Estb democracy in DRC
Dj	Front pour la Restoration de l'Unité Nationale et de la Démocratie (FRUD)	1991	hundreds	C	Dj	Represent Afar population of Dj and estb multi-party elections (Following 1994 split, one faction signed agreement with govt to become legitimate political party, joined 1995 coalition govt)
Er	Alliance of Eritrean National Forces (AENF)	1999	3,000	A	Er	Overthrow Er govt (Coalition of Er armed gps)
Er	Eritrean Islamic Jihad / Islamic Salvation Movement	1990's	hundreds	A	Er, Sdn	Overthrow Er govt; al-Qaeda link
Eth	Ogaden National Liberation Army (ONLA)	1984	n.k.	A	Eth	Restore rights of Ogaden population and obtain right to self-determination (Armed wing of ONLF)
Gui	Movement of the Democratic Forces of Guinea (RFDG)	late 1990's	1,800	Defeated	southern Gui	Anti-govt, possibly composed of ex-army officers
LAR	Libyan Islamic Fighting Group / al-Jama'at al-Islamiyah al-Muqatilah	1995	200+	A	LAR, Middle East	Anti-Libyan government; al-Qaeda link
Lb	Movement for Democracy in Liberia (MODEL)	2003	5,000	C	east, south Lb	Overthrow Charles Taylor's govt, currently disarming
Nga	Al Sunna Wal Jamma	2002	200	A	Nga	Estb an Islamic state in Nga
Nga	Egbesu Boys of Africa	late 1990s	thousands	A	Ijaw regions of Nga	Rid Ijaw regions of Nigerian military and foreign oil co.; armed wing of Ijaw Youth Council
Nga	Federated Niger Delta Ijaw Communities (FNDIC)	2003	3,000	A	south east Nga	Protect Ijaw rights, ensure Ijaw have access to benefits
Nga	Arewa People's Congress (APC)	1999	n.k.	A	north Nga	Defend the rights of the Hausa-Fulani tribe
Nga	Movement for the Actualisation of the Sovereign State of Biafra (MASSOB)	1999	thousands	A	south east Nga	Secession of Biafra
RMM	United Movement and Fronts of Azawad (MFUA)	early1990s	3–10,000	A	N.E RMM	Umbrella group of Arab and Tuareg anti govt rebels
RMM	Patriotic Movement of Ganda Koy (MPGK)	1994	n.k.	A	RMM	Stop northern encroachment against sedentary people in south; anti MFUA
Rwa	Interahamwe	1994	15,000-	A	DRC, Rwa	Reinstate Hutu control of Rwa, armed wg of Party
Rwa	Forces Démocratiques pour la Liberation du Rwanda (FDLR)	2000	3,000+	A	DRC, South Kivu and Katanga	Reinstate Hutu control of Rwa [Consists of refugee survivors of genocide in DRC by the Rwandan Patriotic Army (RPA) in 1996–97]
Rwa	Mai-Mai Militia / Alliance pour la Resistance Democratique (ARD)	1997	n.k.	A	Rw	Indigenous militia aligned with the FDLR

Table 41 Selected Non-State Armed Groups

Origin	Organisation * aka	Estb.	Est. Strength	Status	Operates	Aims (Remarks)
Sen	Mouvement des Forces Démocratiques de Casamance (MFDC)	1982	500–1,000	C	Sen	Independent Casamance (Involved in peace talks with govt since 2000)
SL	Civil Defense Force (CDF)	1990's	37,000+	C	SL	Defense of tribal communities against RUF and govt
SL	Independent RUF (RUF–I)	2002	500-	C	Lb border	Against cease-fire signed between Sipah-I-Sahaba and gov in Jan 2002. (Split from RUF in 2002)
SL	Revolutionary United Front (RUF)	1980s	n.k.	C	Gui, SL	Overthrow SL govt (Signed cease-fire agreement in Nov 2000. Disarmament programme completed in Jan 2002)
RSA	People Against Gangsterism and Drugs (PAGAD)	1995	50	A	Cape Town area	Combat and eradicate crime, gangsterism and drugs (armed wing of PAGAD)
RSA	Qibla	1980s	300-	A	Cape Town area	'Estb an Islamic state in RSA' (Allied to PAGAD); al-Qaeda link
Sdn	The Beja Congress	1993	500-	A	east Sdn	'Overthrow Sdn govt and estb autonomous Beja state' (Controls area of eastern Sdn centred around Garoura and Hamshkoraib)
Sdn	Janjaweed Militias	2002-2003	20,000-	A	W Sdn	Janjaweed is a term for tribal Arab militias displacing the African population of Darfur
Sdn	Justice and Equality Movement (JEM)	2002-2003	thousands	A	Darfur	Defence of Darfur population, protest at regional under-development
Sdn	Sudan Liberation Movement/Army (SLM/A)	2003	thousands	A	Darfur	Defence of the African population of Darfur, self determination for Darfur, democracy in Sudan
Sdn	New Sudan Brigade	1995	2,000-	A	east Sdn	Eastern branch of SPLA
Sdn	Sudan Alliance Forces	1994	500	A	east Sdn	Overthrow Sdn govt and 'estb progressive and secular democracy' (Played major role in opening new war front in east since 1997)
Sdn	Sudan People's Liberation Army (SPLA)	1983	20,000–30,000	C	south Sdn	Secular and democratic Sdn. Armed wing of Sudan People's Liberation Movement (SPLM). Signed cease-fire agreement with govt in July 2002. Largely Christian and southern
SR	Al-Ittihad al-Islami (AIAI)	1992	2,000	A	SR, Eth, Kya	Estb an Islamic regime in Somalia
SR	Somali National Alliance (SNA) / United Somali Congress (USC)	1989	n.k.	A	SR, esp S. Mogadishu	Militia of the Hawiye clan, led by Aideed family, overthrew Siad Barre, struggle for political power
SR	Somali National Front (SNF)	1991	2–3,000	A	SR	Marehans fighting for control of south Gedo region bordering Kenya, pro-Siad Barre
SR	Somali National Movement (SNM)	1982	5,000+	A	north SR	Independence of Somaliland
SR	Somali Patriotic Movement (SPM)	1989	2–3,000	A	SR	Ogaden tribal militia that helped overthrow Barre govt
SR	Rahanweyn Resistance Army (RRA)	1996	n.k.	A	south SR	Local autonomy (Allied to SDM)
SR	Somali Democratic Movement (SDM)	1992	n.k.	A	south SR	Local autonomy (Allied to RRA)
SR	Somali Salvation Democratic Front (SSDF)	1978	3,000-	A	north-east SR	Independence of Puntland
SR	United Somali Congress – ali Mahdi Faction	1990's	10,000	A	North SR	Anti Aideed, Abgal clan militia
Uga	Allied Democratic Front / Uganda Allied Democratic Army	1996	200	A	west Uga	Replace Uga govt with regime based on Sharia law
Uga	Lord's Resistance Army (LRA)	1989	1,500	A	Gulu and Kitgum districts	'Rule Uga according to biblical ten commandments and create Great Nile Republic in northern Uga' (Christian fundamentalist)
Uga	West Nile Bank Front (WNBF)	1995	1,000-	A/D	Uga	Anti government group dominated by west. Nile tribes and former army officers under Idi Amin

PART THREE
Reference

Table 42 Designations of aircraft

NOTES

1 [Square brackets] indicate the type from which a variant was derived: 'Q-5 … [MiG-19]' indicates that the design of the Q-5 was based on that of the MiG-19.

2 (Parentheses) indicate an alternative name by which an aircraft is known, sometimes in another version: 'L-188 … *Electra* (P-3 *Orion*)' shows that in another version the Lockheed Type 188 *Electra* is known as the P-3 *Orion*.

3 Names given in 'quotation marks' are NATO reporting names, e.g., 'Su-27… "*Flanker*".

4 When no information is listed under 'Country of origin' or 'Maker', the primary reference given under 'Name/designation' should be looked up under 'Type'.

5 For country abbreviations, see 'Index of Countries and Territories' (p. 446).

Type	Name/designation	Country of origin/Maker
Fixed-wing		
A-1	AMX	**Br/It** AMX
A-1	*Ching-Kuo*	**ROC** AIDC
A-3	*Skywarrior*	**US** Douglas
A-4	*Skyhawk*	**US** MD
A-5	(Q-5)	
A-7	*Corsair* II	**US** LTV
A-10	*Thunderbolt*	**US** Fairchild
A-36	*Halcón* (C-101)	
A-37	*Dragonfly*	**US** Cessna
A-50	'*Mainstay*' (Il-76)	**RF** Beriev
A300		**UK/Fr/Ge/Sp** Airbus Int
A310		**UK/Fr/Ge/Sp** Airbus Int
A340		**UK/Fr/Ge/Sp** Airbus Int
AC-47	(C-47)	
AC-130	(C-130)	
Air Beetle		**Nga** AIEP
Airtourer		**NZ** Victa
AJ-37	(J-37)	
Alizé	(Br 1050)	**Fr** Breguet
Alpha Jet		**Fr/Ge** Dassault–Breguet/Dornier
AMX		**Br/It** Embraer/Alenia/Aermacchi
An-2	'*Colt*'	**Ukr** Antonov
An-12	'*Cub*'	**Ukr** Antonov
An-14	'*Clod*' (*Pchyelka*)	**Ukr** Antonov
An-22	'*Cock*' (*Antei*)	**Ukr** Antonov
An-24	'*Coke*'	**Ukr** Antonov
An-26	'*Curl*'	**Ukr** Antonov
An-28/M-28	'*Cash*'	**Ukr** Antonov/**Pl** PZL
An-30	'*Clank*'	**Ukr** Antonov
An-32	'*Cline*'	**Ukr** Antonov
An-72	'*Coaler-C*'	**Ukr** Antonov
An-74	'*Coaler-B*'	**Ukr** Antonov
An-124	'*Condor*' (*Ruslan*)	**Ukr** Antonov
Andover	[HS-748]	
Arava		**Il** IAI
AS-202	*Bravo*	**CH** FFA
AT-3	*Tsu Chiang*	**ROC** AIDC
AT-6	(T-6)	
AT-11		**US** Beech
AT-26	EMB-326	
AT-33	(T-33)	
Atlantic	(*Atlantique*)	**Fr** Dassault–Breguet
AU-23	*Peacemaker* [PC-6B]	**US** Fairchild
AV-8	*Harrier* II	**US/UK** MD/BAe
Aztec	PA-23	**US** Piper
B-1	*Lancer*	**US** Rockwell
B-2	*Spirit*	**US** Northrop Grumman
B-5	H-5	
B-6	H-6	
B-52	*Stratofortress*	**US** Boeing
B-65	*Queen Air*	**US** Beech
BAC-167	*Strikemaster*	**UK** BAe
BAe-125		**UK** BAe
BAe-146		**UK** BAe
BAe-748	(HS-748)	**UK** BAe
Baron	(T-42)	
Basler T-67	(C-47)	**US** Basler
Be-6	'*Madge*'	**RF** Beriev
Be-12	'*Mail*' (*Tchaika*)	**RF** Beriev
Beech 50	*Twin Bonanza*	**US** Beech
Beech 95	*Travel Air*	**US** Beech
BN-2	*Islander, Defender, Trislander*	**UK** Britten-Norman
Boeing 707		**US** Boeing
Boeing 727		**US** Boeing
Boeing 737		**US** Boeing
Boeing 747		**US** Boeing
Boeing 757		**US** Boeing
Boeing 767		**US** Boeing
Bonanza		**US** Beech
Bronco	(OV-10)	
BT-5	HJ-5	
Bulldog		**UK** BAe
C-1		**J** Kawasaki
C-2	*Greyhound*	**US** Grumman
C-5	*Galaxy*	**US** Lockheed
C-7	DHC-7	
C-9	*Nightingale* (DC-9)	
C-12	*Super King Air* (*Huron*)	**US** Beech
C-17	*Globemaster* III	**US** McDonnell Douglas
C-18	[Boeing 707]	
C-20	(*Gulfstream* III)	
C-21	(*Learjet*)	
C-22	(Boeing 727)	

Type	Name/designation	Country of origin/Maker
C-23	(Sherpa) ....**UK** Shorts	
C-26	Expediter/Merlin ....**US** Fairchild	
C-27	Spartan .... **It** Alenia	
C-32	[Boeing 757] .... **US** Boeing	
C-37A	[Gulfstream V] .... **US** Gulfstream	
C-38A	(Astra) ....**Il** IAI	
C-42	(Neiva Regente) .... **Br** Embraer	
C-46	Commando .... **US** Curtis	
C-47	DC-3 (Dakota) (C-117 Skytrain) ....**US** Douglas	
C-54	Skymaster (DC-4) ....**US** Douglas	
C-91	HS-748	
C-93	HS-125	
C-95	EMB-110	
C-97	EMB-121	
C-101	Aviojet.................................**Sp** CASA	
C-115	DHC-5 ....**Ca** De Havilland	
C-117	(C-47)	
C-118	Liftmaster (DC-6)	
C-123	Provider ....**US** Fairchild	
C-127	(Do-27) ....**Sp** CASA	
C-130	Hercules (L-100) ....**US** Lockheed	
C-131	Convair 440 ....**US** Convair	
C-135	[Boeing 707]	
C-137	[Boeing 707]	
C-140	(Jetstar) ....**US** Lockheed	
C-141	Starlifter ....**US** Lockheed	
C-160	Transall ....**Fr/Ge** EADS	
C-212	Aviocar ....**Sp** CASA	
C-235	Persuader ....**Sp/Indo** CASA/Airtech	
C-295M	....**Sp** CASA	
Canberra	......................................**UK** BAe	
CAP-10	....**Fr** Mudry	
CAP-20	....**Fr** Mudry	
CAP-230	....**Fr** Mudry	
Caravelle	SE-210 ....**Fr** Aérospatiale	
CC-115	DHC-5....................................	
CC-117	(Falcon 20)	
CC-132	(DHC-7)	
CC-137	(Boeing 707)	
CC-138	(DHC-6)	
CC-144	CL-600/-601 ....**Ca** Canadair	
CF-5a	.............................**Ca** Canadair	
CF-18	F/A-18....................................	
Cheetah	[Mirage III] ....**RSA** Atlas	
Cherokee	PA-28 ....**US** Piper	
Cheyenne	PA-31T [Navajo] ....**US** Piper	
Chieftain	PA-31-350 [Navajo] ....**US** Piper	
Ching-Kuo	A-1 ....**ROC** AIDC	
Citabria	..............................**US** Champion	
Citation	(T-47) .... **US** Cessna	
CJ-5	[Yak-18] ....**PRC** NAMC (Hongdu)	
CJ-6	[Yak-18] ....**PRC** NAMC (Hongdu)	
CL-215	.............................**Ca** Canadair	
CL-415	.............................**Ca** Canadair	
CL-600/604	Challenger ....**Ca** Canadair	
CM-170	Magister [Tzukit] ....**Fr** Aérospatiale	
CM-175	Zéphyr..........................**Fr** Aérospatiale	
CN-212	...........................**Sp/Indo** CASA/IPTN	
CN-235	...........................**Sp/Indo** CASA/IPTN	

Type	Name/designation	Country of origin/Maker
Cochise	T-42	
Comanche	PA-24 ....**US** Piper	
Commander	Aero-/TurboCommander ....**US** Rockwell	
Commodore	MS-893 ....**Fr** Aérospatiale	
CP-3	P-3 Orion	
CP-140	Aurora (P-3 Orion) ....**US** Lockheed	
Acturas		
CT-4	Airtrainer .... **NZ** Victa	
CT-114	CL-41 Tutor ....**Ca** Canadair	
CT-133	Silver Star [T-33] ....**Ca** Canadair	
CT-134	Musketeer	
CT-156	Harvard II .... **US** Beech	
Dagger	(Nesher)	
Dakota	......................................**US** Piper	
Dakota	(C-47)	
DC-3	(C-47) ....**US** Douglas	
DC-4	(C-54) ....**US** Douglas	
DC-6	(C-118) ....**US** Douglas	
DC-7	......................................**US** Douglas	
DC-8	......................................**US** Douglas	
DC-9	......................................**US** MD	
Deepak	(HPT-32)	
Defender	BN-2	
DHC-3	Otter ....**Ca** DHC	
DHC-4	Caribou ....**Ca** DHC	
DHC-5	Buffalo ....**Ca** DHC	
DHC-6	Twin Otter, CC-138 ....**Ca** DHC	
DHC-7	Dash-7 (Ranger, CC-132) ....**Ca** DHC	
DHC-8	......................................**Ca** DHC	
Dimona	H-36 .... **Ge** Hoffman	
Do-27	(C-127) ....**Ge** Dornier	
Do-28	Skyservant ....**Ge** Dornier	
Do-128	......................................**Ge** Dornier	
Do-228	......................................**Ge** Dornier	
E-2	Hawkeye..........................**US** Grumman	
E-3	Sentry ....**US** Boeing	
E-4	[Boeing 747] ....**US** Boeing	
E-6	Mercury [Boeing 707] ....**US** Boeing	
E-26	T-35A (Tamiz) ....**Chl** Enear	
EA-3	[A-3]	
EA-6	Prowler [A-6]	
EC-130	[C-130]	
EC-135	[Boeing 707]	
EF-111	Raven (F-111) .....**US** General Dynamic	
Electra	(L-188)	
EMB-110	Bandeirante	
EMB-111	Maritime Bandeirante ....**Br** Embraer	
EMB-120	Brasilia ....**Br** Embraer	
EMB-121	Xingu ....**Br** Embraer	
EMB-145	(R-99A/-99B) ....**Br** Embraer	
EMB-201	Ipanema ....**Br** Embraer	
EMB-312	Tucano ....**Br** Embraer	
EMB-314	Super Tucano ....**Br** Embraer	
EMB-326	Xavante (MB-326) ....**Br** Embraer	
EMB-810	[Seneca] ....**Br** Embraer	
EP-3	(P-3 Orion)	
ERJ-145	......................................**Br** Embraer	
Etendard/Super Etendard	...........................**Fr** Dassault	
EV-1	(OV-1)	

Type	Name/designation	Country of origin/Maker
F-1	[T-2]	**J** Mitsubishi
F-4	*Phantom*	**US** MD
F-5	*-A/-B Freedom Fighter-E/-F Tiger* II	**US** Northrop
F-6	J-6	
F-7	J-7	
F-8	J-8	
F-10	J-10	
F-11	J-11	
F-14	*Tomcat*	**US** Grumman
F-15	*Eagle*	**US** MD
F-16	*Fighting Falcon*	**US** GD
F-18	[F/A-18], *Hornet*	
F-21	*Kfir*	**Il** IAI
F-22	*Raptor*	**US** Lockheed
F-27	*Friendship*	**Nl** Fokker
F-28	*Fellowship*	**Nl** Fokker
F-35	*Draken*	**Swe** SAAB
F-50/-60		**Nl** Fokker
F-104	*Starfighter*	**US** Lockheed
F-111	EF-111	**US** GD
F-117	*Nighthawk*	**US** Lockheed
F-172	(Cessna 172)	**Fr/US** Reims-Cessna
F-406	*Caravan*	**Fr** Reims
F/A-18	*Hornet*	**US** MD
Falcon	*Mystère-Falcon*	
FB-111	(F-111)	
FBC-1	*Feibao* [JH-7]	
FC-1	(*Sabre* 2, *Super-7*)	**PRC/RF/Pak** CAC/MAPO/Pak
FH-227	(F-27)	**US** Fairchild-Hiller
Firefly	(T-67M)	**UK** Slingsby
Flamingo	MBB-233	
FT-5	JJ-5	
FT-6	JJ-6	
FT-7	JJ-7	
FTB-337	[Cessna 337]	
G-91		**It** Aeritalia
G-115E	*Tutor*	**Ge** Grob
G-222		**It** Alenia
Galaxy	C-5	
Galeb		**FRY** SOKO
Genet	SF-260W	
GU-25	(*Falcon* 20)	
Guerrier	R-235	
Gulfstream		**US** Gulfstream Aviation
Gumhuria	(*Bücker* 181)	**Et** Heliopolis
H-5	[Il-28]	**PRC** HAF
H-6	[Tu-16]	**PRC** XAC
H-36	*Dimona*	
Halcón	[C-101]	
Harrier	(AV-8)	**UK** BAe
Hawk		**UK** BAe
Hawker 800XP	(BAe-125)	**US** Raytheon
HC-130	(C-130)	
HF-24	*Marut*	**Ind** HAL
HFB-320	*Hansajet*	**Ge** Hamburger FB
HJ-5	(H-5)	
HJT-16	*Kiran*	**Ind** HAL
HPT-32	*Deepak*	**Ind** HAL
HS-125	(*Dominie*)	**UK** BAe

Type	Name/designation	Country of origin/Maker
HS-748	[*Andover*]	**UK** BAe
HT-2		**Ind** HAL
HU-16	*Albatross*	**US** Grumman
HU-25	(*Falcon* 20)	
Hunter		**UK** BAe
HZ-5	(H-5)	
IA-50	*Guaraní*	**Arg** FMA
IA-58	*Pucará*	**Arg** FMA
IA-63	*Pampa*	**Arg** FMA
IAI-201/-202	*Arava*	**Il** IAI
IAI-1124	*Westwind, Seascan*	**Il** IAI
IAI-1125	*Astra*	**Il** IAI
Iak-52	(Yak-52)	**R** Aerostar
IAR-28		**R** IAR
IAR-93	*Orao*	**FRY/R** SOKO/IAR
IAR-99	*Soim*	**R** IAR
Il-14	'Crate'	**RF** Ilyushin
Il-18	'Coot'	**RF** Ilyushin
Il-20	'Coot-A' (Il-18)	**RF** Ilyushin
Il-22	'Coot-B' (Il-18)	**RF** Ilyushin
Il-28	'Beagle'	**RF** Ilyushin
Il-38	'May'	**RF** Ilyushin
Il-62	'Classic'	**RF** Ilyushin
Il-76	'Candid' (tpt), 'Mainstay' (AEW)	**RF** Ilyushin
Il-78	'Midas' (tkr)	**RF** Ilyushin
Il-82	'Candid'	**RF** Ilyushin
Il-86	'Camber'	**RF** Ilyushin
Il-87	'Maxdome'	**RF** Ilyushin
Impala	[MB-326]	**RSA** Atlas
Islander	BN-2	
J-5	[MiG-17F]	**PRC** SAF
J-6	[MiG-19]	**PRC** SAF
J-7	[MiG-21]	**PRC** CAC/GAIC
J-8	*Finback*	**PRC** SAC
J-10	[IAI *Lavi*]	**PRC** SAC
J-11	[Su-27]	**PRC** SAC
J-32	*Lansen*	**Swe** SAAB
J-35	*Draken*	**Swe** SAAB
J-37	*Viggen*	**Swe** SAAB
JA-37	(J-37)	
Jaguar		**Fr/UK** SEPECAT
JAS-39	*Gripen*	**Swe** SAAB
Jastreb		**FRY** SOKO
Jetstream		**UK** BAe
JH-7	[FBC-1]	**PRC** XAC
JJ-5	[J-5]	**PRC** CAF
JJ-6	[J-6]	**PRC** SAF
JJ-7	[J-7]	**PRC** GAIC
JZ-6	(J-6)	
K-8		**PRC/Pak/Et** Hongdu/E
KA-3	[A-3]	
KA-6	[A-6]	
KT-1B		**ROK** KAI
KC-10	*Extender* [DC-10]	**US** MD
KC-130	[C-130]	
KC-135	[Boeing 707]	
KE-3A	[Boeing 707]	
KF-16	(F-16)	
Kfir		**Il** IAI

Type	Name/designation	Country of origin/Maker
King Air		US Beech
Kiran	HJT-16	
Kraguj		FRY SOKO
KT-1		ROK KAI
L-4	Cub	
L-18	Super Cub	US Piper
L-19	O-1	
L-21	Super Cub	US Piper
L-29	Delfin	Cz Aero
L-39	Albatros	Cz Aero
L-59	Albatros	Cz Aero
L-70	Vinka	SF Valmet
L-100	C-130 (civil version)	
L-188	Electra (P-3 Orion)	US Lockheed
L-410	Turbolet	Cz LET
L-1011	Tristar	US Lockheed
Learjet	(C-21)	US Gates
LR-1	(MU-2)	J Mitsubishi
M-28	Skytruck/Bryza	Pl MIELEC
Magister	CM-170	
Marut	HF-24	
Mashshaq	MFI-17	Pak/Swe PAC/SAAB
Matador	(AV-8)	
Maule	M-7/MXT-7	US Maule
MB-326		It Aermacchi
MB-339	(Veltro)	It Aermacchi
MBB-233	Flamingo	Ge MBB
MC-130	(C-130)	
Mercurius	(HS-125)	
Merlin		US Fairchild
Mescalero	T-41	
Metro		US Fairchild
MFI-17	Supporter (T-17)	Swe SAAB
MiG-15	'Midget' trg	RF MiG
MiG-17	'Fresco'	RF MiG
MiG-19	'Farmer'	RF MiG
MiG-21	'Fishbed'	RF MiG
MiG-23	'Flogger'	RF MiG
MiG-25	'Foxbat'	RF MiG
MiG-27	'Flogger' D'	RF MiG
MiG-29	'Fulcrum'	RF MiG
MiG-31	'Foxhound'	RF MiG
Mirage		Fr Dassault
Missionmaster	N-22	
Mohawk	OV-1	
MS-760	Paris	Fr Aérospatiale
MS-893	Commodore	
MU-2	LR-1	J Mitsubishi
Musketeer	Beech 24	US Beech
Mystère-Falcon		Fr Dassault
N-22	Floatmaster, Missionmaster	Aus GAF
N-24	Searchmaster B/L	Aus GAF
N-262	Frégate	Fr Aérospatiale
N-2501	Noratlas	Fr Aérospatiale
Navajo	PA-31	US Piper
NC-212	C-212	Sp/Indo CASA/Nurtanio
NC-235	C-235	Sp/Indo CASA/Nurtanio
Nesher	[Mirage III]	Il IAI
NF-5	(F-5)	

Type	Name/designation	Country of origin/Maker
Nightingale	(C-9)	
Nimrod	[Comet]	UK BAe
Nomad		Aus GAF
O-1	Bird Dog	US Cessna
O-2	(Cessna 337 Skymaster)	US Cessna
OA-4	(A-4)	
OA-37	Dragonfly	
Orao	IAR-93	
Ouragan		Fr Dassault
OV-1	Mohawk	US Rockwell
OV-10	Bronco	US Rockwell
P-3	Orion [L-188 Electra]	US Lockheed
P-92		It Teenam
P-95	EMB-110	
P-166		It Piaggio
P-180	Avanti	It Piaggio
PA-18	Super Cub	US Piper
PA-23	Aztec	US Piper
PA-28	Cherokee	US Piper
PA-31	Navajo	US Piper
PA-32	Cherokee Six	US Piper
PA-34	Seneca	US Piper
PA-36	Pawnee Brave	US Piper
PA-38	Tomahawk	US Piper
PA-42	Cheyenne III	US Piper
PBY-5	Catalina	US Consolidated
PC-6	Porter	CH Pilatus
PC-6A/B	Turbo Porter	CH Pilatus
PC-7	Turbo Trainer	CH Pilatus
PC-9		CH Pilatus
PC-12		CH Pilatus
PD-808		It Piaggio
Pillán	T-35	
PL-1	Chien Shou	ROC AIDC
PLZ M-28	[An-28]	Pl PZL
Porter	PC-6	
PS-5	[SH-5]	
PZL M-28	M-28 [An-28]	Pl PZL
PZL-104	Wilga	Pl PZL
PZL-130	Orlik	Pl PZL
Q-5	A-5 'Fantan' [MiG-19]	PRC NAMC (Hongdu)
Queen Air	(U-8)	
R-99A/B	EMB-145	Br Embraer
R-160		Fr Socata
R-235	Guerrier	Fr Socata
RC-21	(C-21, Learjet)	
RC-47	(C-47)	
RC-95	(EMB-110)	
RC-135	[Boeing 707]	
RF-4	(F-4)	
RF-5	(F-5)	
RF-35	(F-35)	
RF-104	(F-104)	
RG-8A		US Schweizer
RT-26	(EMB-326)	
RT-33	(T-33)	
RU-21	(King Air)	
RV-1	(OV-1)	
S-2	Tracker	US Grumman

Type	Name/designation	Country of origin/Maker
S-208	....	**It** SIAI
S-211	....	**It** SIAI
SA 2-37A	....	**US** Schweizer
Saab 340H	....	**Swe** SAAB
Sabreliner	(CT-39)	**US** Rockwell
Safari	MFI-15	
Safir	SAAB-91 (SK-50)	**Swe** SAAB
SB7L-360	(Seeker)	**Aus/HKJ** KADDB/Seabird
SC-7	Skyvan	**UK** Short
SE-210	Caravelle	
Sea Harrier	(Harrier)	
Seascan	IAI-1124	
Searchmaster	N-24 B/L	
Seneca	PA-34 (EMB-810)	**US** Piper
Sentinel	(Global Express)	**Ca** Bombardier
Sentry	(O-2)	**US** Summit
SF-37	(J-37)	
SF-260	(SF-260W Warrior)	**It** SIAI
SH-5	PS-5	**PRC** HAMC
SH-37	(J-37)	
Sherpa	Short 330, C-23	**UK** Short
Short 330	(Sherpa)	**UK** Short
Sierra 200	(Musketeer)	
SK-35	(J-35)	**Swe** SAAB
SK-37	(J-37)	
SK-60	(SAAB-105)	**Swe** SAAB
SK-61	(Bulldog)	
Skyvan	....	**UK** Short
SM-90	....	**RF** Technoavia
SM-1019	....	**It** SIAI
SP-2H	Neptune	**US** Lockheed
SR-71	Blackbird	**US** Lockheed
Su-7	'Fitter-A'	**RF** Sukhoi
Su-15	'Flagon'	**RF** Sukhoi
Su-17/-20/-22	'Fitter-B' - '-K'	**RF** Sukhoi
Su-24	'Fencer'	**RF** Sukhoi
Su-25	'Frogfoot'	**RF** Sukhoi
Su-27	'Flanker'	**RF** Sukhoi
Su-29	....	**RF** Sukhoi
Su-30	'Flanker'	**RF** Sukhoi
Su-33	(Su-27K) 'Flanker-D'	**RF** Sukhoi
Su-34	(Su-27IB) 'Flanker-C2'	**RF** Sukhoi
Su-35	(Su-27) 'Flanker'	**RF** Sukhoi
Su-39	(Su-25T) 'Frogfoot'	**RF** Sukhoi
Super	....	**Fr** Dassault
Shrike Aerocommander	....	**US** Rockwell
Super Galeb	....	**FRY** SOKO
T-1	....	**J** Fuji
T-1A	Jayhawk	**US** Beech
T-2	Buckeye	**US** Rockwell
T-2	....	**J** Mitsubishi
T-3	....	**J** Fuji
T-6A	Texan II	**US** Beech
T-17	(Supporter, MFI-17)	**Swe** SAAB
T-23	Uirapurú	**Br** Aerotec
T-25	Neiva Universal	**Br** Embraer
T-26	EMB-326	
T-27	Tucano	**Br** Embraer

Type	Name/designation	Country of origin/Maker
T-28	Trojan	**US** North American
T-33	Shooting Star	**US** Lockheed
T-34	Mentor	**US** Beech
T-35	Pillán [PA-28]	**Chl** Enaer
T-36	(C-101)	
T-37	(A-37)	
T-38	Talon	**US** Northrop
T-39	(Sabreliner)	**US** Rockwell
T-41	Mescalero (Cessna 172)	**US** Cessna
T-42	Cochise (Baron)	**US** Beech
T-43	(Boeing 737)	
T-44	(King Air)	
T-47	(Citation)	
T-67M	(Firefly)	**UK** Slingsby
T-400	(T-1A)	**US** Beech
TB-20	Trinidad	**Fr** Aérospatiale
TB-21	Trinidad	**Fr** Socata
TB-30	Epsilon	**Fr** Aérospatiale
TB-200	Tobago	**Fr** Socata
TBM-700	....	**Fr** Socata
TC-45	(C-45, trg)	
TCH-1	Chung Hsing	**ROC** AIDC
TL-1	(KM-2)	**J** Fuji
Tornado	....	**UK/Ge/It** Panavia
TR-1	[U-2]	**US** Lockheed
Travel Air	Beech 95	
Trident	....	**UK** BAe
Trislander	BN-2	
Tristar	L-1011	
TS-8	Bies	**Pl** PZL
TS-11	Iskra	**Pl** PZL
Tu-16	'Badger'	**RF** Tupolev
Tu-22	'Blinder'	**RF** Tupolev
Tu-22M	'Backfire'	**RF** Tupolev
Tu-95	'Bear'	**RF** Tupolev
Tu-126	'Moss'	**RF** Tupolev
Tu-134	'Crusty'	**RF** Tupolev
Tu-142	'Bear F'	**RF** Tupolev
Tu-154	'Careless'	**RF** Tupolev
Tu-160	'Blackjack'	**RF** Tupolev
Tucano	(EMB-312/314)	**Br** Embraer
Turbo Porter	PC-6A/B	
Twin Bonanza	Beech 50	
Twin Otter	DHC-6	
Typhoon	....	**Ge,Sp,Ir,UK** Eurofighter
Tzukit	[CM-170]	**Il** IAI
U-2	....	**US** Lockheed
U-3	(Cessna 310)	**US** Cessna
U-4	Gulfstream IV	**US** Gulfstream Aviation
U-7	(L-18)	
U-8	(Twin Bonanza/Queen Air)	**US** Beech
U-9	(EMB-121)	
U-10	Super Courier	**US** Helio
U-17	(Cessna 180, 185)	**US** Cessna
U-21	(King Air)	
U-36	(Learjet)	
U-42	(C-42)	
U-93	(HS-125)	
U-125	BAe 125-800	**UK** BAe

Type	Name/designation	Country of origin/Maker
U-206G	Stationair	US Cessna
UC-12	(King Air)	
UP-2J	(P-2J)	
US-1		J Shin Meiwa
US-2A	(S-2A, tpt)	
US-3	(S-3, tpt)	
UTVA-66		FRY UTVA
UTVA-75		FRY UTVA
UV-18	(DHC-6)	
V-400	Fantrainer 400	Ge VFW
V-600	Fantrainer 600	Ge VFW
Vampire	DH-100	
VC-4	Gulfstream I	
VC-10		UK BAe
VC-11	Gulfstream II	
VC-25	[Boeing 747]	US Boeing
VC-91	(HS-748)	
VC-93	(HS-125)	
VC-97	(EMB-120)	
VC-130	(C-130)	
VFW-614		Ge VFW
Vinka	L-70	
VU-9	(EMB-121)	
VU-93	(HS-125)	
WC-130	[C-130]	
WC-135	[Boeing 707]	US Boeing
Westwind	IAI-1124	
Winjeel	CA-25	
Xavante	EMB-326	
Xingu	EMB-121	
Y-5	[An-2]	PRC Hua Bei
Y-7	[An-24/-26]	PRC XAC
Y-8	[An-12]	PRC STAF
Y-12	Turbo/Twin Panda	PRC HAMC
Yak-11	'Moose'	RF Yakovlev
Yak-18	'Max'	RF Yakovlev
Yak-28	'Firebar' ('Brewer')	RF Yakovlev
Yak-38	'Forger'	RF Yakovlev
Yak-40	'Codling'	RF Yakovlev
Yak-42	'Clobber'	RF Yakovlev
Yak-52	(IAK 52)	R Aerostar
Yak-55		RF Yakovlev
YS-11		J Nihon
Z-142/143		Cz Zlin
Z-226		Cz Zlin
Z-242		Cz Zlin
Z-326		Cz Zlin
Z-526		Cz Zlin
Zéphyr	CM-175	

Tilt-Rotor Wing

Type	Name/designation	Country of origin/Maker
V-22	Osprey	US Bell/Boeing

Helicopters

Type	Name/designation	Country of origin/Maker
A-109	Hirundo	It Agusta
A-129	Mangusta	It Agusta
AB-...	(Bell 204/205/206/212/214, etc.)	It/US Agusta/Bell
AH-1	Cobra/Sea Cobra	US Bell

Type	Name/designation	Country of origin/Maker
AH-2	Rooivalk	RSA Denel
AH-6	(Hughes 500/530)	US MD
AH-64	Apache	US Hughes
ALH	Adv Light Hel	Ind HAL
Alouette II	SA-318, SE-3130	Fr Aérospatiale
Alouette III	SA-316, SA-319	Fr Aérospatiale
AS-61	(SH-3)	US/It Sikorsky/Agusta
AS-313 – AS-365/-366	(ex-SA-313 – SA-365/-366)	
AS-332	Super Puma	Fr Aérospatiale
AS-350	Ecureuil	Fr Aérospatiale
AS-355	Ecureuil II	Fr Aérospatiale
AS-365	Dauphin	Fr Aérospatiale
AS-532	Cougar	Fr Eurocopter
AS-550/555	Fennec	Fr Aérospatiale
AS-565	Panther	Fr Eurocopter
ASH-3	(Sea King)	It/US Agusta/Sikorsky
AUH-76	(S-76)	
Bell 47	(Sioux)	US Bell
Bell 205		US Bell
Bell 206		US Bell
Bell 212		US Bell
Bell 214		US Bell
Bell 222		US Bell
Bell 406		US Bell
Bell 412		US Bell
Bo-105	(NBo-105)	Ge MBB
CH-3	(SH-3)	
CH-34	Choctaw	US Sikorsky
CH-46	Sea Knight	US Boeing-Vertol
CH-47	Chinook	US Boeing-Vertol
CH-53	Stallion (Sea Stallion)	US Sikorsky
CH-54	Tarhe	US Sikorsky
CH-113	(CH-46)	
CH-124	SH-3 (Sea King)	
CH-136	Kiowa	Ca Bell
CH-139	Bell 206	
CH-146	Bell 412	Ca Bell
CH-147	CH-47	
CH-149	Cormorant (Merlin)	
Cheetah	[SA-315]	Ind HAL
Chetak	[SA-319]	Ind HAL
Commando	(SH-3)	UK/US Westland/Sikorsky
EC-120B	Colibri	Fr/Ge Eurocopter
EH-60	(UH-60)	
EH-101	Merlin	UK/It Westland/Agusta
F-28F		US Enstrom
FH-1100	(OH-5)	US Fairchild-Hiller
Gazela	(SA-342)	Fr/FRY Aérospatiale/SOKO
Gazelle	SA-341/-342	
H-34	(S-58)	
H-76	S-76	
HA-15	Bo-105	
HB-315	Gavião (SA-315)	Br/Fr Helibras Aérospatiale
HB-350	Esquilo (AS-350)	Br/Fr Helibras Aérospatiale
HD-16	SA-319	
HH-3	(SH-3)	
HH-34	(CH-34)	
HH-53	(CH-53)	
HH-65	(AS-365)	Fr Eurocopter

Type	Name/designation	Country of origin/Maker
Hkp-2	*Alouette* II/SE-3130	
Hkp-3	AB-204	
Hkp-4	KV-107	
Hkp-5	Hughes 300	
Hkp-6	AB-206	
Hkp-9	Bo-105	
Hkp-10	AS-332	
HR-12	OH-58	
HSS-1	(S-58)	
HSS-2	(SH-3)	
HT-17	CH-47	
HT-21	AS-332	
HU-1	(UH-1)	**J/US** Fuji/Bell
HU-8	UH-1B	
HU-10	UH-1H	
HU-18	AB-212	
Hughes 300		**US** MD
Hughes 500/520	*Defender*	**US** MD
IAR-316/-330	(SA-316/-330)	**R/Fr** IAR/Aérospatiale
Ka-25	'Hormone'	**RF** Kamov
Ka-27/-28	'Helix-A'	**RF** Kamov
Ka-29	'Helix-B'	**RF** Kamov
Ka-32	'Helix-C'	**RF** Kamov
Ka-50	*Hokum*	**RF** Kamov
KH-4	(Bell 47)	**J/US** Kawasaki/ Bell
KH-300	(Hughes 269)	**J/US** Kawasaki/MD
KH-500	(Hughes 369)	**J/US** Kawasaki/MD
Kiowa	OH-58	
KV-107	[CH-46]	**J/US** Kawasaki/Vertol
Lynx		**UK** Westland
MD-500/530	*Defender*	**US** McDonnell Douglas
Merlin	EH-101	**UK/It** Westland/Augusta
MH-6	(AH-6)	
MH-53	(CH-53)	
Mi-2	'Hoplite'	**RF** Mil
Mi-4	'Hound'	**RF** Mil
Mi-6	'Hook'	**RF** Mil
Mi-8	'Hip'	**RF** Mil
Mi-14	'Haze'	**RF** Mil
Mi-17	'Hip-H'	**RF** Mil
Mi-24, -25, -35	'Hind'	**RF** Mil
Mi-26	'Halo'	**RF** Mil
Mi-28	'Havoc'	**RF** Mil
NAS-330	(SA-330)	**Indo/Fr** Nurtanio/Aérospatiale
NAS-332	AS-332	**Indo/Fr** Nurtanio/Aérospatiale
NB-412	Bell 412	**Indo/US** Nurtanio/Bell
NBo-105	Bo-105	**Indo/Ge** Nurtanio/MBB
NH-300	(Hughes 300)	**It/US** Nardi/MD
OH-6	*Cayuse* (Hughes 369)	**US** MD
OH-13	(Bell 47G)	
OH-23	*Raven*	**US** Hiller
OH-58	*Kiowa* (Bell 206)	
OH-58D	(Bell 406)	

Type	Name/designation	Country of origin/Maker
Oryx	(SA-330)	
PAH-1	(Bo-105)	
Partizan	(*Gazela*, armed)	
RH-53	(CH-53)	
S-58	(*Wessex*)	**US** Sikorsky
S-61	SH-3	
S-65	CH-53	
S-70	UH-60	**US** Sikorsky
S-76		**US** Sikorsky
S-80	CH-53	
SA-313	*Alouette* II	**Fr** Aérospatiale
SA-315	*Lama* [*Alouette* II]	**Fr** Aérospatiale
SA-316	*Alouette* III (SA-319)	**Fr** Aérospatiale
SA-318	*Alouette* II (SE-3130)	**Fr** Aérospatiale
SA-319	*Alouette* III (SA-316)	**Fr** Aérospatiale
SA-321	*Super Frelon*	**Fr** Aérospatiale
SA-330	*Puma*	**Fr** Aérospatiale
SA-341/-342	*Gazelle*	**Fr** Aérospatiale
SA-360	*Dauphin*	**Fr** Aérospatiale
SA-365/-366	*Dauphin* II (SA-360)	
Scout	(*Wasp*)	**UK** Westland
SE-316	(SA-316)	
SE-3130	(SA-318)	
Sea King	[SH-3]	**UK** Westland
SH-2	*Sea Sprite*	**US** Kaman
SH-3	(*Sea King*)	**US** Sikorsky
SH-34	(S-58)	
SH-57	Bell 206	
SH-60	*Sea Hawk* (UH-60)	
Sokol	W3	
TH-50	*Esquilo* (AS-550)	
TH-55	Hughes 269	
TH-57	*Sea Ranger* (Bell 206)	
TH-67	*Creek* (Bell 206B-3)	**Ca** Bell
Tiger	AS-665	**Fr** Eurocopter
UH-1	*Iroquois* (Bell 204/205/212)	
UH-12	(OH-23)	**US** Hiller
UH-13	(Bell 47J)	
UH-19	(S-55)	
UH-34T	(S-58T)	
UH-46	(CH-46)	
UH-60	*Black Hawk* (SH-60)	**US** Sikorsky
VH-4	(Bell 206)	
VH-60	(S-70)	
W-3	*Sokol*	**Pl** PZL
Wasp	(*Scout*)	**UK** Westland
Wessex	(S-58)	**US/UK** Sikorsky/Westland
Z-5	[Mi-4]	**PRC** HAF
Z-6	[Z-5]	**PRC** CHAF
Z-8	[AS-321]	**PRC** CHAF
Z-9	[AS-365]	**PRC** HAMC
Z-11	[AS-352]	**PRC** CHAF

Table 43 **Operational Offensive Nuclear Delivery Systems**

Systems with dedicated crews and targeting mechanisms in place. Excludes strategic defence forces. Missile range varies with payload-to-fuel ratio and firing direction. Aircraft range can be extended with in-flight fuelling.

Name/ Designation	AKA	Warhead	Range (km)	Name/ Designation	AKA	Warhead	Range (km)
Land Ballistic Missiles				**RF**			
US				Tu-95M	*Bear*	◆■	12,000
LGM-30G	*Minuteman* III	▲	13,000	Tu-160	*Blackjack*	◆■	4,000
LGM-118	MX/ *Peacekeeper*	▲	9,600	Tu-22M-3	*Backfire*	▼	4,800
RF				Su-24M	*Fencer*	■	2,100
SS-18	*Satan*	▲	15,000	**Fr**			
SS-19	*Stiletto*	▲	10,000	Super Etendard		◆	650
SS-24 Scalpel		▲	10,000	Mirage 2000N		◆	1,200
SS-25 Sickle		●	10,000	Rafale		◆	1,200
SS-27 Topol -M		●	10,500	**PRC**			
PRC				H-6	*Tu-16*	■	5,000
CSS-2	DF-3A	●	2,800	Q-5	*MiG-19*	■	400
CSS-3	DF-4	●	4,750	**Il**			
CSS-4	DF-5A	●▲	13,000	F-4E-2000	*Kumass*	■	2,200
CSS-5	DF-21	●	2,150	F-16A/B/C/D	*Fighting Falcon*	■	2,500
CSS-5	DF-21A	●	2,500	F-15I	*Thunder*	■	2,500
CSS-6	DF-15/M-9	●	600	**Ind**			
CSS-7	DF-11/M-11	●	300	Jaguar S(I)	*Shamsher*	■	1,060
CSS-8	DF-7	●	150	MiG-27M	*Bahadur*	■	1,000
CSS-9	DF-31	●▲	8,000	Mirage 2000H	*Vajra*	■	1,200
Pak				**Pak**			
Ghauri 1	*Hatf* 5	●	1,500	F-16A/B	*Fighting Falcon*	■	1,000
Il				Mirage 5		■	1,200
Jericho 1		●	500	Q-5	*MiG-19*	■	1,200
Jericho 2		●	1,800	**DPRK**			
SLBM				H-5	*Il-28*	■	2,100
US				**SLCM**			
UGM-96	*Trident* I C-4	▲	7,400	**US**			
UGM-133	*Trident* II D-5	▲	12,000	Tomahawk	TLAM-N	●	2,500
UK				**RF**			
UGM-135	*Trident* II D-5	▲	12,000	SS-N-9	*Siren*	●	110
RF				SS-N-12	*Sandbox*	●	550
SS-N-8	*Sawfly*	▲	9,100	SS-N-19	*Shipwreck*	●	550
SS-N-18	*Stingray*	▲	6,500	SS-N-21	*Sampson*	●	2,400
SS-N-20	*Sturgeon*	▲	8,300	SS-N-22	*Sunburn*	●	120
SS-N-23	*Skiff*	▲	8,300	**Il**			
Fr				Turbo-Popeye 3		●	1,500
M-4		▲	4,000	**ALCM**			
M-45		▲	4,000	**US**			
PRC				AGM-86B		●	2,500
CSS-N-3	JL-1	●	2,150	AGM-129		●	3,500
Aircraft				**RF**			
US				AS-4	Kh-22 *Kitchen*	●	310
B-52H	*Stratofortress*	◆	16,000	AS-15A	KH-55 *Kent*	●	2,500
B-2	*Spirit*	■	12,200	AS-15B	Kh-55SM *Kent*	●	3,000
F-15E	*Strike Eagle*	■	2,500	AS-16	Kh-15 *Kickback*	●	150
F-16A/B/C/D	*Fighting Falcon*	■	2,500	**Fr**			
F-117A	*Nighthawk*	■	2,100	ASMP		●	250

KEY ▲ MIRV ● Single ◆ ALCM ■ Bomb ▼ ASM

Table 44 **List of Abbreviations**

- part of unit is detached/less then

* combat capable

" unit with overstated title/ship class nickname

+unit reinforced/more than

<under 100 tonnes

† serviceability in doubt

ε estimated

AAA anti-aircraft artillery

AAM air-to-air missile

AAV amphibious assault Vehicle

AB airborne

ABM anti-ballistic missile

about the total could be higher

ABU sea going buoy tender

ac aircraft

ACCS Air Command and Control System

ACP airborne command post

ACV air cushion vehicle

AD air defence

ADA air defence artillery

adj adjusted

AE auxiliary, ammunition carrier

AEW airborne early warning

AF stores ship with RAS

AFB/S Air Force Base/ Station

AFR Air Force Reserve

AG misc auxiliary

AGB Icebreaker

AGF command ship

AGHS hydrographic survey vessel

AGI intelligence collection vessel

AGL automatic grenade launcher

AGM air-to-ground missile

AGOR oceanographic research vessel

AGOS oceanographic surveillance vessel

AGS survey ship

AH hospital ship/attack helicopter

AIFV armoured infantry fighting vehicle

AK cargo ship

aka also known as

AKR fast sealift ship/ cargo ship

AKSL Stores ship (light)

ALARM air-launched anti-radiation missile

ALCM air-launched cruise missile

amph amphibious/amphibian

AMRAAM advanced medium-range air-to-air missile

AO tanker with RAS capability

AOE auxillary fuel and ammunition, RAS capability

AORH tanker with hel capacity

AORL replenishment oiler light

AORLH oiler light with hel deck

AOT tanker

AP armour-piercing/anti-personnel

APC armoured personnel carrier

APL anti-personnel land-mine

AR Repair Ship

AR/C repair ship/cable

ARG amphibious ready group

ARL airborne reconnaissance low

ARM anti-radiation missile

armd armoured

ARS salvage ship

ARSV armoured reconnaissance/ surveillance vehicle

ARTHUR artillery hunting radar

arty artillery

ARV armoured recovery vehicle

AS anti-submarine

ASaC airborne surveillance and control

ASCM anti-ship cruise missile

ASM air-to-surface missile

ASR submarine rescue craft

ASROC anti-submarine rocket

ASSM anti-surface-ship missile

ASTROS II artillery saturation rocket System

ASTT anti-submarine torpedo tube

ASUW anti-surface unit warfare

ASW anti-submarine warfare

AT tug

ATBM anti-tactical ballistic missile

ATF tug, ocean going

ATGW anti-tank guided weapon

ATK anti-tank / attack

ATTACMS army tactical missile system

ATTC all terrain tracked carrier

ATTU Atlantic to the Urals

AV armoured vehicle

AVB aviation logistic ship

avn aviation

AWACS airborne warning and control system

AWT water tanker

AX training

AXL training craft

AXS training craft, sail

BA budget authority (US)

Bbr bomber

BCT brigade combat team

bde brigade

bdgt budget

BG battle group

BMD ballistic missile defense

bn battalion/billion

bty battery

C2 command and control

C³I command, control, communications and intelligence

C⁴ISR command, control, communication, computers, intelligence, surveillance and reconnaissance

Cal calibration

CALCM conventional air-launched cruise missile

can cannon

CAS close air support

casevac casualty evacuation

CASM conventionally armed stand-off missile

cat category

cav cavalry

cbt combat

CBU cluster bomb unit

CCS command and control systems

cdo commando

CEP circular error probable

CFE Conventional Armed Forces in Europe

CG guided missile cruiser

CGN guided missile cruiser, nuclear powered

cgo cargo (freight) aircraft

CIWS Close in Weapons System

CL light crusier

CLOS command to line of sight

COIN counter insurgency

col collaborative

comb combined/combination

Comd command

COMINT Communications Intelligence

Comms communications

CSAR combat search and rescue

CSG Carrier Strike Group (US)

CTOL conventional take off and landing

CV aircraft carrier

CVBG carrier battlegroup

CVH aircraft carrier, helicopter

CVN aircraft carrier, nuclear powered

CVS aircraft carrier with VSTOL

CW chemical warfare/weapons

DD destroyer

DDG guided missile destroyer

DDGH guided missile destroyer with helicopter

DDS dry dock shelter

def defence

defn definition

demob demobilised

det detachment

div division

dom domestic

DSCS defense satellite communications system

ECM electronic counter measures

econ aid economic aid with a military use

ECR electronic combat and reconnaissance

EDA Excess Defense Articles (US)

EELV evolved expendable launch vehicle

EEZ exclusive economic zone

ELINT electronic intelligence

elm element

EmDA Emergency Drawdown Authority (US)

engr engineer

EOD explosive ordnance disposal

eqpt equipment

ESG Expeditionary Strike Group (US)

ESM electronic support measures

est estimate(d)

EW electronic warfare

excl excludes/excluding

exp expenditure

FAC forward air control

fd field

FF frigate

FFG guided missile frigate

FFH frigate with helicopter

FFL light frigate

FGA fighter ground attack

FHTV family of heavy transport vehicles

flo-flo float-on, float-off

flt flight

FMA/F/S Foreign Military Assistance/ Financing/Sales

FMTV family of medium transport vehicles

FROG free rocket over ground

FS corvette

FSG guided missile corvette

FSSG Force Service Support Group

FSTA future strategic tanker aircraft

FTR fighter

FW fixed-wing

FY fiscal year

g gram

GBAD ground-based air defences

gd guard

GDP gross domestic product

GMLS guided missile launch sytem

GNP gross national product

gp group

GEODSS ground based electro optical deep space surveillance system

GS General Service (UK)

GW guided weapon

HARM high-speed anti-radiation missile

hel helicopter

HIMARS high mobility artillery rocket system

HMMWV high-mobility multi-purpose wheeled vehicle

HOT High-subsonic Optically Teleguided

how howitzer

HQ headquarters

HS Home Service (UK)

HVM high-velocity missile

HWT heavyweight torpedo

hy heavy

IBU inshore boat unit

ICBM inter-continental ballistic missile

IEW Intelligence/Electronic Warfare

IFG Indian Field Gun

IMET International Military Education and Training

imp improved

incl includes/including

indep independent

inf infantry

IRBM intermediate-range ballistic missile

IRLS infra-red line scan

ISTAR intelligence, surveillance, target acquisition and reconnaissance

JDAM Joint Direct Attack Munition

JSF Joint Strike Fighter

JSTARS Joint Surveillance Target Attack Radar System

kg kilogram

KT kiloton

LAM land-attack missile

LAMPS light airborne multi-purpose system

LANTIRN low-altitude navigation and targeting infra-red system night

LASH cargo ship barge

LAV light armoured vehicle

LAW light anti-tank weapon

LC landing craft

LCA landing craft assault

LCC amphibious command ship

LCH landing craft heavy

LCM landing craft medium

LCPA landing craft personnel aircushion

LCPL landing craft personnel small

LCT landing craft tank

LCU landing craft utility

LCVP landing craft vehicles and personnel

LFAV light forces armoured vehicles

LGB laser-guided bomb

LHA landing ship assault

LHD amphibious assault ship

LKA cargo ship

log logistic

LORADS long range radar display system

LP landing platform

LPD landing platform dock

LPH landing platform helicopter

LPV lifespan patrol vessel

LRAR long range artillery rocket

LRSA long-range strike/attack

LS landing ship

LSD landing ship dock

LSL landing ship logistic

LSLH landing ship logistic helicopter

LSM landing ship medium

LST landing ship tank

LWT lightweight torpedo

maint maintenance

MAMBA mobile artillery monitoring battlefield radar

MANPAD man portable air defence

MARDIV marine division

MAW marine aviation wing

MBT main battle tank

MCC mine countermeasure coastal

MCD mine countermeasure diving support

MCDV maritime coastal defence vessel

MCI mine countermeasure inshore

MCLOS manual CLOS

MCM mine countermeasures

MCMV mine countermeasures vessel

MCO mine countermeasures ocean

MCV mine countermeasures vessel

MD military district

MEB marine expeditionary brigade

mech mechanised

med medium

MEF marine expeditionary force

MEU marine expeditionary unit

MG machine gun

MHC mine hunter coastal

MHD mine hunter drone

MHI mine hunter inshore

MHO mine hunter ocean

mil military

MIRV multiple independently targetable re-entry vehicle

MISC miscellaneous

MIUW mobile inshore undersea warfare

mk mark (model number)

ML minelayer

MLRS multiple-launch rocket system

MLU mid-life update

MLV medium launch vehicle

mm millimetre

mne marine

mob mobilisation/ mobile

mod modified/modification

mor mortar

mot motorised/motor

MP maritime patrol

MPA maritime patrol aircraft

MPS marine prepositioning squadron

MR maritime reconnaissance

MRAAM medium-range air-to-air missile

MRBM medium-range ballistic missile

MRD motor rifle division

MRL multiple rocket launcher

MRR motor rifle regiment

MS mine sweeper

MSA mine sweeper auxillary

MSAM medium-range surface-to-air missile

MSC mine sweeper coastal

MSD mine sweeper drone

MSI mine sweeper inshore

msl missile

MSO mine sweeper ocean

MSR mine sweeper riverine

MSTAR manportable surveillance and target acquisition radar

MT megaton

Mtn mountain

NAEW NATO Airborne Early Warning & Control Force

n.a. not applicable

n.k. not known

NBC nuclear biological chemical

NCO non-commissioned officer

nm nautical mile

NMD national missile defence

NMP net material product

nuc nuclear

O & M operations and maintenance

OBS observation

OCU operational conversion unit

OOV objects of verification

op/ops operational/operations

OPFOR opposition training force

OPV off-shore patrol vessel

org organised/organisation

OTH/-B over-the-horizon/backscatter (radar)

OTHR/T over-the-horizon radar/targeting

PAAMS principle anti-air missile system

para paratroop/parachute

pax passenger/passenger transport aircraft

PB patrol boat

PBC patrol boat coastal

PBI patrol boat Inshore

PBR Patrol boat riverine

PC patrol craft

PCC patrol craft coastal

PCI patrol craft inshore

PCM patrol craft with SSM (surfact to surface missiles)

PCO patrol craft offshore

PCR patrol craft riverine

PCT patrol craft with torpedo

PDMS point defence missile system

pdr pounder

pers personnel

PFB fast patrol boat

PFC fast patrol craft coastal

PFI fast patrol craft inshore

PFM fast patrol craft with SSM

PFO fast patrol craft Ocean

PFT fast patrol craftwith torpedo

PGM precision guided munitions

PHM patrol hydrofoil with SSM

PHT patrol hydrofoil with Torpedo

PKO peacekeeping operation

POMCUS prepositioning of material configured to unit sets

PPP purchasing-power parity

PR photo-reconnaissance

prepo pre-positioned

PSO offshore patrol vessel over 60 metres

PSOH offshore patrol vessel over 60 metres with helicopter capability

PTG guided missile patrol craft

PTRL/SURV patrol / surveillance

publ public

PVO anti-aircraft defences

qd quadrillion

R&D research and development

RAM rolling airframe missile

RANGE INST range instrumentation

RAPID Reorganized Army Plains Infantry Division

RAS replenishment at sea

RCL ramped craft logistic

recce reconnaissance

regt regiment

res reserve(d)(s)

RIB rigid inflatable boat

RL rocket launcher

ro-ro roll-on, roll-off

RPV remotely piloted vehicle

RR/C/F rapid-reaction corps/force

RRC rapid raiding craft

RV re-entry vehicle

RY royal yacht

SACLOS semi-automatic CLOS

SAM surface-to-air missile

SAR search and rescue

sat satellite

SDV swimmer- delivery vehicles

SEAD suppression of enemy air defence

SEAL sea-air-land

SEWS satellite early warning station

SF special forces

SH support helicopter

SHORAD short range air defence

SIGINT signal intelligence

SLAM stand-off land-attack missile

SLBM submarine launched ballistic missile

SLCM submarine launched cruise missile

SLEP service life extension programme

SLOCs sea lines of communication

SMAW shoulder-launched multi-purpose assault weapon

SOC special operations capable

SP self propelled

SPEC OP special operations

spt support

sqn squadron

SRAM short-range-attack missile

SRBM short range ballistic missile

SS diesel submarine

SSAN submersible auxilliary support vessel

SSBN ballistic-missile submarine nuclear-fuelled

SSC diesel submarine coastal

SSG attack submarine diesel, non-ballistic missile launchers

SSGN SSN with dedicated non-ballistic missile launchers

SSI diesel submarine inshore

SSK Ptrl submarine with ASW capability

SSM surface-to-surface missile

SSN attack submarine nuclear powered

START Strategic Arms Reduction Talks/ Treaty

STO(V)L short take-off and (vertical) landing

STOBAR short take-off but arrested recovery

str strength

SUGW surface-to-underwater GW

SURV surveillance

SUT surface and underwater target

svc service

sy security

t tonnes

tac tactical

TASM tactical air-to-surface missile

TD tank division

temp temporary

THAAD Theater High Altitude Area Defense (US)

TIPH Temporary International presence in Hebron

tk tank

Tkr tanker

TLE treaty-limited equipment (CFE)

TMD theatre missile defence

torp torpedo

TOW tube launched optically wire guided

Tpt/Tkr transport/tanker

tr trillion

trg training

TRIAD triple AD

TRV torpedo recovery vehicle

TT torpedo tube

UA unit of action

UAV unmanned aerial vehicle

URG under-way replenishment group

USGW underwater to surface guided Weapon

utl utility

V(/S)TOL vertical(/short) take-off and landing

veh vehicle

VLS vertical launch system

VSRAD very short range air defence

wg wing

WGS wideband gapfiller satellite

WLIC Inland construction tenders

WMD weapon(s) of mass destruction

wpn weapon

WTGB Icebreaker tugs

YDG degaussing

YDT diving tender

Index of Countries and Territories

Index of **Country Abbreviations**